# Lecture Notes in Computer Science 16252

Founding Editors

Gerhard Goos
Juris Hartmanis

AF773085

Editorial Board Members

Elisa Bertino, *Purdue University, West Lafayette, IN, USA*
Wen Gao, *Peking University, Beijing, China*
Bernhard Steffen, *TU Dortmund University, Dortmund, Germany*
Moti Yung, *Columbia University, New York, NY, USA*

The series Lecture Notes in Computer Science (LNCS), including its subseries Lecture Notes in Artificial Intelligence (LNAI) and Lecture Notes in Bioinformatics (LNBI), has established itself as a medium for the publication of new developments in computer science and information technology research, teaching, and education.

LNCS enjoys close cooperation with the computer science R & D community, the series counts many renowned academics among its volume editors and paper authors, and collaborates with prestigious societies. Its mission is to serve this international community by providing an invaluable service, mainly focused on the publication of conference and workshop proceedings and postproceedings. LNCS commenced publication in 1973.

Goichiro Hanaoka · Bo-Yin Yang
Editors

# Advances in Cryptology – ASIACRYPT 2025

31st International Conference on the Theory and Application of Cryptology and Information Security
Melbourne, VIC, Australia, December 8–12, 2025
Proceedings, Part VIII

Springer

*Editors*
Goichiro Hanaoka
National Institute of Advanced Industrial Science and Technology
Tokyo, Japan

Bo-Yin Yang
Academia Sinica
Taipei, Taiwan

ISSN 0302-9743 ISSN 1611-3349 (electronic)
Lecture Notes in Computer Science
ISBN 978-981-95-5124-8 ISBN 978-981-95-5125-5 (eBook)
https://doi.org/10.1007/978-981-95-5125-5

© International Association for Cryptologic Research 2026

This work is subject to copyright. All rights are solely and exclusively licensed by the Publisher, whether the whole or part of the material is concerned, specifically the rights of translation, reprinting, reuse of illustrations, recitation, broadcasting, reproduction on microfilms or in any other physical way, and transmission or information storage and retrieval, electronic adaptation, computer software, or by similar or dissimilar methodology now known or hereafter developed.
The use of general descriptive names, registered names, trademarks, service marks, etc. in this publication does not imply, even in the absence of a specific statement, that such names are exempt from the relevant protective laws and regulations and therefore free for general use.
The publisher, the authors and the editors are safe to assume that the advice and information in this book are believed to be true and accurate at the date of publication. Neither the publisher nor the authors or the editors give a warranty, expressed or implied, with respect to the material contained herein or for any errors or omissions that may have been made. The publisher remains neutral with regard to jurisdictional claims in published maps and institutional affiliations.

This Springer imprint is published by the registered company Springer Nature Singapore Pte Ltd.
The registered company address is: 152 Beach Road, #21-01/04 Gateway East, Singapore 189721, Singapore

If disposing of this product, please recycle the paper.

# Preface

The 31st Annual International Conference on the Theory and Application of Cryptology and Information Security (Asiacrypt 2025) was held in Melbourne, Australia, on December 8–12, 2025. The conference covered all technical aspects of cryptology and was sponsored by the International Association for Cryptologic Research (IACR).

We received 533 paper submissions for Asiacrypt from around the world, which is exactly 100 more than last year's record-breaking number, setting a new all-time high. The Program Committee (PC) selected 143 papers for publication in the proceedings of the conference. As in the previous year, the Asiacrypt 2025 program had three tracks. Throughout the entire paper selection process, the ten Area Chairs made significant contributions. The two Program Co-chairs express their sincere gratitude to all the Area Chairs. The Area Chairs were Chris Brzuska for Fundamentals and Complexity Theory, Sherman Chow for Real-World Cryptography, Steven Galbraith for Higher Mathematics in Cryptography, Naofumi Homma for Efficient and Secure Implementations, Feng-Hao Liu for Public-Key Primitives with Advanced Functionalities, Takahiro Matsuda for Multi-party Computation and Zero-Knowledge, Manoj M. Prabhakaran for Information-Theoretic Cryptography, Damien Stehlé for Fully Homomorphic Encryption Theory and Practice, Meiqin Wang for Symmetric-Key Cryptography, and Keita Xagawa for Postquantum Cryptography. The Area Chairs kindly recommended excellent candidates for PC members and, in collaboration with the Discussion Leads, consolidated the opinions of the PC members within their respective areas to reach consensus. They then presented important recommendations regarding the acceptance or rejection of each paper to the Program Co-chairs. Furthermore, for submissions requiring additional reviews, they arranged for extra reviewers and, in some cases, conducted the reviews themselves. Beyond these dedicated contributions, they also provided many valuable insights and suggestions to support the Program Co-chairs in making key decisions. We are deeply grateful for their tremendous efforts. For submissions that the Area Chairs could not handle due to conflicts of interest, we asked the following four individuals to serve as substitute Area Chairs: Christian Rechberger, Yu Sasaki, Renaud Sirdey, and Frederik Vercauteren. We also extend our sincere appreciation to them for their dedicated support.

To review and evaluate the submissions, while keeping the load per PC member manageable, we selected as PC members 117 leading experts from all over the world, in all ten topic areas of cryptology, and we also had approximately 443 external reviewers, whose input was critical to the selection of papers. The review process was conducted using double-blind peer review. The conference operated a two-round review system with a rebuttal phase. This year, we continued the interactive rebuttal from Asiacrypt 2024. After the reviews and first-round discussions, PC members and area chairs selected 318 submissions to proceed to the second round. The remaining 215 papers were rejected, including 15 desk rejections. The authors were then invited to participate in a two-step interactive rebuttal phase, where the authors needed to submit a rebuttal in five days and then interact with the reviewers to address questions and concerns the following week. We believe the interactive form of the rebuttal encouraged discussions between the authors and the reviewers to clarify the concerns and contributions of the submissions and improved the review process. Then, after two weeks of second-round discussions (and more than two weeks of the shepherding process), the committee selected the final 143 papers to appear in these proceedings. Submissions received on average three reviews each during this process.

The PC nominated and voted for papers to receive the Best Paper Awards. The Best Theory Paper Award and the Best Early-Career Paper Award went to Tim Beyne and Michiel Verbauwhede for their paper "Integral cryptanalysis in characteristic *p*," the Best Practical Paper Award went to Charles Bouillaguet, Claire Delaplace, Mickaël Hamdad, and Damien Vergnaud for their paper "Practical cryptanalysis of pseudorandom correlation generators based on quasi-Abelian syndrome decoding," and the Best Early-Career Paper Award went to Thiago Bergamaschi and Naresh Boddu for their paper "On split-state quantum tamper detection." The authors of those three papers were invited to submit extended versions of their papers to the Journal of Cryptology. At Asiacrypt 2025, we were honored to have three Invited Talks delivered by Sherman Chow, Ron Steinfeld, and Peter Schwabe, respectively. We would like to express our sincere gratitude to these invited speakers as well. Following Asiacrypt 2024, we selected three PC members for the Distinguished PC Members Awards, nominated by the area chairs and program chairs. The Distinguished PC Members Awards went to Julia Kastner, Renaud Sirdey, and Jean-Pierre Tillich. As in the previous year, Asiacrypt 2025 included an artifact evaluation process. Authors of accepted papers were invited to submit associated artifacts, such as software or datasets, for archiving alongside their papers; 23 artifacts were submitted. Markku-Juhani O. Saarinen was the Artifact Chair and led an artifact evaluation committee of 12 members listed below. In the interactive review process between authors and reviewers, the goal was not just to evaluate artifacts but also to improve them. Artifacts that passed successfully through the artifact review process were publicly archived by the IACR at https://artifacts.iacr.org/.

Last, but not least, we would like to once again express our deep gratitude to everyone who contributed to Asiacrypt 2025. Without the diverse and extensive cooperation of all involved, the success of Asiacrypt 2025 would not have been possible. First and foremost, we sincerely thank all authors who submitted their valuable research results to Asiacrypt 2025. This year saw a significantly higher number of submissions than last year, and we understand that many authors may not have received the outcome they had hoped for despite the high quality of their work. To those authors as well, we extend our heartfelt thanks and wish them success in their future submissions. We also deeply appreciate the Area Chairs, PC members, and external reviewers, who actively engaged in discussions based on their highly specialized expertise to review this large volume of submissions. In organizing Asiacrypt 2025, we received tremendous support from General Chair Joseph Liu and his organizing team. Despite the unexpectedly large number of presentations, they provided an excellent venue and arrangements, for which we are truly grateful. Additionally, we would like to thank Kevin McCurley and Kay McKelly for their meticulous support in managing the website and review system. We are also deeply grateful to Kai-Min Chung and Yu Sasaki, who, drawing on their experience as

Program Co-chairs of last year's Asiacrypt, provided extremely helpful advice as Chairs at Large & Emeritus. We are also grateful for the helpful advice and organizational material provided to us by Crypto 2024 Program Co-chairs Leonid Reyzin and Douglas Stebila. We also thank the team at Springer for handling the publication of these conference proceedings.

December 2025

Goichiro Hanaoka
Bo-Yin Yang

# Organization

## General Chair

| | |
|---|---|
| Joseph Liu | Monash University, Australia |

## Program Committee Chairs

| | |
|---|---|
| Goichiro Hanaoka | National Institute of Advanced Industrial Science and Technology, Japan |
| Bo-Yin Yang | Academia Sinica, Taiwan |

## Area Chairs

| | |
|---|---|
| Chris Brzuska | Aalto University, Finland |
| Sherman S. M. Chow | Chinese University of Hong Kong, Hong Kong |
| Steven Galbraith | University of Auckland, New Zealand |
| Naofumi Homma | Tohoku University, Japan |
| Feng-Hao Liu | Washington State University, USA |
| Takahiro Matsuda | AIST, Japan |
| Manoj M. Prabhakaran | Indian Institute of Technology Bombay, India |
| Damien Stehlé | CryptoLab Inc., France |
| Meiqin Wang | Shandong University, China |
| Keita Xagawa | Technology Innovation Institute, UAE |

## Chairs at Large and Emeritus

| | |
|---|---|
| Kai-Min Chung | Academia Sinica, Taiwan |
| Yu Sasaki | NTT Social Informatics Laboratories, Japan and NIST, USA |

## Program Committee

| | |
|---|---|
| Adi Akavia | University of Haifa, Israel |
| Navid Alamati | VISA Research, USA |

| | |
|---|---|
| Elena Andreeva | TU Wien, Austria |
| Shi Bai | Florida Atlantic University, USA |
| Zhenzhen Bao | Tsinghua University, China |
| Ward Beullens | IBM Research Zurich, Switzerland |
| Tim Beyne | KU Leuven, Belgium |
| Shivam Bhasin | Nanyang Technological University, Singapore |
| Alexander Block | University of Illinois Chicago, USA |
| Jean-Philippe Bossuat | Gauss Labs, Switzerland |
| Pedro Branco | Bocconi University, Italy |
| Alex Bredariol Grilo | CNRS, France |
| Wouter Castryck | KU Leuven, Belgium |
| Sofía Celi | Brave, Portugal |
| Binyi Chen | Stanford University, USA |
| Shiyao Chen | Nanyang Technological University, Singapore |
| Yilei Chen | Tsinghua University, China |
| Wutichai Chongchitmate | Chulalongkorn University, Thailand |
| Tung Chou | Academia Sinica, Taiwan |
| Arka Rai Choudhuri | Nexus, USA |
| Chitchanok Chuengsatiansup | University of Klagenfurt, Austria |
| Michele Ciampi | University of Edinburgh, UK |
| Valerio Cini | Bocconi University, Italy |
| Alexandru Cojocaru | University of Edinburgh, UK |
| Daniel Collins | Texas A&M University, USA |
| Alain Couvreur | École Polytechnique, France |
| Bernardo David | IT University of Copenhagen, Denmark |
| Jean Paul Degabriele | Technology Innovation Institute, UAE |
| Patrick Derbez | University of Rennes, Inria, CNRS, IRISA, France |
| Jintai Ding | Xi'an Jiaotong-Liverpool University, China |
| Kirsten Eisentraeger | Penn State University, USA |
| Reo Eriguchi | AIST, Japan |
| Thomas Espitau | PQShield, France |
| Jun Furukawa | NEC Corporation, Japan |
| Rachit Garg | New York University, USA |
| Benedikt Gierlichs | KU Leuven, Belgium |
| Aarushi Goel | Purdue University, USA |
| Dawu Gu | Shanghai Jiao Tong University, China |
| Mohammad Hajiabadi | University of Waterloo, Canada |
| Minki Hhan | University of Texas at Austin, USA |
| Kai Hu | Shandong University, China |
| Michael Hutter | University of the Bundeswehr Munich & PQShield, Germany |

| | |
|---|---|
| Yasuhiko Ikematsu | Kyushu University, Japan |
| Takanori Isobe | The University of Osaka, Japan |
| Tibor Jager | Wuppertal University, Germany |
| Ashwin Jha | Ruhr-University of Bochum, Germany |
| Haodong Jiang | Henan Key Laboratory of Network Cryptography Technology, China |
| Zhenzhong Jin | Northeastern University, USA |
| Fatih Kaleoglu | JPMorganChase, USA |
| Chethan Kamath | IIT Bombay, India |
| Matthias J. Kannwischer | Chelpis Quantum Corp, Taiwan |
| Julia Kastner | CWI, Netherlands |
| Miran Kim | Hanyang University, South Korea |
| Elena Kirshanova | Technology Innovation Institute, UAE |
| David Kohel | Aix-Marseille Université, France |
| Srijita Kundu | University of Waterloo, Canada |
| Qiqi Lai | Shaanxi Normal University, China |
| Keewoo Lee | University of California, Berkeley, USA |
| Tancrède Lepoint | Amazon Web Services (Security), USA |
| Xiao Liang | City University of Hong Kong, Hong Kong |
| Wei-Kai Lin | University of Virginia, USA |
| Tianren Liu | Peking University, China |
| Fukang Liu | Science Tokyo, Japan |
| Chen-Da Liu-Zhang | Lucerne University of Applied Sciences and Arts & Web3 Foundation, Switzerland |
| Julian Loss | CISPA, Germany |
| Stefan Lucks | Bauhaus-Universität Weimar, Germany |
| Hemanta Maji | Purdue University, USA |
| Florian Mendel | Infineon Technologies, Germany |
| Bart Mennink | Radboud University, Netherlands |
| Hart Montgomery | Linux Foundation, USA |
| Thorben Moos | UCLouvain, Belgium |
| Tomoyuki Morimae | Kyoto University, Japan |
| Khoa Nguyen | University of Wollongong, Australia |
| Maciej Obremski | National University of Singapore, Singapore |
| Hiroshi Onuki | The University of Tokyo, Japan |
| Anat Paskin-Cherniavsky | Ariel University, Israel |
| Peter Pessl | Infineon Technologies, Germany |
| Christophe Petit | University of Birmingham, UK and Université libre de Bruxelles, Belgium |
| Rachel Player | Royal Holloway, University of London, UK |
| Bertram Poettering | IBM Research Europe – Zurich, Switzerland |

| | |
|---|---|
| Antigoni Polychroniadou | J.P. Morgan AI Research & AlgoCRYPT CoE, USA |
| Manoj M. Prabhakaran | Indian Institute of Technology Bombay, India |
| Luowen Qian | NTT Research, Inc., USA |
| Sebastian Ramacher | AIT Austrian Institute of Technology, Austria |
| Christian Rechberger | TU Graz, Austria |
| Adeline Roux-Langlois | CNRS, GREYC, France |
| Lawrence Roy | Aarhus University, Denmark |
| Sujoy Sinha Roy | Graz University of Technology, Austria |
| Markku-Juhani Saarinen | Tampere University, Finland |
| Amin Sakzad | Monash University, Australia |
| Simona Samardjiska | Radboud University, Netherlands |
| Paolo Santini | Marche Polytechnic University, Italy |
| Pascal Sasdrich | Ruhr University Bochum, Germany |
| André Schrottenloher | Inria Rennes, France |
| Sruthi Sekar | IIT Bombay, India |
| Srinath Setty | Microsoft Research, USA |
| Renaud Sirdey | CEA, France |
| Daniel Slamanig | Universität der Bundeswehr München, Germany |
| Ling Song | Jinan University, China |
| Yongsoo Song | Seoul National University, South Korea |
| Ron Steinfeld | Monash University, Australia |
| Qiang Tang | The University of Sydney, Australia |
| Jean-Pierre Tillich | Inria de Paris, France |
| Ha Tran | University of Alberta, Canada |
| Monika Trimoska | Eindhoven University of Technology, Netherlands |
| Yiannis Tselekounis | Royal Holloway, University of London, UK |
| Rei Ueno | Kyoto University, Japan |
| Frederik Vercauteren | KU Leuven, Belgium |
| Benedikt Wagner | Ethereum Foundation, Germany |
| Mingyuan Wang | NYU Shanghai, China |
| Zhedong Wang | Shanghai Jiao Tong University, China |
| Thom Wiggers | PQShield, Netherlands |
| Shota Yamada | AIST, Japan |
| Takashi Yamakawa | NTT, Japan |
| Yu Yu | Shanghai Jiao Tong University, China |
| Hong-Sheng Zhou | Virginia Commonwealth University, USA |
| Aron van Baarsen | Aarhus University, Denmark |
| Akin Ünal | Institute of Science and Technology Austria, Austria |

## Additional Reviewers

Balthazar Bauer
Sidhant Saraogi
Michel Abdalla
Damiano Abram
Hamza Abusalah
Anasuya Acharya
Amit Agarwal
Aikata Aikata
Nouri Alnahawi
Saed Alsayigh
Hiroaki Anada
Ravi Anand
Yoshinori Aono
Evan Apinis
Sarah Arpin
Roderick Asselineau
Thomas Attema
Benedikt Auerbach
Daniel Augot
Gennaro Avitabile
Karen Azari
Renas Bacho
Kano Bacho
David Balbás
Shalini Banerjee
Fabio Banfi
Laasya Bangalore
Subhadeep Banik
Anaïs Barthoulot
James Bartusek
Andrea Basso
Michele Battagliola
Kit Battarbee
Carsten Baum
Tamar Ben-David
Adda-Akram Bendoukha
Barbara Jiabao Benedikt
Francesco Berti
Rishabh Bhadauria
Amit Singh Bhati
Amit Singh Bhati
Arghya Bhattacharjee
Rishiraj Bhattacharyya
Ritam Bhaumik
Alexander Bienstock
Estelle Blin
Maxime Bombar
Antonina Bondarchuk
Jonathan Bootle
Sebastiano Boscardin
Vincenzo Botta
Samuel Bouaziz-Ermann
Aymen Boudguiga
Alexandre Bouez
Christina Boura
Konstantinos Brazitikos
Pierre Briaud
Colten Brunner
Dung Bui
Jean-Paul Bultel
Julien Béguinot
Luca Campa
Isaac Andres Canales Martínez
Kevin Carrier
Ignacio Cascudo
Gaëtan Cassiers
Enrique Cervero-Martin
Rutchathon Chairattana-Apirom
Avik Chakraborti
Olive Chakraborty
Kaushik Chakraborty
Suvradip Chakraborty
Debasmita Chakraborty
Hubert Chan
Rohit Chatterjee
Marina Checri
Mingjie Chen
Long Chen
Jie Chen
Yincen Chen
Liyan Chen
Clémence Chevignard
James Chiang
James Hsin-yu Chiang
Sohto Chiku
Wonhee Cho

Hyeongmin Choe
Antoine Choffrut
Wonseok Choi
Hao Chung
Pierre-Emmanuel Clet
Léo Colisson
Craig Costello
Jolijn Cottaar
Elizabeth Crites
Miguel Cueto Noval
Shujie Cui
Hongrui Cui
Jiamin Cui
Pierrick Dartois
Dipayan Das
Thomas Debris-Alazard
Thomas Decru
Mathieu Degre
Hugo Delavenne
Pierpaolo Della Monica
Gabriel Dettling
Lalita Devadas
Xiaohui Ding
Lin Ding
Joao Diogoduarte
Christoph Dobraunig
Jack Doerner
Antoine Douteau
Rafael Dowsley
Minxin Du
Qiuyan Du
Li Duan
Léo Ducas
Clement Ducros
Jesko Dujmovic
Jules Dumezy
Dung Hoang Duong
Moumita Dutta
Maria Eichlseder
Fatima Elsheimy
Saroja Erabelli
Daniel Escudero
Andre Esser
Marie Euler
Frederic Ezerman
Zhang Fahong
Sebastian Faller
Antonio Faonio
Joël Felderhoff
Jakob Feldtkeller
Yansong Feng
Hanwen Feng
Houda Ferradi
Chase Fickes
Marc Fischlin
Christian Forler
Tore Kasper Frederiksen
Daniele Friolo
Masayuki Fukumitsu
Hiroki Furue
Philippe Gaborit
Phillip Gajland
Mariana Gama
Shuhong Gao
Gayathri Garimella
Christina Garman
Robin Geelen
Baptiste Germon
Diana Ghinea
Ashrujit Ghoshal
Valerie Gilchrist
Emanuele Giunta
Eli Goldin
Junqing Gong
Boru Gong
Suchetana Goswami
Rishab Goyal
Lorenzo Grassi
Milos Grujic
Jiaxin Guan
Aurore Guillevic
Antonio Guimaraes
Aditya Gulati
Chun Guo
Yue Guo
Hao Guo
Christoph U. Günther
Hosein Hadipour
Mike Hamburg
Shuai Han

Lucas Hanouz
Lucjan Hanzlik
Keisuke Hara
Shingo Hasegawa
Keitaro Hashimoto
Valerian Hatey
Jinye He
Jiahui He
Aditya Hegde
Rachelle Heim
Lena Heimberger
Raphael Heitjohann
Julius Hermelink
Taiga Hiroka
Keitaro Hiwatashi
Christian Holler
Alexander Hoover
Akinori Hosoyamada
Kristina Hostakova
Chengan Hou
Shiqi Hou
Marc Houben
Martha Hovd
Yao-Ching Hsieh
Yuncong Hu
Yu-Hsuan Huang
Akiko Inoue
Akira Ito
Ryoma Ito
Samuel Jose Garcia Garcia
Nikai Jagganath
Fatemeh Jalalvand
Amit Jana
Hansraj Jangir
Jake Januzelli
Weidan Ji
Liheng Ji
Haoxiang Jin
Hyungrok Jo
Eda Kirimli
Daniel Kales
Anders Kallesøe
Dina Kamel
Simon Kamp
Jiayi Kang
Minsik Kang
Bhavana Kanukurthi
Upendra Kapshikar
Alexandr Karenin
Harish Karthikeyan
Shuichi Katsumata
Jonathan Katz
Yutaka Kawai
Andes Y. L. Kei
Mahimna Kelkar
John Kelsey
Mustafa Khairallah
Dmitry Khovratovich
Duhyeong Kim
Taeseong Kim
Fuyuki Kitagawa
Ivana Klasovita
Christian Knabenhans
Lisa Kohl
Sebastian Kolby
Jonathan Komada Eriksen
Swastik Kopparty
Thomas Korak
Gaurish Korpal
Katharina Koschatko
Veronika Kuchta
Naman Kumar
Dilip Kumar S. V.
Simran Kumari
Po-Chun Kuo
Péter Kutas
Paweł Kędzior
Yi-Fu Lai
Nathalie Lang
Roman Langrehr
Oleksandra Lapiha
Jun Bo Lau
Abel Laval
Dania Lazzarini
Jason LeGrow
Joon-Woo Lee
Yongwoo Lee
Changmin Lee
Hyeonbum Lee
Charlotte Lefevre

Anja Lehmann
Dominik Leichtle
Axel Lemoine
Doryan Lesaignoux
Andrea Lesavourey
Jannis Leuther
Laura Lewis
Yu Li
Muzhou Li
Muzhou Li
Afonso Li
Peigen Li
Shiyu Li
Yang Li
Junru Li
Yanan Li
Xiling Li
Zeyong Li
Yao-Ting Lin
Eik List
Zeyu Liu
Xiangyu Liu
Qun Liu
Qipeng Liu
Chen Lotan
Yu-Cheng Lu
Jinyu Lu
Mingqi Lu
George Lu
Vihaan Luhariwala
Ji Luo
Zhongtang Luo
Yingjie Lyu
Shanxiang Lyu
Saswata Mukherjee
Yiping Ma
Lorenzo Magliocco
Bernardo Magri
Luciano Maino
Monosij Maitra
Janmajaya Mal
Mary Maller
Sougata Mandal
Varun Maram
Laurane Marco
Elizabeth Margolin
Chloe Martindale
Christian Matt
Noam Mazor
Willi Meier
Fredrik Meisingseth
Nikolas Melissaris
Fei Meng
Antoine Mesnard
Pierre Meyer
Francesco Migliaro
Kazuhiko Minematsu
Omid Mir
Anuja Modi
Deep Inder Mohan
Charles Momin
Rocco Mora
Tomoki Moriya
Travis Morrison
Tamer Mour
Changrui Mu
Garazi Muguruza
Anisha Mukherjee
Ananta Mukherjee
Guilhem Mureau
Mari Muurman
Gina Muuss
Anne Müller
Jordan Naccache (Ethan)
Michael Naehrig
Marcel Nageler
Yusuke Naito
Kohei Nakagawa
Wenjie Nan
Shintaro Narisada
Shafik Nassar
María Naya-Plasencia
Tom Neuschulten
Tran Ngo
Ruben Niederhagen
Guilhem Niot
Aysan Nishaburi
Ryo Nishimaki
Zhongfeng Niu
Wakaha Ogata

Kazuma Ohara
Ryo Ohashi
Shinya Okumura
Michał Osadnik
Alex Ozdemir
Adam O'Neill
Hugo Pacheco
Tapas Pal
Jiaxin Pan
Lorenz Panny
Charalampos Papamanthou
Eugenio Paracucchi
Jai Hyun Park
Jeongeun Park
Aditi Partap
Alain Passelègue
Sikhar Patranabis
Alice Pellet-Mary
Olivier Pereira
Octavio Perez Kempner
Ray Perlner
Simone Perriello
Thomas Peters
Minh Pham
Duc Tu Pham
Xuanrong Piao
Aurel Pichollet-Mugnier
Rafael del Pino
Simon Pohmann
Guru Vamsi Policharla
Yuriy Polyakov
Thomas Prest
Daniel Pöllmann
Yue Qin
Tian Qiu
Sarawathy R. V.
Seyoon Ragavan
Mostafizar Rahman
Lars Ran
Shahram Rasoolzadeh
Divya Ravi
Michael Reichle
Krijn Reijnders
Marc Renard
Omar Renawi
Emeline Repel
Jan Richter-Brockmann
Peter Rindal
Silvia Ritsch
Michael Rosenberg
Arnab Roy
Ryan Rueger
Yusuke Sakai
Kosei Sakamoto
Samipa Samanta
Giacomo Santato
Bagus Santoso
Santanu Sarkar
Swagata Sasmal
Rahul Satish
Shingo Sato
Leonard Schild
Martin Schläffer
Fabian Schmid
Phil Schmieder
Peter Scholl
Jan Schoone
Jacob C. N. Schuldt
Robert Schädlich
Gabrielle Scullard
Melvin Seitner
Nicolas Sendrier
Hwajeong Seo
Yaobin Shen
Yipeng Shi
Kaiyan Shi
SeongHan Shin
Igor Shparlinski
Mark Simkin
Priyanshu Singh
Satvinder Singh
Adi Sireesh
Mathias Soeken
Nada Somswasdi
Yongha Son
Pratik Soni
Jannik Spiessens
Sebastian A. Spindler
Gabriele Spini
Sriram Sridhar

Adwaiya Srivastav
Oana Stan
Francois-Xavier Standaert
Miha Stopar
Roy Stracovsky
Patrick Struck
Marc Stöttinger
Ling Sun
Shi-Feng Sun
Siwei Sun
Bing Sun
Erkan Tairi
Akira Takahashi
Taisei Takahashi
Atsushi Takayasu
Kaoru Takemure
Ernest Tan
Yuhao Tang
Khai Hanh Tang
Gang Tang
Chengdong Tao
Brady Testa
Lea Thiemt
Tian Tian
Mehdi Tibouchi
Marcel Tiepelt
Tyge Tiessen
Saliha Tokat
Toi Tomita
Daphné Trama
Nam Tran
Stefano Trevisani
Ni Trieu
Ida Tucker
Nirvan Tyagi
Ioannis Tzannetos
Aleksei Udovenko
Dominique Unruh
Bart Van Vulpen
Marloes Venema
Michiel Verbauwhede
Javier Verbel
Psi Vesely
Hilder Vitor Lima Pereira
Jelle Vos
Quoc-Huy Vu
Hendrik Waldner
Alexandre Wallet
Linya Wang
Yuyu Wang
Xiaoyu Wang
Zhiheng Wang
Hongxiao Wang
Qingju Wang
Yuntao Wang
Jianhua Wang
Geng Wang
Libo Wang
Xinzhou Wang
Chenke Wang
Shichang Wang
Gaoli Wang
Haoyang Wang
Jiafan Wang
Violetta Weger
Christian Weinert
Weiqiang Wen
Chenkai Weng
Andreas Weninger
Stella Wohnig
Harry W. H. Wong
David Wu
Ke Wu
Zhili Wu
Yu Xia
Wenwen Xia
Zejun Xiang
Yuting Xiao
Jiajun Xin
Jiayu Xu
Yanhong Xu
Haiyang Xue
Aayush Yadav
Anshu Yadav
Saikumar Yadugiri
Sophia Yakoubov
Kyosuke Yamashita
Yingfei Yan
Luhan Yan
Naoto Yanai

Rupeng Yang
Kang Yang
Yu Yang
Qianqian Yang
Masaya Yasuda
Xiaxi Ye
Randy Yee
Yongdong Yeo
Kevin Yeo
Kazuki Yoneyama
William Youmans
Yuanzhuo Yu
Albert Yu
Aaram Yun
Chak Fai Yung
Álvaro Yángüez
Thomas Zacharias
Hadas Zeilberger
Runzhi Zeng
Yinuo Zhang
Yanhua Zhang
Tianyu Zhang
Liu Zhang
Yingjie Zhang
Kai Zhang
Yinuo Zhang
Ziyu Zhao
Yi Zhao
Raymond Zhao
Mingxun Zhou
Biming Zhou
Zhelei Zhou
Chenzhi Zhu
Floyd Zweydinger
Thomas den Hollander
Wessel van Woerden
Jonas von der Heyden
Marius Årdal
Alper Çakan

## Artifact Chair

| | |
|---|---|
| Markku-Juhani O. Saarinen | Tampere University, Finland |

## Artifact Evaluation Committee

| | |
|---|---|
| Sebastiano Boscardin | Eindhoven University of Technology, Netherlands |
| Charles Bouillaguet | Sorbonne University, France |
| Eros Camacho-Ruiz | Instituto de Microelectrónica de Sevilla, Spain |
| Fabrizio De Santis | Siemens AG, Germany |
| Matthias Kannwischer | Chelpis Quantum Corporation, Taiwan |
| Katharina Koschatko | Graz University of Technology, Austria |
| Pablo Navarro-Torrero | Instituto de Microelectrónica de Sevilla, Spain |
| Reyhaneh Rabbaninejad | Tampere University, Finland |
| Krijn Reijnders | KU Leuven, Belgium |
| Sachin Shukla | Microsoft, USA |
| Mohamed Soliman | Tampere University, Finland |
| Mert Yassi | Monash University, Australia |

# Contents

# Secret Sharing

# A Construction of Evolving $k$-Threshold Secret Sharing Scheme over A Polynomial Ring

Qi Cheng[1,2], Hongru Cao[2], Sian-Jheng Lin[2(✉)], Nenghai Yu[2], Yunghsiang S. Han[3], and Xianhong Xie[1]

[1] School of Information and Artificial Intelligence, Anhui Agricultural University, Hefei 230036, China
{chengqi,xianhxie}@ahau.edu.cn

[2] School of Cyber Science and Technology, University of Science and Technology of China, Hefei 230027, China
chrkeith@mail.ustc.edu.cn, sjlin@ustc.edu.cn

[3] Shenzhen Institute for Advanced Study, University of Electronic Science and Technology of China, Shenzhen 518000, China
ynh@ustc.edu.cn

**Abstract.** The threshold secret sharing scheme enables a dealer to distribute the share to every participant such that the secret is correctly recovered from a certain amount of shares. The traditional $(k, n)$ threshold secret sharing scheme requires that the number of participants $n$ is known in advance. In contrast, the evolving secret sharing scheme allows that $n$ can be uncertain and even ever-growing. In this paper, we consider the evolving secret sharing scenario. Based on the prefix codes, we propose a brand-new construction of evolving $k$-threshold secret sharing scheme for an $\ell$-bit secret over a polynomial ring, with correctness and perfect security. The proposed scheme is the first evolving $k$-threshold secret sharing scheme by generalizing Shamir's scheme onto a polynomial ring. Besides, the proposed scheme also establishes the connection between prefix codes and the evolving schemes for $k \geq 2$. The analysis shows that the size of the $t$-th share is $(k-1)(\ell_t - 1) + \ell$ bits, where $\ell_t$ denotes the length of a binary prefix code of encoding integer $t$. In particular, when $\delta$ code is chosen as the prefix code, the share size is $(k-1)\lfloor \lg t \rfloor + 2(k-1)\lfloor \lg(\lfloor \lg t \rfloor + 1) \rfloor + \ell$, which improves the prior best result $(k-1)\lg t + 6k^4 \ell \lg\lg t \cdot \lg\lg\lg t + 7k^4 \ell \lg k$, where lg denotes the binary logarithm. Specifically, when $k = 2$, the proposal also provides a unified mathematical decryption for prior evolving 2-threshold secret sharing schemes and also achieves the minimal share size for a single-bit secret, which is the same as the best-known scheme.

**Keywords:** Threshold secret sharing · Evolving · Prefix codes · Polynomial ring · Share size · Security

© International Association for Cryptologic Research 2026
G. Hanaoka and B.-Y. Yang (Eds.): ASIACRYPT 2025, LNCS 16252, pp. 3–33, 2026.
https://doi.org/10.1007/978-981-95-5125-5_1

# 1 Introduction

The $(k, n)$ secret sharing scheme encodes the secret into $n$ shares such that the secret can be losslessly recovered from any $k$ out of $n$ shares, and any $k-1$ shares cannot decode any information for the secret. Shamir [1] and Blakley [2] independently proposed the $(k, n)$ secret sharing scheme in 1979. Due to the practicality of secret sharing scheme, it has been widely used and plays a very important role in modern cryptography [3–6]. However, the conventional secret sharing schemes require that the dealer knows the maximum number of participants $n$ in advance. When we allow the dealer can produce the corresponding share for each new participant, the maximum number of $n$ cannot be determined, and hence, most conventional schemes cannot be applied to this scenario.

To solve this issue, Komargodski et al. [7,8] introduced an evolving $k$-threshold secret sharing scheme. In this scheme, the secret can be recovered from any $k$ out of infinitely many participants, and any $k-1$ shares out of these cannot get any information about the secret. Specifically, Komargodski et al. [8] first proposed the construction of an evolving 2-threshold secret sharing scheme based on prefix codes, and showed the equivalence between binary prefix codes for the integers and evolving 2-threshold secret sharing schemes. The results show that when a set of prefix codes is given, there must exist a corresponding construction of the evolving 2-threshold scheme, and vice versa. Later, D'Arco et al. [9] also provided an alternative technique to show the equivalence. These results links prefix codes with evolving 2-threshold scheme, reducing the complex task of constructing such schemes to the simpler task of designing prefix codes, which holds significant research value. By analyzing the corresponding share size, it [8] shows that the share size of the $t$-th share is no more than $\lg t + (\ell + 1) \lg \lg t + 4\ell + 1$ bits for an $\ell$-bit secret. The scheme is optimal for a 1-bit secret. Furthermore, the authors in [8] proposed a general construction of the evolving $k$-threshold secret sharing scheme for arbitrary $k$, and analyzed that the $t$-th share size of the evolving $k$-threshold scheme is $(k-1)\lg t + 6k^4\ell \lg\lg t \cdot \lg\lg\lg t + 7k^4\ell \lg k$.

However, firstly, the evolving schemes in [8] are constructed based on the idea of distributing shares on a generational basis and use an evolving scheme once and Shamir's scheme multiple times. Hence, they will become increasingly complex and even difficult to construct as $k$ increases. The natural idea for constructing the evolving scheme is based on simulating Shamir's scheme. Komargodski et al. [8] attempted this approach but failed. Thus, how to design algebraic-oriented constructions for evolving secret sharing schemes is also left as an open problem in [8]. Secondly, it is unknown whether there are connections between prefix codes and the evolving $k$-threshold secret sharing schemes when $k > 2$. This is also left as an open problem in [8]. Thirdly, the corresponding share size in [8] is not optimal. To further reduce the share size, D'Arco et al. [10] proposed a new construction of the evolving 3-threshold scheme based on the Chinese Remainder Theorem, which is slightly different from the model in [8]. They achieved the share size of the $t$-th participant close to $\lg t + poly(k) \cdot o(\lg t)$. However, the scheme can only be used in the case of $k = 3$. As for $k \geq 4$, there are no related works, to the best of our knowledge.

To this end, we propose a brand-new construction of an evolving $k$-threshold secret sharing scheme for an $\ell$-bit secret over a polynomial ring based on prefix codes, where the size of the $t$-th share is determined by the codeword length for encoding $t$. The proposed schemes achieve algebraic-oriented constructions by generalizing Shamir's scheme and establish the connection between prefix codes and the evolving schemes for $k \geq 2$. Specifically, we first propose the construction of an evolving 2-threshold secret sharing scheme over $\mathbb{F}_2[x]$. We also apply the construction to other complicated binary prefix codes to compare the share size with the scheme proposed in [8]. It shows that the proposed scheme can achieve a smaller size for some binary prefix codes. Second, we extend the scheme to the evolving $k$-threshold secret sharing scheme on $\mathbb{F}_2[x]$ for $k \geq 3$. The analysis of share size shows that the $t$-th share of the proposed scheme is $(k-1)(\ell_t - 1) + \ell$ bits, where $\ell_t$ denotes the length of a prefix code of encoding integer $t$. When using $\delta$ code [11] as the prefix code, the share size is given by $(k-1)\lfloor \lg t \rfloor + 2(k-1)\lfloor \lg(\lfloor \lg t \rfloor + 1) \rfloor + \ell$, which is smaller than the prior result $(k-1)\lg t + 6k^4\ell \lg\lg t \cdot \lg\lg\lg t + 7k^4\ell \lg k$ in [8]. Third, considering the secret $s \in \{0, 1, \cdots, p-1\}^\ell$, we proposed a construction of evolving $k$-threshold scheme over the polynomial ring $\mathbb{F}_p[x]$, where $k \geq 2$. This can be seen as an extension of the proposed scheme. In addition, we also show some $p$-ary prefix codes for positive integers and then apply the construction to these codes.

### 1.1 Our Contributions

Consequently, the above interesting and challenging problems remain open. In this paper, we focus on settling these problems simultaneously. Then the major contributions of this paper are enumerated as follows.

- The proposed brand-new scheme is more direct and concise by using the algebraic structure of polynomial ring. This result addresses the open question raised by [8]. It is the first evolving $k$-threshold secret sharing scheme that generalizes Shamir's scheme to a polynomial ring. Given that Shamir's scheme is the standard in traditional secret sharing, we believe that the proposed scheme has the potential to become the benchmark for evolving schemes.
- The proposed scheme successfully establishes the connection between prefix codes and evolving $k$-threshold secret sharing for arbitrary $k$, where the $t$-th share size is determined by the codeword length of encoding $t$. This demonstrates that there is a corresponding construction of an evolving $k$-threshold secret sharing scheme for any given prefix code. This result can answer another open question raised by [8].
- The share size of the proposed evolving $k$-threshold schemes is $(k-1)(\ell_t-1)+\ell$ bits, where $\ell_t$ denotes the length of a binary prefix code of encoding integer $t$. Specially, when choosing $\delta$ code as the prefix code, the proposed schemes can achieve a smaller share size for thresholds $k = 2$ and $k \geq 4$, compared with all currently known constructions. A comparative summary of share sizes in existing evolving threshold secret sharing schemes is provided in Table 1.

**Table 1.** Share sizes of evolving $k$-threshold schemes, where the value of the lowest share size is in bold for each case of $k$.

| threshold | algorithm | share size |
|---|---|---|
| $k = 2$ | [12] | $\ell \cdot O(2^{1+\varepsilon} \lg t),\ \varepsilon > 0$ |
| | [8] | $\lg t + (\ell + 1) \lg \lg t + 4\ell + 1$ |
| | **ours** | $\boldsymbol{\lfloor \lg t \rfloor + 2\lfloor \lg (\lfloor \lg t \rfloor + 1)\rfloor + \ell}$ |
| $k = 3$ | [12] | $\ell \cdot O(3^{1+\varepsilon} \lg t),\ \varepsilon > 0$ |
| | [8] | $2 \lg t + 486\ell \lg \lg t \cdot \lg \lg \lg t + 567\ell \lg 3$ |
| | ours | $2\lfloor \lg t \rfloor + 4\lfloor \lg(\lfloor \lg t \rfloor + 1)\rfloor + \ell$ |
| | [10] | $\boldsymbol{\lg t + poly(k) \cdot o(\lg t)}$ |
| $k \geq 4$ | [12] | $\ell \cdot O(k^{1+\varepsilon} \lg t),\ \varepsilon > 0$ |
| | [8] | $(k-1) \lg t + 6k^4 \ell \lg \lg t \cdot \lg \lg \lg t + 7k^4 \ell \lg k$ |
| | **ours** | $\boldsymbol{(k-1)\lfloor \lg t \rfloor + 2(k-1)\lfloor \lg (\lfloor \lg t \rfloor + 1)\rfloor + \ell}$ |

- Based on the prefix codes and the properties of polynomial ring, the proposed $k$-threshold secret sharing schemes have correctness and perfect security. Specially, we present an ingenious mathematical proof demonstrating the scheme's perfect security. This innovative approach significantly enhances the clarity and comprehensibility of the proof process.
- It is well known that the evolving 2-threshold secret sharing scheme has been studied comprehensively. When $k = 2$, the proposed scheme provides a unified mathematical description for prior evolving 2-threshold secret sharing schemes. In addition, the proposed scheme also achieves the minimal share size for single-bit secret, as stated in [8].

### 1.2 Technical Overview

We now give a detailed overview of the main techniques we use to obtain our results, explaining the ideas behind each of our constructions. Our approach leverages the algebraic structure of polynomial rings, prefix codes for integers, and innovative proof techniques to achieve a unified and efficient framework for evolving $k$-threshold secret sharing. Below, we elaborate on the core technical components.

**Construction of the Scheme.** Our scheme generalizes Shamir's secret sharing to a polynomial ring, enabling a direct and concise construction for evolving $k$-threshold schemes. The key technical steps are as follows.

*Polynomial Ring Framework.* We work over a polynomial ring $\mathbb{F}_p[x]$. For a secret $s \in \mathbb{F}_p[x]$ with degree $\ell - 1$, we construct a polynomial $f(y)$ of the form $f(y) = \sum_{j=0}^{k-2} r_j y^j + s y^{k-1}$ over $\mathbb{F}_p[x]$, where $\{r_j\}_{j=0}^{k-2}$ are random parameters. Then the shares are encoded as evaluations of polynomials. This algebraic structure allows us to naturally extend Shamir's scheme to an unbounded number of participants.

*Prefix Codes for Integers.* To handle the evolving nature of the scheme, we map each participant index $t$ to a codeword from a prefix code and $\ell_t$ denote the length of the corresponding codeword. The corresponding polynomial form $y_t$ derived from its prefix code is then substituted into the pre-constructed polynomial $f(y)$, and the evaluation result of $f(y_t)$ modulo $x^{(k-1)(\ell_t-1)+\ell}$ is assigned as the corresponding share.

**Correctness and Secrecy Proofs.** The correctness and security of our scheme rely on careful algebraic analysis and combinatorial properties of prefix codes.

*Correctness.* The scheme ensures correctness through the following mechanism. Upon collecting $k$ shares, we can establish a system of $k$ equations containing $k$ unknown variables $(r_0, r_1, \cdots, r_{k-2}, s)$. By leveraging the algebraic structure of polynomial rings and the properties of prefix codes, we solve the secret $s$ using Gaussian elimination, thereby guaranteeing that any $k$ participants can reconstruct $s$.

*Secrecy.* When collecting $k-1$ shares, we can construct a system of $k-1$ equations. To demonstrate security according to the formal definition, we choose two distinct secrets $s_0$ and $s_1$, and denote $\{Z_{i_j}^{(s_0)}\}_{j=1}^{k-1}$ and $\{Z_{i_j}^{(s_1)}\}_{j=1}^{k-1}$ the share sets generated under each secret respectively. Given any fixed $k-1$ shares $\{z_{i_j}\}_{j=1}^{k-1}$, the security proof reduces to showing $P(\{Z_{i_j}^{(s_0)} = z_{i_j}\}_{j=1}^{k-1}) = P(\{Z_{i_j}^{(s_1)} = z_{i_j}\}_{j=1}^{k-1})$. Then, we prove the equality $P(\{Z_{i_j}^{(s_0)} = z_{i_j}\}_{j=1}^{k-1}) = P(\{Z_{i_j}^{(s_1)} = z_{i_j}\}_{j=1}^{k-1})$ by demonstrating that the two equation systems possess an equal number of solutions. By leveraging the algebraic structure of polynomials and the properties of prefix codes, along with techniques for solving equations, we rigorously show that these two equation systems indeed contain identical number of solutions. Therefore, the proposed scheme has perfect security.

## 1.3 Related Works

Shamir [1] and Blakley [2] independently proposed the $(k, n)$ secret sharing scheme in 1979. The construction of Shamir's scheme was based on Lagrange interpolation. Blakley's scheme was established by using the property of points in multidimensional space. In Shamir's scheme, the dealer randomly chose a polynomial in $\mathbb{F}_p[x]$ of degree less than $k$ such that the constant term of this polynomial is the secret and $p > n$. Consequently, the $n$ shares, which are the evaluations of the polynomial at $n$ distinct points, are respectively distributed to $n$ participants. Therefore, each share is an element of $\mathbb{F}_p$ that can be represented with approximately $\lg n$ bits. Later, Karnin et al. [13] proved that the share size of Shamir's scheme is optimal when the length of the secret is $\lg n$ bits. Bogdanov et al. [14] proved that the share size of Shamir's secret sharing scheme is optimal for a 1-bit secret when $n$ is a prime power and $k = n - 1$. Inspired by the Shamir's scheme, many works have constructed secret sharing schemes using different algebraic structures. Cramer and Fehr [15] proposed a black-box secret sharing scheme over any finite Abelian group. Cao et al. [16] proposed a secret sharing scheme based on polynomial rings. Notably, when selecting specific ring structures, the Fast Fourier Transform can be incorporated into the scheme's encoding process, significantly enhancing computational efficiency. This approach established an important framework for subsequent research.

Unlike Shamir [1] uses a finite field to construct a secret sharing scheme, Mignotte [17] and Asmuth et al. [18] independently gave the new constructions of $(k, n)$ threshold secret sharing scheme based on the Chinese Remainder Theorem for integer rings. Both schemes are similar, however, Asmuth-Bloom's scheme improved security compared with Mignotte's scheme. In Asmuth-Bloom's scheme, $n$ integers that are increasing and pairwise coprime are randomly selected, and the product of any $k$ numbers is greater than the value of the secret. Subsequently, the dealer calculated the remainders that module the secret for $n$ integers separately and sent each participant a share consisting of the corresponding integer and its remainder. Due to the superior computational complexity and efficiency of this scheme, it has become a widely studied and highly regarded secret sharing scheme. Then, many works [19–21] utilized the technology of Asmuth-Bloom's scheme to achieve various performances in practical applications.

Due to the significant advantages of secret sharing schemes, they were widely used in other applications, including threshold cryptography [22], multiparty protocol [23] and quantum computation [24]. In 1985, Chor et al. [25] proposed the concept of verifiability for the first time and constructed a verifiable secret sharing scheme. Moreover, Krawczyk's scheme [26] was constructed to achieve computing efficiency with high probability, allowing small statistical errors in security. Ding et al. [27] described a new construction for the communication efficient secret sharing scheme with a small share size to minimize the decoding bandwidth.

However, traditional secret sharing schemes require the dealer to determine the total number of participants $n$ in advance, which cannot adapt to scenarios where new participants dynamically join. To meet practical needs, Komargodski et al. [7,8] introduced the evolving $k$-threshold secret sharing scheme, which allows the total number of participants to dynamically increase. Actually, before Komargodski et al. proposed the scheme, Csirmaz and Tardos [28] had conducted preliminary discussions on similar scenarios, but did not provide a concrete construction. In contrast, Komargodski et al.'s contributions [7,8] not only established a clear definition and design framework for evolving secret sharing but also laid the theoretical foundations for dynamic threshold access structures. On this basis, Komargodski and Paskin-Cherniavsky [29] proposed practical solutions through algebraic operation of detection codes, further promoting the development of evolutionary secret sharing schemes.

The construction of the evolving threshold secret sharing scheme proposed by Komargodski et al. is currently the most commonly used construction method, which establishes a connection between integer prefix codes and evolving 2-threshold secret sharing schemes. This groundbreaking discovery has sparked extensive research interest, and subsequently, numerous scholars have conducted in-depth studies on the evolving 2-threshold schemes based on integer prefix codes. Given a secret with arbitrary length, Okamura et al. [30] first applied the construction of an evolving 2-threshold scheme to more complicated binary codes for positive integers and analyzed the corresponding share size. Furthermore, based on $D$-ary prefix code for $D \geq 3$, the construction of the evolving 2-threshold scheme was also proposed in [30]. To evaluate the quality of the scheme, Yan et al. [31] introduce a metric to evaluate evolving 2-threshold secret sharing schemes. Based on this, D'Arco et al. [32] proposed a new evolving 2-threshold secret sharing scheme improving on the previous best known scheme and making closer the lower bound.

When $k > 2$, the scheme [8] proposed by Komargodski et al. still exhibits significant limitations. It adopts a hierarchical design by combining a one-time evolving scheme with multiple instances of the Shamir scheme. As the threshold $k$ increases, the number of Shamir scheme invocations grows substantially, leading to a sharp rise in complexity eventually. Later, Alon et al. [33] gave a construction of evolving secret sharing schemes for infinite layered branching programs. Tough their scheme can handle any evolving access structure which can be computed by an layered branching program, but choosing the right generation growth is not trivial. To achieve a simpler construction method for evolving $k$-threshold secret sharing schemes, Xing and Yuan [12] proposed a novel scheme based on algebraic geometry codes but larger share size than the scheme [8]. To further reduce the share size, D'Arco et al. [10] proposed a new construction of the evolving 3-threshold scheme based on the Chinese Remainder Theorem, reducing the core term of the $t$-th share size from $\lg t$ to $\lg t$. However, the construction method is a bit complicated and can only be applicable to the case of $k = 3$.

### 1.4 Organization

The rest of the paper is organized as follows. In Sect. 2, we review the traditional secret sharing scheme and evolving secret sharing scheme. In Sect. 3, we first propose a new construction of an evolving 2-threshold secret sharing scheme and elaborate on the security of the scheme. Then, the evolving $k$-threshold secret sharing scheme is given in Sect. 4 for $k \geq 3$. In Sect. 5, we provide a construction of evolving $k$-threshold secret sharing scheme considering the secret $s \in \{0, 1, \cdots, p-1\}^{\ell}$. Finally, Sect. 6 concludes the work and discusses the unresolved issues.

## 2 Models and Notations

Let $\mathbb{N}^+$ denote the set of positive integers. Let $[n] = \{1, 2, \cdots, n\}$ for $n \in \mathbb{N}^+$. Let $|A|$ denote the cardinality of the set $A$. For any $p \in \mathbb{N}^+$ being a prime, let $\mathbb{F}_p$ denote the finite field with $p$ elements. Let $\mathbb{F}_p[x] = \{\sum_{j=0}^{N} a_j x^j | a_j \in \mathbb{F}_p\}$ as the polynomial ring, where $N$ is a finite positive integer. For any $f(x), g(x) \in \mathbb{F}_p[x]$, if $g(x)$ divides $f(x)$, it can be expressed as $g(x) \mid f(x)$. The result of $g(x)$ dividing $f(x)$ is denoted as *quotient*, which is written as $\frac{f(x)}{g(x)}$. For any $i, a \in \mathbb{N}^+$, $f(x) \in \mathbb{F}_p[x]$, if $x^i \mid f(x)$ with any $i \leq a$ and $x^{a+1} \nmid f(x)$, then $a$ be denoted as *the maximal extractable power* of $f(x)$. For any $d \in \mathbb{N}^+$, let $\mathbb{F}_p[x]/x^d$ be a quotient ring, which is composed of polynomials $f(x) \in \mathbb{F}_p[x]$ with the degree less than $d$. For any $f(x) \in \mathbb{F}_p[x]/x^d$, if there exists a polynomial $g(x) \in \mathbb{F}_p[x]/x^d$ such that $f(x)g(x) = 1 \in \mathbb{F}_p[x]/x^d$, then $f(x)$ is called to be *invertible*, which be represented as $f^{-1}(x)$. Equivalently, $f(x)$ has a multiplicative inverse $g(x)$ modulo $x^d$ in the quotient ring $\mathbb{F}_p[x]/x^d$. Let $\mathbb{F}_p[[x]] = \{\sum_{j=0}^{\infty} a_j x^j | a_j \in \mathbb{F}_p\}$.

### 2.1 Secret Sharing Scheme

Let $\mathcal{P}_n = \{P_1, P_2, \cdots, P_n\}$ represent the set of $n$ participants. The power set of $\mathcal{P}_n$ is written as $2^{\mathcal{P}_n}$. The collection $\mathcal{A} \subseteq 2^{\mathcal{P}_n}$ is monotone if for arbitrary $A \in \mathcal{A}$ and $A \subseteq C$, it holds that $C \in \mathcal{A}$. The access structure is defined as follows.

**Definition 1.** *An access structure $\mathcal{A} \subseteq 2^{\mathcal{P}_n}$ is a monotone collection of non-empty sets. The set in $\mathcal{A}$ is called qualified, and the set not in $\mathcal{A}$ is called unqualified.*

**Definition 2.** *For $k, n \in \mathbb{N}^+$ with $k \leq n$, the $(k, n)$-threshold access structure $\mathcal{A}$ refers to the set containing only all elements in $2^{\mathcal{P}_n}$ of size at least $k$, i.e.*

$$\mathcal{A} = \{A \in 2^{\mathcal{P}_n} || A| \geq k\}.$$

Constructing a $(k, n)$ threshold secret sharing scheme requires a dealer, a secret $s \in S$, a set of $n$ participants and a $(k, n)$ access structure $\mathcal{A}$, where $S$ is the domain of the secret. In the scheme, the dealer distributes the shares to all participants such that the shares of any set in $\mathcal{A}$ can correctly recover the secret, while the shares of any set not in $\mathcal{A}$ cannot gain any information about the secret. We denote by $Z_i^{(s)}$ the share of the $i$-th participant. The formal definition is given as follows.

**Definition 3.** *A $(k, n)$ threshold secret sharing scheme consists of a pair of algorithms $(\mathcal{E}, \mathcal{R})$, where $\mathcal{E}$ is used to encode the secret $s$ into shares, and $\mathcal{R}$ is used to reconstruct the secret from a set of shares $H \in 2^{\mathcal{P}_n}$. The following requirements shall be satisfied.*

- ***Correctness.*** *For any qualified set $A \in \mathcal{A}$, the algorithm $\mathcal{R}$ can correctly recover $s$ from the shares of the participants in $A$, that is*

$$P[\mathcal{R}(\{Z_i^{(s)}\}_{P_i \in A}, A) = s] = 1.$$

- ***Secrecy.*** *For any unqualified set $C \notin \mathcal{A}$, there is no information about $s$ leaking to the participants in $C$, that is, for any two different secrets $s_0, s_1 \in S$ and every possible vector of shares $\{z_i\}_{P_i \in C}$, $P(\{Z_i^{(s_0)} = z_i\}_{P_i \in C}) = P(\{Z_i^{(s_1)} = z_i\}_{P_i \in C})$.*

Let $B(Z_i^{(s)})$ represent the bit length of $Z_i^{(s)}$ for $1 \leq i \leq n$. Shamir [1] first proposed a construction for the $(k, n)$-threshold secret sharing scheme. For an $\ell$-bit secret $s$, the scheme uses the polynomial over $\mathbb{F}_p$ for $p \geq n$. The share size satisfies $B(Z_i^{(s)}) \geq \max\{\ell, \lg p\}$ for any $i \in [n]$ in Shamir's scheme.

## 2.2 Evolving Secret Sharing Scheme

When the maximum number of $n$ cannot be determined in advance and can even be infinite, conventional secret sharing schemes cannot be applied directly. In this case, evolving secret sharing schemes are developed. We denote $\mathcal{P} = \{P_1, P_2, \cdots, P_n, \cdots\}$ as the set of participants, where $\mathcal{P}$ is possibly infinite. Then, we give some definitions of the evolving secret sharing scheme.

**Definition 4.** *A collection of sets $\mathcal{A} \subseteq 2^{\mathcal{P}}$ is an evolving access structure if for every $t \in \mathbb{N}^+$, $\mathcal{A}_t := \mathcal{A} \cap 2^{\{P_1, P_2, \cdots, P_t\}}$ is an access structure as defined in Definition 1.*

**Definition 5.** *For $k \in \mathbb{N}^+$, the evolving $k$-threshold access structure $\mathcal{A}$ refers to the set consisting only of all elements in $2^{\mathcal{P}}$ of size at least $k$, i.e.*

$$\mathcal{A} = \{A \in 2^{\mathcal{P}} || A| \geq k\}.$$

Similarly, constructing an evolving $k$-threshold secret sharing scheme requires a dealer, a secret $s \in S$, a set of participants and an evolving $k$-threshold access structure $\mathcal{A}$. The dealer distributes the shares to all participants such that the shares of any set in $\mathcal{A}$ can correctly reconstruct the secret, while the shares of any set not in $\mathcal{A}$ cannot obtain any information about the secret. The formal definition is given as follows.

**Definition 6 ([8]).** *Let $\mathcal{A}$ be an be an evolving access structure and $S$ be a domain of secrets, where $|S| \geq 2$. A secret sharing scheme for $\mathcal{A}$ and $S$ consists of a pair of algorithms $(\mathcal{E}, \mathcal{R})$, where the sharing procedure $\mathcal{E}$ and the reconstruction procedure $\mathcal{R}$ satisfy the following requirements.*

- ***Share procedure.*** *$\mathcal{E}(s, \{Z_1^{(s)}, Z_2^{(s)}, \cdots, Z_{j-1}^{(s)}\})$ gets as input a secret $s \in S$ and the secret shares of participants $P_1, P_2, \cdots, P_{j-1}$. It outputs a share for the $j$-th party. For $j \in \mathbb{N}^+$ and secret shares $Z_1^{(s)}, Z_2^{(s)}, \cdots, Z_{j-1}^{(s)}$ generated for participants $\{P_1, P_2, \cdots, P_{j-1}\}$, respectively, we let*

$$Z_j^{(s)} \leftarrow \mathcal{E}(s, \{Z_1^{(s)}, Z_2^{(s)}, \cdots, Z_{j-1}^{(s)}\}).$$

*be the secret share of participant $P_j$.*
*We abuse notation and sometimes denote by $Z_j^{(s)}$ the random variable that corresponds to the secret share of participant $P_j$ generated as above.*

- ***Correctness***. *For every $s \in S$ and every $t \in \mathbb{N}^+$, every qualified set in $\mathcal{A}_t$ can reconstruct the secret. That is, for $s \in S$, $t \in \mathbb{N}^+$ and $A \in \mathcal{A}_t$, it holds that*

$$P[\mathcal{R}(\{Z_i^{(s)}\}_{P_i \in A}, A) = s] = 1,$$

*where the probability is over the randomness of the sharing and reconstruction procedures.*

- ***Secrecy***. *For every $t \in \mathbb{N}^+$, every unqualified set $C \notin \mathcal{A}_t$, and every two secret $s_0, s_1 \in S$, the distribution of the secret shares of participants in $C$ generated with secret $s_0$ and the distribution of the shares of participants in $C$ generated with secret $s_1$ are identical. Namely, the distributions $(\{Z_i^{(s_0)} = z_i\}_{P_i \in C})$ and $(\{Z_i^{(s_1)} = z_i\}_{P_i \in C})$ are identical.*

## 3 Evolving 2-Threshold Secret Sharing Scheme over $\mathbb{F}_2[x]$

In this section, we propose an evolving 2-threshold secret sharing scheme for an $\ell$-bit secret $s$. The scheme allows the dealer to distribute the share to every participant such that any single share cannot recover $s$.

### 3.1 Proposed Scheme

Before describing the proposed scheme, we first introduce the definition of prefix codes.

**Definition 7.** *A prefix (or more precisely, prefix-free) code is a code in which no codeword is prefix of any other codeword. A prefix code for the integers is an infinite prefix code $C = \{c_1, c_2, \cdots\}$, where $c_i$ is the codeword of encoding integer $i$.*

Given a set of binary prefix codes for integers, the codeword of the integer $i$ is denoted as $c_i = (c_{i,0}, c_{i,1}, \cdots, c_{i,\ell_i - 1})$, where $\ell_i$ represents the length of $c_i$ with $i \in \mathbb{N}^+$. The polynomial form of $c_i$ is defined as $y_i = \sum_{j=0}^{\ell_i - 1} c_{i,j} x^j \in \mathbb{F}_2[x]$. Given an $\ell$-bit binary sequence $s = (s_0, s_1, \cdots, s_{\ell-1})$, the polynomial form of $s$ is defined as $\sum_{j=0}^{\ell-1} s_j x^j \in \mathbb{F}_2[x]$ and the degree is less than $\ell$. Then the $i$-th share is defined as

$$Z_i^{(s)} = r_0 + s y_i \pmod{x^{\ell_i + \ell - 1}}, \tag{1}$$

where $r_0$ is randomly chosen in $\mathbb{F}_2[[x]]$. Notably, $s$ in (1) uses the polynomial form, which would be the default form throughout this paper. As the degree of $r_0$ is infinite in (1), we cannot choose such $r_0 \in \mathbb{F}_2[[x]]$ in practice. However, due to the operation modulo $x^{\ell_i + \ell - 1}$ in (1), the dealer only needs to choose the part of $r_0$ with a degree less than $\ell_i + \ell - 1$.

For any two participants $P_i, P_j \in \mathcal{P}$ with $i < j$, let $L_{i,j}$ represent the maximal extractable power of $(y_i - y_j)$. The algorithm $\mathcal{R}$ finds out that the following equation

$$s(y_i - y_j) \equiv Z_i^{(s)} - Z_j^{(s)} \pmod{x^{\ell_i + \ell - 1}} \tag{2}$$

has a unique solution of $s$ in $\mathbb{F}_2[x]/x^\ell$ as

$$s = \frac{Z_i^{(s)} - Z_j^{(s)}}{x^{L_{i,j}}} \left(\frac{y_i - y_j}{x^{L_{i,j}}}\right)^{-1} \pmod{x^\ell}. \tag{3}$$

The existence and uniqueness of $s$ in $\mathbb{F}_2[x]/x^\ell$ will be provided in the proof of correctness in the next subsection.

Notably, when the dealer generates the $i$-th share via (1), where $i$ is sufficiently large, the dealer needs to construct the corresponding $r_0$. Assuming that the dealer has already distributed shares to the first $i-1$ participants. Therefore, the dealer owns the corresponding $r_0$, which is used to construct the $(i-1)$-th share. The degree of the $r_0$ is $\ell_{i-1}+\ell-2$. We need to update $r_0$ to be a polynomial with degree $\ell_i+\ell-2$. Then the dealer randomly chooses $\ell_i-\ell_{i-1}$ coefficients from $\mathbb{F}_2$ for $x^{\ell_{i-1}+\ell-1}, \cdots, x^{\ell_i+\ell-2}$ such that the degree of $r_0$ is extended from $\ell_{i-1}+\ell-2$ to $\ell_i+\ell-2$. Hence, the corresponding $r_0$, which is used to construct the $i$-th share, is generated.

### 3.2 Proofs of Correctness and Secrecy

In this subsection, we will prove the correctness and secrecy of the proposed scheme. Before that, we first emphasize several lemmas, which provide useful results for the proofs.

**Lemma 1.** *Given any finite field $\mathbb{F}_p$, let $f(x), g(x), h(x), k(x) \in \mathbb{F}_p[x]$ with $f(x) \neq 0$ satisfy the congruence equation*

$$f(x)g(x) \equiv f(x)h(x) \pmod{f(x)k(x)}. \tag{4}$$

*Then we have*

$$g(x) \equiv h(x) \pmod{k(x)}. \tag{5}$$

*Proof.* According to the definition of congruence equation in (4), there exists $h_1(x) \in \mathbb{F}_p[x]$ such that

$$f(x)g(x) - f(x)h(x) = f(x)k(x)h_1(x), \tag{6}$$

since $\mathbb{F}_p$ is a finite field and $f(x) \neq 0$ in $\mathbb{F}_p[x]$, we can further get

$$g(x) - h(x) = k(x)h_1(x). \tag{7}$$

Therefore, we have

$$g(x) \equiv h(x) \pmod{k(x)}. \tag{8}$$

**Lemma 2.** *For any $n, k \in \mathbb{N}^+$, let $f(x) = a_n x^n + a_{n-1}x^{n-1} + \cdots + a_1 x + a_0 \in \mathbb{F}_p[x]$. If $a_0 \neq 0$, then $f(x)$ is invertible in $\mathbb{F}_p[x]/x^k$.*

*Proof.* Let $g(x) = x^k$, then we infer that the factor of $g(x)$ must be the form of $x^d$ for any $0 \leq d \leq k$. However, since $f(0) = a_0 \neq 0$, then $x^d$ is not the factor of $f(x)$. Therefore, we have

$$(g(x), f(x)) = 1. \tag{9}$$

According to Euclidean algorithm, there exists $u(x), v(x) \in \mathbb{F}_p[x]$ such that

$$u(x)f(x) + v(x)x^k = 1. \tag{10}$$

Hence, we further derive

$$u(x)f(x) \equiv 1 \pmod{x^k}. \tag{11}$$

Then $u(x)$ modulo $x^k$ is the inverse of $f(x)$ in $\mathbb{F}_p[x]/x^k$.

**Lemma 3.** *For any $k_1, k_2 \in \mathbb{N}^+$ with $k_1 \leq k_2$, let $f_1(x), g_1(x), f_2(x), g_2(x)$ be polynomials in $\mathbb{F}_p[x]$ satisfying the following congruence equations*

$$\begin{cases} f_1(x) \equiv g_1(x) \pmod{x^{k_1}}, \\ f_2(x) \equiv g_2(x) \pmod{x^{k_2}}. \end{cases} \tag{12}$$

*Then we have*

$$f_2(x) - f_1(x) \equiv g_2(x) - g_1(x) \pmod{x^{k_1}}. \tag{13}$$

*Proof.* According to the definition of congruence equations in (12), there exists $h_1(x), h_2(x) \in \mathbb{F}_p[x]$ such that

$$f_1(x) - g_1(x) = x^{k_1} h_1(x), \tag{14}$$

and

$$f_2(x) - g_2(x) = x^{k_2} h_2(x) = x^{k_1} h_2(x) x^{k_2 - k_1}. \tag{15}$$

Subtracting the equation (14) from the equation (15), we can further get

$$(f_2(x) - f_1(x)) - (g_2(x) - g_1(x)) = x^{k_1}(h_2(x)x^{k_2-k_1} - h_1(x)). \tag{16}$$

From (16), we obtain

$$f_2(x) - f_1(x) \equiv g_2(x) - g_1(x) \pmod{x^{k_1}}. \tag{17}$$

**Lemma 4.** *For any $\ell, \ell_1, k \in \mathbb{N}^+$ with $\ell \leq k$ and $\ell_1 \leq k$, given $f(x), h(x) \in \mathbb{F}_p[x]$ with $f(x) \neq 0$, let $\ell_1$ denote the maximal extractable power of $f(x)$. Let $g(x) \in \mathbb{F}_p[x]$ be a unknown polynomial with the degree no more than $\ell - 1$, and $g(x)$ satisfy the following congruence equation*

$$f(x)g(x) \equiv h(x) \pmod{x^k}. \tag{18}$$

*Then if $\ell + \ell_1 \leq k$, there exists a unique $g(x) \in \mathbb{F}_p[x]$ with the degree no more than $\ell - 1$ satisfying (18), i.e.*

$$g(x) = \frac{h(x)}{x^{\ell_1}} \left(\frac{f(x)}{x^{\ell_1}}\right)^{-1} \pmod{x^{\ell}}. \tag{19}$$

*Proof.* As $\ell_1$ is the maximal extractable power such that $x^{\ell_1} \mid f(x)$ and $x^{\ell_1+1} \nmid f(x)$, then $f(x)$ can be written $f(x) = x^{\ell_1} f_1(x)$, where $f_1(x) = \frac{f(x)}{x^{\ell_1}} \in \mathbb{F}_p[x]$ and the constant term of $f_1(x)$ is nonzero in $\mathbb{F}_p$. Taking $x^{\ell_1} f_1(x)$ to replace $f(x)$ in (18), then

$$x^{\ell_1} f_1(x) g(x) \equiv h(x) \pmod{x^k}. \tag{20}$$

Since $\ell_1 \leq k$, we infer that $x^{\ell_1}$ is a factor of $h(x)$, then

$$x^{\ell_1} f_1(x) g(x) \equiv x^{\ell_1} h_1(x) \pmod{x^{\ell_1} x^{k-\ell_1}}, \tag{21}$$

where $h_1(x) = \frac{h(x)}{x^{\ell_1}} \in \mathbb{F}_p[x]$. By using Lemma 1, we can eliminate the common factor $x^{\ell_1}$ on both sides of (21) and obtain

$$f_1(x) g(x) \equiv h_1(x) \pmod{x^{k-\ell_1}}. \tag{22}$$

As $\ell \leq k - \ell_1$, (22) also holds under modulo $x^\ell$, i.e.

$$f_1(x) g(x) \equiv h_1(x) \pmod{x^\ell}. \tag{23}$$

Since the constant term of $f_1(x)$ is nonzero, by using the conclusion of Lemma 2, there exists the inverse of $f_1(x)$ in $\mathbb{F}_p[x]/x^\ell$, then we have

$$g(x) = h_1(x) f_1(x)^{-1} = \frac{h(x)}{x^{\ell_1}} \left(\frac{f(x)}{x^{\ell_1}}\right)^{-1} \pmod{x^\ell}. \tag{24}$$

Therefore, considering in the polynomial ring $\mathbb{F}_p[x]/x^\ell$, there exists a unique solution $g(x)$ satisfying (18).

**The Proof of Correctness.** For $t \in \mathbb{N}^+, A \in \mathcal{A}_t$, then $|A| \geq 2$. We need to show that the $\ell$-bit secret $s$ can be correctly reconstructed by the shares of the participants in $A$.

Without loss of generality, we take two participants $P_i$ and $P_j$ from $A$ with $i < j \leq t$. Since $y_i$ and $y_j$ are the binary prefix codes of $i$ and $j$, $\ell_i$ and $\ell_j$ are the bit length of $i$ and $j$, thus we have $\ell_i \leq \ell_j$. Then, the $i$-th and $j$-th shares are as follows.

$$\begin{cases} Z_i^{(s)} = r_0 + s y_i \pmod{x^{\ell_i+\ell-1}}, \\ Z_j^{(s)} = r_0 + s y_j \pmod{x^{\ell_j+\ell-1}}. \end{cases} \tag{25}$$

By Lemma 3, subtracting the second equation from the first equation in (25), we can further get

$$(y_i - y_j)s \equiv Z_i^{(s)} - Z_j^{(s)} \pmod{x^{\ell_i+\ell-1}}. \tag{26}$$

As $c_i$ is not a prefix of $c_j$, we have

$$y_i - y_j \neq 0 \pmod{x^{\ell_i}}. \tag{27}$$

Since $L_{i,j}$ denotes the maximal extractable power of $(y_i - y_j)$ satisfying $x^{L_{i,j}} \mid (y_i - y_j)$, by (27), we have

$$L_{i,j} \leq \ell_i - 1. \tag{28}$$

Thus,

$$L_{i,j} + \ell \leq \ell_i + \ell - 1. \tag{29}$$

Using the conclusion of Lemma 4 and combining the bit length of $s$ is $\ell$, the congruence equation (26) has a unique solution in $\mathbb{F}_2[x]/x^\ell$, which can be calculated as

$$s = \frac{Z_i^{(s)} - Z_j^{(s)}}{x^{L_{i,j}}} \left(\frac{y_i - y_j}{x^{L_{i,j}}}\right)^{-1} \pmod{x^\ell}. \tag{30}$$

**The Proof of Secrecy.** For any $t \in \mathbb{N}^+, C \notin \mathcal{A}_t$, i.e. $|C| < 2$. We need to prove that the secret $s$ is unable to be recovered by the shares in $C$. Since the case of $|C| = 0$ is trivial, we only prove the case of $|C| = 1$ in the following.

Assume the only element in $C$ as $P_i$ with $i \leq t$. For any $s$, we have $Z_i^{(s)} = r_0 + sy_i$ in $\mathbb{F}_2[x]/x^{\ell_i+\ell-1}$. As $r_0$ is a random variable uniformly distributed in the additive group $\mathbb{F}_2[x]/x^{\ell_i+\ell-1}$, $Z_i^{(s)}$ is independent from $sy_i$, which makes $Z_i^{(s)}$ independent from $s$. Hence, $Z_i^{(s)}$ is uniformly random in $\mathbb{F}_2[x]/x^{\ell_i+\ell-1}$ for each selection of $s$.

Now, we will provide an example to show the processes of distributing shares and reconstructing the secret.

**Example.** Given a secret $s = 1001$, for the two participants $P_3$, $P_4$, let 101 and 11000 be the binary prefix codes of 3 and 4, respectively. According to $\ell + \ell_4 - 1 = 8$, the algorithm $\mathcal{E}$ randomly chooses an 8-bit binary string $r_0 = 10101001$. Then the share of $P_3$ is given by

$$\begin{aligned} Z_3^{(s)} =& r_0 + sy_3 \pmod{x^6} \\ =& (1 + x^2 + x^4) + (1 + x^3)(1 + x^2) \\ =& x^3 + x^4 + x^5 \pmod{x^6}, \end{aligned}$$

thus, the 3-th share $Z_3^{(s)}$ is 000111.

And the share of $P_4$ is given by

$$\begin{aligned} Z_4^{(s)} =& r_0 + sy_4 \pmod{x^8} \\ =& (1 + x^2 + x^4 + x^7) + (1 + x^3)(1 + x) \\ =& x + x^2 + x^3 + x^7 \pmod{x^8}, \end{aligned}$$

thus, the 4-th share $Z_4^{(s)}$ is 01110001.

Next, we take this example to show how to reconstruct the secret $s$. Let the bit length of $s$ be 4. Let 101 and 11000 be the prefix codes of 3 and 4, respectively. The shares of the two participants $P_3$ and $P_4$ are 000111 and 01110001, respectively. Then we have

$$\begin{cases} Z_3^{(s)} = x^3 + x^4 + x^5 = r_0 + s(1 + x^2) \pmod{x^6}, \\ Z_4^{(s)} = x + x^2 + x^3 + x^7 = r_0 + s(1 + x) \pmod{x^8}. \end{cases}$$

Since $\ell + \ell_3 - 1 = 6$, $y_3 - y_4 = x + x^2 = x(1+x)$ and the bit length of $s$ is 4, the algorithm $\mathcal{R}$ solves the following equation

$$s(y_3 - y_4) \equiv Z_3^{(s)} - Z_4^{(s)} \pmod{x^6}$$

with a unique solution, i.e.

$$\begin{aligned} s =& \frac{Z_3^{(s)} - Z_4^{(s)}}{x} \left(\frac{y_3 - y_4}{x}\right)^{-1} \pmod{x^4} \\ =& \frac{x + x^2 + x^4 + x^5 + x^7}{x} \left(\frac{x + x^2}{x}\right)^{-1} \pmod{x^4} \\ =& \frac{1 + x + x^3}{1 + x} = (1 + x + x^3)(1 + x)^{-1} \pmod{x^4} \\ \overset{(a)}{=}& (1 + x + x^3)(1 + x + x^2 + x^3) = 1 + x^3 \pmod{x^4}. \end{aligned}$$

where (a) holds since $(1 + x)(1 + x + x^2 + x^3) = 1$ in $\mathbb{F}_2[x]/x^4$. Therefore, the algorithm $\mathcal{R}$ outputs $s = 1001$, which is correct.

**Share Size.** We analyze the share size of the proposed scheme. For the $t$-th participant, from (1), the share $Z_t^{(s)}$ can be regarded as a polynomial of $x$ in $\mathbb{F}_2$ with the degree no more than $\ell_t + \ell - 2$, where $\ell_t$ is the length of binary prefix code for the positive integer $t$. Then, the size of the corresponding share is

$$B(Z_t^{(s)}) = \ell_t + \ell - 1. \tag{31}$$

From (31), we find that it may obtain different share sizes when choosing different binary prefix codes.

Next, we show the corresponding share size by using several binary prefix codes. We denote by $L(\cdot)$ the codeword length for encoding $t$ for $t \in \mathbb{N}^+$. Considering $\gamma$ code [11], a widely used integer universal code, the codeword length of $\gamma(t)$ is given by

$$L(\gamma(t)) = 2\lfloor \lg t \rfloor + 1.$$

Therefore, when using $\gamma$ code [11] as the binary prefix code, the size of the $t$-th share satisfies

$$B(Z_t^{(s)}) = 2\lfloor \lg t \rfloor + \ell. \tag{32}$$

Except for $\gamma$ code, we also consider another binary prefix code, $\delta$ code [11]. The codeword length of $\delta(t)$ is given by

$$L(\delta(t)) = \lfloor \lg t \rfloor + 2\lfloor \lg(\lfloor \lg t \rfloor + 1) \rfloor + 1.$$

Therefore, if using $\delta$ code as the binary prefix code, the share size of the $t$-th satisfies

$$B(Z_t^{(s)}) = \lfloor \lg t \rfloor + 2\lfloor \lg(\lfloor \lg t \rfloor + 1) \rfloor + \ell. \tag{33}$$

In all knowns evolving 2-threshold schemes, the best result of share size is $\lg t + (\ell + 1)\lg\lg t + 4\ell + 1$, which is mentioned in [8]. Compared with it, when $\ell = 1$, the result of (33) is approximately equal to the result of [8]. When $\ell \geq 2$, the result is smaller than the result of [8].

# 4 Evolving $k$-Threshold Secret Sharing Scheme over $\mathbb{F}_2[x]$

Based on similar techniques, we extend the prior scheme to the evolving $k$-threshold scheme in this section. We will give the construction of the evolving $k$-threshold scheme over $\mathbb{F}_2[x]$ for an $\ell$-bit secret $s$, where $k \geq 3$. The scheme allows the dealer to distribute the share to each participant such that only no less than $k$ participants can reconstruct $s$.

## 4.1 Proposed Scheme

Given a set of binary prefix codes for integers, the codeword of the integer $i$ is denoted as $c_i = (c_{i,0}, c_{i,1}, \cdots, c_{i,\ell_i-1})$, where $\ell_i$ represents the length of $c_i$ with $i \in \mathbb{N}^+$. The polynomial form of $c_i$ is defined as $y_i$. Given an $\ell$-bit secret $s$. For any $i \in \mathbb{N}^+$, the $i$-th share is defined as

$$Z_i^{(s)} = \sum_{j=0}^{k-2} r_j y_i^j + s y_i^{k-1} \pmod{x^{(\ell_i-1)(k-1)+\ell}}, \tag{34}$$

where $r_j$ is randomly chosen from $\mathbb{F}_2[[x]]$ for $0 \leq j \leq k-2$. However, we cannot choose an $r_j \in \mathbb{F}_2[[x]]$ in practice. Due to the operation modulo $x^{(\ell_i-1)(k-1)+\ell}$ in (34), the dealer only needs to choose a part of $r_j$ with degrees less than $(\ell_i - 1)(k-1) + \ell$.

Given any $k$ participants $P_{i_1}, P_{i_2}, \cdots, P_{i_k} \in \mathcal{P}$ with $i_1 < \cdots < i_k$, let $L_{i_u,i_v}$ denote the maximal extractable power of $y_{i_u} - y_{i_v}$ for any $u, v \in [k]$ with $u \neq v$. Let $L_{i_m} = (\ell_{i_m} - 1)(k-1) + \ell$ for $1 \leq m \leq k$, and $\alpha = \min_{m=1}^{k}\{L_{i_m} + \sum_{\substack{1\leq u<v\leq k \\ u,v\neq m}} L_{i_u,i_v}\}$. The algorithm $\mathcal{R}$ finds out that the following equation

$$s\Big(\prod_{1\leq u<v\leq k}(y_{i_u} - y_{i_v})\Big) \equiv \sum_{m=1}^{k} \prod_{\substack{1\leq u<v\leq k \\ u,v\neq m}} (y_{i_u} - y_{i_v}) Z_{i_m}^{(s)} \pmod{x^\alpha} \tag{35}$$

has a unique solution about $s$ in $\mathbb{F}_2[x]/x^\ell$ as

$$s = \frac{\sum_{m=1}^{k} \prod_{\substack{1\leq u<v\leq k \\ u,v\neq m}} (y_{i_u} - y_{i_v}) Z_{i_m}^{(s)}}{x^{\sum_{1\leq u<v\leq k} L_{i_u,i_v}}} \Big(\frac{\prod_{1\leq u<v\leq k}(y_{i_u} - y_{i_v})}{x^{\sum_{1\leq u<v\leq k} L_{i_u,i_v}}}\Big)^{-1} \pmod{x^\ell}. \tag{36}$$

Similarly, considering in $\mathbb{F}_2[x]/x^\ell$, the existence and uniqueness of $s$ will be provided in the proof of correctness in the next subsection.

When the dealer generates the $i$-th share via (34), where $i$ is sufficiently large, the dealer also needs to construct the corresponding random polynomials $\{r_j\}_{j=0}^{k-2}$. Assume that the dealer has already distributed shares to the first $i-1$ participants. Therefore, the dealer owns the corresponding $\{r_j\}_{j=0}^{k-2}$, which are used to construct the $(i-1)$-th share. For any $0 \leq j \leq k-2$, the degree of $r_j$ is

$(\ell_{i-1}-1)(k-1)+\ell-1$. To obtain the corresponding $\{r_j\}_{j=0}^{k-2}$ used to construct the $i$-th share, the dealer randomly chooses $(\ell_i-\ell_{i-1})(k-1)$ coefficients in $\mathbb{F}_2$ such that the degree of each $r_j$ is extended from $(\ell_{i-1}-1)(k-1)+\ell-1$ to $(\ell_i-1)(k-1)+\ell-1$. Hence, the corresponding $\{r_j\}_{j=0}^{k-2}$ are constructed.

### 4.2 Analysis of Share Size

Next, we discuss the corresponding share size. The share size in the proposed evolving $k$-threshold scheme is analyzed as follows.

For the $t$-th participant, from (34), the share $Z_t^{(s)}$ is a polynomial of $x$ in $\mathbb{F}_2$ and the degree is $(k-1)(\ell_t-1)+\ell-1$, where $\ell_t$ is the length of prefix code to encode positive integer $t$. Hence, the share size satisfies

$$B(Z_t^{(s)}) = (k-1)(\ell_t-1)+\ell. \tag{37}$$

If using $\gamma$ code as the prefix code, the corresponding share size satisfies

$$B(Z_t^{(s)}) = 2(k-1)\lfloor \lg t \rfloor + \ell. \tag{38}$$

However, when using $\delta$ code as the prefix code, then the corresponding share size satisfies

$$B(Z_t^{(s)}) = (k-1)\lfloor \lg t \rfloor + 2(k-1)\lfloor \lg(\lfloor \lg t \rfloor + 1) \rfloor + \ell. \tag{39}$$

We tabulate the share sizes of currently known evolving threshold secret sharing schemes. For the proposed scheme, we show the corresponding share size for using $\delta$ code as the prefix code. In Table 1, we represent the value of the lowest share size in bold for each case of $k$. When $k \geq 2$, the proposed schemes can achieve consistently lower share sizes than the scheme given in [8,12]. When $k=3$, the proposed scheme's share size is larger than the result of [10]. However, the result of [10] is optimized only for the case $k=3$.

### 4.3 Proofs of Correctness and Secrecy

The proofs of the correctness and secrecy of the proposed scheme are given as follows.

**The Proof of Correctness.** For any $t \in \mathbb{N}^+, A \in \mathcal{A}_t$, then $|A| \geq k$, we will prove that the secret $s$ can be correctly recovered by the shares of the participants in $A$. Since the cases of $|A| \geq k$ include the case of $|A| = k$, we only prove the case of $|A| = k$.

Denote the $k$ elements in $A$ as $P_{i_1}, P_{i_2}, \cdots, P_{i_k}$ with $i_1 < \cdots < i_k \leq t$. Since $c_{i_m}$ is the prefix code of $i_m$, $y_{i_m}$ is the polynomial form of $c_{i_m}$ and $\ell_{i_m}$ is the code length of $i_m$, thus $\ell_{i_m}$ is increasing on $m$, where $1 \leq m \leq k$. Recall that the corresponding shares are as follows.

$$\begin{cases} Z_{i_1}^{(s)} = \sum_{j=0}^{k-2} r_j y_{i_1}^j + s y_{i_1}^{k-1} & (\mathrm{mod}\ x^{(\ell_{i_1}-1)(k-1)+\ell}), \\ Z_{i_2}^{(s)} = \sum_{j=0}^{k-2} r_j y_{i_2}^j + s y_{i_2}^{k-1} & (\mathrm{mod}\ x^{(\ell_{i_2}-1)(k-1)+\ell}), \\ \cdots & \\ Z_{i_k}^{(s)} = \sum_{j=0}^{k-2} r_j y_{i_k}^j + s y_{i_k}^{k-1} & (\mathrm{mod}\ x^{(\ell_{i_k}-1)(k-1)+\ell}). \end{cases} \tag{40}$$

In order to calculate $s$, we need to eliminate these elements $r_0, \cdots, r_{k-2}$. Considering each congruence equation in (40), there exists $h_m(x) \in \mathbb{F}_2[x]$ such that the equation

$$\sum_{j=0}^{k-2} r_j y_{i_m}^j + s y_{i_m}^{k-1} - Z_{i_m}^{(s)} = h_m(x) x^{(\ell_{i_m}-1)(k-1)+\ell} \tag{41}$$

holds.
Considering (41), we multiply both sides of the equation by $\prod_{\substack{1\leq u<v\leq k \\ u,v\neq m}} (y_{i_u} - y_{i_v})$. For the convenience of writing, let $H_{i_m}(x) = \prod_{\substack{1\leq u<v\leq k \\ u,v\neq m}} (y_{i_u} - y_{i_v})$, and $L_{i_m} = (\ell_{i_m} - 1)(k-1) + \ell$ for $1 \leq m \leq k$ , then the equation (41) becomes

$$H_{i_m}(x)\Big(\sum_{j=0}^{k-2} r_j y_{i_m}^j + s y_{i_m}^{k-1} - Z_{i_m}^{(s)}\Big) = H_{i_m} h_m(x) x^{L_{i_m}}. \tag{42}$$

Performing the above same steps for each congruent equation in (40), then we can obtain

$$\begin{cases} H_{i_1}(x)\Big(\sum_{j=0}^{k-2} r_j y_{i_1}^j + s y_{i_1}^{k-1} - Z_{i_1}^{(s)}\Big) = H_{i_1} h_1(x) x^{L_{i_1}}, \\ H_{i_2}(x)\Big(\sum_{j=0}^{k-2} r_j y_{i_2}^j + s y_{i_2}^{k-1} - Z_{i_2}^{(s)}\Big) = H_{i_2} h_2(x) x^{L_{i_2}}, \\ \cdots \\ H_{i_k}(x)\Big(\sum_{j=0}^{k-2} r_j y_{i_k}^j + s y_{i_k}^{k-1} - Z_{i_k}^{(s)}\Big) = H_{i_k} h_k(x) x^{L_{i_k}}, \end{cases} \tag{43}$$

Summing all equations in (43), we have

$$\begin{aligned} &\sum_{m=1}^{k} H_{i_m}(x) y_{i_m}^{k-1} s + \sum_{j=0}^{k-2} \sum_{m=1}^{k} H_{i_m}(x) y_{i_m}^j r_j \\ &= \sum_{m=1}^{k} H_{i_m}(x) Z_{i_m}^{(s)} + \sum_{m=1}^{k} H_{i_m}(x) h_m(x) x^{L_{i_m}}. \end{aligned} \tag{44}$$

Consider the coefficient of $s$ as $\sum_{m=1}^{k} H_{i_m}(x) y_{i_m}^{k-1} = \prod_{\substack{1\le u<v\le k \\ u,v\ne m}} (y_{i_u} - y_{i_v}) y_{i_m}^{k-1}$ in $\mathbb{F}_2[x]$, which is equal to the following Vandermonde determinant, i.e.

$$\sum_{m=1}^{k} H_{i_m}(x) y_{i_m}^{k-1} \overset{(b)}{=} \begin{vmatrix} 1 & 1 & \cdots & 1 \\ y_{i_1} & y_{i_2} & \cdots & y_{i_k} \\ \vdots & \vdots & \cdots & \vdots \\ y_{i_1}^{k-1} & y_{i_2}^{k-1} & \cdots & y_{i_k}^{k-1} \end{vmatrix} = \prod_{1\le u<v\le k} (y_{i_u} - y_{i_v}), \tag{45}$$

where (b) holds since $\sum_{m=1}^{k} H_{i_m}(x) y_{i_m}^{k-1}$ is equal to the result of expanding the above determinant based on the last row.

For arbitrary $j$ with $0 \le j \le k-2$, the coefficient of $r_j$ is $\sum_{m=1}^{k} H_{i_m}(x) y_{i_m}^{j}$, then we have

$$\sum_{m=1}^{k} H_{i_m}(x) y_{i_m}^{j} \overset{(c)}{=} \begin{vmatrix} 1 & 1 & \cdots & 1 \\ y_{i_1} & y_{i_2} & \cdots & y_{i_k} \\ \vdots & \vdots & \cdots & \vdots \\ y_{i_1}^{k-2} & y_{i_2}^{k-2} & \cdots & y_{i_k}^{k-2} \\ y_{i_1}^{j} & y_{i_2}^{j} & \cdots & y_{i_k}^{j} \end{vmatrix} = 0, \tag{46}$$

where (c) holds since $\sum_{m=1}^{k} H_{i_m}(x) y_{i_m}^{j}$ is equal to the result of expanding the above determinant based on the last row.

Taking the results of (45) and (46) into (44), we can further obtain

$$\prod_{1\le u<v\le k} (y_{i_u} - y_{i_v}) s = \sum_{m=1}^{k} H_{i_m}(x) Z_{i_m}^{(s)} + \sum_{m=1}^{k} H_{i_m}(x) h_m(x) x^{L_{i_m}}. \tag{47}$$

Since $L_{i_u,i_v}$ denotes the maximal extractable power of $y_{i_u} - y_{i_v}$ for any $u, v \in [k]$ with $u \ne v$, and $L_{i_m} = (\ell_{i_m} - 1)(k-1) + \ell$ for $1 \le m \le k$, we can infer that each polynomial

$$H_{i_m}(x) h_m(x) x^{L_{i_m}} = \prod_{\substack{1\le u<v\le k \\ u,v\ne m}} (y_{i_u} - y_{i_v}) x^{L_{i_m}} h_m(x)$$

has the factor $x^{\alpha}$ for any $m$, where $\alpha = \min_{1\le m\le k}\{L_{i_m} + \sum_{\substack{1\le u<v\le k \\ u,v\ne m}} L_{i_u,i_v}\}$.

Substituting $H_{i_m}(x)$ by $\prod_{\substack{1\le u<v\le k \\ u,v\ne m}} (y_{i_u} - y_{i_v})$ in (47) and simplying the equation, then we obtain

$$s\Big(\prod_{1\le u<v\le k} (y_{i_u} - y_{i_v})\Big) \equiv \sum_{m=1}^{k} \prod_{\substack{1\le u<v\le k \\ u,v\ne m}} (y_{i_u} - y_{i_v}) Z_{i_m}^{(s)} \pmod{x^{\alpha}}. \tag{48}$$

We note that the polynomial $\prod_{1\le u<v\le k} (y_{i_u} - y_{i_v})$ has the maximal extractable power $\sum_{1\le u<v\le k} L_{i_u,i_v}$. If $\sum_{1\le u<v\le k} L_{i_u,i_v} + \ell \le \alpha$, we can use the conclusion of Lemma 4 to recover $s$. Next, our goal is to prove $\sum_{1\le u<v\le k} L_{i_u,i_v} + \ell \le \alpha$.

Without loss of generality, we assume $\alpha = \min_{1\le m\le k}\{L_{i_m} + \sum_{\substack{1\le u<v\le k\\ u,v\ne m}} L_{i_u,i_v}\}$
$= L_{i_q} + \sum_{\substack{1\le u<v\le k\\ u,v\ne q}} L_{i_u,i_v}$ for some $q$. Since $L_{i_q} = (\ell_{i_q}-1)(k-1)+\ell$, then we have

$$\begin{aligned}
&\alpha - \sum_{1\le u<v\le k} L_{i_u,i_v} - \ell\\
=&L_{i_q} + \sum_{\substack{1\le u<v\le k\\ u,v\ne q}} L_{i_u,i_v} - \sum_{1\le u<v\le k} L_{i_u,i_v} - \ell\\
=&(\ell_{i_q}-1)(k-1) - \sum_{\substack{1\le u\le k\\ u\ne q}} L_{i_u,i_q}\\
=&\sum_{\substack{1\le u\le k\\ u\ne q}} (\ell_{i_q} - 1 - L_{i_u,i_q}).
\end{aligned} \tag{49}$$

For any $u \ne q$ with $1 \le u \le k$, since $y_{i_u} - y_{i_q} \ne 0$, $L_{i_u,i_q}$ is the maximal extractable power of $y_{i_u} - y_{i_q}$, and $\ell_{i_q}$ is the prefix codeword length of $y_{i_q}$, then we have $L_{i_u,i_q} \le \ell_{i_q} - 1$. Replacing the result in (49), we get

$$\sum_{1\le u<v\le k} L_{i_u,i_v} + \ell \le \alpha. \tag{50}$$

By using the conclusion of Lemma 4, we can recover the unique solution about $s$ of (48) in $\mathbb{F}_2[x]/x^\ell$ as

$$s = \frac{\sum_{m=1}^{k}\prod_{\substack{1\le u<v\le k\\ u,v\ne m}}(y_{i_u} - y_{i_v})Z_{i_m}^{(s)}}{x^{\sum_{1\le u<v\le k} L_{i_u,i_v}}}\left(\frac{\prod_{1\le u<v\le k}(y_{i_u} - y_{i_v})}{x^{\sum_{1\le u<v\le k} L_{i_u,i_v}}}\right)^{-1} \pmod{x^\ell}. \tag{51}$$

Therefore, the correctness of the proposed scheme has been proved completely.

In the second part of this subsection, we demonstrate the security of this scheme. Before proving the security, we first present a lemma that provides a useful conclusion for proving the security.

**Lemma 5.** *Let $i_1, i_2, \cdots, i_{k-1} \in \mathbb{N}^+$ satisfy $i_1 < i_2 < \cdots < i_{k-1}$, $c_{i_m}$ represent the p-ary codeword of encoding the integer $i_m$ with a p-ary prefix code and $\ell_{i_m}$ denote the codeword length of $c_{i_m}$, where $1 \le m \le k-1$. Let $y_{i_m}$ represent the corresponding polynomial form of $c_{i_m}$. For $\ell \in \mathbb{N}^+$, let $s_0, s_1 \in \mathbb{F}_p[x]/x^\ell$ be two different polynomials. Given $k-1$ polynomials $z_{i_m} \in \mathbb{F}_p[x]/x^{L_{i_m}}$ for $1 \le m \le k-1$, where $L_{i_m} = (\ell_{i_m}-1)(k-1)+\ell$, let $(r_{0,0}, r_{0,1}, \cdots, r_{0,k-2})$ and $(r_{1,0}, r_{1,1}, \cdots, r_{1,k-2})$ respectively be the unknowns of the following two congruence equations*

$$\begin{cases}
z_{i_1} = \sum_{j=0}^{k-2} r_{0,j}y_{i_1}^j + s_0 y_{i_1}^{k-1} \pmod{x^{L_{i_1}}},\\
z_{i_2} = \sum_{j=0}^{k-2} r_{0,j}y_{i_2}^j + s_0 y_{i_2}^{k-1} \pmod{x^{L_{i_2}}},\\
\cdots\\
z_{i_{k-1}} = \sum_{j=0}^{k-2} r_{0,j}y_{i_{k-1}}^j + s_0 y_{i_{k-1}}^{k-1} \pmod{x^{L_{i_{k-1}}}},
\end{cases} \tag{52}$$

*and*

$$\begin{cases} z_{i_1} = \sum_{j=0}^{k-2} r_{1,j} y_{i_1}^j + s_1 y_{i_1}^{k-1} \pmod{x^{L_{i_1}}}, \\ z_{i_2} = \sum_{j=0}^{k-2} r_{1,j} y_{i_2}^j + s_1 y_{i_2}^{k-1} \pmod{x^{L_{i_2}}}, \\ \cdots \\ z_{i_{k-1}} = \sum_{j=0}^{k-2} r_{1,j} y_{i_{k-1}}^j + s_1 y_{i_{k-1}}^{k-1} \pmod{x^{L_{i_{k-1}}}}, \end{cases} \tag{53}$$

*where* $r_{h,j} \in \mathbb{F}_p[x]/x^{L_{i_{k-1}}}$ *for* $0 \leq h \leq 1$, $0 \leq j \leq k-2$.

*Then the equations* (52) *and* (53) *have the same number of solutions.*

*Proof.* We prove the conclusion by contradiction. Without loss of generality, we assume that the congruence equation (52) has $N_0$ solutions and the congruence equation (53) has $N_1$ solutions with $N_0 > N_1$. Let $\mathbb{R}_0$ and $\mathbb{R}_1$ respectively be the solution sets of (52) and (53). According to the definition of congruence equations in (52), there exists $w_{0,j}$ satisfying following equation

$$\begin{cases} z_{i_1} = \sum_{j=0}^{k-2} r_{0,j} y_{i_1}^j + s_0 y_{i_1}^{k-1} + w_{0,1} x^{L_{i_1}}, \\ z_{i_2} = \sum_{j=0}^{k-2} r_{0,j} y_{i_2}^j + s_0 y_{i_2}^{k-1} + w_{0,2} x^{L_{i_2}}, \\ \cdots \\ z_{i_{k-1}} = \sum_{j=0}^{k-2} r_{0,j} y_{i_{k-1}}^j + s_0 y_{i_{k-1}}^{k-1} + w_{0,k-1} x^{L_{i_{k-1}}}, \end{cases} \tag{54}$$

where $w_{0,m} \in \mathbb{F}_p[x]/x^{(\ell_{i_{k-1}}-1)(2k-3)+\ell-L_{i_m}}$ for $1 \leq m \leq k-1$.

Correspondingly, there exists $w_{1,m} \in \mathbb{F}_p[x]/x^{(\ell_{i_{k-1}}-1)(2k-3)+\ell-L_{i_m}}$ such that congruence equation (53) satisfys the following form

$$\begin{cases} z_{i_1} = \sum_{j=0}^{k-2} r_{1,j} y_{i_1}^j + s_1 y_{i_1}^{k-1} + w_{1,1} x^{L_{i_1}}, \\ z_{i_2} = \sum_{j=0}^{k-2} r_{1,j} y_{i_2}^j + s_1 y_{i_2}^{k-1} + w_{1,2} x^{L_{i_2}}, \\ \cdots \\ z_{i_{k-1}} = \sum_{j=0}^{k-2} r_{1,j} y_{i_{k-1}}^j + s_1 y_{i_{k-1}}^{k-1} + w_{1,k-1} x^{L_{i_{k-1}}}. \end{cases} \tag{55}$$

It finds that the number of solutions $(r_{0,0}, r_{0,1}, \cdots, r_{0,k-2}, w_{0,1}, w_{0,2}, \cdots, w_{0,k-1})$ of (54) and the number of solutions $(r_{0,0}, r_{0,1}, \cdots, r_{0,k-2})$ of (52) are same, the numbers of solutions of (55) and (53) are same. Thus, we can prove that (52)) and (53) have the same number of solutions, to show that the conclusion holds. Next, we analyze the solution cases of (54) and (55). According to the assumptions, (52) has solutions. As $\mathbb{R}_0$ is the solution set of (52), we choose one of solutions in $\mathbb{R}_0$ and denote it as $R_0^1 = (r_{0,0}^1, r_{0,1}^1, \cdots, r_{0,k-2}^1)$, then $R_{0,+}^1 = (r_{0,0}^1, r_{0,1}^1, \cdots, r_{0,k-2}^1, w_{0,1}, w_{0,2}, \cdots, w_{0,k-1})$ is the solution of (54), where $w_{0,m} = \frac{\sum_{j=0}^{k-2} r_{0,j}^1 y_{i_m}^j + s_0 y_{i_m}^{k-1} - z_{i_m}}{x^{L_{i_m}}}$ for $1 \leq m \leq k-1$.

Consider the quotient ring $\mathbb{F}_p[x]/x^{(\ell_{i_{k-1}}-1)(2k-3)+\ell}$. Subtracting (55) from (54), then we have

$$\begin{cases} (s_0 - s_1) y_{i_1}^{k-1} = \sum_{j=0}^{k-2} r_j y_{i_1}^j + w_1 x^{L_{i_1}}, \\ (s_0 - s_1) y_{i_2}^{k-1} = \sum_{j=0}^{k-2} r_j y_{i_2}^j + w_2 x^{L_{i_2}}, \\ \cdots \\ (s_0 - s_1) y_{i_{k-1}}^{k-1} = \sum_{j=0}^{k-2} r_j y_{i_{k-1}}^j + w_{k-1} x^{L_{i_{k-1}}}, \end{cases} \tag{56}$$

where $r_j = r_{1,j} - r_{0,j}$ for $0 \leq j \leq k-2$ and $w_m = w_{1,m} - w_{0,m}$ for $1 \leq m \leq k-1$.

Suppose that there exists a solution $R = (r_0, \cdots, r_{k-2}, w_1, \cdots, w_{k-1})$ of (56). Then combining $R$ with the solution $R^1_{0,+}$ of (54), we assert that $R^1_{0,+} + R$ is the solution of (55). Let $R' = (r_0, \cdots, r_{k-2})$ be the part of $R$, combining that $R^1_0 = (r^1_{0,0}, r^1_{0,1}, \cdots, r^1_{0,k-2})$ is the solution of (52), then $R^1_0 + R' = (r^1_{0,0} + r_0, r^1_{0,1} + r_1, \cdots, r^1_{0,k-2} + r_{k-2})$ is a solution of (53). When $R^1_0$ is taken across the whole solution set $\mathbb{R}_0$, (53) has at least $N_0$ different solutions, which contradicts that (53) has $N_1$ solutions. Therefore, (52) and (53) have the same number of solutions. Next, our goal is to show that (56) has solutions.

We first consider the following equations

$$\begin{cases} (s_0 - s_1) y_{i_1}^{k-1} = \sum_{j=0}^{k-2} r_j y_{i_1}^j, \\ (s_0 - s_1) y_{i_2}^{k-1} = \sum_{j=0}^{k-2} r_j y_{i_2}^j, \\ \cdots \\ (s_0 - s_1) y_{i_{k-1}}^{k-1} = \sum_{j=0}^{k-2} r_j y_{i_{k-1}}^j. \end{cases} \tag{57}$$

Let $r = (r_0, r_1, \cdots, r_{k-2})$ be unknowns. Call that a fact, for a monic polynomial $f(y) = y^{k-1} + \sum_{i=1}^{k-1} a_i y^{k-1-i}$ with known $k-1$ roots $(y_1, y_2, \cdots, y_{k-1})$, then the $k-1$ coefficients $(a_1, a_2, \cdots, a_{k-1})$ are uniquely determined. By the formulas of the relation between roots and coefficients, we can calculate $a_i = (-1)^i \sigma_i(y_1, y_2, \cdots, y_{k-1}) = \sum_{\substack{C \subseteq [k-1] \\ |C|=i}} \prod_{g \in C} y_g$. Thus, we can obtain a solution about $r$ in (57), i.e.

$$\begin{aligned} r_j =& (-1)^{k-2-j}(s_0 - s_1)\sigma_{k-1-j}(y_{i_1}, y_{i_2}, \cdots, y_{i_{k-1}}) \\ =& (-1)^{k-2-j}(s_0 - s_1) \sum_{\substack{C \subseteq [k-1] \\ |C|=k-1-j}} \prod_{g \in C} y_{i_g} \end{aligned} \tag{58}$$

for $0 \leq j \leq k-2$.

From above, we can construct a solution of (56) as

$$R = (\{r_j = (-1)^{k-2-j}(s_0 - s_1) \sum_{\substack{C \subseteq [k-1] \\ |C|=k-1-j}} \prod_{g \in C} y_{i_g}\}_{j=0}^{k-2}, \{w_m = 0\}_{m=1}^{k-1}). \tag{59}$$

Thus, the proof is completed.

**The Proof of Secrecy.** For any $t \in \mathbb{N}^+, C \notin \mathcal{A}_t$, we prove that the secret $s$ is unable to be recovered by the shares of participants in $C$. $C$ is unqualified, then $|C| < k$. Since the cases of $|C| < k$ include the case of $|C| = k-1$, we only prove the case of $|C| = k-1$. Other cases can be proved accordingly.

Denote the elements in $C$ as $P_{i_1}, \cdots, P_{i_{k-1}}$ with $i_1 < \cdots < i_{k-1} \leq t$. We choose any two distinct secrets $s_0, s_1$, let $Z^{(s_0)}_{i_m}$ and $Z^{(s_1)}_{i_m}$ be corresponding the $i_m$-th shares for $1 \leq m \leq k-1$. We need to prove that for any $z_{i_m} \in \mathbb{F}_2[x]/x^{L_{i_m}}$, where $L_{i_m} = (\ell_{i_m} - 1)(k-1) + \ell$ for $1 \le m \le k-1$, the following two probabilities are equal, i.e.

$$P(\{Z_{i_m}^{(s_0)} = z_{i_m}\}_{m=1}^{k-1}) = P(\{Z_{i_m}^{(s_1)} = z_{i_m}\}_{m=1}^{k-1}). \tag{60}$$

We first analyze the value of $P(\{Z_{i_m}^{(s_0)} = z_{i_m}\}_{m=1}^{k-1})$. Consider the following congruence equations

$$\begin{cases} z_{i_1} = \sum_{j=0}^{k-2} r_{0,j} y_{i_1}^j + s_0 y_{i_1}^{k-1} \pmod{x^{L_{i_1}}}, \\ z_{i_2} = \sum_{j=0}^{k-2} r_{0,j} y_{i_2}^j + s_0 y_{i_2}^{k-1} \pmod{x^{L_{i_2}}}, \\ \qquad \cdots \\ z_{i_{k-1}} = \sum_{j=0}^{k-2} r_{0,j} y_{i_{k-1}}^j + s_0 y_{i_{k-1}}^{k-1} \pmod{x^{L_{i_{k-1}}}}. \end{cases} \tag{61}$$

Though $r_{0,j} \in \mathbb{F}_2[[x]]$, only the part with degree less than $L_{i_{k-1}}$ participates in the above calculation. Hence, we only need to consider the part of $r_{0,j}$ modulo $x^{L_{i_{k-1}}}$. Therefore, the whole space of the solution vector $(r_{0,0}, r_{0,1}, \cdots, r_{0,k-2})$ can be regarded as $\{\mathbb{F}_2[x]/x^{L_{i_{k-1}}}\}^{k-1}$. The value of $P(\{Z_{i_m}^{(s_0)} = z_{i_m}\}_{m=1}^{k-1})$ is equal to the ratio of the number of solution $(r_{0,0}, r_{0,1}, \cdots, r_{0,k-2})$ of (61) in the whole space $\{\mathbb{F}_2[x]/x^{L_{i_{k-1}}}\}^{k-1}$.

By similar analysis, the value of $P(\{Z_{i_m}^{(s_1)} = z_{i_m}\}_{m=1}^{k-1})$ is equal to the ratio of the number of solution of (62) in the whole space $\{\mathbb{F}_2[x]/x^{L_{i_{k-1}}}\}^{k-1}$.

$$\begin{cases} z_{i_1} = \sum_{j=0}^{k-2} r_{1,j} y_{i_1}^j + s_1 y_{i_1}^{k-1} \pmod{x^{L_{i_1}}}, \\ z_{i_2} = \sum_{j=0}^{k-2} r_{1,j} y_{i_2}^j + s_1 y_{i_2}^{k-1} \pmod{x^{L_{i_2}}}, \\ \qquad \cdots \\ z_{i_{k-1}} = \sum_{j=0}^{k-2} r_{1,j} y_{i_{k-1}}^j + s_1 y_{i_{k-1}}^{k-1} \pmod{x^{L_{i_{k-1}}}}. \end{cases} \tag{62}$$

By Lemma 5, the numbers of solutions of the congruence equations (61) and (62) are same, which implies $P(\{Z_{i_m}^{(s_0)} = z_{i_m}\}_{m=1}^{k-1}) = P(\{Z_{i_m}^{(s_1)} = z_{i_m}\}_{m=1}^{k-1})$. Then, the security of the proposed scheme is completely proved.

## 5 Construction of Evolving $k$-Threshold Secret Sharing Scheme over A Polynomial Ring $\mathbb{F}_p[x]$

As described in the prior sections, for an $\ell$-bit binary sequence $s$, based on binary prefix codes, we have proposed the constructions of evolving $k$-threshold secret sharing scheme over $\mathbb{F}_2[x]$, where $k \ge 2$. When consider the secret $s \in \{0, 1, \cdots, p-1\}^\ell$ for any prime $p \in \mathbb{N}^+$, based on $p$-ary prefix codes, we extend the proposed evolving $k$-threshold secret sharing scheme to $\mathbb{F}_p[x]$.

### 5.1 Proposed Scheme

Given a set of $p$-ary prefix codes for positive integers, the codeword of the integer $i$ is denoted as $c_i = (c_{i,0}, c_{i,1}, \cdots, c_{i,\ell_i - 1})$, where $c_{i,j} \in \mathbb{F}_p$ for $0 \le j \le \ell_i - 1$ and

$\ell_i$ denotes the codeword length of $c_i$. The polynomial form of $c_i$ is defined as $y_i = \sum_{j=0}^{j=\ell_i-1} c_{i,j}x^j \in \mathbb{F}_p[x]$. Given an $\ell$ length $p$-ary sequence $s = (s_0, s_1, \cdots, s_{\ell-1})$, the polynomial form of $s$ is defined as $\sum_{j=0}^{\ell-1} s_j x^j \in \mathbb{F}_p[x]$ and the degree is less than $\ell$. For any $i \in \mathbb{N}^+$, then the $i$-th share is defined as

$$Z_i^{(s)} = \sum_{j=0}^{k-2} r_j {y_i}^j + s{y_i}^{k-1} \pmod{x^{(\ell_i-1)(k-1)+\ell}}, \tag{63}$$

where $r_j$ is randomly chosen from $\mathbb{F}_p[[x]]$ for $0 \le j \le k-2$.

Given any $k$ participants $P_{i_1}, P_{i_2}, \cdots, P_{i_k} \in \mathcal{P}$ with $i_1 < \cdots < i_k$, let $L_{i_u,i_v}$ denote the maximal extractable power of $y_{i_u} - y_{i_v}$ satisfying $x^{L_{i_u,i_v}} \mid (y_{i_u} - y_{i_v})$, for any $u, v \in [k]$ with $u \neq v$. Let $L_{i_m} = (\ell_{i_m} - 1)(k-1) + \ell$ for $1 \le m \le k$ and $\alpha = \min_{1\le m\le k}\{L_{i_m} + \sum_{\substack{1\le u<v\le k \\ u,v\neq m}} L_{i_u,i_v}\}$. The algorithm $\mathcal{R}$ finds out that the following equation

$$s\Big(\prod_{1\le u<v\le k} (y_{i_u} - y_{i_v})\Big) \equiv \sum_{m=1}^{k} (-1)^{m-1} \prod_{\substack{1\le u<v\le k \\ u,v\neq m}} (y_{i_u} - y_{i_v}) Z_{i_m}^{(s)} \pmod{x^\alpha} \tag{64}$$

has a unique solution about $s$ in $\mathbb{F}_p[x]/x^\ell$ as

$$s = \frac{\sum_{m=1}^{k} (-1)^{m-1} \prod_{\substack{1\le u<v\le k \\ u,v\neq m}} (y_{i_u} - y_{i_v}) Z_{i_m}^{(s)}}{x^{\sum_{1\le u<v\le k} L_{i_u,i_v}}} \times \Big(\frac{\prod_{1\le u<v\le k}(y_{i_u} - y_{i_v})}{x^{\sum_{1\le u<v\le k} L_{i_u,i_v}}}\Big)^{-1} \pmod{x^\ell}. \tag{65}$$

The existence and uniqueness of $s$ will be provided in the proof of correctness in next subsection.

Now, we will provide an example to show the processes of distributing shares and reconstructing the secret.

**Example.** In this example, we choose $k = 3$, $p = 3$ the secret $s = 2101$ with $\ell = 4$. For the three participants $P_2$, $P_5$ and $P_8$, let 01, 102 and 112 be the prefix codes of 2, 5 and 8, respectively. As $\ell + (k-1)(\ell_8 - 1) = 8$, the algorithm $\mathcal{E}$ randomly chooses two 8-bit binary strings $r_0 = 01201200$ and $r_1 = 20100010$, then the share of $P_2$ is given by

$$\begin{aligned} Z_2^{(s)} &= r_0 + r_1 y_2 + s{y_2}^2 \\ &= (x + 2x^2 + x^4 + 2x^5) + (2 + x^2)x + (2 + x + x^3)x^2 \\ &= x^2 + 2x^3 + x^4 \pmod{x^6}, \end{aligned}$$

thus, the share $Z_2^{(s)}$ is 001210.

The share of $P_5$ is calculated by

$$\begin{aligned}Z_5^{(s)} =&r_0 + r_1 y_5 + s {y_5}^2\\ =&(x + 2x^2 + x^4 + 2x^5) + (2 + x^2 + x^6)(1 + 2x^2) + (2 + x + x^3)(1 + 2x^2)^2\\ =&1 + 2x + 2x^3 + 2x^4 + x^5 + x^6 + x^7 \pmod{x^8},\end{aligned}$$

thus, the share $Z_5^{(s)}$ is 12022111.

And the share of $P_8$ is given by

$$\begin{aligned}Z_8^{(s)} =&r_0 + r_1 y_8 + s {y_8}^2\\ =&(x + 2x^2 + x^4 + 2x^5) + (2 + x^2 + x^6)(1 + x + 2x^2)\\ &+ (2 + x + x^3)(1 + x + 2x^2)^2\\ =&1 + 2x + x^2 + 2x^4 + 2x^5 + 2x^6 + 2x^7 \pmod{x^8},\end{aligned}$$

thus, the share $Z_8^{(s)}$ is 12102222.

Let 01, 102 and 112 be the prefix codes of 2, 5 and 8, respectively. Let 001210, 12022111 and 12102222 respectively be the shares of the three participants $P_2$, $P_5$, $P_8$. Then we have

$$\begin{cases} Z_{P_2}^{(s)} = x^2 + 2x^3 + x^4 \pmod{x^6},\\ Z_{P_5}^{(s)} = 1 + 2x + 2x^3 + 2x^4 + x^5 + x^6 + x^7 \pmod{x^8},\\ Z_{P_8}^{(s)} = 1 + 2x + x^2 + 2x^4 + 2x^5 + 2x^6 + 2x^7 \pmod{x^8}.\end{cases}$$

As $(y_2 - y_5)(y_2 - y_8)(y_5 - y_8) = x(2 + x + 2x^2 + 2x^3 + 2x^4)$ and the bit length of the secret $s$ is 4, the algorithm $\mathcal{R}$ recovers the secret $s$ as

$$\begin{aligned}s =&\frac{\sum_{m=1}^{3}(-1)^{m-1}\prod_{\substack{1\le u<v\le 3\\ u,v\neq m}}(y_{i_u} - y_{i_v})Z_{i_m}^{(s)}}{x^{\sum_{1\le u<v\le 3} L_{i_u,i_v}}}\left(\frac{\prod_{1\le u<v\le 3}(y_{i_u} - y_{i_v})}{x^{\sum_{1\le u<v\le 3} L_{i_u,i_v}}}\right)^{-1} \pmod{x^4}\\ =&\frac{Z_2^{(s)}(y_5 - y_8) - Z_5^{(s)}(y_2 - y_8) + Z_8^{(s)}(y_2 - y_5)}{x^{\sum_{1\le u<v\le 3} L_{i_u,i_v}}}\left(\frac{(y_2 - y_5)(y_2 - y_8)(y_5 - y_8)}{x^{\sum_{1\le u<v\le 3} L_{i_u,i_v}}}\right)^{-1}\\ =&\frac{x(1 + x + 2x^2 + 2x^3 + x^4 + x^5 + 2x^6 + x^8)}{x}\left(\frac{x(2 + x + 2x^2 + 2x^3 + 2x^4)}{x}\right)^{-1}\\ =&(1 + x + 2x^2 + 2x^3)(2 + x + 2x^2 + 2x^3)^{-1} \pmod{x^4}\\ =&(1 + x + 2x^2 + 2x^3)(2 + 2x + 2x^3) \pmod{x^4}\\ =&2 + x + x^3 \pmod{x^4},\end{aligned}$$

thus, the secret is 2101.

## 5.2 Proofs of Correctness and Secrecy

We will prove the correctness and secrecy of the proposed scheme in this subsection.

**The Proof of Correctness.** For any $t \in \mathbb{N}^+, A \in \mathcal{A}_t$, we will prove that the secret $s$ can be correctly recovered by the shares of the participants in $A$. Similarly, we only need to consider the case of $|A| = k$ when $|A| \geq k$.

Using the similar proof method proposed in Subsect. 4.3, we make slight modifications to the proof. Denote the $k$ elements in $A$ as $P_{i_1}, P_{i_2}, \cdots, P_{i_k}$ with $i_1 < \cdots < i_k \leq t$, the corresponding shares are as follows.

$$\begin{cases} Z_{i_1}^{(s)} = \sum_{j=0}^{k-2} r_j y_{i_1}^j + s y_{i_1}^{k-1} \pmod{x^{(\ell_{i_1}-1)(k-1)+\ell}}, \\ Z_{i_2}^{(s)} = \sum_{j=0}^{k-2} r_j y_{i_2}^j + s y_{i_2}^{k-1} \pmod{x^{(\ell_{i_2}-1)(k-1)+\ell}}, \\ \cdots \\ Z_{i_k}^{(s)} = \sum_{j=0}^{k-2} r_j y_{i_k}^j + s y_{i_k}^{k-1} \pmod{x^{(\ell_{i_k}-1)(k-1)+\ell}}. \end{cases} \tag{66}$$

Considering the congruence equations in (66), there exists $h_m(x) \in \mathbb{F}_p[x]$ satisfying the equation

$$\sum_{j=0}^{k-2} r_j y_{i_m}^j + s y_{i_m}^{k-1} - Z_{i_m}^{(s)} = h_m(x) x^{(\ell_{i_m}-1)(k-1)+\ell}. \tag{67}$$

Then, we multiply both sides of the equation (67) by $H_{i_m}(x)$, where $H_{i_m}(x) = (-1)^{m-1} \prod_{\substack{1 \leq u < v \leq k \\ u,v \neq m}} (y_{i_u} - y_{i_v})$. Let $L_{i_m} = (\ell_{i_m} - 1)(k-1) + \ell$ for $1 \leq m \leq k$. Performing the above steps for each congruent equation in (66), then, we have

$$\begin{cases} H_{i_1}(x)\Big(\sum_{j=0}^{k-2} r_j y_{i_1}^j + s y_{i_1}^{k-1} - Z_{i_1}^{(s)}\Big) = H_{i_1} h_1(x) x^{L_{i_1}}, \\ H_{i_2}(x)\Big(\sum_{j=0}^{k-2} r_j y_{i_2}^j + s y_{i_2}^{k-1} - Z_{i_2}^{(s)}\Big) = H_{i_2} h_2(x) x^{L_{i_2}}, \\ \cdots \\ H_{i_k}(x)\Big(\sum_{j=0}^{k-2} r_j y_{i_k}^j + s y_{i_k}^{k-1} - Z_{i_k}^{(s)}\Big) = H_{i_k} h_k(x)(x) x^{L_{i_k}}, \end{cases} \tag{68}$$

Summing these equations, we can obtain

$$\begin{aligned} &\sum_{m=1}^{k} H_{i_m}(x) y_{i_m}^{k-1} s + \sum_{j=0}^{k-2} \sum_{m=1}^{k} H_{i_m}(x) y_{i_m}^j r_j \\ =& \sum_{m=1}^{k} H_{i_m}(x) Z_{i_m}^{(s)} + \sum_{m=1}^{k} H_{i_m}(x) h_m(x) x^{(\ell_{i_m}-1)(k-1)+\ell}. \end{aligned} \tag{69}$$

Consider the coefficient of $s$ as $\sum_{m=1}^{k} H_{i_m}(x) y_{i_m}^{k-1}$ in $\mathbb{F}_p[x]$, which is equal to the following Vandermonde determinant, i.e.

$$\sum_{m=1}^{k} H_{i_m}(x) y_{i_m}^{k-1} = \begin{vmatrix} 1 & 1 & \cdots & 1 \\ y_{i_1} & y_{i_2} & \cdots & y_{i_k} \\ \vdots & \vdots & \cdots & \vdots \\ y_{i_1}^{k-1} & y_{i_2}^{k-1} & \cdots & y_{i_k}^{k-1} \end{vmatrix} = \prod_{1 \leq u < v \leq k} (y_{i_u} - y_{i_v}). \tag{70}$$

For arbitrary $j$ with $0 \leq j \leq k-2$, the coefficient of $r_j$ is $\sum_{m=1}^{k} H_{i_m}(x) y_{i_m}^j$ in $\mathbb{F}_p[x]$, then we have

$$\sum_{m=1}^{k} H_{i_m}(x) y_{i_m}^j = \begin{vmatrix} 1 & 1 & \cdots & 1 \\ y_{i_1} & y_{i_2} & \cdots & y_{i_k} \\ \vdots & \vdots & \cdots & \vdots \\ y_{i_1}^{k-2} & y_{i_2}^{k-2} & \cdots & y_{i_k}^{k-2} \\ y_{i_1}^j & y_{i_2}^j & \cdots & y_{i_k}^j \end{vmatrix} = 0 \tag{71}$$

for $0 \leq j \leq k-2$. Taking the results of (70) and (71) into (69), we can further obtain

$$\prod_{1 \leq u < v \leq k} (y_{i_u} - y_{i_v}) s = \sum_{m=1}^{k} H_{i_m}(x) Z_{i_m}^{(s)} + \sum_{m=1}^{k} H_{i_m}(x) h_m(x) x^{(\ell_{i_m}-1)(k-1)+\ell}. \tag{72}$$

As $\alpha = \min_{1 \leq m \leq k} \{L_{i_m} + \sum_{\substack{1 \leq u < v \leq k \\ u,v \neq m}} L_{i_u, i_v}\}$ and $L_{i_m} = (\ell_{i_m} - 1)(k-1) + \ell$ for $1 \leq m \leq k$, then that each polynomial

$$H_{i_m}(x) h_m(x) x^{L_{i_m}} = \prod_{\substack{1 \leq u < v \leq k \\ u,v \neq m}} (y_{i_u} - y_{i_v}) x^{L_{i_m}} h_m(x)$$

has the factor $x^\alpha$ for any $m$. Therefore, (72) can be derived into

$$\prod_{1 \leq u < v \leq k} (y_{i_u} - y_{i_v}) s \equiv \sum_{m=1}^{k} (-1)^{m-1} \prod_{\substack{1 \leq u < v \leq k \\ u,v \neq m}} (y_{i_u} - y_{i_v}) Z_{i_m}^{(s)} \pmod{x^\alpha}. \tag{73}$$

As $\prod_{1 \leq u < v \leq k} (y_{i_u} - y_{i_v})$ has the maximal extractable power $\sum_{1 \leq u < v \leq k} L_{i_u, i_v}$, and the codeword length of $s$ is $\ell$, we get $\sum_{1 \leq u < v \leq k} L_{i_u, i_v} + \ell \leq \alpha$ (the proof is proposed in Subsect. 4.3). Using Lemma 4, we can recover the unique solution of $s$ in $\mathbb{F}_p[x]/x^\ell$, which can be written as

$$s = \frac{\sum_{m=1}^{k} (-1)^{m-1} \prod_{\substack{1 \leq u < v \leq k \\ u,v \neq m}} (y_{i_u} - y_{i_v}) Z_{i_m}^{(s)}}{x^{\sum_{1 \leq u < v \leq k} L_{i_u, i_v}}} \times \left( \frac{\prod_{1 \leq u < v \leq k} (y_{i_u} - y_{i_v})}{x^{\sum_{1 \leq u < v \leq k} L_{i_u, i_v}}} \right)^{-1} \pmod{x^\ell}. \tag{74}$$

As for the security of the proposed scheme, a similar proof method has been mentioned in Subsect. 4.3. Therefore, we will no longer describe it here.

**Table 2.** Comparision of evolving $k$-threshold schemes based on $p$-ary prefix codes.

| threshold | scheme | $D(Z_t^{(s)})$ |
|---|---|---|
| $k=2$ | [30] | $(\lfloor \log_p t \rfloor + 2\lfloor \log_p(\lfloor \log_p t \rfloor + 1) \rfloor + 2) \cdot \max\{\lceil \lg (p+1) \rceil, \ell\}$ |
| | **ours** | $\boldsymbol{\lfloor \log_p t \rfloor + 2\lfloor \log_p (\lfloor \log_p t \rfloor + 1) \rfloor + 1 + \ell}$ |
| $k \geq 3$ | none | / |
| | **ours** | $\boldsymbol{(k-1)(\lfloor \log_p t \rfloor + 2\lfloor \log_p (\lfloor \log_p t \rfloor + 1) \rfloor + 1) + \ell}$ |

### 5.3 Construction Based on Two $p$-Ary Prefix Codes

For the proposed scheme over $\mathbb{F}_p[x]$, the $t$-th participant's share $Z_t^{(s)}$ can be regarded as a polynomial of $x$ over $\mathbb{F}_p$. Therefore, we denote by $D(Z_t^{(s)})$ the length of the corresponding $p$-ary codeword of $Z_t^{(s)}$, then we have

$$D(Z_t^{(s)}) = (k-1)(\ell_t - 1) + \ell, \tag{75}$$

where $\ell_t$ is the codeword length of using $p$-ary prefix code to encode positive integer $t$. If choosing different $p$-ary prefix codes, the corresponding $D(Z_t^{(s)})$ may be different.

Now, we introduce two $p$-ary prefix codes named $M_1$ code and $M_2$ code. $M_1$ code is represented by

$$M_1(t) = \overbrace{0, 0, \cdots, 0}^{\lfloor \log_p t \rfloor}[t]_p,$$

where $[t]_p$ is the $p$-ary expression. Thus, we have

$$L(M_1(t)) = 2\lfloor \log_p t \rfloor + 1. \tag{76}$$

Hence, if using $M_1$ code as the prefix code, we have

$$D(Z_t^{(s)}) = 2(k-1)\lfloor \log_p t \rfloor + \ell. \tag{77}$$

$M_2$ code is given by

$$M_2(t) = M_1(\lfloor \log_p t \rfloor + 1)[t]_p.$$

Then the codeword length of $M_2(t)$ is given by

$$L(M_2(t)) = \lfloor \log_p t \rfloor + 2\lfloor \log_p(\lfloor \log_p t \rfloor + 1) \rfloor + 2. \tag{78}$$

Therefore, if using $M_2$ code as the $p$-ary prefix code, we have

$$D(Z_t^{(s)}) = (k-1)(\lfloor \log_p t \rfloor) + 2(k-1)(\lfloor \log_p(\lfloor \log_p t \rfloor + 1) \rfloor) + (k-1) + \ell. \tag{79}$$

We tabulate the currently known evolving threshold secret sharing schemes, which are based on $p$-ary prefix codes and compare the corresponding $D(Z_t^{(s)})$. For the proposed scheme, we analyze the corresponding $D(Z_t^{(s)})$ for using $M_2$ code as the $p$-ary prefix code. In Table 2, we also represent the value of the lowest $D(Z_t^{(s)})$ in bold for each case of $k$. When $k = 2$, the proposed scheme's $D(Z_t^{(s)})$ is lower than the scheme in [30]. When $k \geq 3$, there are no other schemes based on $p$-ary prefix codes. However, the proposed construction is applicable to any $k$.

## 6 Conclusion and Discussion

In this paper, we propose a number of evolving threshold secret sharing schemes. Based on the binary prefix codes, we first propose a construction of evolving 2-threshold scheme for an $\ell$-bit secret over on a polynomial ring $\mathbb{F}_2[x]$. Then we extend the construction to evolving $k$-threshold scheme for $k \geq 3$. Finally, we gave a construction of an evolving $k$-threshold scheme over a polynomial ring $\mathbb{F}_p[x]$ considering the secret $s \in \{0, 1, \cdots, p-1\}^\ell$. In addition, we show that the share size of the $t$-th share is $(k-1)(\ell_t - 1) + \ell$, where $\ell_t$ denotes the codeword length of the integer $t$ encoded by the given binary prefix code. When $\delta$ code is applied, the $t$-th share size is $(k-1)\lfloor \lg t \rfloor + 2(k-1)\lfloor \lg(\lfloor \lg t \rfloor + 1) \rfloor + \ell$, that is smaller than Komargodski's scheme, when $k > 3$ and $\ell > 1$. Third, we consider an $\ell$-bit secret $s \in \{0, 1, \cdots, p-1\}^\ell$ for the first time. Based on the $p$-ary prefix codes, we extend the construction of the evolving $k$-threshold scheme over a polynomial ring $\mathbb{F}_p[x]$. We also show some $p$-ary prefix codes for positive integers and then apply the proposed construction to these codes.

There still exists some thought-provoking and challenging issues that remain unresolved, which are also our future works.

1) The correctness and security of the proposed schemes are perfect. If relaxing correctness or security, can one propose more interesting and efficient schemes to achieve high work efficiency or lower share size?
2) Compared with evolving 3-threshold scheme given in [10], the share size of the proposed scheme is larger than the result of [10]. Check whether the proposed scheme be improved to achieve a smaller share size. If not, check whether the scheme [10] be extended for other cases.

**Acknowledgements.** We would like to thank the anonymous reviewers for their insightful comments. This work was supported by the National Natural Science Foundation of China (Grants No. 62071446).

## References

1. Shamir, A.: How to share a secret. Commun. ACM **22**(11), 612–613 (1979). https://doi.org/10.1145/359168.359176
2. Blakley, G.R.: Safeguarding cryptographic keys. In: 1979 International Workshop on Managing Requirements Knowledge (MARK), p. 313 (1979). https://doi.org/10.1109/MARK.1979.8817296
3. Yang, Z., He, D., Qu, L., Xu, J.: On the security of a lattice-based multi-stage secret sharing scheme. IEEE Trans. Dependable Secure Comput. **20**(5), 4441–4442 (2023). https://doi.org/10.1109/TDSC.2022.3209011
4. Chen, X., Zhang, L., Liu, J.: Verifiable homomorphic secret sharing for low degree polynomials. IEEE Trans. Dependable Secure Comput. **20**(4), 2882–2895 (2023). https://doi.org/10.1109/TDSC.2022.3194321

5. Huo, L., Wu, L., Zhang, Z., Li, C., He, D., Wang, J.: Libras: a fair, secure, verifiable and scalable outsourcing computation scheme based on blockchain. IEEE Trans. Inf. Forensics Secur. **19**, 5725–5737 (2024). https://doi.org/10.1109/TIFS.2024.3403489
6. Xie, Y., Li, R., Huang, Y., Zhang, C., Wei, L., Sun, Y.: A monitoring-free bitcoin payment channel scheme with support for real-time settlement. IEEE Trans. Serv. Comput. **17**(5), 1924–1937 (2024). https://doi.org/10.1109/TSC.2024.3390396
7. Komargodski, I., Naor, M., Yogev, E.: How to share a secret, infinitely. In: Hirt, M., Smith, A. (eds.) TCC 2016. LNCS, vol. 9986, pp. 485–514. Springer, Heidelberg (2016). https://doi.org/10.1007/978-3-662-53644-5_19
8. Komargodski, I., Naor, M., Yogev, E.: How to share a secret, infinitely. IEEE Trans. Inf. Theory **64**(6), 4179–4190 (2017). https://doi.org/10.1109/TIT.2017.2779121
9. D'Arco, P., De Prisco, R., De Santis, A.: On the equivalence of 2-threshold secret sharing schemes and prefix codes. In: Castiglione, A., Pop, F., Ficco, M., Palmieri, F. (eds.) CSS 2018. LNCS, vol. 11161, pp. 157–167. Springer, Cham (2018). https://doi.org/10.1007/978-3-030-01689-0_13
10. D'Arco, P., De Prisco, R., De Santis, A.: Secret sharing schemes for infinite sets of participants: a new design technique. Theoret. Comput. Sci. **859**, 149–161 (2021). https://doi.org/10.1016/j.tcs.2021.01.019
11. Elias, P.: Universal codeword sets and representations of the integers. IEEE Trans. Inf. Theory **21**(2), 194–203 (1975). https://doi.org/10.1109/TIT.1975.1055349
12. Xing, C., Yuan, C.: Evolving secret sharing schemes based on polynomial evaluations and algebraic geometry codes. IEEE Trans. Inf. Theory **70**(5), 3718–3728 (2024). https://doi.org/10.1109/TIT.2024.3379278
13. Karnin, E., Greene, J., Hellman, M.: On secret sharing systems. IEEE Trans. Inf. Theory **29**(1), 35–41 (1983). https://doi.org/10.1109/TIT.1983.1056621
14. Bogdanov, A., Guo, S., Komargodski, I.: Threshold secret sharing requires a linear size alphabet. In: Hirt, M., Smith, A. (eds.) TCC 2016. LNCS, vol. 9986, pp. 471–484. Springer, Heidelberg (2016). https://doi.org/10.1007/978-3-662-53644-5_18
15. Cramer, R., Fehr, S.: Optimal black-box secret sharing over arbitrary abelian groups. In: Yung, M. (ed.) CRYPTO 2002. LNCS, vol. 2442, pp. 272–287. Springer, Heidelberg (2002). https://doi.org/10.1007/3-540-45708-9_18
16. Cao, H., Lin, S., Zhang, W., Han, Y.: On the security of secret sharing over a ring and the fast implementation. IEEE Signal Process. Lett. **26**(5), 705–709 (2019). https://doi.org/10.1109/LSP.2019.2907010
17. Mignotte, M.: How to share a secret. In: Beth, T. (ed.) EUROCRYPT 1982. LNCS, vol. 149, pp. 371–375. Springer, Heidelberg (1983). https://doi.org/10.1007/3-540-39466-4_27
18. Asmuth, C., Bloom, J.: A modular approach to key safeguarding. IEEE Trans. Inf. Theory **29**(2), 208–210 (1983). https://doi.org/10.1109/TIT.1983.1056651
19. Liu, Y., Harn, L., Chang, C.: A novel verifiable secret sharing mechanism using theory of numbers and a method for sharing secrets. Int. J. Commun. Syst. **28**(7), 1282–1292 (2015). https://doi.org/10.1002/dac.2760
20. Harn, L., Hsu, C., Zhang, M., He, T., Zhang, M.: Realizing secret sharing with general access structure. Inf. Sci. **367**, 209–220 (2016). https://doi.org/10.1016/j.ins.2016.06.006
21. Ning, Yu., Miao, F., Huang, W., Meng, K., Xiong, Y., Wang, X.: Constructing ideal secret sharing schemes based on Chinese remainder theorem. In: Peyrin, T., Galbraith, S. (eds.) ASIACRYPT 2018. LNCS, vol. 11274, pp. 310–331. Springer, Cham (2018). https://doi.org/10.1007/978-3-030-03332-3_12

22. Gennaro, R., Rabin, M., Rabin, T.: Simplified VSS and fast-track multiparty computations with applications to threshold cryptography. In: Proceedings of the Seventeenth Annual ACM Symposium on Principles of Distributed Computing, pp. 101–111 (1998). https://doi.org/10.1145/277697.277716
23. Cramer, R., Damgård, I., Maurer, U.: General secure multi-party computation from any linear secret-sharing scheme. In: Preneel, B. (ed.) EUROCRYPT 2000. LNCS, vol. 1807, pp. 316–334. Springer, Heidelberg (2000). https://doi.org/10.1007/3-540-45539-6_22
24. Wang, Yu., Tian, C., Su, Q., Wang, M., Su, X.: Measurement-device-independent quantum secret sharing and quantum conference based on Gaussian cluster state. SCIENCE CHINA Inf. Sci. **62**(7), 1–14 (2019). https://doi.org/10.1007/s11432-018-9705-x
25. Chor, B., Goldwasser, S., Micali, S., Awerbuch, B.: Verifiable secret sharing and achieving simultaneity in the presence of faults. In: 26th Annual Symposium on Foundations of Computer Science, pp. 27–35 (1985). https://doi.org/10.1109/SFCS.1985.64
26. Krawczyk, H.: Secret sharing made short. In: Stinson, D.R. (ed.) CRYPTO 1993. LNCS, vol. 773, pp. 136–146. Springer, Heidelberg (1994). https://doi.org/10.1007/3-540-48329-2_12
27. Ding, J., Lin, C., Wang, H., Xing, C.: Communication efficient secret sharing with small share size. IEEE Trans. Inf. Theory **68**(1), 659–669 (2021). https://doi.org/10.1109/TIT.2021.3123692
28. Csirmaz, L., Tardos, G.: On-line secret sharing. Des. Codes Crypt. **63**(6), 127–147 (2012). https://doi.org/10.1007/s10623-011-9540-y
29. Komargodski, I., Paskin-Cherniavsky, A.: Evolving secret sharing: dynamic thresholds and robustness. In: Kalai, Y., Reyzin, L. (eds.) TCC 2017. LNCS, vol. 10678, pp. 379–393. Springer, Cham (2017). https://doi.org/10.1007/978-3-319-70503-3_12
30. Okamura, R., Koga, H.: New constructions of an evolving 2-threshold scheme based on binary or D-ary prefix codes. In: 2020 International Symposium on Information Theory and Its Applications, pp. 432–436 (2020)
31. Yan, W., Lin, S., Han, Y.: A new metric and the construction for evolving 2-threshold secret sharing schemes based on prefix coding of integers. IEEE Trans. Commun. **71**(5), 2906–2915 (2023). https://doi.org/10.1109/TCOMM.2023.3253720
32. D'Arco, P., Prisco, R.D., Santis, A.D.: Constructions and lower bounds for evolving 2-threshold secret sharing schemes. IEEE Trans. Commun. (2024). https://doi.org/10.1109/TCOMM.2024.3493802
33. Alon, B., Beimel, A., Ben David, T.B., Omri, E., Paskin-Cherniavsky, A.: New upper bounds for evolving secret sharing via infinite branching programs. In: Boyle, E., Mahmoody, M. (eds.) Theory of Cryptography. TCC 2024, LNCS, vol. 15367, pp. 548–580. Springer, Heidelberg (2024). https://doi.org/10.1007/978-3-031-78023-3_18

# New Tight Bounds on the Local Leakage Resilience of the Additive $(n, n)$-Threshold Scheme Determined by the Eigenvalues of Circulant Matrices

Hiroki Koga[1(✉)] and Hiroto Abe[2]

[1] Institute of Systems and Information Engineering, University of Tsukuba, Tsukuba, Ibaraki, Japan
koga@iit.tsukuba.ac.jp

[2] Graduate School of Science and Technology, University of Tsukuba, Tsukuba, Ibaraki, Japan

**Abstract.** Recently, Benhamouda et al. [1] formulate leakage from the $n$ shares $(X_1, X_2, \ldots, X_n)$ of a $(t, n)$-threshold scheme as $\boldsymbol{Y} = (Y_1, Y_2, \ldots, Y_n)$, where $Y_j = \tau_j(X_j)$, $j = 1, 2, \ldots, n$ and $\tau_j$, $j = 1, 2, \ldots, n$ are deterministic functions with the range $\{0, 1, \ldots, L-1\}$ and evaluate the maximum $V_n^*$ of the total variational distance between the conditional distributions $P_{\boldsymbol{Y}|S}(\cdot|s)$ and $P_{\boldsymbol{Y}|S}(\cdot|s')$, where the maximum is taken with respect to $s, s'$ and $\tau_j$, $j = 1, 2, \ldots, n$. In this paper, we propose a new method to evaluate $V_n^*$ more precisely than the existing methods for the $(n, n)$-threshold scheme over a finite field $\mathbb{F}_p$. For the case of $L = 2$, we show that $V_n^*$ converges to zero of order $O((p \sin \frac{\pi}{2p})^{-n})$. We also characterize the class of leakage functions that attain $V_n^*$. For the case of $L \geq 3$, we succeed in obtaining an upper bound of $V_n^*$ by using the theory of majorization. The order of the obtained upper bound is smaller than the upper bound in [1] and is proved to be tight under a certain assumption.

**Keywords:** Secret sharing scheme · local leakage resilience · $(n, n)$-threshold scheme

## 1 Introduction

In secret sharing schemes originating from [2,17], a dealer generates $n \geq 2$ shares $X_1, X_2, \ldots, X_n$ from a secret $S$ and securely distributes the $n$ shares to the respective participants. In a $(t, n)$-threshold scheme, it is required that $S$ is recovered from arbitrary more than or equal to $t$ shares, and no information on $S$ is revealed from any less than $t$ shares, where $t$ is a constant satisfying $2 \leq t \leq n$. Shamir realized the the $(t, n)$-threshold scheme by using a random polynomial of degree at most $t-1$ over a finite field [17]. For the case of $t = n$, Karnin, Greene and Hellman give the additive $(n, n)$-threshold scheme [6]. In the additive $(n, n)$-threshold scheme, given a secret $S$, $n-1$ shares $X_1, X_2, \ldots, X_{n-1}$ are generated subject to the uniform distribution and the $n$-th share $X_n$ is generated as

© International Association for Cryptologic Research 2026
G. Hanaoka and B.-Y. Yang (Eds.): ASIACRYPT 2025, LNCS 16252, pp. 34–66, 2026.
https://doi.org/10.1007/978-981-95-5125-5_2

$X_n = S - (X_1 + X_2 + \cdots + X_{n-1})$. In this paper, we focus on this additive $(n, n)$-threshold scheme over a finite field $\mathbb{F}_p = \{0, 1, \ldots, p-1\}$, where $p$ is an arbitrary prime number.

### 1.1 Background

In recent studies of cryptographic primitives, we need to be careful that real-world implementations of cryptographic systems can be vulnerable to side-channel attacks (e.g., [8,9]). Recently, Benhamouda et al. formulated the problem of the secret sharing scheme secure against independent physical bit leakage [1]. They considered the situation as follows. Let a secret $S$ and $n$ shares $X_1, X_2, \ldots, X_n$ be elements of $\mathbb{F}_p$. We consider $n$ arbitrary mappings $\tau_j : \mathbb{F}_p \to \mathcal{L} \stackrel{\text{def}}{=} \{0, 1, \ldots, L-1\}$ for $j = 1, 2, \ldots, n$, where $2 \le L \le p-1$ is an integer. We regard $Y_j = \tau_j(X_j)$, $j = 1, 2, \ldots, n$ as a leakage from the share $X_j$. It is desirable that a secret sharing scheme be designed to be safe against an adversary who has access to $\boldsymbol{Y} = (Y_1, Y_2, \ldots, Y_n)$. In [1] the authors treat the total variational distance between $P_{\boldsymbol{Y}|S}(\cdot\,|s)$ and $P_{\boldsymbol{Y}|S}(\cdot\,|s')$ as a security criterion and show that its worst-case value with respect to the leakage functions

$$V_n^* = \max_{\tau_1, \tau_2, \ldots, \tau_n} V_n(\tau_1, \tau_2, \ldots, \tau_n)$$

is small enough, where $P_{\boldsymbol{Y}|S}(\boldsymbol{y}\,|s)$ denotes the conditional probability of $\boldsymbol{Y} = \boldsymbol{y}$ given $S = s$, $V_n(\tau_1, \tau_2, \ldots, \tau_n) = \max_{s,s' \in \mathbb{F}_p} d(P_{\boldsymbol{Y}|S}(\cdot\,|s), P_{\boldsymbol{Y}|S}(\cdot\,|s'))$, and the total variational distance is defined as

$$d(P_{\boldsymbol{Y}|S}(\cdot\,|s), P_{\boldsymbol{Y}|S}(\cdot\,|s')) = \frac{1}{2} \sum_{\boldsymbol{y} \in \mathcal{L}^n} \left| P_{\boldsymbol{Y}|S}(\boldsymbol{y}\,|s) - P_{\boldsymbol{Y}|S}(\boldsymbol{y}\,|s') \right|.$$

One of the main results in [1] is that the additive $(n, n)$-threshold scheme satisfies $V_n^* = O((\frac{L \sin \frac{\pi}{L}}{p \sin \frac{\pi}{p}})^n)$. In particular, if $L = 2$, $\frac{L \sin \frac{\pi}{L}}{p \sin \frac{\pi}{p}} \downarrow \frac{2}{\pi}$ as $p \to \infty$.

### 1.2 Problem Statement

In this paper, we focus on the additive $(n, n)$-threshold scheme and investigate the asymptotic behavior of $V_n^*$ as $n \to \infty$ for an arbitrarily fixed prime number $p$. Clearly, the above result in [1] guarantees that $V_n^*$ converges to zero of exponential order of $n$. However, nothing is discussed whether the base $\frac{L \sin \frac{\pi}{L}}{p \sin \frac{\pi}{p}}$ can be improved or not. This motivates us to develop a new method that enables us to evaluate the asymptotic behavior of $V_n^*$ more precisely. Obtaining a tight bound of $V_n^*$ that vanishes exponentially in $n$ is one of the goals of this paper.

We are also interested in the worst-case leakage functions that attain $V_n^*$. We can consider various kinds of leakage functions such as LSB or MSB leakage functions. We want to specify a class of leakage functions such that $V_n(\tau_1, \tau_2, \ldots, \tau_n)$ goes to zero as slowly as possible as $n \to \infty$. We also have the following simple question: do $n$ possibly distinct leakage functions really make the convergence of $V_n^*$ slow compared with using an identical leakage function? Obtaining deep insights into these problems is another goal of this paper.

So far, the Fourier analysis that was introduced by [1] has been a key method for the evaluation of $V_n^*$ in all of the recent papers related to the leakage-resilient secret sharing schemes [4,7,10,11,15]. In this paper, we write $V_n(\tau_1, \tau_2, \ldots, \tau_n)$ by using the eigenvalues of certain $p \times p$ zero-one circulant matrices that are induced by the leakage functions $\tau_1, \tau_2, \ldots, \tau_n$. Characterizing certain properties on the magnitudes of the eigenvalues is a key in our analysis.

### 1.3 Our Contribution

We first consider a simple case where the $n$ leakage functions $\tau_1, \tau_2, \ldots, \tau_n$ are identical to a single leakage function $\tau : \mathbb{F}_p \to \mathcal{L} = \{0, 1, \ldots, L-1\}$. Instead of $V_n^*$, we evaluate

$$V_n^\dagger = \max_\tau V_n(\tau), \quad \text{where} \quad V_n(\tau) = \max_{s,s'} d(P_{\boldsymbol{Y}|S}(\cdot\,|s), P_{\boldsymbol{Y}|S}(\cdot\,|s')).$$

Given $n$ leakages $\boldsymbol{y} = (y_1, y_2, \ldots, y_n) \in \mathcal{L}^n$, we can compute the number $z^{(s)}_{y_1 y_2 \cdots y_n}$ of the $n$ shares $(x_1, x_2, \ldots, x_n) \in \mathbb{F}_p^n$ for a secret $s \in \mathbb{F}_p$ satisfying $y_i = \tau(x_i)$ for all $i = 1, 2, \ldots, n$. Actually, letting $\boldsymbol{z}_{y_1 y_2 \cdots y_n} = [z^{(0)}_{y_1 y_2 \cdots y_n}, z^{(1)}_{y_1 y_2 \cdots y_n}, \ldots, z^{(p-1)}_{y_1 y_2 \cdots y_n}]^T$, it holds that

$$\boldsymbol{z}_{y_1 y_2 \cdots y_n} = C_{y_n} C_{y_{n-1}} \cdots C_{y_2} \boldsymbol{z}_{y_1}, \tag{1}$$

where $C_0, C_1, \ldots, C_{L-1}$ are the circulant matrices induced by $\tau$, the superscript $T$ means the transpose, and $\boldsymbol{z}_{y_1}$ is a certain $p$-dimensional vector. Then, $\boldsymbol{z}_{y_1 y_2 \cdots y_n}$ is obtained by simultaneous diagonalization of $C_0, C_1, \cdots, C_{L-1}$, where, letting $\lambda_{bk}$, $k = 0, 1, \ldots, p-1$ be the $p$ eigenvalues of $C_b$, we have $\mathrm{diag}(\lambda_{b0}, \lambda_{b1}, \ldots, \lambda_{b,p-1}) = P^{-1} C_b P$ for a common regular matrix $P$. Here, for each $b = 0, 1, \ldots, L-1$ we use the notations that $\lambda_{b0}$ is a real-valued eigenvalue and $\lambda_{bk}$, $k = 1, 2, \ldots, p-1$ are complex-valued eigenvalues with nonzero imaginary parts. In fact, $\lambda_{bk}$, $k = 1, 2, \ldots, p-1$ are expressed as a sum of $\zeta^j$ with respect to $j \in S$, where $S \subset \{0, 1, \ldots, p-1\}$ and $\zeta = e^{\frac{2\pi i}{p}}$. Since $P_{\boldsymbol{Y}|S}(\boldsymbol{y}|s) = z^{(s)}_{y_1 y_2 \cdots y_n} / p^{n-1}$, we can obtain the formula of $V_n(\tau)$ from $\boldsymbol{z}_{y_1 y_2 \cdots y_n}$.

For the case of $L = 2$, $V_n(\tau)$ is upper-bounded by a sum of the terms including $(\frac{2|\lambda_{0k}|}{p})^n$ for $k = 1, 2, \ldots, p-1$, where $|z|$ means the magnitude of a complex number $z$. This means that $V_n^\dagger = O((\frac{2|\lambda_{0,\max}|}{p})^n)$, where $|\lambda_{0,\max}| = \max_{1 \le k \le p-1} |\lambda_{0k}|$. We can show that $|\lambda_{0,\max}| = \frac{1}{2\sin\frac{\pi}{2p}}$. In this way, we obtain the following upper bound of $V_n^\dagger$:

$$V_n^\dagger \le 2\cos\frac{\pi}{2p} \frac{1}{(p\sin\frac{\pi}{2p})^n} + o\left(\frac{1}{(p\sin\frac{\pi}{2p})^n}\right) \tag{2}$$

(Theorem 2). We can consider a class $\mathcal{B}_2$ of leakage functions $\tau$ such that $C_0$ has the eigenvalue with the magnitude equal to $\frac{1}{2\sin\frac{\pi}{2p}}$. It is easily verified that the LSB or MSB leakage functions belong to $\mathcal{B}_2$. We can give an upper bound including higher order terms for all $\tau \in \mathcal{B}_2$ (Theorem 2). We can also give the following lower bound of $V_n^\dagger$:

$$V_n^\dagger \geq 2\left(\cos\frac{\pi}{2p}\right)^2 \frac{1}{(p\sin\frac{\pi}{2p})^n} + o\left(\frac{1}{(p\sin\frac{\pi}{2p})^n}\right), \tag{3}$$

which guarantees the tightness of the order $O((p\sin\frac{\pi}{2p})^{-n})$ of the dominant term of $V_n^\dagger$ (Theorem 3). If $p$ is large, the gap between the coefficients of the dominant terms in (2) and (3) is small.

We take the same approach for analyzing the asymptotic behavior of $V_n^\dagger$ for the case of $3 \leq L \leq p-1$. Again, we express $V_n(\tau)$ by using the eigenvalues $\lambda_{bk}$ of $L$ zero-one circulant matrices $C_0, C_1, \ldots, C_{L-1}$. We show that $V_n(\tau)$ can be expressed as a sum of the terms including $(\frac{1}{p}\sum_{b=0}^{L-1}|\lambda_{bk}|)^n$, $k = 1, 2, \ldots, p-1$. Therefore, finding the maximum of $\sum_{b=0}^{L-1}|\lambda_{bk}|$ leads to an upper bound of $V_n^\dagger$. We apply the theory of majorization [14] to find the maximum $g_{L,p}^* = \frac{L_g \sin\frac{u_g\pi}{p} + L_s \sin\frac{u_s\pi}{p}}{\sin\frac{\pi}{p}}$ of $\sum_{b=0}^{L-1}|\lambda_{bk}|$, where $u_g = \lceil p/L \rceil$, $u_s = \lfloor p/L \rfloor$, $L_g = p - Lu_s$ and $L_s = Lu_g - p\, u_s$. In this way, we obtain the following upper bound of $V_n^\dagger$:

$$V_n^\dagger \leq 2\cos\frac{\pi}{2p}\left(\frac{g_{L,p}^*}{p}\right)^n + o\left(\left(\frac{g_{L,p}^*}{p}\right)^n\right) \tag{4}$$

(Theorem 4). This upper bound coincides with the right side of (2) by setting $L = 2$, though we do not need the theory of majorization if $L = 2$. In addition, we can prove the tightness of the order of the dominant term in (4) under a certain assumption (Theorem 5).

Extension of the upper bound in (4) to the case of $n$ non-identical leakage functions is easy. Similarly to the identical case, we can show that $V_n(\tau_1, \tau_2, \ldots, \tau_n)$ is upper bounded by the sum of the terms of orders $\prod_{i=1}^n(\frac{1}{p}\sum_{b=0}^{L-1}|\lambda_{bk}^{[i]}|)$ for $k = 1, 2, \ldots, p-1$, where $\lambda_{bk}^{[i]}$, $k = 1, 2, \ldots, p-1$ are the eigenvalues of the $p \times p$ zero-one circulant matrix that is induced by $\tau_i$. Since $\sum_{b=0}^{L-1}|\lambda_{bk}^{[i]}| \leq g_{L,p}^*$ as before, the product of $\sum_{b=0}^{L-1}|\lambda_{bk}^{[i]}|$ is maximized if $\sum_{b=0}^{L-1}|\lambda_{bk}^{[i]}| = g_{L,p}^*$ at $k = k_0$ for all $i = 1, 2, \ldots, n$. This argument guarantees that not only $V_n^\dagger$ but also $V_n^*$ are upper-bounded by the right side of (4) (Corollary 2).

We can show that the base $g_{L,p}^*/p$ of the exponential term in (4) is less than the base $\frac{L\sin\pi}{p\sin\frac{\pi}{p}}$ in [1]. This fact is clearly explained from a viewpoint of the theory of majorization. In order to find the maximum of $\frac{1}{p}\sum_{b=0}^{L-1}|\lambda_{bk}|$, we need to consider the maximization of the function $g(u_0, u_1, \ldots, u_{L-1}) = \frac{1}{\sin\frac{\pi}{p}}\sum_{b=0}^{L-1}\sin\frac{u_b\pi}{p}$ subject to the constraints of $u_0 + u_1 + \cdots + u_{L-1} = p$ and $u_b$, $b = 0, 1, \ldots, L-1$ are nonnegative integers. This maximum, which equals $g_{L,p}^*$, is attained by $(u_0, u_1, \ldots, u_{L-1})$ such that $L_g$ (resp., $L_s$) out of the $L$ components are equal to $u_g$ (resp., $u_s$). If we drop the integer constraint of $u_b$, $b = 0, 1, \ldots, L-1$, and consider the same maximization problem, the maximum is attained by $(u_0, u_1, \ldots, u_{L-1}) = (p/L, p/L, \ldots, p/L)$, which yields the base $\frac{L \sin \pi}{p \sin \frac{\pi}{p}}$ in [1].

### 1.4 Related Work

Leakage resilience of Shamir's $(t, n)$-threshold scheme is discussed by various authors [1,4,7,11,12,15,16]. Fourier analysis is applied in all of these papers. A sufficient condition on $t$ under which Shamir's $(t, n)$-thresshold scheme is local leakage resilient is discussed by [1,7,11,12,15]. In particular, [7] shows that $(t, n)$-thresshold scheme is local leakage resilient if $t/n > 0.69$. A leakage function based on the quadratic residue is discussed in [15]. Under this leakage function, $t/n$ can be an arbitrary constant. Leakage resilience of Shamir's scheme over an extension field is discussed in [13,16]. Another application of the Fourier analysis to secret sharing can be found in [3].

### 1.5 Organization of This Paper

In Sect. 2, we formulate the problem of the leakage-resilient $(n, n)$-threshold scheme and review basic properties of circulant matrices. Evaluation of $V_n^\dagger$ for the case of $p = 3$ is given in Sect. 3 as a warm-up. The value of $V_n^\dagger$ for an arbitrary prime number $p \geq 3$ is evaluated in Sect. 4. We discuss the cases of $L = 2$ and $3 \leq L \leq p - 1$ separately and obtain upper bounds and lower bounds of $V_n^\dagger$ for the respective cases. A connection between the method developed in this paper and the Fourier analytic method [1] is also discussed. The evaluation of $V_n^*$ is discussed in Sect. 5.

## 2 Preliminaries

### 2.1 Additive $(n, n)$-Threshold Scheme and Leakages

Let $\mathcal{P} = \{1, 2, \ldots, n\}$ be a set of $n$ participants, where $n$ is a positive integer. Letting $S$ be a secret, a dealer generates $n$ shares $X_1, X_2, \ldots, X_n$ from $S$ by using random numbers. Suppose that $S$ and $X_1, X_2, \ldots, X_n$ are random variables taking values in a finite field $\mathbb{F}_p = \{0, 1, \ldots, p-1\}$, where $p$ is a prime number. We define addition, subtraction, multiplication, and division of two elements of $\mathbb{F}_p$ based on the residue modulo $p$. We use $\{0, 1, \ldots, p-1\}$ as the $p$ elements of $\mathbb{F}_p$ as well as the $p$ nonnegative integers less than $p$.

This paper focuses on the additive $(n, n)$-threshold scheme [6]. Given a secret $S$, a dealer generates $X_1, X_2, \ldots, X_{n-1}$ subject to the uniform distribution over $\mathbb{F}_p$ and $X_n$ as the element of $\mathbb{F}_p$ satisfying

$$X_1 + X_2 + \cdots + X_n = S. \tag{5}$$

The share $X_i$ is securely distributed to participant $i$ for $i = 1, 2, \ldots, n$. In the reproduction phase, the $n$ participants reproduce $S$ by adding all their shares.

Although we usually consider the case of $n \geq 2$ in the context of secret sharing schemes, we consider the case of $n = 1$ as well. We define $X_1 = S$ if $n = 1$.

In the problem of the leakage-resilient secret sharing schemes originating from [1], we consider $n$ deterministic mappings called *leakage functions* $\tau_i : \mathbb{F}_p \to \mathcal{L}\,(i = 1, 2, \ldots, n)$, where $\mathcal{L} = \{0, 1, \ldots, L-1\}$. Define

$$Y_i = \tau_i(X_i), \qquad i = 1, 2, \ldots, n. \tag{6}$$

Note that $Y_i$ is a random variable on $\mathcal{L}$ determined by $X_i$ and $\tau_i$ for $i = 1, 2, \ldots, n$. For example, if $L = 2$, $\tau_i$ can be the mapping that gives the most (or least) significant bit of $X_i$ when $X_i$ is expressed in the binary form. Define $\boldsymbol{Y} = (Y_1, Y_2, \ldots, Y_n)$ and call $\boldsymbol{Y}$ a *leakage*. In this paper, we mainly focus on the case where $\tau_1, \tau_2, \ldots, \tau_n$ are identical to a leakage function $\tau : \mathbb{F}_p \to \mathcal{L}$ and develop a method to evaluate $P_{\boldsymbol{Y}|S}(\cdot\,|s)$, the conditional probability distribution of the leakage $\boldsymbol{Y}$ given $S = s \in \mathbb{F}_p$. Without loss of generality, we assume that $L < p$. If $L \geq p$, we can define $\tau_1, \tau_2, \ldots, \tau_n$ as one-to-one mappings, which makes the supports of $P_{\boldsymbol{Y}|S}(\cdot\,|s)$, $s \in \mathbb{F}_p$ disjoint.

Given $n$ leakage functions $\tau_1, \tau_2, \ldots, \tau_n$, define

$$V_n(\tau_1, \tau_2, \ldots, \tau_n) = \max_{s, s' \in \mathbb{F}_p} d(P_{\boldsymbol{Y}|S}(\cdot\,|s), P_{\boldsymbol{Y}|S}(\cdot\,|s')),$$

where

$$d(P_{\boldsymbol{Y}|S}(\cdot\,|s), P_{\boldsymbol{Y}|S}(\cdot\,|s')) = \frac{1}{2} \sum_{\boldsymbol{y} \in \mathcal{L}^n} |P_{\boldsymbol{Y}|S}(\boldsymbol{y}\,|s) - P_{\boldsymbol{Y}|S}(\boldsymbol{y}\,|s')|$$

denotes the total variational distance between $P_{\boldsymbol{Y}|S}(\cdot\,|s)$ and $P_{\boldsymbol{Y}|S}(\cdot\,|s')$. Furthermore, define

$$V_n^* = \max_{\tau_1, \tau_2, \ldots, \tau_n} V_n(\tau_1, \tau_2, \ldots, \tau_n).$$

We regard $V_n^*$ as the measure of the leakage resilience of the $(n, n)$-threshold scheme. For the case where $\tau_1, \tau_2 \ldots, \tau_n$ are identical to some $\tau$, we use the notations $V_n(\tau)$ and $V_n^\dagger$ instead of $V_n(\tau_1, \tau_2, \ldots, \tau_n)$ and $V_n^*$, respectively. For the case of $L = 2$, we use the notation $V_{\mathrm{bin},n}^\dagger$ as well. Obviously, $V_n^\dagger \leq V_n^*$ for all $n \geq 1$. However, in Sect. 5 we will see that an upper bound of $V_n^\dagger$ is also an upper bound of $V_n^*$.

## 2.2 Properties of Circulant Matrices

In the following sections, we evaluate the values of $V_n^*$ and $V_n^\dagger$ by using properties of circulant matrices. We summarize some of these properties in this subsection. See [5] for basic properties of circulant matrices.

Let $p$ be an arbitrary prime number. A $p \times p$ circulant matrix is ordinarily determined by $p$ complex numbers $c_0, c_1, \ldots, c_{p-1}$ as

$$C = \begin{bmatrix} c_0 & c_1 & c_2 & \cdots & c_{p-1} \\ c_{p-1} & c_0 & c_1 & \cdots & c_{p-2} \\ c_{p-2} & c_{p-1} & c_0 & \cdots & c_{p-3} \\ \vdots & \vdots & \vdots & \ddots & \vdots \\ c_1 & c_2 & c_3 & \cdots & c_0 \end{bmatrix}. \quad (7)$$

Hereinafter, we specify the rows and columns of matrices by a zero-indexed way. That is, we call the top row the 0-th row and the bottom row the $(p-1)$-th row. In this terminology, we can say that the $k$-th row of the above $C$ is obtained by the cyclic shift to the right of the 0-th row repeatedly for $k$ times. Similarly, we call the leftmost (resp., rightmost) column the 0-th (resp., $(p-1)$-th) column. The same zero-indexed rule is applied to the components of $p$-dimensional vectors. In this paper, we only treat circulant matrices satisfying $c_0, c_1, \ldots, c_{p-1} \in \{0, 1\}$. We call such circulant matrices *zero-one circulant matrices.* Define a polynomial corresponding to a $p \times p$ zero-one circulant matrix $C$ by

$$f_C(t) = c_0 + c_1 t + \cdots + c_{p-1} t^{p-1},$$

where the coefficients of $f_C(t)$ are determined by the 0-th row of $C$. We can also specify a $p \times p$ zero-one circulant matrix by giving a polynomial $f$ of degree at most $p-1$ with the coefficients equal to either zero or one.

The following fact on the eigenvalues of a circulant matrix $C$ is well-known.

**Lemma 1.** *Let $C$ be a $p \times p$ circulant matrix. Then, the $p$ eigenvalues of $C$ are given by $\lambda_k = f_C(\zeta^k)$ for $k = 0, 1, \ldots, p-1$, where $\zeta = e^{\frac{2\pi i}{p}}$, $i$ means the imaginary unit and $f_C(t)$ is the polynomial corresponding to $C$. In addition, the eigenvector corresponding to the eigenvalue $\lambda_k$ is given by $\boldsymbol{e}_k = [1, \zeta^k, (\zeta^k)^2, \ldots, (\zeta^k)^{p-1}]^T$ for $k = 0, 1, \ldots, p-1$, where the superscript $T$ means the transpose.*

It is obvious that $\lambda_0 = \sum_{j=0}^{p-1} c_j$ is the eigenvalue corresponding to the eigenvector $\boldsymbol{e}_0 = [1, 1, \ldots, 1]^T$. It is easily verifyed that $C\boldsymbol{e}_k = \lambda_k \boldsymbol{e}_k$, $k = 1, 2, \ldots, p-1$ by direct computation using $\zeta^p = 1$.

Define $P = [\boldsymbol{e}_0, \boldsymbol{e}_1, \ldots, \boldsymbol{e}_{p-1}]$. Obviously, $P$ is the Vandermonde matrix. In addition, since $\zeta^k$, $k = 0, 1, \ldots, p-1$ are distinct, the determinant of $P$ is nonzero. This shows that $P$ has the inverse $P^{-1}$. Since neither $P$ nor $P^{-1}$ depends on $C$, we have the following lemma, claiming that any collection of $L$ circulant matrices is simultaneously diagonalized by $P$ and $P^{-1}$.

**Lemma 2.** *Let $C_b$, $b \in \mathcal{L}$ be arbitrary $L$ $p \times p$ circulant matrices. Then, it holds that $\Lambda_b = P^{-1} C_b P$ for all $b \in \mathcal{L}$, where $\Lambda_b = \mathrm{diag}(\lambda_{b0}, \lambda_{b1}, \ldots, \lambda_{b,p-1})$, $\lambda_{bk} = f_{C_b}(\zeta^k)$, $k = 0, 1, \ldots, p-1$, and $\lambda_{bk}$ and $\lambda_{b,k}$ are used in the same sense.*

The following lemma indicates that $P^{-1}$ is expressed in a simple form.

**Lemma 3.** $P^{-1} = \frac{1}{p}[\boldsymbol{e}_0, \boldsymbol{e}_{p-1}, \boldsymbol{e}_{p-2}, \ldots, \boldsymbol{e}_1]$.

Lemma 3 is easily verified by noticing that the $(i, j)$-component of $C$ is given as $\zeta^{ij}$ for all $0 \le i, j \le p-1$ and establishing

$$\boldsymbol{e}_i^T \boldsymbol{e}_j = \begin{cases} p, \text{ if } i+j=0 \text{ or } i+j=p \ , \\ 0, \text{ otherwise.} \end{cases}$$

We use the following lemma to evaluate the magnitudes of the eigenvalues of a circulant matrix. We say that a subset $A \subset \{0, 1, \ldots, p-1\}$ consists of $m$ *consecutive integers modulo* $p$ if there exists an integer $0 \le a \le p-1$ such that $A$ is expressed as $A = \{a, a+1, \ldots, a+(m-1)\}$ under the addition of modulo $p$ (equivalently, the addition of $\mathbb{F}_p$). For example, for the case of $p = 5$ and $m = 3$, both $\{2, 3, 4\}$ and $\{4, 0, 1\}$ consist of 3 consecutive integers modulo 5.

**Lemma 4** ([1])**.** *Let $p \ge 3$ be an arbitrary prime number and $A$ an arbitrary subset of $\mathbb{F}_p$ satisfying $1 \le \#A \le p-1$, where $\#A$ means the cardinality of $A$. Then, it holds that*

$$\left| \sum_{a \in A} \zeta^a \right| \le \left| 1 + \zeta + \cdots + \zeta^{t-1} \right|, \tag{8}$$

*where $t = \#A$ and $| \cdot |$ in (8) means the magnitude of a complex number. The equality in (8) holds if and only if $A$ is the set of $t$ or $p-t$ consecutive integers modulo $p$.*

Notice that the right side of (8) can be expressed as $|1 + \zeta + \cdots + \zeta^{p-t-1}|$ by using $1 + \zeta + \cdots + \zeta^{p-1} = 0$ and $|\zeta| = 1$. In addition, since

$$|1 + \zeta + \cdots + \zeta^{t-1}| = \left| \frac{\zeta^t - 1}{\zeta - 1} \right| = \left| \frac{\zeta^{t/2} - \zeta^{-t/2}}{\zeta^{1/2} - \zeta^{-1/2}} \right| = \frac{\sin \frac{t\pi}{p}}{\sin \frac{\pi}{p}},$$

the right side of (8) is maximized with respect to $t$ if $t \in \{\frac{p-1}{2}, \frac{p+1}{2}\}$.

## 3 The Case of $p = 3$ Under an Identical Leakage Function

In this section, we consider the additive $(n, n)$-threshold scheme for the case where $p = 3$ and $n$ leakage functions $\tau_1, \tau_2, \ldots, \tau_n$ are identical to a mapping $\tau : \mathbb{F}_3 \to \mathcal{L} = \{0, 1\}$. We focus on this case to demonstrate the basic idea that is used throughout this paper.

First, let us consider the case where $\tau$ satisfies $\tau(0) = \tau(1) = 0$ and $\tau(2) = 1$. For $s \in \mathbb{F}_3$ and $y_1, y_2, \ldots, y_n \in \{0, 1\}$, define

$$A^{(s)}_{y_1 y_2 \cdots y_i} = \{(x_1, x_2, \ldots, x_i) \in \mathbb{F}_3^i : \tau(x_j) = y_j \text{ for all } 1 \le j \le i \text{ and } x_1 + x_2 + \cdots + x_i = s\}, \quad i = 1, 2, \ldots, n. \tag{9}$$

Then, for an arbitrarily fixed $\boldsymbol{y} = (y_1, y_2, \ldots, y_n) \in \{0,1\}^n$ we have

$$\begin{aligned} A^{(0)}_{y_1 y_2 \ldots y_i 0} &= (A^{(0)}_{y_1 y_2 \ldots y_i} \times \{0\}) \cup (A^{(2)}_{y_1 y_2 \ldots y_i} \times \{1\}), \\ A^{(1)}_{y_1 y_2 \ldots y_i 0} &= (A^{(0)}_{y_1 y_2 \ldots y_i} \times \{1\}) \cup (A^{(1)}_{y_1 y_2 \ldots y_i} \times \{0\}), \\ A^{(2)}_{y_1 y_2 \ldots y_i 0} &= (A^{(1)}_{y_1 y_2 \ldots y_i} \times \{1\}) \cup (A^{(2)}_{y_1 y_2 \ldots y_i} \times \{0\}) \end{aligned}$$

for all $i = 1, 2, \ldots, n-1$. Setting $z^{(s)}_{y_1 y_2 \cdots y_i} = \# A^{(s)}_{y_1 y_2 \ldots y_i}$, disjointness of $A^{(0)}_{y_1 y_2 \ldots y_i}$, $A^{(1)}_{y_1 y_2 \ldots y_i}$ and $A^{(2)}_{y_1 y_2 \ldots y_i}$ implies that

$$z^{(0)}_{y_1 y_2 \cdots y_i 0} = z^{(0)}_{y_1 y_2 \cdots y_i} + z^{(2)}_{y_1 y_2 \cdots y_i}, \tag{10}$$

$$z^{(1)}_{y_1 y_2 \cdots y_i 0} = z^{(0)}_{y_1 y_2 \cdots y_i} + z^{(1)}_{y_1 y_2 \cdots y_i}, \tag{11}$$

$$z^{(2)}_{y_1 y_2 \cdots y_i 0} = z^{(1)}_{y_1 y_2 \cdots y_i} + z^{(2)}_{y_1 y_2 \cdots y_i}. \tag{12}$$

Similarly, we have

$$z^{(0)}_{y_1 y_2 \ldots y_i 1} = z^{(1)}_{y_1 y_2 \ldots y_i}, \tag{13}$$

$$z^{(1)}_{y_1 y_2 \ldots y_i 1} = z^{(2)}_{y_1 y_2 \ldots y_i}, \tag{14}$$

$$z^{(2)}_{y_1 y_2 \ldots y_i 1} = z^{(0)}_{y_1 y_2 \ldots y_i} \tag{15}$$

for all $i = 1, 2, \ldots, n-1$, which follows from $A^{(0)}_{y_1 y_2 \ldots y_i 1} = A^{(1)}_{y_1 y_2 \ldots y_i} \times \{2\}$, $A^{(1)}_{y_1 y_2 \ldots y_i 1} = A^{(2)}_{y_1 y_2 \ldots y_i} \times \{2\}$, and $A^{(2)}_{y_1 y_2 \ldots y_i 1} = A^{(0)}_{y_1 y_2 \ldots y_i} \times \{2\}$, respectively.

In addition, since $X_1$ is defined as $S$ for the case of $n = 1$, we have $z^{(0)}_0 = z^{(1)}_0 = 1$, $z^{(2)}_0 = 0$ and $z^{(0)}_1 = z^{(1)}_1 = 0$, $z^{(2)}_1 = 1$. Therefore, setting

$$C_0 = \begin{bmatrix} 1\,0\,1 \\ 1\,1\,0 \\ 0\,1\,1 \end{bmatrix}, \quad C_1 = \begin{bmatrix} 0\,1\,0 \\ 0\,0\,1 \\ 1\,0\,0 \end{bmatrix}, \quad \boldsymbol{z}_{y_1 y_2 \ldots y_i} = \begin{bmatrix} z^{(0)}_{y_1 y_2 \cdots y_i} \\ z^{(1)}_{y_1 y_2 \cdots y_i} \\ z^{(2)}_{y_1 y_2 \cdots y_i} \end{bmatrix}, \quad \boldsymbol{z}_0 = \begin{bmatrix} 1 \\ 1 \\ 0 \end{bmatrix}, \quad \boldsymbol{z}_1 = \begin{bmatrix} 0 \\ 0 \\ 1 \end{bmatrix},$$

(10)–(15) lead to the following recurrence relation:

$$\boldsymbol{z}_{y_1 y_2 \ldots y_{i+1}} = C_{y_{i+1}} \boldsymbol{z}_{y_1 y_2 \ldots y_i}, \quad i = 1, 2, \ldots, n-1. \tag{16}$$

Notice that both $C_0$ and $C_1$ are circulant matrices.

*Example 1.* Let us consider the case of $n = 4$. We can easily verify that the following three sets are determined from $y_1 = y_2 = y_3 = 0$:

$$A^{(0)}_{000} = \{000, 111\},\ A^{(1)}_{000} = \{001, 010, 100\} \ \text{and}\ A^{(2)}_{000} = \{011, 101, 110\},$$

where $(x_1, x_2, x_3)$ is simply expressed as $x_1 x_2 x_3$. Only 0 and 1 appear in the above three sets because setting $y_i = 0$ implies that $x_i = 0$ or $x_i = 1$. Notice that if $x_1 x_2 x_3 \in A^{(s)}_{000}$, it holds that $x_1 + x_2 + x_3 = s$. It is important to notice that

$$A^{(0)}_{0000} = \{0000, 1110, 0111, 1011, 1101\} \ \text{and}\ A^{(0)}_{0001} = \{0012, 0102, 1002\}$$

are expressed as

$$A^{(0)}_{0000} = (A^{(0)}_{000} \times \{0\}) \cup (A^{(2)}_{000} \times \{1\}) \text{ and } A^{(0)}_{0001} = A^{(1)}_{000} \times \{2\},$$

respectively, where $(x_1, x_2, x_3) \times \{x_4\}$ means $(x_1, x_2, x_3, x_4)$ and $(x_1, x_2, x_3, x_4)$ is simply expressed as $x_1x_2x_3x_4$. Notice that $y_4 = \tau(x_4)$ restricts the values of the fourth share.

We determine $z_{y_1 y_2 \dots y_n}$ from (16). Obviously, it holds that

$$z_{y_1 y_2 \dots y_n} = C_{y_n} C_{y_{n-1}} \cdots C_{y_2} z_{y_1}. \tag{17}$$

Since $C_0$ and $C_1$ are the circulant matrices, Lemma 2 tells us that $C_0$ and $C_1$ are diagonalized as $\Lambda_0 = P^{-1}C_0P$ and $\Lambda_1 = P^{-1}C_1P$, respectively, where $\zeta = e^{\frac{2\pi i}{3}}$,

$$\Lambda_0 = \begin{bmatrix} \lambda_{00} & 0 & 0 \\ 0 & \lambda_{01} & 0 \\ 0 & 0 & \lambda_{02} \end{bmatrix} = \begin{bmatrix} 2 & 0 & 0 \\ 0 & 1+\zeta^2 & 0 \\ 0 & 0 & 1+\zeta \end{bmatrix}, \quad \Lambda_1 = \begin{bmatrix} \lambda_{10} & 0 & 0 \\ 0 & \lambda_{11} & 0 \\ 0 & 0 & \lambda_{12} \end{bmatrix} = \begin{bmatrix} 1 & 0 & 0 \\ 0 & \zeta & 0 \\ 0 & 0 & \zeta^2 \end{bmatrix},$$

$$P = \begin{bmatrix} 1 & 1 & 1 \\ 1 & \zeta & \zeta^2 \\ 1 & \zeta^2 & \zeta \end{bmatrix} \text{ and } P^{-1} = \frac{1}{3}\begin{bmatrix} 1 & 1 & 1 \\ 1 & \zeta^2 & \zeta \\ 1 & \zeta & \zeta^2 \end{bmatrix}$$

and $\lambda_{bk}$ ($b = 0, 1$ and $k = 0, 1, 2$) are obtained from Lemma 1. We can also check that

$$P^{-1}z_0 = \frac{1}{3}\begin{bmatrix} 2 \\ 1+\zeta^2 \\ 1+\zeta \end{bmatrix} = \frac{1}{3}\begin{bmatrix} \lambda_{00} \\ \lambda_{01} \\ \lambda_{02} \end{bmatrix} \text{ and } P^{-1}z_1 = \frac{1}{3}\begin{bmatrix} 1 \\ \zeta \\ \zeta^2 \end{bmatrix} = \frac{1}{3}\begin{bmatrix} \lambda_{10} \\ \lambda_{11} \\ \lambda_{12} \end{bmatrix}.$$

Therefore, setting

$$\mathcal{Y}_l = \{(y_1, y_2, \dots, y_n) : \#\{1 \le i \le n : y_i = 1\} = l\}, \quad l = 0, 1, \dots, n,$$

$z_{y_1 y_2 \dots y_n}$ in (17) can be expressed as follows:

$$\begin{aligned} z_{y_1 y_2 \dots y_n} &= \frac{1}{3}P\begin{bmatrix} \prod_{i=1}^n \lambda_{y_i 0} \\ \prod_{i=1}^n \lambda_{y_i 1} \\ \prod_{i=1}^n \lambda_{y_i 2} \end{bmatrix} = \frac{1}{3}P\begin{bmatrix} \lambda_{00}^{n-l}\lambda_{10}^l \\ \lambda_{01}^{n-l}\lambda_{11}^l \\ \lambda_{02}^{n-l}\lambda_{12}^l \end{bmatrix} \\ &= \frac{1}{3}\,\mathrm{P}\begin{bmatrix} 2^{n-l} \\ (-1)^{n-l}\zeta^n \\ (-1)^{n-l}\zeta^{2n} \end{bmatrix} \quad \text{for all } (y_1, y_2, \dots, y_n) \in \mathcal{Y}_l, \end{aligned}$$

where we have used $1 + \zeta + \zeta^2 = 0$ and therefore $\zeta_{01} = -\zeta_{11} = \zeta$ and $\zeta_{02} = -\zeta_{12} = -\zeta^2$ to obtain the last equality. Now, we have the following form of $z_{y_1 y_2 \cdots y_n} \in \mathcal{Y}_l$, $l = 0, 1, \dots, n$:

$$z_{y_1 y_2 \dots y_n} = \frac{1}{3}\begin{bmatrix} 2^{n-l} + (-1)^{n-l}(\zeta^n + \zeta^{2n}) \\ 2^{n-l} + (-1)^{n-l}(\zeta^{n+1} + \zeta^{2(n+1)}) \\ 2^{n-l} + (-1)^{n-l}(\zeta^{n+2} + \zeta^{2(n+2)}) \end{bmatrix} \quad \text{for all } (y_1, y_2, \dots, y_n) \in \mathcal{Y}_l, \tag{18}$$

where we have used $\zeta^3 = 1$ as well.

We are ready to evaluate the total variational distance between $P_{\boldsymbol{Y}|S}(\cdot\,|s)$ and $P_{\boldsymbol{Y}|S}(\cdot\,|s')$. Given $S \in \mathbb{F}_3$, $X_1, X_2, \ldots, X_{n-1}$ are independently generated subject to the uniformly distribution over $\mathbb{F}_3$ and $X_n$ is uniquely determined from $S$ and $X_1, X_2, \ldots, X_{n-1}$. This means that

$$P_{\boldsymbol{Y}|S}(\boldsymbol{y}\,|s) = \frac{z^{(s)}_{y_1 y_2 \cdots y_n}}{3^{n-1}} \quad \text{for all } s \in \mathbb{F}_3 \text{ and } \boldsymbol{y} = (y_1, y_2, \ldots, y_n) \in \{0,1\}^n.$$

Therefore, $V_n(\tau)$ can be written in the following form:

$$V_n(\tau) = \max_{s,s' \in \mathbb{F}_3} \frac{1}{2} \sum_{l=0}^{n} \sum_{(y_1,\ldots,y_n)\in\mathcal{Y}_l} \frac{1}{3^{n-1}} \left| z^{(s)}_{y_1 y_2 \cdots y_n} - z^{(s')}_{y_1 y_2 \cdots y_n} \right|. \tag{19}$$

We evaluate the right side of (19) by using the following identity:

$$\zeta^n + \zeta^{2n} = \begin{cases} 2, & \text{if } n \equiv 0 \pmod 3, \\ -1, & \text{otherwise,} \end{cases}$$

which yields

$$\left| z^{(0)}_{y_1 y_2 \cdots y_n} - z^{(1)}_{y_1 y_2 \cdots y_n} \right| = \begin{cases} 1, & \text{if } n \equiv 0 \text{ or } 2 \pmod 3, \\ 0, & \text{otherwise,} \end{cases} \tag{20}$$

$$\left| z^{(1)}_{y_1 y_2 \cdots y_n} - z^{(2)}_{y_1 y_2 \cdots y_n} \right| = \begin{cases} 1, & \text{if } n \equiv 1 \text{ or } 2 \pmod 3, \\ 0, & \text{otherwise,} \end{cases} \tag{21}$$

$$\left| z^{(2)}_{y_1 y_2 \cdots y_n} - z^{(0)}_{y_1 y_2 \cdots y_n} \right| = \begin{cases} 1, & \text{if } n \equiv 0 \text{ or } 1 \pmod 3, \\ 0, & \text{otherwise.} \end{cases} \tag{22}$$

Notice that the value of $|z^{(s)}_{y_1 y_2 \cdots y_n} - z^{(s')}_{y_1 y_2 \cdots y_n}|$ depends only on $s, s' \in \mathbb{F}_3$ and $n$, and is independent of $(y_1, y_2, \ldots, y_n) \in \{0,1\}^n$. Setting $\delta_n(s,s') = |z^{(s)}_{y_1 y_2 \cdots y_n} - z^{(s')}_{y_1 y_2 \cdots y_n}|$, we can evaluate $V_n(\tau)$ in the following way:

$$\begin{aligned} V_n(\tau) &= \max_{s,s' \in \mathbb{F}_3} \frac{1}{2} \sum_{l=0}^{n} \sum_{(y_1,\ldots,y_n)\in\mathcal{Y}_l} \frac{1}{3^{n-1}} \delta_{s,s'} \\ &= \left(\frac{2}{3}\right)^{n-1} \max_{s,s' \in \mathbb{F}_3} \delta_n(s,s') = \left(\frac{2}{3}\right)^{n-1} \quad \text{for all } n \geq 1, \end{aligned} \tag{23}$$

where the last equaltiy holds because (20)–(22) guarantee the existence of a pair $(s,s') \in \mathbb{F}_3$ satisfying $\delta_n(s,s') = 1$ for each $n \geq 1$.

Summarizing, we have the following proposition:

**Proposition 1.** *Consider the additive $(n,n)$-threshold scheme over $\mathbb{F}_3$ under the identical leakage function satisfying $\tau(0) = \tau(1) = 0$ and $\tau(2) = 1$. Then, it holds that $V_n(\tau) = \left(\frac{2}{3}\right)^{n-1}$ for all $n \geq 1$.*

Next, we discuss the value of $V_n(\tau)$ for different identical leakage functions. It is obvious that we also have $V_n(\tau) = \left(\frac{2}{3}\right)^{n-1}$ as in Proposition 1 if $\tau(0) = \tau(1) = 1$ and $\tau(2) = 0$. In this case, only the roles of $C_0$ and $C_1$ are interchanged. So, we need to discuss the two other cases: (A) $\tau(0) = \tau(2) = 0$ and $\tau(1) = 1$, and (B) $\tau(1) = \tau(2) = 0$ and $\tau(0) = 1$.

It is easily verified that for all $0 \le l \le n$ and $(y_1, y_2, \ldots, y_n) \in \mathcal{Y}_l$ we have

$$z_{y_1 y_2 \ldots y_n} = \frac{1}{3}\begin{bmatrix} 2^{n-l} + (-1)^{n+l}(\zeta^n + \zeta^{2n}) \\ 2^{n-l} + (-1)^{n+l}(\zeta^{n+2} + \zeta^{2(n+2)}) \\ 2^{n-l} + (-1)^{n+l}(\zeta^{n+1} + \zeta^{2(n+1)}) \end{bmatrix} \quad \text{and} \quad z_{y_1 y_2 \ldots y_n} = \frac{1}{3}\begin{bmatrix} 2^{n-l} + 2(-1)^n \\ 2^{n-l} - (-1)^n \\ 2^{n-l} - (-1)^n \end{bmatrix}$$

for cases (A) and (B), respectively. In both cases $\delta_n(s, s') = |z^{(s)}_{y_1 y_2 \ldots y_n} - z^{(s')}_{y_1 y_2 \ldots y_n}|$, which depends only on $s, s' \in \mathbb{F}_3$ and $n$, satisfies $\max_{s,s'} \delta_n(s, s') = 1$ for all $n \ge 1$. By repeating the argument in (23) together with the above $z_{y_1 y_2 \ldots y_n}$'s, we have the following theorem:

**Theorem 1.** *For the additive $(n, n)$-threshold scheme over $\mathbb{F}_3$, we have $V^{\dagger}_{\mathrm{bin},n} = \left(\frac{2}{3}\right)^{n-1}$ for all $n \ge 1$.*

# 4 Generalization Under an Arbitrary Identical Leakage Function

In this section, we consider the case where $p \ge 3$ is an arbitrary prime number and $\tau : \mathbb{F}_p \to \mathcal{L} = \{0, 1, \ldots, L-1\}$ is an identical leakage function. We often identify integers belonging to $\{0, 1, \ldots, p-1\}$ to elements of $\mathbb{F}_p$ and apply the arithmetic operations in $\mathbb{F}_p$. In particular, when we use the notion $ab \in \mathbb{F}_p$ for two integers $a, b \in \{0, 1, \ldots, p-1\}$, this means that we identify $a$ and $b$ as the elements $a$ and $b$ in $\mathbb{F}_p$ and apply the multiplication of $\mathbb{F}_p$.

Fix a leakage function $\tau : \mathbb{F}_p \to \mathcal{L} = \{0, 1, \ldots, L-1\}$ arbitrarily and define

$$\begin{aligned} A^{(s)}_{y_1 y_2 \ldots y_i} = \{(x_1, x_2, \ldots, x_i) \in \mathbb{F}_p^i \,:\, \tau(x_j) = y_j \text{ for all } 1 \le j \le i \\ \text{and } x_1 + x_2 + \cdots + x_i = s\}, \quad i = 1, 2, \ldots, n. \end{aligned} \tag{24}$$

Then, the following relationship holds for all $s \in \mathbb{F}_p$ and $(y_1, y_2, \ldots, y_n) \in \mathcal{L}^n$:

$$A^{(s)}_{y_1 y_2 \cdots y_{i+1}} = \bigcup_{j \in \tau^{-1}(y_{i+1})} A^{(s-j)}_{y_1 y_2 \cdots y_i} \times \{j\}, \quad i = 1, 2 \ldots, n-1, \tag{25}$$

where $\tau^{-1}(b) = \{x \in \mathbb{F}_p \,:\, \tau(x) = b\}$ for $b \in \mathcal{L}$. Notice that $s - j \in \mathbb{F}_p$ because both $s$ and $j$ are elements of $\mathbb{F}_p$. Since $A^{(0)}_{y_1 y_2 \cdots y_i}, A^{(1)}_{y_1 y_2 \cdots y_i}, \ldots, A^{(p-1)}_{y_1 y_2 \cdots y_i}$ are disjoint for arbitrarily fixed $y_1, y_2, \ldots, y_i \in \mathcal{L}$, we have

$$z^{(s)}_{y_1 y_2 \cdots y_{i+1}} = \sum_{j \in \tau^{-1}(y_{i+1})} z^{(s-j)}_{y_1 y_2 \cdots y_i} = \sum_{j:\ s-j \in \tau^{-1}(y_{i+1})} z^{(j)}_{y_1 y_2 \cdots y_i}, \quad i = 1, 2 \ldots, n-1. \tag{26}$$

Hence, if we define the $p \times p$ matrix $C_b$ ($b \in \mathcal{L}$) with the $(s, j)$-component given by

$$C_b[s, j] = \begin{cases} 1, \text{ if } s - j \in \tau^{-1}(b), \\ 0, \text{ otherwise}, \end{cases} \tag{27}$$

(26) leads to

$$z^{(s)}_{y_1 y_2 \cdots y_{i+1}} = \sum_{j=0}^{p-1} C_{y_{i+1}}[s, j]\, z^{(j)}_{y_1 y_2 \cdots y_i}, \quad i = 1, 2 \ldots, n-1$$

for each $s \in \{0, 1, \ldots, p-1\}$. This immediately implies that

$$\boldsymbol{z}_{y_1 y_2 \cdots y_{i+1}} = C_{y_{i+1}} \boldsymbol{z}_{y_1 y_2 \cdots y_i}, \quad i = 1, 2 \ldots, n-1, \tag{28}$$

where $\boldsymbol{z}_{y_1 \cdots y_i} = [z^{(0)}_{y_1 y_2 \cdots y_i}, z^{(1)}_{y_1 y_2 \cdots y_i}, \ldots, z^{(p-1)}_{y_1 y_2 \cdots y_i}]^T$. By repeated applications of (28), we obtain

$$\boldsymbol{z}_{y_1 y_2 \cdots y_n} = C_{y_n} C_{y_{n-1}} \cdots C_{y_2} \boldsymbol{z}_{y_1}, \tag{29}$$

where $\boldsymbol{z}_{y_1} = [z^{(0)}_{y_1}, z^{(1)}_{y_1}, \ldots, z^{(p-1)}_{y_1}]^T$ is defined as

$$z^{(s)}_{y_1} = \begin{cases} 1, \text{ if } \tau(s) = y_1, \\ 0, \text{ otherwise}. \end{cases}$$

Recall that $X_1 = S$ by definition for the case of $n = 1$.

Note that, since (27) guarantees that $C_b[s+1, j+1] = C_b[s, j]$, $C_b$ is a circulant matrix for each $b \in \mathcal{L}$. In addition, since $\tau$ is defined as a deterministic mapping, the $(s, j)$-component of $C_b$ is equal to one if $\tau(s - j) = b$ and zero otherwise. This implies that $C_0 + C_1 + \cdots + C_{L-1}$ equals the $p \times p$ all-one matrix. Hereinafter, we call $C_0, C_1, \ldots, C_{L-1}$ the *zero-one circulant matrices induced by* $\tau$.

Denote by $f_{C_b}(t)$ the polynomial corresponding to the circulant matrix $C_b$. Lemma 1 tells us that the $p$ eigenvalues of $C_b$ are expressed as $\lambda_{bk} = f_{C_b}(\zeta^k)$, $k = 0, 1, \ldots, p-1$, where $\zeta = e^{\frac{2\pi \mathrm{i}}{p}}$. Recall that $\zeta$ satisfies $\zeta^p = 1$ and $1+\zeta+\cdots+\zeta^{p-1} = 0$. Clearly, $\lambda_{b0} = |\tau^{-1}(b)|$. In addition, since $\zeta^{p-k} = \overline{\zeta^k}$, it holds that $\lambda_{b,p-k} = \overline{\lambda_{bk}}$, $k = 1, 2, \ldots, p-1$, where $\overline{z}$ denotes the complex conjugate of a complex number $z$. Lemma 2 claims that $C_0, C_1, \ldots, C_{L-1}$ are diagonalized by $P$ and $P^{-1}$. For each $b \in \mathcal{L}$, define $\Lambda_b = P^{-1} C_b P$, where $\Lambda_b = \mathrm{diag}(\lambda_{b0}, \lambda_{b1}, \ldots, \lambda_{b,p-1})$. Therefore, (29) can be expressed as

$$\boldsymbol{z}_{y_1 y_2 \cdots y_n} = P \Lambda_{y_n} \Lambda_{y_{n-1}} \cdots \Lambda_{y_2} P^{-1} \boldsymbol{z}_{y_1}. \tag{30}$$

We use the following lemma to simplify the computation of $\boldsymbol{z}_{y_1 y_2 \cdots y_n}$:

**Lemma 5.** *For any* $b \in \mathcal{L}$, $P^{-1} \boldsymbol{z}_b = \frac{1}{p}[\lambda_{b0}, \lambda_{b1}, \ldots, \lambda_{b,p-1}]^T$.

*Proof.* Fix $b \in \mathcal{L}$ arbitrarily. Then, it holds that $C_b[0, j] = z_b^{(p-j)}$ for any $j \in \{0, 1, \dots, p-1\}$, where $z_b^{(p)}$ is interpreted as $z_b^{(0)}$. In fact, $C_b[0, j] = 1$ holds if $\tau(-j) = \tau(p-j) = b$ is satisfied. Therefore, the $k$-th component of $P^{-1}z_b$ can be evaluated in the following manner:

$$(P^{-1}z_b)[k] = \frac{1}{p}\sum_{j=0}^{p-1}(\zeta^{p-j})^k z_b^{(j)} = \frac{1}{p}\sum_{j=0}^{p-1}(\zeta^j)^k z_b^{(p-j)} = \frac{1}{p}\sum_{j=0}^{p-1} C_b[0, j](\zeta^k)^j$$
$$= \frac{1}{p} f_{C_b}(\zeta^k) = \frac{1}{p}\lambda_{bk},$$

where the first equality follows from Lemma 3 and the second equality follows by setting $j' = p - j$ and using $\zeta^p = \zeta^0 = 1$ and $z_b^{(p)} = z_b^{(0)}$. □

In view of (30) and Lemma 5, the right side of (30) can be written as follows:

$$z_{y_1 y_2 \dots y_n} = \frac{1}{p}P\begin{bmatrix} \prod_{i=1}^n \lambda_{y_i 0} \\ \prod_{i=1}^n \lambda_{y_i 1} \\ \vdots \\ \prod_{i=1}^n \lambda_{y_i, p-1} \end{bmatrix} = \frac{1}{p}P\begin{bmatrix} \prod_{b=0}^{L-1} \lambda_{b0}^{l_b} \\ \prod_{b=0}^{L-1} \lambda_{b1}^{l_b} \\ \vdots \\ \prod_{b=0}^{L-1} \lambda_{b,p-1}^{l_b} \end{bmatrix}$$
$$\text{for any} (l_0, l_1, \dots, l_{L-1}) \in \mathcal{I}_{L,n} \text{and } (y_1, y_2, \dots, y_n) \in \mathcal{Y}_{l_0, l_1, \dots, l_{L-1}}, \tag{31}$$

where

$$\mathcal{I}_{L,n} = \{(l_0, l_1, \dots, l_{L-1}) \in \mathbb{Z}^L : \; l_b \geq 0,\ b = 0, 1, \dots, L-1 \text{ and } l_0 + l_1 + \cdots + l_{L-1} = n\},$$
$$\mathcal{Y}_{l_0, l_1, \dots, l_{L-1}} = \{(y_1, y_2, \dots, y_n) \in \mathcal{L}^n : \; \#\{1 \leq i \leq n : y_i = b\} = l_b \text{ for all } b = 0, 1, \dots, L-1\}$$

for each $(l_0, l_1, \dots, l_{L-1}) \in \mathcal{I}_{L,n}$, and $\mathbb{Z}$ denotes the set of integers.

### 4.1 Evaluation of $V_n^\dagger$ for $L = 2$

For the case of $L = 2$, we can give a simple general formula for $V_n(\tau)$. It is important to notice that $\lambda_{1k} = -\lambda_{0k}$ for $k = 1, 2, \dots, p-1$ because $C_0 + C_1$ is the $p \times p$ all-one matrix and $1 + \zeta + \cdots + \zeta^{p-1} = 0$. In view of (31), we have

$$z_{y_1 y_2 \dots y_n} = \frac{1}{p}P\begin{bmatrix} \lambda_{00}^{n-l_1}\lambda_{10}^{l_1} \\ (-1)^{l_1}\lambda_{01}^n \\ \vdots \\ (-1)^{l_1}\lambda_{0,p-1}^n \end{bmatrix} \quad \text{for all } (l_0, l_1) \in \mathcal{I}_{2,n} \text{and } (y_1, y_2, \dots, y_n) \in \mathcal{Y}_{l_0, l_1}. \tag{32}$$

Since the $(s, k)$-component of the matrix $P$ is expressed as $\zeta^{sk}$, (32) implies that

$$z^{(s)}_{y_1 y_2 \cdots y_n} = \frac{1}{p}\left(\lambda_{00}^{n-l_1}\lambda_{10}^{l_1} + (-1)^{l_1}\sum_{k=1}^{p-1}\zeta^{sk}\lambda_{0k}^{n}\right) \quad \text{for all } s \in \mathbb{F}_p. \tag{33}$$

Hence, for any $s, s' \in \mathbb{F}_p$ it follows from (33) that

$$|z^{(s)}_{y_1 y_2 \cdots y_n} - z^{(s')}_{y_1 y_2 \cdots y_n}| = \frac{1}{p}\left|\sum_{k=1}^{p-1}(\zeta^{sk} - \zeta^{s'k})\lambda_{0k}^{n}\right|, \tag{34}$$

which no longer depends on $(y_1, y_2, \ldots, y_n) \in \{0, 1\}^n$. Then, recalling

$$P_{\boldsymbol{Y}|S}(\boldsymbol{y}|s) = \frac{z^{(s)}_{y_1 \cdots y_n}}{p^{n-1}} \quad \text{for all } s \in \mathbb{F}_p \text{and} \boldsymbol{y} = (y_1, y_2, \ldots, y_n) \in \{0, 1\}^n,$$

in view of (34) the value of $V_n(\tau)$ can be evaluated as follows:

$$\begin{aligned} V_n(\tau) &= \max_{s,s' \in \{0,1,\ldots,p-1\}} \frac{1}{2p^{n-1}} \sum_{(y_1,y_2,\ldots,y_n)\in\{0,1\}^n} \frac{1}{p}\left|\sum_{k=1}^{p-1}(\zeta^{sk} - \zeta^{s'k})\lambda_{0k}^{n}\right| \\ &= \frac{1}{2}\left(\frac{2}{p}\right)^n \max_{s,s' \in \{0,1,\ldots,p-1\}} \left|\sum_{k=1}^{p-1}(\zeta^{sk} - \zeta^{s'k})\lambda_{0k}^{n}\right|. \end{aligned} \tag{35}$$

Summarizing, we have the following proposition.

**Proposition 2.** *For the additive $(n, n)$-threshold scheme over $\mathbb{F}_p$, $V_n(\tau)$ is given by (35) for any identical leakage function $\tau : \mathbb{F}_p \to \{0, 1\}$.*

Hereinafter, we derive an upper bound of $V_n(\tau)$ in (35) that is valid for all $\tau$. By applying the triangle inequality, we have

$$\begin{aligned} \max_{s,s' \in \{0,1,\ldots,p-1\}} \left|\sum_{k=1}^{p-1}(\zeta^{sk} - \zeta^{s'k})\lambda_{0k}^{n}\right| &\le \max_{s,s' \in \{0,1,\ldots,p-1\}} \sum_{k=1}^{p-1} |\zeta^{sk} - \zeta^{s'k}||\lambda_{0k}|^n \\ &\le 4\cos\frac{\pi}{2p}\sum_{k=1}^{\frac{p-1}{2}}|\lambda_{0k}|^n, \end{aligned} \tag{36}$$

where the second inequality follows because $|\zeta^{sk} - \zeta^{s'k}| \le 2\sin\frac{(p-1)\pi}{2p} = 2\cos\frac{\pi}{2p}$ for all $s, s' \in \{0, 1, \ldots, p-1\}$ and $\lambda_{0,p-k} = \overline{\lambda_{0k}}$ for all $k = 0, 1, \ldots, p-1$. Then, the combination of (35) and (36) yields

$$V_n(\tau) \le 2\cos\frac{\pi}{2p}\sum_{k=1}^{\frac{p-1}{2}}\left(\frac{2|\lambda_{0k}|}{p}\right)^n. \tag{37}$$

Note that the dominant term on the right side of (37) is $\left(\frac{2|\lambda_{0,\max}|}{p}\right)^n$, where $|\lambda_{0,\max}| = \max\{|\lambda_{0k}| : k = 1, 2, \ldots, \frac{p-1}{2}\}$.

We use the following lemma that characterizes the magnitude of the eigenvalues of zero-one circulant matrices. Before giving the claim of the lemma, let us introduce the notion of a *set of powers*. Let $C$ be a $p\times p$ zero-one circulant matrix, $f_C(t)$ the polynomial corresponding to $C$, and $\lambda_k = f_C(\zeta^k)$, $k = 0, 1, \ldots, p-1$ the $p$ eigenvalues of $C$. Since $\zeta^p = 1$, for each $k \in \{1, 2, \ldots, p-1\}$ $\lambda_k$ is expresed as a sum of $\zeta^i$ with respect to $i \in T_k$, where $T_k$ is a subset of $\{0, 1, \ldots, p-1\}$. We call $T_k$ a *set of powers* of $\lambda_k$. For example, setting $p = 5$ and letting $C$ be the zero-one circulant matrix with $f_C(t) = t + t^2 + t^3$, the sets of powers of $\lambda_1, \lambda_2, \lambda_3$ and $\lambda_4$ are given by $T_1 = \{1, 2, 3\}$, $T_2 = \{1, 2, 4\}$, $T_3 = \{1, 3, 4\}$ and $T_4 = \{2, 3, 4\}$, respectively. It is obvious that $T_k = \{kj \in \mathbb{F}_p : j \in T_1\}$ for $k = 2, 3, 4$, where $kj \in \mathbb{F}_p$ is interpreted as the multiplication of $j, k \in \mathbb{F}_p$.

**Lemma 6.** *Let $p \geq 3$ be an arbitrary prime number and $u$ an arbitrary integer satisfying $2 \leq u \leq \frac{p-1}{2}$. Then, we have:*

(A) *Let $C^*$ be the $p \times p$ zero-one circulant matrix with $f_{C^*}(t) = 1 + t + \cdots + t^{u-1}$ as the polynomial corresponding to $C^*$. Let $\lambda_k^* = f_{C^*}(\zeta^k)$, $k = 0, 1, \ldots, p-1$ denote the $p$ eigenvalues of $C^*$. Then, $\lambda_0^* = u$ and*

$$\max\{|\lambda_k^*| : k = 1, 2, \ldots, p-1\} = |1 + \zeta + \cdots + \zeta^{u-1}|,$$

*where the above maximum is attained only by $k = 1$ and $k = p-1$.*

(B) *Let $\mathcal{E}(C^*)$ and $\mathcal{E}(C)$ denote the sets of the $p$ eigenvalues of $C^*$ in (A) and an arbitrary $p \times p$ zero-one circulant matrix $C$, respectively. If $\lambda_1^* \in \mathcal{E}(C)$, then $\mathcal{E}(C) = \mathcal{E}(C^*)$.*

(C) *Let $\mathcal{E}(C)$ denote the set of the $p$ eigenvalues of an arbitrary zero-one circulant matrix $C$. If $\lambda^\dagger \stackrel{\text{def}}{=} \zeta^a + \zeta^{a+1} + \cdots + \zeta^{a+u-1} \in \mathcal{E}(C)$ for some $a \in \{1, 2, \ldots, p-1\}$, it holds that*

$$\{|\lambda| : \lambda \in \mathcal{E}(C)\} = \{|\lambda| : \lambda \in \mathcal{E}(C^*)\} = \{|\lambda_0^*|, |\lambda_1^*|, \ldots, |\lambda_{p-1}^*|\}.$$

*Proof.* (A) Since $\overline{\zeta^k} = \zeta^{p-k}$ for all $k = 0, 1, \ldots, p-1$, we have $\overline{\lambda_k^*} = \overline{f_{C^*}(\zeta^k)} = f_{C^*}(\overline{\zeta^k}) = f_{C^*}(\zeta^{p-k}) = \lambda_{p-k}^*$, which implies that $\lambda_{p-1}^* = \overline{\lambda_1^*}$ and $|\lambda_1^*| = |\overline{\lambda_1^*}| = |\lambda_{p-1}^*|$. Lemma 4 guarantees that both $\lambda_1^*$ and $|\lambda_{p-1}^*|$ have the maximum magnitude among $\{\lambda_1^*, \lambda_2^*, \ldots, \lambda_{p-1}^*\}$.

Hereinafter, we prove that $|\lambda_k^*| < |\lambda_1^*|$ for all $k = 2, 3, \ldots, p-2$ by using a contradiction argument. Denote by $T_k$ the set of powers of $\lambda_k^* = f_{C^*}(\zeta^k)$ for $k = 1, 2, \ldots, p-1$. Clearly, $T_k = \{kj \in \mathbb{F}_p : j \in T_1\}$ for all $k = 1, 2, \ldots, p-1$. Suppose that there exists $k_0 \in \{2, 3, \ldots, p-2\}$ such that $T_{k_0}$ consists of $u$ consecutive integers modulo $p$. It is easily verified that $T_{k_0} \neq T_1$. In fact, if $k_0 \geq u$, it is obvious that $k_0 \notin T_0$ and $k_0 \in T_{k_0}$ because $1 \in T_1$. In addition, for the case of $2 \leq k_0 \leq u$, we can check that $k_0\lceil u/k_0\rceil \notin T_1$ and $k_0\lceil u/k_0\rceil \in T_{k_0}$ because $\lceil u/k_0\rceil \in T_1$. Similarly, we can verify that $T_{k_0} \neq T_{p-1}$ by regarding $p-1$ as $-1$.

Now, suppose that $T_{k_0}$ coincides with one of the following $D_l$, where

$$D_l = \left\{p-u+l+1, p-u+l+2, \ldots, p-1, 0, 1, \ldots, l\right\}, \quad l = 1, 2, \ldots, u-2.$$

Since $f_{C^*}(t)$ contains a constant term, $T_{k_0}$ must contain 0. In addition, since $T_{k_0} \neq T_1$ and $T_{k_0} \neq T_{p-1}$, not only 0 but also 1 and $p-1$ must be the elements of $T_{k_0}$. Assume that $T_{k_0}$ equals $D_{l_0}$ for some integer $1 \leq l_0 \leq u-2$. Since $T_{k_0} = \{k_0 j \in \mathbb{F}_p : 0 \leq j \leq u-1\}$ and $\{1, p-1\} \subset D_{l_0}$, there exist $j_1$ and $j_2$ satisfying $0 \leq j_1, j_2 \leq u-1$ and $\{k_0 j_1, k_0 j_2\} = \{1, p-1\}$. However, this implies that $k_0(j_1 + j_2) = p$, which yields a contradiction because $0 < j_1 + j_2 \leq 2u \leq p-1$ by assumption.

(B) Denote by $f_C(t)$ the polynomial corresponding to an arbitrary zero-one circulant matrix $C$. In view of Lemma 1, $\mathcal{E}(C) = \{f(\zeta^k) : k = 0, 1, \ldots, p-1\}$. It is important to notice that $\lambda_1^* \in \mathcal{E}(C)$ implies the existence of $k_0 \in \{1, 2, \ldots, p-1\}$ satisfying $\lambda_1^* = f_C(\zeta^{k_0})$. Notice that $\{k_0 j \in \mathbb{F}_p : j = 0, 1, \ldots, p-1\} = \{0, 1, \ldots, p-1\}$ because $p$ is prime and $k_0 \neq 0$. Hence, $\lambda_1^* = f_{C^*}(\zeta) = f_C(\zeta^{k_0})$ yields

$$\begin{aligned} \mathcal{E}(C) &= \{f_C((\zeta^{k_0})^j) : j = 0, 1, \ldots, p-1\} \\ &= \{f_{C^*}(\zeta^j) : j = 0, 1, \ldots, p-1\} = \mathcal{E}(C^*). \end{aligned}$$

(C) Letting $f_C(t)$ be the polynomial corresponding to a circulant matrix $C$, we have $\mathcal{E}(C) = \{f_C(\zeta^k) : k = 0, 1, \ldots, p-1\}$. Suppose that there exists $k_0 \in \{1, 2, \ldots, p-1\}$ satisfying $f_C(\zeta^{k_0}) = \zeta^a + \zeta^{a+1} + \cdots + \zeta^{a+u-1}$ for some $a \in \{1, 2, \ldots, p-1\}$. Setting $g(t) = t^a + t^{a+1} + \cdots + t^{a+u-1}$ and recalling $\{k_0 j \in \mathbb{F}_p : j = 0, 1, \ldots, p-1\} = \{0, 1, \ldots, p-1\}$, we obtain

$$\begin{aligned} \mathcal{E}(C) &= \{f_C((\zeta^{k_0})^j) : j = 0, 1, \ldots, p-1\} \\ &= \{g(\zeta^j) : j = 0, 1, \ldots, p-1\}. \end{aligned}$$

Then, since

$$g(\zeta^j) = (\zeta^j)^a + (\zeta^j)^{a+1} + \cdots + (\zeta^j)^{a+u-1}, = \zeta^{ja} f_{C^*}(\zeta^j)$$

we have $|g(\zeta^j)| = |\zeta^{ja} f_{C^*}(\zeta^j)| = |\zeta^{ja}||f_{C^*}(\zeta^j)| = |\lambda_j^*|$ for $j = 0, 1, \ldots, p-1$. □

The combination of Lemmas 4 and 6 tells us that (i) the greatest non-real eigenvalue of a $p \times p$ zero-one circulant matrix $C$ is less than or equal to $|1 + \zeta + \cdots + \zeta^{\frac{p-1}{2}}|$, and (ii) if a $p \times p$ zero-one circulant matrix $C$ has the non-real eigenvalue $\lambda$ with the greatest magnitude, then it holds that $\{|\lambda| : \lambda \in \mathcal{E}(C)\} = \{|\lambda^*| : \lambda \in \mathcal{E}(C^*)\}$, where $C^*$ is the zero-one circulant matrix with the polynomial $f_{C^*}(t) = 1 + t + \cdots + t^{\frac{p-1}{2}}$. Notice that Lemma 6 (A) gurantees that $C^*$ has *exactly* two non-real eigenvalues, $f_{C^*}(\zeta)$ and $f_{C^*}(\zeta^{p-1}) = \overline{f_{C^*}(\zeta)}$, with the greatest magnitude.

We define the following class of leakage functions.

**Definition 1.** *A class $\mathcal{B}_2$ of binary worst-case leakage functions is defined as the collection of leakage functions $\tau : \mathbb{F}_p \to \{0,1\}$ such that the zero-one circulant matrix $C_0$ (or, equivalently, $C_1$) in (27) induced by $\tau$ has an eigenvalue $\lambda$ satisfying $|\lambda| = |1 + \zeta + \cdots + \zeta^{\frac{p-1}{2}}|$.*

It is obvious that a leakage function $\tau$ belongs to $\mathcal{B}_2$ if and only if the zero-one circulant matrices $C_0$ (or $C_1$) induced by $\tau$ has an eigenvalue $\lambda$ whose set of powers consists of $\frac{p+1}{2}$ consecutive integers modulo $p$. Clearly, the leakage function that induces $C^*$ with $f_{C^*}(t) = 1 + t + \cdots + t^{\frac{p-1}{2}}$ belongs to $\mathcal{B}_2$. Actually, letting $\tau^*$ denote this leakage function, $\tau^*$ satisfies $\tau^*(0) = \tau^*(p-1) = \tau^*(p-2) = \cdots = \tau^*(\frac{p+1}{2}) = 0$ and $\tau^*(1) = \tau^*(2) = \cdots = \tau^*(\frac{p-1}{2}) = 1$. In addition, the LSB leakage discussed in [4,11] belongs to $\mathcal{B}_2$. In fact, $\tau$ gives the LSB of $X_i$ if $\tau(0) = \tau(2) = \cdots = \tau(p-1) = 0$ and if $\tau(1) = \tau(3) = \cdots = \tau(p-2) = 1$. For this $\tau$, $f_{C_1}(t) = t^2 + t^4 + \cdots + t^{p-1}$ ($f_{C_1}(t)$ has all the even powers of $t$ up to $p-1$ and does not have the constant term), which implies $\lambda_{1,\frac{p+1}{2}} = f_{C_1}(\zeta^{\frac{p+1}{2}}) = \zeta + \zeta^2 + \cdots + \zeta^{\frac{p-1}{2}}$. This means that $\lambda_{0,\frac{p+1}{2}} = 1 + \zeta^{\frac{p+1}{2}} + \cdots + \zeta^{p-1}$, which has the set of powers $\{\frac{p+1}{2}, \cdots, p-1, 0\}$ that consists of $\frac{p+1}{2}$ consecutive integers modulo $p$. Similarly, the MSB leakage, which is defined as $\tau(0) = \tau(1) = \cdots = \tau(\frac{p-1}{2}) = 0$ and $\tau(\frac{p+1}{2}) = \tau(\frac{p+3}{2}) = \cdots = \tau(p-1) = 1$, also belongs to $\mathcal{B}_2$ because $f_{C_0}(t) = 1 + t^{\frac{p+1}{2}} + t^{\frac{p+3}{2}} + \cdots + t^{p-1}$ and $|\lambda_{01}| = |1 + \zeta + \cdots + \zeta^{\frac{p-1}{2}}|$.

The following lemma gives the magnitudes of the eigenvalues of $C^*$.

**Lemma 7.** *Let $C^*$ be the $p \times p$ zero-one circulant matrix with the polynomial $f_{C^*}(t) = 1 + t + \cdots + t^{\frac{p-1}{2}}$. Let $\lambda_k^* = f_{C^*}(\zeta^k)$, $k = 0, 1, \ldots, p-1$ be the $p$ eigenvalues of $C^*$. Then, we have*

$$|\lambda_k^*| = \begin{cases} \frac{1}{2\sin\frac{k\pi}{2p}}, & \text{if } k \text{ is odd,} \\ \frac{1}{2\cos\frac{k\pi}{2p}}, & \text{if } k \text{ is even and } k \neq 0 \ . \end{cases}$$

*In addition, it holds that*

$$|\lambda_1^*| > |\lambda_3^*| > \cdots > |\lambda_{\frac{p-1}{2}}^*| > |\lambda_{\frac{p-3}{2}}^*| > |\lambda_{\frac{p-7}{2}}^*| > \cdots > |\lambda_2^*|, \quad \text{if } \frac{p-1}{2} \text{ is odd, and}$$

$$|\lambda_1^*| > |\lambda_3^*| > \cdots > |\lambda_{\frac{p-3}{2}}^*| > |\lambda_{\frac{p-1}{2}}^*| > |\lambda_{\frac{p-5}{2}}^*| > \cdots > |\lambda_2^*|, \quad \text{if } \frac{p-1}{2} \text{ is even.}$$

*Proof.* The first claim of Lemma 7 follows from

$$|\lambda_k^*| = \left| \frac{1 - (\zeta^k)^{\frac{p+1}{2}}}{1 - \zeta^k} \right| = \frac{\left|\sin\frac{k(p+1)\pi}{2p}\right|}{\sin\frac{k\pi}{p}} \quad \text{for } k = 1, 2, \ldots, p-1,$$

the double angle formula and $\sin\frac{k(p+1)\pi}{2p} = (-1)^{\frac{k-1}{2}}\cos\frac{k\pi}{2p}$ if $k$ is odd and $\sin\frac{k(p+1)\pi}{2p} = (-1)^{\frac{k}{2}}\sin\frac{k\pi}{2p}$ if $k \neq 0$ is even. The second claim is obvious. □

The combination of (37) and Lemma 7 yields the following upper bound on $V^{\dagger}_{\text{bin},n}$.

**Theorem 2.** *Consider the additive $(n, n)$-threshold scheme over $\mathbb{F}_p$, where $p \geq 3$ is an arbitrary prime number. Then, we have*

$$V^{\dagger}_{\text{bin},n} \leq 2\cos\frac{\pi}{2p}\frac{1}{(p\sin\frac{\pi}{2p})^n} + o\left(\frac{1}{(p\sin\frac{\pi}{2p})^n}\right), \tag{38}$$

*where $o(f(n))$ means a collection $g(n)$ of the terms satisfying $g(n)/f(n) \to 0$ as $n \to \infty$. In particular, for any leakage function $\tau \in \mathcal{B}_2$ we can obtain the higher order terms as follows:*

$$V_n(\tau) \leq 2\cos\frac{\pi}{2p}\left[\sum_{\substack{k=1\\k:\text{odd}}}^{\frac{p-1}{2}}\frac{1}{(p\sin\frac{k\pi}{2p})^n} + \sum_{\substack{k=1\\k:\text{even}}}^{\frac{p-1}{2}}\frac{1}{(p\cos\frac{k\pi}{2p})^n}\right] \quad \textit{for all } n \geq 1. \tag{39}$$

The dominant term in both the upper bounds in (38) and (39) is $2\cos\frac{\pi}{2p}/(p\sin\frac{\pi}{2p})^n$. While we can give the upper bound that is valid for all integers $n \geq 1$ if $\tau \in \mathcal{B}_2$, we can give an asymptotic upper bound for a general $\tau$.

We have the following result on a lower bound of $V^{\dagger}_{\text{bin,n}}$, which tells us that the order of the dominant term in the upper bounds in (38) and (39) cannot be improved.

**Theorem 3.** *For the additive $(n, n)$-threshold scheme over $\mathbb{F}_p$, it holds that*

$$V^{\dagger}_{\text{bin},n} \geq 2\left(\cos\frac{\pi}{2p}\right)^2\frac{1}{(p\sin\frac{\pi}{2p})^n} + o\left(\frac{1}{(p\sin\frac{\pi}{2p})^n}\right). \tag{40}$$

*Proof.* Since $V^{\dagger}_{\text{bin},n} \geq V_n(\tau)$ for any $\tau : \mathbb{F}_p \to \{0, 1\}$, it is sufficient to prove that $V_n(\tau^*)$ is lower-bounded by the right side of (40), where $\tau^*$ is the leakage function that induces the zero-one circulant matrix $C^*$ with $f_{C^*}(t) = 1+t+\cdots+t^{\frac{p-1}{2}}$. To this end, let $s \in \{0, 1, \ldots, p-1\}$ be an arbitrary integer and define $\tilde{s} = s+\frac{p-1}{2} \pmod p$. Then, it follows from Proposition 2 that

$$\begin{aligned} V_n(\tau) &= \frac{1}{2}\left(\frac{2}{p}\right)^n \max_{s,s' \in \{0,1,\ldots,p-1\}}\left|\sum_{k=1}^{p-1}(\zeta^{sk} - \zeta^{s'k})(\lambda^*_k)^n\right| \\ &\geq \frac{1}{2}\left(\frac{2}{p}\right)^n \max_{s \in \{0,1,\ldots,p-1\}}\left|\sum_{k=1}^{p-1}\zeta^{sk}(1 - \zeta^{\frac{(p-1)k}{2}})(\lambda^*_k)^n\right|, \end{aligned} \tag{41}$$

where the inequality follows from the definition of $s'$. By using the triangle inequality $|z_1 - z_2| \geq |z_1| - |z_2|$ for complex numbers $z_1$ and $z_2$, we have

$$\begin{aligned} &\left|\sum_{k=1}^{p-1}\zeta^{sk}(1 - \zeta^{\frac{(p-1)k}{2}})(\lambda^*_k)^n\right| \\ &\geq \left|\zeta^{s}(1 - \zeta^{\frac{p-1}{2}})(\lambda^*_1)^n + \zeta^{-s}(1 - \zeta^{-\frac{p-1}{2}})(\overline{\lambda^*_1})^n\right| - \left|\sum_{k=2}^{p-2}\zeta^{sk}(1 - \zeta^{\frac{(p-1)k}{2}})(\lambda^*_k)^n\right|, \end{aligned} \tag{42}$$

where we have used that $\zeta^{p-1} = \zeta^{-1}$ and $\lambda^*_{p-1} = \overline{\lambda^*_1}$. In view of Lemma 7, the first and second terms in (42) are of order $O(|\lambda^*_1|^n)$ and $O(|\lambda^*_3|^n)$, respectively, and therefore the first term is dominant for sufficiently large $n$.

Hereinafter, we evaluate the first term on the right side of (42). Setting $\theta_1 = \arg(\lambda^*_1)$, $r = |1 - \zeta^{\frac{p-1}{2}}|$ and $\beta = \arg(1 - \zeta^{\frac{p-1}{2}})$, where $\arg(z)$ denotes the argument of a complex number $z$, the first term in (42) can be written as follows:

$$\left|\zeta^s(1-\zeta^{\frac{(p-1)}{2}})(\lambda^*_1)^n + \zeta^{-s}(1-\zeta^{-\frac{(p-1)}{2}})(\overline{\lambda^*_1})^n\right| = 2r|\lambda^*_1|^n \left|\cos\left(n\theta_1 + \frac{2s\pi}{p} + \beta\right)\right|. \quad (43)$$

Since it is easily verified that $r = 2\sin\frac{(p-1)\pi}{2p} = 2\cos\frac{\pi}{2p}$, $\theta_1 = \frac{(p-1)\pi}{p}$ and $\beta = -\frac{\pi}{2p}$, the argument of the cosine function is given by

$$n\theta_1 + \frac{2s\pi}{p} + \beta = \frac{[2(p-1)n + 4s - 1]\pi}{2p}.$$

We choose $s = s_n \stackrel{\text{def}}{=} \frac{(p+1)n}{2} \pmod p$ so that $(p-1)n + 2s \equiv 0 \pmod p$ is satisfied for all $n \geq 1$. Clearly, $n\theta_1 + \frac{2s_n\pi}{p} + \beta = m\pi - \frac{\pi}{2p}$, where $m$ is an integer. Hence, we have

$$\begin{aligned} &\max_{s\in\{0,1,\ldots,p-1\}} \left|\zeta^s(1-\zeta^{\frac{(p-1)}{2}})(\lambda^*_1)^n + \zeta^{-s}(1-\zeta^{-\frac{(p-1)}{2}})(\overline{\lambda^*_1})^n\right| \\ &\geq 2r|\lambda^*_1|^n \cos\frac{\pi}{2p} = 4\left(\cos\frac{\pi}{2p}\right)^2 \frac{1}{(2\sin\frac{\pi}{2p})^n}. \end{aligned} \quad (44)$$

The combination of (41), (42) and (44) implies the claim of this theorem. □

Let us compare the lower bound in (40) with the lower bound $V_n(\tau) \geq \frac{1}{2}(\frac{2}{\pi})^n$ for the LSB leakage in [11, Theorem 10] that is valid for all sufficiently large $n$. Let us compare the bases $\frac{1}{p\sin\frac{\pi}{2p}}$ with $\frac{2}{\pi}$ the exponential terms. It is not hard to verify that $\frac{1}{p\sin\frac{\pi}{2p}} > \frac{2}{\pi}$ for all prime numbers $p$ and $\frac{1}{p\sin\frac{\pi}{2p}} \downarrow \frac{2}{\pi}$ as $p \to \infty$. In addition, it is obvious that $2(\cos\frac{\pi}{2p})^2 \geq 1/2$ for all prime numbers $p$. Therefore, if we compare the dominant terms of the two upper bounds, our lower bound in (40) is greater than the lower bound in [11]. We also point out that the same dominant term $(\frac{1}{p\sin\frac{\pi}{2p}})^n$ with a smaller coefficient can be obtained by slightly modifying the proof of [11, Theorem 10].

### 4.2 $V_n^\dagger$ for $L \geq 3$

Next, we consider the case of $3 \leq L \leq p-1$. Fix an identical leakage function $\tau : \mathbb{F}_p \to \mathcal{L} = \{0, 1, \ldots, L-1\}$ arbitrarily. Since the $(s,k)$-component of the matrix $P$ is equal to $\zeta^{sk}$, (31) tells us that

$$z^{(s)}_{y_1 y_2 \ldots y_n} = \frac{1}{p}\left(\prod_{b=0}^{L-1} \lambda_{b0}^{l_b} + \sum_{k=1}^{p-1} \zeta^{sk} \prod_{b=0}^{L-1} \lambda_{bk}^{l_b}\right) \text{ for any } s \in \mathbb{F}_p,\ (l_0, l_1, \ldots, l_{L-1}) \in \mathcal{I}_{L,n}$$
$$\text{and } (y_1, y_2, \ldots, y_n) \in \mathcal{Y}_{l_0, l_1, \ldots, l_{L-1}}. \quad (45)$$

Then, for any $s, s' \in \{0, 1, \ldots, p-1\}$ satisfying $s \neq s'$ it holds that

$$\begin{aligned} |z^{(s)}_{y_1 y_2 \cdots y_n} - z^{(s')}_{y_1 y_2 \cdots y_n}| &= \frac{1}{p}\left|\sum_{k=1}^{p-1}(\zeta^{sk} - \zeta^{s'k})\prod_{b=0}^{L-1}\lambda_{bk}^{l_b}\right| \\ &\leq \frac{1}{p}\sum_{k=1}^{p-1}|\zeta^{sk} - \zeta^{s'k}|\prod_{b=0}^{L-1}|\lambda_{bk}|^{l_b} \\ &\leq \frac{4}{p}\cos\frac{\pi}{2p}\sum_{k=1}^{\frac{p-1}{2}}\prod_{b=0}^{L-1}|\lambda_{bk}|^{l_b}, \end{aligned} \tag{46}$$

where the first inequality follows from the triangle inequality and the second inequality follows from $|\zeta^{sk} - \zeta^{s'k}| \leq 2\sin\frac{(p-1)\pi}{2p} = 2\cos\frac{\pi}{2p}$ for all $s, s', k$ and $\lambda_{b,p-k} = \overline{\lambda_{bk}}$. Notice that the right side of (46) does not depend on $s, s' \in \{0, 1, \ldots, p-1\}$ and $(y_1, \ldots, y_n) \in \mathcal{Y}_{l_0, l_1, \ldots, l_{L-1}}$. Therefore, it follows that

$$\begin{aligned} &d(P_{\mathbf{Y}|S}(\cdot\,|s), P_{\mathbf{Y}|S}(\cdot\,|s')) \\ &= \frac{1}{2p^{n-1}}\sum_{(l_0,l_1,\ldots,l_{L-1})\in\mathcal{I}_{L,n}}\ \sum_{(y_1,y_1,\ldots,y_n)\in\mathcal{Y}_{l_0,l_1,\ldots,l_{L-1}}}|z^{(s)}_{y_1 y_2 \cdots y_n} - z^{(s')}_{y_1 y_2 \cdots y_n}| \\ &\leq \frac{2}{p^n}\cos\frac{\pi}{2p}\sum_{(l_0,l_1,\ldots,l_{L-1})\in\mathcal{I}_{L,n}}\ \sum_{(y_1,y_2,\ldots,y_n)\in\mathcal{Y}_{l_0,l_1,\ldots,l_{L-1}}}\ \sum_{k=1}^{\frac{p-1}{2}}\prod_{b=0}^{L-1}|\lambda_{bk}|^{l_b} \\ &= \frac{2}{p^n}\cos\frac{\pi}{2p}\sum_{k=1}^{\frac{p-1}{2}}\ \sum_{(l_0,l_1,\ldots,l_{L-1})\in\mathcal{I}_{L,n}}\binom{n}{l_0, l_1, \ldots, l_{L-1}}\prod_{b=0}^{L-1}|\lambda_{bk}|^{l_b} \\ &= 2\cos\frac{\pi}{2p}\sum_{k=1}^{\frac{p-1}{2}}\left(\frac{1}{p}\sum_{b=0}^{L-1}|\lambda_{bk}|\right)^n, \end{aligned} \tag{47}$$

where $\binom{n}{l_0, l_1, \ldots, l_{L-1}}$ denotes the multinomial coefficient, the second equality follows from the change of the order of summation, and the last equality follows from the multinomial theorem.

In order to maximize the right side of (47) with respect to $\tau$, we introduce the notion of majorization (see [14]). Define

$$\begin{aligned} \mathcal{U}_L = \{&(u_0, u_1, \ldots, u_{L-1}) \in \mathbb{R}^L : \\ &u_i \geq 0 \text{ for } i = 0, 1, \ldots, L-1 \text{ and } u_0 + u_1 + \cdots + u_{L-1} = p\}, \end{aligned}$$

where $\mathbb{R}$ denotes the set of real numbers. Let $\boldsymbol{u} = (u_0, u_1, \ldots, u_{L-1})$ be an element of $\mathcal{U}_L$. Denote by $(u_{[0]}, u_{[1]}, \ldots, u_{[L-1]})$ the permutation of the components of $\boldsymbol{u}$ in the nonincreasing order, i.e., $u_{[0]} \geq u_{[1]} \geq \cdots \geq u_{[L-1]}$. Letting $\boldsymbol{u}$ and $\boldsymbol{v}$ be two elements of $\mathcal{U}_L$, we say that $\boldsymbol{v}$ dominates $\boldsymbol{u}$ (we use the notation $\boldsymbol{u} \preceq \boldsymbol{v}$) if

$$u_{[0]} + u_{[1]} + \cdots + u_{[j]} \leq v_{[0]} + v_{[1]} + \cdots + v_{[j]} \quad \text{for all } j = 0, 1, \ldots, L-1. \tag{48}$$

Since $\boldsymbol{u}, \boldsymbol{v} \in \mathcal{U}_L$, the inequality in (48) always holds with equality if $j = L-1$. If there exists $\boldsymbol{u}^* \in \mathcal{U}_L$ satisfying $\boldsymbol{u}^* \preceq \boldsymbol{v}$ for all $\boldsymbol{v} \in \mathcal{U}_L$, $\boldsymbol{u}^*$ is called the least element of $\mathcal{U}_L$. If a function $h(\boldsymbol{u})$ with the domain equal to $\mathcal{U}_L$ is Schur concave [14], i.e., $h(\boldsymbol{u}) \geq h(\boldsymbol{v})$ is satisfied for all $\boldsymbol{u}, \boldsymbol{v} \in \mathcal{U}_L$ satisfying $\boldsymbol{u} \preceq \boldsymbol{v}$, and the least element $\boldsymbol{u}^* \in \mathcal{U}_L$ exists, then $h(\boldsymbol{u})$ attains the maximum at $\boldsymbol{u} = \boldsymbol{u}^*$. We also define the subset $\tilde{\mathcal{U}}_L$ of $\mathcal{U}_L$ as the collection of the elements of $\mathcal{U}_L$ all components of which are integers.

We use the following lemma.

**Lemma 8.** *Let $p \geq 3$ be an arbitrary prime number and $L$ an arbitrary integer satisfying $2 \leq L \leq p-1$. Let $\{T_0, T_1, \ldots, T_{L-1}\}$ be a partition of $\{0, 1, \ldots, p-1\}$. Define*

$$f(T_0, T_1, \ldots, T_{L-1}) = \sum_{j=0}^{L-1} \left| \sum_{i \in T_j} \zeta^i \right|, \tag{49}$$

*where $\zeta = e^{\frac{2\pi i}{p}}$. Then, we have:*

(A) *Fix $\boldsymbol{u} = (u_0, u_1, \ldots, u_{L-1}) \in \tilde{\mathcal{U}}_L$ arbitrarily. Then, the maximum of $f(T_0, T_1, \ldots, T_{L-1})$ with respect to $(T_0, T_1, \ldots, T_{L-1})$ satisfying $\#T_i = u_i$, $i = 0, 1, \ldots, L-1$ is attained if and only if all of $T_i$, $i = 0, 1, \ldots, L-1$ consist of consecutive integers modulo $p$.*

(B) *Denote by $g(u_0, u_1, \ldots, u_{L-1})$ the maximum given in (A). Then, the maximum of $g(u_0, u_1, \ldots, u_{L-1})$ with respect to $\boldsymbol{u} = (u_0, u_1, \ldots, u_{L-1}) \in \tilde{\mathcal{U}}_L$ is attained if and only if the components of $\boldsymbol{u}$ consists of $L_g \stackrel{\text{def}}{=} p - Lu_s$ $u_g$'s and $L_s \stackrel{\text{def}}{=} Lu_g - p$ $u_s$'s where $u_g = \lceil p/L \rceil$ and $u_s = \lfloor p/L \rfloor$. The maximum of $g(u_0, u_1, \ldots, u_{L-1})$ is given by*

$$g^*_{L,p} \stackrel{\text{def}}{=} \frac{L_g \sin \frac{u_g \pi}{p} + L_s \sin \frac{u_s \pi}{p}}{\sin \frac{\pi}{p}}. \tag{50}$$

*Proof.* (A) Fix $\boldsymbol{u} = (u_0, u_1, \ldots, u_{L-1})$ arbitrarily. Then, Lemma 4 claims that for every $j \in \{0, 1, \ldots, L-1\}$ satisfying $u_j > 0$ $|\sum_{i \in T_j} \zeta^i|$ is maximized if and only if $T_j$ consists of $u_j$ consequtive integers modulo $p$. Since $f(T_0, T_1, \ldots, T_{L-1})$ is defined as the sum of $|\sum_{i \in T_j} \zeta^i|$, the maximum of $f(T_0, T_1, \ldots, T_{L-1})$ is attained if and only if $|\sum_{i \in T_j} \zeta^i|$ is maximized for every $j$ satisfying $u_j > 0$. This simultaneous maximization is possible by choosing, for example, $T_0 = \{0, 1, \ldots, u_0 - 1\}$, $T_1 = \{u_0, u_0 + 1, \ldots, u_0 + u_1 - 1\}$, $\cdots$, $T_{L-1} = \{\sum_{i=0}^{L-2} u_i, \sum_{i=0}^{L-2} u_i + 1, \ldots, p-1\}$.

(B) Fix $j \in \mathcal{L}$ satisfying $u_j > 0$ arbitrarily and set $T_j = \{k, k+1, \ldots, k+u_j-1\}$. Then, since it holds that

$$\left| \sum_{i \in T_j} \zeta^i \right| = |\zeta|^k \, |1 + \zeta + \cdots + \zeta^{u_j - 1}| = \left| \frac{\zeta^{u_j} - 1}{\zeta - 1} \right| = \frac{\sin \frac{u_j \pi}{p}}{\sin \frac{\pi}{p}},$$

$g(u_0, u_1, \ldots, u_{L-1})$ can be expressed as

$$g(u_0, u_1, \ldots, u_{L-1}) = \frac{1}{\sin \frac{\pi}{p}} \sum_{j=0}^{L-1} \sin \frac{u_j \pi}{p}.$$

Notice that $g(u_0, u_1, \ldots, u_{L-1})$ is Schur concave because $\sin(\pi x)$ is concave in the unit interval $[0, 1]$ and $g(u_0, u_1, \ldots, u_{L-1})$ is defined as the sum of $\sin(t_j \pi)$ where $t_j = u_j/p \in [0, 1]$ for all $j = 0, 1, \ldots, L-1$ [14]. Hence, $g(u_0, u_1, \ldots, u_{L-1})$ attains the maximum at the least element $\tilde{\boldsymbol{u}}^*$ of $\tilde{\mathcal{U}}_L$. In view of (48), all the elements of $\boldsymbol{u}^*$ must be equal to either $u_g = \lceil L/p \rceil$ or $u_s = \lfloor L/p \rfloor$. Letting $L_g$ (resp., $L_s$) be the numbers of the elements of $\boldsymbol{u}^*$ that equal to $u_g$ (resp., $u_s$), we have $L_g + L_s = L$ and $L_g u_g + L_s u_s = p$. By taking $u_g - u_s = 1$ into consideration, we obtain $L_g = p - L u_s$ and $L_s = L u_g - p$. □

*Example 2.* Suppose that $p = 7$ and $L = 3$. In this case, $u_g = 3, u_s = 2, L_g = 1$ and $L_s = 2$. Clearly, $L_g + L_s = L$ and $u_g L_g + u_s L_s = p$ are satisfied. Then, $f(T_0, T_1, T_2)$ in (49) is maximized by, say, $T_0 = \{0, 1, 6\}, T_1 = \{4, 5\}$ and $T_2 = \{2, 3\}$, all of which consist of consecutive integers modulo 7.

We also need the following lemma to evaluate $V_n(\tau)$.

**Lemma 9.** *Let $p \geq 3$ be an arbitrary prime number and $L$ an arbitrary integer satisfying $2 \leq L \leq p-1$. Let $C_0, C_1, \ldots, C_{L-1}$ be arbitrary $p \times p$ zero-one circulant matrices such that $C_0 + C_1 + \cdots + C_{L-1}$ is the all-one matrix. Denote by $f_{C_b}(t)$ the polynomial corresponding to $C_b$ and $\lambda_{bk} = f_{C_b}(\zeta^k)$, $k = 0, 1, \ldots, p-1$ the $p$ eigenvalues of $C_b$. Then, we have:*

*(A) It holds that*

$$\sum_{b=0}^{L-1} |\lambda_{bk}| \leq g^*_{L,p} \quad \text{for all } k = 1, 2, \ldots, p-1. \tag{51}$$

*The inequality in (51) is satisfied with equality at $k = k_0 \in \{1, 2, \ldots, p-1\}$ if and only if $L_g$ (resp., $L_s$) $T_{bk_0}$'s consist of $u_g$ (resp., $u_s$) consecutive integers modulo $p$, where $T_{bk}$ denotes the set of powers of $\lambda_{bk}$.*

*(B) If there exists an integer $k_0 \in \{1, 2, \ldots, p-1\}$ satisfying (51) with equality, then it holds that*

$$\sum_{b=0}^{L-1} |\lambda_{bk}| < g^*_{L,p} \quad \text{for all } k \in \{1, 2, \ldots, p-1\} \backslash \{k_0, p-k_0\}. \tag{52}$$

*Proof.* (A) Since $C_0 + C_1 + \cdots + C_{L-1}$ is assumed to be the all-one matrix, $\{T_{01}, T_{11}, \ldots, T_{L-1,1}\}$ forms a partition of $\{0, 1, \ldots, p-1\}$. Since $T_{bk} = \{ki \in \mathbb{F}_p : i \in T_{b1}\}$ for each $b \in \mathcal{L}$, $\{T_{0k}, T_{1k}, \ldots, T_{L-1,k}\}$ also forms a partition of

$\{0, 1, \ldots, p-1\}$ for all $k = 2, 3, \ldots, p-1$. Therefore, by virtue of Lemma 8, we have

$$\sum_{b=0}^{L-1} |\lambda_{bk}| = \sum_{b=0}^{L-1} \left| \sum_{i \in T_{bk}} \zeta^i \right| \leq g^*_{L,p} \quad \text{for all } k = 1, 2, \ldots, p-1. \tag{53}$$

Lemma 8 also tells us that the inequality in (51) is satisfied with equality at $k = k_0$ if and only if $L_g$ (resp., $L_s$) $T_{bk_0}$'s satisfy $|T_{bk_0}| = u_g$ (resp., $|T_{bk_0}| = u_s$) and all of $T_{bk_0}$, $b \in \mathcal{L}$ consist of consecutive integers modulo $p$.

(B) Denote by $C_0, C_1, \ldots, C_{L-1}$ the $p \times p$ zero-one $L$ circulant matrices satisfying the equality condition of (A) at $k = k_0$. Define $T_{bk}$ as the set of powers of $\lambda_{bk} = f_{C_b}(\zeta^k)$. Fix $b \in \mathcal{L}$ arbitrarily and set $u = |T_{b1}|$. Define $C^*$ as the $p \times p$ zero-one circulant matrix determined by the polynomial $f_{C^*}(t) = 1 + t + \cdots + t^{u-1}$. Define $\lambda^*_k = f_{C^*}(\zeta^k)$, $k = 0, 1, \ldots, p-1$. Recall that Lemma 6 guarantees that

$$\{|\lambda_{bk}| : k = 1, 2, \ldots, p-1\} = \{|\lambda^*_k| : k = 1, 2, \ldots, p-1\},$$

$|\lambda_{bk_0}| = |\lambda_{b,p-k_0}| = |\lambda^*_1|$ and $|\lambda_{bk}| < |\lambda^*_1|$ for all $k \in \{1, 2, 3, \ldots, p-1\} \backslash \{k_0, p-k_0\}$. Since the same argument is valid for all $b \in \mathcal{L}$, the claim of (B) is obvious. □

We continue evaluating the right side of (47). Let $\lambda_{bk} = f_{C_b}(\zeta^k)$, $b = 0, 1, \ldots, L-1$. Then, Lemma 9 (A) guarantees

$$\sum_{b=0}^{L-1} |\lambda_{bk}| \leq g^*_{L,p} \quad \text{for all } k = 1, 2, \ldots, \frac{p-1}{2}. \tag{54}$$

However, if (54) is satisfied with equality by some integer $k = k_0 \in \{1, 2, \ldots, \frac{p-1}{2}\}$, Lemma 9 (B) claims that the inequality (54) strictly holds for all $k \in \{1, 2, \ldots, \frac{p-1}{2}\} \backslash \{k^*\}$. This immediately implies that, letting $\varepsilon > 0$ be an arbitrarily small number, we have

$$d(P_{\mathbf{Y}|S}(\cdot\,|s), P_{\mathbf{Y}|S}(\cdot\,|s')) \leq 2\cos\frac{\pi}{2p}\left(\frac{g^*_{L,p}}{p}\right)^n + o\left(\left(\frac{g^*_{L,p}}{p}\right)^n\right). \tag{55}$$

Since the right side of (55) is independent of $s, s'$ and $\tau : \mathbb{F}_p \to \mathcal{L}$, the following theorem is established.

**Theorem 4.** *Consider the additive $(n,n)$-threshold scheme over $\mathbb{F}_p$ with an identical leakage function $\tau : \mathbb{F}_p \to \{0, 1, \ldots, L-1\}$, where $p \geq 5$ is an arbitrary prime number and $L$ is an arbitrary integer satisfying $3 \leq L \leq p-1$. Then, it holds that*

$$V^\dagger_n \leq 2\cos\frac{\pi}{2p}\left(\frac{g^*_{L,p}}{p}\right)^n + o\left(\left(\frac{g^*_{L,p}}{p}\right)^n\right) \tag{56}$$

*where $g^*_{L,p}$ is defined in (50).*

It is important to notice that the first claim of Theorem 2 is obtained as a corollary to Theorem 4. In fact, in the derivation of Theorem 4 we did not use the assumption of $L \geq 3$ and the argument above is valid even for the case of $L = 2$. In fact, for the case of $L = 2$, we can easily verify that $g^*_{2,p} = \frac{1}{\sin\frac{\pi}{2p}}$ because $L_g = L_s = 1$, $u_g = \frac{p+1}{2}$, $u_s = \frac{p-1}{2}$ and $\sin\frac{(p+1)\pi}{2p} = \sin\frac{(p-1)\pi}{2p}$. We discussed the case of $L = 2$ separately because we do not need the argument of majorization if $L = 2$ and we can obtain a sharper result (39) for the class of $\mathcal{B}_2$.

**Corollary 1.** *The claim of Theorem 4 is valid for any prime $p \geq 3$ and integer $2 \leq L \leq p - 1$.*

The difference between the cases of $L = 2$ and $L \geq 3$ appears in the expressions of $|z^{(s)}_{y_1 y_2 \cdots y_n} - z^{(s')}_{y_1 y_2 \cdots y_n}|$ in (34) and (46), respectively. Although in (34) $|z^{(s)}_{y_1 y_2 \cdots y_n} - z^{(s')}_{y_1 y_2 \cdots y_n}|$ depends on neither $(y_1, y_2, \ldots, y_n) \in \mathcal{Y}_{l_0,l_1}$ nor $(l_0, l_1) \in \mathcal{I}_{2,n}$, the dependency on $(l_0, l_1, \ldots, l_{L-1}) \in \mathcal{I}_{L,n}$ remains in (46). We must say that this dependency makes it difficult to obtain a result on a lower bound of $V^\dagger_n$.

We need the following assumption to establish a lower bound of $V^\dagger_n$:

**Assumption A:** Let $p \geq 3$ be a prime number and $L$ an arbitrary integer satisfying $2 \leq L \leq p - 1$. Define $L_g, L_s, u_g$ and $u_s$ as in Lemma 8. Set $\beta = -\frac{\pi}{2p}$, $\theta^*_b = b\frac{2u_g\pi}{p} + \frac{u_g\pi}{p}$ for $b = 0, 1, \ldots, L_g - 1$ and $\theta^*_{L_g+b} = L_g\frac{2u_g\pi}{p} + b\frac{2u_s\pi}{p} + \frac{u_s\pi}{p}$ for $b = 0, 1, \ldots, L_s - 1$. Then, for an arbitrary (possibly, sufficiently large) integer $n$, there exist $p$ and $s \in \{0, 1, \ldots, p - 1\}$ satisfying

$$\sum_{b=0}^{L-1} l_b\theta^*_b + \beta + \frac{2s\pi}{p} \notin \left\{\frac{\pi}{2} + m\pi \,:\, m \in \mathbb{Z}\right\} \quad \text{for all } (l_0, l_1, \ldots, l_{L-1}) \in \mathcal{I}_{L,n}. \tag{57}$$

We have numerically checked that Assumption A is satisfied if $p$ is relatively large compared with $n$ and $L$. For example, for the case of $n = 5$, $L = 3$ and $p = 13$, we can find $s = 3$ that meets (57). Giving a proof on the exisitence of $s$ satisyfing (57) seems quite difficult.

We have the following result on a lower bound on $V^\dagger_n$:

**Theorem 5.** *Consider the additive $(n, n)$-threshold scheme over $\mathbb{F}_p$ with an identical leakage function $\tau : \mathbb{F}_p \to \{0, 1, \ldots, L - 1\}$, where $p \geq 3$ is a prime number and $L$ is an arbitrary integer satisfying $2 \leq L \leq p-1$. Then, under the assumption of the existence of $p$ and $s \in \{0, 1, \ldots, p-1\}$ satisfying (57) in in Assumption A, it holds that*

$$V^\dagger_n \geq 2\sin\frac{\pi}{p}\left(\frac{g^*_{L,p}}{p}\right)^n + o\left(\left(\frac{g^*_{L,p}}{p}\right)^n\right). \tag{58}$$

*Proof.* Given a sufficiently large $n$, we choose a prime $p$ and $s \in \{0, 1, \ldots, p - 1\}$ satisfying (57). Let $L_g, L_s, u_g$ and $u_s$ be the numbers defined in Lemma 8.

Let $C_0^*, C_1^*, \ldots, C_{L-1}^*$ be zero-one circulant matrices specified by the following polynomials:

$$f_{C_b^*}(t) = t^{bu_g} + t^{bu_g+1} + \cdots + t^{(b+1)u_g-1}, \quad b = 0, 1, \ldots, L_g - 1, \text{ and}$$
$$f_{C_{L_g+b}^*}(t) = t^{L_g u_g}(t^{bu_s} + t^{bu_s+1} + \cdots + t^{(b+1)u_s-1}), \quad b = 0, 1, \ldots, L_s - 1.$$

Denote by $\lambda_{bk}^* = f_{C_b^*}(\zeta^k)$, $k = 0, 1, \ldots, p-1$ the $p$ eigenvalues of $C_b^*$. We also define $\lambda_g^* = 1 + \zeta + \cdots + \zeta^{u_g-1}$ and $\lambda_s^* = 1 + \zeta + \cdots + \zeta^{u_s-1}$. Lemma 4 tells us that

$$|\lambda_g^*| = |\lambda_{b1}^*| = |\lambda_{b,p-1}^*| > \max\{|\lambda_{bk}^*| : k = 2, 3, \ldots, p-2\},$$
$$\text{for all } b = 0, 1, \ldots, L_g - 1 \text{ , and} \tag{59}$$
$$|\lambda_s^*| = |\lambda_{L_g+b,1}^*| = |\lambda_{L_g+b,p-1}^*| > \max\{|\lambda_{L_g+b,k}^*| : k = 2, 3, \ldots, p-2\},$$
$$\text{for all } b = 0, 1, \ldots, L_s - 1. \tag{60}$$

In addition, since $|\lambda_g^*| = \frac{\sin \frac{u_g \pi}{p}}{\sin \frac{\pi}{p}}$ and $|\lambda_s^*| = \frac{\sin \frac{u_s \pi}{p}}{\sin \frac{\pi}{p}}$, $g_{L,p}^*$ defined in (50) is expressed as $g_{L,p}^* = L_g|\lambda_g^*| + L_s|\lambda_s^*|$.

Let $\tau^*$ be the leakage function that induces the above circulant matrices $C_0^*, C_1^*, \ldots, C_{L-1}^*$. We prove that $V_n(\tau_n^*)$ is lower bounded by the right side of (58). We apply a method similar to the proof of Theorem 3. In view of (45), we have

$$\begin{aligned} V_n(\tau^*) &= \frac{1}{2p^n} \max_{s,s' \in \{0,1,\ldots,p-1\}} \sum_{(l_0,l_1,\ldots,l_{L-1}) \in \mathcal{I}_{L,n}} \sum_{(y_1,y_1,\ldots,y_n) \in \mathcal{Y}_{l_0,l_1,\ldots,l_{L-1}}} \\ &\qquad \left| \sum_{k=1}^{p-1} (\zeta^{sk} - \zeta^{s'k}) \prod_{b=0}^{L-1} (\lambda_{bk}^*)^{l_b} \right| \\ &\geq \frac{1}{2p^n} \sum_{(l_0,l_1,\ldots,l_{L-1}) \in \mathcal{I}_{L,n}} \sum_{(y_1,y_1,\ldots,y_n) \in \mathcal{Y}_{l_0,l_1,\ldots,l_{L-1}}} \left| \sum_{k=1}^{p-1} \zeta^{sk} (1 - \zeta^{\frac{(p-1)k}{2}}) \prod_{b=0}^{L-1} (\lambda_{bk}^*)^{l_b} \right|, \end{aligned} \tag{61}$$

where the inequality is obtained by setting $s' = s + \frac{p-1}{2} \pmod p$. By using the triangle inequality, it holds that

$$\begin{aligned} &\left| \sum_{k=1}^{p-1} (1 - \zeta^{\frac{(p-1)k}{2}}) \prod_{b=0}^{L-1} (\lambda_{bk}^*)^{l_b} \right| \\ &\geq \left| \zeta^s (1 - \zeta^{\frac{p-1}{2}}) \prod_{b=0}^{L-1} (\lambda_{b1}^*)^{l_b} + \zeta^{-s} (1 - \zeta^{-\frac{p-1}{2}}) \prod_{b=0}^{L-1} (\overline{\lambda_{b1}^*})^{l_b} \right| \\ &\qquad - \left| \sum_{k=2}^{p-2} \zeta^{sk} (1 - \zeta^{\frac{(p-1)k}{2}}) \prod_{b=0}^{L-1} (\lambda_{bk}^*)^{l_b} \right|, \end{aligned} \tag{62}$$

where we have used that $\zeta^{p-1} = \zeta^{-1}$ and $\lambda_{b,p-1}^* = \overline{\lambda_{b,1}^*}$ for all $b \in \mathcal{L}$.

Hereinafter, we evaluate the first term on the right side of (62). Set $r = |1 - \zeta^{\frac{p-1}{2}}|$, $\beta = \arg(1 - \zeta^{\frac{p-1}{2}})$ and $\theta_b^* = \arg(\lambda_{b1}^*)$ for $b \in \mathcal{L}$. Since it holds that

$$\zeta^s(1 - \zeta^{\frac{p-1}{2}}) \prod_{b=0}^{L-1} (\lambda_{b1}^*)^{l_b} = r \left( \prod_{b=0}^{L-1} |\lambda_{b1}^*|^{l_b} \right) \exp\left[ \mathrm{i} \left( \sum_{b'=0}^{L-1} l_{b'} \theta_{b'}^* + \beta + \frac{2s\pi}{p} \right) \right],$$

we have

$$\begin{aligned} &\zeta^s(1 - \zeta^{\frac{p-1}{2}}) \prod_{b=0}^{L-1} (\lambda_{b1}^*)^{l_b} + \zeta^{-s}(1 - \zeta^{-\frac{p-1}{2}}) \prod_{b=0}^{L-1} (\overline{\lambda_{b1}^*})^{l_b} \\ &= 2r \left( \prod_{b=0}^{L-1} |\lambda_{b1}^*|^{l_b} \right) \cos\left( \sum_{b'=0}^{L-1} l_{b'} \theta_{b'}^* + \beta + \frac{2\,s\pi}{p} \right). \end{aligned} \tag{63}$$

It is easily verified that $r = 2\cos\frac{\pi}{2p}$, $\beta = -\frac{\pi}{2p}$ and $\theta_b^*$, $b = 0, 1, \ldots, L-1$ are given by $\theta_b^* = b\frac{2u_g\pi}{p} + \frac{u_g\pi}{p}$ for $b = 0, 1, \ldots, L_g - 1$ and $\theta_{L_g+b}^* = L_g\frac{2u_g\pi}{p} + b\frac{2u_s\pi}{p} + \frac{u_s\pi}{p}$ for $b = 0, 1, \ldots, L_s - 1$ as are given in Assumption A. Under these definitions, the argument of the cosine in (63) is expressed as

$$\begin{aligned} &\sum_{b=0}^{L-1} l_b \theta_b^* + \beta + \frac{2\,s\pi}{p} \\ &= \frac{\pi}{p} \left[ \sum_{b=0}^{L_g-1} l_b u_g (2b+1) + \sum_{b=0}^{L_s-1} l_{L_g+b} \Big( 2u_g L_g + u_s(2b+1) \Big) + 2s - \frac{1}{2} \right]. \end{aligned}$$

Notice that the number between the above square brackets is a half-integer. Hence, under Assumption A, it holds that

$$\begin{aligned} \min_{(l_0, l_1, \ldots, l_{L-1}) \in \mathcal{I}_{L,n}} \left| \cos\left( \sum_{b'=0}^{L-1} l_{b'} \theta_{b'}^* + \beta + \frac{2s\pi}{p} \right) \right| &\geq \min_{m \in \{1,2,\ldots,p\} \setminus \{\frac{p+1}{2}\}} \left| \cos\frac{(2m-1)\pi}{2p} \right| \\ &= \sin\frac{\pi}{2p}, \end{aligned}$$

where we have used $\cos\frac{(p-1)\pi}{2p} = \sin\frac{\pi}{2p}$. Therefore, (63) leads to

$$2r \left( \prod_{b=0}^{L-1} |\lambda_{b1}^*|^{l_b} \right) \left| \cos\left( \sum_{b'=0}^{L-1} l_{b'} \theta_{b'}^* + \beta + \frac{2\,s\pi}{p} \right) \right| \geq 2r \left( \prod_{b=0}^{L-1} |\lambda_{b1}^*|^{l_b} \right) \sin\frac{\pi}{2p}. \tag{64}$$

By using (64), we can develop a simple lower bound on the sum of the first term in (62) with respect to $(l_0, l_1, \ldots, l_{L-1}) \in \mathcal{I}_{L,n}$ and $(y_1, y_2, \ldots, y_n) \in \mathcal{Y}_{l_0, l_1, \ldots, l_{L-1}}$ in the following way:

$$\sum_{(l_0,l_1,\ldots,l_{L-1})\in \mathcal{I}_{L,n}} \sum_{(y_1,\ldots,y_n)\in \mathcal{Y}_{l_0,l_1,\ldots,l_{L-1}}} \left|(1-\zeta^{\frac{p-1}{2}})\prod_{b=0}^{L-1}(\lambda^*_{b1})^{l_b} + (1-\zeta^{-\frac{p-1}{2}})\prod_{b=0}^{L-1}(\overline{\lambda^*_{b1}})^{l_b}\right|$$

$$\stackrel{a)}{\geq} \sum_{(l_0,l_1,\ldots,l_{L-1})\in \mathcal{I}_{L,n}} \sum_{(y_1,\ldots,y_n)\in \mathcal{Y}_{l_0,l_1,\ldots,l_{L-1}}} 2r\left(\prod_{b=0}^{L-1}|\lambda^*_{b1}|^{l_b}\right)\left|\cos\left(\sum_{b'=0}^{L-1} l_{b'}\theta^*_{b'}+\beta\right)\right|$$

$$\stackrel{b)}{\geq} 2r\sin\frac{\pi}{2p}\sum_{(l_0,l_1,\ldots,l_{L-1})\in \mathcal{I}_{L,n}}\binom{n}{l_0,l_1,\ldots,l_{L-1}}\prod_{b=0}^{L-1}|\lambda^*_{b1}|^{l_b}$$

$$\stackrel{c)}{=} 4\cos\frac{\pi}{2p}\sin\frac{\pi}{2p}\left(\sum_{b=0}^{L-1}|\lambda^*_{b1}|\right)^n$$

$$\stackrel{d)}{=} 2\sin\frac{\pi}{p}(g^*_{L,p})^n, \tag{65}$$

where the marked equality and inequalities follows from:

a): (63),
b): (64) and $\#\mathcal{Y}_{l_0,l_1,\ldots,l_{L-1}} = \binom{n}{l_0,l_1,\ldots,l_{L-1}}$,
c): the multinomial theorem and $r = 2\cos\frac{\pi}{2p}$, and
d): (59), (60), the double angle theorem and $L_g|\lambda^*_g| + L_s|\lambda^*_s| = g^*_{L,p}$ due to the definition of $g^*_{L,p}$.

Consequently, by combining (61), (62) and (65), we obtain the claim of the theorem. □

## 4.3 Connection to the Fourier Analysis

In this subsection, we investigate a connection between the method for analyzing the asymptotic behaviour of $V_n^\dagger$ that is developed in this paper and the Fourier analytic method that originates from [1]. Given a secret $s \in \mathbb{F}_p$, an identical leakage function $\tau : \mathbb{F}_p \to \mathcal{L}$ and $\boldsymbol{y} = (y_1, y_2, \ldots, y_n) \in \mathcal{Y}_{l_0,l_1,\ldots,l_{L-1}}$ for some $(l_0, l_1, \ldots, l_{L-1}) \in \mathcal{I}_{L,n}$, $z^{(s)}_{y_1y_2\cdots y_n}$ in (45) gives the conditional probability $P_{\boldsymbol{Y}|S}(\boldsymbol{y}|s) = \frac{1}{p^{n-1}}z^{(s)}_{y_1y_2\cdots y_n}$. We show that we can obtain a formula similar to (45) by using the Fourier analytic method. To this end, set

$$C_s = \{(x_1, x_2, \ldots, x_n) \in \mathbb{F}_p^n \;:\; x_1 + x_2 + \cdots + x_n = s\}.$$

Then, it holds that

$$\begin{aligned} P_{\boldsymbol{Y}|S}(\boldsymbol{y}|s) &= \mathop{E}_{\boldsymbol{X}\leftarrow C_s}\left[\mathbf{1}_{y_1}(X_1)\mathbf{1}_{y_2}(X_2)\ldots\mathbf{1}_{y_n}(X_n)\right] \\ &= \mathop{E}_{\boldsymbol{X}\leftarrow C_s}\left[\sum_{\boldsymbol{a}\in\mathbb{F}_p^n}\left(\prod_{i=1}^n\hat{\mathbf{1}}_{y_i}(a_i)\right)\zeta^{-\langle \boldsymbol{X},\boldsymbol{a}\rangle}\right] \\ &= \sum_{\boldsymbol{a}\in\mathbb{F}_p^n}\left(\prod_{i=1}^n\hat{\mathbf{1}}_{y_i}(a_i)\right)\mathop{E}_{\boldsymbol{X}\leftarrow C_s}\left[\zeta^{-\langle \boldsymbol{X},\boldsymbol{a}\rangle}\right], \end{aligned} \tag{66}$$

where $\underset{\boldsymbol{X}\leftarrow C_s}{E}$ denotes the expectation with respect to the uniform distribution over $\mathbb{F}_p^n$ with $\boldsymbol{X}$ being restricted to $C_s$, $\mathbf{1}_y(x) = 1$ if $\tau(y) = x$ and 0 otherwise, $\hat{\mathbf{1}}_y(a) = \frac{1}{p}\sum_{x\in\mathbb{F}_p}\mathbf{1}_y(x)\zeta^{ax}$ denotes the Fourier transform of $\mathbf{1}_y(x)$, $\langle \boldsymbol{X}, \boldsymbol{a}\rangle = \sum_{i=1}^n X_i a_i$ means the inner product of $\boldsymbol{a} = (a_1, a_2, \ldots, a_n)$ and $\boldsymbol{X} = (X_1, X_2, \ldots, X_n)$. Notice that the second equality in (66) follows from the Poisson summation formula [1, Lemma 4.15]. In addition, it is not hard to verify that $\underset{\boldsymbol{X}\leftarrow C_s}{E}\left[\zeta^{-\langle \boldsymbol{X},\boldsymbol{a}\rangle}\right] = \frac{1}{p^n}\zeta^{-as}$ if $\boldsymbol{a} = (a, a, \ldots, a)$ for $a \in \mathbb{F}_p$ and 0 otherwise. Therefore, (66) can be expressed as

$$P_{\boldsymbol{Y}|S}(\boldsymbol{y}|s) = \sum_{a\in\mathbb{F}_p}\left(\prod_{i=1}^n \hat{\mathbf{1}}_{y_i}(a)\right)\zeta^{-as} \tag{67}$$

Next, we investigate the meaning of $\hat{\mathbf{1}}_y(a)$. By the definitions of the Fourier transform and $\mathbf{1}_y(x)$, we have

$$\hat{\mathbf{1}}_y(a) = \frac{1}{p}\sum_{x\in\mathbb{F}_p}\mathbf{1}_y(x)\zeta^{ax} = \frac{1}{p}\sum_{x\in\tau^{-1}(y)}\zeta^{ax}.$$

Define the polynomial $f_y(t)$ of order at most $p-1$ by $f_y(t) = \sum_{x\in\tau^{-1}(y)} t^x$. Recall that $f_y(t)$ determines a $p\times p$ zero-one circulant matrix $C_y$. Then, since $\hat{\mathbf{1}}_y(a) = \frac{1}{p}f_y(\zeta^a)$, $\hat{\mathbf{1}}_y(a)$ equals $\frac{\lambda_{ya}}{p}$, where $\lambda_{ya}$ denotes the the $a$-th eigenvalue of the zero-one circulant matrix $C_y$. Consequently, (67) can be expressed as

$$\begin{aligned} P_{\boldsymbol{Y}|S}(\boldsymbol{y}|s) &= \frac{1}{p^n}\sum_{a\in\mathbb{F}_p}\left(\prod_{i=1}^n \lambda_{y_i a}\right)\zeta^{-as} = \frac{1}{p^n}\left(\prod_{i=1}^n \lambda_{y_i 0} + \sum_{\substack{a\in\mathbb{F}_p:\\ a\neq 0}}\zeta^{-as}\prod_{i=1}^n \lambda_{y_i a}\right) \\ &= \frac{1}{p^n}\left(\prod_{b=0}^{L-1}\lambda_{b0}^{l_b} + \sum_{k=1}^{p-1}\zeta^{-as}\prod_{b=0}^{L-1}\lambda_{bk}^{l_b}\right), \end{aligned} \tag{68}$$

where the last equality holds if $(y_1, y_2, \ldots, y_n) \in \mathcal{Y}_{l_0,l_1,\ldots,l_{L-1}}$ and $(l_0, l_1, \ldots, l_{L-1}) \in \mathcal{I}_{L,n}$, which is almost the same form as (45) divided by $p^{n-1}$.

It is interesting that we can obtain the first term in (68) as

$$\begin{aligned} \underset{\boldsymbol{X}\leftarrow\mathbb{F}_p^n}{E}\left[\mathbf{1}_{y_1}(X_1)\mathbf{1}_{y_2}(X_2)\ldots\mathbf{1}_{y_n}(X_n)\right] &= \sum_{\boldsymbol{a}\in\mathbb{F}_p^n}\left(\prod_{i=1}^n \hat{\mathbf{1}}_{y_i}(a_i)\right)\underset{\boldsymbol{X}\leftarrow\mathbb{F}_p^n}{E}\left[\zeta^{-\langle \boldsymbol{X},\boldsymbol{a}\rangle}\right] \\ &= \frac{1}{p^n}\prod_{i=1}^n \lambda_{y_i 0} \end{aligned} \tag{69}$$

similarly to (66), where the last equality is obtained because $\underset{\boldsymbol{X}\leftarrow\mathbb{F}_p^n}{E}\left[\zeta^{-\langle \boldsymbol{X},\boldsymbol{a}\rangle}\right] = 1$ if $\boldsymbol{a} = (0, 0, \ldots, 0)$ and 0 otherwise. Therefore, we can eliminate the effect of the real eigenvalues $\prod_{i=1}^n \lambda_{y_i 0}$ by subtracting the left side of (69) from $P_{\boldsymbol{Y}|S}(\boldsymbol{y}|s)$ in (68) (see [1, Theorem 4.7]).

The difference between the upper bounds of $V_n(\tau)$ obtained in this paper and [1] mainly consists in evaluations of the multiplicity of the terms that become the most dominant (Lemma 6 for $L = 2$ and Lemma 9 for $3 \le L \le p-1$). We also clarified the meaning of the values $\hat{\mathbf{1}}_{y_i}(a)$, $a \in \mathbb{F}_p$ of the Fourier transform in the real (share) domain as the eigenvalues of a certain $p \times p$ zero-one circulant matrix determined by $\tau$. Finally, we also point out that the connection to the Fourier analysis demonstrated in this subsection is valid when the leakage functions $\tau_1, \tau_2, \ldots, \tau_n$ are not identical.

## 5 Extension to Non-identical Leakage Functions

So far, we have considered the case where $n$ leakage functions $\tau_1, \tau_2, \ldots, \tau_n$ are identical to a leakage function $\tau$ and have established that $V_n^\dagger$ vanishes of order $(g^*_{L,p}/p)^n$.

In this section, we show that the results in the preceding section can be easily extended to the case where $\tau_1, \tau_2, \ldots, \tau_n$ are not required to be identical. To this end, let us consider $n$ leakage functions $\tau_1, \tau_2, \ldots, \tau_n$ and define the leakage $\boldsymbol{Y} = (Y_1, Y_2, \ldots, Y_n)$ according to (6). For $s \in \mathbb{F}_p$ and $(y_1, y_2, \ldots, y_n) \in \mathcal{L}^n$ define

$$\begin{aligned} A^{(s)}_{y_1 y_2 \ldots y_i} = \{(x_1, x_2, \ldots, x_i) \in \mathbb{F}_p^i \ :\ \tau_j(x_j) = y_j \text{ for all } 1 \le j \le i \\ \text{and } x_1 + x_2 + \cdots + x_i = s\}, \qquad i = 1, 2, \ldots, n, \end{aligned}$$

which is a modified version of $A^{(s)}_{y_1 y_2 \ldots y_i}$ in (24). Then, similarly to (25), it holds that

$$A^{(s)}_{y_1 y_2 \cdots y_{i+1}} = \bigcup_{j \in \tau_{i+1}^{-1}(y_{i+1})} A^{(s-j)}_{y_1 y_2 \cdots y_i} \times \{j\}, \quad i = 1, 2 \ldots, n-1. \tag{70}$$

Notice that the union in (70) is taken with respect to $j \in \tau_{i+1}^{-1}(y_{i+1})$. It follows from (70) that

$$z_{y_1 y_2 \cdots y_{i+1}} = C^{[i+1]}_{y_{i+1}} z_{y_1 y_2 \cdots y_i}, \quad i = 1, 2 \ldots, n-1, \tag{71}$$

where $C^{(i)}_b$ is the $p \times p$ circulant matrix with the $(s, j)$-component given by

$$C^{[i]}_b[s, j] = \begin{cases} 1, \text{ if } s - j \in \tau_i^{-1}(b), \\ 0, \text{ otherwise,} \end{cases}$$

for $b \in \mathcal{L}$ and $i = 2, 3, \ldots, n$. By using (71) repeatedly, we obtain

$$z_{y_1 y_2 \cdots y_n} = C^{[n]}_{y_n} C^{[n-1]}_{y_{n-1}} \cdots C^{[2]}_{y_2} z_{y_1}. \tag{72}$$

Notice that the circulant matrices in (72) depend not only $y_i \in \mathcal{L}$ but also $i \in \{2, 3, \ldots, n\}$ for the non-identical case. However, Lemma 2 still guarantees that $C^{[i]}_b$ ($b \in \mathcal{L}$, $i = 2, 3, \ldots, n$) are diagonalized by the matrices $P$ and $P^{-1}$ as $\Lambda^{[i]}_b =$

$P^{-1}C_b^{[i]}P$, where $\mathrm{diag}(\lambda_{b0}^{[i]}, \lambda_{b1}^{[i]}, \ldots, \lambda_{b,p-1}^{[i]})$ and $\lambda_{bk}^{[i]} = f_{C_b^{[i]}}(\zeta^k)$, $k = 0, 1, \ldots, p-1$ are eigenvalues of $C_b^{[i]}$. Taking Lemma 5 and (72) into consideration, we obtain the following formula for $z_{y_1 y_2 \ldots y_n}^{(s)}$:

$$z_{y_1 y_2 \ldots y_n}^{(s)} = \frac{1}{p}\left(\prod_{i=1}^{n} \lambda_{y_i 0}^{[i]} + \sum_{k=1}^{p-1} \zeta^{sk} \prod_{i=1}^{n} \lambda_{y_i k}^{[i]}\right)$$
$$\text{for } s \in \{0, 1, \ldots, p-1\} \text{and} (y_1, y_2, \ldots, y_n) \in \mathcal{L}^n.$$

Then, similarly to (46), we can obtain

$$\max_{s,s' \in \{0,1,\ldots,p-1\}} |z_{y_1 y_2 \cdots y_n}^{(s)} - z_{y_1 y_2 \cdots y_n}^{(s')}| \le \frac{4}{p} \cos \frac{\pi}{2p} \sum_{k=1}^{\frac{p-1}{2}} \prod_{i=1}^{n} |\lambda_{y_i k}^{[i]}|.$$

By using the triangle inequality, $V_n^*$ can be evaluated as follows:

$$\begin{aligned} V_n^* &\le \frac{2}{p^n} \cos \frac{\pi}{2p} \sum_{k=1}^{\frac{p-1}{2}} \sum_{(y_1, y_2, \ldots, y_n) \in \mathcal{L}^n} \prod_{i=1}^{n} |\lambda_{y_i k}^{[i]}| \\ &= \frac{2}{p^n} \cos \frac{\pi}{2p} \sum_{k=1}^{\frac{p-1}{2}} \prod_{i=1}^{n} \left(|\lambda_{0k}^{[i]}| + |\lambda_{1k}^{[i]}| + \cdots + |\lambda_{L-1,k}^{[i]}|\right), \end{aligned} \tag{73}$$

where the last equality follows from the change of the order of summation and multiplication. Notice here that, for each $i = 1, 2, \ldots, n$ $C_0^{[i]}, C_1^{[i]}, \ldots, C_{L-1}^{[i]}$ are $p \times p$ zero-one circulant matrices satisfying $C_0^{[i]} + C_1^{[i]} + \cdots + C_{L-1}^{[i]}$ equals the all-one matrix Lemma 9(A) guarantees

$$|\lambda_{0k}^{[i]}| + |\lambda_{1k}^{[i]}| + \cdots + |\lambda_{L-1,k}^{[i]}| \le g_{L,p}^* \quad \text{for all } 1 \le i \le n \text{ and } 1 \le k \le \frac{p-1}{2}. \tag{74}$$

In order to maximize the product in (73), the equality in (74) must be attained at an identical $k = k_0 \in \{1, 2, \ldots, \frac{p-1}{2}\}$ for all $i = 1, 2, \ldots, n$. However, in such a case Lemma 9(B) tells us that the equality in (74) does not hold for all $k \in \{1, 2, \ldots, \frac{p-1}{2}\} \backslash \{k_0\}$. This means that $V_n^*$ is also upper-bounded by the right side of (56). In addition, since we have $V_n^* \ge V_n^\dagger$, the lower bound in (58) is also valid as a lower bound of $V_n^*$.

Summarizing, we have the following corollary:

**Corollary 2.** *Let $p \ge 3$ be an arbitrary prime number and $L$ an arbitrary integer satisfying $2 \le L \le p-1$. Consider the additive $(n, n)$-threshold scheme over $\mathbb{F}_p$ with $n$ leakage functions $\tau_1, \tau_2, \ldots, \tau_n$, where $\tau_i : \mathbb{F}_p \to \mathcal{L} = \{0, 1, \ldots, L-1\}$ for $i = 1, 2, \ldots, n$. Then, $V_n^*$ is upper-bounded by the right side of (56). In addition, under Assumption A, $V_n^*$ is lower-bounded by the right side of (58).*

We can compare the base $\frac{g^*_{L,p}}{p} = \frac{L_g \sin\frac{u_g\pi}{p} + L_s \sin\frac{u_s\pi}{p}}{p\sin\frac{\pi}{p}}$ of the dominant term of $V^*_n$ with the base $\frac{L\sin\frac{\pi}{L}}{p\sin\frac{\pi}{p}}$ in [1, Corollary 4.8]. Recall that $g^*_{L,p}$ obtained by maximization of $g(\boldsymbol{u})$ in Lemma 8 under the constraint of $\boldsymbol{u} = (u_0, u_1, \ldots, u_{L-1}) \in \tilde{\mathcal{U}}_L$. That is, all the components of $\boldsymbol{u}$ are nonnegative integers satisfying $u_0 + u_1 + \cdots + u_{L-1} = p$. Actually, $g(\boldsymbol{u})$ is maximized by the least element $\tilde{\boldsymbol{u}}^* \in \tilde{\mathcal{U}}_L$, which gives $g^*_{L,p} = g(\tilde{\boldsymbol{u}}^*) = \frac{L_g \sin\frac{u_g\pi}{p} + L_s \sin\frac{u_s\pi}{p}}{\sin\frac{\pi}{p}}$. On the other hand, we can also consider the maximization of $g(\boldsymbol{u})$ in $\mathcal{U}_L$. In this case, all the components of $\boldsymbol{u}$ can be nonnegative real numbers satisfying $u_0 + u_1 + \cdots + u_{L-1} = p$. In fact, $g(\boldsymbol{u})$ is maximized by the least element $\boldsymbol{u}^* = (p/L, p/L, \ldots, p/L)$ of $\mathcal{U}_L$, which gives $g(\boldsymbol{u}^*) = \frac{L\sin\frac{\pi}{L}}{\sin\frac{\pi}{p}}$. Since $\tilde{\mathcal{U}}_L \subset \mathcal{U}_L$, it obviously holds that $g(\tilde{\boldsymbol{u}}^*) < g(\boldsymbol{u}^*)$. Therefore, the base in $g^*_{L,p}/p$ in Corollary 2 is smaller than the base $\frac{L\sin\frac{\pi}{L}}{p\sin\frac{\pi}{p}}$ in [1].

## 6 Conclusion

In this paper, we have considered the local leakage resilience of the additive $(n, n)$-threshold scheme defined over a finite field $\mathbb{F}_p$, where $p \geq 3$ is an arbitrary prime number. Letting $(X_1, X_2, \ldots, X_n)$ be the $n$ shares and $\boldsymbol{Y} = (Y_1, Y_2, \ldots, Y_n)$ be a leakage defined by $Y_i = \tau_i(X_i)$ for $i = 1, 2, \ldots, n$, where $\tau_i : \mathbb{F}_p \to \{0, 1, \ldots, L-1\}$ is a deterministic mapping, we have analyzed the worst-case total variational distance $V^*_n$ between the conditional probability distributions $P_{\boldsymbol{Y}|S}(\cdot\,|s)$ and $P_{\boldsymbol{Y}|S}(\cdot\,|s')$ of $\boldsymbol{Y}$ given secrets $s$ and $s'$. We have proposed a new method to evaluate $V^*_n$ more precisely than the existing methods. For the case of $L = 2$, we have shown that $V^*_n$ converges to zero of order $O((p\sin\frac{\pi}{2p})^{-n})$. A class of leakage functions that attain $V^*_n$ is also clarified. For the case of $L \geq 3$, we have obtained an upper bound of $V^*_n$ by using the theory of majorization. The order of the obtained upper bound is smaller than the upper bound in [1] and is proved to be tight under a certain assumption.

**Acknowledgements.** The authors acknowledge constructive comments from anonymous reviewers. The first author is supported in part by JSPS KAKENHI Grant Number 23K10979.

## References

1. Benhamouda, F., Degwekar, A., Ishai, Y., Rabin, T.: On the local leakage resilience of linear secret sharing schemes. J. Cryptology **34**(2), 10 (2021)
2. Blakley, G.: Safeguarding cryptographic keys. In: Proceedings of the AFIPS National Computer Conference, vol. 22, pp. 313–317 (1979)
3. Bogdanov, A., Guo, S., Komargodski, I.: Threshold secret sharing requires a large-size alphabet. Theory Comput. **16**(2), 1–18 (2020)

4. Faust, S., Masure, L., Micheli, E., Orlt, M., Standaert, F.X.: Connecting leakage-resilient secret sharing to practice: scaling trends and physical dependencies of prime field masking. In: Joye, M., Leander, G. (eds.) EUROCRYPT 2024. LNCS, vol. 14654, pp. 316–344. Springer, Cham (2024). https://doi.org/10.1007/978-3-031-58737-5_12
5. Gray, R.M.: Toeplitz and Circulant Matrices: A Review. Now Publishers (2006)
6. Karnin, E., Greene, J., Hellman, M.: On secret sharing systems. IEEE Trans. Inf. Theory **29**(1), 35–41 (1983)
7. Klein, O., Komargodski, I.: New bounds on the local leakage resilience of Shamir's secret sharing scheme. In: Handschuh, H., Lysyanskaya, A. (eds.) CRYPTO 2023. LNCS, vol. 14081, pp. 139–170. Springer, Cham (2023). https://doi.org/10.1007/978-3-031-38557-5_5
8. Kocher, P.C.: Timing attacks on implementations of Diffie-Hellman, RSA, DSS, and other systems. In: Koblitz, N. (ed.) CRYPTO 1996. LNCS, vol. 1109, pp. 104–113. Springer, Heidelberg (1996). https://doi.org/10.1007/3-540-68697-5_9
9. Kocher, P., Jaffe, J., Jun, B.: Differential power analysis. In: Wiener, M. (ed.) CRYPTO 1999. LNCS, vol. 1666, pp. 388–397. Springer, Heidelberg (1999). https://doi.org/10.1007/3-540-48405-1_25
10. Maji, H.K., Nguyen, H.H., Paskin-Cherniavsky, A., Suad, T., Wang, M.: Leakage-resilience of the shamir secret-sharing scheme against physical-bit leakages. In: Canteaut, A., Standaert, F.-X. (eds.) EUROCRYPT 2021. LNCS, vol. 12697, pp. 344–374. Springer, Cham (2021). https://doi.org/10.1007/978-3-030-77886-6_12
11. Maji, H., et al.: Tight estimate of the local leakage resilience of the additive secret-sharing scheme & its consequences. In: Information-Theoretic Cryptography. LIPIcs, vol. 230, pp. 16:1–16:19. Schloss Dagstuhl Leibniz-Zentrum für Informatik (2022)
12. Maji, H., Nguyen, H., Paskin-Cherniavsky, A., Wang, M.: Improved bound on the local leakage-resilience of Shamir's secret sharing. In: Proceedings of the IEEE ISIT 2022, pp. 2678–2683 (2022)
13. Maji, H.K., Nguyen, H.H., Paskin-Cherniavsky, A., Ye, X.: Constructing leakage-resilient Shamir's secret sharing: over composite order fields. In: Joye, M., Leander, G. (eds.) EUROCRYPT 2024. LNCS, vol. 14654, pp. 286–315. Springer, Cham (2024). https://doi.org/10.1007/978-3-031-58737-5_11
14. Marshall, A.W., Olkin, I., Arnold, B.C.: Inequalities: Theory of Majorization and Its Applications, 2nd edn. Springer, Cham (2010)
15. Nguyen, H.H.: Towards breaking the half-barrier of local leakage-resilient Shamir's secret sharing. In: Reyzin, L., Stebila, D. (eds.) Advances in Cryptology – CRYPTO 2024. LNCS, vol. 14924, pp. 257–285. Springer, Cham (2024). https://doi.org/10.1007/978-3-031-68388-6_10
16. Nguyen, H.H.: Physical-bit leakage resilience of linear code-based secret sharing. In: Fehr, S., Fouque, PA. (eds.) EUROCRYPT 2025, Part VIII. LNCS, vol. 15608, pp. 64–93, Springer, Cham (2025). https://doi.org/10.1007/978-3-031-91101-9_3
17. Shamir, A.: How to share a secret. Commun. ACM **22**(11), 612–613 (1979)

# Taming Adaptive Security and New Access Structures in Evolving Secret Sharing

Danilo Francati[1], Sara Giammusso[1,2], and Daniele Venturi[1(✉)]

[1] Sapienza University of Rome, Rome, Italy
venturi@di.uniroma1.it
[2] Banca d'Italia, Rome, Italy

**Abstract.** Evolving secret sharing (Komargodski, Naor, and Yogev, TCC 2016) allows a dealer to share a secret value in an online manner, without knowing the access structure or the maximum number of parties in advance, and without ever updating the shares of older players. In this paper, we continue the study of evolving secret sharing schemes in the computational setting, as first considered by Francati and Venturi (ASIACRYPT 2024), where the number of parties is upper bounded by an unknown polynomial and the privacy property only holds against computationally-bounded adversaries.

Our main results are outlined below:

- We construct secret sharing schemes for new evolving access structures. In particular, we design secret sharing schemes for the so-called dynamic weighted threshold evolving access structure and for all evolving monotone functions in NP.
- We initiate the study of adaptive security for evolving secret sharing, where the attacker can corrupt shareholders in an adaptive manner. In particular, we design adaptively-secure secret sharing schemes for the dynamic weighted threshold evolving access structure and for evolving monotone circuits.

**Keywords:** evolving secret sharing · adaptive security · computational security

## 1 Introduction

*Long ago, in Cryptoland, a grand vault sat at the heart of the citadel, entrusted with the kingdom's deepest lore. From its inception, the vault's keepers realized that the circle of trust could not remain unmodified. Heroes and scholars joined the realm at unpredictable moments, and some fell from grace or were lost to distant realms. To address this, the vault's architects*

D. Francati—Work done in part while at Royal Holloway, University of London, Egham, UK.

© International Association for Cryptologic Research 2026
G. Hanaoka and B.-Y. Yang (Eds.): ASIACRYPT 2025, LNCS 16252, pp. 67–98, 2026.
https://doi.org/10.1007/978-981-95-5125-5_3

*wove a living enchantment: whenever a new guardian arrived, they received a unique rune (share) that intertwined seamlessly with existing runes-no ancient guardian ever needed their rune replaced.*
*On the dawn of each solstice, newcomers gathered before the vault's arcane gates. The Grand Archivist, acting as dealer, whispered a fresh incantation, distributing runes that encoded the secret without revealing it. These runes respected the current council's logic: any coalition declared worthy by the kingdom's decrees could unite their runes to open the vault, but no lesser group gained a single clue. Crucially, the Archivist need not know how many guardians might arrive in future ages-only that the runes would adapt to every new participant.*
*Yet, dark clouds gathered as scary dragons-sly adversaries able to observe guardians and adjust their tactics in real time-sought to breach the vault. They tested every combination of runes they could steal. But the living enchantment was fortified ensuring that even as dragons learned cunning new strategies, the vault's magic remained unbreakable. No matter how the dragons shifted their approach, they could never accumulate a forbidden coalition of runes strong enough to open the gates.*

Secret sharing [6,21] allows a dealer to encode a secret value into shares to be distributed among $n$ players. The access structure of a secret sharing scheme describes the subsets of players that are authorized to reconstruct the secret (by pulling their shares together); access structures must be *monotone* (i.e., if a given subset of parties is authorized, so is any subset containing that subset). At the same time, every unauthorized subset of players has no information about the secret (this is the so-called privacy property).

When the number of parties is not fixed in advance and grows over time, we speak of *evolving* access structures. To deal with this scenario, Komargodski, Naor, and Yogev [16] were the first to consider secret sharing schemes supporting evolving access structures in the information-theoretic setting, where the number of parties can potentially go to infinite and the privacy guarantee holds statistically. In a recent paper, Francati and Venturi [12] explored evolving secret sharing in the computational setting, where the privacy property only holds in the presence of computationally-bounded adversaries, and additionally the number of parties is an arbitrary polynomial (unknown to the dealer) in some relevant security parameter $\lambda \in \mathbb{N}$. Evolving access structures must be *rigid* (i.e., if a given subset of parties is unauthorized when there are $n_1$ players, that subset remains unauthorized when there are $n_2$ players for any $n_2 > n_1$), as otherwise the dealer would need to update the shares of old parties.

While of course weaker than statistical security, computational security allows to obtain evolving secret sharing schemes with shorter shares, where the size of a share is measured as a function of the current number of parties $n$ (and of the security parameter). In fact, in their work, Francati and Venturi beat the share size of all previous constructions; for specific evolving access structures, they are even able to get secret sharing schemes with *succinct* shares, meaning that the share size is much smaller compared to the size of a natural computational representation of the evolving access structure.

### 1.1 Our Contributions

In this paper, we continue the line of research on computationally-secure evolving secret sharing in two directions:

(i) First, we design secret sharing schemes for new evolving access structures that were not considered in previous works.
(ii) Second, we consider for the first time evolving secret sharing schemes with adaptive security, meaning that the adversary can corrupt parties dynamically while the access structure evolves.

Below, we summarize our results in more details. In Sect. 1.2, we provide an informal overview of the main techniques required to obtain our results.

**Part I: New Access Structures.** Perhaps, the most basic evolving access structure is the evolving threshold access structure, in which the number of parties $n$ grows over time, and any subset of parties is of size at least $t$, for a fixed threshold $t \in \mathbb{N}$. As argued in [12], it is rather simple to design a secret sharing scheme for the threshold evolving access structure in the computational setting: it suffices to take Shamir's secret sharing over a field of super-polynomial size; since the number of participants is at most polynomial, the dealer can simply distribute the evaluation of the polynomial over the next point without ever running out of points.

The case of *dynamic* threshold evolving access structures is more challenging. Here, the access structure is described by a sequence of thresholds $\{t_n\}_{n \geq 1}$. The threshold $t_n$ can depend on $n$ and is unknown to the dealer before the $n$-th party arrives. Assuming one-way functions (OWFs), Francati and Venturi [12] gave a secret sharing scheme for dynamic evolving threshold access structures with share size $\lambda(n+1)$.

*Dynamic Weighted Threshold Access Structures.* In this paper, we consider a natural generalization of the dynamic threshold evolving access structure, in which each party is assigned a different weight according to a weight function $w_n$: when there are $n$ parties, a subset of parties is authorized whenever the sum of their weights meets the threshold $t_n$. Hence, both the weights and the threshold change over time. We present a construction based on OWFs yielding a share size that grows linearly with both the weight and the number of parties:

**Theorem 1 (Informal Theorem 5 and Corollary 1).** *Assuming OWFs, there exists a secret sharing scheme for the dynamic weighted threshold evolving access structure in which the share size for party $n \geq 1$ equals $\lambda(1 + W_n)$, where $W_n = W_{n-1} + w_n$ and $w_n$ is the weight associated to the $n$-th party.*

*Monotone* NP *access structures.* As defined in Komargodski et al. [15] a monotone NP access structure is characterized by a monotone NP language, where each subset of parties corresponds to an instance, and the subset is authorized if the instance is in the NP language. Monotonicity ensures that any superset of an authorized subset is also authorized. Intuitively, in a secret sharing scheme for such access structures, reconstruction is possible for qualified subsets via a witness certifying membership in the language provided as an auxiliary input by the parties (as defined in [15]), whereas for unqualified subsets such a witness does not exist and thus the secret cannot be recovered. We extend this notion to the evolving setting, where the access structure is defined by a sequence of monotone NP (mNP) functions $\{f_n\}$, with $n$ being the current number of parties. We present a construction for this access structure based on witness encryption (WE) for NP and OWFs, achieving a share size polynomial in both the number of parties $n$ and the security parameter:

**Theorem 2 (Informal Theorem 6).** *Assuming witness encryption for* NP *and OWFs, there exists a secret sharing scheme for the* mNP *evolving access structure in which the share size for party* $n \geq 1$ *equals* $\mathsf{poly}(\lambda, n)$.

**Part II: Adaptive Security.** We initiate the study of adaptive security in the context of evolving secret sharing. For the class of evolving dynamic weighted threshold access structures, we introduce the first adaptively secure construction, relying on trapdoor permutations in the random oracle model (ROM).

**Theorem 3 (Informal Theorem 7 and Corollary 2).** *Assuming trapdoor permutations, there exists a secret sharing scheme for the dynamic weighted threshold evolving access structure that is adaptively secure in the ROM, with share size for party* $n \geq 1$ *equal to* $\lambda(n + W_n)$*, where* $W_n = W_{n-1} + w_n$ *and* $w_n$ *is the weight of party* $n$.

*Monotone Circuits Access Structures.* In monotone circuits evolving access structures parties correspond to the inputs wires of an evolving boolean circuit made of AND and OR gates with unbounded fan-in. We show that the [12]'s construction supporting the monotone circuits evolving access structures (based on OWFs and projective PRGs) achieves adaptive security when restricted to $\mathsf{NC}^0$ monotone circuits. We demonstrate its adaptivity by leveraging the framework of Jafargholi et al. [14].

**Theorem 4 (Informal Theorem 8).** *Assuming OWFs and RSA (resp., iO and somewhere statistically binding hash functions), there exists a secret sharing scheme for the monotone* $\mathsf{NC}^0$ *circuits evolving access structure that is adaptively secure, with share size for party* $n \geq 1$ *equal to* $m_g \cdot \mathsf{poly}(\lambda)$*, where* $m_g$ *is the number of gates in the circuit.*

In addition to the RSA assumption, we remark that projective PRGs can be instantiated under a variety of other assumptions, namely: (i) indistinguishability obfuscation (iO) combined with somewhere statistically binding (SSB) hash functions; (ii) the Decisional Diffie-Hellman (DDH) and Bilinear Decisional Diffie-Hellman (BDDH) assumptions; and (iii) the Learning With Errors (LWE) assumption. Depending on the specific instantiation of the projective PRGs, we obtain different-though generally larger-share sizes.

## 1.2 Technical Overview

In this section, we give an overview of the techniques used to obtain our results.

**Dynamic Weighted Threshold Access Structures $\hat{\mathcal{A}}^{\mathsf{dwthr}}$.** We study dynamic weighted threshold evolving access structures, denoted $\hat{\mathcal{A}}^{\mathsf{dwthr}}$, which extend classic threshold schemes by assigning weights to parties and allowing the access structure to evolve over time. A subset of parties is authorized at stage $n$ if the sum of their weights—according to a global weight function $w_n$—meets or exceeds a threshold $t_n$. Note that $t_n$ freely varies with $n$. We also allow the function $w_n$ to adapt with $n$, as long as it respects monotonicity and rigidity: once a set becomes authorized, it remains so, and unauthorized sets stay unauthorized unless extended.

We present a construction based on OWFs, yielding linear share size w.r.t. both the number of parties and the weights. The construction, described in Construction 3.1, can be seen as a generalization to that presented by [12] for the case of evolving dynamic threshold, and works as follows. Let $\mathsf{G}$ be a PRG with unbounded polynomial stretch, and let $\mathsf{SS}_{\mathsf{NE}}$ be a (possibly computational) secret sharing scheme for the (non-evolving) weighted threshold access structure. When party $n$ arrives, the dealer samples a random seed $\kappa_n$, then it computes $n$ shares $(\mathsf{sh}_i^n)_{i\in[n]}$ of the message $\mu$ using the $\mathsf{SS}_{\mathsf{NE}}$ scheme over the non-evolving weighted threshold access structure when there are $n$ parties. The (evolving) share $\sigma_n$ of a party $n$ consists of the seed $\kappa_n$, of the share $\mathsf{sh}_n^n$, along with $n-1$ ciphertexts $(\gamma_i)_{i<n}$ where each ciphertext $\gamma_i$ is an encryption of $\mathsf{sh}_i^n$ under the pseudorandom pad $\rho_i = \mathsf{G}(\kappa_i)[n-i]$ ($\mathsf{G}(\kappa_i)[n-i]$ denotes the next unused block output by the PRG $\mathsf{G}(\kappa_i)$ associated to the party $i$). When we instantiate our construction using as non-evolving secret sharing for the weighted threshold access structure Shamir's secret sharing with weight virtualization—where a party of weight $w_i$ holds $w_i$ Shamir shares of size $\lambda$—the construction results in a share size $|\sigma_n| = \lambda(1 + W_n)$, where $W_n$ is the sum of the weights of all the $n$ parties.[1] Reconstruction is straightforward. Any authorized subset can recover at least $t_n$ pads used to encrypt the shares $(\mathsf{sh}_i^n)_{i\in[n]}$, and thus reconstruct the message by means of the $\mathsf{SS}_{\mathsf{NE}}$ reconstruction algorithm.

[1] We highlight that the GIDT technique from [1] can be used to obtain a non-evolving secret sharing scheme for weighted access structures with share size $2^{\mathsf{polylog}(n)}$, i.e., share size independent of the weights' values. However, since we are in the computational setting and $n = \mathsf{poly}(\lambda)$, such a scheme cannot be used to improve the share size of our evolving construction (when used as a replacement for Shamir's secret sharing with weight virtualization), as this would produce shares of superpolynomial size.

Finally, computational privacy follows by observing that: (*i*) all ciphertexts $\gamma_j$ corresponding to honest parties appear as uniformly random strings (due to the security of $\mathsf{G}$ and the fact that the honest seeds are never revealed to the adversary); and (*ii*) the remaining decryptable shares $\mathsf{sh}_j^i$ (for some indices $i$ and $j$) are insufficient to reconstruct the message $\mu_b$, i.e., $\mu_b$ remains hidden as long as the underlying non-evolving secret sharing scheme $\mathsf{SS}_{\mathsf{NE}}$ satisfies (possibly computational) privacy.

**Monotone NP Access Structures $\hat{\mathcal{A}}^{\mathsf{mNP}}$.** We now consider the case of monotone NP evolving access structures, denoted $\hat{\mathcal{A}}^{\mathsf{mNP}}$. In this setting, a subset of parties is authorized to reconstruct the secret if there exists a witness—provided as auxiliary input by the parties—certifying that the subset satisfies a given monotone NP language. Specifically, at each stage $n$, the access structure is defined by a monotone NP function $f_n : \{0,1\}^n \to \{0,1\}$, where each subset of parties $\mathcal{I}_x \subseteq [n]$ is represented by a binary indicator vector $x$, and is considered authorized if and only if $f_n(x) = 1$. Intuitively, the vector $x$ defines a statement in the underlying NP language $L$, and reconstruction of the secret is possible if and only if the participating parties hold a valid witness certifying that $x \in L$. Moreover, the sequence of functions $\{f_n\}_{n \geq 1}$ must satisfy the standard monotonicity and rigidity conditions throughout its evolution. Specifically, if there exists a deterministic input $x = (x_1, \ldots, x_{n-1}) \in \{0,1\}^{n-1}$ such that $f_{n-1}(x) = 1$, then for every $x_n \in \{0,1\}$ it follows that $f_n(x||x_n) = 1$. Conversely, if not such input $x$ exists, then it must hold that $f_n(x||0) = 0$.

Non-evolving monotone NP access structures were studied in [15], where the authors constructed a computational secret sharing scheme for *any* monotone function in NP assuming witness encryption for NP and one-way functions. In their construction, the access structure is encoded into an NP language $L'$, and for any subset of parties, an instance $y$ of this language includes a vector of commitments to the parties' indices. Each party's share contains an opening to the commitment and a witness encryption of the message under the instance $y$.

*From Static to Evolving.* Our contribution is an evolving variant of the secret sharing scheme in [15] where we replace the commitment scheme with a length-doubling PRG $\mathsf{G} : \{0,1\}^\lambda \to \{0,1\}^{2\lambda}$.[2] Similarly to [15], we define a new language $\hat{\mathcal{A}}^{\mathsf{mNP}'}$ mirroring the original monotone NP access structure $\hat{\mathcal{A}}^{\mathsf{mNP}}$ but with statements expressed as a collection of PRG outputs rather than subset of parties. Precisely, the language $\hat{\mathcal{A}}^{\mathsf{mNP}'}$ consists of statements of the forms $(y_1, \ldots, y_n)$ where each $y_i$ is a PRG output. The connection among the two languages is the following: if a subset $\mathcal{I}$ is authorized in $\hat{\mathcal{A}}^{\mathsf{mNP}}$, then the witness for membership in $\hat{\mathcal{A}}^{\mathsf{mNP}'}$ must include the seeds $\kappa_i$ for all $i \in \mathcal{I}$, such that $\mathsf{G}(\kappa_i) = y_i$, together with the witness certifying the membership of $\mathcal{I}$ in $\hat{\mathcal{A}}^{\mathsf{mNP}}$.

Since $\hat{\mathcal{A}}^{\mathsf{mNP}'}$ can be seen as a "wrapper" of $\hat{\mathcal{A}}^{\mathsf{mNP}}$ (indeed, if the correct PRG seeds are known, the two access structures behave in the same manner), we focus ourselves in building an evolving secret sharing scheme for $\hat{\mathcal{A}}^{\mathsf{mNP}'}$. Specifically, given a WE for NP, we can compute the share of the $n$-th party by sampling a

[2] We use a length-doubling PRG to simplify the construction and the related proof.

random seed $\kappa_n$, and evaluating the PRG output $y_n = \mathsf{G}(\kappa_n)$ together with a witness encryption $\mathsf{ct}_n$ of the message over the instance $(y_1, \ldots, y_n)$.

The share $\sigma_n$ for party $n$ consists of the seed $\kappa_n$ and the ciphertext $\mathsf{ct}_n$, resulting in a share size $|\sigma_n| = |\mathsf{ct}_n| + \lambda = \mathsf{poly}(\lambda, n)$ where the polynomial dependency is due to the relation size that depends on $n$.[3]

Correctness follows by observing that (1) the new language $\hat{\mathcal{A}}^{\mathsf{mNP}'}$ preserves the semantics of the original $\hat{\mathcal{A}}^{\mathsf{mNP}}$ since $\mathsf{G}$ is a deterministic and injective and so each output $y_i$ uniquely determines its seed $\kappa_i$, and (2) each of the party $i$ in an authorized subset knows the seed $\kappa_i$, moreover the party $n$ also knows $\mathsf{ct}_n$, thus by the correctness of the $\mathsf{WE}$ scheme, $\mathsf{ct}_n$ can be decrypted given the valid PRG outputs of parties in $\mathcal{I}$ and the original witness $w$. Finally, computational privacy follows from two key observations. First, all PRG outputs $y_i$ corresponding to honest parties appear uniformly random to the adversary, due to the security of $\mathsf{G}$ and the fact that the underlying seeds $\kappa_i$ are never revealed; Second, to leverage the security of the $\mathsf{WE}$ scheme, we must ensure the adversary lacks a valid witness for the associated statement. This is indeed the case: (1) by the definition of valid adversary, it only owns a witness for a statement not in the language; and (2) it cannot forge an alternative statement for which a witness exists, since the probability that a uniformly random string $y_i \in \{0,1\}^{2\lambda}$ has a valid preimage $\kappa_i \in \{0,1\}^{\lambda}$ under $\mathsf{G}$ is negligible. Hence privacy follows by the security of the $\mathsf{WE}$ scheme.

**Adaptive Security.** We then move into considering a stronger security notion. To this end, we initiate a study on the feasibility of adaptive security in the setting of evolving secret sharing schemes. Intuitively, adaptive security refers to the possibility of adaptively corrupting parties over time based on previously obtained information (e.g., parties shares).

Adaptive security is formalized by enhancing the standard computational privacy experiment to give the adversary oracle access to $\mathcal{O}_{\mathsf{share}}$. This oracle allows the adversary to continue the evolution process while simultaneously accessing shares of previously uncorrupted parties. In this way, the adversary can leverage $\mathcal{O}_{\mathsf{share}}$ to evolve the access structure and adaptively corrupt current participants. We refer the reader to Definition 15 for the formal definition.

In terms of results, we present two constructions that achieve (evolving) adaptive security. The first construction supports dynamic weighted threshold evolving access structures $\hat{\mathcal{A}}^{\mathsf{dwthr}}$ and is based on trapdoor permutations in the Random Oracle Model (ROM). The second construction is identical to that of Francati and Venturi [12], supporting monotone circuits evolving access structures. Our contribution lies in proving its adaptive security (using the framework of Jafargholi et al. [14]) when those circuits are restricted to the class $\mathsf{NC}^0$.

*Adaptive Construction for Dynamic Weighted Threshold Evolving Access Structures* $\hat{\mathcal{A}}^{\mathsf{dwthr}}$. We present a secret sharing construction for the evolving dynamic

[3] We highlight that if a succinct witness encryption scheme is used (at least for a particular relation), our construction will inherit the same share size.

weighted threshold $\hat{\mathcal{A}}^{\mathsf{dwthr}}$ access structures that achieves adaptive security in the ROM. This marks a significant step forward, as all prior evolving secret sharing schemes in this setting only achieved static security.

The starting point of our construction is a black-box computational secret sharing scheme for the non-evolving weighted threshold access structures, denoted $\mathsf{SS}_{\mathsf{NE}}$. We assume this underlying scheme is adaptively secure. Moreover, we assume the existence of trapdoor permutations and of a programmable random oracle. Our construction, described in Construction 4.1, mirrors the construction of non-interactive non-committing encryption (NCE) in the ROM presented by Nielsen [19], and proceeds as follows. When party $n$ arrives, the dealer samples a trapdoor permutation $f_n$ and computes shares $(\mathsf{sh}_i^n)_{i\in[n]}$ of the message $\mu$ using the $\mathsf{SS}_{\mathsf{NE}}$ scheme over the non-evolving weighted threshold access structure when there are $n$ parties. These shares are then encrypted, each producing a ciphertext of the form $\gamma_i^n = (f_i(x_i^n), H(x_i^n) \oplus \mathsf{sh}_i^n)$, where $f_i$ is the trapdoor permutation sampled when party $i$-th joined, and $x_i^n$ is a uniformly random element. The share $\sigma_n$ of a party $n$ consists of $f_n^{-1}$, the (non-evolving) share $\mathsf{sh}_n^n$, along with $n-1$ ciphertexts $(\gamma_i)_{i<n}$. Specifically, we instantiate the underlying scheme using Shamir's secret sharing with weight virtualization, i.e., a party of weight $w_i$ holds $w_i$ Shamir shares of size $\lambda$. We rely on Shamir's scheme because it is secure against adaptive adversaries—a crucial property in our setting. Under this instantiation, the resulting share size for party $n$ is $\lambda(n+W_n)$ where $W_n$ is the sum of the weights of all the $n$ parties.

Correctness follows by observing that parties in an authorized subset $\mathcal{I}$ can use their trapdoors to invert the permutations, recover the random values $x_i^n$, and then retrieve the masked non-evolving shares. Since party $n$ holds the necessary ciphertexts and his share, and the other parties contribute their trapdoors, all shares needed to reconstruct the secret can be recovered and used to apply the underlying non-evolving reconstruction algorithm.

The security proof mirrors the core simulation strategy used in the NCE construction by Nielsen [19], where random oracle programmability enables secure recovery of internal states after corruption. We define a sequence of hybrid experiments. First, we show that the adversary cannot query the oracle on inputs $x_i$ hidden in the ciphertexts $\gamma_i$ corresponding to an uncorrupted party $i$ without breaking the one-wayness of trapdoor permutations. Next, we demonstrate that for honest parties $i$ the ciphertext $\gamma_i^k = (f_i(x_i^k), H(x_i^k) \oplus \mathsf{sh}_i^k)$ can be replaced with $\gamma_i^k = (f_i(x_i^k), r_i^k)$ with $r_i^k$ being a uniformly random value without detection, by properly updating the random oracle as soon as parties are corrupted. Finally, we gradually switch the shared message from $\mu_0$ to $\mu_1$ arguing that a distinguisher among two consecutive hybrids could be turned into an adversary attacking the privacy of the non evolving computational secret sharing scheme $\mathsf{SS}_{\mathsf{NE}}$. We note that the ability to simulate shares for newly corrupted parties relies on the adaptive security of the underlying static secret sharing scheme; without this property, it would be impossible to proceed with the simulation.

*Proving the Adaptive Security of* [12]*'s Construction.* We conclude by proving that a previously known secret sharing construction for monotone circuits evolving access structures $\hat{\mathcal{A}}^{\mathsf{ckts}}$—presented in [12] and originally proven secure in the static setting—also achieves adaptive security provided the access structure is implemented by a circuit in the class $\mathsf{NC}^0$. In such an evolving structure, denoted as $\hat{\mathcal{A}}^{\mathsf{ckts}}$, parties arrive in generations rather than one-by-one. The access structure consists of a sequence of monotone formulas $\hat{\varphi}_g$, with $g = \mathsf{poly}(\lambda)$ being the number of generations, where each formula is defined as $\hat{\varphi}_g(x) = \bigvee_g \hat{C}_g(x_1, \ldots, x_n)$, and each $\hat{C}_g : \{0,1\}^n \to \{0,1\}$ is an arbitrary AND-OR circuit satisfying $\hat{C}_g(x_1, \ldots, x_{n-n_g}, 0, \ldots, 0) = 0$.

Our security proof crucially builds on the Jafargholi et al. framework [14] (we refer the reader to the full version of this paper), which enables transforming selective security proofs into adaptive ones with only mild security loss. The key idea is to compress the adversary's full commitment $w \in \mathcal{W}$ (i.e. the set of users to be corrupted) into a succinct representation $h(w) \in \mathcal{U}$, using a pebbling configuration over the monotone circuit. A pebble on a gate indicates that the associated ciphertext or key is replaced with a random value, thereby breaking its dependency on the message. They refer to hybrids depending on this partial information as "partially selective" hybrids, in contrast to the "fully selective" original hybrids. The framework shows that if, for every pair of neighboring fully selective hybrids $\boldsymbol{H}_i$, $\boldsymbol{H}_{i+1}$, there exists a pair of partially selective hybrids $\hat{\boldsymbol{H}}_{i,0}$, $\hat{\boldsymbol{H}}_{i,1}$ (see Fig. 1) that are indistinguishable, then the security loss depends only on $|\mathcal{U}|$ rather than $|\mathcal{W}|$.

Let $C$ be the global circuit representing the access structure $\hat{\mathcal{A}}^{\mathsf{ckts}}$, i.e. $C = \bigvee_{g=1}^{\bar{g}} \hat{C}_g(x_1, ..., x_n)$, where $\bar{g} = \mathsf{poly}(\lambda)$ is chosen by the adversary and $n$ is the number of parties in the access structure when the $\bar{g}$ generation is reached. We apply the pebbling strategy from [14] to each $\hat{C}_g$, and finally to the root OR gate of $C$. The pebbling rules depend on the unauthorized subset of parties $\mathcal{U}$ chosen by the adversary:

1. A pebble can be placed/removed on an AND gate if *at least one* of its input wires is *not in* $\mathcal{U}$ or comes from a *pebbled gate*.
2. A pebble can be placed/removed on an OR gate if *all* its input wires are either *not in* $\mathcal{U}$ or come from *pebbled gates*.

To prove indistinguishability among each pair of $\hat{\boldsymbol{H}}_{i,0}$ and $\hat{\boldsymbol{H}}_{i,1}$, we ensure that they differ by only a single gate and that each pebbling configuration can be described succinctly. We then show that all such hybrids are computationally indistinguishable under standard cryptographic assumptions (e.g., PRG security and robustness of the projective PRG), and apply Jafargholi et al. theorem to bound the overall security loss by $\mathsf{poly}(\lambda)^{\mathcal{O}(d)}$. Notably, the security loss does not depend anymore on the number of possible unauthorized subsets (which could be exponential in the number of parties $n$), but instead grows exponentially in the depth $d$ of the circuit representing $\hat{\mathcal{A}}^{\mathsf{ckts}}$. However, when considering $\mathsf{NC}^0$ such a depth is constant, allowing us to prove the final adaptive security of our construction.

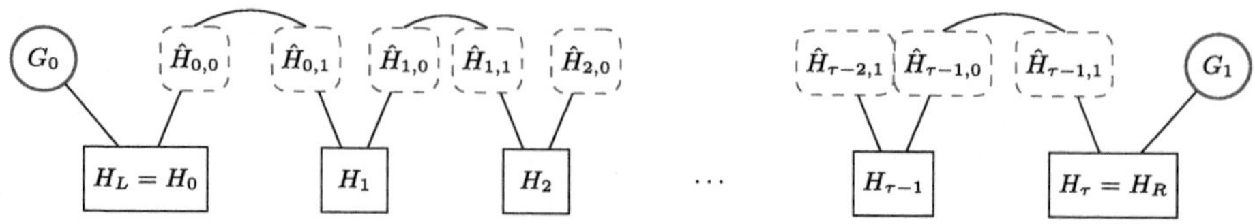


**Fig. 1.** A schematic diagram showing the relationship between adaptive (green circles), fully selective (solid black boxes) and partially selective (dotted blue boxes) hybrids. The arrows indicate indistinguishability. (Color figure online)

### 1.3 Related Work

Evolving secret sharing schemes were first introduced by Komargodski et al. [16], who gave a secret sharing scheme for every evolving access structure with exponential share. Subsequent works focus on improving the share size by targeting specific access structures or switching to the computational assumptions. We begin by reviewing results in the information-theoretic setting.

For *general* access structures, Paskin-Cherniavsky [20] improve the share size (still exponential), assuming the dealer knows the access structure in advance[4], while Desmedt et al. [9] apply techniques from evolving perfect hash families, enabling constructions for schemes with a message space defined over non-abelian groups. For *multi-level* access structures Dutta et al. [10] reduce the share size exponentially compared to [16], again assuming the dealer has full knowledge of the access structure. For *threshold* access structures, Komargodski et al. [16] propose both general and specific constructions, the latter ones are later improved by D'arco et al. [7]. For *dynamic threshold* access structures, where the reconstruction threshold evolves with the number of parties, Komargodski et al. [17] and later Xing et al. [22] propose increasingly efficient schemes, improving the share size to $\mathcal{O}(n^4)$. Xing et al. [22] and Alon et al. [1] further optimize the construction for the case of small and large threshold regimes respectively. *Ramp* access structures, which allow for a gap between privacy and reconstruction thresholds, are studied by Beimel et al. [4,5], who give constructions under various threshold-gap regimes, including for fixed thresholds. For $k$-*slice* access structures, where the behavior on size-$k$ sets is unspecified, Alon et al. [1] present constructions for 2-and 3-slice structures with sub-exponential complexity. For access structures described by *branching programs*, [1] constructs schemes for generalized infinite decision trees (GIDTs), showing that evolving access structures representable as bounded-width layered infinite branching programs (LIBPs) admit non-trivial evolving secret-sharing schemes. Finally, Alon et al. [1] prove lower bounds on share size for *directed st-connectivity* and $k$-*hypergraph* access structures, while Ben David et al. [8] give tight bounds on the message complexity of evolving *conditional disclosure of secrets* (CDS) protocols.

Recently, Francati and Venturi [12] initiated the study of evolving secret-sharing in the computational setting. They construct schemes for *arbitrary* access

[4] These advances only target some structures beyond Mazor's $2^{t-o(t)}$ lower bound [18].

structures under one-way functions, assuming each party appears in few authorized sets. For *dynamic threshold* structures, they give a scheme with share size $\lambda(n+1)$, again assuming OWFs. For *graph-based structures*, they design schemes under RSA or iO+SSB. Finally, for monotone circuits, they provide constructions under various assumptions (RSA, iO+SSB, DDH/BDDH, or LWE), with complexity tied to the size of the evolving circuit.

In the static setting, weighted threshold secret sharing schemes typically achieve share sizes that are either linear in the party weights—e.g., by assigning $w_i$ Shamir shares to a party of weight $w_i$—or quasipolynomial in the number of parties [3]. More recently, Farràs et al. [11] improved efficiency by approximating the access structure using Chow parameters, resulting in share sizes of $n^{1+o(1)}$.

# 2 Preliminaries

## 2.1 Notation

We denote by $[n]$ the set of numbers $\{1, 2, ...n\}$. Capital bold-face letters (such as $\boldsymbol{X}$) are used to denote probability distributions, small letters (such as $x$) to denote concrete values, calligraphic letters (such as $\mathcal{X}$) to denote sets, sans-serif letters (such as $\mathsf{A}$) to denote algorithms. For a string $x \in \{0,1\}^*$, we let $|x|$ be its length; if $\mathcal{X}$ is a set, $|\mathcal{X}|$ represents the cardinality of $\mathcal{X}$. When $x$ is chosen uniformly from a set $\mathcal{X}$, we write $x \xleftarrow{\$} \mathcal{X}$.

If $\mathsf{A}$ is a deterministic algorithm (modeled as a Turing machine), we write $y = \mathsf{A}(x)$ to denote a run of $\mathsf{A}$ on input $x$ and output $y$; if $\mathsf{A}$ is randomized, we write $y \xleftarrow{\$} \mathsf{A}(x)$ (or $y = \mathsf{A}(x; r)$) to denote a run of $\mathsf{A}$ on input $x$ and (uniform) randomness $r$, and output $y$. An algorithm $\mathsf{A}$ is *probabilistic polynomial-time* (PPT) if $\mathsf{A}$ is randomized and for any input $x, r \in \{0,1\}^*$ the computation of $\mathsf{A}(x; r)$ terminates in a polynomial number of steps (in the input size).

We write $\mathsf{negl}(\lambda)$ to denote an arbitrary (unspecified) negligible function of the security parameter $\lambda \in \mathbb{N}$. Similarly, we write $\mathsf{poly}(\lambda)$ to denote an arbitrary (unspecified) polynomial function of the security parameter. We assume all algorithms take the security parameter (in unary) as input.

Let $\boldsymbol{X} = \{\boldsymbol{X}(\lambda)\}_{\lambda \in \mathbb{N}}$ and $\boldsymbol{Y} = \{\boldsymbol{Y}(\lambda)\}_{\lambda \in \mathbb{N}}$ be ensembles of random variables. We say $\boldsymbol{X}$ and $\boldsymbol{Y}$ are computationally indistinguishable (denoted $\boldsymbol{X} \approx_c \boldsymbol{Y}$) if for all PPT adversaries $\mathsf{A}$ we have $|\mathbb{P}[\mathsf{A}(\boldsymbol{X}(\lambda)) = 1] - \mathbb{P}[\mathsf{A}(\boldsymbol{Y}(\lambda)) = 1]| \leq \mathsf{negl}(\lambda)$. The notion of computational indistinguishability immediately extends to (ensembles of) interactive games $\mathbf{G}_{\mathsf{A}}(\lambda)$ featuring a PPT adversary and a challenger, where at the end of the game the adversary outputs a bit given its view.

## 2.2 Pseudorandom Generators

Let $\ell_{\mathsf{in}} = \ell_{\mathsf{in}}(\lambda)$, $\ell_{\mathsf{out}} = \ell_{\mathsf{out}}(\lambda)$, and $\mathsf{G} : \{0,1\}^{\ell_{\mathsf{in}}} \to \{0,1\}^{\ell_{\mathsf{out}}}$ be two polynomials (in the security parameters) such that $\ell_{\mathsf{in}}(\lambda) < \ell_{\mathsf{out}}(\lambda)$ and an efficiently computable function $\mathsf{G}$, respectively. We say that $\mathsf{G}$ is a pseudo-random generator (*PRG*) if $\mathsf{G}(s)$ and $y \xleftarrow{\$} \{0,1\}^{\ell_{\mathsf{out}}}$ are computationally indistinguishable whenever $s \xleftarrow{\$} \{0,1\}^{\ell_{\mathsf{in}}}$.

**Definition 1 (Security of PRG).** *A PRG* $\mathsf{G}: \{0,1\}^{\ell_{\mathsf{in}}} \to \{0,1\}^{\ell_{\mathsf{out}}}$ *is secure if for every* PPT *adversary* A, $|\mathbb{P}[\mathsf{A}(1^\lambda, \mathsf{G}(\kappa)) = 1] - \mathbb{P}[\mathsf{A}(1^\lambda, y) = 1]| \leq \mathsf{negl}(\lambda)$, *where* $\kappa \xleftarrow{\$} \{0,1\}^{\ell_{\mathsf{in}}}$ *and* $y \xleftarrow{\$} \{0,1\}^{\ell_{\mathsf{out}}}$.

Moreover, we say that G has unbounded polynomial stretch if the stretch function $\ell_{\mathsf{out}}(\lambda) - \ell_{\mathsf{in}}(\lambda)$ is unbounded and polynomially large in $\lambda$.

### 2.3 Non-evolving and Evolving Secret Sharing

**Computational Non-evolving Secret Sharing.** Let $n \in \mathbb{N}$. A collection of subsets $\mathcal{A} \subseteq 2^{[n]}$ is *monotone* if for every $\mathcal{I} \in \mathcal{A}$, with $\mathcal{I} \subseteq \mathcal{I}'$, we have $\mathcal{I}' \in \mathcal{A}$.

**Definition 2 (Access structure).** *An access structure* $\mathcal{A} \subseteq 2^{[n]}$ *is a monotone collection of non-empty subsets. Subsets in* $\mathcal{A}$ *are called* qualified, *whereas subsets not in* $\mathcal{A}$ *are called* unqualified.

We may think of $\mathcal{A}$ as a characteristic function $\mathcal{A}: 2^{[n]} \to \{0,1\}$ that outputs 1 given an input $X \subseteq 2^{[n]}$ if and only if $X$ is in the access structure. If $\mathcal{A}$ is an access structure, then a subset $\mathcal{B} \in \mathcal{A}$ is *minimal* if $\mathcal{B}' \notin \mathcal{A}$ whenever $\mathcal{B}' \subset \mathcal{B}$.

Non-evolving secret sharing schemes are typically defined in a setting where the number of parties $n$ is fixed.

**Definition 3 (Secret sharing).** *A computational secret sharing scheme* $\mathsf{CSS} = (\mathsf{CSS.Share}, \mathsf{CSS.Recon})$, *with message space* $\mathcal{M}$ *and share space* $\mathcal{S}$, *for an access structure* $\mathcal{A}$ *consists of two polynomial-time algorithms specified as follows (we implicitly assume all algorithms take as input the security parameter* $1^\lambda$*):*

- $(\sigma_i)_{i\in[n]} \xleftarrow{\$} \mathsf{CSS.Share}(\mu, \mathcal{A})$: *The probabilistic sharing algorithm* $\mathsf{CSS.Share}(\mu, \mathcal{A})$ *takes as input a message* $\mu \in \mathcal{M}$, *and an access structure* $\mathcal{A}$, *and outputs a share* $\sigma_i$ *for every party* $i \in [n]$.
- $\mu \leftarrow \mathsf{CSS.Recon}((\sigma_i)_{i\in\mathcal{I}}, \mathcal{I}, \mathcal{A})$: *The deterministic reconstruction algorithm* $\mathsf{CSS.Recon}((\sigma_i)_{i\in\mathcal{I}}, \mathcal{I}, \mathcal{A})$ *takes as input a collection of shares* $(\sigma_i)_{i\in\mathcal{I}}$, *along with a subset* $\mathcal{I} \subseteq 2^{[n]}$ *of the parties, and the access structure* $\mathcal{A}$ *and output a message* $\mu \in \mathcal{M}$.

Secret sharing schemes are required to satisfy the following two properties. The first property is a correctness requirement saying that qualified subsets of parties can recover the message. The second property is a computational security requirement saying that a PPT adversary knowing the shares corresponding to an unqualified subset of parties obtains no information about the message. This privacy guarantee can be formalized against either a static adversary, which chooses the corrupted parties in advance, or an adaptive adversary, which may choose which parties to corrupt as it learns information during the protocol.

**Definition 4 (Correctness of secret sharing).** *We say that a computational secret sharing scheme* CSS *over message space* $\mathcal{M}$ *for an access structure* $\mathcal{A}$ *is correct if for every message* $\mu \in \mathcal{M}$, *for every qualified subset* $\mathcal{I} \in \mathcal{A}$, *it holds that* $\mathbb{P}\left[\mu = \mu' : \{\sigma_i\}_{i\in[n]} \xleftarrow{\$} \mathsf{CSS.Share}(\mu, \mathcal{A}), \mu' = \mathsf{CSS.Recon}((\sigma_i)_{i\in\mathcal{I}}, \mathcal{I}, \mathcal{A})\right] = 1$.

**Definition 5 (Static computational privacy of secret sharing).** *We say that a secret sharing scheme* $\mathsf{CSS}$ *over message space* $\mathcal{M}$ *for the access structure* $\mathcal{A}$ *is computationally private in the static setting if* $\{\boldsymbol{G}^{\mathsf{priv}}_{\mathsf{CSS},\mathsf{A}}(\lambda,0)\}_{\lambda\in\mathbb{N}} \approx_c \{\boldsymbol{G}^{\mathsf{priv}}_{\mathsf{CSS},\mathsf{A}}(\lambda,1)\}_{\lambda\in\mathbb{N}}$*, where the game* $\{\boldsymbol{G}^{\mathsf{priv}}_{\mathsf{CSS},\mathsf{A}}(\lambda,b)\}$ *is defined as follows:*

- *The adversary* $\mathsf{A}$ *chooses a pair of messages* $\mu_0,\mu_1 \in \mathcal{M}$*, and an unqualified subset* $\mathcal{U} \notin \mathcal{A}$*, and forwards them to the challenger.*
- *The challenger computes* $\{\sigma_i\}_{i\in[n]} \xleftarrow{\$} \mathsf{CSS.Share}(\mu_b,\mathcal{A})$*, and forwards* $(\sigma_i)_{i\in\mathcal{U}}$ *to* $\mathsf{A}$*.*
- *Finally,* $\mathsf{A}$ *outputs a bit* $b' \in \{0,1\}$ *which is also the output of the experiment.*

**Definition 6 (Adaptive computational privacy of secret sharing).** *We say that a secret sharing scheme* $\mathsf{CSS}$ *over message space* $\mathcal{M}$ *for the access structure* $\mathcal{A}$ *is computationally private in the adaptive setting if* $\{\boldsymbol{G}^{\mathsf{priv,adapt}}_{\mathsf{CSS},\mathsf{A}}(\lambda,0)\}_{\lambda\in\mathbb{N}} \approx_c \{\boldsymbol{G}^{\mathsf{priv,adapt}}_{\mathsf{CSS},\mathsf{A}}(\lambda,1)\}_{\lambda\in\mathbb{N}}$*, where the game* $\{\boldsymbol{G}^{\mathsf{priv,adapt}}_{\mathsf{CSS},\mathsf{A}}(\lambda,b)\}$ *is defined as follows:*

- *The adversary* $\mathsf{A}$ *chooses a pair of messages* $\mu_0,\mu_1 \in \mathcal{M}$*.*
- *The challenger picks a random bit* $b \xleftarrow{\$} \{0,1\}^\lambda$ *and computes* $\{\sigma_i\}_{i\in[n]} \xleftarrow{\$} \mathsf{CSS.Share}(\mu_b,\mathcal{A})$*.*
- *The adversary* $\mathsf{A}$ *interacts with the challenger multiple times as follows:*
  - $\mathsf{A}$ *sends an index* $i \in [n]$ *to the challenger.*
  - *If the set of parties requested by* $\mathsf{A}$ *so far is unqualified, the challenger returns the share* $\sigma_i$*. Otherwise, the challenger aborts.*
- *Finally,* $\mathsf{A}$ *outputs a bit* $b' \in \{0,1\}$ *which is also the output of the experiment.*

**Computational Evolving Secret Sharing.** In evolving secret sharing, instead, parties arrive one by one and thus the value $n$ represents the number of parties currently in the system. In this work, we focus on the computationally setting [12] where the number of parties $n$ can grow up while remaining polynomial in the security parameter, i.e., $n = \mathsf{poly}(\lambda)$. Following [12], we denote by $\mathcal{A}_n$ the access structure when there are $n$ parties in the system. We stress, that the dealer does not know the value $n$ (beside the fact that $n$ will be polynomial), neither it knows the access structure $\mathcal{A}_n$ before the $n$-th party enters the system (i.e., the evolution is unknown in advance).[5]

**Definition 7 (Evolving access structure).** *Let* $n \in \mathbb{N}$*, with* $n(\lambda) = \mathsf{poly}(\lambda)$*. An evolving access structure* $\mathcal{A} = \{\mathcal{A}_n\}$ *is a monotone collection of subsets* $\mathcal{A}_n \subseteq 2^{[n]}$ *such that, for every* $n \in \mathbb{N}$*, it holds that* $\mathcal{A}_n \subseteq \mathcal{A}_{n+1}$*.*

[5] As described in [12], knowing the evolution pattern and the parties in advance causes the non-evolving and evolving notions to collapse. If the dealer knows that $n < \tilde{n}$ for some value $\tilde{n}$, along with the access structure $\mathcal{A}_{\tilde{n}}$, it can simply use a non-evolving secret sharing scheme for $\mathcal{A}_{\tilde{n}}$ and distribute the shares to the parties as they arrive.

We stress that, in the computational setting, we implicitly deal with access structures $\mathcal{A}$ that allows for an efficient representation. We refer the reader to [12, Remark 1] for details.

As noted by [12], we focus on rigid monotone evolving access structures, i.e., subsets that were previously unauthorized cannot become authorized later in time. [12] demonstrated that this condition is necessary to avoid updating the shares of previous parties each time a new party arrives (one of the traits of evolving secret sharing). We provide the formal definition below.

**Definition 8 (Rigid evolving access structure).** *A* rigid *evolving access structure $\mathcal{A} = \{\mathcal{A}_n\}_{n\geq 1}$ is a monotone collection of subsets $\mathcal{A}_n \subseteq 2^{[n]}$ such that, for any $n \in \mathbb{N}$, it holds that $\mathcal{A}_n = \mathcal{A} \cap 2^{[n]}$.*

Throughout the paper, we use the hat symbol $\hat{\mathcal{A}}$ to denote access structures that evolve while preserving rigidity.

Next, we give the formal definition of an evolving secret sharing scheme.

**Definition 9 (Evolving secret sharing).** *A secret sharing scheme* $\mathsf{SS} = (\mathsf{SS.Share}, \mathsf{SS.Recon})$*, with message space $\mathcal{M}$ and share space $\mathcal{S}$, for an evolving access structure $\mathcal{A}$ consists of two polynomial-time algorithms specified as follows (we implicitly assume all algorithms take as input the security parameter $1^\lambda$):*

- $\sigma_n \xleftarrow{\$} \mathsf{SS.Share}(\mu, (\sigma_i)_{i\in[n-1]}, \mathcal{A}_n)$*: The probabilistic sharing algorithm* $\mathsf{SS.Share}(\mu, (\sigma_i)_{i\in[n-1]}, \mathcal{A}_n)$ *takes as input a message $\mu \in \mathcal{M}$, a collection of $n-1$ shares $\sigma_1, ..., \sigma_{n-1} \in \mathcal{S}$, and an access structure $\mathcal{A}_n$, and outputs the share $\sigma_n$ for the $n$-the party.*
- $\mu \leftarrow \mathsf{SS.Recon}((\sigma_i)_{i\in\mathcal{I}}, \mathcal{I}, \mathcal{A}_n)$*: The deterministic reconstruction algorithm* $\mathsf{SS.Recon}((\sigma_i)_{i\in\mathcal{I}}, \mathcal{I}, \mathcal{A}_n)$ *takes as input a collection of shares $(\sigma_i)_{i\in\mathcal{I}}$, along with a subset $\mathcal{I} \subseteq 2^{[n]}$ of the parties and the access structure $\mathcal{A}_n$, and outputs a message $\mu \in \mathcal{M}$.*

The share size $s(n, \ell, \lambda)$ of a party $n$ in a secret sharing scheme for evolving access structure $\mathcal{A}$ is defined as the maximum of $|\sigma_n|$ over all messages of length $\ell = \ell(n)$ and over all possible previous assignments $\sigma_1, ..., \sigma_{n-1}$. As considered in [2], we are interested in building *succinct* computational secret sharing schemes, i.e., schemes with share size smaller than the representation of the access structure (see [12, Remark 1]).

Evolving secret sharing schemes are required to satisfy the following two properties: correctness and security.

**Definition 10 (Correctness of evolving secret sharing).** *We say that a secret sharing scheme* $\mathsf{SS}$ *over message space $\mathcal{M}$ for the evolving access structure $\mathcal{A}$ is correct if for every message $\mu \in \mathcal{M}$, for every number of parties $n \geq 1$, and for every qualified subset $\mathcal{I} \in \mathcal{A}_n$ it holds that* $\mathbb{P}[\mu = \mu' : \forall i \leq n : \sigma_i \xleftarrow{\$} \mathsf{SS.Share}(\mu, (\sigma_j)_{j<i}, \mathcal{A}_i), \mu' = \mathsf{SS.Recon}((\sigma_i)_{i\in\mathcal{I}}, \mathcal{I}, \mathcal{A}_n)] = 1$.

**Definition 11 (Static computational privacy of evolving secret sharing).** *We say that a secret sharing scheme* SS *over message space* $\mathcal{M}$ *for the evolving access structure* $\mathcal{A}$ *is computationally private in the static setting if* $\{G^{\mathsf{priv}}_{\mathsf{SS,A}}(\lambda, 0)\}_{\lambda\in\mathbb{N}} \approx_c \{G^{\mathsf{priv}}_{\mathsf{SS,A}}(\lambda, 1)\}_{\lambda\in\mathbb{N}}$*, where the game* $\{G^{\mathsf{priv}}_{\mathsf{SS,A}}(\lambda, b)\}$ *is defined as follows:*

- *The adversary* A *chooses a pair of messages* $\mu_0, \mu_1 \in \mathcal{M}$*, an integer* $n \geq 1$*, and an unqualified subset* $\mathcal{U} \notin \mathcal{A}_n$*, and forwards them to the challenger.*
- *The challenger computes* $\sigma_i \xleftarrow{\$} \mathsf{SS.Share}(\mu_b, (\sigma_j)_{j<i}, \mathcal{A}_i)$ *for all* $i \leq n$*, and forwards* $(\sigma_i)_{i\in\mathcal{U}}$ *to* A*.*
- *Finally,* A *outputs a bit* $b' \in \{0, 1\}$ *which is also the output of the experiment.*

While prior work has primarily focused on static security—where the adversary chooses which parties to corrupt in advance (as defined in the definition above)—this work additionally investigates the stronger notion of adaptive security. Thus, in Sect. 4, we enhance the static security definition by allowing the adversary to: (*i*) adaptively and continuously evolve the access structure over time, and (*ii*) adaptively decide which parties to corrupt.

## 2.4 Monotone NP

We follow the definition of access structures realizing monotone functions in NP (Definition 12) proposed by [15].

A function $f : 2^{[n]} \rightarrow \{0, 1\}$ is said to be monotone if for every $X \subseteq [n]$ such that $f(X) = 1$ it also holds that $\forall Y \subseteq [n]$ such that $X \subseteq Y$ it holds that $f(Y) = 1$. A monotone Boolean circuits is a boolean circuit with AND and OR gates (without negations). A non-deterministic circuit is a boolean circuit whose inputs are divided into two parts: standard inputs and non-deterministic inputs. A non-deterministic circuit accepts a standard input if and only if there is some setting of the non-deterministic input that causes the circuit to evaluate to 1. A monotone non-deterministic circuit is a non-deterministic circuit where the monotonicity requirement applies only to the standard inputs, that is, every path from a standard input wire to the output wire does not have a negation gate.

**Definition 12** ([13]). *A function* $f$ *is in* mNP *if there exists a uniform family of polynomial-size monotone non-deterministic circuit that computes* $f$*.*

**Lemma 1** ([13], **Theorem** 2.2). mNP = NP ∩ mono*, where* mono *is the set of all monotone functions.*

We refer the reader to the full version of this paperfor the formal syntax and security definition of a secret sharing scheme for mNP.

## 2.5 Further Preliminaries

For space reasons, we defer other auxiliary standard definitions to the full version of this paper.

# 3 Constructions of Evolving Secret Sharing

In this section, we present our constructions of evolving secret sharing schemes. All of the constructions presented in this section achieves static security.

## 3.1 Dynamic Weighted Threshold Access Structures

A dynamic weighted threshold evolving access structure is denoted by $\hat{\mathcal{A}}^{\mathsf{dwthr}}$. In these access structures, each party is assigned a weight upon joining, and a subset of parties is authorized at stage $n$ if the sum of their weights is greater or equal to a threshold $t$.

Following [12], we allow the threshold to change over time. We denote by $t_n$ the threshold associated with the arrival of party $n$. Moreover, we study the case of evolving weights, where the weights of parties may change over time with the arrival of new ones. We denote by $\mathsf{weight}_n : [n] \to \mathbb{N}$ the weight function when there are $n$ parties. Since we permit weights to change, we could have that $\mathsf{weight}_n(i) \neq \mathsf{weight}_i(i)$ for some $i < n$. Naturally, this change of threshold and weights should not break the monotonicity and rigidity property.

**Definition 13 (Dynamic Weighted Threshold Evolving Access Structure).** *A dynamic weighted threshold evolving access structure $\hat{\mathcal{A}}^{\mathsf{dwthr}}$ is defined over a sequence of weights functions and threshold pairs $(\mathsf{weight}_n, t_n)$ satisfying the following conditions:*

- *a set $\mathcal{I} = \{i_1, \ldots, i_k, n\}$ is authorized (i.e., $\mathcal{I} \in \hat{\mathcal{A}}^{\mathsf{dwthr}}_n$) if $t_n \leq \sum_{j \in \mathcal{I}} \mathsf{weight}_n(j)$;*
- *(monotonicity) for every $n_1 \in \mathbb{N}$, for every $\mathcal{I} \subseteq 2^{[n_1]}$, for every $n_2 \in \mathbb{N}$ such that $n_2 > n_1$, if $t_{n_1} \leq \sum_{j \in \mathcal{I}} \mathsf{weight}_{n_1}(j)$ then $t_{n_2} \leq \sum_{j \in \mathcal{I}} \mathsf{weight}_{n_2}(j)$;*
- *(rigidity) for every $n_1 \in \mathbb{N}$, for every $\mathcal{I} \subseteq 2^{[n_1]}$, for every $n_2 \in \mathbb{N}$ such that $n_2 > n_1$, if $t_{n_1} > \sum_{j \in \mathcal{I}} \mathsf{weight}_{n_1}(j)$ then $t_{n_2} > \sum_{j \in \mathcal{I}} \mathsf{weight}_{n_2}(j)$.*

The second and third conditions are necessary to ensure that the access structure remains monotone and rigid. In other words, we allow the weights and thresholds to change over time, as long as they comply with these two conditions.

Our definition of the access structure follows the approach described in [12, Remark 4], namely: the thresholds and weights (during reconstruction) are enforced by the party with the largest identifier. For this reason, we do not impose the constraint that the access structure must have increasing thresholds. See [12, Remark 4] for more details.

**Construction from OWFs.** We present a construction of a secret sharing scheme for the weighted threshold evolving access structure $\hat{\mathcal{A}}^{\mathsf{dwthr}}$ over the message space $\{0,1\}^\lambda$. Our construction relies on any black-box computational secret-sharing scheme (Definition 3) for the static (non-evolving) weighted threshold setting and a PRG $\mathsf{G} : \{0,1\}^\lambda \to \{0,1\}^*$ with unbounded polynomial stretch.

Our evolving secret sharing scheme is formally described in Construction 3.1.

**Construction 3.1**

Let $\mathsf{G} : \{0,1\}^\lambda \to \{0,1\}^*$ be a standard PRG with unbounded polynomial stretch. For a seed $\kappa \in \{0,1\}^\lambda$, we parse the output of $\mathsf{G}(\kappa)$ into blocks of size $\lambda$, and we denote with $\mathsf{G}(\kappa)[i]$ the $i$-th such block. Let $\mathsf{SS_{NE}} = (\mathsf{SS_{NE}.Share}, \mathsf{SS_{NE}.Recon})$ be a (non-evolving) secret sharing scheme for the weighted threshold access structure. Consider the following secret sharing scheme $\mathsf{SS} = (\mathsf{SS.Share}, \mathsf{SS.Recon})$ over message space $\mathcal{M} = \{0,1\}^\lambda$ for the dynamic weighted threshold evolving access structure $\hat{\mathcal{A}}^{\mathsf{dwthr}}$ defined over a sequence of weights functions and threshold pairs $(\mathsf{weight}_n, t_n)$.

**Sharing:** When the $n$-th party arrives, the dealer proceeds as follows:

- Compute the shares for all parties $p_i$ with $i \in [n]$, as $(\mathsf{sh}_i^n)_{i\in[n]} \overset{\$}{\leftarrow} \mathsf{SS_{NE}}.\mathsf{Share}(\mu, \hat{\mathcal{A}}_n^{\mathsf{dwthr}})$ where $\hat{\mathcal{A}}_n^{\mathsf{dwthr}}$ denotes the weighted threshold non-evolving access structure when there are $n$ parties with threshold $t_n$ and weight function $\mathsf{weight}_n$.
- For every $i \in [n-1]$, compute $\gamma_i = \mathsf{sh}_i^n \oplus \mathsf{G}(\kappa_i)[n-i]$.
- Finally, set the share of the $n$-th player to $\sigma_n = (\kappa_n, (\gamma_i)_{i<n}, \mathsf{sh}_n^n)$ where $\kappa_n \overset{\$}{\leftarrow} \{0,1\}^\lambda$.

**Reconstruction:** The reconstruction algorithm $\mathsf{SS.Recon}((\sigma_i)_{i\in\mathcal{I}}, \mathcal{I}, \hat{\mathcal{A}}_n^{\mathsf{dthr}})$, given the shares $(\sigma_i)_{i\in\mathcal{I}} = (\kappa_i, (\gamma_j)_{j<i}, \mathsf{sh}_i^i)$, and a (minimal) authorized subset $\mathcal{I} \in \hat{\mathcal{A}}^{\mathsf{dwthr}}$, proceeds as follows:

- For every $i \in \mathcal{I}$, compute $\mathsf{sh}_i'^n = \gamma_i \oplus \mathsf{G}(\kappa_i)[n-i]$ where $(\gamma_k)_{k<n}$ are the ciphertexts contained in $\sigma_n$.
- Compute $\mu' = \mathsf{SS_{NE}}.\mathsf{Recon}((\mathsf{sh}_i'^n)_{i\in\mathcal{I}}, \mathcal{I}, \hat{\mathcal{A}}_n^{\mathsf{dthr}})$

Finally, output $\mu' = \mu$.

Let $\mathcal{I} = \{i_1, ..., i_j, n\} \in \hat{\mathcal{A}}^{\mathsf{dwthr}}$ be a minimal authorized subset, i.e., $\mathcal{I}$ is such that $\sum_{i\in\mathcal{I}} \mathsf{weight}_n(i) \geq t_n$. Correctness follows by observing that, for $j \in [n-1]$, each ciphertext $\gamma_{i_j}$ contained in $\sigma_n$ can be correctly decrypted by means of the seed $\kappa_{i_j}$, contained in $\sigma_{i_j}$, thus yielding $\mathsf{sh}_{i_j}'^n = \gamma_{i_j} \oplus \mathsf{G}(\kappa_{i_j})[n-i_j] = \mathsf{sh}_{i_j}^n$. Hence, the authorized parties can retrieve $|\mathcal{I}|$ shares (as $\mathsf{sh}_n^n$ is included in $\sigma_n$). Thus, by correctness of $\mathsf{SS_{NE}^n}$ (Definition 4), the parties in $\mathcal{I}$ can recover the correct message $\mu' = \mu$. As for security, we prove the following result whose proof appears in the full version of this paper.

**Theorem 5.** *Assuming* $\mathsf{G}$ *is secure (Definition 1), and the secret sharing scheme* $\mathsf{SS_{NE}}$ *is computationally private (Definition 5) in the static setting, the scheme* $\mathsf{SS}$ *described in Construction 3.1 is a computationally private secret sharing scheme in the static setting for the dynamic weighted threshold evolving access structures* $\hat{\mathcal{A}}^{\mathsf{dwthr}}$.

By instantiating the underlying non-evolving secret sharing scheme for weighted thresholds with Shamir's secret sharing using weight virtualization (i.e., each party holds a number of shares proportional to their weight), we obtain the following corollary.

**Corollary 1.** *Assuming OWFs, there exists a computationally private secret sharing scheme over* $\mathcal{M} = \{0,1\}^\lambda$ *in the static setting for the dynamic weighted threshold evolving access structure* $\hat{\mathcal{A}}^{\mathsf{dwthr}}$*, where the share size of party* $n \geq 1$ *is* $\lambda \cdot (1 + W_n)$ *where* $W_n = \sum_{i\in[n]} \mathsf{weight}_n(i)$.

*Proof.* The corollary follows directly by observing that, by instantiating the underlying non-evolving secret sharing scheme for weighted thresholds with Shamir's secret sharing using weight virtualization, we obtain that the underlying $\mathsf{SS_{NE}} = (\mathsf{SS_{NE}.Share}, \mathsf{SS_{NE}.Recon})$ produces shares of size $s_i = \lambda \cdot \mathsf{weight}(i)$ where $i$ is the identifier of the corresponding party and $\mathsf{weight}$ the weight function used on setup. Thus, we conclude that the overall share size in our construction is given by $|\sigma_n| = \lambda + \sum_{i\in[n]} s_i = \lambda \cdot (1 + \sum_{i\in[n]} \mathsf{weight}_n(i)) = \lambda \cdot (1 + W_n)$. □

### 3.2 Monotone NP Access Structures

We extend the notion of monotone NP of Sect. 2.4 to the evolving setting. We model the monotone NP evolving access structures as a sequence $\hat{\mathcal{A}}^{\mathsf{mNP}} = \{\hat{\mathcal{A}}_n^{\mathsf{mNP}}\}_{n\geq 1}$, where each $\hat{\mathcal{A}}_n^{\mathsf{mNP}}$ corresponds to a monotone NP (non-deterministic) function $f_n : \{0,1\}^n \to \{0,1\}$ (i.e., $f_n \in \mathsf{mNP}$). A subset $\mathcal{I}_x \subseteq [n]$ is considered qualified if and only if there exists an input $x \in \{0,1\}^n$ such that $x_i = 1$ iff $i \in \mathcal{I}_x$, and the non-deterministic circuit accepts $x$ if there is some non-deterministic input such that $f_n(x) = 1$. Moreover, the sequence of functions $\{f_n\}_{n\geq 1}$ is required to satisfy the standard monotonicity and rigidity conditions while evolving. Below, we provide the formal definition.

**Definition 14 (mNP evolving access structure).** *A* mNP *evolving access structure is a sequence of access structures* $\hat{\mathcal{A}}^{\mathsf{mNP}} = \{\hat{\mathcal{A}}_n^{\mathsf{mNP}}\}_{n\geq 1}$ *such that, for each* $n \in \mathbb{N}$, $\hat{\mathcal{A}}_n^{\mathsf{mNP}}$ *is defined by a* mNP *function* $f_n : \{0,1\}^n \to \{0,1\}$. *The sequence of functions* $\{f_n\}$ *satisfies the following conditions:*

- *a set* $\mathcal{I} = \{i_1, \ldots, i_k, n\}$ *is authorized (i.e.,* $\mathcal{I} \in \hat{\mathcal{A}}_n^{\mathsf{mNP}}$*) if and only if* $f_n(x) = 1$, *where* $x \in \{0,1\}^n$ *is the indicator vector for* $\mathcal{I}$, *i.e.* $x_i = 1$ *iff* $i \in \mathcal{I}$;
- *(monotonicity) if there exists a deterministic input* $x = (x_1, \ldots, x_{n-1}) \in \{0,1\}^{n-1}$ *such that* $f_{n-1}(x) = 1$, *then for any* $x_n \in \{0,1\}$, *we have that* $f_n(x||x_n) = 1$;[6]
- *(rigidity) for* $x = (x_1, \ldots, x_{n-1}) \in \{0,1\}^{n-1}$, *if* $f_{n-1}(x) = 0$, *then* $f_n(x||0) = 0$.

[6] Recall that $f$ is non-deterministic, so it outputs 1 iff there exists a corresponding non-deterministic input $w$.

*Construction from OWFs and WE.* Let $\hat{\mathcal{A}}^{\mathsf{mNP}} = \{\hat{\mathcal{A}}_n^{\mathsf{mNP}}\}_{n\geq 1}$ be a mNP evolving access structure as defined in Definition 14, where for each new party $n$, the access structure is determined by a monotone NP function $f_n : \{0,1\}^n \rightarrow \{0,1\}$. For a language $L$ in NP let $\mathsf{WE}_L = (\mathsf{Encrypt}_L, \mathsf{Decrypt}_L)$ be a witness encryption scheme and let $\mathsf{G}$ be a length-doubling PRG $\mathsf{G} : \{0,1\}^\lambda \rightarrow \{0,1\}^{2\lambda}$ (Definition 1). We refer the reader to the full version of this paperfor the formal syntax and security definition of a witness encryption scheme.

We define a language $\hat{\mathcal{A}}^{\mathsf{mNP}'}$ that is related to $\hat{\mathcal{A}}^{\mathsf{mNP}}$ as follows. The statement (induced by $\hat{\mathcal{A}}^{\mathsf{mNP}'}$) are vectors of $n$ PRG outputs $(y_i)_{i\in[n]} \in (\{0,1\}^{2\lambda})^n$, and the witness consists of a subset of the seeds that generated them together with the witness $w$ proving that $\mathcal{I}_x \in \hat{\mathcal{A}}^{\mathsf{mNP}}$. In other words, $\mathcal{I}_x \in \hat{\mathcal{A}}^{\mathsf{mNP}'}$ (whose witness is $w$) if and only if $\mathcal{I}_x \in \hat{\mathcal{A}}^{\mathsf{mNP}}$ and there exist $(\kappa_i)_{i\in[n]}$ is such that

$$\forall i \in [n] : \qquad x_i = \begin{cases} 1 & \text{if } \kappa_i \neq \bot \text{ and } \mathsf{G}(\kappa_i) = y_i, \\ 0 & \text{otherwise.} \end{cases} \tag{1}$$

Thus, the witnesses and the statements of $\hat{\mathcal{A}}^{\mathsf{mNP}'}$ can be seen as $(\kappa_1, \ldots, \kappa_n, w)$ and $(y_1, \ldots, y_n)$, respectively.[7]

Each time a new party $n$ arrives, our construction computes shares consisting of two components: (*i*) A random seed $\kappa_n \in \{0,1\}^\lambda$, and (*ii*) a WE ciphertext $\mathsf{ct}_n \xleftarrow{\$} \mathsf{Encrypt}_{\hat{\mathcal{A}}^{\mathsf{mNP}'}}((y_1, \ldots, y_n), \mu)$, where the PRG outputs $y_i = \mathsf{G}(\kappa_i)$ (for $i \in [n]$) form the statement of the relation. Reconstruction proceeds by decrypting $\mathsf{ct}_n$ using a witness $w'$ composed of the known PRG seeds (included in the shares of parties $\mathcal{I}_x$) and the witness $w$ attesting $\mathcal{I}_x \in \hat{\mathcal{A}}^{\mathsf{mNP}}$ (recall that $\hat{\mathcal{A}}^{\mathsf{mNP}}$ is our original mNP access structure used to define $\hat{\mathcal{A}}^{\mathsf{mNP}'}$ as described in Eq. 1).

Below, we present the formal construction. The syntax is adapted from that of the non-evolving case (i.e., the reconstruction algorithm additionally takes a witness $w$ provided as auxiliary input by the parties). We refer the reader to the full version of this paperfor more details regarding the non-evolving notion.

**Construction 3.2**

Let $\hat{\mathcal{A}}^{\mathsf{mNP}'}$ and $\hat{\mathcal{A}}^{\mathsf{mNP}}$ be two evolving mNP access structure as described above. Let $\mathsf{G} : \{0,1\}^\lambda \rightarrow \{0,1\}^{2\lambda}$ be a length-doubling PRG (Definition 1), and let $\mathsf{WE} = (\mathsf{Encrypt}_{\hat{\mathcal{A}}^{\mathsf{mNP}'}}, \mathsf{Decrypt}_{\hat{\mathcal{A}}^{\mathsf{mNP}'}})$ be a witness encryption for $\hat{\mathcal{A}}^{\mathsf{mNP}'}$. Our construction of secret sharing scheme $\mathsf{SS} = (\mathsf{SS.Share}, \mathsf{SS.Recon})$ over message space $\mathcal{M} = \{0,1\}^\lambda$ for the evolving mNP access structure $\hat{\mathcal{A}}^{\mathsf{mNP}}$ is defined as follows.

**Sharing**: When the $n$-th party arrives, the dealer proceeds as follows:

- Sample a random seed $\kappa_n \xleftarrow{\$} \{0,1\}^\lambda$.
- Compute $y_n = \mathsf{G}(\kappa_n)$.

[7] Such a translation from $\hat{\mathcal{A}}^{\mathsf{mNP}}$ to $\hat{\mathcal{A}}^{\mathsf{mNP}'}$ inserts into the relation a form of authentication (implemented through the knowledge of the PRG preimage). This is fundamental in order to leverage the security of WE in the proof of security of our construction.

– Compute $\mathsf{ct}_n \xleftarrow{\$} \mathsf{Encrypt}_{\hat{\mathcal{A}}^{\mathsf{mNP}'}}((y_1, \ldots, y_n), \mu)$.
– Return $\sigma_n = (\kappa_n, \mathsf{ct}_n)$ to the party.

**Reconstruction**: Given the shares $(\sigma_i)_{i \in \mathcal{I}}$ such that $\sigma_i = (\kappa_i, \mathsf{ct}_i)$, and a (minimal) authorized subset $\mathcal{I} = \{i_1, ..., i_{k-1}, n\} \in \hat{\mathcal{A}}_n^{\mathsf{mNP}}$ for some $k \geq 1$, and a witness $w$ (corresponding to $\mathcal{I}$ w.r.t. $\hat{\mathcal{A}}_n^{\mathsf{mNP}}$), the reconstruction algorithm $\mathsf{SS.Recon}((\sigma_i)_{i \in \mathcal{I}}, \mathcal{I}, \hat{\mathcal{A}}_n^{\mathsf{mNP}}, w)$ proceeds as follows:

– Let $\mathsf{ct}_n$ be the $\mathsf{WE}$ ciphertext contained into $\sigma_n$.
– For any $i \in [n]$ let $\kappa_i' = \begin{cases} \kappa_i & \text{if } i \in \mathcal{I} \\ \perp & \text{otherwise.} \end{cases}$
– Output $\mu = \mathsf{Decrypt}_{\hat{\mathcal{A}}^{\mathsf{mNP}'}}(\mathsf{ct}_n, (\kappa_1', \cdots, \kappa_n', w))$.

Recall that, by rigidity, every new authorized subset $\mathcal{I} \in \hat{\mathcal{A}}_n^{\mathsf{mNP}} \setminus \hat{\mathcal{A}}_{n-1}^{\mathsf{mNP}}$ must include the new party $n$. Recall the definition of $\mathsf{SS.Recon}$ in Construction 3.2: $\mathsf{SS.Recon}$ gets as input the shares of a subset of parties $\mathcal{I} = \{i_1, ..., i_{t-1}, n\}$ for some $t \geq 1$, the access structure, and a valid witness $w$. Correctness then follows by the fact that each of the party $i$ in $\mathcal{I}$ knows the seed $\kappa_i$ and the party $n$ also knows $\mathsf{ct}_n$. Thus, $\mathsf{SS.Recon}$ can decrypt $\mathsf{ct}_n$ given the seed of parties in $\mathcal{I}$ and the witness $w$. By the correctness of the $\mathsf{WE}$ scheme, the output of the decryption procedure on $\mathsf{ct}_n$, given a valid $\mathcal{I}$ and a valid witness, is $\mu$.

As for security, we establish the following result whose proof appears in the full version of this paper. Note that the share size of this construction is not succinct due to the ciphertext size of $\mathsf{WE}$ that is bound by $\mathsf{poly}(\lambda, |R|)$, that is $\mathsf{poly}(\lambda, n)$ in our case (see Eq. 1).

**Theorem 6.** *Assuming* $\mathsf{G}$ *is secure (Definition 1) and* $\mathsf{WE}$ *is secure, then the scheme* $\mathsf{SS}$ *described in Construction 3.2 is a computationally private secret sharing scheme in the static setting for the* $\mathsf{mNP}$ *evolving access structure* $\hat{\mathcal{A}}^{\mathsf{mNP}}$*. The share size of the n-party is* $|\sigma_n| = \mathsf{poly}(\lambda, n)$*.*

## 4 Adaptive Security of Evolving Secret Sharing

All constructions so far are secure in the static corruption setting. In this section, we tackle this problem by investigating how to construct evolving secret-sharing schemes that remain secure against *adaptive adversaries*. In contrast to the *static* setting—where the adversary must commit to the set of corrupted parties in advance—the adaptive model captures a significantly stronger and more realistic threat: the adversary can observe shares as they are generated and dynamically choose which parties to corrupt, based on the information previously obtained.

### 4.1 Definition of Adaptive Security

We formally define adaptive computational privacy for evolving secret sharing in Definition 15. In a nutshell, the definition is similar to that of static security except that the adversary has access to an oracle $\mathcal{O}_{\mathsf{share}}$. The latter allows the adversary to adaptively choose the party corrupts, depending on the previously obtained shares. Moreover, since we deal with evolving access structure, such an oracle additionally permits to adaptively increase the number of parties.

**Definition 15 (Adaptive computational privacy of evolving secret sharing).** *We say that a secret sharing scheme* SS *over message space* $\mathcal{M}$ *for the evolving access structure* $\mathcal{A}$ *is computationally private in the adaptive setting if* $\{\boldsymbol{G}^{\mathsf{priv,adapt}}_{\mathsf{SS,A}}(\lambda, 0)\}_{\lambda\in\mathbb{N}} \approx_c \{\boldsymbol{G}^{\mathsf{priv,adapt}}_{\mathsf{SS,A}}(\lambda, 1)\}_{\lambda\in\mathbb{N}}$, *where the game* $\{\boldsymbol{G}^{\mathsf{priv,adapt}}_{\mathsf{SS,A}}(\lambda, b)\}$ *is defined as follows:*

- *The adversary* A *chooses a pair of messages* $\mu_0, \mu_1 \in \mathcal{M}$.
- *The adversary* A *gets oracle access to* $\mathcal{O}_{\mathsf{share}}(\cdot,\cdot)$ *that, on input an integer* $n_g \in \mathbb{N}$ *and a set of indices* $\mathcal{U}$, *proceeds as follows:*
  - *If* $\bigcup_{i\in[q]} \mathcal{U}_i \in \mathcal{A}_{n+n_g}$, *where* $q$ *is the number of oracle queries made so far, the oracle returns* $\perp$ *and aborts.*
  - *Otherwise, it computes* $\sigma_{n+i} \xleftarrow{\$} \mathsf{SS.Share}(\mu_b, (\sigma_j)_{j<n+i}, \mathcal{A}_{n+i})$ *for every* $i \in [n_g]$.
  - *The oracle internally stores* $(\sigma_i)_{i\in[n+n_g]}$ *and updates* $n = n + n_g$.
  - *Finally, it returns* $(\sigma_i)_{i\in\mathcal{U}}$.
- *Finally,* A *outputs a bit* $b' \in \{0,1\}$ *which is also the output of the experiment.*

## 4.2 Adaptive Construction for Dynamic Weighted Threshold Evolving Access Structures

We provide a construction of secret sharing for $\hat{\mathcal{A}}^{\mathsf{dwthr}}$ (Definition 13) with message space $\{0,1\}^\lambda$ in the ROM. The construction relies on (*i*) any adaptively secure computational (non-evolving) secret sharing (Definition 3) for the non-evolving weighted threshold access structure, and (*ii*) on trapdoor permutations. As described in the technical overview, our construction is inspired by the technique introduced by Nielsen [19] to building non-interactive non-committing encryption. We refer the reader to Sect. 1.2 for more details.

**Construction 4.1**

Let $\mathsf{SS}_{\mathsf{NE}} = (\mathsf{SS}_{\mathsf{NE}}.\mathsf{Share}, \mathsf{SS}_{\mathsf{NE}}.\mathsf{Recon})$, $\{f_i\}$, and $H : \{0,1\}^* \to \{0,1\}^*$ be respectively a computational secret sharing scheme for the non-evolving weighted threshold access structure, a familiy of trapdoor permutations, and an hash function modeled as a RO. Consider the following secret sharing scheme $\mathsf{SS} = (\mathsf{SS.Share}, \mathsf{SS.Recon})$ over message space $\mathcal{M} = \{0,1\}^\lambda$ for the evolving dynamic weighted threshold access structure $\hat{\mathcal{A}}^{\mathsf{dwthr}}$ defined over a sequence of weights functions and threshold pairs $(\mathsf{weight}_n, t_n)$.

**Sharing:** When the $n$-th party arrives, the dealer proceeds as follows:

- Randomly sample a trapdoor permutation $f_n$ whose inverse is denoted by $f_n^{-1}$.
- Compute $(\mathsf{sh}_i^n)_{i\in[n]} \xleftarrow{\$} \mathsf{SS}_{\mathsf{NE}}.\mathsf{Share}(\mu, \hat{\mathcal{A}}_n^{\mathsf{dwthr}})$ where $\hat{\mathcal{A}}_n^{\mathsf{dwthr}}$ denotes the non-evolving weighted threshold access structure when there are $n$ parties with threshold $t_n$ and weight function $\mathsf{weight}_n$.

- For every $i \in [n-1]$, compute $\gamma_i^n = (f_i(x_i^n), H(x_i^n) \oplus \mathsf{sh}_i^n)$, where $x_i^n \xleftarrow{\$} \{0,1\}^\lambda$.
- Finally, set the share of the $n$-th player to $\sigma_n = (f_n^{-1}, (\gamma_i^n)_{i<n}, \mathsf{sh}_n^n)$.

**Reconstruction:** The reconstruction algorithm $\mathsf{SS.Recon}((\sigma_i)_{i\in\mathcal{I}}, \mathcal{I}, \hat{\mathcal{A}}_n^{\mathsf{dwthr}})$, given the shares $(\sigma_i)_{i\in\mathcal{I}} = (f_i^{-1}, (\gamma_j^i)_{j<i}, \mathsf{sh}_i^i)$, and a (minimal) authorized subset $\{i_1, ..., i_j, n\} = \mathcal{I} \in \hat{\mathcal{A}}^{\mathsf{dwthr}}$, proceeds as follows:

- From $\sigma_n$ parse $(\gamma_i^n)_{i<n} = (\gamma_{i,1}^n, \gamma_{i,2}^n)_{i<n}$ and set $\mathsf{sh}_n'^n = \mathsf{sh}_n^n$.
- For every $i \in \mathcal{I} \setminus \{n\}$, compute $x_i^n = f_i^{-1}(\gamma_{i,1}^n)$ and $\mathsf{sh}_i'^n = H(x_i^n) \oplus \gamma_{i,2}^n$.
- Compute $\mu' = \mathsf{SS_{NE}.Recon}((\mathsf{sh}_i'^n)_{i\in\mathcal{I}}, \mathcal{I}, \hat{\mathcal{A}}_n^{\mathsf{dwthr}})$

Finally, output $\mu' = \mu$.

Let $\mathcal{I} = \{i_1, ..., i_j, n\} \in \hat{\mathcal{A}}^{\mathsf{dwthr}}$ be an authorized subset, i.e., $\mathcal{I}$ is such that $\sum_{i\in\mathcal{I}} \mathsf{weight}_n(i) \geq t_n$. Correctness follows by observing that, for $j \in [n-1]$, each ciphertext $\gamma_{i_j}^n$ contained in $\sigma_n$ allows retrieval of the corresponding non-evolving share. This is done by computing $x_{i_j}^n$ by means of the $f_{i_j}^{-1}$, which is included in $\sigma_{i_j}$. Hence, the authorized parties can retrieve $|\mathcal{I}|$ shares (as $\mathsf{sh}_n^n$ is included in $\sigma_n$). Thus, by correctness of $\mathsf{SS_{NE}}$ (Definition 4), the parties in $\mathcal{I}$ can recover the correct message $\mu' = \mu$.

As for security, we established the following result whose proof appears in the full version of this paper.

**Theorem 7.** *If the family $\{f_i\}$ is secure and the secret sharing scheme $\mathsf{SS_{NE}}$ is adaptively secure (Definition 6), the scheme $\mathsf{SS}$ described in Construction 4.1 is an adaptively secure secret sharing scheme (Definition 15) for the dynamic weighted threshold evolving access structures $\hat{\mathcal{A}}^{\mathsf{dwthr}}$ in the ROM.*

Note that our construction heavily relies on the adaptive security of the underlying non-evolving secret sharing scheme. In the threshold setting, we can instantiate the latter scheme using Shamir's secret sharing with weight virtualization, i.e., each party $i$ receives $\mathsf{weight}(i)$ shares. The corollary below states the share size of this instantiation.

**Corollary 2.** *Assuming trapdoor permutations, there exists an adaptively secure secret sharing scheme over $\mathcal{M} = \{0,1\}^\lambda$ for the dynamic weighted threshold evolving access structure $\hat{\mathcal{A}}^{\mathsf{dwthr}}$, where the share size of party $n \geq 1$ is $\lambda(n+W_n)$, with $W_n = \sum_{i\in[n]} \mathsf{weight}_n(i)$.*

*Proof.* The corollary follows by using any trapdoor permutation with output space $\{0,1\}^\lambda$ and instantiating $\mathsf{SS_{NE}}$ using Shamir's secret sharing with weight virtualization. The $i$-th share (corresponding to the $i$-th party) in the latter scheme has size $\mathsf{weight}(i) \cdot \lambda$.

Combining the above, we obtain that the share size of the $n$-th party, produced by the evolving Construction 4.1, is $\lambda(n+W_n)$, where $\sum_{i\in[n]} \mathsf{weight}_n(i) = W_n$ and $\mathsf{weight}_n$ is the weight function when $n$ parties are present. □

### 4.3 Monotone Circuits Access Structures

Finally, we study adaptive security of evolving secret sharing schemes for monotone circuits access structures. Our contribution is to prove the adaptiveness of the construction proposed by Francati and Venturi [12] based on projective PRG. Following [12], we define a monotone circuit evolving access structure $\hat{\mathcal{A}}^{\mathsf{ckts}}$ as a sequence of monotone circuits.

**Definition 16 (Monotone Circuits Evolving Access Structure).** *A monotone circuit evolving access structure* $\hat{\mathcal{A}}^{\mathsf{ckts}} = \{\hat{\varphi}_g\}_{g \geq 1}$ *consists of a sequence of monotone formulas* $\hat{\varphi}_g$ *(with* $g = \mathsf{poly}(\lambda)$*) defined as follows:*

$$\hat{\varphi}_g(x) = \bigvee_g \hat{C}_g(x_1, \ldots, x_n), \tag{2}$$

*where* $\hat{C}_g : \{0,1\}^n \rightarrow \{0,1\}$ *is an arbitrary AND-OR circuit such that* $\hat{C}_g(x_1, \ldots, x_{n-n_g}, 0, \ldots, 0) = 0$.

Following [12], let $x = (x_1, \ldots, x_n)$ be the input to the circuit, where each $x_i$ indicates whether the $i$-th player is part of the reconstruction process. The construction employs the following important conventions:

- All outgoing wires of OR gates are connected as incoming wires of AND gates, and vice versa. If this is not the case, we can duplicate a gate's outputs and connect them directly to another gate of the same type.
- Each input wire connects only to an OR gate of fan-in 1; To ensure this, inputs feeding larger AND or OR gates are routed through added fan-in 1 OR (and, if needed, AND) gates.
- We assume that the gates are numbered from 1 to $m$ in topological order, with the first $n$ corresponding to the inputs $x_1, \ldots, x_n$. We use the notation $i \rightarrow j$ to indicate that gate $i$'s output feeds gate $j$.
- The output gates in $\hat{C}_g$ are all AND gates.

Based on the above formalization, they propose an evolving secret sharing scheme for $\hat{\mathcal{A}}^{\mathsf{ckts}}$ based on projective PRGs with bounded polynomial stretch (and standard PRGs with unbounded polynomial stretch). We refer the reader to the full version of this paperfor the formal syntax and security definition of a projective PRG. To make the paper self-contained, we described the formal construction below. We refer the reader to [12] for the formal statements of security and share size.

**Construction 4.2**

Let $\mathsf{pPRG} = (\mathsf{pPRG.Setup}, \mathsf{pPRG.KeyGen}, \mathsf{pPRG.Eval})$ be a block projective PRG with bounded polynomial stretch, and $\mathsf{G} : \{0,1\}^\lambda \rightarrow \{0,1\}^*$ be a standard PRG with unbounded polynomial stretch. For a seed $\kappa \in \{0,1\}^\lambda$, we parse the output of $\mathsf{G}(\kappa)$ into blocks of size equal to the size of a projective key produced by $\mathsf{pPRG}$, and denote with $\mathsf{G}(\kappa)[i]$ the $i$-th such block. Consider the following secret sharing scheme $\mathsf{SS} = (\mathsf{SS.Share}, \mathsf{SS.Recon})$ over message space $\mathcal{M} = \{0,1\}^\lambda$ for the rigid evolving monotone circuits access structure $\hat{\mathcal{A}}^{\mathsf{ckts}}$.

**Sharing:** When the generation $g \geq 1$ begins, the dealer proceeds as follows:

- Let $\hat{C}_g$ be the AND-OR circuit corresponding to the arrival of the $g$-th generation (see Equation 2). Let $m_g = m_g^\wedge + m_g^\vee$ be the number of gates in $\hat{C}_g$, where $m_g^\wedge$ and $m_g^\vee$ are, respectively, the number of AND and OR gates (including the input and output gates).
- Compute $(\mathsf{mpk}_g, \mathsf{msk}_g) \xleftarrow{\$} \mathsf{pPRG.Setup}(1^\lambda, 1^{m_g^\vee})$.
- For each $i \in [m_g^\vee]$, associate to the $i$-th OR gate in $\hat{C}_g$ a key $\kappa_i^{(g)}$ determined as follows:
  - If the gate is an input OR gate, set $\kappa_i^{(g)} = \mathsf{G}(\kappa_i^*)[1]$ where $\kappa_i^* \xleftarrow{\$} \{0,1\}^\lambda$ for each $i \in [n] \setminus [n-n_g]$, and $\kappa_i^{(g)} = \mathsf{G}(\kappa_i^*)[g - g_i + 1]$ for each $i \in [n - n_g]$, where $g_i$ is the generation corresponding to the arrival of party $i \in [n-n_g]$. (Observe that, for every $i \in [n-n_g]$ the key $\kappa_i^*$ corresponds to the PRG seed contained in the shares of parties of previous generations.)
  - If the gate is a non-input OR gate, set $\kappa_i^{(g)} = y_i^{(g)} = \mathsf{pPRG.Eval}(\mathsf{mpk}_g, \alpha_{\{i\}}^{(g)}, \{i\})$, where $\alpha_{\{i\}}^{(g)} = \mathsf{pPRG.KeyGen}(\mathsf{mpk}_g, \mathsf{msk}_g, \{i\})$.
- For each $i \in [m_g^\wedge]$, associate to the $i$-th AND gate in $\hat{C}_g$ a key $\kappa_i^{(g)}$ determined as follows:
  - If the $i$-th gate is a non-output AND gate, set $\kappa_i^{(g)} = \alpha_{\mathcal{T}_i^{(g)}} = \mathsf{pPRG.KeyGen}(\mathsf{mpk}_g, \mathsf{msk}_g, \mathcal{T}_i^{(g)})$, where $\mathcal{T}_i^{(g)} = \{j : i \to j \text{ in } \hat{C}_g\}$ consists of all out-neighbor of the $i$-th AND gate in $\hat{C}_g$.
  - If the $i$-th gate is an output AND gate, set $\kappa_i^{(g)} = \mu$.
- For each $i \in [m_g^\wedge]$, associate to the $i$-th AND gate in $\hat{C}_g$ (including the output gates) the ciphertext $\gamma_i^{(g)} = \kappa_i^{(g)} \oplus \rho_i^{(g)}$, which is viewed as an encryption of $\kappa_i^{(g)}$ under the mask $\rho_i^{(g)} = \bigoplus_{j:j \to i} \mathsf{G}(\kappa_j^{(g)})[i]$. (For each of the output AND gates, we only take the first $\lambda$ bits of the corresponding PRG blocks.)
- Finally, the share of party $i \in [n] \setminus [n-n_g]$ (i.e., the share of the new parties belonging to the $g$-th generation) is defined to be $\sigma_i = (\mathsf{mpk}_g, \kappa_i^*, (\gamma_j^{(g)})_{j \in [m_g^\wedge]})$.

**Reconstruction:** Let $x \in \{0,1\}^n$ be the input corresponding to the parties willing to reconstruct the message. We traverse each generation's circuit $\hat{C}_g$, and recover the key $\kappa_i^{(g)}$ associated to each gate $i$ that is satisfied by $x$ (i.e., the gate is evaluated to 1 under the assignment $x$) in $\hat{C}_g$. In case the latter allows to obtain the key associated to any of the output AND gates in $\hat{C}_g$, output that value as the reconstructed message.

### 4.4 Proving Adaptive Security

We now turn to the security analysis. Using the techniques described in the technical overview (see Sect. 1.2) based on the framework of Jafargholi et al. [14] (we refer the reader to the full version of this paper), we analyze the evolving secret-sharing scheme for $\hat{\mathcal{A}}^{\mathsf{ckts}}$ from [12] (Construction 4.2). We show that the scheme achieves adaptive security with significantly reduced security loss, provided the underlying monotone circuit belongs to the class $\mathsf{NC}^0$. We formalize this in the following theorem.

**Theorem 8.** *Let $\hat{\mathcal{A}}^{\mathsf{ckts}} = \{\hat{\varphi}_g\}_{g\geq 1}$ be a rigid evolving monotone circuits access structure consisting of a sequence of monotone formulas $\hat{\varphi}_g$ (with $g = \mathsf{poly}(\lambda)$) defined as $\hat{\varphi}_g(x) = \bigvee_g \hat{C}_g(x_1, ..., x_n)$, where $\hat{C}_g : \{0,1\}^n \rightarrow \{0,1\}$ is an arbitrary AND-OR circuit such that $\hat{C}_g(x_1, ..., x_{n-n_g}, 0, ...0) = 0$. Assuming that for every $g$, $\hat{C}_g$ is a circuit in the $\mathsf{NC}^0$ class, $\mathsf{pPRG}$ is robust and $\mathsf{G}$ is secure (Definition 1), the scheme $\mathsf{SS}$ described in Construction 4.2 is an adaptively secure secret sharing scheme over $\mathcal{M} = \{0,1\}^\lambda$ for the evolving access structure $\hat{\mathcal{A}}^{\mathsf{ckts}}$.*

*Proof.* We begin by outlining a sketch of the proof. To prove Theorem 8 we rely on the framework introduced in [14]. Our goal is to prove that an adversary cannot distinguish between the challengers $\boldsymbol{G}_L = \boldsymbol{G}_0$ and $\boldsymbol{G}_R = \boldsymbol{G}_1$, corresponding to the adaptive games $\boldsymbol{G}^{\mathsf{priv,adapt}}_{\mathsf{SS,A}}(\lambda, 0)$ and $\boldsymbol{G}^{\mathsf{priv,adapt}}_{\mathsf{SS,A}}(\lambda, 1)$. We define a function $f$ that extracts the adversary's choices from the transcript of the adaptive game. Using this, we construct the selectivized versions of the games as $\boldsymbol{H}_L = \mathsf{SEL}_{2^{[n]}}[\boldsymbol{G}_L, f]$ and $\boldsymbol{H}_R = \mathsf{SEL}_{2^{[n]}}[\boldsymbol{G}_R, f]$, where the adversary is required to commit in advance to the entire unauthorized set of shares it intends to access. Then we construct a sequence of $\ell$ selective hybrid games $\boldsymbol{H}_L = \boldsymbol{H}_0, \boldsymbol{H}_1, ..., \boldsymbol{H}_{\ell-1}, \boldsymbol{H}_\ell = \boldsymbol{H}_R$. For each $\boldsymbol{H}_i$ we define two selective games $\hat{\boldsymbol{H}}_{i,0}$, $\hat{\boldsymbol{H}}_{i,1}$ and show that for every $i \in \{0, ..., \ell - 1\}$, there exists a mapping $h_i$ such that the games $\boldsymbol{H}_{i+b}$ and $\hat{\boldsymbol{H}}_{i,b}$ (for $b \in \{0,1\}$) are equivalent up to the encoding of the inputs to the games (given by $h_i$). In other words, $\boldsymbol{H}_i \equiv \mathsf{SEL}_{\mathcal{V}\rightarrow 2^{[n]}}[\hat{\boldsymbol{H}}_{i,0}, f, h_i]$ and $\boldsymbol{H}_{i+1} \equiv \mathsf{SEL}_{\mathcal{V}\rightarrow 2^{[n]}}[\hat{\boldsymbol{H}}_{i,1}, f, h_i]$, with $h_i$ being the function that extracts from the transcript the $i$-th and the $(i+1)$-th pebbling configurations. Then, we can apply Theorem 4 in [14] and obtain our result.

Let $\mathcal{U}_1, \mathcal{U}_2, ..., \mathcal{U}_q \subseteq [n]$ be the unqualified subsets of parties chosen by the adversary in the queries to $\mathcal{O}_{\mathsf{share}}(\cdot; \cdot)$ during the execution of the adaptive privacy game for $\mathsf{SS}$. Let $\mathcal{U} := \bigcup_{j=1}^q \mathcal{U}_j$ be the union of all such unqualified subsets.

Note that the total number of parties $n$ and the number of generations $\bar{g}$ that arise in the game are not fixed in advance, but depend on the adversary's adaptive choices—specifically, on how many times and with which parameters it queries the oracle $\mathcal{O}_{\mathsf{share}}$. In particular, each query $\mathcal{O}_{\mathsf{share}}(n_g, \mathcal{U}_j)$ will increase the number of parties by $n_g$, adding a new AND-OR circuit $\hat{C}_g$ to the monotone formula of Eq. 2. By validity of the adversary, the unqualified subset $\mathcal{U}$ is associated to an input $x_{\mathcal{U}} \in \{0,1\}^n$ such that $\bigvee_g \hat{C}_g(x_{\mathcal{U}}) = 0$, where $\hat{C}_g$ is the AND-OR circuit corresponding to the $g$-th generation.

We need to prove that $\boldsymbol{G}_0 = \boldsymbol{G}^{\mathsf{priv,adapt}}_{\mathsf{SS,A}}(\lambda, 0) \approx_c \boldsymbol{G}^{\mathsf{priv,adapt}}_{\mathsf{SS,A}}(\lambda, 1) = \boldsymbol{G}_1$.

**Algorithm 1** Return the $t$-th pebbling configuration for circuit $C = \bigvee_{g=1}^{\bar{g}} \hat{C}_g(x_1, ..., x_n)$ representing $\hat{\mathcal{A}}^{\mathsf{ckts}}$.

```
Global variables: T = 0, 𝒫 = ∅
function ComputeTthPebble(C, t, 𝒰)
    Let i* denote the root of the circuit C
    return RecursivePebbleStep(C, t, 𝒰, i*, i*)
function RecursivePebbleStep(C, t, 𝒰, i*, i)        ▷ i* is the root of C; i is the currently visited gate
    for j ∈ children(i, C) do
        RecursivePebbleStep(C, t, 𝒰, i*, j)          ▷ Recursively pebble children
    if i ∈ 𝒫 and CanPebble(C, i, 𝒰, 𝒫) then
        𝒫 := 𝒫 \ {i}                                 ▷ Unpebble if i already pebbled
    else if i ∉ 𝒫 and CanPebble(C, i, 𝒰, 𝒫) then
        𝒫 := 𝒫 ∪ {i}                                 ▷ Place pebble on i
        if i = i* then return 𝒫                      ▷ Return if root is pebbled
    Increment T
    if T = t then return 𝒫                           ▷ Return t-th configuration
    for j ∈ children(i, C) do
        RecursivePebbleStep(C, t, 𝒰, i*, j)          ▷ Unpebble children
function CanPebble(C, i, 𝒰, 𝒫)
    Let g := type of gate i (AND or OR)
    Let in_i := set of input wires to gate i
    if g = AND then
        for each w ∈ in_i do
            if w ∉ 𝒰 or w ∈ 𝒫 then return true
        return false
    else if g = OR then
        for each w ∈ in_i do
            if w ∈ 𝒰 and w ∉ 𝒫 then return false
        return true
```

*Proof.* Let $C$ be the circuit representing the access structure $\hat{\mathcal{A}}^{\mathsf{ckts}}$, i.e. $C = \bigvee_{g=1}^{\bar{g}} \hat{C}_g(x_1, ..., x_n)$, where $\bar{g} = \mathsf{poly}(\lambda)$ is chosen by the adversary. Let $n$ be the number of parties in the access structure when the $\bar{g}$ generation is reached. Let $f : \{0,1\}^* \rightarrow 2^{[n]}$ be the function that extracts from the transcript all the unqualified subsets $\{\mathcal{U}_j\}_{j \in [q]}$ and aggregates them into one set $\mathcal{U} = \bigcup_{j=1}^{q} \mathcal{U}_j$. Let $\boldsymbol{H}_L = \mathsf{SEL}_{2^{[n]}}[\boldsymbol{G}_0, f]$ and $\boldsymbol{H}_R = \mathsf{SEL}_{2^{[n]}}[\boldsymbol{G}_1, f]$ be the selectivized versions of $\boldsymbol{G}_0$ and $\boldsymbol{G}_1$ respectively, where the adversary has to commit to the whole unauthorized set of shares $\mathcal{U}$.

We now construct a sequence of $\ell$ selective hybrid games $\boldsymbol{H}_L = \boldsymbol{H}_0, \boldsymbol{H}_1, ..., \boldsymbol{H}_{\ell-1}, \boldsymbol{H}_\ell = \boldsymbol{H}_R$, where for every $\boldsymbol{H}_i$ with $i \in \{0, ..., \ell - 1\}$, the adversary first commits to the unauthorised set $\mathcal{U}$, and then the challenger executes a new sharing procedure that depends on the $i$-th pebbling configuration.

Our objective is to design a pebbling strategy such that the hybrid experiment $\boldsymbol{H}_0$, corresponding to the configuration where no gates are pebbled, coincides with the experiment $\boldsymbol{H}_L$, while the hybrid $\boldsymbol{H}_\ell$, in which only the root gate is pebbled, matches the experiment $\boldsymbol{H}_R$. Additionally, we aim for the pebbling strategy to be encoded as a succinct sequence of moves, where each configuration can be represented using as few bits as possible. This compact representation is crucial to reduce the complexity of sampling from the configuration space when guessing the adversary's commitment.

Towards this goal we recall that by Lemma 2 in [14], for every subset of parties $\mathcal{U}$ and any monotone circuit of depth $d$, fan-in $k_{\mathsf{in}}$, and $m$ gates, there exists a sequence of $(2k_{\mathsf{in}})^{2d}$ pebbling rules such that every pebbling configuration can be uniquely described by at most $d \cdot (\log m + \log k_{\mathsf{in}} + 1)$ bits.

Now, we can apply the pebbling strategy presented in Jafargholi et al. [14] framework to each circuit $\hat{C}_g$ for $g \in [\bar{g}]$, i.e., every predecessor of the root OR gate of $C$ (recall that $C = \bigvee_{g=1}^{\bar{g}} \hat{C}_g(x_1, ..., x_n)$), and once the root gate of each $\hat{C}_g$ has been pebbled, the final step is to pebble the root OR gate of the overall circuit $C$. This step incurs no additional cost: since the pebbling algorithm is recursive and bottom-up, and all the child gates of the root OR gate (i.e., the output AND gates of the $\hat{C}_g$ circuits) have already been pebbled, placing a pebble on the root OR gate happens automatically and without requiring further steps.

The pebbling strategy is defined in Algorithm 1. The rules of the pebbling game depend on the unauthorized subset of parties chosen by the adversary:

1. A pebble can be placed/removed on an AND gate if *at least one* of its input wires is *not in $\mathcal{U}$* or comes from a *pebbled gate.*
2. A pebble can be placed/removed on an OR gate if *all* its input wires are either *not in $\mathcal{U}$* or come from *pebbled gates.*

Note that for every $\hat{C}_g$, $n_g$, i.e., the number of parties of the $g$-th generation corresponds to the fan-in of the circuit, thus by Lemma 2 in [14] the pebbling sequence length for $C$ will be at most $(2k_{\mathsf{in}})^{2d} = (2\mathsf{max}_{g\in[\bar{g}]} n_g)^{2d} = (2n_{g^*})^{(2d)}$.

**Construction 4.3: Sharing procedure $\mathsf{S}^j$**

Let $\mathcal{P}^j$ be the set of pebbled gates in the $j$-th pebbling configuration. When the generation $g \geq 1$ begins, the dealer proceeds as follows:

- Let $\hat{C}_g$ be the AND-OR circuit corresponding to the arrival of the $g$-th generation (see Equation 2). Let $m_g = m_g^\wedge + m_g^\vee$ be the number of gates in $\hat{C}_g$, where $m_g^\wedge$ and $m_g^\vee$ are, respectively, the number of AND and OR gates (including the input and output gates).
- Compute $(\mathsf{mpk}_g, \mathsf{msk}_g) \xleftarrow{\$} \mathsf{pPRG.Setup}(1^\lambda, 1^{m_g^\vee})$.
- For each $i \in [m_g^\vee]$, associate to the $i$-th OR gate in $\hat{C}_g$ a key $\kappa_i^{(g)}$ determined as follows:

- If the gate is an input OR gate, set

$$\kappa_i^{(g)} = \begin{cases} \{0,1\}^{|\alpha|}, & \text{if } i \in \mathcal{P}^j, \\ \mathsf{G}(\kappa_i^*)[1], & \text{if } i \notin \mathcal{P}^j \text{and } i \in [n] \setminus [n-n_g], \\ \mathsf{G}(\kappa_i^*)[g-g_i+1], & \text{if } i \notin \mathcal{P}^j \text{and } i \in [n-n_g] \end{cases}$$

where $\kappa_i^* \xleftarrow{\$} \{0,1\}^\lambda$, and $|\alpha|$ is the size of a projective key of pPRG.

$$\kappa_i^{(g)} = \begin{cases} \{0,1\}^{|\alpha|}, & \text{if } i \in \mathcal{P}^j, \\ y_i^{(g)} = \mathsf{pPRG.Eval}(\mathsf{mpk}_g, \alpha_{\{i\}}^{(g)}, \{i\}), & \text{if } i \notin \mathcal{P}^j \end{cases}$$

where $\alpha_{\{i\}}^{(g)} = \mathsf{pPRG.KeyGen}(\mathsf{mpk}_g, \mathsf{msk}_g, \{i\})$.

– For each $i \in [m_g^\wedge]$, associate to the $i$-th AND gate in $\hat{C}_g$ a key $\kappa_i^{(g)}$ determined as follows:
  - If the $i$-th gate is a non-output AND gate, set

$$\kappa_i^{(g)} = \alpha_{\mathcal{T}_i^{(g)}} = \mathsf{pPRG.KeyGen}(\mathsf{mpk}_g, \mathsf{msk}_g, \mathcal{T}_i^{(g)}),$$

where $\mathcal{T}_i^{(g)} = \{j : i \to j \text{ in } \hat{C}_g\}$ consists of all out-neighbor of the $i$-th AND gate in $\hat{C}_g$.
  - If the $i$-th gate is an output AND gate, set $\kappa_i^{(g)} = \mu$.

$$\gamma_i^{(g)} = \begin{cases} \{0,1\}^{|\alpha|}, & \text{if } i \in \mathcal{P}^j, \\ \kappa_i^{(g)} \oplus \rho_i^{(g)}, & \text{if } i \notin \mathcal{P}^j \end{cases}$$

where $\rho_i^{(g)} = \bigoplus_{j:j \to i} \mathsf{G}(\kappa_j^{(g)})[i]$. (For each of the output AND gates, we only take the first $\lambda$ bits of the corresponding PRG blocks.)

– Finally, the share of party $i \in [n] \setminus [n-n_g]$ (i.e., the share of the new parties belonging to the $g$-th generation) is defined to be $\sigma_i = (\mathsf{mpk}_g, \kappa_i^*, (\gamma_j^{(g)})_{j \in [m_g^\wedge]})$.

*Proof.* Now, in every $\boldsymbol{H}_i$ with $i \in \{0, ..., \ell-1\}$, the adversary first commits to the unauthorised set $\mathcal{U}$, and then the challenger executes a new sharing procedure $\mathsf{S}^i$ (described in Construction 4.3) that depends on the $i$-th pebbling configuration. The sharing procedure $\mathsf{S}^i$ is identical to the sharing procedure in Construction 4.2 except that for each pebbled gate $k$ in the $i$-th pebbling configuration we replace:

– the key $\kappa_k^{(g)}$ associated to every input OR gate corresponding to an honest party, with a uniformly random string of the appropriate length;
– the key $\kappa_k^{(g)}$ associated to an unsatisfied non-input OR gate with a uniformly random key of the appropriate length;
– the ciphertext $\gamma_k^{(g)}$ associated to an unsatisfied AND gate (including the output AND gates) with a uniformly random ciphertext.

We now define $\hat{\boldsymbol{H}}_{i,0}$ and $\hat{\boldsymbol{H}}_{i,1}$ for every $i \in \{0, ..., \ell-1\}$. In both hybrid games $\hat{\boldsymbol{H}}_{i,0}$ and $\hat{\boldsymbol{H}}_{i,1}$, the adversary first commits to the $i$-th pebbling configuration and the next pebbling rule to apply. By Lemma 2 in [14], the number of total possible pebbling configurations is $Q \leq 2^{d\cdot(\log m+\log k_{\mathsf{in}}+1)} = 2^{d\cdot(\log m+\log n_{g^*}+1)}$. Denote by $j' \in [Q]$ the index of the pebbling configuration resulting from applying the next configuration rule to the $j$-th pebbling configuration. In $\hat{\boldsymbol{H}}_{i,0}$ the challenger samples the shares from $\mathsf{S}^j$ and in $\hat{\boldsymbol{H}}_{i,1}$ the challenger samples the shares from $\mathsf{S}^{j'}$ (but other than this the games do not change). Denote by $\mathcal{V}$ the space of messages that the adversary has to commit in the hybrids $\hat{\boldsymbol{H}}_{i,b}$. This space includes all tuples of pebbling configurations and an additional valid pebbling rule. As noted in [14], there are $Q$ possible pebbling configurations, and the additional valid pebbling rule can be described by a gate name since a pebbling rule is just flipping the color of the pebble on that gate. Thus, for a circuit with $m$ gates this requires additional $\log m$ bits. Thus, $\mathcal{V} = \{(j,t) \mid j \in [Q], t \in [m]\}$ and this means that the size of $\mathcal{V}$ is bounded by $|\mathcal{V}| \leq Q \cdot m \leq 2^{d\cdot(\log m+\log n_{g^*}+1)} \cdot m$.

In order to apply Theorem 4 in [14] we still need to prove that $\hat{\boldsymbol{H}}_{i,0}$ and $\hat{\boldsymbol{H}}_{i,1}$ are indistinguishable for every $i \in \{0, ..., \ell-1\}$. We observe that $\hat{\boldsymbol{H}}_{i,0}$ and $\hat{\boldsymbol{H}}_{i,1}$ differs by only one pebbling rule, meaning that they differ for at most one pebbled gate. Let $h$ be the gate that is pebbled in either $\hat{\boldsymbol{H}}_{i,0}$ or $\hat{\boldsymbol{H}}_{i,1}$, but not in both hybrids, i.e. $h = \mathcal{P}^j \triangle \mathcal{P}^{j+1}$, and let $g$ be the generation gate $h$ belongs to. This gate could be either an input/non-input OR gate or an AND gate or the final OR output (recall that $C = \bigvee_{g=1}^{\bar{g}} \hat{C}_g(x_1, ..., x_n)$). We deal with the four cases separately.

**Case 1: the $h$-th gate is an input OR gate.** If the $h$-th gate has been pebbled it must be the case that $h \notin \mathcal{U}$, so we have that the seed $\kappa_h^*$ is never revealed to the adversary. Hence, $\hat{\boldsymbol{H}}_{i,0}$ and $\hat{\boldsymbol{H}}_{i,1}$ are indistinguishable by the security of the PRG $G$. The reduction is standard, and thus we omit it.

**Case 2: the $h$-th gate is a non-input OR gate.** In this case, we show how to turn any distinguisher $\mathsf{A}$ between $\hat{\boldsymbol{H}}_{i,0}$ and $\hat{\boldsymbol{H}}_{i,1}$ into an adversary attacking the robustness property of the projective PRG $\mathsf{pPRG}$ as follows:

- The reduction initializes the robustness game with parameters $1^{m_g^{\vee}}$. Then, consider the set of output neighbors of every non-output AND gate $k$, $\mathcal{T}_k^{(g)} = \{z : k \to z\}$ in $\hat{C}_g$. The reduction asks to the challenger the projective keys associated to all the sets $\mathcal{T}_k^{(g)}$, except for the sets that contain the index $h$.
- The reduction computes the shares of the players exactly as defined in $\mathsf{S}^j$, except that it replaces the keys $\kappa_h^{(g)}$ with the $y_b$ obtained by the challenger. Also, it uses the projective keys received from the challenger to generate all the other keys $\kappa_i^{(g)}$ with $i \geq h$ that are needed by the sharing algorithm for this generation. Finally, the reduction outputs whatever $\mathsf{A}$ outputs.

**Case 3: the $h$-th gate is an AND gate.** In this case, at least one of the incoming wires of the gate $h$ must be connected to an already pebbled OR gate

$j < h$. The key $\kappa_j^{(g)}$ associated to this gate is chosen at random in both hybrids, so we can turn any distinguisher $\mathsf{A}$ between the two hybrids into an adversary attacking the security of the PRG $\mathsf{G}$ as follows:

- The reduction is given $m_g^\wedge$ blocks of size equal to the dimension of a projective key produced by $\mathsf{pPRG}$, which we denote by $z = (z_1, ..., z_{m_g^\wedge})$, where $z_i$ is uniform for all $i \leq h-1$ and $z_i = \mathsf{G}(\kappa_j^{(g)})[i]$ for all $i \geq h+1$, and where $z_h$ is either uniform or equal to $z_h = \mathsf{G}(\kappa_j^{(g)})[h]$.
- The reduction computes the shares of the players in each generation exactly as defined in $\mathsf{S}^j$, except that it replaces the key $\kappa_i^{(g)}$ with the challenge block $z_i$. Finally, the reduction outputs whatever $\mathsf{A}$ outputs.

**Case 4: the $h$-th gate is the output OR gate.**: Firstly, the $h$-th gate being pebbled does not imply any difference in the sharing procedure $\mathsf{S}^j$; secondly, by the pebbling rules, if the $h$-th gate has been pebbled it must be the case that all the predecessors AND gates (i.e., the output AND gates of every $\hat{C}_g$) are pebbled as well. This means that for every generation $g \in [\bar{g}]$, the ciphertext $\gamma_i^{(g)}$ associated to each pebbled output AND gate in $\hat{C}_g$ is uniform, and the shares' distribution given to the adversary is now independent of the message.

Finally, applying Theorem 4 in [14] with the fact that $\ell \leq (2n_{g^*})^{2d}$ and $|\mathcal{V}| \leq 2^{d\cdot(\log m + \log n_{g^*}+1)} \cdot m$, we get that if $\mathsf{G}$ and $\mathsf{pPRG}$ are secure, then for any polynomial-time adversary $\mathsf{A}$ and any access structure on $n$ parties described by a monotone circuit of depth $d$ and $m$ gates of fan-in $n_{g^*}$, it holds that

$$\begin{aligned}
|\mathbb{P}[\mathsf{A}(1^\lambda, \boldsymbol{G}_0) = 1] - \mathbb{P}[\mathsf{A}(1^\lambda, \boldsymbol{G}_1) = 1]| &\leq |\mathcal{V}| \cdot \ell \cdot \mathsf{negl}(\lambda) \\
&= 2^{d\cdot(\log m + \log n_{g^*}+1)} \cdot m \cdot (2n_{g^*})^{(2d)} \cdot \mathsf{negl}(\lambda) \\
&= (m \cdot n_{g^*} \cdot 2)^d \cdot m \cdot (2n_{g^*})^{(2d)} \cdot \mathsf{negl}(\lambda) \\
&= \mathsf{poly}(\lambda)^d \cdot \mathsf{poly}(\lambda) \cdot \mathsf{poly}(\lambda)^{2d} \cdot \mathsf{negl}(\lambda) = \mathsf{poly}(\lambda)^{O(d)} \cdot \mathsf{negl}(\lambda)
\end{aligned}$$

Notably, the security loss does not depend anymore on the number of possible unauthorized subsets (which could be exponential in the number of parties $n$), but instead grows exponentially in the depth $d$ of the circuit representing $\hat{\mathcal{A}}^{\mathsf{ckts}}$. However, when considering $\mathsf{NC}^0$ such a depth is constant, allowing us to prove the final adaptive security of our construction. □

**Acknowledgements.** Daniele Venturi is member of the Gruppo Nazionale Calcolo Scientifico Istituto Nazionale di Alta Matematica (GNCS-INdAM). His research was supported by project SERICS (PE00000014) and by project PARTHENON (B53D23013000006), under the MUR National Recovery and Resilience Plan funded by the European Union-NextGenerationEU, and by project BEAT, funded by Sapienza University of Rome.

## References


1. Alon, B., Beimel, A., Ben David, T., Omri, E., Paskin-Cherniavsky, A.: New upper bounds for evolving secret sharing via infinite branching programs. In: Boyle, E., Mahmoody, M. (eds.) Theory of Cryptography, pp. 548–580. Springer, Cham (2025). https://doi.org/10.1007/978-3-031-78023-3_18
2. Applebaum, B., Beimel, A., Ishai, Y., Kushilevitz, E., Liu, T., Vaikuntanathan, V.: Succinct computational secret sharing. In: Proceedings of the 55th Annual ACM Symposium on Theory of Computing, STOC 2023, pp. 1553–1566. Association for Computing Machinery, New York (2023). https://doi.org/10.1145/3564246.3585127
3. Beimel, A., Weinreb, E.: Monotone circuits for weighted threshold functions. In: 20th Annual IEEE Conference on Computational Complexity (CCC 2005), pp. 67–75 (2005). https://doi.org/10.1109/CCC.2005.12
4. Beimel, A., Othman, H.: Evolving ramp secret-sharing schemes. In: Catalano, D., De Prisco, R. (eds.) SCN 2018. LNCS, vol. 11035, pp. 313–332. Springer, Cham (2018). https://doi.org/10.1007/978-3-319-98113-0_17
5. Beimel, A., Othman, H.: Evolving ramp secret sharing with a small gap. In: Canteaut, A., Ishai, Y. (eds.) EUROCRYPT 2020. LNCS, vol. 12105, pp. 529–555. Springer, Cham (2020). https://doi.org/10.1007/978-3-030-45721-1_19
6. Blakley, G.R.: Safeguarding cryptographic keys. In: Proceedings of AFIPS 1979 National Computer Conference, vol. 48, pp. 313–317 (1979)
7. D'Arco, P., De Prisco, R., De Santis, A.: Secret sharing schemes for infinite sets of participants: a new design technique. Theor. Comput. Sci. **859**, 149–161 (2021). https://doi.org/10.1016/j.tcs.2021.01.019. https://www.sciencedirect.com/science/article/pii/S0304397521000347
8. David, T.B., Paskin-Cherniavsky, A.: Tight lower bounds and new upper bounds for evolving CDS. Cryptology ePrint Archive, Paper 2025/292 (2025). https://eprint.iacr.org/2025/292
9. Desmedt, Y., Dutta, S., Morozov, K.: Evolving perfect hash families: a combinatorial viewpoint of evolving secret sharing. In: Mu, Y., Deng, R.H., Huang, X. (eds.) CANS 2019. LNCS, vol. 11829, pp. 291–307. Springer, Cham (2019). https://doi.org/10.1007/978-3-030-31578-8_16
10. Dutta, S., Roy, P.S., Fukushima, K., Kiyomoto, S., Sakurai, K.: Secret sharing on evolving multi-level access structure. In: You, I. (ed.) WISA 2019. LNCS, vol. 11897, pp. 180–191. Springer, Cham (2020). https://doi.org/10.1007/978-3-030-39303-8_14
11. Farràs, O., Guiot, M.: Reducing the share size of weighted threshold secret sharing schemes via chow parameters approximation. In: Boyle, E., Mahmoody, M. (eds.) Theory of Cryptography, pp. 517–547. Springer, Cham (2025). https://doi.org/10.1007/978-3-031-78023-3_17
12. Francati, D., Venturi, D.: Evolving secret sharing made short. In: Chung, K.M., Sasaki, Y. (eds.) ASIACRYPT 2024, pp. 69–99. Springer, Singapore (2025). https://doi.org/10.1007/978-981-96-0941-3_3
13. Grigni, M., Sipser, M.: Monotone complexity. In: Proceedings of the London Mathematical Society Symposium on Boolean Function Complexity, pp. 57–75. Cambridge University Press (1992)
14. Jafargholi, Z., Kamath, C., Klein, K., Komargodski, I., Pietrzak, K., Wichs, D.: Be adaptive, avoid overcommitting. In: Katz, J., Shacham, H. (eds.) CRYPTO 2017. LNCS, vol. 10401, pp. 133–163. Springer, Cham (2017). https://doi.org/10.1007/978-3-319-63688-7_5

15. Komargodski, I., Naor, M., Yogev, E.: Secret-sharing for NP. In: Sarkar, P., Iwata, T. (eds.) ASIACRYPT 2014. LNCS, vol. 8874, pp. 254–273. Springer, Heidelberg (2014). https://doi.org/10.1007/978-3-662-45608-8_14
16. Komargodski, I., Naor, M., Yogev, E.: How to share a secret, infinitely. In: Hirt, M., Smith, A. (eds.) TCC 2016. LNCS, vol. 9986, pp. 485–514. Springer, Heidelberg (2016). https://doi.org/10.1007/978-3-662-53644-5_19
17. Komargodski, I., Paskin-Cherniavsky, A.: Evolving secret sharing: dynamic thresholds and robustness. In: Kalai, Y., Reyzin, L. (eds.) TCC 2017. LNCS, vol. 10678, pp. 379–393. Springer, Cham (2017). https://doi.org/10.1007/978-3-319-70503-3_12
18. Mazor, N.: A lower bound on the share size in evolving secret sharing. In: 4th Conference on Information-Theoretic Cryptography (ITC 2023). Schloss Dagstuhl-Leibniz-Zentrum für Informatik (2023). https://doi.org/10.4230/LIPIcs.ITC.2023.2
19. Nielsen, J.B.: Separating random oracle proofs from complexity theoretic proofs: the non-committing encryption case. In: Yung, M. (ed.) CRYPTO 2002. LNCS, vol. 2442, pp. 111–126. Springer, Heidelberg (2002). https://doi.org/10.1007/3-540-45708-9_8
20. Paskin-Cherniavsky, A.: How to infinitely share a secret more efficiently. Cryptology ePrint Archive, Paper 2016/1088 (2016). https://eprint.iacr.org/2016/1088
21. Shamir, A.: How to share a secret. Commun. ACM **22**(11), 612–613 (1979)
22. Xing, C., Yuan, C.: Evolving secret sharing schemes based on polynomial evaluations and algebraic geometry codes. Cryptology ePrint Archive, Paper 2021/1115 (2021). https://eprint.iacr.org/2021/1115

# Succinct Computational Secret Sharing for Monotone Circuits

George Lu[1(✉)], Shafik Nassar[1], and Brent Waters[1,2]

[1] University of Texas at Austin, Austin, TX, USA
georgelu97@gmail.com
[2] NTT Research, Sunnyvale, CA, USA

**Abstract.** Secret sharing is a cornerstone of modern cryptography, underpinning the secure distribution and reconstruction of secrets among authorized participants. In these schemes, succinctness—measured by the size of the distributed shares—has long been an area of both great theoretical and practical interest, with large gaps between constructions and best known lower bounds. In this paper, we present a novel computational secret sharing scheme for monotone Boolean circuits that achieves substantially shorter share sizes than previously known constructions in the standard model. Our scheme attains a public share size of $n + \mathsf{poly}(\lambda, \log |C|)$ and a user share size of $\lambda$, where $n$ denotes the number of users, $C$ is the monotone circuit and $\lambda$ is the security parameter, thus effectively eliminating the dependence on the circuit size. This marks a significant improvement over earlier approaches, which exhibited share sizes that grew with the number of gates in the circuit. Our construction makes use of indistinguishability obfuscation and injective one-way functions.

## 1 Introduction

*Secret sharing* [Sha79, Bla79, ISN89] is a way for an individual with a secret $s$ to distribute $n$ 'shares' of the secret to $n$ parties in a way such that the secret remains hidden to any "unauthorized" subset of parties, while "authorized" subsets of parties can reconstruct the secret. The set of authorized parties is specified by some access policy, which is given as input to both the sharing and reconstruction algorithms. Secret sharing is a fundamental primitive with many applications, most notably in secure multi-party computation [BOGW88, CCD88, RBO89].

Traditionally, secret sharing guarantees information-theoretic privacy: even an unbounded adversary cannot learn anything about the secret from an unauthorized set of shares. It is known that there is a secret sharing scheme for any *monotone access policy* [BL88]. However, this classic construction gets the policy as a truth table of size $2^n$, and produces a scheme where *each* share grows with the size of the truth table of the function, namely $O(2^n/\log n)$. A lot of effort has been put into minimizing the share size, and in recent years, a line of work [LVW18, LV18, ABF+19, ABNP20, AN21] managed to bring it down

© International Association for Cryptologic Research 2026
G. Hanaoka and B.-Y. Yang (Eds.): ASIACRYPT 2025, LNCS 16252, pp. 99–129, 2026.
https://doi.org/10.1007/978-981-95-5125-5_4

to $(1.5)^{n+o(n)}$. However, this remains far from the best known lower bounds [Csi96, Csi97].

More recently, a remarkable work by Applebaum et al. [ABI+23] demonstrated the power of *computational secret sharing* (CSS). As opposed to statistical security, CSS only has computational security and requires the secret to be hidden from *efficient* adversaries that hold an unauthorized set of shares. They show that CSS offers a dramatic advantage in terms of share size, by constructing a *succinct* CSS for arbitrary monotone functions with share size $\mathsf{poly}(n)$, as opposed to the exponential size of information-theoretic constructions. However, a crucial limitation is the work of [ABI+23] requires work proportional to the number of clauses in order to reconstruct the circuit. Indeed, *both* algorithms in the construction of [ABI+23] (may in general) run in time proportional to $2^n$. And thus might only be efficiently computable when $n$ is logarithmic in the security parameter. This may hold *even* if the function encoded in the truth table is efficiently computable (e.g., is derived from a monotone circuit).

In this work, we study succinct CSS for efficient representations of access policies. Specifically, we consider policies that are represented by *monotone circuits.* In this setting, we consider a CSS to be succinct if the share size is independent of the circuit size, up to polylogarithmic factors. The classic Yao construction [Yao89, VNS+03] for monotone circuits gets shares and run time that grow with the number of *wires* in the circuit. The same work of [ABI+23] managed to improve upon that construction as well, and got the share size down to grow with the number of AND gates. To be precise, their construction achieves shares of size $\mathsf{poly}(\lambda, \log \ell)$ and public information of size $\ell_\wedge \cdot \lambda$, where $\ell$ is the number of gates and $\ell_\wedge$ is the number of AND gates. However, that construction does not offer an improvement for all monotone circuits, and is still, in fact, dependent on the size of the representation. So the following question remains open: *Is it possible to construct a succinct CSS scheme for monotone circuits, where the share size does not depend on the size of the circuit?*

We answer this question positively and prove the following theorem:

**Theorem 1.1.** *Assuming polynomially secure indistinguishability obfuscation and one-way injective functions, there exists a (standard model) succinct computational secret sharing scheme for general monotone circuits where the share size is $\lambda$ and the public information size is $\mathsf{poly}(\lambda, \log \ell) + n$, where $\lambda$ is the security parameter, $n$ is the number of parties and $\ell$ is the size of the circuit. The sharing and reconstruction algorithms run in time $\mathsf{poly}(\lambda, \ell)$.*

We emphasize that $n$ is the number of parties and not the circuit size, thus we get the first succinct CSS for general monotone circuits. Moreover, we only have an additive factor of $n$, which is not multiplied by any polylogarithmic factors or $\lambda$ (as in [ABI+23]).

### 1.1 Technical Overview

The conceptual starting point of our construction is the classic computational secret sharing scheme of Yao [Yao82, VNS+03] for monotone Boolean circuits.

Let $C$ be a monotone circuit that has $\ell$ gates, including $n$ special *input gates* that correspond to the input bits of the circuit. Each gate gets an index $i \in [\ell]$, and the indices $1, \ldots, n$ correspond to those input gates, while index $\ell$ corresponds to the output gate. Finally, we say that a gate $i$ is a *child* of gate $j$ if $i$ computes a wire that feeds into $j$. Throughout this work, we assume that the indices are a topological order of the gates, which means that if $i$ is a child of $j$ then $i < j$.

In a very high level, each gate $i < \ell$ in the policy circuit $C$ is assigned a random secret key $K_i$. The output gate $\ell$ is assigned the secret $K_\ell = s$. The keys must satisfy the following invariant: one can obtain $K_i$ if and only if they posses sufficient keys of the children gates $i_0, i_1$, where the meaning of "sufficient" depends on the operation of the gate $i$:

- If $i$ is an AND gate, then the two keys $K_{i_0}, K_{i_1}$ are required to obtain $K_i$.
- If $i$ is an OR gate, then any single one of the keys $K_{i_0}, K_{i_1}$ is required to obtain $K_i$.

Each player $i \in [n]$ gets the key $K_i$ as its private share. As a result, if any authorized set of players, represented by an $n$-bit string $x$, put their shares together, then by definition $C(x) = 1$ and they would manage to obtain the secret $K_\ell = s$.

Without going into details, the aforementioned invariant is facilitated using a symmetric key encryption scheme, but requires publishing as public information a ciphertext for *each wire* in the circuit. This results in public information that grows with the number of wires in the circuit.

Let us try to view the idea more abstractly: initially, each share $i$ is a "proof" that whoever possesses it can satisfy input gate $i$. Similarly, each internal gate $i$ has a similar proof attesting that it can be satisfied. The public information allows the initial proofs to be inductively combined to derive proofs on the subsequent gates, until we reach the output gate and retrieve the secret.

*Natural iO-Based Construction.* Through this perspective, we propose the following iO-based idea: replace the approximately $\ell$ ciphertexts with a single obfuscated program that generates gate proofs, if given sufficient proofs for its children gates. Since we plan to use iO, we start by suggesting an "iO friendly" proof for each gate. This proof is simply the classic symmetric-key puncturable signature scheme based on a puncturable pseudorandom function (PPRF) $F : \{0,1\}^\lambda \times [|C|] \to \{0,1\}^\lambda$ and a pseudorandom generator (PRG) $G : \{0,1\}^\lambda \to \{0,1\}^{2\lambda}$. We recall it:

- The key is a PPRF key $K$.
- The signature on an index $i$ is simply $\sigma_i = F(K, i)$.
- The verification algorithm on a key $K$, a message $i$ and a signature $\sigma_i$ simply checks that $G(F(K,i)) = G(\sigma_i)$.

The obfuscated program needs access to the description of the circuit, but we cannot afford to embed the entire circuit in the program. Instead, we use a succinct hash with succinct local openings and embed the digest of the circuit $C$.

For now, imagine we use a somewhere-statistically binding hash (SSB) [HW15] to compress the circuit description. We justify later that we can replace the SSB with a pure iO primitive, like a positional accumulator [KLW15]. We represent the circuit $C$ as a vector of gate descriptions, where the description of gate $i$ specifies the children of gate $i$ and the operation that gate $i$ performs.

The dealer generates a program $P_{\mathsf{SS}}$ that has hardcoded the secret $s$, a hash key, a signature key and a succinct hash of the circuit $C$ using the SSB. The program gets as input a gate index $i$, a description $(g_i, i_0, i_1)$ of gate $i$, an opening to that gate in the hash of $C$ and signatures on its children gates $\sigma_{i_0}, \sigma_{i_1}$, and does the following:

1. Verifies the opening of the hash in position $i$ to the given gate description $(g_i, i_0, i_1)$.
2. Computes a bit $v_0$ (resp. $v_1$) that indicates whether the signature $\sigma_{i_0}$ (resp. $\sigma_{i_1}$) verifies w.r.t. index $i_0$ (resp. $i_1$).
3. Computes the bit evaluated by gate $i$ as $v = g_i(v_0, v_1)$.
4. If $v = 0$, the program outputs $\perp$. Else,
5. If $i$ is an internal gate, it outputs the signature on gate $i$. If $i$ is the output gate it outputs the secret $s$.

The public information consists of the obfuscated program $i\mathcal{O}(P_{\mathsf{SS}})$ and the hash key. As in [Yao82, VNS+03], share $i$ is the signature (proof) on input wire $i$ (which we view as an input gate). The reconstruction algorithm gets the circuit description $C$ for free, and uses it to compute the openings to the hash of $C$ w.r.t. the given hash key. It then uses the shares it possesses (alongside the hash openings) to inductively generate gate signatures using the obfuscated program until the program reveals the secret.

Regarding efficiency, we note that this construction is fully succinct. Each private player share is still a single signature. The public information consists only of a hash key and the obfuscation of the program $P_{\mathsf{SS}}$: this program includes a succinct hash of C, and is otherwise independent of C or the number of players, therefore this share has size $\mathsf{poly}(\lambda, \log |C|)$.

*Difficulty of Proving Security.* We quickly recall the (selective) security game of a secret sharing scheme: an adversary $\mathcal{A}$ submits a policy $C : \{0,1\}^n \to \{0,1\}$, an unauthorized set $x \in \{0,1\}^n$ and a pair of secrets $s_0, s_1$. The challenger chooses one secret $s_b$ randomly, secret shares it, and sends to $\mathcal{A}$ the shares $\{\mathsf{sh}_i\}_{x_i=1}$ corresponding to the set $x$. The adversary wins if it can guess the secret that was shared.

Intuitively, our construction seems secure because the adversary does not have enough shares to force the evaluation of the circuit to be 1. By the monotonicity of the circuit $C$, the only way to flip a gate value from 0 to 1, is to flip one of its children gates. Hence, the task boils down to proving that the adversary cannot compute signatures on gates that are supposedly 0 in the evaluation of $C$ on $x$. If we have ideal obfuscation then it is straightforward to do this task.

Unfortunately, assuming "just" iO, it is not clear how to do so without having the program size depend on the circuit. We elaborate further. The proof strategy is to use a hybrid argument to gradually transition to a game where the signature is punctured on the output gate, thus $P_{\mathsf{SS}}$ would be equivalent to a program that never outputs $s_b$, therefore we can substitute it out by relying on iO security.

An input gate $i$ (corresponding to a share that was not requested by the adversary) can be punctured using the standard PRG and iO trick: first we switch $P_{\mathsf{SS}}$ to a program that has $z = G(F(K, i))$ hardcoded using iO security, then we switch $z$ to a uniform string over $\{0,1\}^{2\lambda}$ using PRG and PPRF security, and finally switch the program to one that always fails the check on index $i$ using iO security and the fact that with all but negligible probability, the uniform $z$ is not in the image of the PRG.

Now imagine we want to puncture an internal gate $i$, and assume it is an OR gate. To do so, we need to switch from a functionally equivalent program that never outputs the signature on $i$ in the first place, and this can only be done if both children gates to $i$ are punctured simultaneously. This step crucially relies on the monotonicity of the circuit: we ensure $i$ cannot be flipped by ensuring that its children cannot be flipped.

The problem is that those children gate indices should remain punctured until all of their "parents" (the gates into which the punctured children directly feed) are also punctured. Even if we assume a layered circuit (wires from gates in layer $i$ feed only into gates in layer $i+1$), we would have to puncture the signature on an entire layer, which results in punctured PPRF keys of size $\mathsf{poly}(W)$ (where $W$ is the width of the circuit $C$).

*Warm Up: Additive Dependence on The Circuit Size.* Let $x \in \{0,1\}^n$ be the challenge set submitted by the adversary. If the adversary is admissible, then $C(x) = 0$. We extend $x$ to $\mathbf{x} = x_1 \cdots x_\ell$ as follows: for each $i \in [\ell]$, let $x_i$ be the value of gate $i$ in the evaluation of $C$ on $x$. We view $\mathbf{x}$ as the *honest circuit evaluation* of the challenge set $x$.

Now imagine the obfuscated program has access to $\mathbf{x}$. Then we can modify it to gradually refuse to give out signatures on gates such that $x_i = 0$. That is, for each $i^* \in [\ell]$ we define a program $P_{\mathsf{SS}}^{i^*}$ (which takes the same inputs as program $P_{\mathsf{SS}}$) as follows:

1. Verifies the opening of the hash in position $i$ to the given gate description $(g_i, i_0, i_1)$.
2. Computes a bit $v_0$ (resp. $v_1$) that indicates whether the signature $\sigma_{i_0}$ (resp. $\sigma_{i_1}$) verifies w.r.t. index $i_0$ (resp. $i_1$).
3. Computes the bit evaluated by gate $i$ as $v = g_i(v_0, v_1)$.
4. If $i < i^*$ and $x_i = 0$ then overwrite $v \leftarrow 0$.
5. If $v = 0$, the program outputs $\perp$. Else,
6. If $i$ is an internal gate, it outputs the signature on gate $i$. If $i$ is the output gate it outputs the secret $s$.

The idea is that the string $\mathbf{x}$ encodes what gate indices need to be punctured, and the index $i^*$ keeps track of what has been punctured so far. Together, $\mathbf{x}$ and $i^*$ actually enforce the puncturing in the obfuscated program. This mechanism allows us to overcome the obstacle of puncturing an internal gate, without having to simultaneously puncture the signature key on its input gates.

In more detail, imagine we are already in Hybrid $i^*$ that uses $P_{\mathsf{SS}}^{i^*}$. Now, in order to enforce the honest circuit evaluation on gate $i^*$ (assuming that gate $i^*$ should evaluate to 0 given the shares in the possession of the adversary, i.e., $x_{i^*} = 0$), we do the following:

- First, we make the hash key statistically binding on position $i^*$. This ensures that the program $P_{\mathsf{SS}}^{i^*}$ only verifies the correct gate description in Step 1.
- Next, we puncture the signature on the relevant children gates of $i^*$, i.e., denote the children of $i^*$ by $i_0^*$ and $i_1^*$ and puncture on the set $S = \{i_b^* : x_{i_b^*} = 0\}$. The idea is that since $i_b^* < i^*$, then the program $P_{\mathsf{SS}}^{i^*}$ never signs the indices in $S$ by the check in Step 4, so we can safely puncture the signing key on $S$.
- Now that the signing key is punctured on the set $S$, bit $v$ will never be assigned the value 1 by the definition of the set $S$ and the fact that $x_{i^*} = g_i(x_{i_0^*}, x_{i_1^*}) = 0$, therefore we can safely extend the check in Step 4 to include index $i^*$, meaning that we advance to using program $P_{\mathsf{SS}}^{i^*+1}$.
- Finally, we undo the changes we made to the hash and signature key: return the hash key to be in normal mode and the signature key to be unpunctured. Now, we are in Hybrid $i^* + 1$.

This process continues inductively until we reach Hybrid $\ell+1$. By the admissibility of the adversary, it must be that $x_\ell = C(x) = 0$. Therefore, when we switch to program $P_{\mathsf{SS}}^{\ell+1}$, we know that it will never output the secret. This allows us to switch to a program $P_{\mathsf{SS}}^{\perp}$ that does not have the secret $s$ hardcoded at all.

Now, we address the long string in the room. Of course, we cannot hardcode all of $\mathbf{x}$ in the program, since that would blow up the size of the program. Instead, in the real construction:

- The dealer gives out a uniform random string $\mathbf{w}$ as public information.
- A hash $h_{\mathbf{w}}$ of $\mathbf{w}$ is hardcoded into the program $P_{\mathsf{SS}}$. Imagine, for now, that we use an SSB hash here as well.
- Program $P_{\mathsf{SS}}$ now expects a valid opening of $h_{\mathbf{w}}$ on index $i$ whenever it is asked to sign gate $i$.

In the security proof, the first step is to switch the way the dealer samples $\mathbf{w}$ to a pseudorandom one-time pad of $\mathbf{x}$ using a PRF, i.e., the dealer samples a PRF key $K_{\mathsf{bit}}$ and sets $w_i = x_i \oplus F(K_{\mathsf{bit}}, i)$. Next, the dealer hardcodes the key $K_{\mathsf{bit}}$ into the obfuscated program, which allows it to decode $x_i$ given the opening of $h_{\mathbf{w}}$ on index $i$.

*Why SSB is Not Necessary.* Although our construction requires a somewhere-statistically binding property of the hash in order to be compatible with iO, we point out that the honest dealer (i.e., the challenger in the security game) generates the hash keys *after* the adversary has already declared the message to be hashed. This allows us to use a weaker non-adaptive notion of security, similar to that of *positional accumulators* [KLW15]. Koppula et al. [KLW15] showed that positional accumulators can be constructed from iO and OWFs.

*Fully Succinct CSS in the CRS Model.* Our warm up construction already gives a fully succinct computational secret sharing in the common (unstructured) random string model. This is due to the fact that $\mathbf{w}$ is uniformly random in the actual construction and is pseudorandom in the security analysis, which allows us to program the CRS in the security proof and argue indistinguishability. With the string $\mathbf{w}$ out of the way, this leaves us with shares of size $\lambda$ and public information of size $\mathsf{poly}(\lambda, \log |C|)$. The CRS can be further "compressed" in the random oracle model. The fact that we can get iO-based fully succinct CSS in the CRS model was already pointed out in [ABI+23] as a consequence of [HW15] and other follow up works [HIJ+16, BCG+19, ASY22, BFK+19] that can generically compress shares on existing secret sharing schemes. Here, we just point out that our techniques (so far) give an alternative construction of succinct CSS in the CRS model, which is both simpler and only requires OWFs in addition to iO, as opposed to SSB and iO. However, this is not satisfying since the CRS in our warm up construction and previous constructions is long and grows with the circuit size, therefore does not yield a succinct CSS in the standard model.

*Abstraction: Circuit Evaluation Embedding.* We now describe how to replace $\mathbf{w}$ with a shorter string. Recall that our technique requires embedding the evaluation of a circuit over $\ell$ gates. Furthermore, the embedded string has to be hidden from the adversary. While at first it may seem like we need at least $\ell$ bits since we are effectively encrypting an $\ell$-bit string $\mathbf{x}$, we recall that $\mathbf{x}$ admits a very short description *given* the circuit $C$: it is merely the evaluation of every gate in $C$ on an input $x$ of length $n$. In other words, given a string $x \in \{0,1\}^n$, we need a way to compress an encryption $\mathbf{w}$ of the full evaluation $\mathbf{x}$ into a short string $\alpha$ in a way that allows anyone with access to $\alpha$ and $C$ to expand back to $\mathbf{w}$. At the same time, we want the string $\alpha$ to completely hide the $x$. In addition, there should be a trapdoor $\mathsf{td}$ that allows for recovering $x_i$ from each $w_i$. We call this a *circuit evaluation embedding scheme* (CEE) and define it formally in Sect. 3.

*Simple CEE from Fully Homomorphic Encryption.* Although our goal is to construct succinct CSS purely from iO, it is useful to see first a simple CEE construction based on *fully homomorphic encryption* (FHE) and PRFs. The natural idea is to encrypt the input string using fully homomorphic *hybrid* encryption [GGI+15], and then homomorphically evaluate a ciphertext for each gate value. We recall that hybrid encryption works as follows: to encrypt a string $x$, we use the underlying encryption scheme to encrypt a PRF key $K$, then use the PRF as a "one-time pad" to hide $x$. We describe the construction:

- To embed the evaluation of a circuit $C$ on a string $x \in \{0,1\}^n$, the embedding algorithm samples a PRF key $K$ with domain $[n]$ and codomain $\{0,1\}$ and a FHE key pair $(\mathsf{pk}, \mathsf{sk})$, computes $w = x \oplus F(K,1) \cdots F(K,n)$ and encrypts $K$ under the FHE to produce a ciphertext $\mathsf{ct}_K$. It then outputs $\alpha = (\mathsf{pk}, \mathsf{ct}_K, w)$ which is simply a public key $\mathsf{pk}$ and "hybrid FHE" ciphertext hiding the string $x$. The trapdoor is the secret key $\mathsf{sk}$.

- We can expand $\alpha$ into an *encryption* of $\mathbf{w}$ as follows: define the function $f_{C_i,w}(K) = C_i(w \oplus F(K,1) \cdots F(K,n))$, where $C_i : \{0,1\}^n \to \{0,1\}$ is the circuit computing gate $i$ in the circuit $C$. Anyone with access to $\alpha = (\mathsf{pk}, \mathsf{ct}_K, w)$ can homomorphically compute $\mathsf{ct}_i = \mathsf{Eval}(\mathsf{pk}, \mathsf{ct}_K, f_{C_i,w})$.
- To extract a bit $x_i$ from $\mathsf{ct}_i$ using the trapdoor $\mathsf{sk}$, we simply decrypt the ciphertext $w_i = \mathsf{Dec}(\mathsf{sk}, \mathsf{ct}_i)$ and $K = \mathsf{Dec}(\mathsf{sk}, \mathsf{ct}_K)$, and then compute $x_i = F(K,i) \oplus w_i$.

The hiding property of the CEE follows by the semantic security of the hybrid FHE scheme.

Note that already, this gives us the first succinct CSS for monotone circuits based on iO and FHE: the public information has size $\mathsf{poly}(\lambda, \log|C|) + n$, where $\mathsf{poly}(\lambda, \log|C|)$ comes from the FHE public key and the encryption of the PRF key as well as the obfuscated program described in the warm up, and the $n$ term is the string $w$. Each share remains of size $\lambda$ as in the warm up[1].

*iO-Based Construction of CEE.* At a high level, the construction of our CEE looks similar to the construction of our secret sharing scheme. Our CEE scheme consists of a short input-encoding digest $w$ and the obfuscation of a small program $P_{\mathsf{CEE}}$ which evaluates $w$ with respect to the policy circuit $C$. In the same way our secret sharing program $P_{\mathsf{SS}}$ is tasked with iteratively verifying the honest circuit evaluation $\mathbf{x}$ bit by bit from a challenge input $x$, our CEE program $P_{\mathsf{CEE}}$ has the task of computing evaluation embedding $\mathbf{w}$ bit by bit from input-encoding digest $w$. On the surface, it seems like we run into the same issues as our secret sharing scheme, having simply delayed the problem. However, the key difference here is that since an adversary can potentially try to decrypt with any subset of the shares they are given, $P_{\mathsf{SS}}$ needs to support correctly validating $\mathbf{x}$ on potentially exponential subsets of the challenge input $x$. However, $w$ is the *only* input which program $P_{\mathsf{CEE}}$ needs to be evaluated on. Thus, instead of producing signatures for individual wire values, we can instead compute a signature attesting to the *entire* computation of $w_1, \dots w_i$ thus far.

Concretely, for any $i \in [\ell]$, to compute $w_i$, our program $P_{\mathsf{CEE}}$ takes as input a hash $h_{\mathbf{w}_{[i-1]}}$ of the first $i-1$ bits of $\mathbf{w}$ computed thus far, along with a signature from the previous invocation of $P_{\mathsf{CEE}}$ that this was computed correctly. This way, when looking at gate $C_i = (g_i, i_0, i_1)$, rather than checking that for signatures directly on bits $w_{i_0}$, $w_{i_1}$, our program can instead directly verify a signature on $h_{\mathbf{w}_{[i-1]}}$ in conjunction with local openings of this hash on indices $i_0, i_1$. Of course, to enable computation to continue for larger values of $i$, we also need $P_{\mathsf{CEE}}$ to output a signature of the hash of our extended prefix, $\mathbf{w}_{[i]}$. Since $P_{\mathsf{CEE}}$ needs to be small, it cannot represent $\mathbf{w}_{[i]}$ directly, despite the decoder having already recovered the first $i-1$ bits in the clear. Fortunately, we can take advantage of the 'writeability' of positional accumulators, which allows our program to directly compute $h_{\mathbf{w}_{[i]}}$ from $h_{\mathbf{w}_{[i-1]}}$ and $w_i$.

[1] Note while this construction doesn't yield a uniform 'uncompressed' string unlike our prior toy example and our full iO construction, it is sufficient for our purposes as secret sharing program $P_{\mathsf{SS}}$ can contain the hard-coded FHE key $\mathsf{sk}$ in the proof.

Putting everything together, to compute bit $w_i$, our program $P_{\mathsf{CEE}}$ hard codes a hash key, signature key, hash $h_C$ of circuit $C$, PRF key $K_{\mathsf{bit}}$. It takes as input the local opening of $h_C$ on gate $i$ to a gate description $(g_i, i_0, i_1)$, the 'prefix hash' $h_{\mathbf{w}_{[i-1]}}$ of the first $i-1$ bits of $\mathbf{w}$, and a signature $\sigma_{i-1}$ on this hash, and local openings of $h_{\mathbf{w}_{[i-1]}}$ on bits $i_0, i_1$.

1. Verify the local opening of $h_C$ as a gate description $(g_i, i_0, i_1)$.
2. Verify that $\sigma_{i-1}$ is a valid signature of $h_{\mathbf{w}_{[i-1]}}$.
3. Verify local openings of $h_{\mathbf{w}_{[i-1]}}$ to bits $i_0, i_1$, producing bit values $w_{i_0}, w_{i_1}$ respectively.
4. Recover honest circuit evaluation $x_{i_b} = w_{i_b} \oplus F(K_{\mathsf{bit}}, i_b)$ for $b \in \{0, 1\}$ and compute $x_i = g_i(x_{i_0}, x_{i_1})$.
5. Reencode $w_i = x_i \oplus F(K_{\mathsf{bit}}, i)$, and compute $h_{\mathbf{w}_{[i]}}$ from $h_{\mathbf{w}_{[i-1]}}, w_i$.
6. Compute signature $\sigma_i$ of $h_{\mathbf{w}_{[i]}}$ and output $w_i, \sigma_i$.

Now if we set input $w = x \oplus F(K_{\mathsf{bit}}, 1), \ldots F(K_{\mathsf{bit}}, n)$, this program exactly recovers the "additive dependence on circuit size" construction described previously.

Just like with secret sharing, the primary technical challenge here will be arguing computational hiding of our embedded 'message', in this case, the challenge input $x$. While this is simple to see when $\mathbf{w}$ is given out directly, now our program $P_{\mathsf{CEE}}$ includes the PRF key $K_{\mathsf{bit}}$ used to mask honest evaluation $\mathbf{x}$. While we cannot hope to argue that $\mathbf{w}$ appears pseudorandom, since we are giving a compact representation of it, we *can* argue that $\mathbf{w}$ is indistinguishable from a simple PRF evaluation $F(K_{\mathsf{bit}}, 1) \ldots F(K_{\mathsf{bit}}, \ell)$ independent of challenge input $x$. The indistinguishability of $F(K_{\mathsf{bit}}, 1) \ldots F(K_{\mathsf{bit}}, \ell)$ to our 'true' encoded input $\mathbf{w}$ proceeds via a series of hybrids. At a high level, our goal will be to ensure that on Hybrid $i$, the local openings to the gate $(g_i, i_0, i_1)$ and encoding bits $w_{i_0}, w_{i_1}$ are statistically fixed. To achieve this, we will need two properties:

1. On input hash $h_{i-1}$ and signature $\sigma_{i-1}$, the signature will *only* verify if $h_{i-1} = h_{\mathbf{w}_{[i-1]}}$.
2. Hash $h_C$ is statistically binding on index $i$, and hash $h_{\mathbf{w}_{[i-1]}}$ is statistically binding on indices $i_0, i_1$.

Once we statistically fix $w_{i_0}, w_{i_1}$, it is easy to see that whether $w_i$ is computed with or without circuit embedding, $P_{\mathsf{CEE}}$ there is only one bit value which $P_{\mathsf{CEE}}$ can output on index $i$. This allows us to leverage $i\mathcal{O}$ security to puncture $K_{\mathsf{bit}}$ at index $i$, giving us indistinguishability of the two cases. Finally, to tie all our hybrids together, we require a pebbling argument [GPSZ17] to ensure the total number of points in which we need to hard code property 1 in our obfuscated program is logarithmic in $\ell$. We refer to Sect. 5 for the full construction and analysis of our circuit evaluation embedding.

## 1.2 Related Approaches

*Non-interactive Batch Arguments.* A *non-interactive batch argument for* NP (BARG) [CJJ21a,CJJ21b] is a proof system allowing for the verification of a batch of $\mathsf{NP}$ statements essentially at the price of one, meaning that the proof size grows sub-linearly in the batch size. A *monotone-policy BARG* [BBK+23, NWW24] allows the verifier to check that the set of true statements satisfies some monotone policy, described by a monotone circuit. Brakerski et al. [BBK+23] show how to get monotone policy BARGs from FHE with a CRS of size roughly $n \cdot \ell_{\mathsf{FHE}}$, where $\ell_{\mathsf{FHE}}$ is the size of a single FHE ciphertext. We observe that their CRS size can be reduced to $n + \ell_{\mathsf{FHE}}$ using the standard hybrid FHE technique used in the FHE-based CEE construction we described before.

The notion of monotone-policy BARGs bears a structural resemblance to secret sharing, as both involve enforcing monotone access structures; in both settings, a monotone circuit determines whether a given set of inputs (witnesses for BARGs, shares for secret sharing) satisfies the access policy. Despite these similarities, techniques from monotone-policy BARGs do not directly translate to succinct CSS. We believe it would be interesting to establish formal connections or generic compilers between the two settings.

*iO for Turing Machines.* From a high level, our tools and techniques are somewhat similar to those used in the context of iO for Turing machines [BGL+15, CHJV15, KLW15]. As a first attempt, one might try to use iO for Turing machines in a "black-box" way to get succinct CSS. Indeed, if we consider access policies that can be computed by a Turing machine of size $M$, using iO for TMs with unbounded space [KLW15], would give us an obfuscated program, and thus secret sharing scheme, of size $\mathsf{poly}(\lambda, n, M)$. This approach has two significant drawbacks: first, since the public information is polynomial in $M$, it limits the class of circuits that we can handle to circuits with a short Turing Machine description, as opposed to our general result that handles any circuit. Second, even for small $M$, the public information of the CSS would be polynomial in $n$, as opposed to just having a simple additive factor of $n$ as in our result.

Still, the problem we tackle here resembles the problem of constructing iO for TMs: in both cases, a 'large' computation is compressed into a compact, circuit-based obfuscated program that locally computes an encoding of the next tape cell (in the Turing machine setting) or circuit wire (in our setting). The output of this program is then used as input in subsequent invocations of the obfuscated program to further advance the computation. To ensure an adversary does not deviate from this intended evaluation path, the obfuscated program attaches a signature to each encoding which is later verified when that encoding is used as input. Despite the similarities, our setting differs in a couple of key ways, which are reflected in our construction:

- **Succinctness in circuit size** - iO for TMs achieves succinctness in runtime and space usage, while our goal is to compress the description of the circuit. Indeed, the obfuscated program in iO for TMs *does* grow with the description of the machine, making it unlikely that a direct application of iO for TMs would yield the desired succinctness. We overcome this problem using the fact that the circuit description is given 'for free' to the sharing and reconstruction algorithms, and utilizing the succinctness of PAs/SSB hash to embed a binding succinct description of the circuit into the obfuscated program.

- **Iterating over input space** - In the iO for TMs setting, security reductions typically iterate over the entire input space, thus causing the obfuscated program size to be polynomial in the input length, as well as incur a subexponential loss in security. On the surface, our construction of secret sharing looks like it could necessitate a similar exhaustive approach, as our security proof needs to argue the verification program remains secure when evaluated on *any* subset of corrupted shares. However, we crucially rely on the monotonicity of the access policy to prove a weaker but still sufficient property in the CSS security game: that the adversary is not able to flip the evaluation of any gate from 0 to 1. Extending this invariant to the output gate suffices to show overall security.[2]

Our construction can be viewed as being inspired by the KLW [KLW15] "machine hiding encodings" as a starting point where we make important modifications to (1) handle circuit descriptions (instead of Turing Machine descriptions), (2) simplified to only write memory once and (3) replacing the splittable signatures and their related security used in Koppula, Lewko and Waters [KLW15] with a pebbling argument [GPSZ17]. We remark that one could potentially also arrive at a circuit evaluation embedding by starting from other machine or randomized encoding schemes such as Garg and Srinivasan [GS18].

*Signature-Based Witness Encryption* Finally, we note our work shares some technical similarities in that the work of Avitabile et al. [ADM+25] in building *signature-based witness encryption (SbWE) with compact ciphertexts*, both using $i\mathcal{O}$ based techniques from the $i\mathcal{O}$ for TMs literature discussed previously to realize succinct cryptography. Furthermore, since signature-based witness encryption can be viewed as a reusable generalization of secret sharing, constructions of compact SbWE can directly be translated to a (succinct) secret sharing scheme. However, their work only considers threshold policies, a domain where succinct secret sharing is easy to construct. We think it is an interesting open question to try and extend our techniques to the setting of SbWE for general policies.

## 2 Preliminaries

*Notation.* We use $[n]$ to refer to the set $\{1, 2, \dots n\}$. For a subset $S \subseteq [n]$, we say $x \in \{0,1\}^n$ is the characteristic vector of $S$ if the $i^{th}$ bit of $x$ is 1 iff $i \in S$. Given a string $x \in \{0,1\}^n$, we use $S_x$ to denote the set for which $x$ is the characteristic vector.

[2] One notable exception that constructs iO for TMs without iterating over the input space is the work of Jain and Jin [JJ22] which utilizes *mathematical proofs of equivalence* between TMs to argue security. An intriguing direction for future work is exploring whether the mathematical proofs framework could eliminate the additive dependence on $n$ in our setting.

*Boolean Circuits.* We represent boolean circuits $C : \{0,1\}^n \to \{0,1\}$ with $\ell$ gates (including inputs) as an ordered list of $\ell - n$ tuples of the form $C_i = (g_i, i_0, i_1)$. The indices $i \in [n]$ are reserved for input wires, while each internal gate gets a unique index $i \in [n+1, \ell]$. For each $C_i = (g_i, i_0, i_1)$, the variable $g_i \in \{\mathsf{AND}, \mathsf{OR}, \mathsf{NOT}\}$ denotes the operation that is computed by gate $i$ and the indices $i_0, i_1 < i$ denote the indices of the gates that compute the input wires to gate $i$ (only $i_0$ for NOT gates). The gates $i_0, i_1$ are referred to as the children of gate $i$. We take the $\ell^{th}$ gate $C_\ell$ to be the output of the circuit. For convenience, we extend the representation of $C$ to an ordered list of length $\ell$, where the first $n$ elements are simply the indices $1, \ldots, n$ denoting the input gates. We refer to boolean circuits without NOT gates as monotone boolean circuits. For any input $x \in \{0,1\}^n$ and index $i \in [\ell]$, we denote by $C(x)[i]$ the value that gate $i$ takes in the evaluation of $C$ on input $x$. We let $g(b_0, b_1)$ to denote the evaluation function evaluating a gate $g$ on bits $b_0, b_1$.

### 2.1 Computational Secret Sharing

**Definition 2.1 (Access Structure [Bei96]).** *For any set $S = \{s_1, \ldots, s_n\}$, let $2^S$ denote the power set of $S$ (the set of all subsets of $S$). An access structure on $S$ is a set $\mathbb{A} \subseteq 2^S \setminus \varnothing$ of non-empty subsets of $S$. We refer to the elements of $\mathbb{A}$ as the* authorized *sets and those not in $\mathbb{A}$ as the* unauthorized *sets. We say an access structure is* monotone *if for all sets $S_1, S_2 \in 2^S$, if $S_1 \in \mathbb{A}$ and $S_1 \subseteq S_2$, then $S_2 \in \mathbb{A}$. We say a program $P$ implements an access structure if $P$ takes as input a string $x \in \{0,1\}^n$ and $P(x) = 1$ iff $\{s_i \mid x_i = 1\} \in \mathbb{A}$ (and $P(x) = 0$ otherwise).*

We now define the main notion of computational secret sharing. While (computational) secret sharing has been defined in many prior works, our definition most closely follows that of [ABI+23].

**Definition 2.2 (Computational Secret Sharing).** *Let $\lambda$ be a security parameter. A computational secret sharing (CSS) scheme with supporting programs $\mathcal{P} = \{\mathcal{P}_\lambda\}$, secret space $\mathcal{S} = \{\mathcal{S}_\lambda\}$ is a tuple of efficient algorithms $\Pi_{\mathsf{CSS}} = (\mathsf{Share}, \mathsf{Recon})$:*

- $\mathsf{Share}(1^\lambda, C, s) \to (\mathsf{sh}_0, \mathsf{sh}_1, \ldots, \mathsf{sh}_n)$*: On input security parameter $\lambda$, a monotone Boolean circuit $C : \{0,1\}^n \to \{0,1\}$, and secret $s \in \mathcal{S}$, the share algorithm generates a set of shares $(\mathsf{sh}_0, \mathsf{sh}_1, \ldots, \mathsf{sh}_n)$ where $\mathsf{sh}_0$ is the public information, and $\mathsf{sh}_1, \ldots, \mathsf{sh}_n$ are the shares distributed to the n parties.*
- $\mathsf{Recon}(C, x, \mathsf{sh}_0, \{\mathsf{sh}_i\}_{i \in S_x}) \to s \cup \bot$*: On input monotone Boolean circuit $C : \{0,1\}^n \to \{0,1\}$, input $x$, public information $\mathsf{sh}_0$, and set of user shares $\{\mathsf{sh}_i\}$ on indices $\in S_x$, the reconstruction algorithm outputs the secret $s$ (or $\bot$ for a reconstruction error).*

*We refer to share size* $\mathsf{shsize} = \mathsf{shsize}(\lambda, |C|)$ *to denote the maximum size of individual shares* $\max\{\mathsf{sh}_i \mid i \in [n]\}$ *in the above scheme and public information size to denote the size of* $\mathsf{sh}_0$. *We require the following properties:*

- **Correctness:** *For all security parameters* $\lambda$*, secrets* $s \in \mathcal{S}$*, monotone Boolean circuits* $C : \{0,1\}^n \to \{0,1\}$ *and inputs* $x$ *where* $C(x) = 1$*, we have that*

$$\Pr[\mathsf{Recon}(C, x, \mathsf{sh}_0, \{\mathsf{sh}_i\}_{i \in S_x}) = s : \mathsf{Share}(1^\lambda, C, s) \to (\mathsf{sh}_0, \mathsf{sh}_1, \dots, \mathsf{sh}_n)] = 1$$

- **Security:** *For a bit* $b \in \{0,1\}$ *and an adversary* $\mathcal{A}$*, define the secret sharing security game* $\mathsf{ExptCSS}_{\mathcal{A}}(\lambda, b)$ *as follows:*
  1. *Algorithm* $\mathcal{A}(1^\lambda)$ *chooses a policy* $C$*, an unauthorized input* $x$ *where* $C(x) = 0$ *and a pair of secrets* $s_0, s_1$*.*
  2. *The challenger samples* $(\mathsf{sh}_0, \mathsf{sh}_1, \dots, \mathsf{sh}_n) \leftarrow \mathsf{Share}(1^\lambda, C, s_b)$ *and returns* $\mathsf{sh}_0, \{\mathsf{sh}_i\}_{i \in S_x}$.
  3. *Algorithm* $\mathcal{A}$ *outputs a bit* $b' \in \{0,1\}$*, which is the output of the experiment.*

  *We say* $\Pi_{\mathsf{CSS}}$ *is secure if, for all efficient adversaries* $\mathcal{A}$*, there exists a negligible function* $\mathsf{negl}(\cdot)$ *such that for all* $\lambda \in \mathbb{N}$*,*

$$|\Pr[\mathsf{ExptCSS}_{\mathcal{A}}(\lambda, 0) = 1] - \Pr[\mathsf{ExptCSS}_{\mathcal{A}}(\lambda, 1) = 1]| = \mathsf{negl}(\lambda).$$

*Without loss of generality, we may assume that the first step that* $\mathcal{A}$ *runs is deterministic. That is, once* $\mathcal{A}$ *is fixed then* $P, x$ *and the pair* $s_0, s_1$ *are fixed.*

## 2.2 Building Blocks

In this section, we will review the ingredients we will use to build our secret sharing scheme.

**Definition 2.3 (Indistinguishability Obfuscation** [BGI+12, GGH+13]**).** *Let* $\mathcal{C} = \{\mathcal{C}_\lambda\}_{\lambda \in \mathbb{N}}$ *be a family of polynomial-size circuits. An indistinguishability obfuscator* $i\mathcal{O}$ *is an efficient algorithm that takes as input the security parameter* $\lambda$*, a circuit* $C \in \mathcal{C}_\lambda$ *and outputs a circuit* $C'$*. An* $i\mathcal{O}$ *scheme should satisfy the following properties:*

- **Functionality-preserving:** *For all security parameters* $\lambda \in \mathbb{N}$*, all* $C \in \mathcal{C}_\lambda$*, and all inputs* $x$*, we have that* $C'(x) = C(x)$ *where* $C' \leftarrow i\mathcal{O}(1^\lambda, C)$*.*
- **Security:** *For all efficient ( non-uniform) adversaries* $\mathcal{A} = (\mathsf{Samp}, \mathcal{A}')$*, there exists a negligible function* $\mathsf{negl}(\cdot)$ *such that the following holds: if for all security parameters* $\lambda \in \mathbb{N}$*,*

$$\Pr[\forall x, C_0(x) = C_1(x) : (C_0, C_1, \mathsf{st}) \leftarrow \mathsf{Samp}(1^\lambda)] = 1 - \mathsf{negl}(\lambda),$$

  *then*

$$\left| \Pr[\mathcal{A}'(\mathsf{st}, i\mathcal{O}(1^\lambda, C_0)) = 1] - \Pr[\mathcal{A}'(\mathsf{st}, i\mathcal{O}(1^\lambda, C_1)) = 1] \right| = \mathsf{negl}(\lambda),$$

  *where* $(C_0, C_1, \mathsf{st}) \leftarrow \mathsf{Samp}(1^\lambda)$.

**Definition 2.4 (Pseudorandom Generator).** *Let $\lambda$ be a security parameter, $n = n(\lambda)$ be a seed length, and $\ell = \ell(\lambda)$ be an output length. A pseudorandom generator* $\mathsf{PRG}\colon \{0,1\}^n \to \{0,1\}^\ell$ *is an efficiently-computable function such that for all efficient adversaries $\mathcal{A}$, there exists a negligible function* $\mathsf{negl}(\cdot)$ *such that for all $\lambda \in \mathbb{N}$,*

$$\left|\Pr\left[\mathcal{A}(\mathsf{PRG}(s)) = 1 : s \xleftarrow{R} \{0,1\}^n\right] - \Pr\left[\mathcal{A}(r) = 1 : r \xleftarrow{R} \{0,1\}^\ell\right]\right| = \mathsf{negl}(\lambda).$$

*We extend the security game to adversaries that request a constant number of samples $c \in \mathbb{N}$, that is, for all efficient adversaries $\mathcal{A}$, there exists a negligible function* $\mathsf{negl}(\cdot)$ *such that for all $\lambda \in \mathbb{N}$,*

$$|\Pr[\mathcal{A}(\mathsf{PRG}(s_1), \ldots, \mathsf{PRG}(s_c)) = 1] - \Pr[\mathcal{A}(r_1, \ldots, r_c) = 1]| = \mathsf{negl}(\lambda),$$

*where $s_i \xleftarrow{R} \{0,1\}^n$ and $r_i \xleftarrow{R} \{0,1\}^\ell$. The two security games are computationally equivalent by a standard hybrid argument.*

**Definition 2.5 ((Injective) One Way Functions and Hardcore Bits).** *Let $\lambda$ be a security parameter, $n = n(\lambda)$ be a seed length, and $\ell = \ell(\lambda)$ be an output length. We say a function* $\mathsf{hcb}(x)$ *is a hardcore bit [BM82, Yao82, GM82] of a one way function $F\colon \{0,1\}^n \to \{0,1\}^\ell$ if for all efficient adversaries $\mathcal{A}$, there exists a negligible function* $\mathsf{negl}(\cdot)$ *such that for all $\lambda \in \mathbb{N}$,*

$$|\Pr[\mathcal{A}(F(x), \mathsf{hcb}(x)) = 1] - \Pr[\mathcal{A}(F(x), \mathsf{hcb}(x) \oplus 1) = 1]| = \mathsf{negl}(\lambda),$$

*where $x \xleftarrow{R} \{0,1\}^n$.*

**Theorem 2.6 (Generic Hardcore Bits (informal) [GL89]).** *There exists a randomized hardcore bit* $\mathsf{hcb}(x; r)$ *for any one way function $F$.*

**Definition 2.7 (Positional Accumulator [KLW15]).** *Let $\lambda$ be a security parameter. A positional accumulator with block length $\ell_{\mathsf{blk}} = \ell_{\mathsf{blk}}(\lambda)$, output length $\ell_{\mathsf{hash}} = \ell_{\mathsf{hash}}(\lambda)$, and opening length $\ell_{\mathsf{open}} = \ell_{\mathsf{open}}(\lambda)$ is a tuple of efficient algorithms $\Pi_{\mathsf{PA}} =$ (Setup, SetupEnforce, Hash, Open, Verify) with the following properties:*

- $\mathsf{Setup}(1^\lambda, 1^{\ell_{\mathsf{blk}}}, 1^{|I|}) \to \mathsf{hk}$*: On input the security parameter $\lambda$, the block size $\ell_{\mathsf{blk}}$, the enforcing set size $|I|$, the setup algorithm outputs a hash key* $\mathsf{hk}$. *We let $\Sigma = \{0,1\}^{\ell_{\mathsf{blk}}}$ denote the block alphabet. We omit parameter enforcing set size $1^{|I|}$ when $|I| = 1$, i.e. when we are enforcing on a single index.*
- $\mathsf{SetupEnforce}(1^\lambda, 1^{\ell_{\mathsf{blk}}}, \mathbf{x}, I^*) \to \mathsf{hk}$*: On input security parameter $\lambda$, block size $\ell_{\mathsf{blk}}$, a tuple of inputs $\mathbf{x} \in \Sigma^N$, and an enforcing index set $I^*$, the enforcing setup algorithm outputs a hash key* $\mathsf{hk}$.
- $\mathsf{Hash}(\mathsf{hk}, \mathbf{x}) \to h$*: On input the hash key* $\mathsf{hk}$ *and a message $\mathbf{x} \in \Sigma^N$, the hash algorithm* deterministically *outputs a hash $h \in \{0,1\}^{\ell_{\mathsf{hash}}}$.*
- $\mathsf{Append}(\mathsf{hk}, h, x) \to h'$*: On input hash key* $\mathsf{hk}$*, hash $h$, and an input block $x \in \Sigma$, the hash algorithm* deterministically *outputs an updated hash $h' \in \{0,1\}^{\ell_{\mathsf{hash}}}$.*

- $\mathsf{Open}(\mathsf{hk}, \mathbf{x}, i) \to \pi_i$: *On input the hash key* hk*, an input* $\mathbf{x} \in \Sigma^N$*, and an index* $i \in [N]$*, the open algorithm outputs an opening* $\pi_i \in \{0,1\}^{\ell_{\mathsf{open}}}$.
- $\mathsf{Verify}(\mathsf{hk}, h, i, x_i, \pi_i) \to \{0,1\}$: *On input the hash key* hk*, a hash value* $h \in \{0,1\}^{\ell_{\mathsf{hash}}}$*, an index* $i \in [N]$*, a value* $x_i \in \Sigma$*, and an opening* $\pi_i \in \{0,1\}^{\ell_{\mathsf{open}}}$*, the verification algorithm outputs a bit* $b \in \{0,1\}$ *indicating whether it accepts or rejects.*

*We require the following properties:*

- **Correctness:** *For all security parameters* $\lambda \in \mathbb{N}$*, all block sizes* $\ell_{\mathsf{blk}} = \ell_{\mathsf{blk}}(\lambda)$*, all integers* $N \leq 2^\lambda$*, all indices and enforcing set sizes* $i, |I| \in [N]$*, and any* $\mathbf{x} \in \Sigma^N$,

$$\Pr\left[\mathsf{Verify}(\mathsf{hk}, h, i, x_i, \pi_i) = 1 : \begin{array}{c} \mathsf{hk} \leftarrow \mathsf{Setup}(1^\lambda, 1^{\ell_{\mathsf{blk}}}, 1^{|I|}); \\ h \leftarrow \mathsf{Hash}(\mathsf{hk}, \mathbf{x}); \pi_i \leftarrow \mathsf{Open}(\mathsf{hk}, \mathbf{x}, i) \end{array}\right] = 1.$$

- **Setup Indistinguishability:** *For a bit* $b \in \{0,1\}$ *and an adversary* $\mathcal{A}$*, define the index hiding game* $\mathsf{ExptIH}_{\mathcal{A}}(\lambda, b)$ *as follows:*
  1. *Algorithm* $\mathcal{A}(1^\lambda)$ *chooses a block length* $1^{\ell}_{\mathsf{blk}}$*, input sequence* $\mathbf{x}$ *an index set* $I^* \subseteq [N]$.
  2. *The challenger samples*

  $$\mathsf{hk}_0 \leftarrow \mathsf{Setup}(1^\lambda, 1^{\ell_{\mathsf{blk}}}, 1^{|I^*|}) \text{ and } \mathsf{hk}_1 \leftarrow \mathsf{SetupEnforce}(1^\lambda, 1^{\ell}_{\mathsf{blk}}, \mathbf{x}, I^*)$$

  *and gives* $\mathsf{hk}_b$ *to* $\mathcal{A}$.
  3. *Algorithm* $\mathcal{A}$ *outputs a bit* $b' \in \{0,1\}$*, which is also the output of the experiment.*

  *We require that for all polynomials* $\ell_{\mathsf{blk}} = \ell_{\mathsf{blk}}(\lambda)$ *and all efficient adversaries* $\mathcal{A}$*, there exists a negligible function* $\mathsf{negl}(\cdot)$ *such that for all* $\lambda \in \mathbb{N}$,

$$|\Pr[\mathsf{ExptSI}_{\mathcal{A}}(\lambda, 0) = 1] - \Pr[\mathsf{ExptSI}_{\mathcal{A}}(\lambda, 1) = 1]| = \mathsf{negl}(\lambda).$$

- **Read Enforcing:** *We say that a hash key* hk *is read enforcing for an input* $\mathbf{x} = (x_1, \ldots, x_N)$ *and index set* $I^* \in [N]$ *if there does not exist* $i^* \in I^*$ *and* $x' \neq x_{i^*} \in \Sigma$*, and* $\pi'$ *where* $\mathsf{Verify}(\mathsf{hk}, h, i^*, x', \pi') = 1$ *for* $h \leftarrow \mathsf{Hash}(\mathsf{hk}, \mathbf{x})$*. We require that for all polynomials* $\ell_{\mathsf{blk}} = \ell_{\mathsf{blk}}(\lambda)$*, there exists a negligible function* $\mathsf{negl}(\cdot)$ *such that for all* $\lambda \in \mathbb{N}$*, all inputs* $\mathbf{x} \in \Sigma^N$*, and all* $I^* \subseteq [N]$,

$$\Pr[\mathsf{hk} \text{ is read enforcing for } (\mathbf{x}, I^*)] = 1 - \mathsf{negl}(\lambda),$$

  *where* $\mathsf{hk} \leftarrow \mathsf{SetupEnforce}(1^\lambda, 1^{\ell_{\mathsf{blk}}}$.
- **Write Enforcing:** *For all security parameters* $\lambda \in \mathbb{N}$*, all block sizes* $\ell_{\mathsf{blk}} = \ell_{\mathsf{blk}}(\lambda)$*, all inputs* $\mathbf{x} = (x_1, \ldots x_N) \in \Sigma^N$ *and blocks* $x_{N+1}$*, we require that*

$$\Pr\left[\mathsf{Hash}(\mathsf{hk}, (x_1, \ldots x_N, x_{N+1})) = \mathsf{Append}(\mathsf{hk}, h, x_{N+1})\right] = 1,$$

  *where* $\mathsf{hk} \leftarrow \mathsf{Setup}(1^\lambda, 1^{\ell_{\mathsf{blk}}}, 1^{|I^*|})$ *and* $h \leftarrow \mathsf{Hash}(\mathsf{hk}, \mathbf{x})$.
- **Succinctness:** *The hash length* $\ell_{\mathsf{hash}}$*, and opening length* $\ell_{\mathsf{open}}$ *are all fixed polynomials in the security parameter* $\lambda$ *and the block size* $\ell_{\mathsf{blk}}$ *(and notably independent of the number of blocks hashed* $N$*).*

**Theorem 2.8 (Positional Accumulators** [KLW15]**).** *Assuming the existence of an indistinguishability obfuscation scheme and one-way functions, there exists a positional accumulator for arbitrary polynomial input lengths* $\ell = \ell(\lambda)$.

*Remark 2.9.* We present a simpler definition of positional accumulators modifying that given in [GSWW22] compared to the original definition of [KLW15], and is more reminiscent of the abstraction of somewhere statistically binding (SSB) hashes [HW15,OPWW15]. We do not require the full ability of arbitrary read/write sequences and instead only need the ability to 'append' to the end of a hash input.

**Definition 2.10 (Puncturable PRF** [BW13,KPTZ13,BGI14]**).** *A* $t$*-puncturable pseudorandom function consists of a tuple of efficient algorithms* $\Pi_{\mathsf{PPRF}} = (\mathsf{KeyGen}, \mathsf{Eval}, \mathsf{Puncture})$ *with the following syntax:*

- $\mathsf{KeyGen}(1^\lambda, 1^{\ell_{\mathsf{in}}}, 1^{\ell_{\mathsf{out}}}) \to K$*: On input a security parameter* $\lambda$*, an input length* $\ell_{\mathsf{in}}$*, and an output length* $\ell_{\mathsf{out}}$*, the key generation algorithm outputs a key* $K$*. We assume the key contains an implicit description of* $\ell_{\mathsf{in}}$ *and* $\ell_{\mathsf{out}}$*.*
- $\mathsf{Puncture}(K, S) \to K^{(S)}$*: On input a key* $K$ *and a set* $S \subseteq \{0,1\}^{\ell_{\mathsf{in}}}$ *of size* $t$*, the puncture algorithm outputs a punctured key* $K^{(S)}$*. We assume the punctured key contains an implicit description of* $\ell_{\mathsf{in}}$ *and* $\ell_{\mathsf{out}}$*.*
- $\mathsf{Eval}(K, x) \to y$*: On input a key* $K$ *and an input* $x \in \{0,1\}^{\ell_{\mathsf{in}}}$*, the evaluation algorithm outputs a value* $y \in \{0,1\}^{\ell_{\mathsf{out}}}$*. We sometimes write* $F(K, x)$ *to denote* $\mathsf{Eval}(K, x)$*.*

*In addition,* $\Pi_{\mathsf{PPRF}}$ *should satisfy the following properties:*

- ***Functionality-preserving:*** *For all* $\lambda, \ell_{\mathsf{in}}, \ell_{\mathsf{out}} \in \mathbb{N}$*, every set* $S \subseteq \{0,1\}^{\ell_{\mathsf{in}}}$ *of size* $t$*, and every* $x \in \{0,1\}^{\ell_{\mathsf{in}}} \setminus S$*,*

$$\Pr\left[\mathsf{Eval}(K, x) = \mathsf{Eval}\left(K^{(S)}, x\right) : \begin{array}{c} K \leftarrow \mathsf{KeyGen}(1^\lambda, 1^{\ell_{\mathsf{in}}}, 1^{\ell_{\mathsf{out}}}) \\ K^{(S)} \leftarrow \mathsf{Puncture}(K, S) \end{array}\right] = 1$$

- ***Punctured pseudorandomness:*** *For a bit* $b \in \{0,1\}$ *and a security parameter* $\lambda$*, we define the (selective) punctured pseudorandomness game between an adversary* $\mathcal{A}$ *and a challenger as follows:*
  - *On input a parameter* $\lambda$*, the adversary outputs an input length* $1^{\ell_{\mathsf{in}}}$ *and an output length* $1^{\ell_{\mathsf{out}}}$*, and commits to a set* $S \subseteq \{0,1\}^{\ell_{\mathsf{in}}}$ *of size* $t$*.*
  - *The challenger samples a key* $K \leftarrow \mathsf{KeyGen}(1^\lambda, 1^{\ell_{\mathsf{in}}}, 1^{\ell_{\mathsf{out}}})$ *and gives the punctured key* $K^{(S)} \leftarrow \mathsf{Puncture}(K, S)$ *to* $\mathcal{A}$*.*
  - *If* $b = 0$*, then the challenger sets* $y_i^* = \mathsf{Eval}(K, x_i^*)$ *for each* $x_i^* \in S$*. Otherwise it samples* $y_i^* \xleftarrow{\mathrm{R}} \{0,1\}^{\ell_{\mathsf{out}}}$ *for each* $i \in [t]$*. In any case, the challenger gives* $(y_i^*)_{i \in [t]}$ *to* $\mathcal{A}$*.*
  - *The adversary outputs a guess* $b' \in \{0,1\}$*, which is the output of the experiment.*

  *We say that* $\Pi_{\mathsf{PPRF}}$ *satisfies punctured pseudorandomness if for all polynomial time adversaries* $\mathcal{A}$*, there exists a negligible function* $\mathsf{negl}(\lambda)$ *such that*

$$|\Pr[\mathsf{ExptPP}_{\mathcal{A}}(\lambda, 0) = 1] - \Pr[\mathsf{ExptPP}_{\mathcal{A}}(\lambda, 1) = 1]| \leq \mathsf{negl}(\lambda)$$

**Definition 2.11.** *Let $\Pi_{\mathsf{PPRF}} = (\mathsf{KeyGen}, \mathsf{Eval}, \mathsf{Puncture})$ be a puncturable PRF. For a bit $b \in \{0,1\}$ and a security parameter $\lambda$, we define the (selective) pseudorandomness game between an adversary $\mathcal{A}$ and a challenger as follows:*

- *On input a parameter $\lambda$, the adversary outputs an input length $1^{\ell_{\mathsf{in}}}$ and an output length $1^{\ell_{\mathsf{out}}}$, and commits to a point $x^* \in \{0,1\}^{\ell_{\mathsf{in}}}$.*
- *The challenger samples a key $K \leftarrow \mathsf{KeyGen}(1^\lambda, 1^{\ell_{\mathsf{in}}}, 1^{\ell_{\mathsf{out}}})$. If $b = 0$, then the challenger sets $y^* = \mathsf{Eval}(K, x^*)$. Otherwise it sets $y^* \xleftarrow{R} \{0,1\}^{\ell_{\mathsf{out}}}$. In any case, the challenger gives $y^*$ to $\mathcal{A}$.*
- *The adversary $\mathcal{A}$ is allowed to make polynomially many queries $x \in \{0,1\}^{\ell_{\mathsf{in}}}$ and the challenger responds with $\mathsf{Eval}(K, x)$.*
- *The adversary outputs a guess $b' \in \{0,1\}$, which is the output of the experiment.*

*We say that $\Pi_{\mathsf{PRF}} := (\mathsf{KeyGen}, \mathsf{Eval})$ satisfies pseudorandomness if for all polynomial time adversaries $\mathcal{A}$, there exists a negligible function $\mathsf{negl}(\lambda)$ such that*

$$|\Pr[b' = 1 : b = 0] - \Pr[b' = 1 : b = 1]| \leq \mathsf{negl}(\lambda).$$

**Fact 2.12.** *If $\Pi_{\mathsf{PPRF}} = (\mathsf{KeyGen}, \mathsf{Eval}, \mathsf{Puncture})$ is a puncturable PRF, then $\Pi_{\mathsf{PRF}} = (\mathsf{KeyGen}, \mathsf{Eval})$ satisfies pseudorandomness.*

## 3 Circuit Evaluation Embedding

In this section, we define the new notion of circuit evaluation embeddings which we will use to build our secret sharing scheme. We can view this as a way to secretly embed the computation of a public circuit $C$ and its evaluation on a hidden input $x$ into a short digest $\alpha$, which can be publicly expanded into a local encoding of the gates of $C$ evaluated on $x$.

**Definition 3.1. (Circuit Evaluation Embedding).** *A circuit evaluation embedding is a tuple of efficient algorithms $(\mathsf{Gen}, \mathsf{EmbedGen}, \mathsf{Expand}, \mathsf{Extract})$ with the following syntax:*

- $\mathsf{Gen}(1^\lambda, 1^n, C) \rightarrow \alpha$ : *On input a security parameter $\lambda$, an input length $n$ and a description of a circuit $C : \{0,1\}^n \rightarrow \{0,1\}$, the generation algorithm outputs a seed $\alpha$.*
- $\mathsf{EmbedGen}(1^\lambda, 1^n, C, x) \rightarrow (\alpha^*, \mathsf{td})$ : *On input a security parameter $\lambda$, an input length $n$, a description of a circuit $C : \{0,1\}^n \rightarrow \{0,1\}$ and a string $x \in \{0,1\}^n$, the embedding generation algorithm outputs a seed $\alpha^*$ and a trapdoor* $\mathsf{td}$.
- $\mathsf{Expand}(C, \alpha) \rightarrow \mathbf{w}$ : *On input the description of a circuit $C : \{0,1\}^n \rightarrow \{0,1\}$ and a seed $\alpha$, the expansion algorithm* deterministically *outputs a string $\mathbf{w} \in \{0,1\}^\ell$ of length $\ell$, where $\ell$ is the number of gates in the circuit $C$.*
- $\mathsf{Extract}(\mathsf{td}, i, b) \rightarrow 0/1$ : *On input a trapdoor* $\mathsf{td}$, *an index $i \in [\ell]$ and a bit $b \in \{0,1\}$, the extraction algorithm outputs a bit.*

*We require $\Pi_{\mathsf{CEE}}$ to satisfy the following properties:*

- ***Computational mode indistinguishability:*** *We define the mode indistinguishability experiment between an attacker $\mathcal{A}$ and the challenger, parameterized by a bit $b \in \{0,1\}$, as follows:*
  1. *The attacker $\mathcal{A}$ on input $1^\lambda$ chooses a circuit $C : \{0,1\}^n \to \{0,1\}$ with $\ell$ wires and a string $x \in \{0,1\}^n$, and sends $(C, x)$ to the challenger.*
  2. *If $b = 0$ then the challenger samples $\alpha \leftarrow \mathsf{Gen}(1^\lambda, 1^n)$. Otherwise, the challenger samples $(\alpha, \mathsf{td}) \leftarrow \mathsf{EmbedGen}(1^\lambda, 1^n, C, x)$. In any case, it sends $\alpha$ to $\mathcal{A}$.*
  3. *Algorithm $\mathcal{A}$ outputs a bit $b'$ which is the output of the experiment.*

  *We say that $\Pi_{\mathsf{CEE}}$ satisfies computational mode indistinguishability if for any efficient $\mathcal{A}$ there exists a negligible function $\mathsf{negl}(\lambda)$ such that*

$$|\Pr[b' = 1 : b = 0] - \Pr[b' = 1 : b = 1]| \leq \mathsf{negl}(\lambda).$$

- ***Statistical extraction:*** *for any $\lambda, n, \ell \in \mathbb{N}$, circuit $C : \{0,1\}^n \to \{0,1\}$ of size $\ell$, $x \in \{0,1\}^n$ and $(\alpha^*, \mathsf{td})$ in the support of $\mathsf{EmbedGen}(1^\lambda, 1^n, C, x)$, it holds that $\mathsf{Extract}(\mathsf{td}, i, w_i) = C(x)[i]$, where $w_i$ is the $i^{th}$ bit of $\mathbf{w} = \mathsf{Expand}(C, \alpha^*)$ and $C(x)[i]$ is the value of wire $i$ when evaluation $C$ on $x$.*
- ***Succinctness:*** *Let $m := m(\lambda, n, \ell)$ be any function. We say that $\Pi_{\mathsf{CEE}}$ is $m$-succinct if for any $\lambda, n, \ell \in \mathbb{N}$ and any circuit $C : \{0,1\}^n \to \{0,1\}$ with $\ell$ gates, the seed $\alpha$ output by algorithm $\mathsf{Gen}(1^\lambda, 1^n, C)$ is an $m$-bit string.*
- ***Succinct trapdoors:*** *We say that $\Pi_{\mathsf{CEE}}$ has succinct trapdoors if there exists a polynomial $\mathsf{poly}(\lambda)$ such that for any $\lambda, n, \ell \in \mathbb{N}$, any circuit $C : \{0,1\}^n \to \{0,1\}$ and any $x \in \{0,1\}^n$, the trapdoor $\mathsf{td}_{\mathsf{CEE}}$ output by algorithm $\mathsf{EmbedGen}(1^\lambda, 1^n, C, x)$ is $\mathsf{poly}(\lambda)$ bits long.*

## 4 Computational Secret Sharing From Circuit Evaluation Embeddings

In this section, we construct a computational secret sharing scheme for monotone boolean circuits based on iO, OWFs and a circuit evaluation embedding. Instantiating our circuit evaluation embedding scheme with the construction in Sect. 5 our scheme has public information size $n + \mathsf{poly}(\lambda, \log|C|)$ and share size $\lambda$.

**Construction 4.1 (Computational Secret Sharing).** We construct a computational secret sharing scheme over secret space $\mathcal{S}$ and policy class of polynomial size monotone boolean circuits given the following primitives:

1. A puncturable PRF $\Pi_{\mathsf{PPRF}} = (\mathsf{KeyGen}, \mathsf{Eval}, \mathsf{Puncture})$.
2. A PRG $\mathsf{PRG}$ from $\{0,1\}^\lambda \to \{0,1\}^{2\lambda}$.
3. A positional accumulator $\Pi_{\mathsf{PA}} = (\mathsf{Setup}, \mathsf{SetupEnforce}, \mathsf{Hash}, \mathsf{Open}, \mathsf{Verify})$.
4. An indistinguishability obfuscator for circuits $i\mathcal{O}$.
5. A circuit evaluation embedding $\Pi_{\mathsf{CEE}} = (\mathsf{Gen}, \mathsf{EmbedGen}, \mathsf{Expand}, \mathsf{Extract})$ for the class of monotone boolean circuits.

Apart from circuit evaluation embeddings, which we will discuss in the following section, these primitives can all be built from indistinguishability obfuscation and one way functions.

At a high level, our construction assigns a secret key to each gate $i$ in the policy circuit as the output of a PRF on index $i$, then gives each player the secret key of the corresponding input wire. To allow players to derive the secret keys of internal gates, the share generation algorithm produces an obfuscated program that outputs the secret key of gate $i$, if given sufficient secret keys of the children gates. To ensure security, our construction requires publishing a string $\mathbf{w}$ that (secretly) embeds the evaluation of the policy on the challenge input (i.e., the unauthorized set). Then, we gradually change our obfuscated program to output secret keys of gates only if they are permitted by the evaluation embedded in $\mathbf{w}$. We now describe our construction formally:

- $\mathsf{Share}(1^\lambda, C, s) \rightarrow (\mathsf{sh}_0, \mathsf{sh}_1, \ldots, \mathsf{sh}_n)$: On input security parameter $\lambda$, a monotone policy circuit $C : \{0,1\}^n \rightarrow \{0,1\}$ of size $\ell$, and secret $s \in \mathcal{S}$. Denote by $\ell_{\mathsf{gate}} = 1 + 2\log \ell$ the size of the representation of a single gate $C_i$ in $C$. Our sharing algorithm does the following:
  1. Samples the hash keys $\mathsf{hk}_{\mathbf{w}} \leftarrow \Pi_{\mathsf{PA}}.\mathsf{Setup}(1^\lambda, 1)$ and $\mathsf{hk}_C \leftarrow \Pi_{\mathsf{PA}}.\mathsf{Setup}(1^\lambda, 1^{\ell_{\mathsf{gate}}})$.
  2. Samples the PPRF key $K_\lambda \leftarrow \Pi_{\mathsf{PPRF}}.\mathsf{KeyGen}(1^\lambda, 1^{\log \ell}, 1^\lambda)$.
  3. Samples the CEE seed $\alpha \leftarrow \Pi_{\mathsf{CEE}}.\mathsf{Gen}(1^\lambda, 1^n, C)$.
  4. Expands $\mathbf{w} = \Pi_{\mathsf{CEE}}.\mathsf{Expand}(C, \alpha)$.
  5. Hashes $h_{\mathbf{w}} = \Pi_{\mathsf{PA}}.\mathsf{Hash}(\mathsf{hk}_{\mathbf{w}}, \mathbf{w})$ and $h_C = \Pi_{\mathsf{PA}}.\mathsf{Hash}(\mathsf{hk}_C, C)$.
  6. Obfuscates the program from Fig. 1
  $$P \leftarrow i\mathcal{O}(\mathsf{ComputePolicy}[\mathsf{hk}_C, \mathsf{hk}_{\mathbf{w}}, h_C, h_{\mathbf{w}}, K_\lambda, s]).$$
  7. Sets $\mathsf{sh}_0 = (P, \alpha, \mathsf{hk}_C, \mathsf{hk}_{\mathbf{w}})$, and $\mathsf{sh}_i = \Pi_{\mathsf{PPRF}}.\mathsf{Eval}(K_\lambda, i)$ for each $i \in [n]$.
  8. Outputs $(\mathsf{sh}_0, \ldots, \mathsf{sh}_n)$.
- $\mathsf{Recon}(C, x, \mathsf{sh}_0, \{\mathsf{sh}_i\}_{i \in S_x}) \rightarrow s \cup \bot$: On input a monotone policy circuit $C : \{0,1\}^n \rightarrow \{0,1\}$ of size $\ell$, input $x \in \{0,1\}^n$, public information $\mathsf{sh}_0$, and set of user shares $\{\mathsf{sh}_i\}_{i \in S_x}$, our reconstruction algorithm does the following:
  1. Parses $\mathsf{sh}_0 = (P, \alpha, \mathsf{hk}_C, \mathsf{hk}_{\mathbf{w}})$.
  2. Expands $\mathbf{w} = \Pi_{\mathsf{CEE}}.\mathsf{Expand}(C, \alpha)$.
  3. Computes openings for all indices on both hashes, that is for all $i \in [\ell]$:
     - $\pi_i^{(C)} \leftarrow \Pi_{\mathsf{PA}}.\mathsf{Open}(\mathsf{hk}_C, C, i)$.
     - $\pi_i^{(\mathbf{w})} \leftarrow \Pi_{\mathsf{PA}}.\mathsf{Open}(\mathsf{hk}_{\mathbf{w}}, \mathbf{w}, i)$.
  4. Compute the following values for $i \in [n]$:
  $$\sigma_i = \begin{cases} \mathsf{sh}_i & i \in S_x \\ \bot & i \notin S_x \end{cases}$$
  5. For $i = n+1, \ldots, \ell$, computes $\sigma_i = P(i, C_i, \pi_i^{(C)}, w_i, \pi_i^{(\mathbf{w})}, \sigma_{i_0}, \sigma_{i_1})$, where $C_i = (g_i, i_0, i_1)$ is the description of gate $i$ in the representation of $C$.
  6. Output $\sigma_\ell$.

**Constants:** Hash keys $\mathsf{hk_w}, \mathsf{hk}_C$, hashes $h_\mathbf{w}, h_C$, puncturable PRF key $K_\lambda$, and the secret $s$.
**Inputs:** Gate index $i$, gate description $C_i = (g_i, i_0, i_1)$, local opening $\pi_i^{(C)}$, a bit $w_i$, local opening $\pi_i^{(\mathbf{w})}$ and for each $b \in \{0,1\}$, a signature $\sigma_{i_b}$.

1. Verify inputs are well formed. Abort with $\perp$ if any checks do not pass.
   (a) Check $i \in [n+1, \ell]$.
   (b) Check $\mathsf{Verify}(\mathsf{hk}_C, h_C, i, C_i, \pi_i^{(C)}) = 1$.
   (c) Check $\mathsf{Verify}(\mathsf{hk_w}, h_\mathbf{w}, i, w_i, \pi^{(\mathbf{w})}) = 1$.
2. For $b \in \{0,1\}$, set $v_{i_b} = 1$ if and only if $\mathsf{PRG}(\Pi_{\mathsf{PPRF}}.\mathsf{Eval}(K_\lambda, i_b)) = \mathsf{PRG}(\sigma_{i_b})$.
3. Compute $v_i = g_i(v_{i_0}, v_{i_1})$.
4. If $i < \ell$, set $\sigma_i = \Pi_{\mathsf{PPRF}}.\mathsf{Eval}(K_\lambda, i)$ if $v_i = 1$ and $\sigma_i = \perp$ otherwise. Output $\sigma_i$.
5. Otherwise, if $v_i = 1$, output the secret $s$. If $v_i = 0$, output $\perp$.

**Fig. 1.** Program $\mathsf{ComputePolicy}[\mathsf{hk}_C, \mathsf{hk_w}, h_C, h_\mathbf{w}, K_\lambda, s]$.

### 4.1 Correctness and Efficiency

**Theorem 4.2 (Correctness).** *Suppose $i\mathcal{O}$ is a functionality preserving obfuscator and $\Pi_{\mathsf{PA}}$ is a correct positional accumulator. Then Construction 4.1 is a correct CSS scheme.*

*Proof.* Consider any $s \in \mathcal{S}$ and monotone Boolean circuit $C : \{0,1\}^n \to \{0,1\}$. Let $x \in \{0,1\}^n$ be an authorized set, i.e., $C(x) = 1$. Let $\mathsf{sh}_0 = (P, \alpha, \mathsf{hk}_C, \mathsf{hk_w})$ and $\mathsf{sh}_1, \ldots, \mathsf{sh}_n$ be some shares output by $\mathsf{Share}(1^\lambda, C, s)$.

Now consider the values $\sigma_1, \ldots, \sigma_\ell$ as defined in $\mathsf{Recon}(C, x, \mathsf{sh}_0, \{\mathsf{sh}_i\}_{i \in S_x})$. We prove that $\sigma_i = \Pi_{\mathsf{PPRF}}.\mathsf{Eval}(K_\lambda, i)$ for each $i \in [\ell - 1]$ such that $C(x)[i] = 1$ by induction on $i$. For the input gates $i \in [n]$, the claim follows directly by Step 4. Let $i \in [n+1, \ell-1]$ and assume the invariant holds for all $j < i$. By construction of the program in Fig. 1 and the functionality preserving of $i\mathcal{O}$, if we prove that all checks in Step 1 pass and that $v_i = 1$ in Step 3 then the program will output $\sigma_i = \Pi_{\mathsf{PPRF}}.\mathsf{Eval}(K_\lambda, i)$.

- Check 1a passes by the fact that $i \in [n+1, \ell-1]$.
- Checks 1b and 1c pass by the correctness of $\Pi_{\mathsf{PA}}$.
- Let be an internal gate, $g_i \in \{\mathsf{AND}, \mathsf{OR}\}$ be the operation it computes and $i_0, i_1$ be its children gates. By the induction hypothesis and since $i_0, i_1 < i$, we have $\sigma_{i_b} = \Pi_{\mathsf{PPRF}}.\mathsf{Eval}(K_\lambda, i_b)$, therefore $v_{i_b} \geq C(x)[i_b]$ by the way we compute $v_{i_b}$ in Step 2. Finally, if $C(x)[i] = 1$, then $g_i(C(x)[i_0], C(x)[i_1]) = 1$ and by the monotonicity of $g_i$, we have $v_i = g_i(v_{i_0}, v_{i_0}) = 1$.

Therefore the claim holds for all gates $i < \ell$. By an analogous argument, we prove that the program does not output $\perp$ when evaluated on the output gate $\ell$. In that case, it will output $\sigma_\ell = s$ and thus the secret will be output by $\mathsf{Recon}$ and correctness follows.

**Theorem 4.3 (Succinctness).** *If* $\Pi_{\mathsf{CEE}}$ *is* $m$*-succinct and has succinct trapdoors and* $\Pi_{\mathsf{PA}}$ *is succinct, Construction 4.1 has public information of size* $m + \mathsf{poly}(\lambda, \log |C|)$ *and shares of size* $\lambda$.

*Proof.* Consider any $s \in \mathcal{S}$ and monotone Boolean circuit $C : \{0,1\}^n \to \{0,1\}$ of size $\ell$. Let $x \in \{0,1\}^n$ be an authorized set, i.e., $C(x) = 1$. Let $\mathsf{sh}_0 = (P, \alpha, \mathsf{hk}_C, \mathsf{hk}_{\mathbf{w}})$ be some public information and $\mathsf{sh}_1, \ldots, \mathsf{sh}_n$ be some shares output by $\mathsf{Share}(1^\lambda, C, s)$. By construction, each share $\mathsf{sh}_i$ for $i < 0$ is exactly $\lambda$ bits long since it is the output of a PRF on range $\{0,1\}^\lambda$. The public information consists of the following:

- The seed $\alpha$ is $m$ bits long by the $m$-succinctness of $\Pi_{\mathsf{CEE}}$.
- The hash keys $\mathsf{hk}_C$ and $\mathsf{hk}_{\mathbf{w}}$ are bounded by $\mathsf{poly}(\lambda, \ell_{\mathsf{gate}}) = \mathsf{poly}(\lambda, \log \ell)$ by the efficiency of $\Pi_{\mathsf{PA}}.\mathsf{Setup}$.
- The program $P$ has the following hardcoded in it:
  - The hash keys $\mathsf{hk}_C$ and $\mathsf{hk}_{\mathbf{w}}$ of size $\mathsf{poly}(\lambda, \log \ell)$.
  - The hashes $h_C, h_{\mathbf{w}}$ of size $\mathsf{poly}(\lambda, \log \ell)$ by the succinctness of $\Pi_{\mathsf{PA}}$.
  - The PPRF key $K_\lambda$ of size $\mathsf{poly}(\lambda, \log \ell)$ by the efficiency of $\Pi_{\mathsf{PPRF}}.\mathsf{Eval}$.
  - The secret $s$ which we assume is of size $\mathsf{poly}(\lambda)$.
  - Indices on number in $[\ell]$ which have size $\log \ell$.

  Therefore the program has size $\mathsf{poly}(\lambda, \log \ell)$. Furthermore, by inspecting the security proof in the full version of this paper, we see that the programs used there also have size $\mathsf{poly}(\lambda, \log \ell)$, and by the efficiency of $i\mathcal{O}$, the obfuscated programs would also have size $\mathsf{poly}(\lambda, \log \ell)$.

Therefore the public information has total size of $m + \mathsf{poly}(\lambda, \log \ell)$.

### 4.2 Security

To show security of our CSS scheme, rather than attempting to use our obfuscated program to enforce some global validity property on the computation of the access policy, which is restricted by the small size of the obfuscated program, we instead leverage our circuit evaluation embedding and the monotonicity of our policy circuit to enforce a *local* property on the relationship between the circuit embedding $\mathbf{w}$ and the ability of our obfuscated program to produce a signature $\sigma$ on a particular index. Using this, we are able to incrementally rule out the ability for our program to produce a signature $\sigma$ on any wire for which $\mathbf{w}$ (when encoding the adversary's challenge input $x$) encodes a 0 bit. Once this reaches the output gate, since any valid adversary's challenge input $x$ cannot satisfy the policy circuit, we can directly remove our program's ability to generate and verify $\sigma_\ell$, allowing us to remove secret $s$ as well.

**Theorem 4.4 (Security).** *If* $\mathsf{PRG}$ *is a secure PRG,* $\Pi_{\mathsf{PPRF}}$ *is a secure and correct puncturable PRF,* $\Pi_{\mathsf{PA}}$ *is a setup indistinguishable and read enforcing positional accumulator,* $\Pi_{\mathsf{CEE}}$ *is a mode indistinguishable and extractable circuit evaluation embedding, and* $i\mathcal{O}$ *is a secure indistinguishability obfuscator, then Construction 4.1 is a secure CSS scheme.*

*Proof.* To show security, we define a sequence of experiments, beginning with $\mathsf{Exp}^{(\beta)}_{\mathsf{real}}$, which is the real secret sharing $\mathsf{ExptCSS}_{\mathcal{A}}(\lambda, \beta)$ using secret $s_\beta$ and ending in $\mathsf{Exp}^{(\beta)}_{\mathsf{final}}$, an experiment where the adversary's inputs are independent of secret $s_\beta$. We will argue indistinguishability of this sequence of experiments.

- $\mathsf{Exp}^{(\beta)}_{\mathsf{real}}$: This is the real CSS security when using our scheme Construction 4.1.
  1. The adversary $\mathcal{A}(1^\lambda)$ chooses a policy $C : \{0,1\}^n \to \{0,1\}$, an unauthorized input $x \in \{0,1\}^n$ where $C(x) = 0$ and a pair of secrets $s_0, s_1$. Let $\ell = |C|$ be the number of gates in $C$.
  2. The challenger samples and outputs the following:
     (a) Samples the hash keys $\mathsf{hk}_{\mathbf{w}} \leftarrow \Pi_{\mathsf{PA}}.\mathsf{Setup}(1^\lambda, 1)$ and $\mathsf{hk}_C \leftarrow \Pi_{\mathsf{PA}}.\mathsf{Setup}(1^\lambda, 1^{\ell_{\mathsf{gate}}})$.
     (b) Samples the PPRF key $K_\lambda \leftarrow \Pi_{\mathsf{PPRF}}.\mathsf{KeyGen}(1^\lambda, 1^{\log \ell}, 1^\lambda)$.
     (c) Samples the CEE seed $\alpha \leftarrow \Pi_{\mathsf{CEE}}.\mathsf{Gen}(1^\lambda, 1^n, C)$.
     (d) Expands $\mathbf{w} = \Pi_{\mathsf{CEE}}.\mathsf{Expand}(C, \alpha)$.
     (e) Hashes $h_{\mathbf{w}} = \Pi_{\mathsf{PA}}.\mathsf{Hash}(\mathsf{hk}_{\mathbf{w}}, \mathbf{w})$ and $h_C = \Pi_{\mathsf{PA}}.\mathsf{Hash}(\mathsf{hk}_C, C)$.
     (f) Obfuscates the program from Fig. 1
     $$P \leftarrow i\mathcal{O}(\mathsf{ComputePolicy}[\mathsf{hk}_C, \mathsf{hk}_{\mathbf{w}}, h_C, h_{\mathbf{w}}, K_\lambda, s_\beta]).$$
     (g) Sets $\mathsf{sh}_0 = (P, \alpha, \mathsf{hk}_C, \mathsf{hk}_{\mathbf{w}})$, and $\mathsf{sh}_i = \Pi_{\mathsf{PPRF}}.\mathsf{Eval}(K_\lambda, i)$ for each $i \in [n]$.
     (h) Gives $\mathsf{sh}_0, \{\mathsf{sh}\}_{i \in S_x}$ to $\mathcal{A}$.
  3. The adversary $\mathcal{A}$ outputs a guess $\beta'$.
  4. The output of the experiment is 1 if $\beta' = \beta$ and 0 otherwise.

The next step is replacing the string $\mathbf{w}$ with an embedding of the true gate values of the evaluation of the circuit $C(x)$, where $x$ is the unauthorized input submitted by the adversary. We do this by sampling $\alpha$ using $\Pi_{\mathsf{CEE}}.\mathsf{EmbedGen}$ and embedding $x$, instead of $\Pi_{\mathsf{CEE}}.\mathsf{Gen}$. Formally, we define the following experiment:

- $\mathsf{Exp}^{(\beta)}_{\mathsf{embed}}$: same as $\mathsf{Exp}^{(\beta)}_{\mathsf{real}}$, but the challenger samples $\mathbf{w}$ as follows:
  (c) The challenger samples $(\alpha, \mathsf{td}_{\mathsf{CEE}}) \leftarrow \Pi_{\mathsf{CEE}}.\mathsf{EmbedGen}(1^\lambda, 1^n, C, x)$, for the unauthorized input $x \in \{0,1\}^n$ submitted by the adversary in the first Step 1.

The output of this experiment is negligibly close to the previous one by the computational mode indistinguishability of the circuit evaluation embedding as per Definition 3.1.

We next define hybrid experiments for $i^* \in [n+1, \ell+1]$ as follows:

- $\mathsf{Exp}^{(\beta)}_{i^*}$: Same as $\mathsf{Exp}^{(\beta)}_{\mathsf{embed}}$ with the following changes:
  (f) Obfuscates the program from Fig. 2
  $$P \leftarrow i\mathcal{O}(\mathsf{ComputePolicy}'[i^*, \mathsf{hk}_C, \mathsf{hk}_{\mathbf{w}}, h_C, h_{\mathbf{w}}, K_\lambda, \mathsf{td}_{\mathsf{CEE}}, s_\beta]).$$

**Constants:** Hash keys $\mathsf{hk}_{\mathbf{w}}, \mathsf{hk}_C$, hashes $h_{\mathbf{w}}, h_C$, puncturable PRF key $K_\lambda$ and CEE trapdoor $\mathsf{td}_{\mathsf{CEE}}$, the secret $s$, and index $i^*$.
**Inputs:** Gate index $i$, gate description $C_i = (g_i, i_0, i_1)$, local opening $\pi_i^{(C)}$, a bit $w_i$, local opening $\pi_i^{(\mathbf{w})}$ and for each $b \in \{0,1\}$, a signature $\sigma_{i_b}$.

1. Verify inputs are well formed. Abort with $\perp$ if any checks do not pass.
   (a) Check $i \in [n+1, \ell]$.
   (b) Check $\mathsf{Verify}(\mathsf{hk}_C, h_C, i, C_i, \pi_i^{(C)}) = 1$.
   (c) Check $\mathsf{Verify}(\mathsf{hk}_{\mathbf{w}}, h_{\mathbf{w}}, i, w_i, \pi^{(\mathbf{w})}) = 1$.
2. For $b \in \{0,1\}$, set $v_{i_b} = 1$ if and only if $\mathsf{PRG}(\Pi_{\mathsf{PPRF}}.\mathsf{Eval}(K_\lambda, i_b)) = \mathsf{PRG}(\sigma_{i_b})$.
3. Compute $v_i = g_i(v_{i_0}, v_{i_1})$.
4. If $i < i^*$ and $\Pi_{\mathsf{CEE}}.\mathsf{Extract}(\mathsf{td}_{\mathsf{CEE}}, i, w_i) = 0$ then check that $v_i = 0$. If the check fails, abort with $\perp$.
5. If $i < \ell$, set $\sigma_i = \Pi_{\mathsf{PPRF}}.\mathsf{Eval}(K_\lambda, i)$ if $v_i = 1$ and $\sigma_i = \perp$ otherwise. Output $\sigma_i$.
6. Otherwise, if $v_i = 1$, output the secret $s$. If $v_i = 0$, output $\perp$.

**Fig. 2.** Program $\mathsf{ComputePolicy}'[i^*, \mathsf{hk}_C, \mathsf{hk}_{\mathbf{w}}, h_C, h_{\mathbf{w}}, K_\lambda, \mathsf{td}_{\mathsf{CEE}}, s]$.

Due to space constraints, the proofs are deferred to the full version of this paper.

## 5 Constructing Circuit Evaluation Embeddings

In this section, we construct a circuit evaluation embedding Definition 3.1 for all monotone Boolean circuits with seed size $n + \mathsf{poly}(\lambda, \log |C|)$.

**Construction 5.1.** Our construction makes use of the following ingredients:

- An indistinguishability obfuscator for circuits $i\mathcal{O}$.
- A positional accumulator $\Pi_{\mathsf{PA}} = (\mathsf{Setup}, \mathsf{SetupEnforce}, \mathsf{Hash}, \mathsf{Open}, \mathsf{Verify})$.
- A puncturable PRF $\Pi_{\mathsf{PPRF}} = (\mathsf{KeyGen}, \mathsf{Eval}, \mathsf{Puncture})$.
- An injective one way function $F$ and associated hard core predicate $\mathsf{hcb}(\cdot)$. We assume any randomness for $\mathsf{hcb}$ is implicitly hard-coded where $\mathsf{hcb}$ is used.

Apart from injective one way functions, these primitives all follow from a combination of indistinguishability obfuscation and one way functions. Our use of injective one way functions can be realized via subexponential one way functions and $i\mathcal{O}$ [BPW15] or non-uniformly secure one way functions [WW24].

We compress our representation of the string $\mathbf{w}$ by generating it via an $i\mathcal{O}$ program. While initially, our $i\mathcal{O}$ program simply produces the output of a PRF, we incrementally switch our program to homomorphically compute the evaluation of the policy circuit on the challenge input. We use a combination of positional accumulators and another puncturable PRF to ensure that the obfuscated program is only able to follow the 'honest' evaluation path, despite being much smaller than the policy circuit.

**Constants:** Hash keys $\mathsf{hk}_{\mathbf{w}}, \mathsf{hk}_C$, hash $h_C$, puncturable PRF keys $K_\lambda, K_{\mathsf{bit}}$, hash $h_{\mathsf{sd}}$
**Inputs:** Hash $h_{\mathbf{w}_{[i-1]}}$, string $\sigma_{i-1}$, wire index $i$, gate description $C_i = (g_i, i_0, i_1)$, local opening $\pi_i^{(C)}$, wire value $w_{i_b}$ and $\pi_{i_b}^{(\mathbf{w})}$ for $b \in \{0,1\}$.

1. Verify inputs are well formed. Abort with $\bot$ if any checks do not pass.
   (a) Check $i \in [n+1, \ell]$.
   (b) Check $\Pi_{\mathsf{PA}}.\mathsf{Verify}(\mathsf{hk}_C, h_C, i, C_i, \pi_i^{(C)}) = 1$.
   (c) For $b \in \{0,1\}$, check $\Pi_{\mathsf{PA}}.\mathsf{Verify}(\mathsf{hk}_{\mathbf{w}}, h_{\mathbf{w}_{[i-1]}}, i_b, \pi_{i_b}^{(\mathbf{w})}) = w_{i_b}$.
   (d) Check $\sigma_{i-1}$ is well formed:
      - Compute $(y_{i-1}, r'_{i-1}) \leftarrow \Pi_{\mathsf{PPRF}}.\mathsf{Eval}(K_\lambda, i-1)$ (parse as 2 strings $\in \{0,1\}^\lambda$).
      - Compute $K'_{i-1} \leftarrow \Pi_{\mathsf{PPRF}}.\mathsf{KeyGen}(1^\lambda, 1^{|h|}, 1^\lambda; r'_{i-1})$
      - Check that $y_{i-1} = \Pi_{\mathsf{PPRF}}.\mathsf{Eval}(K'_{i-1}, h_{\mathbf{w}_{[i-1]}}) \oplus \sigma_{i-1}$.
2. Set $w_i = \Pi_{\mathsf{PPRF}}.\mathsf{Eval}(K_{\mathsf{bit}}, i)$.
3. Compute $h_{\mathbf{w}_{[i]}} = \Pi_{\mathsf{PA}}.\mathsf{Append}(\mathsf{hk}_{\mathbf{w}}, h_{\mathbf{w}_{[i-1]}}, w_i)$
   - If $i - 1 = n$, check $h_{\mathbf{w}_{[i-1]}} = h_{\mathsf{sd}}$.
4. Compute $\sigma_i$ as:
   - Compute $(y_i, r'_i) \leftarrow \Pi_{\mathsf{PPRF}}.\mathsf{Eval}(K_\lambda, i-1)$.
   - Compute $K'_i \leftarrow \Pi_{\mathsf{PPRF}}.\mathsf{KeyGen}(1^\lambda, 1^{|h|}, 1^\lambda; r'_i)$
   - Set $\sigma_i = y_{i-1} \oplus \Pi_{\mathsf{PPRF}}.\mathsf{Eval}(K'_{i-1}, h_{\mathbf{w}_{[i-1]}})$.
5. Output $(w_i, \sigma_i)$

**Fig. 3.** Program $\mathsf{RefGen}[\mathsf{hk}_C, \mathsf{hk}_{\mathbf{w}}, h_C, K_\lambda, K_{\mathsf{bit}}, h_{\mathsf{sd}}]$.

- $\mathsf{Gen}(1^\lambda, 1^n, C) \to \alpha$: On input security parameter $\lambda$, input length $n$, and circuit $C$, the Gen algorithm does as follows:
  1. Sample the following hash and PRF keys:
     (a) $\mathsf{hk}_{\mathbf{w}} \leftarrow \Pi_{\mathsf{PA}}.\mathsf{Setup}(1^\lambda, 1, 1^2)$ is a positional accumulator key on one bit blocks which can bind on 2 positions.
     (b) $\mathsf{hk}_C \leftarrow \Pi_{\mathsf{PA}}.\mathsf{Setup}(1^\lambda, 1^{1+2\log\ell})$ is a positional accumulator key on blocks of the form $C_i = g_i \times [\ell] \times [\ell]$.
        - Set $h_C \leftarrow \Pi_{\mathsf{PA}}.\mathsf{Hash}(\mathsf{hk}_C, C)$.
     (c) $K_{\mathsf{bit}} \leftarrow \Pi_{\mathsf{PPRF}}.\mathsf{KeyGen}(1^\lambda, 1^{\log\ell}, 1)$ is a puncturable PRF key with domain $[\ell]$ and one bit outputs.
     (d) $K_\lambda \leftarrow \Pi_{\mathsf{PPRF}}.\mathsf{KeyGen}(1^\lambda, 1^{\log\ell}, 1^{2\lambda})$ is a puncturable PRF key with domain $[\ell]$ and outputs of the form $\{0,1\}^\lambda \times \{0,1\}^\lambda$.
  2. For $i \in [n]$, set $w_i = \Pi_{\mathsf{PPRF}}.\mathsf{Eval}(K_{\mathsf{bit}}, i)$. Let $\mathsf{sd} = w_1 w_2 \ldots w_n$.
     (a) Set $h_{\mathsf{sd}} \leftarrow \Pi_{\mathsf{PA}}.\mathsf{Hash}(\mathsf{hk}_{\mathbf{w}}, \mathsf{sd})$.
     (b) Compute $(y_n, r'_n) \leftarrow \Pi_{\mathsf{PPRF}}.\mathsf{Eval}(K_\lambda, n)$.
     (c) Compute $K'_n \leftarrow \Pi_{\mathsf{PPRF}}.\mathsf{KeyGen}(1^\lambda, 1^{|h|}, 1^\lambda; r'_n)$.
     (d) Set $\sigma_n = y_n \oplus \Pi_{\mathsf{PPRF}}.\mathsf{Eval}(K'_n, h_{\mathsf{sd}})$.
  3. Output $(\mathsf{hk}_{\mathbf{w}}, \mathsf{hk}_C, \mathsf{sd}, \sigma_n, i\mathcal{O}(1^\lambda, \mathsf{RefGen}[\mathsf{hk}_C, \mathsf{hk}_{\mathbf{w}}, h_C, K_\lambda, K_{\mathsf{bit}}, h_{\mathsf{sd}}]))$.

- $\mathsf{EmbedGen}(1^\lambda, 1^n, C, x) \rightarrow (\alpha^*, \mathsf{td})$: On input security parameter $\lambda$, input length $n$, circuit $C$ of size $\ell$ and input $x = x_1 \dots x_n$, the $\mathsf{EmbedGen}$ algorithm does as follows:
  1. Sample the following hash and PRF keys:
     (a) $\mathsf{hk}_{\mathbf{w}} \leftarrow \Pi_{\mathsf{PA}}.\mathsf{Setup}(1^\lambda, 1, 1^2)$ is a positional accumulator key on one bit blocks which can bind on 2 positions.
     (b) $\mathsf{hk}_C \leftarrow \Pi_{\mathsf{PA}}.\mathsf{Setup}(1^\lambda, 1^{1+2\log \ell})$ is a positional accumulator key on blocks of the form $C_i = g_i \times [\ell] \times [\ell]$.
        - Set $h_C \leftarrow \Pi_{\mathsf{PA}}.\mathsf{Hash}(\mathsf{hk}_C, C)$.
     (c) $K_{\mathsf{bit}} \leftarrow \Pi_{\mathsf{PPRF}}.\mathsf{KeyGen}(1^\lambda, 1^{\log \ell}, 1)$ is a puncturable PRF key with domain $[\ell]$ and one bit outputs.
     (d) $K_\lambda \leftarrow \Pi_{\mathsf{PPRF}}.\mathsf{KeyGen}(1^\lambda, 1^{\log \ell}, 1^{2\lambda})$ is a puncturable PRF key with domain $[\ell]$ and outputs of the form $\{0,1\}^\lambda \times \{0,1\}^\lambda$.
  2. For $i \in [n]$, set $w_i = \Pi_{\mathsf{PPRF}}.\mathsf{Eval}(K_{\mathsf{bit}}, i) \oplus x_i$. Let $\mathsf{sd} = w_1 w_2 \dots w_n$.
     (a) Set $h_{\mathsf{sd}} \leftarrow \Pi_{\mathsf{PA}}.\mathsf{Hash}(\mathsf{hk}_{\mathbf{w}}, \mathsf{sd})$.
     (b) Compute $(y_n, r'_n) \leftarrow \Pi_{\mathsf{PPRF}}.\mathsf{Eval}(K_\lambda, n)$.
     (c) Compute $K'_n \leftarrow \Pi_{\mathsf{PPRF}}.\mathsf{KeyGen}(1^\lambda, 1^{|h|}, 1^\lambda; r'_n)$.
     (d) Set $\sigma_n = y_n \oplus \Pi_{\mathsf{PPRF}}.\mathsf{Eval}(K'_n, h_{\mathsf{sd}})$.
  3. Output

$$\alpha^* = (\mathsf{hk}_{\mathbf{w}}, \mathsf{hk}_C, \mathsf{sd}, \sigma_n, i\mathcal{O}(1^\lambda, \mathsf{RefGen}_{\mathsf{embed}}[\mathsf{hk}_C, \mathsf{hk}_{\mathbf{w}}, h_C, K_\lambda, K_{\mathsf{bit}}, h_{\mathsf{sd}}]))$$

  and $\mathsf{td} = K_{\mathsf{bit}}$.
- $\mathsf{Expand}(C, \alpha) \rightarrow \mathbf{w}$: On input circuit $C$, and seed $\alpha$, the $\mathsf{Expand}$ algorithm does as follows
  1. Parse seed $\alpha = (\mathsf{hk}_{\mathbf{w}}, \mathsf{hk}_C, \mathsf{sd}, \sigma_n, \tilde{P})$.
  2. Parse circuit $C$ as a sequence of gate descriptions $C_i$ for $i \in [n+1, \ell]$.
  3. Let $\mathbf{w}_{[i]}$ denote the first $i$ elements of $\mathbf{w}$, where for we set the first $n$ elements to that of $\mathsf{sd}$ as $w_1, \dots w_n = w_1, \dots w_n$.
  4. Compute hash $h_{\mathbf{w}_{[n]}} = \Pi_{\mathsf{PA}}.\mathsf{Hash}(\mathsf{hk}_{\mathbf{w}}, \mathsf{sd})$.
  5. For $i = [n+1, \ell]$, iteratively compute $w_i$ as:
     (a) Parse $C_i = (g_i, i_0, i_1)$.
     (b) Compute hash $h_{\mathbf{w}_{[i-1]}} = \Pi_{\mathsf{PA}}.\mathsf{Hash}(\mathsf{hk}_{\mathbf{w}}, \mathbf{w}_{[i-1]})$
     (c) Compute local opening $\pi_i^{(C)} \leftarrow \Pi_{\mathsf{PA}}.\mathsf{Open}(\mathsf{hk}_C, C, i)$.
     (d) For $b \in \{0,1\}$, compute local openings

$$\pi_{i_b}^{(\mathsf{sd})} \leftarrow \Pi_{\mathsf{PA}}.\mathsf{Open}(\mathsf{hk}_C, \mathbf{w}_{[i-1]}, i_b).$$

     (e) Evaluate

$$(w_i, \sigma_i) \leftarrow \tilde{P}(h_{\mathbf{w}_{[i-1]}}, \sigma_{i-1}, i, C_i, \pi_i^{(C)}, \{(i_b, w_{i_b}, \pi_{i_b}^{(\mathsf{sd})})\}_{b \in \{0,1\}}).$$

  6. Output string $\mathbf{w}$.
- $\mathsf{Extract}(\mathsf{td}, i, b) \rightarrow \{0,1\}$: On input trapdoor $\mathsf{td}$, index $i$ and bit $b$, the $\mathsf{Extract}$ algorithm does as follows:
  1. Parse $\mathsf{td} = K_{\mathsf{bit}}$.
  2. Output $\Pi_{\mathsf{PPRF}}.\mathsf{Eval}(K_{\mathsf{bit}}, i) \oplus b$.

**Constants:** Hash keys $\mathsf{hk}_{\mathbf{w}}, \mathsf{hk}_C$, hash $h_C$, puncturable PRF keys $K_\lambda, K_{\mathsf{bit}}$, hash $h_{\mathsf{sd}}$.
**Inputs:** Hash $h_{\mathbf{w}_{[i-1]}}$, string $\sigma_{i-1}$, wire index $i$, gate description $C_i = (g_i, i_0, i_1)$, local opening $\pi_i^{(C)}$, wire value $w_{i_b}$ and $\pi_{i_b}^{(\mathbf{w})}$ for $b \in \{0,1\}$.

1. Verify inputs are well formed. Abort with $\perp$ if any checks do not pass.
   (a) Check $i \in [n+1, \ell]$.
   (b) Check $\Pi_{\mathsf{PA}}.\mathsf{Verify}(\mathsf{hk}_C, h_C, i, C_i, \pi_i^{(C)}) = 1$.
   (c) For $b \in \{0,1\}$, check $\Pi_{\mathsf{PA}}.\mathsf{Verify}(\mathsf{hk}_{\mathbf{w}}, h_{\mathbf{w}_{[i-1]}}, i_b, \pi_{i_b}^{(\mathbf{w})}) = w_{i_b}$.
   (d) Check $\sigma_{i-1}$ is well formed:
      - Compute $(y_{i-1}, r'_{i-1}) \leftarrow \Pi_{\mathsf{PPRF}}.\mathsf{Eval}(K_\lambda, i-1)$.
      - Compute $K'_{i-1} \leftarrow \Pi_{\mathsf{PPRF}}.\mathsf{KeyGen}(1^\lambda, 1^{|h|}, 1^\lambda; r'_{i-1})$
      - Check that $y_{i-1} = \Pi_{\mathsf{PPRF}}.\mathsf{Eval}(K'_{i-1}, h_{\mathbf{w}_{[i-1]}}) \oplus \sigma_{i-1}$.
2. Set $v_b = w_{i_b} \oplus \Pi_{\mathsf{PPRF}}.\mathsf{Eval}(K_{\mathsf{bit}}, i_b)$, and $w_i = \Pi_{\mathsf{PPRF}}.\mathsf{Eval}(K_{\mathsf{bit}}, i) \oplus g(v_0, v_1)$.
3. Compute $h_{\mathbf{w}_{[i]}} = \Pi_{\mathsf{PA}}.\mathsf{Append}(\mathsf{hk}_{\mathbf{w}}, h_{\mathbf{w}_{[i-1]}}, w_i)$
   - If $i - 1 = n$, check $h_{\mathbf{w}_{[i-1]}} = h_{\mathsf{sd}}$.
4. Compute $\sigma_i$ as:
   - Compute $(y_i, r'_i) \leftarrow \Pi_{\mathsf{PPRF}}.\mathsf{Eval}(K_\lambda, i-1)$.
   - Compute $K'_i \leftarrow \Pi_{\mathsf{PPRF}}.\mathsf{KeyGen}(1^\lambda, 1^{|h|}, 1^\lambda; r'_i)$
   - Set $\sigma_i = y_{i-1} \oplus \Pi_{\mathsf{PPRF}}.\mathsf{Eval}(K'_{i-1}, h_{\mathbf{w}_{[i-1]}})$.
5. Output $(w_i, \sigma_i)$

**Fig. 4.** Program $\mathsf{RefGen}_{\mathsf{embed}}[\mathsf{hk}_C, \mathsf{hk}_{\mathbf{w}}, h_C, K_\lambda, K_{\mathsf{bit}}, h_{\mathsf{sd}}]$.

### 5.1 Correctness and Succinctness

**Theorem 5.2 (Statistical Extraction).** *Suppose $i\mathcal{O}$ is a functionality preserving indistinguishability obfuscator $\Pi_{\mathsf{PA}}$ is a correct positional accumulator, then Construction 5.1 satisfies statistical extraction.*

*Proof.* Consider any circuit $C : \{0,1\}^n \to \{0,1\}$ and input $x \in \{0,1\}^n$. Let $\alpha^* = (\mathsf{hk}_{\mathsf{sd}}, \mathsf{hk}_C, \mathsf{sd}, \sigma_n, \tilde{P}), \mathsf{td} = K_{\mathsf{bit}}$ be some output of $\mathsf{EmbedGen}(1^\lambda, 1^n, C, x)$. Define the string $\mathbf{w}$ as in program $\mathsf{RefGen}_{\mathsf{embed}}$ (Fig. 4), where

$$w_i = \begin{cases} F_{K_{\mathsf{bit}}}(i) \oplus x_i & \text{for } i \in [n] \\ F_{K_{\mathsf{bit}}}(i) \oplus g_i(w_{i_0} \oplus F_{K_{\mathsf{bit}}}(i_0), w_{i_1} \oplus F_{K_{\mathsf{bit}}}(i_1)) & \text{for } i \in [n+1, \ell] \end{cases}$$

where $F_{K_{\mathsf{bit}}}(j) := \Pi_{\mathsf{PPRF}}.\mathsf{Eval}(K_{\mathsf{bit}}, j)$ and $C_i = (g_i, i_0, i_1)$ for $i \in [n+1, \ell]$.

We will first observe that this is in fact the string output by $\mathsf{Expand}(C, \alpha^*)$. First, we observe that for $i \in [n]$, this is true by definition, as $w_i = w_i$, which is set to $\Pi_{\mathsf{PPRF}}.\mathsf{Eval}(K_{\mathsf{bit}}, i) \oplus x_i$ by construction. Next, we can see for $i \in [n+1, \ell]$, this is indeed what is output in the final step of $\mathsf{RefGen}_{\mathsf{embed}}$, so this is true so long as $\tilde{P}$ does not abort in prior steps.

- Check 1a passes by construction, as only $i \in [n+1, \ell]$ is passed into program $\tilde{P}$.

- Checks 1b and 1c follow from correctness of $\Pi_{\mathsf{PA}}$.
- We can inductively argue check 1d passes, as $\sigma_{i-1}$ is simply output by the previous invocation to $\tilde{P}$, and is computed in the same way as it is checked.
- Check 3 passes as both EmbedGen and Expand compute hash $h_{\mathsf{sd}} = h_{\mathbf{w}_{[n]}} = \Pi_{\mathsf{PA}}.\mathsf{Hash}(\mathsf{hk}_{\mathsf{sd}}, \mathsf{sd})$.

Taking these together with the functionality preservation of $i\mathcal{O}$, we get that $\mathbf{w}$ is indeed output as above. Statistical extractability now follows from a simple inductive argument. For gates $i \in [n]$, since $w_i = \Pi_{\mathsf{PPRF}}.\mathsf{Eval}(K_{\mathsf{bit}}, i) \oplus x_i$, we can see since Extract simply xor's $\Pi_{\mathsf{PPRF}}.\mathsf{Eval}(K_{\mathsf{bit}}, i)$, it returns $x_i$. For $i \in [n+1, \ell]$, using our inductive hypothesis on $w_{i_0}, w_{i_1}$, we can see that $g_i(w_{i_0} \oplus \Pi_{\mathsf{PPRF}}.\mathsf{Eval}(K_{\mathsf{bit}}, i_0), w_{i_1} \oplus \Pi_{\mathsf{PPRF}}.\mathsf{Eval}(K_{\mathsf{bit}}, i_1))$ is exactly the wire value of $C(x)[i]$. This is also equal to $w_i \oplus \Pi_{\mathsf{PPRF}}.\mathsf{Eval}(K_{\mathsf{bit}}, i)$ return by Extract.

**Theorem 5.3 (Succinctness).** *If $\Pi_{\mathsf{PA}}$ is succinct then Construction 5.1 is a $n + \mathsf{poly}(\lambda, \log |C|)$-succinct circuit evaluation embedding.*

*Proof.* Recall seed $\alpha$ consists of components $\mathsf{hk}_{\mathsf{sd}}, \mathsf{hk}_C, \mathsf{sd}, \sigma_n, \tilde{P}$, where program $\tilde{P}$ is an obfuscation of program RefGen (Fig. 3).

- Components $\mathsf{hk}_{\mathsf{sd}}, \mathsf{hk}_C, \sigma_n$ are all of size $\mathsf{poly}(\lambda, \log |C|)$ simply by efficiency of their setup algorithms and by definition respectively.
- String sd is an $n$ bit string by construction.
- Finally, we can observe that of the constants and inputs of RefGen, all hash keys, hashes, and local openings are $\mathsf{poly}(\lambda, \log |C|)$ by succinctness of $\Pi_{\mathsf{PA}}$, punctured PRF keys $K_\lambda, K_{\mathsf{bit}}$ are $\mathsf{poly}(\lambda, \log |C|)$ by efficiency of $\Pi_{\mathsf{PPRF}}.\mathsf{KeyGen}$, and inputs $\sigma_{i-1}, C_i, i, (i_b, w_{i_b})$ are $\mathsf{poly}(\lambda, \log |C|)$ by construction. Thus, program RefGen is of size $\mathsf{poly}(\lambda, \log |C|)$, as is its obfuscation. We observe in the security analysis (deferred to the full version), that the size of programs in the security proof also never exceed $\mathsf{poly}(\lambda, \log |C|)$, bounding the amount of padding we need to give our obfuscation to argue security.

Taking these together, our total seed size can be bound by $n + \mathsf{poly}(\lambda, \log |C|)$.

## 5.2 Security

**Theorem 5.4 (Mode Indistinguishability).** *Suppose $\Pi_{\mathsf{PPRF}}$ is a secure and perfectly correct puncturable PRF, $i\mathcal{O}$ is a secure indistinguishability obfuscator $\Pi_{\mathsf{PA}}$ is a setup enforcing indistinguishable and read and write enforcing positional accumulator, then Construction 5.1 satisfies mode indistinguishability.*

*Proof.* To show mode indistinguishability, we define a sequence of experiments, beginning with $\mathsf{Exp}_{\mathsf{real}}$, which is the real mode indistinguishability game when $b = 0$ - i.e. using Gen, and ending in $\mathsf{Exp}_{\mathsf{embed}}$, the mode indistinguishability game when $b = 1$ or using EmbedGen. We will argue indistinguishability of this sequence of experiments.

At a high level, our proof proceeds by leveraging the puncturability of PRF $K_{\mathsf{bit}}$ to incrementally switch the bits of $\mathbf{w}$ from a simple PRF evaluation to an embedding of the evaluation of our circuit. Since the PRF evaluation in Gen on a bit $i$ is independent of the particular value of input wire bits $\{w_{i_b}\}$ while EmbedGen is not, the challenge now is to move to an experiment where input wire bits can only statistically verify to one value. This effectively makes our program 'input independent', allowing us to leverage the classic $i\mathcal{O}$ in conjunction with puncturable PRF to hard code the output bit $w_i$. To accomplish this statistical input binding, we need the following to be true:

- The hard coded hash $h_C$ is binding on index $i$, statistically binding to the tuple $(g_i, i_0, i_1)$.
- The input hash $h_{\mathbf{w}_{[i-1]}}$ is statistically binding on indices $i_0, i_1$. Moreover, these bits are open to wire values $w_{i_0}, w_{i_1}$ respectively.

For both requirements, the binding indices are easy to guarantee via simple mode indistinguishability of our hash. However, because hash $h_{\mathbf{w}_{[i-1]}}$ is taken as *input*, we also need to rule out the ability for an adversary to generate a dishonest input hash $h$ which opens $i_0, i_1$ to different bits. We achieve this by (implicitly) constructing a simplified version of splittable signatures [KLW15], allowing us to replace our verification process for $\sigma_{i-1}$ with one that only works on a fixed hash value $h_{i-1}$. Unfortunately, unlike mode indistinguishability in our hash function, the verification of $\sigma_{i-1}$ is naturally only indistinguishable when our program is *not* able to generate signatures for any other hash $h'_{i-1} \neq h_{i-1}$. This in turn means that to argue such indistinguishability, our signature needs to be 'split' on index $i-1$ as well, hard coding hash $h_{i-2}$. Argued naively, this blows up the obfuscated program in our experiments to be of size $O(\ell)$, meaning we would require $O(\ell)$ padding in our original obfuscations of RefGen, $\mathsf{RefGen}_{\mathsf{embed}}$ to attempt to argue security. Fortunately, we can employ a combinatorial 'pebbling argument' [GPSZ17] where we can bound the number of hard coded hash locations at $\mathsf{poly}(\log \ell)$, bounding the total obfuscation padding required similarly. For more details on how we define our inner hybrids, how to proceed with our pebbling argument, and formal proofs, we refer the reader to the full version of this paper.

**Acknowledgments.** Brent Waters is supported by NSF CNS-2318701 and a Simons Investigator award.

## References

[ABF+19] Applebaum, B., Beimel, A., Farràs, O., Nir, O., Peter, N.: Secret-sharing schemes for general and uniform access structures. In: Ishai, Y., Rijmen, V. (eds.) EUROCRYPT 2019. LNCS, vol. 11478, pp. 441–471. Springer, Cham (2019). https://doi.org/10.1007/978-3-030-17659-4_15

[ABI+23] Applebaum, B., Beimel, A., Ishai, Y., Kushilevitz, E., Liu, T., Vaikuntanathan, V.: Succinct computational secret sharing. In: STOC. ACM (2023)

[ABNP20] Applebaum, B., Beimel, A., Nir, O., Peter, N.: Better secret sharing via robust conditional disclosure of secrets. In: STOC. ACM (2020)

[ADM+25] Avitabile, G., Döttling, N., Magri, B., Sakkas, C., Wohnig, S.: Signature-based witness encryption with compact ciphertext. In: Chung, K.M., Sasaki, Y. (eds.) ASIACRYPT 2024. LNCS, vol. 15484, pp. 3–31. Springer, Singapore (2025). https://doi.org/10.1007/978-981-96-0875-1_1

[AN21] Applebaum, B., Nir, O.: Upslices, downslices, and secret-sharing with complexity of $1.5^n$. In: Malkin, T., Peikert, C. (eds.) CRYPTO 2021. LNCS, vol. 12827, pp. 627–655. Springer, Cham (2021). https://doi.org/10.1007/978-3-030-84252-9_21

[ASY22] Abram, D., Scholl, P., Yakoubov, S.: Distributed (correlation) samplers: how to remove a trusted dealer in one round. In: Dunkelman, O., Dziembowski, S. (eds.) EUROCRYPT 2022. LNCS, vol. 13275, pp. 790–820. Springer, Cham (2022). https://doi.org/10.1007/978-3-031-06944-4_27

[BBK+23] Brakerski, Z., Brodsky, M.F., Kalai, Y.T., Lombardi, A., Paneth, O.: SNARGs for monotone policy batch NP. In: Handschuh, H., Lysyanskaya, A. (eds.) Advances in Cryptology – CRYPTO 2023. Lecture Notes in Computer Science, vol. 14082, pp. 252–283. Springer, Cham (2023). https://doi.org/10.1007/978-3-031-38545-2_9

[BCG+19] Boyle, E., Couteau, G., Gilboa, N., Ishai, Y., Kohl, L., Scholl, P.: Efficient pseudorandom correlation generators: silent OT extension and more. In: Boldyreva, A., Micciancio, D. (eds.) CRYPTO 2019. LNCS, vol. 11694, pp. 489–518. Springer, Cham (2019). https://doi.org/10.1007/978-3-030-26954-8_16

[Bei96] Beimel, A.: Secure schemes for secret sharing and key distribution. Ph.D. thesis, Technion (1996)

[BFK+19] Badrinarayanan, S., Fernando, R., Koppula, V., Sahai, A., Waters, B.: Output compression, MPC, and iO for turing machines. In: Galbraith, S.D., Moriai, S. (eds.) ASIACRYPT 2019. LNCS, vol. 11921, pp. 342–370. Springer, Cham (2019). https://doi.org/10.1007/978-3-030-34578-5_13

[BGI+12] Barak, B., et al.: On the (im)possibility of obfuscating programs. J. ACM (2012)

[BGI14] Boyle, E., Goldwasser, S., Ivan, I.: Functional signatures and pseudorandom functions. In: Krawczyk, H. (ed.) PKC 2014. LNCS, vol. 8383, pp. 501–519. Springer, Heidelberg (2014). https://doi.org/10.1007/978-3-642-54631-0_29

[BGL+15] Bitansky, N., Garg, S., Lin, H., Pass, R., Telang, S.: Succinct randomized encodings and their applications. In: STOC (2015)

[BL88] Benaloh, J., Leichter, J.: Generalized secret sharing and monotone functions. In: Goldwasser, S. (ed.) CRYPTO 1988. LNCS, vol. 403, pp. 27–35. Springer, New York (1990). https://doi.org/10.1007/0-387-34799-2_3

[Bla79] Blakley, G.R.: Safeguarding cryptographic keys. In: International Workshop on Managing Requirements Knowledge, MARK, p. 1979. IEEE (1979)

[BM82] Blum, M., Micali, S.: How to generate cryptographically strong sequences of pseudo random bits. In: FOCS. IEEE Computer Society (1982)

[BOGW88] Ben-Or, M., Goldwasser, S., Wigderson, A.: Completeness theorems for non-cryptographic fault-tolerant distributed computation. In: Proceedings of the Twentieth Annual ACM Symposium on Theory of Computing (1988)

[BPW15] Bitansky, N., Paneth, O., Wichs, D.: Perfect structure on the edge of chaos. In: Kushilevitz, E., Malkin, T. (eds.) TCC 2016. LNCS, vol. 9562, pp.

474–502. Springer, Heidelberg (2016). https://doi.org/10.1007/978-3-662-49096-9_20

[BW13] Boneh, D., Waters, B.: Constrained pseudorandom functions and their applications. In: Sako, K., Sarkar, P. (eds.) ASIACRYPT 2013. LNCS, vol. 8270, pp. 280–300. Springer, Heidelberg (2013). https://doi.org/10.1007/978-3-642-42045-0_15

[CCD88] Chaum, D., Crépeau, C., Damgard, I.: Multiparty unconditionally secure protocols. In: Proceedings of the Twentieth Annual ACM Symposium on Theory of Computing (1988)

[CHJV15] Canetti, R., Holmgren, J., Jain, A., Vaikuntanathan, V.: Succinct garbling and indistinguishability obfuscation for RAM programs. In: STOC (2015)

[CJJ21a] Choudhuri, A.R., Jain, A., Jin, Z.: Non-interactive batch arguments for NP from standard assumptions. In: Malkin, T., Peikert, C. (eds.) CRYPTO 2021. LNCS, vol. 12828, pp. 394–423. Springer, Cham (2021). https://doi.org/10.1007/978-3-030-84259-8_14

[CJJ21b] Choudhuri, A.R., Jain, A., Jin, Z.: SNARGs for P from LWE. In: FOCS (2021)

[Csi96] Csirmaz, L.: The dealer's random bits in perfect secret sharing schemes. Stud. Sci. Math. Hungarica (1996)

[Csi97] Csirmaz, L.: The size of a share must be large. J. cryptol. (1997)

[GGH+13] Garg, S., Gentry, C., Halevi, S., Raykova, M., Sahai, A., Waters, B.: Candidate indistinguishability obfuscation and functional encryption for all circuits. In: FOCS (2013)

[GGI+15] Gentry, C., Groth, J., Ishai, Y., Peikert, C., Sahai, A., Smith, a.: Using fully homomorphic hybrid encryption to minimize non-interative zero-knowledge proofs. *J. Cryptol.* (2015)

[GL89] Goldreich, O., Levin, L.A.: A hard-core predicate for all one-way functions. In: STOC. ACM (1989)

[GM82] Goldwasser, S., Micali, S.: Probabilistic encryption & how to play mental poker keeping secret all partial information. In: Proceedings of the Fourteenth Annual ACM Symposium on Theory of Computing (1982)

[GPSZ17] Garg, S., Pandey, O., Srinivasan, A., Zhandry, M.: Breaking the sub-exponential barrier in obfustopia. In: Coron, J.-S., Nielsen, J.B. (eds.) EUROCRYPT 2017. LNCS, vol. 10212, pp. 156–181. Springer, Cham (2017). https://doi.org/10.1007/978-3-319-56617-7_6

[GS18] Garg, S., Srinivasan, A.: A simple construction of iO for turing machines. In: Beimel, A., Dziembowski, S. (eds.) TCC 2018. LNCS, vol. 11240, pp. 425–454. Springer, Cham (2018). https://doi.org/10.1007/978-3-030-03810-6_16

[GSWW22] Garg, R., Sheridan, K., Waters, B., Wu, D.J.: Fully succinct batch arguments for np from indistinguishability obfuscation. In: Kiltz, E., Vaikuntanathan, V. (eds.) TCC 2022. LNCS, vol. 13747, pp. 526–555. Springer, Cham (2022). https://doi.org/10.1007/978-3-031-22318-1_19

[HIJ+16] Halevi, S., Ishai, Y., Jain, A., Kushilevitz, E., Rabin, T.: Secure multiparty computation with general interaction patterns. In: Proceedings of the 2016 ACM Conference on Innovations in Theoretical Computer Science (2016)

[HW15] Hubácek, P., Wichs, D.: On the communication complexity of secure function evaluation with long output. In: ITCS (2015)

[ISN89] Ito, M., Saito, A., Nishizeki, T.: Secret sharing scheme realizing general access structure. Electron. Commun. Jpn. Part III-Fundam. Electron. Sci. (1989)

[JJ22] Jain, A., Jin, Z.: Indistinguishability obfuscation via mathematical proofs of equivalence. In: FOCS (2022)

[KLW15] Koppula, V., Lewko, A.B., Waters, B.: Indistinguishability obfuscation for turing machines with unbounded memory. In: STOC. ACM (2015)

[KPTZ13] Kiayias, a., Papadopoulos, S., Triandopoulos, N., Zacharias, T.: Delegatable pseudorandom functions and applications. In: Proceedings of the 2013 ACM SIGSAC Conference on Computer & Communications Security (2013)

[LV18] Liu, T., Vaikuntanathan, V.: Breaking the circuit-size barrier in secret sharing. In: Proceedings of the 50th Annual ACM SIGACT Symposium on Theory of Computing (2018)

[LVW18] Liu, T., Vaikuntanathan, V., Wee, H.: Towards breaking the exponential barrier for general secret sharing. In: Nielsen, J.B., Rijmen, V. (eds.) EUROCRYPT 2018. LNCS, vol. 10820, pp. 567–596. Springer, Cham (2018). https://doi.org/10.1007/978-3-319-78381-9_21

[NWW24] Nassar, S., Waters, B., Wu, D.J.: Monotone policy BARGs from BARGs and additively homomorphic encryption. In: Boyle, E., Mahmoody, M. (eds.) TCC 2024. LNCS, vol. 15365, pp. 399–430. Springer, Cham (2025). https://doi.org/10.1007/978-3-031-78017-2_14

[OPWW15] Okamoto, T., Pietrzak, K., Waters, B., Wichs, D.: New realizations of somewhere statistically binding hashing and positional accumulators. In: Iwata, T., Cheon, J.H. (eds.) ASIACRYPT 2015. LNCS, vol. 9452, pp. 121–145. Springer, Heidelberg (2015). https://doi.org/10.1007/978-3-662-48797-6_6

[RBO89] Rabin, T., Ben-Or, M.: Verifiable secret sharing and multiparty protocols with honest majority. In: Proceedings of the Twenty-First Annual ACM Symposium on Theory of Computing (1989)

[Sha79] Shamir, A.: How to share a secret. ACM Commun. (1979)

[VNS+03] Vinod, V., Narayanan, A., Srinathan, K., Rangan, C.P., Kim, K.: On the power of computational secret sharing. In: Johansson, T., Maitra, S. (eds.) INDOCRYPT 2003. LNCS, vol. 2904, pp. 162–176. Springer, Heidelberg (2003). https://doi.org/10.1007/978-3-540-24582-7_12

[WW24] Waters, B., Wu, D.J.: A pure indistinguishability obfuscation approach to adaptively-sound SNARGs for NP. IACR Cryptol. ePrint Arch. (2024)

[Yao82] Yao, A.C.: Theory and application of trapdoor functions. In: 23rd Annual Symposium on Foundations of Computer Science (SFCS 1982). IEEE (1982)

[Yao89] Yao, A.C.-C.: Unpublished manuscript (1989)

# Succinct Witness Encryption for Batch Languages and Applications

Lalita Devadas[1(✉)], Abhishek Jain[2,3], Brent Waters[3,4], and David J. Wu[4]

[1] MIT, Cambridge, MA, USA
lali@mit.edu
[2] Johns Hopkins University, Baltimore, MD, USA
[3] NTT Research, Sunnyvale, CA, USA
[4] UT Austin, Austin, TX, USA

**Abstract.** Witness encryption allows one to encrypt a message to an $\mathsf{NP}$ relation $\mathcal{R}$ and a statement $x$. The corresponding decryption key is any valid $\mathsf{NP}$ witness $w$. In a *succinct* witness encryption scheme, we require that the size of the ciphertext be sublinear in the size of the $\mathsf{NP}$ relation. Currently, all realizations of succinct witness encryption for $\mathsf{NP}$ rely on strong assumptions such as pseudorandom obfuscation, extractable witness encryption, or differing-inputs obfuscation. Notably, none of these notions are known from standard assumptions.

In this work, we consider a relaxation of succinct witness encryption for $\mathsf{NP}$ to the setting of *batch* $\mathsf{NP}$. In this setting, one encrypts to an $\mathsf{NP}$ relation $\mathcal{R}$ together with $K$ statements $x_1, \ldots, x_K$. In the basic version, one can decrypt if they have a witness $w_1, \ldots, w_K$ for all $K$ statements. The succinctness requirement is that the size of the ciphertext should be *sublinear* in the number of instances $K$, but is allowed to grow with the size of the $\mathsf{NP}$ relation (i.e., the size of a *single* instance). More generally, we can also impose a (monotone) policy $P\colon \{0,1\}^K \to \{0,1\}$ over the $K$ instances. In this case, decryption is possible only if there exists $w_1, \ldots, w_K$ such that $P(\mathcal{R}(x_1, w_1), \ldots, \mathcal{R}(x_K, w_K)) = 1$.

In this work, we initiate a systematic study of succinct witness encryption for batch languages. We start with two simple constructions that support CNF and DNF policies based on plain witness encryption in conjunction with a somewhere statistically sound batch argument for $\mathsf{NP}$ or a function-binding hash function. Then, using indistinguishability obfuscation, we show how to support policies that can be computed by read-once bounded-space Turing machines. The latter construction is in fact a unique witness map for monotone-policy batch $\mathsf{NP}$, and as such, also gives a SNARG for monotone-policy batch $\mathsf{NP}$ where the size of the common reference string is *sublinear* in the number of instances.

Finally, we demonstrate some immediate applications of succinct witness encryption for batch languages. We construct new succinct computational secret sharing schemes for CNFs, DNFs, and weighted threshold policies. We also show how to build distributed monotone-policy encryption, a notion that generalizes recent trustless primitives like distributed broadcast encryption and threshold encryption with silent setup.

© International Association for Cryptologic Research 2026
G. Hanaoka and B.-Y. Yang (Eds.): ASIACRYPT 2025, LNCS 16252, pp. 130–162, 2026.
https://doi.org/10.1007/978-981-95-5125-5_5

# 1 Introduction

In a witness encryption scheme (for NP) [32], a user can encrypt a message to an NP statement $x$. Anyone who knows an associated witness $w$ can decrypt the ciphertext and recover the message. If the statement is false, then the message is computationally hidden. Witness encryption has been used to build a broad set of cryptographic primitives such as public-key encryption and generalizations such as identity-based encryption, attribute-based encryption, broadcast encryption [29,32,52], oblivious transfer [7], laconic arguments [9,28,45], and null obfuscation [38,56].

**The Witness Size Barrier.** In witness encryption, the size of the ciphertext generally scales with the size of the NP witness. This is true for constructions based on indistinguishability obfuscation ($i\mathcal{O}$) [31], multilinear maps [32,36], and lattice-based assumptions [22,50,51]. At a high level, we can view a witness encryption ciphertext as a program that takes an NP witness as input, checks if the witness is valid, and if so, outputs the message. Since this program takes the NP witness as input, the ciphertext size in existing constructions of witness encryption scale with the witness size (and more broadly, the size of the circuit computing the NP relation).

A natural approach to overcome this witness-size dependency in the ciphertext size is to represent the NP relation as a Turing machine, where the description length of the machine is independent of the witness size. For instance, the ciphertext could be an obfuscated Turing machine that reads the witness and outputs the message if the witness is valid. While we can build witness encryption in this way using $i\mathcal{O}$ for Turing machines [8,17,35,44], for general computations, the size of the obfuscated Turing machine still scales with the length of the input to the machine. Thus, these approaches still run into the witness size barrier. Using differing-inputs obfuscation [4] or extractable witness encryption [37], we can overcome this input-size barrier for $i\mathcal{O}$ for Turing machines. However, neither of these notions are currently known from standard assumptions.

**Succinct Witness Encryption.** Very recently, Branco et al. [15] introduced the notion of *succinct* witness encryption where the size of the ciphertext is sublinear in the witness size. Moreover, they show how to overcome the witness size barrier and construct succinct witness encryption for general NP relations from a notion called *pseudorandom obfuscation*, which can be viewed as an ideal obfuscation for pseudorandom functions (i.e., the obfuscated program is computationally independent of the input program). While [15] shows the feasibility of succinct witness encryption for NP, it relies on the new notion of pseudorandom obfuscation which we do not know how to instantiate using standard assumptions. The only such instantiations from [2,15] is based on learning with errors (LWE) together with the *private-coin* evasive LWE assumption. The work of [15] also shows that pseudorandom obfuscation for arbitrary pseudorandom functions is impossible. As such, the security of their specific construction necessarily relies on a carefully-tailored formulation of private-coin evasive LWE. Moreover, a sequence of recent works [3,15,16,27,40,41,51] have raised significant questions on the plausibility of private-coin evasive LWE. Thus, a natural question to ask is whether we can build succinct witness encryption from standard cryptographic assumptions.

## 1.1 Our Results

In this work, we conduct a systematic study of succinct witness encryption for *subclasses* of NP. Specifically, we consider batch languages, where instead of encrypting to a single NP statement, one instead encrypts to a batch of $K$ statements $x_1, \ldots, x_K$. Decryption succeeds if one knows valid witnesses $w_i$ for some subset of the statements. The succinctness requirement is that the ciphertext scales *sublinearly* with the total number of statements $K$, but we do allow the ciphertext to scale with the size of a *single* witness. In some sense, this is the same type of relaxation considered in the study of batch arguments (BARGs) for NP [13], where the goal is to give a succinct proof of a batch of statements with a proof whose size scales sublinearly with the number of instances.

The basic version of our notion requires the decrypter to know a witness for *every* statement in order to decrypt. However, we can consider more general decryption policies such as a threshold policy where one needs to know $t$-out-of-$n$ witnesses in order to decrypt. Most generally, we consider monotone policies where the encryption algorithm takes the statements $x_1, \ldots, x_K$ together with a monotone policy $P\colon \{0,1\}^K \to \{0,1\}$, and decryption is successful only if there exist witnesses $w_1, \ldots, w_K$ such that $P(C(x_1, w_1), \ldots, C(x_K, w_K)) = 1$. Here $C$ is the circuit that implements the associated NP relation. This setting is the analog of monotone-policy batch arguments [12,47,48] in the setting of succinct witness encryption.

The recent work of [6] considers a conceptually-similar notion of succinct witness encryption for batch languages, but their work has two key restrictions. First they focus on witness encryption for a *specific* cryptographic relation (namely, knowledge of a signature) and second, they only consider threshold policies. Their work gives a construction from $i\mathcal{O}$ for Turing machines. In this work, our focus is on constructing succinct witness encryption for batch NP and we also explore broader policy classes. We give constructions for simple policy families using plain witness encryption and constructions for more expressive policies (e.g., monotone policies that can be computed by read-once bounded-space Turing machines) using $i\mathcal{O}$.

**Constructions of Succinct Witness Encryption.** In this work, we provide three constructions of succinct witness encryption for batch languages for different policy families. Our first two constructions support CNF and DNF policies and are based on (plain) witness encryption. Our third construction relies on $i\mathcal{O}$ and supports any monotone policy that can be computed by a read-once log-space Turing machine as well as policies like weighted thresholds (with $\mathsf{poly}(\lambda)$-bit weights). We summarize the key features of our constructions below:

- **Conjunctions of local predicates.** Our first construction of succinct witness encryption supports conjunctions of local monotone predicates. Specifically, consider a policy $P \colon \{0,1\}^K \to \{0,1\}$ of the form

$$P(\beta_1, \ldots, \beta_K) := P_1(\vec{\beta}_{S_1}) \wedge \cdots \wedge P_c(\vec{\beta}_{S_c}),$$

  where each $P_i$ is a monotone predicate that depends on a subset $S_i \subseteq [K]$ of the inputs, and we write $\vec{\beta}_{S_i}$ to denote the subset of $\beta_1, \ldots, \beta_K$ indexed by $S_i$. An encryption of a message $\mu$ with respect to a Boolean relation $C \colon \{0,1\}^n \times \{0,1\}^h \to \{0,1\}$, policy $P$, and instances $x_1, \ldots, x_K \in \{0,1\}^n$ has size $|\mu| + \mathsf{poly}(\lambda, |C|, s, \log c)$, where $s$ is the size of the largest predicate $P_i$. For instance, when each predicate $P_i$ depends on a constant number of input variables, then $s = O(1)$ and the size of the ciphertext is $\mathsf{poly}(\lambda, |C|, \log |P|)$, which scales with the size of a *single* instance and only polylogarithmically with the number of instances. This captures important special cases where the predicate $P$ is a conjunction or a 3-CNF formula. We construct our succinct witness encryption scheme for conjunctions of local predicates from plain witness encryption and a *somewhere-statistically-sound* batch argument for $\mathsf{NP}$ (e.g., [53]; see Sect. 1.2 for a description of the somewhere-statistically-soundness requirement).
- **Disjunction of local predicates.** We then consider the dual notion of succinct witness encryption for *disjunctions* of local monotone predicates.[1] Specifically, our construction supports policies of the form

$$P(\beta_1, \ldots, \beta_K) := P_1(\vec{\beta}_{S_1}) \vee \cdots \vee P_c(\vec{\beta}_{S_c}),$$

  where each $P_i$ is a monotone predicate that depends on a subset $S_i \subseteq [K]$ of the inputs. An encryption of a message $\mu$ with respect to a Boolean relation $C$, policy $P$, and instances $x_1, \ldots, x_K$ has size $|\mu| + \mathsf{poly}(\lambda, |C|, s, \log c)$, where $s$ is the size of the largest predicate $P_i$. Once again, the ciphertext size scales with the size of a single instance and the size of the largest predicate, and only polylogarithmically with the number of predicates. This constructions captures notions like DNF formulas as a special case. We construct our succinct witness encryption scheme for disjunctions of local predicates from plain witness encryption and a function-binding hash function [29]; the latter can be built from any leveled homomorphic encryption scheme.
- **Read-once bounded-space Turing machine policies from $i\mathcal{O}$.** Our final construction supports monotone policies that can be computed by a read-once

[1] Technically, this construction only supports "trapdoor $\mathsf{NP}$ relations" (see Definition 4.4) where we assume there is an efficient algorithm that can decide the instance with the help of a trapdoor. This is a subclass of $\mathsf{NP}$, but one that suffices for the cryptographic applications of succinct witness encryption we consider in this work (Sect. 6).

bounded-space Turing machine. Specifically, suppose $P\colon \{0,1\}^K \to \{0,1\}$ is a policy that can be computed by a read-once Turing machine with $S$-bits of space. Then an encryption of a message $\mu$ with respect to a Boolean relation $C$, policy $P$, and instances $x_1, \dots, x_K$ has size $|\mu| + \mathsf{poly}(\lambda, |C|, 2^S)$. Note that the size of the ciphertext scales *exponentially* with the space usage, so this scheme is tailored for policies that can be computed by read-once Turing machines with $O(\log \lambda)$-bits of space. For instance, this captures policies such as threshold policies. Technically, our scheme is more general and can support monotone policies computable by read-once Turing machines where the set of unreachable states has a compact description. For instance, this allows our scheme to also support *weighted* threshold policies with $\lambda$-bit weights (i.e., weights with magnitude $2^\lambda$). Our construction here relies on $i\mathcal{O}$ for circuits together with somewhere-statistically-binding (SSB) hash functions [42].

**Succinct Unique Witness Maps for Monotone-Policy Batch NP.** Our $i\mathcal{O}$-based construction for read-once bounded-space Turing machines is more general and in particular, gives a succinct *unique witness map* [18] for monotone-policy batch NP with respect to policies computable by read-once bounded-space Turing machines. A unique witness map for an NP relation deterministically maps all witness for an NP statement onto a single "canonical" witness. There is a public verification algorithm that decides whether a candidate witness is the canonical witness for a statement. The soundness requirement is that for a false statement, an efficient adversary cannot produce a witness that satisfies the verification relation. In this work, we show how to construct a *succinct* unique witness map for monotone-policy batch NP where the policy can be computed by a read-once bounded-space Turing machine. The succinctness requirement is that the size of the common reference string (CRS) for the unique witness map is sublinear in $K$ and the size of the canonical witness for $K$ instances has size $\mathsf{poly}(\lambda, \log K)$. Notably, the size of the canonical witness is *fully* succinct (independent of the size of the NP relation). A succinct unique witness map for monotone-policy batch NP with policy family $\mathcal{P}$ immediately yields the following:

- A succinct witness encryption scheme for batch NP with policy family $\mathcal{P}$ (see Remark 5.3). This follows via the same "or-proof with hard-core predicate" transformation in [18] (who described the implication from a unique witness map for NP to witness encryption for NP).
- A succinct non-interactive argument (SNARG) for monotone-policy batch NP with policy family $\mathcal{P}$ where the size of the CRS is sublinear in the number of instances (see Remark 5.2). Previously, SNARGs for batch NP with a sublinear-size CRS were only known for conjunction policies [26,30]. Our work gives the first construction that supports policies like weighted thresholds. Even *without* full succinctness (i.e., monotone-policy BARGs where the proof size can scale with the size of the NP relation and just needs to be sublinear in the number of instances), previous constructions [12,47,48] also required a CRS whose size scales linearly with the number of instances.

**Applications of Succinct Witness Encryption for Batch Languages.** We then highlight two immediate applications of succinct witness encryption for batch languages. The first is to succinct computational secret sharing [5] and the second is a notion we call distributed monotone-policy encryption, which is a generalization of notions like distributed broadcast encryption [10,57] and threshold encryption with silent setup [6,33]:

**Succinct Computational Secret Sharing.** In a succinct computational secret sharing scheme [5], a dealer can share a secret with $K$ parties with respect to a monotone access policy $P$. Thereafter, any subset of parties that satisfies the access policy can come together and reconstruct the secret while the shares of any unauthorized set of users should computationally hide the message. The succinctness requirement is that the size of each share should be sublinear in the number of parties and the description size of $P$. A succinct witness encryption scheme for batch $\mathsf{NP}$ with policy family $\mathcal{P}$ immediately implies a computational secret sharing scheme for the same family $\mathcal{P}$. Thus, our work gives a succinct computational secret sharing scheme for monotone CNF and DNF formulas from plain witness encryption (together with the LWE assumption) as well as for monotone policies computable by read-once log-space Turing machines from $i\mathcal{O}$ (and SSB hash functions). Our construction for DNFs additionally assumes the parties share a long, but reusable common random string, which can be compressed using a random oracle.

Previously, the works of [1,11,39] show how to use pseudorandom correlation generators based on $i\mathcal{O}$ to build succinct computational secret sharing for general monotone policies in a setting where parties have access to a long, reusable common random string (or alternatively, in the random oracle model). In the plain model, the work of [5] shows how to construct succinct computational secret sharing for CNFs using either RSA or $i\mathcal{O}$. For DNF policies, the work of [5] give a construction with a *public* share whose size is *linear* in the policy size. Our constructions improve upon these approaches as follows:

- For $k$-CNF policies (with constant $k$), we give a construction based on witness encryption in the plain model. This is the first construction that does not use $i\mathcal{O}$ or the RSA assumption.
- For $k$-DNF policies (for any constant $k$), we obtain a construction from witness encryption in the random oracle model. Previous constructions either relied on $i\mathcal{O}$ in the random oracle model [1,11,39] or on one-way functions but with a long (message-dependent) public share [5]. Strictly speaking, the construction of [5] does not satisfy the standard succinctness requirement for succinct computational secret sharing which requires all shares to be sublinear in the size of the policy.
- Using $i\mathcal{O}$, we obtain the first succinct computational secret sharing scheme for weighted threshold policies where the share size is $\mathsf{poly}(\lambda, \log W)$ in the plain model and $W$ is the magnitude of the weights. Previously, this was only known from $i\mathcal{O}$ in the random oracle model [1,11,39]. Technically, our

construction supports any policy family that can be computed by a read-once, log-space Turing machine.[2]

**Distributed Monotone-Policy Encryption.** Distributed monotone-policy encryption is a generalization of distributed broadcast encryption [10,57] and threshold encryption with silent setup [6,33]. Specifically, in a threshold encryption scheme with silent setup, individual users each choose a public/secret key-pair $(\mathsf{pk}_i, \mathsf{sk}_i)$. Each user publishes their public key $\mathsf{pk}_i$ in a public key directory. Later on, an encrypter can select any subset of public keys $\{\mathsf{pk}_i\}_{i \in S}$ and a threshold $t \le |S|$ and encrypt a message $\mu$ to this set. The guarantee is that any set of at least $t$ users in the set $S$ can decrypt and recover the message $\mu$, while any subset of less than $t$ users are unable to do so. Moreover, the size of the ciphertext should be succinct (scaling independently of the size of the number of public keys in $S$). Distributed broadcast encryption is the special case where the threshold $t = 1$ (i.e., any individual user in the set $S$ can decrypt).

Existing constructions of distributed monotone-policy encryption have thus far been limited to simple policies: threshold encryption [6,33] or distributed broadcast encryption [10,20,21,29,43,55]. Using succinct witness encryption for batch languages, we immediately obtain the first constructions that can support more general policies including CNFs and DNFs from witness encryption, and weighted thresholds and more from $i\mathcal{O}$.

### 1.2 Technical Overview

We begin with an overview of our constructions and show how to use succinct witness encryption for batch languages to realize other cryptographic primitives.

**Succinct Witness Encryption for Conjunctions.** As a warm-up, we show how to construct succinct witness encryption for conjunctions from plain witness encryption and a *somewhere-statistically-sound* batch argument (BARG). In a somewhere-statistically-sound BARG for $\mathsf{NP}$ [53], a prover can prove a batch of $K$ $\mathsf{NP}$ statements $x_1, \ldots, x_K$ with a proof whose size scales sublinearly with $K$. Moreover, the public parameters for the BARG can be programmed with a special index $i$ such that the BARG is *statistically* sound on index $i$. In other words, when the CRS is binding on index $i$, with overwhelming probability over the choice of $i$, there does not exist[3] an accepting proof for any batch of instances $(x_1, \ldots, x_K)$ where $x_i$ is false. The special index $i$ is computationally hidden from the view of the prover. In some sense, a BARG proof $\pi$ can be viewed as a "compressed" witness for the tuple $(x_1, \ldots, x_K)$. We leverage this to construct a succinct witness encryption scheme for conjunctions:

[2] The actual class we capture is more general (see Sect. 1.2), and includes weighted thresholds (which is not captured generically by a read-once, log-space Turing machine when the weights are $\omega(\log \lambda)$-bits).

[3] Other BARG constructions such as [23,24] only ensure somewhere *computational* soundness which stipulates that such proofs are hard to find for an efficient adversary.

- Suppose we want to encrypt a message $\mu$ to instances $(x_1, \ldots, x_K)$ for an $\mathsf{NP}$ relation $\mathcal{R}$. We want decryption to be possible only if the user knows a witness for *all* $K$ instances.
- We compress the instances by hashing them. Let $\mathsf{h}$ be a hash of $(x_1, \ldots, x_K)$. We assume that the hash function supports local openings (i.e., it is possible to open $\mathsf{h}$ to any $x_i$ with an opening of size $\mathsf{poly}(\lambda, \log K, |x_i|)$).
- The ciphertext is a witness encryption ciphertext for the $\mathsf{NP}$ relation that verifies a BARG proof on $K$ instances, where the witness for instance $i$ consists of a purported statement $x_i$, a local opening of $x_i$ with respect to the hash $\mathsf{h}$, and a witness $w_i$ for $x_i$. The BARG relation would check the validity of the local opening to $x_i$ and then check that $\mathcal{R}(x_i, w_i) = 1$.

Correctness follows immediately from completeness of the BARG. Succinctness follows from succinctness of the BARG and the hash function. Security relies on security of the underlying witness encryption scheme and somewhere-statistical-soundness of the BARG. Specifically, we show that if any individual instance $x_i$ is false, then there does not *exist* a BARG proof that verifies (with respect to the hash digest $\mathsf{h}$). To argue this, we require that the hash function be somewhere statistically binding [42] (namely, the hash key can be programmed at a hidden index $i$ such that any hash $\mathsf{h}$ can only be opened to one particular value at position $i$) and the BARG to be somewhere statistically sound. Then, we proceed as follows:

- Take any $(x_1, \ldots, x_K)$ where $x_i$ is false. First, we program the hash function to be statistically binding at index $i$ and similarly, we program the BARG to be somewhere statistically sound on index $i$.
- Let $\mathsf{h}$ be an SSB hash of $(x_1, \ldots, x_K)$. The encryption algorithm encrypts with respect to the honestly-computed hash $\mathsf{h}$. Since $\mathsf{h}$ is statistically binding on index $i$, there does not exist a valid opening $\sigma_i$ of $\mathsf{h}$ to any string $x_i' \neq x_i$ at index $i$.
- Now, the $i^{\text{th}}$ instance of the BARG is false, since it consists of either an invalid local opening of $\mathsf{h}$ to some $x_i' \neq x_i$, or a valid opening of $\mathsf{h}$ to the false statement $x_i$. Since the BARG is statistically sound on index $i$, there does not exist an accepting BARG proof.
- Thus, the plain witness encryption scheme is being applied to a false statement (since a witness would be an accepting BARG proof), so we can appeal to semantic security of the plain witness encryption scheme.

This immediately gives a succinct witness encryption for conjunctions. The construction naturally generalizes to CNFs and conjunctions of local predicates, and we give the details in Sect. 4.1.

**Succinct Witness Encryption for Disjunctions.** Next, we turn to the setting of disjunctions. Here, we show how to combine plain witness encryption with a *function-binding hash function* [29] to obtain a succinct witness encryption scheme for disjunctions. Essentially, the function-binding hash function plays the role of the index BARG for compressing the instances. Function-binding hash function (for disjunctions) generalize SSB hash functions by (statistically) binding to a function of the input. Specifically, they have the following syntax:

- Like SSB hash functions, a user can use the hash key to compute a hash $\mathsf{h}$ of an input $(x_1, \ldots, x_K)$ and produce a succinct local opening of $x_i$ with respect to the hash.
- Next, the hash key can be sampled to be function binding for a specific function $g$. Like [29], we consider disjunctions of the form

$$f(x_1, \ldots, x_K) := \bigvee_{i \in [K]} g(x_i),$$

  where $g$ is some predicate. The function binding property now states that if $\mathsf{h}$ is a hash of $(x_1^*, \ldots, x_n^*)$ where $f(x_1^*, \ldots, x_n^*) = 0$, then there does *not* exist an opening to any $\hat{x}_{i^*}$ at any index $i^* \in [K]$ where $g(\hat{x}_{i^*}) = 1$. Moreover, the hash key *hides* the associated function $f$.

To construct a succinct witness encryption scheme for disjunctions, we now proceed as follows:

- Suppose we want to encrypt $\mu$ to instances $(x_1, \ldots, x_K)$ with respect to an $\mathsf{NP}$ relation $\mathcal{R}$. We want to support decryption if the user know a witness $w_i$ for any instance $x_i$.
- The encrypter starts by computing a hash $\mathsf{h}$ of $(x_1, \ldots, x_K)$ using the function-binding hash function. Then, the encrypter prepares a witness encryption of the message $\mu$ with respect to the $\mathsf{NP}$ relation that takes as input a purported statement $x_i$, an opening of $x_i$ with respect to the hash $\mathsf{h}$, and a witness $w_i$ for $x_i$. The witness encryption simply checks that the local opening is valid and that $\mathcal{R}(x_i, w_i) = 1$. The size of the ciphertext grows with the size of the verification circuit for the function-binding hash function and the size of the $\mathsf{NP}$ relation $|\mathcal{R}|$.

Security of the above construction relies on the function-binding property of the hash function. Here, we will need to additionally assume that the $\mathsf{NP}$ relation $\mathcal{R}$ is a "trapdoor $\mathsf{NP}$ relation:" namely, given some trapdoor information, there is an efficient algorithm that decides membership in the $\mathsf{NP}$ language. Many cryptographic languages are trapdoor $\mathsf{NP}$ relations (e.g., the set of strings that are encryptions of 1 under a public-key encryption scheme). As we discuss later (see also Sect. 6), when using witness encryption to build other cryptographic primitives, it is typically applied to a cryptographic language. Indeed, both of the applications we consider in this work (to succinct computational secret sharing and to distributed monotone-policy encryption) can be instantiated from succinct witness encryption for batch trapdoor $\mathsf{NP}$ relations.

To prove security of this construction, we start by fixing a false instance $(x_1, \ldots, x_K)$. Let $C_{\mathsf{td}}$ be the trapdoor-decision algorithm associated with $\mathcal{R}$. Namely, $C_{\mathsf{td}}(x) = 1$ if and only if there exists a witness $w$ where $\mathcal{R}(x, w) = 1$. Since $(x_1, \ldots, x_K)$ is false, this means $C_{\mathsf{td}}(x_i) = 0$ for all $i \in [K]$. Suppose we now program the function-binding hash function to be function-binding on the function $f(x_1, \ldots, x_K) = \bigvee_{i \in [K]} C_{\mathsf{td}}(x_i)$. Now, if $\mathsf{h}$ is a hash of $(x_1, \ldots, x_K)$, the function-binding property says there cannot be *any* opening of $\mathsf{h}$ to a statement $\tilde{x}_i$ where $C_{\mathsf{td}}(\tilde{x}_i) = 1$. Correspondingly, the only openings that exist for $\mathsf{h}$ are to statements $\tilde{x}_i$ where $\mathcal{R}(\tilde{x}_i, \tilde{w}_i) = 0$ for all $\tilde{w}_i$. Thus, there does not exist a valid witness for the witness encryption relation, and security follows from security of the witness encryption scheme.

Similar to our construction for conjunctions, this scheme readily generalizes to support disjunctions of arbitrary local monotone predicates. We provide the full details and formal analysis in Sect. 4.2.

**Unique Witness Maps for Read-once Turing Machines.** Our main construction is a unique witness map based on $i\mathcal{O}$ for monotone-policy batch $\mathsf{NP}$ that supports any policy that can be computed by a read-once bounded-space Turing machine. For our applications, we require two types of succinctness: the common reference string for the unique witness map must be sublinear in the number of instances $K$, and the size of the canonical witness for a batch of statements $(x_1, \ldots, x_K)$ should be $\mathsf{poly}(\lambda, \log K)$, and be essentially independent of the size of the $\mathsf{NP}$ relation or the size of the associated policy. In our construction, the size of the public parameters will scale with $2^S$ where $S$ is the space usage of the Turing machine. As we see later, the size actually scales with the description length of the set of unreachable states associated with the policy, which for certain policy families, is much smaller than $2^S$. An important example of this is the class of weighted thresholds (see Remark 5.7).

The common reference string (CRS) for our unique witness map consists of two (obfuscated) programs: (1) a prover program that is used to map witnesses for a batch of $K$ statements together with an associated policy onto a canonical witness; and (2) a verification program for verifying a canonical witness. Since we require the CRS size to be sublinear in $K$, we cannot publish an obfuscated program that reads all $K$ instances at once. Instead, similar to [26,30] (which consider SNARGs for batch $\mathsf{NP}$ with respect to conjunction policies), the prover program reads one statement/witness at a time. After reading each statement/witness, it then outputs a representation of its internal state together with a signature on it. The evaluator then invokes the prover program on the next instance. More concretely, the programs behave as follows:

- First, we assume the $\mathsf{NP}$ relation (expressed as a Boolean circuit $C$ that computes the $\mathsf{NP}$ relation) is hard-coded in the prover and verification programs.
- We model a policy $P \colon \{0,1\}^K \to \{0,1\}$ as a read-once Turing machine with $S$ bits of space. Concretely, we represent it as $(\mathsf{Step}_1, \ldots, \mathsf{Step}_K, c_{\mathsf{init}}, c_{\mathsf{acc}})$, where $\mathsf{Step}_i \colon \{0,1\}^S \times \{0,1\} \to \{0,1\}^S$ is a Boolean circuit that takes the current configuration and the next bit of the input and outputs the next state, $c_{\mathsf{init}} \in \{0,1\}^S$ is the initial configuration, and $c_{\mathsf{acc}} \in \{0,1\}^S$ is the accepting configuration. Let $\mathsf{h}$ be a hash on the tuple $((x_1, \mathsf{Step}_1), \ldots, (x_K, \mathsf{Step}_K))$.[4]

[4] In the actual construction (Construction 5.8), we separate these into two separate hashes in order to support a local evaluation property that is useful for applications

- To compute the canonical witness, the evaluator runs the obfuscated proving program $K$ times. On the $i^{\text{th}}$ iteration, the evaluator passes in the hash $\mathsf{h}$, the instance $x_i$, the step function $\mathsf{Step}_i$ together with an opening for $(x_i, \mathsf{Step}_i)$ relative to $\mathsf{h}$, the associated witness $w_i$, the configuration $c_{i-1}$ from the first $i-1$ steps of the evaluation (with $c_0 := c_{\mathsf{init}}$), and a signature $\sigma_{i-1}$ on $(\mathsf{h}, i-1, c_{i-1})$.
- If the signature $\sigma_{i-1}$ is valid, then the proving program computes the bit $\beta_i = C(x_i, w_i)$ and the updated state of the Turing machine $c_i = \mathsf{Step}_i(c_{i-1}, \beta_i)$. It outputs a signature $\sigma_i$ on $(\mathsf{h}, i, c_i)$.
- The canonical witness for the batch of $K$ statements is a signature on $(\mathsf{h}, K, c_{\mathsf{acc}})$, where $c_{\mathsf{acc}}$ is the accepting configuration.
- The verification algorithm calls the obfuscated verification program which checks whether it was given a valid signature on $(\mathsf{h}, K, c_{\mathsf{acc}})$ or not.

For any tuple of statements $(x_1, \ldots, x_K)$ and policy $P$, the canonical witness is a (deterministic) signature on $(\mathsf{h}, K, c_{\mathsf{acc}})$. This depends solely on the statements and the policy, and is *independent* of the witnesses used to derive the signature. Thus, this constructive gives a unique witness map for batch instances.

Proving security of this construction is very delicate. Recall that the security requirement for a unique witness map says that an efficient adversary cannot come up with a proof that passes verification for any tuple $(x_1, \ldots, x_K)$ that does not satisfy the policy $P$. The general approach we take combines the chaining approach from [26,30] with the pebbling arguments from [34,35]. Notably, the latter was used for analyzing $i\mathcal{O}$ for Turing machines. We highlight some of the key features of our reduction and refer to Sect. 5 for the formal description:

- First, we consider selective security where the statements $(x_1, \ldots, x_K)$ and the monotone policy $P$ are fixed in advance. Now, for each $i \in [K]$, we define the set $S_i$ of reachable configurations after $i$ steps of $P$. Specifically, let $S_0 = \{c_{\mathsf{init}}\}$ be the initial configuration. Then, for each $i \in [K]$, $S_i$ contains all $c_i$ where $c_i = \mathsf{Step}(c_{i-1}, 0)$ and $c_{i-1} \in S_{i-1}$ (i.e., the states that are reachable by starting from a reachable state after $i-1$ steps and then reading a 0). In addition, if the $i^{\text{th}}$ statement is true, then $S_i$ also contains all $c_i$ where $c_i = \mathsf{Step}(c_{i-1}, 1)$ where $c_{i-1} \in S_{i-1}$ (i.e., the states that are reachable from a reachable state after $i$ steps and then reading a 1).
- Let $\mathsf{h}^*$ be the hash on $((x_1, \mathsf{Step}_1) \ldots, (x_K, \mathsf{Step}_K))$. Our general strategy in the security proof is to propagate the following invariant: at step $i$ of the computation, the only possible signatures on tuples of the form $(\mathsf{h}^*, i, c_i)$ are those where $c_i \in S_i$. Namely, signatures should only exist on *reachable* configurations. We show that if the invariant holds for an index $i$, then using punctured programming techniques [49], we can establish the invariant for index $i+1$. To carry out this step, we need to embed within the obfuscated program a description of the reachable states after the first $i$ states (i.e., a description of the set $S_i$). For this reason, the size of the obfuscated program

(see the full version of this paper [25]). For ease of exposition in this overview, we describe things using a single hash.

in our construction grows exponentially with the space of the Turing machine, limiting us to log-space computations. However, in settings where the sets $S_i$ have a compact description, then the size of the programs only scales with the size of the compact description of $S_i$. This captures important policies families such as weighted threshold policies (see Remark 5.7).

- The next challenge comes from the need to "unpuncture." Specifically, the way we establish our invariant that signatures do not exist on any unreachable configuration is we "puncture" away the ability to generate signatures on inputs of the form $(\mathsf{h}^*, i, c_i)$ for all $c_i \notin S_i$. If we have to hard-code all of these inputs into the program across all indices $i \in [K]$, then the size of the program scales linearly with the number of instances, which is precisely what we want to avoid. Thus, once we have established the invariant on an index $i$, we need a way to unpuncture previous points. We can model this unpuncturing step as a pebbling game [34,35], which provides a way to propagate our invariant while ensuring that at any point in time, we only need to program in the sets $S_i$ for at most $O(\log K)$ indices. We refer to the full version of this paper [25] for the full details.
- A second challenge that arises in our analysis is within the propagation step itself. Recall that on step $i$, our goal is to puncture away all signatures on inputs of the form $(\mathsf{h}^*, i, c_i)$ where $c_i \notin S_i$. A natural approach would be to step through each of the $2^S$ possible configurations one-by-one and leverage punctured programming (and indeed, this is our overall proof strategy). This would result in $2^S$ hybrids in total, and if done naïvely, would lead to signatures whose size now scales with the space-bound $S$. Once again, this would no longer meet our succinctness requirements. Thus, we need to design our hybrids so that the dependence on the space usage $S$ is entirely absorbed by the programs in the common reference string and not in the size of the output signatures. To support this, we use the randomization techniques developed recently in the context of constructing and batching adaptively-sound SNARGs for $\mathsf{NP}$ from $i\mathcal{O}$ [26,54].

Taken together, we obtain a succinct witness map for batch languages from $i\mathcal{O}$ and SSB hash functions. The size of the CRS scales with the description length of the set of reachable states for the Turing machine. Note that if we directly use $i\mathcal{O}$ for Turing machines to build a unique witness map (i.e., read all $K$ statements/witnesses and output a signature if the policy is satisfied), then the size of the CRS grows linearly with the number of instances $K$ (because the size of the obfuscated program in existing constructions of $i\mathcal{O}$ for Turing machines from standard assumptions [8,17,35,44] all grow with the input length). These approaches would in turn not suffice for either of our applications to succinct witness encryption or for SNARGs for monotone-policy batch NP with a sublinear-size CRS. Our approach shows how to overcome this input-size barrier for a particular class of computations.

**Application to Succinct Computational Secret Sharing.** A succinct witness encryption scheme for a policy $\mathcal{P}$ immediately gives a succinct computational secret sharing scheme for $\mathcal{P}$. The construction is straightforward:

- Let $\mathsf{pk}$ be the public-key for a public-key encryption scheme. Suppose there are $K$ parties in the system. Each party's share consists of a pair $(\mathsf{ct}_i, r_i)$ where $\mathsf{ct}_i = \mathsf{Encrypt}(\mathsf{pk}, 1; r)$ is encryption of 1 under $\mathsf{pk}$ using randomness $r_i$.
- Let $\mathcal{R}_{\mathsf{pk}}(\mathsf{ct}, r)$ be an $\mathsf{NP}$ relation that outputs 1 if $\mathsf{ct} = \mathsf{Encrypt}(\mathsf{pk}, 1; r)$. To share a message $\mu$ with respect to a policy $P$, the dealer publishes a witness encryption ciphertext with message $\mu$, statement $(\mathsf{ct}_1, \ldots, \mathsf{ct}_K)$, policy $P$, and $\mathcal{R}_{\mathsf{pk}}$ as the associated $\mathsf{NP}$ relation.

Both the parties' individual shares as well as the public information are succinct (the latter by succinctness of the witness encryption scheme). Moreover, any set of users that satisfies the policy is able to decrypt and recover $\mu$.[5] Security follows readily from security of the succinct witness encryption scheme. We refer to the full version of this paper [25] for the full details. An appealing feature of our construction is that the party's individual shares are *reusable*. Whenever the dealer wants to share a new message, it only needs to publish a short *public* share (i.e., the witness encryption ciphertext).

**Application to Distributed Monotone-Policy Encryption.** Our second application is to distributed monotone-policy encryption. In this notion, users generate their own public keys $\mathsf{pk}$ and post them to a public-key directory. Thereafter, one can encrypt to a collection of public keys $\{\mathsf{pk}_i\}_{i \in S}$ together with a monotone policy $P$ (on the set $S$ of public keys). Any authorized set of users can pool their decryption keys to decrypt and learn the message. We can construct a distributed monotone-policy encryption scheme in the same manner as our succinct computational secret sharing construction. Namely, the public parameters for the monotone-policy encryption scheme will be the public key $\mathsf{pk}$ for a public-key encryption scheme. Each user's public key will be an encryption of 1 under $\mathsf{pk}$ and their secret key is the associated encryption randomness. An encryption of a message $\mu$ to a set of public keys $\{\mathsf{pk}_i\}_{i \in S}$ and access policy $P$ is precisely a succinct witness encryption of $\mu$ where the statement corresponds to $\{\mathsf{pk}_i\}_{i \in S}$ and the policy corresponds to $P$. Correctness and security follow as in the case of succinct computational secret sharing.

In the basic version described here, users have to share their decryption keys in order to decrypt. We can also consider a stronger model where instead of users exchanging secret keys to decrypt they instead publish a one-time partial decryption of the message. This is standard in settings like multi-key homomorphic encryption [46] or threshold encryption with silent setup [6,33]. Using similar techniques as in [6,33], we can easily extend our construction to support this. Namely, we let each user's long-term secret key be a signing key for

[5] Technically, this requires that decryption is possible even if the users do *not* know the full statement (i.e., the public keys of all users in the system). As we discuss in Sects. 4 and 5, the schemes in this work support this "local" decryption property.

a digital signature scheme. Their public key is the associated verification key. Next, we associate a (random) tag with each ciphertext. Instead of checking for possession of the associated decryption key, the witness encryption scheme now checks that the decrypter provides a valid signature for a set of users that satisfy the access policy. The signatures now serves as the "decryption key." Security of the signature scheme ensures that the decryption hint for one ciphertext does not help break semantic security of an unrelated ciphertext. We provide the full details in the full version of this paper [25].

## 2 Preliminaries

Throughout this work, we write $\lambda$ to denote the security parameter. For a positive integer $n \in \mathbb{N}$, we write $[n] := \{1, \ldots, n\}$. We say a function $f(\lambda)$ is negligible if $f = o(\lambda^{-c})$ for all $c \in \mathbb{N}$, and write $\mathsf{negl}(\lambda)$ to denote a negligible function. We say an algorithm is efficient if it runs in probabilistic polynomial time in the length of its input. We write $\mathsf{poly}(\lambda)$ to denote a fixed function that is bounded by some polynomial in $\lambda$. We model an efficient non-uniform algorithm $\mathcal{A}$ as a pair of algorithms $\mathcal{A} = (\mathcal{A}_0, \mathcal{A}_1)$ where $\mathcal{A}_0$ is a (possibly unbounded) algorithm that takes as input $1^\lambda$ and outputs an advice string $\rho_\lambda$ of polynomial length, and algorithm $\mathcal{A}_1$ is an efficient algorithm. The output of $\mathcal{A}$ on an input $x \in \{0,1\}^\lambda$ is defined as first computing the advice string $\rho_\lambda \leftarrow \mathcal{A}_0(1^\lambda)$ and then taking the output to be $\mathcal{A}_1(\rho_\lambda, x)$. Throughout this work, we will consider efficient non-uniform adversaries. In the full version of this paper [25], we recall the definitions of the standard cryptographic primitives we use in our constructions.

**Witness Encryption.** We now recall the notion of a witness encryption scheme for $\mathsf{NP}$ [32].

**Definition 2.1 (Witness Encryption [32, adapted]).** *Let $\mathcal{M}$ be a message space. A witness encryption scheme $\Pi_{\mathsf{WE}}$ for $\mathsf{NP}$ with message space $\mathcal{M}$ is a pair of efficient algorithms $\Pi_{\mathsf{WE}} = (\mathsf{Encrypt}, \mathsf{Decrypt})$ with the following syntax:*

- $\mathsf{Encrypt}(1^\lambda, C, \mu) \to \mathsf{ct}$*: On input the security parameter $\lambda \in \mathbb{N}$, a circuit $C \colon \{0,1\}^h \to \{0,1\}$, and a message $\mu \in \mathcal{M}$, the encryption algorithm outputs a ciphertext* $\mathsf{ct}$.
- $\mathsf{Decrypt}(\mathsf{ct}, C, w) \to \mu$*: On input a ciphertext* $\mathsf{ct}$*, a Boolean relation $C \colon \{0,1\}^h \to \{0,1\}$, a witness $w \in \{0,1\}^h$, the decryption algorithm outputs a message $\mu$.*

*Moreover, we require that* $(\mathsf{Encrypt}, \mathsf{Decrypt})$ *satisfy the following two properties:*

- **Correctness:** *For all $\lambda \in \mathbb{N}$, all Boolean circuits $C \colon \{0,1\}^h \to \{0,1\}$, all witnesses $w \in \{0,1\}^h$ where $C(w) = 1$, and all messages $\mu \in \mathcal{M}$,*

$$\Pr[\mathsf{Decrypt}(\mathsf{ct}, C, w) = \mu : \mathsf{ct} \leftarrow \mathsf{Encrypt}(1^\lambda, C, \mu)] = 1.$$

- **Semantic security:** *For a security parameter $\lambda \in \mathbb{N}$, a bit $b \in \{0,1\}$, and an adversary $\mathcal{A}$, we define the semantic security game as follows:*
  - *On input the security parameter $1^\lambda$, algorithm $\mathcal{A}$ outputs a Boolean relation $C\colon \{0,1\}^h \to \{0,1\}$ and a pair of messages $\mu_0, \mu_1 \in \mathcal{M}$.*
  - *If there exists $w \in \{0,1\}^h$ such that $C(w) = 1$, then the challenger outputs $0$. Otherwise, the challenger responds with $\mathsf{ct} \leftarrow \mathsf{Encrypt}(1^\lambda, C, \mu_b)$.*
  - *Algorithm $\mathcal{A}$ outputs a bit $b' \in \{0,1\}$ which is also the output of the experiment.*

  *The witness encryption scheme is semantically secure if for all efficient adversaries $\mathcal{A}$, there exists a negligible function $\mathsf{negl}(\cdot)$ such that for all $\lambda \in \mathbb{N}$, $|\Pr[b' = 1 \mid b = 0] - \Pr[b' = 1 \mid b = 1]| = \mathsf{negl}(\lambda)$ in the semantic security game.*

## 3 Succinct Witness Encryption for Batch Languages

We begin by introducing the notion of succinct witness encryption for batch languages. This is the main cryptographic notion we consider in this work, and in Sect. 6, we show how it can be used to realize applications to computational secret sharing and monotone-policy encryption.

**Definition 3.1 (Succinct Witness Encryption for Batch Languages).** *Let $\mathcal{M}$ be a message space and $\mathcal{P}$ be a family of policies. A succinct witness encryption scheme $\Pi_{\mathsf{WE}}$ for batch languages with message space $\mathcal{M}$ and policy family $\mathcal{P}$ is a pair of efficient algorithms $\Pi_{\mathsf{WE}} = (\mathsf{Encrypt}, \mathsf{Decrypt})$ with the following syntax:*

- $\mathsf{Encrypt}(1^\lambda, C, P, (x_1, \ldots, x_K), \mu) \to \mathsf{ct}$: *On input the security parameter $\lambda \in \mathbb{N}$, a Boolean relation $C\colon \{0,1\}^n \times \{0,1\}^h \to \{0,1\}$, a Boolean policy $P \in \mathcal{P}$ where $P\colon \{0,1\}^K \to \{0,1\}$, instances $x_1, \ldots, x_K \in \{0,1\}^n$, and a message $\mu$, the encryption algorithm outputs a ciphertext* $\mathsf{ct}$.
- $\mathsf{Decrypt}(\mathsf{ct}, C, P, (x_1, \ldots, x_K), (w_1, \ldots, w_K)) \to \mu$: *On input a ciphertext* $\mathsf{ct}$, *a Boolean relation $C\colon \{0,1\}^n \times \{0,1\}^h \to \{0,1\}$, a Boolean policy $P \in \mathcal{P}$ where $P\colon \{0,1\}^K \to \{0,1\}$, statements $(x_1, \ldots, x_K) \in \{0,1\}^n$, and witnesses $w_1, \ldots, w_K \in \{0,1\}^h$, the decryption algorithm outputs a message $\mu$.*

*Moreover, we require that $\Pi_{\mathsf{WE}}$ satisfy the following properties:*

- **Correctness:** *For all security parameters $\lambda \in \mathbb{N}$, all Boolean relations $C\colon \{0,1\}^n \times \{0,1\}^h \to \{0,1\}$, all Boolean policies $P \in \mathcal{P}$ where $P\colon \{0,1\}^K \to \{0,1\}$, all tuples of statements $x_1, \ldots, x_K \in \{0,1\}^n$, all witnesses $w_1, \ldots, w_K \in \{0,1\}^h$ where $P(C(x_1, w_1), \ldots, C(x_K, w_K)) = 1$, and all messages $\mu \in \mathcal{M}$,*

$$\Pr[\mathsf{Decrypt}(\mathsf{ct}, C, P, (x_1, \ldots, x_K), (w_1, \ldots, w_K)) = \mu : \\ \mathsf{ct} \leftarrow \mathsf{Encrypt}(1^\lambda, C, P, (x_1, \ldots, x_K), \mu)] = 1.$$

- **Semantic security:** *For a security parameter* $\lambda \in \mathbb{N}$*, a bit* $b \in \{0,1\}$*, and an adversary* $\mathcal{A}$*, we define the semantic security game as follows:*
  - *On input the security parameter* $1^\lambda$*, algorithm* $\mathcal{A}$ *outputs a Boolean relation* $C\colon \{0,1\}^n \times \{0,1\}^h \to \{0,1\}$*, a policy* $P \in \mathcal{P}$ *where* $P\colon \{0,1\}^K \to \{0,1\}$*, a tuple of statements* $x_1, \ldots, x_K \in \{0,1\}^n$*, and a pair of messages* $\mu_0, \mu_1 \in \mathcal{M}$*.*
  - *If there exists* $w_1, \ldots, w_K \in \{0,1\}^h$ *such that* $P(C(x_1, w_1), \ldots, C(x_K, w_K)) = 1$*, then the challenger outputs* 0*. Otherwise, the challenger responds with the ciphertext* $\mathsf{ct} \leftarrow \mathsf{Encrypt}(1^\lambda, C, P, (x_1, \ldots, x_K), \mu)$*.*
  - *Algorithm* $\mathcal{A}$ *outputs a bit* $b' \in \{0,1\}$*, which is the output of the experiment.*

  *The succinct witness encryption scheme for batch languages is semantically secure if for all efficient adversaries* $\mathcal{A}$*, there exists a negligible function* $\mathsf{negl}(\cdot)$ *such that for all* $\lambda \in \mathbb{N}$*,*

$$|\Pr[b' = 1 \mid b = 0] - \Pr[b' = 1 \mid b = 1]| = \mathsf{negl}(\lambda)$$

  *in the semantic security game.*
- **Succinctness:** *There exists a polynomial* $\mathsf{poly}$ *such that for all* $\lambda \in \mathbb{N}$*, circuits* $C\colon \{0,1\}^n \times \{0,1\}^h \to \{0,1\}$*, policies* $P \in \mathcal{P}$ *(on* $n$*-bit inputs), instances* $x_1, \ldots, x_K \in \{0,1\}^n$*, and messages* $\mu \in \mathcal{M}$*, the size of the ciphertext* $\mathsf{ct}$ *output by* $\mathsf{ct} \leftarrow \mathsf{Encrypt}(1^\lambda, C, P, (x_1, \ldots, x_K), \mu)$ *satisfies* $|\mathsf{ct}| \le o(|P|) \cdot \mathsf{poly}(\lambda, |C|, \log K)$*.*

**Local Decryption.** In Definition 3.1, the decryption algorithm requires knowledge of *all* of the statements associated with the ciphertext. When considering applications of succinct witness encryption to computational secret sharing and monotone policy encryption, it will be important to consider a decryption algorithm that only requires knowledge of a *subset* of statements that satisfy the policy (as opposed to all of the statements). Similar to the setting of batch arguments [24] and locally verifiable signatures, we can support this property by decomposing the decryption algorithm into a preprocessing algorithm which takes as input the policy $P$ together with *all* of the statements and outputs a short "hint" associated with each statement. The preprocessing algorithm only depends on the statement and not the witnesses. Then, there is a local decryption algorithm that takes as input the ciphertext together with a subset of statements and their associated hints and witnesses and outputs the message. Notably, the local decryption algorithm only requires knowledge of the statements and hints that satisfy the policy. We define this property formally below:

**Definition 3.2 (Local Decryption).** *A succinct witness encryption scheme* $\Pi_{\mathsf{WE}} = (\mathsf{Encrypt}, \mathsf{Decrypt})$ *with message space* $\mathcal{M}$ *and policy family* $\mathcal{P}$ *supports local decryption if there exist a pair of efficient algorithms* $(\mathsf{Preprocess}, \mathsf{DecryptLocal})$ *with the following syntax:*

- $\mathsf{Preprocess}(\mathsf{ct}, C, P, (x_1, \dots, x_K)) \to (\mathsf{ht}_1, \dots, \mathsf{ht}_K)$: *On input a ciphertext* $\mathsf{ct}$*, a Boolean relation* $C: \{0,1\}^n \times \{0,1\}^h \to \{0,1\}$*, a Boolean policy* $P \in \mathcal{P}$*, and the statements* $x_1, \dots, x_K \in \{0,1\}^n$*, the preprocessing algorithm outputs a tuple of hints* $\mathsf{ht}_1, \dots, \mathsf{ht}_K$*. This algorithm is deterministic.*
- $\mathsf{DecryptLocal}(\mathsf{ct}, C, P, \{(i, \mathsf{ht}_i, w_i)\}_{i \in S}) \to \mu$: *On input a ciphertext* $\mathsf{ct}$*, a Boolean relation* $C: \{0,1\}^n \times \{0,1\}^h \to \{0,1\}$*, a Boolean policy* $P \in \mathcal{P}$*, and a collection of hints and witnesses* $(\mathsf{ht}_i, w_i)$ *for* $i \in S$*, the local decryption algorithm outputs a message* $\mu$*. This algorithm is also deterministic.*

*We require* ($\mathsf{Preprocess}, \mathsf{DecryptLocal}$) *satisfy the following properties:*

- **Correctness:** *For all security parameters* $\lambda \in \mathbb{N}$*, all Boolean relations* $C: \{0,1\}^n \times \{0,1\}^h \to \{0,1\}$*, all Boolean policies* $P \in \mathcal{P}$ *where* $P: \{0,1\}^K \to \{0,1\}$*, all inputs* $\beta_1, \dots, \beta_K \in \{0,1\}$ *where* $P(\beta_1, \dots, \beta_K) = 1$*, all statements* $x_1, \dots, x_K \in \{0,1\}^n$*, all witnesses* $w_1, \dots, w_K \in \{0,1\}^h$ *where* $C(x_i, w_i) = 1$ *for all* $i$ *where* $\beta_1 = 1$*, and for all messages* $\mu \in \mathcal{M}$*,*

$$\Pr\left[\mathsf{DecryptLocal}(\mathsf{ct}, C, P, \{(i, \mathsf{ht}_i, w_i)\}_{i \in [K]: \beta_i = 1}) = \mu\right] = 1,$$

*where* $\mathsf{ct} \leftarrow \mathsf{Encrypt}(1^\lambda, C, P, (x_1, \dots, x_K), \mu)$ *and*

$$(\mathsf{ht}_1, \dots, \mathsf{ht}_K) = \mathsf{Preprocess}(\mathsf{ct}, C, P, (x_1, \dots, x_K)).$$

- **Succinct hints:** *There exists a polynomial* $\mathsf{poly}$ *such that for all* $\lambda \in \mathbb{N}$*, circuits* $C: \{0,1\}^n \times \{0,1\}^h \to \{0,1\}$*, policies* $P \in \mathcal{P}$ *(on* $n$*-bit inputs), instances* $x_1, \dots, x_K \in \{0,1\}^n$*, messages* $\mu \in \mathcal{M}$*, and all ciphertexts* $\mathsf{ct}$ *in the support of* $\mathsf{Encrypt}(1^\lambda, C, P, (x_1, \dots, x_K), \mu)$*, the hints* $(\mathsf{ht}_1, \dots, \mathsf{ht}_K) = \mathsf{Preprocess}(\mathsf{ct}, C, P, (x_1, \dots, x_K))$ *satisfy*

$$\forall i \in [K] : |\mathsf{ht}_i| \le o(|P|) \cdot \mathsf{poly}(\lambda, |C|, \log K).$$

# 4 Succinct Witness Encryption for CNFs and DNFs

In this section, we show how to construct succinct witness encryption with succinct ciphertexts that support CNF and DNF policies from witness encryption (in conjunction with either somewhere statistically sound batch arguments for NP [53] or function-binding hash functions [29]).

## 4.1 Succinct Witness Encryption for CNF Policies

We start by constructing a succinct witness encryption scheme that supports CNF policies. The size of the ciphertext scales with the maximum number of variables that can appear in a single clause but polylogarithmically in the total number of clauses. For the particular setting where each clause contains a constant number of variables, the size of the ciphertext (and public parameters) scale polylogarithmically with the description length of the CNF.

**Construction 4.1 (Succinct Witness Encryption for CNF Policies).** Let $\lambda$ be a security parameter, $\mathcal{M}$ be a message space, and $\mathcal{P}$ be the set of Boolean formulas in conjunctive normal form. Our construction relies on the following:

- Let $\Pi_{\mathsf{SSB}} = (\mathsf{SSB.Setup}, \mathsf{SSB.Hash}, \mathsf{SSB.Verify})$ be a somewhere statistically binding hash function.
- Let $\Pi_{\mathsf{BARG}} = (\mathsf{BARG.Setup}, \mathsf{BARG.Prove}, \mathsf{BARG.Verify})$ be a somewhere statistically sound index BARG.
- Let $\Pi_{\mathsf{WE}} = (\mathsf{WE.Encrypt}, \mathsf{WE.Decrypt})$ be a witness encryption scheme with message space $\mathcal{M}$.

We construct a succinct witness encryption scheme with message space $\mathcal{M}$ and policy space $\mathcal{P}$ as follows:

- $\mathsf{Encrypt}(1^\lambda, C, P, (x_1, \ldots, x_K), \mu)$: On input the security parameter $\lambda$, the Boolean relation $C\colon \{0,1\}^n \times \{0,1\}^h \to \{0,1\}$, the Boolean policy $P \in \mathcal{P}$ where $P\colon \{0,1\}^K \to \{0,1\}$, instances $x_1, \ldots, x_K \in \{0,1\}^n$, and the message $\mu \in \mathcal{M}$, the encryption algorithm proceeds as follows:
  - Let $c$ be the number of clauses in $P$ and let $t \leq K$ be the maximum number of variables that appears in any clause of $P$.
  - Sample $\mathsf{hk}_{\mathsf{inst}} \leftarrow \mathsf{SSB.Setup}(1^\lambda, 1^n, 1^t, K, \varnothing)$. Let $\ell_{\mathsf{cl}} = \ell_{\mathsf{cl}}(\lambda)$ be a bound on the description of a single clause. Sample $\mathsf{hk}_{\mathsf{cl}} \leftarrow \mathsf{SSB.Setup}(1^\lambda, 1^{\ell_{\mathsf{cl}}}, 1^1, c, \varnothing)$.
  - Compute a hash of the instances
$$(\mathsf{h}_{\mathsf{inst}}, \pi_{\mathsf{inst},1}, \ldots, \pi_{\mathsf{inst},K}) = \mathsf{SSB.Hash}(\mathsf{hk}_{\mathsf{inst}}, (x_1, \ldots, x_K)).$$
  - For $i \in [c]$, let $S_i \subseteq [K]$ denote the variables that appear in clause $i$ of $P$ (under a canonical ordering of the variables). Compute a hash of the clauses $(\mathsf{h}_{\mathsf{cl}}, \pi_{\mathsf{cl},1}, \ldots, \pi_{\mathsf{cl},c}) = \mathsf{SSB.Hash}(\mathsf{hk}_{\mathsf{cl}}, (S_1, \ldots, S_c))$.

**Fixed values:** hash keys $\mathsf{hk}_{\mathsf{inst}}, \mathsf{hk}_{\mathsf{cl}}$, a circuit $C\colon \{0,1\}^n \times \{0,1\}^h \to \{0,1\}$, and hashes $\mathsf{h}_{\mathsf{inst}}, \mathsf{h}_{\mathsf{cl}}$
**Statement:** index $i \in \mathbb{N}$
**Witness:** a set $S$, an opening $\pi_{\mathsf{cl}}$, an index $j$, an $\mathsf{NP}$ statement $x$, an opening $\pi_{\mathsf{inst}}$, and an $\mathsf{NP}$ witness $w$

On input a statement $i \in \mathbb{N}$ and a tuple $(S, \pi_{\mathsf{cl}}, j, x, \pi_{\mathsf{inst}}, w)$, output 1 if the following conditions hold:

* $\mathsf{SSB.Verify}(\mathsf{hk}_{\mathsf{cl}}, \mathsf{h}_{\mathsf{cl}}, i, S, \pi_{\mathsf{cl}}) = 1$.
* $j \in S$ and $\mathsf{SSB.Verify}(\mathsf{hk}_{\mathsf{inst}}, \mathsf{h}_{\mathsf{inst}}, j, x, \pi_{\mathsf{inst}}) = 1$ and $C(x, w) = 1$.

**Fig. 1.** The $\mathsf{NP}$ relation $\mathcal{R}_{\mathsf{ClauseSAT}}[\mathsf{hk}_{\mathsf{inst}}, \mathsf{hk}_{\mathsf{cl}}, C, \mathsf{h}_{\mathsf{inst}}, \mathsf{h}_{\mathsf{cl}}]$

- Define the index relation $\mathcal{R}_{\mathsf{ClauseSAT}}$:
- Let $s$ be the size of the Boolean circuit $C_{\mathsf{ClauseSAT}}$ that computes $\mathcal{R}_{\mathsf{ClauseSAT}}[\mathsf{hk}_{\mathsf{inst}}, \mathsf{hk}_{\mathsf{cl}}, C, \mathsf{h}_{\mathsf{inst}}, \mathsf{h}_{\mathsf{cl}}]$ from Fig. 1. Sample

$$\mathsf{crs}_{\mathsf{BARG}} \leftarrow \mathsf{BARG.Setup}(1^\lambda, 1^c, 1^s).$$

- Let $C_{\mathsf{ValidBARG}}$ be the Boolean circuit that takes as input a BARG proof $\pi$ and outputs

$$\mathsf{BARG.Verify}(\mathsf{crs}_{\mathsf{BARG}}, C_{\mathsf{ClauseSAT}}, c, \pi).$$

In particular, the values of $\mathsf{crs}_{\mathsf{BARG}}$, $C_{\mathsf{ClauseSAT}}$, and $c$ are hard-wired in the circuit $C_{\mathsf{ValidBARG}}$. Compute the ciphertext

$$\mathsf{ct}_{\mathsf{WE}} \leftarrow \mathsf{WE.Encrypt}(1^\lambda, C_{\mathsf{ValidBARG}}, \mu).$$

Output the ciphertext $\mathsf{ct} = (\mathsf{crs}_{\mathsf{BARG}}, \mathsf{hk}_{\mathsf{inst}}, \mathsf{hk}_{\mathsf{cl}}, \mathsf{ct}_{\mathsf{WE}})$.

– $\mathsf{Decrypt}(\mathsf{ct}, C, P, (x_1, \ldots, x_K), (w_1, \ldots, w_K))$: On input a ciphertext $\mathsf{ct} = (\mathsf{crs}_{\mathsf{BARG}}, \mathsf{hk}_{\mathsf{inst}}, \mathsf{hk}_{\mathsf{cl}}, \mathsf{h}_{\mathsf{inst}}, \mathsf{h}_{\mathsf{cl}}, \mathsf{ct}_{\mathsf{WE}})$, a Boolean relation $C\colon \{0,1\}^n \times \{0,1\}^h \to \{0,1\}$, a policy $P \in \mathcal{P}$ where $P\colon \{0,1\}^K \to \{0,1\}$, instances $x_1, \ldots, x_K \in \{0,1\}^n$, and witnesses $w_1, \ldots, w_K \in \{0,1\}^h$, the decryption algorithm proceeds as follows:
  - If $P(C(x_1, w_1), \ldots, C(x_K, w_K)) = 0$, output $\perp$.
  - Otherwise, compute a hash of the instances $(\mathsf{h}_{\mathsf{inst}}, \pi_{\mathsf{inst},1}, \ldots, \pi_{\mathsf{inst},K}) = \mathsf{SSB.Hash}(\mathsf{hk}_{\mathsf{inst}}, (x_1, \ldots, x_K))$. Let $c$ be the number of clauses that appear in $P$. For $i \in [c]$, let $S_i \subseteq [K]$ denote the variables that appear in clause $i$ of $P$ (under a canonical ordering of the variables). Compute a hash of the clauses $(\mathsf{h}_{\mathsf{cl}}, \pi_{\mathsf{cl},1}, \ldots, \pi_{\mathsf{cl},c}) = \mathsf{SSB.Hash}(\mathsf{hk}_{\mathsf{cl}}, (S_1, \ldots, S_c))$.
  - Since $P(C(x_1, w_1), \ldots, C(x_K, w_K)) = 1$ and $P$ is a CNF, every clause of $P$ must contain a satisfied literal. In other words, for every $i \in [c]$, there exists an index $j_i \in S_i$ where $C(x_{j_i}, w_{j_i}) = 1$. Let $j_i$ be the smallest such index and define $w_{\mathsf{BARG},i} = (S_i, \pi_{\mathsf{cl},i}, j_i, x_{j_i}, \pi_{\mathsf{inst},j_i}, w_{j_i})$.
  - Let $C_{\mathsf{ClauseSAT}}$ be the Boolean circuit that computes the $\mathsf{NP}$ relation $\mathcal{R}_{\mathsf{ClauseSAT}}[\mathsf{hk}_{\mathsf{inst}}, \mathsf{hk}_{\mathsf{cl}}, C, \mathsf{h}_{\mathsf{inst}}, \mathsf{h}_{\mathsf{cl}}]$ from Fig. 1. Construct a proof $\pi_{\mathsf{BARG}} \leftarrow \mathsf{BARG.Prove}(\mathsf{crs}_{\mathsf{BARG}}, C_{\mathsf{ClauseSAT}}, c, (w_{\mathsf{BARG},1}, \ldots, w_{\mathsf{BARG},c}))$.
  - Let $C_{\mathsf{ValidBARG}}$ be the circuit that takes as input a proof $\pi$ and outputs $\mathsf{BARG.Verify}(\mathsf{crs}_{\mathsf{BARG}}, C_{\mathsf{ClauseSAT}}, c, \pi)$. Output

$$\mathsf{WE.Decrypt}(\mathsf{ct}_{\mathsf{WE}}, C_{\mathsf{ValidBARG}}, \pi_{\mathsf{BARG}}).$$

In the full version of this paper [25], we show that Construction 4.1 is correct, semantically-secure, and supports local decryption.

**Instantiation.** Construction 4.1 yields a succinct witness encryption scheme for CNF policies from plain witness encryption in conjunction with somewhere statistically binding hash functions and somewhere statistically sound (index) BARGs for NP [53]. When encrypting to a Boolean circuit $C: \{0,1\}^n \times \{0,1\}^h \to \{0,1\}$, a CNF policy $P: \{0,1\}^K \to \{0,1\}$ with $c$ clauses and where each clauses has size at most $t$, the size of the ciphertext in Construction 4.1 is $\mathsf{poly}(\lambda, |C|, t, \log c)$. In particular, the size of the ciphertext scales with the size of a *single* clause and polylogarithmically with the total number of clauses. In particular, when the size of each clause is constant, then the overall ciphertext size is polylogarithmic in the size of the policy. We summarize the efficiency properties of our instantiation in the following corollary:

**Corollary 4.2 (Succinct Witness Encryption for CNF Policies).** *Let $\lambda$ be a security parameter. Assuming the existence of somewhere statistically binding hash functions, somewhere statistically sound BARGs for* NP*, and witness encryption for* NP*, there exists a succinct witness encryption scheme for CNF policies (that supports local decryption). An encryption of a message $\mu$ with respect to a Boolean circuit $C: \{0,1\}^n \times \{0,1\}^h \to \{0,1\}$ and a CNF policy $P: \{0,1\}^K \to \{0,1\}$ with $c$ clauses and maximum clause size $t$ has size $|\mu| + \mathsf{poly}(\lambda, |C|, t, \log c)$. In particular, when consider CNFs where each clause contains a constant number of variables (e.g., $t = O(1)$), the ciphertext size scales polylogarithmically with the size of the policy $P$.*

*Remark 4.3 (Conjunctions of Local Monotone Predicates).* Construction 4.1 immediately generalizes to yield a succinct witness encryption scheme for conjunctions of arbitrary (local) monotone predicates.

We defer the details to the full version of this paper [25].

### 4.2 Succinct Witness Encryption for DNF Policies

In this section, we show how to construct a succinct witness encryption scheme for DNF policies by combining a witness encryption scheme together with a function-binding hash function. Our scheme is limited to trapdoor NP relations where there is an efficiently-computable algorithm that can decide membership in the language (given some trapdoor information). Specifically, we define a trapdoor NP relation as follows:

**Definition 4.4 (Trapdoor NP Relation).** *Let $\mathcal{R} = \{\mathcal{R}_n\}_{n\in\mathbb{N}}$ be a family of* NP *relations where $\mathcal{R}_n: \{0,1\}^n \times \{0,1\}^h \to \{0,1\}$ is an efficiently-computable relation. We say $\mathcal{R}$ is a trapdoor* NP *relation if there exists an efficiently-computable family of circuits $\mathcal{C} = \{C_n\}_{n\in\mathbb{N}}$ such that for all $n \in \mathbb{N}$ and all $x \in \{0,1\}^n$,*

$$C_n(x) = 1 \qquad \textit{if and only if} \qquad \exists w \in \{0,1\}^h : \mathcal{R}_n(x, w) = 1.$$

Importantly for our applications, the construction itself does not require knowledge of the trapdoor circuits $\mathcal{C}$. Otherwise, the language is in P and witness encryption is trivial. The *existence* of the trapdoor relation is only needed in the security proof (where the circuit family could be provided to the reduction algorithm as non-uniform advice). As we show in Sect. 6, succinct witness encryption for trapdoor languages suffices for applications to both computational secret sharing and the notion of monotone-policy encryption we introduce in this work.

**Construction 4.5 (Succinct Witness Encryption for DNF Policies).** Let $\lambda$ be a security parameter, $\mathcal{M}$ be a message space, and $\mathcal{P}$ be the set of Boolean formulas in disjunctive normal form. Our construction relies on the following:

- Let $\Pi_{\mathsf{FBH}} = (\mathsf{FBH.Setup}, \mathsf{FBH.Hash}, \mathsf{FBH.Verify})$ be a function-binding hash function for disjunctions of block functions.
- Let $\Pi_{\mathsf{WE}} = (\mathsf{WE.Encrypt}, \mathsf{WE.Decrypt})$ be a witness encryption scheme with message space $\mathcal{M}$.

Let $\mathcal{R} = \{\mathcal{R}_n\}_{n \in \mathbb{N}}$ be a family of trapdoor $\mathsf{NP}$ relations, where the associated family of trapdoor circuits $C_{\mathsf{td}} = \{C_{\mathsf{td},n}\}_{n \in \mathbb{N}}$ can be computed by a circuit of depth at most $d_{\mathsf{td}} = d_{\mathsf{td}}(n)$ and size at most $s_{\mathsf{td}}(n)$. We construct a succinct witness encryption scheme for $\mathcal{R}$ with message space $\mathcal{M}$ and policy space $\mathcal{P}$ as follows:

- $\mathsf{Encrypt}(1^\lambda, C, P, (x_1, \ldots, x_K), \mu)$: On input the security parameter $\lambda$, the Boolean relation $C \colon \{0,1\}^n \times \{0,1\}^h \to \{0,1\}$, the Boolean policy $P \in \mathcal{P}$ where $P \colon \{0,1\}^K \to \{0,1\}$, instances $x_1, \ldots, x_K \in \{0,1\}^n$, and the message $\mu \in \mathcal{M}$, the encryption algorithm proceeds as follows:
  - Let $c$ be the number of min-terms in $P$, and let $t \leq K$ be the maximum number of variables that appears in any min-term of $P$. For each min-term $\varphi_j$ of $P$ over instances with indices $i_{j,1}, \ldots, i_{j,t} \in [K]$, let $X_j = (x_{i_{j,1}}, \ldots, x_{i_{j,t}})$. In the following, we assume that the indices $i_{j,1}, \ldots, i_{j,t}$ of the instances that appear in $\varphi_j$ are in lexicographic order, so for every $\varphi_j$, there is a canonical description of $X_j$.
  - Define the circuit
  $$C^{(t)}_{\mathsf{td},n}(x_1, \ldots, x_t) := \bigwedge_{\tau \in [t]} C_{\mathsf{td},n}(x_\tau). \tag{4.1}$$
  Let $d_{\max}$ be its depth and let $s_{\max}$ be its size.
  - Sample $\mathsf{hk} \leftarrow \mathsf{FBH.Setup}(1^\lambda, 1^{nt}, 1^{d_{\max}}, 1^{s_{\max}}, c, \bot)$.
  - Compute a hash of the instances $(\mathsf{h}, \pi_1, \ldots, \pi_c) = \mathsf{FBH.Hash}(\mathsf{hk}, (X_1, \ldots, X_c))$.
  - Let $C_{\mathsf{DNFSat}}$ be the Boolean circuit computing the following functionality (Fig. 2):
  Compute the ciphertext $\mathsf{ct}_{\mathsf{WE}} \leftarrow \mathsf{WE.Encrypt}(1^\lambda, C_{\mathsf{DNFSat}}[\mathsf{hk}, C, \mathsf{h}], \mu)$ and output the ciphertext $\mathsf{ct} = (\mathsf{hk}, \mathsf{h}, \mathsf{ct}_{\mathsf{WE}})$.
- $\mathsf{Decrypt}(\mathsf{ct}, C, P, (x_1, \ldots, x_K), (w_1, \ldots, w_K))$: On input a ciphertext $\mathsf{ct} = (\mathsf{hk}, \mathsf{h}, \mathsf{ct}_{\mathsf{WE}})$, a Boolean relation $C \colon \{0,1\}^n \times \{0,1\}^h \to \{0,1\}$, a policy $P \in \mathcal{P}$ where $P \colon \{0,1\}^K \to \{0,1\}$, instances $x_1, \ldots, x_K \in \{0,1\}^n$, and witnesses $w_1, \ldots, w_K \in \{0,1\}^h$, the decryption algorithm proceeds as follows:

**Fixed values:** a hash key $\mathsf{hk}$, a circuit $C: \{0,1\}^n \times \{0,1\}^h \to \{0,1\}$, a hash $\mathsf{h}$

**Input:** an index $j \in \mathbb{N}$, instances $\tilde{x}_1, \ldots, \tilde{x}_t$, witnesses $\tilde{w}_1, \ldots, \tilde{w}_t$, and an opening $\pi$

On input the index $j \in \mathbb{N}$, instances $\tilde{x}_1, \ldots, \tilde{x}_t$, witnesses $\tilde{w}_1, \ldots, \tilde{w}_t$, and an opening $\pi$, output 1 if the following conditions hold:

* For all $\tau \in [t]$, it is the case that $C(\tilde{x}_\tau, \tilde{w}_\tau) = 1$.
* Check that $\mathsf{FBH.Verify}(\mathsf{hk}, \mathsf{h}, j, (\tilde{x}_1, \ldots, \tilde{x}_t), \pi) = 1$.

**Fig. 2.** The $C_{\mathsf{DNFSat}}[\mathsf{hk}, C, \mathsf{h}]$ circuit

- Let $c$ be the number of min-terms in $P$, and let $t \leq K$ be the maximum number of variables that appears in any min-term of $P$. For each min-term $\varphi_j$ of $P$ over instances with indices $i_{j,1}, \ldots, i_{j,t} \in [K]$, let $X_j = (x_{i_{j,1}}, \ldots, x_{i_{j,t}})$.
- Compute a hash of the instances $(\mathsf{h}, \pi_1, \ldots, \pi_c) = \mathsf{FBH.Hash}(\mathsf{hk}, (X_1, \ldots, X_c))$.
- Since $P$ is satisfied, there must exist an index $j \in [c]$ such that $\varphi_j$ is satisfied. Let $w = (j, x_{i_{j,1}}, \ldots, x_{i_{j,t}}, w_{i_{j,1}}, \ldots, w_{i_{j,t}}, \pi_j)$. Output $\mathsf{WE.Decrypt}(\mathsf{ct}, w)$.

In the full version of this paper [25], we show that Construction 4.5 is correct and semantically secure.

**Instantiation.** Construction 4.5 yields a succinct witness encryption scheme for DNF policies from plain witness encryption in conjunction with a function-binding hash function (for disjunction of block functions). The latter can be built from standard lattice assumptions (e.g., [14,29]). When encrypting to a Boolean circuit $C: \{0,1\}^n \times \{0,1\}^h \to \{0,1\}$, a DNF policy $P: \{0,1\}^K \to \{0,1\}$ with $c$ min-terms, each of size at most $t$, the size of the ciphertext in Construction 4.5 is $\mathsf{poly}(\lambda, |C|, t, \log c)$. Similar to the case with CNFs (Constructions 4.1 and 4.2), the size of the ciphertext scales with the size of a single min-term and polylogarithmically with the number of min-terms. When each min-term is over a constant number of variables, then the overall ciphertext is polylogarithmic in the policy size. We summarize our instantiation with the following corollary:

**Corollary 4.6 (Succinct Witness Encryption for DNF Policies).** *Let $\lambda$ be a security parameter. Assuming the existence of leveled homomorphic encryption, function-binding hash functions for disjunction of block functions, and witness encryption for* NP, *there exists a succinct witness encryption scheme for*

*DNF policies over a* trapdoor $\mathsf{NP}$ *relation. An encryption of a message* $\mu$ *with respect to a Boolean circuit* $C\colon \{0,1\}^n \times \{0,1\}^h \to \{0,1\}$ *and a DNF policy* $P\colon \{0,1\}^K \to \{0,1\}$ *with* $c$ *min-terms of size at most* $t$ *is* $|\mu| + \mathsf{poly}(\lambda, |C|, t, \log c)$. *When each min-term is over a constant number of variables (e.g.,* $t = O(1)$*), then the ciphertext size scales polylogarithmic with the size of* $P$.

*Remark 4.7 (Disjunction of Local Monotone Predicates).* Much like the case for Construction 4.1 (see Remark 4.3), Construction 4.5 readily generalizes to yield a succinct witness encryption scheme for disjunctions of arbitrary (local) monotone predicates.

We defer the details to the full version of this paper [25].

## 5 Succinct Unique Witness Map for Read-Once Bounded-Space Policies

In this section, we show how to construct a succinct unique witness map for batch $\mathsf{NP}$ languages [18]. Unique witness maps can also be viewed as a publicly-verifiable witness PRF [19,58]. As discussed in Sect. 1 (see also Remarks 5.3 and 5.2), a succinct unique witness map for batch $\mathsf{NP}$ immediately implies a succinct witness encryption for batch $\mathsf{NP}$ as well as a SNARG for monotone-policy batch $\mathsf{NP}$ (relative to the same policy class). We begin with the definition.

**Definition 5.1 (Succinct Unique Witness Map for Batch Languages).** *Let* $\mathcal{P}$ *be a family of policies. A succinct unique witness map for batch* $\mathsf{NP}$ *with policy family* $\mathcal{P}$ *is a tuple of efficient algorithms* $\Pi_{\mathsf{UWM}} = (\mathsf{Setup}, \mathsf{Map}, \mathsf{Verify})$ *with the following syntax:*

- $\mathsf{Setup}(1^\lambda, C, K) \to \mathsf{crs}$: *On input the security parameter* $1^\lambda \in \mathbb{N}$, *a Boolean relation* $C\colon \{0,1\}^n \times \{0,1\}^h \to \{0,1\}$, *and a bound on the number of instances* $K$, *the setup algorithm outputs a common reference string* $\mathsf{crs}$.
- $\mathsf{Map}(\mathsf{crs}, P, (x_1, \ldots, x_K), (w_1, \ldots, w_K)) \to \sigma$: *On input the common reference string* $\mathsf{crs}$, *a Boolean policy* $P \in \mathcal{P}$ *where* $P\colon \{0,1\}^K \to \{0,1\}$, *instances* $x_1, \ldots, x_K \in \{0,1\}^n$, *and witnesses* $w_1, \ldots, w_K \in \{0,1\}^h$, *the mapping algorithm* deterministically *outputs a canonical witness* $\sigma$.
- $\mathsf{Verify}(\mathsf{crs}, P, (x_1, \ldots, x_K), \sigma) \to b$: *On input the common reference string* $\mathsf{crs}$, *instances* $x_1, \ldots, x_K \in \{0,1\}^n$, *and a canonical witness* $\sigma$, *the deterministic verification algorithm outputs a bit* $b \in \{0,1\}$.

*Moreover, we require that* $\Pi_{\mathsf{UWM}}$ *satisfy the following properties:*

- **Completeness:** *For all* $\lambda \in \mathbb{N}$, *all Boolean circuits* $C\colon \{0,1\}^n \times \{0,1\}^h \to \{0,1\}$, *all Boolean policies* $P \in \mathcal{P}$ *where* $P\colon \{0,1\}^K \to \{0,1\}$, *and all tuples of instances* $\vec{x} = (x_1, \ldots, x_K)$ *and witnesses* $\vec{w} = (w_1, \ldots, w_K)$ *where* $P(C(x_1, w_1), \ldots, C(x_K, w_K)) = 1$, *we have that*

$$\Pr\left[\mathsf{Verify}(\mathsf{crs}, P, \vec{x}, \sigma) = 1 : \begin{array}{c} \mathsf{crs} \leftarrow \mathsf{Setup}(1^\lambda, C, K) \\ \sigma = \mathsf{Map}(\mathsf{crs}, P, \vec{x}, \vec{w}) \end{array}\right] = 1.$$

– **Uniqueness:** *For all* $\lambda \in \mathbb{N}$*, all Boolean circuits* $C\colon \{0,1\}^n \times \{0,1\}^h \to \{0,1\}$*, all Boolean policies* $P \in \mathcal{P}$ *where* $P\colon \{0,1\}^K \to \{0,1\}$*, all tuples of instances* $\vec{x} = (x_1, \ldots, x_K)$*, all tuples of witnesses* $\vec{w} = (w_1, \ldots, w_K)$*,* $\vec{w}' = (w'_1, \ldots, w'_K)$ *where* $P\big(C(x_1, w_1), \ldots, C(x_K, w_K)\big) = P\big(C(x_1, w'_1), \ldots, C(x_K, w'_K)\big) = 1$*, we have that*

$$\Pr\left[\mathsf{Map}(\mathsf{crs}, P, \vec{x}, \vec{w}) = \mathsf{Map}(\mathsf{crs}, P, \vec{x}, \vec{w}') : \mathsf{crs} \leftarrow \mathsf{Setup}(1^\lambda, C, K)\right] = 1.$$

– **Selective soundness:** *For a security parameter* $\lambda \in \mathbb{N}$ *and an adversary* $\mathcal{A}$*, we define the selective soundness game as follows:*
  - *On input the security parameter* $1^\lambda$*, algorithm* $\mathcal{A}$ *outputs a Boolean circuit* $C\colon \{0,1\}^n \times \{0,1\}^h \to \{0,1\}$*, a Boolean policy* $P \in \mathcal{P}$ *where* $P\colon \{0,1\}^K \to \{0,1\}$*, and challenge instances* $x_1^*, \ldots, x_K^* \in \{0,1\}^n$*.*
  - *If there exists* $w_1, \ldots, w_K \in \{0,1\}^h$ *such that* $P(C(x_1^*, w_1), \ldots, C(x_K^*, w_K)) = 1$*, then the challenger outputs 0. Otherwise, the challenger sends* $\mathsf{crs} \leftarrow \mathsf{Setup}(1^\lambda, C, K)$ *to* $\mathcal{A}$*.*
  - *Algorithm* $\mathcal{A}$ *outputs* $\sigma$*.*
  - *The output of the experiment is the bit* $b' = \mathsf{Verify}\big(\mathsf{crs}, (x_1^*, \ldots, x_K^*), \sigma\big)$*.*

  *The unique witness map satisfies selective soundness if for all efficient adversaries* $\mathcal{A}$*, there exists a negligible function* $\mathsf{negl}(\cdot)$ *such that for all* $\lambda \in \mathbb{N}$*,* $\Pr[b' = 1] = \mathsf{negl}(\lambda)$ *in the selective soundness game.*

– **Succinctness:** *There exists universal polynomials* $\mathsf{poly}_1, \mathsf{poly}_2$ *such that for all* $\lambda \in \mathbb{N}$*, all Boolean circuits* $C\colon \{0,1\}^n \times \{0,1\}^h \to \{0,1\}$*, all Boolean policies* $P \in \mathcal{P}$ *where* $P\colon \{0,1\}^K \to \{0,1\}$*, all tuples of instances* $\vec{x} = (x_1, \ldots, x_K)$*, all tuples of witnesses* $\vec{w} = (w_1, \ldots, w_K)$ *where* $P(C(x_1, w_1), \ldots, C(x_K, w_K)) = 1$*, the following properties hold:*
  - *The size of the reference string* $\mathsf{crs}$ *output by* $\mathsf{Setup}(1^\lambda, C, K)$ *satisfies* $|\mathsf{crs}| \le o(|P|) \cdot \mathsf{poly}_1(\lambda, |C|, \log K)$*.*
  - *The size of the canonical witness* $\sigma$ *output by* $\mathsf{Map}(\mathsf{crs}, \vec{x}, \vec{w})$ *satisfies* $|\sigma| \le \mathsf{poly}_2(\lambda, \log K)$*.*

*Remark 5.2 (Succinct Witness Encryption).* The work of [18] shows how to obtain witness encryption by composing a unique witness map with a hardcore predicate. The same transformation extends to the batch setting (and preserves succinctness). This means a unique witness map for batch NP and policy family $\mathcal{P}$ (satisfying Definition 5.1) directly implies a succinct witness encryption for batch languages with the same policy family $\mathcal{P}$.

*Remark 5.3 (Non-Adaptive SNARG for Monotone-Policy Batch* NP*).* By definition, any unique witness map for (batch) NP is also a non-interactive argument for (batch) NP (namely, the proof for a statement $x$ is simply the unique witness $w$ associated with $x$). Thus, a succinct unique witness map for batch NP with policy family $\mathcal{P}$ immediately gives a succinct non-interactive argument (SNARG) for batch NP with policy family $\mathcal{P}$ (also called a "fully-succinct" batch argument [26,30]). The size of the common reference string for the corresponding SNARG is precisely the size of the reference string for the unique witness map.

Selective security for the unique witness map then corresponds to non-adaptive soundness for the resulting SNARG. A construction satisfying the succinctness properties in Definition 5.1 gives a fully succinct monotone-policy BARG where the size of the CRS is sublinear in the policy size.

**Construction.** In this section, we show how to use indistinguishability obfuscation (together with a somewhere statistically binding hash function and an injective PRG) to construct a succinct unique witness map for monotone policies that can be implemented by a read-once bounded-space Turing machine. In particular, this captures policies like weighted thresholds.

**Definition 5.4 (Monotone Read-Once Bounded-Space Policy).** *Let $P\colon \{0,1\}^K \to \{0,1\}$ be a monotone policy. We say that $P$ can be computed by a read-once Turing machine $\Gamma$ with $S$ bits of space if there exists a tuple $\Gamma = (\mathsf{Step}_1, \ldots, \mathsf{Step}_K, c_{\mathsf{init}}, c_{\mathsf{acc}})$ with the following properties:*

- $\mathsf{Step}_i\colon \{0,1\}^S \times \{0,1\} \to \{0,1\}^S$ *is a Boolean circuit that implements the $i^{\text{th}}$ step of the Turing machine evaluation;*
- $c_{\mathsf{init}} \in \{0,1\}^S$ *is the initial configuration; and*
- $c_{\mathsf{acc}} \in \{0,1\}^S$ *is the accepting configuration.*

*Moreover, $P(\vec{\beta}) = 1$ if and only if $c_K = c_{\mathsf{acc}}$ where we define $c_0 = c_{\mathsf{init}}$ and for all $i \in [K]$, $c_i = \mathsf{Step}_i(c_{i-1}, \beta_i)$.*

**Reachable States for Read-once Turing Machines.** Our construction of a succinct unique witness map will rely on a notion of the set of reachable states for a given input. Specifically, for a string $\vec{\beta} = (\beta_1, \ldots, \beta_K) \in \{0,1\}^K$ and an index $i \in [K]$, we associate a set of states $T_{\vec{\beta},i} \subseteq \{0,1\}^S$ that are *potentially* reachable after $i$ evaluation steps. In our model, if $\beta_i = 0$, then the evaluator must use the value 0 in position $i$, but if $\beta_i = 1$, then the evaluator can choose *either* the value 0 *or* the value 1 as its input in position $i$. In the following, we will sometimes say that $\vec{\beta}' \in \{0,1\}^K$ is "consistent" with $\vec{\beta}$ if for all $i \in [K]$ where $\vec{\beta}_i = 0$, we also have $\vec{\beta}'_i = 0$. We now give the precise characterization of reachable states that we use in our analysis:

**Definition 5.5 (Reachable States for a Read-Once Turing Machines).** *Let $P\colon \{0,1\}^K \to \{0,1\}$ be a monotone policy that can be computed by a read-once Turing machine $(\mathsf{Step}_1, \ldots, \mathsf{Step}_K, c_{\mathsf{init}}, c_{\mathsf{acc}})$ with space $S$. We say an ensemble of sets $\{T_{\vec{\beta},i}\}_{\vec{\beta}\in\{0,1\}^K, i\in[0,K]}$ represents an admissible set of reachable states if it satisfies the following properties:*

- *For all $\vec{\beta} \in \{0,1\}^K$, $c_{\mathsf{init}} \in T_{\vec{\beta},0}$.*
- *For all $\vec{\beta} \in \{0,1\}^K$, $i \in [K]$, and $c \in \{0,1\}^S$ where $c \in T_{\vec{\beta},i-1}$, we have $\mathsf{Step}_i(c, 0) \in T_{\vec{\beta},i}$.*
- *For all $\vec{\beta} \in \{0,1\}^K$, $i \in [K]$, and $c \in \{0,1\}^S$ where $c \in T_{\vec{\beta},i-1}$ and $\beta_i = 1$, we have $\mathsf{Step}_i(c, 1) \in T_{\vec{\beta},i}$.*

- *For all* $\vec{\beta} \in \{0,1\}^K$ *where* $P(\vec{\beta}) = 0$, *it holds that* $c_{\mathsf{acc}} \notin T_{\vec{\beta},K}$.

*We also associate a Boolean function* $\mathsf{Reachable}_{\vec{\beta},i} \colon \{0,1\}^S \to \{0,1\}$ *with each set* $T_{\vec{\beta},i}$ *where* $\mathsf{Reachable}_{\vec{\beta},i}(c) = 1$ *if and only if* $c \in T_{\vec{\beta},i}$. *In some settings of interest (e.g., weighted thresholds; see Remark 5.7), the Boolean circuit computing* $\mathsf{Reachable}_{\vec{\beta},i}(c)$ *has a much more compact description than enumerating the elements of* $T_{\vec{\beta},i}$.

The first property in Definition 5.5 states that the initial state must be reachable. The second property says that if a configuration $c_{i-1} \in \{0,1\}^S$ is reachable after $i-1$ steps, then the state $c_i = \mathsf{Step}_i(c_{i-1}, 0)$ must also be reachable after $i$ steps. This corresponds to the case of the evaluator taking a reachable configuration $c_{i-1}$ from the first $i-1$ steps and reading the bit 0 on Step $i$. When $\beta_i = 1$, the second property says that the state $\mathsf{Step}_i(c_{i-1}, 1)$ must also be reachable after $i$ steps. This corresponds to the evaluator taking $c_{i-1}$ and reading the bit 1 on Step $i$. The final property says that if $\vec{\beta} \in \{0,1\}^K$ does not satisfy the policy, then the accepting states should *not* be reachable. Finally, Definition 5.5 allows the set $T_{\vec{\beta},i}$ to be a super-set of the actual set of reachable states that can arise from honest executions of $P$ on inputs $\vec{\beta}' \in \{0,1\}^t$ that are consistent with $\vec{\beta} \in \{0,1\}^t$. The only requirement is that $T_{\vec{\beta},K}$ does *not* contain any accepting state (but could contain non-accepting states that are technically not reachable from an honest evaluation of $P$).

*Remark 5.6 (CRS Size).* In our unique witness map construction, the size of the common reference string grows with the maximum size of the description of $\mathsf{Reachable}_{\vec{\beta},i}(c)$ rather than the cardinality of the set $T_{\vec{\beta},i}$. In settings where the description length of $T_{\vec{\beta},i}$ is much smaller than the size of the set itself (e.g., the case of weighted thresholds; see Remark 5.7), this yields constructions with a more compact CRS.

*Remark 5.7 (Reachable States for Weighted Threshold Policies).* A simple example of a monotone policy that can be computed by a read-once bounded-space Turing machine is a weighted threshold policy. A weighted threshold policy is parameterized by a set of (non-negative) weights $w_1, \ldots, w_K \in \mathbb{N}$ and a threshold $t \in \mathbb{N}$. An input $\vec{\beta} \in \{0,1\}^K$ satisfies the policy if $\sum_{i \in [K]} \beta_i w_i > t$. Suppose the maximum weight is $W$. It is easy to implement a weighted threshold policy with a read-once Turing machine with $S = \log(KW)$ bits of space. The state $c \in \{0,1\}^S$ is an accumulator that stores the current (weighted) sum and the $\mathsf{Step}_i(c_{i-1}, \beta_i)$ circuit updates the accumulated value from $c_{i-1}$ to $c_{i-1} + \beta_i w_i$. The set of accepting states consists of all values greater than the threshold. Moreover, this Turing machine has a simple and admissible set of reachable states $\{T_{\vec{\beta},i}\}_{\vec{\beta} \in \{0,1\}^K, i \in [K]}$ where $T_{\vec{\beta},i} = \left\{ t \in \{0,1\}^S : t \leq \sum_{j \leq i} \beta_j w_j \right\}$. Here, $\sum_{j \leq i} \beta_j w_j$ is the *maximum* possible value that can arise after reading the first $i$ bits of the input. As such, *every* valid configuration will be a value in the set $T_{\vec{\beta},i}$. It is easy to see that this ensemble of sets satisfies all of the admissibility requirements from Definition 5.5. Moreover, we can check membership in the set $T_{\vec{\beta},i}$ with a Boolean circuit $\mathsf{Reachable}_{\vec{\beta},i}$ of size $\mathsf{poly}(\log(KW))$ by simply hard-coding the threshold $\sum_{j \leq i} \beta_j w_j$ within $\mathsf{Reachable}_{\vec{\beta},i}$.

**Construction 5.8 (Succinct Unique Witness Map for Read-Once Bounded-Space Policies).** Let $\lambda$ be a security parameter and $\mathcal{P}$ be a family of read-once bounded-space monotone policies that can be computed by read-once space-$S$ Turing machines (see Definition 5.5). Let $s = s(\lambda, S)$ be a bound on the size of the Boolean circuit that computes a step functions $\mathsf{Step}_i$ associated with policies in $\mathcal{P}$. Without loss of generality, we assume that all of the Turing machines $\Gamma$ computing a policy in $\mathcal{P}$ share the same initial state $c_{\mathsf{init}}$ and same accepting state $c_{\mathsf{acc}}$. This is without loss of generality since we can always relabel the states of the Turing machine and apply the same relabeling to the step functions. Our construction relies on the following ingredients:

- Let $i\mathcal{O}$ be an indistinguishability obfuscator for Boolean circuits.
- Let $\Pi_{\mathsf{SSB}} = (\mathsf{SSB.Setup}, \mathsf{SSB.Hash}, \mathsf{SSB.Verify})$ be a somewhere statistically binding hash function.
- Let $\Pi_{\mathsf{PPRF}} = (\mathsf{F.KeyGen}, \mathsf{F.Eval}, \mathsf{F.Puncture})$ be a puncturable PRF. For a key $k$ and an input $x$, we will write $\mathsf{F}(k, x)$ to denote $\mathsf{F.Eval}(k, x)$.
- Let $\mathsf{G} \colon \{0,1\}^\ell \to \{0,1\}^m$ be an injective PRG with seed length $\ell = \ell(\lambda)$ and output length $m = m(\lambda)$.

Let $\lambda_{\mathsf{obf}} = \lambda_{\mathsf{obf}}(\lambda, S)$ and $\lambda_{\mathsf{PRF}} = \lambda_{\mathsf{PRF}}(\lambda, S)$ be polynomials in the security parameter which we will set in the security analysis. We construct a succinct unique witness map for batch $\mathsf{NP}$ and policy family $\mathcal{P}$ as follows:

- $\mathsf{Setup}(1^\lambda, C, K)$: On input the security parameter $\lambda$, a Boolean relation $C \colon \{0,1\}^n \times \{0,1\}^h \to \{0,1\}$, and a bound on the number of instances $K$, the setup algorithm proceeds as follows:
  - Sample two hash keys $\mathsf{hk}_{\mathsf{step}} \leftarrow \mathsf{SSB.Setup}(1^\lambda, 1^s, 1^1, K, \varnothing)$ and $\mathsf{hk}_{\mathsf{inst}} \leftarrow \mathsf{SSB.Setup}(1^\lambda, 1^n, 1^1, K, \varnothing)$ for hashing the step functions and the instances, respectively.
  - Let $s'$ be the output length of $\mathsf{SSB.Hash}(\mathsf{hk}_{\mathsf{step}}, \cdot)$ and let $n'$ be the output length of $\mathsf{SSB.Hash}(\mathsf{hk}_{\mathsf{inst}}, \cdot)$. Sample a PRF key
  $$k \leftarrow \mathsf{F.KeyGen}\big(1^{\lambda_{\mathsf{PRF}}}, 1^{s'+n'+\lceil \log K \rceil + S}, 1^\ell\big).$$
  We will denote domain elements for the PRF by a tuple $(\mathsf{h}_{\mathsf{step}}, \mathsf{h}_{\mathsf{inst}}, i, c)$ where $\mathsf{h}_{\mathsf{step}}$ is a hash of the step functions, $\mathsf{h}_{\mathsf{inst}}$ is a hash of the instances, $i \in [K]$ is an index, and $c \in \{0,1\}^S$ is a configuration of the Turing machine computing the policy.
  - Define the program $\mathsf{MapProg}$ as follows (Fig. 3):
  Let $\mathsf{size}_{\mathsf{MapProg}}$ be the maximum size of the program $\mathsf{MapProg}[C, K, \mathsf{hk}_{\mathsf{step}}, \mathsf{hk}_{\mathsf{inst}}, c_{\mathsf{init}}, k]$ and the corresponding programs appearing in the proof (see the full version of this paper [25]). Compute the obfuscated program
  $$\mathsf{ObfMap} \leftarrow i\mathcal{O}(1^{\lambda_{\mathsf{obf}}}, 1^{\mathsf{size}_{\mathsf{MapProg}}}, \mathsf{MapProg}[C, K, \mathsf{hk}_{\mathsf{step}}, \mathsf{hk}_{\mathsf{inst}}, c_{\mathsf{init}}, k]).$$
  - Define the program $\mathsf{VerProg}$ as follows (Fig. 4):
  Let $\mathsf{size}_{\mathsf{VerProg}}$ be the maximum size of the program $\mathsf{VerProg}[K, c_{\mathsf{acc}}, k]$ and

**Fixed values:** Boolean relation $C\colon \{0,1\}^n \times \{0,1\}^h \to \{0,1\}$, number of instances $K$, hash keys $\mathsf{hk}_{\mathsf{step}}, \mathsf{hk}_{\mathsf{inst}}$, the initial configuration $c_{\mathsf{init}} \in \{0,1\}^S$, and a PRF key $k$

**Input:** an index $i \in [K]$, a configuration $c \in \{0,1\}^S$, a step function $\mathsf{Step}\colon \{0,1\}^S \times \{0,1\} \to \{0,1\}$, an instance $x \in \{0,1\}^n$, hash values $\mathsf{h}_{\mathsf{step}}, \mathsf{h}_{\mathsf{inst}}$, openings $\pi_{\mathsf{step}}, \pi_{\mathsf{inst}}$, a witness $w \in \{0,1\}^h$, and a signature $\sigma \in \{0,1\}^t$

On input $(i, c, \mathsf{Step}, x, \mathsf{h}_{\mathsf{step}}, \mathsf{h}_{\mathsf{inst}}, \pi_{\mathsf{step}}, \pi_{\mathsf{inst}}, w, \sigma)$:

1. If $\mathsf{SSB.Verify}(\mathsf{hk}_{\mathsf{step}}, \mathsf{h}_{\mathsf{step}}, i, \mathsf{Step}, \pi_{\mathsf{step}}) = 0$, output $\perp$.
2. If $i = 1$ and $c \neq c_{\mathsf{init}}$, output $\perp$.
3. If $i > 1$ and $\mathsf{G}(\sigma) \neq \mathsf{G}(\mathsf{F}(k, (\mathsf{h}_{\mathsf{step}}, \mathsf{h}_{\mathsf{inst}}, i-1, c)))$, output $\perp$.
4. Compute the next configuration $c_i \in \{0,1\}^S$ as follows:

$$c_i = \begin{cases} \mathsf{Step}(c, 1) & \text{if } \mathsf{SSB.Verify}(\mathsf{hk}_{\mathsf{inst}}, \mathsf{h}_{\mathsf{inst}}, i, x, \pi_{\mathsf{inst}}) = 1 \\ & \quad \text{and } C(x, w) = 1 \\ \mathsf{Step}(c, 0) & \text{otherwise.} \end{cases}$$

5. Output $(c_i, \mathsf{F}(k, (\mathsf{h}_{\mathsf{step}}, \mathsf{h}_{\mathsf{inst}}, i, c_i)))$.

**Fig. 3.** The mapping program $\mathsf{MapProg}[C, K, \mathsf{hk}_{\mathsf{step}}, \mathsf{hk}_{\mathsf{inst}}, c_{\mathsf{init}}, k]$.

the corresponding programs appearing in the proof (see the full version of this paper [25]). Compute the obfuscated program

$$\mathsf{ObfVer} \leftarrow i\mathcal{O}(1^{\lambda_{\mathsf{obf}}}, 1^{\mathsf{size}_{\mathsf{VerProg}}}, \mathsf{VerProg}[K, c_{\mathsf{acc}}, k]).$$

- Output $\mathsf{crs} = (\mathsf{hk}_{\mathsf{step}}, \mathsf{hk}_{\mathsf{inst}}, \mathsf{ObfMap}, \mathsf{ObfVer})$.

– $\mathsf{Map}(\mathsf{crs}, P, (x_1, \ldots, x_K), (w_1, \ldots, w_K))$: On input $\mathsf{crs} = (\mathsf{hk}_{\mathsf{step}}, \mathsf{hk}_{\mathsf{inst}}, \mathsf{ObfMap}, \mathsf{ObfVer})$, a policy $P \in \mathcal{P}$ computed by a Turing machine $\Gamma = (\mathsf{Step}_1, \ldots, \mathsf{Step}_K, c_{\mathsf{init}}, c_{\mathsf{acc}})$, instances $x_1, \ldots, x_K \in \{0,1\}^n$, and witnesses $w_1, \ldots, w_K \in \{0,1\}^h$, the mapping algorithm proceeds as follows:

- Compute hashes of the step functions and the instances:

$$(\mathsf{h}_{\mathsf{step}}, \pi_{\mathsf{step},1}, \ldots, \pi_{\mathsf{step},K}) = \mathsf{SSB.Hash}(\mathsf{hk}_{\mathsf{step}}, (\mathsf{Step}_1, \ldots, \mathsf{Step}_K))$$
$$(\mathsf{h}_{\mathsf{inst}}, \pi_{\mathsf{inst},1}, \ldots, \pi_{\mathsf{inst},K}) = \mathsf{SSB.Hash}(\mathsf{hk}_{\mathsf{inst}}, (x_1, \ldots, x_K)).$$

- Initialize $c_0 = c_{\mathsf{init}}$ and $\sigma_0 = \perp$. For each $i \in [K]$, compute

$$(c_i, \sigma_i) = \mathsf{ObfMap}(i, c_{i-1}, \mathsf{Step}_i, x_i, \mathsf{h}_{\mathsf{step}}, \mathsf{h}_{\mathsf{inst}}, \pi_{\mathsf{step},i}, \pi_{\mathsf{inst},i}, w_i, \sigma_{i-1}).$$

- Output $\sigma_K$.

**Fixed values:** number of instances $K$, the accepting configuration $c_{\mathsf{acc}}$, and a PRF key $k$
**Input:** hash values $\mathsf{h}_{\mathsf{step}}, \mathsf{h}_{\mathsf{inst}}$, and a signature $\sigma \in \{0,1\}^t$
On input $(\mathsf{h}_{\mathsf{step}}, \mathsf{h}_{\mathsf{inst}}, \sigma)$:

1. If $\mathsf{G}(\sigma) = \mathsf{G}(\mathsf{F}(k, (\mathsf{h}_{\mathsf{step}}, \mathsf{h}_{\mathsf{inst}}, K, c_{\mathsf{acc}})))$, output 1.
2. Else, output 0.

**Fig. 4.** The verification program $\mathsf{VerProg}[K, c_{\mathsf{acc}}, k]$.

- $\mathsf{Verify}(\mathsf{crs}, P, (x_1, \ldots, x_K), \sigma)$: On input $\mathsf{crs} = (\mathsf{hk}_{\mathsf{step}}, \mathsf{hk}_{\mathsf{inst}}, \mathsf{ObfMap}, \mathsf{ObfVer})$, a policy $P \in \mathcal{P}$ computed by a Turing machine $\Gamma = (\mathsf{Step}_1, \ldots, \mathsf{Step}_K, c_{\mathsf{init}}, c_{\mathsf{acc}})$, instances $x_1, \ldots, x_K \in \{0,1\}^n$, and a signature $\sigma$, the verification algorithm proceeds as follows:
  - Compute $\mathsf{h}_{\mathsf{step}}$ and $\mathsf{h}_{\mathsf{inst}}$ from $(\mathsf{Step}_1, \ldots, \mathsf{Step}_k)$ and $(x_1, \ldots, x_k)$ as in $\mathsf{Prove}$.
  - Output $\mathsf{ObfVer}(\mathsf{h}_{\mathsf{step}}, \mathsf{h}_{\mathsf{inst}}, \sigma)$.

We give the correctness and security analysis of Construction 5.8 in the full version of this paper [25].

## 6 Applications

In the full version of this paper [25], we describe two immediate applications of succinct witness encryption for batch languages. The first application is to succinct computational secret sharing [5] and the second is to distributed monotone-policy encryption, a generalization of notions like distributed broadcast encryption [10,57] and threshold encryption with silent setup [6,33].

**Acknowledgments.** We thank Yuval Ishai for extensive discussions in an early phase of this project. We thank the anonymous Asiacrypt reviewers for helpful feedback. Brent Waters is supported by NSF CNS-2318701, and a Simons Investigator award. David J. Wu is supported by NSF CNS-2140975, CNS-2318701, a Sloan Fellowship, a Microsoft Research Faculty Fellowship, a Google Research Scholar Award, and an Amazon Research Award.

## References

1. Abram, D., Scholl, P., Yakoubov, S.: How to remove a trusted dealer in one round. In: Dunkelman, O., Dziembowski, S. (eds.) EUROCRYPT 2022. LNCS, vol. 13275, pp. 790–820. Springer, Cham (2022). https://doi.org/10.1007/978-3-031-06944-4_27

2. Agrawal, S., Kumari, S., Yamada, S.: Pseudorandom multi-input functional encryption and applications. IACR Cryptol. ePrint Arch. (2024)
3. Agrawal, S., Modi, A., Yadav, A., Yamada, S.: Evasive LWE: attacks, variants & obfustopia. IACR Cryptol. ePrint Arch., p. 375 (2025)
4. Ananth, P., Boneh, D., Garg, S., Sahai, A., Zhandry, M.: Differing-inputs obfuscation and applications. IACR Cryptol. ePrint Arch. (2013)
5. Applebaum, B., Beimel, A., Ishai, Y., Kushilevitz, E., Liu, T., Vaikuntanathan, V.: Succinct computational secret sharing. In: STOC (2023)
6. Avitabile, G., Döttling, N., Magri, B., Sakkas, C., Wohnig, S.: Signature-based witness encryption with compact ciphertext. In: Chung, K.M., Sasaki, Y. (eds.) ASIACRYPT 2024. LNCS, vol. 15484, pp. 3–31. Springer, Singapore (2024). https://doi.org/10.1007/978-981-96-0875-1_1
7. Badrinarayanan, S., Garg, S., Ishai, Y., Sahai, A., Wadia, A.: Two-message witness indistinguishability and secure computation in the plain model from new assumptions. In: Takagi, T., Peyrin, T. (eds.) ASIACRYPT 2017. LNCS, vol. 10626, pp. 275–303. Springer, Cham (2017). https://doi.org/10.1007/978-3-319-70700-6_10
8. Bitansky, N., Garg, S., Lin, H., Pass, R., Telang, S.: Succinct randomized encodings and their applications. In: STOC (2015)
9. Boneh, D., Ishai, Y., Sahai, A., Wu, D.J.: Quasi-optimal SNARGs via linear multi-prover interactive proofs. In: Nielsen, J.B., Rijmen, V. (eds.) EUROCRYPT 2018. LNCS, vol. 10822, pp. 222–255. Springer, Cham (2018). https://doi.org/10.1007/978-3-319-78372-7_8
10. Boneh, D., Zhandry, M.: Multiparty key exchange, efficient traitor tracing, and more from indistinguishability obfuscation. In: Garay, J.A., Gennaro, R. (eds.) CRYPTO 2014. LNCS, vol. 8616, pp. 480–499. Springer, Heidelberg (2014). https://doi.org/10.1007/978-3-662-44371-2_27
11. Boyle, E., Couteau, G., Gilboa, N., Ishai, Y., Kohl, L., Scholl, P.: Efficient pseudorandom correlation generators: silent OT extension and more. In: Boldyreva, A., Micciancio, D. (eds.) CRYPTO 2019. LNCS, vol. 11694, pp. 489–518. Springer, Cham (2019). https://doi.org/10.1007/978-3-030-26954-8_16
12. Brakerski, Z., Brodsky, M.F., Kalai, Y.T., Lombardi, A., Paneth, O.: SNARGs for Monotone Policy Batch NP. In: Handschuh, H., Lysyanskaya, A. (eds.) CRYPTO 2023. LNCS, vol. 14082, pp. 252–283. Springer, Cham (2023). https://doi.org/10.1007/978-3-031-38545-2_9
13. Brakerski, Z., Holmgren, J., Kalai, Y.T.: Non-interactive delegation and batch NP verification from standard computational assumptions. In: STOC (2017)
14. Brakerski, Z., Vaikuntanathan, V.: Efficient fully homomorphic encryption from (standard) LWE. In: FOCS (2011)
15. Branco, P., et al.: Pseudorandom Obfuscation and Applications. In: Tauman Kalai, Y., Kamara, S.F. (eds.) CRYPTO 2025. LNCS, vol. 16004, pp. 663–698. Springer, Cham (2025). https://doi.org/10.1007/978-3-032-01901-1_21
16. Brzuska, C., Ünal, A., Woo, I.K.Y.: Evasive LWE assumptions: definitions, classes, and counterexamples. In: Chung, K.M., Sasaki, Y. (eds.) ASIACRYPT 2024. LNCS, vol. 15487, pp. 418–449. Springer, Singapore (2025). https://doi.org/10.1007/978-981-96-0894-2_14
17. Canetti, R., Holmgren, J., Jain, A., Vaikuntanathan, V.: Succinct garbling and indistinguishability obfuscation for RAM programs. In: STOC (2015)
18. Chakraborty, S., Prabhakaran, M., Wichs, D.: Witness maps and applications. In: PKC (2020)

19. Chakraborty, S., Prabhakaran, M., Wichs, D.: A Map of Witness Maps: New Definitions and Connections. In: Boldyreva, A., Kolesnikov, V. (eds.) PKC 2023. LNCS, vol. 13941, pp. 635–662. Springer, Cham (2023). https://doi.org/10.1007/978-3-031-31371-4_22
20. Champion, J., Hsieh, Y.C., Wu, D.J.: Registered ABE and adaptively-secure broadcast encryption from succinct LWE. In: Tauman Kalai, Y., Kamara, S.F. (eds.) CRYPTO 2025. LNCS, vol. 16002, pp. 3–34. Springer, Cham (2025). https://doi.org/10.1007/978-3-032-01881-6_1
21. Champion, J., Wu, D.J.: Distributed broadcast encryption from lattices. In: Boyle, E., Mahmoody, M. (eds.) TCC 2024. LNCS, vol. 15366, pp. 156–189. Springer, Cham (2025). https://doi.org/10.1007/978-3-031-78020-2_6
22. Chen, Y., Vaikuntanathan, V., Wee, H.: GGH15 beyond permutation branching programs: proofs, attacks, and candidates. In: Shacham, H., Boldyreva, A. (eds.) CRYPTO 2018. LNCS, vol. 10992, pp. 577–607. Springer, Cham (2018). https://doi.org/10.1007/978-3-319-96881-0_20
23. Choudhuri, A.R., Garg, S., Jain, A., Jin, Z., Zhang, J.: Correlation intractability and SNARGs from sub-exponential DDH. In: Handschuh, H., Lysyanskaya, A. (eds.) CRYPTO 2023. LNCS, vol. 14084, pp. 635–668. Springer, Cham (2023). https://doi.org/10.1007/978-3-031-38551-3_20
24. Choudhuri, A.R., Jain, A., Jin, Z.: SNARGs for $\mathcal{P}$ from LWE. In: FOCS (2021)
25. Devadas, L., Jain, A., Waters, B., Wu, D.J.: Succinct witness encryption for batch languages and applications. IACR Cryptol. ePrint Arch. (2025). https://eprint.iacr.org/2025/944.pdf
26. Devadas, L., Waters, B., Wu, D.J.: Batching adaptively-sound SNARGs for NP. In: Boyle, E., Mahmoody, M. (eds.) TCC 2024. LNCS, vol. 15365, pp. 339–370. Springer, Cham (2025). https://doi.org/10.1007/978-3-031-78017-2_12
27. Döttling, N., Jain, A., Malavolta, G., Mathialagan, S., Vaikuntanathan, V.: Simple and general counterexamples for private-coin evasive LWE. In: Tauman Kalai, Y., Kamara, S.F. (eds.) CRYPTO 2025. LNCS, vol. 16006, pp. 73–92. Springer, Cham (2025). https://doi.org/10.1007/978-3-032-01907-3_3
28. Faonio, A., Nielsen, J.B., Venturi, D.: Predictable arguments of knowledge. In: Fehr, S. (ed.) PKC 2017. LNCS, vol. 10174, pp. 121–150. Springer, Heidelberg (2017). https://doi.org/10.1007/978-3-662-54365-8_6
29. Freitag, C., Waters, B., Wu, D.J.: How to use (plain) witness encryption: registered ABE, flexible broadcast, and more. In: Handschuh, H., Lysyanskaya, A. (eds.) CRYPTO 2023. LNCS, vol. 14084, pp. 498–531. Springer, Cham (2023). https://doi.org/10.1007/978-3-031-38551-3_16
30. Garg, R., Sheridan, K., Waters, B., Wu, D.J.: Fully succinct batch arguments for NP from indistinguishability obfuscation. In: Kiltz, E., Vaikuntanathan, V. (eds.) TCC 2022. LNCS, vol. 13747, pp. 526–555. Springer, Cham (2022). https://doi.org/10.1007/978-3-031-22318-1_19
31. Garg, S., Gentry, C., Halevi, S., Raykova, M., Sahai, A., Waters, B.: Candidate indistinguishability obfuscation and functional encryption for all circuits. In: FOCS (2013)
32. Garg, S., Gentry, C., Sahai, A., Waters, B.: Witness encryption and its applications. In: STOC (2013)
33. Garg, S., Kolonelos, D., Policharla, G.V., Wang, M.: Threshold encryption with silent setup. In: Reyzin, L., Stebila, D. (eds.) CRYPTO 2024. LNCS, vol. 14926, pp. 352–386. Springer, Cham (2024). https://doi.org/10.1007/978-3-031-68394-7_12

34. Garg, S., Pandey, O., Srinivasan, A., Zhandry, M.: Breaking the sub-exponential barrier in obfustopia. In: Coron, J.-S., Nielsen, J.B. (eds.) EUROCRYPT 2017. LNCS, vol. 10212, pp. 156–181. Springer, Cham (2017). https://doi.org/10.1007/978-3-319-56617-7_6
35. Garg, S., Srinivasan, A.: A simple construction of iO for turing machines. In: Beimel, A., Dziembowski, S. (eds.) TCC 2018. LNCS, vol. 11240, pp. 425–454. Springer, Cham (2018). https://doi.org/10.1007/978-3-030-03810-6_16
36. Gentry, C., Lewko, A., Waters, B.: Witness encryption from instance independent assumptions. In: Garay, J.A., Gennaro, R. (eds.) CRYPTO 2014. LNCS, vol. 8616, pp. 426–443. Springer, Heidelberg (2014). https://doi.org/10.1007/978-3-662-44371-2_24
37. Goldwasser, S., Kalai, Y.T., Popa, R.A., Vaikuntanathan, V., Zeldovich, N.: How to run turing machines on encrypted data. In: Canetti, R., Garay, J.A. (eds.) CRYPTO 2013. LNCS, vol. 8043, pp. 536–553. Springer, Heidelberg (2013). https://doi.org/10.1007/978-3-642-40084-1_30
38. Goyal, R., Koppula, V., Waters, B.: Lockable obfuscation. In: FOCS (2017)
39. Halevi, S., Ishai, Y., Jain, A., Kushilevitz, E., Rabin, T.: Secure multiparty computation with general interaction patterns. In: ITCS (2016)
40. Hsieh, Y.-C., Jain, A., Lin, H.: Lattice-based post-quantum iO from circular security with random opening assumption (part II: zeroizing attacks against private-coin evasive LWE assumptions). In: CRYPTO (2025)
41. Huang, T.-H., Hung, W.-H., Yamada, S.: A note on obfuscation-based attacks on private-coin evasive LWE. IACR Cryptol. ePrint Arch., p. 421 (2025)
42. Hubácek, P., Wichs, D.: On the communication complexity of secure function evaluation with long output. In: ITCS (2015)
43. Kolonelos, D., Malavolta, G., Wee, H.: Distributed broadcast encryption from bilinear groups. In: Guo, J., Steinfeld, R. (eds.) ASIACRYPT 2023. LNCS, vol. 14442, pp. 407–441. Springer, Singapore (2023). https://doi.org/10.1007/978-981-99-8733-7_13
44. Koppula, V., Lewko, A.B., Waters, B.: Indistinguishability obfuscation for Turing machines with unbounded memory. In: STOC (2015)
45. Liu, Y., Mazor, N., Pass, R.: On witness encryption and laconic zero-knowledge arguments. IACR Cryptol. ePrint Arch. (2024)
46. Mukherjee, P., Wichs, D.: Two round multiparty computation via multi-key FHE. In: Fischlin, M., Coron, J.-S. (eds.) EUROCRYPT 2016. LNCS, vol. 9666, pp. 735–763. Springer, Heidelberg (2016). https://doi.org/10.1007/978-3-662-49896-5_26
47. Nassar, S., Waters, B., Wu, D.J.: Monotone policy BARGs from BARGs and additively homomorphic encryption. In: Boyle, E., Mahmoody, M. (eds.) TCC 2024. LNCS, vol. 15365, pp. 399–430. Springer, Cham (2025). https://doi.org/10.1007/978-3-031-78017-2_14
48. Nassar, S., Waters, B., Wu, D.J.: Monotone-policy BARGs and more from BARGs and quadratic residuosity. In: Jager, T., Pan, J. (eds.) PKC 2025. LNCS, vol. 15677, pp. 283–313. Springer, Cham (2025). https://doi.org/10.1007/978-3-031-91829-2_9
49. Sahai, A., Waters, B.: How to use indistinguishability obfuscation: deniable encryption, and more. In: STOC (2014)
50. Tsabary, R.: Candidate witness encryption from lattice techniques. In: Dodis, Y., Shrimpton, T. (eds.) CRYPTO 2022. LNCS, vol. 13507, pp. 535–559. Springer, Cham (2022). https://doi.org/10.1007/978-3-031-15802-5_19

51. Vaikuntanathan, V., Wee, H., Wichs, D.: Witness encryption and null-IO from evasive LWE. In: Agrawal, S., Lin, D. (eds.) ASIACRYPT 2022. LNCS, vol. 13791, pp. 195–221. Springer, Cham (2022). https://doi.org/10.1007/978-3-031-22963-3_7
52. Waters, B., Wichs, D.: Adaptively secure attribute-based encryption from witness encryption. In: Boyle, E., Mahmoody, M. (eds.) TCC 2024. LNCS, vol. 15366, pp. 65–90. Springer, Cham (2025). https://doi.org/10.1007/978-3-031-78020-2_3
53. Waters, B., Wu, D.J.: Batch arguments for NP and more from standard bilinear group assumptions. In: Dodis, Y., Shrimpton, T. (eds.) CRYPTO 2022. LNCS, vol. 13508, pp. 433–463. Springer, Cham (2022). https://doi.org/10.1007/978-3-031-15979-4_15
54. Waters, B., Wu, D.J.: A pure indistinguishability obfuscation approach to adaptively-sound SNARGs for NP. In: Tauman Kalai, Y., Kamara, S.F. (eds.) CRYPTO 2025. LNCS, vol. 16006, pp. 292–326. Springer, Cham (2025). https://doi.org/10.1007/978-3-032-01907-3_10
55. Wee, H., Wu, D.J.: Unbounded distributed broadcast encryption and registered ABE from succinct LWE. In: Tauman Kalai, Y., Kamara, S.F. (eds.) CRYPTO 2025. LNCS, vol. 16002, pp. 204–235. Springer, Cham (2025). https://doi.org/10.1007/978-3-032-01881-6_7
56. Wichs, D., Zirdelis, G.: Obfuscating compute-and-compare programs under LWE. In: FOCS (2017)
57. Wu, Q., Qin, B., Zhang, L., Domingo-Ferrer, J.: Ad hoc broadcast encryption. In: ACM CCS (2010)
58. Zhandry, M.: How to avoid obfuscation using witness PRFs. In: Kushilevitz, E., Malkin, T. (eds.) TCC 2016. LNCS, vol. 9563, pp. 421–448. Springer, Heidelberg (2016). https://doi.org/10.1007/978-3-662-49099-0_16

# Quantum

# On Split-State Quantum Tamper Detection

Thiago Bergamaschi[1(✉)] and Naresh Goud Boddu[2]

[1] UC Berkeley, Berkeley, USA
thiagob@berkeley.edu
[2] NTT Research, Sunnyvale, USA
naresh.boddu@ntt-research.com

**Abstract.** Tamper-detection codes (TDCs) are fundamental objects at the intersection of cryptography and coding theory. A TDC encodes messages in such a manner that tampering the codeword causes the decoder to either output the original message, or reject it. In this work, we study quantum analogs of one of the most well-studied adversarial tampering models: the so-called $t$-split-state tampering model, where the codeword is divided into $t$ shares, and each share is tampered with "locally".

It is impossible to achieve tamper detection in the split-state model using classical codewords. Nevertheless, we demonstrate that the situation changes significantly if the message can be encoded into a multipartite quantum state, entangled across the $t$ shares. Concretely, we define a family of quantum TDCs defined on any $t \geq 3$ shares, which can detect arbitrary split-state tampering so long as the adversaries are unentangled, or even limited to a finite amount of pre-shared entanglement. Previously, this was only known in the limit of asymptotically large $t$.

As our flagship application, we show how to augment threshold secret sharing schemes with similar tamper-detecting guarantees. We complement our results by establishing connections between quantum TDCs and quantum encryption schemes.

## 1 Introduction

The split-state tampering model, originally studied by Dziembowski, Pietrzak, and Wichs (ICS 2010) [27] and Liu and Lysyanskaya (Crypto 2012) [42], is by now a staple in information-theoretic cryptography. It corresponds to an adversarial coding scenario in which a message is encoded into a codeword divided into $t$ *shares*, $c = (c_1, c_2, \cdots, c_t)$, and each part is sent to one of $t$ different, non-communicating adversaries. The goal of the adversaries is to independently corrupt the codeword, transforming $(c_1, c_2, \cdots, c_t)$ into $(f_1(c_1), f_2(c_2), \cdots, f_t(c_t))$, in order to change the underlying message. While apriori somewhat abstract, this model connects naturally to many other cryptographic settings, including secret sharing [30], commitment schemes [32], multi-source extractors [22], etc.

Arguably, what makes the split-state model interesting is that simple goals such as error-correction (where the message is recovered) or tamper-detection

© International Association for Cryptologic Research 2026
G. Hanaoka and B.-Y. Yang (Eds.): ASIACRYPT 2025, LNCS 16252, pp. 165–192, 2026.
https://doi.org/10.1007/978-981-95-5125-5_6

(where the receiver can additionally reject) are clearly impossible, at least with classical codewords (bits).[1] Nevertheless, [27,42] showed that a weaker, but related goal known as *non-malleability* is possible, wherein the receiver is allowed to output the original message, or a completely uncorrelated message. This spurred a prolific line of work in the last decade on the design of split-state non-malleable codes with several desiderata, including smaller number of shares $t$, high coding rate, small security error, and even post-quantum security (see Sect. 1.2). However, only recently have coding schemes with quantum capabilities have been considered [2,14,16].

**Quantum Tamper Detection in the Split-State Model.** In this work, we consider a quantum analog of the split-state model, where the adversaries are non-communicating, nor are they allowed to share entanglement. However, the message is encoded into a quantum state entangled across the $t$ shares. We show, perhaps surprisingly, that *tamper detection* is possible in this model, and arises naturally as a consequence of (classical or quantum) non-malleability [16]. Concretely, we design a family of codes defined on any $t \geq 3$ shares, which can detect arbitrary adversarial unentangled tampering. Previously, this was only known in an assymptotically large limit of $t$ [14] (Eurocrypt 2024).

At first glance, it may seem that this is only possible by giving the (entangled) decoder much more power over the (unentangled) adversaries.[2] However, our conclusions are robust to a finite amount of pre-shared entanglement between the adversaries, up to a constant fraction of the blocklength $n$ in qubits of the code. This is near-optimal, in the sense that tamper-detection is impossible if the adversaries have $n$ qubits of entanglement (by the substitution attack!). Thus, we offer an alternative interpretation: The adversaries can only tamper with the message unnoticeably, if they share a macroscopic $\Omega(n)$ amount of entanglement.

**Applications.** The inspiration for our work lies in the study of non-locality in quantum systems, and their consequences to quantum cryptography. However, we find more concrete cryptographic motivation by complementing our results in two directions. First, we initiate the study of a new type of "tamper-detecting" quantum secret sharing scheme, which always detects unentangled adversarial attacks. The most technical part of our work lies in constructing such a secret sharing scheme from our new 3-split TDCs, combined with techniques from a long literature of non-malleable and leakage-resilient secret-sharing schemes [3,20,30,31]. Second, we draw connections between split-state quantum TDCs, quantum non-malleable codes, and quantum encryption schemes.

---

[1] After all, the adversaries can always replace the ciphertext with a valid codeword of a pre-agreed message. The so-called substitution attack.

[2] To some extent, an asymmetry between the decoder and adversaries is inherent even to the classical split-state setting.

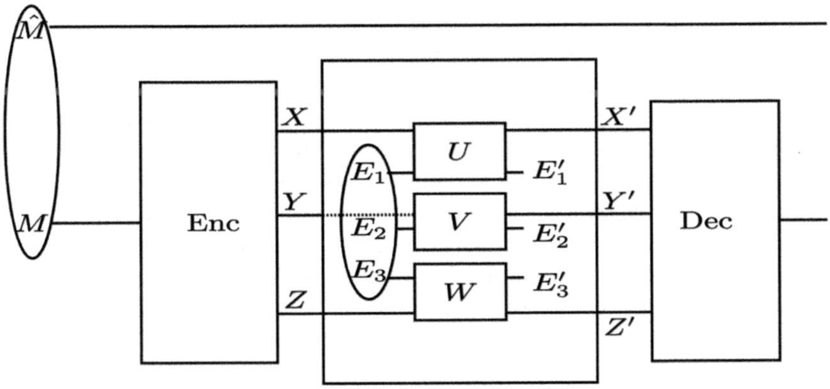


**Fig. 1.** The Quantum Split-State Tampering Model, $t = 3$ [16]. A (possibly entangled) message $M$ is encoded, and subsequently tampered with using quantum channels $U, V, W$, jointly with an entangled state on registers $E_1, E_2, E_3$.

### 1.1 Summary of Contributions

To begin, we first summarize the split-state models considered in this work. See Fig. 1 for a diagram of the tampering setup. The "amount" of pre-shared entanglement between the adversaries simply refers to the size of registers $E_1E_2E_3$.

- $\mathsf{LO}^t$: Local (unentangled) quantum operations on $t$ registers.
- $\mathsf{LO}^t_*$: Local quantum operations on $t$ registers with arbitrary pre-shared entanglement.
- $\mathsf{LO}^t_a$: Local quantum operations on $t$ registers, with at most $\leq a$ qubits of pre-shared entanglement.

While we discuss rigorous definitions shortly (Sect. 2), the underlying intuition behind a Tamper-Detection code [36] is that after the decoding operation $\mathsf{Dec}$, the receiver obtains a mixture (i.e. a convex combination) of the original message (while preserving entanglement with $\hat{M}$) *or* an abort flag $\perp$.

**Main Code Construction.** Our main result is a construction showing that tamper detection is possible in the quantum split-state model $\mathsf{LO}^t_a$, even with a constant number of shares $t \geq 3$. Moreover, our construction has constant rate, and inverse sub-exponential error.

**Theorem 1 (3-Split Tamper Detection Codes).** *For every $n \in \mathbb{N}$, $\gamma \in (0, \frac{1}{20})$, there exists a quantum tamper detection code secure against the 3-split-state tampering model $\mathsf{LO}^3_{\Theta(\gamma n)}$, of blocklength $n$, rate $\frac{1}{11} - \gamma$, and error $2^{-n^{\Omega(1)}}$.*

Again, we emphasize that such a tamper-detection code is fundamentally impossible if the message were encoded into a classical codeword. Nonetheless, we achieve tamper detection (at high rate) by appealing to a modern line of work on quantum and post-quantum non-malleable codes and extractors [2,14,16], in combination with quantum authentication schemes.

Unfortunately, our TDCs do not offer any security when composed in parallel. This is somewhat unsurprising: For instance, our TDCs against local adversaries $\mathsf{LO}^3$ involve entangled code-states. Given two TDCs, shared among the same set of parties, can the entanglement in one of them be used to break the security of the other?[3] Nevertheless, the main application (and technical challenge) in our work shows how to augment secret sharing schemes with tamper-detection guarantees, by carefully reasoning about composition in combination with new ideas in *leakage-resilient* secret sharing.

**Applications to Tamper-Resilient Secret Sharing.** In a $t$-out-of-$p$ secret sharing scheme, a dealer encodes a secret into $p$ shares and distributes them among $p$ parties, satisfying the following privacy guarantee: the shares of any (unauthorized) subset of $< t$ parties don't reveal any information about the secret, while the shares of any (authorized) subset of $\geq t$ parties are enough to uniquely reconstruct it.

As we discuss shortly, our construction from Theorem 1 is both a tamper-detection code and a 3-out-of-3 secret sharing scheme. In a natural generalization, we introduce the notion of a *tamper-detecting secret sharing scheme* or TDSSs, strengthening the *non-malleable* secret sharing schemes (NMSSs) introduced by Goyal and Kumar (STOC 2018) [30]. TDSS simulatenously strengthens both quantum secret sharing and tamper-detection codes: In a TDSSs, even if all the $p$ parties tamper with each share (locally, but without entanglement), the tampered shares of *an authorized set* are always enough to either recover the secret or reject, declaring adversaries have tampered with the shares.

Here, we present a construction of a TDSSs with a *ramp* access structure, a generalization of threshold secret sharing where the privacy and robust reconstruction thresholds differ:

**Theorem 2 (Tamper-Detecting Quantum Secret Sharing).** *For every $p, t$ s.t. $4 \leq t \leq p-2$, there exists a $t$-out-of-$p$ quantum secret sharing scheme for $k$ bit secrets, of share size $k \cdot \mathsf{poly}(p)$ qubits, where even if all the shares are tampered with an $\mathsf{LO}^p$ channel, an authorized set of size $\geq (t+2)$ either reconstructs the secret or rejects with error $2^{-(kp)^{\Omega(1)}}$.*

Our secret sharing schemes are inspired by a well-known result by Aggarwal et al. [3] (Crypto 2019), who showed how to compile generic secret sharing schemes into a leakage-resilient and non-malleable secret sharing schemes. Informally, their approach to NMSS can be viewed as "concatenating" secret sharing schemes with 2-split NMCs. Here, we revisit their compiler by combining it with our new (3-split) tamper-detection code. As previously mentioned, proving the security of our compilers is the main challenge in this work and requires a number

[3] Similar contraints arise in the parallel composition of (entangled) quantum data-hiding schemes against LOCC (unentangled) adversaries.

of new ideas, including relying on new quantum secure forms of leakage-resilient secret sharing schemes (see Sect. 2).

**Connections to Quantum Encryption Schemes.** The notion of tamper detection studied in this work closely resembles the guarantees of quantum authentication schemes (QAS) [7,12,19,29,35]. In a QAS, a sender and receiver (who share a secret key), are able to communicate a private quantum state while detecting arbitrary man-in-the-middle attacks. A remarkable feature of *quantum* authentication schemes, in contrast to their classical counterparts, is that they encrypt the message from the view of adversaries who do not know the key. Here, we similarly show that split-state TDCs must encrypt their shares:

**Theorem 3 (Tamper-Detection Codes Encrypt their Shares).** *The reduced density matrix of each share of a quantum tamper-detection code against* $\mathsf{LO}^t$ *with error* $\varepsilon$*, is* $4\sqrt{\varepsilon}$ *close to a state which doesn't depend on the message.*

This follows from the simple but fundamental idea that adversaries that can distinguish between code-states of two known orthogonal messages, $|x\rangle, |y\rangle$, can also map between their superpositions $(|x\rangle \pm |y\rangle)/\sqrt{2}$ [1,12,34], breaking tamper-detection.

### 1.2 Related Work

**Comparison to Prior Work.** Closely related to our results on tamper detection is work by [14], who introduced the notion of a Pauli Manipulation Detection code, in a quantum analog to the well-studied classical algebraic manipulation detection (AMD) codes [25]. By combining these codes with stabilizer codes, he constructed tamper-detection codes in a "qubit-wise" setting, a model which can be understood as the unentangled $t$-split-state model $\mathsf{LO}^t$ for assymptotically large $t$ (and each share is a single qubit). However, to achieve tamper detection (and high rate), [14] relied on strong quantum circuit lower bounds for stabilizer codes [10]. In contrast, as we will see shortly, we simply leverage Bell basis measurements.

Even though TDCs are infeasible in entangled split-state model ($\mathsf{LO}^t_*$), NMCs are still feasible. [2] studied *quantum secure* versions of classical non-malleable codes in the $\mathsf{LO}^2_*$ model. [16] introduced quantum non-malleable codes, and constructed codes with inverse-polynomial rate in the $\mathsf{LO}^2_*$ model. [13], leveraging constructions of quantum secure non-malleable *randomness encoders*, showed how to construct constant rate non-malleable codes in the $\mathsf{LO}^3_*$ model.

**Other Classical Non-malleable Codes and Secret Sharing Schemes.** NMCs were originally introduced by Dziembowski, Pietrzak and Wichs [27], in the context of algebraic and side-channel attacks to tamper-resilient hardware. In the past decade, the split-state and closely related tampering models for NMCs and secret sharing schemes have witnessed a flurry of work [3–6,11,17,18,20, 21,23,24,26,28,30,31,33,36,38–42], culminating in recent explicit constructions of classical split-state NMCs of explicit constant rate 1/3 [5] and constructions with (small) constant rate but also smaller error [41].

**Non-malleable Quantum Encryption.** Other notions of non-malleability for quantum messages have previously been studied in the context of quantum encryption schemes. Ambainis, Bouda, and Winter [9], and later Alagic and Majenz [8], introduced related notions of quantum non-malleable encryption schemes which (informally) can be understood as a keyed version of the NMCs we study here. [8] showed that in the keyed setting, non-malleability actually implies encryption in a strong sense. We view the connections we raise to encryption schemes as analogs to these results in a coding-theoretic setting.

## 2 Our Techniques

We begin in Sect. 2.1 by presenting definitions of the various tampering guarantees we consider, and a reduction from non-malleability to quantum tamper-detection, which highlights the intuition behind our results. We proceed in Sect. 2.2 by describing how to construct our 3-split tamper-detection codes of Theorem 1 from classical, quantum-secure non-malleable codes. Finally, in Sect. 2.3 we describe our constructions of tamper-detection secret sharing schemes (Theorem 2) based on our 3-split TDCs.

### 2.1 Non-malleability Implies Quantum Tamper Detection

Consider the following tampering experiment. Given some message $M$, encode it into a coding scheme $c \leftarrow \mathsf{Enc}(M)$, tamper with it using a function $f$, and finally decode it to $M' = \mathsf{Dec}(f(c))$. Dziembowski, Pietrzak, and Wichs [27] formalized a coding-theoretic notion of non-malleability using a simulation paradigm: $M'$ can be simulated by a distribution $\mathcal{D}_f$ that depends only on $f$:

$$M' \approx_\varepsilon p_f \cdot M + (1 - p_f) \cdot \mathcal{D}_f, \text{ for some } p_f \in [0, 1]. \tag{1}$$

In words, the distribution over $M'$ is a convex combination of the original message $M$, and a completely uncorrelated message.

Recently, [16] introduced the notion of a *quantum non-malleable code*, where both the messages and the codewords can be quantum states, and showed how to construct them from certain *quantum-secure* versions of classical non-malleable codes. The main difference to their classical counterparts lies in the notion of an "uncorrelated message": which must either preserve, or completely break entanglement with any side-information (a property also known as *decoupling*).

**Definition 1 (Quantum Non-Malleable Codes [16]).** *A pair of CPTP channels* (Enc, Dec) *is a* quantum non-malleable code *against a tampering channel $\Lambda$ with error $\varepsilon$ if the "effective channel" satisfies*

$$\forall \psi \in \mathcal{D}(\mathcal{H}_M \otimes \mathcal{H}_{\hat{M}}) : (\mathsf{Dec} \circ \Lambda \circ \mathsf{Enc} \otimes \mathbb{I}_{\hat{M}})(\psi_{M\hat{M}}) \approx_\varepsilon p \cdot \psi_{M\hat{M}} + (1-p) \cdot \sigma \otimes \psi_{\hat{M}}, \tag{2}$$

*where $p \in [0, 1]$ and $\sigma \in \mathcal{D}(\mathcal{H}_M)$ depend only on $\Lambda$, and are independent of $\psi$.*

If instead of the arbitrary state $\sigma$, the decoder rejected by outputting a fixed flag $\sigma = \perp$, then we would refer to $(\mathsf{Enc}, \mathsf{Dec})$ as a *tamper-detection code* for $\Lambda$.

**Tamper Detection in the Unentangled Split-State Model.** The starting point of our work lies in the observation that the decoupling nature of non-malleability actually implies strong tamper-detecting guarantees in the split-state model. Here, we sketch a reduction which converts any quantum non-malleable code $(\mathsf{Enc}^t, \mathsf{Dec}^t)$ for the unentangled $t$-split model, $\mathsf{LO}^t$, into a tamper-detection code for the unentangled $(t+1)$-split model $\mathsf{LO}^{t+1}$.

Given a message state $\psi$ and some integer parameter $\lambda$, the channel $\mathsf{Enc}_\lambda(\psi)$ simply prepares $\lambda$ EPR pairs, $\Phi_{E\hat{E}}^{\otimes\lambda}$, and encodes $\psi$ and half of the EPR pairs into $\mathsf{Enc}^t$ (see Fig. 2):

$$\mathsf{Enc}_\lambda(\psi) = [\mathsf{Enc}^t_{ME} \otimes \mathbb{I}_{\hat{E}}](\psi \otimes \Phi_{E\hat{E}}^{\otimes\lambda}). \tag{3}$$

The remaining EPR halves $\hat{E}$ are placed in the additional $(t+1)$st share.

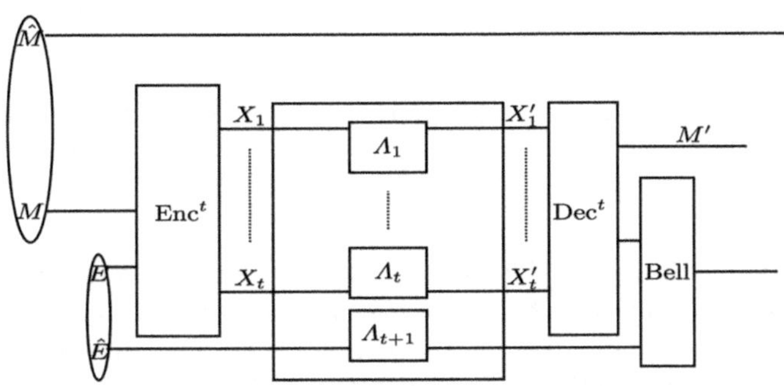


**Fig. 2.** Quantum TDC against $\mathsf{LO}^{t+1}$.

To decode (after tampering), we first decode the non-malleable code on the first $t$ shares using $\mathsf{Dec}^t$, and then measure the EPR registers in the Bell basis. Since the adversaries in $\mathsf{LO}^{t+1}$ are unentangled, the decoder $\mathsf{Dec}^t$ always either receives $\psi$ back, or a *product state* with the $(t+1)$st share. However, the Bell basis measurement is guaranteed to reject product states, and therefore can be used to verify (and reject) if the adversaries have tampered with their shares.

Unfortunately, our reduction only takes us so far. The reason is two-fold: First, to construct constant rate 3-split TDCs, we require 2-split quantum NMCs of constant rate, which remains an open problem [16]. More importantly, it is somewhat unclear whether this compiler can even be used to construction codes in the bounded storage model, or secret sharing schemes.

## 2.2 Tamper-Detection Codes in the Bounded Storage Model

Instead, to construct our 3-split TDCs in the 'bounded storage' model $\mathsf{LO}_a^3$ (with high rate), we appeal to recent constructions of split-state quantum non-malleable codes by [13,16] against $\mathsf{LO}_*$. They observed that a certain *augmented* property of classical non-malleable codes could be used to achieve non-malleability for quantum states. Here we briefly overview their approach and highlight our modifications.

**The 3-Split Quantum Non-Malleable Codes by** [13,16] combined:

(a) $(\mathsf{Enc}_{\mathsf{NM}}, \mathsf{Dec}_{\mathsf{NM}})$: A quantum secure *augmented* 2-split non-malleable code.

(b) A family of unitary 2-designs $\{C_R\}_{R\in K}$[6].

To encode a message $\psi$, their encoding channel

1. Samples a uniformly random key $R$ and encodes it into the non-malleable code, $(X, Y) = \mathsf{Enc}_{\mathsf{NM}}(R)$
2. Authenticates $\psi$: $C_R \psi C_R^\dagger$ (on some register $Q$), using the family of 2-designs keyed by $R$.

2 of the 3 parties hold the classical registers $X, Y$, and the last holds $Q$: $(Q, X, Y)$.

The non-malleability of this scheme against local adversaries with shared entanglement, $\mathsf{LO}_*^3$, relies crucially on the *augmented* security of the quantum-proof non-malleable code. Informally, suppose the two shares $X, Y$ are tampered to $X', Y'$ using shared entanglement, and $W$ denotes any quantum side-information held by one of the adversaries. By definition, the resulting joint distribution (state) over the original uniformly random key, the recovered key $R' = \mathsf{Dec}_{\mathsf{NM}}(X', Y')$, *and the side-information*, is a convex combination of the original key and a fixed, independent key:

$$R, R', W \approx p \cdot U_{R=R'} \otimes W + (1-p) \cdot U_R \otimes (R', W), \tag{4}$$

where $p \in [0,1]$ is independent of $R$, and $U_{R=R'}$ denotes the recovered key is the same as the original and uniformly random.

It turns out that the non-malleability of the secret key, suffices to achieve non-malleability for the quantum message. In the first case above, the key is recovered and is independent of the side information. By the properties of the two-design unitaries, the message is authenticated [7], and thereby we either recover it, or reject. In the second case, the key is lost to the decoder. Thereby, from the decoder's perspective, it receives a message scrambled by a random

[6] Here we point out that any Quantum Authentication Scheme (QAS) would suffice [12,19,29,35], as would a non-malleable *randomness encoder* in place of a non-malleable code [13,37]. For background on these components, refer to Section A of the full version.

unitary $C_R$, and therefore 'looks' encrypted and independent of the original message.

Inspired by our reductions, we differ from the outline above in only one detail: we encrypt the message state $\psi$ *together* with $\lambda$ halves of EPR pairs. The remaining EPR halves are handed to one of the other two adversaries, together with one of the NMC splits. In detail,

**Our Construction of 3-Split Tamper-Detection Codes** is defined by an encoding channel $\mathsf{Enc}^{\lambda}_{\mathsf{TD}}$, parametrized by an integer $\lambda$, which:

1. Prepares $\lambda$ EPR pairs, on quantum registers $E, \hat{E}$.
2. Samples a uniformly random key $R$ and encodes it into the 2-split non-malleable code $(X, Y) = \mathsf{Enc}_{\mathsf{NM}}(R)$
3. Encrypts $E$ together with the message $\psi$, using a family of 2-design unitaries keyed by $R$. Let the resulting register be $Q$.

The final 3 shares are $(Q, Y\hat{E}, X)$.

By combining the properties of the quantum secure non-malleable code with a Bell basis measurement (on states of low Schmidt rank), we prove that the construction above is a secure tamper-detection code against an even stronger 'bounded storage' adversarial model, which we refer to as $\mathsf{LO}^3_{(a,*,*)}$. In $\mathsf{LO}^3_{(a,*,*)}$, the 3 adversaries hold a pre-shared entangled state on registers $A_1, A_2, A_3$, where the 1st party (the one holding the register $Q$) is limited to $|A_1| \leq a$ qubits, but the other two may be unbounded. As we will see shortly, this model plays a particularly important role in our constructions of tamper-detecting secret sharing schemes.

### 2.3 Tamper-Detecting Secret Sharing Schemes Against LO

We dedicate this section to an overview of our construction of ramp secret sharing schemes (for classical messages) that detect local tampering. At a very high level, our secret sharing schemes are based on the concatenation of classical secret sharing schemes, with our tamper-detection codes. The key challenge lies in reasoning about the security of our tamper-detection codes when composed in parallel, which we address by combining them with extra leakage-resilient properties of the underlying classical scheme.

The outline of our construction lies in a compiler by [3]. Their compiler takes secret sharing schemes for arbitrary access structures as input, and produces either leakage-resilient or non-malleable secret sharing schemes for the same access structure. We begin with a brief description:

**The Compiler by** [3]. To encode a message $m$, they begin by

1. Encoding it into the base secret sharing scheme $(M_1, \cdots, M_p) \leftarrow \mathsf{Share}(m)$.
2. Then, each share $M_i$ is encoded into some (randomized) *bipartite* coding scheme $(\mathsf{Enc}, \mathsf{Dec})$, to obtain two shares $L_i$ and $R_i$.
3. For each $i \in [n]$, the new compiled shares amount to giving $L_i$ to the $i$-th party, and a copy of $R_i$ to every other party. At the end of this procedure, the $i$-th party has a compiled share $S_i$, where

$$S_i = (R_1, \cdots, R_{i-1}, L_i, R_{i+1}, \cdots, R_p) \tag{5}$$

The natural decoding algorithm takes all pairs of shares $(L_i, R_i)$ within an authorized set of parties, recovers $M_i \leftarrow \mathsf{Dec}(L_i, R_i)$, and then uses the reconstruction algorithm for the secret sharing scheme to recover the message $m$. By instantiating this compiler using different choices of the underlying bipartite coding scheme (strong seeded extractors or non-malleable extractors), they construct secret sharing schemes satisfying different properties (leakage resilience or non-malleability).

**Our Construction** attempts a tripartite version of the compiler by [3]. We combine

(a) $(\mathsf{Enc}^{\lambda}_{\mathsf{TD}}, \mathsf{Dec}^{\lambda}_{\mathsf{TD}})$, our 3-split-state TDC in the bounded storage model.

(b) $(\mathsf{Share}, \mathsf{Rec})$, a classical $t$-out-of-$p$ secret sharing scheme, which is additionally leakage-resilient against a certain local quantum leakage model.

On input a classical message $m$, we similarly begin by

1. Encoding it into the base secret sharing scheme $(M_1, \cdots, M_p) \leftarrow \mathsf{Share}(m)$.
2. Then, every triplet of parties $a < b < c \in [n]$ encodes a copy of their shares $M_a, M_b, M_c$ into a certain 3-out-of-3 "gadget", $\mathsf{Enc}_{\triangle}(M_a, M_b, M_c)$, which is then re-distributed between the three parties.

**Fig. 3.** A "Tamper-Detecting" Secret Sharing Scheme

We refer the reader to Fig. 3 for a description of our compiler. The most technical part of our work is to find a choice of $\mathsf{Enc}_{\triangle}$ which guarantees a local version of tamper detection for the shares in the gadget, and can be combined with the leakage-resilience of the underlying secret sharing scheme to ensure tamper detection of the actual message. We motivate this challenge and our choice of $\mathsf{Enc}_\triangle$ below.

**Weak Tamper Detection and the Selective Bot Problem.** The most natural tripartite candidate for $\mathsf{Enc}_\triangle$ would directly be our tamper-detection code. That is, $M_a, M_b, M_c$ are jointly encoded into $\mathsf{Enc}_{\mathsf{TD}}(M_a||M_b||M_c)$, resulting in 3 (entangled) quantum registers $A, B, C$, which are handed to parties $a, b, c$ respectively.

One can readily verify that this construction already offers a certain "weak" tamper detection guarantee. If any three parties $a, b, c$, were to tamper with their shares, then by the properties of $\mathsf{Enc}_{\mathsf{TD}}$[5], one can show that the *marginal* distribution over the recovered shares $M'_a, M'_b, M'_c$ is near a convex combination of the original shares $M_a, M_b, M_c$, or rejection. Similarly, given tampered shares of any authorized subset of parties $T \subset [p]$, after decoding all the copies of $\mathsf{Enc}_{\mathsf{TD}}$ in $T$, by a standard union bound we either reject or recover all the honest shares of $T$. By the correctness of the secret sharing scheme, this implies we either recover the message, or reject, $\mathsf{Dec} \circ \Lambda \circ \mathsf{Enc}(m) \in \{m, \perp\}$ with high probability.

The reason this code only offers "weak" tamper detection is that *the probability the decoder rejects may depend on the message.* That is, whether the gadgets in $T$ reject may correlate with all the shares of $T$, and therefore the message itself, violating tamper detection/non-malleability. This "selective bot" problem is a fundamental challenge in the design of non-malleable secret sharing schemes [30], and we combine two new ideas to overcome it.

**A Multipartite Encoder with staggered Entanglement.** One might hope that instead of simply relying on the privacy of the underlying secret sharing scheme, one could leverage stronger properties to simplify the tampering process (to some other effective tampering on the classical shares). While this is indeed roughly the approach we undertake, the main obstacle lies in that to implement $\mathsf{Enc}_{\mathsf{TD}}(M_a||M_b||M_c)$, one of the parties $i \in \{a, b, c\}$ will contain a register with an encryption of all three shares. Any simulation[6] of $\mathsf{Enc}_{\mathsf{TD}}$ acting directly on the shares would then seem to require communication, which is too strong to impose on the classical secret sharing scheme.

Our first idea is to instead use independent tamper-detection codes $\mathsf{Enc}_{\mathsf{TD}}^{\lambda_i}(M_i)$ for each $i \in \{a, b, c\}$, using different numbers $\lambda_i$ of "trap" EPR pairs $(E_i\hat{E}_i)$. This new gadget $\mathsf{Enc}_\triangle$ can be implemented using only *local knowledge* of $m_i$ and pre-shared entanglement between the parties, but no communication.

We find it illustrative to imagine parties $a, b, c$ in a triangle, where each party $i$ hands the EPR halves $\hat{E}_i$ to the party immediately to their left in the ordering $c > b > a$. As we will see shortly, the locality in this scheme plays an important role in addressing the selective bot problem, however, it also comes

---

[5] Technically, we additionally require $\mathsf{Enc}_{\mathsf{TD}}$ to satisfy a strong form of 3-out-of-3 secret sharing, where any two shares are maximally mixed.

[6] By simulation, we mean that the joint distribution over the recovered shares is the same as that of the quantum process.

$\mathsf{Enc}_\triangle(M_a, M_b, M_c)$: Each party $i \in \{a, b, c\}$,

1. Encodes their share into $\mathsf{Enc}_{\mathsf{TD}}^{\lambda_i}(M_i)$, resulting in registers $(Q_i, Y_i\hat{E}_i, X_i)$.
2. Party $i$ keeps the register $Q_i$, hands $X_i$ to party $i-1$, and both $Y_i, \hat{E}_i$ to party $i+1$.

The decoding channel $\mathsf{Dec}_\triangle$ simply runs $\mathsf{Dec}_{\mathsf{TD}}^{\lambda_i}$ on the 3 TDCs, and rejects if anyone of them does.

at a cost. Suppose we tamper with $\mathsf{Enc}_\triangle(M_a, M_b, M_c)$ using a channel in $\mathsf{LO}^3$. Since $\mathsf{Enc}_\triangle$ is comprised of 3 copies of $\mathsf{Enc}_{\mathsf{TD}}$ "in parallel", we apriori have no global guarantee on all 3 of them.

Nevertheless, we prove that we can recover *two out of the three shares* by picking an increasing sequence of EPR pairs, say, $\lambda_a, \lambda_b, \lambda_c = \lambda, 2\cdot\lambda, 3\cdot\lambda$ (where $a < b < c$). This follows by carefully inspecting the marginal distribution on any single recovered share $M_i'$. We observe that the effective tampering channel on the $i$th tamper-detection code can be simulated by a channel in the bounded storage model $\mathsf{LO}^3_{(\lambda_{i-1},*,*)}$: where the other two copies of $\mathsf{Enc}_{\mathsf{TD}}$ act as pre-shared entanglement which can aid the adversaries.[7] Since $\mathsf{Enc}_{\mathsf{TD}}^{\lambda_i}$ is secure against $\mathsf{LO}_{(\lambda_{i-1},*,*)}$ whenever $\lambda_i > \lambda_{i-1}$, we acquire weak tamper detection for both $M_b$ and $M_c$ (but not $M_a$).[8]

We point out that this is the main technical reason for which we relax our model to ramp secret sharing (instead of threshold): our decoder will have essentially no guarantees on the smallest share of $T$. Nevertheless, by the same union bound, all the other shares of $T$ except for the smallest are "weak" tamper-detected. If we assume $|T| \geq t+1$, we acquire weak tamper detection for the message as well.

**Correlations Between Triangles and Leakage-Resilient Secret Sharing.** To conclude our construction, we show how to leverage leakage-resilient secret sharing to ensure the probability the decoder rejects doesn't depend on the message. Together with the weak tamper detection guarantee inherited by the outer tamper-detection codes, this implies the secret sharing scheme is actually (strongly) tamper detecting.

At a high level, we devise a *bipartite* decoder which captures the following scenario. Suppose we partition an authorized subset $T = A \cup B$ into disjoint, unauthorized sets of size $\geq 3$. After independent tampering on the shares of $T$, suppose we use $\mathsf{Dec}_\triangle$ to decode all the triplets $a, b, c$ contained entirely in $A$ or

[7] Recall from Sect. 2.2 that $\mathsf{LO}^3_{(e,*,*)}$ corresponds to the set of 3-split-state adversaries aided by a pre-shared entangled state where only one of the parties is limited to $\leq e$ qubits, but the other two may have unbounded sized registers.

[8] This idea resembles [30] approach to non-malleable secret sharing by combining secret sharing schemes with different privacy parameters to acquire one-sided independence.

$B$, but we completely ignore the gadgets which cross between $A$ and $B$. What is the probability any of the gadgets rejects? Can it correlate with $m$?

It turns out this scenario is cleanly captured by a model of quantum leakage-resilience between $A$ and $B$ on the underlying classical secret sharing scheme. Note that the amount of shared entanglement between $A$, $B$ comprises $\mu = O(p^3 \cdot \lambda)$ qubits, due to all the EPR pairs in the triplets of $A \cup B$. Using the locality of the gadget $\mathsf{Enc}_\triangle$, we claim that the joint measurement performed to decide whether $A$ or $B$ reject in our compiler (a binary outcome POVM), can be simulated directly on the underlying classical secret sharing scheme by a $\mu$ qubit "leakage channel" from $A$ to $B$.

In slightly more detail, this leakage channel comprises the following experiment on the classical secret sharing scheme. The parties in $A$ are allowed to jointly process their classical shares $M_A$ into a (small) $\mu \ll |M_A|$ qubit quantum state $\sigma_{M_A}$, which is then sent to the parties in $B$. In turn, the parties in $B$ are allowed to jointly use their own shares $M_B$, together with the leakage $\sigma_{M_A}$, to attempt to guess the message. If $B$ can't distinguish between any two messages $m^0, m^1$ with bias more than $\varepsilon_{\mathsf{LR}}$, that is,

$$M_B^0, \sigma_{M_A^0} \approx_{\varepsilon_{\mathsf{LR}}} M_B^1, \sigma_{M_A^1} \text{ where } M_A^b, M_B^b = \left(\mathsf{Share}_{\mathsf{LRSS}}(m^b)\right)_{A \cup B}, \tag{6}$$

then we say the secret sharing scheme is leakage-resilient (to this bipartite quantum leakage model) with error $\varepsilon_{\mathsf{LR}}$. In the context of our compiler, if we choose the underlying secret sharing scheme to be such an LRSS, we conclude that the probability $A, B$ reject is (roughly) $\varepsilon_{\mathsf{LR}}$ close to independent of the message. Together with the weak tamper detection guarantee, we all but conclude the proof.

It only remains to construct such classical leakage-resilient secret sharing schemes. Unfortunately, this bipartite quantum leakage model is slightly non-standard, and to the best of our knowledge, there are no "off-the-shelf" solutions in the literature. This is due in part to the joint nature of the leakage model, but also to its security against quantum adversaries. In Appendix E of the full version [15], we show how to construct leakage-resilient secret sharing schemes in this model following simple modifications to a classical LRSS compiler by [20].

### 2.4 Discussion

We dedicate this section to a discussion on the future directions raised in our work.

**Optimal Tamper Detection in the Bounded Storage Model.** Our TDCs against $\mathsf{LO}_a^3$ achieve tamper detection even against adversaries whose amount of pre-shared entanglement is at most a constant fraction of the blocklength $n$. Can one design codes robust against $(1 - o(1)) \cdot n$ qubits of pre-shared entanglement, approaching the non-malleability threshold?

**Is Tamper Detection Against LO Possible in the 2-Split Model?** Based on our constructions for LO, there are a number of "natural" 2-split candidates which combine classical 2-split non-malleable codes with entanglement across the cut. Nevertheless, they all seem to fall short of tamper detection, due in part to adversaries which correlate their attack on the entangled state with their attack *on both of the shares* of the non-malleable code.

**Stronger Secret Sharing Schemes.** Can one extend our results to quantum secret sharing schemes, where the messages are quantum states? Extending [30] or [11] approach to tamper-detecting secret sharing schemes for quantum messages seems to require completely new ideas, including at the very least a definition of leakage resilient quantum secret sharing.

**Paper Organization.** In the interest of conciseness, we defer all the basic definitions to the full version [15], along with many of the proofs. In this paper, we present our main result on the construction of the TDSS.

# 3 Tamper-Detecting Secret Sharing Schemes

In this section, we prove our main result on the construction of secret sharing schemes which detect local tampering, restated below. See the subsection below for formal definitions.

**Theorem 4 (Theorem 2, restatement).** *For every $p, t$ s.t. $4 \leq t \leq p - 2$, there exists a $(p, t, 0, 0)$ secret sharing scheme for $k$ bit messages which is $(\mathsf{LO}^p, t + 2, 2^{-\max(p,k)^{\Omega(1)}})$-tamper detecting.*

In other words, no $t - 1$ shares reveal any information about the message, any $t$ honest shares uniquely determine the message, and one can detect $\mathsf{LO}$ tampering on any $(t + 2)$ shares.

We organize this section as follows. We begin by presenting definitions of the relevant secret sharing schemes. In Sect. 3.2, we introduce the relevant code components, and overview the construction, as well as presenting the construction and analysis of the "triangle gadgets" discussed in Sect. 2.3. Next, in Sect. 3.3 we present our secret sharing scheme, and in the subsequent Sect. 3.4 we present its analysis.

## 3.1 Definitions

Informally, in a $t$-out-of-$p$ secret sharing scheme, any $t$ honest shares suffice to reconstruct the secret, but no $t - 1$ shares offer any information about it.

**Definition 2 ($(p, t, \varepsilon_{\mathsf{priv}}, \varepsilon_c)$-Secret Sharing Scheme).** *Let $\mathcal{M}$ be a finite set of secrets, where $|\mathcal{M}| \geq 2$. Let $[p] = \{1, 2, \cdots, p\}$ be a set of identities (indices) of $p$ parties. A sharing channel* $\mathsf{Enc}$ *with domain of secrets $\mathcal{M}$ is a $(p, t, \varepsilon_{\mathsf{priv}}, \varepsilon_c)$* threshold secret sharing scheme *if the following two properties hold:*

1. ***Correctness:*** *the secret can be reconstructed by any set of parties* $T \subset [p], |T| \geq t$. *That is, for every such* $T$, *there exists a reconstruction channel* $\mathsf{Dec}_T$ *such that*

$$\forall m \in \mathcal{M}: \ \mathbb{P}[\mathsf{Dec}_T \circ \mathsf{Enc}(m)_T \neq m] \leq \varepsilon_c \tag{7}$$

2. ***Statistical Privacy:*** *Any collusion of* $|T| \leq t-1$ *parties has "almost" no information about the underlying secret. That is, for every distinguisher* $D$ *with binary output:*

$$\forall m_0, m_1 \in \mathcal{M}: \ |\mathbb{P}[D(\mathsf{Enc}(m_0)_T) = 1] - \mathbb{P}[D(\mathsf{Enc}(m_1)_T) = 1]| \leq \varepsilon_{\mathsf{priv}} \tag{8}$$

We point out that we use the same syntactic definition of secret sharing for schemes which hide classical messages into classical or quantum ciphers. Integral in our constructions are classical secret sharing schemes which offer privacy guarantees even if unauthorized subsets are allowed to leak information about their shares to each other in an attempt to distinguish the message.

**Definition 3 (Leakage-Resilient Secret Sharing).** *Let* $(\mathsf{Share}, \mathsf{Rec})$ *be a secret sharing scheme with randomized sharing function* $\mathsf{Share} : \mathcal{M} \to \{\{0,1\}^{l'}\}^p$, *and let* $\mathcal{F}$ *be a family of leakage channels. Then* $\mathsf{Share}$ *is said to be* $(\mathcal{F}, \varepsilon_{lr})$ *leakage-resilient if, for every channel* $\Lambda \in \mathcal{F}$,

$$\forall m_0, m_1 \in \mathcal{M}: \ \Lambda(\mathsf{Share}(m_0)) \approx_{\varepsilon_{lr}} \Lambda(\mathsf{Share}(m_1)) \tag{9}$$

As an example, the standard local leakage model in the context of classical secret sharing schemes allows bounded leakage queries $\{f_i : \{0,1\}^{l'} \to \{0,1\}^{\mu}\}_{i \in K}$, on each share corresponding to an arbitrary set of indices $K \subset [n]$, and further allows full share queries corresponding to an unauthorised subset $T \subset [n]$:

$$\mathsf{Leak}(\mathsf{Share}(m)) = \mathsf{Share}(m)_T, \{f_i(\mathsf{Share}(m)_i)\}_{i \in K}. \tag{10}$$

In our constructions, we unfortunately require a slight modification to this setting, where the leakage parties $K$ are an unauthorized subset, but are allowed to *jointly* leak a small quantum state (dependent on their shares) to $T$. We formally introduce this model as follows:

**Definition 4 (Quantum $k$-Local Leakage Model).** *For any integer sizes* $p, t, k$ *and leakage length (in qubits)* $\mu$, *we define the* $(p,t,k,\mu)$*-local leakage model to be the collection of channels specified by*

$$\mathcal{F}^{p,t}_{k,\mu} = \left\{ (T, K, \Lambda) : T, K \subset [p], |T| < t, |K| \leq k, \ \text{and } \Lambda : \{0,1\}^{l' \cdot |K|} \to \mathsf{L}(\mathcal{H}) \right\}, \tag{11}$$

*where* $\log \dim(\mathcal{H}) = \mu$. *A leakage query* $(T, K, \Lambda) \in \mathcal{F}^{p,t}_{k,\mu}$ *on a secret* $m$ *is the density matrix:*

$$(\mathbb{I}_T \otimes \Lambda_K)(\mathsf{Share}(m)_{T \cup K}) \tag{12}$$

In other words, the parties in $K$ perform a quantum channel on their (classical) shares and send the $\mu$ qubit output state to $T$. To the extent of our knowledge, in the literature we do not know of LRSS constructions in this model (even with classical leakage). In the full version [15], we show that simple modifications to a construction of LRSS against local leakage by [20] provides such guarantees.

**Theorem 5.** *For every $\mu, k, t, p, l \in \mathbb{N}$ such that $k < t, t + k \leq p$, and $p \leq l$, there exists an $(p, t, 0, 0)$ threshold secret sharing scheme on messages of $l$ bits and shares of size $l + \mu + o(l, \mu)$ bits, which is perfectly correct and private and $p \cdot 2^{-\tilde{\Omega}(\sqrt[3]{\frac{l+\mu}{p}})}$ leakage-resilient against $\mathcal{F}^{p,t}_{k,\mu}$.*

Below we formalize the tamper detection properties for the secret sharing schemes that we consider in this section. In a (generic) tamper-detecting secret sharing scheme, we stipulate that the distribution over the recovered message is near convex combination of the original $m$ and $\perp$, which doesn't depend on $m$:

**Definition 5 (Tamper-Detecting Ramp Secret Sharing Schemes).** *Let a family of CPTP maps* (Enc, Dec) *be a $(p, t, \varepsilon_{\mathsf{priv}}, \varepsilon_c)$ secret sharing scheme over $k$ bit messages and $\mathcal{F}$ a family of tampering channels. We refer to* (Enc, Dec) *as $(\mathcal{F}, r, \varepsilon_{\mathsf{TD}})$* tamper-detecting *if, for every subset $R \subset [p]$ of size $|R| \geq r$ and tampering channel $\Lambda \in \mathcal{F}$, there exists a constant $p_\Lambda \in [0, 1]$ such that*

$$\forall m \in \{0,1\}^k, \quad \mathsf{Dec}_R \circ \Lambda \circ \mathsf{Enc}(m) \approx_{\varepsilon_{\mathsf{TD}}} p_\Lambda \cdot m + (1 - p_\Lambda) \cdot \perp \qquad (13)$$

### 3.2 Code Components and the Triangle Gadget

In Sect. 3.2, we describe the ingredients in our secret sharing scheme, in Sect. 3.2 we introduce the "triangle gadget", and in Sect. 3.2 we prove that it inherits two basic properties: (weak) tamper detection, and 3-out-of-3 secret sharing.

**Ingredients and Overview.** We combine:

1. $(\mathsf{Share}_{\mathsf{LRSS}}, \mathsf{Rec}_{\mathsf{LRSS}})$: A classical $(p, t, 0, 0)$-secret sharing scheme which is $\varepsilon_{lr}$-leakage resilient to $\mu$ qubits of the 3-local leakage model $\mathcal{F}^{p,t}_{3,\mu}$, such as that of Section F of the full version [15].
2. $(\mathsf{Enc}^{\lambda}_{\mathsf{TD}}, \mathsf{Dec}^{\lambda}_{\mathsf{TD}})$, $\lambda \in \mathbb{N}$: The 3-split-state quantum tamper-detection code in the bounded storage model of Theorem 1 with $\lambda$ EPR pairs, comprised of:
   (a) $\mathsf{nmExt} : \{0,1\}^q \times \{0,1\}^{\delta \cdot q} \to \{0,1\}^r$, a quantum secure two source non-malleable extractor, with error $\varepsilon_{\mathsf{NM}} = 2^{-q^{\Omega_\delta(1)}}$ and output size $r = (1/2 - \delta)q$, see Section A [15].
   (b) A family of 2-design unitaries $C_R$ on $\frac{1}{5} \cdot r$ qubits.

   From Theorem 1, $(\mathsf{Enc}^{\lambda}_{\mathsf{TD}}, \mathsf{Dec}^{\lambda}_{\mathsf{TD}})$ has message length $\frac{r}{5} - \lambda$ and is $\varepsilon_{\mathsf{TD}} \leq 2(\varepsilon_{\mathsf{NM}} + 2^{a-\lambda})$ secure against $\mathsf{LO}_{(a,*,*)}$.

A recollection of all these code components can be found in Section A of the full version.

Our approach to secret sharing attempts to extend the compiler of [3] to a tripartite setting. First, the classical message $m$ is shared into the secret sharing scheme, resulting in classical shares $(M_1, \cdots, M_p) \leftarrow \mathsf{Share}_{\mathsf{LRSS}}(m)$. Then every triplet of parties $a < b < c$ jointly encodes their shares $M_a, M_b, M_c$ into a code $\mathsf{Enc}_{\triangle}$ supported on a tripartite register, the shares of which are redistributed among $a, b, c$.

In this subsection, we present our gadget code $\mathsf{Enc}_{\triangle}$ and prove two of its relevant properties: a strong form of 3-out-of-3 secret sharing, as well as a weak form of tamper detection. In the next subsections, we show how to leverage these gadget properties together with that of the underlying leakage-resilient secret sharing scheme to achieve tamper detection, globally.

**The Triangle Gadget.** The central building block of our construction is the following 3-out-of-3 secret sharing scheme, described in Algorithm 1.

**Algorithm 1:** $\mathsf{Enc}_{\triangle}$: The "triangle gadget"

**Input:** Three parties $p_0 < p_1 < p_2 \in [p]$, three messages $M_0, M_1, M_2$, and an integer parameter $\lambda$.

**Output:** A quantum state $\mathsf{Enc}^{\lambda}_{\triangle}(M_0, M_1, M_2)$ on a tripartite register $A, B, C$.

1: Each party $i \in \{0, 1, 2\}$ encrypts their message $M_i$ into the tamper-detection code of Theorem 1, into a tripartite register $(Q_i, Y_i\hat{E}_i, X_i)$. Explicitly, party $i$:

1. Samples uniformly random classical registers $X_i, Y_i$ and evaluates the key $R_i = \mathsf{nmExt}(X_i, Y_i)$.
2. Prepares $\lambda_i = (i+1) \cdot \lambda$ EPR pairs, on a bipartite register $E_i\hat{E}_i$.
3. Samples the pseudo-random Clifford unitary $C_{R_i}$ using the sampling process $\mathsf{Samp}$. Applies $C_{R_i}$ on registers $M_i, E_i$ to generate $Q_i$.
4. Hands register $X_i$ to party $i-1 \pmod 3$, registers $Y_i, \hat{E}_i$ to party $i+1 \pmod 3$, and keeps the authenticated register $Q_i$.

2: Output registers $A, B, C$ for parties $p_0, p_1, p_2$ respectively, where

$$A = (Q_0, Y_2\hat{E}_2, X_1), B = (Q_1, Y_0\hat{E}_0, X_2), C = (Q_2, Y_1\hat{E}_1, X_0) \tag{14}$$

To decode this gadget in the presence of tampering, we use the following decoding algorithm.

$\mathsf{Dec}_{\triangle}$: We simply run the decoder $\mathsf{Dec}_{\mathsf{TD}}$ for the tamper-detection code on the registers $(Q_i, Y_i\hat{E}_i, X_i)$ corresponding to $\mathsf{Enc}_{\mathsf{TD}}(M_i)$. If any of the three are

$\perp$, output $\perp$. If otherwise, output the resulting messages $(M'_0, M'_1, M'_2)$. Note that if no tampering is present, then from the perfect correctness of the tamper-detection code $(\mathsf{Enc}_\triangle, \mathsf{Dec}_\triangle)$ is also perfectly correct.

**Analysis of the Triangle Gadget.** Before moving on to our global construction, we prove two important properties of the gadget $(\mathsf{Enc}_\triangle, \mathsf{Dec}_\triangle)$. The first is that not only is $\mathsf{Enc}_\triangle$ 3-out-of-3 secret sharing, but in fact any two shares $\mathsf{Enc}_\triangle$ are near maximally mixed. Note that 3-out-of-3 secret sharing only implies that the two-party reduced density matrices are independent of the message, but apriori they could still be entangled.

**Lemma 1 (Pairwise Independence).** *For every share $W \in \{A, B, C\}$ and fixed strings $m_0, m_1, m_2$, the two party marginal of $\mathsf{Enc}_\triangle(m_0, m_1, m_2)$ without $W$ is $\delta_{\mathsf{PI}}$-close to maximally mixed, where $\delta_{\mathsf{PI}} \leq 6 \cdot (\varepsilon_{\mathsf{NM}} + 2^{-\lambda})$.*

*Proof.* Recall that $\mathsf{Enc}^e_{\mathsf{TD}}$ is pairwise independent with error $\leq 2(\varepsilon_{\mathsf{NM}} + 2^{-e})$. The result follows from a triangle inequality. □

The second property concerns the resilience of $\mathsf{Enc}_\triangle$ to tampering in $\mathsf{LO}^3$. We prove that two of the three inputs, namely $m_1, m_2$, are individually tamper-detected:

**Lemma 2 (Share-wise Tamper Detection).** *Fix $\Lambda \in \mathsf{LO}^3$, three strings $m_0, m_1, m_2$, and an integer $\lambda$. Let $(M'_0, M'_1, M'_2) \leftarrow \mathsf{Dec}_\triangle \circ \Lambda \circ \mathsf{Enc}_\triangle(m_0, m_1, m_2)$ denote the distribution over the recovered shares. Then for both $i \in \{1, 2\}$,*

$$\mathbb{P}[M'_i \notin \{m_i, \perp\}] \leq \varepsilon_{\mathsf{Share}}, \tag{15}$$

*where $\varepsilon_{\mathsf{Share}} \leq \varepsilon_{\mathsf{NM}} + 2^{4-\lambda}$.*

By a union bound, we have $\mathbb{P}[(M'_1, M'_2) \notin \{(m_1, m_2), \perp\}] \leq 2 \cdot \varepsilon_{\mathsf{Share}}$. However, here we already exhibit the selective bot problem. The event $M'_1 = \perp$ may correlate with $M'_2$, breaking the tamper detection guarantee.

*Proof.* [of Lemma 2] Fix $m_0, m_1, m_2$, the tampering channel $\Lambda \in \mathsf{LO}^3$, and $i \in \{1, 2\}$. In Algorithm 1, note that the $i$th share of $\mathsf{Enc}_\triangle$ is comprised of registers $(Q_i, Y_{i-1}\hat{E}_{i-1}, X_{i+1})$, where

1. $Q_i$ is a share of $\mathsf{Enc}^{\lambda_i}_{\mathsf{TD}}(m_i)$
2. The only other quantum register contains $|\hat{E}_{i-1}| \leq \lambda_{(i-1)\bmod 3}$ qubits.

We can now consider the marginal distribution over the $i$th message $m_i$ after the tampering channel. The marginal distribution over the recovered share $m'_i$ in the gadget $\mathsf{Enc}_\triangle$ can be simulated using a channel $\Lambda'$ directly on $\mathsf{Enc}_{\mathsf{TD}}(m_i)$:

$$\mathrm{Tr}_{\neq i}\mathsf{Dec}_\triangle \circ \Lambda \circ \mathsf{Enc}_\triangle(m_1, m_2, m_3) = \mathsf{Dec}_{\mathsf{TD}} \circ \Lambda' \circ \mathsf{Enc}_{\mathsf{TD}}(m_i), \tag{16}$$

where $\Lambda'$ consists of a local tampering channel on $(Q_i, Y_i\hat{E}_i, X_i)$ aided by pre-shared entanglement in a particular form: the adversary who receives share $Q_i$

holds at most $a = \lambda_{i-1}$ qubits of pre-shared entanglement (but the other two may hold unbounded-size registers). This is precisely the model $\mathsf{LO}^3_{(a,*,*)}$, and we recall by Theorem 1 that $\mathsf{Enc}^e_{\mathsf{TD}}$ detects tampering against $\mathsf{LO}^3_{(a,*,*)}$ with error $2\varepsilon_{\mathsf{NM}} + 2^{4+a-e}$. Since parties $i \in \{1, 2\}$ hold more EPR pairs in their tamper-detection codes than the corresponding adversaries pre-shared, i.e. $\lambda_i - \lambda_{i-1} = \lambda > 0$ when $i \in \{1, 2\}$, we conclude their shares are tamper-detected:

$$i \in \{1,2\} : \mathbb{P}[M_i' \notin \{m_i, \perp\}] \leq 2\varepsilon_{\mathsf{NM}} + 2^{4-\lambda}. \tag{17}$$

□

### 3.3 Code Construction

We describe our encoding algorithm in Algorithm 2 below:

**Algorithm 2:** Enc: A Tamper-Detecting Ramp Secret Sharing Scheme

**Input:** A $k$ bit message $m$.

1: Encode $m$ into the LRSS, $(M_1, \cdots, M_p) \leftarrow \mathsf{Share}_{\mathsf{LRSS}}(m)$.

2: For every triplet of parties $a < b < c \in [p]$,

1. Encode the shares $(M_a, M_b, M_c)$ into the "triangle gadget" described in Algorithm 1 supported on triplets of quantum registers

$$A_{(a,b,c)}, B_{(a,b,c)}, C_{(a,b,c)} \leftarrow \mathsf{Enc}_{\triangle}(M_a, M_b, M_c) \tag{18}$$

2. Hand the $A_{(a,b,c)}$ register to party $a$, $B_{(a,b,c)}$ to $b$, and $C_{(a,b,c)}$ to $c$.

3: Let the resulting $i$th share be the collection of quantum registers

$$S_i = \{A_{(i,b,c)} : \forall b, c \text{ s.t. } i < b < c\} \bigcup \tag{19}$$

$$\{B_{(a,i,c)} : \forall a, c \text{ s.t. } a < i < c\} \bigcup \tag{20}$$

$$\{C_{(a,b,i)} : \forall a, b \text{ s.t. } a < b < i\} \tag{21}$$

We are now in a position to describe our decoding algorithm. Upon receiving the locally tampered shares of any authorized subset $T$ of size equal to $t+2$, our decoder partitions $T$ into two un-authorized subsets, and decodes the gadgets only within each partition.

**Algorithm 3:** Dec: A Bipartite Decoding Algorithm.

**Input:** An (authorized) subset $T$ of size $t+2$, and a collection of tampered quantum registers $S'_i : i \in T$.

**Output:** A $k$ bit message $M'$

1: Partition $T$ into a subset $U$ of the three smallest indexed shares, and $T \setminus U$.

2: For every triplet of parties $a < b < c$ contained entirely in $T \setminus U$ or entirely in $U$:

1. Apply the triangle gadget decoding algorithm $\mathsf{Dec}_{\triangle}$ on registers $A_{(a,b,c)}, B_{(a,b,c)}, C_{(a,b,c)}$.
2. Output $\perp$ if so does the decoder. Otherwise, let $M'_{(a,bc)}, M'_{(b,ac)}, M'_{(c,ab)}$ be the recovered shares.

3: If $M'_{(a,bc)} \neq M'_{(a,de)}$ for any two triangles $(a,b,c),(a,d,e)$ on the same side of the partition, output $\perp$. Otherwise, let $M'_U$, $M'_{T\setminus U}$ be the recovered shares from either side of the partition.

4: Remove the lowest index share of $U$ to obtain $V \subset U$ and $T \setminus U$ to obtain $W \subset T \setminus U$. Note $|V \cup W| \geq t$.

5: Run the decoder $M' \leftarrow \mathsf{Rec}_{\mathsf{LRSS}}(M'_V, M'_W)$ on the classical shares of $V \cup W$.

The main result of this section proves that the secret sharing scheme described in Algorithm 2 and Algorithm 3 above detects unentangled tampering, when handed at least $t+2$ shares.

**Lemma 3.** *Assuming the* LRSS *is* $\varepsilon_{lr}$*-resilient to* $\mu \geq 10 \cdot p^2 \cdot \lambda$ *qubits of leakage, then* (Enc, Dec) *described above is a* $(p,t,0,0)$*-secret sharing scheme which is* $(\mathsf{LO}^p, t+2, \varepsilon)$*-tamper-detecting with error* $\varepsilon = O(\varepsilon_{lr} + p^4 \cdot (\varepsilon_{\mathsf{NM}}^{1/2} + 2^{-\lambda/2}))$.

We dedicate the next subsection to its proof. By instantiating Lemma 3 above,

**Theorem 6.** *There exists an efficient* $(p,t,0,0)$ *secret sharing scheme for* $k$ *bit messages which is* $(\mathsf{LO}^p, t+3, 2^{-\max(k,p)^{\Omega(1)}})$*-tamper-detecting.*

*Proof.* We use the construction of the $(p,t,0,0)$ LRSS from Section F of [15] with message length $k$ bits, shares of length $s = k + p^2 \cdot \lambda$ bits, and error $2^{-\Omega(\lambda)}$; together with the tamper-detection codes $\mathsf{Enc}^{\lambda}$ from Theorem 1 with message size $s$, error $2^{-\lambda} + 2^{-s^{\Omega(1)}}$, and selecting $\lambda = \max(k,p)$, we conclude the corollary. □

### 3.4 Analysis

Our proof is comprised of two key lemmas, which we state and use to prove Lemma 3 and then analyze in the subsequent sections. We begin by arguing that our secret sharing scheme inherits a weak form of tamper detection from the "outer" split-state tamper-detection codes.

**Lemma 4 (Weak Tamper Detection).** *For every tampering channel $\Lambda \in \mathsf{LO}^p$, authorized subset $T \subset [p]$ of size $\geq t+2$ and message $m$, the distribution over the recovered message $M' \leftarrow \mathsf{Dec}_T \circ \Lambda \circ \mathsf{Enc}(m)$ satisfies*

$$\mathbb{P}[M' \notin \{m, \bot\}] \leq \eta_{\mathsf{TD}} = O(p^3 \cdot (\varepsilon_{\mathsf{Share}} + \delta_{\mathsf{PI}} \cdot p)) = O(p^4(\varepsilon_{\mathsf{NM}} + 2^{-\lambda})) \quad (22)$$

*In fact, all the shares of $V \cup W$ are recovered whp:*

$$\mathbb{P}[\exists i \in V \cup W : M_i' \notin \{m_i, \bot\}] \leq \eta_{\mathsf{TD}} \quad (23)$$

In other words, $(\mathsf{Enc}, \mathsf{Dec})$ is a secret sharing scheme which is weak tamper-detecting against $\mathsf{LO}^p$, so long as the decoder receives at least $t+2$ shares. As previously discussed, the reason this is only *weak* tamper detecting is due to the selective bot problem - the probability with which we reject may apriori depend on $m$. We leverage the leakage resilience of the underlying secret sharing scheme to ensure this cannot occur:

**Lemma 5 (The Selective Bot Problem).** *For every tampering channel $\Lambda \in \mathsf{LO}^p$ and authorized subset $T \subset [p]$ of size $\geq t+2$, the probability the decoding algorithm* $\mathsf{Dec}$ *in Algorithm 3 rejects is near independent of the message. That is, $\forall \Lambda \in \mathsf{LO}^p, m_0, m_1$ :*

$$\left|\mathbb{P}[\mathsf{Dec}_T \circ \Lambda \circ \mathsf{Enc}(m_0) = \bot] - \mathbb{P}[\mathsf{Dec}_T \circ \Lambda \circ \mathsf{Enc}(m_1) = \bot]\right| \leq \eta_{lr}, \quad (24)$$

*where $\eta_{lr} = O(\varepsilon_{lr} + p^2 \cdot \sqrt{\delta_{\mathsf{PI}} + \varepsilon_{\mathsf{Share}}}) = O(\varepsilon_{lr} + p^2(\varepsilon_{\mathsf{NM}}^{1/2} + 2^{-\lambda/2}))$.*

Put together, we now conclude the proof:

*Proof.* [of Lemma 3] Let the random variable $M$ denote the uniform distribution over messages, and let $m$ be any fixed value of $M$. From Lemma 4, for a fixed $\Lambda \in \mathsf{LO}^p$ and $T \subset [p]$ the distribution over the recovered message $M'$ is near a convex combination of $M$ and rejection, with bias $\gamma_m$ (dependent on $m$):

$$M'|_{M=m} \approx_{\eta_{\mathsf{TD}}} \gamma_m \cdot m + (1 - \gamma_m) \cdot \bot. \quad (25)$$

However, by Lemma 5, the probability of $\bot$ can barely depend on $M$:

$$1 - \gamma_m \approx_{\eta_{\mathsf{TD}}} \mathbb{P}[M' = \bot | M = m] \approx_{\eta_{lr}} \mathbb{P}[M' = \bot] \equiv p_{\mathsf{Adv}} \quad (26)$$

By the triangle inequality, $M'|_{M=m} \approx_{3 \cdot \eta_{\mathsf{TD}} + 2\eta_{lr}} (1 - p_{\mathsf{Adv}}) \cdot m + p_{\mathsf{Adv}} \cdot \bot$, for some fixed $p_{\mathsf{Adv}}$ dependent on $\Lambda, T$. With $\eta_{\mathsf{TD}}, \eta_{lr}$ as in the lemmas above we conclude the theorem. □

**Proof of Weak Tamper Detection (Lemma 4)**

*Proof.* [of Lemma 4] Consider any triangle $a < b < c \in [p]$ contained on the same side of the partition $(U, T \setminus U)$, and let $(m_a, m_b, m_c)$ be any fixing of their classical shares. Note that the reduced density matrix on their quantum registers $(S_a, S_b, S_c)|((M_a, M_b, M_c) = (m_a, m_b, m_c))$ contains the triangle $\mathsf{Enc}_\triangle(m_a, m_b, m_c)$, as well as the registers of all the triangles $(a', b', c')$ which intersect $(a, b, c)$. However, since each individual register of $\mathsf{Enc}_\triangle$ is maximally mixed, and all pairs of registers of $\mathsf{Enc}_\triangle$ are $\delta_{\mathsf{PI}}$ approximately pairwise independent (Lemma 1), we have

$$(S_a, S_b, S_c)|_{((M_a, M_b, M_c)=(m_a, m_b, m_c))} \approx_{3\cdot\delta_{\mathsf{PI}}\cdot p} \mathsf{Enc}_\triangle(m_a, m_b, m_c) \otimes \frac{\mathbb{I}}{\mathrm{Tr}\mathbb{I}} \tag{27}$$

The copies $\sigma = \frac{\mathbb{I}}{\mathrm{Tr}\mathbb{I}}$ of the maximally mixed state are separable across the shares $a, b, c$, and independent of $m$, and act as ancillas. Therefore, any channel $\Lambda \in \mathsf{LO}^3$ which tampers with the registers $(S_a, S_b, S_c)$ using $\sigma$ can be simulated in $\mathsf{LO}^3$ without them:

$$\begin{aligned}
&\mathsf{Dec}_\triangle \circ \Lambda \circ (S_a, S_b, S_c)|_{((M_a, M_b, M_c)=(m_a, m_b, m_c))} \\
&\approx_{3\cdot\delta_{\mathsf{PI}}\cdot p} \mathsf{Dec}_\triangle \circ \Lambda(\mathsf{Enc}_\triangle(m_a, m_b, m_c) \otimes \sigma) \\
&= \mathsf{Dec}_\triangle \circ \Lambda' \circ \mathsf{Enc}_\triangle(m_a, m_b, m_c)
\end{aligned}$$

By Lemma 2 and the triangle inequality, this implies that two of the three shares in each triangle $(a, b, c)$ are weak tamper detected:

$$\mathbb{P}[(M'_a, M'_b) \notin \{(m_a, m_b), \perp\}] \leq 2\varepsilon_{\mathsf{Share}} + 3 \cdot \delta_{\mathsf{PI}} \cdot p \tag{28}$$

By a union bound over all the triangles, either all the shares in $V \subset U, W \subset (T \setminus U)$ are recovered, or we reject with probability

$$\mathbb{P}[\forall i \in V \cup W : M'_i \notin \{m_i, \perp\}] \leq t^3 \cdot (2\varepsilon_{\mathsf{Share}} + 3 \cdot \delta_{\mathsf{PI}} \cdot p). \tag{29}$$

Since $|V \cup W|$ contains $t$ (honest) shares,

$$\mathbb{P}[M' \notin \{m, \perp\}] \leq t^3 \cdot (2\varepsilon_{\mathsf{Share}} + 3 \cdot \delta_{\mathsf{PI}} \cdot p). \tag{30}$$

□

**Proof of Leakage-Resilience (Lemma 5).** The decoder $\mathsf{Dec}_T$ of Algorithm 3 rejects a tampered message $\Lambda \circ \mathsf{Enc}(m)$ if either subset $U$ or $(T \setminus U)$ reject (up to step 3), or if the decoder for the LRSS rejects.

We begin by analyzing the first of these two possibilities. In Lemma 6, we use the leakage resilience of the underlying secret sharing scheme to argue that the event that either subset $U$ or $(T \setminus U)$ rejects cannot depend on the message $m$. To do so, we show that the measurement of whether either $U$ or $(T \setminus U)$ reject can be simulated by a leakage channel from $U$ to $(T \setminus U)$ on the shares of the classical LRSS.

**Lemma 6.** *Fix a tampering channel $\Lambda$ and subsets $T \subset [n]$, $|T| \geq t+2$ and $U \subset T$ of the smallest 3 shares in $T$. The probability $\mathsf{Dec}_T$ Algorithm 3 has rejected before step 4, does not depend on the message: $\forall m_0, m_1$ :*

$$\Big| \mathbb{P}[\mathsf{Dec}_T \textit{ aborts before Step 4 } | M = m_0] - \tag{31}$$

$$\mathbb{P}[\mathsf{Dec}_T \textit{ aborts before Step 4 } | M = m_1] \Big| \leq p^3 \cdot \delta_{\mathsf{PI}} + \varepsilon_{lr}. \tag{32}$$

*Proof.* Fix a message $m$, and let us condition on the classical $\mathsf{LRSS}$ shares $M_T$ of $m$ in $T \subset [p]$ being a fixed value $M_T = m_T = \{m_i : i \in T\}$. Now, consider the reduced density matrix $(\mathsf{Enc}(m)_T|_{M_T=m_T})$ on the shares of $T \subset [p]$ conditioned on the classical shares. It is comprised of multiple shares of $\mathsf{Enc}_\triangle$, for every triangle $a < b < c$ which intersects $T$. However, similarly to the proof of Lemma 4, the pairwise independence of $\mathsf{Enc}_\triangle$ (Lemma 1) ensures any less than three shares are near maximally mixed. It suffices to then consider the triangles contained entirely in $T$:

$$\left\| (\mathsf{Enc}(m)_T|_{M_T=m_T}) - \Big( \bigotimes_{a,b,c \in T} \mathsf{Enc}_\triangle(m_a, m_b, m_c) \Big) \otimes \frac{\mathbb{I}}{\mathrm{Tr}\mathbb{I}} \right\|_1 \leq p^3 \cdot \delta_{\mathsf{PI}} \tag{33}$$

Now, recall that $\mathsf{Enc}_\triangle^\lambda$ can be implemented using local operations between the three parties and at most $O(\lambda)$ qubits of shared entanglement. This implies that the parties in $U$ and $T \setminus U$ could prepare the reduced density matrix $T$, $(\mathsf{Enc}(m)_T|_{M_T=m_T})$, using only their own shares $m_U, m_{T\setminus U}$ and

1. Joint operations within the subsets $U, T \setminus U$.
2. At most $\mu = O(\lambda \cdot p^2)$ qubits of one-way communication from $U$ to $T \setminus U$.

If we denote $L$ as the $\mu$ qubit "leakage" register, then one can formalize the above by defining two channels $\mathcal{E}_{L,U}$ and $\mathcal{E}_{T\setminus U,L}$. $\mathcal{E}_{L,U}$ acts on the shares of $U$ producing the leakage register $L$, and $\mathcal{E}_{T\setminus U,L}$ acts on $L, T \setminus U$ respectively:

$$(\mathsf{Enc}(m)_T|_{M_T=m_T}) \approx_{p^3\delta_{\mathsf{PI}}} (\mathcal{E}_{T\setminus U,L} \otimes \mathbb{I}_U) \circ (\mathbb{I}_{T\setminus U} \otimes \mathcal{E}_{L,U}) \circ (m_{T\setminus U}, m_U) \tag{34}$$

Moreover, before step 4 in Algorithm 3 the decoding channel $\mathsf{Dec}_T$ factorizes as a tensor product of channels $\mathsf{Dec}_U \otimes \mathsf{Dec}_{T\setminus U}$, as does the tampering channel $\Lambda_U \otimes \Lambda_{T\setminus U}$. The output of the decoder (up to step 4), conditioned on the message $m$ and its shares $M_T = m_T$ can thereby be simulated using

$$(\mathsf{Dec}_T \circ \Lambda_T \circ \mathsf{Enc}(m)_T \big|_{M_T=m_T}) \tag{35}$$

$$\approx_{p^3\delta_{\mathsf{PI}}} (\mathcal{N}_{T\setminus U,L} \otimes \mathbb{I}_U) \circ (\mathbb{I}_{T\setminus U} \otimes \mathcal{N}_{L,U}) \circ (m_{T\setminus U}, m_U) \tag{36}$$

$$\text{where } \mathcal{N}_{U,L} = \mathsf{Dec}_U \circ \Lambda_U \circ \mathcal{E}_{U,L} \text{ and } \mathcal{N}_{L,T\setminus U} = \mathsf{Dec}_{T\setminus U} \circ \Lambda_{T\setminus U} \circ \mathcal{E}_{T\setminus U,L} \tag{37}$$

Let $\mathcal{N}'_{U,L}$ denote the channel which applies $\mathcal{N}_{U,L}$ on $m_U$ and then checks whether the decoder rejected (a bit $b$), leaks $b$ and $L$ to $T \setminus U$, and traces out $U$. Note that $\mathcal{N}'_{U,L}$ is in the leakage family $\mathcal{F}^{p,t}_{3,\mu+1}$, since $|U| = 3$ leaks $\mu + 1$ qubits to a subset of size $|T \setminus U| < t$. We conclude that for any two messages $m_0, m_1$, by monotonicity of trace distance under CPTP maps:

$$\Big|\mathbb{P}[\mathsf{Dec}_T \text{ aborts before Step 4 } |M = m_0] - \mathbb{P}[\mathsf{Dec}_T \text{ aborts before Step 4 } |M = m_1]\Big|$$
$$\leq 2 \cdot p^3 \cdot \delta_{\mathsf{PI}} + \|(\mathcal{N}'_{U,L} \otimes \mathbb{I}_{T\setminus U}) \circ \mathsf{Share}(m_0)_T - (\mathcal{N}'_{U,L} \otimes \mathbb{I}_{T\setminus U}) \circ \mathsf{Share}(m_1)_T\|_1$$

$\leq 2 \cdot p^3 \cdot \delta_{\mathsf{PI}} + \varepsilon_{lr}$, where last we leverage the leakage resilience of the LRSS against $\mathcal{F}^{p,t}_{3,\mu}$. □

Observe that in Algorithm 3 the LRSS can only reject if the subsets $U$ or $(T \setminus U)$ did not already reject. However, from Lemma 4, we know that if $U$ or $(T \setminus U)$ didn't reject, then (roughly) with high probability we must have recovered honest shares from the subsets $V \subset U, W \subset (T \setminus U)$ - which the LRSS must accept. We can now conclude the proof of Lemma 5:

*Proof.* [of Lemma 5] The decoder $\mathsf{Dec}_T$ rejects a tampered message $\Lambda \circ \mathsf{Enc}(m)$ with probability

$$\mathbb{P}[\mathsf{Dec} \circ \Lambda \circ \mathsf{Enc}(M) = \bot | M = m] = \mathbb{P}[\mathsf{Dec}_T \text{ aborts before Step 4 } |M = m] +$$
$$+ \mathbb{P}[\mathsf{Dec}_T \text{ doesn't abort before Step 4 and } \mathsf{Rec}_{\mathsf{LRSS}}(M'_V, M'_W) = \bot | M = m].$$

From Lemma 6, the probability either half of the partition $U$ or $T \setminus U$ rejects is $\gamma = 2p^3 \cdot \delta_{\mathsf{PI}} + \varepsilon_{lr}$ close to independent of the message:

$$\mathbb{P}[\mathsf{Dec}_T \text{ aborts before Step 4 } |M = m_0] \approx_\gamma \quad (38)$$
$$\mathbb{P}[\mathsf{Dec}_T \text{ aborts before Step 4 } |M = m_1] \quad (39)$$

Fix a real parameter $\delta$. We divide into two cases on

$$\mathbb{P}[\mathsf{Dec}_T \text{ aborts before Step 4 } |M = m_0] \quad (40)$$

**Case 1.** $\mathbb{P}[\mathsf{Dec}_T \text{ doesn't abort before Step 4 } |M = m_0] \leq \delta$, then $\forall m$,

$$\mathbb{P}\Big[\mathsf{Dec}_T \text{ doesn't abort before Step 4, and } \mathsf{Rec}_{\mathsf{LRSS}}(M'_V, M'_W) = \bot \Big| M = m\Big] \leq$$
$$\leq \mathbb{P}\Big[\mathsf{Dec}_T \text{ doesn't abort before Step 4 } \Big| M = m\Big] \leq \delta + \gamma.$$

By the triangle inequality,

$$\mathbb{P}[\mathsf{Dec} \circ \Lambda \circ \mathsf{Enc}(m_0) = \bot] \approx_{\delta+\gamma} \mathbb{P}[\mathsf{Dec} \circ \Lambda \circ \mathsf{Enc}(m_1) = \bot]. \quad (41)$$

**Case 2.** $\mathbb{P}[\mathsf{Dec}_T \text{ doesn't abort before Step 4 } |M = m_0] \geq \delta$. From the weak tamper detection guarantee in Lemma 4, $\forall m$:

$$\mathbb{P}[\mathsf{Dec}_T \text{ doesn't abort before Step 4,}$$
$$\text{and } (M'_V, M'_W) \neq (m_V, m_W) | M = m] \leq \eta_{\mathsf{TD}}.$$

Since under message $m_0$, $\mathsf{Dec}_T$ doesn't abort before Step 4 with non-negligible probability, then conditioned on that event, the shares of $V, W$ are untampered with high probability:

$$\mathbb{P}\Big[(M'_V, M'_W) = (m_V, m_W)\Big| \text{ (conditioned on)} \tag{42}$$

$$\mathsf{Dec}_T \text{ doesn't abort before Step 4}, M = m_0\Big] \geq 1 - \frac{\eta_{\mathsf{TD}}}{\delta}. \tag{43}$$

A similar statement holds for $m_1$ since

$$\mathbb{P}[\mathsf{Dec}_T \text{ doesn't abort before Step 4 } |M = m_1] \geq \delta - \gamma,$$

and consequently,

$$\mathbb{P}\Big[(M'_V, M'_W) = (m_V, m_W)\Big| \text{ (conditioned on)} \tag{44}$$

$$\mathsf{Dec}_T \text{ doesn't abort before Step 4}, M = m_1] \geq 1 - \frac{\eta_{\mathsf{TD}}}{\delta - \gamma}. \tag{45}$$

Finally, since $\mathsf{Rec}_{\mathsf{LRSS}}$ has perfect correctness, if we condition on $(M'_V, M'_W) = (m_V, m_W)$, $\mathsf{Rec}_{\mathsf{LRSS}}$ recovers the message with probability 1. Thus,

$$\forall m : \mathbb{P}\Big[\mathsf{Dec}_T \text{ doesn't abort before Step 4}, \tag{46}$$

$$\text{and } \mathsf{Rec}_{\mathsf{LRSS}}(M'_V, M'_W) \neq \bot \Big| M = m\Big] \approx_{\frac{\eta_{\mathsf{TD}}}{\delta-\gamma}} \tag{47}$$

$$\approx \mathbb{P}\Big[\mathsf{Dec}_T \text{ doesn't abort before Step 4}\Big| M = m\Big]. \tag{48}$$

We conclude

$$|\mathbb{P}[\mathsf{Dec} \circ \Lambda \circ \mathsf{Enc}(m_0) = \bot] - \mathbb{P}[\mathsf{Dec} \circ \Lambda \circ \mathsf{Enc}(m_1) = \bot]| \leq \eta_{lr}, \tag{49}$$

where, by the triangle inequality and optimizing over $\delta$ :

$$\eta_{lr} \leq \gamma + \max(\delta, \frac{\eta_{\mathsf{TD}}}{\delta - \gamma}) \leq 2\gamma + \sqrt{\eta_{\mathsf{TD}}} \leq O(\varepsilon_{lr} + p^2 \cdot \sqrt{\delta_{\mathsf{PI}} + \varepsilon_{\mathsf{Share}}}), \tag{50}$$

where we used the values of $\gamma$ and $\eta_{\mathsf{TD}}$ from Lemma 6 and Lemma 4. □

**Acknowledgements.** A preliminary version of this work appeared on arxiv at the reference [15]. We thank João Ribeiro for insights on his compilers for secret sharing schemes, Venkat Guruswami and Rahul Jain for discussions on the capacity of split-state classical and quantum non-malleable codes, and Marshall Ball for conversations on augmented quantum non-malleable codes during the early stages of this work. Finally, Umesh Vazirani and Nathan Ju for comments on the manuscript and presentation.

TB acknowledges support by the National Science Foundation Graduate Research Fellowship under Grant No. DGE 2146752. The entire work was carried out while NGB was a postdoctoral research fellow at NTT Research, Sunnyvale, USA.

## References


1. Aaronson, S., Atia, Y., Susskind, L.: On the hardness of detecting macroscopic superpositions. Electron. Colloquium Comput. Complex. **TR20** (2020)
2. Aggarwal, D., Boddu, N.G., Jain, R.: Quantum secure non-malleable-codes in the split-state model (2022). arXiv:2202.13354
3. Aggarwal, D., et al.: Stronger leakage-resilient and non-malleable secret sharing schemes for general access structures. In: Boldyreva, A., Micciancio, D. (eds.) CRYPTO 2019. LNCS, vol. 11693, pp. 510–539. Springer, Cham (2019). https://doi.org/10.1007/978-3-030-26951-7_18
4. Aggarwal, D., Dodis, Y., Lovett, S.: Non-malleable codes from additive combinatorics. SIAM J. Comput. **47**(2), 524–546 (2018). https://doi.org/10.1137/140985251, preliminary version in STOC 2014 version in STOC 2014
5. Aggarwal, D., Kanukurthi, B., Obbattu, S.L.B., Obremski, M., Sekar, S.: Rate one-third non-malleable codes. In: Proceedings of the 54th Annual ACM SIGACT Symposium on Theory of Computing, STOC 2022, pp. 1364–1377. Association for Computing Machinery, New York (2022). https://doi.org/10.1145/3519935.3519972
6. Aggarwal, D., Obremski, M.: A constant rate non-malleable code in the split-state model. In: 2020 IEEE 61st Annual Symposium on Foundations of Computer Science (FOCS), pp. 1285–1294. IEEE Computer Society, Los Alamitos, CA, USA (2020). https://doi.org/10.1109/FOCS46700.2020.00122. https://doi.ieeecomputersociety.org/10.1109/FOCS46700.2020.00122
7. Aharonov, D., Ben-Or, M., Eban, E.: Interactive proofs for quantum computations. In: International Conference on Supercomputing (2008)
8. Alagic, G., Majenz, C.: Quantum non-malleability and authentication. In: Katz, J., Shacham, H. (eds.) CRYPTO 2017. LNCS, vol. 10402, pp. 310–341. Springer, Cham (2017). https://doi.org/10.1007/978-3-319-63715-0_11
9. Ambainis, A., Bouda, J., Winter, A.: Nonmalleable encryption of quantum information. J. Math. Phys. **50**(4), 042106 (2009). https://doi.org/10.1063/1.3094756
10. Anshu, A., Nirkhe, C.: Circuit lower bounds for low-energy states of quantum code hamiltonians. arXiv abs/2011.02044 (2020). https://api.semanticscholar.org/CorpusID:226299885
11. Badrinarayanan, S., Srinivasan, A.: Revisiting non-malleable secret sharing. In: Ishai, Y., Rijmen, V. (eds.) EUROCRYPT 2019. LNCS, vol. 11476, pp. 593–622. Springer, Cham (2019). https://doi.org/10.1007/978-3-030-17653-2_20
12. Barnum, H., Crépeau, C., Gottesman, D., Smith, A.D., Tapp, A.: Authentication of quantum messages. In: The 43rd Annual IEEE Symposium on Foundations of Computer Science, 2002. Proceedings, pp. 449–458 (2001)
13. Batra, R., Boddu, N.G., Jain, R.: Quantum secure non-malleable randomness encoder and its applications (2023)
14. Bergamaschi, T.: Pauli manipulation detection codes and applications to quantum communication over adversarial channels (2023)
15. Bergamaschi, T., Boddu, N.G.: On split-state quantum tamper detection and non-malleability (2023)
16. Boddu, N.G., Goyal, V., Jain, R., Ribeiro, J.: Split-state non-malleable codes and secret sharing schemes for quantum messages (2023)
17. Brian, G., Faonio, A., Obremski, M., Simkin, M., Venturi, D.: Non-malleable secret sharing against bounded joint-tampering attacks in the plain model. In: Micciancio, D., Ristenpart, T. (eds.) CRYPTO 2020. LNCS, vol. 12172, pp. 127–155. Springer, Cham (2020). https://doi.org/10.1007/978-3-030-56877-1_5

18. Brian, G., Faonio, A., Venturi, D.: Continuously non-malleable secret sharing: joint tampering, plain model and capacity. In: Nissim, K., Waters, B. (eds.) Theory of Cryptography, pp. 333–364. Springer, Cham (2021)
19. Broadbent, A., Wainewright, E.: Efficient simulation for quantum message authentication. In: Nascimento, A.C., Barreto, P. (eds.) Information Theoretic Security, pp. 72–91. Springer, Cham (2016)
20. Chandran, N., Kanukurthi, B., Obbattu, S.L.B., Sekar, S.: Short leakage resilient and non-malleable secret sharing schemes. In: Dodis, Y., Shrimpton, T. (eds.) Advances in Cryptology - CRYPTO 2022, pp. 178–207. Springer (2022). https://doi.org/10.1007/978-3-031-15802-5_7
21. Chattopadhyay, E., Goyal, V., Li, X.: Nonmalleable extractors and codes, with their many tampered extensions. SIAM J. Comput. **49**(5), 999–1040 (2020). https://doi.org/10.1137/18M1176622, preliminary version in STOC 2016
22. Cheraghchi, M., Guruswami, V.: Non-malleable coding against bit-wise and split-state tampering. J. Cryptol. **30**, 191–241 (2013). https://api.semanticscholar.org/CorpusID:1470207
23. Cheraghchi, M., Guruswami, V.: Non-malleable coding against bit-wise and split-state tampering. In: Proceedings of Theory of Cryptography Conference (TCC). pp. 440–464 (2014), extended version in Journal of Cryptology
24. Cheraghchi, M., Guruswami, V.: Capacity of non-malleable codes. IEEE Trans. Inf. Theory **62**(3), 1097–1118 (2016). https://doi.org/10.1109/TIT.2015.2511784
25. Cramer, R., Dodis, Y., Fehr, S., Padró, C., Wichs, D.: Detection of algebraic manipulation with applications to robust secret sharing and fuzzy extractors. In: International Conference on the Theory and Application of Cryptographic Techniques (2008). https://api.semanticscholar.org/CorpusID:5864621
26. Dziembowski, S., Kazana, T., Obremski, M.: Non-malleable codes from two-source extractors. In: Canetti, R., Garay, J.A. (eds.) CRYPTO 2013. LNCS, vol. 8043, pp. 239–257. Springer, Heidelberg (2013). https://doi.org/10.1007/978-3-642-40084-1_14
27. Dziembowski, S., Pietrzak, K., Wichs, D.: Non-malleable codes. J. ACM **65**(4) (2018). https://doi.org/10.1145/3178432, preliminary version in ICS 2010
28. Faonio, A., Venturi, D.: Non-malleable secret sharing in the computational setting: adaptive tampering, noisy-leakage resilience, and improved rate. In: Boldyreva, A., Micciancio, D. (eds.) CRYPTO 2019. LNCS, vol. 11693, pp. 448–479. Springer, Cham (2019). https://doi.org/10.1007/978-3-030-26951-7_16
29. Garg, S., Yuen, H., Zhandry, M.: New security notions and feasibility results for authentication of quantum data (2016)
30. Goyal, V., Kumar, A.: Non-malleable secret sharing. In: Proceedings of the 50th Annual ACM SIGACT Symposium on Theory of Computing, STOC 2018, pp. 685–698. Association for Computing Machinery, New York (2018). https://doi.org/10.1145/3188745.3188872
31. Goyal, V., Kumar, A.: Non-malleable secret sharing for general access structures. In: Shacham, H., Boldyreva, A. (eds.) CRYPTO 2018. LNCS, vol. 10991, pp. 501–530. Springer, Cham (2018). https://doi.org/10.1007/978-3-319-96884-1_17
32. Goyal, V., Pandey, O., Richelson, S.: Textbook non-malleable commitments. In: Proceedings of the Forty-Eighth Annual ACM Symposium on Theory of Computing, STOC 2016, pp. 1128–1141. Association for Computing Machinery, New York (2016). https://doi.org/10.1145/2897518.2897657
33. Goyal, V., Srinivasan, A., Zhu, C.: Multi-source non-malleable extractors and applications. In: Canteaut, A., Standaert, F.-X. (eds.) EUROCRYPT 2021. LNCS, vol.

12697, pp. 468–497. Springer, Cham (2021). https://doi.org/10.1007/978-3-030-77886-6_16
34. Gunn, S., Ju, N., Ma, F., Zhandry, M.: Commitments to quantum states. In: Proceedings of the 55th Annual ACM Symposium on Theory of Computing (2022)
35. Hayden, P.M., Leung, D.W., Mayers, D.: The universal composable security of quantum message authentication with key recyling. arXiv, Quantum Physics (2016)
36. Jafargholi, Z., Wichs, D.: Tamper detection and continuous non-malleable codes. In: Theory of Cryptography Conference (2015). https://api.semanticscholar.org/CorpusID:1165875
37. Kanukurthi, B., Obbattu, S.L.B., Sekar, S.: Non-malleable randomness encoders and their applications. In: Nielsen, J.B., Rijmen, V. (eds.) Advances in Cryptology - EUROCRYPT 2018, pp. 589–617. Springer, Cham (2018)
38. Li, X.: Three-source extractors for polylogarithmic min-entropy. In: 2015 IEEE 56th Annual Symposium on Foundations of Computer Science, pp. 863–882 (2015). https://doi.org/10.1109/FOCS.2015.58
39. Li, X.: Improved non-malleable extractors, non-malleable codes and independent source extractors. In: Proceedings of the 49th Annual ACM SIGACT Symposium on Theory of Computing, STOC 2017, pp. 1144–1156. Association for Computing Machinery, New York (2017). https://doi.org/10.1145/3055399.3055486
40. Li, X.: Non-malleable extractors and non-malleable codes: partially optimal constructions. In: Proceedings of the 34th Computational Complexity Conference. CCC 2019, Schloss Dagstuhl–Leibniz-Zentrum fuer Informatik, Dagstuhl, DEU (2019). https://doi.org/10.4230/LIPIcs.CCC.2019.28
41. Li, X.: Two source extractors for asymptotically optimal entropy, and (many) more (2023). https://arxiv.org/abs/2303.06802. To appear at FOCS 2023
42. Liu, F.-H., Lysyanskaya, A.: Tamper and leakage resilience in the split-state model. In: Safavi-Naini, R., Canetti, R. (eds.) CRYPTO 2012. LNCS, vol. 7417, pp. 517–532. Springer, Heidelberg (2012). https://doi.org/10.1007/978-3-642-32009-5_30

# On Quantum Query Complexities of Collision-Finding in Non-uniform Random Functions

Tianci Peng[1,2], Shujiao Cao[1,2](✉), and Rui Xue[1,2]

[1] State Key Laboratory of Cyberspace Security Defense, Institute of Information Engineering, Chinese Academy of Sciences, Beijing 100093, China
{pengtianci,caoshujiao,xuerui}@iie.ac.cn
[2] School of Cyber Security, University of CAS, Beijing 100049, China

**Abstract.** Collision resistance and collision finding are now extensively exploited in Cryptography, especially in the case of quantum computing. For any function $f : [M] \to [N]$ with $f(x)$ uniformly distributed over $[N]$, Zhandry has shown that the number $\Theta(N^{1/3})$ of queries is both necessary and sufficient for finding a collision in $f$ with constant probability. However, there is still a gap between the upper and the lower bounds of query complexity in general non-uniform distributions.

In this paper, we investigate the quantum query complexity of the collision-finding problem with respect to general non-uniform distributions. Inspired by previous work, we pose the concept of collision domain and a new parameter $\gamma$ that heavily depends on the underlying non-uniform distribution. We then present a quantum algorithm that expectedly uses $O(\gamma^{1/6})$ quantum queries to find a collision for any non-uniform random function. By transforming a problem in a non-uniform setting into a problem in a uniform setting, we are also able to show that $\Omega(\gamma^{1/6} \log^{-1/2} \gamma)$ quantum queries are necessary for collision-finding in any non-uniform random function.

The upper bound and the lower bound in this work indicate that the proposed algorithm is nearly optimal with query complexity in the general non-uniform case.

**Keywords:** Quantum · Query complexity · Collision-finding algorithm · Compressed oracle technique · Non-uniform distribution · Lower bound

## 1 Introduction

Quantum computation has brought threats to classical cryptography since Shor's seminal article [32]. In the black-box model, the advantage of quantum computing embodied the fact that a quantum adversary may take input or output in the form of a quantum superposition, which potentially allows for gaining advantages that might not be possible in traditional computations. As a result, many

© International Association for Cryptologic Research 2026
G. Hanaoka and B.-Y. Yang (Eds.): ASIACRYPT 2025, LNCS 16252, pp. 193–223, 2026.
https://doi.org/10.1007/978-981-95-5125-5_7

classical public key encryption systems, including Diffie-Hellman protocol [15] and RSA cryptosystem [31], are broken by Shor's factoring and discrete-log algorithms [32]. The Grover's algorithm [22] allows greatly improves the efficiency of the adversary by accelerating the speed for solving the search problems. Many cryptographic schemes that are secure in classical computation may no longer be applicable to the quantum world [7,16,23,26].

Faced with the threats from quantum computing, people widely investigate, as in classical computation, the complexity of quantum computing. One expects to figure out, to each problem, the problem-solving capabilities and the limitations of quantum computing by considering the number of queries in the black-box model.

In this work, we manage to further explore both the upper and lower bounds of quantum query complexity of the collision-finding problem in generally non-uniform random functions.

Collision resistance is one of the important properties in cryptography. For any positive integers $M, N$, let $[M]$ be the set $\{1, \ldots, M\}$. A collision to a function $f$ from $[M]$ to $[N]$ is a couple of distinct inputs $x_1, x_2 \in [M]$ such that $f(x_1) = f(x_2)$. The collision-resistant hash functions in cryptography emphasize the difficulty in finding collisions. They are broadly employed in various cryptographic primitives [9,10,18].

It has been well studied on the complexity of finding a collision in the quantum setting. In view of the upper bounds, Brassard et al.[12] showed that $O(N^{1/3})$ queries are sufficient to find a collision in a two-to-one function. Ambainis[4] proved that $O(M^{2/3})$ quantum queries are sufficient to achieve a collision with constant probability in a function $f : [M] \to [N]$ by quantum walk, in which $f$ should be guaranteed to have at least one pair of collisions.

Zhandry[38] proposed an algorithm that takes $O(N^{1/3})$ quantum queries to find a collision in a uniformly random function. Targhi et al.[17] and Balogh et al.[8] proved, separately, that $O(2^{\beta/3})$ quantum queries are sufficient to find a collision in a non-uniform random function, where $\beta$ is the collision-entropy of distribution $D$ (cf. Definition 1).

In terms of lower bounds, Aaronson and Shi [1] proved that $\Omega(N^{1/3})$ quantum query is necessary to find a collision in any function $f : [N] \to [N]$, where $f$ is a two-to-one function. The result was further extended to the case of small range by Kutin [27] and Ambainis[5] independently. Yuen[36] proved that $\Omega(N^{1/5}/\texttt{poly}\log N)$ quantum queries are necessary to find a collision in a uniformly random function $f : [N] \to [N]$. Zhandry [38] improved this bound further to $\Omega(N^{1/3})$ in a uniform function from $[M]$ to $[N]$.

Targhi et al. proved a lower bound $\Omega(2^{\mathtt{k}/9})$ in a non-uniform random function[33], in the case that for any $x \in [M]$ the output of $f(x)$ is selected according to a distribution $D$ over $[N]$, which possesses the min-entropy $\mathtt{k}$. Targhi and Unruh improved the previous lower bound to $\Omega(2^{\mathtt{k}/5})$[17]. Balogh et al.[8] recently improved that lower bound to $\Omega(2^{\mathtt{k}/3})$.

One should note that Zhandry's results claim that, in a uniform random function $f$ from $[M]$ to $[N]$, $\Theta(N^{1/3})$ quantum queries are both necessary and sufficient to find a collision[38], and thus give the tight upper and lower bounds in uniform case.

In the research of the collision-finding problem with respect to general non-uniform distributions, however, from the reviews above and also the summarization in Table 1, we see that there lacks currently a tight upper and lower query complexity bound characterizing as in uniform settings.

**Table 1.** Recent complexity results to collision-finding problem

| Literatures | Distribution | Upper Bound | Lower Bound |
|---|---|---|---|
| [Zha15][38] | uniform | $O(N^{1/3})$ | $\Omega(N^{1/3})$ |
| [TTU16][33] | non-uniform | | $\Omega(2^{k/9})$ |
| [EU18][17] | non-uniform | $O(\min\{2^{\beta/3}, 2^{k/2}\})$ | $\Omega(\max\{2^{\beta/9}, 2^{k/5}\})$ |
| [BES18][8] | non-uniform | $O(\min\{2^{\beta/3}, 2^{k/2}\})$ | $\Omega(\max\{2^{\beta/6}, 2^{k/3}\})$ |

Existing algorithms in this setting, for example in [8], gain optimum bounds valid to some special distributions, as is pointed out later in the context, not in generally non-uniform distributions. Hence, exploiting further characterization of query complexity of collision-finding in non-uniform functions is deserved from the theoretical point of view as well as in practical applications in cryptography. For example, non-uniform functions were used in cryptographic systems such as the famous Fujisaki-Okamoto construction[19] and further discussions in [6,34].

This work aims to work out (almost) optimal upper and lower bounds on numbers of quantum queries for collision-finding problem in general non-uniform random functions.

### 1.1 Contributions

In this work, we first propose two collision-finding algorithms and analyze their quantum query complexity, and then show a quantum query complexity lower bound in any non-uniform function. Both the upper bound and the lower bound are characterized by a newly proposed collision parameter, and finally, result in tighter bounds.

In [17], Targhi et al. showed that, provided that only min-entropy is used in describing the collision-finding complexity in non-uniform random functions, the upper bound $O(2^{k/2})$ and the lower bound $\Omega(2^{k/3})$ are both the best possible ones. The gap between the upper and lower bounds there hints to us that min-entropy might not be good enough in describing the query complexity of the collision-finding problem.

This leads us to seek finer parameter that may reflect more properties of underlying distributions. In this work, we propose a new collision parameter $\gamma$ in investigating the quantum query complexity of collision-finding in non-uniform random functions.

For any constant $c > 1$, we start with a partition, called $c$-partition which is somewhat similar as in [20], to divide the domain $[N]$ into a sequence of subsets $\{S_1, \ldots, S_\ell\}$ according to the weight of distribution $D : \{p_1, \cdots, p_N\}$. To denote $p(S_i)$ as the maximal probability of elements in $S_i$ of size $n_i$, then $\gamma(c)$ is defined to be the minimum one among all $1/n_i p^3(S_i)$. Although the value of $\gamma(c)$ is dependent on $c$, later in Proposition 5, we show that the concrete value of constant $c$ does not affect the magnitude of query complexity, and hence we may mention $\gamma$ now and then rather than $\gamma(c)$.

In terms of this parameter, we can compose two algorithms that succeed in collision-finding with $O(\gamma^{1/6})$ quantum queries for some specific kind of functions which we call them well-behaved and also propose a mixed algorithm that works for arbitrary functions with expected queries $O(\gamma^{1/6})$. On the other side, we prove the number $\Omega(\gamma^{1/6}/\sqrt{\log \gamma})$ of quantum queries are necessary for any collision-finding algorithms over non-uniform distributions. Since the two bounds almost meet, we believe parameter $\gamma$ is one of appropriate parameters in describing the query complexity of collision-finding.

It is important to note that our upper bound is stated in terms of expected query complexity, rather than guaranteeing that a collision can be found with constant probability using only $O(\gamma^{1/6})$ queries in the worst case. This limitation is common as in prior works [8, 17] becase bad points is usually unavoidable for a general random distribution without additional structural requirement(e.g., for those functions that only have few collisions).

Besides, in previous work minimum entropy and collision entropy are employed as indicators of the complexity of this problem. Here a new entropy(i.e. $\log \gamma$) is proposed, and accordingly almost tight upper and lower quantum query complexities are obtained to the collision-finding problem with non-uniform oracles. It might be expected the new entropy proposed here be applied in the future works. Compared to min-entropy, the new parameter $\gamma$ depends on finer information about the distribution to calculate as the collision-entropy does (cf. Definition 1). Indeed, before running the proposed collision-finding algorithm, it needs to find the right collision domain $S_i$ at first, which is somewhat different from existing algorithms which only take the min-entropy as input. This is based on the observation that the key to improving the acceleration in an algorithm is to find the most suitable collision search range (which is called collision domain in the context, cf. Definition 3), and that should be inevitable to make use of the information of underlying distribution. This might also be understood as a trade-off between getting a finer algorithm and using neat properties like the min-entropy.

This requirement is often implicitly assumed (or by default) in practice. An example is in the CCA quantum security proof to the famous Fujisaki-Okamoto transformation [6, 34]. In that proof one has to ensure that it is hard for any polynomial quantum algorithm to find collisions $(c, c')$ in non-uniform random function $g = f \circ H = f(\delta, H(\delta, c))$, where $H$ is a uniform random function and $f$ is the encryption algorithm in the asymmetric encryption scheme. An adversary not only has oracle access to $f$, but also knows the underlying structure of the encryption algorithm (for example, the adversary knows in advance that $f$ is the ElGamal encryption algorithm, which means the construction of this scheme is based on DDH assumptions). This means, the adversary is able to analyze the distribution of pre-image of the encryption algorithm (namely for any $\delta \in \{0,1\}^m$ and $y \in \{0,1\}^n$, to calculate $\Pr[y = f(\delta, H(\delta, c)) : c \leftarrow \texttt{coin}]$). That implies the adversary is capable and likely to know all the information about the corresponding distribution of the non-uniform random function $g$. In addition, the enhanced lower bound here can be used in the CCA security proof of FO transformation as the replacement of the corresponding component in the proof (such as Lemma 11, in the full version of [6]), which will result in a tighter reducible bound in the CCA security of FO transformation.

### 1.2 Technical Overview

Here we describe the main ideas and techniques in this work.

**The Parameter $\gamma$ and its Properties.** A novel parameter $\gamma$ is proposed in this work, aiming at accurately describing the quantum computational complexity of the collision-finding problem in general non-uniform random functions.

There is a significant difference between quantum and classical computing in solving the collision-finding problem in the non-uniform case. Specifically, the acceleration effects in quantum computing in a more restricted search scope may be performed better. This fact is counterintuitive to the classical setting. That means, in the classical case it is always easier to find any collision in a set than in any of its subsets.

Based on this observation, the key point to effectively find a collision is to seek the most suitable search range, which is referred to as the collision domain in this work. Given non-uniform distribution $D$ with weight sequence $\{p_1, \ldots, p_N\}$, assuming without loss of generality that $p_1 \geq p_2 \geq \cdots \geq p_N$, we choose a constant threshold $c > 1$ (which is proved not essential to the complexity and will be discussed later in Proposition 5), and partition domain $[D]$ accordingly into a series of subsets.

For any non-uniform distribution $D$ over $[N]$, we want to make a partition of $[N]$. For this purpose, a constant $c$ is chosen to control the size of the partition, so that in each part $S$ of the partition, the ratio $p_j/p_i$ for any $i, j \in S$ does not exceed the threshold $c > 1$. The larger $c$ is, the finer the partition is.

Given the threshold $c > 1$, we start to collect all index $j \in [N]$ satisfying $p_1 \geq p_j > p_1/c$ as a set $S_1$. Let $n_1 := |S_1|$ and $p(S_1) := p_1$. And then let $S_2$ be the collection of all $j \in [N]$ such that $p(S_2) \geq p_j > p(S_2)/c$, where $p(S_2) := p_{n_1+1}$. Continuing this process, it finally divides $[N]$ into a series of subsets $S_1, S_2, \ldots, S_\ell$ with $|S_i| = n_i$ for $i = 1, \ldots, \ell$. We name this partition as $c$-partition. If let $\gamma_i(c) := 1/n_i p^3(S_i)$ for each $i \in [\ell]$, the parameter $\gamma(c)$ is defined as the smallest one among $\gamma_i(c)$. Suppose $\gamma(c) = \gamma_{k_0}(c)$, the subset $S_{k_0}$ is named as the collision domain and $k_0$ is the smallest such index among $[\ell]$.

The relations of $\gamma(c)$ with the min-entropy $\mathtt{k}$ and collision-entropy $\beta$ used in existing algorithms are explored in Sect. 5 (see Proposition 2 and 3). It shows that both the upper bound and lower bound in this work are at least as good as the best prior result in [8]. An example is also presented there to indicate the superiority of our result to existing ones such that $\max\{\beta^{1/6}, 2^{k/3}\} \ll \gamma^{1/6} \ll \min\{\beta^{1/3}, 2^{k/2}\}$.

The proposed collision-finding algorithm in this work will take the collision domain as input, compared to previous algorithms which mainly take min-entropy or collision-entropy as inputs. To make the computation of the collision domain simpler in the application, a result is shown in Proposition 4 in order to reduce the actual range to locate the collision domain.

Although $\gamma(c)$ depends on the classification of discrete sequence with constant $c$, we are able to show, in Proposition 5, the relative error between $\gamma(c_1)$ and $\gamma(c_2)$ is $O(1)$ as long as $c_1, c_2 > 1$ are constants. That claims that the parameter $\gamma(c)$ is NOT affected by concrete $c$ in the magnitude of query complexity bounds, provided $c > 1$ is a constant.

**The Algorithm and Complexity Upper Bound.** We present two collision-finding algorithms in contexts. In general, the two algorithms are consistent in terms of query complexity, but there are some differences in details. The first algorithm is the quantum walk algorithm, which requires quantum memory but can successfully find collision even if there is only one collision in the collision domain. The second algorithm is a BHT-type algorithm, this algorithm only requires classical memory, but it has certain requirements for the input random function domain $[M]$. Informally, it works if there is enough collision in the collision domain.

The first algorithm can be seen as a variation of Ambainis's element distinctness algorithm[4]. Johnson graph is a standard graph on which we perform quantum random walk (QRW). Including the element distinctness problem we mentioned, many problems with the form: given $x_1, \ldots, x_n \in \Omega$ and a relation $R \subset \Omega^k$, find $x_{i_1}, \ldots, x_{i_k}$ such that $(x_{i_1}, \ldots, x_{i_k}) \in R$, can be solved using the quantum walk over the Johnson graph $J(n, r)$ (here $r$ is the number of quantum registers required)[2,13,21].

In our setting, we have to modify the graph that performs the quantum walk in Ambainis's algorithm. When finding a collision in a random function $f : [M] \to [N]$, we employ, instead of the general Johnson graph $J(M, r)$ for QRW in Ambainis's algorithm, the subgraph of $J(M, r)$ to which QRW is restricted by some additional operations, thanks the collision domain in hand. With this modification, the expected query complexity of the algorithm can be reduced.

Our second algorithm is intuitively designed as follows. First, to use Grover's algorithm to find a list $L$ of elements in collision domain $S_{k_0}$, and then to adopt a standard collision algorithm to find a collision in $L$. It uses an adaptively adjusted search domain according to the underlying distribution to achieve acceleration, which has been missed in previous algorithms.

For this purpose, some changes to BBHT algorithm must be made to be used in our algorithm. BBHT algorithm in [11] gives the expected number of queries when the algorithm succeeds, while we expect to get a relation, depending on the number of queries, to indicate the success probability of the algorithm. The modified BBHT algorithm here is actually a de-randomized version of BBHT algorithm.

Finally, since the former two algorithms only succeed over average function $f$, by integrating the two aforementioned algorithms, we propose a mix algorithm. Distinguished from the previous two, this algorithm is characterized by its ability to find a collision with constant probability for any function $f$, while maintaining an expected query complexity of $O(\gamma^{1/6}(c))$. To some extent it implies that the parameter $\gamma(c)$ exploits the more significant information of a non-uniform distribution in collision-finding, resulting in better acceleration.

**The Lower Bound.** Exploring the lower bound in terms of $\gamma(c)$ is a little bit involved. To obtain the lower bound of query complexity, we first estimate the success probability restricted over each $S_r$ (Problem 1 in Sect. 4.2), where $S_r$ is any subset partitioned in $c$-partition. Then, the success probability of the problem is bounded by the sum of the upper bounds of the success probabilities over all $S_r$. In such a way, we are able to calculate a lower bound.

To attack the restricted problem, one idea is to adapt techniques like Zhandry's compressed oracle. That technique makes a quantum algorithm capable of "recording" when accesses to a quantum random oracle. That is useful to derive a quantum lower bound because of its "recording property". However, Zhandry's technique in [39] is with respect to uniform random functions. Therefore we transform the problem into another one (Problem 2), a problem with respect to uniform distributions. In such a way, the compressed oracle technique in the quantum random oracle model (QROM) proposed by Zhandry can be exploited.

The transformed problem splits into several sub-problems of the same type according to $c$-partition, and each sub-problem can be calculated as the corresponding upper bound of the success probability after $q$ quantum queries by the compressed oracle technique. From this, we can show $\Omega(\gamma^{1/6}(c) \cdot \delta_c^{-1/2})$ as a quantum lower bound.

At last, by the properties of $c$-partition, we show $\delta_c = O(\mathtt{k})$, where $\mathtt{k}$ is the min-entropy of distribution $D$. On the other hand, we prove in Sect. 5 that $\mathtt{k} = \Theta(\log \gamma(c))$ (Proposition 2). We hence obtain $\Omega(\gamma^{1/6}(c)/\sqrt{\log \gamma(c)})$ as a quantum query complexity lower bound for the collision-finding problem in general non-uniform distributions.

The transformation technique in this work might be of independent interest in lower bound explorations in non-uniform random settings.

The structure of the paper is as follows. In Sect. 2, we give some definitions (including $c$-partition) and preliminaries. In Sect. 3, our collision-finding algorithms and their correctness are presented. The quantum query complexity of the algorithm is also analyzed. In Sect. 4, a lower bound to the collision-finding problem is proved by adapting Zhandry's compressed oracle technique. In the last section, the relations of parameter $\gamma(c)$ with min-entropy and collision-entropy are shown, and some other properties are discussed.

## 2 Preliminaries

### 2.1 Notations and Definitions

In this paper, $M, N$ are positive integers, and $[N]$ is the set $\{1, \ldots, N\}$ and $[M..N]$ is the set $\{M, M+1, \ldots, N\}$ if $M \leq N$. The set $N^M$ is the collection of all functions from $[M]$ to $[N]$, and $f \leftarrow N^M$ refers to the uniformly random sampling from $N^M$. If $D$ is a distribution over $[N]$, then $D^M$ represents the distribution over $N^M$ such that $\Pr_{f \leftarrow D^M}[f(x) = y] = D(y)$ for any $x \in [M]$ independently. We denote $p_i := D(i)$ and assume, without loss of generality, that $p_1 \geq p_2 \geq \cdots \geq p_N$ due to the property of symmetry.

The following definitions appeared in the prior works and will be cited later.

**Definition 1 (Min-Entropy & Collision-Entropy**[8]**).** *The* min-entropy *of a probabilistic distribution $D$ is* $\mathtt{k} := -\log_2(\max_y D(y))$ *which is* $-\log_2 p_1$ *in our setting. The* collision-entropy *of $D$ is defined as* $\beta := -\log_2(\sum_{i=1}^{N} p_i^2)$.

In the literature of collision-finding, the upper and lower bounds of query complexities were described in terms of min-entropy $\mathtt{k}$ or collision-entropy $\beta$. For example, in classical computation, the best upper bound is $O(2^{\beta/2})$, and the lower bound is $\Omega(2^{\mathtt{k}/2})$. In this paper, however, we show that in the quantum world, the complexity of collision-finding in non-uniform distribution may not be completely characterized by these two parameters. In order to narrow the gap between the upper and lower bounds mentioned above, more properties of non-uniform distributions have to be considered. With such a point of view, we divide the set $[N]$ into several parts according to $\{p_1, \ldots, p_n\}$, which is described as follows.

For any $c > 1$, we divide $[N]$ into a series of subsets $S_1, S_2, \ldots, S_\ell$ with respect to $D$: $S_1$ is the collection of index $i \in [N]$ such that $p_i > p_1/c$, with $p(S_1) := p_1$ and $|S_1| = n_1$; $S_2$ then contains all indexes $j \in [N] - S_1$ such that $p_j > p(S_2)/c$, and $p(S_2)$ is the largest one among $\{p_i \mid i \in S_2\}$, hence $p(S_2) = p_{n_1+1}$ (since $p_1 \geq p_2 \geq \cdots \geq p_N$), and so forth. In other words, the subset $S_i$'s are in some sense the maximal sets of indexes whose corresponding weight differ by a constant factor $c > 1$. Formally,

**Definition 2 ($c$-partition).** *Given constant $c > 1$ and a distribution $D$ over $[N]$ as above. The* $c$-partition of $[N]$ with respect to $D$ *is a partition* $\{S_1, \ldots, S_\ell\}$ *of $[N]$ such that*

$$|S_i| := n_i, \qquad [N] = \cup_{i=1}^{\ell} S_i, \qquad S_i \cap S_j = \emptyset \ (\textit{for any} \quad i \neq j),$$

*where $S_i$ is recursively defined as follows:*

- *Let* $S_1 := \{j \in [N] \mid p_1 \geq p_j > p_1/c\}$. *To denote* $n_1 := |S_1|$ *and* $p(S_1) := p_1$.
- *For* $i \geq 2$, *let*

$$S_i := \{j \in [N] \mid p(S_i) \geq p_j > \frac{p(S_i)}{c}\}, \qquad n_i := |S_i|. \tag{1}$$

*Where* $p(S_i) \in \{p_1, \ldots, p_N\}$ *satisfies*

$$p(S_i) := \max\{p_j : j \in [N] - \bigcup_{k=1}^{i-1} S_k\}. \quad (2)$$

For any constant $c > 1$ and a (non-uniform) distribution $D$ over $[N]$, we define the collision parameter $\gamma(c)$ with respect to $c$-partition in the same notations as above, as follows.

**Definition 3 (Collision Parameter & Collision Domain).** *For any real number* $c > 1$ *and a probabilistic distribution over [N], let c-partition of* $[N]$ *with respect to D as above. The* $\gamma(c)$ *defined as follows is called* the collision parameter *of D with respect to c, for* $i = 1, \ldots, \ell$,

$$\gamma_i(c) := 1/n_i p^3(S_i), \quad \gamma(c) := \min_{i \in [\ell]}\{\gamma_i(c)\}. \quad (3)$$

*Let* $k_0$*, referred to as the index of collision domain later in context, be the smallest* $k_0 \in [\ell]$ *such that* $\gamma(c) = \gamma_{k_0}(c)$*, then* $S_{k_0}$ *is called* the collision domain *of D with respect to c.*

*Remark 1.* The notion "collision parameter" proposed here will be in place of "min-entropy and collision-entropy" that appeared in current literature. It heavily depends on the distribution $D$ in evaluations. This is similar to "collision-entropy" in prior work, which also needs the whole information of $D$ to calculate. In addition, it is not hard to check that for any uniform distribution $D$ and $c > 1$, $\gamma^{1/6}(c)$ is just the same as $2^{\beta/3}$ and $2^{\mathrm{k}/2}$ in magnitude, the latter is proved optimal in that case.

In the general case (namely in arbitrary non-uniform distribution), compared with existing collision variables, the collision parameter proposed here will give more concise characterizations for both upper and lower query bounds to the collision-finding problem. Moreover, although the parameter $\gamma(c)$ is formally related to the classification of discrete sequence, we are able to prove the fact that the query complexity in $\gamma(c)$ is NOT affected by the value of constant $c > 1$ in the magnitude. The analysis of these two points is presented in Sect. 5.

### 2.2 Grover's Algorithm and BBHT Algorithm

Grover proposed a quantum algorithm for the database search problem [22], demonstrating the powerful acceleration effect of quantum computing on this issue.

**Lemma 1 (Grover's Algorithm[22]).** *Given a boolean function* $f : [N] \to \{0, 1\}$ *such that there is only one* $x_0 \in [N]$ *satisfying* $f(x_0) = 1$*, there is a quantum algorithm that requires* $O(\sqrt{N})$ *queries to find* $x_0$ *in constant probability.*

Boyer et al. [11] proposed a generalized algorithm to be applied to the case of multiple solutions to the search problem even without knowing the number of solutions in advance. That surmounts the restriction in Grover's algorithm that there exists only one $x_0 \in [N]$ satisfying $f(x_0) = 1$. The generalized algorithm is now referred to as BBHT algorithm.

**Lemma 2 (BBHT[11]).** *Given a boolean function $f : [N] \to \{0,1\}$ and $t = |f^{-1}(1)|$, there is a quantum algorithm that may find $x_0 \in [N]$ with $f(x_0) = 1$ with $\Theta(\sqrt{N/t})$ expected queries.*

BBHT algorithm starts with uniform superposition state $|\psi_0\rangle = \sum_{i=0}^{N-1} \frac{1}{\sqrt{N}}|i\rangle$ in the workspace. If $\mathcal{T}$ is the solution space of $f$ and $\mathcal{F} := [N]\backslash\mathcal{T}$, the input can be written as

$$|\psi_0\rangle = \alpha_0 \sum_{i\in\mathcal{T}} \frac{1}{\sqrt{t}}|i\rangle + \beta_0 \sum_{j\in\mathcal{F}} \frac{1}{\sqrt{N-t}}|j\rangle .$$

Where $\alpha_0 = \sqrt{\frac{t}{N}} = \sin\theta$.

After $q$ quantum queries, one gets the superposition

$$|\psi_q\rangle = \alpha_q \sum_{i\in\mathcal{T}} \frac{1}{\sqrt{t}}|i\rangle + \beta_q \sum_{j\in\mathcal{F}} \frac{1}{\sqrt{N-t}}|j\rangle .$$

Where $\alpha_q = \sin(2q+1)\theta$. It was proved that $\alpha_q = \Theta(1)$ when $q = \Theta(\sqrt{N/t})$, namely the algorithm may find the pre-image of 1 with constant probability.

### 2.3 Quantum Random Walk

We now brief recall quantum random walk (QRW). To facilitate understanding, we will focus on the special case of QRW over Johnson graphs, since it's suffice to us. There are several variants of QRW and our presentation is mostly based on [29] and [25].

Suppose we have a connected unweighted undirected simple graph $G = (V, E)$ and a subset of marked vertices $M \subset V$, the goal is to find a vertex $v \in M$.

The problem can be solved using a quantum random walk algorithm. Intuitively, a one-step classical random walk represents the process of randomly moving from a vertex in the graph to its neighbors. The quantum random walk differs from the classical case in that its initial input can be a superposition state $\frac{1}{\sqrt{|V|}} \sum_{v\in V} |v\rangle$ rather than a vertex $v_0$. To denote $N_G(u) := \{v \in V | \{u, v\} \in E\}$ as the set of $u$'s neighbors, the costs of a quantum random walking algorithm consist of three categories:

**Setup Cost S**: it's the cost of constructing

$$|\pi\rangle := \sum_{u\in V} \sqrt{\pi_u}|u\rangle_L|0\rangle_R|D(u)\rangle_d$$

(here $D(u)$ is a data structure used to assist in the check process and $\pi := \{\pi_u\}$ is the stationary distribution of the transition matrix corresponding to our quantum random walk).

**Update Cost U**: it's the cost of perform one-step QRW. Specifically, it contains the cost of implementing the following two operators:

$$U_P : |u\rangle_L|0\rangle_R \to |u\rangle_L \sum_{v \in V} \frac{1}{\sqrt{|N_G(u)|}}|v\rangle_R$$

and

$$U_D : |u\rangle_L|v\rangle_R|D(u)\rangle_d \to |v\rangle_L|u\rangle_R|D(v)\rangle_d.$$

**Check Cost C**: it's the cost of checking whether a vertex $v$ is marked with the assistance of data structure, namely the cost of constructing:

$$|u\rangle_L|D(u)\rangle_d \to (-1)^{F(u)}|u\rangle_L|D(u)\rangle_d.$$

Here $F(u) = 1$ if $u \in M$, otherwise $F(u) = 0$.

Suppose there is $\epsilon > 0$ that satisfies $\frac{|M|}{|V|} \geq \epsilon$ and $\delta$ be the spectral gap of $G$, we have:

**Lemma 3** ([29]). *If the fraction of marked vertices is at least $\epsilon$, there is a QRW algorithm to find a marked vertex with constant probability. The cost incurred is*

$$O(\mathbf{S} + \frac{1}{\sqrt{\epsilon}}(\frac{1}{\sqrt{\delta}} \cdot \mathbf{U} + \mathbf{C})).$$

If we restrict ourselves to QRW over Johnson graphs, it will be more convenient in practical applications. The definition of Johnson graphs is as follows:

**Definition 4.** *The Johnson graph $J(n, r)$ is an (undirected) graph in which the vertex set is the set of all subsets of $r$-elements of $[n]$. $(u, v) \in E$ iff $u := \{u_1, \ldots, u_r\}$ and $v := \{v_1, \ldots, v_r\}$ satisfy that $|u \cap v| = r - 1$.*

The QRW over Johnson graphs has a nice property: the initial state $|\pi\rangle$ mentioned above can be constructed as the superposition state

$$\sum_{\substack{|u|=r, u_i \in [n] \\ u_i \neq u_j}} \frac{1}{\sqrt{C(n,r)}}|u\rangle_L|0\rangle_R|D(u)\rangle_d.$$

Where $C(n, r)$ is the binomial coefficient. That enables $|u\rangle_L = \bigotimes_{i \in [r]} |u_i\rangle_L$ to be prepared efficiently in the setup process. In addition, the spectral gap $\delta$ of $J(n, r)$ satisfies $\delta \approx \frac{1}{r}$, so later on in the discussion of algorithmic complexity, we're left with the analysis of $\mathbf{S}$, $\mathbf{U}$, $\mathbf{C}$ and $\epsilon$.

### 2.4 Some Probabilistic Inequalities

The following are some probabilistic inequalities used in subsequent sections.

**Lemma 4. (Höffding's Inequality).** *Let $X_1, \ldots, X_n$ be a sequence of independent random variables such that $X_i$ with values in $[a_i, b_i]$ for $i \in [n]$ and $X = \sum_{i=1}^n X_i$. If the expectation $\mathrm{E}(X) = \mu$, we have, for any $t$,*

$$\Pr[\mu - X \geq t] \leqslant \exp\left(\frac{-2\,t^2}{\sum_{i=1}^n (a_i - b_i)^2}\right).$$

*and*

$$\Pr[X - \mu \geq t] \leqslant \exp\left(\frac{-2\,t^2}{\sum_{i=1}^n (a_i - b_i)^2}\right).$$

If we know something about the variance of random variables in addition to the expectation, in some cases, we can get a tighter bound.

**Lemma 5. (Bernstein's Inequality).** *Let $X_1, \ldots, X_n$ be a sequence of independent random variables with values in $[0, 1]$ and $X = \sum_{i=1}^n X_i$. If the expectation $\mathrm{E}(X) = \mu$ and the variances $\mathrm{Var}(X) = \sigma^2$, we then have, for any $t$,*

$$\Pr[\mu - X \geq t] \leqslant \exp\left(\frac{-t^2/2}{\sigma^2 + t/3}\right)$$

*and*

$$\Pr[X - \mu \geq t] \leqslant \exp\left(\frac{-t^2/2}{\sigma^2 + t/3}\right).$$

## 3 Collision-Finding Algorithms and Their Query Complexity

This section is organized as follows. Subsection 3.1, reviews prior collision-finding algorithms in the non-uniform setting and motivate key ideas for improvement. In Subsect. 3.2, we propose a quantum walk-based algorithm, and analyze its correctness in the average case in Subsect. 3.3. Subsection 3.4 presents a BHT-type algorithm and its performance is analyzed in Subsect. 3.5. Finally, in Subsect. 3.6, we integrate the two algorithms above to construct a mix algorithm that finds a collision with constant probability for any function $f$, with an expected query complexity $O(\gamma^{1/6}(c))$.

### 3.1 Warming up

Balogh, Eaton and Song [8] proposed a collision-finding algorithm (referred as BES algorithm) based on the collision-entropy $\beta$. It applies Ambainis's quantum walk algorithm[4] as a subroutine for element distinctness, which may be sketched (among others) as follows:

**BES Algorithm (sketch).**

1. Choose subset $M' \subset [M]$ arbitrarily such that $|M'| = 2^{\beta/2}$.
2. Run Ambainis's algorithm for function $f|_{M'} : M' \to [N]$.
3. Output $(x, x')$ if Ambainis's algorithm output $(x, x')$; Otherwise output $\perp$.

Though with very well performance in many cases, however after careful inspection, the approach is found to have space to improve the acceleration effect in some settings. The following is an example, though somewhat artificial. For $M, N > 1$, let $D$ be a distribution over $[N]$ such that

$$p_1 := \frac{1}{2^n}, p_2 = p_3 = \cdots = p_N := \frac{2^n - 1}{(N-1)2^n}$$

for any integer $n > 0$. Then for $N = 2^{2n}$, to find a collision by BES algorithm requires $\Theta(2^{\beta/3}) = \Theta(2^{2n/3}) = \Theta(2^{2\mathtt{k}/3})$ queries since the min-entropy $\mathtt{k} = n$ in this case. The query complexity is even much higher than the other bound $2^{\mathtt{k}/2}$ by Grover's algorithm at this time.

**Observations and Motivations.** The random distribution will bring us more information when exploring the query complexity, which is reflected in the fact that a random function provides additional specific information about the sampling distribution, namely $D$: $\{p_1, p_2, \ldots, p_N\}$, and how to optimally make use of this information to a random function should be the key point to finding more efficient algorithm than to an arbitrary given function.

For a uniform random function $f \leftarrow N^M$, the information is expressed in a concise manner, namely $p_1 = p_2 = \cdots = p_N = \frac{1}{N}$. All the information now can be explained by the sole parameter $N$, so the query complexity of a uniform function is only determined by $N$ (and the other parameter $M$ is to guarantee the existence of collision). While in the case of general non-uniform random functions, the probabilistic weights of the non-uniform distribution avoid this advantage. The query complexity of a non-uniform function would be heavily dependent on $p_1, \ldots, p_N$. That is the main ingredient in comparing a non-uniform distribution with a uniform distribution.

Let's try to figure out the obstacle in the non-uniform case when investigating the query complexity. For uniformly chosen $f \leftarrow N^M$ and for any $S_1, S_2 \subseteq [N]$ with $|S_1| = |S_2|$, we have

$$\Pr_{f \leftarrow N^M}[f(x) = f(x'), f(x) \in S_1] = \Pr_{f \leftarrow N^M}[f(x) = f(x'), f(x) \in S_2]$$

for any $x, x' \in [M]$. However, the equation would not hold with non-uniform distributions. This fact may conduct a problem when the former collision-finding algorithm is adopted to achieve acceleration: For any two sets $S_1, S_2 \subseteq [N]$ such that $|S_1| = |S_2|$, when a quantum collision-finding algorithm is adopted, the cost for finding a collision in $S_1$ may be much less than the cost for finding a collision in $S_2$. Therefore, it's necessary to try to avoid spending numerous quantum queries which may not have much effect on collision-finding. An effective approach might be to use Grover's algorithm while limiting the search scope, which means that the search range $S$ should not be too large.

On the other side, the search domain $S$ should not be too small. Informally, the reason why the collision-finding problem is (arguably) potentially easier than the inverting problem is that there is no prefixed point in the collision problem, which allows the collision problem to have greater searching freedom, and hence might reduce its computational complexity to a certain extent.

Above all, a balance should be taken when selecting the research domain $S$, and the specific equilibrium result depends on the underlying non-uniform distribution.

In view of current algorithms in the literature, the BES algorithm introduced above sets $[N]$ as the search domain, while the others set the search domain to $S = \{1\}$ using Grover's algorithm. All of them do not make full use of the information provided by the distributions.

That motivates us to propose the notion of $c$-partition in this work. By dividing $[N]$ into a sequence of subsets, the part with the best quantum acceleration effect is determined according to distribution. An (almost) optimal quantum collision-finding algorithm is designed for non-uniform functions based on these arguments.

### 3.2 A Quautum Random Walk Algorithm

In this subsection, we propose our quantum random walk algorithm for collision-finding in non-uniform random functions. As mentioned in the previous overview, compared with directly using Ambainis's algorithm to solve the problem, the main improvement we have made is the modification of the graph that performs the quantum walk.

Now we give our QRW algorithm, all the parameters that occur in the algorithm are analyzed in the next subsection. The key point of how to modify is the property of non-uniform. Since we can calculate the collision domain $S_{k_0}$, namely if we find a collision $(x_1, x_2)$, it has a maximum probability satisfying $f(x_1) = f(x_2) \in S_{k_0}$ compared to other $S_i \subset [n]$. So our idea is to focus only on vertices $u := (u_1, \dots, u_r)$ which satisfy $f(u_i) \in S_{k_0}$ for all $i \in [r]$, and quantum random walk over the subgraph induced on the Johnson graph $J(M, r)$ by the set of these vertices. As far as we know, the idea of limiting quantum walks to subgraphs has not appeared in previous quantum walk algorithms, we hope our idea can be applied to other problems.

There are two main obstacles to this idea. There is some convenience in performing the quantum walk directly on $J(M, r)$. First, the uniform superposition state

$$\sum_{\substack{|u|=r, u_i \in [M] \\ u_i \neq u_j}} \frac{1}{\sqrt{C(M, r)}} |u\rangle_L$$

can be prepared efficiently without any query to $f$ by default, so $\mathbf{S}$ is actually the cost of constructing the data structure $|D(u)\rangle_d$. Second, when performing

**Algorithm 1.** QRW Algorithm for Collision-Finding in Non-uniform Functions

**Input:** Collision domain $S_{k_0}$ and a function $f : [M] \to [N]$ with $f \leftarrow D^M$.
**Output:** A collision $(x_1, x_2)$ or $\perp$.

1: Choose $M' \subset [M]$ arbitrarily such that $|M'| = \frac{12c^2}{\sqrt{n_{k_0} p^2(S_{k_0})}}$.
2: Run **Init**$(S_{k_0}, f, M')$ to generate the initial state

$$|\pi_0\rangle = \sum_{\substack{u_i \in |M_f| \\ u_i \neq u_j \text{ if } i \neq j \\ f(u_i) \in S_{k_0}}} \frac{1}{\sqrt{C(|M_f|, r)}} \bigotimes_{i \in [r]} |u_i\rangle_L |0\rangle_R |D(u)\rangle_d$$

here $|D(u)\rangle_d := \bigotimes_{i\in[r]} |f(u_i)\rangle_d$ and $M_f$ be the collection of all $x \in M'$ such that $f(x) \in S_{k_0}$.
3: $O(1/\sqrt{\epsilon})$ times repeat:
(a) Perform the transformation $|u\rangle_L|v\rangle_R|D(u)\rangle_d \to -|u\rangle_L|v\rangle_R|D(u)\rangle_d$ for $u := (u_1, \ldots, u_r)$ satisfy that there exist $f(u_{i_1}) = f(u_{i_2})$ for some $u_{i_1}, u_{i_2} \in [M_f]$ (it's easy to see that a vertex $u$ is marked iff there is a collision in $|u\rangle_L$).
(b) Perform $O(1/\sqrt{\delta})$ steps of the quantum random walk over the Johnson graph $J(|M_f|, r)$.
4: Measure $|D(u)\rangle_d$, if there exist $f(u_{i_1}) = f(u_{i_2})$ for some $u_{i_1}, u_{i_2} \in [M_f]$ then output $(u_{i_1}, u_{i_2})$ which can be find in $|u\rangle_L$, otherwise $\perp$.

QRW on $J(M, r)$, the query complexity of implementing $U_P$ is also 0 by default. So the previous quantum walk algorithm only needs to focus on changes in the data structure $D(u)$, and it's easy to get $\mathbf{S} = r$ and $\mathbf{U} = 2$ (only need to perform $|u_i\rangle_L|0\rangle_d \to |u_i\rangle_L|f(u_i)\rangle_d$ for all $i \in [r]$ to get $D(u)$ and only an un-compute and a compute operation is required to implement $U_D$).

But if we constrain the quantum walk, what we have mentioned above needs to be considered carefully. We can't get to the initial state $\sum \alpha_u |u\rangle_L$ without any queries, since we can't determine whether $f(u_i) \in S_{k_0}$ for any $i \in [r]$. Similarly, we need additional queries to check whether $v \in N_G(u)$ meets our additional constraints. In the next subsection, we show how to solve these two problems with additional queries.

### 3.3 Analysis of Algorithm 1

Now we analyze the query complexity of our algorithm in the previous subsection. First of all, we estimate $|M_f|$, which will help us with some of our proofs later on. Let $f$ is *well-behaved* if $6c\sqrt{n_{k_0}} < |M_f| < 18c^2\sqrt{n_{k_0}}$.

**Lemma 6.** *For any c-partition with constant* $c > 1$, $f \leftarrow D^M$ *is well-behaved with probability at least* $1 - \exp(-\frac{18c^2\sqrt{n_{k_0}}}{12c^2+2c})$.

*Proof.* Since for any $x \in [M]$, $f(x) \in S_{k_0}$ with probability $P = \sum_{i \in S_{k_0}} p_i$, by the binomial distribution it's easy to see that $\mathrm{E}(|M_f|) = M'P$ and $\mathrm{Var}(|M_f|) =$

$M'P(1-P) < M'P$. According to the definition $|M'| = \frac{12c^2}{\sqrt{n_{k_0} p^2(S_{k_0})}}$ and $n_{k_0} p(S_{k_0})/c \leq \sum_{i \in S_{k_0}} p_i \leq n_{k_0} p(S_{k_0})$, we have:

$$12c\sqrt{n_{k_0}} \leq \mathrm{E}(|M_f|) \leq 12c^2\sqrt{n_{k_0}} \quad \text{and} \quad \mathrm{Var}(|M_f|) < 12c^2\sqrt{n_{k_0}}.$$

Therefore, by Bernstein's inequality, we have:

$$\Pr_{f \leftarrow D^M}[(|M_f| \leq 6c\sqrt{n_{k_0}}) \vee (|M_f| \geq 18c^2\sqrt{n_{k_0}})] \leq \Pr_f \left[ |\mathrm{E}[M_f] - |M_f|| \geq 6c\sqrt{n_{k_0}} \right]$$
$$\leq 2 \exp\Big( - \frac{18c^2\sqrt{n_{k_0}}}{12c^2 + 2c} \Big).$$

That hence completes that lemma. □

Here, the purpose of defining 'well-behaved' is to control the cost at each step of executing the quantum walk algorithm within a bounded range. Now we explicitly give estimates of the parameters in the algorithm.

**Check Cost C**: It's easy to see that $\mathbf{C} = 0$.

**The Spectral Gap** $\delta$: $\delta \approx 1/r$ by the property of Johnson graph [35].

**The Fraction of Marked Vertices** $\epsilon$: We show the following theorem.

**Theorem 1.** *If $f$ is well-behaved, $\epsilon = \Omega(\frac{n_{k_0}}{r^2})$ with constant probability.*

**The Setup Cost:** We get $\mathbf{S} = \Theta(\frac{r}{\sqrt{n_{k_0} p(S_{k_0})}})$ by the following theorem.

**Theorem 2.** *If $f$ is well-behaved, there exists an algorithm that constructs the initial state with $\Theta(\frac{r}{\sqrt{n_{k_0} p(S_{k_0})}})$ expected queries.*

**The Update Cost:** By the conclusion of following theorem, we obtain

$$\mathbf{U} = U_P + U_D = \Theta(\frac{1}{\sqrt{n_{k_0} p(S_{k_0})}}) + 2 = \Theta(\frac{1}{\sqrt{n_{k_0} p(S_{k_0})}}),$$

since $n_{k_0} p(S_{k_0}) < c$ in $c$-partition.

**Theorem 3.** *If $f$ is well-behaved, the expected number of queries required to implement $U_P$ is $\Theta(\frac{1}{\sqrt{n_{k_0} p(S_{k_0})}})$.*

The proofs of the Theorem 1, 2, 3 can be found in the full version [30].

Put these results together, according to Lemma 3, Algorithm 1 succeeds with constant probability. The expected number of queries required is

$$\begin{aligned}\mathrm{E}(Q) &:= O(\frac{r}{\sqrt{n_{k_0} p(S_{k_0})}} + \sqrt{\frac{n_{k_0}}{r^2}} \cdot \sqrt{r} \cdot \frac{1}{\sqrt{n_{k_0} p(S_{k_0})}}) \\ &= O(\frac{r}{\sqrt{n_{k_0} p(S_{k_0})}} + \frac{1}{\sqrt{r p(S_{k_0})}}).\end{aligned}$$

Let $r = \Theta(\sqrt[3]{n_{k_0}})$, the equation above gives $\mathrm{E}(Q) = O(\gamma^{1/6}(c))$.

We therefore shows that Algorithm 1 finds a collision with constant probability in a well-behaved non-uniform random function $f \leftarrow D^M$, and requires $O(\gamma^{1/6}(c))$ queries and $O(r) = O(\sqrt[3]{n_{k_0}})$ qubits of memory.

### 3.4 A BHT-Type Collision-Finding Algorithm

In this subsection, we propose another BHT-type collision-finding algorithm for random functions. Let's start by making some minor modification to BBHT algorithm. In our collision-finding algorithm, the modified BBHT algorithm will be loaded as a subroutine. It expects to have a relation depending on the number of queries to describe the success probability, while BBHT in [11] provides only the expected number of queries when the algorithm succeeds. Actually, the modification can be seen as a de-randomized version of BBHT algorithm.

The modified algorithm can be found in the full version [30] and the success probability of the modified BBHT algorithm is concluded as follows.

**Theorem 4.** *For any boolean function* $f : [N] \to \{0, 1\}$ *and* $t_0 := |f^{-1}(1)| > 0$, *the modified BBHT algorithm makes at most* $3.6q$ *queries to find a pre-image of* 1 *with probability at least* $\min\{1/2, \frac{q^2 t_0}{3N}\}$.

The proof also can be found in the full version [30]. With the above preparations, the algorithm is presented in Algorithm 2.

The parameters $t$, $q_1$ and $q_2$ in Algorithm 2 will be discussed and determined later in the context. Essentially, $t = \sqrt[3]{n_{k_0}}$ (see discussions after Theorem 6), $q_1 = O(1/\sqrt{n_{k_0} p(S_{k_0})})$ (Theorem 5) and $q_2 = O(1/\sqrt{t\, p(S_{k_0})})$ (Theorem 6).

Now we justify the correctness and the complexity of the algorithm in the Subsect. 3.5.

### 3.5 Analysis of Algorithm 2

From Definition 2 of $c$-partition, we know that $p(S_i)$ is $p_{n_1+\ldots n_{i-1}+1}$ for any $i \in [\ell]$, and is, in fact, the maximum one in $\{p_j, j \in S_i\}$. Also, we have that $p(S_i)/c \leq p_j \leq p(S_i)$ for arbitrary $j \in S_i$.

Let $T_f$ be the set of all the $x$ such that $f(x) \in S_{k_0}$, and its size as $|T_f|$. Similarly, we call a function $f \leftarrow D^M$ *well-behaved* if and only if $|T_f| > \frac{2M n_{k_0} p(S_{k_0})}{3c}$. We then have the following conclusion.

**Algorithm 2.** Collision-Finding Algorithm in Non-uniform Functions

**Input:** Collision domain $S_{k_0}$ and a function $f : [M] \to [N]$ with $f \leftarrow D^M$.
**Output:** A collision $(x_1, x_2)$ or $\perp$.

1: Construct a function $F_1 : [M] \to \{0,1\}$ such that $F_1(x) = 1$ iff $f(x) \in S_{k_0}$. Let $L$ be a dynamic constructed set which initially is emptyset $L = \emptyset$.
2: Run the modified BBHT algorithm with $F_1$ and $q_1$ to search for $x$ such that $F_1(x) = 1$. Query $y := f(x)$ and check whether $y \in S_{k_0}$. If yes, add $(x, y)$ into $L$; otherwise discard it. The process repeats until $L$ contains $t$ pairs of elements and to go to the next step; or repeats $4t$ times, and the Algorithm halts with $|L| < t$ and outputs $\perp$.
3: Check the elements in $L$. If there exist $(x_1, y_1), (x_2, y_2) \in L$ such that $x_1 \neq x_2$ and $y_1 = y_2$, output $(x_1, x_2)$ and halt. Otherwise to go to the next step.
4: Construct a function $F_2 : [M] \to \{0,1\}$ such that $F_2(x) = 1$ iff there exists $(x_0, y_0) \in L$ such that $f(x) = y_0$ and $x \neq x_0$. Invoke the modified BBHT algorithm with $F_2$ and $q_2$ to get an $x_1 \in [M]$.
5: If there is $(x_2, y_2) \in L$ such that $f(x_1) = y_2$, then output $(x_1, x_2)$; otherwise $\perp$.

**Lemma 7.** *For any constant $c > 1$, the random function $f \leftarrow D^M$ is well-behaved with probability at least $1 - \exp(-\frac{Mn_{k_0}p(S_{k_0})}{18c^2+2c})$.*

The Lemma 7 is proved in the full version [30]. Then, let suc denote the event that Algorithm 2 successfully finds a collision. We have

$$\begin{aligned}\Pr_{f \leftarrow D^M}[\text{suc}] &= \sum_f \Pr[f] \cdot \Pr[\text{suc} \mid f] \geq \sum_{f\text{: well-behaved}} \Pr[f] \cdot \Pr[\text{suc} \mid f] \\ &\geq \Big( \sum_{f\text{: well-behaved}} \Pr[f] \Big) \cdot \min_f \{\Pr[\text{suc} \mid f \text{ is well-behaved}]\} \\ &> ((1 - \exp(-\frac{Mn_{k_0}p(S_{k_0})}{18c^2 + 2c})) \cdot \min_f \{\Pr[\text{suc} \mid f \text{ is well-behaved}]\}.\end{aligned} \tag{4}$$

The last inequality is inherited from the proof of Lemma 7.

Notice that the key to the success of the algorithm is whether step 2 can successfully find $t$ pairs (to denote as $\text{suc}_2$) and whether step 3 or step 4 can find a collision pair (to denote as $\text{suc}_3$ and $\text{suc}_4$ respectively). Namely our algorithm succeeds iff $\text{suc}_2$ happens and one of $\text{suc}_3$ and $\text{suc}_4$ happens. That is,

$$\begin{aligned}&\min_f \{\Pr[\text{suc} \mid f \text{ is well-behaved}]\} \\ &= \min_{f\text{:well-behaved}} \big\{ \Pr[\text{suc}_2 \mid f] \cdot \Pr[\text{suc}_3 \vee \text{suc}_4 \mid f \wedge \text{suc}_2] \big\} \\ &\geq \min_{f\text{:well-behaved}} \Pr[\text{suc}_2 \mid f] \cdot \min_{f\text{:well-behaved}} \Pr[\text{suc}_3 \vee \text{suc}_4 \mid f \wedge \text{suc}_2].\end{aligned} \tag{5}$$

Note that the probabilities in the equation above are determined by $f$ and the query number $q$ in the corresponding step. For convenience, let

$$P_1^q := \min_{f:\text{well-behaved}} \Pr[\mathrm{suc}_2 \mid f], \tag{6}$$

$$P_2^q := \min_{f:\text{well-behaved}} \Pr[\mathrm{suc}_3 \vee \mathrm{suc}_4 \mid f \wedge \mathrm{suc}_2]. \tag{7}$$

We are going to show, for sufficiently large $q$, that $P_1^q$ and $P_2^q$ have lower bounds asymptotically to 1. Which, in turn from (5), implies that promised $f$ is well-behaved, Algorithm 2 finds the collision with bounded error.

**Estimations of $P_1^q$ and $P_2^q$.** We show the following two results.

**Theorem 5.** *For any constant $c > 1$ and $f \leftarrow D^M$, if $f$ is well-behaved, Algorithm 2 succeeds in Step 2 with the probability at least $1 - \exp(-\frac{t}{2})$ after making at most $21.6t\sqrt{c}/\sqrt{n_{k_0}p(S_{k_0})}$ queries.*

**Theorem 6.** *Suppose it has successfully obtained $t$ pairs in Step 2 of Collision-Finding Algorithm, then for $f \leftarrow D^M$, if $f$ is well-behaved, the algorithm, which makes at most $32.4\sqrt{c}/\sqrt{t\,p(S_{k_0})}$ queries, will find a collision with the probability at least $\frac{1}{2} \cdot (3/4 - e^{-t/2})$.*

The formal proofs of Theorem 5, 6 may refer to the full version of this paper. According to the two conclusions, the algorithm will find a collision with high probability with at most $O(\max(t/\sqrt{n_{k_0}p(S_{k_0})}, 1/\sqrt{tp(S_{k_0})}))$ queries. It's easy to see that when $t := O(\sqrt[3]{n_{k_0}})$, namely $\frac{t}{\sqrt{n_{k_0}p(S_{k_0})}} = \Theta(\frac{1}{\sqrt{t\,p(S_{k_0})}})$, the order of magnitude of the number of queries reaches the minimum, which will be

$$O(\frac{t}{\sqrt{n_{k_0}p(S_{k_0})}}) = O(\frac{1}{\sqrt{t\,p(S_{k_0})}}) = O((n_{k_0}p^3(S_{k_0}))^{-1/6}) = O(\gamma^{1/6}(c)).$$

Overall, combining the conclusions from (4), (5), (6), (7) along with Theorem 5 and Theorem 6, we ultimately obtain the result in Theorem 7 below.

**Theorem 7.** *For any constant $c > 1$, suppose $D$ be a probabilistic distribution over $[N]$ with $M > 12c^2/p(S_{k_0})$, where $k_0$ is the index of collision domain defined in Definition 3, then in the case that $f$ is well-behaved, with $O(\gamma^{1/6}(c))$ queries, Algorithm 2 will find a collision to $f \leftarrow D^M$ with probability $\Omega(1)$.*

*Remark 2.* The algorithm's requirements for $M$ are described in terms of $p(S_{k_0})$, which may not be particularly intuitive. In Sect. 5, we will show that $M$ can be relaxed to $M = \Omega(2^{3\mathrm{k}/2})$ or $M = \Omega(N)$.

### 3.6 Strategies to Avoid Algorithm Invalidity

We note that the complexity analysis of the algorithms in the previous section is carried out only in the average case over $f$. In other words, the success probability is evaluated for "well-behaved" functions $f$ (recall that, in the two algorithms respectively, well-behaved $f$ satisfy $6c\sqrt{n_{k_0}} < |M_f| < 18c^2\sqrt{n_{k_0}}$ and $|T_f| > \frac{2Mn_{k_0}p(S_{k_0})}{3c}$). To handle functions $f$ that do not satisfy these conditions, we give the following lemma to estimate the probability that unwanted $f$ occurs.

**Lemma 8.** *Suppose $D$ be a probabilistic distribution over $[N]$, $\{S_1, \ldots, S_\ell\}$ is the c-partition and $n_{k_0}p(S_{k_0})^3 := \max_i\{n_i p(S_i)^3\}$, then one of the following condition holds*

- $n_{k_0} \geq (\log N)^2$;
- $n_{k_0}p(S_{k_0}) \geq \frac{18c^2 \log N}{N}$.

The proof of Lemma 8 can be found in the full version[30]. We now present the mixed algorithm in Algorithm 3.

---

**Algorithm 3.** A Mixed Algorithm for Non-uniform Collision Finding

---

**Input:** Collision domain $S_{k_0}$, a function $f : [M] \to [N]$ drawn as $f \leftarrow D^M$, and a query bound $q_f$.

**Output:** A collision $(x_1, x_2)$ or $\perp$.

1: With probability 0.99, check whether (a) $n_{k_0} \geq (\log N)^2$ or (b) $n_{k_0}p(S_{k_0}) \geq \frac{18c^2 \log N}{N}$:

2: if (a) holds, run Algorithm 1 and output its return value;

3: if (b) holds, run Algorithm 2 and output its return value;

4: With probability 0.01, sample a random subset $M' \subseteq M$ with $|M'| = O(\gamma^{1/6}(c))$, find and output a collision in $M'$ if exists.

5: If no collision is found, check whether the query number $q$ exceeds $q_f$. If not, repeat from Step 1; otherwise, return $\perp$.

---

To calculate the expected query complexity, we denote by $q_f$ the number of queries that Algorithm 3 succeeds with constant probability on function $f$. By Lemma 8, Lemma 6, and Lemma 7, when $M = \Omega(N)$, either $f$ is well-behaved for Algorithm 1 with probability at least $1 - \exp(-\log N) > 1 - 1/N$, or $f$ is well-behaved for Algorithm 2 with probability at least $1 - \exp(-0.9 \log N) > 1 - 1/N$. Combining Theorems 1 and 7, Algorithm 3 (Step 2 and 3) succeeds with constrant probability on well-behaved $f$ via expected query complexity $O(\gamma^{1/6}(c))$. Step 4 of Algorithm 3 works for nonwell-behaved $f$. To achieve constant success probability on such $f$, it might need as large as $O(N)$ queries. Since non-well-behaved $f$ occurs with probability at most $O(1/N)$, the overall expected query complexity of Algorithm 3 is $\mathrm{E}_f\, q_f = O(\gamma^{1/6}(c)) + O(N \cdot 1/N) = O(\gamma^{1/6}(c))$.

# 4 The Lower Bound

In this section, we are going to exploit a query complexity lower bound, during which the compressed oracle technique is adopted. For this purpose, we first introduce Zhandry's compressed oracle in Sect. 4.1. We then turn the collision-finding problem with respect to non-uniform functions into another problem with uniform functions, for which we are able to use compressed oracle technique to give a lower bound to the transformed problem as shown in Theorem 9 in Sect. 4.3. The relation of their success probabilities for two problems is then shown in Sect. 4.2. With Corollary 1 (a variant of Theorem 9), we explore the lower bound and get the main result in Theorem 10. In the last subsection, we discuss the parameter $\delta_c$ that appeared in Theorem 10, which leads to an almost tight lower bound.

## 4.1 Zhandry's Compressed Oracle

There are two models of oracles in quantum computing called, respectively, the standard oracle and phase oracle. These two are widely used in quantum computation in the black-box setting. By using the Hadamard transformation, these two oracles have been shown to be completely equivalent, so only the phase oracle will be introduced here.

Let $\mathcal{A}^{\mathcal{O}}$ be a $q$-query quantum algorithm which is given oracle access to a function $\mathcal{O}$ from $N^M$. Let $|\psi_0\rangle$ be the input state for $\mathcal{A}^{\mathcal{O}}$ and $|\psi_i\rangle$ the output state before the $i$'th measurement. A quantum computation performed by $\mathcal{A}$ with $i$ queries is generally described as the product of a series of unitary transformations, in the following form:

$$|\psi_i\rangle = U_i\mathcal{O}\ldots U_1\mathcal{O}U_0|\psi_0\rangle.$$

where $U_0, \ldots, U_i$ are some unitary operators independent of the input $x$.

**A Phase Oracle** is a unitary transformation as follows:

$$\sum_{x,y,z} a_{x,y,z}|x,y,z\rangle \rightarrow \sum_{x,y,z} (-1)^{y\cdot f(x)} a_{x,y,z}|x,y,z\rangle.$$

For any random function $f \leftarrow N^M$. Here $x$ denotes the input register, $y$ is the output register and $z$ is some auxiliary bits.

Zhandry discovered that $\mathcal{O}$ could be written in another form, in which $f$ would be written as a truth table $|f\rangle = |f(0), f(1)\ldots f(M-1)\rangle$, and a query to $\mathcal{O}$ should be considered as a quantum entanglement as follows:

$$\sum_{x,y,z} a_{x,y,z}|x,y,z\rangle \otimes \sum_f \frac{1}{\sqrt{N^M}}|f\rangle \rightarrow \sum_{x,y,z} (-1)^{y\cdot f(x)} a_{x,y,z}|x,y,z\rangle \otimes \sum_f \frac{1}{\sqrt{N^M}}|f\rangle.$$

**Compressed Phase Oracle:** In the model of compressed phase oracle[39], the superposition state $\sum|f\rangle$ in phase oracle above will be replaced by a database $\mathbf{D}$

which records $q$ binary and initialize as $\mathbf{D} := \{(0, \perp), ..., (0, \perp)\}$(for convenience, for any $x \in [M]$, if there is $(x, y)$ in $\mathbf{D}$, we denote $\mathbf{D}(x) := y$, otherwise we denote $D(x) = \perp$). When the adversary makes a query to the compressed phase oracle $\mathcal{O}$ on $|x, y, z, \mathbf{D}\rangle$, a binary pair in D is modified accordingly. More specifically, it performs in a sequence of the following steps:

1. If $\mathbf{D}(x) = \perp$, we denote $\mathbf{D}' \cup (0, \perp) = \mathbf{D}$, then it performs the map:

$$|x, y, z\rangle \otimes |\mathbf{D}' \cup (0, \perp)\rangle \rightarrow |x, y, z\rangle \otimes \frac{1}{\sqrt{2^n}} \sum_w |\mathbf{D}' \cup (x, w)\rangle.$$

   If $\mathbf{D}(x) = y_0$, then check whether binary pairs in $\mathbf{D}$ should be deleted. More specifically, if we denote $\mathbf{D}' \cup (x, y_0) = \mathbf{D}$, it performs the map:

$$\frac{1}{\sqrt{2^n}} \sum_{y_0} (-1)^{z' \cdot y_0} |\mathbf{D}' \cup (x, y_0)\rangle \rightarrow \begin{cases} \frac{1}{\sqrt{2^n}} \sum_{y_0} (-1)^{z' \cdot y_0} |\mathbf{D}' \cup (x, y_0)\rangle, & \text{if } z' \neq 0; \\ |\mathbf{D}' \cup (0, \perp)\rangle, & \text{if } z' = 0. \end{cases}$$

2. If $\mathbf{D}(x) \neq \perp$, perform the following unitary transformation:

$$|x, y, z\rangle \otimes |\mathbf{D}' \cup (x, w)\rangle \rightarrow (-1)^{y \cdot w} |x, y, z\rangle \otimes |\mathbf{D}' \cup (x, w)\rangle.$$

   If $\mathbf{D}(x) = \perp$, this step performs the identity transformation.
3. Perform Step 1 again.

Zhandry proved that the two random oracles are equivalent. That is, for any adversary $\mathcal{A}$, phase oracle and compressed phase oracle are perfectly indistinguishable. Moreover, under the compressed oracle model, the database attached is very likely to record the information obtained by the adversary. The details, verbatim quoted from the original paper, are as follows:

**Lemma 9 (Lemma 5 in** [39]**).** *Consider a quantum algorithm $\mathcal{A}$ making queries to a random oracle $H$ and outputting tuples $(x_1 \ldots x_k, y_1, \ldots y_k, z)$. Let $R$ be a collection of such tuples. Suppose with probability $p$, $\mathcal{A}$ outputs a tuple such that (1) the tuple is in $R$ and (2) $H(x_i) = y_i$ for all $i$. Now consider running $A$ with the compressed phase oracle, and suppose the database $\mathbf{D}$ is measured after $\mathcal{A}$ produces its output. Let $p'$ be the probability that (1) the tuple is in $R$, and (2) $\mathbf{D}(x_i) = y_i$ for all $i$ (and in particular $\mathbf{D}(x_i) \neq \perp$). Then $\sqrt{p} < \sqrt{p'} + \sqrt{k/2^n}$.*

This indicates compressed oracle's record reliability to ensure that if $\mathcal{A}$ can find a solution to a problem with a non-negligible probability, it can also be found in $\mathbf{D}$ with a non-negligible probability (provided that $k$ is small enough).

In the collision-finding problem, the output of any quantum algorithm will be a binary pair, namely $k = 2$. This hints us a new way to seek lower bound. Although the quantum adversary method[3] and the polynomials[37] approaches are usually adapted to derive the quantum lower bound proofs. Zhandry's technique allows us to turn attention to the changes in $\mathbf{D}$ after each query (notice any unitary operators $U_i$ can not change the database $\mathbf{D}$), which would be, in some cases, more intuitive and convenient[24,28].

## 4.2 Transformation from Non-uniform Case to Uniform Case

Since the compressed oracle is equivalent to the phase oracle only for the uniform random functions and it might not be easy directly to apply in the non-uniform setting, therefore we have to turn the collision-finding problem in the non-uniform setting into another problem in the uniform setting with a larger range.

For a given random distribution $D$ over $[N]$, we have $c$-partition defined as in Definition 2 and Definition 3. With the same notations as in definitions, we pose the following problem.

*Problem 1* For any $r \in [\ell]$, let $f : [M] \to [N]$ be a function chosen according to non-uniform distribution $D^M$, the problem is to find a collision $(x, x')$ such that $f(x) = f(x') \in S_r$.

The problem is the same as the general collision-finding problem except that a constraint $f(x) \in S_r$ is posed. It is easy to see that if an adversary $\mathcal{A}$ successfully finds a collision in general, then Problem 1 should be solved for some $S_r$. Hence, the success probability of $\mathcal{A}$ is bounded by the SUM of the upper bounds of the success probabilities for solving Problem 1 overall $S_r$ (as shown in (8) in Sect. 4.3). In this way, we will show the number of queries necessary for collision-finding.

In order to estimate the success probabilities for Problem 1, we turn to the following corresponding problem.

*Problem 2* For the $r \in [\ell]$, let $g : [M] \to [KN]$ be a function chosen from $(KN)^M$ uniformly at random, where $K$ is a large integer (cf. Theorem 8 for the possible values of $K$). To define $s_i \subseteq [KN]$ as follows $(i = 1, \ldots, N+1)$.

$$s_i := \begin{cases} [1 \mathrel{..} \lfloor KNp_1 \rfloor], & \text{for } i = 1; \\ [1 + \sum_{j=1}^{i-1} \lfloor KNp_j \rfloor \mathrel{..} \sum_{j=1}^{i} \lfloor KNp_j \rfloor], & \text{for } i \in [2, N]; \\ [KN] \setminus (\bigcup_{i=1}^{N} s_i), & \text{for } i = N+1. \end{cases}$$

The problem is to find two distinct inputs $x, x'$ such that $g(x), g(x') \in s_k$ for some $k \in S_r$.

The following result reveals the relationship between these two problems above:

**Theorem 8** *If there exists a q-query quantum algorithm $\mathcal{A}$ that solves Problem 1 with probability $\mathbf{P}_1$, then there exists a q-query quantum algorithm $\mathcal{B}$ that solves Problem 2 with probability $\mathbf{P}_2$ such that*

$$\mathbf{P}_1 - \mathbf{P}_2 < O(\frac{q^2}{K}).$$

It tells us that, for large enough $K$, if there exists an algorithm $\mathcal{A}$ solving Problem 1 with success probability $\Omega(1)$, then there will have an algorithm $\mathcal{B}$ solving Problem 2 successfully with probability $\Omega(1)$.

In other words, if we get an upper bound of success probability with $q$ queries solving Problem 2, we will get an upper bound of success probability with $q$ queries solving Problem 1. That is, we use Problem 2 to functions with uniform distributions to simulate the Problem 1 to functions with non-uniform distributions. Moreover, the larger the $K$ is, the better the simulation does.

The proof of Theorem 8 can be found in the full version[30]. The result in Theorem 8 allows us, when considering the collision-finding problem, to focus on Problem 2, which is with respect to uniform random functions. That also makes the compressed oracle technology useful for our purpose.

*Remark 3.* In our work, by transforming a non-uniform problem into a uniform one, we can apply Zhandry's compressed oracle technique in our proof. However, we note that in [14], a more generalized version of the compressed oracle technique was proposed, which can be directly applied to the non-uniform setting studied in our paper. Using their technique directly may lead to a more concise proof, and we encourage interested readers to explore this possibility.

### 4.3 The Lower Bound for Collision-Finding

The main result in this subsection is the following theorem.

**Theorem 9.** *Given $r > 0$ and distribution $D$ as in the last section, for any quantum algorithm, $\Omega(\gamma_r^{1/6}(c))$ quantum queries are necessary to solve Problem 2 with constant probability.*

Due to the limitation of spcae, we put the proof of Theorem 9 in the full version [30]. Moreover, as a variant of Theorem 9, the following result is obtained directly from the proof of Theorem 9.

**Corollary 1.** *For any quantum algorithm making $q$ queries, the success probability in solving Problem 2 is at most $O(\max\{q^3 n_r^{1/2} p^{3/2}(S_r), q^2 n_r^{1/4} p(S_r)\})$.*

According to Corollary 1, we now explore a quantum query lower bound for the collision-finding problem with respect to non-uniform distributions.

Let's denote $S_r' := \bigcup_{j \in S_r} s_j$, we get

$$\begin{aligned}
&\Pr_{f \leftarrow D^M}\left[f(x) = f(x'), x \neq x' : (x, x') \leftarrow \mathcal{A}^f\right] \\
&= \Pr_{f \leftarrow D^M}[f(x) = f(x'), x \neq x', f(x) \in \bigcup_{r=1}^{\ell} S_r : (x, x') \leftarrow \mathcal{A}^f] \qquad (8) \\
&\leq \sum_{r=1}^{\ell} \Pr_{f \leftarrow D^M}[f(x) = f(x'), x \neq x', f(x) \in S_r : (x, x') \leftarrow \mathcal{A}^f].
\end{aligned}$$

According to Theorem 8, there is an algorithm $\mathcal{B}$ such that

$$\Pr_{f \leftarrow D^M}[f(x) = f(x'), x \neq x', f(x) \in S_r : (x, x') \leftarrow \mathcal{A}^f]$$
$$\leq \Pr_{g \leftarrow (KN)^M}[g(x), g(x') \in s_j, x \neq x', s_j \subset S'_r : (x, x') \leftarrow \mathcal{B}^g] + O(\frac{q^2}{K}),$$

which in turn implies from (8)

$$\Pr_{f \leftarrow D^M}\left[f(x) = f(x'), x \neq x' : (x, x') \leftarrow \mathcal{A}^f\right]$$
$$\leq \sum_{r=1}^{\ell} \Pr_{g \leftarrow (KN)^M}[g(x), g(x') \in s_j, x \neq x', s_j \subset S'_r : (x, x') \leftarrow \mathcal{B}^g] + O(\frac{\ell q^2}{K}).$$

By Corollary 1, we have

$$\begin{aligned} &\Pr[g(x), g(x') \in s_j, x \neq x', s_j \subset S'_r : (x, x') \leftarrow \mathcal{B}^g, g \leftarrow (KN)^M] \\ &\qquad \leq O(\max\{q^3 n_r^{1/2} p^{3/2}(S_r), q^2 n_r^{1/3} p(S_r)\}) \end{aligned} \tag{9}$$

for any $i \in [\ell]$. To combine (8) and (9), we have

$$\begin{aligned} &\Pr[f(x) = f(x'), x \neq x' : (x, x') \leftarrow A^f, f \leftarrow D^M] \\ &\leq O(\frac{\ell q^2}{K}) + \sum_{r=1}^{\ell} O\big(\max\{q^3 n_r^{1/2} p^{3/2}(S_r), q^2 n_r^{1/3} p(S_r)\}\big) \qquad (10) \\ &\leq O\Big(\sum_{r=1}^{\ell} \max\{q^3 n_r^{1/2} p^{3/2}(S_r), q^2 n_r^{1/3} p(S_r)\}\Big). \end{aligned}$$

The last inequality holds since $\ell/K$ can be as small as required with large enough $K$. In fact, when distribution $D$ is given, $\ell$ is fixed.

By the upper bound for $q$ in Theorem 7, we assume $q < \gamma^{1/6}(c) \leq \gamma_r^{1/6}(c)$. That implies

$$\max\{q^3 n_r^{1/2} p^{3/2} p(S_r), q^2 n_r^{1/3} p(S_r)\} = q^2 n_r^{1/3} p(S_r).$$

for any any $r \in [\ell]$. Hence from (10), we have:

$$\begin{aligned} \Pr_{f \leftarrow D^M}[f(x) = f(x'), x \neq x' : (x, x') \leftarrow A^f] &\leq O(q^2 \sum_{r=1}^{\ell} n_r^{1/3} p(S_r)) \\ &= O(q^2 \cdot \delta_c \max_r\{(n_r p^3(S_r))^{1/3}\}) = O(\delta_c q^2 \gamma^{-1/3}(c)). \end{aligned} \tag{11}$$

where

$$\delta_c := \frac{\sum_{r=1}^{\ell} (n_r p^3(S_r))^{1/3}}{\max_r\{(n_r p^3(S_r))^{1/3}\}} = \frac{\sum_{r=1}^{\ell} \gamma_r^{-1/3}(c)}{\gamma^{-1/3}(c)}.$$

(11) implies that if the success probability for collision-finding is a constant, then $q = \Omega(\gamma^{1/6}(c) \cdot \delta_c^{-1/2})$. Now we give the main conclusion of this section is as follows.

**Theorem 10.** *For any quantum collision-finding algorithm with respect to a non-uniform distribution, $\Omega(\gamma^{1/6}(c) \cdot \delta_c^{-1/2})$ queries are necessary to find a collision with constant probability.*

Specially, when $D$ is a uniform distribution, for any constant $c > 1$, one can easily get $\delta_c = 1$ and $\gamma(c) = N^2$, and hence the upper bound and lower bound here meet as $\Theta(\gamma^{1/6}(c)) = \Theta(N^{1/3})$ as shown in [38].

We let readers convince themselves that the upper bound and the lower bound here also meets on flat-$\mathtt{k}$-distribution and $\delta$-$\mathtt{k}$ distribution (cf. [8]). Here we refer to these two distributions to illustrate our algorithm's optimality. It hint that the upper bound and lower bound obtained in this work possess more generality.

In the following section, we will estimate the value of $\delta_c$ to derive a concise lower bound.

### 4.4 Estimation of Upper Bound of $\delta_c$

We now estimate $\delta_c$ appeared in the lower bound in the last section. We prove the following upper bound for $\delta_c$ mentioned above. That will lead to a nearly tight lower bound.

**Proposition 1.** *We have $\delta_c = O(\mathtt{k})$ for any non-uniform distribution $D$ and any constant $c > 1$. Where $\mathtt{k} = -\log p_1$ is the min-entropy of $D$.*

*Proof.* Let $b_i := \gamma_i^{-1/3}(c)/\gamma^{-1/3}(c)$ for all $i \in [\ell]$. We rearrange the list $b_1, \ldots, b_\ell$ in non-increasing order and denote it as $a_1, \ldots, a_\ell$ with $a_1 = 1, a_i \leq 1$ for any $i \in [\ell]$ and obviously

$$\sum_{i=1}^{\ell} a_i = \sum_{i=1}^{\ell} b_i = \frac{\sum_{r=1}^{\ell} \gamma_r^{-1/3}(c)}{\gamma^{-1/3}(c)} = \delta_c. \tag{12}$$

Let $a_k = b_{i_k} = \gamma_{i_k}^{-1/3}(c)/\gamma^{-1/3}(c)$, and hence $a_k^3 = n_{i_k} p^3(S_{i_k})/n_{k_0} p^3(S_{i_{k_0}})$, where $k_0$ is the collision domain index in Definition 3. By $c$-partition, it holds that $n_{i_k} p(S_{i_k}) \leq c$. Hence we have

$$c p(S_{i_k})^2 \geq n_{i_k} p(S_{i_k})^3 = a_k^3 \gamma^{-1} \geq a_k^3 \cdot 2^{-3\mathtt{k}}.$$

The last inequality is by Proposition 2 that $\gamma^{1/6}(c) \leq 2^{\mathtt{k}/2}$ for any constant $c > 1$. It implies, for any $k \in [\ell]$

$$p(S_{i_k}) \geq \frac{1}{\sqrt{c}} \cdot a_k^{3/2} \cdot 2^{-3\mathtt{k}/2}. \tag{13}$$

It is easy to see that $\delta_c \leq \ell$, otherwise $\delta_c = \sum_{i=1}^{\ell} a_i \leq \ell \cdot a_1 < \delta_c$ for decreasing sequence $a_i$ with $a_1 = 1$, which is impossible.

Next, we show there is a $j \leq \lfloor \frac{\ell}{\lfloor \delta_c/2 \rfloor} \rfloor$ that satisfies $a_{j\lfloor \delta_c/2 \rfloor} \geq 1/(j+1)^4$. Otherwise, if $a_{j\lfloor \delta_c/2 \rfloor} < 1/(j+1)^4$ for all $j \leq \lfloor \frac{\ell}{\lfloor \delta_c/2 \rfloor} \rfloor$, then by (12),

$$\delta_c = \sum_{i=1}^{\ell} a_i = \sum_{i=1}^{\lfloor \frac{\delta_c}{2} \rfloor} a_i + \sum_{i=\lfloor \frac{\delta_c}{2} \rfloor + 1}^{2\lfloor \frac{\delta_c}{2} \rfloor} a_i + \cdots + \sum_{i=\lfloor \frac{\ell}{\lfloor \delta_c/2 \rfloor} \rfloor \cdot \lfloor \frac{\delta_c}{2} \rfloor + 1}^{\ell} a_i$$
$$< \lfloor \frac{\delta_c}{2} \rfloor \cdot \left(1 + \frac{1}{2^4} + \cdots + \frac{1}{(\lfloor \frac{\ell}{\lfloor \delta_c/2 \rfloor} \rfloor + 1)^4}\right) < \lfloor \frac{\delta_c}{2} \rfloor \cdot \sum_{j=1}^{\infty} \frac{1}{j^4} < \frac{9}{8} \cdot \lfloor \delta_c/2 \rfloor < \delta_c.$$

This is a contradiction. Let $j_0$ be the smallest $j \leq \lfloor \frac{\ell}{\lfloor \delta_c/2 \rfloor} \rfloor$ that satisfies the inequality $a_{j\lfloor \delta_c/2 \rfloor} \geq 1/(j+1)^4$. Together with (13), it implies, for all $k \in [j_0 \lfloor \frac{\delta_c}{2} \rfloor]$

$$\begin{aligned} p(S_{i_k}) &\geq \frac{1}{\sqrt{c}} \cdot a_k^{3/2} \cdot 2^{-3\mathtt{k}/2} \\ &\geq \frac{1}{\sqrt{c}} \cdot a_{j_0 \lfloor \frac{\delta_c}{2} \rfloor}^{3/2} \cdot 2^{-3\mathtt{k}/2} \geq \frac{1}{\sqrt{c} \cdot (j_0+1)^6 \cdot 2^{3\mathtt{k}/2}}. \end{aligned} \tag{14}$$

On the other hand, from the definition of min-entropy $\mathtt{k}$, for all $k \in [j_0 \lfloor \frac{\delta_c}{2} \rfloor]$,

$$1/2^{\mathtt{k}} = p_1 \geq p(S_{i_k}). \tag{15}$$

According to (14) and (15), we get, by definition of $c$-partition,

$$\frac{1}{2^{\mathtt{k}}} \cdot \sqrt{c} \cdot (j_0+1)^6 \cdot 2^{\frac{3\mathtt{k}}{2}} \geq \frac{\max\{p(S_{i_k})\}_{k \in j_0 \lfloor \frac{\delta_c}{2} \rfloor}}{\min\{p(S_{i_k})\}_{k \in j_0 \lfloor \frac{\delta_c}{2} \rfloor}} \geq c^{j_0 \lfloor \frac{\delta_c}{2} \rfloor}.$$

Namely, we have

$$\delta_c \leq \frac{\mathtt{k} + 12 \log_2(j_0+1) + \log_2 c}{j_0 \log_2 c} + 2 = O(\mathtt{k}).$$

As desired. □

Together with Theorem 10, this concludes that $\Omega(\gamma^{1/6}(c)/\sqrt{\mathtt{k}})$ quantum queries are necessary to find a collision for any non-uniform random function and any constant $c > 1$. In combination with Proposition 2, which we will prove in the next section, we can get our final answer to the lower bound: $\Omega(\gamma^{1/6}(c)/\sqrt{\log \gamma(c)})$. Compared with the upper bound $O(\gamma^{1/6}(c))$ in Theorem 7, it is a nearly tight lower bound.

## 5 An Analysis on the Properties of $\gamma(c)$

In this section, we will give some properties of $\gamma(c)$, proofs of all Propositions in this section can be found in the full version [30]. We will present the relations of $\gamma$ with the min-entropy $\mathtt{k}$ and collision-entropy $\beta$, respectively. An upper bound of $p(S_{k_0})$ is given so as to help to simplify the calculation of collision parameter and collision domain whenever using Algorithm 2. In the last, we show that the constant $c$ in partition does not affect the magnitude of query complexity in collision-finding.

First, we point out a fact that will be frequently used in the subsequent proofs. Since $\sum_{i=1}^{N} p_i = 1$, we have by $c$-partition that, for any $k \in [\ell]$:

$$n_k p(S_k) \leq \sum_{i=1}^{\ell} n_i p(S_i) = c \sum_{i=1}^{\ell} \frac{n_i p(S_i)}{c} \leq c \sum_{i=1}^{N} p_i = c. \tag{16}$$

Now we show a relation between parameter $\gamma$ and min-entropy $\mathtt{k}$.

**Proposition 2.** *For any non-uniform distribution $D$ and any constant $c > 1$, it holds that $2^{2\mathtt{k}}/c \leq \gamma(c) \leq 2^{3\mathtt{k}}$. Where $\mathtt{k} = -\log p_1$ is the min-entropy.*

The results in Proposition 1, Proposition 2 and Theorem 10 claim the following conclusion.

**Corollary 2.** *The number $\Omega(\gamma^{1/6}(c)/\sqrt{\log \gamma(c)})$ of quantum queries are necessary for any algorithms of collision-finding in random functions.*

We show the relation between $\gamma$ and collision-entropy $\beta$ as follows.

**Proposition 3.** *For any non-uniform distribution $D$ and any constant $c > 1$, we have $\frac{1}{c} \cdot 2^{\beta} \leq \gamma(c) < \frac{16c^3}{(c-1)^2} \cdot 2^{2\beta}$.*

From Table 1, we see Proposition 2 and 3 show that, in general non-uniform distribution, the upper bound and lower bound here in the parameter $\gamma$ are always at least as good as the best prior results. Moreover, in the full version [30], we present an example to show that the results here can be better in general.

The following technique result will allow us to simplify the calculation of the collision domain in $c$-partition.

**Proposition 4.** *For any non-uniform distribution $D$, we have*

$$p(S_{k_0}) \geq \max\left\{c^{-1/2} \cdot 2^{-\frac{3\mathtt{k}}{2}}, \frac{c^2-1}{c^2 N}\right\}.$$

*Where $p(S_{k_0})$ satisfies $n_{k_0} p^3(S_{k_0}) = \gamma^{-1}(c)$, and $\mathtt{k} = -\log p_1$ is the min-entropy.*

The result above also implies that in the calculation of the collision parameter and the collision domain, one only needs to seek for the sets $S_i$ satisfying $p(S_i) = \Omega(2^{-3\mathtt{k}/2})$ or $p(S_i) = \Omega(N^{-1})$.

The following proposition indicates that the choice of $c$ does not affect the order of magnitude of $\gamma(c)$ (as long as $c > 1$ is a constant).

**Proposition 5.** *For any non-uniform distribution $D$ and constants $c_1, c_2$ satisfying $c_2 > c_1 > 1$, we have* $\frac{c_1^3-1}{c_1^3 c_2^3} \cdot \gamma(c_1) < \gamma(c_2) \leq 2c_1^3 \cdot \gamma(c_1)$.

**Acknowledgement.** We thank the anonymous reviewers, especially the shepherd of this article, for helpful comments that significantly improved the quality of this paper. This work is supported by National Natural Science Foundation of China (62302496, 62172405), and the Key Research Program of the Chinese Academy of Science, Grant No. ZDRW-XX-2022-1.

## References

1. Aaronson, S., Shi, Y.: Quantum lower bounds for the collision and the element distinctness problems. J. ACM **51**(4), 595–605 (2004)
2. Akmal, S., Jin, C.: Near-optimal quantum algorithms for string problems, 10 (2021)
3. Ambainis, A.: Quantum lower bounds by quantum arguments. In Proceedings of the Thirty-Second Annual ACM Symposium on Theory of Computing, May 21-23, 2000, Portland, OR, USA, pages 636–643 (2000)
4. Ambainis, A.: Quantum walk algorithm for element distinctness. In: FOCS 2004, pages 22–31. IEEE Comput. Soc. (2004)
5. Ambainis, A.: Polynomial degree and lower bounds in quantum complexity: collision and element distinctness with small range. Theory Comput. **1**(1), 37–46 (2005)
6. Ambainis, A., Hamburg, M., Unruh, D.: Quantum security proofs using semi-classical oracles. In: CRYPTO 2019, pages 269–295. Springer (2019)
7. Ambainis, A., Rosmanis, A., Unruh, D.: Quantum attacks on classical proof systems: the hardness of quantum rewinding. In: 55th IEEE Annual Symposium on Foundations of Computer Science, FOCS 2014, Philadelphia, PA, USA, October 18-21, 2014, pages 474–483 (2014)
8. Balogh, M., Eaton, E., Song, F.: Quantum collision-finding in non-uniform random functions. In: PQCrypto 2018, pages 467–486. Springer (2018)
9. Berman, I., Degwekar, A., Rothblum, R.D., Vasudevan, P.N.: Multi-collision resistant hash functions and their applications. In: Advances in Cryptology - EUROCRYPT 2018, pages 133–161 (2018)
10. Boldyreva, A., Kumar, V.: A new pseudorandom generator from collision-resistant hash functions. In: CT-RSA 2012, vol. 7178 of Lecture Notes in Computer Science, pages 187–202. Springer (2012)
11. Boyer, M., Brassard, G., Høyer, P., Tapp, A.: Tight bounds on quantum searching. Fortschritte der Physik: Prog. Phys. **46**(4–5), 493–505 (1998)
12. Brassard, G., Høyer, P., Tapp, A.: Quantum cryptanalysis of hash and claw-free functions. SIGACT News **28**(2), 14–19 (1997)
13. Chailloux, A., Loyer, J.: Lattice sieving via quantum random walks. In Mehdi Tibouchi and Huaxiong Wang, editors, ASIACRYPT 2021, pages 63–91. Springer (2021)
14. Chung, K.-M., Fehr, S., Huang, Y.-H., Liao, T.-N.: On the compressed-oracle technique, and post-quantum security of proofs of sequential work. Cryptology ePrint Archive, Paper 2020/1305 (2020)
15. Diffie, W., Hellman, M.E.: New directions in cryptography. IEEE Trans. Inf. Theory **22**(6), 644–654 (1976)

16. Dong, X., Dong, B., Wang, X.: Quantum attacks on some Feistel block ciphers. Des. Codes Cryptogr. **88**(6), 1179–1203 (2020)
17. Ebrahimi, E., Unruh, D.: Quantum collision-resistance of non-uniformly distributed functions: upper and lower bounds. Quantum Inf. Comput. **18**(15&16), 1332–1349 (2018)
18. Fischlin, M., Lehmann, A.: Security-amplifying combiners for collision-resistant hash functions. In: Alfred Menezes, editor, Advances in Cryptology - CRYPTO 2007, 27th Annual International Cryptology Conference, Santa Barbara, CA, USA, August 19-23, 2007, Proceedings, volume 4622 of Lecture Notes in Computer Science, pages 224–243. Springer (2007)
19. Fujisaki, E., Okamoto, T.: Secure integration of asymmetric and symmetric encryption schemes. In: CRYPTO 99, pages 537–554. Springer (1999)
20. Fuller, B., Reyzin, L., Smith, A.D.: When are fuzzy extractors possible? In ASIACRYPT **2016**, 277–306 (2016)
21. Gall, F.L.: Improved quantum algorithm for triangle finding via combinatorial arguments. In: 2014 IEEE 55th Annual Symposium on Foundations of Computer Science, pages 216–225 (2014)
22. Grover, L.K.: A fast quantum mechanical algorithm for database search. In: Proceedings of the Twenty-Eighth Annual ACM Symposium on the Theory of Computing, Philadelphia, Pennsylvania, USA, May 22-24, 1996, pages 212–219 (1996)
23. Hallgren, S., Smith, A.D., Song, F.: Classical cryptographic protocols in a quantum world. CoRR, abs/1507.01625 (2015)
24. Hosoyamada, A., Iwata, T.: 4-round luby-rackoff construction is a qprp. In: ASIACRYPT 2019, pages 145–174. Springer (2019)
25. Jeffery, S., Kothari, R., Magniez, F.: Nested quantum walks with quantum data structures. In: Proceedings of the Twenty-Fourth Annual ACM-SIAM Symposium on Discrete Algorithms. Soc. Indus. Appl. Math. (2013)
26. Kaplan, M., Leurent, G., Leverrier, A., Naya-Plasencia, M.: Breaking symmetric cryptosystems using quantum period finding. In: CRYPTO 2016, pages 207–237. Springer (2016)
27. Kutin, S.: Quantum lower bound for the collision problem with small range. Theory Comput. **1**(1), 29–36 (2005)
28. Liu, Q., Zhandry, M.: On finding quantum multi-collisions. In Yuval Ishai and Vincent Rijmen, editors, EUROCRYPT, pages 189–218. Springer (2019)
29. Magniez, F., Nayak, A., Roland, J., Santha, M.: Search via quantum walk. SIAM J. Comput. **40**(1), 142–164 (2011)
30. Peng, T., Cao, S., Xue, R.: On quantum query complexities of collision-finding in non-uniform random functions. Cryptology ePrint Archive, Paper 2021/1578 )(2021)
31. Rivest, R.L., Shamir, A., Adleman, L.M.: A method for obtaining digital signatures and public-key cryptosystems. Commun. ACM **21**(2), 120–126 (1978)
32. Shor, P.W.: Polynomial-time algorithms for prime factorization and discrete logarithms on a quantum computer. SIAM J. Comput. **26**(5), 1484–1509 (1997)
33. Targhi, E.E., Tabia, G.N., Unruh, D.: Quantum collision-resistance of non-uniformly distributed functions. In: Takagi, T., ed., PQCrypto 2016, pages 79–85. Springer (2016)
34. Targhi, E.E., Unruh, D.: Post-quantum security of the fujisaki-okamoto and OAEP transforms. In: TCC 2016-B, pages 192–216 (2016)
35. Wolf, R.: Quantum computing: Lecture notes, 07 (2019)
36. Yuen, H.: A quantum lower bound for distinguishing random functions from random permutations. Quantum Inf. Comput. **14**(13–14), 1089–1097 (2014)

37. Zhandry, M.: How to construct quantum random functions. In: FOCS 2012, pages 679–687. IEEE Comput. Soc. (2012)
38. Zhandry, M.: A note on the quantum collision and set equality problems. Quan. Inf. Comput. **15**(7&8), 557–567 (2015)
39. Zhandry, M.: How to record quantum queries, and applications to quantum indifferentiability. In: Advances in Cryptology - CRYPTO 2019,August 18-22, 2019, pages 239–268 (2019)

# Quantum Periodic Distinguisher Construction: Symbolization Method and Automated Tool

Qun Liu[1,2,4], Haoyang Wang[3], Jinliang Wang[1,2,4], Boyun Li[1,2,4], and Meiqin Wang[1,2,4](✉)

[1] School of Cyber Science and Technology, Shandong University, Qingdao, China
qunliu@sdu.edu.cn, {jinliangwang,boyunli}@mail.sdu.edu.cn
[2] State Key Laboratory of Cryptography and Digital Economy Security, Shandong University, Qingdao, China
mqwang@sdu.edu.cn
[3] Shanghai Jiao Tong University, Shanghai, China
haoyang.wang@sjtu.edu.cn
[4] Key Laboratory of Cryptologic Technology and Information Security, Ministry of Education, Shandong University, Jinan, China

**Abstract.** As one of the famous quantum algorithms, Simon's algorithm enables the efficient derivation of the period of periodic functions in polynomial time. However, the complexity of constructing periodic functions has hindered the widespread application of Simon's algorithm in symmetric-key cryptanalysis. Currently, aside from the exhaustive search-based testing method introduced by Canale et al. at CRYPTO 2022, there is no unified model for effectively searching for periodic distinguishers. Although Xiang et al. established a link between periodic functions and truncated differential theory at ToSC 2024, their approach lacks the ability to construct periods using unknown differentials and does not provide automated tools. This limitation underscores the inadequacy of existing methods in identifying periodic distinguishers for complex structures. In this paper, we address the challenge of advancing periodic distinguishers for symmetric-key ciphers. First, we propose a more generalized method for constructing periodic distinguishers, addressing the limitations of Xiang et al.'s theory in handling unknown differences. We further extend it to probabilistic periodic distinguishers. As a result, our method can cover a wider range of periodic distinguishers. Second, we introduce a novel symbolic representation to simplify the search for periodic distinguishers, and propose the first fully automated SMT-based search model, which efficiently addresses the challenges of manual searching in complex structures. Based on our method, we have achieved new quantum distinguishers with the following round configurations: 10 rounds for GFS-4F, 10 rounds for LBlock, 10 rounds for TWINE, and 16 rounds for Skipjack-B, improving the previous best results by 1, 2, 2, and 3 rounds, respectively. Our model also identifies the first 7/8/9-round periodic distinguishers for SKINNY. Compared with existing distinguishers (Hadipour et al., CRYPTO 2024) with the

© International Association for Cryptologic Research 2026
G. Hanaoka and B.-Y. Yang (Eds.): ASIACRYPT 2025, LNCS 16252, pp. 224–255, 2026.
https://doi.org/10.1007/978-981-95-5125-5_8

same round in the classical setting, our distinguishers achieve lower data complexity.

**Keywords:** Quantum cryptanalysis · Automated search model · Simon's algorithm · Generalized Feistel structure · SPN structure

## 1 Introduction

Quantum computing represents a significant paradigm shift in computation, with the potential to solve specific classes of problems with exponential speedup compared to classical computing systems. Among its most significant implications is its impact on cryptography, where quantum algorithms challenge the foundation of classical cryptographic security.

Grover's algorithm [13], which provides a quadratic speedup for unstructured search problems, has played an important role in evaluating the quantum threat to symmetric-key ciphers. The theoretical perspective suggests that the primary quantum vulnerability for symmetric-key ciphers arises from Grover's algorithm, necessitating a doubling of key lengths to maintain security levels equivalent to those in classical systems. However, this strategy may not fully address the broader spectrum of quantum attacks. Simon's algorithm [28], on the other hand, introduces new considerations by reducing the complexity of the exponential-time Boolean period-finding problem in classical computing to polynomial time in the quantum setting. Despite its theoretical importance, Simon's algorithm has not been extensively applied in the cryptanalysis of primitives. This gap is largely attributable to the incomplete theoretical framework and the lack of robust methodologies for constructing periodic functions of symmetric-key ciphers.

Addressing this gap is essential for advancing the theoretical foundations of symmetric cryptography. In recent years, the cryptographic community has directed significant efforts toward exploring the construction of periodic functions for various cryptographic primitives based on Simon's algorithm. A seminal contribution was made at CRYPTO 2016 by Kaplan et al. [19], who demonstrated for the first time that widely deployed modes of operation for authentication and authenticated encryption, such as CBC-MAC, GCM, and OCB etc., are completely compromised utilizing Simon's algorithm. Subsequently, at ASIACRYPT 2017, Leander and May [22] made a pioneering advance by proposing the Grover-meet-Simon algorithm. Another progress was achieved at ASIACRYPT 2019 by Bonnetain et al. [4], who refined the Grover-meet-Simon algorithm to achieve an optimized trade-off between quantum time complexity and classical data requirements for EM and FX constructions. Then, Bonnetain et al. [5] also introduced a novel methodology for applying Simon's algorithm at ASIACRYPT 2021, successfully compromising numerous parallelizable MACs that were previously considered secure. The core principle underlying these attacks is that the successful construction of a periodic function enables the execution of an attack on the cryptographic structure with significantly reduced computational complexity.

The central challenge in quantum cryptanalysis with Simon's algorithm lies in the construction of periodic functions for complex structures. For the Feistel structure with two branches, it is relatively easy to construct the periodic function. Kuwakado and Morii [21] proposed a 3-round periodic distinguisher, while Ito et al. [18] introduced a 4-round periodic distinguisher for the Feistel structure using the quantum chosen-ciphertext attack. In contrast, constructing periodic functions for more intricate designs, such as the Generalized Feistel Structure (GFS) with increased number of branches, presents significant challenges. While several heuristic manual deduction methods [8,9,11,12,16,24,29,31] have been used to identify periodic functions of various GFS instances, these approaches are inherently limited. Such manual methods become increasingly impractical for identifying periodic functions as the number of branches in the structure grows. Furthermore, these techniques are unsuitable for analyzing newly designed structures.

There is a need for a generalized and automated framework to efficiently evaluate the security of various cryptographic structures against quantum attacks with Simon's algorithm. Currently, three main approaches have been explored in the literature. First, in 2020, Hodžić et al. [15] attempted to summarize the general properties of periodic function construction. However, their work was not able to encompass many effective periodic functions. Second, at CRYPTO 2022, Canale et al. [6] proposed the first automated algorithm to identify periodic functions. Their method involved examining all possible circuits and testing each one for periodicity by instantiating the function in small dimensions. Although this approach is effective for structures with few branches, it suffers from scalability issues as the number of branches increases, making it impractical for more complex designs. Third, in order to simplify the construction of periodic distinguishers, Xiang et al. [33] established the links between periodic functions and truncated differentials at ToSC 2024. Although their framework can be used to identify periodic distinguishers for various GFSs, it lacks the ability for constructing periods using unknown differences and does not provide automated tools, limiting its practical utility.

Substitution-Permutation Network (SPN) is one fundamental structure for block ciphers, prominently exemplified by AES [10] and SKINNY [1]. SPN structures exhibit stronger avalanche properties compared to Feistel networks. However, it is more difficult to identify effective periodic distinguishers for SPN-based ciphers. Consequently, existing methods for searching effective periodic distinguishers are difficult to be applied to SPN structures. For example, for SKINNY block cipher with $4 \times 4$ branch configuration, the fact that all branches pass through the S-box in each round leads to unknown differences to appear very quickly. This renders the truncated differential theory [33] proposed by Xiang et al. inapplicable, as it relies on predictable differential propagation patterns. Additionally, the use of Maximum Distance Separable (MDS) matrices in SPN structures further complicates the search for periodic distinguishers by introducing strong diffusion properties that disrupt traditional analytical approaches. Furthermore, the automated method proposed by Canale et al. [6], which involves examining all input circuits, instantiating them, and testing each for periodicity, becomes impractical for SPN structures due to their increased complexity. This limitation underscores the inadequacy of existing methods in addressing the unique challenges of searching periodic distinguishers for SPN-based ciphers.

### 1.1 Our Contributions

In this paper, we address the challenges of constructing periodic distinguishers for symmetric-key primitives. We propose a new generalized theoretical framework for building periodic distinguishers and, based on this framework, present the first efficient automated search model tailored for GFSs. Additionally, we extend this model to SPN-based block ciphers. Our key contributions are summarized as follows:

**More Generalized Method for Constructing Periodic Distinguishers.** Our method consists of two parts, the polynomial-time periodic distinguisher (see Theorem 3) and the probabilistic periodic distinguisher (see Theorem 4). The polynomial-time periodic distinguisher not only accounts for the input difference value of $x$ and $\alpha_b$ ($\alpha_0$ and $\alpha_1$ are two distinct constants) for the input branches, but also incorporates the values and difference value after the round functions. This advancement addresses the limitation of information loss inherent in Xiang et al.'s truncated differential theory [33], enabling the construction of periodic functions even in the presence of certain unknown differences. As a direct consequence, we achieve a one-round improvement in the distinguisher for GFS-2F [26]. Furthermore, we extend the theory to probabilistic periodic distinguishers based on the collisions of $\alpha_b$. While previous approaches typically involved an arbitrary selection of $\alpha_b$, our work demonstrates that when $\alpha_b$ satisfies certain properties (see Definition 3), it becomes possible to identify the potential new periodic function. This extends the separability property in [15]. The periodicity occurs only for particular choices of $\alpha_0$ and $\alpha_1$, which we can search for using Grover's algorithm. This turns the distinguisher into a Grover-meet-Simon algorithm [4,22].

**First Fully Automated SMT-Based Search Model for Periodic Distinguishers.** Based on our generalized method, we implement the first fully automated SMT-based search model for periodic distinguishers, which significantly differs from the circuit instantiations method in [6]. Our model utilizes simplified symbol representations to identify the differences of $x$, $\alpha_b$, and the output values of the round functions, while ensuring that the output satisfies the periodicity. As a broad application of our model, we discover the first quantum periodic distinguishers with the following round configurations: 10 rounds for GFS-4F [26], 16-round Skipjack-B [3,9,20], 10 rounds for LBlock [32], and 10 rounds for TWINE [30], improving the previous best results by 1, 3, 2 and 2 rounds, respectively. Table 1 summarizes the periodic distinguishers. As the first example, the 16-round periodic distinguisher we present for Skipjack-B outperforms all known classical distinguishers in the classical setting. Based on the birthday problem, we prepare $2^{\frac{16}{2}}$ values of $x$. For each $x$, we encrypt $x$ for $\alpha_0$ and $\alpha_1$, and store the corresponding outputs to identify a pair of $x$ that satisfies the possible period. The computational complexity is about $2^9$. In contrast, the classical impossible differential distinguisher requires a complexity of at least $2^{32}$ [3]. Moreover, our periodic distinguishers exhibit lower complexity compared to the differential-linear distinguishers reported at CRYPTO 2024 [14] over the same number of rounds, as shown in Table 2.

**Extending the Periodic Distinguishers to More Ciphers.** As another significant application of the automated model, this paper presents the first construction of periodic distinguishers for SPN structure. For SKINNY, we discover the first 7-round polynomial-time periodic distinguisher and the first 9-round exponential-time periodic distinguisher. For the Feistel-SP structure, such as Piccolo with MDS matrices, we extend the models to incorporate the propagation through the MDS. Furthermore, for CRAFT, Type-1/2/3 GFS, SM4, MARS, and SIMON, our method can also identify periodic distinguishers. These

**Table 1.** The periodic distinguishers of different structures and ciphers. qCPA is the quantum chosen-plaintext attack. qCCA is the quantum chosen-ciphertext attack. $N$ is the size of the internal state of the structure.

| Structure/Cipher | Type | Attack | #Rounds | Probability | Reference |
|---|---|---|---|---|---|
| GFS-2F | GFS | qCPA | 5 | 1 | [34] |
| | | | 6 | $2^{-\frac{N}{2}}$ | [34] |
| | | | **6** | **1** | **Section** 5.1 |
| GFS-4F | GFS | qCPA | 8 | 1 | [34] |
| | | | 9 | 1 | [7] |
| | | | **10** | **1** | **Section** 5.1 |
| Skipjack-B-type | GFS | qCPA | 13 | 1 | [9] |
| | | | **16** | **1** | **Section** 5.2 |
| LBlock | Feistel | qCPA | 3 | 1 | [21] |
| | | qCCA | 4 | 1 | [18] |
| | | qCPA | 8 | 1 | [33] |
| | | qCPA | **8** | 1 | **Section** 5.3 |
| | | qCPA | **10** | $\mathbf{2^{-8}}$ | **Section** 5.3 |
| TWINE | GFS | qCPA | 8 | 1 | [7] |
| | | | **8** | **1** | **Section** 5.3 |
| | | | **10** | $\mathbf{2^{-8}}$ | **Section** 5.3 |
| SKINNY-64/128 | SPN | qCPA | **7** | **1** | **Section** 6.1 |
| | | | **9** | $\mathbf{2^{-16}/2^{-32}}$ | **Section** 6.1 |

**Table 2.** The comparisons with [14] in the classical setting. DL is the differential-linear distinguisher. PD is the periodic distinguisher.

| Cipher | Type | Attack | #Rounds | Complexity | Reference |
|---|---|---|---|---|---|
| TWINE | GFS | DL | 8 | $2^{4.36}$ | [14] |
| | | **PD** | 8 | $\mathbf{2^{3}}$ | **Section** 5.3 |
| | | DL | 9 | $2^{12.64}$ | [14] |
| | | **PD** | 9 | $\mathbf{2^{2+5}}$ | **Section** 5.3 |
| | | DL | 10 | $2^{16.7}$ | [14] |
| | | **PD** | 10 | $\mathbf{2^{8+5}}$ | **Section** 5.3 |
| LBlock | Feistel | DL | 8 | $2^{5}$ | [14] |
| | | **PD** | 8 | $\mathbf{2^{3}}$ | **Section** 5.3 |
| | | DL | 9 | $2^{8.78}$ | [14] |
| | | **PD** | 9 | $\mathbf{2^{2+5}}$ | **Section** 5.3 |
| | | DL | 10 | $2^{13}$ | [14] |
| | | **PD** | 10 | $\mathbf{2^{8+5}}$ | **Section** 5.3 |
| SKINNY-64 | SPN | DL | 7 | $2^{5.64}$ | [14] |
| | | **PD** | 7 | $\mathbf{2^{3}}$ | **Section** 6.1 |
| | | DL | 8 | $2^{14.5}$ | [14] |
| | | **PD** | 8 | $\mathbf{2^{4+5}}$ | **Section** 6.1 |
| | | DL | 9 | $2^{22.72}$ | [14] |
| | | **PD** | 9 | $\mathbf{2^{16+5}}$ | **Section** 6.1 |

advancements broaden the applicability of Simon's algorithm in symmetric-key cryptanalysis and are expected to influence the design of future structures.

### 1.2 Organization

In Sect. 2, we provide essential definitions and an introduction to quantum algorithms. In Sect. 3, we present the approach for constructing periodic distinguishers. The automated SMT-based searching model is introduced in Sect. 4. Section 5 and Sect. 6 introduce the application of the model. Section 7 concludes the paper with a summary of our method.

## 2 Preliminaries

### 2.1 Notation

We define $E : \{0,1\}^N \rightarrow \{0,1\}^N$ as a block cipher with a block size of $N$. We also define $f : \{0,1\}^n \rightarrow \{0,1\}^n$ as a Boolean function. The unitary operator $U_f$ is defined as $U_f : \sum_{x,y} |x\rangle|y\rangle \rightarrow \sum_{x,y} |x\rangle|y \oplus f(x)\rangle$. For a cipher, $f_j^i$ denotes the $j$-th round function applied in the $i$-th round. When there is only one function in each round, we denote it as $f^i$ instead of $f_0^i$.

### 2.2 Simon's Algorithm

Consider a function $f : \{0,1\}^n \to \{0,1\}^n$ that is guaranteed to be periodic with period $s$, meaning $f(x) = f(x \oplus s)$ for a non-zero $s$. The goal of Simon's algorithm is to determine the period $s$. The algorithm is shown in Algorithm 1. Kaplan et al. [19] show that after $cn$ queries, the period $s$ can be recovered.

---

**Algorithm 1.** The process of Simon's algorithm

---

1: Prepare two $n$-qubit registers initialized to the zero state $|0\rangle^{\otimes n}|0\rangle^{\otimes n}$.

2: Apply a Hadamard transform to the first register:

$$(H^{\otimes n} \otimes I)|0\rangle^{\otimes n}|0\rangle^{\otimes n}.$$

3: Apply the oracle $U_f$, we have

$$|\psi_1\rangle = \frac{1}{\sqrt{2^n}} \sum_x |x\rangle|f(x)\rangle.$$

4: Measure the second register in the computational basis yields a value $f(z)$ and collapses the first register to the state:

$$|\psi_2\rangle = \frac{1}{\sqrt{2}}(|z\rangle + |z \oplus s\rangle).$$

5: Apply again the Hadamard transform $H^{\otimes n}$ to the first register yields

$$|\psi_3\rangle = \frac{1}{\sqrt{2}} \frac{1}{\sqrt{2^n}} \sum_{y \in \{0,1\}^n} (-1)^{y \cdot z} \left(1 + (-1)^{y \cdot s}\right) |y\rangle.$$

6: Measure the first register to get the output value $y$, which is guaranteed to satisfy $y \cdot s = 0$.

---

**Theorem 1** ([19]). *If* $p_0 = \max_{t \in \{0,1\}^n \setminus \{0,s\}} \Pr_x[f(x) = f(x \oplus t)] < 1$, *then Simon's algorithm returns* $s$ *with* $cn$ *queries and* $O(n)$ *qubits, with probability at least* $1 - (2(\frac{1+p_0}{2})^c)^n$.

Usually, we have $p_0 < \frac{1}{2}$. Otherwise, $f$ will exhibit highly non-random characteristics. Under this assumption, when we apply Simon's algorithm to $f$, it returns $s$ with a probability of at least $1 - 2^n \cdot \left(\frac{3}{4}\right)^{cn}$.

**Distinguisher Without Recovering the Period.** Ito et al. [18] further relax the condition by focusing on the dimension of the vector space. Let $C$ be a block cipher $E$ or a random permutation $\Pi$ ($\{0,1\}^n \to \{0,1\}^n$). Obtaining $\eta = O(n)$ vectors, if the dimension of $Y$ is not $n$, we can distinguish $E$ from $\Pi$ with a high probability. Algorithm 2 shows the process. The algorithm simplifies the analysis by removing the requirement to bound the probability of collisions other than the period, which is adopted by this paper to search for the period of the function.

**Algorithm 2.** Distinguisher without recovering the period

```
1: Prepare an empty set Y.
2: for 1 ≤ i ≤ η do
3:     Following the process of Simon's algorithm, measure the first register and add
       the obtained vector y to Y.
4: end for
5: Calculate the dimension d of the vector space spanned by Y.
6: if d = n then
7:     return C is Π.
8: else
9:     return C is E.
10: end if
```

**Truncated Outputs of Quantum Oracles.** Hosoyamada and Sasaki [17] introduced the truncated outputs of quantum oracles, which can be used to obtain truncated outputs $E|_u$, where $E|_u$ represents the output of $E$ truncated to the branch $u$. This paper focuses more on how to search for periods and therefore does not emphasize circuit implementation.

**Q1 and Q2 Setting.** In the Q1 setting, the adversary is allowed to perform quantum computations online but can only make classical queries to the cryptographic oracle, while the Q2 setting permits superposition queries. This work focuses on attacks in the Q2 setting, while attacks in the Q1 setting can be derived using the techniques proposed in [4].

### 2.3 Grover-Meet-Simon Algorithm

At ASIACRYPT 2017, Leander and May [22] proposed the Grover-meet-Simon algorithm, which combines Simon's algorithm with Grover's algorithm. Based on this work, Bonnetain et al. [4] reduced the number of queries by reusing internal states. We now provide a brief introduction to the problem.

**Definition 1 (Grover-meet-Simon problem).** *Let $f : \{0,1\}^m \times \{0,1\}^n \rightarrow \{0,1\}^d$ be a function such that there exists some $u \in \{0,1\}^m$ for which $f(u,\cdot)$ hides a non-trivial period $s_u$ with a probability of $2^{-m}$. The goal is to find any tuple $(u, s_u) \in U_s$, where $U_s := \{(u, s_u) : u \in \{0,1\}^m, s_u \text{ is the period of } f(u,\cdot)\}$.*

The Grover-meet-Simon algorithm operates as follows:

- Attacker makes a guess for $u$ (this forms the Grover part of the algorithm).
- For the correct guess, the attacker identifies a periodic function, which is then detected using Simon's algorithm.

Grover's algorithm serves as an outer loop with a running time of approximately $O(2^{m/2})$, while Simon's algorithm acts as an inner loop with polynomial complexity.

**Theorem 2 (Proposition 2 in [4]).** *Suppose that $m$ is in $O(n)$. The computation of finding $u$ is done in time $O\left((n^3 + nT_f)2^{m/2}\right)$, where $T_f$ is the time required to evaluate $f$ once.*

In this paper, we are more focused on how to automate the search for periodic distinguishers. Thus, we assume that there exists a $O(1)$-time quantum circuit capable of efficiently implementing a function $f$ or a structure $E$ and simplify the complexity as $O(2^{\frac{m}{2}})$, ignoring the polynomial factors in Theorem 2.

### 2.4 Link Between Periodic Functions and Truncated Differentials

We first introduce the distinguisher from Kuwakado and Morii [21], and then provide a simple example of Xiang et al.'s technique below. Kuwakado and Morii's work distinguishes the Feistel structure (see Fig. 1) from a random permutation. The three-round Feistel structure is defined by $(x_L^3, x_R^3) = E(x_L^0, x_R^0)$, where $E : \{0,1\}^{2n} \rightarrow \{0,1\}^{2n}$ and the two halves of the input are denoted as $x_L^0$ and $x_R^0$, then for round $i$, the transformation is given by:

$$x_L^i = x_R^{i-1} \oplus f^i(x_L^{i-1}), \quad x_R^i = x_L^{i-1},$$

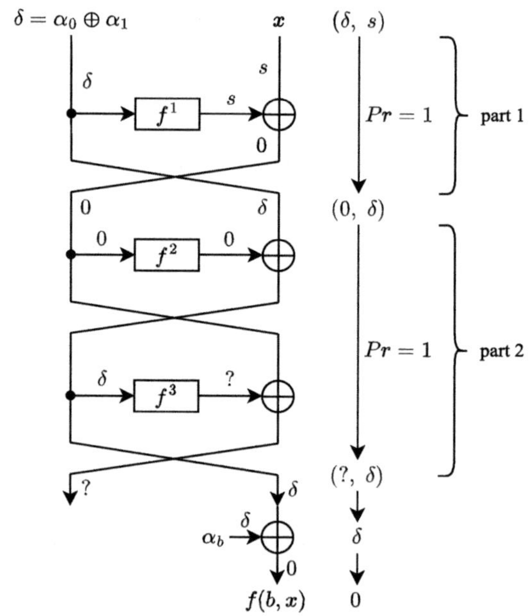


**Fig. 1.** 3-round Feistel structure with the truncated differential periodicity.

where $f^i$ is the round function. They define a function $f(b, x)$ that takes as input a bit $b$ and a string $x$, XORed with two arbitrary constants $\alpha_0$ and $\alpha_1$:

$$f : \{0,1\} \times \{0,1\}^n \to \{0,1\}^n,$$
$$b, x \mapsto x_R^3 \oplus \alpha_b,$$
$$f(b, x) = f^2(x \oplus f^1(\alpha_b)).$$

$f(b, x)$ satisfies the periodic property required by Simon's algorithm and $s = 1\|(f^1(\alpha_0) \oplus f^1(\alpha_1))$ is the period of $f$:

$$f(b, x) = f(b \oplus 1, x \oplus f^1(\alpha_0) \oplus f^1(\alpha_1)).$$

At ToSC 2024, Xiang et al. studied the link between periodic functions and truncated differentials [33]. In Xiang et al.'s theory [33], the distinguisher is divided into two parts. Part 1 is a truncated differential $(\delta, s) \to (s \oplus f^1(\delta), \delta)$, where $\delta = \alpha_0 \oplus \alpha_1$ and Part 2 is a truncated differential $(0, \delta) \to (?, \delta)$, where $f^1(\delta)$ is defined by $f^1(\alpha_0) \oplus f^1(\alpha_1)$. By setting $x = f^1(\alpha_0) \oplus f^1(\alpha_1)$, the output of the truncated differential in Part 1 will connect with the input of the truncated differential in Part 2. Then, we can find a 3-round periodic distinguisher $(\delta, s) \to (?, \delta)$. The second $\delta$ is used to construct the periodic function in Xiang et al.'s truncated differential theory.

## 3 Generalized Method of Periodic Construction

In this section, we present a generalized method for constructing periodic distinguishers. It consists of two theorems:

- Theorem 3: A unified method to construct quantum periodic distinguishers in polynomial time.
- Theorem 4: New probabilistic periodic distinguisher. The distinguisher holds when $\alpha_0$ and $\alpha_1$ satisfy certain properties, where $\alpha_0$ and $\alpha_1$ are distinct constants.

### 3.1 A General Method for Constructing Periodic Distinguishers

We notice that there are various methods for constructing periodic functions, which complicates the automatic search for suitable distinguishers. To address this, we first define the concepts of periodic functions and periodic distinguishers.

Let $E^r : (u_0^0, u_1^0, \ldots, u_{t-1}^0) \to (u_0^r, u_1^r, \ldots, u_{t-1}^r)$ denote an $r$-round function with $t$ branches, where the size of each branch is $n$ bits, and $u_j^i$ represents the $j$-th branch during the $i$-th round. Assume that the input of $E^r$ can be written with disjoint variables as

$$(x, \alpha_b, c) \in \{0,1\}^n \times \{0,1\}^{e_1} \times \{0,1\}^{e_2}, \;\; n + e_1 + e_2 = tn = N, \;\; e_1 \geq 1, e_2 \geq 0,$$

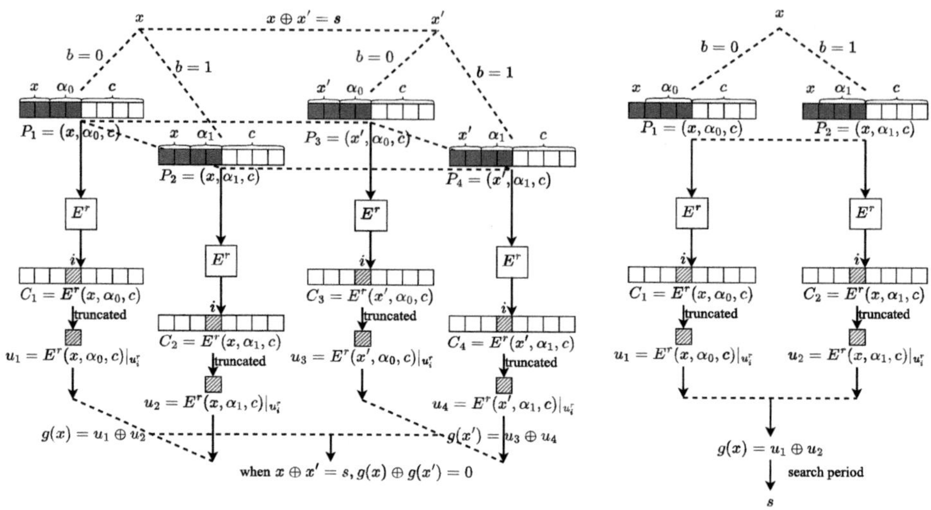

**Fig. 2.** The process of the construction of periodic distinguisher.

where $x$ is a variable, while $\alpha_b$ and $c$ are constants. For convenience, we use $\Delta\alpha_b$ and $\Delta f(\alpha_b)$ to represent the differences of $\alpha_0 \oplus \alpha_1$ and $f(\alpha_0) \oplus f(\alpha_1)$, respectively. For any constant $t$, we have $\Delta t = 0$. Figure 2-left illustrates the core idea of the periodic distinguisher. Define the periodic function $g$:

$$\begin{aligned} g : \{0,1\}^n &\rightarrow \{0,1\}^n, \\ x &\mapsto \Delta u_i^r, \\ g(x) = E^r(x, \alpha_0, c)|_{u_i^r} &\oplus E^r(x, \alpha_1, c)|_{u_i^r}, \end{aligned} \tag{1}$$

where $\Delta u_i^r$ is the difference of the values $u_i^r$ when $b = 0$ and $b = 1$. The construction method of the periodic function will be explained in Theorem 3. We notice that a similar function is used for Type-1 GFS in [29].

Once the period has been identified, Algorithm 3 can be applied in the distinguishing attack.

In the quantum setting, this process can be simplified (see Fig. 2-right). The period $s$ does not need to be predetermined, and the quartet of plaintexts is not required. For $b = 0$ and $b = 1$, the encryption function $E$ is accessed separately, and the outputs are XORed to obtain the periodic function $g$. Simon's algorithm can then be used to search for $s$ from $g(x)$.

Based on the method shown in Fig. 2-right, we define the periodic distinguisher represented by

$$(s, \delta, 0) \rightarrow (?, \ldots, ?, 0, ?, \ldots, ?). \tag{2}$$

In the input, $s$ denotes the site of $x$ as $g(x) \oplus g(x \oplus s) = 0$, $\delta = \Delta\alpha_b$ represents the difference of $\alpha_b$, and $0 = \Delta c$ is the difference of $c$. In the output, 0 corresponds

**Algorithm 3.** The process of the distinguishing attack.

1: Choose $\alpha_0 \neq \alpha_1$ and $c$ randomly.
2: Construct a quartet of plaintexts $(P_1, P_2, P_3, P_4)$. For $b = 0$, $P_1 = (x, \alpha_0, c)$; for $b = 1$, $P_2 = (x, \alpha_1, c)$. Assume that $s \in \{0,1\}^n$ is the possible period. Let $x' = x \oplus s$. Then, $P_3 = (x', \alpha_0, c)$ and $P_4 = (x', \alpha_1, c)$.
3: The ciphertexts are $C_1 = E^r(x, \alpha_0, c), C_2 = E^r(x, \alpha_1, c),, C_3 = E^r(x', \alpha_0, c)$, and $C_4 = E^r(x', \alpha_1, c)$.
4: We focus solely on the $i$-th branch, thus truncating the ciphertext to this branch. $u_1 = C_1|_{u_i^r}$, $u_2 = C_2|_{u_i^r}$, $u_3 = C_3|_{u_i^r}$, and $u_4 = C_4|_{u_i^r}$.
5: Compute $g(x) \oplus g(x')$. If $s$ is the period of $g$, we have $g(x) \oplus g(x') = 0$ for any $x \in \{0,1\}^n$. Otherwise, this probability is negligible.

to the branch $u_i^r$ and can be used to construct the periodic function $g(x)$, while ? indicates a branch without periodicity.

In this paper, each periodic function corresponds to a unique periodic distinguisher. Therefore, unless otherwise specified, we assume that the two are interchangeable without ambiguity. Next, we introduce how to search for periodic distinguishers, or construct periodic functions.

### 3.2 Polynomial-Time Periodic Distinguisher

At PQCrypto 2020, Hodžić et al. [15] presented the separability property based on an observation regarding the construction of Simon's algorithm, including the strong separability property, semi-strong separability property, and weak separability property. However, the types of periodic functions are still limited, and it remains unclear which weak separability properties can be used for periodic construction.

We define four functions: $F, G, P, Q : \{0,1\}^* \rightarrow \{0,1\}^n$. Each function takes an input of arbitrary length and produces an $n$-bit output. For example, $F(x, y)$ is defined as a function that depends only on the input $x$ and $y$. The same definition applies to $G, P$ and $Q$. We now present the following definition.

**Definition 2 (Differential separability property).** *A branch $u_i^r$ satisfies the differential separability property if $u_i^r$ is represented as*

$$u_i^r = E^r(x, \alpha_b, c)|_{u_i^r} = F(x \oplus G(\alpha_b, c), c) \oplus P(x, c) \oplus Q(\alpha_b, c).$$

Compared with Hodžić et al.'s definition [15], our definition allows any unknown values caused individually by $\alpha_b$ or $x$. It directly leads to their inability to construct a polynomial-time 5-round distinguisher (only 4 rounds in [15]), whereas our definition allows for the 5-round distinguisher.

In the following, Theorem 3 establishes that if a branch $u_i^r$ satisfies the differential separability property, it can always be used to construct a periodic function. Next, we focus solely on the existence of a branch that satisfies the differential separability property.

**Theorem 3 (Polynomial-time periodic distinguisher).** *Given a block cipher $E^r$, if an output branch $u_i^r$ satisfies the differential separability property, $g(x)$ is always a periodic function.*

*Proof.* $g(x)$ is defined by Eq. (1). We have

$$\begin{aligned} g(x) &= E^r(x,\alpha_0,c)|_{u_i^r} \oplus E^r(x,\alpha_1,c)|_{u_i^r} \\ &= \Delta F(x\oplus G(\alpha_b,c),c) \oplus \Delta P(x,c) \oplus \Delta Q(\alpha_b,c) \\ &= \Delta F(x\oplus G(\alpha_b,c),c) \oplus \Delta Q(\alpha_b,c). \end{aligned}$$

Set $s = \Delta G(\alpha_b,c) = G(\alpha_0,c)\oplus G(\alpha_1,c)$, then for any $x$:

$$\begin{aligned} g(x\oplus s) &= \Delta F(x\oplus s\oplus G(\alpha_b,c),c) \oplus \Delta Q(\alpha_b,c) \\ &= \Delta F(x\oplus G(\alpha_b,c),c) \oplus \Delta Q(\alpha_b,c) \\ &= g(x). \end{aligned}$$

Through our construction, aside from $F(x\oplus G(\alpha_b,c),c)$, the other terms either depend only on $x$ and thus get canceled out, or depend only on $\alpha_b$, resulting in a fixed differential value $Q(\alpha_0,c)\oplus Q(\alpha_1,c)$. The period can always be set to $s=\Delta G(\alpha_b,c)$ to satisfy $g(x\oplus s)=g(x)$. □

*Remark 1.* As shown in Eq. (2) and Theorem 3, we are only interested in the differences of $x$, $c$, and $\alpha_b$, rather than their specific values. The following explains this in detail:

- Only when $x\oplus x' = s$, we can find $g(x)\oplus g(x') = 0$. The function $F(x\oplus G(\alpha_b,c),c)$ is the essential characteristic determining periodicity. For any $\alpha_0\neq\alpha_1$, the difference of $x$ equals $\Delta G(\alpha_b,c)$, which is the period $s$.
- For $\alpha_0$ and $\alpha_1$, the constraint is $\Delta\alpha_b=\alpha_0\oplus\alpha_1\neq 0$.
- The difference $\Delta c$ is always zero, meaning that $c$ does not affect the construction of the periodicity in $g(x)$. Thus, we can omit $c$ in our theory and set it as a constant 0 in the periodic distinguisher.

*Example 1 (Improvement to Xiang et al.'s truncated differential theory in* [33]*).* GFS-2F [26] is a type of GFS, proposed by Nyberg at ASIACRYPT 1996. Using the truncated differential theory from [33], a 5-round distinguisher $(s,\delta,0,0)\xrightarrow{5r}(0,0,?,?)$ is found. In the subsequent round, every branch has an unknown difference.

For the same input, a 6-round distinguisher $(s,\delta,0,0)\xrightarrow{6r}(0,?,?,?)$ is identified based on Theorem 3. $u_0^6$ satisfies the differential separability property:

$$u_2^0\oplus f_1^3(u_1^0\oplus f_0^1(u_2^0))\oplus f_0^4(u_3^0\oplus f_1^2(u_2^0)\oplus f_0^3(u_0^0\oplus f_1^1(u_3^0)\oplus f_0^2(u_1^0\oplus f_0^1(u_2^0)))).$$

The corresponding periodic function is

$$\begin{aligned} g(x) &= E^6(x,\alpha_0,u_2^0,u_3^0)|_{u_0^6} \oplus E^6(x,\alpha_1,u_2^0,u_3^0)|_{u_0^6} \\ &= \Delta f_1^3(\alpha_b\oplus C_1)\oplus\Delta f_0^4(C_2\oplus f_0^3(x\oplus f_0^2(\alpha_b\oplus C_3)\oplus C_4)), \end{aligned}$$

where $u_2^0, u_3^0$ are random constants, $C_1=f_0^1(u_2^0)$, $C_2=u_3^0\oplus f_1^2(u_2^0)$, $C_3=f_0^1(u_2^0)$, and $C_4=f_1^1(u_3^0)$ are also constants. Then, set the period as $s=\Delta f_0^2(\alpha_b\oplus C_3)$. For any $x$, we have $g(x\oplus s)\oplus g(x)=0$. Figure 3 shows the difference.

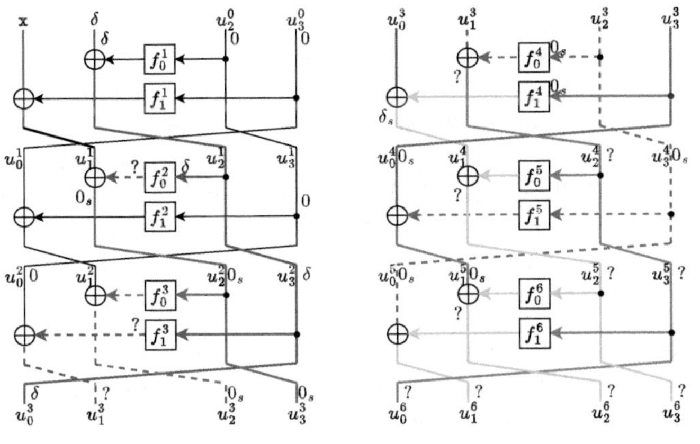

**Fig. 3.** The 6-round periodic distinguisher for GFS-2F.

### 3.3 Probabilistic Periodic Distinguisher

In this section, we utilize the collisions of $\Delta\alpha_b$ to enhance the periodic distinguisher. The difference of initial $\Delta\alpha_b$ affects the propagation of the periodic distinguisher, even though these values were chosen randomly in Kuwakado and Morii's work [21]. Thus, we propose a method to construct the probabilistic periodic distinguisher, which can be solved by the Grover-meet-Simon algorithm.

**Definition 3 (Probabilistic periodic distinguisher problem).** *For any $x, \alpha_0, \alpha_1, c$, let $f : \{0,1\}^n \times \{0,1\}^{e_1} \times \{0,1\}^{e_1} \times \{0,1\}^{e_2} \rightarrow \{0,1\}^n$ be a function such that there exists some $(\alpha_0, \alpha_1) \in \{0,1\}^{2e_1}$ for which $f(\cdot, \alpha_0, \alpha_1, c)$ hides a non-trivial period $s_u$ with a probability of $2^{-p}$. The goal is to find any tuple $(\alpha_0, \alpha_1, s_u) \in U_s$, where $U_s := \{(\alpha_0, \alpha_1, s_u) : (\alpha_0, \alpha_1) \in \{0,1\}^{2e_1}, s_u$ is the period of $f(\cdot, \alpha_0, \alpha_1, c)\}$.*

The simple example below is a demonstration of the probabilistic periodic distinguisher.

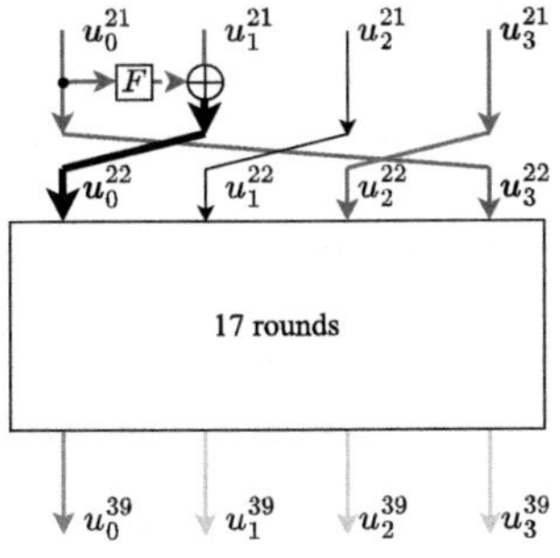


**Fig. 4.** An example for CAST-256.

*Example 2.* In [29], Sun et al. proposed a 17-round periodic distinguisher of CAST-256: $(0, 0, s, \delta) \to (0, ?, ?, ?)$ from $(u_0^{22}, u_1^{22}, u_2^{22}, u_3^{22})$ to $(u_0^{39}, u_1^{39}, u_2^{39}, u_3^{39})$.

With the new technique, we found a 18-round probabilistic periodic distinguisher $(\delta^0, \delta^1, 0, s) \to (0, ?, ?, ?)$, as shown in Fig. 4, where $\delta$ is from two branches by $\delta = \delta^0 || \delta^1$. We have $\delta^0 = \alpha_0^0 \oplus \alpha_1^0$, $\delta^1 = \alpha_0^1 \oplus \alpha_1^1$, and $\alpha_b = \alpha_b^0 || \alpha_b^1$. Once the constraint $\Delta F(\alpha_b^0) = \Delta \alpha_b^1$ holds, $u_0^{22}$ is 0 in the distinguisher because of $\Delta u_0^{22} = 0$. Then, $u_0^{39}$ can satisfy the differential separability property. The probability is $2^{-n}$, where $n$ is the length of one branch. The full distinguishers are shown in the full version [23].

We refer to this phenomenon, in which $\alpha_0, \alpha_1$ must satisfy specific conditions, as *a collision*. The collision resets the zero difference in the periodic function.

Accordingly, we propose the following theorem about the probabilistic periodic distinguisher using the same periodic function. The proof is similar to Theorem 3.

**Theorem 4 (Probabilistic periodic distinguisher).** *If after some collisions with probability $2^{-p}$, a branch $u_i^r$ satisfies the differential separability property, $u_i^r$ can be used to construct an $r$-round periodic distinguisher with probability $2^{-p}$.*

**Discussion on the Theoretical Probability and the Practical Collision Probability.** Given the randomness of the key, for any two arbitrary functions $f_1$ and $f_2$, the values $f_1(\alpha_0)$, $f_1(\alpha_1)$, $f_2(\alpha_0)$, and $f_2(\alpha_1)$ are unpredictable. On average, the probability of a collision, where $\Delta f_1(\alpha_b) = \Delta f_2(\alpha_b)$ in two $n$-bit branches, is about $2^{-n}$. We use this average probability as an estimate of complexity. On the other hand, if multiple collisions need to be satisfied, it is essential to determine which constraints are necessary. Therefore, we provide two algorithms to evaluate the probability (see the full version [23]).

**Applying Periodic Distinguishers in the Q2 Settings.** Simon's algorithm can be directly applied to polynomial-time periodic distinguishers, where the periodicity condition can be efficiently verified in time $O(n)$.

For probabilistic periodic distinguishers, we use Grover-meet-Simon algorithm to search for input pairs $(\alpha_0, \alpha_1)$ that satisfy the periodicity condition. Assume that, for any distinct $n$-bit pair $(\alpha_0 \neq \alpha_1)$, the probability of satisfying the periodicity condition is about $2^{-n}$. Define the search space as $\{(\alpha_0, \alpha_1) \in \{0,1\}^n \times \{0,1\}^n\}$, which has size $2^{2n}$. In the Grover-meet-Simon algorithm, we execute $cn$ parallel instances of Simon's algorithm. The dimension of the resulting output space reveals whether a candidate pair satisfies the periodicity condition. For the case where $\alpha_0 = \alpha_1$, the function $g(x) = E^r(x, \alpha_0, c)|_{u_i^r} \oplus E^r(x, \alpha_1, c)|_{u_i^r} \equiv 0$ is constant. In Simon's algorithm, each run outputs a vector $y \in \mathbb{F}_2^n$ such that $y \cdot s = 0$ for all $s \in S$. Since $S = \mathbb{F}_2^n$, the only possible output is the zero vector. Thus, its impact can be neglected. The overall search complexity is approximately $O(2^{\frac{n}{2}})$.

**Applying Periodic Distinguishers in the Classical Settings.** The periodic distinguishers are effective in the classical setting. For a polynomial-time periodic distinguisher, assume that the size of each branch $x$ is $n$ bits. Based on the birthday paradox, we prepare $2^{\frac{n}{2}}$ values of $x$ and store the corresponding outputs in order to find a pair of $x$ that satisfies the periodicity condition. For each $x$, we perform one encryption for $b = 0$ and another for $b = 1$. Only a small number of additional tests are needed to verify whether the periodicity condition is met. The total complexity is about $2^{\frac{n}{2}+1}$, with a success probability exceeding 50%.

For probabilistic periodic distinguishers with probability $2^{-p}$, we perform encryption for each $x$ and check whether a period exists. For each choice of $\alpha_0$ and $\alpha_1$, we iterate over all $n$-bit values $x \in \{0, 1, 2, \ldots, 2^n - 1\}$, and encrypt them to obtain the corresponding ciphertexts. If the chosen $\alpha_0$ and $\alpha_1$ are correct, the resulting ciphertexts will satisfy the expected periodicity condition and reveal the hidden period. This process will be repeated $2^p$ times. The total complexity is about $2^{p+n+1}$.

## 4 Automated SMT-Based Searching Model

Automating the search for periodic distinguishers remains an open problem for complex structures.

- As the number of rounds increases, the cipher function becomes more complex, making it increasingly difficult to determine the existence of a period by exhaustively searching all possible inputs.
- Manually deriving a probabilistic periodic distinguisher is also extremely challenging.

In this section, we achieve the automated search for periods for complex structures. We first introduce several symbols that represent all types of states in a distinguisher, simplifying the search process. With these new symbols, all states and their combinations can be easily represented. We then propose the first automated SMT-based model to address this open problem.

### 4.1 Symbols in Our Model

Before introducing the model, we define all relevant operations and specify the three operations used in it.

- `R`: the keyed round function $R$ taking a round key.
- `XOR`: the XOR operation between two branches.
- `SPLIT`: the branching operation.

We omit the round key and constant in our model, which does not affect the periodicity of the function.

To identify the separability property, 7 types of states are defined based on Definition 2 (see Table 3). We use the symbol $\perp$ (the state that loses its periodic properties) and 5-bit variables (the leftmost bit is the least significant bit), corresponding to $(\mathtt{0_s}, \mathtt{R(x)}, \mathtt{x}, \mathtt{R}(\delta), \delta)$, where $\mathtt{0_s}$ indicates a function like "$F(x \oplus G(\alpha_b, c), c)$", to represent all the states. Through this approximate

**Table 3.** Notations for used symbols in our model.

| Symbol | Encoding | Meaning |
|---|---|---|
| $\mathtt{0}$ | $(0,0,0,0,0)$ | The zero difference |
| $\delta$ | $(0,0,0,0,1)$ | $\delta = \Delta\alpha_b$ where $\alpha_0, \alpha_1$ are chosen randomly |
| $\mathtt{x}$ | $(0,0,1,0,0)$ | The period difference $s$ between $x$ and $x \oplus s$ |
| $\mathtt{R(x)}$ | $(0,1,0,0,0)$ | Indicating a function like "$P(x,c)$" |
| $\mathtt{R}(\delta)$ | $(0,0,0,1,0)$ | Indicating a function like "$Q(\alpha_b,c)$" |
| $\mathtt{0_s}$ | $(1,0,0,0,0)$ | Indicating a function like "$F(x \oplus G(\alpha_b,c),c)$" |
| ? | $\perp$ | The unknown state |

representation, the complex problem of constructing periodic functions is transformed into the interaction among a limited set of symbols.

According to Definition 2 and Theorem 3, a branch $u^i_j$ has the periodicity when it can be represented by $u^i_j = F(x \oplus G(\alpha_b,c),c) \oplus P(x,c) \oplus Q(\alpha_b,c)$. States $\mathtt{0_s}$, $\mathtt{R(x)}$, and $\mathtt{R}(\delta)$ represent $F(x \oplus G(\alpha_b,c),c)$, $P(x,c)$, and $Q(\alpha_b,c)$, respectively. $u^i_j$ can be written by $\mathtt{0_s} \oplus \mathtt{R(x)} \oplus \mathtt{R}(\delta)$, which is encoded by $(1,1,0,1,0)$, where the meaning of the encoding is the XOR value of the terms corresponding to the bits being 1. In general, $(1,*,*,*,*)$ always satisfies the separability property, where $*$ represents either 0 or 1. We can always obtain a path that uses our symbols

$$(\mathtt{x}, \delta, \mathtt{0}) \to (?, \dots, ?, \mathtt{0_s} \oplus *, ?, \dots, ?),$$

where $*$ represents any state except from ?. The path corresponds to a periodic distinguisher $(s, \delta, 0) \to (?, \dots, ?, 0, ?, \dots, ?)$ (see Eq. (2)).

**Further Discussion.** This approximate representation significantly reduces the search space by mapping terms with similar properties to corresponding symbols. While this approximation introduces some loss of precision, it maintains the ability to effectively analyze complex structures. By using our symbolic representation, the process of searching for periods becomes more efficient, eliminating the need to handle numerous algebraic equations. Even without an automated model, employing these symbols enables faster identification of periodic distinguishers compared to manual methods.

### 4.2 SMT-Based Automated Model

In this section, we propose a unified automated model to identify branches that satisfy the separability property from complex polynomials derived from multiple inputs. Our approach mainly uses the SMT solver, STP, to solve these models.

The complete propagation rules of our model are provided below, including the initial constraints and the propagation rules of `SPLIT`, `R`, and `XOR`.

**Modelling the Initial Constraints.** Assume that there is an $r$-round path with $n$ branches: $(u^0_0, u^0_1, \dots, u^0_{n-1}) \xrightarrow{r} (u^r_0, u^r_1, \dots, u^r_{n-1})$. The model is subject to the following constraints:

1. Each $u_i^0$ $(0 \le i \le n-1)$ must be one of $\{\mathtt{x}, \delta, \mathtt{0}, \mathtt{x} \oplus \delta\}$.
2. At least one element in $(u_0^0, u_1^0, \dots, u_{n-1}^0)$ must be $\delta$, and $\mathtt{x}$ or $\mathtt{x} \oplus \delta$ can appear only once.
3. At least one element in $(u_0^r, u_1^r, \dots, u_{n-1}^r)$ must be $(1, *, *, *, *)$ or $(0, 0, 1, *, *)$.

Constraints 1 and 2 ensure that the initial values are valid. Constraint 3 ensures that the output satisfies the separability property or still maintains a direct relationship with the input. The encoding $(0, 0, 1, *, *)$ actually represents a weakened function "$F(x \oplus G(\alpha_b, c), c)$", where $F$ is identify function. Since $(0, 0, 1, *, *)$ only occurs in the case of a small number of rounds, we ignore it in the end of our model. Based on these constraints, we can always find a path from $\{\mathtt{x}, \delta, \mathtt{0}, \mathtt{x} \oplus \delta\}$ to $\mathtt{0_s} \oplus *$.

**Modelling the Propagation Rules of SPLIT.** Let SPLIT duplicate a state without modifying it. That is, for each state $u$, the output states $v$, $w$ of SPLIT satisfy $u = v = w$.

**Modelling the Propagation Rules of R.** R indicates that the current state undergoes a round function. The following property shows the rules.

*Property 1.* The complete rules of R are:

$$\mathtt{x},\ \mathtt{R(x)},\ \mathtt{R(x)} \oplus \mathtt{x} \xrightarrow{\mathtt{R}} \mathtt{R(x)}, \tag{3}$$

$$\delta,\ \mathtt{R}(\delta),\ \mathtt{R}(\delta) \oplus \delta \xrightarrow{\mathtt{R}} \mathtt{R}(\delta), \tag{4}$$

$$\mathtt{0} \xrightarrow{\mathtt{R}} \mathtt{0},\ \mathtt{0_s} \xrightarrow{\mathtt{R}} \mathtt{0_s}, \tag{5}$$

$$\mathtt{x} \oplus \delta,\ \mathtt{x} \oplus \mathtt{R}(\delta),\ \mathtt{x} \oplus \mathtt{R}(\delta) \oplus \delta \xrightarrow{\mathtt{R}} \mathtt{0_s} \text{ (only once) or } \perp \text{ (others)}, \tag{6}$$

$$\text{others} \xrightarrow{\mathtt{R}} \perp. \tag{7}$$

*Proof.* After applying the round function R, the new states $\mathtt{R(x)}$ and $\mathtt{R}(\delta)$ represent the outputs for $\mathtt{x}$ and $\delta$, respectively. Assume that $\mathtt{R(x)} \oplus \mathtt{x}$ represents $P(x, c) \oplus x$. $\mathtt{R(R(x)} \oplus \mathtt{x)}$ is also $\mathtt{R(x)}$, representing $P'(x, c) := R(P(x, c) \oplus x)$, where $P'$ is a function. In general, we define any function that only contains $x$ and $c$ as $\mathtt{R(x)}$. Although this may result in $R(x)$ not being a permutation, it generally does not affect the propagation of the period. Our model is more concerned with which initial values are included in this branch. The same rule applies to $\delta$. Thus, Eqs. (3) and (4) are proved.

Next, we prove Eq. (5). The transformation $\mathtt{0} \xrightarrow{\mathtt{R}} \mathtt{0}$ is trivial. By definition, assume that $\mathtt{0_s}$ represents a term $F(x \oplus G(\alpha_b, c), c)$, where the period is $\Delta G(\alpha_b, c)$. The output of R is $F'(x \oplus G(\alpha_b, c), c) := R(F(x \oplus G(\alpha_b, c), c))$, where $F'$ is a function. This still satisfies the definition of $\mathtt{0_s}$, and the period $\Delta G(\alpha_b, c)$ remains unchanged.

Then, we prove Eq. (6). We assume that multiple occurrences can happen from $\mathtt{x} \oplus \delta$, $\mathtt{x} \oplus \mathtt{R}(\delta)$, $\mathtt{x} \oplus \mathtt{R}(\delta) \oplus \delta$ to $\mathtt{0_s}$. Let us consider a counterexample:

- A branch $u$ with the state $\mathtt{x} \oplus \mathtt{R}(\delta)$ represents the term $x \oplus G_1(\alpha_b, c)$. After R, we have $u' = R(x \oplus G_1(\alpha_b, c))$, where the implied period is $\Delta G_1(\alpha_b, c)$.

- A branch $v$ with the state $\mathtt{x} \oplus \mathtt{R}(\delta)$ represents $x \oplus G_2(\alpha_b, c)$. After R, we have $v' = R(x \oplus G_2(\alpha_b, c))$, where the implied period is $\Delta G_2(\alpha_b, c)$.

If two branches $u'$ and $v'$ have the states $\mathtt{0_s}$, errors may arise in state propagation. Let us discuss this case by case.

- $\Delta G_1(\alpha_b, c) = \Delta G_2(\alpha_b, c)$. The two branches have the same period. $w := u' \oplus v' = R(x \oplus G_1(\alpha_b, c)) \oplus R(x \oplus G_2(\alpha_b, c))$. We construct the periodic function $g(x) = \Delta R(x \oplus G_1(\alpha_b, c)) \oplus \Delta R(x \oplus G_2(\alpha_b, c))$. Setting $s = \Delta G_1(\alpha_b, c) = \Delta G_2(\alpha_b, c)$, we have $g(x \oplus s) = R(x \oplus s \oplus G_1(\alpha_0, c)) \oplus R(x \oplus s \oplus G_1(\alpha_1, c)) \oplus R(x \oplus s \oplus G_2(\alpha_0, c)) \oplus R(x \oplus s \oplus G_2(\alpha_1, c)) = \Delta R(x \oplus G_2(\alpha_b, c)) \oplus \Delta R(x \oplus G_1(\alpha_b, c)) = g(x)$. $u' \oplus v' \to w$ implies the rule $\mathtt{0_s} \oplus \mathtt{0_s} \to \mathtt{0_s}$.
- $\Delta G_1(\alpha_b, c) \neq \Delta G_2(\alpha_b, c)$. The two branches have different periods. $w := u_1 \oplus u_2 = R(x \oplus G_1(\alpha_b, c)) \oplus R(x \oplus G_2(\alpha_b, c))$ loses its periodicity. This situation must be avoided, as $\mathtt{0_S}$ from different branches should not interact.

Thus, we allow the occurrence of $\mathtt{x} \oplus \delta,\ \mathtt{x} \oplus \mathtt{R}(\delta),\ \mathtt{x} \oplus \mathtt{R}(\delta) \oplus \delta \xrightarrow{\mathtt{R}} \mathtt{0_s}$ through R to happen only once, which ensures that the case $\Delta G_1(\alpha_b, c) \neq \Delta G_2(\alpha_b, c)$ will not happen. Although we may lose some precision for certain special structures, this constraint ensures that the $\mathtt{0_s}$ in the model always implicitly share the same period. As a generalized model, we consider this to be necessary.

Now, we can ensure that the first $\mathtt{0_s}$ is always generated by Eq. (6) and all other $\mathtt{0_s}$ are either copies or combinations of $\mathtt{0_s}$ by $\mathtt{0_s} \xrightarrow{\mathtt{R}} \mathtt{0_s}$ and $\mathtt{0_s} \oplus \mathtt{0_s} = \mathtt{0_s}$, containing the same periods.

Equation (7) shows that for all branches where the period cannot be identified, we denote them by $\perp$. □

In the proof, we need to add new constraints for Eq. (6). We assign a Boolean variable $s_i$ for each application of R, let $\Sigma(s_i) = 1$, and set

$$\begin{cases} s_i = 1, & \text{if } \mathtt{x} \oplus \delta \xrightarrow{\mathtt{R}} \mathtt{0_s} \text{ or } \mathtt{x} \oplus \mathtt{R}(\delta) \xrightarrow{\mathtt{R}} \mathtt{0_s} \text{ or } \mathtt{x} \oplus \mathtt{R}(\delta) \oplus \delta \xrightarrow{\mathtt{R}} \mathtt{0_s}, \\ s_i = 0, & \text{if } \mathtt{x} \oplus \delta \xrightarrow{\mathtt{R}} \perp \text{ or } \mathtt{x} \oplus \mathtt{R}(\delta) \xrightarrow{\mathtt{R}} \perp \text{ or } \mathtt{x} \oplus \mathtt{R}(\delta) \oplus \delta \xrightarrow{\mathtt{R}} \perp. \end{cases}$$

**Modelling the Propagation Rules of XOR.** For XOR, we need to consider the possibility of collisions. Let the input states be $u = (u_0, u_1, u_2, u_3, u_4)$ and $v = (v_0, v_1, v_2, v_3, v_4)$, and the output state be $w = (w_0, w_1, w_2, w_3, w_4)$.

Note that only $w_3$ and $w_4$ may be affected by the collisions. We first consider the rules for $w_0, w_1, w_2$, which are established in Property 2.

*Property 2.* If $u = \perp$ or $v = \perp$, then $w = \perp$. Otherwise, the complete rules of $(w_0, w_1, w_2)$ are:

$$w_0 = \max(u_0, v_0), \quad w_1 = \max(u_1, v_1), \quad w_2 = u_2 \oplus v_2.$$

*Proof.* Figure 5 shows the propagation of states. In the proof of Property 1, we have proven $\mathtt{0_s} \oplus \mathtt{0_s} = \mathtt{0_s}$. As long as the two branches with states $\mathtt{0_s}$ imply the same period, the equation $\mathtt{0_s} \oplus \mathtt{0_s} = \mathtt{0_s}$ always holds. The constraint is satisfied by Eq. (6). We prove a more generalized case for different round functions:

- $u$ has the state $0_s$, representing $F_1(x \oplus G(\alpha_b, c), c)$,
- $v$ has the state $0_s$, representing $F_2(x \oplus G(\alpha_b, c), c)$,

where $F_1$ and $F_2$ are different functions. Equation (6) states that $u$ and $v$ have the same implied period $\Delta G(\alpha_b, c)$. Let $w := u \oplus v = F_1(x \oplus G(\alpha_b, c), c) \oplus F_2(x \oplus G(\alpha_b, c), c)$. We prove that the branch $w$ also has the same period. The periodic function is $g(x) = \Delta F_1(x \oplus G(\alpha_b, c), c) \oplus \Delta F_2(x \oplus G(\alpha_b, c), c)$. Setting $s = \Delta G(\alpha_b, c)$, $g(x \oplus s) = F_1(x \oplus s \oplus G(\alpha_0, c), c) \oplus F_1(x \oplus s \oplus G(\alpha_1, c), c) \oplus F_2(x \oplus s \oplus G(\alpha_0, c), c) \oplus F_2(x \oplus s \oplus G(\alpha_1, c), c) = g(x)$. Thus, $w = u \oplus v$ can be written by $F'(x \oplus G(\alpha_b, c), c)$ and also has the state $0_s$. On the other hand, if the periods of $u$ and $v$ are different, this rule does not hold.

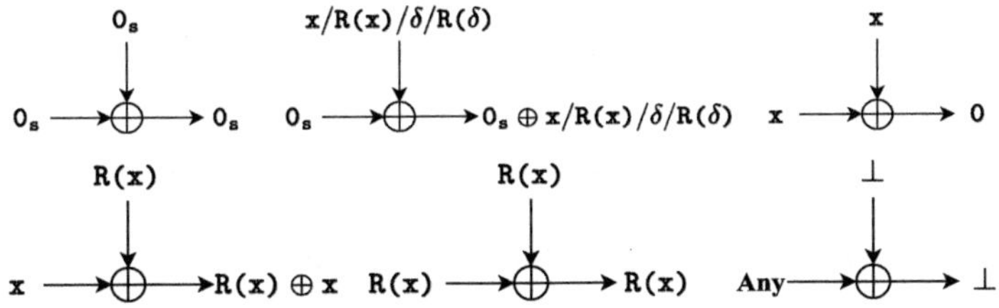


**Fig. 5.** The rules of $(w_0, w_1, w_2)$.

The state x represents the term $x$. Thus, we have $\mathtt{x} \oplus \mathtt{x} \to \mathtt{0}$. According to the definition of $\mathtt{R(x)}$, $\mathtt{R(x)} \oplus \mathtt{R(x)} \to \mathtt{R(x)}$ is also trivial. □

Now, we consider the rules of $w_3, w_4$, i.e., $\mathtt{R}(\delta)$ and $\delta$. In order to compute the number of collisions, we assign a Boolean variable $x_i$ for each XOR operation. $x_i = 1$ indicates that the collision occurs. We first consider the rules without collisions. That is, $x_i$ always be 0.

*Property 3.* The rules of $(u_3, u_4, v_3, v_4) \to (w_3, w_4, x_i)$ without collisions are:

$$\begin{cases} (0,0,v_3,v_4) => (v_3,v_4,0), \quad (u_3,u_4,0,0) => (u_3,u_4,0), \\ (0,1,0,1) => (0,0,0), \quad (0,1,1,1) => (1,0,0), \quad (1,1,0,1) => (1,0,0). \end{cases}$$

The proof is similar and therefore omitted. Figure 6 shows the rules.

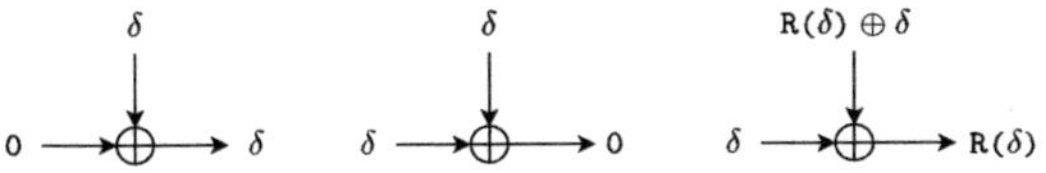


**Fig. 6.** The rules of $(w_3, w_4, x_i)$ without collisions.

Next, we consider the propagation rules where collisions may occur.

*Property 4.* The rules of $(u_3, u_4, v_3, v_4) \rightarrow (w_3, w_4, x_i)$ with collisions are:

$$\begin{cases} ((1,0,0,1) \text{ OR } (0,1,1,0)) => ((1,1,0) \text{ OR } (0,0,1)), \\ ((1,1,1,1) \text{ OR } (1,0,1,0)) => ((1,0,0) \text{ OR } (0,0,1)), \\ ((1,1,1,0) \text{ OR } (1,0,1,1)) => ((1,1,0) \text{ OR } (0,0,1) \text{ OR } (0,1,1)). \end{cases}$$

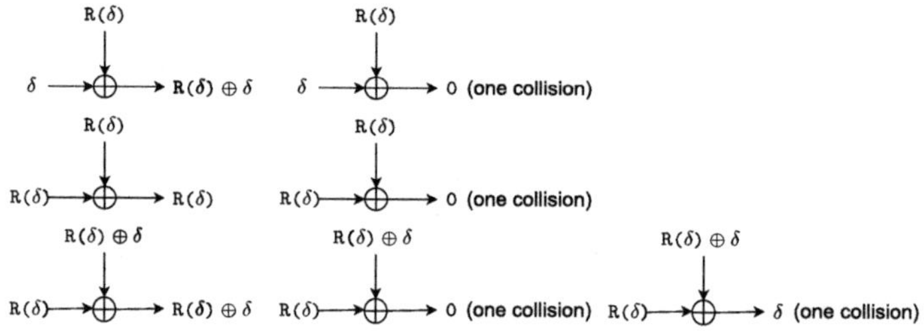


**Fig. 7.** The rules of $(w_3, w_4, x_i)$ with collisions.

*Proof.* If there is no collision, the rule is the same as R(x) (see Fig. 7). When a collision occurs, we have the following properties. The output of $\delta \oplus \mathtt{R}(\delta)$ is 0. The output of $\mathtt{R}(\delta) \oplus \mathtt{R}(\delta)$ is 0. For the states $\mathtt{R}(\delta)$ and $\mathtt{R}(\delta) \oplus \delta$, there are two cases. First, $\mathtt{R}(\delta)$ and $\mathtt{R}(\delta)$ has a collision, the output is $\delta$. Second, $\mathtt{R}(\delta)$ and $\mathtt{R}(\delta) \oplus \delta$ has a collision, the output is 0. □

For Property 4, we define an integer variable $X$ to count the number of collisions and set $\Sigma(x_i) = X$. On average, the probability of a collision occurring in each $n$-bit branch is $2^{-n}$. Thus, the required probability of collisions is calculated by $2^{-n \cdot X}$. Additionally, we impose the constraint $X \leq t - 1$, where $t$ denotes the number of branches. If $X = 0$, a distinguisher with polynomial time complexity is returned.

## 5 Application on GFS-2F/4F, Skipjack-Type Structure, LBlock, and TWINE

In this section, we apply the automated model to GFS-2F/4F, Skipjack-type structure, LBlock, and TWINE, improving the distinguishers.

### 5.1 Application on GFS-2F/4F

GFS-2F and GFS-4F [26] are two types of GFSs proposed by Nyberg at ASIACRYPT 1996 that are resistant to both differential and linear attacks. In [34], the authors provided a 5-round periodic distinguisher for GFS-2F and a 8-round periodic distinguisher for GFS-4F. They also obtained a 6-round distinguisher for GFS-2F with complexity $O(2^{\frac{N}{4}})$.

Using our model, we find a new 6-round periodic distinguisher of GFS-2F without the need for probability, as well as the first 10-round periodic distinguisher of GFS-4F in complexity $O(N)$. The 6-round periodic distinguisher has been explained in Sect. 3.1. We introduce the 10-round distinguisher below.

**The 10-Round Periodic Distinguisher of GFS-4F.** We extensively use colors while depicting distinguishers. In order to have a better explanation, we take the 10-round distinguisher of GFS-4F (see Fig. 8) for illustration.

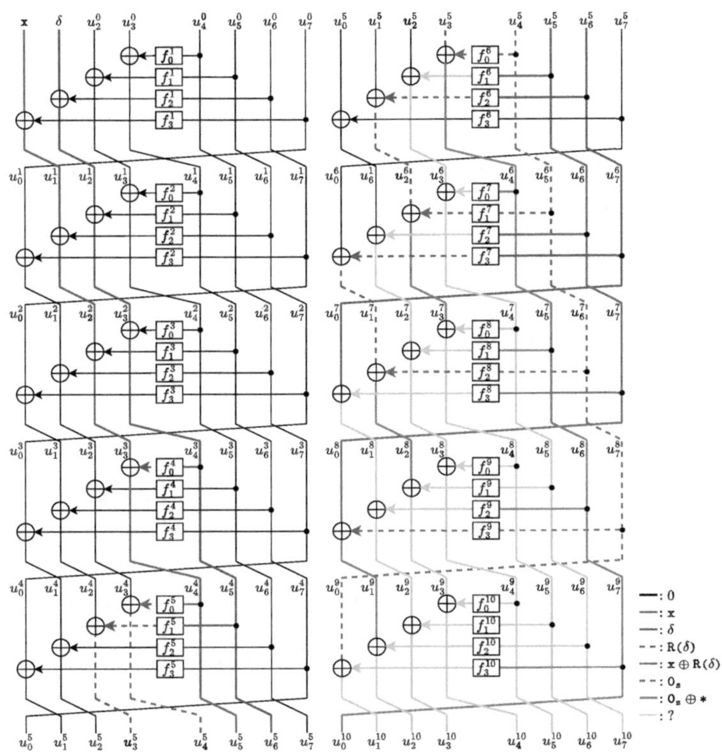


**Fig. 8.** The 10-round periodic distinguisher for GFS-4F.

Solid red, blue, and black lines represent x, $\delta$ and 0 in the model, respectively. Red and blue lines become dashed lines after passing through the round function R. A solid purple line represents $\mathtt{x} \oplus \mathtt{R}(\delta)$, indicating the existence of an explicit period. After passing through R, the explicit period will be hidden within the dashed purple line ($0_s$). According to Property 6, the rule of (the solid purple line $\rightarrow$ the dashed purple line) occurs only once. Finally, A solid gray line ($0_s \oplus *$) indicates which branch still retains the separability property. According to

Theorem 3, we can construct the periodic function. The period $s$ is $\Delta f_0^4(\alpha_b \oplus C_2)$, where $C_2 = f_2^1(u_6^0) \oplus f_1^2(u_4^0) \oplus f_0^3(u_2^0 \oplus f_1^1(u_5^0) \oplus f_0^2(u_3^0 \oplus f_0^1(u_4^0)))$ is a constant.

The complete periodic function is provided as follows.

We can see that the advantage of symbolic representation lies in transforming complexity into simplicity, which greatly expands the applicability of periodic distinguishers. For the 10-round distinguisher for GFS-4F, we have

$$\begin{aligned} u_0^{10} = {} & u_6^0 \oplus f_3^3(u_5^0) \oplus f_2^4(u_3^0 \oplus f_0^1(u_4^0)) \\ & \oplus f_1^5(u_1^0 \oplus f_2^1(u_6^0) \oplus f_1^2(u_4^0) \oplus f_0^3(u_2^0 \oplus f_1^1(u_5^0) \oplus f_0^2(u_3^0 \oplus f_0^1(u_4^0)))) \\ & \oplus f_0^6(u_7^0 \oplus f_3^2(u_6^0) \oplus f_2^3(u_4^0) \oplus f_1^4(u_2^0 \oplus f_1^1(u_5^0) \oplus f_0^2(u_3^0 \oplus f_0^1(u_4^0))) \\ & \oplus f_0^5(u_0^0 \oplus f_3^1(u_7^0) \oplus f_2^2(u_5^0) \oplus f_1^3(u_3^0 \oplus f_0^1(u_4^0)) \\ & \oplus f_0^4(u_1^0 \oplus f_2^1(u_6^0) \oplus f_1^2(u_4^0) \oplus f_0^3(u_2^0 \oplus f_1^1(u_5^0) \oplus f_0^2(u_3^0 \oplus f_0^1(u_4^0)))))). \end{aligned}$$

The periodic function is constructed by

$$\begin{aligned} g(x) &= E^{10}(x, \alpha_0, u_2^0, u_3^0, u_4^0, u_5^0, u_6^0, u_7^0)|_{u_0^{10}} \oplus E^{10}(x, \alpha_1, u_2^0, u_3^0, u_4^0, u_5^0, u_6^0, u_7^0)|_{u_0^{10}} \\ &= \Delta f_1^5(\alpha_b \oplus C_1) \oplus \Delta f_0^6(f_0^5(x \oplus f_0^4(\alpha_b \oplus C_2) \oplus C_3) \oplus C_4), \end{aligned}$$

where $u_2^0, u_3^0, u_4^0, u_5^0, u_6^0, u_7^0$ are constants, $C_1 = f_2^1(u_6^0) \oplus f_1^2(u_4^0) \oplus f_0^3(u_2^0 \oplus f_1^1(u_5^0) \oplus f_0^2(u_3^0 \oplus f_0^1(u_4^0)))$, $C_2 = f_2^1(u_6^0) \oplus f_1^2(u_4^0) \oplus f_0^3(u_2^0 \oplus f_1^1(u_5^0) \oplus f_0^2(u_3^0 \oplus f_0^1(u_4^0)))$, $C_3 = f_3^1(u_7^0) \oplus f_2^2(u_5^0) \oplus f_1^3(u_3^0 \oplus f_0^1(u_4^0))$, $C_4 = u_7^0 \oplus f_3^2(u_6^0) \oplus f_2^3(u_4^0) \oplus f_1^4(u_2^0 \oplus f_1^1(u_5^0) \oplus f_0^2(u_3^0 \oplus f_0^1(u_4^0)))$ are also constants.

## 5.2 Application on Skipjack-Type Structure

Skipjack [25] is the encryption algorithm developed by the NSA for the Clipper chip and Fortezza PC card. The published description of Skipjack characterizes the rounds as either Rule A or Rule B (see Fig. 9). In [20], Knudsen and Wagner considered different combinations of the two rules. Furthermore, in [3], Blondeau et al. used the impossible differential attack and zero-correlation linear attack to show the 16-round distinguishers for two common variants:

- Skipjack-A: only use Rule A as the round function,
- Skipjack-B: only use Rule B as the round function.

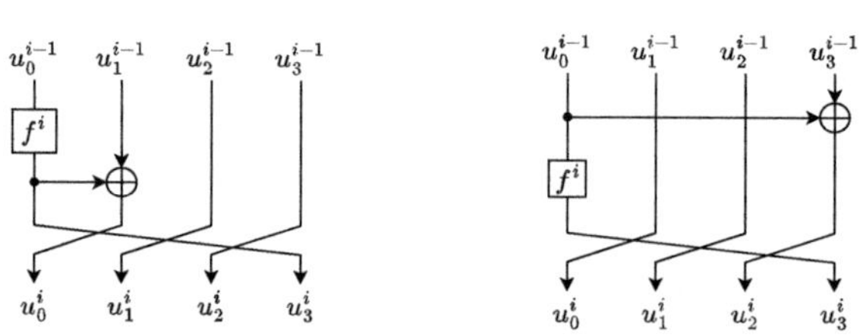


**Fig. 9.** The round function of Rule A (left) and Rule B (right).

Cui et al. [9] provided the first 13-round periodic distinguishers for the two variants Skipjack-A and Skipjack-B. In this section, we apply our model to Skipjack-A and Skipjack-B, and find the first 16-round polynomial-time periodic distinguisher of Skipjack-A/B. Based on the following observation, we present only the results for Skipjack-B, as the periodic distinguishers of both variants can be transformed into each other.

**Observation 1.** *As Rule B is basically the inverse of Rule A with minor positioning differences, any periodic distinguisher of Skipjack-B based on qCPA can be transformed into the periodic distinguisher of Skipjack-A based on qCCA.*

**The First 16-Round Polynomial-Time Distinguisher of Skipjack-B with qCPA.** Our model finds a 16-round periodic distinguisher of Skipjack-B (see Fig. 10):

$$(\delta, 0, 0, s \oplus \delta) \stackrel{16r}{\to} (0, ?, ?, ?).$$

Since the initial difference can be controlled by the adversary, the XOR of the two $\delta$ results in 0 based on Property 3. This distinguisher is three rounds longer than the previous quantum distinguisher and is the longest distinguisher of Skipjack-B in polynomial time. It can be transformed into a 16-round distinguisher of Skipjack-A based on qCCA.

**Applying the 16-Round Periodic Distinguisher in the Classical Setting.** Usually, for GFS, impossible differential and zero-correlation linear distinguishers are the most effective attacks. For Skipjack-B, in [3], Blondeau et al. showed a 16-round zero-correlation distinguisher $(u, u, 0, 0) \xrightarrow{\text{16r}} (0, v, 0, 0)$ and a 16-round impossible differential distinguisher $(\delta, \delta, 0, 0) \xrightarrow{\text{16r}} (\gamma, 0, 0, 0)$. The complexity is not less than $2^{32}$. Our distinguisher can be achieved within the complexity $2^9$ in the classical setting.

**Further Discussion.** Our results demonstrate that the proposed distinguisher is not only more effective in the quantum setting but also outperforms traditional distinguishers in the classical setting. This has significant implications for future structural designs. If periodic distinguishers are not considered during the design phase, they may become the primary form of cryptanalysis against the cipher.

### 5.3 Application on LBlock and TWINE

LBlock [32] is a variant of Feistel structures with the only difference that a left circular shift is performed on the right branch. TWINE [30] is a variant of GFS and is designed for multiple platforms.

Our model provides a 8-round periodic distinguisher of LBlock. Furthermore, with 4 collisions, the first 10-round distinguisher is discovered for both LBlock and TWINE. Table 4 summarizes the results. The conditions of 10-round periodic distinguisher for LBlock are $\Delta u_0^1 = 0$, $\Delta u_3^1 = 0$, $\Delta u_0^2 = 0$, and $\Delta u_5^4 = 0$, and the conditions of 10-round periodic distinguisher for TWINE are $\Delta u_8^1 = 0$,

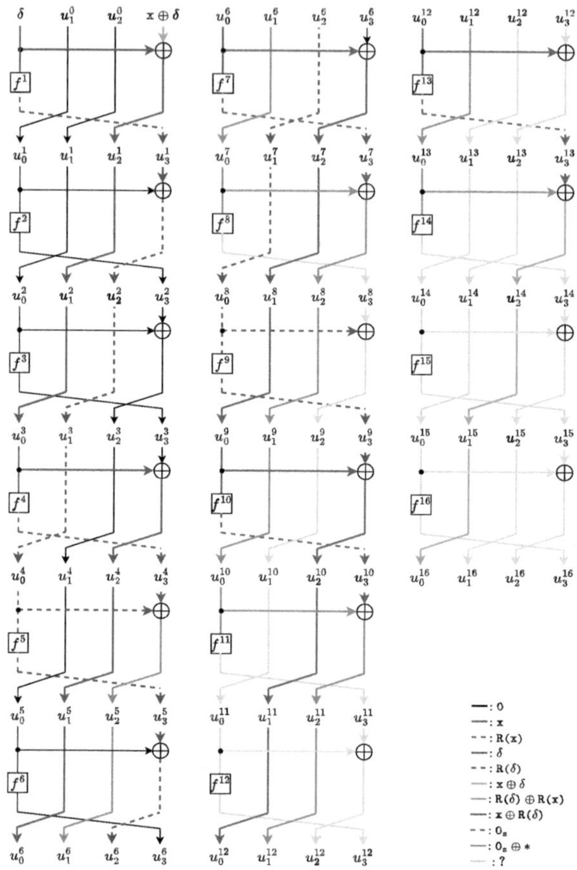


**Fig. 10.** 16-round distinguisher of Skipjack-B.

$\Delta u_{14}^1 = 0$, $\Delta u_4^2 = 0$, and $\Delta u_0^4 = 0$. The other distinguishers are explained in the full version [23].

**Considering the Difference Distribution Table (DDT) in the Distinguishers.** We observed that the collisions arise from specific differences of $\Delta\alpha_b$. In structural attacks, differential transitions through the S-box happen with random probabilities. To increase the success probability of the attack, we utilize the DDT by selecting the high-probability entries. If the two input branches are freely chosen, the output can be determined and propagated using the DDT. Figure 11 illustrates this property. For TWINE, the input to the 10-round distinguisher is:

$$(0x0, 0x0, 0x0, 0x0, 0x0, 0x0, 0x9, 0x8, 0x0, s, 0x0, 0x7, 0x0, 0x0, 0x9, 0x8).$$

According to the DDT, the probability of each collision is $2^{-2}$, thus, the probability of satisfying 4 collisions is $2^{-8}$.

**Table 4.** The periodic distinguishers of LBlock and TWINE.

| Cipher | #Rounds | Input | Output | Probability | Reference |
|---|---|---|---|---|---|
| LBlock | 3 | – | – | 1 | [21] |
| | 4 | – | – | 1 | [18] |
| | 8 | – | – | 1 | [33] |
| | **8** | $(0,0,0,0,0,0,s,0,0,0,0,0,0,0,\delta)$ | $(?,?,?,?,?,?,?,?,?,0,?,?,?,?,?,?)$ | **1** | **Our model** |
| | **10** | $(0,\delta,\delta,0,0,0,0,0,0,s,\delta,\delta,0,\delta,0,0)$ | $(?,?,?,?,?,?,?,?,?,0,?,?,?,?,?,?)$ | $\mathbf{2^{-8}}$ | **Our model** |
| TWINE | 8 | – | – | 1 | [7] |
| | **8** | $(0,0,\delta,s,0,0,0,\delta,0,0,0,0,0,0,0,0)$ | $(?,?,?,?,?,?,?,?,?,?,?,?,?,?,?,0)$ | **1** | **Our model** |
| | **10** | $(0,0,0,0,0,0,\delta,\delta,0,s,0,\delta,0,0,\delta,\delta)$ | $(?,0,?,?,?,?,?,?,?,?,?,?,?,?,?,?)$ | $\mathbf{2^{-8}}$ | **Our model** |

Then, we choose the input of the 10-round distinguisher for LBlock as:

$$(0x0, 0x5, 0x4, 0x0, 0x0, 0x0, 0x0, 0x0, 0x0, s, 0x4, 0x4, 0x0, 0x9, 0x0, 0x0).$$

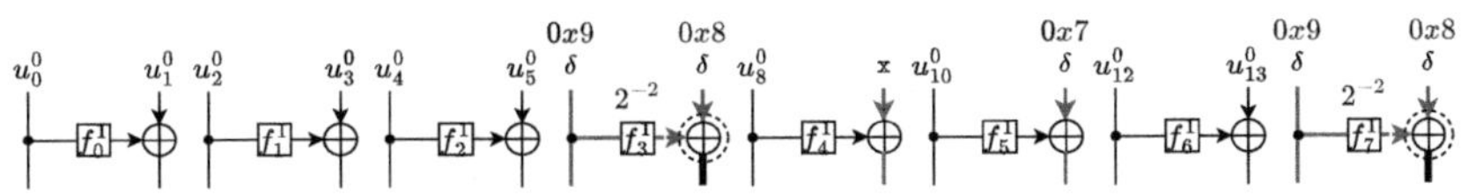

**Fig. 11.** The example of using DDT.

**Improvement in the Classical Setting.** To demonstrate the effectiveness of periodic distinguishers, we apply them in the classical setting and compare the results with the best known differential-linear distinguishers in [14]. Table 2 shows that our distinguishers achieve better performance over the same number of rounds. For example, the complexities of the 8/9/10-round distinguishers for TWINE is reduced from $2^{4.36}/2^{12.64}/2^{16.7}$ to $2^3/2^7/2^{13}$.

## 6 Extending Periodic Distinguishers to SKINNY and Other Ciphers

To date, no periodic distinguisher has been proposed for any SPN structure. In this section, we successfully apply the automated model to the SPN structure, such as SKINNY. Then, we extend the model to many other ciphers and show its effectiveness, including CRAFT, Piccolo, SM4, MARS, and SIMON. Note that we adopt an assumption from traditional distinguisher searches: The constraints of differences in different rounds are assumed to be independent after passing through the random round keys and S-boxes.

### 6.1 New Periodic Distinguishers of SKINNY

SKINNY [1] is a family of lightweight block ciphers which adopt the SPN structure. The internal states are represented as $4 \times 4$ arrays of cells with each cell being a nibble in case of 64-bit internal state or a byte in case of 128-bit internal state. The round function is described in Fig. 12. The transformation `MixColumns` maps a column $(a, b, c, d)^T$ into $(a \oplus c \oplus d, a, b \oplus c, a \oplus c)^T$, the word-based operations can be used to generate probabilistic distinguishers. For `SubCells`, let it be the operation `R` in our model. Since constants and keys do not affect the difference of the output of the periodic distinguisher, the two transformations `AddConstants` and `AddRoundTweakey` can be omitted.

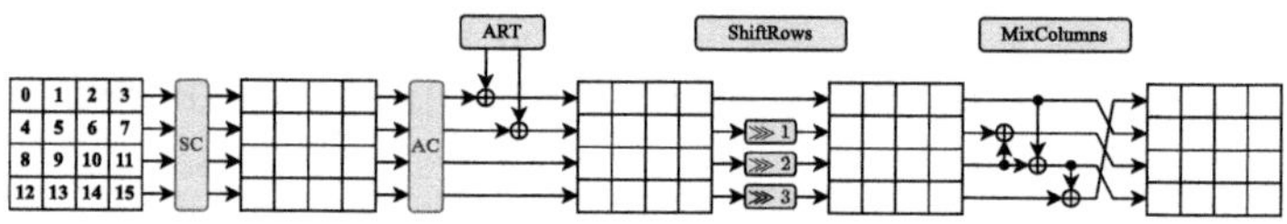


**Fig. 12.** The SKINNY round function: `SubCells`(SC), `AddConstants`(AC), `AddRoundTweakey`(ART), `ShiftRows`(SR), `MixColumns`(MC).

We use superscripts to indicate the positions in the cipher. For example, let the values be $\alpha_b = (\alpha_b^4, \alpha_b^7, \alpha_b^{10}, \alpha_b^{11}, \alpha_b^{13}, \alpha_b^{14}, \alpha_b^{15})$ in the 7-round distinguisher of SKINNY, and the difference be $\delta = (\delta^4, \delta^7, \delta^{10}, \delta^{11}, \delta^{13}, \delta^{14}, \delta^{15})$.

We provide a detailed explanation of the 7-round periodic distinguisher. Due to the structure of SKINNY, where `SubCells` precedes `AddRoundTweakey`, we adopt the method of searching for periodic distinguishers in the FK construction proposed in [6,9]. Firstly, because the first operation is `SubCells`, it is necessary to construct the state $\mathtt{x} \oplus \delta$ at the input. After passing through the `SubCells`, the state $\mathtt{x} \oplus \delta$ is transformed into $\mathtt{0_s}$. Next, $\alpha_0^4, \alpha_1^4, \alpha_0^7, \alpha_1^7, \alpha_0^{15}, \alpha_1^{15}$ are chosen randomly ($\alpha_0^4 \neq \alpha_1^4, \alpha_0^7 \neq \alpha_1^7, \alpha_0^{15} \neq \alpha_1^{15}$). Let $\alpha_b^{11} = \alpha_b^4, \alpha_b^{14} = \alpha_b^4, \alpha_b^{10} = \alpha_b^7, \alpha_b^{13} = \alpha_b^7$. Then, we can construct a 7-round periodic distinguisher.

Using the same method, we provide a detailed explanation of the 9-round periodic distinguisher. It is also necessary to construct the state $\mathtt{x} \oplus \delta$ at the input. After passing through the `SubCells`, the state $\mathtt{x} \oplus \delta$ is transformed into $\mathtt{0_s}$. Next, $\alpha_0^0, \alpha_1^0, \alpha_0^3, \alpha_1^3, \alpha_0^6, \alpha_1^6, \alpha_0^{13}, \alpha_1^{13}, \alpha_0^{14}, \alpha_1^{14}$ are chosen randomly ($\alpha_0^0 \neq \alpha_1^0, \alpha_0^3 \neq \alpha_1^3$, $\alpha_0^6 \neq \alpha_1^6, \alpha_0^{13} \neq \alpha_1^{13}, \alpha_0^{14} \neq \alpha_1^{14}$). Let $\alpha_b^7 = \alpha_b^0, \alpha_b^{10} = \alpha_b^0, \alpha_b^9 = \alpha_b^3$. Then, we can construct a 9-round periodic distinguisher.

Let the $j$-th branch before and after the $i$-th round of `MixColumns` be denoted by $SR_j^i$ and $MC_j^i$, respectively. The 9-round distinguisher imposes the following constraints: In Round 2: $\Delta SR_1^2 = \Delta SR_5^2, \Delta SR_1^2 = \Delta SR_9^2$. In Round 3: $\Delta SR_6^3 = \Delta SR_{10}^3$. In Round 5: $\Delta SR_1^5 = \Delta SR_{13}^5$. Based on our assumption, the constraints of different rounds are considered independent after `AddRoundTweakey` and `SubCells` operations, which are used to calculate the theoretical probability. Experiments have verified that this probability is reasonable. The distinguishers are provided in the full version [23].

**Improvement in the Classical Setting.** We apply our distinguishers in the classical setting and compare them with the best known differential-linear distinguishers in [14]. The complexity of 7-/8-/9-round differential-linear distinguisher for SKINNY-64 is $2^{5.64}/2^{14.5}/2^{22.72}$, respectively. In contrast, our distinguishers achieve significantly lower complexities of $2^3/2^9/2^{21}$ for the same number of rounds.

## 6.2 New Periodic Distinguishers of CRAFT

CRAFT [2] is a lightweight tweakable block cipher, the internal states are represented as $4 \times 4$ arrays of cells with each cell being a nibble. The round function is described in Fig. 13. For stronger diffusion, `PermuteNibbles` uses different methods, such as `RShift`, `Shuffle`, and `LShift`. `S-box` is not included in the last round.

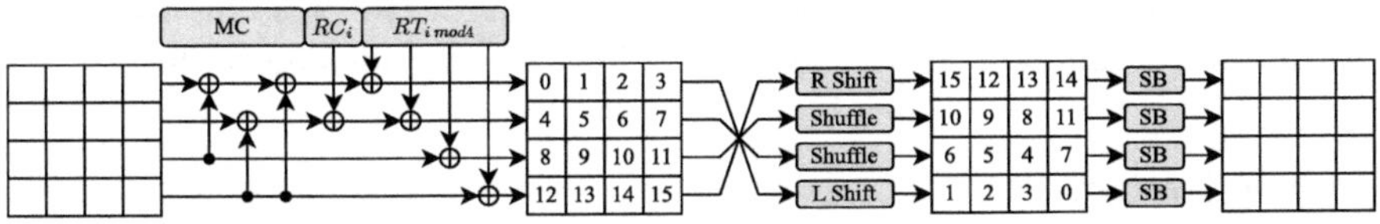


**Fig. 13.** The CRAFT round function, including `MixColumns`(MC), `AddRoundConstants`(RC), `AddTweakey`(RT), `PermuteNibbles`(PN), and `S-box`(SB).

`MixColumns` maps a column $(a, b, c, d)^T$ into $(a \oplus c \oplus d, b \oplus d, c, d)^T$. Then, `AddRoundConstants` and `AddTweakey` can be omitted, and we let `S-box` be the operation `R` in our model. However, if the difference with unknown values passes `R`, the periodicity will vanish. Since our model requires that the input is `x` or $\delta$ and the period is included in $\mathtt{R}(\mathtt{x} \oplus \delta)$ or $\mathtt{R}(\mathtt{x} \oplus \mathtt{R}(\delta))$, `x` must occur in the first two lines. The periodic point $\mathtt{0_s}$ always occurs in the first round. This is similar to SKINNY. The full version [23] provides more details.

## 6.3 Further Application on Piccolo

We have proven that the model is highly applicable to various structures and ciphers. However, for ciphers that include MDS matrices, there is currently no effective method to describe periodic attacks. We take Piccolo [27] as an example to illustrate how our model can be applied to this type of cipher.

Piccolo is a lightweight block cipher using the Feistel-SP structure, proposed by Shibutani et al. for extremely constrained devices. For Feistel-SP structure, there exists a 3-round periodic distinguisher based on qCPA and a 4-round distinguisher based on qCCA [18]. The more complex permutation used in Piccolo makes it difficult for these attacks to be directly applied. It remains unknown whether a better distinguisher can be found by decomposing the round function. Finally, based on our modified model, we successfully identify the first 4-round polynomial-time periodic distinguisher. The full version [23] provides more details.

### 6.4 Applications on Type-1/2/3 GFS, SM4, MARS, and SIMON

For Type-1/2/3 GFS, there are many periodic distinguishers. Using our method, all longest-round periodic distinguishers can be reconstructed. In [9,33], the periodic distinguishers for SM4, MARS, and SIMON are proposed. For each cipher, we can find the periodic distinguisher, which has the same rounds with [9,33]. For SM4 and MARS, our method can be used to search for the 7-round periodic distinguishers with only slight modifications. Notably, for MARS, we also use a particular property in [9]:

$$u_0^4 \oplus u_1^4 \oplus u_2^4 = u_0^5 \oplus u_1^5 \oplus u_3^5 = u_0^6 \oplus u_2^6 \oplus u_3^6 = u_1^7 \oplus u_2^7 \oplus u_3^7 \quad (8)$$

Thus, our goal is to search for a 4-round periodic distinguisher such that $u_0^4$, $u_1^4$, and $u_2^4$ are the state $\mathtt{0_s} \oplus *$. Then, using Eq. (8), we can construct a 7-round periodic distinguisher. For SIMON, we use the property in [33] when two states are combined by an AND operation, and can search for the periodic distinguisher with the same rounds as [33]. The full version [23] provides more details.

## 7 Conclusion

This paper presents a significant advancement in quantum cryptanalysis of symmetric-key schemes by introducing an automated approach for discovering periodic distinguishers. The proposed methodology for Simon's algorithm offers a more refined and systematic framework compared to existing techniques. A key contribution is the development of probabilistic periodic distinguishers using the Grover-meet-Simon algorithm, which enhances the identification of effective periodic distinguishers through optimized strategies for selecting initial differences. This theoretical framework significantly broadens the scope of detectable periodic distinguishers. The SMT-based model demonstrates extensive applicability, achieved through significant advancements in the analysis of both generalized Feistel structures and substitution-permutation network (SPN) ciphers. This framework enables the discovery of optimized periodic distinguishers for numerous cryptographic constructions, including generalized Feistel structures (e.g., GFS-2F/4F, Skipjack-type structures, LBlock, and TWINE) as well as SPN-based designs (e.g., SKINNY). Our findings reveal that periodic distinguishers, as identified through our automated model, demonstrate effects that differ from traditional methods. Notably, these distinguishers not only prove effective in quantum cryptanalysis but also exhibit new insight in classical cryptanalysis settings. We anticipate that future research will further explore these distinguishers and potentially extend their application to a wider range of cryptographic primitives by providing improved periodic analysis methodologies. The results from our automated model suggest that periodic analysis may establish a novel cryptanalytic technology. However, some challenges remain, particularly in developing more precise analytical models for ciphers with MDS matrices, which represents a critical direction for future investigation.

**Acknowledgements.** The authors would like to thank the anonymous reviewers and shepherd for their valuable comments and suggestions to improve the quality of the paper. This work is supported by the National Key R&D Program of China (Grant No. 2024YFA1013000, 2023YFA1009500), the National Natural Science Foundation of China (Grant No. 62032014, U2336207, 623B2067), and the National Cryptologic Science Fund of China (Grant No. 2025NCSF01013). In addition, Haoyang Wang is supported by the National Natural Science Foundation of China (Grant No. 62302293). We used generative AI tools (OpenAI's ChatGPT) for grammar checking and spell correction. All content was written and verified by the authors, who take full responsibility for the final text.

## References

1. Beierle, C., et al.: The SKINNY family of block ciphers and its low-latency variant MANTIS. In: Robshaw, M., Katz, J. (eds.) CRYPTO 2016, Part II. LNCS, vol. 9815, pp. 123–153. Springer, Heidelberg (2016). https://doi.org/10.1007/978-3-662-53008-5_5
2. Beierle, C., Leander, G., Moradi, A., Rasoolzadeh, S.: CRAFT: lightweight tweakable block cipher with efficient protection against DFA attacks. IACR Trans. Symmetric Cryptol. **2019**(1), 5–45 (2019). https://doi.org/10.13154/TOSC.V2019.I1.5-45
3. Blondeau, C., Bogdanov, A., Wang, M.: On the (In)equivalence of impossible differential and zero-correlation distinguishers for Feistel- and Skipjack-type ciphers. In: Boureanu, I., Owesarski, P., Vaudenay, S. (eds.) ACNS 2014. LNCS, vol. 8479, pp. 271–288. Springer, Cham (2014). https://doi.org/10.1007/978-3-319-07536-5_17
4. Bonnetain, X., Hosoyamada, A., Naya-Plasencia, M., Sasaki, Yu., Schrottenloher, A.: Quantum attacks without superposition queries: the offline Simon's algorithm. In: Galbraith, S.D., Moriai, S. (eds.) ASIACRYPT 2019, Part I. LNCS, vol. 11921, pp. 552–583. Springer, Cham (2019). https://doi.org/10.1007/978-3-030-34578-5_20
5. Bonnetain, X., Leurent, G., Naya-Plasencia, M., Schrottenloher, A.: Quantum linearization attacks. In: Tibouchi, M., Wang, H. (eds.) ASIACRYPT 2021, Part I. LNCS, vol. 13090, pp. 422–452. Springer, Cham (2021). https://doi.org/10.1007/978-3-030-92062-3_15
6. Canale, F., Leander, G., Stennes, L.: Simon's algorithm and symmetric crypto: Generalizations and automatized applications. In: Dodis, Y., Shrimpton, T. (eds.) CRYPTO 2022, Part III. LNCS, vol. 13509, pp. 779–808. Springer, Cham (2022). https://doi.org/10.1007/978-3-031-15982-4_26
7. Chen, J., Liu, Q., Li, B., Qiao, J., Wang, J.: Simplified periodic distinguishers searching: application to GFS-4F/2F and TWINE. In: Lin, D., Wang, M., Yung, M. (eds.) Information Security and Cryptology. LNCS, pp. 425–443. Springer, Singapore (2025). https://doi.org/10.1007/978-981-96-4734-7_21
8. Cid, C., Hosoyamada, A., Liu, Y., Sim, S.M.: Quantum cryptanalysis on contracting Feistel structures and observation on related-key settings. In: Bhargavan, K., Oswald, E., Prabhakaran, M. (eds.) INDOCRYPT 2020. LNCS, vol. 12578, pp. 373–394. Springer, Cham (2020). https://doi.org/10.1007/978-3-030-65277-7_17
9. Cui, J., Guo, J., Ding, S.: Applications of Simon's algorithm in quantum attacks on Feistel variants. Quantum Inf. Process. **20**(3), 117 (2021). https://doi.org/10.1007/S11128-021-03027-X

10. Daemen, J., Rijmen, V.: The Design of Rijndael - The Advanced Encryption Standard (AES), Second Edition. Information Security and Cryptography, Springer (2020). https://doi.org/10.1007/978-3-662-60769-5
11. Dong, X., Dong, B., Wang, X.: Quantum attacks on some Feistel block ciphers. Des. Codes Cryptogr. **88**(6), 1179–1203 (2020). https://doi.org/10.1007/S10623-020-00741-Y
12. Dong, X., Li, Z., Wang, X.: Quantum cryptanalysis on some generalized Feistel schemes. Sci. China Inf. Sci. **62**(2), 22501:1–22501:12 (2019). https://doi.org/10.1007/S11432-017-9436-7
13. Grover, L.K.: A fast quantum mechanical algorithm for database search. In: Miller, G.L. (ed.) Proceedings of the Twenty-Eighth Annual ACM Symposium on the Theory of Computing, Philadelphia, Pennsylvania, USA, 22–24 May 1996, pp. 212–219. ACM (1996)
14. Hadipour, H., Derbez, P., Eichlseder, M.: Revisiting differential-linear attacks via a boomerang perspective with application to AES, Ascon, CLEFIA, SKINNY, PRESENT, KNOT, TWINE, WARP, LBlock, Simeck, and SERPENT. In: Reyzin, L., Stebila, D. (eds.) CRYPTO 2024, Part IV. LNCS, vol. 14923, pp. 38–72. Springer, Cham (2024). https://doi.org/10.1007/978-3-031-68385-5_2
15. Hodžić, S., Knudsen Ramkilde, L., Brasen Kidmose, A.: On quantum distinguishers for type-3 generalized Feistel network based on separability. In: Ding, J., Tillich, J.-P. (eds.) PQCrypto 2020. LNCS, vol. 12100, pp. 461–480. Springer, Cham (2020). https://doi.org/10.1007/978-3-030-44223-1_25
16. Hosoyamada, A., Aoki, K.: On Quantum Related-Key Attacks on Iterated Even-Mansour Ciphers. In: Obana, S., Chida, K. (eds.) IWSEC 2017. LNCS, vol. 10418, pp. 3–18. Springer, Cham (2017). https://doi.org/10.1007/978-3-319-64200-0_1
17. Hosoyamada, A., Sasaki, Yu.: Quantum Demiric-Selçuk meet-in-the-middle attacks: applications to 6-round generic Feistel constructions. In: Catalano, D., De Prisco, R. (eds.) SCN 2018. LNCS, vol. 11035, pp. 386–403. Springer, Cham (2018). https://doi.org/10.1007/978-3-319-98113-0_21
18. Ito, G., Hosoyamada, A., Matsumoto, R., Sasaki, Yu., Iwata, T.: Quantum chosen-ciphertext attacks against Feistel ciphers. In: Matsui, M. (ed.) CT-RSA 2019. LNCS, vol. 11405, pp. 391–411. Springer, Cham (2019). https://doi.org/10.1007/978-3-030-12612-4_20
19. Kaplan, M., Leurent, G., Leverrier, A., Naya-Plasencia, M.: Breaking symmetric cryptosystems using quantum period finding. In: Robshaw, M., Katz, J. (eds.) CRYPTO 2016, Part II. LNCS, vol. 9815, pp. 207–237. Springer, Heidelberg (2016). https://doi.org/10.1007/978-3-662-53008-5_8
20. Knudsen, L.R., Wagner, D.A.: On the structure of skipjack. Discret. Appl. Math. **111**(1–2), 103–116 (2001). https://doi.org/10.1016/S0166-218X(00)00347-4
21. Kuwakado, H., Morii, M.: Quantum distinguisher between the 3-round Feistel cipher and the random permutation. In: IEEE International Symposium on Information Theory, ISIT 2010, Austin, Texas, USA, 13–18 June 2010, Proceedings, pp. 2682–2685. IEEE (2010). https://doi.org/10.1109/ISIT.2010.5513654
22. Leander, G., May, A.: Grover meets Simon – quantumly attacking the FX-construction. In: Takagi, T., Peyrin, T. (eds.) ASIACRYPT 2017, Part II. LNCS, vol. 10625, pp. 161–178. Springer, Cham (2017). https://doi.org/10.1007/978-3-319-70697-9_6
23. Liu, Q., Wang, H., Wang, J., Li, B., Wang, M.: Quantum periodic distinguisher construction: symbolization method and automated tool. Cryptology ePrint Archive, Paper 2025/681 (2025). https://eprint.iacr.org/2025/681

24. Ni, B., Ito, G., Dong, X., Iwata, T.: Quantum attacks against type-1 generalized Feistel ciphers and applications to CAST-256. In: Hao, F., Ruj, S., Sen Gupta, S. (eds.) INDOCRYPT 2019. LNCS, vol. 11898, pp. 433–455. Springer, Cham (2019). https://doi.org/10.1007/978-3-030-35423-7_22
25. NIST: Skipjack and kea algorithm specifications (1998). https://csrc.nist.gov/CSRC/media//Projects/Cryptographic-Algorithm-Validation-Program/documents/skipjack/skipjack.pdf
26. Nyberg, K.: Generalized Feistel networks. In: Kim, K., Matsumoto, T. (eds.) ASIACRYPT 1996. LNCS, vol. 1163, pp. 91–104. Springer, Heidelberg (1996). https://doi.org/10.1007/BFB0034838
27. Shibutani, K., Isobe, T., Hiwatari, H., Mitsuda, A., Akishita, T., Shirai, T.: *Piccolo*: an ultra-lightweight blockcipher. In: Preneel, B., Takagi, T. (eds.) CHES 2011. LNCS, vol. 6917, pp. 342–357. Springer, Heidelberg (2011). https://doi.org/10.1007/978-3-642-23951-9_23
28. Simon, D.R.: On the power of quantum computation. In: 35th Annual Symposium on Foundations of Computer Science, Santa Fe, New Mexico, USA, 20–22 November 1994, pp. 116–123. IEEE Computer Society (1994). https://doi.org/10.1109/SFCS.1994.365701
29. Sun, H.W., Cai, B.B., Qin, S.J., Wen, Q.Y., Gao, F.: Quantum attacks on type-1 generalized feistel schemes. Adv. Quant. Technol. **6**(10), 2300155 (2023)
30. Suzaki, T., Minematsu, K., Morioka, S., Kobayashi, E.: *TWINE*: a lightweight block cipher for multiple platforms. In: Knudsen, L.R., Wu, H. (eds.) SAC 2012. LNCS, vol. 7707, pp. 339–354. Springer, Heidelberg (2013). https://doi.org/10.1007/978-3-642-35999-6_22
31. Wang, X., Xiang, Z., Zhang, S., Chen, S., Zeng, X.: Quantum chosen-ciphertext attacks based on Simon's algorithm against unified structures. In: Patra, A. (ed.) CT-RSA 2025. LNCS, vol. 15598, pp. 99–122. Springer, Cham (2025). https://doi.org/10.1007/978-3-031-88661-4_5
32. Wu, W., Zhang, L.: LBlock: a lightweight block cipher. In: Lopez, J., Tsudik, G. (eds.) ACNS 2011. LNCS, vol. 6715, pp. 327–344. Springer, Heidelberg (2011). https://doi.org/10.1007/978-3-642-21554-4_19
33. Xiang, Z., et al.: Links between quantum distinguishers based on Simon's algorithm and truncated differentials. IACR Trans. Symmetric Cryptol. **2024**(2), 296–321 (2024). https://doi.org/10.46586/TOSC.V2024.I2.296-321
34. Xu, Y., Du, X., Jia, M., Wang, X., Zou, J.: Quantum attacks on generalized Feistel networks based on the strong-weak separability. Quantum Inf. Process. **22**(10), 375 (2023). https://doi.org/10.1007/S11128-023-04135-6

# Hybrid-query bounds with partial input control – framework and application to tight M-eTCR

Andreas Hülsing[1,2(✉)], Mikhail Kudinov[1(✉)], and Christian Majenz[3(✉)]

[1] Eindhoven University of Technology, Eindhoven, Netherlands
[2] SandboxAQ, Paolo Alto, USA
[3] Technical University of Denmark, Kongens Lyngby, Denmark
andreas@huelsing.net, mishel.kudinov@gmail.com, chmaj@dtu.dk

**Abstract.** In this paper, we revisit the security of randomized hash& sign. More precisely, we present an improved security analysis for the underlying hash function property *multi-target extended target collision resistance (M-ETCR)* in the quantum random oracle model (QROM). While prior work relied on reprogramming techniques to handle adversarial challenge queries, we leverage the hybrid compressed oracle framework of Hamoudi, Liu, and Sinha [19] to formulate an adaptive search problem. To do so, we had to extend their framework to cover partially randomized classical adversary queries. We conjecture that this extension will also allow to analyze further hash function properties that allow adversaries to define challenges via a classical oracle.

By applying the extended framework to M-ETCR, we give an improved upper bound on the adversary's success probability. Our results show that the required key size for M-ETCR can be reduced by more than half (from 192 to 72 bits), and we prove the tightness of our bound in the number of queries via matching attacks. To illustrate practical impact, we optimize parameters for Falcon in the hash&sign paradigm, enabling more efficient instantiations with reduced salt sizes resulting in smaller signature lengths. For the example of multiple signatures aggregation, we achieve a signature size improvement of 30 kB for typical parameters.

**Keywords:** QROM · Hybrid QROM · TCR · Hash & Sign.

## 1 Introduction

Hash functions are one of the most widely used primitives in modern cryptography. One of the first steps in analyzing a given security property for a hash function is to analyze the property for a random function. To do so, we model the hash function as a random oracle [3, 14] (Random Oracle Model, ROM). The ROM

A.H. and M.K. were supported by an NWO VIDI grant (Project No. VI.Vidi.193.066). C.M. acknowledges support by the Independent Research Fund Denmark via a DFF Sapere Aude grant (IM-3PQC, grant ID 10.46540/2064-00034B)

Date: December 5, 2025

© International Association for Cryptologic Research 2026
G. Hanaoka and B.-Y. Yang (Eds.): ASIACRYPT 2025, LNCS 16252, pp.256–286, 2026.
https://doi.org/10.1007/978-981-95-5125-5_9

is the standard tool for characterizing generic attacks against hash functions: attacks that only depend on the input-output behavior of the hash function rather than the details of the algorithm. In the ROM, the number of queries required to break a certain security property is used as a proxy for the real (time-)complexity of an attack. On the other hand, such analysis gives a bound on the maximum possible level of security for real-world hash functions for a given property.

The desire for security against quantum computing attacks requires revisiting many cryptographic techniques, including the ROM. A quantum adversary possesses a large-scale quantum computer and may perform local quantum computations, while the honest users remain classical. Such a quantum adversary can implement any publicly available primitive as a quantum circuit and run it on a superposition of inputs. As hash functions are public primitives, we need to model them as being quantumly accessible. This also applies to the ROM, resulting in the quantum-accessible random oracle model (QROM) [6].

While we consider a quantum adversary for post-quantum security, the honest parties remain classical. Thus, any interaction between an honest user and the adversary must be classical. If an adversary has access to a keyed functionality which, in turn, queries a random oracle, such access thus remains classical. A typical example would be pseudorandomness of a keyed hash function. An honest user generates a secret key. The adversary may query the user for outputs of the hash function instantiated with the secret key and needs to determine whether the responses are generated by actual evaluation of the hash function or if they are just random strings. In this case, the adversary needs to perform classical queries to the honest user while still being able to do quantum queries (containing both the key and the message) to the hash function.

In this work we aim to improve the security analysis of extended target collision resistance (eTCR) in the multi-target setting (m-eTCR). Loosely speaking, an eTCR-adversary must find a collision for a message of their choice, but the key for that message is chosen uniformly at random: $\mathcal{A}$ chooses $\mathsf{m}$, and then given a uniformly random $k$, must find $(k', \mathsf{m}' \neq \mathsf{m})$, such that $F(k', \mathsf{m}') = F(k, \mathsf{m})$. For the multi-target case the adversary gets a new key for each submitted message. Most importantly, m-eTCR is underlying the security of signature schemes in the hash & sign paradigm [1, 10, 29]. However, it also relates to the security of keyed-hash message authentication codes [23].

The analysis of properties with adaptively chosen challenges remains challenging in the QROM despite the recent surge in new QROM-proof techniques. While we have optimal bounds for most important non-adaptive properties like collision resistance or one-wayness [2, 4, 9, 20], the best known result for m-eTCR is non-optimal as it uses reprogramming techniques [16] to handle adaptive queries. Intuitively, the bound is obtained by first bounding the case of non-adaptive, random challenges and then using reprogramming to map the adversaries queries to these random challenges. The bound for random challenges can be obtained using the recent transition capacity framework [9] by Chung, Fehr, Huang, and Liao. This framework helps to analyze quantum query progress using only classical reasoning. In their work, the authors view the QRO as a database, which is updated with each query. Such an approach is possible because of the compressed random oracle (CRO) – a technique introduced by Zhandry [30] that allows the investigation of queries made to the oracle. The CRO largely resembles the classical lazy sampling technique.

A recent advancement to the transition capacity framework introduced by Hamoudi, Liu, and Sinha in [19] potentially offers an alternative strategy. Motivated by the limited resources of near-term quantum computing, Hamoudi, Liu, and Sinha sought to enable fine-grained analysis of hybrid algorithms that make a mixture of classical and quantum queries. The aim of [19] was to show lower bounds on the complexities of certain problems. For example, the authors showed that the optimal success probability of an algorithm making $q$ quantum and $c$ classical queries for solving the Collision Finding problem is $\Theta((c^2+cq^2+q^3)/N)$. One might hope to use this new hybrid framework to directly cover the full M-ETCR problem with the transition capacity approach, avoiding the need for reprogramming which was the source of looseness so far. While their framework's ability to separate classical and quantum queries is powerful, it sadly is not directly applicable to the M-ETCR setting for two key reasons:

First and foremost, the role of classical queries differ between [19] and our work. In [19], classical and quantum queries model different ways to access the same public primitive. Especially, regardless of the type of query, they do not in any way influence the success condition of the adversary. In our setting of M-ETCR, however, classical queries adaptively change the success condition of the adversary.

Second, in our setting the classical query interface models adversarial access to a (secretly-)keyed cryptographic functionality while in [19] it simply models classical access to a fully public object. Consequently, in our case the adversary might only get partial control over the query input while part of it is sampled / controlled by another procedure.

An important open question is thus:

*Can we upgrade the hybrid compressed oracle technique to allow tight query bounds for partial-input-control query access and achieve better bounds for the security of M-ETCR?*

**Our contribution.** In this paper, we develop a framework for proving QROM query bounds for algorithms with standard quantum access and an additional classical query interface with partially randomized input that supports adaptively changing success conditions based on classical queries. Towards this end, we extend the techniques of [19]. In their work, the authors introduced two distinct databases: one stores the results of classical queries, while the other is used for quantum queries. Additionally, they provide a detailed analysis of how the amplitudes change after each query type. A key insight is that the separate databases for quantum and classical queries in the framework of [19] allow the analysis of problems where input-output pairs obtained from the classical query interface are treated differently from other pairs.

Concretely, we develop a framework for proving query bounds in settings where an adversary can provide part of the input to the classical query interface of a QRO, and the remaining part is sampled at random. Starting from the work of [19], our technique bounds the "progress", as measured by a database predicate projector, that the adversary can achieve with such partial-control classical queries. While this does not require fundamentally new techniques, it does require additional non-trivial analysis, which we cover in Lemma 5.

We apply the new framework to analyze the multi-target extended target collision resistance property (M-ETCR) in the QROM (Definition 6). The security of this property has been analyzed in the QROM in [16]. We give it another look. Using the techniques from [19] and the ones we develop in this paper, we were able to improve the state-of-the-art bound for QROM security of M-ETCR. The proof requires an analysis of the progress a quantum and a classical query can make. This is done with the use of our extension and careful inspection of possible amplitude growth.

The new bound allows us to reduce key size by more than half, resulting in a reduction from 192 to 72 bits for category one security level in the NIST call [26, Section 4]. Moreover, our proof is tight in the number of queries. We provide an attack with a matching number of queries for each term in the bound, essentially closing the question of the security analysis of M-ETCR for random functions.

We expect the new technique to be useful across various other hash function properties that allow the adversary to adaptively define targets, including M-ETCR with nonce [16], or the single target TCR notion for tweakable hash functions [5]. The new tools may also contribute to the study of Interleaved Target Subset Resilience [5], a crucial property used by schemes such as SPHINCS$^+$ [5].

We also discuss the implications of our new M-ETCR bound. We take a closer look at one of the typical use cases – randomized hashing in the hash & sign paradigm. It is often the case that we want to hash the message before signing it. Adding randomness to the hash function input allows us to decrease the security requirement from collision resistance to M-ETCR. This usually allows us to use a smaller digest length but forces us to append the used randomness (often called a 'salt') to the signature. Hence, using smaller salt gives us smaller signature sizes. This becomes especially important in the case of multiple signature aggregation. By applying our bound to a recent proposal [1], we achieve a significant reduction in the size of the aggregated signature. In case the aggregated signature is formed from 2000 signatures, our analysis enables a size reduction from 165 kB to 136 kB.

**Organization.** We introduce necessary definitions and discuss CRO in Sect. 2. Sect. 3 is devoted to the description of the hybrid CRO framework. In Sect. 3.1, we improve the framework by presenting a bound on the progress for a new type of query. The security proof for M-ETCR that uses the results obtained in the previous section is given in Sect. 4. Sect. 5 discuss the use of M-ETCR in signature schemes.

## 2 Preliminaries: Compressed Random Oracle

In this section, we revisit the quantum-accessible random oracle model (QROM) and Zhandry's Compressed Oracle (CRO) [30]. The random oracle methodology effectively helps designing and proving the security of cryptographic protocols by treating hash functions as external oracles. We focus on keyed hash functions, $F : \mathcal{K} \times \mathcal{M} \rightarrow \mathcal{N}$. Although it is acknowledged that this methodology can potentially fail [8, 22], experience suggests that this rarely occurs for naturally designed protocols. The key difference between the classical ROM and QROM is that in the classical setting, security reductions can examine queries, whereas in the quantum setting, superposition queries are difficult to inspect without disrupting the adversary's state.

To deal with this, Zhandry introduced the Compressed Oracle framework (CRO) [30]. The CRO provides an approach that is useful for establishing lower bounds against quantum algorithms with black-box access to a uniformly random function $F$, which maps $\mathcal{M}$ to $\mathcal{N}$ (in our case $\mathcal{K} \times \mathcal{M}$ to $\mathcal{N}$). The CRO enables the storage of a compressed representation of the random function, conditional on the knowledge obtained from previous queries. Conceptually, the technique resembles the classical "lazy sampling" method. Technically, it considers a quantum purification of the random function $F$ and then analyzes the internal state of the random oracle in the Fourier domain.

Here, we are going to closely follow the description of QROM and CRO from [9]. In our model, it is sufficient to work with three different registers $|x, y, z\rangle$, where $x$ will contain a concatenation of elements from $\mathcal{K}$ and $\mathcal{M}$, $y$ is the output register, and $z$ is the work register. We will omit the work register in most cases. The standard approach for an ordinary QROM defined with unitary $\mathsf{StO}$ works the following way: $\mathsf{StO} \sum_{x,y} \alpha_{x,y} |x, y\rangle \rightarrow \sum_{x,y} \alpha_{x,y} |x, y + F(x)\rangle$.

To switch to the CRO, we first need to consider a superposition $\sum_F |F\rangle$ of all possible functions $F$ in the defined domain and range. So, the initial state will be $|\Pi_0\rangle = \sum_F |F\rangle$. Now, we want to look at it in a Fourier basis, which we will denote with a hat symbol "^".

$$|\Pi_0\rangle = \sum_F |F\rangle = \bigotimes_x (\sum_y |y\rangle) = \bigotimes_x |\hat{0}\rangle$$

The idea is that we can compress these $|\hat{0}\rangle$ states in a new special state $|\bot\rangle$. This will imply some error for decompressing, but we can make it small enough for our use cases. So, we will define compression in the following way:

$$\mathsf{Comp}_x = |\bot\rangle \langle\hat{0}| + \sum_{\hat{w}\neq 0} |\hat{w}\rangle \langle\hat{w}|, \text{i.e.} \quad |\hat{y}\rangle \rightarrow \begin{cases} |\bot\rangle & \text{if } \hat{y} = \hat{0} \\ |\hat{y}\rangle & \text{if } \hat{y} \neq \hat{0} \end{cases}$$

Now, we can apply this isometry to every register $x \in \mathcal{X}$ and obtain the compression operator $\mathsf{Comp} = \otimes_x \mathsf{Comp}_x$. If we apply $\mathsf{Comp}$ to the $|\Pi_0\rangle$, we will get all the $|\bot\rangle$ states.

$$\mathsf{Comp}\,|\Pi_0\rangle = (\bigotimes_x \mathsf{Comp}_x)(\bigotimes_x |\hat{0}\rangle) = \bigotimes_x \mathsf{Comp}_x |\hat{0}\rangle = \bigotimes_x |\bot\rangle$$

This can be viewed as a trivial database that maps everything to $|\bot\rangle$. This compression will work mostly the same as just working with the Fourier basis, i.e. $\mathsf{Comp}\,|\hat{F}\rangle = |\hat{D}\rangle$, where $\hat{D}$ is such that $\hat{D}(x) = \hat{F}(x)$ whenever $\hat{F}(x) \neq 0$ and $\hat{D}(x) = \bot$ whenever $\hat{F}(x) = 0$. As a result, after $q$ queries, we will have the internal state of the Compressed Oracle consisting of several state vectors, where $D(x) = \bot$ for all but (at most) $q$ choices of $x$. The last step is to efficiently store it in terms of the number of qubits. We omit this technical detail. For more information, we refer to [30]. We now use an updated definition of $\mathsf{StO}$ to accommodate the superposition of functions:

$$\mathsf{StO} \sum_{x,y,F} \alpha_{x,y,F} |x, y\rangle |F\rangle \to \sum_{x,y,F} \alpha_{x,y,F} |x, y + F(x)\rangle |F\rangle$$

As a result, we have the compressed random oracle: $\mathsf{cO} :- \mathsf{Comp} \circ \mathsf{StO} \circ \mathsf{Comp}^\dagger$.

Here, we implicitly refer to $F$ representation as database $D$, which is a common approach. Intuitively, a database $D$ represents a classical lazy sampling technique. The original state is $D_0$, where for any input, the output is the $\bot$ symbol. After a query, we check if the input is in the database or not. In the first case, we respond with the value assigned to that input in $D$; otherwise, we sample a uniformly random value for the output and update $D$, i.e., $D_i = D_{i-1}[x_i \to y_i]$. So $D_i(x_i) = y_i$. In the case of superposition queries, we have a superposition of such databases.

According to [12], we bound the difference in working with QROM rather than CRO by the following corollary.

**Corollary 1 ( [12, Corollary 2.8]).** *Let $R \subseteq \mathcal{X}^\ell \times \mathcal{Y}^\ell \times \mathcal{Z}$ be a relation, where $|\mathcal{Y}| = N$. Let $\mathcal{A}$ be an oracle quantum algorithm that outputs $\mathbf{x} = (x_1, \ldots, x_\ell) \in \mathcal{X}^\ell$ and $z \in \mathcal{Z}$. Let $\tilde{\mathcal{A}}$ be the oracle quantum algorithm that runs $\mathcal{A}$, makes $\ell$ classical queries on the outputs $x_i$ to obtain $\mathbf{y} = (y_1 = F(x_1), \ldots, y_l = F(x_l)) = F(\mathbf{x})$, and then outputs $(\mathbf{x}, \mathbf{y}, z)$. Let*

$$p_\circ(\mathcal{A}) := \Pr[(\mathbf{x}, F(\mathbf{x}), z) \in R]$$

*be the considered probability when $\mathcal{A}$ has interacted with the RO. Furthermore, let $p(\tilde{\mathcal{A}})$ be the probability that $\mathbf{y} = F(\mathbf{x})$ and $(\mathbf{x}, \mathbf{y}, z) \in R$ when $\tilde{\mathcal{A}}$ has interacted with the standard random oracle, initialized with a uniformly random function $F$, and $p'(\tilde{\mathcal{A}})$ be the probability that $\mathbf{y} = D(\mathbf{x})$ and $(\mathbf{x}, \mathbf{y}, z) \in R$ when $\tilde{\mathcal{A}}$ has interacted with the compressed oracle instead and $D$ is obtained by measuring its internal state (in the computational basis). Then*

$$p_\circ(\mathcal{A}) = p(\tilde{\mathcal{A}}) \leq p'(\tilde{\mathcal{A}}) + \frac{2\ell}{N}.$$

In our work, we actually need extra features. We need to be able to distinguish classical queries from quantum. This is implemented as a hybrid random oracle [19], which we present in Sect. 3.

## 3 Hybrid Compressed Oracle

In this section, we briefly recall the construction of the Hybrid Compressed Random Oracle (HCRO) and its properties from [19]. We then discuss our extension of the existing techniques in Sect. 3.1.

As presented in [19], a hybrid compressed random oracle is a framework that allows us to analyze the success probability of hybrid algorithms that perform a mix of quantum and classical queries. The HCRO framework is built upon the CROM. While in [19], this framework was used to develop general lower-bound techniques that characterize the tradeoffs between the number of quantum queries and classical queries, we use it to address specific properties of hash functions. We focus on the properties, where the adversary get the challenges through the oracle interaction.

The hybrid oracle is built by replacing both classical and quantum query operators with new recording query operators that maintain a coherent log of all classical-quantum interactions during the algorithm's execution. Importantly, this framework naturally generalizes existing approaches: when restricted to purely classical queries, it simplifies to the classical lazy sampling method, while for purely quantum queries, it reduces to the compressed oracle technique.

The main addition of the Hybrid Compressed Oracle framework is a history register. HCRO contains the quantum database register $\mathsf{D}$ that is dedicated to store the results of all the queries. Additionally, the history register $\mathsf{H}$ is added. $\mathsf{H}$ is dedicated to recording all the classical queries $(x, D(x))$. The contents of the recorded query stay unchanged throughout the algorithm's entire run. To incorporate it with the CROM, new compression and uncompression operations are defined. The new ones are conditioned on the content of the history register. If an input $x$ is recorded in history, then it is never compressed or uncompressed for the database again.

Let us recall the notation, that will be used in this paper: $D$ represents the query database for the function $F$, and is stored in the register $\mathsf{D}$. $H$ represents the input-output pares obtained through classical queries and is stored in the register $\mathsf{H}$.

**Hybrid CRO overview.** Below, we formally present the Hybrid CRO framework [19].

**Memory.** The memory of an algorithm accessing an oracle $D : \mathcal{M}' \to \mathcal{N}$ is made of three quantum registers defined as follows:

- Index register $\mathsf{X}$ holding $x \in \mathcal{M}'$. We will sometimes partition register $\mathsf{X}$ into two: register $\mathsf{K}$ and register $\mathsf{M}$ representing the division of the space $\mathcal{M}'$ into two subspaces. $\mathsf{K}$ holds $k \in \mathcal{K}$ and $\mathsf{M}$ holds $\mathsf{m} \in \mathcal{M}$.
- Phase register $\mathsf{Y}$ holding $y \in \mathcal{N}$.
- Workspace register $\mathsf{Z}$ holding $z \in \{0,1\}^*$ (the register size may increase during the computation as we allow appending new qubits to it).
- Denote the size of message space, key space, and output space as: $|\mathcal{M}'| = M'$, $|\mathcal{M}| = M$, $|\mathcal{K}| = K$, $|\mathcal{N}| = N$,

We use $\mathsf{A} = \mathsf{XYZ}$ to denote the registers on which the algorithm operates. The initial state of the memory is the all-zero basis state $|0,0,0\rangle_{\mathsf{A}}$. We consider phase oracle, which returns the value $D(x)$ in the phase, but it is equivalent to the standard oracle that maps $|x,y,z\rangle_{\mathsf{A}}$ to $|x, y \oplus D(x), z\rangle_{\mathsf{A}}$ up to a unitary transformation. For now lets assume that we fix a random database $D$.

**Quantum Phase Oracle.** The quantum oracle $\mathcal{O}_0^D$ is defined as the unitary operator acting on the memory of the algorithm as follows.

$$\mathcal{O}_0^D : |x,y,z\rangle_{\mathsf{A}} \mapsto \omega_N^{y \cdot D(x)} |x,y,z\rangle_{\mathsf{A}} \quad \text{where} \quad \omega_N = e^{\frac{2i\pi}{N}}.$$

**Classical Oracle.** A classical oracle query can be viewed as a query to the standard oracle that maps $|x,y,z\rangle_{\mathsf{A}}$ to $\omega_N^{yD(x)} |x,y,z\rangle_{\mathsf{A}}$ followed by a measurement on the index register $\mathsf{X}$ and phase register $\mathsf{Y}$.

To represent the measurement, the *history* register $\mathsf{H}$ is added. In our work we consider that the number of classical queries is limited (for example at most $t$), so the history register can be represented as $\mathsf{H} = \mathsf{H}_1 \cdots \mathsf{H}_t$ where the $c$-th subregister $\mathsf{H}_c$ is used to purify the $c$-th classical query and stores a value in $(\mathcal{M}' \times \mathcal{N}) \cup \{\star\}$, where $\star$ is a new state that represents that the query has not happened yet. This purification resemble the delegation of measurement technique in quantum algorithms through the controlled NOT operator. The initial state of that register is $|\star, \ldots, \star\rangle_{\mathsf{H}}$. The classical oracle $\mathcal{O}_1^D$ is defined as the unitary operator acting as follows

$$\begin{aligned}\mathcal{O}_1^D \; : \quad & |x,y,z\rangle_{\mathsf{A}} |(x_1,y_1), \ldots, (x_c,y_c), \star, \ldots, \star\rangle_{\mathsf{H}} \\ \mapsto \omega_N^{yD(x)} & |x,y,z\rangle_{\mathsf{A}} |(x_1,y_1), \ldots, (x_c,y_c), (x, D(x)), \star, \ldots, \star\rangle_{\mathsf{H}} .\end{aligned}$$

We will denote the list of history records $((x_1,y_1), \ldots, (x_c,y_c), \star, \ldots, \star)$ by $H$ and we say $x \in H$ if and only if there exists $1 \le i \le c$ such that $x_i = x$.

**Definition 1** **($H_{x \leftarrow y}$ [19]).** *Given a history $H = ((x_1,y_1), \ldots, (x_c,y_c), \star, \ldots, \star)$ with at least one star entry, we define the appendment of a new pair $(x,y)$ to $H$ as*

$$H_{x \leftarrow y} = ((x_1,y_1), \ldots, (x_c,y_c), (x,y), \star, \ldots, \star)$$

*where the leftmost star has been replaced with $(x,y)$.*

Sometimes, we will identify the above list with a function $H : \mathcal{M}' \to \mathcal{N} \cup \{\star\}$ if there are no ambiguous pairs, i.e., no pairs of the form $(x,y)$ and $(x,y')$ where $y \neq y'$. We also let $\mathscr{H}$ denote the set of all possible histories $H$.

**Hybrid Oracle.**The above definitions are extended by allowing for probabilistic choices between the two oracles. This is represented by a channel that applies the quantum oracle $\mathcal{O}_0^D$ with probability $1-b$, for some $b \in [0,1]$, and applies the classical oracle $\mathcal{O}_1^D$ otherwise. Additionally, we assume that the algorithm is provided with a query type bit (or "flag") indicating which oracle has been applied. We represent this operation by an isometry$\mathcal{O}_b^D$ acting as

$$\begin{aligned}&\mathcal{O}_b^D : |x,y,z\rangle_{\mathsf{A}} |H\rangle_{\mathsf{H}} \mapsto \\ &\qquad \omega_N^{yD(x)} |x,y\rangle_{\mathsf{XY}} \left(\sqrt{1-b} \cdot |z0\rangle_{\mathsf{Z}} |H\rangle_{\mathsf{H}} + \sqrt{b} \cdot |z1\rangle_{\mathsf{Z}} |H_{x \leftarrow D(x)}\rangle_{\mathsf{H}}\right)\end{aligned}$$

where the bit appended to the workspace $z$ indicates the nature of the oracle. We recover the quantum and classical oracles when $b = 0$ and $b = 1$, respectively (ignoring the query type bit). We will not use $b \notin \{0,1\}$ in the analysis, but sometimes it is more convenient to use this representation.

**Hybrid Algorithm.** An algorithm with $t$ queries is defined as a sequence $U_0, \ldots, U_t$ of unitary transformations acting on the memory register $\mathsf{A}$ and a list of real numbers $b(1), \ldots, b(t) \in \{0,1\}$ that specifies which type of query is used. The state $|\psi_t^D\rangle$ of the algorithm after $t$ queries is

$$|\psi_t^D\rangle = U_t\, \mathcal{O}^D_{b(t)}\, U_{t-1} \cdots U_1\, \mathcal{O}^D_{b(1)}\, U_0\, |0\rangle_{\mathsf{A}} |\star, \ldots, \star\rangle_{\mathsf{H}}.$$

The function $D$ is chosen uniformly at random from the set of all functions: $\{D : \mathcal{M}' \to \mathcal{N}\}$. This is modeled by adding another purification register (the *database*) $\mathsf{D} = \mathsf{D}_0 \ldots \mathsf{D}_{M-1}$ where each subregister $\mathsf{D}_x$ for $x \in \mathcal{M}'$ holds a value $D(x) \in \mathcal{N}$ and we define the following joint state,

$$|\psi_t\rangle = \frac{1}{N^{M'/2}} \sum_{D \in \mathcal{N}^{\mathcal{M}'}} |\psi_t^D\rangle_{\mathsf{AH}} \otimes |D\rangle_{\mathsf{D}} = U_t\, \mathcal{O}_{b(t)}\, U_{t-1} \cdots U_1\, \mathcal{O}_{b(1)}\, U_0\, |\psi_0\rangle,$$

where $\mathcal{O}_b := \sum_D \mathcal{O}_b^D \otimes |D\rangle\langle D|_{\mathsf{D}}$ and $|\psi_0\rangle := |0\rangle_{\mathsf{A}} \otimes |\star, \cdots, \star\rangle_{\mathsf{H}} \otimes \frac{1}{N^{M'/2}} \sum_D |D\rangle_{\mathsf{D}}$.

**Output.** The output of a hybrid algorithm is obtained by performing a computational basis measurement on the final state $|\psi_t\rangle$ where we measure a designated part of the workspace register $\mathsf{Z}$.

As we mentioned, we only consider the algorithms that make only two types of queries: quantum and classical. One can further distinguish whether the algorithm is static or adaptive. We say that the algorithm is static if the order of quantum and classical queries is fixed. An adaptive algorithm can adaptively choose the query type of each individual query as long as the total number of quantum (classical) queries is unchanged. Theorem 1 shows that without loss of generality, we can always consider the algorithm to be static.

**Theorem 1 ( [11,19]).** *In the hybrid random oracle model, for any adaptive hybrid quantum algorithm making at most $q$ quantum queries and $c$ classical, there exists a static hybrid algorithm making at most $2q$ quantum queries and $2c$ classical queries such that their outputs are always identical.*

**Construction.** Now, we present the actual construction from [19]. While we include it to give a self-contained presentation, the reader might want to skip this subsection, proceed with the Sect. 3, and return to this one later.

To begin, it is necessary to define a compressed encoding for the database that is compatible with the history register. This involves expanding the alphabet used for the database register, allowing $\mathsf{D}_x$ to hold values from the set $\{\perp\} \cup \mathcal{N}$, where $D(x)$ represents the value associated with $x$. We state that $\omega_N^{yD(x)} = 1$ when $D(x) = \perp$. The initial state of the database is set as $|\perp, \ldots, \perp\rangle_{\mathsf{D}}$, implying all entries are initially undefined. The history register's alphabet is also expanded to accommodate tuples of the form $(x, \perp)$, where $x$ belongs to $\mathcal{M}'$. Denote $x \in H$ if a tuple $(x, y)$ exists in $H$, with $y \in \{\perp\} \cup \mathcal{N}$. In cases where no ambiguous pairs are present in the list, $H$ can be viewed as a function that maps elements from $\mathcal{M}'$ to the extended set $\{\bot, \star\} \cup \mathcal{N}$.

We define the uncompression operator $S$. Let

$$|\hat{y}\rangle_{\mathsf{D}_x} = \frac{1}{\sqrt{N}} \sum_{p\in\mathcal{N}} \omega_N^{yp} |p\rangle_{\mathsf{D}_x}$$

for $y = 0, \ldots, N-1$, denote the Fourier basis states and let $S_x$ be the unitary operator acting on $\mathsf{D}_x$ such that

$$S_x : \begin{cases} |\bot\rangle_{\mathsf{D}_x} \longmapsto |\hat{0}\rangle_{\mathsf{D}_x} \\ |\hat{0}\rangle_{\mathsf{D}_x} \longmapsto |\bot\rangle_{\mathsf{D}_x} \\ |\hat{y}\rangle_{\mathsf{D}_x} \longmapsto |\hat{y}\rangle_{\mathsf{D}_x} \quad \text{for } y = 1, \ldots, N-1. \end{cases}$$

$S_x$ is unitary and Hermitian. A controlled unitary $S_{x,H}$ acting on $\mathsf{D}_x$ is defined as:

$$S_{x,H} = \begin{cases} \mathbb{I} & \text{if } x \in H \\ S_x & \text{otherwise.} \end{cases}$$

Define the Hermitian unitary operator $S$ acting on $\mathsf{AHD}$ such that:

$$S = \sum_{x\in\mathcal{M}', H\in\mathscr{H}} |x\rangle\langle x|_{\mathsf{X}} \otimes \mathbb{I}_{\mathsf{YZ}} \otimes |H\rangle\langle H|_{\mathsf{H}} \otimes (\mathbb{I}_{\mathsf{D}_0\ldots\mathsf{D}_{x-1}} \otimes S_{x,H} \otimes \mathbb{I}_{\mathsf{D}_{x+1}\ldots\mathsf{D}_{M-1}}).$$

The hybrid compressed oracle $\mathcal{R}_b$ is defined as follows,

$$\mathcal{R}_b = S\mathcal{O}_b S \quad \text{where} \quad \mathcal{O}_b = \sum_{D\in(\{\bot\}\cup\mathcal{N})^M} \mathcal{O}_b^D \otimes |D\rangle\langle D|_{\mathsf{D}}, \text{ for } b \in [0,1].$$

We acquired an oracle that, for any basis state $|x,y,z\rangle_{\mathsf{A}} |H,D\rangle_{\mathsf{HD}}$ satisfies the following:

- If the queried input $x$ is contained in the history register: $x \in H$, it means that $x$ has been queried classically before; then we stop (un)compressing $\mathsf{D}_x$, and it behaves like a regular phase oracle on input $x$.
- If $x \notin H$, then $\mathsf{D}_x$ is simulated as a compressed oracle.

The quantum query through the oracle $\mathcal{R}_0$ only acts on the register $\mathsf{H}$ as control and does not change its records. The joint state $|\phi_t\rangle$ of the algorithm and the oracle after $t$ queries in the hybrid compressed oracle model is defined as

$$|\phi_t\rangle = U_t \,\mathsf{R}_{b(t)}\, U_{t-1} \cdots U_1 \,\mathsf{R}_{b(1)}\, U_0 \,(|0\rangle_{\mathsf{A}} |\star, \ldots, \star\rangle_{\mathsf{H}} |\bot, \ldots, \bot\rangle_{\mathsf{D}}).$$

The initial state is defined as $|\phi_0\rangle = |0\rangle_{\mathsf{A}} \otimes |\star, \cdots, \star\rangle_{\mathsf{H}} \otimes |\bot, \ldots, \bot\rangle_{\mathsf{D}}$.

**Basic results regarding HCRO.** Below, we will present the main properties and results for HCRO obtained in [19]. We start with a definition of the

History-Database Consistent state. Each query can increase the size of the quantum database by no more than one input. And a history database query also increases the number of records maximally by one. The history database must be unambiguous: there should not be two pairs $(x, y)$, $(x, y')$, where $y \neq y'$. We also want the quantum part to coincide with the classical part: $H(x) = D(x)$, where $H(x) \neq \star$. We note that the history database can have multiple records with the same pair $(x, y)$. This happens if the same classical query is performed multiple times.

**Definition 2 (History-Database Consistent State [19]).** *Given an integer $t$, we say that $(H, D)$ is a history-database $t$-consistent pair if it has the following properties:*

1. *(Database SIZE) The database satisfies $D(x) \neq \bot$ for at most $t$ different values of $x$.*
2. *(History SIZE) The history is of the form*

$$H = ((x_1, y_1), \ldots, (x_c, y_c), \star, \ldots, \star),$$

   *where $x_1, \ldots, x_c \in \mathcal{M}'$ and $y_1, \ldots, y_c \in \{\bot\} \cup \mathcal{N}$ for some $c \leq t$.*
3. *(Uniqueness) We can identify the history with a function $H : \mathcal{M}' \to \{\star, \bot\} \cup \mathcal{N}$ where $H(x_j) = y_j$ for all $j \in \{1, 2, \cdots c\}$ (meaning no two pairs in the history can differ on the second coordinate only) and $H(x) = \star$ for $x \notin \{x_1, \ldots, x_c\}$.*
4. *(Equality) The database coincides with the history on non-$\star$ values, meaning that $H(x) \neq \star$ implies $D(x) = H(x)$.*

*We let $\mathbb{H}_t$ denote the vector space spanned by all basis states $|x, y, z\rangle_{\mathsf{A}} |H, D\rangle_{\mathsf{HD}}$ where $(H, D)$ is history-database $t$-consistent. We say that a basis state is history-database consistent if it is in $\mathbb{H}_t$ for some integer $t$.*

**Proposition 1 (Consistency [19]).** *Any state $|\phi_t\rangle$ obtained after $t$ queries in the hybrid compressed oracle model satisfies $|\phi_t\rangle \in \mathbb{H}_t$.*

The following lemmas describe what happens after a quantum or a classical query. Note that a quantum query never changes the history part. For a classical query with an input that is not in the history database, but in the quantum database, there is a small chance of resampling, but most probably the database will remain the same.

**Lemma 1 (Quantum Query $\mathcal{R}_0$ [19]).** *Let $|x, y, z\rangle |H, D\rangle$ be a history-database consistent basis state. Then, $\mathcal{R}_0$ maps this state to $|x, y, z0\rangle |H\rangle |\varphi\rangle$ where the state $|\varphi\rangle$ of the database register is*

- $\omega^{yD(x)} |D\rangle$ (if $H(x) \neq \star$ or $y = 0$)
- $\displaystyle\sum_{p \in \mathcal{N}} \frac{\omega^{yp}}{\sqrt{N}} |D_{x \leftarrow p}\rangle$ (if $H(x) = \star$, $D(x) = \bot$, $y \neq 0$)
- $\displaystyle\omega^{yD(x)} |D\rangle + \frac{\omega^{yD(x)}}{\sqrt{N}} |D_{x \leftarrow \bot}\rangle + \sum_{p \in \mathcal{N}} \frac{1 - \omega^{yD(x)} - \omega^{yp}}{N} |D_{x \leftarrow p}\rangle$

  (if $H(x) = \star$, $D(x) \neq \bot$, $y \neq 0$)

**Lemma 2 (Classical Query $\mathcal{R}_1$ [19] ).** *Let $|x, y, z\rangle |H, D\rangle$ be a history-database consistent basis state. Then, $\mathcal{R}_1$ maps this state to $|x, y, z1\rangle |\varphi\rangle$, where $z1$ represents the attachment of the query type bit, and the state $|\varphi\rangle$ of the history-database registers is*

- $\omega^{yD(x)} |H_{x \leftarrow D(x)}, D\rangle$ (if $H(x) \neq \star$)
- $\sum_{p \in \mathcal{N}} \frac{\omega^{yp}}{\sqrt{N}} |H_{x \leftarrow p}, D_{x \leftarrow p}\rangle$ (if $H(x) = \star$, $D(x) = \perp$)
- $\omega^{yD(x)} |H_{x \leftarrow D(x)}, D\rangle + \frac{1}{\sqrt{N}} |H_{x \leftarrow \perp}, D_{x \leftarrow \perp}\rangle - \sum_{p \in \mathcal{N}} \frac{\omega^{yp}}{N} |H_{x \leftarrow p}, D_{x \leftarrow p}\rangle$ (if $H(x) = \star$, $D(x) \neq \perp$)

To clarify the outcomes of classical queries:

- If the input exists in $H$, then it also exists in $D$. A new record is still added to $H$ using the corresponding output value from $D$, that must be consistent with $H$;
- If the input is not found in either the quantum database $D$ or the history $H$, a new output value is sampled and stored in both $D$ and $H$;
- If the input is only present in the quantum database $D$, its associated output value will likely be retrieved and added to the history $H$.

**Progress measure.** In the following, we present the results from [19] that help us measure the amount of progress an algorithm can make towards solving a given task. In Sect. 3.1, we add a new result to the already existing framework. To define the task, we use predicates. In this paper, all progress measures will be defined in terms of the norm of the projection onto basis states satisfying certain predicates.

**Definition 3 (Basis-State Predicate [19]).** *Let $\mathrm{P} : (x, y, z, H, D) \mapsto \{False, True\}$ be a predicate function over all basis states $|x, y, z\rangle_{\mathsf{A}} |H, D\rangle_{\mathsf{HD}}$. We define the projection*

$$\Pi_{\mathrm{P}} = \sum_{(x,y,z,H,D) \in \mathrm{P}^{-1}(True)} |x, y, z, H, D\rangle \langle x, y, z, H, D|$$

*over all basis states satisfying* $\mathrm{P}$. *We let $\overline{\mathrm{P}}$ denote the negation of* $\mathrm{P}$ *and, given two predicates $\mathrm{P}_1$ and $\mathrm{P}_2$, we let $\mathrm{P}_1 \cdot \mathrm{P}_2$ denote their conjunction and $\mathrm{P}_1 + \mathrm{P}_2$ denote their disjunction.*

For the basis-state predicates the following fact will be used in our proofs.

*Remark 1 ( [19]).* Let $\mathrm{P}_1$ and $\mathrm{P}_2$ be two basis-state predicates. Then, the projections $\Pi_{\mathrm{P}_1}$ and $\Pi_{\mathrm{P}_2}$ are commuting operators. We have $\Pi_{\overline{\mathrm{P}_1}} = \mathbb{I} - \Pi_{\mathrm{P}_1}, \Pi_{\mathrm{P}_1 \cdot \mathrm{P}_2} = \Pi_{\mathrm{P}_1} \Pi_{\mathrm{P}_2}$ and $\Pi_{\mathrm{P}_1 + \mathrm{P}_2} = \Pi_{\mathrm{P}_1} + \Pi_{\mathrm{P}_2} - \Pi_{\mathrm{P}_1} \Pi_{\mathrm{P}_2}$. Moreover, $P_1 \Rightarrow P_2$ if and only if $\Pi_{\mathrm{P}_1} \preceq \Pi_{\mathrm{P}_2}$, where $\preceq$ is the Loewner order.

We define the following general notions of progress measure and overlap. Loosely speaking, the progress measure gives a bound on the improvement gained after a query, and the progress overlap represents how the query interacts with the part of the state that did not satisfy some property. We will utilize these notions to derive a bound on the increase in success probability of an adversary after performing query.

**Definition 4 (Progress Measure and Progress Overlap [19]).** *Given a state $|\phi\rangle$, a real $b \in [0,1]$ and a projector $\Pi$ over* AHD, *we define progress measure ($\Delta_b$) and progress overlap ($\Gamma_b$) as*

$$\Delta_b(\Pi, |\phi\rangle) = \|\Pi \mathcal{R}_b |\phi\rangle \|^2 - \|\Pi |\phi\rangle \|^2$$

*and*

$$\Gamma_b(\Pi, |\phi\rangle) = \frac{\|\Pi \mathcal{R}_b (\mathbb{I} - \Pi) |\phi\rangle \|^2}{\|(\mathbb{I} - \Pi) |\phi\rangle \|^2},$$

*with the convention that $\Gamma_b(\Pi, |\phi\rangle) = 0$ if $\|(\mathbb{I} - \Pi) |\phi\rangle \| = 0$.*

In this work, we formally define predicates that evaluate whether a given database state satisfies certain properties. While these predicates could in principle operate on arbitrary database states (including those with inconsistent inputs), we restrict our attention to a special class called History-Database predicates, which satisfy three key requirements: We want the predicate to be satisfied only on the pairs $(H, D)$ that can be obtained through oracle interaction. According to Proposition 1, every such pair is history-database consistent. Next, we want that the order of the history database inputs does not affect the predicate mapping. Lastly, we want that adding new values to the quantum database (making queries on inputs that were not in the quantum database) should not turn a satisfied predicate into unsatisfied.

**Definition 5 (History-Database Predicate [19]).** *Consider a predicate $\mathrm{P} : (H, D) \mapsto \{False,\ True\}$ to be a function over all history-database pairs. We say that it is a history-database predicate if for every true-pair $(H, D) \in \mathrm{P}^{-1}(True)$ it satisfies the following conditions:*

- *(Consistent) The pair $(H, D)$ is history-database consistent (see Definition 2).*
- *(History Invariant) For every list $H'$ such that $(H', D)$ is history-database consistent and $H(x') = H'(x')$ for all $x' \in \mathcal{M}'$, we have $(H', D) \in \mathrm{P}^{-1}(True)$.*
- *(Database Monotone) For every database $D'$ that is obtained by replacing a $\perp$ in $D$ with another value (i.e. $D = D'_{x' \leftarrow \perp}$ for some $x' \in \mathcal{M}'$ ), we have $(H, D') \in \mathrm{P}^{-1}(True)$.*

*By extension, we say that $\mathrm{P} : (x, y, z, H, D) \mapsto \{False,\ True\}$ is a history-database predicate if it does not depend on $(x, y, z)$ and its restriction to $(H, D)$ satisfies the above properties.*

The next lemmas are used to bound the progress overlap that an algorithm can gain after a query. To bound this, we want to use the probability that the database will turn into one that satisfies the predicate. The analysis of the quantum query case is similar to the analysis in [9,30], the classical query analysis was introduced in [19]. The restriction for the classical query bound is that the database can not turn into a satisfying one by adding an existing input from the quantum database into the history register. This restriction is reasonable when there is no logical distinction between the two databases. For example, in [19], a collision finding problem was analyzed. The hybrid compressed random oracle model allowed a fine-grained analysis of an algorithm that uses both quantum and classical queries. In our work, the classical queries serve the purpose of challenge definition. Hence, having an input in the quantum database is not the same as having an input in the history register. In Sect. 3.1, we present our extension of the existent framework by giving a bound on progress overlap that is more suitable for such scenarios.

**Lemma 3 (Progress Overlap, Quantum Query [19]).** *Let* $\mathrm{P}$ *be a history-database predicate,* $t$ *be an integer, and* $\gamma \in [0,1]$ *be a real parameter. Suppose that, for every false-state* $(H, D) \in \mathrm{P}^{-1}(\mathrm{False}) \cap \mathbb{H}_t$ *where* $D(x) = \perp$*, the probability to make the predicate true by replacing* $D(x)$ *with a random value* $p$ *is at most*

$$\Pr_{p \leftarrow \mathcal{N}} \left[(H, D_{x \leftarrow p}) \in \mathrm{P}^{-1}(\mathit{True})\right] \leq \gamma.$$

*Then, the quantum progress overlap is at most* $\Gamma_0(\Pi_P, |\phi\rangle) \leq 10\gamma$ *for all* $|\phi\rangle \in \mathbb{H}_t$*.*

**Lemma 4 (Progress Overlap, Classical Query [19]).** *Let* $\mathrm{P}$ *be a history-database predicate,* $t$ *be an integer, and* $\gamma \in [0,1]$ *be a real parameter. Suppose that, for every false-state* $(H, D) \in \mathrm{P}^{-1}(\mathrm{False}) \cap \mathbb{H}_t$ *where* $D(x) = \perp$*, the probability to make the predicate true by replacing* $H(x)$ *and* $D(x)$ *with the same random value* $p$ *is at most*

$$\Pr_{p \leftarrow \mathcal{N}} \left[(H_{x \leftarrow p}, D_{x \leftarrow p}) \in \mathrm{P}^{-1}(\mathrm{True})\right] \leq \gamma.$$

*Assume further that, for every false-state* $(H, D) \in \mathrm{P}^{-1}(\mathit{False})$*, the predicate does not become true when* $(x, D(x))$ *is appended to the history, i.e.*

$$(H, D) \in \mathrm{P}^{-1}(\mathrm{False}) \quad \Rightarrow \quad (H_{x \leftarrow D(x)}, D) \in \mathrm{P}^{-1}(\mathrm{False})$$

*Then, the classical progress overlap is at most* $\Gamma_1(\Pi_\mathrm{P}, |\phi\rangle) \leq 2\gamma$ *for all* $|\phi\rangle \in \mathbb{H}_t$*.*

Note that $\gamma$ will often depend on the number of queries that have been performed (equivalently, the maximum number $t$ of values contained in the database and in the history). If Lemma 3 and Lemma 4 hold with parameters $\gamma_0$ and $\gamma_1$ respectively, then the combined progress can be written as $\Gamma_b(\Pi_P, |\phi\rangle) \leq 10(1-b)\gamma_0 + 2b\gamma_1$.

### 3.1 Progress overlap with partially random inputs

As we discussed before, we want to analyze properties that use classical queries as challenge setting. An example can be target collision resistance: the adversary makes a classical query with a message $m$ and gets $\{k, F(k,m)\}$ in response. Here, the $k$ is chosen uniformly at random for each query. Then, the adversary is asked to find a collision for one of the messages used in the classical queries. This example shows a typical structure: an adversary is given quantum access to the function, but to get information about the challenges, the adversary must make classical queries to an oracle. Note that these classical queries have a part of the input that is not controlled by the adversary and is usually uniformly random. To address these types of properties, we extend the framework. We bound the probability of success of pulling a value from the quantum database into the history register, which allows us to analyze a wider range of queries. The proof of Lemma 5 is inspired by the proof of Lemma 4 in [19]. The core difference is precisely when a query input exists in the quantum database but not in the history register.

**Lemma 5 (Progress Overlap, Classical Query with randomness).** *Let* $\mathrm{P}$ *be a history-database predicate,* $t$ *be an integer, and* $\gamma \in [0,1]$ *be a real parameter. Suppose that, for every false-state* $(H, D) \in \mathrm{P}^{-1}(\mathrm{False}) \cap \mathbb{H}_t$ *where* $D(x) = \perp$*, the probability to make the predicate true by replacing* $H(x)$ *and* $D(x)$ *with the same random value* $p$ *is at most*

$$\Pr_{p \leftarrow \mathcal{N}}\left[(H_{x\leftarrow p}, D_{x\leftarrow p} \in \mathrm{P}^{-1}(\mathrm{True})\right] \leq \gamma.$$

*Assume* $\mathcal{M}' = \mathcal{K} \times \mathcal{M}$ *and we can write* $x = (k,m) \in \mathcal{K} \times \mathcal{M}$. *Suppose that, for every false-state* $(H, D) \in \mathrm{P}^{-1}(\mathrm{False}) \cap \mathbb{H}_t$ *the probability to make the predicate true by adding a value* $((k,m), D(k,m))$ *to the history database, where* $k$ *is chosen uniformly at random, is at most*

$$\Pr_{k \leftarrow \mathcal{K}}\left[(H_{(k,m)\leftarrow D(k,m)}, D) \in \mathrm{P}^{-1}(\mathrm{True})\right] \leq \varepsilon.$$

*Then, the classical progress overlap with a partially random input is at most* $\Gamma_1(\Pi_{\mathrm{P}}, |\phi\rangle) \leq 3\gamma + 2\varepsilon$ *for all* $|\phi\rangle \in \mathbb{H}_t$.

*Proof.* Let $\Pi_{\overline{\mathrm{P}}} |\phi\rangle = \sum_{x,y,z,H,D} \alpha_{x,y,z,H,D} |x,y,z\rangle |H,D\rangle \in \mathbb{H}_t \cap \mathrm{supp}(\Pi_{\overline{\mathrm{P}}})$ be any state supported over consistent basis-states evaluating the predicate $\mathrm{P}$ to false. We show that, after making a classical query, the probability of satisfying $\mathrm{P}$ is at most $\|\Pi_{\mathrm{P}} \mathcal{R}_1 \Pi_{\overline{\mathrm{P}}} |\phi\rangle\|^2 \leq (3\gamma + 2\varepsilon) \cdot \|\Pi_{\overline{\mathrm{P}}} |\phi\rangle\|^2$. We define three projections $\Pi_1, \Pi_2, \Pi_3$ such that $\Pi_1 + \Pi_2 + \Pi_3 = \Pi_{\overline{\mathrm{P}}}$.

- $\Pi_1$ : all basis states $|x,y,z,H,D\rangle \in \mathbb{H}_t \cap \mathrm{supp}(\Pi_{\overline{\mathrm{P}}})$ such that $H(x) = \star$ and $D(x) = \perp$.
- $\Pi_2$ : all basis states $|x,y,z,H,D\rangle \in \mathbb{H}_t \cap \mathrm{supp}(\Pi_{\overline{\mathrm{P}}})$ such that $H(x) = \star$ and $D(x) \neq \perp$.
- $\Pi_3$ : all basis states $|x,y,z,H,D\rangle \in \mathbb{H}_t \cap \mathrm{supp}(\Pi_{\overline{\mathrm{P}}})$ such that $H(x) \neq \star$.

Below, we prove the (in)equalities

- $\|\Pi_{\mathrm{P}} \mathcal{R}_1 \Pi_1 |\phi\rangle\|^2 \leq \gamma \|\Pi_1 |\phi\rangle\|^2$
- $\|\Pi_{\mathrm{P}} \mathcal{R}_1 \Pi_2 |\phi\rangle\|^2 \leq 2(\gamma + \varepsilon) \|\Pi_2 |\phi\rangle\|^2$

– $\|\Pi_{\mathrm{P}}\mathcal{R}_1\Pi_3 |\phi\rangle \| = 0$

Hence, by the triangle inequality and Cauchy-Schwarz inequality, we conclude that

$$\begin{aligned}\|\Pi_{\mathrm{P}}\mathcal{R}_1\Pi_{\overline{\mathrm{P}}} |\phi\rangle \|^2 &\leq (\|\Pi_{\mathrm{P}}\mathcal{R}_1\Pi_1 |\phi\rangle \| + \|\Pi_{\mathrm{P}}\mathcal{R}_1\Pi_2 |\phi\rangle \| + \|\Pi_{\mathrm{P}}\mathcal{R}_1\Pi_3 |\phi\rangle \|)^2 \\ &\leq (3\gamma + 2\varepsilon)\|\Pi_{\overline{\mathrm{P}}} |\phi\rangle \|^2.\end{aligned}$$

The analysis of the cases for $\Pi_1$ and $\Pi_3$ matches the analysis in the proof of Lemma 4. The case for $\Pi_2$ needs some extra work, since we are now allowed to pull the values from the quantum database.

**Analysis of $\Pi_1$.** The analysis of this case matches the case for Lemma 4. We present it below.

$$\begin{aligned}&\|\Pi_{\mathrm{P}}\mathcal{R}_1\Pi_1 |\phi\rangle \|^2 \\ &= \|\Pi_{\mathrm{P}}\mathcal{R}_1 \sum_{\substack{x,y,z,H,D:\\ H(x)=\star, D(x)=\perp}} \alpha_{x,y,z,H,D} |x,y,z\rangle |H,D\rangle \|^2 \\ &= \|\Pi_{\mathrm{P}} \sum_{\substack{x,y,z,H,D:\\ H(x)=\star, D(x)=\perp}} \alpha_{x,y,z,H,D} |x,y,z1\rangle \big(\sum_{p\in\mathcal{N}} \frac{\omega^{yp}}{\sqrt{N}} |H_{x\leftarrow p}, D_{x\leftarrow p}\rangle\big)\|^2 \\ &= \sum_{\substack{x,y,z,H,D:\\ H(x)=\star, D(x)=\perp}} \|\alpha_{x,y,z,H,D}\|^2 \cdot \Pr_{p\leftarrow\mathcal{N}}\left[(H_{x\leftarrow p}, D_{x\leftarrow p}) \in \mathrm{P}^{-1}(\mathrm{True})\right] \\ &\leq \gamma\|\Pi_1 |\phi\rangle \|^2\end{aligned}$$

The first equality obtained from the definition of $\Pi_1$. The second equality is from Lemma 2. The third equality is based on the orthogonality of the basis states. Finally, the last inequality is based on the Lemma 5.

**Analysis of $\Pi_2$.** This is the main difference compared to Lemma 4. The projection $\Pi_2$ corresponds to all basis states $|x,y,z,H,D\rangle \in \mathbb{H}_t \cap \mathrm{supp}(\Pi_{\overline{\mathrm{P}}})$ such that $H(x) = \star$ and $D(x) \neq\perp$. According to Lemma 2, we have the following result of the classical query:

$$\begin{aligned}\mathcal{R}_1 |x,y,z\rangle |H,D\rangle = |x,y,z1\rangle \big(\omega^{yD(x)} &|H_{x\leftarrow D(x)}, D\rangle + \\ &\frac{1}{\sqrt{N}} |H_{x\leftarrow\perp}, D_{x\leftarrow\perp}\rangle - \sum_{p\in\mathcal{N}} \frac{\omega^{yp}}{N} |H_{x\leftarrow p}, D_{x\leftarrow p}\rangle\big)\end{aligned}$$

So, we have three terms that correspond to three possible scenarios:

1. $D(x)$ remains unchanged in the database: $|H_{x\leftarrow D(x)}, D\rangle$.
2. $D(x)$ gets removed: $|H_{x\leftarrow\perp}, D_{x\leftarrow\perp}\rangle$.
3. $D(x)$ is resampled to a new value $p$: $|H_{x\leftarrow p}, D_{x\leftarrow p}\rangle$.

The third option can be analyzed the same way as in Lemma 4. Loosely speaking, this case is the same as adding a new input. The second option can not make the predicate turn from False to True according to the Monotone property from Definition 5. The first option is now possible. This corresponds to the case when we pull a value from a quantum database into the history register. We aim to bound it with $\varepsilon$.

Now, remember, since we are doing a classical query, we know that there is a part of $x = (k, m)$ that is distributed uniformly at random. Hence, we can write the initial state as

$$|\phi\rangle = \sum_{k,m,y,z,H,D} \frac{1}{\sqrt{K}} \alpha_{m,y,z,H,D} |k, m, y, z\rangle |H, D\rangle .$$

We proceed by applying $\Pi_2$. We need to include only the inputs that exist in the quantum database. Hence, we need $(k, \cdot) \in D$ and $D(k, m) \neq \perp$. Notice that if $D(k, m) \neq \perp$, then $k$ is guaranteed to be in the database. So we can write

$$\Pi_2 |\phi\rangle = \sum_{\substack{k,m,y,z,H,D:\\ H(k,m)=\star, D(k,m)\neq\perp}} \frac{1}{\sqrt{K}} \alpha_{m,y,z,H,D} |k, m, y, z\rangle |H, D\rangle .$$

Now, let us look at how the query behaves for $\Pi_2 |\phi\rangle$.

$$\begin{aligned}
&\|\Pi_{\mathrm{P}} \mathcal{R}_1 \Pi_2 |\phi\rangle \|^2 \\
&= \|\Pi_{\mathrm{P}} \mathcal{R}_1 \sum_{\substack{k,m,y,z,H,D:\\ H(k,m)=\star, D(k,m)\neq\perp}} \frac{1}{\sqrt{K}} \alpha_{m,y,z,H,D} |k, m, y, z\rangle |H, D\rangle \|^2 \\
&= \|\Pi_{\mathrm{P}} \sum_{\substack{k,m,y,z,H,D:\\ H(k,m)=\star, D(k,m)\neq\perp}} \frac{1}{\sqrt{K}} \alpha_{m,y,z,H,D} |k, m, y, z1\rangle \\
&\quad \cdot \Big(\omega^{yD(k,m)} |H_{(k,m)\leftarrow D(k,m)}, D\rangle + \frac{1}{\sqrt{N}} |H_{(k,m)\leftarrow\perp}, D_{(k,m)\leftarrow\perp}\rangle \\
&\quad - \sum_{p\in\mathcal{N}} \frac{\omega^{yp}}{N} |H_{(k,m)\leftarrow p}, D_{(k,m)\leftarrow p}\rangle\Big) \|^2 \\
&= \|\Pi_{\mathrm{P}} \sum_{\substack{k,m,y,z,H,D:\\ H(k,m)=\star, D(k,m)\neq\perp}} \frac{1}{\sqrt{K}} \alpha_{m,y,z,H,D} |k, m, y, z1\rangle \\
&\quad \cdot \Big(\omega^{yD(k,m)} |H_{(k,m)\leftarrow D(k,m)}, D\rangle - \sum_{p\in\mathcal{N}} \frac{\omega^{yp}}{N} |H_{(k,m)\leftarrow p}, D_{(k,m)\leftarrow p}\rangle\Big) \|^2 \\
&\leq 2\|\Pi_{\mathrm{P}} \sum_{\substack{k,m,y,z,H,D:\\ H(k,m)=\star, D(k,m)\neq\perp}} \\
&\quad \frac{1}{\sqrt{K}} \alpha_{m,y,z,H,D} \Big( (\omega^{yD(k,m)} - \frac{\omega^{yD(k,m)}}{N}) |x, y, z1\rangle |H_{(k,m)\leftarrow D(k,m)}, D\rangle \Big) \|^2 \\
&\quad + 2\|\Pi_{\mathrm{P}} \sum_{\substack{k,m,y,z,H,D:\\ H(k,m)=\star, D(k,m)\neq\perp}}
\end{aligned}$$

$$\frac{1}{\sqrt{K}}\alpha_{m,y,z,H,D}\left(\sum_{p\in\mathcal{N}\setminus D(k,m)}\frac{\omega^{yp}}{N}|x,y,z1\rangle|H_{(k,m)\leftarrow p},D_{(k,m)\leftarrow p}\rangle\right)\|^2$$

The first equality is by definition of $\Pi_2$. The second equation is by Lemma 2. The third equation is due to the fact that $|H_{x\leftarrow\bot},D_{x\leftarrow\bot}\rangle$ can not make the predicate turn from False to True. The last inequality is based on the triangle inequality $(a+b)^2\leq 2a^2+2b^2$.

Let us analyze the last two terms separately. We start with the second one since it has already been analyzed for Lemma 4. Following the reasoning from [19, Analysis of $\Pi_2$ in Lemma 4.13] we get

$$\begin{aligned}&\|\Pi_{\mathrm{P}}\sum_{\substack{k,m,y,z,H,D:\\H(k,m)=\star,D(k,m)\neq\bot}}\\&\quad\frac{1}{\sqrt{K}}\alpha_{m,y,z,H,D}\left(\sum_{p\in\mathcal{N}\setminus D(k,m)}\frac{\omega^{yp}}{N}|x,y,z1\rangle|H_{(k,m)\leftarrow p},D_{(k,m)\leftarrow p}\rangle\right)\|^2\\&\leq\gamma\|\Pi_2|\phi\rangle\|^2\end{aligned}$$

Now, we need to prove that

$$\begin{aligned}&\|\Pi_{\mathrm{P}}\sum_{\substack{k,m,y,z,H,D:\\H(k,m)=\star,D(k,m)\neq\bot}}\\&\quad\frac{1}{\sqrt{K}}\alpha_{m,y,z,H,D}((\omega^{yD(k,m)}-\frac{\omega^{yD(k,m)}}{N})|x,y,z1\rangle|H_{(k,m)\leftarrow D(k,m)},D\rangle)\|^2\\&\leq\varepsilon\|\Pi_2|\phi\rangle\|^2\end{aligned}$$

To do so, let us first remove the subtraction from the coefficient.

$$\begin{aligned}&\|\Pi_{\mathrm{P}}\sum_{\substack{k,m,y,z,H,D:\\H(k,m)=\star,D(k,m)\neq\bot}}\\&\quad\frac{1}{\sqrt{K}}\alpha_{m,y,z,H,D}((\omega^{yD(k,m)}-\frac{\omega^{yD(k,m)}}{N})|x,y,z1\rangle|H_{(k,m)\leftarrow D(k,m)},D\rangle)\|^2\\&\leq\|\Pi_{\mathrm{P}}\sum_{\substack{k,m,y,z,H,D:\\H(k,m)=\star,\\D(k,m)\neq\bot}}\alpha_{m,y,z,H,D}(\frac{1}{\sqrt{K}}\omega^{yD(k,m)})|x,y,z1\rangle|H_{(k,m)\leftarrow D(k,m)},D\rangle\|^2\end{aligned}$$

This holds as we can take a factor $\left(1-\frac{1}{N}\right)$ out of the norm expression. Since we started with the state

$$\sum_{\substack{x,y,z,H,D:\\H(x)=\star,D(x)\neq\bot}}\alpha_{x,y,z,H,D}|x,y,z\rangle|H,D\rangle,$$

where every term represents an orthogonal state, adding a value to the history databases does not change orthogonality. This is because if we have a history database of the same size, then we are adding different values, and the order of the inputs in the history database matters for orthogonality; hence, we get orthogonal vectors. If the history database has different sizes, we have different vectors $z$. Hence, every term in the result represents an orthogonal vector. Note that $\Pi_{\mathrm{P}}$ does not spoil the orthogonality since it is diagonal in the computational basis. Hence, we get:

$$\begin{aligned}&\|\Pi_{\mathrm{P}} \sum_{\substack{k,m,y,z,H,D:\\ H(k,m)=\star,\\ D(k,m)\neq\perp}} \alpha_{m,y,z,H,D}(\frac{1}{\sqrt{K}}\omega^{yD(k,m)}) |x,y,z1\rangle |H_{(k,m)\leftarrow D(k,m)}, D\rangle \|^2\\ &\leq \sum_{\substack{k,m,y,z,H,D:\\ H(k,m)=\star,\\ D(k,m)\neq\perp}} \|\alpha_{m,y,z,H,D}\|^2 \cdot \Pr_{k\leftarrow\mathcal{K}}\left[(H_{(k,m)\leftarrow D(k,m)}, D) \in \mathrm{P}^{-1}(\mathrm{True})\right]\\ &\leq \varepsilon\|\Pi_2 |\phi\rangle \|^2\end{aligned}$$

**Analysis of $\Pi_3$.** The analysis of this case matches the case for Lemma 4. By Lemma 2, and since $H(x) \neq \star$, the operator $\mathcal{R}_1$ maps any state

$$|x,y,z\rangle |H,D\rangle \in \mathrm{supp}(\Pi_3) \overset{\mathcal{R}_1}{\to} \omega^{yD(x)} |x,y,z1\rangle |H_{x\leftarrow D(x)}, D\rangle .$$

Moreover, $H$ and $H_{x\leftarrow D(x)}$ have the same function representation (since the initial state is history-database consistent we append the same pair (x, D(x))). Thus, by the history invariant property (see Definition 5), we have $\mathrm{P}(H_{x\leftarrow D(x)}, D) = False$ and $\|\Pi_{\mathrm{P}}\mathcal{R}_1\Pi_3 |\phi\rangle \| = 0$.

This concludes the proof.

In this section, we established bounds on the potential improvement in an adversary's success probability when making classical queries with uniformly random keys. This result will be instrumental in the following section, where we apply our techniques to the analysis of M-ETCR security, incorporating both existing methods and the new bounds developed here.

## 4 The security of m-eTCR

In this section, we show how to apply the improved framework. We choose the M-ETCR notion (see Definition 6) as a good example to illustrate the utility of our technique.

We start by recalling the definition of the keyed hash function family. In the following let $\mathcal{F}_N = \{F_k : \mathcal{M} \to \mathcal{N}\}_{k\in\mathcal{K}}$ be a keyed family of hash functions. We will also write $F(k,m)$ to denote $F_k(m)$.

We define the Multi-target extended target collision resistance (M-ETCR) property for a keyed hash function family.

**Definition 6 (Multi-target extended Target Collision Resistance (m-eTCR) [20]).** *Let* $F : \mathcal{K} \times \mathcal{M} \to \mathcal{N}$ *be a keyed hash function. Let* $\mathcal{A} = (\mathcal{A}_1, \mathcal{A}_2)$ *be a two-staged algorithm. Consider the following experiment* $\textbf{m-eTCR}_{F,c}(\mathcal{A})$*:*

1. *Prepare an empty list* $Q$*.*
2. *Run the first stage of* $\mathcal{A}$ *called* $\mathcal{A}_1$ *with (classical) access to an oracle* $\mathcal{O}(\cdot)$ *that takes* $\mathsf{m} \in \mathcal{M}$ *and works as follows:*
   - *If* $|Q| \geq c$*, return* $\perp$*.*
   - *Generate a random key* $k \leftarrow_\$ \mathcal{K}$*.*
   - *Insert* $(k, \mathsf{m})$ *into the list* $Q$*.*
   - *Return* $(k, F(k, \mathsf{m}))$*.*
3. *When* $\mathcal{A}$ *signals to continue, then continue to the second stage of* $\mathcal{A}$ *called* $\mathcal{A}_2$*, without the oracle access.*
4. *Obtain an output from* $\mathcal{A}_2$*:* $(k^*, \mathsf{m}^*, j) \leftarrow \mathcal{A}_2(Q)$*, where* $k^* \in \mathcal{K}$*,* $\mathsf{m}^* \in \mathcal{M}$*, and* $j \in [|Q|]$*. Denote the* $j$*th entry in* $Q$ *by* $(k_j, \mathsf{m}_j)$*.*
5. *Output* 1 *if* $F(k_j, \mathsf{m}_j) = F(k^*, \mathsf{m}^*)$ *and* $\mathsf{m}^* \neq \mathsf{m}_j$*.*
   *Otherwise, output* 0*.*

*For any such algorithm* $\mathcal{A}$*, we define the success probability against multi-target target collision resistance of* $F$ *as:*

$$\mathrm{Succ}_{F,c}^{\textit{M-ETCR}}(\mathcal{A}) = \Pr\left[\textbf{m-eTCR}_{F,c}(\mathcal{A}) \Rightarrow 1\right]$$

For M-ETCR, the adversary is allowed to obtain up to $c$ challenges for a given hash function family. The challenges are generated for a random key. The best-known bound for the M-ETCR in the QROM was obtained in [16]:

$$\mathrm{Succ}_{\mathcal{F}_N,c}^{\text{M-ETCR}}(\mathcal{A}) \leq \frac{8c(c+q+2)^2}{N} + \frac{3c}{2}\sqrt{\frac{q+c+1}{K}},$$

where $q$ is the number of (quantum) queries to $F(\cdot,\cdot)$.

The second term in this inequality comes from the reprogramming of the random oracle. The main idea is that previously, it was hard to deal with a mix of classical and quantum queries. One of the possible approaches was to learn the outputs of all the challenge queries before any quantum query happens. This was done by choosing all the responses uniformly at random and then reprogramming them into the hash function as a challenge query happens. Intuitively, the reprogramming was not needed to alter the response but rather to move the challenge queries to the very beginning. We can overcome this difficulty and get a tight bound with the new technique. We get the following theorem:

**Theorem 2.** *The success probability of an algorithm* $\mathcal{A}$*, that makes at most* $q$ *quantum queries to the function family* $\mathcal{F}_N$ *and* $c$ *classical challenge queries and outputs a solution of* M-ETCR *is at most:*

$$\mathrm{Succ}_{\mathcal{F}_N,c}^{\textit{M-ETCR}}(\mathcal{A}) \leq 46(\frac{cq+c^2}{N} + q\sqrt{\frac{c}{N}} + \frac{cq^{3/2}+c^{3/2}}{KN^{1/2}} + \frac{c}{K}\frac{q^3}{N}) + \frac{4}{N}$$

$$= O(\frac{c^2}{N} + q\sqrt{\frac{c}{N}} + \frac{c}{K}\sqrt{\frac{q^3}{N}}).$$

Before we proceed to the proof, let us discuss this result. First, we highlight that the bound is tight on the number of queries up to a constant factor as demonstrated by matching attacks, detailed below.

The first term $\frac{cq+c^2}{N}$ comes from a probability that we get either a collision in the challenge queries or we make a challenge query, and it collides with an input that is already in the quantum database. Next, $q\sqrt{\frac{c}{N}}$ is obtained by setting $c$ classical targets and searching for a solution using quantum queries (similar to Grover search [17]). The last terms come from the following attack strategy: First, find a collision for some message $\mathsf{m}$ and different keys. Then do challenge queries with this message and hope that the sampled key will match one of your prepared collisions. The terms $\sqrt{\frac{q^3}{N}}$ and $\frac{q^3}{N}$ give a bound on the number of queries for finding collisions, and there is a chance of $\frac{c}{K}$ that one of the challenge queries will hit the needed key.

We have the following implications from the new bound compared to the previous one:

1. Previously, $K$, the size of the randomness space, had to match the bound $K \geq c^2 \cdot (q+c)$. So, for example, for $q = c = 2^{64}$ (which matches the requirements of category one in the NIST call [26, Section 4]), $K$ would have to be greater than $2^{192}$. Now we bound $K$ as $K \geq 46(\sqrt{cq}+c+q)$ (assuming $N = q^2 \cdot c$). This will allow us to use $K \geq 2^{72}$ for the same security level. Hence, we can use keys almost 2/3 smaller than with the previous bound.
2. Given the bound of $K$, the number of allowed challenge queries now influence $N$ as $c^2$ instead of $c^3$ compared to the previous bound. This is important because we may allow the number of challenges as big as $2^{64}$ in some applications. For example, in the NIST post-quantum standardization process, the security bound for signature schemes was required to assume that the attacker has access to signatures for up to $2^{64}$ chosen messages [26, Section 4].
3. Our bound includes a term $q\sqrt{\frac{c}{N}}$ which is larger than the corresponding term $\frac{cq^2}{N}$ in the bound from [16]. Nevertheless, we argue that the query complexity for constant success probability remains the same: $\Omega(\sqrt{N/c})$. As this is what is usually used to inform parameter choices, our result constitutes a significant improvement.

Before proving Theorem 2, we need to define different predicates on basis states and different types of collisions.

**Definition 7 (Collision Type).** *Given a history-database consistent pair $(H, D)$, we say that it contains a collision if there exist two values $x_1 \neq x_2$ such that $D(x_1) = D(x_2) \neq \perp$. Additionally, if $x_1, x_2 \notin H$, the collision is said to be quantum, if $x_1, x_2 \in H$, it is said to be classical, and if $x_1 \notin H, x_2 \in H$ (or $x_2 \notin H, x_1 \in H$), it is said to be hybrid.*

Given the three types of collisions, we define the corresponding predicates. We also define a $k$-collision predicate for the quantum database. The $k$Q predicate represents our ability to track how many times a query formed a new collision. Each new query that forms a collision can either collide with an existing collision or create a new one. In the first case, the number of inputs in the database for which there exists a collision increases by one, and in the second case, by two.

**Definition 8.** *The predicates, presented below, evaluate a basis state* $|x, y, z, H, D\rangle$ *to True if and only if it is history-database consistent (see Definition 2) and satisfies the next conditions:*

- Q, H, C: *there is respectively at least one quantum, one hybrid, or one classical collision contained in* $(H, D)$.
- $k$Q - *There are* $k \leq l \leq 2k$ *distinct inputs* $x_1, \ldots, x_l$*, such that there exists a quantum collision for each of them:* $x_i \neq x_j,\ i \neq j\ i, j \in [1, l]; \forall x_i\ \exists x_j :$ $D(x_i) = D(x_j) \neq \perp,\ x_i,\ x_j \notin H,\ i, j \in [1, l]$.

The proof of Theorem 2 relies on the results of Lemma 6 and Lemma 8. These lemmas limit the progress that can be achieved with quantum and classical queries. Using these results, we bound the success probability of the whole algorithm.

*Proof (Proof of Theorem 2).* Before analyzing M-ETCR, we need to reflect that working with the CRO introduces a slight disturbance. According to Corollary 1, working with the CRO introduces an error that is dependent on the number of the output values of the algorithm. The output of the algorithm for M-ETCR consists of 2 values. Hence, we can limit the error with an additive term of $\frac{4}{N}$.

First, let us observe that a solution for M-ETCR results in a database that either contains a classical collision or a hybrid one. Let $|\phi_t\rangle = |x, y, z, H, D\rangle$ denote a state that is obtained after $t$ queries, where $q$ queries are quantum and $c$ classical ($t = q + c$). Hence, we need to bound $\|\Pi_{\mathrm{H+C}} |\phi_t\rangle\|^2$. It will also be convenient to keep track of the following progress measure:

$$\Phi_t = \|\Pi_{\mathrm{C}} |\phi_t\rangle\|^2 + \|\Pi_{\mathrm{H}\overline{\mathrm{C}}} |\phi_t\rangle\|^2$$

Observe that $\|\Pi_{\mathrm{H+C}} |\phi_t\rangle\|^2 = \Phi_t$. We claim the following recurrence holds for the potential $\Phi_t$ if the $t$-th query is made to the oracle $\mathcal{R}_b$, $b \in \{0, 1\}$.

$$\begin{aligned}
\Phi_t =& \Phi_{t-1} \\
&+ (1-b)(\Delta_b(\Pi_{\mathrm{C}}, |\phi_{t-1}\rangle) + \Delta_b(\Pi_{\mathrm{H}\overline{\mathrm{C}}}, |\phi_{t-1}\rangle)) \\
&+ b(\Delta_b(\Pi_{\mathrm{H+C}}, |\phi_{t-1}\rangle)) \\
\leq& \Phi_{t-1} + \Delta_0(\Pi_{\mathrm{C}}, |\phi_{t-1}\rangle) + \Delta_0(\Pi_{\mathrm{H}\overline{\mathrm{C}}}, |\phi_{t-1}\rangle) + \Delta_1(\Pi_{\mathrm{H+C}}, |\phi_{t-1}\rangle)
\end{aligned}$$

From the initial condition $\Phi_0 = 0$ and Lemma 6, Lemma 8 we get:

$$\begin{aligned}\Phi_t \leq &\frac{10cq}{N} + 3q\sqrt{\frac{10c}{N}} + \frac{3(q+c)c}{N} \\ &+ 36\frac{c}{K}\sqrt{\frac{q^3}{N}} + 44\frac{c}{K}\frac{q^3}{N} + 10\frac{c\sqrt{q+c}}{K\sqrt{N}} + 10\frac{c(q+c)}{KN^{3/2}} \\ \leq &\frac{23cq + 13c^2}{N} + 3q\sqrt{\frac{10c}{N}} + 36\frac{c}{K}\sqrt{\frac{q^3}{N}} + 44\frac{c}{K}\frac{q^3}{N} + 10\frac{c\sqrt{q+c}}{K\sqrt{N}} \\ \leq &23\frac{cq+c^2}{N} + 12q\sqrt{\frac{c}{N}} + 46\frac{cq^{3/2}+c^{3/2}}{KN^{1/2}} + 44\frac{cq^3}{KN}\end{aligned}$$

To establish the second inequality, we combine the first, third, and seventh (blue) terms, using the fact that $KN^{3/2} > N$. For the third inequality, we combine the third and fifth (green) terms, using the observation that $cq^{1/2} \leq cq^{3/2}$.

**Lemma 6 (Progress Measure, Quantum Query).** *Given an integer $t = q + c$, where $q$ is the number of quantum queries and $c$ is the number of classical queries, and a state $|\phi\rangle \in \mathbb{H}_t$ with the norm at most 1, the progress made by one quantum query of $\phi$ satisfies:*

$$\Delta_0(\Pi_{\mathrm{C}}, |\phi\rangle) = 0 \qquad\qquad \Delta_0(\Pi_{\mathrm{H}\overline{\mathrm{C}}}, |\phi\rangle) \leq \frac{10c}{N} + 2\sqrt{\frac{10c}{N}}$$

*Proof.* $\Delta_0(\Pi_{\mathrm{C}}, |\phi\rangle) = 0$ comes from a simple observation that quantum query does not affect the History part of the database (see Lemma 1). Hence, we are left to prove $\Delta_0(\Pi_{\mathrm{H}\overline{\mathrm{C}}}, |\phi\rangle) \leq \frac{10c}{N} + 2\sqrt{\frac{10c}{N}}$. To do so first lets expand $\Delta_0(\Pi_{\mathrm{H}\overline{\mathrm{C}}}, |\phi\rangle)$:

$$\begin{aligned}&\Delta_0(\Pi_{\mathrm{H}\overline{\mathrm{C}}}, |\phi\rangle) \\ &= \|\Pi_{\mathrm{H}\overline{\mathrm{C}}}\mathcal{R}_0 |\phi\rangle \|^2 - \|\Pi_{\mathrm{H}\overline{\mathrm{C}}} |\phi\rangle \|^2 \\ &= \|\Pi_{\mathrm{H}\overline{\mathrm{C}}}\mathcal{R}_0(\Pi_{\mathrm{H}\overline{\mathrm{C}}} + \Pi_{\overline{\mathrm{H}}+\mathrm{C}}) |\phi\rangle \|^2 - \|\Pi_{\mathrm{H}\overline{\mathrm{C}}} |\phi\rangle \|^2 \\ &\leq (\|\Pi_{\mathrm{H}\overline{\mathrm{C}}}\mathcal{R}_0\Pi_{\mathrm{H}\overline{\mathrm{C}}} |\phi\rangle \| + \|\Pi_{\mathrm{H}\overline{\mathrm{C}}}\mathcal{R}_0\Pi_{\overline{\mathrm{H}}+\mathrm{C}} |\phi\rangle \|)^2 - \|\Pi_{\mathrm{H}\overline{\mathrm{C}}} |\phi\rangle \|^2 \\ &= \|\Pi_{\mathrm{H}\overline{\mathrm{C}}}\mathcal{R}_0\Pi_{\mathrm{H}\overline{\mathrm{C}}} |\phi\rangle \|^2 + 2\|\Pi_{\mathrm{H}\overline{\mathrm{C}}}\mathcal{R}_0\Pi_{\mathrm{H}\overline{\mathrm{C}}} |\phi\rangle \| \cdot \|\Pi_{\mathrm{H}\overline{\mathrm{C}}}\mathcal{R}_0\Pi_{\overline{\mathrm{H}}+\mathrm{C}} |\phi\rangle \| \\ &\qquad + \|\Pi_{\mathrm{H}\overline{\mathrm{C}}}\mathcal{R}_0\Pi_{\overline{\mathrm{H}}+\mathrm{C}} |\phi\rangle \|^2 - \|\Pi_{\mathrm{H}\overline{\mathrm{C}}} |\phi\rangle \|^2 \\ &\leq 2 \cdot \|\Pi_{\mathrm{H}\overline{\mathrm{C}}}\mathcal{R}_0\Pi_{\overline{\mathrm{H}}+\mathrm{C}} |\phi\rangle \| + \|\Pi_{\mathrm{H}\overline{\mathrm{C}}}\mathcal{R}_0\Pi_{\overline{\mathrm{H}}+\mathrm{C}} |\phi\rangle \|^2\end{aligned}$$

The first equation comes from the definition of $\Delta_0$. Next we use that $\mathbb{I} = (\Pi_{\mathrm{H}\overline{\mathrm{C}}} + \Pi_{\overline{\mathrm{H}}+\mathrm{C}})$. In the third inequality, we use the triangle inequality. The equality in line 4 is obtained by opening the brackets. For the last inequality we use $\|\Pi_{\mathrm{H}\overline{\mathrm{C}}}\mathcal{R}_0\Pi_{\mathrm{H}\overline{\mathrm{C}}} |\phi\rangle \|^2 \leq \|\Pi_{\mathrm{H}\overline{\mathrm{C}}} |\phi\rangle \|^2$.

The last step is to bound $\|\Pi_{\mathrm{H}\overline{\mathrm{C}}}\mathcal{R}_0\Pi_{\overline{\mathrm{H}}+\mathrm{C}}\left|\phi\right\rangle\|$ we look at $\Gamma_0(\Pi_{\mathrm{H}\overline{\mathrm{C}}}, \left|\phi\right\rangle)$. According to Lemma 3 we have:

$$\Gamma_0(\Pi_{\mathrm{H}\overline{\mathrm{C}}}, \left|\phi\right\rangle) = \frac{\|\Pi_{\mathrm{H}\overline{\mathrm{C}}}\mathcal{R}_0(\mathbb{I} - \Pi_{\mathrm{H}\overline{\mathrm{C}}})\left|\phi\right\rangle\|^2}{\|(\mathbb{I} - \Pi_{\mathrm{H}\overline{\mathrm{C}}})\left|\phi\right\rangle\|^2} \leq 10\gamma$$
$$\|\Pi_{\mathrm{H}\overline{\mathrm{C}}}\mathcal{R}_0(\mathbb{I} - \Pi_{\mathrm{H}\overline{\mathrm{C}}})\left|\phi\right\rangle\|^2 = \|\Pi_{\mathrm{H}\overline{\mathrm{C}}}\mathcal{R}_0(\Pi_{\overline{\mathrm{H}}+\mathrm{C}})\left|\phi\right\rangle\|^2$$
$$= \|\Pi_{\mathrm{H}\overline{\mathrm{C}}}\mathcal{R}_0(\Pi_{\overline{\mathrm{H}\mathrm{C}}})\left|\phi\right\rangle\|^2 \leq 10\gamma \cdot \|\Pi_{\overline{\mathrm{H}}+\mathrm{C}}\left|\phi\right\rangle\|^2 \leq 10\gamma = \frac{10c}{N},$$

where

$$\gamma = \Pr_{y \leftarrow \mathcal{N}}\left[(H, D_{x\leftarrow y}) \in \mathrm{H}\overline{\mathrm{C}}\right] \leq \frac{c}{N},$$

for a $(D, H) \in \overline{\mathrm{HC}}$.

Here the equality $\|\Pi_{\mathrm{H}\overline{\mathrm{C}}}\mathcal{R}_0(\Pi_{\overline{\mathrm{H}}+\mathrm{C}})\left|\phi\right\rangle\|^2 = \|\Pi_{\mathrm{H}\overline{\mathrm{C}}}\mathcal{R}_0(\Pi_{\overline{\mathrm{H}\mathrm{C}}})\left|\phi\right\rangle\|^2$ comes from the fact that a quantum query can not turn the predicate C from True to False. Hence, we do not need to take into consideration the databases that satisfy the C predicate; after a quantum query, they will still satisfy it.

Before analyzing the classical case, we first establish an intermediate result by deriving a bound on the classical progress overlap. Later, we employ a proof strategy analogous to our quantum query analysis, using this classical progress overlap bound to obtain a corresponding bound on the progress measure.

**Lemma 7 ($\Pi_{\mathrm{H}+\mathrm{C}}$ classical progress overlap).** *Given an integer $t = q + c$, where $q$ is the number of quantum queries and $c$ is the number of classical queries, and a state $\left|\phi\right\rangle \in \mathbb{H}_t$ with the norm at most 1, the progress overlap obtained through one classical query on $\phi$ satisfies:*

$$\Gamma_1(\Pi_{\mathrm{H}+\mathrm{C}}, \left|\phi\right\rangle) \leq (3\gamma + 2\varepsilon),$$

*where $\gamma \leq \frac{q+c}{N}$ and $\varepsilon \leq \frac{18q^{3/2}}{KN^{1/2}} + \frac{22q^3}{KN}$.*

*Proof.* According to Lemma 5 we have:

$$\Gamma_1(\Pi_{\mathrm{H}+\mathrm{C}}, \left|\phi\right\rangle) = \frac{\|\Pi_{\mathrm{H}+\mathrm{C}}\mathcal{R}_1(\mathbb{I} - \Pi_{\mathrm{H}+\mathrm{C}})\left|\phi\right\rangle\|^2}{\|(\mathbb{I} - \Pi_{\mathrm{H}+\mathrm{C}})\left|\phi\right\rangle\|^2} \leq 3\gamma + 2\varepsilon$$
$$\|\Pi_{\mathrm{H}+\mathrm{C}}\mathcal{R}_1(\mathbb{I} - \Pi_{\mathrm{H}+\mathrm{C}})\left|\phi\right\rangle\|^2 = \|\Pi_{\mathrm{H}+\mathrm{C}}\mathcal{R}_1\Pi_{\overline{\mathrm{H}}\cdot\overline{\mathrm{C}}}\left|\phi\right\rangle\|^2$$
$$\leq (3\gamma + 2\varepsilon) \cdot \|\Pi_{\overline{\mathrm{H}}\cdot\overline{\mathrm{C}}}\left|\phi\right\rangle\|^2 \leq (3\gamma + 2\varepsilon),$$

where

$$\gamma = \Pr_{y \leftarrow \mathcal{N}}\left[(H_{x\leftarrow y}, D_{x\leftarrow y}) \in (\mathrm{H} + \mathrm{C})\right] \leq \frac{q+c}{N}$$

for false-state $(H, D) \in \overline{\mathrm{H}} \cdot \overline{\mathrm{C}} \cap \mathbb{H}_t$ where $D(x) = \perp$; and

$$\varepsilon = \Pr_{k \leftarrow \mathcal{K}}\left[(H_{(k,m)\leftarrow D(k,m)}, D) \in (\mathrm{H} + \mathrm{C})\right],$$

for false-state $(H, D) \in \overline{\mathrm{H}} \cdot \overline{\mathrm{C}} \cap \mathbb{H}_t$.

Note that $\varepsilon$ depends on the state of the quantum part of the database. We need to analyze when adding a value from $D$ turns $\overline{\mathrm{H}} \cdot \overline{\mathrm{C}}$ into $(\mathrm{H} + \mathrm{C})$. In this case, we get either a hybrid collision or a classical one. Assume we move a value from $D$ to $H$ and get a classical collision. This means that before, we had a collision between $D$ and $H$, which is excluded (we start from $\overline{\mathrm{H}} \cdot \overline{\mathrm{C}}$). Hence, the only possibility is to get a hybrid collision. If we move a value from $D$ to $H$ and get a hybrid collision, this means there was a collision in $D$ before the classical query.

Our classical query contains a chosen input $m$ and a random key $k$: $x = (k||m)$. Denote with $j$ maximum number of different keys $k_1, \ldots, k_j$ for which there exists a colliding pair of the following type: $[D(k_1, m) = D(k'_1, m'_1)]$, ..., $[D(k_j, m) = D(k'_j, m'_j)]$, where $(k_i, m) \neq (k'_i, m'_i)$. Note that we do not have any extra requirement for the $k'_i, m'_i$. If we can bound the probability that after $q$ queries, we know $j$ colliding inputs, then the maximum number of different keys we can obtain from these collisions is $2j$.

In [24, Section 4.3], the authors give a bound on finding $j$ distinct collisions. However, their argument actually works by bounding the probability that a new query collides with some input that is already in the database. They do not distinguish whether it is a new collision or if we have formed a 3-collision, for example. Hence, we can use their bound and claim that $\|\Pi_{j\mathrm{Q}} |\phi_t\rangle \|^2 \leq \min\{(\frac{e \cdot q^{3/2}}{j \cdot \sqrt{N}})^j; 1\}$.

Using this result, we deduce the bound on $\varepsilon$ :

$$\begin{aligned}
\varepsilon &= \Pr_{k \leftarrow \mathcal{K}} \left[ (H_{(k,m) \leftarrow D(k,m)}, D) \in (\mathrm{H} + \mathrm{C}) \right] \\
&\leq \sum_{j=1}^{q-1} \left( \frac{2j}{K} \cdot \|\Pi_{j\mathrm{Q}} |\phi_t\rangle \|^2 \right) \leq \sum_{j=1}^{q-1} \frac{2j}{K} \cdot \left( \frac{e \cdot q^{3/2}}{j \cdot \sqrt{N}} \right)^j \\
&\leq e \cdot \frac{2}{K} \left( \frac{q^3}{N} \right)^{1/2} + \frac{2e \cdot q^{3/2}}{K\sqrt{N}} \sum_{j=2}^{q-1} \left( \frac{e \cdot q^{3/2}}{j \cdot \sqrt{N}} \right)^{j-1}.
\end{aligned}$$

We analyze the last sum separately.

$$\begin{aligned}
&\sum_{j=2}^{q-1} \left( \frac{e \cdot q^{3/2}}{j \cdot \sqrt{N}} \right)^{j-1} \\
&= \sum_{j=0}^{q-3} \left( \frac{e \cdot q^{3/2}}{(j+2) \cdot \sqrt{N}} \right)^{j+1} \leq \frac{e \cdot q^{3/2}}{\sqrt{N}} \sum_{j=0}^{q-3} \left( \frac{e \cdot q^{3/2}}{(j+2) \cdot \sqrt{N}} \right)^j \\
&\leq \frac{e \cdot q^{3/2}}{\sqrt{N}} \sum_{j=0}^{q-3} \left( \frac{e \cdot q^{3/2}}{j \cdot \sqrt{N}} \right)^j \leq \frac{e \cdot q^{3/2}}{\sqrt{N}} \sum_{j=0}^{q-3} \left( \frac{e \cdot q^{3/2}}{\sqrt{N}} \right)^j (j!)^{-1} \\
&\leq \frac{e \cdot q^{3/2}}{\sqrt{N}} \sum_{j=0}^{\infty} \left( \frac{e \cdot q^{3/2}}{\sqrt{N}} \right)^j (j!)^{-1} = \frac{e \cdot q^{3/2}}{\sqrt{N}} \exp\left( \frac{e \cdot q^{3/2}}{\sqrt{N}} \right).
\end{aligned}$$

For the first inequality, we have used $j+2 \geq 1$ for all $j \geq 0$. In the second inequality, we have used $j+2 \geq j$. In the third inequality we have used $j! \leq j^j$ for all $j \geq 0$ (note that by convention, $0^0 = 1$). In the fourth inequality, we have extended the domain of the sum.

We are striving to bound the progress overlap, which is trivially upper-bonded by 1. Assume now $\frac{e^2 \cdot q^{3/2}}{\sqrt{N}} < 1$. Then $\exp\left(\frac{e \cdot q^{3/2}}{\sqrt{N}}\right) \leq \exp\left(\frac{1}{e}\right)$. In summary, we get

$$\varepsilon \leq \frac{2e}{K}\left(\frac{q^3}{N}\right)^{1/2} + \exp\left(\frac{1}{e}\right)\frac{2e^2 \cdot q^3}{K \cdot N} \leq \frac{6}{K}\left(\frac{q^3}{N}\right)^{1/2} + \frac{22 \cdot q^3}{K \cdot N}$$

Now consider $\frac{e \cdot q^{3/2}}{\sqrt{N}} \geq 1$, set $j_0 = \frac{e \cdot q^{3/2}}{\sqrt{N}}$. For $j \leq j_0$ we get $\min\{(\frac{e \cdot q^{3/2}}{j \cdot \sqrt{N}})^j; 1\} = 1$.

$$\varepsilon = \Pr_{k \leftarrow [K]}\left[(H_{(k,m) \leftarrow D(k,m)}, D) \in (\mathrm{H}+\mathrm{C})\right] \leq$$

$$\sum_{j=1}^{q-1}\left(\frac{2j}{K} \cdot \|\Pi_{j\mathrm{Q}} |\phi_t\rangle\|^2\right) \leq \sum_{j=1}^{q-1}\left(\frac{2j}{K} \cdot \min\{(\frac{e \cdot q^{3/2}}{j \cdot \sqrt{N}})^j; 1\}\right) \leq$$

$$\sum_{j=1}^{\lfloor j_0 \rfloor}\left(\frac{2j}{K}\right) + \sum_{j=\lfloor j_0+1 \rfloor}^{q-1}\left(\frac{2j}{K} \cdot (\frac{e \cdot q^{3/2}}{j \cdot \sqrt{N}})^j\right) \leq \frac{{j_0}^2}{K} + \sum_{j=\lfloor j_0+1 \rfloor}^{q-1}\left(\frac{2j}{K} \cdot (\frac{e \cdot q^{3/2}}{j \cdot \sqrt{N}})^j\right) =$$

$$\frac{e^2 q^3}{KN} + \sum_{\lfloor j_0+1 \rfloor}^{q-1}\left(\frac{2j}{K} \cdot (\frac{j_0}{j})^j\right) = \frac{e^2 q^3}{KN} + \sum_{j=\lfloor j_0+1 \rfloor}^{q-1}\left(\frac{2jj_0}{Kj} \cdot (\frac{j_0}{j})^{j-1}\right) =$$

$$\frac{e^2 q^3}{KN} + \frac{2j_0}{K}\sum_{j=\lfloor j_0+1 \rfloor}^{q-1}\left((\frac{j_0}{j})^{j-1}\right) \leq \frac{e^2 q^3}{KN} + \frac{2j_0}{K}\sum_{j=\lfloor j_0+1 \rfloor}^{q-1}\left((\frac{j_0}{j-1})^{j-1}\right) \leq$$

$$\frac{e^2 q^3}{KN} + \frac{2j_0}{K}\sum_{j=\lfloor j_0+1 \rfloor}^{q-1}\left((1 - \frac{j-1-j_0}{j-1})^{j-1}\right) \leq \frac{e^2 q^3}{KN} + \frac{2j_0}{K}\sum_{j=\lfloor j_0+1 \rfloor}^{q-1} e^{j-1-j_0} \leq$$

$$\frac{e^2 q^3}{KN} + \frac{2j_0}{K}\sum_{j'=0}^{q-j_0} e^{-j'} \leq \frac{e^2 q^3}{KN} + \frac{2j_0}{K}\frac{e}{e-1} \leq \frac{e^2 q^3}{KN} + \frac{6j_0}{K} \leq$$

$$\frac{9q^3}{KN} + \frac{18q^{3/2}}{KN^{1/2}}$$

Combining two bounds and taking maximum of the terms we get $\varepsilon \leq \frac{18q^{3/2}}{KN^{1/2}} + \frac{22q^3}{KN}$.

**Lemma 8 (Progress Measure, Classical Query).** *Given an integer $t = q+c$, where $q$ is the number of quantum queries and $c$ is the number of classical queries, and a state $|\phi\rangle \in \mathbb{H}_t$ with the norm at most 1, the progress made by one classical query of $\phi$ satisfies:*

$$\Delta_1(\Pi_{\mathrm{H}+\mathrm{C}}, |\phi\rangle) = \frac{3(q+c)}{N} + 2\varepsilon + 10\left(\frac{\sqrt{q+c}}{K\sqrt{N}} + \frac{q+c}{KN^{3/2}}\right),$$

*where $\varepsilon \leq \frac{18q^{3/2}}{KN^{1/2}} + \frac{22q^3}{KN}$.*

*Proof.* Lets expand $\Delta_1(\Pi_{\mathrm{H+C}}, |\phi\rangle)$:

$$\begin{aligned}
&\Delta_1(\Pi_{\mathrm{H+C}}, |\phi\rangle) \\
&= \|\Pi_{\mathrm{H+C}}\mathcal{R}_1 |\phi\rangle \|^2 - \|\Pi_{\mathrm{H+C}} |\phi\rangle \|^2 \\
&= \|\Pi_{\mathrm{H+C}}\mathcal{R}_1(\Pi_{\mathrm{H+C}} + \Pi_{\overline{\mathrm{H}}\cdot\overline{\mathrm{C}}}) |\phi\rangle \|^2 - \|\Pi_{\mathrm{H+C}} |\phi\rangle \|^2 \\
&= \|\Pi_{\mathrm{H+C}}\mathcal{R}_1\Pi_{\mathrm{H+C}} |\phi\rangle + \Pi_{\mathrm{H+C}}\mathcal{R}_1\Pi_{\overline{\mathrm{H}}\cdot\overline{\mathrm{C}}} |\phi\rangle \|^2 - \|\Pi_{\mathrm{H+C}} |\phi\rangle \|^2 \\
&= \| |\phi_1\rangle + |\phi_2\rangle \|^2 - \|\Pi_{\mathrm{H+C}} |\phi\rangle \|^2 \\
&= \langle\phi_1|\phi_1\rangle + \langle\phi_1|\phi_2\rangle + \langle\phi_2|\phi_1\rangle + \langle\phi_2|\phi_2\rangle - \|\Pi_{\mathrm{H+C}} |\phi\rangle \|^2 \\
&= \|\Pi_{\mathrm{H+C}}\mathcal{R}_1\Pi_{\mathrm{H+C}} |\phi\rangle \|^2 + \|\Pi_{\mathrm{H+C}}\mathcal{R}_1\Pi_{\overline{\mathrm{H}}\cdot\overline{\mathrm{C}}} |\phi\rangle \|^2 \\
&+ \langle\phi_1|\phi_2\rangle + \langle\phi_2|\phi_1\rangle - \|\Pi_{\mathrm{H+C}} |\phi\rangle \|^2 \\
&\leq \|\Pi_{\mathrm{H+C}}\mathcal{R}_1\Pi_{\overline{\mathrm{H}}\cdot\overline{\mathrm{C}}} |\phi\rangle \|^2 + \langle\phi_1|\phi_2\rangle + \langle\phi_2|\phi_1\rangle ,
\end{aligned}$$

where $|\phi_1\rangle = \Pi_{\mathrm{H+C}}\mathcal{R}_1\Pi_{\mathrm{H+C}} |\phi\rangle$ and $|\phi_2\rangle = \Pi_{\mathrm{H+C}}\mathcal{R}_1\Pi_{\overline{\mathrm{H}}\cdot\overline{\mathrm{C}}} |\phi\rangle$. The first equality comes from the definition. In the next equality we use that $\mathbb{I} = (\Pi_{\mathrm{H+C}} + \Pi_{\overline{\mathrm{H}}\cdot\overline{\mathrm{C}}})$. The fifth equality comes from the fact that $\|\psi\|^2 = \langle\psi|\psi\rangle$ and distributivity and associativity of the inner product. The last inequality comes from the fact $\|\Pi_{\mathrm{H+C}}\mathcal{R}_1\Pi_{\mathrm{H+C}} |\phi\rangle \|^2 \leq \|\Pi_{\mathrm{H+C}} |\phi\rangle \|^2$.

To bound $\|\Pi_{\mathrm{H+C}}\mathcal{R}_1\Pi_{\overline{\mathrm{H}}\cdot\overline{\mathrm{C}}} |\phi\rangle \|^2$ we look at $\Gamma_1(\Pi_{\mathrm{H+C}}, |\phi\rangle)$. According to our result from Lemma 7 we can deduce that

$$\|\Pi_{\mathrm{H+C}}\mathcal{R}_1\Pi_{\overline{\mathrm{H}}\cdot\overline{\mathrm{C}}} |\phi\rangle \|^2 \leq (3\gamma + 2\varepsilon),$$

where $\gamma \leq \frac{q+c}{N}$ and $\varepsilon \leq \frac{18q^{3/2}}{KN^{1/2}} + \frac{22q^3}{KN}$.

The last step is to bound $\langle\phi_1|\phi_2\rangle + \langle\phi_2|\phi_1\rangle$.

A detailed proof of this step is provided in the full version of the paper [21]. The key idea involves analyzing the non-orthogonal components of of $\phi_1$ and $\phi_2$ and characterizing the types of queries that can generate these components. After careful handling of different cases we show that

$$\langle\phi_1|\phi_2\rangle \leq \sqrt{16\frac{t}{K^2N} + 16\frac{t^2}{K^2N^3}} + \frac{2}{KN} \leq 5(\frac{\sqrt{t}}{K\sqrt{N}} + \frac{t}{KN^{3/2}})$$

Note that $\langle\phi_1|\phi_2\rangle = \langle\phi_2|\phi_1\rangle^\dagger$. Hence, we can use that $\langle\phi_1|\phi_2\rangle + \langle\phi_2|\phi_1\rangle \leq 2|\langle\phi_1|\phi_2\rangle|$. Combining all the results, we obtain the bound from the theorem.

In this section, we establish a security bound for the M-ETCR notion by analyzing the maximal advantage an adversary can gain through additional oracle queries. Our proof technique combines an adaptation of existing framework from prior work to handle quantum queries, and an introduced extension to handle classical challenge queries with randomly sampled keys.

## 5 Applications

In this section, we discuss the practical implications of our result on the M-ETCR security of a hash function under generic attacks. The main application of

M-ETCR is the analysis of the hash & sign transform [10, 29]. The hash & sign transform allows to turn a fixed message-length signature scheme into a variable message-length signature by first computing a message digest and then signing the digest: $\sigma = \text{Sign}(H(m))$. This plain version requires a collision-resistant hash function for security. When SHA1 was broken, collision-resistance was considered an unfavorable requirement that was to be avoided where possible. Such avoidance usually also comes with shorter digest sizes as other properties are not vulnerable to birthday attacks, improving efficiency too.

For hash & sign, it was suggested to randomize the digest computation [18] to avoid the need for collision resistance. In this case, the message is hashed with a random salt $r$, which is then attached to the signature of the original scheme: $\sigma = (r, \text{Sign}(H(r, m)))$. The authors introduced the extended target collision resistance notion (eTCR) to analyze the security of this construction. eTCR matches the M-ETCR notion if we make just one challenge query. By a plug & play argument, eTCR implies M-ETCR up to the number of challenge queries. While adding randomization to the message hashing allows us to reduce the security requirements from collision resistance to M-ETCR, potentially reducing the digest size, it also increases the signature size since the salt must be added to the signature. In total, this is usually still beneficial. However, to optimize the scheme's performance, we aim for a M-ETCR bound that allows to use minimal-length salts.

The hash & sign paradigm is often used to allow the signing of arbitrary long messages. An example of such an application can be found in [7, Section 14.1.1]. The authors show how the hashing of the message can improve the efficiency of one-time hash-based digital signatures. They also rely on randomized hashing and eTCR security. Note that for one-time hash-based signatures, the signed digest's size directly affects the scheme's overall efficiency and signature sizes. By requiring only M-ETCR security, we can avoid using long digests, which we would have to use if we did rely on collision resistance. Due to our analysis, we can also use short salts, shrinking the total size of the signature.

The hash & sign paradigm is also widely used in lattice-based signature schemes. For example, Falcon [28] - a lattice-based digital signature scheme, recently chosen for standardization by NIST [27]. The authors suggest randomized hashing of the message (see [28, Section 2.2.2]). Since the security of Falcon is based on the GPV framework [15], it is important that two different signatures are never generated for the same digest. To achieve this, the authors require the size of the salt to be 320 bits. Note that the M-ETCR property covers the required properties for message hashing. If we aim for the highest security level for the NIST parameters, we can estimate the number of classical queries as $2^{64}$ and the number of quantum queries as $2^{128}$. The hashing in Falcon is done with the SHAKE256 hash function [25]. Hence, we set $N = 2^{256}$. Using these parameters, we get that 200 bits is enough for the salt space. This is significantly smaller than the sizes used by the Falcon team.

The salt part may not play a big role in the signature sizes, especially for post-quantum schemes. While this is true, salts can play a significant role when we look at signature aggregation. In [1], the authors analyze the aggregation of multiple Falcon signatures. This approach is very useful when sending a large number of signatures over a low bandwidth network – a typical case for large-scale blockchains. Due to a conflict between the random oracle model and viewing a hash function as a circuit (see [22]), the authors decided to include the salts from all the signatures in the final aggregated signature (so the verifier can compute $H(r, m)$ locally). If we require salts of size 200, instead of 320 bits, for the parameters that the authors suggest (see [1, Table 1]), for 2000 signatures, we get a total size reduction from 165 kB to 136 kB, which is an almost 18% decrease in signature size.

Sometimes, it is possible to include the salt in the aggregation. For example, a recent work [13] did this for their hash-based multi-signatures construction. In this case, the effect on the signature size will be minimal. However, a general approach to aggregate signatures involves building a circuit that verifies multiple signatures and then producing a succinct argument for this circuit. Larger salt increases this circuit's complexity, affecting the singing and verification efficiency.

## References


1. Aardal, M.A., Aranha, D.F., Boudgoust, K., Kolby, S., Takahashi, A.: Aggregating falcon signatures with LaBRADOR. In: Reyzin, L., Stebila, D. (eds.) Advances in Cryptology – CRYPTO 2024, Part I. Lecture Notes in Computer Science, vol. 14920, pp. 71–106. Springer, Cham, Switzerland, Santa Barbara, CA, USA (Aug 18–22, 2024). https://doi.org/10.1007/978-3-031-68376-3_3
2. Ambainis, A.: Polynomial degree and lower bounds in quantum complexity: Collision and element distinctness with small range. Theory of Computing **1**(3), 37–46 (2005). https://doi.org/10.4086/toc.2005.v001a003, https://theoryofcomputing.org/articles/v001a003
3. Bellare, M., Rogaway, P.: Random oracles are practical: A paradigm for designing efficient protocols. In: Denning, D.E., Pyle, R., Ganesan, R., Sandhu, R.S., Ashby, V. (eds.) ACM CCS 93: 1st Conference on Computer and Communications Security. pp. 62–73. ACM Press, Fairfax, Virginia, USA (Nov 3–5, 1993). https://doi.org/10.1145/168588.168596
4. Bennett, C.H., Bernstein, E., Brassard, G., Vazirani, U.: Strengths and weaknesses of quantum computing. SIAM Journal on Computing **26**(5), 1510–1523 (1997). https://doi.org/10.1137/S0097539796300933, https://doi.org/10.1137/S0097539796300933
5. Bernstein, D.J., Hülsing, A., Kölbl, S., Niederhagen, R., Rijneveld, J., Schwabe, P.: The SPHINCS$^+$ signature framework. In: Cavallaro, L., Kinder, J., Wang, X., Katz, J. (eds.) ACM CCS 2019: 26th Conference on Computer and Communications Security. pp. 2129–2146. ACM Press, London, UK (Nov 11–15, 2019). https://doi.org/10.1145/3319535.3363229
6. Boneh, D., Dagdelen, Ö., Fischlin, M., Lehmann, A., Schaffner, C., Zhandry, M.: Random oracles in a quantum world. In: Lee, D.H., Wang, X. (eds.) Advances in Cryptology – ASIACRYPT 2011. Lecture Notes in Computer Science, vol. 7073, pp. 41–69. Springer Berlin Heidelberg, Germany, Seoul, South Korea (Dec 4–8, 2011). https://doi.org/10.1007/978-3-642-25385-0_3

7. Boneh, D., Shoup, V.: A Graduate Course in Applied Cryptography (2023), https://toc.cryptobook.us/
8. Canetti, R., Goldreich, O., Halevi, S.: The random oracle methodology, revisited (preliminary version). In: 30th Annual ACM Symposium on Theory of Computing. pp. 209–218. ACM Press, Dallas, TX, USA (May 23–26, 1998). https://doi.org/10.1145/276698.276741
9. Chung, K.M., Fehr, S., Huang, Y.H., Liao, T.N.: On the compressed-oracle technique, and post-quantum security of proofs of sequential work. In: Canteaut, A., Standaert, F.X. (eds.) Advances in Cryptology – EUROCRYPT 2021, Part II. Lecture Notes in Computer Science, vol. 12697, pp. 598–629. Springer, Cham, Switzerland, Zagreb, Croatia (Oct 17–21, 2021). https://doi.org/10.1007/978-3-030-77886-6_21
10. Diffie, W., Hellman, M.E.: New directions in cryptography. IEEE Transactions on Information Theory **22**(6), 644–654 (1976). https://doi.org/10.1109/TIT.1976.1055638
11. Don, J., Fehr, S., Huang, Y.H.: Adaptive versus static multi-oracle algorithms, and quantum security of a split-key PRF. In: Kiltz, E., Vaikuntanathan, V. (eds.) TCC 2022: 20th Theory of Cryptography Conference, Part I. Lecture Notes in Computer Science, vol. 13747, pp. 33–51. Springer, Cham, Switzerland, Chicago, IL, USA (Nov 7–10, 2022). https://doi.org/10.1007/978-3-031-22318-1_2
12. Don, J., Fehr, S., Majenz, C., Schaffner, C.: Efficient NIZKs and signatures from commit-and-open protocols in the QROM. In: Dodis, Y., Shrimpton, T. (eds.) Advances in Cryptology – CRYPTO 2022, Part II. Lecture Notes in Computer Science, vol. 13508, pp. 729–757. Springer, Cham, Switzerland, Santa Barbara, CA, USA (Aug 15–18, 2022). https://doi.org/10.1007/978-3-031-15979-4_25
13. Drake, J., Khovratovich, D., Kudinov, M.A., Wagner, B.: Hash-based multi-signatures for post-quantum ethereum. IACR Communications in Cryptology (CiC) **2**(1), 13 (2025). https://doi.org/10.62056/aey7qjp10
14. Fiat, A., Shamir, A.: How to prove yourself: Practical solutions to identification and signature problems. In: Odlyzko, A.M. (ed.) Advances in Cryptology – CRYPTO'86. Lecture Notes in Computer Science, vol. 263, pp. 186–194. Springer Berlin Heidelberg, Germany, Santa Barbara, CA, USA (Aug 1987). https://doi.org/10.1007/3-540-47721-7_12
15. Gentry, C., Peikert, C., Vaikuntanathan, V.: Trapdoors for hard lattices and new cryptographic constructions. In: Ladner, R.E., Dwork, C. (eds.) 40th Annual ACM Symposium on Theory of Computing. pp. 197–206. ACM Press, Victoria, BC, Canada (May 17–20, 2008). https://doi.org/10.1145/1374376.1374407
16. Grilo, A.B., Hövelmanns, K., Hülsing, A., Majenz, C.: Tight adaptive reprogramming in the QROM. In: Tibouchi, M., Wang, H. (eds.) Advances in Cryptology – ASIACRYPT 2021, Part I. Lecture Notes in Computer Science, vol. 13090, pp. 637–667. Springer, Cham, Switzerland, Singapore (Dec 6–10, 2021). https://doi.org/10.1007/978-3-030-92062-3_22
17. Grover, L.K.: A fast quantum mechanical algorithm for database search. In: 28th Annual ACM Symposium on Theory of Computing. pp. 212–219. ACM Press, Philadephia, PA, USA (May 22–24, 1996). https://doi.org/10.1145/237814.237866
18. Halevi, S., Krawczyk, H.: Strengthening digital signatures via randomized hashing. In: Dwork, C. (ed.) Advances in Cryptology – CRYPTO 2006. Lecture Notes in Computer Science, vol. 4117, pp. 41–59. Springer Berlin Heidelberg, Germany, Santa Barbara, CA, USA (Aug 20–24, 2006). https://doi.org/10.1007/11818175_3
19. Hamoudi, Y., Liu, Q., Sinha, M.: The NISQ complexity of collision finding. In: Joye, M., Leander, G. (eds.) Advances in Cryptology – EUROCRYPT 2024,

Part IV. Lecture Notes in Computer Science, vol. 14654, pp. 3–32. Springer, Cham, Switzerland, Zurich, Switzerland (May 26–30, 2024). https://doi.org/10.1007/978-3-031-58737-5_1

20. Hülsing, A., Rijneveld, J., Song, F.: Mitigating multi-target attacks in hash-based signatures. In: Cheng, C.M., Chung, K.M., Persiano, G., Yang, B.Y. (eds.) PKC 2016: 19th International Conference on Theory and Practice of Public Key Cryptography, Part I. Lecture Notes in Computer Science, vol. 9614, pp. 387–416. Springer Berlin Heidelberg, Germany, Taipei, Taiwan (Mar 6–9, 2016). https://doi.org/10.1007/978-3-662-49384-7_15
21. Hülsing, A., Kudinov, M., Majenz, C.: Hybrid-query bounds with partial input control - framework and application to tight m-eTCR. Cryptology ePrint Archive, Paper 2025/633 (2025), https://eprint.iacr.org/2025/633
22. Khovratovich, D., Rothblum, R.D., Soukhanov, L.: How to prove false statements: Practical attacks on fiat-shamir. In: Tauman Kalai, Y., Kamara, S.F. (eds.) Advances in Cryptology – CRYPTO 2025. pp. 3–26. Springer Nature Switzerland, Cham (2025)
23. Krawczyk, H., Bellare, M., Canetti, R.: HMAC: Keyed-Hashing for Message Authentication. RFC 2104 (Feb 1997). https://doi.org/10.17487/RFC2104, https://www.rfc-editor.org/info/rfc2104
24. Liu, Q., Zhandry, M.: On finding quantum multi-collisions. In: Ishai, Y., Rijmen, V. (eds.) Advances in Cryptology – EUROCRYPT 2019, Part III. Lecture Notes in Computer Science, vol. 11478, pp. 189–218. Springer, Cham, Switzerland, Darmstadt, Germany (May 19–23, 2019). https://doi.org/10.1007/978-3-030-17659-4_7
25. National Institute of Standards and Technology (NIST): FIPS publication 202: Sha-3 standard: Permutation-based hash and extendable-output functions (August 2015), https://nvlpubs.nist.gov/nistpubs/FIPS/NIST.FIPS.202.pdf
26. National Institute of Standards and Technology (NIST), Computer Security Resource Center (CSRC): Call for proposals: Additional digital signature schemes for the nist post-quantum cryptography standardization process (September 2022), https://csrc.nist.gov/csrc/media/Projects/pqc-dig-sig/documents/call-for-proposals-dig-sig-sept-2022.pdf
27. National Institute of Standards and Technology (NIST), Computer Security Resource Center (CSRC): Post-quantum cryptography. Webpage, NIST Computer Security Resource Center (2025), https://csrc.nist.gov/projects/post-quantum-cryptography, accessed: 2025-09-09
28. Prest, T., Fouque, P.A., Hoffstein, J., Kirchner, P., Lyubashevsky, V., Pornin, T., Ricosset, T., Seiler, G., Whyte, W., Zhang, Z.: FALCON. Tech. rep., National Institute of Standards and Technology (2022), available at https://csrc.nist.gov/Projects/post-quantum-cryptography/selected-algorithms-2022
29. Rivest, R.L., Shamir, A., Adleman, L.M.: A method for obtaining digital signatures and public-key cryptosystems. Communications of the Association for Computing Machinery **21**(2), 120–126 (Feb 1978). https://doi.org/10.1145/359340.359342
30. Zhandry, M.: How to record quantum queries, and applications to quantum indifferentiability. In: Boldyreva, A., Micciancio, D. (eds.) Advances in Cryptology – CRYPTO 2019, Part II. Lecture Notes in Computer Science, vol. 11693, pp. 239–268. Springer, Cham, Switzerland, Santa Barbara, CA, USA (Aug 18–22, 2019). https://doi.org/10.1007/978-3-030-26951-7_9

# Nonadaptive One-Way to Hiding Implies Adaptive Quantum Reprogramming

Joseph Jaeger(✉)

School of Cybersecurity and Privacy, Georgia Institute of Technology, Atlanta, GA, USA
josephjaeger@gatech.edu

**Abstract.** An important proof technique in the random oracle model involves reprogramming it on hard to predict inputs and arguing that an attacker cannot detect that this occurred. In the quantum setting, a particularly challenging version of this considers adaptive reprogramming wherein the points to be reprogrammed (or the output values they should be programmed to) are dependent on choices made by the adversary. Some quantum frameworks for analyzing adaptive reprogramming were given by Unruh (CRYPTO 2014, EUROCRYPT 2015), Grilo-Hövelmanns-Hülsing-Majenz (ASIACRYPT 2021), and Pan-Zeng (PKC 2024). We show, counterintuitively, that these adaptive results follow from the *non-adaptive* one-way to hiding theorem of Ambainis-Hamburg-Unruh (CRYPTO 2019). These implications contradict beliefs (whether stated explicitly or implicitly) that some properties of the adaptive frameworks cannot be provided by the Ambainis-Hamburg-Unruh result.

## 1 Introduction

Hash functions are a pillar of modern practical cryptography. Many of the most efficient algorithms for a given task (public key encryption, digital signatures, authenticated key exchange, ...) crucially rely on hash functions for their security. Often the security cannot be reduced to standard model assumptions about the hash function and is instead justified by modeling it as a random oracle [4]. A variety of methods of expressing random oracle model proofs are known which can make it easy to express analyses based on basic probabilistic analysis [5,8,18,21,22]. An important aspect of this is bounding the probability that an attacker notices if we adaptively modify the behavior of the oracle on inputs which are statistically/computationally hard for the attacker to guess.

As we prepare for a post-quantum future, there is a natural desire to port these benefits over to the quantum random oracle model [7] which captures that an attacker locally computing a hash function may use a quantum computer to do so in superposition. With this change in model, existing classical proofs no longer apply and, more importantly, the standard proof techniques no longer work. Motivated by this challenge, many techniques have been introduced for quantum random oracle model analysis [3,6,11–13,15,17,20,24–26,30–32].

© International Association for Cryptologic Research 2026
G. Hanaoka and B.-Y. Yang (Eds.): ASIACRYPT 2025, LNCS 16252, pp. 287–319, 2026.
https://doi.org/10.1007/978-981-95-5125-5_10

Rather than providing new analysis tools, we show that an existing tool by Ambainis, Hamburg, and Unruh [3] (AHU) is more broadly applicable than previously realized.[1] This "one-way to hiding" (O2H) theorem (building on earlier versions [11,15,24–26]) bounds an attacker's advantage in distinguishing between a pair of randomly chosen functions based on the probability a related algorithm can extract an input on which they differ. The common impression [3,12,20] seems to be that this result is highly non-adaptive because these two functions must be fixed at the beginning of the experiment, and thus it cannot be used for adaptive analysis where the definitions of the functions can update throughout the experiment (except in a few special corner cases where an adaptive problem can cleverly be expressed non-adaptively).

We dispel this notion, showing that through a change of viewpoint we can easily analyze many highly adaptive problems. As concrete applications of this we prove that an "adaptive reprogramming framework" of Pan and Zeng [20], a "tight adaptive reprogramming theorem" of Grilo, Hövelmanns, Hülsing, Majenz [12], and "adaptive O2H" lemmas of Unruh [24,25] are all implied by the AHU O2H result. We use straightforward proofs that largely rely on classical-like reasoning. The proofs of the "tight adaptive reprogramming theorem" and one of Unruh's "adaptive O2H" lemmas start by representing a random oracle sparsely with Zhandry's technique [32]. The concrete bounds we establish are essentially equivalent to or better than the existing bounds.

Our approach uses a proof technique of Jaeger, Song, and Tessaro [14] which applied a variant of AHU's O2H with fixed permutations to analyze the quantum security of a key-length extension technique they call FFX. We show that this technique is broadly applicable for proving adaptive reprogramming results. The main idea underlying this technique is to switch away from viewing the pair of O2H functions in AHU's theorem as strictly applied to the attacker's input. We instead use permutations that take a combined input containing both the attacker's input and the current state of the "security game", using the latter to respond to the former. Updating the state of the game thereby adaptively changes the inputs on which the oracles differ *from the attacker's perspective*, but actually the set of *combined* inputs on which the permutations differ is fixed from the beginning. In essence, we view the O2H distinguisher as internally running both the attacker and the security game, only exporting very specific pieces of the computation to an oracle. The idea of having the O2H distinguisher run both the attacker and the security game is the core technical idea that allows adaptive proofs using AHU's O2H.

## 1.1 Technique Overview

Consider a setting where an attacker $\mathcal{A}$ makes $q$ queries $x_1, \ldots, x_q$ to random oracle $H$. It's allowed to adaptively select points $x_i^*$, asking for $H(x_i^*)$ to be

[1] In fact, AHU provide multiple O2H theorems. We focus on applying their Theorem 3, which is derived from the Semi-classical O2H theorem (their Theorem 1) which is the focus of their work.

| $\underline{O_b(x_j)}$ | $\underline{P_b(X, Y : H, X^*, Y^*, I)}$ |
|---|---|
| If $\exists i, x_i^* = x_j$: | If $\exists i \leqslant I, X_i^* = X$ // $\mathsf{bad}$ |
| $\quad$ $\mathsf{bad} \leftarrow \mathtt{true}$ | $\quad$ If $b = 1$: $Y \leftarrow Y \oplus Y_i^*$ |
| $\quad$ If $b = 1$: Return $y_i^*$ | $\quad$ If $b = 0$: $Y \leftarrow Y \oplus H(X_i^*)$ |
| Return $H(x_j)$ | Else $Y \leftarrow Y \oplus H(X)$ |
| | Return $(X, Y : H, X^*, Y^*, I)$ |

**Fig. 1. Left:** Expression of oracle as pseudocode for classical equivalent-until-bad analysis. **Right:** Expression of oracle as a classical permutation queried in superposition for quantum Fixed Permutation O2H analysis.

redefined to some $y_i^*$ up to $n$ times. Let $p_1$ be the probability it outputs 1 at the end of its execution and $p_0$ be the probability it outputs 1 if instead $H$ is never redefined. Our goal is to bound $|p_1 - p_0|$.

This setting is adaptive in two senses. First, the differences between the oracles in the experiment change over time, rather than being chosen at the beginning of the experiment. Second, the particular ways in which the oracles are changed may depend on earlier queries of the adversary.

**Classical Analysis.** To analyze this classically, we might use a Bellare-Rogaway style "equivalent-until-bad" approach [5] (or analogous approaches by Maurer [18] or Shoup [22]). Therein we express this setting as a pair of pseudocode games, parameterized by a bit $b$, which are syntactically identical except after a flag $\mathsf{bad}$ is set. This could, for example, be captured by using the pseudocode oracle $O_b$ on the left of Fig. 1. Now the fundamental lemma of game playing tells us that $|p_0 - p_1| \leq \Pr[\mathsf{bad}]$.

At this point, we would bound $\Pr[\mathsf{bad}]$ based on some assumption about $\mathcal{A}$ (e.g., that the $x_i^*$ are statistically or computationally unpredictable). Applying a union bound across all of the queries of $\mathcal{A}$ gives

$$\Pr[\mathsf{bad}] \leq \sum_j \Pr[x_j \in \{x_i^*\}] = q \mathop{\mathbb{E}}_j[\Pr[x_j \in \{x_i^*\}]].$$

For example, if the $x_i^*$ are from adaptively chosen distributions that always have min-entropy at least $\mu$ and the $x_i^*$ are used nowhere else we get $|p_0 - p_1| \leq nq2^{-\mu}$. Notably, (treating the fundamental lemma of game playing as given) the analysis consists entirely of syntactic rewriting of the setting as pseudocode combined with basic probability calculation.

**Non-Adaptive O2H.** Now consider a setting where $x_i^*, y_i^*$ are still chosen classically, but the attacker has quantum access to $H$. The standard formalization of this allows computing the classical permutation $H[\oplus] : (x, y) \mapsto (x, y \oplus H(x))$ in superposition. We can no longer apply the approach above, as the oracle can be queried in a superposition over all $x$ at once so the bad event that it was queried on some $x_i^*$ is not even well defined. One approach to this are "one-way to hiding" (O2H) results [3,11,15,24–26] which can be thought of as a quantum analog to equivalent-until-bad analysis. Consider using an O2H lemma of AHU [3, Theorem 3], which (when simplified) considers a distribution over functions $H_0$, $H_1$ and tells us that

$$|p_{H_0} - p_{H_1}| \leq 2q\sqrt{\mathop{\mathbb{E}}_{j}[\mathsf{Pr}[\text{Measure}(X_j) \in S]]}.$$

Here $p_{H_b}$ is the probability an adversary outputs 1 when interacting with $H_b[\oplus]$ and the last probability considers running the adversary $\mathcal{A}$ with access to either oracle $H_b$, measuring its $j$-th query to the oracle, and checking whether the resulting measured value $x_j$ is in the set $S = \{x : H_0(x) \neq H_1(x)\}$.

Unfortunately, this result is non-adaptive. The two functions $H_0$ and $H_1$ (and thus the points where they differ) are fixed at the beginning of the game. Consequently, it *seems* that the result can only be applied in the limited case that all $x_i^*, y_i^*$ are chosen at the beginning of the game and thus the programming of $H$ occurs immediately. (For this, consider the distribution that samples the $x_i^*, y_i^*$, then defines $H_0$ to be a random oracle, and then defines $H_1$ to equal $H_0$ except it is reprogrammed so $H_1(x_i^*) = y_i^*$ for all $i$.) For example, if the $x_i^*$ are from distributions that have min-entropy at least $\mu$ and the $x_i^*$ are used nowhere else we get $|p_0 - p_1| \leq \sqrt{nq^2 2^{-\mu}}$.

**Fixed Permutation O2H.** This impression is incorrect. We can analyze many adaptive reprogramming settings using AHU's O2H. Start by simplifying it so that rather than considering distributions over permutations of the form $H_b[\oplus]$ we consider two fixed permutations $P_0$ and $P_1$. It follows from Jaeger, Song, and Tessaro [14] variant of AHU's O2H lemma that

$$|p_{P_0} - p_{P_1}| \leq 2q\sqrt{\mathop{\mathbb{E}}_{j}[\mathsf{Pr}[\text{Measure}(\ P_0(X_j) \neq P_1(X_j)\ )]]}.$$

We call this variant of AHU's O2H the Fixed Permutation O2H. To apply this result, we switch our viewpoint. Rather than thinking of $P_b$ being the functions the attacker $\mathcal{A}$ might have access to (and so the O2H distinguisher is essentially identical to the attacker) we will think of building a distinguisher $\mathcal{D}$ that jointly runs both $\mathcal{A}$ and the "security game" $\mathcal{A}$ is interacting with. Then the permutations $P_b$ will be permutations that process oracle queries as a function of both the attacker's input and the game's state.

In our running example, to simulate the game the distinguisher will store the random function in a quantum register $H$ and the reprogramming points $x_i^*, y_i^*$ in registers $X_i^*$ and $Y_i^*$ (together with a register $I$ counting how many points have been chosen so far). Then when the original attacker $\mathcal{A}$ wants to query $H_b[\oplus]$ with registers $X, Y$ while being run internally by the distinguisher $\mathcal{D}$, the distinguisher forwards this together with the game registers $H, X^*, Y^*, I$ as a query $(X, Y, H, X^*, Y^*, I)$ to its own oracle $P_b$ defined on the right side of Fig. 1. It then returns just the $X$ and $Y$ registers to $\mathcal{A}$. Notationally, we use a colon as syntactic sugar to distinguish the input registers controlled by the attacker $\mathcal{A}$ or

```
CRo(x)                              FRo(X, Y : H)
If T[x] = ⊥:                        H[X] ← H[X] ⊕ Y
  Sample T[x]                       Return (X, Y : H)
Return T[x]
                                    FRep_b(X* : H, I, Z)
CRep_b(x_i*)                        If H[X*] ≠ Z[I]: // bad
If T[x_i*] ≠ ⊥:                       If b = 1: Swap H[X*] and Z[I]
  bad ← true                        I ← I + 1 mod n
  If b = 1: Sample T[x_i*]          Return (X* : H, I, Z)
Return
```

**Fig. 2. Left:** Pseudocode for classical proof using lazily sampled random function. **Right:** Permutations for Fixed Permutation O2H proof using sparse representation of random function. Tables $H$ and $Z$ are initially all zero.

the game it is interacting with. We emphasize, however, that $P_b$ is a permutation on six inputs, *all* of which are controlled by the distinguisher.

In this way, the distinguisher perfectly simulates the view of the attacker and the two permutations only differ on inputs for which $X$ is one of the reprogrammed points (as specified by $X^*$ and $I$). Thus the above bound on $|p_{P_0} - p_{P_1}|$ gives a bound on $|p_0 - p_1|$. For example, if the $x_i^*$ are from adaptively chosen distributions that always have min-entropy at least $\mu$ and the $x_i^*$ are used nowhere else we get $|p_0 - p_1| \leq \sqrt{nq^2 2^{-\mu}}$. Notably, (treating the Fixed Permutation O2H as given) the analysis consisted entirely of syntactic rewriting of the oracles as permutations, combined with basic probability calculation.

If we considered an arbitrary distinguisher $\mathcal{D}$, the Fixed Permutation O2H would be vacuous because $\mathcal{D}$ could always just make all its queries with $I > 1$ and $X = X_i^*$, making the right sight of the bound equal to one. However, we will *not* apply the bound with arbitrary distinguishers. We apply it with distinguishers of the particular form described above for whom the value of the right side of the bound depends on $\mathcal{A}$.

**Backwards Bounds from Sparse Functions.** Thinking classically, if each $y_i^*$ is uniformly random, then swapping it with $H(x_i^*)$ will only actually be detectable if the attacker queries its oracle at $x_i^*$ *both* before and after the reprogramming. This can be important because in some settings $x_i^*$ may be hard to query to $H$ before the reprogramming occurred but easy to query afterwards. Our approach so far only considering the probability of $x_i^*$ being queried after reprogramming and thus could not be applied.

Fortunately, the solution to this in the classical setting can be applied to the Fixed Permutation O2H approach as well. The core idea is to consider the "bad event" as occurring when $x_i^*$ is chosen. Then we will look backwards in time to see if $x_i^*$ was previously queried to the random oracle. To do this, we lazily sample the random oracle using a table and then check whether a new $x_i^*$ matches any of the values currently in the table. This is captured by the pseudocode oracles CRo and CRep$_b$ on the left of Fig. 2 for querying the random oracle and reprogramming it to a random value on a specified input. Applying the fundamental lemma of game playing and union bounds gives.

$$|p_0 - p_1| \leq \sum_i \mathsf{Pr}[x_i^* \in T] = n \mathop{\mathbb{E}}_i[\mathsf{Pr}[x_i^* \in T]].$$

If the $x_i^*$ are from adaptively chosen distributions that always have min-entropy at least $\mu$ we get $|p_0 - p_1| \leq nq2^{-\mu}$. Notably, (treating the fundamental lemma of game playing as given) the analysis consists entirely of straightforward syntactic rewriting of the setting as pseudocode combined with basic probability calculation.

For porting this idea over to the quantum regime, the important aspect of lazy sampling was that the random oracle was represented by a sparse table (one which had been written to in at most $q$ locations after $q$ queries). Zhandry [32] showed that we can similarly represent quantum random oracles with (superpositions over) sparse tables. Thereby, we can move from the traditional quantum random oracle which does $y \leftarrow y \oplus H(x)$ for an $H$ initialized at random to the Fourier random oracle which does $H(x) \leftarrow y \oplus H(x)$ for an $H$ initialized to be all zero. In this domain, reprogramming $H(x_i^*)$ to a random output can be performed by swapping its register with a fresh register initialized to be zero. This is captured by the permutations FRo and FRep$_b$ on the right of Fig. 2. Here registers $H$, $I$, and $Z$ are initialized as 0.

We can now apply the Fixed Permutation O2H. The distinguisher runs the attacker, internally storing the game registers and simulating FRo for the attacker. Whenever the original attacker $\mathcal{A}$ wants to reprogram on the value in register $X^*$, the O2H distinguisher $\mathcal{D}$ adds the game registers and then forwards this as a query $(X^*, H, I, Z)$ to its own oracle FRep$_b$, then returns $X^*$ to the attacker. Note that the FRep$_b$ permutations differ only if $H[X^*]$ and $Z[I]$ differ (and $Z[I]$ is necessarily zero), so we get

$$|p_0 - p_1| \leq 2n\sqrt{\mathop{\mathbb{E}}_i[\mathsf{Pr}[\text{Measure}(H[X_i^*] \neq 0)]]}.$$

This result can give better bounds in the natural setting that $q \gg n$ because it (implicitly) switches a factor of $q\sqrt{n}$ with $n\sqrt{q}$. For example, if the $x_i^*$ are from adaptively chosen distributions that always have min-entropy at least $\mu$ we get $|p_0 - p_1| \leq \sqrt{n^2 q 2^{-\mu}}$. Notably, (treating the Fixed Permutation O2H as given) the analysis consisted entirely of straightforward syntactic rewriting of the oracles as permutations combined with basic probability calculation.[2]

## 1.2 Applications of The Technique

To show the broad applicability of the Fixed Permutation O2H [14] for adaptive proofs, we use it to imply an "adaptive reprogramming framework" of Pan and

[2] Prior to Zhandry's work, rewriting quantum random functions as sparse tables was not known to be straightforward. In light of the work, it is quite simple to do so for our purposes.

Zeng [20], a "tight adaptive reprogramming theorem" of Grilo, Hövelmanns, Hülsing, Majenz [12] (GHHM), and "adaptive O2H" lemmas of Unruh [24,25]. We summarize these below.

For some of these results, the concrete bounds we establish have to be parameterized slightly differently than the original results, but we show that they are essentially equivalent (or better) in actual use. Moreover, AHU's O2H shows that their upper bound also applies to the difference of square roots $|\sqrt{p_0} - \sqrt{p_1}|$. This gives better bounds when used to prove $p_0$ is small based on a $p_1$ which is known to be small. For example, if $p_1 = 0$ and the upper bound is $\varepsilon$ we get $p_0 = (\sqrt{p_0} - \sqrt{p_1})^2 \leq \varepsilon^2$ which improves over $p_0 = p_0 - p_1 \leq \varepsilon$. We get the square root versions of all the results we consider for free.[3]

**Pan-Zeng Adaptive Reprogramming Framework.** Pan and Zeng [20] introduced an adaptive reprogramming framework which they use to analyze the selective-opening security of Fujisaki-Okamoto-style public key encryption algorithms. They express a belief that AHU's O2H result lacked the properties needed for these proofs, saying that,

> Our core technical contribution is a computational adaptive reprogramming framework in the QROM that enables a security reduction to adaptively and simultaneously reprogram polynomially many RO-queries which are computationally hidden from a quantum adversary. This is a property that *cannot be provided* by previous techniques in the QROM, such as ...the semi-classical O2H lemma [3]...[4]

We prove that their computational adaptive reprogramming result is implied by the Fixed Permutation O2H with a short proof, thereby establishing that the O2H lemma *can* provide this property.[5] Their framework considers arbitrary reprogramming of the oracle and upper bounds distinguishing advantage by the probability that measuring the input of a random query gives a value at which the function differ. In essence, their result follows directly from the first use of Fixed Permutation O2H that we described above.

**GHHM Adaptive Reprogramming Framework.** GHHM [12] gave a tight adaptive reprogramming theorem for information theoretic settings where the reprogrammed points are from adaptively chosen distributions with high min-entropy, but are immediately given to the attacker. Consequently, the distinguishing advantage must be bound by the probability that one of the reprogrammed points is queried before being selected and does not seem to imply

[3] As pointed out by an Asiacrypt reviewer, a bound of $|p_0 - p_1| \leq \varepsilon$, generically implies a square root bound via $\sqrt{p_0} - \sqrt{p_1} \leq \sqrt{p_1 + \varepsilon} - \sqrt{p_1} \leq \sqrt{p_1} + \sqrt{\varepsilon} - \sqrt{p_1} \leq \sqrt{\varepsilon}$. Our bounds improve on this by getting $\sqrt{p_0} - \sqrt{p_1} \leq \varepsilon$.

[4] This quote is from p.4 (aka p.95) of the proceedings version or p.3 of the current ePrint version. Emphasis ours. We've changed the citation to match our numbers.

[5] Technically, the mentioned semi-classical O2H lemma is a different O2H result of AHU, but AHU showed [3] it directly implies the O2H lemma we prove equivalent to the Fixed Permutation O2H in Sect. 2.

or be implied by the Pan-Zeng result.[6] Our proof of GHHM's theorem follows from our second use of Fixed Permutation O2H by using Zhandry's technique for sparsely representing functions to provide "backwards bounds". GHHM used their tool for tighter proofs of hash and sign techniques (e.g., used by XMSS), tighter proofs for Fiat Shamir signatures, and fault resistance for the hedged Fiat-Shamir transform. Their theorem was later used by [1,9,10,16,19,28,29].

**Unruh's Adaptive O2H.** Unruh [24,25] gave adaptive variants of early O2H results for reprogramming on a single statistically hidden input. These results obtain improved concrete bounds by separately considering the probability that reprogrammed point is queried before or after it is sampled. Consequently, they do not seem to imply or be implied by either the Pan-Zeng or the GHHM result.

Notably, AHU proved a theorem (their Theorem 4) that had previously been shown using the first adaptive O2H result [24]. While doing so, they note that "at least in the proof from [23]" they could replace the adaptive O2H result with their nonadaptive version by programming the random oracle on many points. Our proof of the [24] result applies the Fixed Permutation O2H two times, one of which similarly programs the random oracle on many points. Thereby we show that the approach of AHU actually extends to any application of the adaptive O2H, not just that particular proof.

We reprove the [25] result through two applications of the Fixed Permutation O2H using "backwards bounds". The setting of this result is more general than in [24], but the concrete bounds based on collision-entropy of the input distribution are incomparable. Our proof gives a bound in terms of min-entropy which implies both the collision-entropy bound [25] and an improved version of the bound in [24] (replacing a $q_0$ factor with $\sqrt{q_0}$).

**A Non-Application.** The Fixed Permutation O2H is not a panacea. We conclude the paper by discussing two results that seem out of reach of the Fixed Permutation O2H with current techniques. The first result, by Alagic, Bai, Katz, and Majenz [1], gives a variant of the GHHM result for random permutations reprogrammed on uniformly random points. The result proves an $O(\sqrt{q/2^n})$ bound while we are only able to prove $O(\sqrt{q^2/2^n})$. The second result, by Alagic, Bai, Katz, Majenz, and Struck [2], generalizes the result when a reprogrammed point comes from an adaptively chosen, high entropy distribution. For both, we identify that the gap between our success in proving the GHHM result and inability to prove these results stems from lacking techniques for expressing quantum random permutations sparsely.

[6] The paper [20] erroneously implies that the GHHM theorem is captured by the Pan-Zeng framework. We pointed this error out to the authors who agreed that the current result does not capture the GHHM theorem.

### 1.3 Implications of the Results

Formally, the claim that Fixed Permutation O2H implies any of these other theorems is essentially tautological. The results were already unconditionally proven to be true, so it is vacuously the case that any statement implies them. The essence of the result is not that the implications hold, but rather that the proofs thereof are straightforward and require almost exclusively classical reasoning. (The quantum complexity is instead hidden inside of the O2H result we take as assumed.)

There are two ways we imagine this being used in future work. If one likes to have a "toolbox" of adaptive reprogramming results each targeted narrowly at a particular type of problem that they are well suited to expressing, then our results show that the Fixed Permutation O2H is useful to build such tools. Alternatively, because of the simplicity of our proofs, one could choose to jettison the use of individual adaptive reprogramming results and instead use Fixed Permutation O2H directly in security proofs as a single powerful "multi-tool".[7]

### 1.4 Overview

In Sect. 2 we describe notation conventions, summarize necessary background on quantum computation, and provide the Fixed Permutation O2H lemma we use throughout the paper. In Sect. 3 we prove that the lemma implies the adaptive programming result of Pan and Zeng [20]. In Sect. 4 we prove that the lemma implies the tight adaptive programming result of GHHM [12]. In Sect. 5 we prove that the lemma implies two adaptive one-way-to-hiding results of Unruh [24, 25]. We conclude in Sect. 6 by discussing the challenges in proving the random permutation resampling results of Alagic, Bai, Katz, and Majenz [1] or Alagic, Bai, Katz, Majenz, and Struck [2].

## 2 Preliminaries

**Notation.** We write $y \leftarrow\!\!\$\ \mathcal{A}[O](x)$ for randomized execution of $\mathcal{A}$ with input $x$ and oracle access to $O$ which produces output $y$. We consider quantum $\mathcal{A}$ that can access $O$ in superposition. We let $\Pr[\mathsf{G}]$ denote the probability that game $\mathsf{G}$ returns `true`. Registers are implicitly initialized to store the all zero string.

If $\mathcal{S}$ is a set, then $y \leftarrow\!\!\$\ \mathcal{S}$ denotes sampling $y$ uniformly from $\mathcal{S}$. We let $\mathsf{Fcs}(n, m)$ denote the set of all functions mapping $\{0,1\}^n$ to $\{0,1\}^m$. Sampling $H \leftarrow\!\!\$\ \mathsf{Fcs}(n, m)$ gives a uniform random function.

[7] As an example, we note that several works [10,12,16,28] use both GHHM's result and O2H theorems from AHU.

### 2.1 Quantum Computation Background

We assume familiarity with basic quantum computation, as performing unitary operations on registers which each contain a fixed number of qubits that can be measured in the computational basis. Our main results are primarily based on a "one-way to hiding" theorem (defined soon) which when treated as a blackbox allow us to primarily think "classically". We summarize the most important ideas used in our proofs.

**Computing Permutations.** If $P$ is a permutation, then there is a quantumly computable unitary $U_P$ which maps according to $U_P |x\rangle = |P(x)\rangle$ for $x \in \{0,1\}^n$. The runtime of this unitary grows with the time required to compute both $P$ and $P^{-1}$ classically. We write $P$ in place of $U_P$. If $f : \{0,1\}^n \rightarrow \{0,1\}^m$ is a function, we define the permutation $f[\oplus]$ by $f[\oplus](x, y) = (x, f(x) \oplus y)$.

We define permutations O that will be provided as (possibly quantum accessible) oracles using the following notation.

$$\begin{array}{l} \underline{\mathrm{O}(X_1, \ldots, X_m : Z_1, \ldots, Z_n)} \\ //\text{Code updating } X_1, \ldots, X_m \text{ and } Z_1, \ldots, Z_n \\ \text{Return } (X_1, \ldots, X_m : Z_1, \ldots, Z_n) \end{array}$$

Writing $\mathcal{A}[O]$ will denote the variables/registers before the colon $(X_1, \ldots, X_m)$ are controlled by $\mathcal{A}$ while variables/registers after the colon $(Z_1, \ldots, Z_n)$ are controlled by its surrounding security game. Writing $\mathcal{D}[O_{\Leftrightarrow}]$ will denote that $\mathcal{D}$ controls all of the variables/registers. We use this for one-way-to-hiding distinguishers (which when used for reductions will internally run code of *both* the attacker and the game the attacker expects to interact with).

**Principle of Deferred Measurement.** In proofs, we find it convenient to defer any classical measurements until the end of execution by writing the result of the measurement (in superposition) into an auxiliary register that will otherwise be unused. In the case that $T'$ is the end of an experiment and we only care about the measured value of some other register, then the measurement can be deferred indefinitely.

**Sparse Representation of a Uniformly Random Function.** In two proofs we make use of Zhandry's [32] technique for representing random functions with sparse tables. It lets us replace access to an oracle for which $(x, y)$ is mapped to $(x, y \oplus T[x])$ for a uniformly random $T$ with an oracle for which $(x, y)$ is unchanged and $T[x]$ is updated by $T[x] \leftarrow T[x] \oplus y$ for an initially all-zero $T$.

The full compressed oracle technique of Zhandry combines the above with the ability to represent such a sparse table compactly (with $q$ registers). We do not need this compactness. When we first make use of this approach we will, in an appendix, provide a rigorous breakdown of the technique into individual steps for readers unfamiliar with the technique.

| Game $\mathsf{G}^{\mathsf{hide}}_{O}(\mathcal{D})$ | Game $\mathsf{G}^{\mathsf{ow}}_{P,P'}(\mathcal{D})$ |
|---|---|
| $b \leftarrow\$ \mathcal{D}[O_{\Leftrightarrow}]$ | $i \leftarrow\$ \{1, \ldots, q\}$ |
| Return $b = 1$ | Run $\mathcal{D}[P_{\Leftrightarrow}]$ until its $i$-th query |
| | Measure the input $x$ to this query |
| | Return $(P(x) \neq P'(x))$ |

**Fig. 3.** Games used for O2H Theorem 1

Unruh [27] gives a generalization of Zhandry's technique, exhibiting that the particular choices of using the Fourier domain or the Hadamard transform are inessential for the result. However, for our analysis it is more convenient to concretely work with the Hadamard transform because it allows us to concretely write simple pseudocode for the sparse random oracle. Unruh's presentation does not seem to easily allow this.

**(Fixed Permutation) One-way to Hiding.** Ambainis, Hamburg, and Unruh (AHU) [3] proved a "one-way to hiding" (O2H) theorem which bounds the ability of a distinguisher to distinguish between two oracles by the probability that the distinguisher can be used to find an input on which the two oracles differ. Their theorem and typical uses thereof consider distributions over the oracles. We focus on using a variant where the oracles are permutations that are fixed ahead of time as first used by Jaeger, Song, and Tessaro [14]. We will define both and show that they are essentially equivalent.

Consider the game $\mathsf{G}^{\mathsf{hide}}$ defined in Fig. 3 wherein the distinguisher $\mathcal{D}$ is given access to an oracle $O$ and then outputs a bit $b$. For $e \in \{1, 1/2\}$, we measure the ability of $\mathcal{D}$ to distinguish between permutations $P$ and $P'$ by

$$\mathsf{Adv}^{\mathsf{hide}}_{P,P',e}(\mathcal{D}) = \left(\Pr[\mathsf{G}^{\mathsf{hide}}_{P}(\mathcal{D})]\right)^{e} - \left(\Pr[\mathsf{G}^{\mathsf{hide}}_{P'}(\mathcal{D})]\right)^{e}.$$

The O2H theorem bounds this in terms of the game $\mathsf{G}^{\mathsf{ow}}$ shown in the same figure. There the distinguisher is run with access to oracle $P$. One of its oracle queries (chosen at random) is measured and the game returns `true` is the permutations $P$ and $P'$ would give different outputs on this input. We define

$$\mathsf{Adv}^{\mathsf{ow}}_{P,P'}(\mathcal{D}) = \Pr[\mathsf{G}^{\mathsf{ow}}_{P,P'}(\mathcal{D})].$$

**Theorem 1 (Fixed Permutation O2H,** [14]**).** *Let $P, P'$ be permutations, $\mathcal{D}$ be an distinguisher making at most $q$ oracle queries, and $e \in \{1, 1/2\}$. Then*

$$\left|\mathsf{Adv}^{\mathsf{hide}}_{P,P',e}(\mathcal{D})\right| \leq 2q\sqrt{\mathsf{Adv}^{\mathsf{ow}}_{P,P'}(\mathcal{D})}.$$

Note that the two permutations are a priori fixed. Assuming $P \neq P'$, there trivially exist distinguishers which can distinguish between the two permutations by simply querying them on an input where they differ. Thus, when making productive use of this theorem we will always be considering some restricted class of distinguishers. Generally, the distinguisher will internally be running both an adversary and a security game it is interacting with. The permutations will be used to process when the adversary makes an oracle query to its game, with the distinguisher's query to the permutation consisting both of query variables chosen by the attacker and internal state variables of the security game.

The original result of AHU considered distributions over oracles of the form $f[\oplus]$, rather than arbitrary permutations.[8] Let $\mathbf{D}$ be a distribution over $(f, f', \mathcal{D})$ where $f, f'$ are functions and $\mathcal{D}$ is a distinguisher (for comparison to AHU's original statements, think of it as a fixed distinguisher on input a random string $z$).[9] Then we define

$$\mathsf{Adv}_e^{\mathsf{hide}}(\mathbf{D}) = \left(\mathbb{E}\left[\Pr[\mathsf{G}_{f[\oplus]}^{\mathsf{hide}}(\mathcal{D})]\right]\right)^e - \left(\mathbb{E}\left[\Pr[\mathsf{G}_{f'[\oplus]}^{\mathsf{hide}}(\mathcal{D})]\right]\right)^e \quad \text{and}$$
$$\mathsf{Adv}^{\mathsf{ow}}(\mathbf{D}) = \mathbb{E}\left[\Pr[\mathsf{G}_{f[\oplus],f'[\oplus]}^{\mathsf{ow}}(\mathcal{D})]\right]$$

where the expectations are over $(f, f', \mathcal{D}) \leftarrow\!\!\$\ \mathbf{D}$.

We can capture the relevant parts of their theorem as follows.

**Theorem 2** **([3] , Thm. 3).** *Let* $\mathbf{D}$ *be a distribution as above where* $\mathcal{D}$ *makes at most* $q$ *oracle queries. Let* $e \in \{1, 1/2\}$. *Then*

$$\left|\mathsf{Adv}_e^{\mathsf{hide}}(\mathbf{D})\right| \leq 2q\sqrt{\mathsf{Adv}^{\mathsf{ow}}(\mathbf{D})}.$$

The following result notes that these are essentially equivalent.

**Proposition 1** *Theorem 1 and Theorem 2 directly imply each other (up to constant factors).*

*Proof* Let $\mathbf{D}$ be given. Then define the permutations

$$P(X, Y : f, f') = (X, f(X) \oplus Y : f, f')$$
$$P'(X, Y : f, f') = (X, f'(X) \oplus Y : f, f').$$

We views these as permutations applied to four inputs (three of which are output unmodified by the permutation). Then let $\mathcal{D}^*$ sample $(f, f', \mathcal{D}) \leftarrow \mathbf{D}$ and start running $\mathcal{D}$ internally. Whenever $\mathcal{D}$ makes an oracle query with registers $(X, Y)$, the distinguisher $\mathcal{D}^*$ will query its oracle with $(X, Y : f, f')$. When $\mathcal{D}$ halts and outputs $b$, $\mathcal{D}^*$ halts and outputs $b$ as well. It is clear that

$$\Pr[\mathsf{G}_P^{\mathsf{hide}}(\mathcal{D}^*)] = \mathbb{E}\left[\Pr[\mathsf{G}_{f[\oplus]}^{\mathsf{hide}}(\mathcal{D})]\right], \Pr[\mathsf{G}_{P'}^{\mathsf{hide}}(\mathcal{D}^*)] = \mathbb{E}\left[\Pr[\mathsf{G}_{f'[\oplus]}^{\mathsf{hide}}(\mathcal{D})]\right], \text{ and}$$
$$\Pr[\mathsf{G}_{P,P'}^{\mathsf{ow}}(\mathcal{D}^*)] = \mathbb{E}\left[\Pr[\mathsf{G}_{f[\oplus],f'[\oplus]}^{\mathsf{ow}}(\mathcal{D})]\right] \tag{1}$$

[8] It additionally gave a slightly better bound for distinguishers that can make multiple queries in parallel, but we omit this for simplicity.

[9] AHU's original statement had $\mathbf{D}$ pick a set $S$ satisfying $f'(x) = f(x)$ for all $x \notin S$ and defined $\mathsf{G}^{\mathsf{ow}}$ to check whether $x \in S$. Our formalism essentially fixes the special case $S = \{x : f'(x) \neq f(x)\}$. As this is the smallest possible choice of $S$, it only makes $\mathsf{G}^{\mathsf{ow}}$ harder and hence immediately implies the results for general $S$.

and $\mathcal{D}^*$ makes $q$ queries. Hence Theorem 1 implies Theorem 2.

Now let $P$, $P'$, and $\mathcal{D}^*$ be given where $\mathcal{D}^*$ makes $q$ oracle queries. Define $\mathbf{D}$ to be the distribution which always outputs $(P_\pm, P'_\pm, \mathcal{D})$ where $P_\pm(d, X) = P(X)$ if $d = 1$ and $P^{-1}(X)$ if $d = 0$. Permutation $P'_\pm$ is defined likewise. Distinguisher $\mathcal{D}$ runs $\mathcal{D}^*$ internally. Whenever $\mathcal{D}^*$ makes an oracle query to its oracle with register $X$, $\mathcal{D}$ prepares a register $Y = 0^{|X|}$, queries $O[\oplus](1, X, Y)$ and $O[\oplus](0, Y, X)$ then swaps $X$ and $Y$ before returning $X$ to $\mathcal{D}^*$. If the permutation underlying $O$ was $F$ and $(X, Y)$ initially contained $(x, 0^{|x|})$, then the two oracle queries result in them containing $(0^{|x|}, F(x))$, and so the final swap result is $(F(x), 0^{|x|})$. Because the second register began an ended as containing all 0's, this is indistinguishable from an oracle that just applied $F$ to $X$ from $\mathcal{D}$'s perspective. When $\mathcal{D}^*$ halts and outputs $b$, $\mathcal{D}$ halts and outputs $b$ as well.

It is clear that the equalities in Eq. 1 hold again, but now $\mathcal{D}$ makes $2q$ oracle queries. Hence Theorem 2 implies Theorem 1 up to an additional multiplicative factor of 2 being added to the latter theorem's bound. □

As claimed by Jaeger, Song, and Tessaro [14], a direct emulation of the original proof for Theorem 2 in [3] gives the constant claimed in Theorem 1.

## 3 Pan-Zeng Adaptive Reprogramming Framework

In this section we prove that (a version of) the Pan-Zeng framework for computational adaptive reprogramming [20] is directly implied by the Fixed Permutation O2H (Theorem 1). We start by recalling their framework in Sect. 3.1. In Sect. 3.2, we state and prove our variant of the framework. The bounds provided by the results are complex and hard to compare. In Sect. 3.3 we apply the same simplifications that Pan and Zeng use when applying their result in theorems and show that our theorem provides better concrete bounds in this case.

### 3.1 Pan-Zeng Framework and Security Theorem

In the Pan-Zeng framework for computational adaptive reprogramming we consider multi-stage adversary $\mathcal{A} = (\mathcal{A}_0, \ldots, \mathcal{A}_n)$ trying to distinguish a non-adaptive world from an adaptive world. This world is parameterized by an environment $\mathcal{E}$ which specifies $\mathsf{Init}$, $\mathsf{Orac}$, and $\mathsf{Repro}$. The interactions are defined by the game $\mathsf{G}^{\mathsf{pz\text{-}hide}}$ defined in Fig. 4.

First $\mathsf{Init}$ samples parameter string $s$ (later given to $\mathsf{Orac}$ and $\mathsf{Repro}$ to make them act in a coordinated manner), an initial input $x$ for $\mathcal{A}$, and two functions $H_0$ and $H_1$. In the nonadaptive world ($b = 0$) each stage of $\mathcal{A}$ is given oracle access to $H_0[\oplus]$, produces outputs $y$, and is given inputs $x$ from $\mathsf{Orac}$. In the adaptive world ($b = 1$) it is instead given access to $H_1[\oplus]$ and this function $H_1$ is adaptively updated by $\mathsf{Repro}$ in between each stage of $\mathcal{A}$ based on an auxiliary string passed to it by $\mathsf{Orac}$. In particular, $\mathcal{A}$ passing $y$ to $\mathsf{Orac}$ represents $\mathcal{A}$ having some sort of influence over how $H_1$ will be reprogrammed and $\mathsf{Orac}$ passing $x$ back represents some sort of leakage that $\mathcal{A}$ learns about how its influence work.

| Game $\mathsf{G}^{\text{pz-hide}}_{\mathcal{E},b}(\mathcal{A})$ | Game $\mathsf{G}^{\text{pz-ow}}_{\mathcal{E},i}(\mathcal{A})$ |
|---|---|
| $(\mathsf{Init}, \mathsf{Orac}, \mathsf{Repro}) \leftarrow \mathcal{E}$ | $t \leftarrow_{\$} \{1, \ldots, q_i\}$ |
| $(s, x, H_0, H_1) \leftarrow_{\$} \mathsf{Init}$ | Run $\mathsf{G}^{\text{pz-hide}}_{\mathcal{E},1}$ until $\mathcal{A}_i$ is initiated |
| $y \leftarrow_{\$} \mathcal{A}_0[H_b[\oplus]](x)$ | Run $\mathcal{A}_i[H_1[\oplus]](x)$ until its $t$-th query |
| For $i = 1, \ldots, n$ do | Measure the input $X$ to this query |
| $\quad(x, a) \leftarrow_{\$} \mathsf{Orac}(s, y)$ | Return $(H_0(X) \neq H_1(X))$ |
| $\quad H_1 \leftarrow \mathsf{Repro}(s, a, H_1)$ | |
| $\quad y \leftarrow_{\$} \mathcal{A}_i[H_b[\oplus]](x)$ | |
| Return $y = 1$ | |

**Fig. 4.** Games used for the Pan-Zeng computational adaptive reprogramming framework. Different stages of $\mathcal{A}$ implicitly share state.

The auxiliary information $a$ passed from Orac to Repro contains "instructions" on specifically how Repro should reprogram $H_1$. The concrete details of how Init, Orac, and Repro will depend specifically on what the Pan-Zeng framework is being used to analyze. However, we are analyzing the framework as a whole and so can be agnostic to the specifics of what they do.

Note that the only quantum behavior of this game is internal computation by $\mathcal{A}$ and its superposition queries to its $H_b[\oplus]$ oracle. For $e \in \{1, 1/2\}$, we define $\mathsf{Adv}^{\text{pz-hide}}_{\mathcal{E},e}(\mathcal{A}) = \left(\Pr[\mathsf{G}^{\text{pz-hide}}_{\mathcal{E},1}(\mathcal{A})]\right)^e - \left(\Pr[\mathsf{G}^{\text{pz-hide}}_{\mathcal{E},0}(\mathcal{A})]\right)^e$.

The Pan-Zeng framework (similar to O2H results) bounds the distinguishing advantage of $\mathcal{A}$ in relation to an experiment where one of $\mathcal{A}$'s queries are measured at random and we see if that query differentiates the two oracles. Let $i \in \{0, \ldots, n\}$ and define $q_i$ to be the number of oracle queries that $\mathcal{A}_i$ makes. This is captured by the game $\mathsf{G}^{\text{pz-ow}}$ which is parameterized by $\mathcal{E}$ and the choice of $i$. In it, we run $\mathcal{A}$ in the adaptive world until stage $i$. A random one of its queries in that stage are measured to see if $H_0$ and $H_1$ differ on that input. We define $\mathsf{Adv}^{\text{pz-ow}}_{\mathcal{E},i}(\mathcal{A}) = \Pr[\mathsf{G}^{\text{pz-ow}}_{\mathcal{E},i}(\mathcal{A})]$.

Pan and Zeng proved the following (Lemma 2 in the proceedings version or Lemma 3.1 in the current ePrint version).

**Theorem 3 (Pan-Zeng Adaptive Reprogramming, [20]).** *Let $\mathcal{E}$ be an environment and $\mathcal{A} = (\mathcal{A}_0, \ldots, \mathcal{A}_n)$ be an adversary for which $\mathcal{A}_i$ makes at most $q_i$ oracle queries. Then*

$$\left|\mathsf{Adv}^{\text{pz-hide}}_{\mathcal{E},1}(\mathcal{A})\right| \leq \sum_{k=0}^{n} \sum_{i=0}^{k} 2q_i \sqrt{\mathsf{Adv}^{\text{pz-ow}}_{\mathcal{E},i}(\mathcal{A})}.$$

### 3.2 The Pan-Zeng Theorem Is Implied by O2H

Now we state and prove a variant of Theorem 3 which follows from the Fixed Permutation O2H (Theorem 1).

**Theorem 4.** *Let $\mathcal{E}$ be an environment and $\mathcal{A} = (\mathcal{A}_0, \ldots, \mathcal{A}_n)$ be an adversary for which $\mathcal{A}_i$ makes at most $q_i \geq 1$ oracle queries. Let $q = q_0 + \cdots + q_n$. Then*

$$\left|\mathsf{Adv}^{\mathsf{pz\text{-}hide}}_{\mathcal{E},e}(\mathcal{A})\right| \leq 2q\sqrt{\sum_{i=0}^{n} \frac{q_i}{q} \mathsf{Adv}^{\mathsf{pz\text{-}ow}}_{\mathcal{E},i}(\mathcal{A})}$$

*for $e \in \{1, 1/2\}$.*

*Proof.* To apply the Fixed Permutation O2H (Theorem 1) we will define appropriate $P$, $P'$, and $\mathcal{D}$ from $\mathcal{E}$ and $\mathcal{A}$. We define the permutations as follows.

$$P(X, Y : H_0, H_1) = (X, Y \oplus H_1(X) : H_0, H_1)$$
$$P'(X, Y : H_0, H_1) = (X, Y \oplus H_0(X) : H_0, H_1)$$

We views these as permutations with four inputs (three of which are returned unchanged). Note that $P(X, Y : H_0, H_1) \neq P'(X, Y : H_0, H_1)$ if and only if $H_1(X) \neq H_0(X)$.

Now our distinguisher **D** for $P$ and $P'$ will simply run $\mathsf{G}^{\mathsf{pz\text{-}hide}}_{\mathcal{E},b}(\mathcal{A})$ (that is, internally running both $\mathcal{A}$ and the algorithms of $\mathcal{E}$) except whenever $\mathcal{A}$ would query $(X, Y)$ to $H_b[\oplus]$ it will query $(X, Y : H_0, H_1)$ to its own oracle then return the resulting $(X, Y)$ to $\mathcal{A}$. When $\mathcal{A}$ produces its final output $y$, $\mathcal{D}$ halts and outputs that as well. Formal pseudocode for $\mathcal{D}$ is given in Fig. 5.

By Theorem 1 we get $\left|\mathsf{Adv}^{\mathsf{hide}}_{P,P',e}(\mathcal{D})\right| \leq 2q\sqrt{\mathsf{Adv}^{\mathsf{ow}}_{P,P'}(\mathcal{D})}$. Note that $\mathcal{D}$ perfectly simulated the view of $\mathcal{A}$. This holds because $\mathcal{D}$'s oracle $O$ on input $(X, Y : H_0, H_1)$ returns $(X, Y \oplus H_b(X) : H_0, H_1)$ and hence $\mathcal{D}$ returns $(X, Y \oplus H_b(X))$ to $\mathcal{A}$. Note that $\mathcal{A}$ expects access to $H_b[\oplus]$ which provides the identical behavior of mapping $(x, Y)$ to $(X, Y \oplus H_b(X))$. Hence $\mathsf{Adv}^{\mathsf{hide}}_{P,P',e}(\mathcal{D}) = \mathsf{Adv}^{\mathsf{pz\text{-}hide}}_{\mathcal{E},e}(\mathcal{A})$.

It remains to compute $\mathsf{Adv}^{\mathsf{ow}}_{P,P'}(\mathcal{D})$. Let $I$ denote a random variable taking the value of $i$ sampled inside of $\mathsf{G}^{\mathsf{ow}}_{P,P'}(\mathcal{D})$. Define $Q_0 = 1$, recursively define $Q_{j+1} = Q_j + q_j + 1$, and define the intervals $R_j = \{Q_j, \ldots, Q_{j+1} - 1\}$. Note that if $I \in R_j$, then $\mathcal{D}$ was halted when $\mathcal{A}_j$ made its $I - Q_j + 1$-th query. Then,

$$\begin{aligned}\mathsf{Adv}^{\mathsf{ow}}_{P,P'}(\mathcal{D}) = \Pr[\mathsf{G}^{\mathsf{ow}}_{P,P'}(\mathcal{D})] &= \sum_{j=0}^{n} \Pr[I \in R_j] \Pr[\mathsf{G}^{\mathsf{ow}}_{P,P'}(\mathcal{D}) | I \in R_j] \\ &= \sum_{j=0}^{n} (q_j/q) \cdot \mathsf{Adv}^{\mathsf{pz\text{-}ow}}_{\mathcal{E},j}(\mathcal{A}).\end{aligned}$$

This completes the proof. □

| Distinguisher $\mathcal{D}[O_{\Leftrightarrow}]$ | Oracle $S(X,Y)$ |
|---|---|
| $(\mathsf{Init},\mathsf{Orac},\mathsf{Repro}) \leftarrow \mathcal{E}$ | Call $O_{\Leftrightarrow}$ with input $(X,Y:H_0,H_1)$ |
| $(s,x,H_0,H_1) \leftarrow\$ \mathsf{Init}$ | Return $(X,Y)$ to $\mathcal{A}_i$ |
| $y \leftarrow\$ \mathcal{A}_0[S](x)$ | |
| For $i=1,\ldots,n$ do | |
| $(x,a) \leftarrow\$ \mathsf{Orac}(s,y)$ | |
| $H_1 \leftarrow \mathsf{Repro}(s,a,H_1)$ | |
| $y \leftarrow\$ \mathcal{A}_i[S](x)$ | |
| Return $y$ | |

**Fig. 5.** Distinguisher used in proof of Theorem 4.

### 3.3 Comparing the Pan-Zeng and O2H-Based Theorems

By depending on $q_j$ and $\mathsf{Adv}^{\mathsf{pz\text{-}ow}}_{\mathcal{E},i}(\mathcal{A})$, the bounds in Theorem 3 and Theorem 4 can be hard to parse. When applying Theorem 3 in proofs, Pan and Zeng simplified as follows. Let $\varepsilon = \max_i \mathsf{Adv}^{\mathsf{pz\text{-}ow}}_{\mathcal{E},i}(\mathcal{A})$ and note $q_i \le q$. Then,

$$\sum_{k=0}^{n}\sum_{i=0}^{k} 2q_i\sqrt{\mathsf{Adv}^{\mathsf{pz\text{-}ow}}_{\mathcal{E},i}(\mathcal{A})} \le \sum_{k=0}^{n}\sum_{i=0}^{k} 2q\sqrt{\varepsilon} \le 2(n+1)^2 q\sqrt{\varepsilon}.$$

We can do a little better by noting $q = \sum_{i=0}^{n} q_i$ and calculating,

$$\sum_{k=0}^{n}\sum_{i=0}^{k} 2q_i\sqrt{\mathsf{Adv}^{\mathsf{pz\text{-}ow}}_{\mathcal{E},i}(\mathcal{A})} \le \sum_{k=0}^{n}\sum_{i=0}^{n} 2q_i\sqrt{\varepsilon} = 2(n+1)q\sqrt{\varepsilon}.$$

Performing similar simplifications to the bound from Theorem 4 we get the improved result that

$$2q\sqrt{\sum_{i=0}^{n}\frac{q_i}{q}\mathsf{Adv}^{\mathsf{pz\text{-}ow}}_{\mathcal{E},i}(\mathcal{A})} \le 2q\sqrt{\sum_{i=0}^{n}\frac{q_i}{q}\varepsilon} \le 2q\sqrt{\varepsilon}.$$

This analysis implicitly shows that $\mathsf{Adv}^{\mathsf{ow}}_{P,P'}(\mathcal{D}) \le \varepsilon$ for the $\mathcal{D}$ defined in our proof. We might as well then have stuck with the bound $\left|\mathsf{Adv}^{\mathsf{pz\text{-}hide}}_{\mathcal{E},e}(\mathcal{A})\right| \le 2q\sqrt{\mathsf{Adv}^{\mathsf{ow}}_{P,P'}(\mathcal{D})}$ in the theorem where the latter term could have been expressed in terms of measuring one of $\mathcal{A}$'s $q$ queries chosen uniformly at random. Our result is for $e \in \{1, 1/2\}$ where that of Pan and Zeng only applied for $e = 1$.

## 4 GHHM Adaptive Reprogramming Framework

In this section we prove that (a version of) the Grilo, Hövelmanns, Hülsing, Majenz (GHHM) framework for tight adaptive reprogramming [12] is implied by Fixed Permutation O2H (Theorem 1). We start by recalling their setting in Sect. 4.1. We discuss why their security result seems not to imply or be implied by that of Pan and Zeng [20]. In Sect. 4.2, we state and prove our variant of the framework. The bounds provided by the results are complex and hard to compare directly. In Sect. 4.3 we apply the same simplifications that GHHM use when applying their result in theorems and show that our theorem provides essentially the same concrete bounds in this case.

### 4.1 GHHM Framework and Security Theorem

The GHHM framework for tight adaptive program can syntactically be captured by the $\mathsf{G}^{\mathsf{pz\text{-}hide}}$ game from Fig. 4. Let $(\mathsf{Init}, \mathsf{Orac}, \mathsf{Repro}) = \mathcal{E}$ be an environment as follows.

- $\mathsf{Init}$ outputs $(s, x, H_0, H_1)$ where $H_0$ and $H_1$ are two copies of the same truly random functions from $\mathcal{X}$ to $\mathcal{Y}$. We will assume without loss of generality that $\mathcal{X} = \{0,1\}^l$ and $\mathcal{Y} = \{0,1\}^m$. Outputs $s$ and $x$ are empty strings.
- $\mathsf{Orac}$ interprets its input $y$ as specifying a probability distribution $p$ over $\mathcal{X}$ and samples $x \leftarrow\!\!\$\; p$ and $y \leftarrow\!\!\$\; \mathcal{Y}$, then outputs $(x, a) = (x, (x, y))$.[10]
- $\mathsf{Repro}$ given $a = (x, y)$ and $H_1$ outputs a function defined identically to $H_1$ except it maps $x$ to $y$.

Call such an environment a "GHHM environment". Then GHHM proved the following information theoretic result (their Theorem 1).

**Theorem 5. (GHHM Adaptive Reprogramming, [12]).** *Let $\mathcal{E}$ be a GHHM environment and $\mathcal{A} = (\mathcal{A}_0, \ldots, \mathcal{A}_n)$ be an adversary for which $\mathcal{A}_i$ makes at most $q_i$ oracle queries. Then*

$$\left|\mathsf{Adv}^{\mathsf{pz\text{-}hide}}_{\mathcal{E},1}(\mathcal{A})\right| \le \sum_{i=1}^{n} \left(\sqrt{\hat{q}_i p_{i,\max}} + 0.5 \hat{q}_i p_{i,\max}\right).$$

*Here $\hat{q}_i = q_0 + \cdots + q_{i-1}$ and $p_{i,\max} = \mathbb{E}[\max_{x \in \mathcal{X}} p_i(x)]$ where the expectation is over the behavior of the game up until the i-th oracle query and $p_i$ is a random variable denoting the probability distribution chosen by $\mathcal{A}_i$.*

Even though we expressed this result using the same game from the Pan and Zeng framework, it's not clear that Theorem 3 or Theorem 5 implies the other. The GHHM result seems weaker because it requires reprogrammed points to be information-theoretically (rather than computationally) hidden and requires the initial functions and reprogrammed output to be uniform. On the other hand, the Pan and Zeng result gives a bound in terms of the probability that $\mathcal{A}$ finds a point where $H_1$ differs from $H_0$. To get a meaningful bound we need this

[10] The most general version of GHHM's framework has $p$ output a second "side-information" string $x'$. They already showed (Appendix A in the current ePrint version) that the weaker version we use implies this stronger version with side information.

probability to be small, so the reprogrammed point must be hard to predict even after the reprogramming occurred. GHHM (by Orac giving $x$ to $\mathcal{A}$) is explicitly not such a setting. It instead works for cases where the reprogrammed point is hard to predict ahead of time. Pan and Zeng stated that their result "generalizes and improves" the GHHM result. We notified them that this does not seem to be the case, and they acknowledged that their current result does not capture that of GHHM.

Notably Pan and Zeng are able to apply their result to analyze the selective-opening security of an encryption scheme, a result that a priori would seem like guessing the reprogrammed point should be easy afterwards. They achieve this by choosing an order of programming that differs from what one's first instinct would use. In essence, the "trick" they use is that in the settings they consider, they can predict ahead of time a small set $S$ such that only points in $S$ will ever be programmed. Then they arrange ahead of time for the initial functions $H_0$ and $H_1$ to be different on all of these points and for later reprogramming to switch the functions to being consistent on the reprogrammed point. It does not seem possible in general to capture the GHHM setting in this manner.

### 4.2 The GHHM Theorem Is Implied by O2H

Now we state and prove a variant of Theorem 3 which follows from the O2H result Theorem 1.

**Theorem 6.** *Let $\mathcal{E}$ be a GHHM environment and $\mathcal{A} = (\mathcal{A}_0, \dots, \mathcal{A}_n)$ be an adversary for which $\mathcal{A}_i$ makes at most $q_i$ oracle queries. Let $q = q_0 + \cdots + q_n$. Define $\hat{q}_i$ and $p_{i,\max}$ as in Theorem 5. Let $e \in \{1, 1/2\}$. Then*

$$\left|\mathsf{Adv}^{\mathsf{pz\text{-}hide}}_{\mathcal{E},e}(\mathcal{A})\right| \le 2n\sqrt{\sum_{i=1}^{n} \hat{q}_i p_{i,\max}/n}.$$

There are two challenges that make it surprising this theorem can be proven from the Fixed-Permutation O2H theorem. The first is that all of the dependence on $q$ is inside the square root, whereas O2H gives us a bound with $q$ outside of the square root. Secondly, (and similarly to our comparison with Pan and Zeng's theorem) after a reprogramming the adversary is told the point $x$ at which the oracle was redefined. Consequently, we can only hope to rely on the hardness of querying the oracle on input $x$ before it was reprogrammed. But because the distribution for choosing $x$ is not fixed ahead of time, if we tried to naively apply O2H it's not clear how to make the permutations differ on this unknown $x$ ahead of time.

The same insights tackle both of these challenges. Rather than thinking of the "bad event" happening during queries to $H$, we are going to think of the reprogramming process as being performed inside an oracle and the "bad event" is querying that oracle on inputs that make it reprogram $H$ on places where it has "already been queried". Note that "already been queried" is not a well defined notion because the adversary could have queried all of $H$ in superposition. To formalize this idea, we use the techniques of Zhandry [32] to represent the quantum accessible random oracle $H$ as a "sparse" table which is only non-zero on a few entries that "have been queried" by the attacker. (More precisely, it will be a superposition over such tables.) Then reprogramming at point $x$ can be viewed as a fixed permutation which swaps $H(x)$ with an auxiliary all-zero register. We can apply the Fixed Permutation O2H to compare that reprogramming permutation and a permutation which leaves $H$ untouched. Because the other register is all-zero, the permutations will only differ on inputs where the random $x$ happens to equal one of the few non-zero entries of $H$.

In Sect. 6, we recall more recent variants of this result for reprogramming of random permutations [1,2]. Because no permutation analog for Zhandry's result is known, we are unable to show they follow from Fixed-Permutation O2H.

*Proof.* Our first step will be moving to a setting where queries to the hash and requests for reprogramming are both quantum queries to oracles. Consider the game $\mathsf{G}_0^b$ for $b \in \{0, 1\}$ defined in Fig. 6 which we will use to emulate the execution of $\mathsf{G}_{\mathcal{E},b}^{\mathsf{pz\text{-}hide}}(\mathcal{A})$ for the given $\mathcal{A}$ and $\mathcal{E}$. The behavior of $\mathcal{E}$ is embedded into the oracles. The game stores ahead of time the list of random outputs $Z$ that will be programmed into new locations of the hash function and random strings $R$ that will seed sampling the programmed point from the distributions chosen by the attacker. It uses the following quantum registers.

- $W$: The local work space of $\mathcal{A}$. Its final output guess is obtained by measuring $W[1]$.
- $X, Y$: The registers intended for $\mathcal{A}$ to provide input and receive output, respectively, from its oracles.
- $H$: The register storing the table specifying the random oracle.
- $R$: The registers storing randomness used to seed the choice of $x$'s according to distributions $p$.
- $Z$: The registers storing random strings to be programmed into $H$.
- $I$: The register storing a counter tracking how many reprogramming queries have occurred. It determines which entries of $R$ and $Z$ are used.

We think of $\mathcal{B}$ having direct access to the registers $W, X, Y$. All other registers are controlled exclusively by the game and may not directly be modified by $\mathcal{B}$. Note that both oracles of the game are defined by classical permutations.

Given $\mathcal{A} = (\mathcal{A}_0, \ldots, \mathcal{A}_n)$ we can map it to an algorithm $\mathcal{B}$ playing $\mathsf{G}_0^b$ as follows. It initially runs on $\mathcal{A}_0$ on input $\varepsilon$. Whenever it queries $X, Y$ to its hash oracle, $\mathcal{B}$ forwards this to its RO oracle. When $\mathcal{A}_i$ would end a stage, outputting probability distributions $p$, $\mathcal{B}$ puts the representation of this into $X$ and prepares $Y$ on in the all-zero state. It makes a $\text{REP}_b$ query and returns the result to the next phase of $\mathcal{A}$. When $\mathcal{A}_n$ halts with output $y$, $\mathcal{B}$ stores that in $W[1]$ and halts.

When $b = 1$, each reprogram oracle query programs a fresh random output (from $Z$) into the location of $H$ chosen according to $p$. When $b = 0$, nothing is ever programmed into $H$. These match the behaviors of $H_1$ and $H_0$ in $\mathsf{G}^{\mathsf{pz\text{-}hide}}$ so $\mathcal{B}$ perfectly simulates the view of $\mathcal{A}$, giving $\mathsf{Adv}_{\mathcal{E},e}^{\mathsf{pz\text{-}hide}}(\mathcal{A}) = (\Pr[\mathsf{G}_0^1(\mathcal{B})])^e - (\Pr[\mathsf{G}_0^0(\mathcal{B})])^e$.

| | |
|---|---|
| Games $\mathsf{G}_0^b(\mathcal{B})$ | $\text{Ro}(X, Y : H)$ |
| $\mathbf{H} \leftarrow_\$ \mathsf{Fcs}(l, m)$ | $Y \leftarrow Y \oplus H[X]$ |
| $\mathbf{Z} \leftarrow_\$ \mathsf{Fcs}(\lceil \lg q \rceil, m)$ | Return $(X, Y : H)$ |
| $\mathbf{R} \leftarrow_\$ \mathsf{Fcs}(\lceil \lg q \rceil, \infty)$ | $\text{FRo}(X, Y : H)$ |
| $\lvert H, Z, R\rangle \leftarrow \lvert \mathbf{H}, \mathbf{Z}, \mathbf{R}\rangle$ | $H[X] \leftarrow H[X] \oplus Y$ |
| Run $\mathcal{B}[\text{Ro}, \text{Rep}_b]$ | Return $(X, Y : H)$ |
| Measure $W[1]$ | $\text{Rep}_b(X, Y : H, I, Z, R)$ |
| Return $W[1] = 1$ | Interpret $X$ as prob. dist. $p$ |
| Games $\mathsf{G}_1^b(\mathcal{B})$ | $x \leftarrow p(R[I])$ |
| $\mathbf{R} \leftarrow_\$ \mathsf{Fcs}(\lceil \lg q \rceil, \infty)$ | If $b = 1$ then |
| $\lvert R\rangle \leftarrow \lvert \mathbf{R}\rangle$ | $(H[x], Z[I]) \leftarrow (Z[I], H[x])$ |
| Run $\mathcal{B}[\mathcal{H}^Y \circ \text{FRo} \circ \mathcal{H}^Y, \text{Rep}_b]$ | $Y \leftarrow Y \oplus x$ |
| Measure $W[1]$ | $I \leftarrow I + 1 \bmod 2^{\lceil \lg q \rceil}$ |
| Return $W[1] = 1$ | Return $(X, Y : H, I, Z, R)$ |

**Fig. 6.** Games used in the analysis of Theorem 6. Registers not explicitly initialized are initialized to all 0.

Next we will transition to the games $\mathsf{G}_1^b$. In these games, rather than being sampled at random, the registers $H$ and $Z$ are initialized to zeros. The oracle Ro which writes $H[X]$ into $Y$ has instead been replaced with $\mathcal{H}^Y \circ \text{FRo} \circ \mathcal{H}^Y$ here $\mathcal{H}^Y$ is the Hadamard transform applied to register $Y$ and FRo is the Fourier version of Ro where instead $Y$ is written into $H[X]$.

By the sparse QROM representation technique of Zhandry, these games are completely identical so $\mathsf{Adv}^{\mathsf{pz\text{-}hide}}_{\mathcal{E},e}(\mathcal{A}) = (\Pr[\mathsf{G}_1^1(\mathcal{B})])^e - (\Pr[\mathsf{G}_1^0(\mathcal{B})])^e$ and the view of $\mathcal{A}$ inside of $\mathcal{B}$ is unchanged. In Appendix A we break this claim into smaller atomic steps for those unfamiliar with the technique.

Now we can compare the behavior of the permutations $\text{Rep}_1$ and $\text{Rep}_0$. They only differ in whether $H[x]$ and $Z[I]$ are swapped ($b = 1$) or not ($b = 0$). Thus $\text{Rep}_1$ and $\text{Rep}_0$ will only differ on inputs for which $H[x] \neq Z[I]$.

We bound the difference between the $b = 1$ and $b = 0$ worlds of the game using the Fixed Permutation O2H (Theorem 1). Let $P = \text{Rep}_0$, $P' = \text{Rep}_1$, and $\mathcal{D}$ be the distinguisher that runs all of $\mathsf{G}_1^b$ internally, except it calls its oracle on $(X, Y : H, I, Z, R)$ whenever $\mathcal{B}$ calls its reprogramming oracle on $X, Y$. Note that it makes $n$ oracle queries. We have that $\mathsf{Adv}^{\mathsf{pz\text{-}hide}}_{\mathcal{E},e}(\mathcal{A}) = \mathsf{Adv}^{\mathsf{hide}}_{P,P',e}(\mathcal{D})$.

We complete the proof by analyzing $\mathsf{Adv}^{\mathsf{ow}}_{P,P'}(\mathcal{D})$.[11] Consider a fixed choice of $i \in \{1, \ldots, n\}$ in $\mathsf{G}^{\mathsf{ow}}_{P,P'}(\mathcal{D})$. The permutations differ on the measured input iff $H[x] \neq Z[i-1]$ (because $I$ will have value $i$). By construction of the game $Z[i-1]$ is necessarily all zeros so this is equivalent to asking whether $H[x]$ is zero. Note that $H$ is independent of $R[i-1]$ so we can think of $H$ being measured first, then $R[i-1]$ being measured and so $x = p(R[i-1])$ looks like a fresh sample from $p$. At this point, $\mathcal{B}$ inside of $\mathcal{D}$ has made at most $\hat{q}_i$ queries to FRo so $H$

[11] Leaving the bound in terms of $\mathsf{Adv}^{\mathsf{ow}}_{P,P'}(\mathcal{D})$ would make it applicable to settings where the reprogrammed points are only computationally hard to predict.

is a superposition of tables each of which has at most $\hat{q}_i$ non-zero entries. The result of measuring $H$ will consequently be such a table. The we obtain a fresh sample from $p$ and so the probability of a non-zero entry being hit can be bound by $\hat{q}_i \cdot p_{i,\max}$ via a union bound over the non-zero entries of the measured value of $H$.

Thus, averaging over the possible choice of $i$ we have

$$\mathsf{Adv}^{\mathsf{ow}}_{P,P'}(\mathcal{D}) = \sum_{i=1}^{n} \mathsf{Pr}[i]\mathsf{Pr}[\mathsf{G}^{\mathsf{ow}}_{P,P'}(\mathcal{D})|i] \leq \sum_{i=1}^{n}(1/n)\hat{q}_i \cdot p_{i,\max}.$$

Applying Theorem 1 gives the claimed bound □

### 4.3 Comparing the GHHM and O2H-Based Theorems

By depending on $\hat{q}_j$ and $p_{i,\max}$, the bounds in Theorem 5 and Theorem 6 can be hard to parse. Consequently, when applying Theorem 5 in proofs, GHMM simplified as follows (e.g., from their proposition 2). Let $p_{\max} = \max_i p_{i,\max}$. Note that $\hat{q}_i \leq q$, and $qp_{\max} \leq \sqrt{qp_{\max}}$. Then,

$$\sum_{i=1}^{n}\left(\sqrt{\hat{q}_i p_{i,\max}} + 0.5\hat{q}_i p_{i,\max}\right) \leq \sum_{i=1}^{n} 1.5\sqrt{qp_{\max}} = 1.5n\sqrt{qp_{\max}}.$$

Performing analogous simplifications from the bound in Theorem 6 gives

$$2n\sqrt{\sum_{i=1}^{n} \hat{q}_i p_{i,\max}/n} \leq 2n\sqrt{\sum_{i=1}^{n} qp_{\max}/n} = 2n\sqrt{qp_{\max}}.$$

Our result is for $e \in \{1, 1/2\}$ where that of GHHM only applied for $e = 1$.

## 5 Unruh's Adaptive O2H

In this section, we show that Unruh's Adaptive O2H's results [24,25] (which generalize an earlier result Unruh [26]) are implied by the Fixed Permutation O2H (Theorem 1). To proving the stronger version [25] we emulate the ideas from our proof in Sect. 4.

### 5.1 First Adaptive O2H

The first adaptive O2H result we analyze bounds how well an adversary can distinguish between $H(x, m)$ and a random string where the attacker chooses $m$ and $x$ is uniformly random. This is defined by the games shown in Fig. 7 for which we define

$$\mathsf{Adv}^{\mathsf{un\text{-}hide}}_{e}(\mathcal{A}) = \left(\mathsf{Pr}[\mathsf{G}^{\mathsf{un\text{-}hide}}_{1}(\mathcal{A})]\right)^{e} - \left(\mathsf{Pr}[\mathsf{G}^{\mathsf{un\text{-}hide}}_{0}(\mathcal{A})]\right)^{e}.$$

| Game $\mathsf{G}^{\mathsf{un\text{-}hide}}_b(\mathcal{A})$ | Game $\mathsf{G}^{\mathsf{un\text{-}ow}}(\mathcal{A})$ |
|---|---|
| $H \leftarrow\!\!\$\ \mathsf{Fcs}(l+k,n)$ | $i \leftarrow\!\!\$\ \{1,\ldots,q_1\}$ |
| $m \leftarrow\!\!\$\ \mathcal{A}_0[H[\oplus]]$ | $H \leftarrow\!\!\$\ \mathsf{Fcs}(l+k,n)$ |
| $x \leftarrow\!\!\$\ \{0,1\}^l$ | $m \leftarrow\!\!\$\ \mathcal{A}_0[H[\oplus]]$ |
| $B_0 \leftarrow H(x,m)$ | $x \leftarrow\!\!\$\ \{0,1\}^l$ |
| $B_1 \leftarrow\!\!\$\ \{0,1\}^n$ | $B_1 \leftarrow\!\!\$\ \{0,1\}^n$ |
| $b' \leftarrow\!\!\$\ \mathcal{A}_1[H[\oplus]](x,B_b)$ | Run $\mathcal{A}_1[H[\oplus]](x,B_1)$ until its $i$-th query |
| Return $b'=1$ | Measure the input $(x',m')$ to this query |
| | Return $(x,m)=(x',m')$ |

**Fig. 7.** Games used for Unruh's adaptive O2H [24]. Different stages of $\mathcal{A}$ implicitly share state.

The bound will consist of two terms. Intuitively, the first information theoretically bounds the how much $\mathcal{A}_0$ can contribute the advantage because $x$ is independent of its view. The second terms bounds in terms of how likely $\mathcal{A}_1$ is to query $(x,m)$ to its oracle, captured formally by $\mathsf{Adv}^{\mathsf{un\text{-}ow}}(\mathcal{A}) = \Pr[\mathsf{G}^{\mathsf{un\text{-}ow}}(\mathcal{A})]$.

Of these advantages, Unruh proves the following relationship (Lemma 14 in the current ePrint version).

**Theorem 7. (Unruh Adaptive O2H,** [24]**).** *Let $\mathcal{A}=(\mathcal{A}_0,\mathcal{A}_1)$ be an adversary for which $\mathcal{A}_i$ makes at most $q_i$ oracle queries. Then*

$$\left|\mathsf{Adv}^{\mathsf{un\text{-}hide}}_1(\mathcal{A})\right| \le q_0 2^{-l/2+2} + 2q_1\sqrt{\mathsf{Adv}^{\mathsf{un\text{-}ow}}(\mathcal{A})}.$$

We prove this result for $\mathsf{Adv}^{\mathsf{un\text{-}hide}}_e(\mathcal{A})$ with $e \in \{1, 1/2\}$ from the Fixed Permutation O2H (Theorem 1). Starting from the real world, the proof will first use O2H to program $\mathcal{A}_0$'s oracle to be different on *all* inputs starting with $x$. Then $H(x,m)$ will only ever be used to as input to $\mathcal{A}_1$ and in response to its oracle queries. We switch both uses to use $B_1$ instead, which is equivalent. Then we apply O2H again to switch $\mathcal{A}_1$'s oracle back to using $H(x,m)$.

In Sect. 5.2 our proof of Unruh's second result will actually imply this theorem with a better concrete bound, replacing $q_0 2^{-l/2+2}$ with $\sqrt{q_0}2^{-l/2+1}$. We find it pedagogically useful to start with this proof first. Our proof of Unruh's second result will apply the ideas we used for proving GHHM's result in Sect. 4—in particular, using a sparse representation of the random oracle so that we can check for whether $\mathcal{A}_0$ "queried" $x$ only after it has stopped executing.

AHU [3] used their O2H theorem to prove post-quantum security of a Fujisaki-Okamoto variant—a result previously proven by using Unruh's adaptive O2H result [23].[12] While discussing the differences AHU say,

> While our O2H Theorem is not adaptive (in the sense that the input where the oracle is reprogrammed has to be fixed at the beginning of the game),

[12] In fact, both the proofs had flaws (see the ePrint version of [3]). This is orthogonal to our discussion here.

| Hybrids $\mathsf{H}_{(a,b,c)}$ | $\mathrm{Ro}_a^0(X, M, Y : H, h, x)$ |
|---|---|
| $H \leftarrow\!\!\$\ \mathsf{Fcs}(l+k, n)$ | If $X = x$ then |
| $h \leftarrow\!\!\$\ \mathsf{Fcs}(k, n)$ | $\quad Y \leftarrow Y \oplus H[X, M]$ // $a = 0$ |
| $x \leftarrow\!\!\$\ \{0,1\}^l$ | $\quad Y \leftarrow Y \oplus h[M]$ // $a = 1$ |
| $m \leftarrow\!\!\$\ \mathcal{A}_0[\mathrm{Ro}_a^0]$ | Else $Y \leftarrow Y \oplus H[X, M]$ |
| $B \leftarrow H(x, m)$ // $b = 0$ | Return $(X, M, Y : H, h, x)$ |
| $B_1 \leftarrow\!\!\$\ \{0,1\}^n$ | $\mathrm{Ro}_c^1(X, M, Y : H, B_1, x, m)$ |
| $B \leftarrow B_1$ // $b = 1$ | If $(X, M) = (x, m)$ then |
| $b' \leftarrow\!\!\$\ \mathcal{A}_1[\mathrm{Ro}_c^1](x, B)$ | $\quad Y \leftarrow Y \oplus H[X, M]$ // $c = 0$ |
| Return $b' = 1$ | $\quad Y \leftarrow Y \oplus B_1$ // $c = 1$ |
| | Else $Y \leftarrow Y \oplus H[X, M]$ |
| | Return $(X, M, Y : H, B_1, x, m)$ |

**Fig. 8.** Hybrid games used for proof of Theorem 7.

> it turns out that in the present case our new O2H Theorem can replace the adaptive one. This is because our new O2H Theorem allows us to reprogram the oracle at a large number of inputs (not just a single one). It turns out we do not need to adaptively choose the one input to reprogram, we just reprogram all potential inputs. At least in the proof from [23], this works without problems.

Our proof uses this idea of reprogramming the oracle at a large number of points, showing that the O2H theorem can replace Theorem 7 in *any* proof, not just the one from [3]. Our stronger proof in Sect. 5.2 will only require reprogramming at a single point.

*Proof.* Our proof will use the hybrid games $\mathsf{H}_{(a,b,c)}$ shown in Fig. 8 which are parameterized by $(a, b, c) \in \{0,1\}^3$. Informally, we will show the following.

$$\mathsf{G}_0^{\mathsf{hide}} \equiv \mathsf{H}_{(0,0,0)} \underset{2q_0\sqrt{2^{-l}}}{\approx} \mathsf{H}_{(1,0,0)} \equiv \mathsf{H}_{(1,1,1)} \underset{2q_0\sqrt{2^{-l}}}{\approx} \mathsf{H}_{(0,1,1)} \underset{2q_1\sqrt{\varepsilon^{\mathsf{ow}}}}{\approx} \mathsf{H}_{(0,1,0)} \equiv \mathsf{G}_1^{\mathsf{hide}}.$$

We proceed from left to right. Compared to $\mathsf{G}_0^{\mathsf{un\text{-}hide}}$, hybrid $\mathsf{H}_{(0,0,0)}$ samples an additional (unused) random function $h$ and samples $x$ at the beginning of the game. All three parameters being zero means both random oracles respond correctly using $H$ and that $\mathcal{A}_1$ is given $H(x, m)$ as input. So game $\mathsf{G}_0^{\mathsf{un\text{-}hide}}$ is equivalent to game $\mathsf{H}_{(0,0,0)}$.

Now compare $\mathsf{H}_{(0,0,0)}$ to $\mathsf{H}_{(1,0,0)}$. The change to $a$ means that $\mathcal{A}_0$'s oracle will return $h(M)$ on any input of the form $(x, M)$. Consider a distinguisher $\mathcal{D}$ for the Fixed Permutation O2H (Theorem 1) which runs all of $\mathsf{H}_{(?,0,0)}$ except it forwards $\mathcal{A}_0$'s oracle queries to its own oracle which is either $P = \mathrm{Ro}_0^0$ or $P' = \mathrm{Ro}_1^0$. The adversary provides $X, M, Y$ while $\mathcal{D}$ provides the rest of the inputs. It outputs the same bit $\mathcal{A}_1$ does. Clearly $\mathcal{D}$ correctly simulates the view of $\mathcal{A}$.

Note that the permutations only differ on inputs for which $X = x$ and that $\mathcal{A}_0$'s view is independent of $x$ when interacting with $\mathrm{Ro}_0^0$. Consequently, $\mathsf{Adv}_{P,P'}^{\mathsf{ow}}(\mathcal{D}) \le 1/2^l$ and so $\left|\left(\Pr[\mathsf{H}_{(0,0,0)}]\right)^e - \left(\Pr[\mathsf{H}_{(1,0,0)}]\right)^e\right| \le 2q_0\sqrt{2^{-l}}$.

In $\mathsf{H}_{(1,0,0)}$, $\mathcal{A}_1$ is given the random string $H(x,m)$ as input and then its oracle returns $H(x,m)$ on input $(x,m)$. In $\mathsf{H}_{(1,1,1)}$, $\mathcal{A}_1$ is given the random string $B_1$ as input and then its oracle returns $B_1$ on input $(x,m)$. Note that these variables are otherwise unused because $\mathcal{A}_0$ cannot access $H(x,m)$. Consequently the games are perfectly equivalent. Then we can move back to $\mathsf{H}_{(0,1,1)}$ with analysis analogous to the transition from $\mathsf{H}_{(0,0,0)}$ to $\mathsf{H}_{(1,0,0)}$. Putting these steps together gives $\left|\left(\Pr[\mathsf{H}_{(1,0,0)}]\right)^e - \left(\Pr[\mathsf{H}_{(0,1,1)}]\right)^e\right| \leq 2q_0\sqrt{2^{-l}}$.

Now comparing $\mathsf{H}_{(0,1,1)}$ and $\mathsf{H}_{(0,1,0)}$ we see that they differ only in the behavior of $\mathcal{A}_1$'s oracle. The former will return $B_1$ on input $(x,m)$ while the latter will return $H(x,m)$. Consider a distinguisher $\mathcal{D}'$ for the Fixed Permutation O2H (Theorem 1) which runs all of $\mathsf{H}_{(0,1,?)}$ except it forwards $\mathcal{A}_1$'s oracle queries to its own oracle which is either $P = \mathrm{Ro}_1^1$ or $P' = \mathrm{Ro}_0^1$. The adversary provides $X, M, Y$ while $\mathcal{D}$ provides the rest of the inputs. It outputs the same bit $\mathcal{A}_1$ does. Clearly $\mathcal{D}$ correctly simulates the view of $\mathcal{A}$.

We have $\left|\left(\Pr[\mathsf{H}_{(0,1,1)}]\right)^e - \left(\Pr[\mathsf{H}_{(0,1,0)}]\right)^e\right| \leq 2q_1\sqrt{\mathsf{Adv}^{\mathsf{ow}}_{P,P'}(\mathcal{D}')}$. Note that the permutations only differ on inputs for which $(X,M) = (x,m)$ and that the view of $\mathcal{A}$ run by $\mathcal{D}'$ in $\mathsf{G}^{\mathsf{ow}}_{P,P'}$ matches the view it would get in $\mathsf{G}^{\mathsf{un\text{-}ow}}$. Consequently, $\mathsf{Adv}^{\mathsf{ow}}_{P,P'}(\mathcal{D}') \leq \mathsf{Adv}^{\mathsf{un\text{-}ow}}(\mathcal{A})$.

Finally, we can compare $\mathsf{H}_{(0,1,0)}$ and $\mathsf{G}^{\mathsf{un\text{-}hide}}_0$ to see that they are equivalent. Putting together our claims and using the triangle inequality gives the bound

$$\left|\mathsf{Adv}^{\mathsf{un\text{-}hide}}_e(\mathcal{A})\right| \leq 4q_0\sqrt{2^{-l}} + 2q_1\sqrt{\mathsf{Adv}^{\mathsf{ow}}_{P,P'}(\mathcal{D}')}.$$

This completes the proof. □

### 5.2 Second Adaptive O2H

In [25], Unruh improved on his adaptive O2H result with a version that allowed the hidden point to be chosen according to a arbitrary adaptively chosen distribution, as long as this distribution has sufficient entropy. We can capture the result using games $\mathsf{G}^{\mathsf{un\text{-}hide2}}$ and $\mathsf{G}^{\mathsf{un\text{-}ow2}}$ defined in Fig. 9. In both, sampling $x$ is now done with the classical algorithm $\mathcal{A}_C$. It cannot access $\mathcal{A}_0$'s state beyond the input $m$ passed to it. Algorithm $\mathcal{A}_1$ is allowed allow access the state of both $\mathcal{A}_0$ and $\mathcal{A}_1$. Defining $\mathsf{Adv}^{\mathsf{un\text{-}hide2}}_e(\mathcal{A}) = \left(\Pr[\mathsf{G}^{\mathsf{un\text{-}hide2}}_1(\mathcal{A})]\right)^e - \left(\Pr[\mathsf{G}^{\mathsf{un\text{-}hide2}}_0(\mathcal{A})]\right)^e$ and $\mathsf{Adv}^{\mathsf{un\text{-}ow2}}(\mathcal{A}) = \Pr[\mathsf{G}^{\mathsf{un\text{-}ow2}}(\mathcal{A})]$.

We define the collision entropy $k$ and min-entropy $\mu$ of $\mathcal{A}_C$ by

$$k = \min_{m} -\log_2 \Pr[x = y \ :\ x \leftarrow\!\!\$\ \mathcal{A}_C(m), y \leftarrow\!\!\$\ \mathcal{A}_C(m)]$$
$$\mu = \min_{m,x} -\log_2 \Pr[x = y \ :\ y \leftarrow\!\!\$\ \mathcal{A}_C(m)].$$

| Game $\mathsf{G}_b^{\text{un-hide2}}(\mathcal{A})$ | Game $\mathsf{G}^{\text{un-ow2}}(\mathcal{A})$ |
|---|---|
| $H \leftarrow\$ \mathsf{Fcs}(l, n)$ | $i \leftarrow\$ \{1, \ldots, q_1\}$ |
| $m \leftarrow\$ \mathcal{A}_0[H[\oplus]]$ | $H \leftarrow\$ \mathsf{Fcs}(l, n)$ |
| $x \leftarrow\$ \mathcal{A}_C(m)$ | $m \leftarrow\$ \mathcal{A}_0[H[\oplus]]$ |
| $B_0 \leftarrow H(x)$ | $x \leftarrow\$ \mathcal{A}_C(m)$ |
| $B_1 \leftarrow\$ \{0,1\}^n$ | $B_1 \leftarrow\$ \{0,1\}^n$ |
| $b' \leftarrow\$ \mathcal{A}_1[H[\oplus]](x, B_b)$ | Run $\mathcal{A}_1[H[\oplus]](x, B_1)$ until its $i$-th query |
| Return $b' = 1$ | Measure the input $x'$ to this query |
| | Return $x = x'$ |

**Fig. 9.** Games used for Unruh's second adaptive O2H [25]. Algorithm $\mathcal{A}_C$ is classical. Algorithm $\mathcal{A}_1$ can access the final state of $\mathcal{A}_0$ and $\mathcal{A}_C$.

Note that $2\mu \geq k \geq \mu$.

Then we can state Unruh's result (Lemma 9 in the current ePrint version).

**Theorem 8. (Unruh Adaptive O2H, [25]).** *Let $\mathcal{A} = (\mathcal{A}_0, \mathcal{A}_1)$ be an adversary for which $\mathcal{A}_i$ makes at most $q_i$ oracle queries and $\mathcal{A}_C$ be a classical algorithm with collision entropy $k$. Then*

$$\left|\mathsf{Adv}_1^{\text{un-hide2}}(\mathcal{A})\right| \leq 2q_1\sqrt{\mathsf{Adv}^{\text{un-ow2}}(\mathcal{A})} + (4 + \sqrt{2})\sqrt{q_0}2^{-k/4}.$$

We prove the following slightly generalized result.

**Theorem 9.** *Let $\mathcal{A} = (\mathcal{A}_0, \mathcal{A}_1)$ be an adversary for which $\mathcal{A}_i$ makes at most $q_i$ oracle queries and $\mathcal{A}_C$ be a classical algorithm with min-entropy $\mu$ and collision entropy $k$. Then for $e \in \{1, 1/2\}$.*

$$\begin{aligned}\left|\mathsf{Adv}_e^{\text{un-hide2}}(\mathcal{A})\right| &\leq 2q_1\sqrt{\mathsf{Adv}^{\text{un-ow2}}(\mathcal{A})} + 2\sqrt{q_0}2^{-\mu/2}\\ &\leq 2q_1\sqrt{\mathsf{Adv}^{\text{un-ow2}}(\mathcal{A})} + 2\sqrt{q_0}2^{-k/4}.\end{aligned}$$

Unruh conjectured that the $2^{-k/4}$ factor is an artifact of their proof technique. If so, our proof technique has the same artifact but removes it when min-entropy is an acceptable replacement. This, for example, allows us to directly imply a version of Theorem 7 with the bound improved to replace $q_0$ with $\sqrt{q_0}$.

Our proof combines the ideas from our proof of Unruh's first adaptive O2H (Theorem 7) and our proof of the GHHM adaptive reprogramming result (Theorem 5). We first move to a hybrid where we reprogram $H(x)$ to equal $B_1$ before $\mathcal{A}_1$ is executed (more precisely, we swap the values of $H(x)$ and $B_1$). To obtain a tighter bound for this step than in Theorem 7, we switch to a sparse representation of $H$ and bound the "bad event" at the time of the swap, as in our Theorem 5 proof. Then we show the difference between this hybrid and the final game by reprogramming $\mathcal{A}_1$'s access to $H$ on input $x$.

Games $\mathsf{G}_b(\mathcal{A})$
$\mathbf{H} \leftarrow\!\!{\scriptstyle\$}\ \mathsf{Fcs}(l, n)$
$\mathbf{B} \leftarrow\!\!{\scriptstyle\$}\ \{0,1\}^n$
$\mathbf{R} \leftarrow\!\!{\scriptstyle\$}\ \{0,1\}^\infty$
$|H, B, R\rangle \leftarrow |\mathbf{H}, \mathbf{B}, \mathbf{R}\rangle$
Run $\mathcal{A}_0[\text{Ro}]$
Run $\text{SAMP}_b$
Run $\mathcal{A}_1[\text{Ro}]$
Measure $W[1]$
Return $W[1] = 1$

$\text{SAMP}_b(X, Y : H, B, V, R, X^*)$
$V \leftarrow V \oplus X$
$X^* \leftarrow X^* \oplus \mathcal{A}_C(X; R[I])$
$Y \leftarrow Y \oplus H[X^*]$ // If $b = 0$
$Y \leftarrow Y \oplus B$ // If $b = 1$
Return $(X, Y : H, B, V, R, X^*)$

$\text{Ro}(X, Y : H)$
$Y \leftarrow Y \oplus H[X]$
Return $(X, Y : H)$

Hybrids $\mathsf{H}_{(a,b,c)}$
$\mathbf{R} \leftarrow\!\!{\scriptstyle\$}\ \mathsf{Fcs}(\lceil \lg q \rceil, m)$
$|R\rangle \leftarrow |\mathbf{R}\rangle$
Run $\mathcal{A}_0[\mathcal{H}^Y \circ \text{FRo}^0 \circ \mathcal{H}^Y]$
Run $\mathcal{H}^Y \circ \text{FSAMP}_{a,b} \circ \mathcal{H}^Y$
Run $\mathcal{A}_1[\mathcal{H}^Y \circ \text{FRo}^1_c \circ \mathcal{H}^Y]$
Measure $W[1]$
Return $W[1] = 1$

$\text{FRo}^0(X, Y : H)$
$H[X] \leftarrow Y \oplus H[X]$
Return $(X, Y : H)$

$\text{FSAMP}_{a,b}(X, Y : H, B, V, R, X^*)$
$V \leftarrow V \oplus X$
$X^* \leftarrow X^* \oplus \mathcal{A}_C(X; R[I])$
$(B, H[X^*]) \leftarrow (H[X^*], B)$ // If $a = 1$
$H[X^*] \leftarrow Y \oplus H[X^*]$ // If $b = 0$
$B \leftarrow Y \oplus B$ // If $b = 1$
Return $(X, Y : H, B, V, R, X^*)$

$\text{FRo}^1_c(X, Y : H, B)$
If $X = X^*$ then
  $H[X^*] \leftarrow Y \oplus H[X^*]$ // If $c = 0$
  $B \leftarrow Y \oplus B$ // If $c = 1$
Else $H[X] \leftarrow Y \oplus H[X]$
Return $(X, Y : H, B)$

**Fig. 10.** Hybrid games for proof of Theorem 9, implying the adaptive O2H result of Unruh [25]. Algorithm $\mathcal{A}_1$, but not $\mathcal{A}_0$, may access register $R$.

*Proof.* For this proof we use the games shown in Fig. 10. We start with $\mathsf{G}_b$ which is simply a rewritten version of $\mathsf{G}_b^{\text{un-hide2}}$. It writes the use of $\mathcal{A}_C$ as a single query to an oracle SAMP and make everything quantum. Algorithm $\mathcal{A}_0$ acts on registers $W, X, Y$, while $\mathcal{A}_1$ may additionally act on $R$. (Here $R$ stores the randomness that will be used by $\mathcal{A}_C$. Giving it to $\mathcal{A}_1$ is equivalent for our purposes to letting $\mathcal{A}_1$ access the final state of $\mathcal{A}_C$ and additionally allows $\mathcal{A}_1$ to recompute the $x$ which is stored in $X^*$.) Registers $H$ and $B$ are controlled by the game. To enforce that the SAMP query is classical, it writes the query $X$ (which stores $m$ at this time) into the otherwise unused register $V$. So we have $\Pr[\mathsf{G}_b^{\text{un-hide2}}(\mathcal{A})] = \Pr[\mathsf{G}_b(\mathcal{A})]$.[13]

Our proof will use the hybrid games $\mathsf{H}_{(a,b,c)}$ shown in Fig. 10 which are parameterized by $(a, b, c) \in \{0,1\}^3$. Informally, we will show the following.

$$\mathsf{G}_0 \equiv \mathsf{H}_{(0,0,0)} \underset{2\sqrt{q_0 2^{-\mu}}}{\approx} \mathsf{H}_{(1,0,0)} \equiv \mathsf{H}_{(0,1,1)} \underset{2q_1\sqrt{\varepsilon^{\text{ow}}}}{\approx} \mathsf{H}_{(0,1,0)} \equiv \mathsf{G}_1.$$

[13] Formally, the syntax of $\mathcal{A}$ changed, so on the right-hand side it should have been replaced with an appropriately defined $\mathcal{A}'$.

We proceed from left to right. Consider $\mathsf{H}_{(0,0,0)}$, In this game, rather than being sampled at random, the registers $H$ and $B$ are initialized to zeros. The oracle Ro which writes $H[X]$ into $Y$ has instead been replaced with two (for now equivalent) oracles $\mathcal{H}^Y \circ \text{FRO}^i \circ \mathcal{H}^Y$ where $\mathcal{H}^Y$ is the Hadamard transform applied to register $Y$ and FRo is the Fourier version of Ro where instead $Y$ is written into $H[X]$. Similarly, FSAMP which writes $H[X^*]$ or $B$ into $Y$ has been replaced with $\mathcal{H}^Y \circ \text{SAMP}_{a,b} \circ \mathcal{H}^Y$ which writes $Y$ into $H[X^*]$ or $B$. By the sparse QROM representation technique of Zhandry, these games are completely equivalent, giving $\mathsf{Pr}[\mathsf{G}_b(\mathcal{A})] = \mathsf{Pr}[\mathsf{H}_{(0,b,0)}(\mathcal{A})]$. See our proof of Theorem 6 and in particular Appendix A for an example of how to break this equivalence claims into smaller atomic steps.

Now in $\mathsf{H}_{(0,1,0)}$ we perform an additional swap of $B$ and $H[X^*]$. Note that $\text{FSAMP}_{a,0}$ and $\text{FSAMP}_{a,1}$ differ as permutations only if $B \neq H[X^*]$.

We apply the Fixed Permutation O2H (Theorem 1) with $\mathcal{D}$ that runs all of $\mathsf{H}_{(0,?,0)}$ internally, except it calls its oracle to emulate FSAMP. Note that $\mathcal{D}$ makes one oracle query and at that time $H$ has at most $q_0$ non-zero entries (which thus differ from $B$ which is zero). Thus $\mathsf{Adv}^{\mathsf{ow}}_{\text{FSAMP}_{0,0},\text{FSAMP}_{1,0}}(\mathcal{D}) \leq q_0/2^{-\mu}$ from the min-entropy of $\mathcal{A}_C$ and $|(\mathsf{Pr}[\mathsf{H}_{(0,0,0)}(\mathcal{A})])^e - (\mathsf{Pr}[\mathsf{H}_{(0,1,0)}(\mathcal{A})])^e| \leq 2\sqrt{q_0/2^{\mu}}$.

Hybrid $\mathsf{H}_{(0,1,0)}$ swaps the registers $B$ and $H[X^*]$ before $\mathcal{A}_1$ is run. Note $\mathcal{A}_1$ does not have direct access to these registers, so it would be equivalent to leave $B$ and $H[X^*]$ unswapped, but instead switch which of the two is used in all future accesses to the registers. The is what's done in the equivalent game $\mathsf{H}_{0,1,1}$.

Now $\mathsf{H}_{(0,1,1)}$ differs from $\mathsf{H}_{(0,1,0)}$ only when $X^*$ is queried to $\text{FRO}^1$. Apply the Fixed Permutation O2H (Theorem 1) with $\mathcal{D}'$ that runs all of $\mathsf{H}_{(0,1,?)}$ internally except it uses its own oracle to respond to $\text{FRO}^1$. We get $|(\mathsf{Pr}[\mathsf{H}_{(0,1,0)}(\mathcal{A})])^e - (\mathsf{Pr}[\mathsf{H}_{(0,1,1)}(\mathcal{A})])^e| \leq 2q_1\sqrt{\mathsf{Adv}^{\mathsf{ow}}_{\text{FRO}^1_1,\text{FRO}^1_0}(\mathcal{D}')}$.

The previously discussed equivalence between $\mathsf{H}_{(0,1,0)}$, $\mathsf{G}_1$, and $\mathsf{G}_1^{\mathsf{un\text{-}hide2}}(\mathcal{A})$ allows us to conclude that $\mathsf{Adv}^{\mathsf{ow}}_{\text{FRO}^1_1,\text{FRO}^1_0}(\mathcal{D}') = \mathsf{Adv}^{\mathsf{un\text{-}ow2}}(\mathcal{A})$ and complete the proof using the triangle inequality. □

## 6 Limitations of Fixed Permutation O2H

Alagic, Bai, Katz, and Majenz [1] gave a result for the resampling of random permutations which they call an extension of the GHHM adaptive reprogramming lemma (Theorem 5) to the case of two-way accessible random permutations which we cannot reproduce from Fixed-Permutation O2H because it is not known if quantumly accessible random permutations can be sparsely represented.

Define the swap permutation $S_{s,s'}$ by $S(s) = s'$, $S(s') = s$, and $S(x) = x$ otherwise. Let $\mathsf{Perm}(n)$ denote the set of all permutations on $\{0,1\}^n$. Then the relevant security game is shown in Fig. 11 for which we define $\mathsf{Adv}^{\mathsf{perm}}_e(\mathcal{A}) = (\mathsf{Pr}[\mathsf{G}^{\mathsf{perm}}_1(\mathcal{A})])^e - (\mathsf{Pr}[\mathsf{G}^{\mathsf{perm}}_0(\mathcal{A})])^e$.

Of this game, they prove the following bound (their Lemma 5).

| Game $\mathsf{G}_b^{\mathsf{perm}}(\mathcal{A})$ |
|---|
| $\Pi_0 \leftarrow\!\!\$\ \mathsf{Perm}(n)$ |
| $\mathcal{A}_0[\Pi_0[\oplus], \Pi_0^{-1}[\oplus]]$ |
| $s, s' \leftarrow\!\!\$\ \{0,1\}^n$ |
| $\Pi_1 \leftarrow \Pi_0 \circ S_{s,s'}$ |
| $b' \leftarrow\!\!\$\ \mathcal{A}_1[\Pi_b[\oplus], \Pi_b^{-1}[\oplus]](s, s')$ |
| Return $b' = 1$ |

**Fig. 11.** Game for ABKH resampling for permutations result

**Theorem 10. (ABKH Permutation Resampling,** [1]**).** *Let* $\mathcal{A} = (\mathcal{A}_0, \mathcal{A}_1)$ *be an adversary for which* $\mathcal{A}_0$ *makes at most* $q_0$ *oracle queries. Then*

$$|\mathsf{Adv}^{\mathsf{perm}}(\mathcal{A})| \leq 4\sqrt{q_0/2^n}.$$

While this result is intuitively related to the GHHM adaptive reprogramming result, we cannot port over our proof from Sect. 4, because it relied on Zhandry's technique for sparse representation of a random oracle. No sufficiently analogous technique is currently known for random permutations. (Indeed it is a notoriously difficult problem [27].)

Below for comparison, we prove a bound of the form $2q_0\sqrt{2/2^n}$ for Theorem 10 using Fixed-Permutation O2H by exploiting the fact that $s, s'$ are non-adaptively chosen.

In essence, the issues here correspond to the differences between the two proofs in Sect. 5. The proof we provide here is analogous to our proof of Theorem 7, and we are unable to prove an analog of Theorem 8 because we lack techniques for sparsely representing permutations.

*Proof. (Weakened Theorem* 10*).* First note that $s, s' \leftarrow\!\!\$\ \{0,1\}^n$ could have been sampled at the beginning of the game. Then it would have been completely equivalent to give $\mathcal{A}_0$ access to $\Pi_b$ and $\mathcal{A}_1$ access to $\Pi_0$. We can define the fixed permutations $\textsc{Perm}_b(X, Y, d : \Pi, s, s')$ to implement $\Pi_b$ if $d = 1$ and $\Pi_b^{-1}$ if $d = 0$. They differ only on inputs for which $(X, d) \in \{(s, 1), (s', 1), (\Pi_0(s), 0), (\Pi(s'), 0)\}$. So applying Theorem 1 with these two permutations and $\mathcal{D}$ that picks $s, s'$, runs $\mathcal{A}_0$ with access to the permutation, then internally simulates the rest of the game and outputs whatever $\mathcal{A}$ does we get

$$\mathsf{Adv}_e^{\mathsf{perm}}(\mathcal{A}) = \mathsf{Adv}^{\mathsf{hide}}_{\textsc{Perm}_1,\textsc{Perm}_0,e}(\mathcal{D}) \leq 2q_0\sqrt{\mathsf{Adv}^{\mathsf{ow}}_{\textsc{Perm}_1,\textsc{Perm}_0}(\mathcal{D})} = 2q_0\sqrt{2/2^n}.$$

The last equality comes from noting the view of $\mathcal{A}_0$ is independent of $s, s'$ and that for a given choice of $d$ there are at most two uniformly random $X$'s on which the permutations differ. □

Alagic, Bai, Katz, Majenz, and Struck [2] introduced a stronger version of this theorem which allows $s$ to be sampled according to an adaptively chosen distribution with high min-entropy ($s'$ is still uniform). For this version, the proof

| | |
|---|---|
| Games $\mathsf{G}_0^b(\mathcal{B})$ | $\textsc{Ro}(X, Y : H)$ |
| $\mathbf{H} \leftarrow\$ \mathsf{Fcs}(l, m)$ | $Y \leftarrow Y \oplus H[X]$ |
| $\mathbf{Z} \leftarrow\$ \mathsf{Fcs}(\lceil \lg q \rceil, m)$ | Return $(X, Y : H)$ |
| $\mathbf{R} \leftarrow\$ \mathsf{Fcs}(\lceil \lg q \rceil, \infty)$ | $\textsc{FRo}(X, Y : H)$ |
| $\lvert H, Z, R\rangle \leftarrow \lvert \mathbf{H}, \mathbf{Z}, \mathbf{R}\rangle$ | $H[X] \leftarrow H[X] \oplus Y$ |
| Run $\mathcal{B}[\textsc{Ro}, \textsc{Rep}_b]$ | Return $(X, Y : H)$ |
| Measure $W[1]$ | $\textsc{Rep}_b(X, Y : H, I, Z, R)$ |
| Return $W[1] = 1$ | Interpret $X$ as prob. dist. $p$ |
| Games $\mathsf{G}_1^b(\mathcal{B})$ | $x \leftarrow p(R[I])$ |
| $\mathbf{R} \leftarrow\$ \mathsf{Fcs}(\lceil \lg q \rceil, m)$ | If $b = 1$ then |
| $\lvert R\rangle \leftarrow \lvert \mathbf{R}\rangle$ | $(H[x], Z[I]) \leftarrow (Z[I], H[x])$ |
| Run $\mathcal{B}[\mathcal{H}^Y \circ \textsc{FRo} \circ \mathcal{H}^Y, \textsc{Rep}_b]$ | $Y \leftarrow Y \oplus x$ |
| Measure $W[1]$ | $I \leftarrow I + 1 \bmod 2^{\lceil \lg q \rceil}$ |
| Return $W[1] = 1$ | Return $(X, Y : H, I, Z, R)$ |

```
Hybrid H_κ^b
R ←$ Fcs(⌈lg q⌉, ∞)
|R⟩ ← |R⟩
|H, Z⟩ ← H|H, Z⟩   // H1,H2
Run B[Ro, Rep_b]   // H1
Run B[H^{Y,H} ∘ FRo ∘ H^{Y,H}, H^{Z,H} ∘ Rep_b ∘ H^{Z,H}]   // H2
Run B[H^Y ∘ FRo ∘ H^Y, Rep_b]   // H3
|H, Z⟩ ← H|H, Z⟩   // H3
Measure W[1]
Return W[1] = 1
```

**Fig. 12. Above:** Reproduction of games from the proof of Theorem 6. **Below:** Hybrid games for using Zhandry's sparse representation technique. Registers not explicitly initialized are initialized to all 0.

technique above would not work because we cannot sample $s$ at the beginning of the game. At best, we could prove a variant in which $\mathcal{A}_1$ is never told $s, s'$ and so we can bound its success based its ability to query the permutations on the bad points after they are chosen.

# A Details of Sparse QROM Representation in Theorem 4.2

We provide a detailed analysis of why the games $\mathsf{G}_0^b$ and $\mathsf{G}_1^b$ as defined in Fig. 12 (reproduced from Fig. 6 in the proof of Theorem 6) are equivalent.

We will consider a sequence of hybrid games $\mathsf{H}_1^b$ through $\mathsf{H}_3^b$ for which we justify that $\mathsf{G}_0^b$ is equivalent to $\mathsf{H}_1$, $\mathsf{G}_1^b$ is equivalent to $\mathsf{H}_3^b$, and $\mathsf{H}_\kappa$ is equivalent to $\mathsf{H}_{\kappa+1}$ for each $\kappa$. Formal pseudocode for the games is given in Fig. 12.

**Hybrid 1.** First we define $\mathsf{H}_1^b$ identically to $\mathsf{G}_0^b$ except that $H$ and $Z$ are initialized by applying the Hadamard transform to the all zeros strings. Recall that

$\mathcal{H}|x\rangle = 1/\sqrt{2^n} \cdot \sum_{x'}(-1)^{x \cdot x'}|x'\rangle$ if $x$ is a bitstring $x \in \{0,1\}^n$. When $x$ is the all zeros string, this gives the uniform superposition $1/\sqrt{2^n} \cdot \sum_{x'}|x'\rangle$. Thus, if we measured $H$ and $Z$ immediately, we would be assigning them a uniformly random function as in $\mathsf{G}_0^b$. Values in $H$ and $Z$ are only ever swapped with each other or used to control xor's into other registers. So by the principle of joint deferred measurement, leaving them unmeasured is equivalent.

**Hybrid 2.** Next we define $\mathsf{H}_2^b$ identically to $\mathsf{H}_1^b$ except the oracles $\textsc{Ro}$ and $\textsc{Rep}_b$ have been replaced with $\mathcal{H}^{Y,H} \circ \textsc{FRo} \circ \mathcal{H}^{Y,H}$ and $\mathcal{H}^{Z,H} \circ \textsc{Rep}_b \circ \mathcal{H}^{Z,H}$. These do not change the behavior of the game because $\textsc{Ro} = \mathcal{H}^{Y,H} \circ \textsc{FRo} \circ \mathcal{H}^{Y,H}$ and $\textsc{Rep}_b = \mathcal{H}^{Z,H} \circ \textsc{Rep}_b \circ \mathcal{H}^{Z,H}$. These equalities follow from the following lemma (and the fact that $\mathcal{H}$ is its own inverse).

**Lemma 1.** *Define permutations $P(x,y) = (x \oplus y, y)$, $P'(x,y) = (x, x \oplus y)$, $S(x,y) = (y,x)$, and $I(x,y) = (x,y)$. Then*

$$\begin{aligned} P &= \mathcal{H} \circ P' \circ \mathcal{H} \\ S &= (U \otimes U) \circ S \circ (U^{-1} \otimes U^{-1}) \\ I &= (U \otimes U) \circ I \circ (U^{-1} \otimes U^{-1}) \end{aligned}$$

*where $U$ is an arbitrary unitary with inverse $U^{-1}$.*

**Hybrid 3.** We define $\mathsf{H}_3^b$ by cancelling out many Hadamard transforms in $\mathsf{H}_2$, using that it is its own inverse. First note that $\mathcal{B}$ does not act on register $H$ so transform $\mathcal{H}^H$ will commute with it. Thereby, the initial $\mathcal{H}^H$ used to setup $H$ cancels with the $\mathcal{H}^H$ before the first oracle call. The $\mathcal{H}^H$'s between any two oracle queries cancel with each other. This leaves only the $\mathcal{H}^H$ after the last oracle query, which we've deferred to the end of the game.

Similarly, neither $\mathcal{B}$ nor $\textsc{FRo}$ act on register $Z$ so transform $\mathcal{H}^Z$ will commute with them. This similarly allows us to cancel out all $\mathcal{H}^Z$ except the one after the last query which is deferred until the end of the game.

Finally, comparing $\mathsf{H}_3^b$ with $\mathsf{G}_1^b$ we see they are identical except the former has an additional $|H,Z\rangle \leftarrow \mathcal{H}|H,Z\rangle$ at the end. At that point of execution all that matters is the measurement of $W[1]$ which is unaffected by this operation, so it can be removed.

## References

1. Alagic, G., Bai, C., Katz, J., Majenz, C.: Post-quantum security of the Even-Mansour cipher. In: Dunkelman, O., Dziembowski, S. (eds.) EUROCRYPT 2022, Part III. LNCS, vol. 13277, pp. 458–487. Springer, Cham (2022). https://doi.org/10.1007/978-3-031-07082-2_17
2. Alagic, G., Bai, C., Katz, J., Majenz, C., Struck, P.: Post-quantum security of tweakable Even-Mansour, and applications. In: Joye, M., Leander, G. (eds.) EUROCRYPT 2024, Part I. LNCS, vol. 14651, pp. 310–338. Springer, Cham (2022). https://doi.org/10.1007/978-3-031-58716-0_11

3. Ambainis, A., Hamburg, M., Unruh, D.: Quantum security proofs using semi-classical oracles. In: Boldyreva, A., Micciancio, D. (eds.) CRYPTO 2019. LNCS, vol. 11693, pp. 269–295. Springer, Cham (2019). https://doi.org/10.1007/978-3-030-26951-7_10
4. Bellare, M., Rogaway, P.: Random oracles are practical: a paradigm for designing efficient protocols. In: Denning, D.E., Pyle, R., Ganesan, R., Sandhu, R.S., Ashby, V. (eds.) ACM CCS 93, pp. 62–73. ACM Press (1993). https://doi.org/10.1145/168588.168596
5. Bellare, M., Rogaway, P.: The security of triple encryption and a framework for code-based game-playing proofs. In: Vaudenay, S. (ed.) EUROCRYPT 2006. LNCS, vol. 4004, pp. 409–426. Springer, Berlin, Heidelberg (2006). https://doi.org/10.1007/11761679_25
6. Bindel, N., Hamburg, M., Hövelmanns, K., Hülsing, A., Persichetti, E.: Tighter proofs of CCA security in the quantum random oracle model. In: Hofheinz, D., Rosen, A. (eds.) TCC 2019. LNCS, vol. 11892, pp. 61–90. Springer, Cham (2019). https://doi.org/10.1007/978-3-030-36033-7_3
7. Boneh, D., Dagdelen, Ö., Fischlin, M., Lehmann, A., Schaffner, C., Zhandry, M.: Random oracles in a quantum world. In: Lee, D.H., Wang, X. (eds.) ASIACRYPT 2011. LNCS, vol. 7073, pp. 41–69. Springer, Heidelberg (2011). https://doi.org/10.1007/978-3-642-25385-0_3
8. Chen, S., Steinberger, J.: Tight security bounds for key-alternating ciphers. In: Nguyen, P.Q., Oswald, E. (eds.) EUROCRYPT 2014. LNCS, vol. 8441, pp. 327–350. Springer, Heidelberg (2014). https://doi.org/10.1007/978-3-642-55220-5_19
9. Devevey, J., Fallahpour, P., Passelègue, A., Stehlé, D.: A detailed analysis of Fiat-Shamir with aborts. In: Handschuh, H., Lysyanskaya, A. (eds.) CRYPTO 2023, Part V. LNCS, vol. 14085, pp. 327–357. Springer, Cham (2023). https://doi.org/10.1007/978-3-031-38554-4_11
10. Don, J., Fehr, S., Huang, Y.H., Struck, P.: On the (in)security of the BUFF transform. In: Reyzin, L., Stebila, D. (eds.) CRYPTO 2024, Part I. LNCS, vol. 14920, pp. 246–275. Springer, Cham (2024). https://doi.org/10.1007/978-3-031-68376-3_8
11. Eaton, E.: Leighton-Micali hash-based signatures in the quantum random-oracle model. In: Adams, C., Camenisch, J. (eds.) SAC 2017. LNCS, vol. 10719, pp. 263–280. Springer, Cham (2017). https://doi.org/10.1007/978-3-319-72565-9_13
12. Grilo, A.B., Hövelmanns, K., Hülsing, A., Majenz, C.: Tight adaptive reprogramming in the QROM. In: Tibouchi, M., Wang, H. (eds.) ASIACRYPT 2021, Part I. LNCS, vol. 13090, pp. 637–667. Springer, Cham (2021). https://doi.org/10.1007/978-3-030-92062-3_22
13. Hülsing, A., Rijneveld, J., Song, F.: Mitigating multi-target attacks in hash-based signatures. In: Cheng, C.-M., Chung, K.-M., Persiano, G., Yang, B.-Y. (eds.) PKC 2016. LNCS, vol. 9614, pp. 387–416. Springer, Heidelberg (2016). https://doi.org/10.1007/978-3-662-49384-7_15
14. Jaeger, J., Song, F., Tessaro, S.: Quantum key-length extension. In: Nissim, K., Waters, B. (eds.) TCC 2021. LNCS, vol. 13042, pp. 209–239. Springer, Cham (2021). https://doi.org/10.1007/978-3-030-90459-3_8
15. Jiang, H., Zhang, Z., Chen, L., Wang, H., Ma, Z.: IND-CCA-secure key encapsulation mechanism in the quantum random oracle model, revisited. In: Shacham, H., Boldyreva, A. (eds.) CRYPTO 2018. LNCS, vol. 10993, pp. 96–125. Springer, Cham (2018). https://doi.org/10.1007/978-3-319-96878-0_4

16. Kosuge, H., Xagawa, K.: Probabilistic hash-and-sign with retry in the quantum random oracle model. In: Tang, Q., Teague, V. (eds.) PKC 2024, Part I. LNCS, vol. 14601, pp. 259–288. Springer, Cham (2024). https://doi.org/10.1007/978-3-031-57718-5_9
17. Kuchta, V., Sakzad, A., Stehlé, D., Steinfeld, R., Sun, S.-F.: Measure-rewind-measure: tighter quantum random oracle model proofs for one-way to hiding and CCA security. In: Canteaut, A., Ishai, Y. (eds.) EUROCRYPT 2020. LNCS, vol. 12107, pp. 703–728. Springer, Cham (2020). https://doi.org/10.1007/978-3-030-45727-3_24
18. Maurer, U.: Indistinguishability of random systems. In: Knudsen, L.R. (ed.) EUROCRYPT 2002. LNCS, vol. 2332, pp. 110–132. Springer, Heidelberg (2002). https://doi.org/10.1007/3-540-46035-7_8
19. Morimae, T., Yamakawa, T.: Classically verifiable NIZK for QMA with preprocessing. In: Agrawal, S., Lin, D. (eds.) ASIACRYPT 2022, Part IV. LNCS, vol. 13794, pp. 599–627. Springer, Cham (2022). https://doi.org/10.1007/978-3-031-22972-5_21
20. Pan, J., Zeng, R.: Selective opening security in the quantum random oracle model, revisited. In: Tang, Q., Teague, V. (eds.) PKC 2024, Part II. LNCS, vol. 14603, pp. 92–122. Springer, Cham (2024). https://doi.org/10.1007/978-3-031-57725-3_4
21. Patarin, J.: The "coefficients H" technique (invited talk). In: Avanzi, R.M., Keliher, L., Sica, F. (eds.) SAC 2008. LNCS, vol. 5381, pp. 328–345. Springer, Berlin, Heidelberg (2009). https://doi.org/10.1007/978-3-642-04159-4_21
22. Shoup, V.: Sequences of games: a tool for taming complexity in security proofs. Cryptology ePrint Archive, Report 2004/332 (2004). https://eprint.iacr.org/2004/332
23. Targhi, E.E., Unruh, D.: Post-quantum security of the Fujisaki-Okamoto and OAEP transforms. In: Hirt, M., Smith, A. (eds.) TCC 2016. LNCS, vol. 9986, pp. 192–216. Springer, Heidelberg (2016). https://doi.org/10.1007/978-3-662-53644-5_8
24. Unruh, D.: Quantum position verification in the random oracle model. In: Garay, J.A., Gennaro, R. (eds.) CRYPTO 2014. LNCS, vol. 8617, pp. 1–18. Springer, Heidelberg (2014). https://doi.org/10.1007/978-3-662-44381-1_1
25. Unruh, D.: Non-interactive zero-knowledge proofs in the quantum random oracle model. In: Oswald, E., Fischlin, M. (eds.) EUROCRYPT 2015. LNCS, vol. 9057, pp. 755–784. Springer, Heidelberg (2015). https://doi.org/10.1007/978-3-662-46803-6_25
26. Unruh, D.: Revocable quantum timed-release encryption. J. ACM **62**(6) (2015). https://doi.org/10.1145/2817206
27. Unruh, D.: Towards compressed permutation oracles. In: Guo, J., Steinfeld, R. (eds.) ASIACRYPT 2023, Part IV. LNCS, vol. 14441, pp. 369–400. Springer, Singapore (2023). https://doi.org/10.1007/978-981-99-8730-6_12
28. Yuan, Q., Sun, C., Takagi, T.: Revisiting the security of fiat-shamir signature schemes under superposition attacks. In: Tianqing Zhu, Y.L. (ed.) ACISP 24, Part II. LNCS, vol. 14896, pp. 164–184. Springer, Singapore (2024). https://doi.org/10.1007/978-981-97-5028-3_9
29. Yuan, Q., Tibouchi, M., Abe, M.: Quantum-access security of hash-based signature schemes. In: Simpson, L., Baee, M.A.R. (eds.) ACISP 23. LNCS, vol. 13915, pp. 343–380. Springer, Cham (2023). https://doi.org/10.1007/978-3-031-35486-1_16
30. Zhandry, M.: How to construct quantum random functions. In: 53rd FOCS, pp. 679–687. IEEE Computer Society Press (2012). https://doi.org/10.1109/FOCS.2012.37

31. Zhandry, M.: Secure identity-based encryption in the quantum random oracle model. In: Safavi-Naini, R., Canetti, R. (eds.) CRYPTO 2012. LNCS, vol. 7417, pp. 758–775. Springer, Heidelberg (2012). https://doi.org/10.1007/978-3-642-32009-5_44
32. Zhandry, M.: How to record quantum queries, and applications to quantum indifferentiability. In: Boldyreva, A., Micciancio, D. (eds.) CRYPTO 2019. LNCS, vol. 11693, pp. 239–268. Springer, Cham (2019). https://doi.org/10.1007/978-3-030-26951-7_9

# Signatures From Pseudorandom States via ⊥-PRFs

Mohammed Barhoush[1(✉)], Amit Behera[2], Lior Ozer[2], Louis Salvail[1], and Or Sattath[1,2]

[1] Université de Montréal (DIRO), Montréal, Canada
mohammed.barhoush@umontreal.ca, salvail@iro.umontreal.ca, sattath@bgu.ac.il

[2] Department of Computer Science, Ben-Gurion University of the Negev, Beersheba, Israel
behera@post.bgu.ac.il, lioroz@post.bgu.ac.il

**Abstract.** Different flavors of quantum pseudorandomness have proven useful for various cryptographic applications, with the compelling feature that these primitives are potentially weaker than post-quantum one-way functions. Notably, Ananth, Lin, and Yuen (2023) have shown that logarithmic pseudorandom states can be used to construct a pseudo-deterministic PRG: informally, for a fixed seed, the output is the same with $1 - 1/poly$ probability.

In this work, we introduce new definitions for $\perp$-PRG and $\perp$-PRF. The correctness guarantees are that, for a fixed seed, except with negligible probability, the output is either the same (with probability $1 - 1/poly$) or recognizable abort, denoted $\perp$. Our approach admits a natural definition of multi-time PRG security, as well as the adaptive security of a PRF. We construct a $\perp$-PRG from any pseudo-deterministic PRG and, from that, a $\perp$-PRF.

While many Minicrypt primitives–such as symmetric encryption, commitments, MACs, and length-restricted one-time digital signatures–have been realized from quantum pseudorandomness assumptions, constructing full digital signatures remained an open challenge, and was explicitly posed as an open question by Morimae and Yamakawa (Crypto 2022). We resolve this by presenting the first (quantum) digital signature scheme with classical public keys and signatures from logarithmic pseudorandom states, utilizing our construction of $\perp$-PRFs. Additionally, we construct CPA secure public-key encryption with tamper-resilient quantum public keys. Combined with a recent work of Barhoush, Nishimaki, and Yamakawa (2025), our results demonstrate that these applications can be realized under assumptions that are separated from quantum evaluatable one-way functions.

**Keywords:** Quantum Cryptography · Quantum Pseudorandomness · Pseudodeterminism · Pseudorandom States · Digital Signatures

© International Association for Cryptologic Research 2026
G. Hanaoka and B.-Y. Yang (Eds.): ASIACRYPT 2025, LNCS 16252, pp. 320–349, 2026.
https://doi.org/10.1007/978-981-95-5125-5_11

# 1 Introduction

Introduced by Ji, Liu, and Song in [18], pseudorandom quantum state (PRS) generators capture pseudorandomness in the quantum realm similar to pseudorandom generators (PRG) in the classical setting [8].

Intuitively, a $m$-PRS generator [18] is a quantum polynomial-time algorithm that takes an input $k \in \{0,1\}^\lambda$ and outputs an $m$-qubit state $|\phi_k\rangle$ that is indistinguishable from a random Haar state, even when provided with polynomially many copies of $|\phi_k\rangle$. We consider three PRS sizes:

1. $m = c \cdot \log(\lambda)$ with $c \ll 1$.
2. $m = c \cdot \log(\lambda)$ with $c \geq 1$, which we call *short pseudorandom states (*SPRS*s).*
3. $m = \Omega(\lambda)$, which we call *long pseudorandom states (*LPRS*s).*

These different cases behave quite differently and provide different applications. The first type of PRSs can be constructed unconditionally [11] and are cryptographically inept, similar to how PRGs of output size logarithmic in input size. However, despite the small output size, this is not the case for the second type, i.e., SPRSs because many cryptographic primitives such as symmetric encryption and bit commitments with classical communications can be built from SPRSs [3]. Finally, LPRSs have shown numerous applications including quantum pseudo-encryption, quantum bit-commitments, length-restricted one-time signatures with quantum public keys, and private-key quantum money [4,18,23]. Unlike the classical analogues, the relationship between SPRS and LPRS is not very well understood since no implication is known in either direction.

In relation to PRGs, both LPRSs and SPRSs can be constructed from PRGs [11,18]. In the other direction, Kretschmer [20] showed a black-box separation between PRGs and LPRSs[1], but this separation does not imply a separation between PRGs and SPRSs.

Despite the plethora of cryptographic application of PRS, a significant gap persists between the cryptographic applications of PRGs and these quantum pseudorandom notions in cryptography. Specifically, (many-time) Digital Signatures (DS), arguably one of the most fundamental primitives in cryptography, can be based on PRGs [7,12], but there are no construction of DS based solely on PRSs (of any size). Moreover, due to the separation results, quantum pseudorandomness provides potential avenues to achieve cryptographic tasks even in a world without quantum evaluatable one-way functions. Even though SPRSs are not separated from quantum evaluatable one-way functions, they or their derivatives such as pseudodeterministic PRG (PD-PRG) or their variants can very well be a weaker cryptographic primitive than quantum evaluatable one-way functions, and hence constructing cryptographic applications from SPRSs may shed more light on achieving these tasks from assumptions weaker than quantum evaluatable one-way functions. Indeed, in a subsequent work, Barhoush, Nishimaki, and Yamakawa [5] showed that OWSGs and hence quantum evaluatable one-way

[1] The separation is with respect to quantum evaluatable one-way function, but since any PRG is also a one-way function, the separation holds for PRGs as well.

functions are separated from $\perp$-PRGs, which combined with one of our results (Theorem 1) and [3,11] imply that the existence of $\perp$-PRG a close variant of PD-PRG is a potentially weaker cryptographic assumption than the existence of quantum evaluatable one-way functions.

Concurrent to our work, it was shown in [13] that DS[2] cannot be constructed in a black-box manner from LPRSs. This leaves the question of whether we can construct DS based on SPRSs, which is the main question that we study in this work.

### 1.1 Our Results

Since DS are known to be separated from LPRSs [13], it is natural to ask why it might be possible to build it from PRS with smaller output size such as SPRS. So what makes SPRS more useful than LPRS in constructing DS? The main advantage that SPRS has over LPRS is that the logarithmic output size of the SPRS unlocks the possibility to deterministically extract randomness by doing efficient tomography on the random state using only polynomial number of copies of the state. This property of SPRS was utilized in the work of Ananth, Lin, and Yuen [3] to generate pseudorandom strings, yielding a cryptographically useful primitive known as pseudodeterministic PRGs (PD-PRG) [3]. These functions have classical inputs and outputs yet incorporate quantum computations, which imply that the output is pseudo-deterministic (see Definition 2). Similarly, they define pseudodeterministic pseudorandom functions (PD-PRF) and show a construction based on logarithmic size PRFS.

Our work further extends the cryptographic utility of PD-PRG by achieving many of the cryptographic applications of PRG (such as DS), from PD-PRG. To this end, we first address the following question: under what circumstances can a PRG be replaced with a PD-PRG?

Unfortunately, in many cryptographic constructions involving PRGs, the pseudodeterminism is problematic and prevents us from substituting PRGs with PD-PRG. While completely eliminating the pseudodeterminism appears difficult, we show that the non-deterministic evaluations, i.e., those that are obtained with small probability, can be recognized. This recognizability allows us to replace these evaluations with $\perp$, naturally leading to the novel notion of PRG with recognizable abort[3], denoted as $\perp$-PRG. These functions, except with negligible probability, yield fixed outputs on the majority of inputs, and for the rest, the output is either some fixed value or $\perp$. We construct $\perp$-PRG from PD-PRG with multi-time $\perp$-pseudorandomness guarantees, which ensures security even if the same seed is evaluated multiple times (see the technical overview for further details), providing the following result:

**Theorem 1 (Informal Version of Theorem 8).** PD-PRG *implies* $\perp$-PRG.

[2] The separation in [13] also works for the case of digital signatures with quantum public keys.

[3] The term *recognizable abort* was used to describe a similar phenomenon in [4], which we follow.

An important example where the PRGs are invoked on structured inputs is the GGM construction [15], which constructs a PRF from a PRG. Indeed, we utilize the multi-time ⊥-pseudorandomness of our ⊥-PRG and show, for the first time, a reduction similar to that of the GGM reduction in the pseudodeterministic setting, yielding the following result.

**Theorem 2 (Informal Version of Theorem** 11)**.** ⊥-PRG *implies* ⊥-PRF.

Just like the definition of ⊥-PRG provides additional security compared to PD-PRG in the form of multi-time ⊥-pseudorandomness, the definition of ⊥-PRF, unlike the nonadaptive definition of PD-PRF [3], provides security even against adaptive queries, which plays a crucial role in achieving new applications.

Furthermore, ⊥-PRG is, in some sense, easier to use than PD-PRG. This enables us to use them to build a ⊥-version of universal one-way hash functions, which we denote as ⊥-UOWHF (see Definition 10). Our proof follows a similar template to the deterministic construction given in [16]. However, non-trivial adaptations and generalizations of entropy notions are required to deal with the nondeterminism of ⊥ evaluations. We obtain the following result.

**Theorem 3.** ⊥-PRG *implies* ⊥-UOWHF.

With ⊥-PRF and ⊥-UOWHF in hand, we build digital signatures with some desirable properties as follows.

**Theorem 4 (Informal Version of Theorem** 13)**.** ⊥-PRG *implies an existentially unforgeable (many-time) digital signature scheme with a classical secret key, a classical public key, and classical signatures.*

The construction follows an approach similar to that of the classical construction of digital signatures from PRFs and UOWHFs [21,25,26] (see [14, Chapter 6] for a modern presentation).

We then turn to public-key encryption. Notably, [19] have constructed QPKE with tamper-resilient quantum public keys from *deterministic* strongly unforgeable digital signatures. Remarkably, in their definition, security is guaranteed even if an adversary can tamper with the quantum public keys, provided a classical verification key can be authentically distributed. Our digital signatures are not deterministic due to the potential ⊥ evaluations of the ⊥-PRF. Nevertheless, we show that their approach can be tweaked to fit the pseudodeterministic nature of our signature scheme, hence showing:

**Theorem 5.** ⊥-PRG *implies CPA-secure* QPKE *with reusable (tamper-resilient) quantum public keys.*

*Ramifications of Our Results* The broader consequence of our results is that SPRSs can serve as replacements for PRGs in the two fundamental tasks of public authentication and encryption, with security guaranteed against adversaries making classical queries to the signing or encryption oracle, following the security model used in previous works [2,4,23].

Moreover, as mentioned before, a subsequent work by Barhoush, Nishimaki, and Yamakawa [5] showed that one-way state generators (OWSGs) are separated from ⊥-PRGs. A OWSG is the quantum analog of one-way functions that can be built from a PRS with output length $m \geq \log(\lambda)$ (Theorem C1 [24]). Since every one-way function is itself a OWSG, Theorem 13, and Theorem 5 in combination with [5] imply the following corollaries.

**Corollary 1 (Signatures with Classical Keys and Signatures Separated From OWF).** *There is no classical construction of a one-way function from an unforgeable digital signature scheme, with classical keys and signatures, even though there is a black box construction in the other direction [14,21,25,26]. Hence, digital signatures of the above-mentioned kind are separated from one-way functions.*

**Corollary 2 (Tamper-Proof QPKE Separated From OWF).** *There is no black box construction of a one-way function from a CPA-secure* QPKE *with reusable (tamper-resilient) quantum public keys, even though there is a black box construction in the other direction [19]. Hence,* QPKE *of the above-mentioned kind are separated from one-way functions.*

An interesting avenue for future work is to upgrade the security of ⊥-PRF, or variants thereof, in order to permit adversaries quantum oracle access to the function. In our work, we have only demonstrated security against QPT adversaries that are given *classical* access to the various functionalities. This limitation has implications for our applications as well. This would allow stronger notions of encryption and signatures (see [1,9]) to become attainable.

### 1.2 Related Works

Ever since the introduction of PRSs [18] as a potentially weaker assumption than PRGs, a series of works have attempted to replace PRGs with PRSs. Non-interactive statistically binding commitments [23], non-interactive statistically hiding [17,27] commitments as well as quantum MPC were shown (see [23] and references therein).

Morimae and Yamakawa [23] constructed length-restricted one-time signatures with quantum verification keys from PRSs. Notably, they left an intriguing question unanswered, which is whether digital signatures—the only major missing protocol in MiniCrypt—could be constructed based on PRSs (or variants thereof). We answer this question affirmatively in Theorem 4.

As mentioned before, a recent work [13] has shown that digital signatures are separated from linear-length PRS, which in conjunction with Theorem 4 implies a black-box separation between SPRS and LPRS. In fact, a follow-up work [10] also shows a black-box separation between SPRS and LPRS more directly using our results.

The difficulty of replacing PRGs with LPRSs in cryptography also prompted the introduction of the (potentially) stronger assumption of *pseudorandom function-like states* (PRFSs)[4] [4]. This primitive was used to construct CPA-secure symmetric encryption, message-authentication codes, and quantum public-key encryption (QPKE) with non-reusable keys (each encryption necessitates a new public-key copy) [3,4,7]. Note that this QPKE scheme is not resistant to tampering attacks. This is a drawback because a quantum state cannot be signed [6], implying that their construction requires secure quantum channels for the distribution of the quantum public keys, which is a very strong setup assumption. This motivated the work [19], which provides a QPKE scheme with quantum public-keys that is resistant to tampering attacks based on OWFs. Our scheme is the first to achieve this based on an assumption that is potentially weaker than OWFs – thereby answering a question posed in the same work [19] regarding the possibility of this result.

Most important for our work is the recent paper by Ananth, Lin, and Yuen [3], where they demonstrated how to construct PD-PRG from SPRSs and PD-PRF from logarithmic PRFSs. It should be noted that the definition of PD-PRF considered in [3] only satisfies selective security with unique queries. Consequently, they provide as applications, commitments with classical communication and CPA-secure symmetric encryption with classical ciphertexts. We leverage their construction for PD-PRG to construct ⊥-PRF. Notably, our ⊥-PRF are based on SPRSs, whereas their PD-PRF are based on logarithmic PRFSs which is a potentially stronger assumption than SPRSs. Moreover, our ⊥-PRF provides an easier and more structured definition to work with, thereby enabling the development of more powerful cryptographic applications.

Shortly after our work, Barhoush, Nishimaki, and Yamakawa [5] showed that OWSGs are separated from ⊥-PRGs. As mentioned in Sect. 1.1, OWSGs are the quantum analogues of one-wayness and every one-way function is a OWSG. Combining [5] with our results (Theorems 5 and 4), we conclude that DSs and QPKE as primitives separated from OWF(see Corollaries 1 and 2).

### 1.3 Technical Overview

We will first recall the definition of a PD-PRG. Informally, this is an efficient quantum algorithm $G$, that takes a classical seed of length $\lambda$, and outputs a string $y$ of length $\ell > \lambda$. Unlike a standard PRG, the PD-PRG output need not be deterministic. The correctness guarantee is as follows: There exists a large set of good keys $\mathcal{K}$ consisting of $1 - 1/\mathsf{poly}(\lambda)$ fraction of all keys, such that for every good key $k \in K$, there exists a string $y \in \{0,1\}^\ell$ s.t. $\Pr(G(k) = y) \geq 1 - 1/\mathsf{poly}(\lambda)$. The pseudorandomness property is defined as standard PRGs: A QPT adversary cannot distinguish between $G(k)$, where $k \xleftarrow{\$} \{0,1\}^\lambda$ and a

[4] An $m$-PRFS is a generator $G$ which takes a seed $k \in \{0,1\}^\lambda$ and an input $x \in \{0,1\}^\ell$ and outputs an $m$-qubit state such that oracle access to $G$ is indistinguishable from oracle access to a truly random Haar state generator. It was shown that PRFS with $\ell = O(\log(\lambda))$ can be constructed from PRS, but PRFS with $\ell = \omega(\log(\lambda))$ seems like a stronger assumption and is more useful for applications.

random string $r \xleftarrow{\$} \{0,1\}^\ell$. The formal details are given in Definition 2. Ref. [3] proved that SPRS implies PD-PRG, in some parameter regimes (see Theorem 9).

Following the classical template to construct digital signatures, the first step would be to construct universal one-way hash functions (UOWHF) from a PRG in the psuedodeterministic setting in order to lift a one-time signature scheme to a many-time stateful scheme. The next step would be to construct an adaptively secure PRF from a PRG to enable a full-fledged stateless signature scheme, as we discuss in further detail later.

To achieve the goals mentioned above, we need to develop appropriate notions for PRFs and UOWHFs that can be realized from PD-PRG.

*Need for* $\perp$-PRF. A natural attempt would be to build pseudodeterministic PRFs from PD-PRG, following the constructions in the deterministic setting. However, even if we could do so, the guarantees of a pseudodeterministic PRF may not be enough to construct digital signatures, due to the following obstacles:

1. *Need for Stronger Notions of Security.* In the classical template to construct digital signatures, the signing algorithm chooses a random leaf in the authentication tree, and the corresponding one-time signing key of the leaf finally signs the message, where the one-time signing and public keys for each of the internal node are obtained by evaluating the PRF on the node. Therefore, signing multiple messages would involve evaluating the PRF evaluation of the same string (especially the string representing the root and some of its nearest successors) multiple times. Hence, it is crucial that the PRF satisfies multi-time security, i.e., the adversary in the distinguishing game is allowed to query on the same input twice. Of course, multiple evaluations do not affect security for classical PRFs since they are deterministic, but it is harder to achieve multi-time security in the pseudodeterministic setting. Indeed, the only definition of PD-PRF studied in [3] is not multi-time secure since the security game only allows unique queries from the adversary. This is a necessary restriction because querying a PD-PRF on the same input twice may result in two different outcomes, which will trivially make the PD-PRF distinguishable from a random function.
   Secondly, it is also desirable to make the signing algorithm deterministic. In the classical template, the signing algorithm is derandomized by replacing the randomness required to choose the leaf in the authentication tree for signing the message, with the PRF evaluation of the PRF on the message. With this modification, it becomes crucial in order to argue CMA security that the PRF is secure even when the adversary can make adaptive queries. Alongside the construction of digital signatures with deterministic signing, adaptively secure PRF is widely used in simple constructions of other fundamental primitives. For instance, one of the simplest constructions of Message Authentication Codes (MAC) is where signing a message $m$ is simply evaluating the PRF on $m$ and verification of an alleged message tag pair $(m, \sigma)$ is to evaluate the PRF on $m$ and checking if it the output is same as $\sigma$. Clearly, the adaptive security of PRF is crucial to argue the CMA-security of the MAC thus constructed. However, the (only) PD-PRF definition studied in [3] considers only selective

security. Furthermore, the proof techniques used in [3] to construct PD-PRF seem inadequate to prove adaptive security.

2. *Need for Structured Pseudodeterminism.* The psuedodeterminism in PD-PRF prevents us from utilizing them in the construction of digital signatures. Recall that in the classical template, the public key of the digital signature is associated with the public key of the one-time digital signature scheme at the root of the authentication tree. This public key is used to sign the public keys of its two children, which are the $\mathsf{PRF}_k(0)$ and $\mathsf{PRF}_k(1)$. However, the pseudodeterministic errors of the PD-PRF may cause the one-time signature scheme to sign two different messages using the same secret key, which may compromise the security of the one-time scheme and, thus, of the entire authentication tree. For instance, if the adversary queries the signing oracle twice, and during the signing of the two messages, the two different evaluations of the root yield different outputs, then the adversary would learn two signatures under the same one-time signature secret key at the root.

The main conceptual contribution of our work is solving these issues by introducing the notion of recognizable abort. Recognizable abort for PRF means that for every input $x$, the evaluation either outputs a fixed string $y$ or aborts by outputting the special symbol $\perp$. This clearly provides a more structured form of pseudodeterminism that solves the issues mentioned in Item 2. above. Surprisingly, the structured pseudodeterminism thus obtained also leads us to natural definitions for stronger security guarantees, namely, multi-time security and adaptive security, as discussed above in Item 1. More generally, we believe that this notion provides a simpler route toward achieving applications from pseudodeterministic primitives.

Formally, a $\perp$-PRF family is a family of quantum algorithms $\{f_k\}_{k\in\{0,1\}^\lambda}$, with $m$ bits of inputs, which always yield a *classical* output from the set $\{0,1\}^\ell \cup \{\perp\}$ (i.e., the algorithm can abort). For every key $k$ and input $x$, there exists $y$ such the evaluation $f_k$ is in $\{y, \perp\}$ except with negligible probability. Moreover for every $x \in \{0,1\}^m$, $\Pr(f_k(x) \neq \perp : k \xleftarrow{\$} \{0,1\}^\lambda) \geq 1 - \frac{1}{\mathsf{poly}(\lambda)}$. The recognizable abort property lets us define multi-time adaptive security (i.e., the adversary can adaptively query as well query at the same input more than once) for $\perp$-PRF in the following way, which suffices for constructing digital signatures in the classical template. The challenger samples a key $k \xleftarrow{\$} \{0,1\}^\lambda$, a random function $f : \{0,1\}^m \to \{0,1\}^\ell$, and a bit $b \xleftarrow{\$} \{0,1\}$. If $b$ equals 0, it provides (classical) oracle access to $f_k(\cdot)$. If $b = 1$, the oracle that the challenger provides behaves as follows. Given an input $x$, the oracle outputs $\perp$ if $f_k(x)$ evaluates to $\perp$, and $f(x)$ otherwise. Note that the adversary may query the same element $x$ many times.

Now that we have an multi-time adaptively secure definition of PRF in the pseudodeterministic setting, the next challenge is how to construct $\perp$-PRF from SPRS.

*Construction of* $\perp$-PRF, *and the Need for* $\perp$-PRG A naïve attempt to construct $\perp$-PRF would be to instantiate the famous Goldreich, Goldwasser, and Micali

(GGM) transformation [15] from PRG-to-PRF with a PD-PRG. Note that in the proof of pseudorandomness for the GGM construction, the reduction uses multiple evaluations of the PRG at the same random seed. Of course, multiple evaluations do not affect security in the classical setting since the PRG there is deterministic, but in the pseudodeterministic setting, multiple evaluations may output distinct values, and hence security does not hold for PD-PRG if multiple evaluations are allowed. Indeed, even if two evaluations of a PD-PRG on the same seed are allowed, then with non-negligible probability, we will get different outputs for different evaluations, which is trivially distinguishable from giving a uniformly random string twice.

As a remedy, we attempt to define an intermediate primitive called PRG with recognizable abort or $\perp$-PRG. Similarly, to PD-PRG, a $\perp$-PRG is a quantum algorithm $G$ mapping $\{0,1\}^\lambda$ to $\{0,1\}^\ell$, except the algorithm can also output a special string $\perp$, which represents aborting. We require $\ell > \lambda$, for non-triviality, as all forms of PRG. As for the output, it is guaranteed that for every $k \in \{0,1\}^\lambda$, there exists a string $y \in \{0,1\}^\ell$ s.t. $\Pr(G(k) \in \{y, \perp\}) \geq 1 - \mathsf{negl}(\lambda)$, for some negligible function $\mathsf{negl}(\lambda)$. Moreover, just-like PD-PRG, there exists a good set $\mathcal{K}$ consisting of $1 - 1/\mathsf{poly}(\lambda)$ fraction of all keys, such that for every good key $k \in \mathcal{K}$, $\Pr(G(k) = \perp)$ is negligible. A $\perp$-PRG can be easily distinguished from a random string since a random string is never $\perp$. Therefore, standard pseudorandomness cannot hold for $\perp$-PRG.

A natural alternative would be to demand conditional pseudorandomness, i.e., indistinguishability from a random string conditioned on the evaluation of the $\perp$-PRG not being $\perp$. We will refer to it as $\perp$-pseudorandomness. An advantage of this alternate definition is that it can be extended to incorporate $\perp$-pseudorandomness, even when the $\perp$-PRG is evaluated multiple times on the same random $k$. This extended form of $\perp$-pseudorandomness that we call multi-time $\perp$-pseudorandomness can be explained via the following indistinguishability game, where we demand a negligible distinguishing advantage. For some $q(\lambda) \in \mathsf{poly}(\lambda)$ denoting the number of repeated evaluations, the challenger samples a key $k \xleftarrow{\$} \{0,1\}^\lambda$, and then either provides $q$ evaluations of $G(k)$ to the adversary or sends $y_1, \ldots, y_q$ to the adversary where $y_1, \ldots, y_q$ are generated as follows: The challenger samples a string $y \xleftarrow{\$} \{0,1\}^\ell$, evaluates $G(k)$ $q$-times and if the $i^{th}$ evaluation is successful (i.e., the evaluation did not abort) sets $y_i$ to $y$ else sets $y_i$ to $\perp$. It can be verified that for $q = 1$, the above indistinguishability game coincides with the conditional pseudorandomness or (single-time) $\perp$-pseudorandomness. Note that a $\perp$-PRG satisfying single-time $\perp$-pseudorandomness (i.e., $q = 1$) does not generically satisfy multi-time $\perp$-pseudorandomness. In particular, the multi-time $\perp$-pseudorandomness game, unlike the single-time $\perp$-pseudorandomness game, allows the distinguisher to learn the probability of outputting $\perp$ for the sampled key, which can leak information regarding the non-$\perp$ output of the key. For example, consider a boolean output $\perp$-PRG $G$ and, for simplicity, assume that there are only four keys $k_1, \ldots, k_4$, out of which the only key outside the good set is $k_4$ which evaluates to $\perp$ with probability $\frac{1}{2}$, and outputs 0 with the remaining probability. For $i \in [3]$, $k_i$ outputs 0 with probability $\frac{5}{12}$ and 1 with the remaining probabibility. It can be easily checked that $G$ satisfies the conditional pseudorandomness or single-time ⊥-pseudorandomness. However, $G$ does not satisfy multi-time ⊥-pseudorandomness because, using polynomial evaluations, the distinguisher in the multi-time ⊥-pseudorandomness game can learn the probability of outputting ⊥ for the key $k$ that was sampled by the challenger and, in particular, distinguish between the case when $k$ is from the good set, i.e., $k \in \{k_1, k_2, k_3\}$ or $k$ is not from the good set, i.e., $k = k_4$. Since there is an asymmetry between the output distribution of keys from the good set and the key not from the good set, the distinguisher can guess the non-⊥ output of the key with a constant advantage, using which he can distinguish if the non-⊥ evaluations provided to him were from the ⊥-PRG or if they were provided using a uniformly random string. Concretely, in this example, if the distinguisher learns that the key is from the good set and the non-⊥ evaluation is 1 or if she learns that the key is not from the good set and the non-⊥ evaluation is 1, then she outputs 0 and otherwise outputs 1. Clearly, the distinguisher outputs 1 with a significantly larger probability in the random string case than in the ⊥-PRG case.

Intuitively, the security of ⊥-PRF is an extension of the multi-time ⊥-pseudorandomness property of ⊥-PRG to ⊥-PRF similar to the relation between the pseudorandomness of PRG and PRF in the classical setting. This enables the construction of ⊥-PRF from ⊥-PRG via the GGM transform, via the same classical arguments in the security proof up to adaptations required due to the pseudodeterminism. Interestingly, the main technical difficulty in proving the GGM transformation for ⊥-PRG-to-⊥-PRF is the proof of the correctness for the resulting ⊥-PRF (i.e., it satisfies the relevant ⊥ properties), for which we had to use the security properties, i.e., ⊥-pseudorandomness along with the correctness of the underlying ⊥-PRG, see the full version for more details. This is in contrast to the classical GGM construction, where correctness holds trivially.

⊥-PRG *from* PD-PRG. We show a construction of ⊥-PRG from any PD-PRG, in two steps. In the first step, we run the PD-PRG with the same seed $\lambda$ times, output the outcome that appeared in at least 60% of the evaluations, and output ⊥ if no such outcome occurs. Note that for a good seed $k \in \mathcal{K}$, the generator will not output ⊥, except with negligible probability. A standard argument is used to prove that this construction satisfies the standard notion of weak-PRG pseudorandomness (the output can easily be distinguished from random whenever the output is ⊥, which may occur when a bad seed is picked with probability $1/\mathsf{poly}(\lambda)$).

The goal of the second step is to kill two birds with one stone: to reduce the (weak) pseudorandomness guarantees from $1/\mathsf{poly}(\lambda)$ advantage to a negligible advantage and achieve that in the multi-time ⊥-pseudorandomness setting, thereby achieving both security amplification and security enhancement to multi-time ⊥-pseudorandomness. To achieve that, we use Levin's version of Yao's XOR lemma adapted to the quantum setting. Our construction works as follows. The new ⊥-PRG uses $\lambda$ times longer seeds compared to the previous one, which we use as $k_1, \ldots, k_\lambda$. We first evaluate $G(k_1), \ldots, G(k_\lambda)$ and output ⊥ if any of them aborts, and continue to output the XOR of all of the values otherwise. Note that any seed of the new $\perp$-PRG that consists of $\lambda$ original good seeds is a good seed.

$\perp$-UOWHF *and its Construction From* $\perp$-PRG Toward building digital signatures, we will need to construct some form of UOWHFs. Intuitively, a UOWHF is a OWF that also satisfies a hashing property. Prior works [16,26] have shown how to build a UOWHF from any OWF. Naturally, we would like to adapt these deterministic constructions [16,26], so that it can be instantiated with a pseudodeterministic form of OWFs.

We first introduce the notion of $\perp$-OWFs. Analogous to $\perp$-PRGs, a $\perp$-OWF $F$ (formally defined in the full version) satisfies the following: for every input $x$, there exists an output $y$ s.t. $\Pr(F(x) \in \{y, \perp\}) \geq 1 - \mathsf{negl}(\lambda)$, for some negligible function $\mathsf{negl}(\lambda)$. Moreover, there exists a good set $\mathcal{X}$ consisting of $1 - 1/\mathsf{poly}(\lambda)$ fraction of all inputs, such that for any good input $x \in \mathcal{X}$, $\Pr(F(x) = \perp)$ is negligible. For security, we require that it is difficult for an efficient adversary to find an inverse to a non-$\perp$ image. This is sufficient for our applications of $\perp$-OWFs, as we can simply abort when encountering a $\perp$. Similar to the classical setting, we show that every $\perp$-PRG with sufficient stretch yields a $\perp$-OWF. This extension requires only minor adaptations to handle the presence of $\perp$ evaluations.

However, adapting the classical UOWHF constructions [16,26] to work with $\perp$-OWFs poses new challenges. These constructions crucially rely on structural properties of standard OWFs that fail to hold in the pseudodeterministic setting. For instance, the constructions require intricately working with the entropy of a uniformly random preimage of an image element under the OWF. This is problematic for pseudodeterministic functions, where multiple inputs may map to the same output with some probability, making preimage sets ill-defined and rendering many standard entropy arguments inapplicable.

In the psuedodeterministic case, when we consider the inverses to an element $y$ for a $\perp$-OWF, we are interested in inputs that evaluate to $y$ with non-negligible probability, as these are the inputs that can potentially pass as valid inverses for $y$. This set is more restricted since for each input $x$, there exists a value $y$ such that $F(x) \in \{\perp, y\}$, except with negligible probability. This structure allows us to define entropy notions for $\perp$-OWFs that mirror those of deterministic functions.

Using these insights, we construct $\perp$-UOWHFs from $\perp$-OWFs by following the overall structure of the deterministic approach in [16]. Our proof, however, requires additional care: handling entropy in the $\perp$-OWF context is more delicate, and the presence of $\perp$ outputs complicates the analysis. For example, a key step in [16] uses the observation that if a $\beta$ fraction of inputs map to outputs starting with 0 under an OWF, then the remaining $1 - \beta$ fraction must map to outputs starting with 1. This argument breaks down for $\perp$-OWFs, where a significant portion of inputs may map to $\perp$ with high probability. As a result, several steps in the original proof require alternate reasoning to account for these nuances. See the full version for our proof.

*How to Use Pseudo-Determinism with Recognizable Abort.* Suppose primitive A (e.g., MAC) can be constructed from a deterministic primitive $B$ (e.g., PRF). How can we achieve a similar result using a pseudodeterministic version of $B$ (for example, MAC based on ⊥-PRF)? We use the following template in our work: In the first step, we replace the underlying deterministic primitive (e.g., the PRF) in that construction with its recognizable abort counterpart (e.g., a ⊥-PRF), which, in most cases can easily be shown to be secure[5], but only with $(1 - \frac{1}{\mathsf{poly}(\lambda)})$-correctness, due to ⊥ errors. In the next step of the template, we consider a variant of a $\lambda$-repetition of the $(1 - \frac{1}{\mathsf{poly}(\lambda)})$-correct but secure construction at the end of the previous step to amplify the correctness to $(1 - \mathsf{negl}(\lambda))$. Using standard techniques, we then show that the resulting $\lambda$-fold construction is secure if the underlying base construction is secure. For example, to show a MAC based on ⊥-PRF, we sample $\lambda$ signing keys, and signing a message $m$ would be done by evaluating the ⊥-PRF on this message using all the keys. The verification procedure applies the ⊥-PRF on the message with all the signing keys, and accepts if at least one of the successful un-aborted evaluations agrees with the signature.

*Digital Signatures.* In the classical setting, basing (stateless) digital signatures (DS) on the minimal assumption of OWFs took a sequence of works [14,21,25, 26], culminating in a complex final scheme. We first briefly describe this effort and how we adapt it to our work, replacing OWFs with ⊥-PRGs.

Lamport [21] first showed how to construct a simple one-time signature scheme from any OWF. For single-bit messages, the secret key is two randomly sampled inputs $\mathsf{sk} := (x_0, x_1)$, while the verification key is the images $\mathsf{vk} := (F(x_0), F(x_1))$ under a OWF $F$. The signer can simply reveal $x_b$ to sign message $b$; unforgeability follows easily from the difficulty of inverting $F$.

Furthermore, as shown in [14], by using a UOWHF instead of an OWF, we can ensure that the adversary cannot generate a new signature for a message $m$ even given a signature of $m$. This property is called *strong unforgeability* and is used in the application of QPKE, see the full version for more details.

Next, Naor and Young [25] showed how to sign many-time signature scheme using UOWHFs. However, in their scheme, the signer needs to remember all previous signatures produced. As a result, this scheme is called "*stateful.*" They also show how to construct a UOWHF from any injective OWF. Rompel in [26] then showed that UOWHF can be constructed from any OWF and, therefore, from any PRG. Rompel's proof is quite involved, prompting a follow-up work [16] that provides a simpler construction.

Later, Goldreich [14] leveraged PRFs to achieve the final result: a many-time "*stateless*" DS scheme, where the signer does not need to store previous signatures.

With ⊥-PRFs and ⊥-UOWHF, we carefully adapt the techniques used in the aforementioned works to our setting. The overall construction of the digital signature follows the same template as mentioned above on Page 12. On the downside, by relying on pseudodeterministic functions, our signatures have a

[5] Note that this step may not work if we have pseudodeterminism without recognizable abort because the security proof may require multi-time adaptive security from $B$ (e.g., PRF) that may not hold for the pseudodeterministic version of $B$ (e.g. PD-PRF).

non-negligible probability of failing verification. This issue can be addressed by repetition, however, the resulting scheme is no longer strongly unforgeable and only satisfies standard unforgeability – it is easy to modify one of the 'bad' signatures in the repeated scheme without being detected. Hence, our work gives the option to choose between statistical correctness and strong unforgeability. In conclusion, we achieve statistical correct unforgeable (many-time) stateless DSs from SPRSs and (1/4)-correct strongly unforgeable signatures from SPRSs.

*Tamper-proof QPKE.* A generic construction of CPA secure tamper-proof QPKE from strongly unforgeable digital signatures with unique signatures was shown in [19]. We use their generic construction to show that tamper-proof QPKE can be constructed based on ⊥-PRG as follows. First, we show that instantiating the construction in [19] with a $(1-\frac{1}{\mathsf{poly}(\lambda)})$-correct digital signature scheme that can be based on ⊥-PRG results in a $(1-\frac{1}{\mathsf{poly}(\lambda)})$-correct QPKE scheme $\Pi$ that is IND-pkT-CPA secure, i.e., CPA security in the tamper-proof setting as defined in [19]. Next, we do a variant of $\lambda$-parallel repetition of $\Pi$ to get a QPKE scheme $\Pi^\lambda$ that satisfies negligible correctness error. In the repeated scheme $\Pi^\lambda$, we use $\lambda$ independently generated secret keys, public keys, and verification keys of $\Pi$ as the new secret key, public key, and verification key, respectively. Encryption is performed by encrypting the message $\lambda$ times using the $\lambda$ public keys independently. The decryption interprets the cipher as $\lambda$ ciphers of $\Pi$ runs the decryption of $\Pi$ on each of them with the respective secret keys and outputs $\perp$ if all of them are $\perp$. Else, checks if all the decrypted messages that are non-$\perp$ are the same or not. If they are the same, output that message, else output $\perp$. We show that $\Pi^\lambda$ is IND-pkT-CPA secure if $\Pi$ is IND-pkT-CPA secure, via a standard reduction similar to that used in the black-box construction of secure multi-bit encryption from secure single-bit encryption via parallel repetition. The full proof is given in the full version.

## 2 Preliminaries

### 2.1 Notations

We denote the density matrix of a quantum state in a register $E$ is denoted as $\rho_E$. The trace distance is given as $\delta(\rho,\sigma) := \frac{1}{2}\|\rho-\sigma\|$.

We say $x \leftarrow X$ if $x$ is chosen from the values in $X$ according to the distribution $X$. If $X$ is a set, then $x \leftarrow X$ denotes an element chosen uniformly at random from the set.

We use the notation and convention in [3] to define quantum algorithms. We say that a quantum algorithm $A$ is *QPT* if it consists of a family of generalized quantum circuits (i.e., circuits that have an additional subset of input qubits called ancillae qubits that are initialized to 0) $\{A_\lambda\}_\lambda$ such that each circuit $A_\lambda$ is bounded a polynomial $p(\lambda)$. We call a QPT algorithm $A$ non-uniform if it consists of a family $\{A_\lambda, \rho_\lambda\}_\lambda$ where $\{A_\lambda\}_\lambda$ are circuits of polynomial size (not necessarily uniformly generated), such that for each $\lambda$, there is additionally a subset of input qubits of $A_\lambda$ that are designated to be initialized with the density matrix $\rho_\lambda$ of polynomial length. All the algorithms used in the security definitions are non-uniform unless mentioned otherwise.

We let $A^P$ mean that $A$ is given access to a polynomial number of oracle queries to $P$. We let $[n] \equiv \{1, 2, \ldots, n\}$ for every $n \in \mathbb{N}$ and $\mathsf{negl}(x)$ denote any function that is asymptotically smaller than the inverse of any polynomial. As in [3], we work in the non-uniform setting, meaning all the security guarantees in this work are against non-uniform QPT adversaries, i.e., the adversaries are quantum poly time algorithms with quantum advice states.

We let $\mathsf{Haar}(\mathbb{C}^d)$ denote the Haar measure over $\mathbb{C}^d$ which is the uniform measure over all $d$-dimensional unit vectors. For simplicity, we let $\mathsf{Haar}_m$ denote the Haar measure over $m$-qubit space i.e. $\mathsf{Haar}((\mathbb{C}^2)^{\otimes m})$. We let $\mathcal{O}_{\mathsf{Haar}_m}$ denote an oracle that generates random $m$-qubit Haar states.

### 2.2 Probability Theorems

**Theorem 6 (Chernoff Bound for $n$ Independent Poisson Trials Cited from Theorems 4.4,4.5 [22]).** *Let $X_1, \ldots, X_n$ be independent Poisson trials such that $\Pr[X_i] = p_i$. Let $X = \sum_{i=1}^n X_i$ and $\mu = E[X]$. Then, for $0 < \delta < 1$:*

1. $\Pr[X \geq (1+\delta)\mu] \leq e^{-\mu\delta^2/2}$
2. $\Pr[X \leq (1-\delta)\mu] \leq e^{-\mu\delta^2/2}$

### 2.3 Pseudorandom States and Variants

We recall the definitions of pseudorandom states (PRSs) [18]. In a follow up work [3], SPRSs were used to construct PD-PRG which we define as well.

**Definition 1 (Pseudorandom State Generator).** *A family of QPT algorithms $G = \{G_\lambda\}_{\lambda \in \mathbb{N}}$ is called $m(\lambda)$-*pseudorandom state generator (PRS), *if the following conditions hold:*

- *For all $\lambda \in \mathbb{N}$ and $k \in \{0,1\}^\lambda$, $G_\lambda(k) = \rho_k$ for some $m(\lambda)$-qubit state $\rho_k$.*
- *For any polynomial $t(\cdot)$ and QPT distinguisher $\mathcal{A}$:*

$$\left| \Pr_{k \leftarrow \{0,1\}^\lambda}[\mathcal{A}_\lambda(G_\lambda(k)^{\otimes t(\lambda)}) = 1] - \Pr_{|\phi\rangle \leftarrow \mathsf{Haar}_{m(\lambda)}}[\mathcal{A}_\lambda(|\phi\rangle^{\otimes t(\lambda)}) = 1] \right| \leq \mathsf{negl}(\lambda).$$

*We divide* PRS *into three regimes, based on the state size $m(\lambda)$:*

1. *$m = c \cdot \log(\lambda)$ with $c \ll 1$.*
2. *$m = c \cdot \log(\lambda)$ with $c \geq 1$, which we call* short pseudorandom states (SPRSs).
3. *$m = \Omega(\lambda)$, which we call* long pseudorandom states (LPRSs).

**Definition 2 (Pseudodeterministic Pseudorandom Generators, Adapted From Definition 4.1 in [3]).** *A family of QPT algorithms $G = \{G_\lambda\}_{\lambda \in \mathbb{N}}$ which on input seed $k \in \{0,1\}^\lambda$ $G_\lambda(k)$ outputs a string of length $\ell(\lambda)$ is a* pseudodeterministic pseudorandom generator *(*PD-PRG*) if the following conditions hold:*

- ***Pseudodeterminism:*** *There exists a constant* $c > 0$ *and functions* $\mu(\lambda), \nu(\lambda) = O(\lambda^{-c})$ *such that for sufficiently large* $\lambda \in \mathbb{N}$, *there exists a set* $\mathcal{K}_\lambda \subset \{0,1\}^\lambda$ *such that:*
  1. $\Pr_{k \xleftarrow{\$} \{0,1\}^\lambda}[k \in \mathcal{K}_\lambda] \geq 1 - \mu(\lambda)$.
  2. *For every* $k \in \mathcal{K}_\lambda$*:*

$$\max_{y \in \{0,1\}^{\ell(\lambda)}} \Pr[Y \leftarrow G_\lambda(k) : Y = y] \geq 1 - \nu(\lambda). \quad (1)$$

- ***Stretch:*** *The output length of* $G_\lambda$, *namely* $\ell(\lambda)$, *is strictly greater than* $\lambda$.

*We let* $(\mu, \nu, \ell) - \mathsf{PD\text{-}PRG}$ *denote a generator with stretch* $\ell = \ell(\lambda)$ *satisfying pseudodeterminism with the functions* $\mu = \mu(\lambda), \nu = \nu(\lambda)$.

**Definition 3 (Weak/Strong Pseudorandomness for PD-PRG, Adapted From Definition 4.1 in [3]).** *For every non-uniform QPT distinguisher* $\mathcal{A}$, *there exists a function* $\epsilon$ *such that:*

$$\left| \Pr_{k \leftarrow \{0,1\}^\lambda}[y \leftarrow G_\lambda(k) : \mathcal{A}(y) = 1] - \Pr_{y \leftarrow \{0,1\}^{\ell(\lambda)}}[\mathcal{A}(y) = 1] \right| \leq \epsilon(\lambda). \quad (2)$$

*We say that* $G$ *is a strong* PD-PRG *if for every* $\mathcal{A}$, $\epsilon(\lambda)$ *is a negligible function, and is a weak* PD-PRG *if for every* $\mathcal{A}$, $\epsilon(\lambda) \leq \frac{1}{v(\lambda)}$ *for some polynomial* $v$. *We say that the* PD-PRG *is* $\epsilon$*-pseudorandom for a function* $\epsilon$ *if for every* $\mathcal{A}$ *there is a* $\lambda_0 \in \mathbb{N}$ *such that the bound holds with the* same *function* $\epsilon$ *for all* $\lambda > \lambda_0$.

## 3 ⊥ Pseudorandom Generators

### 3.1 Definitions

Next, we introduce a different notion of pseudo-deterministic PRG , with a recognizable abort property.

**Definition 4 (Pseudorandom Generator with Recognizable Abort (⊥-PRG)).** *A family of QPT algorithms* $G = \{G_\lambda\}_{\lambda \in \mathbb{N}}$ *which on input seed* $k \in \{0,1\}^\lambda$, $G_\lambda(k)$ *outputs a string of length* $\ell(\lambda)$ *is a* pseudodeterministic pseudorandom generator with recognizable abort *(⊥-PRG) if the following conditions hold:*

1. ***Pseudodeterminism:*** *There exist a constant* $c > 0$ *and a function* $\mu(\lambda) = O(\lambda^{-c})$ *such that for sufficiently large* $\lambda \in \mathbb{N}$ *there exists a set* $\mathcal{K}_\lambda \subset \{0,1\}^\lambda$ *such that the following holds:*
   *(a)*

$$\Pr_{k \xleftarrow{\$} \{0,1\}^\lambda}[k \in \mathcal{K}_\lambda] \geq 1 - \mu(\lambda).$$

(b) *For every* $k \in \mathcal{K}_\lambda$ *there exists a* $y \in \{0,1\}^{\ell(\lambda)}$ *and a negligible function such that:*

$$\Pr\left[Y \leftarrow G_\lambda(k) : Y = y\right] \geq 1 - \mathsf{negl}(\lambda). \tag{3}$$

(c) *For every* $k \in \{0,1\}^\lambda$ *there exists a* $y \in \{0,1\}^{\ell(\lambda)}$ *and a negligible function such that:*

$$\Pr\left[Y \leftarrow G_\lambda(k) : Y \in \{y, \bot\}\right] \geq 1 - \mathsf{negl}(\lambda). \tag{4}$$

2. ***Stretch:*** *The output length of* $G_\lambda$*, namely* $\ell(\lambda)$*, is strictly greater than* $\lambda$*.*

*We let* $(\mu,\ell)$-$\bot$-PRG *denote a* $\bot$-PRG *with stretch* $\ell = \ell(\lambda)$ *and* $\mu = \mu(\lambda)$ *pseudodeterminism.*

A $\bot$-PRG differs from a pseudodeterministic pseudorandom generator in two ways. First, for every input $x$, there exists a $y$ such that the output is either $y$ or $\bot$, except with negligible probability. Second, it has better pseudodeterminism for keys in the good set: For those keys, the $\bot$ probability is negligible.

Next, we address the pseudorandomness property of the $\bot$-PRG. Since the $\bot$-PRG may often output the $\bot$ value, there is no hope of achieving the strong security as defined in Definition 3. We modify the pseudorandomness definition to make sure that the adversary cannot obtain any advantage from seeing abort, by providing the abort value both in the pseudorandom, and in the truly random case.

**Definition 5 (Is-⊥).** *We define the operator*

$$\mathsf{Is}\text{-}\bot(a,b) := \begin{cases} \bot & \text{if } a = \bot \\ b & \text{otherwise.} \end{cases}$$

**Definition 6 (Multi-time ⊥-Pseudorandomness for ⊥-PRG).** *Let* $G = \{G_\lambda\}_{\lambda\in\mathbb{N}}$ *be a* $\bot$-PRG*.* $G$ *has multi-time* $\bot$*-pseudorandomness if for any non-uniform QPT distinguisher* $\mathcal{A}$ *and for any polynomial* $q = q(\lambda)$ *there exists a negligible function* $\epsilon$ *such that:*

$$\left| \Pr\begin{bmatrix} k \leftarrow \{0,1\}^\lambda \\ y_1 \leftarrow G_\lambda(k) \\ \vdots \\ y_q \leftarrow G_\lambda(k) \end{bmatrix} : \mathcal{A}(y_1,\dots,y_q) = 1 \right] - \Pr\left[\begin{matrix} k \leftarrow \{0,1\}^\lambda \\ y \leftarrow \{0,1\}^{\ell(\lambda)} \\ y_1 \leftarrow \mathsf{Is}\text{-}\bot(G_\lambda(k), y) \\ \vdots \\ y_q \leftarrow \mathsf{Is}\text{-}\bot(G_\lambda(k), y) \end{matrix} : \mathcal{A}(y_1,\dots,y_q) = 1\right] \right| \leq \epsilon(\lambda)$$

*Similarly,* $G$ *has* $t$*-fold multi-time* $\bot$*-pseudorandomness for a polynomial* $t(\lambda)$ *if for every adversary* $\mathcal{A}$*, the distinguishing advantage in the* $t$*-fold parallel repetition of the above indistinguishability game is negligible.*

**Theorem 7.** *A* $\bot$-PRG *that satisfies multi-time* $\bot$ *pseudorandomness, also satisfies the* $t$*-fold parallel version of multi-sample* $\bot$ *pseudorandomness for* $t \equiv t(\lambda) \in \mathsf{poly}(\lambda)$.

*Proof.* The proof follows by standard hybrid arguments for parallel repetition of indistinguishability games. ∎

### 3.2 Multi-time ⊥-PRG From Weak PD-PRG

The main result of this section is as follows.

**Theorem 8 (Multi-time** $\bot$**-PRG from weak PD-PRG).** *Assuming weak* $(\mu, \nu, \ell)$-PD-PRG *exists for which* $\ell(\lambda) > \lambda^2$ *and there exist a constant* $c > 1$ *such that* $\mu(\lambda) = O(\lambda^{-c})$*, then there exists multi-time* $(\lambda\mu, \ell') - \bot$-PRG*, where* $\ell'(\lambda^2) = \ell(\lambda)$.

The proof is given in the full version.

Ananth, Lin and Yuen proved that a SPRS implies a weak PD-PRG:

**Theorem 9 (Theorem 4.2 in [3]).** *Assuming the existence of* $(c \log \lambda)$*-PRS for some constant* $c > 6$*, then there exists a* $O(\lambda^{-c/6})$*-pseudorandom* $(\mu = O(\lambda^{-c/12}), \nu = O(\lambda^{-c/12}), \ell = \lambda^{c/6})$-PD-PRG.

By combining Theorems 8 and 9, we conclude:

**Corollary 3.** *Assuming the existence of* $(c \log \lambda)$*-PRS for some constant* $c > 12$*, then there exists multi-time* $(\mu = O(\lambda^{-c/12+1}), \ell = \lambda^{c/12}) - \bot$-PRG.

Note that $c$ in the corollary above must satisfy $c > 12$, so that the stretch $\ell(\lambda)$ of the $\bot$-PRG would satisfy $\ell(\lambda) > \lambda$. Even though this would not be used in our work, we mention that Ref. [3] shows that the exact same assumption as in the above, also implies a strong PD-PRG:

**Theorem 10 (Corollary 4.6 in [3]).** *Assuming the existence of* $(c \log \lambda)$*-PRS for some constant* $c > 12$*, then there exists a strong pseudorandom* $(\mu = O(\lambda^{-(c/12-1)}), \nu = O(\lambda^{-(c/12-1)}), \ell = \lambda^{c/6})$-PD-PRG.

## 4 ⊥ Pseudorandom Functions

**Definition 7.** *Let* $\bot$ *be a special symbol called* $\bot$. *A family of quantum algorithms (i.e., the output on a fixed input is a random variable)* $\mathcal{F} = \{f_k\}_{k\in\{0,1\}^\lambda}$ *with domain* $\{0,1\}^m$ *and co-domain* $\{0,1\}^\ell$ *where* $m = m(\lambda)$ *and* $\ell = \ell(\lambda)$ *is called a* $\bot$*-function family. Efficient Implementation: There exists a QPT algorithm A that implements* $\mathcal{F}$*. Correctness: There exists an inverse polynomial* $\mu(\lambda)$,

1. ***Pointwise Far From bot:*** *For every* $x \in \{0,1\}^m$,

$$\Pr[k \xleftarrow{\$} \{0,1\}^\lambda : f_k(x) \neq \bot] \geq 1 - \mu(\lambda).$$

2. ***Bot-Pseudodeterminism:*** *There exists a negligible function* $\mathsf{negl}(\lambda)$ *such that for every* $x \in \{0,1\}^m$ *and* $k \in \{0,1\}^\lambda$*, there exists a* $y \in \{0,1\}^\ell$ *and negligible function* $\mathsf{negl}(\lambda)$ *such that* $\Pr[f_k(x) \in \{y, \perp\}] \geq 1 - \mathsf{negl}(\lambda)$.

*The inverse polynomial* $\mu(\lambda)$ *is the* $\perp$*-error, and the negligible function* $\mathsf{negl}(\lambda)$ *is the pseudodeterminism error. We use* $(\mu, m, \ell)$-$\perp$-PRF *to denote a* $\perp$-PRF *family with* $\perp$*-error* $\mu(\lambda)$*, input length* $m(\lambda)$ *and output length* $\ell(\lambda)$.

**Definition 8.** *A* $\perp$*-function family* $\mathcal{F} = \{f_k\}_{k \in \{0,1\}^\lambda}$ *with domain* $\{0,1\}^m$ *and co-domain* $\{0,1\}^\ell$ *is (adaptively) pseudorandom if for every QPT distinguisher* $D$*, there exists a negligible function* $\mathsf{negl}(\lambda)$ *such that*

$$\Pr[\mathsf{Distinguish\text{-}Expt}_D^{\mathcal{F}}(\lambda) = 1] \leq \frac{1}{2} + \mathsf{negl}(\lambda),$$

*where* $\mathsf{Distinguish\text{-}Expt}_D^{\mathcal{F}}(\lambda)$ *is as defined in Fig. 1.*

$\underline{\mathsf{Distinguish\text{-}Expt}_D^{\mathcal{F}}(\lambda)}$:

1. Challenger Ch samples a bit $b \xleftarrow{\$} \{0,1\}$ and a key $K \xleftarrow{\$} \{0,1\}^\lambda$.
2. Ch samples a random function $F \xleftarrow{\$} \left(\{0,1\}^{\ell(\lambda)}\right)^{\{0,1\}^{m(\lambda)}}$.
3. Let $G$ be the function that on input $x$, runs $f_K(x)$ and if the outcome is $\perp$, outputs $\perp$, else outputs $F(x)$.
4. If $b = 0$, Ch gives $D$ oracle access to $f_K(\cdot)$, and if $b = 1$, gives oracle access to $G(\cdot)$.
5. $D$ outputs a bit $b'$.
6. Output 1 (i.e., distinguisher wins) if $b' = b$.

**Fig. 1.** $\perp$-PRF pseudorandomness experiment

## 4.1 Construction of ⊥-PRF From Multi-time ⊥-PRG

Our construction of $\perp$-PRF from $\perp$-PRG is the same as the classical construction of PRF from PRG by Goldreich, Goldwasser, and Micali [15]. In short, we will be referring to this construction as the GGM construction.

**Theorem 11.** *Assume* $\mu(\lambda) \in \frac{1}{\mathsf{poly}(\lambda)}$ *and* $m(\lambda) \in \mathsf{poly}(\lambda)$ *be such that* $m(\lambda) \cdot \mu(\lambda) \in \frac{1}{\mathsf{poly}(\lambda)}$. *Then, there exists a black box construction of a* $(m\mu + \delta, m, \lambda)$-$\perp$-PRF *family (see Definitions 7 and 8) from any multi-time* $\perp$*-pseudorandom* $(\mu, 2\lambda)$-$\perp$-PRG *(see Definitions 7), for some negligible function* $\delta(\lambda)$.

The construction is the same as the [15] construction. The proof is given in the full version. Combining Theorem 11 with Corollary 3, we get the following result.

**Corollary 4.** *Assume* $m(\lambda) \in \mathsf{poly}(\lambda)$ *and a constant* $c$ *be such that* $m(\lambda) \cdot \lambda^{-c/6+1} \in \frac{1}{\mathsf{poly}(\lambda)}$. *Let* $\eta(\lambda) \equiv m(\lambda) \cdot \lambda^{-c/6+1}$. *Then, there exists a black box construction of a* $(\eta, m, \lambda)$-$\perp$-PRF *family (see Definitions 7 and 8) from any* $(c \log \lambda)$*-PRS (see Definition 7), for some negligible function* $\delta(\lambda)$.

# 5 Digital Signatures

In this section, we construct digital signatures from SPRS. This is done in several steps. In Sect. 5.1, we adapt strong unforgeability for deterministic one-time signatures to the non-deterministic setting yielding what we call *one-message signatures (OMS)*. In Sect. 5.2, we build length-restricted OMSs using our construction for $\perp$-UOWHF (see Sect. 10). In Sect. 5.3, we enable signing long messages using $\perp$-UOWHFs. We build $\perp$-UOWHFs from $\perp$-PRGs in the full version.. This requires multiple adaptions from the classical construction. First, we introduce the notion of $\perp$-OWFs and $\perp$-UOWHF. We further introduce notions of entropy that capture the size of collision sets under any $\perp$-function. Next, we build $\perp$-OWF from a $\perp$-PRG. With these tools at hand, we are able to adapt the proof of [16] (which shows how to construct UOWHFs from OWFs via inaccessible entropy) to our setting achieving $\perp$-UOWHFs from $\perp$-PRGs. Then, in Sect. 5.5, we enable signing many messages but where the signer needs to store previous signatures. As a result, we get a stateful signature scheme. Finally, in Sect. 5.6, we use the construction for $\perp$-PRFs to enable signing without storing previous signatures, resulting in a full-fledged stateless digital signature scheme.

## 5.1 Definition (One-Message) Signatures

One-time SUF requires that an adversary which receives a signature of a message of its choice, cannot forge a new valid message-signature pair. However, in our case, the signing algorithm may be non-deterministic. This causes issues since the scheme may be insecure if the same message is signed multiple times, which occurs in our application of OMSs to many-time signatures. Hence, we need to guarantee SUF against an adversary that receives multiple signatures of a single message of its choice. We call this experiment one-message SUF.

**Experiment** $\mathsf{Sign}^{\text{OM-SUF}}_{\Pi,\mathcal{A}}(\lambda)$:

1. Sample $(\mathsf{sk}, \mathsf{vk}) \leftarrow \mathsf{Gen}(1^\lambda)$.
2. $\mathcal{A}$ is given $\mathsf{vk}$ and classical access to the signing oracle $\mathsf{Sign}(\mathsf{sk}, \cdot)$.
3. Let $\mathcal{Q}$ denote the set of messages-signature pairs returned by the signing oracle.
4. $\mathcal{A}$ outputs a forgery $(m^*, \sigma^*)$.
5. The output of the experiment is 1 if:
   (a) All of the queries were on the same message.
   (b) $(m^*, \sigma^*) \notin \mathcal{Q}$.
   (c) $\mathsf{Verify}(\mathsf{vk}, m^*, \sigma^*) = 1$.
6. Otherwise, the output is 0.

**Definition 9.** *A signature scheme $\Pi$ is* one-message strongly unforgeable (OM-SUF), *if for any QPT $\mathcal{A}$,*

$$\Pr[\mathit{Sign}^{OM\text{-}SUF}_{\Pi,\mathcal{A}}(\lambda) = 1] \le \mathsf{negl}(\lambda).$$

Next, we define the following tool that we use in our construction of OM-SUF.

**Definition 10** **(⊥-UOWHF).** *Let $n = n(\lambda)$ and $m = m(\lambda)$ be polynomials in the security parameter $\lambda \in \mathbb{N}$. A family of QPT algorithms*[6] $\mathcal{H}_\lambda := \{H_\lambda(k, \cdot)\}_{k \in \{0,1\}^\ell}$ *that on input in $\{0,1\}^n$ output an element in $\{0,1\}^m \cup \{\bot\}$ is a $(\mu, \ell, d = n/m, m)$*-pseudodeterministic universal one-way hash family with recognizable abort (⊥-UOWHF) *if the following conditions hold:*

- ***Compression:*** *$d(\lambda) > 1$ for all $\lambda \in \mathbb{N}$.*
- ***Pseudodeterminism:*** *There exist a constant $c > 0$ such that $\mu(\lambda) = O(\lambda^{-c})$ and for sufficiently large $\lambda \in \mathbb{N}$ and $F \in \mathcal{H}_\lambda$, there exists a set $\mathcal{G} \subseteq \{0,1\}^n$ such that the following holds:*
  1. $$\Pr_{x \leftarrow \{0,1\}^n}[x \in \mathcal{G}] \geq 1 - \mu(\lambda).$$
  2. *For every $x \in \mathcal{G}$ there exists a non-⊥ value $y \in \{0,1\}^m$ such that:*
  $$\Pr[F(x) = y] \geq 1 - \mathsf{negl}(\lambda). \tag{5}$$
  3. *For every $x \in \{0,1\}^n$, there exists a non-⊥ value $y \in \{0,1\}^m$ such that:*
  $$\Pr[F(x) \in \{y, \bot\}] \geq 1 - \mathsf{negl}(\lambda). \tag{6}$$
- ***Security:*** *Two conditions need to be satisfied:*
  1. ***One-wayness:*** *For any QPT algorithm $\mathcal{A}$ and $F \in \mathcal{H}_\lambda$,*
  $$\Pr_{x \leftarrow \{0,1\}^n}[F(\mathcal{A}(F(x))) = F_\top(x)] \leq \mathsf{negl}(\lambda).$$
  2. ***Collision-resistance:*** *For every QPT algorithm $\mathcal{A}$, if $\mathcal{A}$ outputs $x \in \{0,1\}^n$, then is given $F \leftarrow \mathcal{H}_\lambda$, and then outputs $x' \neq x$, then*
  $$\Pr[F(x) = F_\top(x')] \leq \mathsf{negl}(\lambda).$$

### 5.2 (Length-Restricted) One-Message Signatures

We now provide a construction for a signature scheme on length-restricted messages satisfying OM-SUF using ⊥-UOWHF (see Definition 10).

**Construction 1.** *Let $\lambda \in \mathbb{N}$ be the security parameter. Let $q$ be polynomial in $\lambda$. Let $\mu = O(1/q^2)$. Let $\mathcal{H}_\lambda = \{H_\lambda(k, \cdot)\}_{k \in \{0,1\}^\ell}$ be a $(\mu, \ell, 2, \lambda)$-⊥-UOWHF family for some polynomial $\ell$ in $\lambda$. The construction for a OMS scheme on $q$-bit messages is as follows:*

[6] We emphasize that even though we call ⊥-UOWHFs as ⊥-functions they are actually algorithms. The term *function* is used to emphasize their similarity to classical notions upto ⊥-determinism.

- $\mathsf{KeyGen}(1^\lambda)$ :
  1. *For each* $j \in [q]$*, and* $b \in \{0,1\}$ :
     (a) *Sample* $k_{j,b} \leftarrow \{0,1\}^\ell$.
     (b) *Sample* $x_{j,b} \leftarrow \{0,1\}^{2\lambda}$.
     (c) *Sample* $y_{j,b} \leftarrow H(k_{j,b}, x_{j,b})$.
  2. *Set* $\mathsf{sk} := (x_{j,b})_{j\in[q],b\in\{0,1\}}$ *and* $\mathsf{vk} := (k_{j,b}, y_{j,b})_{j\in[q],b\in\{0,1\}}$.
  3. *Output* $(\mathsf{sk}, \mathsf{vk})$.
- $\mathsf{Sign}(\mathsf{sk}, m)$ : *Output* $\sigma := (x_{j,m_j})_{j\in[q]}$.
- $\mathsf{Verify}(\mathsf{vk}, m, \sigma)$ :
  1. *Interpret* $\sigma$ *as* $(\tilde{x}_j)_{j\in[q]}$.
  2. *For each* $j \in [q]$*, compute* $\tilde{y}_j \leftarrow H(k_{j,m_j}, \tilde{x}_j)$.
  3. *If* $\tilde{y}_j = y_{j,m_j} \neq \perp$ *for all* $j \in [q]$*, then output* $\top$.
  4. *Otherwise, output* $\perp$.

**Lemma 1 (Correctness).** *Construction 1 is* $(1-\mu)^{4q}$*-correct OMS scheme on q-bit messages assuming the existence of* $\perp$-UOWHF*s.*

*Proof.* Fix $m \in \{0,1\}^q$ and sample $(\mathsf{sk}, \mathsf{vk}) \leftarrow \mathsf{KeyGen}(1^\lambda)$, where $\mathsf{sk} := (x_{j,b})_{j\in[q],b\in\{0,1\}}$ and $\mathsf{vk} := (k_{j,b}, y_{j,b})_{j\in[q],b\in\{0,1\}}$. Let $\mathcal{G}_{j,b}$ denote the good set of inputs for $H(k_{j,b}, \cdot)$.

By the pseudodeterminism of $\perp$-UOWHFs, the probability that $x_{j,b} \in \mathcal{G}_{j,b}$ for all $j \in [q]$ and $b \in \{0,1\}$ is at least $p := (1-\mu)^{2q}$. In this case, there is a negligible function $\mathsf{negl}(\lambda)$ such that for any $j \in [q]$ and $b \in \{0,1\}$, there exists values $(\hat{y}_{j,b})_{j,b}$ such that $\Pr[H_{j,b}(k_{j,b}, x_{j,b}) = \hat{y}_{j,b}] \geq 1 - \mathsf{negl}(\lambda)$. In which case, the verification algorithm will accept with probability at least $(1 - \mathsf{negl}(\lambda))^{2q}$. Hence, the scheme is correct with probability at least $p(1-\mathsf{negl}(\lambda))^{2q} \geq (1-\mu)^{4q}$. ■

**Lemma 2 (Security).** *Construction 1 is OM-SUF signature scheme on q-bit messages assuming the existence of* $\perp$-UOWHF*s.*

The proof is the same as in the classical case given in Sect. 6.5.2 in [14]. Notice that in this scheme, access to multiple signatures of the same message does not affect the experiment since the signing algorithm is deterministic.

### 5.3 One-Message Signatures

We now show how to transform a *length-restricted* OM-SUF signature scheme into a OM-SUF signature scheme based on the approach in the classical case given in Sect. 6.5.2 of [14]. This is important since we will need to sign messages that are double the length of the verification key in order to build many-message signatures in the following sections.

**Construction 2.** *Let* $\lambda \in \mathbb{N}$ *be the security parameter. Let* $q$ *be polynomial in* $\lambda$ *and* $\mu = O(1/q^2)$. *Let* $\mathcal{H}_\lambda = \{H_\lambda(k, \cdot)\}_{k\in\{0,1\}^\ell}$ *be a* $(\mu, \ell, q/\lambda, \lambda)$-$\perp$-UOWHF *family for some polynomial* $\ell$ *in* $\lambda$ *such that* $\ell+\lambda < q/2$. *Let* $(\overline{\mathsf{KeyGen}}, \overline{\mathsf{Sign}}, \overline{\mathsf{Verify}})$ *be the algorithms of Construction 1 on* $(\ell+\lambda)$*-bit messages. The construction for a OMS scheme on q-bit messages is as follows:*

- *KeyGen*$(1^\lambda)$ :
  1. *Sample* $(\overline{\mathsf{sk}}, \overline{\mathsf{vk}}) \leftarrow \overline{\mathit{KeyGen}}(1^\lambda)$.
  2. *Sample* $k \leftarrow \{0,1\}^\ell$.
  3. *Set* $\mathsf{sk} := (\overline{\mathsf{sk}}, k)$ *and* $\mathsf{vk} := \overline{\mathsf{vk}}$.
  4. *Output* $(\mathsf{sk}, \mathsf{vk})$.
- *Sign*$(\mathsf{sk}, m)$ :
  1. *Compute* $y \leftarrow H(k, m)$. *If* $y = \bot$, *output* $\bot$.
  2. *Otherwise, compute* $s \leftarrow \overline{\mathit{Sign}}(\overline{\mathsf{sk}}, k\|y)$.
  3. *Output* $\sigma := (k, s)$.
- *Verify*$(\mathsf{vk}, m, \sigma)$ :
  1. *If* $\sigma = \bot$, *output* $\bot$.
  2. *Otherwise, interpret* $\sigma$ *as* $(k, s)$.
  3. *Compute* $y \leftarrow H(k, m)$. *If* $y = \bot$, *output* $\bot$.
  4. *Otherwise, output* $\overline{\mathit{Verify}}(\mathsf{vk}, k\|y, s)$.

**Lemma 3 (Correctness).** *Construction 2 is* $(1-\mu)^{2q+3}$*-correct OMS scheme assuming the existence of* $\bot$*-*UOWHF*s.*

*Proof.* Fix $m \in \{0,1\}^q$ and sample $(\mathsf{sk}, \mathsf{vk}) \leftarrow \mathsf{KeyGen}(1^\lambda)$ as described in the construction. Let $\mathcal{G}$ denote the good set of inputs for $H(k, \cdot)$. The probability that $m \in \mathcal{G}$ is at least $1 - \mu$.

If $m \in \mathcal{G}$, there is a negligible function $\mathsf{negl}(\lambda)$ and value $\hat{y}$ such that $\Pr[H(k,m) = \hat{y}] \geq 1 - \mathsf{negl}(\lambda)$. In this case, it is clear that the verification algorithm accepts with high probability if and only if $\overline{\mathsf{Verify}}(\mathsf{vk}, k\|\hat{y}, \overline{\mathsf{Sign}}(\mathsf{sk}, k\|\hat{y}))$ accepts. By Lemma 1, this occurs with at least $(1-\mu)^{4(\lambda+\ell)}$ probability.

All in all, the scheme is correct with probability at least $(1-\mu)^{4(\lambda+\ell)}(1-\mu)(1-\mathsf{negl}(\lambda))^2 \geq (1-\mu)^{2q+3}$. ■

**Lemma 4 (Security).** *Construction 2 is OM-SUF signature scheme assuming the existence of* $\bot$*-*UOWHF*s.*

*Proof.* Assume there exists a QPT algorithm $\mathcal{A}$ such that $\Pr[\mathsf{Sign}_{\Pi,\mathcal{A}}^{OM\text{-}SUF}(\lambda) = 1]$ is non-negligible. The experiment samples a key pair $(\mathsf{sk}, \mathsf{vk}) \leftarrow \mathsf{KeyGen}(1^\lambda)$. Let $m$ be the message queried by $\mathcal{A}$. We assume that $\mathcal{A}$ queries the same message as, otherwise, the experiment outcome is 0. There exists a negligible function $\mathsf{negl}(\lambda)$ and value $y$ such that $\Pr[H(k,m) \in \{\bot, y\}] \geq 1 - \mathsf{negl}(\lambda)$. Let $s = \overline{\mathsf{Sign}}(\overline{\mathsf{sk}}, k\|y)$. With high probability, the signing oracle will respond to all queries submitted by $\mathcal{A}$ with either $\bot$ or $(k, s)$.

Let $(\tilde{m}, (\tilde{k}, \tilde{s}))$ be the forgery submitted at the end of the experiment and let $\tilde{y} \leftarrow H(\tilde{k}, \tilde{m})$ be the evaluation computed by the experiment during verification. If the output of the experiment is 1, then there are 2 cases to consider:

- $(\tilde{k}, \tilde{y}, \tilde{s}) \neq (k, y, s)$ : In this case, $\mathcal{A}$ has produced a new valid message-signature pair under the the OMS scheme, contradicting SUF (Lemma 2).
- $(\tilde{k}, \tilde{y}, \tilde{s}) = (k, y, s)$ and $m \neq \tilde{m}$ : In this case, the pair $(m, \tilde{m})$ act as a collision on $H(k, \cdot)$. Given that $\mathcal{A}$ must choose $m$ prior to knowing $k$, this implies that $\mathcal{A}$ breaks the collision-resistance property of $H$.

Hence, both cases contradict security assumptions, yielding a contradiction. ■

### 5.4 Definition (Many-Message) Signatures

We recall the definition of a (many-message) signature scheme.

**Definition 11 (Digital Signatures).** *A digital signature* ($\mathsf{DS}$) *scheme over classical message space* $\mathcal{M}$ *consists of the following QPT algorithms:*

- $\mathsf{Gen}(1^\lambda)$*: Outputs a secret key* $\mathsf{sk}$ *and a verification key* $\mathsf{vk}$.
- $\mathsf{Sign}(\mathsf{sk}, \mu)$ *: Outputs a signature* $\sigma$ *for* $\mu \in \mathcal{M}$ *using* $\mathsf{sk}$.
- $\mathsf{Verify}(\mathsf{vk}, \mu', \sigma')$*: Verifies whether* $\sigma'$ *is a valid signature for* $\mu' \in \mathcal{M}$ *using* $\mathsf{vk}$ *and correspondingly outputs* $\top / \perp$.

**Definition 12 (Correctness).** *A digital signature scheme is* $p$-correct *if for any message* $\mu \in \mathcal{M}$*:*

$$\Pr\left[\mathsf{Verify}(\mathsf{vk}, \mu, \sigma) = \top \;\middle|\; \begin{array}{rl}(\mathsf{sk}, \mathsf{vk}) & \leftarrow \mathsf{Gen}(1^\lambda) \\ \sigma & \leftarrow \mathsf{Sign}(\mathsf{sk}, \mu)\end{array}\right] \geq p.$$

*If* $p \geq 1 - \mathsf{negl}(\lambda)$, *then we simply say that the scheme is* statistically correct.

We recall the security experiment testing *strong unforgeability* (SUF) of a digital signature scheme.

**Experiment** $\mathsf{Sign}^{\mathrm{SUF}}_{\Pi,\mathcal{A}}(\lambda)$:

1. Sample $(\mathsf{sk}, \mathsf{vk}) \leftarrow \mathsf{Gen}(1^\lambda)$.
2. $\mathcal{A}$ is given $\mathsf{vk}$ and classical access to the signing oracle $\mathsf{Sign}(\mathsf{sk}, \cdot)$.
3. Let $\mathcal{Q}$ denote the set of messages-signature pairs returned by the signing oracle.
4. $\mathcal{A}$ outputs a forgery $(m^*, \sigma^*)$.
5. The output of the experiment is 1 if

$$(m^*, \sigma^*) \notin \mathcal{Q} \text{ and } \mathsf{Verify}(\mathsf{vk}, m^*, \sigma^*) = 1.$$

6. Otherwise, the output is 0.

**Definition 13.** *A signature scheme* $\Pi$ *is* strongly unforgeable (SUF), *if for any QPT* $\mathcal{A}$,

$$\Pr[\mathsf{Sign}^{SUF}_{\Pi,\mathcal{A}}(\lambda) = 1] \leq \mathsf{negl}(\lambda).$$

### 5.5 Stateful (Many-Message) Signatures

We upgrade a OMS scheme to a many-message scheme following the approach given in [25] with minimal modifications. The signer needs to store previous signatures so this approach is called *stateful*.

The idea is to construct a tree where each node contains a pair of keys sampled from a one-time $\mathsf{DS}$ scheme. In any non-leaf node, the secret key is used to sign the verification keys of the children nodes. Meanwhile, the leaf keys are used to sign messages. We let $\alpha$ signify the label of the root node in the authentication tree. More generally, we label the rest of the nodes in a natural way: for any node labeled $\alpha v$, we label its left child and right child by $\alpha v0$ and $\alpha v1$, respectively.

**Construction 3.** *Let $n := n(\lambda)$ be even and polynomial in the security parameter $\lambda \in \mathbb{N}$. Let $(\mathsf{OT.Gen}, \mathsf{OT.Sign}, \mathsf{OT.Ver})$ be the algorithms of the OTS scheme given in Construction 2 on messages of length at least twice the length of the verification key*[7]. *Let $\boldsymbol{M}$ denote the signer's memory, which evolves as more messages are signed. The construction for a many-message (stateful) signature scheme on n-bit messages is as follows:*

- $\mathsf{KeyGen}(1^\lambda)$ : *Sample $(\mathsf{s}_\alpha, \mathsf{v}_\alpha) \leftarrow \mathsf{OT.Gen}(1^\lambda)$ and set $\boldsymbol{M} = \emptyset$.*
- $\mathsf{Sign}(\mathsf{sk}, \boldsymbol{M}, m)$ : *At any point in the procedure, if any computation returns $\bot$, then abort and output $\bot$.*
  1. *For each $i \in [n]$:*
     (a) *For $\tau = 0, 1$, try to retrieve the key pair associated to the node labeled $\alpha m_1 m_2 \ldots m_{i-1}\tau$. If the node is not found, then generate a key pair:*
     $$(\mathsf{s}_{\alpha m_1 m_2 \ldots m_{i-1}\tau}, \mathsf{v}_{\alpha m_1 m_2 \ldots m_{i-1}\tau}) \leftarrow \mathsf{OT.Gen}(1^\lambda).$$
     *and store it in node $\alpha m_1 m_2 \ldots m_{i-1}\tau$ in $\boldsymbol{M}$.*
     (b) *Try to retrieve a signature in node $\alpha m_1 m_2 \ldots m_{i-1}$. If no signature is found then generate one:*
     $$\sigma_{\alpha m_1 m_2 \ldots m_{i-1}} \leftarrow \mathsf{OT.Sign}(\mathsf{s}_{\alpha m_1 m_2 \ldots m_{i-1}}, (\mathsf{v}_{\alpha m_1 m_2 \ldots m_{i-1}0}, \mathsf{v}_{\alpha m_1 m_2 \ldots m_{i-1}1})).$$
     *and store it in node $\alpha m_1 m_2 \ldots m_{i-1}$ in $\boldsymbol{M}$.*
  2. *Sign the message $\sigma_{\alpha m} \leftarrow \mathsf{OT.Sign}(\mathsf{s}_{\alpha m}, m)$.*
  3. *Output $(\sigma_{\alpha m_1 \ldots m_{i-1}}, \mathsf{v}_{\alpha m_1 \ldots m_{i-1}0}, \mathsf{v}_{\alpha m_1 \ldots m_{i-1}1})_{i \in [n]}$.*
- $\mathsf{Verify}(\mathsf{vk}, m, \sigma)$ :
  1. *If $\sigma = \bot$, then output $\bot$.*
  2. *Otherwise, interpret $\sigma$ as*
  $$(\sigma_{\alpha m_1 \ldots m_{i-1}}, \mathsf{v}_{\alpha m_1 \ldots m_{i-1}0}, \mathsf{v}_{\alpha m_1 \ldots m_{i-1}1})_{i \in [n]}.$$
  3. *Output $\top$ if the following conditions are satisfied:*
     (a) *For each $i \in [n]$:*
     $$\mathsf{OT.Ver}(\mathsf{v}_{\alpha m_1 \ldots m_{i-1}}, (\mathsf{v}_{\alpha m_1 \ldots m_{i-1}0}, \mathsf{v}_{\alpha m_1 \ldots m_{i-1}1}), \sigma_{\alpha m_1 \ldots m_{i-1}}) = \top.$$
     (b) *$\mathsf{OT.Ver}(\mathsf{v}_{\alpha m}, m, \sigma_{\alpha m}) = \top$.*
  4. *Otherwise, output $\bot$.*

The security proof follows similarly to the proof in the classical case [14].

**Lemma 5 (Sect. 6.4.2.2. of [14]).** *Construction 3 is a SUF many-message (stateful) signature scheme on n-bit messages assuming the existence of $\bot$-$\mathsf{UOWHF}$s.*

[7] This can be achieved using a ⊥-UOWHF with sufficient compression in Construction 2.

### 5.6 Stateless Digital Signatures

We upgrade Construction 3 to a stateless digital signature scheme using our construction for $\bot$-PRFs following a similar approach to [14], which is based on traditional PRFs. The idea is to use a $\bot$-PRF to determine the output of the coin tosses used in the OMS key generation procedures employed in the authentication tree. Specifically, let $\mathsf{OT.Gen}(1^\lambda)$ be a pseudodeterministic QPT algorithm for Construction 2. The algorithm first classically samples random inputs and keys for appropriate $\bot$-UOWHFs. We let $\mathsf{OT.Gen}(1^\lambda; r)$ denote the algorithm where these random decisions are instead determined by $r$.

Instead of choosing $r$ randomly each time, it can be set to the outcome of a $\bot$-PRF, allowing the signer to generate any key-pair in the authentication key on demand without needing to store previous signatures. While the keys generated in this fashion are not deterministic and may sometimes include $\bot$, we simply abort and output $\bot$ in this scenario.

**Construction 4.** *Let $\lambda \in \mathbb{N}$ be the security parameter and $n := n(\lambda)$ be an even polynomial on $\lambda$. Let ($\mathsf{OT.Gen}$, $\mathsf{OT.Sign}$, $\mathsf{OT.Ver}$) be the algorithms of the OTS scheme given in Construction 2 on messages at least twice the length of the verification key such that the key generation algorithm makes $q$ coin tosses ($q$ polynomial in $\lambda$). For $i \in [n]$, let $\mathsf{PRF}^i$ be a $(\mu, i+q, q)$-$\bot$-PRF. The algorithms for a (stateless) DS scheme on $n$-bit messages is as follows:*

- *$\mathsf{KeyGen}(1^\lambda)$ :*
  1. *Sample $(\mathsf{s}_\alpha, \mathsf{v}_\alpha) \leftarrow \mathsf{OT.Gen}(1^\lambda)$.*
  2. *For each $i \in [n]$ and $\tau = 0,1$, sample $k_i \leftarrow \{0,1\}^\lambda$ and $r_{i,\tau} \leftarrow \{0,1\}^{i+q}$.*
  3. *Set $\mathsf{sk} := (\mathsf{s}_\alpha, k_i, r_{i,\tau})_{i\in[n],\tau\in\{0,1\}}$ and $\mathsf{vk} := \mathsf{v}_\alpha$.*
  4. *Output $(\mathsf{sk}, \mathsf{vk})$.*
- *$\mathsf{Sign}(\mathsf{sk}, m)$ : At any point in the procedure, if any computation returns $\bot$, then abort and output $\bot$.*
  1. *For each $i \in [n]$ :*
     *(a) For $\tau = 0, 1$, generate the key pair:*

     $$(\mathsf{s}_{\alpha m_1 m_2 \dots m_{i-1}\tau}, \mathsf{v}_{\alpha m_1 m_2 \dots m_{i-1}\tau}) \leftarrow \mathsf{OT.Gen}(1^\lambda; \mathsf{PRF}^i(k_i, m_1 m_2 \dots m_{i-1}\tau 0^{q-1} \oplus r_{i,\tau})).$$

     *(b) Sign the verification keys:*

     $$\sigma_{\alpha m_1 m_2 \dots m_{i-1}} \leftarrow \mathsf{OT.Sign}(\mathsf{s}_{\alpha m_1 m_2 \dots m_{i-1}}, (\mathsf{v}_{\alpha m_1 m_2 \dots m_{i-1}0}, \mathsf{v}_{\alpha m_1 m_2 \dots m_{i-1}1})).$$

  2. *Sign the message $\sigma_{\alpha m} := \mathsf{OT.Sign}(\mathsf{s}_{\alpha m}, m)$.*
  3. *Output $(\sigma_{\alpha m_1 \dots m_{i-1}}, \mathsf{v}_{\alpha m_1 \dots m_{i-1}0}, \mathsf{v}_{\alpha m_1 \dots m_{i-1}1})_{i\in[n]}$.*
- *$\mathsf{Verify}(\mathsf{vk}, m, \sigma)$ :*
  1. *If $\sigma = \bot$, then output $\bot$.*
  2. *Otherwise, interpret $\sigma$ as $(\sigma_{\alpha m_1 \dots m_{i-1}}, \mathsf{v}_{\alpha m_1 \dots m_{i-1}0}, \mathsf{v}_{\alpha m_1 \dots m_{i-1}1})_{i\in[n]}$.*
  3. *Output $\top$ if the following conditions are satisfied:*
     *(a) For each $i \in [n]$:*

     $$\mathsf{OT.Ver}(\mathsf{v}_{\alpha m_1 \dots m_{i-1}}, (\mathsf{v}_{\alpha m_1 \dots m_{i-1}0}, \mathsf{v}_{\alpha m_1 \dots m_{i-1}1}), \sigma_{\alpha m_1 \dots m_{i-1}}) = \top.$$

(b) $\mathsf{OT.Ver}(v_{\alpha m}, m, \sigma_{\alpha m}) = \top$.
4. *Otherwise, output* $\bot$.

**Lemma 6.** *Construction 4 is* $(1-\mu)^p$*-correct where* $p = 4n\lambda + 10n$ *assuming the existence of* $\bot$-PRF*s and* $\bot$-UOWHF*s.*

*Proof.* Fix $m \in \{0,1\}^n$ and sample $(\mathsf{sk}, \mathsf{vk}) \leftarrow \mathsf{KeyGen}(1^\lambda)$. To sign $m$, for each $j \in [n]$ and $\tau = 0, 1$, we evaluate $\mathsf{PRF}^j$ on the input $(k_j, x^{j,\tau})$ where $x^{j,\tau} := m_1 m_2 \ldots m_{j-1} \tau 0^{q-1} \oplus r_{j,\tau}$. Let $\mathcal{G}_j$ denote the good set of inputs for $\mathsf{PRF}^j(k_j, \cdot)$. By the pseudodeterminism of the $\bot$-PRFs and the randomness of the inputs $x^{j,\tau}$, there is at least $(1-\mu)^{2n}$ probability that $x^{j,\tau} \in \mathcal{G}_j$ for all $j \in [n]$ and $\tau = 0, 1$.

Next, we also need correctness of $n$ OMSs employed in the signing procedure. By Lemma 3, Construction 2 satisfies $(1-\mu)^{2\lambda+3}$-correctness using a $\bot$-UOWHF with sufficient compression.

A small issue is that in our setting, we use pseudorandomness through $\bot$-PRFs instead of actual randomness when generating the key pairs for the OMSs. This may affect the pseudodeterminism of the $\bot$-UOWHF utilized in the OTS scheme. However, if using pseudorandomness significantly worsens the correctness of the OTS scheme, then this easily gives an adversary that can distinguish between the outputs of a $\bot$-PRF and a random $\bot$-function, which yields a contradiction. Hence, the correctness error of the pseudorandom based OTS is within $(1-\mathsf{negl}(\lambda))$ factor from $(1-\mu)^{4\lambda+3}$. We generate $2n$ one-message signatures when signing $m$.

To sum up, the probability that a signature of $m$ passes verification is $(1-\mu)^{2n}(1-\mu)^{4n\lambda+6n}(1-\mathsf{negl}(\lambda))^{2n} \leq (1-\mu)^{4n\lambda+10n}$. ■

**Theorem 12.** *Construction 4 is a SUF digital signature scheme assuming the existence of* $\bot$-PRF*s and* $\bot$-UOWHF*s.*

*Proof.* Let $\mathbf{H}_0$ be the actual scheme. For $i \in [n]$, let $\mathbf{H}_i$ be the hybrid that is the same as $\mathbf{H}_{i-1}$ except $\mathsf{PRF}^j(k_i, \cdot)$ is replaced with the $\bot$-random function $R_{\mathsf{PRF}^i}$, where $R_{\mathsf{PRF}^i}$ is defined as the algorithm which evaluates $\mathsf{PRF}^i(k_i, \cdot)$ and if the result is $\bot$, it returns $\bot$, and otherwise outputs a random string (see Definition 8). Such a hybrid is efficient since to evaluate $R_{\mathsf{PRF}^i}$, the experiment does not need to sample an entire random function, but rather it can compute $\mathsf{PRF}^i(k_i, \cdot)$ and if the result is $\bot$, it returns $\bot$, and otherwise it outputs a random output and stores the evaluation in its memory for future use.

We first argue that the final hybrid is secure. Then, we argue that if there exists $j \in [n]$ such that there exists a QPT distinguisher that can differentiate between hybrids $\mathbf{H}_{j-1}$ and $\mathbf{H}_j$, then there exists QPT distinguisher that can distinguish $\mathsf{PRF}^j$ and $R_{\mathsf{PRF}^j}$, contradicting the security of $\bot$-PRFs. Let $\Pi_{\mathsf{stf}}$ be the stateful scheme (Construction 3).

The scheme $\mathbf{H}_n$ is the same as $\Pi_{\mathsf{stf}}$ except the key generation algorithm uses random $\bot$-functions instead of making random choices during key generation. Now if no random $\bot$-function evaluates to $\bot$ during the procedure, then a valid signature is generated in the same way as in $\Pi_{\mathsf{stf}}$. Alternatively, if there is a

$\perp$, then the process is aborted and the signature is $\perp$. Informally, this scenario clearly does not aid the adversary in forging signatures since whether the signature is $\perp$ or not is independent of the signing key.

To prove this formally, assume for contradiction that there exists a QPT $\mathcal{A}$ such that $\Pr[\mathsf{Sign}^{\text{SUF}}_{\mathbf{H}_n,\mathcal{A}}(\lambda) = 1]$ is non-negligible. We can construct an adversary $\mathcal{B}$ such that $\Pr[\mathsf{Sign}^{\text{SUF}}_{\Pi_{\mathsf{stf}},\mathcal{B}}(\lambda) = 1]$ is non-negligible.

$\mathcal{B}$ in the SUF security experiment for $\Pi_{\mathsf{stf}}$ gets query access to the signing oracle and a verification key $\mathsf{vk}$. $\mathcal{B}$ samples $k_i \leftarrow \{0,1\}^\lambda$ for each $i \in [n]$ and runs $\mathcal{A}$ on $\mathsf{vk}$. Assume $\mathcal{A}$ requests the signature of a message $m$. $\mathcal{B}$ queries the oracle on $m$ and gets as response $\sigma_m$. $\mathcal{B}$ computes $\mathsf{PRF}^i(k_i, m_1m_2\ldots m_i\tau0^{q-1} \oplus r_{i,\tau})$ for all $i \in [n]$ and $\tau \in \{0,1\}$, and if any of the evaluations return $\perp$, then $\mathcal{B}$ returns $\perp$ to $\mathcal{A}$ and otherwise returns $\sigma_m$. $\mathcal{A}$ submits an output $(m^*, \sigma^*)$. $\mathcal{B}$ simply outputs the same pair $(m^*, \sigma^*)$. Clearly, $\Pr[\mathsf{Sign}^{\text{SUF}}_{\Pi_{\mathsf{stf}},\mathcal{B}}(\lambda) = 1]$ is non-negligible which contradicts Lemma 5. Hence, $\mathbf{H}_n$ is a SUF scheme.

Now assume there exists a QPT adversary $\mathcal{A}$ that can distinguish between hybrid $\mathbf{H}_{j-1}$ and $\mathbf{H}_j$ with non-negligible advantage. We construct a QPT algorithm $\mathcal{D}$ with oracle access to a function $G$ which distinguishes whether $G$ is a $\perp$-random function or a $\perp$-$\mathsf{PRF}$ with non-negligible probability. First, $\mathcal{D}$ generates $(\mathsf{sk}, \mathsf{vk}) \leftarrow \mathsf{KeyGen}(1^\lambda)$ and runs $\mathcal{A}(\mathsf{v})$. Whenever $\mathcal{A}$ queries the signing oracle, $\mathcal{D}$ answers the query by following the signing procedure, except it replaces any computation of $\mathsf{PRF}^i(k_i, \cdot)$ with $R_{\mathsf{PRF}^i}$ if $i < j$ and with $G$ if $i = j$.

$\mathcal{A}$ succeeds in distinguishing the two hybrids with non-negligible probability meaning $\mathcal{D}$ distinguishes whether between a $\perp$-$\mathsf{PRF}$ and a random $\perp$-function, yielding a contradiction. Therefore, no QPT adversary can distinguish between any two consecutive hybrids with non-negligible advantage. Hence, by the triangle inequality, $H_0$ is a SUF signature scheme. ■

We can improve correctness, reducing the error to a negligible value, through repetition. In particular, Construction 4 is $(1-\mu)^p$-correct where $p = (1-\mu)^{4n\lambda+10n}$. As long as use $\perp$-$\mathsf{UOWHF}$s and $\perp$-$\mathsf{PRF}$s with pseudodeterminism error of $\mu < 1/p^2$, then $(1-\mu)^p \geq \frac{1}{4}$.

Therefore, by signing a message under $4\lambda$ independent keys, then one of the signatures will pass verification except with negligible probability. In the resulting scheme, the verifier accepts as long as one of the signatures is valid. It is easy to see that this scheme satisfies statistical correctness and unforgeability. However, it does not satisfy strong unforgeability since it is easy to create a new signature given a valid signature. It seems difficult to achieve strong unforgeability along with statistical correctness through our approach and, hence, this is left as an open problem. Nevertheless, our results give the option to choose between statistical correctness and strong unforgeability.

To sum up, the existence of a stateless $\mathsf{DS}$ satisfying UF and statistical correctness based on $\perp$-$\mathsf{PRF}$ and $\perp$-$\mathsf{UOWHF}$ is implied by Theorem 12 and 5 and 4. Furthermore, by Corollaries 3 and 4 and the construction of $\perp$-$\mathsf{UOWHF}$ given in the full-version, $\perp$-$\mathsf{PRF}$ and $\perp$-$\mathsf{UOWHF}$ respectively can be based on $\mathsf{SPRS}$. All in all, we get the following:

**Theorem 13 (Digital Signatures from SPRS).** *Let $\lambda \in \mathbb{N}$ be the security parameter. Assuming the existence of $c\log(\lambda)$-PRS with large enough $c \in \mathbb{N}$, there exists stateless (many-message) digital signatures on $\lambda$-bit messages with classical keys satisfying UF as well as statistical correctness.*

A direct application of our digital signature scheme pertains to symmetric encryption. It is well-known that a CPA-secure symmetric encryption scheme can be constructed from PRFs. This construction can be adapted to ⊥-PRFs without difficulty. Another well-known point is that a CPA-secure scheme can be upgraded to enable CCA-security by signing the ciphertexts. Hence, as a corollary to Corollary 4 and Theorem 13, we obtain the following result:

**Corollary 5.** *Assuming the existence of* SPRS*, there exists a CCA-secure symmetric encryption scheme with classical ciphertexts.*

**Acknowledgments.** We wish to thank an anonymous reviewer for helpful suggestions regarding a previous version of this manuscript. The work was funded by the European Union (ERC-2022-COG, ACQUA, 101087742). Views and opinions expressed are however those of the author(s) only and do not necessarily reflect those of the European Union or the European Research Council Executive Agency. Neither the European Union nor the granting authority can be held responsible for them.

Funded by the European Union

European Research Council Established by the European Commission

## References

1. Alagic, G., Jeffery, S., Ozols, M., Poremba, A.: On quantum chosen-ciphertext attacks and learning with errors. Cryptography **4**(1), 10 (2020)
2. Ananth, P., Gulati, A., Qian, L., Yuen, H.: Pseudorandom (function-like) quantum state generators: new definitions and applications. In: Theory of Cryptography: 20th International Conference, TCC 2022, Chicago, IL, USA, November 7–10, 2022, Proceedings, Part I, pp. 237–265. Springer (2022)
3. Ananth, P., Lin, Y.T., Yuen, H.: Pseudorandom strings from pseudorandom quantum states. arXiv preprint arXiv:2306.05613 (2023)
4. Ananth, P., Qian, L., Yuen, H.: Cryptography from pseudorandom quantum states. In: Advances in Cryptology–CRYPTO 2022: 42nd Annual International Cryptology Conference, CRYPTO 2022, Santa Barbara, CA, USA, August 15–18, 2022, Proceedings, Part I, pp. 208–236. Springer (2022)
5. Barhoush, M., Nishimaki, R., Yamakawa, T.: Microcrypt assumptions with quantum input sampling and pseudodeterminism: Constructions and separations. Cryptology ePrint Archive (2025)
6. Barnum, H., Crépeau, C., Gottesman, D., Smith, A., Tapp, A.: Authentication of quantum messages. In: The 43rd Annual IEEE Symposium on Foundations of Computer Science, 2002. Proceedings, pp. 449–458. IEEE (2002)
7. Barooti, K., et al.: Public-key encryption with quantum keys. In: Rothblum, G.N., Wee, H. (eds.) Theory of Cryptography - 21st International Conference, TCC 2023, Taipei, Taiwan, November 29 - December 2, 2023, Proceedings, Part IV. Lecture Notes in Computer Science, vol. 14372, pp. 198–227. Springer (2023). https://doi.org/10.1007/978-3-031-48624-1_8

8. Blum, M., Micali, S.: How to generate cryptographically strong sequences of pseudorandom bits. SIAM J. Comput. **13**(4), 850–864 (1984)
9. Boneh, D., Zhandry, M.: Quantum-secure message authentication codes. In: Johansson, T., Nguyen, P.Q. (eds.) EUROCRYPT 2013. LNCS, vol. 7881, pp. 592–608. Springer, Heidelberg (2013). https://doi.org/10.1007/978-3-642-38348-9_35
10. Bouaziz-Ermann, S., Muguruza, G.: Quantum pseudorandomness cannot be shrunk in a black-box way (2024). https://doi.org/10.48550/arXiv.2402.13324
11. Brakerski, Z., Shmueli, O.: Scalable pseudorandom quantum states. In: Annual International Cryptology Conference, pp. 417–440. Springer (2020)
12. Carter, J.L., Wegman, M.N.: Universal classes of hash functions. In: Proceedings of the Ninth Annual ACM Symposium on Theory of Computing, pp. 106–112 (1977)
13. Coladangelo, A., Mutreja, S.: On black-box separations of quantum digital signatures from pseudorandom states. arXiv preprint arXiv:2402.08194 (2024)
14. Goldreich, O.: The Foundations of Cryptography - Volume 2: Basic Applications. Cambridge University Press (2004)
15. Goldreich, O., Goldwasser, S., Micali, S.: How to construct random functions. J. ACM **33**(4), 792–807 (1986)
16. Haitner, I., Holenstein, T., Reingold, O., Vadhan, S., Wee, H.: Universal one-way hash functions via inaccessible entropy. In: Gilbert, H. (ed.) EUROCRYPT 2010. LNCS, vol. 6110, pp. 616–637. Springer, Heidelberg (2010). https://doi.org/10.1007/978-3-642-13190-5_31
17. Hhan, M., Morimae, T., Yamakawa, T.: From the hardness of detecting superpositions to cryptography: quantum public key encryption and commitments. In: Hazay, C., Stam, M. (eds.) Advances in Cryptology - EUROCRYPT 2023 - 42nd Annual International Conference on the Theory and Applications of Cryptographic Techniques, Lyon, France, April 23-27, 2023, Proceedings, Part I. Lecture Notes in Computer Science, vol. 14004, pp. 639–667. Springer (2023). https://doi.org/10.1007/978-3-031-30545-0_22
18. Ji, Z., Liu, Y.-K., Song, F.: Pseudorandom quantum states. In: Shacham, H., Boldyreva, A. (eds.) CRYPTO 2018. LNCS, vol. 10993, pp. 126–152. Springer, Cham (2018). https://doi.org/10.1007/978-3-319-96878-0_5
19. Kitagawa, F., Morimae, T., Nishimaki, R., Yamakawa, T.: Quantum public-key encryption with tamper-resilient public keys from one-way functions (2023)
20. Kretschmer, W.: Quantum pseudorandomness and classical complexity. In: 16th Conference on the Theory of Quantum Computation, Communication and Cryptography (2021)
21. Lamport, L.: Constructing Digital Signatures From a One Way Function (1979)
22. Mitzenmacher, C.M.M., Upfal, E.: probability and Computing: Randomized Algorithms and Probabilistic Analysis. Cambridge University Press, Cambridge (2005)
23. Morimae, T., Yamakawa, T.: Quantum commitments and signatures without one-way functions. In: Advances in Cryptology–CRYPTO 2022: 42nd Annual International Cryptology Conference, CRYPTO 2022, Santa Barbara, CA, USA, August 15–18, 2022, Proceedings, Part I, pp. 269–295. Springer (2022)
24. Morimae, T., Yamakawa, T.: One-wayness in quantum cryptography. In: 19th Conference on the Theory of Quantum Computation, Communication and Cryptography (2024)
25. Naor, M., Yung, M.: Universal one-way hash functions and their cryptographic applications. In: Symposium on the Theory of Computing (1989). https://api.semanticscholar.org/CorpusID:14383498

26. Rompel, J.: One-way functions are necessary and sufficient for secure signatures. In: Proceedings of the Twenty-Second Annual ACM Symposium on Theory of Computing, pp. 387–394 (1990)
27. Yan, J.: General properties of quantum bit commitments (extended abstract). In: Agrawal, S., Lin, D. (eds.) Advances in Cryptology - ASIACRYPT 2022 - 28th International Conference on the Theory and Application of Cryptology and Information Security, Taipei, Taiwan, December 5-9, 2022, Proceedings, Part IV. Lecture Notes in Computer Science, vol. 13794, pp. 628–657. Springer (2022). https://doi.org/10.1007/978-3-031-22972-5_22

# Round-Efficient Composable Two-Party Quantum Computation

Vipul Goyal[1,2](✉), Xiao Liang[3], Omkant Pandey[4], Yuhao Tang[4], and Takashi Yamakawa[5]

[1] NTT Research, Sunnyvale, USA
vipul@cmu.edu
[2] Carnegie Mellon University, Pittsburgh, USA
[3] The Chinese University of Hong Kong, Sha Tin, Hong Kong
xiaoliang@cuhk.edu.hk
[4] Stony Brook University, Stony Brook, USA
omkant@cs.stonybrook.edu, yuhtang@cs.stonybrook.edu
[5] NTT Social Informatics Laboratories, Yokosuka, Japan
takashi.yamakawa@ntt.com

**Abstract.** We study secure computation in the plain model against fully concurrent quantum adversaries. While classical simulation-based notions—such as Super-Polynomial Simulation (SPS) security—have enabled meaningful forms of concurrent security, very little is known about their quantum counterparts, particularly under standard polynomial-time hardness assumptions.

Our main result is the first post-quantum two-party computation protocol that achieves concurrent SPS security, based solely on the minimal assumption of semi-honest post-quantum oblivious transfer (PQ-OT). Moreover, our protocol has constant round complexity when the underlying PQ-OT protocol is constant-round. This can be viewed as a post-quantum analog of the classical result by Garg et al. [Eurocrypt'12], but with a crucial difference: our security proof completely avoids rewinding, making it suitable for quantum settings where rewinding is notoriously challenging due to the no-cloning principle.

By leveraging a compiler of Bartusek et al. [Crypto'21], we further extend our result to the fully quantum setting, yielding the first constant-round concurrent SPS two-party computation for *quantum* functionalities in the plain model.

Additionally, we construct a two-round, public-coin, concurrent SPS post-quantum zero-knowledge protocol for languages in **NP** ∩ **coNP**, under the quantum polynomial-time hardness of LWE. This result is notable even in the classical setting.

---

X. Liang—The work described in this paper was partially supported by a grant from the Research Grants Council of the Hong Kong Special Administrative Region, China [Project No.: CUHK 24208025].

O. Pandey—Supported in part by AFOSR Award FA9550-24-1-0156, NSF CAREER Award 2144303, and NSF grant 2106263. Any opinions, findings and conclusions or recommendations expressed in this material are those of the author(s) and do not necessarily reflect the views of the United States Government, AFOSR, or NSF.

© International Association for Cryptologic Research 2026
G. Hanaoka and B.-Y. Yang (Eds.): ASIACRYPT 2025, LNCS 16252, pp. 350–380, 2026.
https://doi.org/10.1007/978-981-95-5125-5_12

**Keywords:** Two-Party Computation · Post-Quantum · Concurrency · Super-Polynomial Simulation · Zero-Knowledge

## 1 Introduction

*Secure multi-party computation* (MPC) [26,49] is a cryptographic protocol that enables multiple parties to jointly compute a function over their private inputs, while ensuring that no party learns anything about the others' inputs beyond what can be inferred from the final output. Traditionally, MPC has been studied in the stand-alone setting, where only a single execution of the protocol is considered. However, in real-world applications, it is more realistic to assume that multiple protocol instances, possibly of different protocols, may be executed concurrently.

To model and ensure security in such concurrent environments, Canetti [13] introduced the framework of *Universally Composable* (UC) security. UC security provides strong guarantees: it ensures that a protocol remains secure even when composed with arbitrary other protocols running concurrently. Despite its desirable properties, achieving UC security is known to be impossible in the plain model (i.e., without trusted setup) for most non-trivial functionalities. This impossibility result holds even when restricted to concurrent executions of the *same* protocol (a setting known as *self-concurrency*) [39,40].

These strong negative results have led to the exploration of alternative notions of security that can still provide meaningful guarantees in concurrent settings. Notable (simulation-based) notions include: (1) *Super-Polynomial Simulation* (SPS) security [45], a variant of the standard simulation-based security that permits the simulator to run in super-polynomial time, (2) *Angel-Based Simulation* [47] and its extension to (interactive) super-polynomial helpers [14], where the simulator itself is polynomial time but has access to an super-polynomial-time oracle, (3) *Shielded-Oracle Model* [12] which offers a middle ground between the first two notions, and (4) *Multiple Ideal-Queries Model* [27] where the simulator is polynomial time but can make multiple queries to the ideal functionality.

While early works in this direction required super-polynomial hardness assumptions [6,38,43,47], Canetti, Lin, and Pass [14] proposed techniques to achieve angel-based simulation under (standard) polynomial-time assumptions. Later, similar results were also achieved for other variants such as SPS and Shielded-oracle [12,24,25]. These concurrency models are extensively studied and offer a range of robust solutions with different trade-offs when standard polynomial-time simulation becomes unachievable.

**Concurrent Security in the Post-quantum Setting.** The above positive results consider only classical security, and it remains unclear whether they hold against quantum adversaries. In fact, it has been observed that classical proofs of simulation-based security often do not directly extend to the post-quantum setting [20,31]. A central obstacle in the post-quantum setting is the no-cloning principle, which prevents duplication of the quantum adversary's internal state and thus undermines classical *rewinding*-based proof techniques. It is worth noting that rewinding techniques are critical to achieve security under polynomial hardness **even when super-polynomial simulators are allowed**, e.g., in SPS and angel-based notions of security mentioned above.

These challenges have motivated a growing line of research, yielding exciting development of quantum simulation techniques. These include the construction of post-quantum zero-knowledge proofs (PQ-ZK) [10,19,41,48], post-quantum secure two-party computation protocols (PQ-2PC) protocols [18,21,33,42], and even post-quantum secure MPC protocols (PQ-MPC) [2,17,35].

However, all of these results were obtained in the *stand-alone* setting. When it comes to concurrent quantum security, rather surprisingly, very little is known[1]. Two works [4,28] address the so-called *bounded-concurrent* setting, but this model is limited: it requires the protocol designer to know an a priori bound on the total number of concurrent sessions; if the number of sessions exceeds this bound in a real-world concurrent scenario, no security guarantees are provided.

It is also worth noting that some classical works achieve concurrent SPS 2PC under only the Learning with Errors (LWE) assumption and using only straight-line simulators (e.g., [1], or [5] combined with [11]). These constructions would naturally remain secure even against quantum adversaries. However, they rely on the *super-polynomial* hardness of LWE, and we know almost nothing under standard *polynomial-time* hardness assumptions. This situation is quite unsatisfactory, especially when contrasted with the rich literature on classical concurrent security as described earlier.

As the primary goal of this work, we aim to improve this unsatisfactory state of affairs by developing techniques that can effectively address (fully) concurrent attacks by a quantum adversary. More specifically, we focus on the following fundamental question:

> **Question:** *Does there exist setup-free PQ-2PC from standard* **polynomial hardness** *assumptions in any meaningful concurrent model (and ideally in a small number of rounds)?*

Note that we aim for a *fully* concurrent model here, in contrast to the bounded concurrency setting studied in prior works [4,28].

### 1.1 Our Results

In this work, we affirmatively answer the above question. We also obtain additional positive results for the case of PQ-ZK.

**Post-quantum SPS-2PC.** Our first result is a construction of constant-round concurrently SPS-secure PQ-2PC (PQ-SPS-2PC) *under the minimal assumption* that post-quantum oblivious transfers (PQ-OTs) exists:

[1] This work focuses on constructions without trusted setup assumptions. If such assumptions are allowed (e.g., a common reference string), there exist known classical UC-MPC protocols that remain secure in the quantum setting, provided they are based on quantum-secure building blocks and admit a straight-line simulator.

**Theorem 1.** *Assuming the existence of constant-round semi-honest PQ-OTs, there exists a constant-round concurrent SPS post-quantum two-party computation.*

Our result can be seen as a post-quantum analog of the result of [24]. Our main technical innovation lies in developing a new proof of security that, roughly speaking, avoids the use of any rewinding[2]. The use of rewinding was critical in [24] in order to achieve a construction under polynomial hardness. Thus, in avoiding the use of any rewinding, our proof departs significantly from that of [24]. Establishing the concurrent post-quantum security of our protocol turns out to be highly nontrivial.

**Post-quantum SPS-ZK.** Our second result is concerned with the construction of concurrent PQ-ZK with super-polynomial simulation (PQ-SPS-ZK). While PQ-SPS-ZK is a special case of PQ-SPS-2PC, and thus follows from it, our focus is on a (tighter) two-round construction. A two-round construction of PQ-SPS-ZK under quantum *subexponential* hardness of LWE already follows as a corollary of the results in [1]. (In the full version of this work [29, Section 6], we also present a direct construction that additionally satisfies the public-coin property.) In contrast, almost nothing is known for this object under **polynomial** hardness assumption.

We show that two-round PQ-SPS-ZK can be achieved under quantum **polynomial** hardness of LWE if we focus on languages in $\mathbf{NP} \cap \mathbf{coNP}$:

**Theorem 2.** *Assuming the quantum polynomial-time hardness of LWE, there exist two-round, public-coin, concurrent PQ-SPS-ZK for* $\mathbf{NP} \cap \mathbf{coNP}$.

We remark that such a result was not known even in the classical setting (even without requiring the public-coin property).

**Extension to Quantum Functionalities.** The discussion so far has focused on the post-quantum setting, where honest parties and their communication channels remain classical. In the quantum regime, however, it is also desirable to grant honest parties quantum computational and communication capabilities, enabling them to securely compute quantum functionalities (e.g., preparing entanglement or performing quantum key distribution).

Indeed, this is a compelling direction that has attracted significant research attention [3,7,8,21–23,32,33,35,42]. However, this line of work focuses on the stand-alone setting, and none of these results address the concurrent setting in the plain model (i.e., without trusted setup assumptions). The closest attempts are again the works of [4] and [28], whose respective limitations have been discussed earlier. *Thus, almost nothing is known about the (unbounded) concurrency of plain-model secure quantum computation!*

We observe that our Thm. 1 can be extended to the fully quantum setting using the compiler developed in [7]. In particular, [7, Theorem 5.1] presents a

[2] Technically speaking, our reduction relies on secure primitives such as non-malleable commitments and zero-knowledge proofs, and the security proofs for those primitives may use rewinding. However, our reduction does not introduce rewinding of its own.

compiler that transforms any post-quantum secure two-party computation (PQ-2PC) protocol into a secure two-party *quantum* computation (2PQC) protocol (i.e., for computing quantum functionalities), incurring only a constant number of additional rounds. Moreover, the security proof of this compiler is "straight-line", in the sense that the simulator for the resulting 2PQC protocol does not rely on rewinding techniques *when viewed in the PQ-2PC hybrid model.* Thanks to this feature, we observe the following: as long as the underlying PQ-2PC protocol is concurrently secure and admits a straight-line SPS simulator, the 2PQC protocol produced via the [7] compiler will also be concurrently secure with a straight-line SPS simulator. This observation, combined with Thm. 1, yields the following corollary:

**Corollary 1.** *Assuming the existence of constant-round semi-honest PQ-OTs, there exists a constant-round concurrent SPS two-party quantum computation.*

### 1.2 Related Work

In the classical setting, constant-round concurrent SPS-MPC (as opposed to 2PC) has been constructed under standard polynomial-time assumptions in [25] (building upon [30,34,37]). Notably, their construction relies only on black-box use of cryptographic primitives, in contrast to ours (which follows the approach of [24]). An important open question is whether a post-quantum analog of [25] can be achieved, that is, whether it is possible to construct a constant-round concurrent PQ-SPS-MPC protocol based on a polynomial-time assumption, ideally using a black-box construction.

We note that Angel-based UC [14,47] and Shielded Oracle UC [12] are closely related generalizations of SPS-security. Unlike concurrent SPS security, these notions have the advantage of supporting a universal composition theorem. However, they often require either more rounds or somewhat stronger assumptions than SPS-security. The state-of-the-art protocols under these security notions include an $\widetilde{O}(\log \lambda)$-round black-box construction based on constant-round semi-honest OT for Angel-based UC [16], and a constant-round black-box construction under stronger polynomial-time assumptions for Shielded Oracle UC [12].

## 2 Technical Overview

### 2.1 Concurrent SPS PQ-2PC

#### 2.1.1 Starting Point: the [24] Protocol

Before presenting our post-quantum, constant-round, concurrently secure two-party computation (2PC) protocol, we first review the *classical-secure* constant-round concurrent 2PC protocol introduced by [24]. It is worth mentioning that, prior to [24], all known constructions of secure computation protocols achieving SPS security either rely critically on a super-polynomial time simulator to break some underlying cryptographic primitives and extract the trapdoor or, in an effort to avoid complexity-leveraging, have to deal with *concurrent rewinding* in some forms, which is often challenging and leads to a substantial increase in round complexity.

To bypass the need for concurrent rewinding, the key idea of [24] is to ensure that the simulator $\mathcal{S}$ can always extract the trapdoor before it begins to "cheat" for the rest of the protocol session, even in the complex setting where multiple instances of the protocol is running concurrently, and proceeds with a straight-line simulation for the rest of the protocol session. More concretely, [24] employs a non-malleable zero-knowledge argument (NMZK) scheme to set up a trapdoor, which enables safe extraction even in the concurrent setting.[3] Following this, the protocol proceeds with a semi-honest two-party computation, where each party proves—at every step—that it is behaving honestly, using a witness-indistinguishable (WI) proof.

A high-level overview of their construction is provided in Protocol 1.

**Protocol 1: Classical-Secure Constant-Round Concurrent 2PC**

**Phase I: Trapdoor Generation**[a]

1. **(Preamble Phase of** $\mathsf{NMZK}$**)** $P_A$ "sends" an extractable commitment ($\mathsf{ExtCom}$) of a random string $\sigma$ to $P_B$; $P_B$ acts symmetrically.
2. **(Trapdoor)** $P_A$ sends $\mathsf{com}_1$, a commitment of bit 0 to $P_B$.
3. **(Post-preamble Phase of** $\mathsf{NMZK}$**)** The two parties execute the "post-preamble phase" of $\mathsf{NMZK}$, where $P_A$ proves to $P_B$ that $com_1$ is a commitment to bit 0.
4. $P_B$ acts symmetrically.

**Phase II: Input Commitment**[b]

In this phase, the parties commit to their inputs and random coins (to be used in the next phase) using $\mathsf{ExtCom}$, and each party attaches a witness-indistinguishable (WI) proof showing that it either "knows" the trapdoor or has sent a valid extractable commitment.

**Phase III: Secure Computation**

In this phase, $P_A$ and $P_B$ engage in an execution of the semi-honest two-party protocol, and each party attaches a WI proof after every semi-honest 2PC message, proving that it either "knows" the trapdoor or behaviors honestly "so far" in the protocol.

[a] The purpose of **Phase I** is to aid the simulator $\mathcal{S}$ in obtaining a "trapdoor" to be used during the simulation of the protocol.

[b] The purpose of **Phase II** is to aid the $\mathcal{S}$ in extracting the adversary's input and randomness.

[3] We remark that a special NMZK scheme is used here, which can be divided into a *preamble phase* and a *post-preamble phase*. Roughly speaking, the preamble phase consists of an extractable commitment to some "trapdoor", while the post-preamble phase is where the actual proof takes place.

Before delving into the security analysis of [24], we first briefly recall a canonical classically-secure extractable commitment scheme ExtCom (e.g., [24, 46]). The first message of ExtCom statistically binds the committed value, and extraction is achieved by rewinding the committer multiple times with different second-message challenges and collecting the corresponding responses. The committed value can then be recovered using these transcripts. Additionally, each such execution—consisting of a second message and its corresponding response—is referred to as a look-ahead thread.

In the security proof of [24], the simulator $\mathcal{S}$ performs rewinding only within dedicated look-ahead threads to extract the trapdoor from ExtCom, and proceeds with a straight-line simulation in the main thread. Crucially, within look-ahead threads, [24] allows $\mathcal{S}$ to use *honest parties' secret inputs* (in intermediate hybrid experiments). More specifically, if $\mathcal{S}$ initiates multiple look-ahead threads to extract the trapdoor committed in the ExtCom of protocol session $j$, then for each session $i \neq j$, it proceeds as follows: if the trapdoor for session $i$ is available, $\mathcal{S}$ performs straight-line simulation for session $i$ within the look-ahead threads; otherwise, $\mathcal{S}$ uses the honest party's input for session $i$ within look-ahead threads. Additionally, in their security proof, [24] introduced a novel approach for organizing the sequence of hybrid experiments. The conventional approach organizes hybrids in a "session-by-session" manner, wherein all modifications to a given session $i$ are completed consecutively (through a sequence of successive hybrids) before proceeding to any other session, independent of the adversary's scheduling. In contrast, [24] designed a sequence of hybrids that interleave across multiple sessions, with transitions "jumping" between sessions as dictated by the adversary's message scheduling. As a result, the exact order of hybrids depends dynamically on the adversary's scheduling decisions. By leveraging the above techniques, [24] avoids dealing with complex concurrent rewinding used in previous works and instead relies solely on "local rewindings" within look-ahead threads. As a result, their protocol achieves constant-round while relying only on polynomial-time assumptions.

### 2.1.2 Challenges in the Post-quantum Setting

However, achieving post-quantum security presents several challenges. First, recall that in [24], the simulator $\mathcal{S}$ must rewind the adversary $\mathcal{A}$ in "look-ahead threads" in order to extract the trapdoor—or, alternatively, $\mathcal{A}$'s input and randomness. This technique is generally incompatible with the quantum setting: due to the no-cloning theorem, $\mathcal{S}$ cannot record $\mathcal{A}$'s internal quantum state between look-ahead threads, and performing intermediate measurements would also disturb $\mathcal{A}$'s internal quantum state. As a result, even if extraction succeeds, $\mathcal{S}$ may not be able to faithfully simulate $\mathcal{A}$'s output state, breaking the simulation. In recent years, there has been significant progresses in quantum rewinding and simulatable-extraction techniques [18, 19, 41, 48]. This naturally raises the question: can these new quantum rewinding techniques be combined with the structured rewinding order used in the original proof of [24] to lift their security analysis to the quantum setting?

Upon closer examination, this approach appears to be quite challenging—if not fundamentally impossible. There are new obstacles that have not been addressed in the existing quantum rewinding literature. In particular, these techniques are not applicable in the concurrent setting due to the adversary's ability to arbitrarily schedule messages. We elaborate on this in the following discussion.

In [24], after the simulator $\mathcal{S}$ initiates multiple look-ahead threads to extract the trapdoor (or the adversary $\mathcal{A}$'s input), it must return to the execution of the main thread. More precisely, $\mathcal{S}$ must first "enter" a look-ahead thread from a specific "entering-point" in the concurrent schedule—namely, the second message of $\mathsf{ExtCom}$, and return to the "entering-point" to begin its execution of the main thread. As we mentioned earlier, to perform extraction, $\mathcal{S}$ sends a different second-message challenge, records the corresponding response, and then rewinds $\mathcal{A}$ to *return to the same "entering-point"*. This process is repeated multiple times to gather sufficient transcripts for extraction.

While this is an easy task in the classical setting, in sharp contrast, this becomes significantly more challenging in the quantum setting—rather surprisingly, no quantum rewinding techniques in existing literature are know to achieve this effect! Indeed, this task seems impossible as we explain below: a direct quantum analog of this requirement would, at the very least, demand the ability to estimate $\mathcal{A}$'s probability of aborting while simultaneously simulating $\mathcal{A}$'s internal state at the entering point—that is, prior to initiating the rewinding procedure. This seems inherently infeasible: for example, if $\mathcal{A}$'s internal state at the "entering-point" is an equal superposition of an honest committer and an always-aborting adversary, then there is no hope to recover $\mathcal{A}$'s original initial state after we collapse its "aborting or not" decision.

There is another, less obvious obstacle, which is more subtle and harder to describe at this point. We defer a detailed discussion to the next subsection, where it will arise naturally in the context of our main ideas.

### 2.1.3 Our Approach

In this work, we aim to construct post-quantum constant-round concurrent secure two-party computation under the minimal assumption that constant-round oblivious transfer (OT) exists. Rather than tackling the seemingly harder problem of building post-quantum simulatable-extraction that remains robust against arbitrary message scheduling, we make a key observation: rewinding is, in fact, entirely unnecessary and can be removed from all intermediate hybrids. For simplicity, we refer to the $2m$ occurrences of $\mathsf{ExtCom}$ across the $m$ sessions as *special commitments* throughout the remainder of this technical overview. In [24], roughly speaking, the authors considered a numbered ordering over all $2m$ special commitments[6] across $m$ sessions (2 special commitments for each session), and associated each occurrence of special commitment with a corresponding hybrid. For every $i \in [2m]$, the hybrid $H_i$ (associated with the $i_{\mathsf{th}}$

[6] In [24], the authors actually considered $4m$ special *messages*; we simplify this to $2m$ special commitments for clarity.

special commitment) will start multiple look-ahead threads to extract the trapdoor (or $\mathcal{A}$'s input) committed in the $i_{\mathsf{th}}$ special commitment. A key structural property of the hybrids is that any future hybrids $H_j$ (for $j > i$) will never make any modifications to the look-ahead threads initiated by $H_i$. Moreover, in $H_i$, no look-ahead threads are initiated after the $i_{\mathsf{th}}$ special commitment has been sent. That is, in hybrid $H_i$, all values committed in the first $i$ special commitment are extracted via look-ahead threads. Since the final simulator $\mathcal{S}$ does not perform any rewindings and instead runs in super-polynomial time to extract trapdoors (or $\mathcal{A}$'s input and randomness), we are likewise allowed to use super-polynomial power to extract trapdoors (or $\mathcal{A}$'s input and randomness) from the first $i_{\mathsf{th}}$ special commitment in $H_i$, for any $i \in [2m]$, provided that we can demonstrate indistinguishability between the hybrids. This crucial observation allows us to avoid the need for any quantum rewinding or simulatable extraction. Consequently, we can significantly weaken the requirements on the underlying commitment scheme and replace each occurrence of ExtCom with a non-interactive, statistical binding commitment[7].

Additionally, since $H_i$ extracts trapdoors using super-polynomial power instead of relying on look-ahead threads, we eliminate the need for a post-quantum, constant-round, public-coin non-malleable commitment NMCom scheme (which serves as a building block in the NMZK construction). Notably, the existence of such a primitive in the post-quantum setting remains an open problem.

In hybrid $H_i$, once $\mathcal{S}$ extracts the trapdoor for session $i$, it begins to "cheat" in the remainder of session $i$. However, we must argue that, when $\mathcal{S}$ begins to "cheat" in session $i$ (viewed as a left interaction), the adversary $\mathcal{A}$ cannot "cheat" simultaneously in any other session (viewed as right interactions). Intuitively, this can be reduced to the non-malleability of NMCom. Nevertheless, several subtleties arise in making this reduction precise.

- The standard security guarantee of non-malleability holds only in settings where a man-in-the-middle adversary $\mathcal{M}$ participates in two executions of the *same* protocol. Consequently, when $H_i$ begins to "cheat" using the extracted trapdoor in session $i$, we cannot directly invoke non-malleability to argue that to argue that the adversary $\mathcal{A}$ cannot simultaneously cheat in other sessions. To address this, [24] relies on the statistical security of the underlying primitives, In our work, we resolve this issue by leveraging an additional property of NMCom known as *robustness*, first introduced by [36] and has recently become a key ingredient in the design of post-quantum non-malleable commitments [9,17,35]. Robustness ensures that non-malleability holds regardless of which protocol is used in the left interaction, allowing us to rule out any cheating behavior by $\mathcal{A}$ in other sessions—even when $\mathcal{S}$ is "cheating" in session $i$.
- To reduce $\mathcal{A}$'s cheating behavior to the (robust) non-malleability of NMCom, we need to construct a man-in-the-middle adversary $\mathcal{M}$ that runs $\mathcal{A}$ internally and interacts with an external committer $C$ and a receiver $R$. However, in

[7] Similar to [24], the non-interactive property is not strictly necessary for our construction, but is chosen for simplicity of presentation.

[24], the hybrid $H_i$ initiates multiple look-ahead threads to extract trapdoor from session $i$. Due to $\mathcal{A}$'s arbitrary message scheduling, it is possible that in some session $j \neq i$, the first message of $\mathsf{NMCom}$ of session $j$ is sent *before* the $i_{\mathsf{th}}$ special commitment. In such cases, $\mathcal{S}$ would need to rewind the external receiver $R$ in the look-ahead threads. This presents a problem, as $R$ is a standalone external party and only responds in a single thread of execution. [24] resolves this issue by leveraging the *public-coin* property of $\mathsf{NMCom}$. In their approach, all $\mathsf{NMCom}$ messages on the main-thread are forwarded between $\mathcal{A}$ and the external receiver $R$; On the other hand, in look-ahead threads, any message that would have been sent by $R$ to $\mathcal{A}$ is instead replaced with a random string by $\mathcal{M}$, and this is valid only because $\mathsf{NMCom}$ is a public-coin protocol.
In contrast, our protocol eliminates rewinding entirely, thereby removing the need for look-ahead threads. As a result, we no longer require $\mathsf{NMCom}$ to be public-coin. However, this leads to a new issue: in our new approach, $H_i$ uses super-polynomial power to extract trapdoors (or $\mathcal{A}$'s input and randomness) from the first $i$ special commitment. Similarly, if there exists a session $j \neq i$ such that the first message of $\mathsf{NMCom}$ of session $j$ is sent before the $i_{\mathsf{th}}$ special commitment, then we cannot reduce this to the non-malleability of $\mathsf{NMCom}$, simply because we are still using super-polynomial power during the execution of $\mathsf{NMCom}$. We resolve this issue by requiring an additional property of $\mathsf{NMCom}$ called *first-message binding*, which requires the first message of $\mathsf{NMCom}$ should be always sent by the committer $C$ and additionally binds the value of $\mathsf{NMCom}$[8]. Thus, for session $j \neq i$, if $\mathsf{NMCom}$ of session $j$ starts before the $i_{\mathsf{th}}$ special commitment, the value of $\mathsf{NMCom}$ is already bound and thus independent of $\mathcal{S}$'s "cheating behavior".

For the detailed construction and security proof of our protocol, please refer to Sect. 4.

## 2.2 Concurrent SPS PQ-ZK for NP ∩ coNP

Although a post-quantum two-round SPS-ZK protocol can be obtained via a variant of the construction proposed by [45] (plase refer to the full version of this work [29, Section 6]), this approach inherently relies on super-polynomial assumptions.

Our construction relies on a collision resistant hash function (against QPT adversary) and a post-quantum function-hiding (also referred as circuit-private) secure function evaluation (SFE). The notion of circuit privacy requires that for any two functionally-equivalent circuits $C_0$ and $C_1$ of the same size, and

[8] For simplicity and clarity, we assume that $\mathsf{NMCom}$ begins with a non-interactive, statistically binding commitment. However, the non-interactive property can be relaxed by having both parties exchange the first message of Naor's commitment at the beginning of the protocol. This allows the commitment used within $\mathsf{NMCom}$ to be treated as effectively non-interactive in the remainder of the protocol.

any $\mathsf{ct}^* \in \{0,1\}^*$, no QPT adversary can distinguish between $\mathsf{Eval}(C_0, \mathsf{ct}^*)$ and $\mathsf{Eval}(C_1, \mathsf{ct}^*)$. We provide a high-level description of our protocol in the following:

- $V \rightarrow P$**:** $V$ sends a hash key $s$ for CRHF, an SFE encryption $\mathsf{ct}$ of 0, and the first message of ZAP to $P$.
- $P \rightarrow V$**:** The prover $P$ begins by computing $\widehat{\mathsf{ct}} \leftarrow \mathsf{Eval}(C^0, \mathsf{ct})$, where $C^0$ is a constant-0 circuit that always outputs 0s. Then, $P$ sends the second message of ZAP, proving that either $x \in \mathcal{L}$, or that it "knows" a collision for the collision-resistant hash function and that $\widehat{\mathsf{ct}} = \mathsf{Eval}(C', \mathsf{ct})$, where $C'$ is a circuit that checks whether the input is a no-witness for $\mathcal{L}$, and if so, outputs the collision; otherwise, it outputs 0.

The round complexity is clear from the description above. Moreover, as long as the underlying SFE protocol is public-coin, our construction remains public-coin as well. The soundness property follows from a standard reduction to collision-resistance. The proof of the super-polynomial-time simulatable zero-knowledge property is provided below.

*Proof (Sketch).* The simulator $\mathcal{S}$ begins by using brute force to find a collision for the collision-resistant hash function. Such a collision is guaranteed to exist due to the compressing property of the CRHF. Then, $\mathcal{S}$ computes $\widehat{\mathsf{ct}}$ as $\mathsf{Eval}(C', \mathsf{ct})$. Given that $x \in \mathcal{L}$, there exists no no-witness for $\mathcal{L}$, and thus $C'$ and $C$ are functionally equivalent. By the circuit privacy of SFE, $\widehat{\mathsf{ct}}$ is statistically indistinguishable from that in the real execution. Finally, $\mathcal{S}$ computes the second message of ZAP using the fact that $\widehat{\mathsf{ct}} = \mathsf{Eval}(C', \mathsf{ct})$ and it "knows" a collision as the witness. By the witness indistinguishability (WI) property of the ZAP, the simulated proof is indistinguishable from a real one. □

Note that for the second message of ZAP, the prover $P$ must prove $(x, \widehat{\mathsf{ct}}) \in \mathcal{L} \vee \mathcal{L}_{\mathsf{ct}}$, where $\widehat{\mathsf{ct}} \in \mathcal{L}_{\mathsf{ct}}$ if and only if $\widehat{\mathsf{ct}} = \mathsf{Eval}(C', \mathsf{ct})$ and it "knows" a collision. At first glance, this seems to require a ZAP for general **NP**, since $\mathcal{L}_{\mathsf{ct}} \notin \mathbf{NP} \cap \mathbf{coNP}$. However, by exploiting the fact that $x \in \mathbf{NP} \cap \mathbf{coNP}$, we observe that it suffices to use a ZAP with certain structural properties tailored to this setting.

- If $x \in \mathcal{L}$, we place no requirement on the soundness of the ZAP. Otherwise, we require that no valid second message $\mathsf{zap}_2$ exists unless $\widehat{\mathsf{ct}} \in \mathcal{L}_{\mathsf{ct}}$.
- If $x \in \mathcal{L}$, we require the ZAP to satisfy witness indistinguishability. Otherwise, no such requirement is imposed.

We refer to ZAPs with the above properties as *ZAPs for Controlled-OR Languages*, and provide a formal definition in Definition 3. Such ZAPs can be instantiated via the construction given in [15][9], under the polynomial-time hardness of LWE.

For the detailed construction and security proof of our protocol, please refer to Sect. 5.

[9] In [15], the authors define and construct ZAPs for super-complement languages. While their definition does not directly imply our notion of ZAPs for Controlled-OR Languages, we emphasize that their construction satisfies our definition, and the corresponding security proof remains essentially unchanged.

# 3 Preliminaries

We use standard notations from the (quantum) cryptography literature. Due to space limitations, we will recall only the most essential preliminaries here. Additional preliminaries are provided in the full version of this work [29, Section 3].

## 3.1 Post-quantum Secure Function Evaluation

We recall the definition of secure function evaluation protocols with statistical circuit privacy and post-quantum input privacy (e.g., defined in [10]).

**Definition 1 (Post-Quantum 2-Message Function-Hiding SFE).** *A post-quantum two-message* function hiding secure function evaluation *(SFE) protocol* SFE *consists of four algorithms* $(\mathsf{Gen}, \mathsf{Enc}, \mathsf{Eval}, \mathsf{Dec})$. *They satisfy the following syntax:*

- $\mathsf{k} \leftarrow \mathsf{Gen}(1^\lambda)$*: a PPT algorithm that takes as input a security parameter* $1^\lambda$*, and outputs a secret key* $\mathsf{k}$*;*
- $\mathsf{ct} \leftarrow \mathsf{Enc}(\mathsf{k}, x)$*: a PPT algorithm that takes as input a key* $\mathsf{k}$ *a string* $x$*, and outputs a ciphertext* $\mathsf{ct}$*;*
- $\widehat{\mathsf{ct}} \leftarrow \mathsf{Eval}(C, \mathsf{ct})$*: a PPT algorithm that takes as input a classical polynomial-size circuit* $C$ *and ciphertext* $\mathsf{ct}$*, and outputs an evaluated ciphertext* $\widehat{\mathsf{ct}}$*;*
- $\widehat{x} = \mathsf{Dec}(\mathsf{k}, \widehat{\mathsf{ct}})$*: a deterministic algorithm that takes as input a ciphertext* $\widehat{\mathsf{ct}}$*, and outputs a string* $\widehat{x}$*.*

*The scheme satisfies the following properties:*

1. **Correctness:** *For all polynomial* $s(\cdot)$*, all* $\lambda \in \mathbb{N}$*, all size-*$s(\lambda)$ *circuit* $C$*, and input* $x$ *for* $C$*, it holds that*

$$\Pr[\mathsf{Dec}(\mathsf{k}, \widehat{\mathsf{ct}}) = C(x) : \mathsf{k} \leftarrow \mathsf{Gen}(1^\lambda); \mathsf{ct} \leftarrow \mathsf{Enc}(\mathsf{k}, x); \widehat{\mathsf{ct}} \leftarrow \mathsf{Eval}(C, \mathsf{ct})] = 1.$$

2. **Post-Quantum Input Privacy:** *For any polynomial* $\ell(\cdot)$*,*

$$\{\mathsf{ct} \;:\; \mathsf{k} \leftarrow \mathsf{Gen}(1^\lambda);\; \mathsf{ct} \leftarrow \mathsf{Enc}(\mathsf{k}, x_0)\}_{\lambda, x_0, x_1} \overset{c}{\approx} \{\mathsf{ct} \;:\; \mathsf{k} \leftarrow \mathsf{Gen}(1^\lambda);\; \mathsf{ct} \leftarrow \mathsf{Enc}(\mathsf{k}, x_1)\}_{\lambda, x_0, x_1}$$

*where* $\lambda \in \mathbb{N}$ *and* $x_0, x_1 \in \{0,1\}^{\ell(\lambda)}$.

3. **Statistical Circuit Privacy:** *For all polynomial* $s(\cdot)$*,*

$$\{\mathsf{Eval}(C_0, \mathsf{ct}^*)\}_{\lambda, C_0, C_1, ct^*} \overset{s}{\approx} \{\mathsf{Eval}(C_1, \mathsf{ct}^*)\}_{\lambda, C_0, C_1, \mathsf{ct}^*},$$

*where* $\lambda \in \mathbb{N}$*,* $C_0$ *and* $C_1$ *are two size-*$s(\lambda)$*, functionally-equivalent circuits, and* $\mathsf{ct}^* \in \{0,1\}^*$.

**Instantiation.** Secure function evaluation schemes satisfying Definition 1 are known from the quantum hardness of LWE [11, 44].

## 4 Post-quantum Constant-Round Concurrent 2PC

We construct a post-quantum constant-round concurrent 2PC, $\Pi(\mathcal{F})$, from standard assumptions. Its description is given in Protocol 2. This construction is based on the following building blocks:

- A non-interactive statistically-binding commitment scheme $\mathsf{Com}$; We use $\mathsf{Com}(m; r)$ to denote the message where a string $m$ is committed using randomness $r$[10].
- A constant-round $\varepsilon$-simulatable zero-knowledge argument of knowledge $\varepsilon$-$\mathsf{ZKAoK}$ without post-extraction simulation.
- A constant-round witness indistinguishable argument $\mathsf{WI}$.
- A constant-round non-malleable commitment scheme $\mathsf{NMCOM}$ with first-message binding property and $k$-robustness. (See the full version for the formal definition [29, Section 3]).
- A constant-round semi-honest two party computation protocol $\langle P_A^{\mathsf{sh}}, P_B^{\mathsf{sh}}\rangle$ that securely computes $\mathcal{F}$.

**Protocol 2: Post-Quantum Constant-Round Concurrent 2PC**

**Parameter:** Let $k$ be $\mathsf{MAX}(\mathsf{rc}(\varepsilon\text{-}\mathsf{ZKAoK}) + 1, 2 * t * (1 + \mathsf{rc}(\mathsf{WI})) + 2)$, where $\mathsf{rc}(\cdot)$ denotes the round complexity.

**Phase I: Trapdoor Generation**

1. $P_A$ uniformly samples a random string $\tau_A$ where $\tau_A \xleftarrow{\$} \{0,1\}^\lambda$. $P_A$ samples a random tape $r_A^{\mathcal{T}}$ and sends $\mathsf{c}_A^{\mathcal{T}} = \mathsf{Com}(\tau_A; r_A^{\mathcal{T}})$ to $P_B$.
2. $P_B$ acts symmetrically as $P_A$ did in Step 1 of **Phase I**. That is, $P_B$ sends $\mathsf{c}_B^{\mathcal{T}} = \mathsf{Com}(\tau_B; r_B^{\mathcal{T}})$ to $P_A$.
3. $P_A$ samples a random tape $r_A^{\mathsf{trap}}$ and sends $\mathsf{c}_A^{\mathsf{trap}} = \mathsf{Com}(0; r_A^{\mathsf{trap}})$ to $P_B$.
4. (a) $P_A$ samples a random tape $r_A^{\mathsf{prove}}$ and sends $\mathsf{c}_A^{\mathsf{prove}} = \mathsf{Com}(0; r_A^{\mathsf{prove}})$ to $P_B$.
   (b) $P_A$ proves to $P_B$ that it "knows" the value committed in $\mathsf{c}_A^{\mathsf{prove}}$ using $\varepsilon$-$\mathsf{ZKAoK}$.
   Formally, $P_A$ proves that $\mathsf{c}_A^{\mathsf{prove}} \in \mathcal{L}_{\mathsf{prove}}$, where
   $$\mathcal{L}_{\mathsf{prove}} := \{\mathsf{c}_A^{\mathsf{prove}} \mid \exists (m, r)\ s.t.\ \mathsf{c}_A^{\mathsf{prove}} = \mathsf{Com}(m; r)\}. \quad (1)$$
   Note that $P_A$ uses the $(0, r_A^{\mathsf{prove}})$ as the witness when executing this $\varepsilon$-$\mathsf{ZKAoK}$.
   (c) $P_B$ sends $\tau_B$ and $r_B^{\mathcal{T}}$ to $P_A$ as the decommit information for $\mathsf{c}_B^{\mathcal{T}}$. $P_A$ aborts if the decommitment is not valid.
   (d) **(NMCOM.)** $P_A$ and $P_B$ engage in an execution of $\mathsf{NMCOM}$, where $P_A$ commits to the value $r_A^{\mathsf{trap}}$ defined in Step 3 Note that the value

[10] Similar to [24], we use a non-interactive, statistically binding commitment scheme in the presentation of our protocol for simplicity. Alternatively, one can replace it with Naor's interactive scheme by requiring both parties to send the first message of Naor's commitment at the onset of the protocol.

$r_A^{\mathsf{trap}}$ serves as a valid witness for the statement that "the $\mathsf{c}_A^{\mathsf{trap}}$ in Step 3 of **Phase I** is a commitment to the value 0." Formally, $r_A^{\mathsf{trap}}$ is a valid witness for the fact that $\mathsf{c}_A^{\mathsf{trap}} \in \mathcal{L}_{\mathsf{Com}(0)}$ where

$$\mathcal{L}_{\mathsf{Com}(0)} := \{\mathsf{c} \mid \exists r \ s.t. \ \mathsf{c} = \mathsf{Com}(0; r)\}. \quad (2)$$

We use $\mathsf{c}_A^{\mathsf{NM}}$ to refer to (the transcript of) this $\mathsf{NMCOM}$.

(e) **(WI.)** $P_A$ and $P_B$ engage in an execution of $\mathsf{WI}$, where $P_A$ proves that *either*
  i. **(honest statement.)** $P_A$ behaves honestly in Step 4d (namely, $\mathsf{c}_A^{\mathsf{NM}}$ is indeed a valid $\mathsf{NMCOM}$ to the value $r_A^{\mathsf{trap}}$, which is a valid witness for the fact that $\mathsf{c}_A^{\mathsf{trap}} \in \mathcal{L}_{\mathsf{Com}(0)}$), *or*
  ii. **(trapdoor statement.)** the $\mathsf{c}_A^{\mathsf{prove}}$ sent by $P_A$ in Step 4a is a commitment to the value $\tau_B$ defined in Step 4c.

Note that when executing this $\mathsf{WI}$, the honest $P_A$ uses the witness corresponding to the **honest statement** above.

5. $P_B$ acts symmetrically as $P_A$ did in Step 3 of this phase. (That is, $P_B$ samples a random tape $r_B^{\mathsf{trap}}$ and sends $\mathsf{c}_B^{\mathsf{trap}} = \mathsf{Com}(0; r_B^{\mathsf{trap}})$ to $P_A$.)
6. Similarly, $P_B$ acts symmetrically as $P_A$ did in Step 4 of this phase.

**Phase II: Input Commitment**

1. $P_A$ samples $r'_A$ (which will be used in the secure computation phase). It sends $\mathsf{c}_A = \mathsf{Com}((x_A, r'_A); r_A^{\mathsf{com}})$
2. Similarly, $P_B$ acts symmetrically. $P_B$ samples $r'_B$ and sends $\mathsf{c}_B = \mathsf{Com}((x_B, r'_B); r_B^{\mathsf{com}})$

**Phase III: Secure Computation**

1. $P_A$ samples $r''_B$ and sends it to $P_B$, where $|r''_B| = |r'_B|$. Similarly, $P_B$ samples $r''_A$ and sends it to $P_A$. Let $r_A = r'_A \oplus r''_A$ and $r_B = r'_B \oplus r''_B$. $r_A$ and $r_B$ are the random coins that $P_A$ and $P_B$ will use during the execution of $\langle P_A^{\mathsf{sh}}, P_B^{\mathsf{sh}} \rangle$.
2. Let $t$ be the number of rounds in $\langle P_A^{\mathsf{sh}}, P_B^{\mathsf{sh}} \rangle$, where one round consists of a message from $P_A^{\mathsf{sh}}$ followed by a reply from $P_B^{\mathsf{sh}}$. Let transcript $T_{A,j}$ (resp., $T_{B,j}$) be defined to contain all the messages exchanged between $P_A^{\mathsf{sh}}$ and $P_B^{\mathsf{sh}}$ before the point $P_A^{\mathsf{sh}}$ (resp., $P_A^{\mathsf{sh}}$ ) is supposed to send a message in round $j$. For $j = 1, \ldots, t$:
  (a) $P_A \Rightarrow P_B$ : Compute $m_{A,j} = P_A^{\mathsf{sh}}(T_{A,j}, x_A, r_A)$ and send it to $P_B$. $P_A$ and $P_B$ then engage in an execution of $\mathsf{WI}$ where $P_A$ proves that *either*
    – **(honest statement)** $\mathsf{c}_A$ is a commitment of $\widehat{x_A}, \widehat{r_A}'$ such that $m_{A,j} = P_A^{\mathsf{sh}}(T_{A,j}, \widehat{x_A}, \widehat{r_A}' \oplus r''_A)$, *or*
    – **(trapdoor statement)** $\mathsf{c}_A^{\mathsf{trap}}$ is a commitment to bit 1.

  Formally, $P_A$ proves that $((m_{A,j}, \mathsf{c}_A), \mathsf{c}_A^{\mathsf{trap}}) \in \mathcal{L}_{\mathsf{sh}}^{T_{A,j}} \vee \mathcal{L}_{\mathsf{trap}}$, and $\mathcal{L}_{\mathsf{sh}}^{T_{A,j}} \vee \mathcal{L}_{\mathsf{trap}}$ denotes the OR-composed language, where

$$\mathcal{L}_{\mathsf{sh}}^{T_{A,j}} := \left\{ (m_{A,j}, \mathsf{c}_A) \mid \wedge \begin{array}{l} \exists \widehat{x_A}, \widehat{r_A}', r \ s.t. \ \mathsf{c}_A = \mathsf{Com}((\widehat{x_A}, \widehat{r_A}'); r) \\ m_{A,j} = P_A^{\mathsf{sh}}(T_{A,j}, \widehat{x_A}, \widehat{r_A}' \oplus r''_A) \end{array} \right\}. \quad (3)$$

and

$$\mathcal{L}_{\mathsf{trap}} := \{\mathsf{c}_A^{\mathsf{trap}} \mid \exists r \; s.t. \; \mathsf{c}_A^{\mathsf{trap}} = \mathsf{Com}(1; r)\}. \tag{4}$$

Note that $P_A$ uses $((x_A, r'_A, r_A^{\mathsf{com}}), \perp)$ the as the witness when executing this WI.

(b) $P_B \Rightarrow P_A$: $P_B$ now acts symmetrically.

### 4.1 Proof of Security

**Theorem 3.** $\Pi(\mathcal{F})$ *(Protocol 2) UC-SPS-realizes* $\mathcal{F}$ *for every well-formed functionality* $\mathcal{F}$.

*Proof.* Note that we aim to prove security in the concurrent setting, where an (unbounded) polynomial number of sessions (also referred to as *instances*) of Protocol 2 may execute concurrently. The adversary is allowed to corrupt exactly one party per session (without loss of generality). We emphasize that this is an "interchangeable-role" corruption model, meaning the adversary may corrupt, for example, party $P_A$ in one session and party $P_B$ in another.

We now describe the simulator. The simulator, dubbed $\mathcal{S}$, operates similarly across all sessions in the concurrent execution. Therefore, it suffices to specify its behavior in a single session (keeping in mind that the simulator is simultaneously handling all sessions in the concurrent setting). Moreover, we assume that in this specific session, $P_B$ is corrupted. The simulator's behavior is symmetric in sessions where $P_A$ is corrupted instead. We present the simulator in Algorithm 4.1.

**Algorithm 4.1: Simulator $\mathcal{S}$ (in a session where $P_B$ is corrupted):**

**Phase I: Trapdoor Generation**

1. In Step 1, $\mathcal{S}$ follows the protocol specification and behaves exactly like the honest $P_A$. Namely, it generates and sends $\mathsf{c}_A^{\mathcal{T}}$ honestly to $P_B$, and receives $\mathsf{c}_B^{\mathcal{T}}$. However, after receiving $\mathsf{c}_B^{\mathcal{T}}$, $\mathcal{S}$ extracts $\tau_B$ by running in super-polynomial time.
2. If the extraction is successful, in Step 3, $\mathcal{S}$ commits to 1 in $\mathsf{c}_A^{\mathsf{trap}} = \mathsf{Com}(1; r_A^{\mathsf{trap}})$ instead of 0. Otherwise, $\mathcal{S}$ outputs $\perp$.
3. In Step 4a, $\mathcal{S}$ commits to $\tau_B$ (instead of 0) in $\mathsf{c}_A^{\mathsf{prove}}$.
4. In Step 4b, $\mathcal{S}$ follows the protocol with an honest execution of $\varepsilon$-ZKAoK to prove knowledge of the decommitment value of $\mathsf{c}_A^{\mathsf{prove}}$ (use $(\tau_B, r_A^{\mathsf{prove}})$ as witness).
5. In Step 4c, $\mathcal{S}$ acts honestly and check the decommit value of $\mathsf{c}_B^{\mathcal{T}}$ sent by malicious $P_B$. If the decommit value is incorrect, $\mathcal{S}$ aborts.
6. In Step 4d, $\mathcal{S}$ commits to 0 (instead of the value $r_A^{\mathsf{trap}}$).
7. In Step 4e, $\mathcal{S}$ participates in the execution of WI, using the witness for the **trapdoor statement** defined in Step 4e in Prot. 2. Note that $\mathcal{S}$ commits

to $\tau_B$ in Step 3 above, therefore the witness for the **trapdoor statement** is available to $\mathcal{S}$.

**Phase II: Input Commitment**
$\mathcal{S}$ commits to string of all zeros instead of $x_A||r'_A$ in $\mathsf{c}_A$, and after receiving $\mathsf{c}_B$, $\mathcal{S}$ extracts $x_B||r'_B$ by running in super-polynomial time. If the extraction fails, $\mathcal{S}$ outputs $\perp$.
**Phase III: Secure Computation Phase**
Let $\mathcal{S}_{\mathsf{sh}}$ denote the simulator for the semi-honest protocol $\langle P_A^{\mathsf{sh}}, P_B^{\mathsf{sh}}\rangle$ that securely computes $\mathcal{F}$. $\mathcal{S}$ internally emulates $\mathcal{S}_{\mathsf{sh}}$ against a malicious $P_B$, using the $x_B$ (extracted in the last step via brute force) as $P_B$'s input. When $\mathcal{S}_{\mathsf{sh}}$ makes a query to the ideal functionality $\mathcal{F}$, $\mathcal{S}$ forwards the query (along with its session ID) to the (external) ideal functionality $\mathcal{F}$, and returns the output to $\mathcal{S}_{\mathsf{sh}}$. $\mathcal{S}_{\mathsf{sh}}$ outputs a transcript

$$(m_{A,1}, m_{B,1}, \ldots, m_{A,t}, m_{A,t})$$

and an associated randomness $r_B$ for malicious party $P_B$. Then, the simulator $\mathcal{S}$ now performs the following steps:

1. In Step 1 of **Phase III**, $\mathcal{S}$ sends $r''_B := r_B \oplus r'_B$ to $P_B$ (instead of sampling it randomly).
2. For each round $i \in [t]$:
   (a) $\mathcal{S}$ sends $m_{A,i}$ to $P_B$
   (b) $\mathcal{S}$ uses the trapdoor witness $r_A^{\mathsf{trap}}$ when it participates in the $\mathsf{WI}$ in Step 2 of **Phase III**. Note that $\mathcal{S}$ commits to 1 in $\mathsf{c}_A^{\mathsf{trap}}$ using randomness $r_A^{\mathsf{trap}}$ in the simulated view.
   (c) On receiving $P_B$'s message $\widetilde{m_{B,i}}$, $\mathcal{S}$ checks if $\widetilde{m_{B,i}} = m_{B,i}$. $\mathcal{S}$ outputs $\perp$ if $\widetilde{m_{B,i}} \neq m_{B,i}$, otherwise it continues.
   (d) $\mathcal{S}$ act as an honest verifier when it engages with $P_B$ in an execution of $\mathsf{WI}$, and output $\perp$ if the proof is not valid.

In order to argue the indistinguishability between the real world execution and the simulated interaction produced by $\mathcal{S}$ running in super-polynomial time, we first consider the following two hybrids.

- **Hybrid $H_0$:** This is the real experiment where $m$ sessions (aka instances) of *Protocol* 2 are running concurrently. The adversary $\mathcal{A}_{\Pi(\mathcal{F})}$ corrupts exactly one party in each session. The output of this hybrid consists the output of the environment $Z$, the output of the honest parties and view of the adversary $\mathcal{A}_{\Pi(\mathcal{F})}$.
- **Hybrid $H_1$:** This corresponds to the simulated execution of the ideal world where $\mathcal{S}$ simulates the honest parties (using the strategy defined in Algorithm 4.1). The honest parties, in each session, receive input from the environment, query the ideal functionality on their input and output the response they receive from the ideal functionality as their output. Again, the output of this

hybrid consists the output of the environment $Z$, the output of the honest parties and view of the adversary $\mathcal{A}_{\Pi(\mathcal{F})}$.

Next, we define a sequence of hybrids $H_{i:j}$ where $i \in [2m]$ and $j \in [6]$. We also define two additional hybrids $H_{0:6}$ and $H_{2m+1:0}$, where $H_{0:6}$ is equivalent to $H_0$ and $H_{2m+1:0}$ is equivalent to $H_1$. Before we give the descriptions of these hybrids, we give some additional notation that will be useful later.

**Special Messages.** As mentioned above, we use $m$ to denote the total number of concurrent sessions. Without loss of generality, we use a single number $i \in [m]$ to denote the session identification number (sid).

For every session with sid $i \in [m]$, we define two special messages:

- **The 1st special message:** This is the commitment to the random string $\tau$ made by the corrupted party in session $i$. That is:
  - If $P_A$ is corrupted in session $i$, then the 1st special special message is the $\mathsf{c}^{\mathcal{T}}_A$ sent by the malicious $P_A$ in Step 1 of **Phase I** in of Protocol 2.
  - if $P_B$ is corrupted in session $i$, then the 1st special special message is the $\mathsf{c}^{\mathcal{T}}_B$ sent by the malicious $P_B$ in Step 2 of **Phase I** in of Protocol 2.
- **The 2nd special message:** This is the **Phase-II** commitment to the input and randomness made by the corrupted party in session $i$. That is:
  - If $P_A$ is corrupted in session $i$, then the 2nd special special message is the $\mathsf{c}_A$ sent by the malicious $P_A$ in Step 1 of **Phase II** in of Protocol 2.
  - If $P_B$ is corrupted in session $i$, then the 2nd special special message is the $\mathsf{c}_B$ sent by the malicious $P_B$ in Step 2 of **Phase II** in of Protocol 2.

In the following, for simplicity of notation, we will refer the honest party in every session as $H$ and the malicious party in every session as $\mathcal{A}$. We consider two special commitments $\mathsf{c}^{\mathcal{T}}_{\mathcal{A}}$ and $\mathsf{c}_{\mathcal{A}}$ sent by $\mathcal{A}$, and refer them as $\mathsf{c}^{\mathcal{T},i}_{\mathcal{A}}$ and $\mathsf{c}^{i}_{\mathcal{A}}$ (with sid in superscript). Note that there are exactly two special commitments in every session. We consider a numbered ordering of all the $2m$ commitments across the $m$ sessions. In the following, we use $s(i)$ to denote the sid of the protocol session that contains $i^{\text{th}}$ special commitment; Note that $\mathsf{c}^{\mathcal{T},i}_{\mathcal{A}}$ always appears before $\mathsf{c}^{i}_{\mathcal{A}}$ for any sid $i \in [m]$, but not necessarily consecutively.

**Invariant Condition.** Similar to [24], we need to prove that the trapdoor condition of $\mathsf{WI}$ in the secure computation phase is false for every session and all intermediate hybrids. More formally, we need to show that, for all sid $i \in [m]$, $\mathsf{c}^{\mathsf{trap}}_{\mathcal{A}} \notin \mathcal{L}_{\mathsf{trap}}$ in Language (4). Therefore, $\mathsf{c}^{\mathsf{NM}}_{\mathcal{A}}$ must be a valid non-malleable commitment to the value $r^{\mathsf{trap}}_{\mathcal{A}}$. We define $m$ variable $\{v^{\ell}_{i:j}\}^{m}_{\ell=1}$ for each intermediate hybrid, where $v^{\ell}_{i:j}$ is the value committed in $\mathsf{c}^{\mathsf{NM}}_{\mathcal{A}}$ in session sid $\ell$, hybrid $H_{i:j}$, and we need to show that $v^{\ell}_{i:j}$ is a valid decommitment of $\mathsf{c}^{\mathsf{trap},\ell}_{\mathcal{A}}$ to the value $r^{\mathsf{trap},\ell}_{\mathcal{A}}$, for every session $\ell \in [m]$.

Now, before we give the description of our hybrids, and argue that the invariant condition still holds as we move from one hybrid to another, we first claim that the invariant condition holds in the real execution.

**Lemma 1.** *In hybrid $H_0$ which corresponds to the real execution of Protocol 2, for every $\ell \in [m]$, it holds that $v_0^\ell = r_{\mathcal{A}}^{\mathsf{trap},\ell}$. That is, $\mathsf{c}_{\mathcal{A}}^{\mathsf{NM}}$ is indeed a valid* NMCOM *to the value $r_{\mathcal{A}}^{\mathsf{trap}}$, which is a valid witness for the fact that $\mathsf{c}_{\mathcal{A}}^{\mathsf{trap}} \in \mathcal{L}_{\mathsf{Com}(0)}$.*

*Proof.* We first show that the trapdoor statement defined in Step 4e is false, for every $\ell \in [m]$. For the sake of contradiction, assume there exists an $\ell \in [m]$ such that the trapdoor statement for $\mathcal{A}$ is true, namely, $\mathsf{c}_{\mathcal{A}}^{\mathsf{prove},\ell}$ is a commitment of $\tau_H^\ell$ in session $\ell$. Levering this $\mathcal{A}$, we construct in Algorithm 4.2 a non-uniform QPT algorithm $\mathcal{A}^*$ breaks the hiding of Com.

| **Algorithm 4.2:** $\mathcal{A}^*$ **against hiding of** Com |
|---|
| $\mathcal{A}'$ internally emulates the algorithm $A$, while externally interacting with a challenger of the hiding property of Com. In particular, $\mathcal{A}^*$ proceeds as follows.<br><br>1. At the beginning, $\mathcal{A}^*$ makes a random guess $\ell^* \in [m]$ about the session number where the trapdoor statement for $\mathcal{A}$ is true.<br>2. $\mathcal{A}^*$ follows the Protocol 2 using honest parties' inputs (received as a non-uniform advice) in every session $\ell \in [m]$ where $\ell \neq \ell^*$<br>3. $\mathcal{A}^*$ samples $\tau_{\mathcal{A}^*,0}^{\ell^*}, \tau_{\mathcal{A}^*,1}^{\ell^*} \xleftarrow{\$} \{0,1\}^\lambda$ and sends $\tau_{\mathcal{A}^*,0}^{\ell^*}$ and $\tau_{\mathcal{A}^*,1}^{\ell^*}$ to the external challenger.<br>4. $\mathcal{A}^*$ receives $\mathsf{c}_{\mathcal{A}^*}^{\tau,\ell^*}$ from the external challenger.<br>5. In session $\ell^*$, instead of generates $\mathsf{c}_H^{\tau,\ell^*}$ honestly, $\mathcal{A}^*$ sends $\mathsf{c}_{\mathcal{A}^*}^{\tau,\ell^*}$ it received from external challenger to $\mathcal{A}$, and follows the Protocol 2 until $\mathcal{A}$ sends $\mathsf{c}_{\mathcal{A}}^{\mathsf{prove},\ell^*}$ to $\mathcal{A}^*$ (as the honest party) in Step 4a.<br>6. Once $\mathcal{A}$ starts its $\varepsilon$-ZKAoK with $\mathcal{A}^*$ (as the honest party) in Step 4b, $\mathcal{A}^*$ invokes $\mathcal{K}$, the knowledge extractor for $\varepsilon$-ZKAoK, to extract the witness that $\mathcal{A}$ used when executing $\varepsilon$-ZKAoK in Step 4b, which is also the value committed in $\mathsf{c}_{\mathcal{A}}^{\mathsf{prove},\ell^*}$. If the extraction succeeds, then $\mathcal{A}^*$ outputs 0 if $\mathsf{val}(\mathsf{c}_{\mathcal{A}}^{\mathsf{prove},\ell^*}) = \tau_{\mathcal{A}^*,0}^{\ell^*}$, and outputs 1 if $\mathsf{val}(\mathsf{c}_{\mathcal{A}}^{\mathsf{prove},\ell^*}) = \tau_{\mathcal{A}^*,1}^{\ell^*}$; Otherwise outputs a random bit. |

Clearly, $\mathcal{A}$ runs in polynomial time, and notice that $\tau_{\mathcal{A}^*,0}^{\ell^*}$ and $\tau_{\mathcal{A}^*,1}^{\ell^*}$ are sampled uniformly, therefore, from $\mathcal{A}$'s perspective, this is exactly the same execution as Protocol 2, and thus by assumption, there exists an $\ell \in [m]$ such that the trapdoor statement for $\mathcal{A}$ is true with non-negligible probability. The probability that $\ell^* = \ell$, is $1/m$, then by the knowledge soundness of $\varepsilon$-ZKAoK, $\mathcal{K}$ returns $\tau_{\mathcal{A}^*,0}^{\ell^*}$ or $\tau_{\mathcal{A}^*,1}^{\ell^*}$ is non-negligible. This breaks the hiding of Com and therefore leads to a contradiction.

Since we just showed that the trapdoor statement is false, for every $\ell \in [m]$, by the soundness of WI, the honest statement must be true with overwhelming probability, namely $\mathsf{c}_{\mathcal{A}}^{\mathsf{NM}}$ is indeed a valid NMCOM to the value $r_{\mathcal{A}}^{\mathsf{trap}}$, which is a valid witness for the fact that $\mathsf{c}_{\mathcal{A}}^{\mathsf{trap}} \in \mathcal{L}_{\mathsf{Com}(0)}$. Therefore, for every $\ell \in [m]$, it holds that $v_0^\ell = r_{\mathcal{A}}^{\mathsf{trap},\ell}$. □

**Description of $H_{i:j}$:** Now, we are ready to describe our sequence of hybrids $H_{i:j}$, where $j \in [6]$ and $i \in [2m]$, which corresponds the numbered ordering of all $2m$ special commitments across $m$ sessions. Recall that we use $s(i)$ to denote the session number of the $i_{\mathsf{th}}$ special commitment.

- Hybrid $H_{i:1}$: This is identical to $H_{i-1:6}$ (for every $i \in [2m]$) except that it runs in super-polynomial time to extract values from the $i_{\mathsf{th}}$ special commitment across all $m$ sessions. Note that it runs in polynomial time after extracting the $i_{\mathsf{th}}$ special commitment. If extraction fails, it outputs $\perp$, and otherwise works similarly to the previous hybrid. We note that this experiment obtains values from the $i_{\mathsf{th}}$ special commitment but does not use it. Thus, by the statistical binding property of $\mathsf{Com}$, we have

$$H_{i:1} \overset{\mathsf{s}}{\approx} H_{i-1:6}. \tag{5}$$

$$\forall \ell \in [m],\ v^{\ell}_{i:1} \overset{\mathsf{s}}{\approx} v^{\ell}_{i-1:6} \tag{6}$$

*Remark 1.* An alternative way to interpret hybrid $H_{i:*}$ is to consider a "super-polynomial time line" placed right after the $i_{\mathsf{th}}$ special commitment, and $H_{i:*}$ runs in super-polynomial time to extract values from the first $i$ (out of $2m$) special commitments above this line, and runs in polynomial time afterwards.

- Hybrid $H_{i:2}$: This is identical to $H_{i:1}$ except if the $i_{\mathsf{th}}$ special commitment corresponds to $\mathsf{c}_{\mathcal{A}}^{\tau,s(i)}$ for session $s(i)$, then $\mathcal{S}$ follows Steps 3 to 7 in the trapdoor generation phase of our description of the final simulator, using $\tau_{\mathcal{A}}^{s(i)}$ extracted from $\mathsf{c}_{\mathcal{A}}^{\tau,s(i)}$ for session $s(i)$.
  In more detail, in the trapdoor generation phase of session $s(i)$:
  1. In Step 1, $\mathcal{S}$ commits to $\tau_{\mathcal{A}}^{s(i)}$ instead of 0 in $\mathsf{c}_H^{\mathsf{prove},s(i)}$;
  2. In Step 4b, $\mathcal{S}$ follows the protocol with an honest execution of $\varepsilon$-$\mathsf{ZKAoK}$ to prove knowledge of the decommitment value of $\mathsf{c}_H^{\mathsf{prove},s(i)}$ (use $(\tau_{\mathcal{A}}^{s(i)}, r_H^{\mathsf{prove},s(i)})$ as witness).
  3. In Step 4c, $\mathcal{S}$ acts honestly and check the decommit value of $\mathsf{c}_{\mathcal{A}}^{\tau,s(i)}$ sent by malicious $P_{\mathcal{A}}$. If the decommit value is incorrect, $\mathcal{S}$ aborts.
  4. In Step 4d, $\mathcal{S}$ commits to 0 instead of decommitment of $\mathsf{c}_H^{\mathsf{trap},s(i)}$ in $\mathsf{c}_H^{\mathsf{MN},s(i)}$.
  5. In Step 4e, $\mathcal{S}$ participates in the execution of $\mathsf{WI}$ using $(\perp, r_H^{\mathsf{prove},s(i)})$ as the witness. Note that $\mathcal{S}$ commits to $\tau_{\mathcal{A}}^{s(i)}$ in the simulated view, therefore the (trapdoor) witness corresponding to the second part of the statement is available to $\mathcal{S}$.

**Claim 4.**

$$H_{i:2} \overset{\mathsf{c}}{\approx} H_{i:1} \tag{7}$$

$$\forall \ell \in [m],\ v^{\ell}_{i:2} \overset{\mathsf{c}}{\approx} v^{\ell}_{i:1} \tag{8}$$

*Proof.* We consider the following sequence of hybrids.

- Hybrid $H_{i:1:1}$: This is identical to $H_{i:1}$ except in session $s(i)$, $\mathcal{S}$ commits to $\tau_{\mathcal{A}}^{s(i)}$ instead of 0 in $\mathsf{c}_H^{\mathsf{prove},s(i)}$, and in Step 4b of session $s(i)$, $\mathcal{S}$ follows the protocol with an honest execution of $\varepsilon$-ZKAoK to prove knowledge of the decommitment value of $\mathsf{c}_H^{\mathsf{prove},s(i)}$ (use $(\tau_{\mathcal{A}}^{s(i)}, r_H^{\mathsf{prove},s(i)})$ as witness).
Note that $\mathcal{S}$ finishes the super-polynomial time extraction before the start of Step 1 in session $s(i)$ and because $\varepsilon$-Zero-Knowledge property imply strong witness-indistinguishability. Thus, by the non-uniform hiding property of Com and the strong non-uniform witness-indistinguishability property of $\varepsilon$-ZKAoK, we have

$$H_{i:1:1} \stackrel{c}{\approx} H_{i:1} \tag{9}$$

Additionally, in order to show $\forall \ell \in [m],\ v_{i:1:1}^{\ell} \stackrel{c}{\approx} v_{i:1}^{\ell}$, $\forall \ell \in [m]$, we consider the following two cases:
  1. if the first message of $\mathsf{c}_{\mathcal{A}}^{\mathsf{NM},\ell}$ of session $\ell$ is sent before $\mathsf{c}_H^{\mathsf{prove},s(i)}$ of session $s(i)$, then by the first-message-binding property of NMCOM, we have $v_{i:1:1}^{\ell} = v_{i:1}^{\ell}$.
  2. if the first message of $\mathsf{c}_{\mathcal{A}}^{\mathsf{NM},\ell}$ of session $\ell$ is sent after (or simultaneously) $\mathsf{c}_H^{\mathsf{prove},s(i)}$ of session $s(i)$. Recall that in session $s(i)$, $H_{i:1:1}$ only made modifications in $\mathsf{c}_H^{\mathsf{prove},s(i)}$ and $\varepsilon$-ZKAoK, then by the $k$-robust property of NMCOM (recall that we set $k \geq \mathsf{rc}(\varepsilon\text{-ZKAoK}) + 1$), we have $v_{i:1:1}^{\ell} \stackrel{c}{\approx} v_{i:1}^{\ell}$.

  Therefore, we have

$$\forall \ell \in [m],\ v_{i:1:1}^{\ell} \stackrel{c}{\approx} v_{i:1}^{\ell} \tag{10}$$

- Hybrid $H_{i:1:2}$: This is identical to $H_{i:1:1}$ except in Step 4e, $\mathcal{S}$ participates in the execution of WI using trapdoor witness $(\perp, r_H^{\mathsf{prove},s(i)})$. Since $\varepsilon$-Zero-Knowledge property imply witness-indistinguishability, by the non-uniform witness-indistinguishability property of $\varepsilon$-ZKAoK, we have

$$H_{i:1:2} \stackrel{c}{\approx} H_{i:1:1} \tag{11}$$

Additionally, by the same proof for Eq. (10), we have

$$\forall \ell \in [m],\ v_{i:1:2}^{\ell} \stackrel{c}{\approx} v_{i:1:1}^{\ell} \tag{12}$$

- Hybrid $H_{i:1:3}$: This is identical to $H_{i:1:2}$ except in Step 4e session $s(i)$, $\mathcal{S}$ commits to 0 instead of decommitment of $\mathsf{c}_H^{\mathsf{trap},s(i)}$ in $\mathsf{c}_H^{\mathsf{MN},s(i)}$. Note that $\mathcal{S}$ finishes the super-polynomial time extraction before the start of Step 4e in session $s(i)$. Thus, by the non-uniform hiding property of NMCOM, we have

$$H_{i:1:3} \stackrel{c}{\approx} H_{i:1:2} \tag{13}$$

Additionally, by the same proof for Eq. (10), except we rely on standard non-malleability of NMCOM instead of $k$-robustness, we have

$$\forall \ell \in [m],\ v_{i:1:3}^{\ell} \stackrel{c}{\approx} v_{i:1:2}^{\ell} \tag{14}$$

□

- Hybrid $H_{i:3}$: This is identical to $H_{i:2}$ except if the $i_{\mathsf{th}}$ special commitment corresponds to $\mathsf{c}_{\mathcal{A}}^{\tau,s(i)}$ for session $s(i)$, then $\mathcal{S}$ commits to 1 instead of 0 in $\mathsf{c}_{H}^{\mathsf{trap},s(i)}$ in the trapdoor generation phase of session $s(i)$. Note that $\mathcal{S}$ finishes the super-polynomial time extraction before the start of Step 3 in session $s(i)$. Thus, by the non-uniform hiding property of $\mathsf{Com}$, we have

$$H_{i:3} \overset{c}{\approx} H_{i:2} \tag{15}$$

Additionally, by a similar proof as for Eq. (10), we have

$$\forall \ell \in [m],\ v_{i:3}^{\ell} \overset{c}{\approx} v_{i:2}^{\ell} \tag{16}$$

- Hybrid $H_{i:4}$: This is identical to $H_{i:3}$ except if the $i_{\mathsf{th}}$ special commitment corresponds to $\mathsf{c}_{\mathcal{A}}^{\tau,s(i)}$ for session $s(i)$, then $\mathcal{S}$ use the trapdoor witness to finish **every** execution of $\mathsf{WI}$ in the secure computation phase. More specifically, use $\mathsf{c}_{\mathcal{A}}^{\mathsf{trap},s(i)} \in \mathcal{L}_{\mathsf{trap}}$ in Language (4) as the witness to finish all $\mathsf{WI}$ instances in the secure computation phase. Since in $H_{i:3}$, $\mathcal{S}$ commits to 1 in $\mathsf{c}_{H}^{\mathsf{trap},s(i)}$ in the trapdoor generation phase of session $s(i)$, the trapdoor witness for $\mathsf{WI}$ is available to $\mathcal{S}$.
Again, observe that $\mathcal{S}$ finishes the super-polynomial time extraction before the start of secure computation phase in session $s(i)$. Thus, by the non-uniform witness-indistinguishability property of $\mathsf{WI}$, we have

$$H_{i:4} \overset{c}{\approx} H_{i:3} \tag{17}$$

Furthermore, by a similar proof to that for Eq. (10), we have

$$\forall \ell \in [m],\ v_{i:4}^{\ell} \overset{c}{\approx} v_{i:3}^{\ell} \tag{18}$$

*Remark 2.* More formally, we can only change the usage of trapdoor witness in $\mathsf{WI}$ one instance at a time, but by a standard hybrid argument, we can extend this proof to multiple $\mathsf{WI}$ cases.

- Hybrid $H_{i:5}$: This is identical to $H_{i:4}$ except if the $i_{\mathsf{th}}$ special commitment corresponds to $\mathsf{c}_{\mathcal{A}}^{\tau,s(i)}$ for session $s(i)$, then $\mathcal{S}$ commits to $0_s$ instead of $x_H||r_H$ in $\mathsf{c}_{H}^{s(i)}$ in the input commitment phase of session $s(i)$.
Note that $\mathcal{S}$ finishes the super-polynomial time extraction before the start of the input commitment phase of session $s(i)$. Thus, by the non-uniform hiding property of $\mathsf{Com}$, we have

$$H_{i:5} \overset{c}{\approx} H_{i:4} \tag{19}$$

Additionally, by the same proof for Eq. (10), we have

$$\forall \ell \in [m],\ v_{i:5}^{\ell} \overset{c}{\approx} v_{i:4}^{\ell} \tag{20}$$

– Hybrid $H_{i:6}$: This is identical to $H_{i:5}$ except if the $i_{\mathsf{th}}$ special commitment corresponds to $\mathsf{c}_{\mathcal{A}}^{s(i)}$ (in the Input Commitment Phase) for session $s(i)$, then $\mathcal{S}$ follows the steps in Phase 4.1 of the final simulator (except for Steps 2b, which is done in $H_{i:4}$).

**Claim 5.**

$$H_{i:6} \stackrel{c}{\approx} H_{i:5} \tag{21}$$

$$\forall \ell \in [m],\ v_{i:6}^{\ell} \stackrel{c}{\approx} v_{i:5}^{\ell} \tag{22}$$

*Proof.* In order to show Eq. (21), for the sake of contradiction, assume that there exists a non-uniform QPT distinguisher $\mathcal{D}$, such that it distinguishes $H_{i:6}$ from $H_{i:5}$ with non-negligible probability, then we build in Algorithm 4.3, a non-uniform QPT adversary $\mathcal{A}^*$ for the semi-honest security of $\langle P_A^{\mathsf{sh}}, P_B^{\mathsf{sh}}\rangle$. Moreover, we assume that in this specific session $s(i)$, $P_B$ is corrupted. $\mathcal{A}^*$'s behavior is symmetric in sessions where $P_A$ is corrupted instead. We present the simulator in Algorithm 4.1.

**Algorithm 4.3: $\mathcal{A}$ against semi-honest security of $\langle P_A^{\mathsf{sh}}, P_B^{\mathsf{sh}}\rangle$**

$\mathcal{A}^*$ internally emulates the algorithm $\mathcal{D}_\lambda^*(\rho_\lambda)$ (dubbed $\mathcal{D}$ henceforth), while externally interacting with a challenger of the semi-honest security of $\langle P_A^{\mathsf{sh}}, P_B^{\mathsf{sh}}\rangle$. In particular, $\mathcal{A}^*$ proceeds as follows.

1. $\mathcal{A}^*$ acts identical to $H_{i:5}$ until the beginning of Phase 4.1 of the final simulator.
2. $\mathcal{A}^*$ queries the ideal functionality $\mathcal{F}$ using $x_B^{s(i)}$ (extracted in previous hybrids) together with sid $s(i)$, and receives $y^{s(i)}$ from $\mathcal{F}$.
3. $\mathcal{A}^*$ sends $s(i), y^{s(i)}, x_A^{s(i)}, x_B^{s(i)}$ to the external challenger, where $x_A^{s(i)}$ is the honest party's input in session $s(i)$.
4. $\mathcal{A}^*$ receives a transcript for $\langle P_A^{\mathsf{sh}}, P_B^{\mathsf{sh}}\rangle$ and randomness $r_A$ from the challenger.
5. $\mathcal{A}^*$ forces this transcript and randomness on $P_B$ (follows the steps in Phase 4.1 of the final simulator except for Step 2b)
6. $\mathcal{A}^*$ finishes the rest of simulation (with $\mathcal{A}_{\Pi(\mathcal{F})}$) identical to $H_{i:5}$
7. $\mathcal{A}^*$ sends its transcript with $\mathcal{A}_{\Pi(\mathcal{F})}$ to internal distinguisher $\mathcal{D}$, and outputs its decision bit.

Clearly, $\mathcal{A}^*$ runs in polynomial time, and notice that

- if external challenger computes the transcript and output using $x_A^{s(i)}$ and $x_A^{s(i)}$, by all previous hybrids, the invariant condition still holds at this point, then $\mathcal{A}^*$'s transcript with $\mathcal{A}_{\Pi(\mathcal{F})}$ is identical to the one generated in $H_{i:5}$, from $\mathcal{D}$'s perspective.
- if external challenger computes the transcript and output using $y^{s(i)}$ and $x_B^{s(i)}$, then $\mathcal{A}^*$'s transcript with $\mathcal{A}_{\Pi(\mathcal{F})}$ is identical to the one generated in $H_{i:6}$, from $\mathcal{D}$'s perspective.

Therefore, by the assumption that $\mathcal{D}$ distinguishes $H_{i:6}$ from $H_{i:5}$ with non-negligible probability, $\mathcal{A}^*$ breaks the non-uniform semi-honest security of $\langle P_A^{\mathsf{sh}}, P_B^{\mathsf{sh}} \rangle$, and this leads to a contradiction. Therefore, $H_{i:6} \overset{c}{\approx} H_{i:5}$.

The proof for Eq. (22) is similar to the proof for Eq. (10), $\forall \ell \in [m]$, we consider the following two cases:

1. if the first message of $\mathsf{c}_{\mathcal{A}}^{\mathsf{NM},\ell}$ of session $\ell$ is sent before the start of the **Phase III** of session $s(i)$, then by the first-message-binding property of $\mathsf{NMCOM}$, we have $v_{i:6}^{\ell} = v_{i:5}^{\ell}$.
2. if the first message of $\mathsf{c}_{\mathcal{A}}^{\mathsf{NM},\ell}$ of session $\ell$ is sent after (or simultaneously) the start of the **Phase III** of session $s(i)$. The total number of messages sent in **Phase III** of session $s(i)$ is $2 * t * (1 + \mathsf{rc}(\mathsf{WI})) + 2$, then by the $k$-robust property of $\mathsf{NMCOM}$ (recall that we set $k \geq 2 * t * (1 + \mathsf{rc}(\mathsf{WI})) + 2$), we have $v_{i:6}^{\ell} \overset{c}{\approx} v_{i:5}^{\ell}$

□

Combining all previous hybrids, it is obvious that $H_{2m+1:0}$ $(H_1)$ is indistinguishable from $H_0$ and therefore finishes the proof of security. □

## 5 Two-Round SPS-ZK for NP ∩ coNP

In this section, we construct a two-round SPS-ZK protocol for **NP**∩**coNP** from polynomial hardness assumptions.

### 5.1 Building Blocks

#### 5.1.1 ZAPs for Controlled-OR Languages

**Definition 2 (Controlled-OR Languages).** *Let $\mathcal{L}_{\mathsf{c}}$ be a language in* **NP** ∩ **coNP**. *Let $\mathcal{L}$ be a language in* **NP**. *We call the following language $\widetilde{\mathcal{L}}$ the $\mathcal{L}_{\mathsf{c}}$-Controlled-OR language*

$$\widetilde{\mathcal{L}} = \mathcal{L}_{\mathsf{c}} \vee \mathcal{L} := \{(x_{\mathsf{c}}, x) \mid x_{\mathsf{c}} \in \mathcal{L}_{\mathsf{c}} \vee x \in \mathcal{L}\}.$$

For the languages define in Definition 2, it is straightforward to see that $\widetilde{L} \in$ **NP**. It is also worth noting that $\widetilde{L}$ may not be in **coNP**, because $\mathcal{L}$ is not necessarily contained in **coNP**.

**Definition 3 (ZAPs for Controlled-OR Languages).** *Let $\mathcal{L}_{\mathsf{c}} \in$* **NP** ∩ **coNP**, *$\mathcal{L} \in$* **NP**, *and $\widetilde{\mathcal{L}} \in$* **NP** *be as in Definition 2. Let $\overline{\mathcal{L}_{\mathsf{c}}}$ be the complement of $\mathcal{L}_{\mathsf{c}}$. A* ZAP *for the* $\mathcal{L}_{\mathsf{c}}$-controlled language *$\widetilde{\mathcal{L}}$ consists of the following three algorithms:*

- $V_1(1^\lambda, 1^{|x_{\mathsf{c}}|})$ : *This is a PPT algorithm that on input the security parameter $1^\lambda$ and an $x_{\mathsf{c}} \in \mathcal{L}_{\mathsf{c}}$, outputs the* first ZAP message $\mathsf{zap}_1$.
- $P((x_{\mathsf{c}}, x), \widetilde{w}, \mathsf{zap}_1)$ : *This is a PPT algorithm that on input a statement pair $(x_{\mathsf{c}}, x)$, a witness $\widetilde{w}$ for the fact that $(x_{\mathsf{c}}, x) \in \widetilde{\mathcal{L}}$, and the first ZAP message $\mathsf{zap}_1$, outputs the* second ZAP message $\mathsf{zap}_2$.

- $V_2((x_c, x), \mathsf{zap}_1, \mathsf{zap}_2)$ : *This is a deterministic polynomial-time algorithm that on input a statement pair* $(x_c, x)$ *and the two ZAP messages* $\mathsf{zap}_1$ *and* $\mathsf{zap}_2$*, and outputs a* decision symbol $d \in \{\top, \bot\}$*, indicating acceptance (when* $d = \top$*) or rejection (when* $d = \bot$*).*

*The following properties are satisfied:*

1. *Completeness: For all* $x_c \in \mathcal{L}_c$*, all* $x$*, and all witness* $\widetilde{w}$ *for* $(x_c, x) \in \widetilde{\mathcal{L}}$*, it holds that*

$$Pr[\mathsf{zap}_1 \leftarrow V_1(1^\lambda, x_c);\ \mathsf{zap}_2 \leftarrow P((x_c, x), \widetilde{w}, \mathsf{zap}_1)\ :\ V_2((x_c, x), \mathsf{zap}_1, \mathsf{zap}_2) = \top] = 1 - \mathsf{negl}(\lambda).$$

   *Note that we do not require that* $x \in \mathcal{L}$*. But as long as* $x_c \in \mathcal{L}_c$*, it must hold that* $(x_c, x) \in \widetilde{\mathcal{L}}$ *(and thus the* $\widetilde{w}$ *specified above must exist).*
2. *NO-Controlled Adaptive Soundness: For all* $x_c \in \overline{\mathcal{L}}_c$ *and all PPT adversary* $P^*$*, it holds that*

$$\Pr\left[\begin{array}{l}\mathsf{zap}_1 \leftarrow V_1(1^\lambda, x_c); \\ (x^*,\ \mathsf{zap}_2) \leftarrow P^*(x_c, \mathsf{zap}_1)\end{array}\ :\ (x^* \notin \mathcal{L})\ \wedge\ \big(V_2((x_c, x^*_t), \mathsf{zap}_1, \mathsf{zap}_2) = \top\big)\right] \leq \mathsf{negl}(\lambda).$$

3. *YES-Controlled Statistical WI: For all* $x_c \in \mathcal{L}_c$ *and all (potentially unbounded) adversarial verifier* $V^*$*, it holds that*

$$\left|\Pr[\mathsf{Expr}^{\mathrm{WI}}_{\mathcal{L}_c,\mathcal{L}}(V^*, x_c) = 1] - \frac{1}{2}\right| \leq \mathsf{negl}(\lambda),$$

   *where* $\mathsf{Expr}^{\mathrm{WI}}_{\mathcal{L}_c,\mathcal{L}}(V^*, x_c)$ *denotes the output of Experiment 1.*

**Experiment 1: Statistical WI Experiment** $\mathsf{Expr}^{\mathrm{WI}}_{\mathcal{L}_c,\mathcal{L}}(V^*, x_c)$

1. $V^*$, on input $x_c$, generates and sends $(\mathsf{zap}_1, x^*, \widetilde{w}_0, \widetilde{w}_1)$.
2. The experiment checks if *both* $\widetilde{w}_0$ and $\widetilde{w}_1$ are valid witnesses for the fact that $(x_c, x^*) \in \widetilde{\mathcal{L}}$ (recall from Definition 2 that the language $\widetilde{\mathcal{L}}$ is defined as $\widetilde{\mathcal{L}} := \mathcal{L}_c \vee \mathcal{L}$):
   - If so, it samples $b \xleftarrow{\$} \{0, 1\}$, executes $\mathsf{zap}_2 \leftarrow P((x_c, x^*), \mathsf{zap}_1, \widetilde{w}_b)$, and sends $\mathsf{zap}_2$ to $V^*$;
   - Otherwise, it halts immediately and outputs a random bit.
3. $V^*$ outputs a bit $b^*$. If $b^* = b$, the experiment outputs 1; otherwise it outputs 0.

As we mentioned earlier, although the definition of *ZAPs for super-complement languages* in [15] does not directly imply Definition 2, their construction nonetheless satisfies Definition 2, and the corresponding security proof remains essentially unchanged.

**Lemma 2** ([15]). *Assuming QLWE, for any controlled-OR language* $\widetilde{\mathcal{L}} = \mathcal{L}_c \vee \mathcal{L}$ *as per Definition 2, there exist ZAPs for* $\widetilde{\mathcal{L}}$ *as per Definition 3.*

### 5.2 Construction

We present our construction of two-round SPS-ZK for **NP** $\cap$ **coNP** in Protocol 3, which is based on the following building blocks:

- A collision-resistant hash function $(\mathsf{Gen}, \mathsf{H})$ with input length $\ell^{\mathsf{in}}(\lambda)$ and output length $\ell^{\mathsf{out}}(\lambda)$.
- A ZAP for Controlled-OR Languages (as per Definition 3).
- A two-message function-hiding SFE (as per Definition 1).

As mentioned earlier, all these building blocks can be instantiated based on the polynomial-hardness of QLWE.

**Protocol 3: Post-Quantum Two-Round SPS ZK for NP $\cap$ coNP**

**Parameter:** Let $\ell^{\mathsf{out}}(\lambda) := \frac{\lambda}{k}$ for some constant $k > 2$.
**Input:** For any $\mathcal{L} \in \mathbf{NP} \cap \mathbf{coNP}$, $x \in \mathcal{L} \cap \{0,1\}^\lambda$, and $w \in \mathcal{R}_{\mathcal{L}}(x)$ denote $P$'s private input.

- **Round 1:** $V$ proceeds as follows:
  1. $V$ samples a SFE key $\mathsf{k} \leftarrow \mathsf{SFE.Gen}(1^\lambda)$ and generates $\mathsf{ct} \leftarrow \mathsf{SFE.Enc}(\mathsf{k}, 0^{\ell(|x|)})$, where $\ell(|x|)$ denotes the length of no-witness of the language[a].
  2. $V$ samples a hash key $s \leftarrow \mathsf{Gen}(1^\lambda)$;
  3. $V$ generates the first ZAP message $\mathsf{zap}_1 \leftarrow V_1(1^\lambda, x)$.

  $V$ sends $(\mathsf{ct}, s, \mathsf{zap}_1)$.
- **Round 2:** $P$ proceeds as follows:
  1. $P$ generates $\widehat{\mathsf{ct}} \leftarrow \mathsf{Eval}(C^0, \mathsf{ct})$, where $C^0$ is a constant-0 circuit that always output 0s.
  2. Additionally, $P$ computes $\mathsf{zap}_2 \leftarrow P((x, \widehat{\mathsf{ct}}), \widetilde{w}, \mathsf{zap}_1)$ proving that either $x \in \mathcal{L}$, or $H^s(x_1) = H^s(x_2)$ and $\widehat{\mathsf{ct}}$ is an output of $\mathsf{Eval}(C^{x_1,x_2}, \mathsf{ct})$, where the description of $C^{x_1,x_2}$ is given in Algorithm 5.1.
     Formally, $\mathsf{zap}_2$ proves that $(x, \widehat{\mathsf{ct}}) \in \mathcal{L} \vee \mathcal{L}_{\mathsf{ct}}$, and $\mathcal{L} \vee \mathcal{L}_{\mathsf{ct}}$ denotes the controlled-OR Language (also as $\mathcal{L}$-Controlled-OR language), and

$$\mathcal{L}_{\mathsf{ct}} := \left\{ \widehat{\mathsf{ct}} \mid \exists x_1, x_2 \ s.t. \ \wedge \begin{array}{c} \widehat{\mathsf{ct}} = \mathsf{Eval}(C^{x_1,x_2}, \mathsf{ct}) \\ H^s(x_1) = H^s(x_2) \end{array} \right\}. \tag{23}$$

  $P$ sends $(\widehat{\mathsf{ct}}, \mathsf{zap}_2)$.

**$V$'s Decision:** $V$ outputs the value of $V_2((x, \widehat{\mathsf{ct}}), \mathsf{zap}_1, \mathsf{zap}_2)$.

[a] (W.l.o.g., we assume that for any given language, the length of its witness/no-witness is some fixed, public polynomial on the length of the instance.)

**Algorithm 5.1: Description of $C^{x_1,x_2}$**

**Input:** $\mathsf{Inp}$
**Hardwire:** instance $x$, $x_1, x_2 \in \{0,1\}^{\ell^{\mathsf{in}}(\lambda)}$

- Check if $\mathsf{Inp} \in \mathcal{R}_{\overline{\mathcal{L}}}(x)$
  - **If true:** outputs $x_1, x_2$;
  - **Otherwise:** outputs 0s.

*Remark 3.* Protocol 3 can in fact be made public-coin, provided that the first message containing the ciphertext $\mathsf{ct}$ of the SFE protocol is itself public-coin. Such an SFE instantiation is known under specific LWE-based constructions, as shown in [11].

### 5.3 Proof of Security

**Theorem 6.** *Protocol 3 is a super-polynomial time simulatable zero-knowledge argument.*

Completeness and round complexity are straightforward from the description of Protocol 3, and the rest of the proof of Theorem 6 is given in Sect. 5.4 and 5.5.

### 5.4 Proof of Soundness

**Lemma 3.** *The protocol described in Protocol 3 is sound against any non-uniform QPT prover* $\{P_\lambda^*, \rho_\lambda\}_{\lambda\in\mathbb{N}}$.

*Proof.* For the sake of contradiction, assume the existence of a non-uniform QPT prover $\{P_\lambda^*, \rho_\lambda\}_{\lambda\in\mathbb{N}}$ and $x \notin L$, such that $V_2((x, \widehat{\mathsf{ct}}), \mathsf{zap}_1, \mathsf{zap}_2) = 1$ with non-negligible probability.

Levering this $\{P_\lambda^*, \rho_\lambda\}_{\lambda\in\mathbb{N}}$, we construct in Algorithm 5.2 a (non-uniform) QPT algorithm $\mathcal{A} = \{\mathcal{A}_\lambda, \rho_\lambda\}_{\lambda\in\mathbb{N}}$ breaking the collision-resistant property of $(\mathsf{Gen}, \mathsf{H})$:

**Algorithm 5.2: $\mathcal{A}$ against collision-resistance**

$\mathcal{A}$ internally emulates the algorithm $\{P_\lambda^*, \rho_\lambda\}_{\lambda\in\mathbb{N}}$ (dubbed $P^*$ henceforth), while externally interacting with a challenger of the collision-resistance of $(\mathsf{Gen}, \mathsf{H})$. In particular, $\mathcal{A}$ proceeds as follows.

1. $\mathcal{A}$ receives a hash key $s$ from the external challenger.
2. $\mathcal{A}$ samples a SFE key $\mathsf{k} \leftarrow \mathsf{SFE}$, computes $\mathsf{zap}_1 \leftarrow V_1(1^\lambda, x)$, and $\mathsf{ct} \leftarrow \mathsf{SFE.Enc}(\mathsf{k}, \overline{w})$, where $\overline{w} \in \mathcal{R}_{\overline{\mathcal{L}}}(x)$ (by the assumption that $x \notin \mathcal{L}$).
3. $\mathcal{A}$ sends $s, \mathsf{ct}, \mathsf{zap}_1$ to $P^*$.
4. $\mathcal{A}$ invokes $P^*$ internally to receive $\widehat{\mathsf{ct}}, \mathsf{zap}_2$. If $V_2((x, \widehat{\mathsf{ct}}), \mathsf{zap}_1, \mathsf{zap}_2) = 1$, then $\mathcal{A}$ outputs $\mathsf{Dec}(\mathsf{k}, \widehat{\mathsf{ct}})$; Otherwise outputs $\bot$.

Clearly, $\mathcal{A}$ runs in polynomial time, and notice that the hash key $s$ is sampled uniformly by the external challenger. By the post-quantum input privacy of $\mathsf{SFE}$ (as per Property 2), $\mathsf{ct}$ is indistinguishable from $\mathsf{SFE.Enc}(\mathsf{k}, 0^{\ell(|x|)})$. Therefore, from the $P^*$'s perspective, this is exactly the same execution as Protocol 3, and thus it will output $\widehat{\mathsf{ct}}, \mathsf{zap}_2$, where $V_2((x, \widehat{\mathsf{ct}}), \mathsf{zap}_1, \mathsf{zap}_2) = 1$ with non-negligible probability due to our assumption.

Since $x \notin \mathcal{L}$, by the NO-Controlled adaptive soundness of ZAP (Property 2), $\widehat{\mathsf{ct}} \in \mathcal{L}_{\mathsf{ct}}$ with a non-negligible probability. By definition of $\mathcal{L}_{\mathsf{ct}}$, $\mathsf{Dec}(\mathsf{k}, \widehat{\mathsf{ct}}) = x_1, x_2$, and $x_1, x_2$ form a collision, with a non-negligible probability. By the fact that $(\mathsf{Gen}, \mathsf{H})$ is collision-resistant, this leads to a contradiction.

### 5.5 Proof of Zero-Knowledge

**Lemma 4.** *The protocol described in Protocol 3 is super-polynomial time simulatable zero-knowledge.*

*Proof.* We first construct a $2^{(2\cdot\lambda/k)}$ time simulator $\mathcal{S}$. $\mathcal{S}$ works as follow:

- **First Message:** $\mathcal{S}$ receives $s, \mathsf{ct}, \mathsf{zap}_1$ from $V^*$
- **Second Message:**
  1. $\mathcal{S}$ first runs in $2^{(2\cdot\lambda/k)}$[12] time to brute-force search for a collision $x_1$ and $x_2$, such that $H^s(x_1) = H^s(x_2)$.
  2. $\mathcal{S}$ computes $\widehat{\mathsf{ct}} \leftarrow \mathsf{Eval}(C^{x_1,x_2}, \mathsf{ct})$
  3. $\mathcal{S}$ computes $\mathsf{zap}_2$ using $x_1, x_2$ as the witness.
  4. $\mathcal{S}$ sends $\widehat{\mathsf{ct}}, \mathsf{zap}_2$ to the verifier

We now consider the following sequence of hybrids.

- **Hybrid** $H_0$: This is the real experiment where $P$ computes $\widehat{\mathsf{ct}} \leftarrow \mathsf{Eval}(C^0, \mathsf{ct})$, and use $w$ in ZAP. It outputs the final output of malicious verifier $V^*_\lambda(\rho_\lambda)$.
- **Hybrid** $H_1$: This is identical to $H_0$ except that it runs in $2^{(2\cdot\lambda/k)}$ time to brute-force search for a collision $x_1$ and $x_2$ such that $H^s(x_1) = H^s(x_2)$. If a collision does not exist, it outputs $\perp$, and otherwise works similarly to the previous hybrid. We note that this experiment obtains a collision but does not use it. By the compressing property of $(\mathsf{Gen}, \mathsf{H})$, the probability that this hybrid outputs $\perp$ is 0. Thus, we have

$$H_1 = H_0 \tag{24}$$

- **Hybrid** $H_2$: This is identical to $H_1$ except that it computes $\widehat{\mathsf{ct}} = \mathsf{Eval}(C^{x_1,x_2}, \mathsf{ct})$ instead of $\mathsf{Eval}(C^0, \mathsf{ct})$. Note that $x \in \mathcal{L}$, no $\overline{w} \in \mathcal{R}_{\overline{\mathcal{L}}}(x)$ exists, therefore $C^0$ and $C^{x_1,x_2}$ are functionally-equivalent, then by the statistical circuit privacy property of $\mathsf{SFE}$ (defined in Property 3), we have

$$H_2 \overset{s}{\approx} H_1 \tag{25}$$

[12] One way to find a collision in time $2^{(2\lambda/k)}$ is to check, for each possible image $y$ (out of $2^{\lambda/k}$ values), whether there exist two or more distinct preimages (among the first $2^{\lambda/k}+1$ inputs) that map to $y$ under the hash function.

– **Hybrid** $H_3$: This is identical to $H_2$ except that it uses the fact that $\widehat{\mathsf{ct}} = \mathsf{Eval}(C^{x_1,x_2}, \mathsf{ct}) \wedge H^s(x_1) = H^s(x_2)$, as the witness to compute $\mathsf{zap}_2$. By the YES-Controlled Statistical WI property of ZAP (Property 3), we have

$$H_3 \overset{s}{\approx} H_2 \tag{26}$$

Note that $H_3$ is equivalent to the simulated output of $\mathcal{S}$, therefore combining Eq. (24) to (26), we obtain Lemma 4.

**Acknowledgment.** Generative AI has been used for grammar/spell checking and basic editing for some parts of the writing.

## References

1. Abdolmaleki, B., Badrinarayanan, S., Fernando, R., Malavolta, G., Rahimi, A., Sahai, A.: Two-round concurrent 2PC from sub-exponential LWE. In: Guo, J., Steinfeld, R. (eds.) ASIACRYPT 2023, Part I. LNCS, vol. 14438, pp. 71–105. Springer, Singapore (2023). https://doi.org/10.1007/978-981-99-8721-4_3
2. Agarwal, A., Bartusek, J., Goyal, V., Khurana, D., Malavolta, G.: Post-quantum multi-party computation. In: Canteaut, A., Standaert, F.-X. (eds.) EUROCRYPT 2021, Part I. LNCS, vol. 12696, pp. 435–464. Springer, Cham (2021). https://doi.org/10.1007/978-3-030-77870-5_16
3. Alon, B., Chung, H., Chung, K.-M., Huang, M.-Y., Lee, Y., Shen, Y.-C.: Round efficient secure multiparty quantum computation with identifiable abort. In: Malkin, T., Peikert, C. (eds.) CRYPTO 2021, Part I. LNCS, vol. 12825, pp. 436–466. Springer, Cham (2021). https://doi.org/10.1007/978-3-030-84242-0_16
4. Ananth, P., Chung, K.-M., Placa, R.L.L.: On the concurrent composition of quantum zero-knowledge. In: Malkin, T., Peikert, C. (eds.) CRYPTO 2021, Part I. LNCS, vol. 12825, pp. 346–374. Springer, Cham (2021). https://doi.org/10.1007/978-3-030-84242-0_13
5. Badrinarayanan, S., Garg, S., Ishai, Y., Sahai, A., Wadia, A.: Two-message witness indistinguishability and secure computation in the plain model from new assumptions. In: Takagi, T., Peyrin, T. (eds.) ASIACRYPT 2017, Part III. LNCS, vol. 10626, pp. 275–303. Springer, Cham (2017). https://doi.org/10.1007/978-3-319-70700-6_10
6. Barak, B., Sahai, A.: How to play almost any mental game over the net - concurrent composition via super-polynomial simulation. In: 46th Annual Symposium on Foundations of Computer Science, pp. 543–552. IEEE Computer Society Press, Pittsburgh (2005). https://doi.org/10.1109/SFCS.2005.43
7. Bartusek, J., Coladangelo, A., Khurana, D., Ma, F.: On the round complexity of secure quantum computation. In: Malkin, T., Peikert, C. (eds.) CRYPTO 2021, Part I. LNCS, vol. 12825, pp. 406–435. Springer, Cham (2021). https://doi.org/10.1007/978-3-030-84242-0_15
8. Bartusek, J., Coladangelo, A., Khurana, D., Ma, F.: One-way functions imply secure computation in a quantum world. In: Malkin, T., Peikert, C. (eds.) CRYPTO 2021, Part I. LNCS, vol. 12825, pp. 467–496. Springer, Cham (2021). https://doi.org/10.1007/978-3-030-84242-0_17

9. Bitansky, N., Lin, H., Shmueli, O.: Non-malleable commitments against quantum attacks. In: Dunkelman, O., Dziembowski, S. (eds.) EUROCRYPT 2022, Part III. LNCS, vol. 13277, pp. 519–550. Springer, Cham (2022). https://doi.org/10.1007/978-3-031-07082-2_19
10. Bitansky, N., Shmueli, O.: Post-quantum zero knowledge in constant rounds. In: Makarychev, K., Makarychev, Y., Tulsiani, M., Kamath, G., Chuzhoy, J. (eds.) 52nd Annual ACM Symposium on Theory of Computing, pp. 269–279. ACM Press, Chicago (2020). DOIurlhttps://doi.org/10.1145/3357713.3384324
11. Brakerski, Z., Döttling, N.: Two-message statistically sender-private OT from LWE. In: Beimel, A., Dziembowski, S. (eds.) TCC 2018, Part II. LNCS, vol. 11240, pp. 370–390. Springer, Cham (2018). https://doi.org/10.1007/978-3-030-03810-6_14
12. Broadnax, B., Döttling, N., Hartung, G., Müller-Quade, J., Nagel, M.: Concurrently composable security with shielded super-polynomial simulators. In: Coron, J.-S., Nielsen, J.B. (eds.) EUROCRYPT 2017, Part I. LNCS, vol. 10210, pp. 351–381. Springer, Cham (2017). https://doi.org/10.1007/978-3-319-56620-7_13
13. Canetti, R.: Universally composable security: a new paradigm for cryptographic protocols. In: 42nd Annual Symposium on Foundations of Computer Science, pp. 136–145. IEEE Computer Society Press, Las Vegas (2001). https://doi.org/10.1109/SFCS.2001.959888
14. Canetti, R., Lin, H., Pass, R.: Adaptive hardness and composable security in the plain model from standard assumptions. In: 51st Annual Symposium on Foundations of Computer Science, pp. 541–550. IEEE Computer Society Press, Las Vegas (2010). https://doi.org/10.1109/FOCS.2010.86
15. Chatterjee, R., et al.: Compact ring signatures from learning with errors. In: Malkin, T., Peikert, C. (eds.) CRYPTO 2021, Part I. LNCS, vol. 12825, pp. 282–312. Springer, Cham (2021). https://doi.org/10.1007/978-3-030-84242-0_11
16. Chatterjee, R., Liang, X., Pandey, O.: Improved black-box constructions of composable secure computation. In: Czumaj, A., Dawar, A., Merelli, E. (eds.) ICALP 2020: 47th International Colloquium on Automata, Languages and Programming. Leibniz International Proceedings in Informatics (LIPIcs), vol. 168, pp. 28:1–28:20. Schloss Dagstuhl - Leibniz-Zentrum fuer Informatik, Saarbrücken (2020). https://doi.org/10.4230/LIPIcs.ICALP.2020.28
17. Chatterjee, R., Liang, X., Pandey, O., Yamakawa, T.: The round complexity of black-box post-quantum secure computation. In: Tauman Kalai, Y., Kamara, S.F. (eds.) CRYPTO 2025. LNCS, vol. 16003, pp. 3–35. Springer, Cham (2025). https://doi.org/10.1007/978-3-032-01884-7_1
18. Chia, N.H., Chung, K.M., Liang, X., Yamakawa, T.: Post-quantum simulatable extraction with minimal assumptions: black-box and constant-round. In: Dodis, Y., Shrimpton, T. (eds.) CRYPTO 2022, Part III. LNCS, vol. 13509, pp. 533–563. Springer, Cham (2022). https://doi.org/10.1007/978-3-031-15982-4_18
19. Chia, N.-H., Chung, K.-M., Yamakawa, T.: A black-box approach to post-quantum zero-knowledge in constant rounds. In: Malkin, T., Peikert, C. (eds.) CRYPTO 2021, Part I. LNCS, vol. 12825, pp. 315–345. Springer, Cham (2021). https://doi.org/10.1007/978-3-030-84242-0_12
20. Damgård, I., Fehr, S., Salvail, L.: Zero-knowledge proofs and string commitments withstanding quantum attacks. In: Franklin, M. (ed.) CRYPTO 2004. LNCS, vol. 3152, pp. 254–272. Springer, Heidelberg (2004). https://doi.org/10.1007/978-3-540-28628-8_16

21. Damgård, I., Lunemann, C.: Quantum-secure coin-flipping and applications. In: Matsui, M. (ed.) ASIACRYPT 2009. LNCS, vol. 5912, pp. 52–69. Springer, Heidelberg (2009). https://doi.org/10.1007/978-3-642-10366-7_4
22. Dulek, Y., Grilo, A.B., Jeffery, S., Majenz, C., Schaffner, C.: Secure multi-party quantum computation with a dishonest majority. In: Canteaut, A., Ishai, Y. (eds.) EUROCRYPT 2020, Part III. LNCS, vol. 12107, pp. 729–758. Springer, Cham (2020). https://doi.org/10.1007/978-3-030-45727-3_25
23. Dupuis, F., Nielsen, J.B., Salvail, L.: Actively secure two-party evaluation of any quantum operation. In: Safavi-Naini, R., Canetti, R. (eds.) CRYPTO 2012. LNCS, vol. 7417, pp. 794–811. Springer, Heidelberg (2012). https://doi.org/10.1007/978-3-642-32009-5_46
24. Garg, S., Goyal, V., Jain, A., Sahai, A.: Concurrently secure computation in constant rounds. In: Pointcheval, D., Johansson, T. (eds.) EUROCRYPT 2012. LNCS, vol. 7237, pp. 99–116. Springer, Heidelberg (2012). https://doi.org/10.1007/978-3-642-29011-4_8
25. Garg, S., Kiyoshima, S., Pandey, O.: A new approach to black-box concurrent secure computation. In: Nielsen, J.B., Rijmen, V. (eds.) EUROCRYPT 2018, Part II. LNCS, vol. 10821, pp. 566–599. Springer, Cham (2018). https://doi.org/10.1007/978-3-319-78375-8_19
26. Goldreich, O., Micali, S., Wigderson, A.: How to play any mental game or a completeness theorem for protocols with honest majority. In: Aho, A. (ed.) 19th Annual ACM Symposium on Theory of Computing, pp. 218–229. ACM Press, New York City (1987). https://doi.org/10.1145/28395.28420
27. Goyal, V., Jain, A.: On concurrently secure computation in the multiple ideal query model. In: Johansson, T., Nguyen, P.Q. (eds.) EUROCRYPT 2013. LNCS, vol. 7881, pp. 684–701. Springer, Heidelberg (2013). https://doi.org/10.1007/978-3-642-38348-9_40
28. Goyal, V., Liang, X., Malavolta, G.: On concurrent multi-party quantum computation. In: Handschuh, H., Lysyanskaya, A. (eds.) CRYPTO 2023, Part V. LNCS, vol. 14085, pp. 129–161. Springer, Cham (2023).https://doi.org/10.1007/978-3-031-38554-4_5
29. Goyal, V., Liang, X., Pandey, O., Tang, Y., Yamakawa, T.: Round-efficient composable two-party quantum computation. Cryptology ePrint Archive, Paper 2025/1595 (2025). https://eprint.iacr.org/2025/1595
30. Goyal, V., Lin, H., Pandey, O., Pass, R., Sahai, A.: Round-efficient concurrently composable secure computation via a robust extraction lemma. In: Dodis, Y., Nielsen, J.B. (eds.) TCC 2015, Part I. LNCS, vol. 9014, pp. 260–289. Springer, Heidelberg (2015). https://doi.org/10.1007/978-3-662-46494-6_12
31. Graaf, J.V.D.: Towards a formal definition of security for quantum protocols. Ph.D. thesis, University of Montreal, Montreal, Canada (1997)
32. Grilo, A.B., Lin, H., Song, F., Vaikuntanathan, V.: Oblivious transfer is in MiniQCrypt. In: Canteaut, A., Standaert, F.-X. (eds.) EUROCRYPT 2021, Part II. LNCS, vol. 12697, pp. 531–561. Springer, Cham (2021). https://doi.org/10.1007/978-3-030-77886-6_18
33. Hallgren, S., Smith, A., Song, F.: Classical cryptographic protocols in a quantum world. In: Rogaway, P. (ed.) CRYPTO 2011. LNCS, vol. 6841, pp. 411–428. Springer, Heidelberg (2011). https://doi.org/10.1007/978-3-642-22792-9_23
34. Kiyoshima, S.: Round-efficient black-box construction of composable multi-party computation. In: Garay, J.A., Gennaro, R. (eds.) CRYPTO 2014, Part II. LNCS, vol. 8617, pp. 351–368. Springer, Heidelberg (2014). https://doi.org/10.1007/978-3-662-44381-1_20

35. Liang, X., Pandey, O., Yamakawa, T.: A new approach to post-quantum non-malleability. In: 64th Annual Symposium on Foundations of Computer Science, pp. 568–579. IEEE Computer Society Press, Santa Cruz (2023). https://doi.org/10.1109/FOCS57990.2023.00041
36. Lin, H., Pass, R.: Non-malleability amplification. In: Mitzenmacher, M. (ed.) 41st Annual ACM Symposium on Theory of Computing, pp. 189–198. ACM Press, Bethesda (2009). https://doi.org/10.1145/1536414.1536442
37. Lin, H., Pass, R.: Black-box constructions of composable protocols without set-up. In: Safavi-Naini, R., Canetti, R. (eds.) CRYPTO 2012. LNCS, vol. 7417, pp. 461–478. Springer, Heidelberg (2012). https://doi.org/10.1007/978-3-642-32009-5_27
38. Lin, H., Pass, R., Venkitasubramaniam, M.: A unified framework for concurrent security: universal composability from stand-alone non-malleability. In: Mitzenmacher, M. (ed.) 41st Annual ACM Symposium on Theory of Computing, pp. 179–188. ACM Press, Bethesda (2009). https://doi.org/10.1145/1536414.1536441
39. Lindell, Y.: Bounded-concurrent secure two-party computation without setup assumptions. In: 35th Annual ACM Symposium on Theory of Computing, pp. 683–692. ACM Press, San Diego (2003). https://doi.org/10.1145/780542.780641
40. Lindell, Y.: Lower bounds for concurrent self composition. In: Naor, M. (ed.) TCC 2004. LNCS, vol. 2951, pp. 203–222. Springer, Heidelberg (2004). https://doi.org/10.1007/978-3-540-24638-1_12
41. Lombardi, A., Ma, F., Spooner, N.: Post-quantum zero knowledge, revisited or: how to do quantum rewinding undetectably. In: 63rd Annual Symposium on Foundations of Computer Science, pp. 851–859. IEEE Computer Society Press, Denver (2022). https://doi.org/10.1109/FOCS54457.2022.00086
42. Lunemann, C., Nielsen, J.B.: Fully simulatable quantum-secure coin-flipping and applications. In: Nitaj, A., Pointcheval, D. (eds.) AFRICACRYPT 2011. LNCS, vol. 6737, pp. 21–40. Springer, Heidelberg (2011). https://doi.org/10.1007/978-3-642-21969-6_2
43. Malkin, T., Moriarty, R., Yakovenko, N.: Generalized environmental security from number theoretic assumptions. In: Halevi, S., Rabin, T. (eds.) TCC 2006. LNCS, vol. 3876, pp. 343–359. Springer, Heidelberg (2006). https://doi.org/10.1007/11681878_18
44. Ostrovsky, R., Paskin-Cherniavsky, A., Paskin-Cherniavsky, B.: Maliciously circuit-private FHE. In: Garay, J.A., Gennaro, R. (eds.) CRYPTO 2014, Part I. LNCS, vol. 8616, pp. 536–553. Springer, Heidelberg (2014). https://doi.org/10.1007/978-3-662-44371-2_30
45. Pass, R.: Simulation in quasi-polynomial time, and its application to protocol composition. In: Biham, E. (ed.) EUROCRYPT 2003. LNCS, vol. 2656, pp. 160–176. Springer, Heidelberg (2003). https://doi.org/10.1007/3-540-39200-9_10
46. Pass, R., Wee, H.: Black-box constructions of two-party protocols from one-way functions. In: Reingold, O. (ed.) TCC 2009. LNCS, vol. 5444, pp. 403–418. Springer, Heidelberg (2009). https://doi.org/10.1007/978-3-642-00457-5_24
47. Prabhakaran, M., Sahai, A.: New notions of security: achieving universal composability without trusted setup. In: Babai, L. (ed.) 36th Annual ACM Symposium on Theory of Computing, pp. 242–251. ACM Press, Chicago (2004). https://doi.org/10.1145/1007352.1007394
48. Watrous, J.: Zero-knowledge against quantum attacks. SIAM J. Comput. **39**(1), 25–58 (2009)
49. Yao, A.C.C.: How to generate and exchange secrets (extended abstract). In: 27th Annual Symposium on Foundations of Computer Science, pp. 162–167. IEEE Computer Society Press, Toronto (1986). https://doi.org/10.1109/SFCS.1986.25

# Non-Interactive Zero-Knowledge Arguments with Certified Deletion

Kasra Abbaszadeh[1(✉)] and Jonathan Katz[2]

[1] University of Maryland, Maryland, USA
kasraz@umd.edu
[2] Google, Washington DC, USA
jkatz2@gmail.com

**Abstract.** We introduce the notion of non-interactive zero-knowledge (NIZK) arguments with *certified deletion*, a new primitive that enables the recipient of a (quantum) NIZK argument to delete it and obtain a (classical) certificate proving such deletion. We formalize this notion and propose two candidate constructions from standard cryptographic assumptions. Our first construction is based on classical NIZK arguments and quantum-hard one-way functions, but requires both the prover and verifier to run quantum algorithms. We then present an extension based on the learning with errors problem that allows the prover to be classical.

Our results have applications to signatures of knowledge and anonymous credentials with certified deletion, which we also define and construct.

**Keywords:** quantum cryptography · certified deletion · zero-knowledge arguments · signatures of knowledge · anonymous credentials

## 1 Introduction

Quantum computation enables novel cryptographic capabilities that are known to be impossible in the classical world. These include primitives such as quantum money [46], unconditionally secure key agreement [14], one-shot signatures [6], copy protection [1], unclonable encryption [18,25], and certified deletion [10,17].

*Quantum copy protection* [1] ensures that, given a single copy of a function $f$, no adversary can generate two copies of $f$. Although this has many applications (e.g., public-key quantum money [2]), building copy protection from standard assumptions remains a challenging open problem. Motivated by this, Ananth et al. [7] introduced the weaker notion of *secure software leasing*. At a high level, this notion enables a function $f$ to be encoded in a quantum state that can be given to a user; later, the user can generate a deletion certificate proving that it deleted its copy, at which point the user is no longer able to execute $f$. Roughly

Work supported in part by NSF award CNS-2154705.

© International Association for Cryptologic Research 2026
G. Hanaoka and B.-Y. Yang (Eds.): ASIACRYPT 2025, LNCS 16252, pp. 381–410, 2026.
https://doi.org/10.1007/978-981-95-5125-5_13

speaking, then, copy protection prevents cloning altogether, whereas software leasing prevents cloning only for users who produce a valid deletion certificate.

Several prior works studied software leasing—also known as revocation—for specific cryptographic functionalities. Ananth et al. [8] and Agrawal et al. [5] independently introduced revocable public-key encryption, where a decryption key is leased to a user; when the key is returned, the user loses the ability to decrypt. Morimae et al. [36] studied digital signature schemes where either the signing key or signatures can be revoked. We extend this line of research and consider revocable non-interactive zero-knowledge (NIZK) arguments [15]. An NIZK argument system enables a prover holding a witness for an NP statement to generate a proof of the statement without revealing any information about the witness. A classical NIZK argument can be verified arbitrarily many times by anyone who obtains it. In some settings, however, a prover may wish to allow verification only for a limited time. To address this, we introduce *NIZK with certified deletion* (NIZK-CD), which enables recipients to certifiably delete arguments they are given. The certificate can be validated by the prover; once a recipient returns such a certificate, it can no longer output a valid argument.

### 1.1 Our Contributions

We define NIZK-CD and propose constructions in the common reference string (CRS) model based on quantum-secure NIZK arguments and one-way functions. Deletion certificates and their corresponding validation algorithm are classical. In our first construction, however, the prover and verifier are required to run quantum algorithms. We then extend this construction, based on the learning with errors (LWE) assumption [42], to allow the prover to be implemented by a classical algorithm that remotely prepares the proof for a (quantum) verifier.

As a natural application, we construct *signatures of knowledge* with certified deletion from NIZK-CD and use them to construct *anonymous credentials* with certified deletion, without blocklisting or expiration-based techniques [4,13]. Goyal et al. [26] and Jawale et al. [30] previously built (anonymous) revocable credentials from unclonable NIZKs. Unlike ours, their schemes are based on iO and require quantum communication for credential generation and deletion.

### 1.2 Related Work

We discuss prior and concurrent work on copy protection and certified deletion.

**Copy Protection and Unclonable Primitives.** Aaronson [1] defined copy protection and presented a copy-protection scheme for any unlearnable Boolean function relative to a quantum oracle. Later [3], it was shown that a classical oracle suffices. Coladangelo et al. [22] proposed copy protection for (multi-bit) point and compute-and-compare functions in the quantum random-oracle model. Copy protection for decryption schemes and pseudorandom functions can be realized from compute-and-compare obfuscation for unpredictable distributions, indistinguishability obfuscation (iO), and one-way functions [5]. Liu et al. [34]

built bounded collusion-resistant copy protection for functionalities including pseudorandom functions based on iO and the LWE assumption.

Recently, Goyal et al. [26], and Jawale et al. [30] studied copy protection for NIZK arguments, also called *unclonable NIZK*. They showed that this notion is equivalent to public-key quantum money [2], which is currently only known to exist under the assumption of iO.

**Certified Deletion and Revocable Cryptography.** Unruh [45] introduced the notion of revocable encryption where the recipient of a quantum ciphertext can delete the ciphertext and lose all information about the message. Broadbent et al. [17] studied certified deletion for quantum one-time pad encryption. There have been several subsequent works [9–11,20,28,40] extending these ideas to other primitives such as public-key and attribute-based encryption. Kitagawa et al. [33] and Bartusek et al. [11] replaced privately verifiable certificates with publicly verifiable ones under the assumption of one-way functions and one-way state generators [37]. Certified deletion has also been studied for the revocation of cryptographic keys [5,8,20], digital signatures [36], secret sharing [12,31], and obfuscation [9]. We remark that revocation has also been considered for general programs by Ananth et al. [7] based on quantum-secure iO.

**Concurrent Work.** Concurrent work by Çakan et al. [19] defines *NIZK with certified deniability*, a stronger guarantee than certified deletion. Roughly, NIZK with certified deletion guarantees that once a user certifiably deletes a proof, the user cannot generate a proof that will be accepted by the honest verification algorithm; NIZK with certified deniability ensures that once a user certifiably deletes a proof, they have no advantage in convincing even a dishonest verifier (who uses an arbitrary verification algorithm) about the truth of the statement. Çakan et al. [19] proposed a construction of NIZK with certified deniability in the random-oracle model. Their construction has quantum deletion certificates; that is, certificate validation in their scheme must be done by a quantum algorithm. An open problem is to realize NIZKs with certified deniability where the deletion certificate is classical. Çakan et al. [19] further showed the impossibility of NIZK with certified deniability in the plain model under black-box security reductions. We believe the same result holds in the presence of a classical common reference string (CRS). Another open problem is to bypass this impossibility result.

## 2 Technical Overview

In this section, we give a high-level overview of our techniques.

### 2.1 Definition of NIZK-CD

An NIZK-CD scheme consists of algorithms $\langle \mathsf{Setup}, \mathsf{Prove}, \mathsf{Verify}, \mathsf{Delete}, \mathsf{Certify} \rangle$. The first three algorithms, $\mathsf{Setup}$, $\mathsf{Prove}$, and $\mathsf{Verify}$, are defined as for standard NIZK. In particular, $\mathsf{Setup}$ generates a CRS and its trapdoor, and $\mathsf{Prove}$ and $\mathsf{Verify}$ are used, respectively, to generate and verify a quantum proof $\pi$. The only difference is that $\mathsf{Prove}$ additionally outputs a (classical) certification key $\mathsf{ck}$ that is kept private. The $\mathsf{Delete}$ algorithm collapses $\pi$ into a (classical) deletion certificate $\mathsf{cert}$ that can be validated by running $\mathsf{Certify}$ on $\mathsf{cert}$ and $\mathsf{ck}$.

A NIZK-CD satisfies the standard requirements of a standard NIZK, i.e., completeness, soundness, and zero knowledge. For deletion security, a natural definition is as follows. Consider $\mathcal{D}$ as an efficiently sampleable quantum-hard distribution over instance-witness pairs. Then we could simply require that if we sample $(x, w) \leftarrow \mathcal{D}$ and give an adversary $x$ and an NIZK-CD proof $\pi$ generated using $x, w$, it should be infeasible for the adversary to output both a valid deletion certificate $\mathsf{cert}$ as well as a valid proof $\pi^*$ for $x$. This definition, however, does not capture an adversary who receives more than one proof, and it does not offer any security guarantees against malleability attacks. To address these limitations, we strengthen the definition to ensure that for any adversary given oracle access to the prover algorithm, if the adversary outputs both a valid deletion certificate and an accepting proof, then it is possible to extract a corresponding witness.

## 2.2 Constructions of NIZK-CD

We propose a generic compiler that transforms any NIZK to a NIZK-CD using a non-interactive commitment scheme with statistical binding and computation hiding (against quantum algorithms); these commitments can be realized from quantum-hard one-way functions [23] in the CRS model. Let $c \leftarrow \mathsf{Com}(\mathsf{crs}, m, r)$ be a commitment to a message $m$ under randomness $r$ using CRS string $\mathsf{crs}$.

Our construction proceeds as follows. Given an NP relation $R$, we generate a NIZK-CD proof for an instance-witness pair $(x, w) \in R$ by having the prover sample strings $r_0$ and $r_1$ and then generate $c_b = \mathsf{Com}(\mathsf{crs}, b, r_b)$ for $b \in \{0, 1\}$. The prover then produces an NIZK proof $\sigma$ that

$$\exists w, r_0, r_1 : \; (x, w) \in R \bigvee \left( \bigwedge_{b \in \{0,1\}} c_b = \mathsf{Com}(\mathsf{crs}, 1 - b, r_b) \right).$$

Given $\sigma$, $c_0$, and $c_1$, one can validate that $\exists w : (x, w) \in R$ if $\sigma$ is valid and some $c_b$ is proved to be a commitment to $b$ (rather than $1 - b$). To achieve the latter, the prover generates $|\psi\rangle := |0\rangle|r_0\rangle|0\rangle + |1\rangle|r_1\rangle|0\rangle$ and sends the NIZK-CD proof $\pi := (|\psi\rangle, \sigma, \{c_b\}_{b\in\{0,1\}})$. It also outputs certification key $\mathsf{ck} := (r_0, r_1)$.

Given a proof $(|\psi\rangle, \sigma, \{c_b\}_{b\in\{0,1\}})$, define $U_{c_0,c_1}$ via

$$|b\rangle|r\rangle|0\rangle \xrightarrow{U_{c_0,c_1}} |b\rangle|r\rangle|\mathsf{Cmt\text{-}Cmp}(\mathsf{crs}, b, r, c_b)\rangle,$$

where $\mathsf{Cmt\text{-}Cmp}$ is a commit-and-compare function that commits to $b$ using randomness $r$, and returns 1 iff the result is equal to the hardcoded string $c_b$. The verifier can verify the proof by verifying $\sigma$ and then applying $U_{c_0,c_1}$ to $|\psi\rangle$ and measuring the third register. For honestly generated proofs, the result is always 1 and the post-measurement state is unchanged; therefore, the proof $\pi$ can be re-verified multiple times. Conversely, if the result is 1 then at least one of the commitments $c_b$ is a commitment to $b$ and so $x$ is in the language.

The verifier can delete $|\psi\rangle$ by applying a Hadamard measurement, which yields a string $d$ such that $d \cdot (r_0 \oplus r_1) = 0$; note that $d$ can be verified using $\mathsf{ck}$. This measurement causes all other information about $r_0, r_1$ to be lost as the state collapses to $|0\rangle + (-1)^{d \cdot (r_0 \oplus r_1)}|1\rangle$.

Formally, deletion security follows from the adaptive hardcore-bit property of one-way functions [11,36]. This property states that for any one-way function $f$, no efficient adversary on input $y_0 = f(r_0)$, $y_1 = f(r_1)$, and a superposition $|r_0\rangle + |r_1\rangle$ can output both a preimage $r$ such that $f(r) \in \{y_0, y_1\}$ and a string $d$ such that $d \cdot (r_0 \oplus r_1) = 0$ with advantage significantly better than 1/2. (The advantage can be reduced to negligible via parallel repetition.) Moreover, since the commitment scheme satisfies hiding and binding, one can view $\mathsf{Com}$ as a one-way function for which the adaptive hardcore-bit property holds.

**Classical prover.** We observe that the prover only needs quantumness to create the state $|\psi\rangle$ and send it to the verifier. Other components of proof generation and deletion require only classical computation and communication. We present an extension of our construction that allows for remote preparation of $|\psi\rangle$ at the verifier; this can be done before $x, w$ are known.

We first recall the notion of *noisy trapdoor claw-free (NTCF)* functions. For a key $k$ and a pair of functions $f_{k,0}, f_{k,1} : \mathcal{X} \to \mathcal{Y}$ of an NTCF family, it is computationally hard to find a *claw*, i.e., a pair $(r_0, r_1)$ where $f_{k,0}(r_0) = f_{k,1}(r_1)$. On the other hand, there is a trapdoor $\mathsf{td}$ that allows for efficient computation of preimages $r_0$ and $r_1$ of any image point $y$, i.e., such that $f_{k,b}(r_b) = y$ for $b \in \{0, 1\}$. Moreover, the adaptive hardcore-bit property holds, i.e., given $y$ and $|r_0\rangle + |r_1\rangle$, where $r_0$ and $r_1$ are preimages of $y$, no adversary can return one of the preimages along with a string $d$ such that $d \cdot (r_0 \oplus r_1) = 0$. An NTCF family can be constructed under the LWE assumption [16].

We now define the following protocol:

1. The prover generates $(k, \mathsf{td})$ for an NTCF family and sends $k$ to the verifier.
2. The verifier generates $|\phi\rangle := \sum_{r \in \mathcal{X}} |0\rangle|r\rangle|0\rangle + |1\rangle|r\rangle|0\rangle$. Define $U_{f_{k,0}, f_{k,1}}$ via
$$|b\rangle|r\rangle|0\rangle \xrightarrow{U_{f_{k,0}, f_{k,1}}} |b\rangle|r\rangle|f_{k,b}(r)\rangle.$$
The verifier applies $U_{f_{k,0}, f_{k,1}}$ to $|\phi\rangle$ and measures the third register to obtain an image $y$ and a state $|\psi\rangle = |0\rangle|r_0\rangle + |1\rangle|r_1\rangle$. It sends $y$ to the prover.
3. The prover uses $\mathsf{td}$ to recover $r_0, r_1$ from $y$, and generates $\sigma, \{c_b\}$ as before.

Although the state-preparation phase is interactive, it is independent of $x, w$ (i.e., it is *instance-independent*); moreover, the final proof $(|\psi\rangle, \sigma, \{c_b\})$ can be verified by anyone. We stress in particular, that soundness holds even if $|\psi\rangle$ is generated by a malicious prover, rather than via the process above. Thus, the prover need not perform state preparation with the eventual verifier, but could instead rely on any untrusted third party.

### 2.3 Signatures of Knowledge with Certified Deletion

A signature of knowledge is a digital signature in which messages are signed with respect to an instance of an NP language using the corresponding witness as signing key. Informally, it requires that if an adversary, given a signature on a message $m$ with respect to an instance $x$, can output two signatures for $m$ with respect to the same instance, they must know the witness. Signatures of knowledge with certified deletion enable the recipient of a signature to delete the signature after it has been verified. This primitive can be constructed from simulation extractable NIZK-CD by incorporating the message $m$ to the proved instance. These signatures can be used to build anonymous credentials with certified deletion, where the signed messages represent access tokens.

## 3 Preliminaries

We use $\lambda$ to denote the security parameter. We use negl as a generic negligible function. For a set $S$, we use $x \leftarrow S$ to indicate that $x$ is sampled uniformly from $S$. We define $[n] := \{0, 1, \dots, n-1\}$. The term PPT stands for probabilistic polynomial time and QPT stands for quantum polynomial time.

**Quantum Conventions.** A register $X$ is a Hilbert space $\mathbb{C}^{2n}$. An $n$-qubit pure state on register $X$ is a unit vector $|\psi\rangle \in \mathbb{C}^{2n}$. A mixed state on register $X$, described by a density matrix $\rho \in \mathbb{C}^{2n \times 2n}$, is a positive semi-definite Hermitian operator with trace 1. Also, a quantum operation $F$ is a completely positive trace-preserving map from a register $X$ to a register $Y$, i.e., on input a density matrix $\rho$ on register $X$, the operation $F$ returns $F(\rho)$ on register $Y$. A unitary operation $U : X \to X$ is a quantum operation that satisfies $U^\dagger U = UU^\dagger = I^X$, where $I^X$ is identity. A projector $\Pi$ is a Hermitian operator such that $\Pi^2 = \Pi$. A projective measurement is a collection of projectors $\{\Pi_i\}_i$ with $\sum_i \Pi_i = I$.

**Densities and Distances.** Let $\mathcal{X}$ be a finite domain. A density on $\mathcal{X}$ is a function $f : \mathcal{X} \to [0, 1]$ such that $\sum_{x \in \mathcal{X}} f(x) = 1$. $\mathcal{D}_\mathcal{X}$ denotes the set of densities on $\mathcal{X}$. For any $f \in \mathcal{D}_\mathcal{X}$, $\mathsf{Supp}(f) = \{x \in \mathcal{X} : f(x) > 0\}$. Given two densities $f_0$ and $f_1$ on $\mathcal{X}$, the Hellinger distance is defined as

$$H^2(f_0, f_1) := 1 - \sum_{x \in \mathcal{X}} \sqrt{f_0(x) f_1(x)}.$$

For two density matrices $\rho$ and $\sigma$, their trace distance is defined as

$$\|\rho - \sigma\|_{\mathsf{tr}} = \frac{1}{2}\|\rho - \sigma\|_1 = \frac{1}{2}\mathsf{Tr}\left[\sqrt{(\rho - \sigma)^2}\right],$$

where $\|\cdot\|_1$ is the trace norm.

**Lemma 3.1.** *Let $\mathcal{X}$ be a finite set, $f_0, f_1 \in \mathcal{D}_\mathcal{X}$, and $|\psi_b\rangle := \sum_{x \in \mathcal{X}} \sqrt{f_b(x)}\,|x\rangle$ for $b \in \{0, 1\}$. We have*

$$\| |\psi_0\rangle\langle\psi_0| - |\psi_1\rangle\langle\psi_1| \|_{\mathsf{tr}} = \sqrt{1 - (1 - H^2(f_0, f_1))^2}.$$

**Theorem 3.2. (Holevo-Helstrom** [27, 29]**).** *Consider the experiment in which one of two quantum states $\rho$ and $\sigma$ is given to some distinguisher, each with probability $\frac{1}{2}$. The advantage of any distinguisher in correctly determining which state was sent is at most $\frac{1}{2} + \frac{1}{2}\|\rho - \sigma\|_{\mathsf{tr}}$.*

### 3.1 The Learning with Errors Assumption

We recall the definition of the learning with errors (LWE) problem. For real positive $B$ and integer $q$, the discrete truncated Gaussian distribution over $\mathbb{Z}_q$ with parameter $B$ is a distribution on $\{x \in \mathbb{Z}_q : \|x\| \leq B\}$ with density

$$D_{\mathbb{Z}_q,B}(x) := \frac{e^{\frac{-\pi\|x\|^2}{B}}}{\sum_{x' \in \mathbb{Z}_q, \|x'\| \leq B} e^{\frac{-\pi\|x'\|^2}{B}}}.$$

For $d > 1$, the truncated discrete Gaussian distribution over $\mathbb{Z}_q^d$ with parameter $B$ is a distribution on $\{x \in \mathbb{Z}_q^d : \|x\| \leq B\sqrt{d}\}$ with density

$$\forall x = (x_1, x_2, \ldots, x_d) \in \mathbb{Z}_q^d : \quad D_{\mathbb{Z}_q^d,B}(x) = D_{\mathbb{Z}_q,B}(x_1) D_{\mathbb{Z}_q,B}(x_2) \cdots D_{\mathbb{Z}_q,B}(x_d).$$

We now define the LWE problem.

**Definition 3.3. (LWE).** *Let $n(\lambda), m(\lambda), q(\lambda)$ be polynomials in $\lambda$. Moreover, let $\mathcal{X} = \mathcal{X}(\lambda)$ be a distribution over $\mathbb{Z}$. The $\mathsf{LWE}_{m,n,q,\mathcal{X}}$ problem is to distinguish between the distributions $(A, As + e)$ and $(A, u)$, where $A \leftarrow \mathbb{Z}_q^{m \times n}$, $s \leftarrow \mathbb{Z}_q^n$, $e \leftarrow \mathcal{X}^m$, $u \leftarrow \mathbb{Z}_q^m$.*

We assume that no QPT algorithm can solve $\mathsf{LWE}_{m,n,q,\mathcal{X}}$ with non-negligible advantage, even given access to a quantum polynomial-size advice depending on the parameters $m$, $n$, $q$, and $\mathcal{X}$ of the problem. We refer to this as the $\mathsf{LWE}_{m,n,q,\mathcal{X}}$ assumption. It can be shown [38,42] that for any $\alpha > 0$ such that $\sigma = \alpha q \geq 2\sqrt{n}$, the $\mathsf{LWE}_{m,n,q,D_{\mathbb{Z}_q,\sigma}}$ problem is at least as hard as solving the shortest independent vector problem on $n$-dimensional lattices within a factor of $\gamma = \tilde{O}(n/\alpha)$ in the *worst case*, where $\tilde{O}$ hides logarithmic factors. The best known algorithm to solve the problem runs in time $2^{\tilde{O}(n/\log \gamma)}$. We assume hardness against QPT adversaries for $\gamma$ super-polynomial in $n$.

### 3.2 Noisy Trapdoor Claw-Free Hash Function Families

We recall noisy trapdoor claw-free (NTCF) hash functions [16]. Given two finite sets $\mathcal{X}$ and $\mathcal{Y}$, a trapdoor claw-free family of functions satisfies the following properties. For a public key $k$, the functions $\{f_{k,b} : \mathcal{X} \rightarrow \mathcal{Y}\}_{b \in \{0,1\}}$ are both injective and have the same range and are invertible given a trapdoor $\mathsf{td}$, i.e., on input $\mathsf{td}$ and an image $y \in \mathcal{Y}$ it is feasible to efficiently output $x_0, x_1 \in \mathcal{X}$ such that $f_0(x_0) = f_1(x_1) = y$. Furthermore, the pair of functions should be claw-free, i.e., it is computationally hard for an attacker to find two preimages $x_0, x_1$ such that $f_0(x_0) = f_1(x_1)$ without the trapdoor. The functions also satisfy the adaptive hardcore bit property, which states that it is computationally hard for an attacker to output a non-trivial $(b, d, x_b)$ with a probability non-negligibly greater than $\frac{1}{2}$ the such that the equation $d \cdot (x_0 \oplus x_1) = 0$ is satisfied; note that $x_{1-b}$ is a unique element such that $f_{1-b}(x_{1-b}) = f_b(x_b)$.

Unfortunately, we are not aware of any exact constructions of the trapdoor claw-free functions. Instead, Brakerski et al. [16] proposed a construction for noisy trapdoor claw-free functions, which relaxes the requirements as follows. First, the range of functions is not $\mathcal{Y}$, but instead $\mathcal{D}_{\mathcal{Y}}$, the set of probability densities over $\mathcal{Y}$. The trapdoor injective pair property is then defined according to the support of the output densities. The use of densities as the output of the functions requires considering additional requirements. In this paper, we need a quantum polynomial-time algorithm that efficiently prepares a superposition over the range of the function, i.e., given a function key $k$ and a bit $b \in \{0,1\}$, the algorithm can prepare the following quantum state:

$$\frac{1}{\sqrt{\mathcal{X}}} \sum_{x \in \mathcal{X}, y \in \mathcal{Y}} \sqrt{f_{k,b}(x)y}|x\rangle|y\rangle.$$

The construction proposed in [16] is unable to exactly produce the above state; however, it is possible to create a superposition with coefficients such that $f_{k,b}(x)$ is approximated by another function $f'_{k,b}(x)$ and the resulting state is within a negligible distance from the above state. $f'_{k,b}(x)$ supports membership checks efficiently without the need for the trapdoor, and the inversion algorithm should operate properly on the images in the support of $f'_{k,b}(x)$. The adaptive hardcore bit property needs to also be slightly modified. The set $\mathcal{X}$ might not be a subset of binary strings. We first assume the existence of an injective, efficiently invertible map $J : \mathcal{X} \to \{0,1\}^w$ and consider the adaptive hardcore bit property to hold for a subset of all non-zero strings. The formal definition is as follows.

**Definition 3.4. (NTCF** *[16]***).** $\mathcal{F} := \{f_{k,b} : \mathcal{X} \to \mathcal{D}_{\mathcal{Y}}\}_{k \in \mathcal{K}, b \in \{0,1\}}$ *is a NTCF hash function family if the following properties are satisfied.*

***Key generation:*** $\mathsf{NTCF.Gen}_{\mathcal{F}}$ *samples a key* $k \in \mathcal{K}$ *and a trapdoor* $\mathsf{td}$.

***Trapdoor Injective Pair:*** *For all* $k \in \mathcal{K}$, $b \in \{0,1\}$, *distinct* $x, x' \in \mathcal{X}$, $\mathsf{Supp}(f_{k,b}(x)) \cap \mathsf{Supp}(f_{k,b}(x')) = \emptyset$. *An efficient deterministic algorithm* $\mathsf{Inv}_{\mathcal{F}}$ *exists such that for all* $k \in \mathcal{K}$, $b \in \{0,1\}$, $x \in \mathcal{X}$, *and* $y \in \mathsf{Supp}(f_{k,b}(x))$, *it holds that* $\mathsf{Inv}(td, b, y) = x$. *Moreover, given a key* $k \in \mathcal{K}$, *there exists a perfect matching* $\mathcal{R}_k \subseteq \mathcal{X} \times \mathcal{X}$ *such that* $f_{k,0}(x_0) = f_{k,1}(x_1)$ *if and only if* $(x_0, x_1) \in \mathcal{R}_k$.

***Range Superposition:*** *For all* $k \in \mathcal{K}$, $b \in \{0,1\}$, $f'_{k,b} : \mathcal{X} \to \mathcal{D}_{\mathcal{Y}}$ *exists where:*

- *For any claw* $(x_0, x_1) \in \mathcal{R}_k$ *with image* $y \in \mathsf{Supp}(f'_{k,b}(x_b))$ *it holds that* $\mathsf{Inv}_{\mathcal{F}}(\mathsf{td}, b, y) = x_b$ *as well as* $\mathsf{Inv}_{\mathcal{F}}(\mathsf{td}, b \oplus 1, y) = x_{b \oplus 1}$.
- *There exists an efficient deterministic algorithm* $\mathsf{Chk}_{\mathcal{F}}$ *where on input* $k \in \mathcal{K}$, $b \in \{0,1\}$, $x \in \mathcal{X}$, $y \in \mathcal{Y}$, *it outputs* 1 *if* $y \in \mathsf{Supp}(f'_{k,b}(x))$ *and* 0 *otherwise.*
- *For all* $k \in \mathcal{K}$, $b \in \{0,1\}$, *we have* $\mathbb{E}_{x \leftarrow X}[H^2(f_{k,b}(x), f'_{k,b}(x))] \leq \mathsf{negl}(\lambda)$. *In addition, there exists a* $\mathsf{QPT}$ *algorithm* $\mathsf{Samp}_{\mathcal{F}}$ *such that on input* $k \in \mathcal{K}$ *and* $b \in \{0,1\}$ *outputs the following quantum state.*

$$|\psi'\rangle = \frac{1}{\sqrt{|\mathcal{X}|}} \sum_{x \in \mathcal{X}, y \in \mathcal{Y}} \sqrt{(f'_{k,b}(x))(y)}|x\rangle|y\rangle.$$

*Given* $|\psi\rangle = \frac{1}{\sqrt{|\mathcal{X}|}} \sum_{x \in \mathcal{X}, y \in \mathcal{Y}} \sqrt{(f_{k,b}(x))(y)}|x\rangle|y\rangle$, *Lemma 3.1 implies that*

$$\| |\psi\rangle\langle\psi| - |\psi'\rangle\langle\psi'| \|_{\mathsf{tr}} \leq \mathsf{negl}(\lambda).$$

***Adaptive Hardcore Bit:*** *For all keys* $k \in \mathcal{K}$ *and a polynomial* $\ell(\lambda)$*:*

- *For all* $b \in \{0,1\}$, $x \in \mathcal{X}$, *there exists a subset of strings* $\mathcal{G}_{k,b,x} \subseteq \{0,1\}^{\ell(\lambda)}$ *such that* $\Pr_{d \leftarrow \{0,1\}^{\ell(\lambda)}}[d \notin \mathcal{G}_{k,b,x}] \leq \mathsf{negl}(\lambda)$. *Moreover, there exists a* PPT *algorithm to efficiently check membership in* $\mathcal{G}_{k,b,x}$ *given* $k, b, x$ *and* td.
- *There exists an efficiently computable injection* $J : \mathcal{X} \to \{0,1\}^{\ell(\lambda)}$ *such that* $J$ *can also be efficiently inverted on its range, and the following holds. Let*

$$H_k := \{(b, x_b, d, d \cdot (J(x_0) \oplus J(x_1))| b \in \{0,1\}, (x_0, x_1) \in R_k, d \in \mathcal{G}_{k,0,x} \cap \mathcal{G}_{k,1,x}\},$$
$$\bar{H}_k := \{(b, x_b, d, u \oplus 1)|(b, x_b, d, u) \in H_k\}.$$

*For any* QPT *algorithm* $\mathcal{A}$ *it holds that*

$$\left| \Pr_{\mathsf{td},k \leftarrow \mathsf{NTCF.Gen}(1^\lambda)}[\mathcal{A}(k) \in H_k] - \Pr_{\mathsf{td},k \leftarrow \mathsf{NTCF.Gen}(1^\lambda)}[\mathcal{A}(k) \in \bar{H}_k] \right| \leq \mathsf{negl}(\lambda).$$

**Theorem 3.5. (** *[16]***).** *Assuming the polynomial-time quantum hardness of LWE, there is an* NTCF *hash function family.*

One can consider an amplified adaptive hardcore bit property such that the adversary cannot return a set $\{(b_i, x_{i,b_i}, d_i, u_i)\}_{i \in [n]}$ where $n$ is polynomial in the security parameter $\lambda$, and each tuple satisfies $d_i \cdot (x_{i,b_i} \oplus x_{i,1-b_i}) = u_i$, so that $(x_{i,b_i}, x_{i,1-b_i})$ is a claw. The property is formally defined as follows.

**Definition 3.6. (Amplified Adaptive Hardcore Bit).** *An* NTCF *function family* $\mathcal{F}$ *satisfies the amplified adaptive hardcore bit property if, for any* QPT *algorithm* $\mathcal{A}$ *and a polynomial* $n = \ell(\lambda)$, *the following is negligible:*

$$\Pr\left[\begin{array}{c} \forall i \in [n] : (k_i, \mathsf{td}_i) \leftarrow \mathsf{NTCF.Gen}(1^\lambda) \\ \{(b_i, x_{i,b_i}, d_i, u_i)\}_{i \in [n]} \leftarrow \mathcal{A}(\{k_i\}_{i \in [n]}) \\ \forall \beta \in \{0,1\} : x_{i,\beta} = \mathsf{Inv}(\mathsf{td}_i, \beta, y_i) \end{array} : \begin{array}{c} \forall i \in [n] : d_i \in \mathcal{G}_{k,0,x} \cap \mathcal{G}_{k,1,x} \\ \wedge \\ u_i = d_i \cdot (J(x_{i,0}) \oplus J(x_{i,1})) \end{array}\right]$$

**Theorem 3.7.** *[32,41] Any* NTCF *family of functions satisfies the amplified adaptive hardcore bit property.*

Morimae et al. [36] introduced a similar notion for general one-way functions (OWFs) and showed the following result.

**Theorem 3.8.** *Given $\ell(\lambda), \kappa(\lambda), n(\lambda) \in \mathbb{N}$, for any quantum-hard OWF $f : \{0,1\}^{\ell(\lambda)} \to \{0,1\}^{\kappa(\lambda)}$, and any* QPT *adversary $\mathcal{A}$,*

$$\Pr\left[\begin{array}{c} \forall i \in [n] : x_{i,0}, x_{i,1} \leftarrow \{0,1\}^{2\ell(\lambda)}, u_i \leftarrow \{0,1\} \\ \{(x_i, d_i)\}_{i\in[n]} \leftarrow \mathcal{A}(\otimes_{i\in[n]} \frac{|x_{i,0}\rangle + (-1)^{u_i}|x_{i,1}\rangle}{\sqrt{2}}, \{f(x_{i,b})\}_{i,b}) \end{array} \right.$$

$$\left. : \begin{array}{c} \wedge_{i\in[n]} f(x_i) \in \{f(x_{i,0}), f(x_{i,1})\} \\ \wedge \\ \wedge_{i\in[n]} d_i \cdot (x_{i,0} \oplus x_{i,1}) = u_i \end{array} \right] \leq \mathsf{negl}(\lambda).$$

### 3.3 Other Useful Cryptographic Primitives and Lemmas

We recall the notion of commitment schemes in the CRS model, which is a central building block for our NIZK-CD constructions throughout this paper.

**Definition 3.9. (Commitment).** *Let $n(\lambda), \ell(\lambda), \kappa(\lambda)$ be polynomials.* Com *is a quantum-secure commitment if the following syntax and properties hold.*

- $(\mathsf{crs}, \mathsf{td}) \leftarrow \mathsf{Setup}(1^\lambda)$*: on input $\lambda$, output* crs, *and trapdoor* td.
- $c \leftarrow \mathsf{Com}(\mathsf{crs}, m, r)$*: on input* crs, *a message $m \in \{0,1\}^{n(\lambda)}$, and randomness $r \in \{0,1\}^{\ell(\lambda)}$, output a commitment $c \in \{0,1\}^{\kappa(\lambda)}$.*

***Statistical Binding:*** *For any algorithm $\mathcal{A}$,*

$$\Pr\left[\begin{array}{c} (\mathsf{crs}, \mathsf{td}) \leftarrow \mathsf{Setup}(1^\lambda) \\ (m_0, r_0, m_1, r_1) \leftarrow \mathcal{A}(\mathsf{crs}) \end{array} : \begin{array}{c} \mathsf{Com}(\mathsf{crs}, m_0, r_0) = \mathsf{Com}(\mathsf{crs}, m_1, r_1) \\ \wedge\, m_0 \neq m_1 \end{array}\right] \leq \mathsf{negl}(\lambda).$$

***Computational Hiding:*** *For any* QPT *distinguisher $\mathcal{D}$ and $m_0, m_1$,*

$$\left| \Pr\left[\begin{array}{c} (\mathsf{crs}, \mathsf{td}) \leftarrow \mathsf{Setup}(1^\lambda) \\ r_0 \leftarrow \{0,1\}^{\ell(\lambda)} \\ c_0 \leftarrow \mathsf{Com}(\mathsf{crs}, m_0, r_0) \end{array} : \mathcal{D}(\mathsf{crs}, c_0) = 1\right] \right.$$

$$\left. - \Pr\left[\begin{array}{c} (\mathsf{crs}, \mathsf{td}) \leftarrow \mathsf{Setup}(1^\lambda) \\ r_1 \leftarrow \{0,1\}^{\ell(\lambda)} \\ c_1 \leftarrow \mathsf{Com}(\mathsf{crs}, m_1, r_1) \end{array} : \mathcal{D}(\mathsf{crs}, c_1) = 1\right] \right| \leq \mathsf{negl}(\lambda).$$

**Theorem 3.10.** ( *[23]*). *Assuming a quantum-hard one-way function, there is a statistically binding, computationally hiding commitment scheme in the CRS model.*

We recall the notion of non-interactive zero-knowledge (NIZK) arguments in the CRS model. We provide two definitions of NIZK as follows. The first one is a single-theorem definition and ensures that no efficient adversary can output an accepting proof for any unsatisfied instance. The second one is a multi-theorem definition and ensures that from any efficient adversary that can output an accepting proof, one can efficiently extract a valid witness to the relation.

**Definition 3.11. (NIZK for NP).** *Let $R$ be an* NP *relation with a corresponding language $L$. $\Pi = \langle \mathsf{Setup}, \mathsf{Prove}, \mathsf{Verify} \rangle$ is a quantum-secure NIZK for* NP *in the CRS model if it satisfies the following syntax and security properties.*

- $(\mathsf{crs}, \mathsf{td}) \leftarrow \mathsf{Setup}(1^\lambda)$ : *on input $\lambda$, output* crs *and a trapdoor* td.
- $\pi \leftarrow \mathsf{Prove}(\mathsf{crs}, x, w)$ : *on input* crs *and a pair $(x, w) \in R$, output a proof $\pi$.*
- $\{0,1\} \leftarrow \mathsf{Verify}(\mathsf{crs}, x, \pi)$ : *on input* crs, *$x$, and $\pi$, output accept or reject.*

***Perfect Completeness:*** *For every security parameter $\lambda \in \mathbb{N}$ and $(x, w) \in R$,*

$$\Pr\left[\begin{array}{c}(\mathsf{crs}, \mathsf{td}) \leftarrow \mathsf{Setup}(1^\lambda) \\ \pi \leftarrow \mathsf{Prove}(\mathsf{crs}, x, w)\end{array} : \mathsf{Verify}(\mathsf{crs}, x, \pi)\right] = 1.$$

***Adaptive Computational Soundness:*** *For any* QPT *adversary algorithm $\mathcal{A}$*

$$\Pr\left[\begin{array}{c}(\mathsf{crs}, \mathsf{td}) \leftarrow \mathsf{Setup}(1^\lambda) \\ (x, \pi) \leftarrow \mathcal{A}(\mathsf{crs})\end{array} : \mathsf{Verify}(\mathsf{crs}, x, \pi) = 1 \wedge x \notin L\right] \leq \mathsf{negl}(\lambda).$$

***Adaptive Computational Zero-Knowledge:*** *There exists a* QPT *simulator* $\mathsf{Sim} = (\mathsf{Sim}_0, \mathsf{Sim}_1)$ *where for every* QPT *adversary $\mathcal{A}$ and distinguisher $\mathcal{D}$,*

$$\left| \Pr\left[\begin{array}{c}(\mathsf{crs}, \mathsf{td}) \leftarrow \mathsf{Setup}(1^\lambda) \\ (x, w, \xi) \leftarrow \mathcal{A}(\mathsf{crs}) \\ \pi \leftarrow \mathsf{Prove}(\mathsf{crs}, x, w)\end{array} : \mathcal{D}(\mathsf{crs}, x, \pi, \xi) = 1\right] - \right.$$
$$\left. \Pr\left[\begin{array}{c}(\mathsf{crs}, \mathsf{td}) \leftarrow \mathsf{Sim}_0(1^\lambda) \\ (x, w, \xi) \leftarrow \mathcal{A}(\mathsf{crs}) \\ \pi \leftarrow \mathsf{Sim}_1(\mathsf{crs}, \mathsf{td}, x)\end{array} : \mathcal{D}(\mathsf{crs}, x, \pi, \xi) = 1\right] \right| \leq \mathsf{negl}(\lambda).$$

**Theorem 3.12.** ( *[39]*). *Assuming quantum hardness of the LWE assumption, there is a quantum-secure non-interactive, adaptively computationally sound, and adaptively computationally zero-knowledge argument for NP.*

**Definition 3.13.** *[Simulation-Extractable NIZK for NP] Let $R$ be an $NP$ relation for language $L$. Then, $\Pi = \langle \mathsf{Setup}, \mathsf{Prove}, \mathsf{Verify} \rangle$ is a quantum-secure simulation-extractable NIZK for NP in the CRS model if it satisfies the properties of Definition 3.11 and also the following additional properties.*

***Adaptive Multi-Theorem Computational Zero-Knowledge:*** *There is a* QPT *simulator* $\mathsf{Sim} = (\mathsf{Sim}_0, \mathsf{Sim}_1)$ *such that for any* QPT *adversary $\mathcal{A}$,*

$$\left| \Pr\left[(\mathsf{crs}, \mathsf{td}) \leftarrow \mathsf{Setup}(1^\lambda) : \mathcal{A}^{\mathsf{Prove}(\mathsf{crs}, \cdot, \cdot)}(\mathsf{crs}) = 1\right] - \right.$$
$$\left. \Pr\left[(\mathsf{crs}, \mathsf{td}) \leftarrow \mathsf{Sim}_0(1^\lambda) : \mathcal{A}^{\mathsf{Sim}_1(\mathsf{crs}, \mathsf{td}, \cdot, \cdot)}(\mathsf{crs}) = 1\right] \right| \leq \mathsf{negl}(\lambda),$$

*where the simulator algorithm* $\mathsf{Sim}_1$ *discards its fourth input value.*

***Simulation Soundness:*** *Let* $\mathsf{Sim} = (\mathsf{Sim}_0, \mathsf{Sim}_1)$ *be the simulator given by the adaptive multi-theorem computational zero-knowledge. For every* QPT *algorithm* $\mathcal{A}$*, the following is negligible:*

$$\Pr\left[\begin{array}{c}(\mathsf{crs}, \mathsf{td}) \leftarrow \mathsf{Sim}_0(1^\lambda)\\ (x, \pi) \leftarrow \mathcal{A}^{\mathsf{Sim}_1(\mathsf{crs},\mathsf{td},\cdot,\cdot)}(\mathsf{crs})\end{array} : \mathsf{Verify}(\mathsf{crs}, x, \pi) = 1 \wedge x \notin L \wedge x \notin Q\right],$$

*where* $Q$ *is the list of queries from* $\mathcal{A}$ *to* $\mathsf{Sim}_1$.

***Simulation Extractability:*** *Let* $\mathsf{Sim} = (\mathsf{Sim}_0, \mathsf{Sim}_1)$ *be the simulator given by adaptive multi-theorem computational zero knowledge. There is a* QPT *extractor* Ext *such that for every* QPT *algorithm* $\mathcal{A}$ *the following is negligible:*

$$\Pr\left[\begin{array}{c}(\mathsf{crs}, \mathsf{td}) \leftarrow \mathsf{Sim}_0(1^\lambda)\\ (x, \pi) \leftarrow \mathcal{A}^{\mathsf{Sim}_1(\mathsf{crs},\mathsf{td},\cdot,\cdot)}(\mathsf{crs})\\ b \leftarrow \mathsf{Verify}(\mathsf{crs}, x, \pi)\\ w \leftarrow \mathsf{Ext}(\mathsf{crs}, \mathsf{td}, x, \pi)\end{array} : b = 1 \wedge (x, w) \notin R \wedge x \notin Q\right],$$

*where* $Q$ *is the list of queries from* $\mathcal{A}$ *to* $\mathsf{Sim}_1$.

*Remark 3.14.* It is known [24,30,43,44] that multi-theorem simulation-extractable NIZK (i.e., Definition 3.11) satisfies Definition 3.13; multi-theorem zero-knowledge implies single-theorem zero-knowledge, and simulation-soundness also implies adaptive computational soundness and simulation soundness.

**Theorem 3.15.** ( *[30,44]*). *Assuming a quantum-secure one-way function and a quantum-secure IND-CPA encryption scheme, any quantum-secure NIZK for NP can be transformed into a quantum-secure simulation-extractable NIZK.*

**corollary 3.16.** *Assuming the quantum hardness of LWE, there exists a quantum-secure simulation-extractable NIZK for NP.*

*Proof.* This follows from Theorems 3.12 and 3.15; IND-CPA encryption can be achieved from the quantum hardness of learning with errors [42].

Finally, we define signatures of knowledge.

**Definition 3.17. (Signature of Knowledge).** *Let* $R$ *be an* NP *relation with language* $L$ *and message space* $\mathcal{M}$. $\Sigma = \langle \mathsf{Setup}, \mathsf{Sign}, \mathsf{Verify}\rangle$ *is a quantum-secure* SimExt*-secure signature of knowledge if the following syntax and properties hold.*

- $(\mathsf{crs}, \mathsf{td}) \leftarrow \mathsf{Setup}(1^\lambda)$ : *on input* $\lambda$*, output a* crs *and trapdoor* td.
- $\sigma \leftarrow \mathsf{Sign}(\mathsf{crs}, x, w, m)$ : *on input* crs*, pair* $(x, w) \in R$*, and message* $m \in \mathcal{M}$*, output a signature of knowledge* $\sigma$ *to the message* $m$.
- $\{0, 1\} \leftarrow \mathsf{Verify}(\mathsf{crs}, x, m, \sigma)$ : *on input* crs*,* $x$*,* $m$*, and* $\sigma$*, accept or reject.*

***Correctness:*** *For every* $\lambda \in \mathbb{N}$, *pair* $(x, w) \in R$ *and message* $m \in \mathcal{M}$,

$$\Pr\left[\begin{array}{c}(\mathsf{crs}, \mathsf{td}) \leftarrow \mathsf{Setup}(1^\lambda) \\ \sigma \leftarrow \mathsf{Sign}(\mathsf{crs}, x, w, m)\end{array} : \mathsf{Verify}(\mathsf{crs}, x, m, \sigma) = 1\right] = 1.$$

***Simulation:*** *There is a* QPT *simulator algorithm* $\mathsf{Sim} = (\mathsf{Sim}_0, \mathsf{Sim}_1)$ *such that for every* QPT *algorithm* $\mathcal{A}$,

$$\Big| \Pr\left[(\mathsf{crs}, \mathsf{td}) \leftarrow \mathsf{Setup}(1^\lambda) : \mathcal{A}^{\mathsf{Sign}(\mathsf{crs},\cdot,\cdot,\cdot)}(\mathsf{crs}) = 1\right] - \Pr\left[(\mathsf{crs}, \mathsf{td}) \leftarrow \mathsf{Sim}_0(1^\lambda) : \mathcal{A}^{\mathsf{Sim}_1(\mathsf{crs},\mathsf{td},\cdot,\cdot,\cdot)}(\mathsf{crs}) = 1\right] \Big| \leq \mathsf{negl}(\lambda),$$

*where the simulator algorithm* $\mathsf{Sim}_1$ *discards its fifth input value.*

***Extraction:*** *Let* $\mathsf{Sim} = (\mathsf{Sim}_0, \mathsf{Sim}_1)$ *be the simulators given by the simulation property. There exist a* QPT *extractor algorithm* $\mathsf{Ext}$ *such that for every* QPT *algorithm* $\mathcal{A}$

$$\Pr\left[\begin{array}{c}(\mathsf{crs}, \mathsf{td}) \leftarrow \mathsf{Sim}_0(1^\lambda) \\ (x, m, \sigma) \leftarrow \mathcal{A}^{\mathsf{Sim}_1(\mathsf{crs},\mathsf{td},\cdot,\cdot,\cdot)}(\mathsf{crs}) \\ b \leftarrow \mathsf{Verify}(\mathsf{crs}, x, m, \sigma) \\ w \leftarrow \mathsf{Ext}(\mathsf{crs}, \mathsf{td}, x, m, \sigma)\end{array} : \begin{array}{c} b = 1 \ \wedge \ (x, w) \notin R \\ \wedge \ (x, m) \notin Q\end{array}\right] \leq \mathsf{negl}(\lambda).$$

*where* $Q$ *is the list of queries from* $\mathcal{A}$ *to* $\mathsf{Sim}_1$.

**Theorem 3.18.** ( *[21, 30]*). *Given quantum-secure simulation extractable NIZK for NP, there exists a quantum-secure* SimExt*-secure signature of knowledge.*

## 4 Defining NIZK Arguments with Certified Deletion

In this section, we introduce the notion of a non-interactive zero-knowledge with certified deletion (NIZK-CD) and define its security properties. This primitive allows to transform any NIZK argument for NP to a NIZK construction where proofs can be deleted by the recipients after being verified, and deletion can be substantiated via a deletion certificate. We provide two different definitions of NIZK-CD. The first one is motivated by simplicity, establishes a single-theorem NIZK-CD, and guarantees that no adversary receiving honestly generated proofs for hard NP instances can output both an accepting proof and a valid deletion certificate. In the second definition, we present a multi-theorem NIZK-CD with a guarantee that from any adversary, even having the oracle access to NIZK-CD simulators, returning both an accepting proof and deletion certificate for some instance, one can extract a valid witness corresponding to the instance.

**Definition 4.1. (Hard Distribution).** *Given an NP relation* $R$, *an efficiently samplable distribution* $(\mathcal{X}, \mathcal{W})$ *over* $R$ *is hard if for every* QPT *algorithm* $\mathcal{A}$

$$\Pr[(x, w) \leftarrow (\mathcal{X}, \mathcal{W}) : (x, \mathcal{A}(x)) \in R] \leq \mathsf{negl}(\lambda).$$

**Definition 4.2. (NIZK with Certified Deletion).** *Let any* NP *relation $R$ with language $L$. $\Gamma = \langle \mathsf{Setup}, \mathsf{Prove}, \mathsf{Verify}, \mathsf{Delete}, \mathsf{Certify} \rangle$ is a NIZK-CD if it satisfies the following syntax and properties.*

- $(\mathsf{crs}, \mathsf{td}) \leftarrow \mathsf{Setup}(1^\lambda)$*: on input $\lambda$, output a classical* crs *and trapdoor* td.
- $(\pi, \mathsf{ck}) \leftarrow \mathsf{Prove}(\mathsf{crs}, x, w)$*: on input* crs *and a hard NP instance-witness pair $(x, w) \in \mathcal{R}$, output a quantum proof $\pi$ and a classical certification key* ck.
- $\{0, 1\} \leftarrow \mathsf{Verify}(\mathsf{crs}, x, \pi)$*: on input* crs*, $x$, and $\pi$, output accept or reject.*
- $\mathsf{cert} \leftarrow \mathsf{Delete}(\pi)$*: on input $\pi$, output a classical deletion certificate* cert.
- $\{0, 1\} \leftarrow \mathsf{Certify}(\mathsf{ck}, \mathsf{cert})$*: on input* ck *and* cert*, output accept or reject.*

***Perfect Completeness:*** *For every $\lambda \in \mathbb{N}$ and every $(x, w) \in R$,*

$$\Pr\left[\begin{array}{c}(\mathsf{crs}, \mathsf{td}) \leftarrow \mathsf{Setup}(1^\lambda)\\ (\pi, \mathsf{ck}) \leftarrow \mathsf{Prove}(\mathsf{crs}, x, w)\\ \mathsf{cert} \leftarrow \mathsf{Delete}(\pi)\end{array} : \begin{array}{c}\mathsf{Verify}(\mathsf{crs}, x, \pi) = 1\\ \wedge\\ \mathsf{Certify}(\mathsf{ck}, \mathsf{cert}) = 1\end{array}\right] = 1.$$

***Adaptive Computational Soundness:*** *For every* QPT *algorithm $\mathcal{A}$*

$$\Pr\left[\begin{array}{c}(\mathsf{crs}, \mathsf{td}) \leftarrow \mathsf{Setup}(1^\lambda)\\ (x, \pi) \leftarrow \mathcal{A}(\mathsf{crs})\end{array} : \mathsf{Verify}(\mathsf{crs}, x, \pi) = 1 \wedge x \notin L\right] \leq \mathsf{negl}(\lambda).$$

***Adaptive Computational Zero-Knowledge:*** *There exists a* QPT *algorithm* $\mathsf{Sim} = (\mathsf{Sim}_0, \mathsf{Sim}_1)$ *such that for every* QPT *algorithm $\mathcal{A}$,* QPT *distinguisher $\mathcal{D}$,*

$$\left|\Pr\left[\begin{array}{c}(\mathsf{crs}, \mathsf{td}) \leftarrow \mathsf{Setup}(1^\lambda)\\ (x, w, \xi) \leftarrow \mathcal{A}(\mathsf{crs})\\ (\pi, \mathsf{ck}) \leftarrow \mathsf{Prove}(\mathsf{crs}, x, w)\end{array} : \mathcal{D}(\mathsf{crs}, x, \pi, \xi) = 1\right] - \right.$$
$$\left.\Pr\left[\begin{array}{c}(\mathsf{crs}, \mathsf{td}) \leftarrow \mathsf{Sim}_0(1^\lambda)\\ (x, w, \xi) \leftarrow \mathcal{A}(\mathsf{crs})\\ (\pi, \mathsf{ck}) \leftarrow \mathsf{Sim}_1(\mathsf{crs}, \mathsf{td}, x)\end{array} : \mathcal{D}(\mathsf{crs}, x, \pi, \xi) = 1\right]\right| \leq \mathsf{negl}(\lambda).$$

***Deletion Security:*** *For every* QPT *algorithm $\mathcal{A}$ and hard distribution $(\mathcal{X}, \mathcal{W})$ over $\mathcal{R}$,*

$$\Pr\left[\begin{array}{c}(\mathsf{crs}, \mathsf{td}) \leftarrow \mathsf{Setup}(1^\lambda)\\ (x, w) \leftarrow (\mathcal{X}, \mathcal{W})\\ (\pi, \mathsf{ck}) \leftarrow \mathsf{Prove}(\mathsf{crs}, x, w)\\ (\pi^*, \mathsf{cert}) \leftarrow \mathcal{A}(\mathsf{crs}, x, \pi)\end{array} : \begin{array}{c}\mathsf{Verify}(\mathsf{crs}, x, \pi^*) = 1\\ \wedge\\ \mathsf{Certify}(\mathsf{ck}, \mathsf{cert}) = 1\end{array}\right] \leq \mathsf{negl}(\lambda).$$

We present the definition of multi-theorem simulation-extractable NIZK-CD.

**Definition 4.3. (Simulation-Extractable NIZK-CD).** *Let $R$ be an* NP *with language $L$. $\Gamma = \langle \mathsf{Setup}, \mathsf{Prove}, \mathsf{Verify}, \mathsf{Delete}, \mathsf{Certify} \rangle$ is a simulation-extractable NIZK-CD if it satisfies Definition 4.2 and the following properties.*

***Adaptive Multi-Theorem Computational Zero-Knowledge:*** *There is a* QPT *simulator algorithm* $\mathsf{Sim} = (\mathsf{Sim}_0, \mathsf{Sim}_1)$ *(where* $\mathsf{Sim}_1$ *discards its fourth input) such that for every* QPT *algorithm* $\mathcal{A}$,

$$\Big|\Pr\Big[(\mathsf{crs}, \mathsf{td}) \leftarrow \mathsf{Setup}(1^\lambda) : \mathcal{A}^{\mathsf{Prove}(\mathsf{crs},\cdot,\cdot)}(\mathsf{crs}) = 1\Big] - \Pr\Big[(\mathsf{crs}, \mathsf{td}) \leftarrow \mathsf{Sim}_0(1^\lambda) : \mathcal{A}^{\mathsf{Sim}_1(\mathsf{crs},\mathsf{td},\cdot,\cdot)}(\mathsf{crs}) = 1\Big]\Big| \leq \mathsf{negl}(\lambda),$$

*where* $\mathcal{A}$ *only receives proofs from the oracles and certifying keys are discarded..*

***Simulation Extractability:*** *Let* $\mathsf{Sim} = (\mathsf{Sim}_0, \mathsf{Sim}_1)$ *be the simulator given by the adaptive multi-theorem computational zero-knowledge property. There is a* QPT *extractor* Ext *such that for any* QPT *adversary* $\mathcal{A}$,

$$\Pr\left[\begin{array}{c} (\mathsf{crs}, \mathsf{td}) \leftarrow \mathsf{Sim}_0(1^\lambda) \\ (x, \pi) \leftarrow \mathcal{A}^{\mathsf{Sim}_1(\mathsf{crs},\mathsf{td},\cdot,\cdot)}(\mathsf{crs}) \\ b \leftarrow \mathsf{Verify}(\mathsf{crs}, x, \pi) \\ w \leftarrow \mathsf{Ext}(\mathsf{crs}, \mathsf{td}, x, \pi) \end{array} : \begin{array}{c} b = 1 \wedge (x, w) \notin R \\ \wedge\, x \notin Q \end{array}\right] \leq \mathsf{negl}(\lambda),$$

*where* $Q$ *is the list of queries from* $\mathcal{A}$ *to* $\mathsf{Sim}_1$*, and* $\mathcal{A}$ *only receives the proof.*

***Simulation Extractability with Deletion:*** *Let* $(\mathsf{Sim}_0, \mathsf{Sim}_1)$ *be the simulator given by the adaptive multi-theorem computational zero-knowledge propery. There exists a* QPT *extractor* Ext-Del *s.t. for every* QPT *algorithm* $\mathcal{A} = (\mathcal{A}_0, \mathcal{A}_1)$,

$$\Pr\left[\begin{array}{c} (\mathsf{crs}, \mathsf{td}) \leftarrow \mathsf{Sim}_0(1^\lambda) \\ (x, \xi) \leftarrow \mathcal{A}_0^{\mathsf{Sim}_1(\mathsf{crs},\mathsf{td},\cdot,\cdot)}(\mathsf{crs}) \\ (\pi, \mathsf{ck}) \leftarrow \mathsf{Sim}_1(\mathsf{crs}, \mathsf{td}, x, \bot) \\ (\pi^*, \mathsf{cert}) \leftarrow \mathcal{A}_1^{\mathsf{Sim}_1(\mathsf{crs},\mathsf{td},\cdot,\cdot)}(\mathsf{crs}, \xi, x, \pi) \\ b_1 \leftarrow \mathsf{Certify}(\mathsf{ck}, \mathsf{cert}),\ b_2 \leftarrow \mathsf{Verify}(\mathsf{crs}, x, \pi^*) \\ w \leftarrow \mathsf{Ext\text{-}Del}(\mathsf{crs}, \mathsf{td}, x, \pi^*, \mathsf{cert}) \end{array} : \begin{array}{c} b_1 = b_2 = 1 \wedge \\ x \notin Q \wedge (x, w) \notin R \end{array}\right]$$

*where* $Q$ *is the list of queries, and* $\mathcal{A}$ *only receives the proof from* $\mathsf{Sim}_1$.

*Remark 4.4.* In the definition of simulation extractability with deletion, $\pi^*$ is a quantum proof output by an adversary and so it may change when operated on by a general quantum algorithm. (Prior work [26,30] was not explicit about this point.) For concreteness, our definition requires $\pi^*$ to be verified before the extractor tries to extract a witness from the (possibly modified) $\pi^*$. We thank an anonymous reviewer from Asiacrypt 2025 for pointing out this subtlety.

The connections between different notions of zero-knowledge, soundness, and extraction for NIZK arguments that are described in Remark 3.14 also hold for NIZK-CD. The following states that the simulation extractability with deletion implies both simulation extractibility and deletion security.

**Theorem 4.5.** *Simulation extractability with deletion defined in Definition 4.3 implies simulation extractibility as defined in Definition 4.3 and deletion security as defined in Definition 4.2.*

*Proof.* First, consider an adversary $\mathcal{B}$ that breaks simulation extractibility with a non-negligible advantage. One can build an adversary $\mathcal{A} = (A_0, A_1)$ that breaks simulation extractibility with deletion with the same advantage. In particular, $A_0$ runs $B$ to get an instance $x$ and a corresponding proof $\pi^*$. The instance $x$ is submitted to the simulator $\mathsf{Sim}_1$, and $\pi^*$ is included in $\xi$. The algorithm $A_1$ receives a proof $\pi$ from $\mathsf{Sim}_1$, which can be deleted to generate a valid deletion certificate $\mathsf{cert}$. Afterwards, $A_1$ can return produced $\mathsf{cert}$ as a valid certificate and $\pi^*$ included in $\xi$ as an accepting proof corresponding to the instance $x$.

Similarly, consider an adversary $\mathcal{B}$ that can break the deletion security with a non-negligible advantage. One can build an adversary $\mathcal{A} = (A_0, A_1)$ where $A_0$ samples a hard instance $x$ and submits it to $\mathsf{Sim}_1$. $A_1$ receives a proof $\pi$ corresponding to the instance $x$ from the oracle. Then, $A_1$ runs $B$ on input $x$ and $\pi$ to get a valid deletion certificate and an accepting transcript where the success probability is the same as the success probability of $\mathcal{B}$.

# 5 Constructions of NIZK-CD from Standard Assumptions

In this section, we propose NIZK-CD constructions from standard cryptographic assumptions. First, we propose a construction with a quantum prover based on quantum-hard one-way functions and standard NIZK proofs. Then, we show how to make the prover classical under the LWE assumption.

## 5.1 NIZK-CD with a Quantum Prover

**Theorem 5.1.** *Assuming quantum-hard one-way functions and quantum-secure simulation-extractable NIZK, there exists a simulation-extractable NIZK-CD.*

*Proof.* Assume $\Sigma = \langle \mathsf{Setup}, \mathsf{Com} \rangle$ to be a quantum secure, statistically binding and computationally hiding which can be realized from one-way functions [23], and $\Pi = \langle \mathsf{Setup}, \mathsf{Prove}, \mathsf{Verify} \rangle$ to be any simulation-extractable NIZK. Our NIZK-CD construction is as follows.

- $(\mathsf{crs}, \mathsf{td}) \leftarrow \mathsf{Setup}(1^\lambda)$: $\mathsf{crs}_\Sigma, \mathsf{td}_\Sigma \leftarrow \Sigma.\mathsf{Setup}(1^\lambda)$ and $\mathsf{crs}_\Pi, \mathsf{td}_\Pi \leftarrow \Pi.\mathsf{Setup}(1^\lambda)$, and output the parameters $\mathsf{crs} := (\mathsf{crs}_\Sigma, \mathsf{crs}_\Pi)$ and $\mathsf{td} := (\mathsf{td}_\Sigma, \mathsf{td}_\Pi)$.
- $(\pi, \mathsf{ck}) \leftarrow \mathsf{Prove}(\mathsf{crs}, x, w)$: For $n(\lambda), \ell(\lambda)$, sample randomness $r_{i,b} \leftarrow \{0,1\}^{\ell(\lambda)}$, and $\forall i \in [n], \forall b \in \{0,1\}$ compute $c_{i,b} = \mathsf{Com}(\mathsf{crs}_\Sigma, b^{n(\lambda)}, r_{i,b})$. Then, given the instance $x^* := (x, \{c_{i,b}\}_{i\in[n], b\in\{0,1\}})$ and witness $w^* := (w, \{r_{i,b}\}_{i\in[n], b\in\{0,1\}})$, invoke $\Pi.\mathsf{Prove}(\mathsf{crs}, x^*, w^*)$ and generate a NIZK proof $\sigma$ for the relation $R^*$,

$$((x, w) \in R) \quad \bigvee_{i\in[n]} \quad \left(\wedge_{b\in\{0,1\}} c_{i,b} = \mathsf{Com}(\mathsf{crs}_\Sigma, (1-b)^{n(\lambda)}, r_{i,b})\right). \qquad (1)$$

Given uniform bits $u_i \leftarrow \{0,1\}$ for all $i \in [n]$, prepare

$$|\psi\rangle := \bigotimes_{i\in[n]} \frac{1}{\sqrt{2}} \left(|0\rangle|r_{i,0}\rangle + (-1)^{u_i}|1\rangle|r_{i,1}\rangle\right). \tag{2}$$

Output $\pi := (\{c_{i,b}\}_{i\in[n],b\in\{0,1\}}, \sigma, |\psi\rangle)$ and $\mathsf{ck} := \{u_i, r_{i,b}\}_{i\in[n],b\in\{0,1\}}$.

- $\{0,1\} \leftarrow \mathsf{Verify}(\mathsf{crs}, x, \pi)$: Parse $\pi$ as $\{c_{i,b}\}_{i\in[n],b\in\{0,1\}}, \sigma, |\psi\rangle$, run the verifier $v_\sigma \leftarrow \Pi.\mathsf{Verify}(\mathsf{crs}, x^*, \sigma)$, where $x^* := (x, \{c_{i,b}\}_{i\in[n],b\in\{0,1\}})$. Let $U_{c_0,c_1}$ be a unitary operation with respect to the commitments $c_0$ and $c_1$ as follows.

$$|b\rangle|r\rangle|0\rangle \xrightarrow{U_{c_0,c_1}} |b\rangle|r\rangle|\mathsf{Cmt\text{-}Cmp}(\mathsf{crs}_\Sigma, b, r, c_b)\rangle, \tag{3}$$

where the commit-and-compare function is defined as:

$$\mathsf{Cmt\text{-}Cmp}(\mathsf{crs}_\Sigma, b, r, c_b) = \left\{ \begin{array}{ll} 1 & \mathsf{Com}(\mathsf{crs}_\Sigma, b^{n(\lambda)}, r) = c_b \quad \text{otherwise.} \end{array} \right. \tag{4}$$

Add ancilla qubits, and apply $U = \bigotimes_{i\in[n]} U_{c_{i,0},c_{i,1}}$ to $|\psi\rangle$,

$$\xrightarrow{U} \bigotimes_{i\in[n]} \frac{1}{\sqrt{2}}(|0\rangle|r_{i,0}\rangle|\mathsf{Cmt\text{-}Cmp}(\mathsf{crs}_\Sigma, 0, r_{i,0}, c_{i,0})\rangle$$
$$+ (-1)^{u_i}|1\rangle|r_{i,1}\rangle|\mathsf{Cmt\text{-}Cmp}(\mathsf{crs}_\Sigma, 1, r_{i,1}, c_{i,1})\rangle). \tag{5}$$

$\forall i \in [n]$, measure the right-most registers $v_i = \mathsf{Cmt\text{-}Cmp}(\mathsf{crs}_\Sigma, b, r_{i,b}, c_{i,b})$. Output $v = v_\sigma \bigwedge_{i\in[n]} v_i$, where $v = 1$ indicates accept and $v = 0$ otherwise.

- $\mathsf{cert} \leftarrow \mathsf{Delete}(\pi)$: Parse $\pi$ as $\{c_{i,b}\}_{i\in[n],b\in\{0,1\}}, \sigma, |\psi\rangle = \bigotimes_{i\in[n]}|\psi_i\rangle$ such that $|\psi_i\rangle = \sum_{b\in\{0,1\}} \frac{1}{\sqrt{2}}(-1)^{b\cdot u_i}|b\rangle|r_{i,b}\rangle$. $\forall i \in [n]$, measure each state $|\psi_i\rangle$ in the Hadamard basis, yielding an outcome string $d_i \in \{0,1\}^{\ell(\lambda)}$ such that it holds that $d_i \cdot (r_{i,0} \oplus r_{i,1}) = u_i$. We define the deletion certificate $\mathsf{cert} := \{d_i\}_{i\in[n]}$.
- $\{0,1\} \leftarrow \mathsf{Certify}(\mathsf{ck}, \mathsf{cert})$: Parse $\mathsf{ck}$ as $\{u_i, r_{i,b}\}_{i\in[n],b\in\{0,1\}}$ and $\mathsf{cert}$ as $\{d_i\}_{i\in[n]}$. Validate whether for all $i \in [n]$ it holds that $d_i \cdot (r_{i,0} \oplus r_{i,1}) = u_i$.

Next, we prove each of the security properties of the proposed construction.

**Perfect Completeness:** Completeness must be shown with respect to both proof verification and certificate validation. Consider the former case. Following the perfect completeness of $\Pi$, we ensure that the proof $\sigma$ is accepting and $v_\sigma = 1$ with a probability of 1. Then, it suffices to show that for all $i \in [n]$, $v_i = 1$. As the commitment algorithm $\mathsf{Com}$ is deterministic, and the commitments are generated honestly, i.e., $c_i = \mathsf{Com}(\mathsf{crs}_\Sigma, b_i^{n(\lambda)}, r_{i,b})$, we ensure that $\forall i \in [n]$ and $\forall b \in \{0,1\}$, we have $\mathsf{Cmt\text{-}Cmp}(\mathsf{crs}_\Sigma, b_i, r_{i,b}, c_{i,b}) = 1$. Therefore, the bit $v_i$ is measured as one with a probability of 1. Consider completeness with respect to deletion. We parse the sate $|\psi\rangle$ as $\bigotimes_{i\in[n]}|\psi_i\rangle$, s.t. $|\psi_i\rangle = \sum_{b\in\{0,1\}} \frac{1}{\sqrt{2}}(-1)^{b\cdot u_i}|b\rangle|r_{i,b}\rangle$. The verifier measures each $|\psi_i\rangle$ in the Hadamard basis, which yields an outcome string $d_i \in \{0,1\}^{\ell(\lambda)}$, and it holds that $u_i = d_i \cdot (r_{i,0} \oplus r_{i,1})$. Therefore, the Certify algorithm always accepts the deletion certificate cert.

**Adaptive Multi-Theorem Computational Zero-Knowledge:** Consider the simulators $\Pi.Sim = (\Pi.Sim_0, \Pi.\mathsf{Sim}_1)$. We then show $\mathsf{Sim} = (\mathsf{Sim}_0, \mathsf{Sim}_1)$ for adaptive multi-theorem computational zero-knowledge of our construction.

- $(\mathsf{crs}, \mathsf{td}) \leftarrow \mathsf{Sim}_0(1^\lambda)$ : Run the algorithms $(\mathsf{crs}_\Pi, \mathsf{td}_\Pi) \leftarrow \Pi.\mathsf{Sim}_1(1^\lambda)$ and $(\mathsf{crs}_\Sigma, \mathsf{td}_\Sigma) \leftarrow \Sigma.\mathsf{Setup}(1^\lambda)$. Output $\mathsf{crs} := (\mathsf{crs}_\Pi, \mathsf{crs}_\Sigma)$ and $\mathsf{td} := (\mathsf{td}_\Pi, \mathsf{td}_\Sigma)$.
- $(\pi, \mathsf{ck}) \leftarrow \mathsf{Sim}_1(\mathsf{crs}, \mathsf{td}, x)$ : Sample $r'_{i,b} \leftarrow \{0,1\}^{\ell(\lambda)}$ and $\forall i \in [n], \forall b \in \{0,1\}$ compute $c'_{i,b} = \mathsf{Com}(\mathsf{crs}_\Sigma, b^{n(\lambda)}, r'_{i,b})$. Given $x^* := (x, \{c'_{i,b}\}_{i\in[n],b\in\{0,1\}})$, query $\Pi.\mathsf{Sim}_1$ on input $x^*$ to get $\sigma'$. Sample $u'_i \leftarrow \{0,1\}$, prepare $|\psi'\rangle$, and output the proof $\pi := (\{c'_{i,b}\}_{i\in[n],b\in\{0,1\}}, \sigma', |\psi'\rangle)$ and certificate $\mathsf{ck} := \{u'_i, r'_{i,b}\}_{i\in[n],b\in\{0,1\}}$.

<u>Reduction:</u> Suppose that there exists a QPT adversary algorithm $\mathcal{A}$ such that for some polynomial $p(\lambda)$,

$$\Big| \Pr\Big[\mathsf{crs}, \mathsf{td} \leftarrow \mathsf{Setup}(1^\lambda) : \mathcal{A}^{\mathsf{Prove}(\mathsf{crs},\cdot,\cdot)}(\mathsf{crs}) = 1\Big] - \Pr\Big[\mathsf{crs}, \mathsf{td} \leftarrow \mathsf{Sim}_0(1^\lambda) : \mathcal{A}^{\mathsf{Sim}_1(\mathsf{crs},\mathsf{td},\cdot,\cdot)}(\mathsf{crs}) = 1\Big] \Big| \geq \frac{1}{p(\lambda)}.$$

We construct a QPT adversary $\mathcal{B}$ for the adaptive multi-theorem computational ZK property of the underlying NIZK $\Pi$ as follows: Receive $\mathsf{crs}_\Pi$ from $\Pi.\mathsf{Setup}$ or $\Pi.\mathsf{Sim}_0$, $\mathsf{crs}_\Sigma$ from $\Sigma.\mathsf{Setup}$, and then send $\mathsf{crs} := (\mathsf{crs}_\Pi, \mathsf{crs}_\Sigma)$ to the adversary $\mathcal{A}$. For each query $(x, w)$, $r_{i,b} \leftarrow \{0,1\}^{\ell(\lambda)}$, $c_{i,b} = \mathsf{Com}(\mathsf{crs}_\Sigma, b^{n(\lambda)}, r_{i,b})$ for all $i \in [n]$ and $b \in \{0,1\}$. Then, given instance $x^* := (x, \{c_{i,b}\}_{i\in[n],b\in\{0,1\}})$ and witness $w^* := (w, \{r_{i,b}\}_{i\in[n],b\in\{0,1\}})$, receive the real or simulated proof $\sigma$ by query either Prove on input $(x^*, w^*)$ or $\Pi.\mathsf{Sim}_1$ on input $x^*$. Moreover, sample bits $u_i \leftarrow \{0,1\}$ and prepares $|\psi\rangle$ as defined in Eq. 2. The proof $\pi = \{c_{i,b}\}_{i\in[n],b\in\{0,1\}}, \sigma, |\psi\rangle$ is sent to the adversary algorithm $\mathcal{A}$. Output the result of $\mathcal{A}$.

As commitment randomness $\{r_{i,b}\}_{i\in[n],b\in\{0,1\}}$ and exponents $\{u_i\}_{i\in[n],b\in\{0,1\}}$ are uniformly sampled, the real and simulated quantum states, i.e., $|\psi\rangle$ and $|\psi'\rangle$, respectively, are statistically indistinguishable. Moreover, computational hiding of the commitment scheme Com ensures that two sets $\{c_{i,b}\}_{i\in[n],b\in\{0,1\}}$ and $\{c'_{i,b}\}_{i\in[n],b\in\{0,1\}}$ are computationally indistinguishable. Thus, $\mathcal{B}$ would have a similar and non-negligible polynomial advantage to $\mathcal{A}$ in breaking the adaptive multi-theorem computational zero-knowledge property of $\Pi$, i.e., $\frac{1}{p(\lambda)} - \mathsf{negl}(\lambda)$.

**Simulation Extractability with Deletion:** One can view the commitment algorithm $\mathsf{Com} : \{0,1\}^{\ell(\lambda)+1}$ as one-way function. Assume that there exists an adversary that, on input $\mathsf{Com}(\mathsf{crs}_\Sigma, b^{n(\lambda)}, r)$, can invert the function and extract $b$ and $r$ with a non-negligible probability. Then, the adversary can break the hiding or binding properties with the same advantage. Lemma 3.8 implies that,

$$\Pr\left[\begin{array}{c} \forall i \in [n] : r_{i,0}, r_{i,1} \leftarrow \{0,1\}^{2\ell(\lambda)}, u_i \leftarrow \{0,1\} \\ \forall i \in [n] : c_{i,0} = \mathsf{Com}(\mathsf{crs}_\Sigma, 0^{n(\lambda)}, r_{i,0}) \wedge c_{i,1} = \mathsf{Com}(\mathsf{crs}_\Sigma, 1^{n(\lambda)}, r_{i,1}) \\ \{(b_i, r_i, d_i)\}_{i\in[n]} \leftarrow \mathcal{A}(\otimes_{i\in[n]} \frac{|0, r_{i,0}\rangle + (-1)^{u_i}|1, r_{i,1}\rangle}{\sqrt{2}}, \{c_{i,b}\}_{i,b}) \end{array} : \begin{array}{c} \wedge_{i\in[n]} \mathsf{Com}(\mathsf{crs}_\Sigma, b_i^{n(\lambda)}, r_i) \in \{c_{i,0}, c_{i,1}\} \\ \wedge \\ \wedge_{i\in[n]} d_i \cdot (r_{i,0} \oplus r_{i,1}) = u_i \end{array}\right] \leq \mathsf{negl}(\lambda)$$

Let $\Pi.\mathsf{Sim} = (\Pi.\mathsf{Sim}_0, \Pi.\mathsf{Sim}_1)$ be the simulators of $\Pi$ and $\mathsf{Sim} = (\mathsf{Sim}_0, \mathsf{Sim}_1)$ be the simulators of our construction given by the corresponding multi-theorem zero-knowledge. Let $\Pi.\mathsf{Ext}$ be the extractor given by the simulation extractibility of $\Pi$. We show an extractor Ext-Del that satisfies simulation extractibility with deletion for our proposed construction as follows.

1. On input crs, td, $x$, $\pi$, and cert, parse the proof $\pi$ as $\{c_{i,b}\}_{i\in[n],b\in\{0,1\}}, \sigma, |\psi\rangle$.
2. Query $\Pi.\mathsf{Ext}$ on input $x^*$ and $\sigma$ and receive the witness $w^*$.
3. Output $w^*$ as $w$.

Reduction: Consider the case that simulation extractibility with deletion does not hold, i.e., there exists a QPT adversary algorithm $A = (A_0, A_1)$ such that given the extractor Ext-Del, and some polynomial $p(\lambda)$,

$$\Pr\left[\begin{array}{c} (\mathsf{crs}, \mathsf{td}) \leftarrow \mathsf{Sim}_0(1^\lambda) \\ (x, \xi) \leftarrow \mathcal{A}_0^{\mathsf{Sim}_1(\mathsf{crs},\mathsf{td},\cdot,\cdot)}(\mathsf{crs}) \\ (\pi, \mathsf{ck}) \leftarrow \mathsf{Sim}_1(\mathsf{crs}, \mathsf{td}, x) \\ (\pi^*, \mathsf{cert}) \leftarrow \mathcal{A}_1^{\mathsf{Sim}_1(\mathsf{crs},\mathsf{td},\cdot,\cdot)}(\mathsf{crs}, \xi, x, \pi) \\ w \leftarrow \mathsf{Ext\text{-}Del}(\mathsf{crs}, \mathsf{td}, x, \pi^*, \mathsf{cert}) \end{array} : \begin{array}{c} \mathsf{Verify}(\mathsf{crs}, x, \pi^*) = 1 \\ \wedge \\ [\mathsf{Certify}(\mathsf{ck}, \mathsf{cert}) = 1 \ \vee \ (x, w) \notin R] \wedge \ x \notin Q \end{array}\right] \geq \frac{1}{p(\lambda)},$$

Since $\mathsf{Sim}_1$ forwards queries to $\Pi.\mathsf{Sim}_1$, we know that $x^*$ is not queried to $\Pi.\mathsf{Sim}_1$. We parse $\pi^*$ as $\{c_{i,b}\}_{i\in[n],b\in\{0,1\}}, \sigma, |\psi\rangle$. Since $\mathsf{Verify}(\mathsf{crs}, x, \pi^*) = 1$, we know that $v_\sigma = \Pi.\mathsf{Verify}(\mathsf{crs}_\Pi, x^*, \sigma) = 1$. The witness $w^*$ returned by $\Pi.\mathsf{Ext}$ is a valid witness for $R^*$. Thus, $w^*$ must include $w$ s.t. $(x, w) \in R$, or, for an $i \in [n]$, it includes $\{r_{i,b}\}_{b\in\{0,1\}}$ s.t. $c_{i,0} = \mathsf{Com}(\mathsf{crs}_\Sigma, 1^{n(\lambda)}, r_{i,0})$ and $c_{i,1} = \mathsf{Com}(\mathsf{crs}_\Sigma, 0^{n(\lambda)}, r_{i,1})$. As $\mathsf{Verify}(\mathsf{crs}, x, \pi^*) = 1$, we can conclude that the measurement outcomes are accepted, i.e., $v_i = 1$ for all $i \in [n]$. According to the definition of $U$ in Eq. 5, each commitment $c_{i,b}$ is statistically bound to the message $b$. Thus, $w^*$ must include a satisfying witness $w$ for $R$; otherwise, the statistical binding property of the commitment scheme can be broken by running $\mathsf{Ext\text{-}Del}$ to obtain one of the openings and measuring $|\psi\rangle$ in the standard basis to obtain the other opening for the same commitment value.

Then, as $(x, w) \in R$, the adversary needs to output a valid $\mathsf{cert} = \{d_i\}_{i\in[n]}$ to pass the experiment, that is, $\forall i \in [n], d_i \cdot (r_{i,0} \oplus r_{i,1}) = u_i$. In this case, measuring $|\psi\rangle$ in the standard basis yields $\{r_{i,b}\}_{i\in[n]}$ such that $c_{i,0} = \mathsf{Com}(\mathsf{crs}_\Sigma, b^{n(\lambda)}, r_{i,b})$; This contradicts the adaptive hard-core bit property. More precisely, we can build an algorithm $\mathcal{B}$ to break adaptive hard-core bit, where on input $\{c_{i,b}\}_{i\in[n],b\in\{0,1\}}$, $|\psi\rangle = \otimes_{i\in[n]} \frac{|r_{i,0}\rangle + (-1)^{u_i}|r_{i,1}\rangle}{\sqrt{2}}$, for an instance $x$, queries $x^* = (x, \{c_{i,b}\}_{i\in[n],b\in\{0,1\}})$ to $\Pi.\mathsf{Sim}_1$ and obtains a proof $\sigma$, generates $\pi := (\{c_{i,b}\}_{i\in[n],b\in\{0,1\}}, \sigma, |\psi\rangle)$, and queries $(x, \pi)$ to $\mathcal{A}_1$ to receive an accepting proof $\pi^*$ and a valid certificate $\mathsf{cert}$. $\mathcal{B}$ can parse $\pi^*$ as $\{c^*_{i,b}\}_{i\in[n],b\in\{0,1\}}, \sigma^*, |\psi^*\rangle$ and $\mathsf{cert}$ as $\{d_i\}_{i\in[n]}$. Measuring $|\psi^*\rangle$ in the standard basis yields $\{r^*_i\}_{i\in[n]}$ such that $c^*_{i,0} = \mathsf{Com}(\mathsf{crs}_\Sigma, 0^{n(\lambda)}, r^*_i)$ or $c^*_{i,1} = \mathsf{Com}(\mathsf{crs}_\Sigma, 1^{n(\lambda)}, r^*_i)$. $\mathcal{B}$ returns $\{(b_i, r^*_i, d_i)\}_{i\in[n]}$ to pass the experiment. This completes the proof.

## 5.2 NIZK-CD with a Classical Prover

In this section, we present our NIZK-CD with a classical prover.

**Theorem 5.2.** *Assuming quantum hardness of LWE and any quantum-secure simulation-extractable NIZK, there exists a simulation-extractable NIZK-CD s.t. the prover algorithm is classical.*

*Proof.* Based on the LWE assumption there is a statistically binding, computationally hiding, and computationally equivocal commitment scheme [35] that we denote by $\Sigma = \langle \mathsf{Setup}, \mathsf{Com}\rangle$. Let $\mathcal{F} := \{f_{k,b} : \mathcal{X} \to \mathcal{D_Y}\}_{k\in\mathcal{K},b\in\{0,1\}}$ be an NTCF family. Let $\Pi = \langle \mathsf{Setup}, \mathsf{Prove}, \mathsf{Verify}\rangle$ be a simulation-extractable NIZK. Our NIZK-CD construction with classical prover is described as follows.

- $(\mathsf{crs}, \mathsf{td}) \leftarrow \mathsf{Setup}(1^\lambda)$: $\mathsf{crs}_\Sigma, \mathsf{td}_\Sigma \leftarrow \Sigma.\mathsf{Setup}(1^\lambda)$ and $\mathsf{crs}_\Pi, \mathsf{td}_\Pi \leftarrow \Pi.\mathsf{Setup}(1^\lambda)$, and output the parameters $\mathsf{crs} := (\mathsf{crs}_\Sigma, \mathsf{crs}_\Pi)$ and $\mathsf{td} := (\mathsf{td}_\Sigma, \mathsf{td}_\Pi)$.
- $(\mathsf{ck}, \pi) \leftarrow \mathsf{Prove}(\mathsf{crs}, x, w)$: For $n(\lambda), \ell(\lambda)$, it proceeds in two phases.

**State preparation:** The prover and verifier run the following.

1. The prover runs $\mathsf{NTCF.Gen}_\mathcal{F}$ to generate $\{k_i\}_{i\in[n]}$, $\{\mathsf{td}_{k_i}\}_{i\in[n]}$, and sends the keys to the verifier. The verifier prepares the state

$$|\phi\rangle := \bigotimes_{i\in[n]} \frac{1}{\sqrt{|\mathcal{X}|}} \sum_{x\in\mathcal{X}} |0\rangle|x\rangle + |1\rangle|x\rangle. \tag{6}$$

From Definition 3.4, $|\phi'\rangle$ can be turned into the following superposition.

$$|\phi'\rangle := \bigotimes_{i\in[n]} \frac{1}{\sqrt{2|\mathcal{X}|}} \sum_{x\in\mathcal{X},y\in\mathcal{Y}} \sqrt{(f'_{k_i,0}(x))(y)}|0\rangle|x\rangle|y\rangle$$
$$+ \frac{1}{\sqrt{2|\mathcal{X}|}} \sum_{x\in\mathcal{X},y\in\mathcal{Y}} \sqrt{(f'_{k_i,1}(x))(y)}|1\rangle|x\rangle|y\rangle \quad (7)$$

The verifier measures the images in the standard basis, obtaining the results $\{y_i\}$ and state

$$\bigotimes_{i\in[n]} \frac{1}{\sqrt{2}} \left(|0\rangle|x_{i,0}\rangle + |1\rangle|x_{i,1}\rangle\right). \quad (8)$$

Here, for all $i \in [n]$, the tuple $(x_{i,0}, x_{i,1}) \in \mathcal{X}^2$ is a claw with respect to the measured image $y_i \in \mathcal{Y}$. Finally, the verifier sends the images $\{y_i\}_{i\in[n]}$ to the prover and applies the injection $J : \mathcal{X} \to \{0,1\}^{\ell(\lambda)}$, as defined in Definition 3.4, to the above superposition and prepares the state $|\psi\rangle$ as

$$|\psi\rangle := \bigotimes_{i\in[n]} \frac{1}{2} \left(|0\rangle|r_{i,0}\rangle + |1\rangle|r_{i,1}\rangle\right)$$
$$\forall i \in [n], b \in \{0,1\} : r_{i,b} = J(x_{i,b}). \quad (9)$$

2. For $i \in [n]$, $b \in \{0,1\}$, the prover runs $\mathsf{Inv}(\mathsf{td}_k, b, y_i)$ and $J(x_{i,b})$ to get $r_{i,b}$.

**Proof Generation:** The remaining parts are similar to the construction in the previous section. The prover generates $c_{i,b} = \mathsf{Com}(\mathsf{crs}_\Sigma, b^{n(\lambda)}, r_{i,b})$ for all $i \in [n], b \in \{0,1\}$. Given $x^* := (x, \{c_{i,b}\})$, $w^* := (w, \{r_{i,b}\})$, the prover runs $\Pi.\mathsf{Prove}(\mathsf{crs}, x^*, w^*)$ and generates a NIZK proof $\sigma$ for $R^*$, as defined in Eq. 1. It outputs $\{c_{i,b}\}_{i\in[n],b\in\{0,1\}}, \sigma$ and $\mathsf{ck} = \{r_{i,b}\}_{i\in[n],b\in\{0,1\}}$.

In the following, define $\pi = (\{c_{i,b}\}_{i\in[n],b\in\{0,1\}}, \sigma, |\psi\rangle)$. Note that $|\psi\rangle$ is needed for verification, but the prover never needs access to it.

- $\{0,1\} \leftarrow \mathsf{Verify}(\mathsf{crs}, x, \pi)$: The verifier runs $v_\sigma \leftarrow \Pi.\mathsf{Verify}(\mathsf{crs}, x^*, \sigma)$. Let $U'_{c_0,c_1}$ and $U$ be as before (cf. Equation 3). Using $U$, the state in Eq. 5 is prepared. Then, the verifier for all $i \in [n]$, measures the commit-and-compare registers $v_i = \mathsf{Cmt\text{-}Cmp}(\mathsf{crs}_\Sigma, 0, r_{i,0}, c_{i,0})$. The outcome is $v = v_\sigma \bigwedge_{i\in[n]} v_i$.
- $\mathsf{cert} \leftarrow \mathsf{Delete}(\pi)$: The proof $\pi$ is parsed as $\{c_{i,b}\}_{i\in[n],b\in\{0,1\}}, \sigma, |\psi\rangle$ and also the state $|\psi\rangle$ as $\bigotimes_{i\in[n]}|\psi_i\rangle$ such that $|\psi_i\rangle = \sum_{b\in\{0,1\}} \frac{1}{2}|b\rangle|r_{i,b}\rangle$. The verifier then for all $i \in [n]$ measures the state $|\psi_i\rangle$ in the Hadamard basis to get strings $d_i \in \{0,1\}^{\ell(\lambda)}$ such that $d_i \cdot (r_{i,0} \oplus r_{i,1}) = 0$. We define $\mathsf{cert} := \{d_i\}_{i\in[n]}$.
- $\{0,1\} \leftarrow \mathsf{Certify}(\mathsf{ck}, \mathsf{cert})$: The key $\mathsf{ck}$ is parsed as $\{r_{i,b}\}_{i\in[n],b\in\{0,1\}}$ and $\mathsf{cert}$ as $\{d_i\}_{i\in[n]}$. Validate whether for all $i \in [n]$ it holds $d_i \cdot (r_{i,0} \oplus r_{i,1}) = 0$.

Then, we prove each of the security properties of our NIZK-CD. Reductions for perfect completeness, adaptive multi-theorem computational zero-knowledge, and simulation extractability with deletion work basically similar to Sect. 5.1.

**Perfect Completeness:** Again, we first show completeness with respect to proof verification and then certificate validation. Consider the former case. The perfect completeness of $\Pi$ ensures that $v_\sigma = 1$ with a probability of 1. As the inversion function $\mathsf{Inv}$ and the map $J$ are deterministic, the randomnesses computed by the prover using trapdoor $\mathsf{td}_k$ and the map $J$ are the same as the randomnesses encoded in the state $|\psi\rangle$. Moreover, as $\mathsf{Com}$ is deterministic and the commitments are generated honestly, we have $\mathsf{Cmt\text{-}Cmp}(\mathsf{crs}_\Sigma, b_i, r_{i,b}, c_{i,b}) = 1$. For all $i \in [n]$, $v_i$ is measured as 1. For completeness with respect to deletion, we have $|\psi\rangle = \bigotimes_{i\in[n]} |\psi_i\rangle$, s.t. $|\psi_i\rangle = \sum_{b\in\{0,1\}} \frac{1}{2}|b\rangle|r_{i,b}\rangle$. The verifier measures each $|\psi_i\rangle$ in the Hadamard basis to obtain $d_i \in \{0,1\}^{\ell(\lambda)}$, where $d_i \cdot (r_{i,0} \oplus r_{i,1}) = 0$.

**Adaptive Multi-Theorem Computational Zero-Knowledge:** Algorithms $\Pi.\mathsf{Sim} = (\Pi.\mathsf{Sim}_0, \Pi.\mathsf{Sim}_1)$ are simulators of $\Pi$. $\mathsf{Sim} = (\mathsf{Sim}_0, \mathsf{Sim}_1)$ is as:

- $(\mathsf{crs}, \mathsf{td}) \leftarrow \mathsf{Sim}_0(1^\lambda)$ : Run the algorithms $(\mathsf{crs}_\Pi, \mathsf{td}_\Pi) \leftarrow \Pi.\mathsf{Sim}_1(1^\lambda)$ and $(\mathsf{crs}_\Sigma, \mathsf{td}_\Sigma) \leftarrow \Sigma.\mathsf{Setup}(1^\lambda)$. Output $\mathsf{crs} := (\mathsf{crs}_\Pi, \mathsf{crs}_\Sigma)$ and $\mathsf{td} := (\mathsf{td}_\Pi, \mathsf{td}_\Sigma)$.
- $(\pi, \mathsf{ck}) \leftarrow \mathsf{Sim}_1(\mathsf{crs}, \mathsf{td}, x)$ : Run $\mathsf{NTCF.Gen}_\mathcal{F}$, generate $\{k'_i\}_{i\in[n]}$, $\{\mathsf{td}_{k'_i}\}_{i\in[n]}$, and send the key $k'$ to the adversary. For all $i \in [n]$, on input the image $y'_i \in \mathcal{Y}$, compute $x'_{i,0} \leftarrow \mathsf{Inv}(\mathsf{td}_{k'}, 0, y'_i)$ and $x'_{i,1} \leftarrow \mathsf{Inv}(\mathsf{td}_{k'}, 1, y'_i)$, and the randomnesses $r'_{i,0} = J(x'_{i,0})$ and $r'_{i,1} = J(x'_{i,1})$. Compute $\forall i \in [n], \forall b \in \{0,1\}$, $c'_{i,b} = \mathsf{Com}(\mathsf{crs}_\Sigma, b^{n(\lambda)}, r'_{i,b})$. Let $x^* := (x, \{c'_{i,b}\}_{i\in[n],b\in\{0,1\}})$. Query $\Pi.\mathsf{Sim}_1$ on input $x^*$ to get a proof $\sigma'$. Prepare $|\psi'\rangle$, as in Eq. 9, and output the proof $\pi := (\{c'_{i,b}\}_{i\in[n],b\in\{0,1\}}, \sigma', |\psi'\rangle)$ and the certificate $\mathsf{ck} := \{u'_i, r'_{i,b}\}_{i\in[n],b\in\{0,1\}}$.

  Reduction: It proceeds similarly to the reduction in Sect. 5.1. The additional note is that the keys $k'$ are uniformly sampled by $\mathsf{NTCF.Gen}_\mathcal{F}$; therefore, they are indistinguishable from the real key $k$.

**Simulation Extractability with Deletion:** We can build an extractor $\mathsf{Ext\text{-}Del}$ that satisfies simulation extractibility with deletion and present the reduction the same as Sect. 5.1. The adaptive hard-core bit property of NTCF hash functions, as defined in Definition 3.4, prevents the adversary from deviating from the protocol. Otherwise, one can use adversary $\mathcal{A}$ to violate at least one of these properties: the statistical binding of the commitment, the simulation extractability of $\Pi$, or the adaptive hard-core bit of the NTCF functions.

# 6 Applications

In this section, we discuss applications of NIZK-CD to signatures of knowledge and anonymous credentials with certified deletion.

## 6.1 Signature of Knowledge with Certified Deletion

We formalize and construct the signature of knowledge with certified deletion. This primitive enables the recipient of a signature of knowledge to delete it and generate a deletion certificate. The certificate serves as proof that the recipient no longer retains access to a valid signature.

**Definition 6.1.** *[Signature of Knowledge with Certified Deletion] For a relation $R$ and a message space $\mathcal{M}$, $\Sigma_R = \langle \mathsf{Setup}, \mathsf{Sign}, \mathsf{Verify}, \mathsf{Delete}, \mathsf{Certify} \rangle$ is a signature of knowledge with certified deletion if it satisfies the following.*

- $(\mathsf{crs}, \mathsf{td}) \leftarrow \mathsf{Setup}(1^\lambda)$ : *on input* $\lambda$, *output* $\mathsf{crs}$ *and trapdoor* $\mathsf{td}$.
- $(\sigma, \mathsf{ck}) \leftarrow \mathsf{Sign}(\mathsf{crs}, x, w, m)$ : *on input* $\mathsf{crs}$, $(x, w) \in R$, $m \in \mathcal{M}$, *output a signature of knowledge* $\sigma$ *and a certification key* $\mathsf{ck}$.
- $\{0,1\} \leftarrow \mathsf{Verify}(\mathsf{crs}, x, m, \sigma)$ : *on input* $\mathsf{crs}$, $x$, $m$, $\sigma$, *accept or reject.*
- $\mathsf{cert} \leftarrow \mathsf{Delete}(\sigma)$: *on input* $\sigma$, *output a deletion certificate* $\mathsf{cert}$.
- $\{0,1\} \leftarrow \mathsf{Certify}(\mathsf{ck}, \mathsf{cert})$: *on input* $\mathsf{ck}$ *and* $\mathsf{cert}$, *output accept or reject.*

***Correctness:*** *For every $\lambda \in \mathbb{N}$, pair $(x, w) \in R$ and message $m \in \mathcal{M}$,*

$$\Pr\left[\begin{array}{c} \mathsf{crs} \leftarrow \mathsf{Setup}(1^\lambda) \\ (\sigma, \mathsf{ck}) \leftarrow \mathsf{Sign}(\mathsf{crs}, x, w, m) \\ \mathsf{cert} \leftarrow \mathsf{Delete}(\sigma) \end{array} : \begin{array}{c} \mathsf{Verify}(\mathsf{crs}, x, m, \sigma) = 1 \\ \wedge \\ \mathsf{Certify}(\mathsf{ck}, \mathsf{cert}) = 1 \end{array}\right] = 1.$$

***Simulation:*** *There is a* QPT *simulator* $\mathsf{Sim} = (\mathsf{Sim}_0, \mathsf{Sim}_1)$ *such that for every* QPT *algorithm* $\mathcal{A}$,

$$\Big| \Pr\left[\mathsf{crs} \leftarrow \mathsf{Setup}(1^\lambda) : \mathcal{A}^{\mathsf{Sign}(\mathsf{crs},\cdot,\cdot,\cdot)}(\mathsf{crs}) = 1\right] -$$
$$\Pr\left[(\mathsf{crs}, \mathsf{td}) \leftarrow \mathsf{Sim}_0(1^\lambda) : \mathcal{A}^{\mathsf{Sim}_1(\mathsf{crs},\mathsf{td},\cdot,\cdot,\cdot)}(\mathsf{crs}) = 1\right] \Big| \leq \mathsf{negl}(\lambda).$$

*where* $\mathsf{Sim}_1$ *discards its fifth input value.*

***Extraction with Deletion:*** *Let* $\mathsf{Sim} = (\mathsf{Sim}_0, \mathsf{Sim}_1)$ *be from the simulation property. There is a* QPT *extractor algorithm* $\mathsf{Ext\text{-}Del}$ *such that for every* QPT *algorithm* $\mathcal{A} = (\mathcal{A}_0, \mathcal{A}_1)$,

$$\Pr\left[\begin{array}{c} (\mathsf{crs}, \mathsf{td}) \leftarrow \mathsf{Sim}_0(1^\lambda) \\ (x, m) \leftarrow \mathcal{A}_0^{\mathsf{Sim}_1(\mathsf{crs},\mathsf{td},\cdot,\cdot)}(\mathsf{crs}) \\ (\sigma, \mathsf{ck}) \leftarrow \mathsf{Sim}_1(\mathsf{crs}, \mathsf{td}, x, m) \\ (\sigma^*, \mathsf{cert}) \leftarrow \mathcal{A}_1^{\mathsf{Sim}_1(\mathsf{crs},\mathsf{td},\cdot,\cdot)}(\mathsf{crs}, \sigma) \\ w \leftarrow \mathsf{Ext\text{-}Del}(\mathsf{crs}, \mathsf{td}, x, m, \sigma^*, \mathsf{cert}) \end{array} : \right.$$
$$\left. \begin{array}{c} \mathsf{Verify}(\mathsf{crs}, x, m, \sigma^*) = 1 \\ \wedge \\ [\mathsf{Certify}(\mathsf{ck}, \mathsf{cert}) = 1 \vee (x, w) \notin R] \wedge (x, m) \notin Q \end{array}\right] \leq \mathsf{negl}(\lambda),$$

*where $Q$ is the list of queries from $\mathcal{A}$ to* $\mathsf{Sim}_1$.

*Remark 6.2.* Similarly to NIZK-CD, in our constructions, $\mathsf{Setup}$ and $\mathsf{Certify}$ are classical, while $\mathsf{Sign}$, $\mathsf{Verify}$, and $\mathsf{Delete}$ are quantum algorithms. Except for $\sigma$, which includes quantum information, other parameters are classical. Moreover, $\mathsf{Sign}$ might be interactive between a classical signer and a quantum verifier.

*Remark 6.3.* Extraction with deletion as defined in Definition 6.1 implies extraction as defined in Definition 3.17; this can be proved similarly to Theorem 4.5.

**Theorem 6.4.** *Assuming any non-interactive simulation-extractable, adaptive multi-theorem computational zero-knowledge with certified deletion, there exists a signature of knowledge with certified deletion.*

*Proof.* Let $\Gamma = \langle \mathsf{Setup}, \mathsf{Prove}, \mathsf{Verify}, \mathsf{Delete}, \mathsf{Certify} \rangle$ be a simulation-extractable NIZK-CD. We build a signature of knowledge with certified deletion as below.

- $\mathsf{crs} \leftarrow \mathsf{Setup}(1^\lambda)$: Output $\mathsf{crs} \leftarrow \Gamma.\mathsf{Setup}(1^\lambda)$.
- $(\sigma, \mathsf{ck}) \leftarrow \mathsf{Sign}(\mathsf{crs}, x, w, m)$: Let $x^* = (x, m)$ be instance, $w^* = w$ witness for
$$L^* = \{(x, m) : \exists w \text{ s.t. } (x, w) \in R\}.$$
Then, we have $(\sigma, \mathsf{ck}) \leftarrow \Gamma.\mathsf{Prove}(\mathsf{crs}, x^*, w^*)$ with respect to $L^*$.
- $\{0,1\} \leftarrow \mathsf{Verify}(\mathsf{crs}, x, m, \sigma)$: Given $x^* = (x, m)$, output $v = \Gamma.\mathsf{Verify}(\mathsf{crs}, x^*, \sigma)$.
- $\mathsf{cert} \leftarrow \mathsf{Delete}(\sigma)$: Output $\mathsf{cert} = \Gamma.\mathsf{Delete}(\sigma)$.
- $\{0,1\} \leftarrow \mathsf{Certify}(\mathsf{ck}, \mathsf{cert})$: Output $v = \Gamma.\mathsf{Certify}(\mathsf{ck}, \mathsf{cert})$.

Next, we prove the correctness, simulation, and extraction with deletion.

***Correctness:*** Since the scheme $\Gamma$ satisfies perfect completeness, for any honestly generated $\sigma$ and cert, both satisfy Verify and Certify, respectively.

***Simulation:*** Let $\Gamma.Sim = (\Gamma.Sim_0, \Gamma.\mathsf{Sim}_1)$ be the simulators of $\Gamma$. We build $\mathsf{Sim} = (\mathsf{Sim}_0, \mathsf{Sim}_1)$ for our construction as follows.

- $(\mathsf{crs}, \mathsf{td}) \leftarrow \mathsf{Sim}_0(1^\lambda)$ : Output $(\mathsf{crs}_\Gamma, \mathsf{td}_\Gamma) \leftarrow \Gamma.\mathsf{Sim}_1(1^\lambda)$.
- $\sigma, \mathsf{ck} \leftarrow \mathsf{Sim}_1(\mathsf{crs}, \mathsf{td}, x, m)$ : Output $(\sigma, \mathsf{ck}) \leftarrow \Gamma.\mathsf{Sim}_1(\mathsf{crs}, \mathsf{td}, x^* := (x, m))$.

<u>Reduction:</u> Suppose a QPT adversary $\mathcal{A}$ exists such that for polynomial $p(\lambda)$, it breaks the simulation property of $\Sigma_R$ with an advantage greater than $\frac{1}{p(\lambda)}$. We construct a QPT adversary $\mathcal{B}$ for the zero-knowledge property of $\Gamma$ as follows.

1. Receive real or simulated $\mathsf{crs}_\Gamma$ and send it to the adversary $\mathcal{A}$.
2. For each query $(x, m, w)$, define $x^* := (x, m)$ and witness $w^* := w$, receive the signature $\sigma$ by a query to Sign or $\Gamma.\mathsf{Sim}_1$, and send $\sigma$ to $\mathcal{A}$.
3. Output the result of $\mathcal{A}$.

$\mathcal{B}$ has the same advantage $\frac{1}{p(\lambda)}$ in breaking the zero-knowledge property of $\Gamma$.

***Extraction with Deletion:*** Let $\Gamma.\mathsf{Sim} = (\Gamma.\mathsf{Sim}_0, \Gamma.\mathsf{Sim}_1)$ be the simulators of $\Gamma$ and $\mathsf{Sim} = (\mathsf{Sim}_0, \mathsf{Sim}_1)$ be the simulators of our construction. Let $\Gamma.\mathsf{Ext}$ be the extractor of $\Gamma$. We show an extractor Ext-Del for extractibility with deletion.

1. On input crs, td, $x$, $m$, $\sigma$, and cert, run $\Pi.\mathsf{Ext}(\mathsf{crs}, \mathsf{td}, (x, m), \sigma, \mathsf{cert})$, and receive the witness $w^*$.
2. Output $w^*$ as $w$.

Reduction: Let $A = (A_0, A_1)$ a QPT algorithm such that given the extractor Ext-Del, and a polynomial $p(\lambda)$, it breaks the extraction with deletion property of $\Sigma_R$ with an advantage greater than $\frac{1}{p(\lambda)}$. Then, one can build an adversary algorithm $\mathcal{B} = (\mathcal{B}_0, \mathcal{B}_1)$ to break the simulation extractibility with deletion of $\Gamma$; $\mathcal{B}_0$ outputs $x^* = (x, m)$ from $\mathcal{A}_0$ and $\mathcal{B}_1$ outputs $(\sigma^*, \mathsf{cert})$ from $\mathcal{A}_1$.

**corollary 6.5.** *Assuming one-way functions and simulation-extractable NIZK, there exists a signature of knowledge with certified deletion.*

*Proof.* This follows from Theorem 5.1 and Theorem 6.4.

**corollary 6.6.** *Assuming LWE and simulation-extractable NIZK, there exists a signature of knowledge with certified deletion and classical signing algorithms.*

*Proof.* This follows from Theorem 5.2 and Theorem 6.4.

### 6.2 Anonymous Credentials with Certified Deletion

We construct anonymous credentials with certified deletion [30], where the recipient of a credentials can provably delete it and generate a deletion certificate, ensuring that they no longer have access to the credential.

**Definition 6.7. (Anonymous Credentials with Certified Deletion).** *A tuple of algorithms* $\langle \mathsf{Setup}, \mathsf{Sign}, \mathsf{Verify}, \mathsf{Delete}, \mathsf{Certify} \rangle$ *is an anonymous credential scheme with certified deletion with respect to a set of accesses* $\{S_\lambda\}_{\lambda \in \mathbb{N}}$ *if it satisfies the following.*

- $(\mathsf{nym}, \mathsf{sk}) \leftarrow \mathsf{IssuerSetup}(1^\lambda)$ : *output a pseudonym* nym *with a secret key* sk.
- $(\mathsf{cred}, \mathsf{ck}) \leftarrow \mathsf{Issue}(\mathsf{nym}, \mathsf{sk}, \mathsf{access})$ : *on input* nym, sk *and requested access* $\mathsf{access} \in S_\lambda$, *output an anonymous credential* cred *and a certification key* ck.
- $\{0,1\} \leftarrow \mathsf{VerifyCred}(\mathsf{nym}, \mathsf{access}, \mathsf{cred})$ : *on input* nym, access, *and* cred, *output* 1 *as accept or* 0 *as reject for validating the anonymous credentials.*
- $\mathsf{cert} \leftarrow \mathsf{Delete}(\mathsf{cred})$: *on input* cred, *output a deletion certificate* cert.
- $\{0,1\} \leftarrow \mathsf{Certify}(\mathsf{ck}, \mathsf{cert})$: *on input* ck *and* cert, *accept or reject.*

***Correctness:*** *For every* $\lambda \in \mathbb{N}$, *pair* $(x, w) \in R$ *and* $m \in \mathcal{M}$,

$$\Pr\left[\begin{array}{c} (\mathsf{nym}, \mathsf{sk}) \leftarrow \mathsf{IssuerSetup}(1^\lambda) \\ (\mathsf{cred}, \mathsf{ck}) \leftarrow \mathsf{Issue}(\mathsf{nym}, \mathsf{sk}, \mathsf{access}) \\ \mathsf{cert} \leftarrow \mathsf{Delete}(\mathsf{cred}) \end{array} : \begin{array}{c} \mathsf{VerifyCred}(\mathsf{nym}, \mathsf{access}, \mathsf{cred}) = 1 \\ \wedge \\ \mathsf{Certify}(\mathsf{ck}, \mathsf{cert}) = 1 \end{array}\right] = 1.$$

***Certified Deletion:*** *For every* QPT *algorithm* $\mathcal{A}$ *and* access, *the following* *probability is negligible:*

$$\Pr\left[\begin{array}{c}(\mathsf{nym},\mathsf{sk})\leftarrow\mathsf{IssuerSetup}(1^\lambda)\\(\mathsf{cred},\mathsf{ck})\leftarrow\mathsf{Issue}(\mathsf{nym},\mathsf{sk},\mathsf{access})\\(\mathsf{cred}^*,\mathsf{cert})\leftarrow\mathcal{A}(\mathsf{nym},\mathsf{cred})\end{array}:\begin{array}{c}\mathsf{VerifyCred}(\mathsf{nym},\mathsf{access},\mathsf{cred}^*)=1\\\wedge\mathsf{Certify}(\mathsf{ck},\mathsf{cert})=1\end{array}\right]$$

**Theorem 6.8.** *Assuming any signature of knowledge with certified deletion, there exist anonymous credentials with certified deletion.*

*Proof.* Let $(\mathcal{X},\mathcal{W})$ be some hard NP distribution. Let $\Sigma_R$ be a signature of knowledge with certified deletion. Our construction of anonymous credentials with certified deletion is presented as follows.

- $(\mathsf{nym},\mathsf{sk})\leftarrow\mathsf{IssuerSetup}(1^\lambda)$: Generate $\mathsf{crs}\leftarrow\Sigma_R.\mathsf{Setup}(1^\lambda)$, sample a pair $(x,w)\leftarrow(\mathcal{X},\mathcal{W})$, and output $\mathsf{nym}=(\mathsf{crs},x)$ and $\mathsf{sk}=w$.
- $(\mathsf{cred},\mathsf{ck})\leftarrow\mathsf{Issue}(\mathsf{nym},\mathsf{sk},\mathsf{access})$: Output $\mathsf{cred},\mathsf{ck}\leftarrow\Sigma_R.\mathsf{Sign}(\mathsf{crs},x,\mathsf{access},w)$.
- $\{0,1\}\leftarrow\mathsf{VerifyCred}(\mathsf{nym},\mathsf{access},\mathsf{cred})$: Output $v=\Gamma.\mathsf{Verify}(\mathsf{crs},x,\mathsf{access},\sigma)$.
- $\mathsf{cert}\leftarrow\mathsf{Delete}(\mathsf{cred})$: Output $\mathsf{cert}=\Gamma.\mathsf{Delete}(\sigma)$.
- $\{0,1\}\leftarrow\mathsf{Certify}(\mathsf{ck},\mathsf{cert})$: Output $v=\Gamma.\mathsf{Certify}(\mathsf{ck},\mathsf{cert})$.

Next, we prove the correctness and certified deletion of the construction.

**Correctness:** Since $\Sigma_R$ satisfies correctness, for honestly generated credentials $\mathsf{cred}$ and certificate $\mathsf{cert}$, both satisfy $\mathsf{VerifyCred}$ and $\mathsf{Certify}$, respectively.

**Certified Deletion:** Suppose that there exists a QPT adversary algorithm $\mathcal{A}$ such that for some polynomial $p(\lambda)$, it breaks certified deletion property of $\Delta$. We construct a QPT adversary $\mathcal{B}$ to break the extraction with deletion of $\Sigma_R$ as described below.

1. Receive simulated $\mathsf{crs}_{\Sigma_R}$ from $\Sigma_R.\mathsf{Sim}_0$, sample a pair $(x,w)\leftarrow(\mathcal{X},\mathcal{W})$, sample an access $\mathsf{access}$, query $\Sigma_R.\mathsf{Sim}_1$ on input $(x,\mathsf{access})$ to get $\sigma$, and send $\mathsf{nym}=(\mathsf{crs},x),\mathsf{cred}=\sigma$ to $\mathcal{A}$.
3. Output the credential $\mathsf{cred}^*$ as signature and $\mathsf{cert}$ as deletion certificate.

$\mathcal{B}$ has the same advantage $\frac{1}{p(\lambda)}$ in breaking the extraction with deletion of $\Sigma_R$.

**corollary 6.9.** *Assuming one-way functions and simulation-extractable NIZK, there exist anonymous credentials with certified deletion.*

*Proof.* This follows from Corollary 6.5 and Theorem 6.8.

**corollary 6.10.** *Assuming LWE and simulation-extractable NIZK, there exist anonymous credentials with certified deletion and classical issuer.*

*Proof.* This follows from Corollary 6.6 and Theorem 6.8.

## References


1. Aaronson, S.: Quantum copy protection and quantum money. In: 24th Annual IEEE Conference on Computational Complexity. IEEE (2009). https://doi.org/10.1109/ccc.2009.42
2. Aaronson, S., Christiano, P.: Quantum money from hidden subspaces. In: 44th Annual ACM Symposium on Theory of Computing (STOC), pp. 41–60. ACM, New York (2012). https://doi.org/10.1145/2213977.2213983
3. Aaronson, S., Liu, J., Liu, Q., Zhandry, M., Zhang, R.: New approaches for quantum copy protection. In: Malkin, T., Peikert, C. (eds.) Advances in Cryptology—Crypto 2021, pp. 526–555. Springer (2021)
4. Acar, T., Nguyen, L.: Revocation for Delegatable anonymous credentials. In: Catalano, D., Fazio, N., Gennaro, R., Nicolosi, A. (eds.) PKC 2011. LNCS, vol. 6571, pp. 423–440. Springer, Heidelberg (2011). https://doi.org/10.1007/978-3-642-19379-8_26
5. Agrawal, S., Kitagawa, F., Nishimaki, R., Yamada, S., Yamakawa, T.: Public key encryption with secure key leasing. In: Hazay, C., Stam, M. (eds.) Advances in Cryptology—Eurocrypt 2023, pp. 581–610. Springer (2023)
6. Amos, R., Georgiou, M., Kiayias, A., Zhandry, M.: One-shot signatures and applications to hybrid quantum/classical authentication. In: 52nd Annual ACM Symposium on Theory of Computing (STOC), pp. 255–268. ACM, New York (2020). https://doi.org/10.1145/3357713.3384304
7. Ananth, P., La Placa, R.L.: Secure Software Leasing. In: Canteaut, A., Standaert, F.-X. (eds.) EUROCRYPT 2021. LNCS, vol. 12697, pp. 501–530. Springer, Cham (2021). https://doi.org/10.1007/978-3-030-77886-6_17
8. Ananth, P., Poremba, A., Vaikuntanathan, V.: Revocable cryptography from learning with errors. In: Rothblum, G., Wee, H. (eds.) Theory of Cryptography, pp. 93–122. Springer (2023)
9. Bartusek, J., Goyal, V., Khurana, D., Malavolta, G., Raizes, J., Roberts, B.: Software with certified deletion. In: Joye, M., Leander, G. (eds.) Advances in Cryptology—Eurocrypt 2024, pp. 85–111. Springer (2024)
10. Bartusek, J., Khurana, D.: Cryptography with certified deletion. In: Handschuh, H., Lysyanskaya, A. (eds.) Advances in Cryptology—Crypto 2023, pp. 192–223. Springer (2023)
11. Bartusek, J., Khurana, D., Malavolta, G., Poremba, A., Walter, M.: Weakening assumptions for publicly-verifiable deletion. In: Rothblum, G., Wee, H. (eds.) Theory of Cryptography, pp. 183–197. Springer (2023)
12. Bartusek, J., Raizes, J.: Secret sharing with certified deletion. In: Reyzin, L., Stebila, D. (eds.) Advances in Cryptology—Crypto 2024, pp. 184–214. Springer (2024)
13. Belenkiy, M., Camenisch, J., Chase, M., Kohlweiss, M., Lysyanskaya, A., Sha, H.: Randomizable proofs and delegatable anonymous credentials. In: Halevi, S. (ed.) Advances in Cryptology—Crypto 2009, pp. 108–125. Springer (2009)
14. Bennett, C.H., Brassard, G.: Quantum cryptography: public key distribution and coin tossing. Theoret. Comput. Sci. **560**, 7–11 (2014). https://doi.org/10.1016/j.tcs.2014.05.025
15. Blum, M., Feldman, P., Micali, S.: Non-interactive zero-knowledge and its applications. In: 20th Annual ACM Symposium on Theory of Computing (STOC), pp. 103–112. ACM, New York (1988). https://doi.org/10.1145/62212.62222
16. Brakerski, Z., Christiano, P., Mahadev, U., Vazirani, U., Vidick, T.: A cryptographic test of quantumness and certifiable randomness from a single quantum

device. In: 2018 IEEE 59th Annual Symposium on Foundations of Computer Science (FOCS), pp. 320–331 (2018). https://doi.org/10.1109/FOCS.2018.00038
17. Broadbent, A., Islam, R.: Quantum encryption with certified deletion. In: Pass, R., Pietrzak, K. (eds.) Theory of Cryptography, pp. 92–122. Springer (2020)
18. Broadbent, A., Lord, S.: Uncloneable quantum encryption via oracles. In: Flammia, S.T. (ed.) 15th Conference on the Theory of Quantum Computation, Communication and Cryptography (TQC 2020). Leibniz International Proceedings in Informatics (LIPIcs), vol. 158, pp. 4:1–4:22. Schloss Dagstuhl – Leibniz-Zentrum für Informatik, Dagstuhl, Germany (2020). https://drops.dagstuhl.de/entities/document/10.4230/LIPIcs.TQC.2020.4
19. Çakan, A., Goyal, V., Raizes, J.: How to delete without a trace: certified deniability in a quantum world. Cryptology ePrint Archive, Paper 2024/1832 (2024). https://eprint.iacr.org/2024/1832
20. Chardouvelis, O., Goyal, V., Jain, A., Liu, J.: Quantum key leasing for PKE and FHE with classical lessor. In: Advances in Cryptology – Eurocrypt 2025: 44th Annual International Conference on the Theory and Applications of Cryptographic Techniques. Madrid, Spain, May 4–8, 2025, Proceedings, Part III, pp. 248–277. Springer-Verlag, Berlin, Heidelberg (2025)
21. Chase, M., Lysyanskaya, A.: On signatures of knowledge. In: Dwork, C. (ed.) Advances in Cryptology—Crypto 2006, pp. 78–96. Springer (2006)
22. Coladangelo, A., Majenz, C., Poremba, A.: Quantum copy protection of compute-and-compare programs in the quantum random oracle model (2022). https://ia.cr/2020/1194
23. Di Crescenzo, G., Ishai, Y., Ostrovsky, R.: Non-interactive and non-malleable commitment. In: 30th Annual ACM Symposium on Theory of Computing (STOC), pp. 141–150. ACM (1998). https://doi.org/10.1145/276698.276722
24. Feige, U., Lapidot, D., Shamir, A.: Multiple non-interactive zero knowledge proofs based on a single random string. In: 31st Annual Symposium on Foundations of Computer Science, pp. 308–317. IEEE (1990). https://doi.org/10.1109/FSCS.1990.89549
25. Gottesman, D.: Uncloneable encryption. Quantum Inf. Comput. **3**(6), 581–602 (2003)
26. Goyal, V., Malavolta, G., Raizes, J.: Unclonable commitments and proofs. In: Boyle, E., Mahmoody, M. (eds.) Theory of Cryptography, pp. 193–224. Springer Nature Switzerland, Cham (2025)
27. Helstrom, C.W.: Quantum detection and estimation theory. J. Statist. Phys. **1**, 231–252 (1969). https://doi.org/10.1007/BF01007479
28. Hiroka, T., Morimae, T., Nishimaki, R., Yamakawa, T.: Quantum encryption with certified deletion, revisited: public key, attribute-based, and classical communication. In: Tibouchi, M., Wang, H. (eds.) Advances in Cryptology—Asiacrypt 2021, pp. 606–636. Springer (2021)
29. Holevo, A.: Statistical decision theory for quantum systems. J. Multivar. Anal. **3**(4), 337–394 (1973). https://doi.org/10.1016/0047-259X(73)90028-6, https://www.sciencedirect.com/science/article/pii/0047259X73900286
30. Jawale, R., Khurana, D.: Unclonable non-interactive zero-knowledge. In: Advances in Cryptology – Asiacrypt 2024: 30th International Conference on the Theory and Application of Cryptology and Information Security. Kolkata, India, December 9–13, 2024, Proceedings, Part IX, pp. 94–128. Springer-Verlag, Berlin, Heidelberg (2024)

31. Katz, J., Sela, B.: Secret sharing with publicly verifiable deletion. In: Advances in Cryptology—Eurocrypt 2025, Part III. LNCS, vol. 15603, pp. 278–304. Springer (2025)
32. Kitagawa, F., Nishimaki, R., Yamakawa, T.: Secure software leasing from standard assumptions. In: Nissim, K., Waters, B. (eds.) Theory of Cryptography, pp. 31–61. Springer (2021)
33. Kitagawa, F., Nishimaki, R., Yamakawa, T.: Publicly verifiable deletion from minimal assumptions. In: Rothblum, G., Wee, H. (eds.) Theory of Cryptography. pp. 228–245. Springer (2023)
34. Liu, J., Liu, Q., Qian, L., Zhandry, M.: Collusion resistant copy-protection for watermarkable functionalities. In: Kiltz, E., Vaikuntanathan, V. (eds.) Theory of Cryptography, pp. 294–323. Springer (2022)
35. Lombardi, A., Schaeffer, L.: A note on key agreement and non-interactive commitments. Cryptology ePrint Archive, Paper 2019/279 (2019), https://eprint.iacr.org/2019/279
36. Morimae, T., Poremba, A., Yamakawa, T.: Revocable quantum digital signatures. In: Magniez, F., Grilo, A.B. (eds.) 19th Conference on the Theory of Quantum Computation, Communication and Cryptography (TQC 2024). Leibniz International Proceedings in Informatics (LIPIcs), vol. 310, pp. 5:1–5:24. Schloss Dagstuhl – Leibniz-Zentrum für Informatik, Dagstuhl, Germany (2024). https://doi.org/10.4230/LIPIcs.TQC.2024.5, https://drops.dagstuhl.de/entities/document/10.4230/LIPIcs.TQC.2024.5
37. Morimae, T., Yamakawa, T.: Quantum commitments and signatures without one-way functions. In: Advances in Cryptology—Crypto 2022, Part I, pp. 269–295. Springer (2022). https://doi.org/10.1007/978-3-031-15802-5_10
38. Peikert, C., Regev, O., Stephens-Davidowitz, N.: Pseudorandomness of ring-LWE for any ring and modulus. In: 49th Annual ACM SIGACT Symposium on Theory of Computing, pp. 461–473. STOC 2017, ACM, New York (2017). https://doi.org/10.1145/3055399.3055489
39. Peikert, C., Shiehian, S.: Noninteractive zero knowledge for NP from (plain) learning with errors. In: Boldyreva, A., Micciancio, D. (eds.) Advances in Cryptology—Crypto 2019, pp. 89–114. Springer (2019)
40. Poremba, A.: Quantum proofs of deletion for learning with errors. In: Tauman Kalai, Y. (ed.) 14th Innovations in Theoretical Computer Science Conference (ITCS 2023). Leibniz International Proceedings in Informatics (LIPIcs), vol. 251, pp. 90:1–90:14. Schloss Dagstuhl – Leibniz-Zentrum für Informatik, Dagstuhl, Germany (2023). https://doi.org/10.4230/LIPIcs.ITCS.2023.90, https://drops.dagstuhl.de/entities/document/10.4230/LIPIcs.ITCS.2023.90
41. Radian, R., Sattath, O.: Semi-quantum money. In: 1st ACM Conference on Advances in Financial Technologies (AFT), pp. 132–146. ACM, New York (2019). https://doi.org/10.1145/3318041.3355462
42. Regev, O.: On lattices, learning with errors, random linear codes, and cryptography. J. ACM **56**(6) (2009). https://doi.org/10.1145/1568318.1568324
43. Sahai, A.: Non-malleable non-interactive zero knowledge and adaptive chosen-ciphertext security. In: 40th Annual Symposium on Foundations of Computer Science, pp. 543–553 (1999). https://doi.org/10.1109/SFFCS.1999.814628
44. Santis, A.D., Crescenzo, G.D., Ostrovsky, R., Persiano, G., Sahai, A.: Robust non-interactive zero knowledge. In: Advances in Cryptology—Crypto 2001, pp. 566–598. Springer (2001)

45. Unruh, D.: Revocable quantum timed-release encryption. In: Nguyen, P.Q., Oswald, E. (eds.) EUROCRYPT 2014. LNCS, vol. 8441, pp. 129–146. Springer, Heidelberg (2014). https://doi.org/10.1007/978-3-642-55220-5_8
46. Wiesner, S.: Conjugate coding. SIGACT News **15**(1), 78–88 (1983). https://doi.org/10.1145/1008908.1008920

# Almost-Total Puzzles and Their Applications

Xiao Liang[1(✉)], Omkant Pandey[2], Yuhao Tang[2], and Takashi Yamakawa[3]

[1] The Chinese University of Hong Kong, Sha Tin, Hong Kong, China
xiao.crypto@gmail.com
[2] Stony Brook University, Stony Brook, USA
{omkant,yuhtang}@cs.stonybrook.edu
[3] NTT Social Informatics Laboratories, Tokyo, Japan
takashi.yamakawa@ntt.com

**Abstract.** Public-coin protocols are cryptographic protocols in which all messages sent by a specific party (typically the receiver or verifier) consist solely of random bits. These protocols have been extensively studied *in the classical setting* due to their advantageous properties in several scenarios, such as the parallel repetition of interactive arguments, and the design of secure multi-party computation with low round complexity, among others. Curiously, *post-quantum constructions* of public-coin protocols remain limited, particularly when optimization is sought in additional factors like round complexity or hardness assumptions.

We introduce the concept of *almost-total puzzles*, a novel cryptographic primitive characterized by two key properties: (i) hardness against any efficient adversary, and (ii) an "almost-total" guarantee of the existence of solutions, even when the puzzle generator is malicious. We demonstrate that this primitive can be derived from one-way functions in public-coin, requiring only two rounds. By leveraging this primitive, we obtain a family of new *public-coin* results in both the classical and post-quantum settings, based on the *minimal assumption* of (post-quantum) one-way functions, including:

- five-round post-quantum extractable commitments and witness-indistinguishable arguments of knowledge, where the (knowledge) extractors achieve the *coherently expected quantum-polynomial-time* ($\mathsf{EQPT}_c$) simulation proposed by Lombardi, Ma, and Spooner [FOCS'22];
- five-round classical extractable commitments that *do not suffer from over extraction*;

X. Liang—The work described in this paper was partially supported by a grant from the Research Grants Council of the Hong Kong Special Administrative Region, China [Project No.: CUHK 24208025].

O. Pandey—Supported in part by AFOSR Award FA9550-24-1-0156, NSF CAREER Award 2144303, NSF grants 2106263, and 2028920. Any opinions, findings and conclusions or recommendations expressed in this material are those of the author(s) and do not necessarily reflect the views of the United States Government, AFOSR, or NSF.

© International Association for Cryptologic Research 2026

G. Hanaoka and B.-Y. Yang (Eds.): ASIACRYPT 2025, LNCS 16252, pp. 411–443, 2026.
https://doi.org/10.1007/978-981-95-5125-5_14

- five-round classical delayed-input strong witness-indistinguishable arguments of knowledge, and delayed-input witness-hiding arguments of knowledge;
- the five-round post-quantum analogue of the last item, but with the difference that (1) the input can be delayed until the third round, and (2) post-quantum arguments of knowledge are again defined w.r.t. $\mathsf{EQPT}_c$-simulation;
- $O(\log^* \lambda)$-round post-quantum non-malleable commitments.

**Keywords:** Post-Quantum · Public-Coin · Extraction · Simulation · Round Complexity

## 1 Introduction

Public-coin protocols are cryptographic schemes in which all messages from a specific party, typically the verifier, consist solely of random bits. Such protocols offer distinct advantages over private-coin protocols in certain scenarios. For instance, parallel repetition can reduce the soundness error, at an exponential speed, for public-coin *interactive arguments* of an arbitrary (polynomial) number of rounds [22,23,44]. In contrast, [8] constructed a four-round *private-coin* interactive argument for which parallel repetition does not reduce the soundness error at all. Another key example is the renowned Fiat-Shamir transform [33], which applies exclusively to public-coin protocols. Additional advantages of the public-coin property are found in the literature on non-malleability and (concurrent) secure multi-party computation, particularly in the low-round-complexity settings (e.g., [21,24–26,35,36]), where the public-coin property enables rewinding-based techniques in settings where rewinding opportunities are very limited due to round constraints.

Given these valuable properties, public-coin protocols have been extensively studied *in the classical settings*. Public-coin constructions, even round-optimal and from minimal assumptions, are known for foundational cryptographic primitives such as extractable commitments (ExtCom) [65], non-malleable commitments (NMCom) [41,42] and witness-indistinguishable (WI) proofs [11,31]. Furthermore, a seminal body of work explores the limitations of zero-knowledge protocols, articulating an "impossible trinity" among constant-round complexity, black-box simulators, and public-coin verifiers [5,6,38].

**The Curious Post-quantum Case.** In contrast, public-coin protocols remain underexplored[1] in the so-called *post-quantum* setting, where honest parties and their communication channels are entirely classical, but the adversary is granted quantum computing power. Post-quantum protocols offer significant efficiency

[1] We remark that the claim here applies only to the plain model, where no trusted setup is available. There are studies that focus on lifting classical results to the post-quantum regime using trusted setups, such as (quantum-accessible) random oracles, which represents a different direction from the focus of the current work.

benefits, as they do not require honest parties to perform quantum operations. Also, they ensure that even if adversaries gain early access to quantum computing capabilities, the honest parties need not adopt quantum technologies to maintain security.

In recent years, significant progress has been made in post-quantum simulation and extraction techniques. However, somewhat unexpectedly, most of the proposed solutions rely on private-coin property, while public-coin constructions and techniques remain relatively underdeveloped, as we will elaborate next.

On Zero-Knowledge. Watrous [70] constructed the first public-coin post-quantum zero-knowledge (PQ-ZK) protocol in a polynomial[2] number of rounds. On the other hand, [18] demonstrated the impossibility of constant-round public-coin PQ-ZK,[3] unless one resorts to *non-black-box simulation* or assumes that $\mathbf{NP} \subseteq \mathbf{BQP}$. However, curiously, existing non-black-box PQ-ZK protocols [2,10] remain private-coin. This stands in contrast to the classical setting, where Barak [5] presented a method for achieving public-coin ZK in constant rounds via non-black-box simulation, complementing the impossibility result of [38].

On Simulatable Extraction. For primitives defined with *explicit* (knowledge) extractors, we emphasize that there are two different definitions in the (post-)quantum setting. A naive definition is to simply require the extractor to extract the secret from the malicious party successfully (e.g., [19,68]). Alternatively, a stronger definition will, in addition to the "successful extraction" guarantee, require the extractor to simulate the post-extraction view of the malicious party (e.g., [17]).

In the classical setting, these two definitions are essentially equivalent. However, in the (post-)quantum setting, achieving the stronger notion, referred to as *simulatable extraction*, is surprisingly non-trivial due to the quantum no-cloning theorem—it requires substantial technical ideas to enable extraction without disturbing the adversary's internal *quantum* state.

We emphasize that the stronger notion of simulatable extraction is more desirable and serves as the correct quantum analogue of the classical extraction requirement. This is particularly important because primitives such as extractable commitments and arguments of knowledge are often used as building blocks in larger protocols, such as secure two-party computation (2PC), where simulating the adversary's post-extraction view is often crucial for ensuring overall security (e.g., in constructing the 2PC simulator).

The current state-of-the-art results w.r.t. simulatable extraction are summarized in Table 1 (see Remark 1 for notations). Notably, the construction of public-coin witness-indistinguishable arguments of knowledge (WIAoK) or ExtCom

---

[2] In fact, it can be optimized to $\omega(1)$ number of rounds. We can do $O(\log \lambda)$ times parallel repetition to reduce soundness error to $1/\mathsf{poly}(\lambda)$ and then do $\omega(1)$ times sequential repetition to reduce the soundness error to $\mathsf{negl}(\lambda)$.

[3] Indeed, this (public-coin) impossibility holds even for PQ-ZK *with $\varepsilon$-simulation* which is a relaxed notion of ZK that allows for an arbitrarily small noticeable simulation error $\varepsilon$.

with standard simulation remains an open problem, *even without restrictions on (polynomial) round complexity.* If we relax the simulation requirement to $\mathsf{EQPT}_c$-simulation (see Sect. 3.1 for a more detailed comparison), constant-round constructions are known. However, these results are either private-coin or rely on assumptions stronger than the minimal, i.e., post-quantum one-way functions (PQ-OWFs). This intriguing state-of-the-art scenario raises fundamental questions:

**Question**: *In the post-quantum regime, is it possible to have public-coin simulatable extraction from the minimal assumption of PQ-OWFs? Is it possible if we relax the simulation requirement to* $\mathsf{EQPT}_c$*-simulation or* $\varepsilon$*-simulation?*

**Table 1.** Summary of Post-Quantum Simulatable Extraction (See Remark 1)

| | Citation | Round Complexity | Public-Coin | Simulation | Assumption |
|---|---|---|---|---|---|
| WIAoK | [3, Thm. 2] | $\mathsf{poly}(\lambda)$ | ✗ | standard | QLWE |
| ExtCom | [2, Sec. 5] | 7 | ✗ | standard | QFHE and more |
| WIAoK & ExtCom | [55, Thm. 1.9, Cor. 1.10] | 4 | ✓ | $\mathsf{EQPT}_c$ | Collapsing Hash |
| | [55, Thm. 1.9, Cor. 1.10] | 4 | ✓ | $\mathsf{EQPT}_c$ | super-poly OWF |
| | [55, Thm. 1.9, Cor. 1.10] | 3 | ✓ | $\mathsf{EQPT}_c$ | super-poly NIC |
| | [55, Cor. 2.7] | 12 | ✗ | $\mathsf{EQPT}_c$ | OWF |
| | Corollary 1, this work | 5 | ✓ | $\mathsf{EQPT}_c$ | OWF |

*Remark 1.* Some remarks regarding Table 1 follow:

1. It should be clear that all results presented are in the post-quantum setting, though for brevity, we omit the prefix "PQ-" in front of terms like WIAoK, OWF, etc.
2. $\mathsf{EQPT}_c$-simulation, introduced in [55], is a relaxed simulation notion. It allows the simulator to *coherently* execute expected QPT procedures, resulting in a superposition of computations with different runtimes, and then "revert" the runtime by executing the computation in reverse.

   It is worth mentioning that $\mathsf{EQPT}_c$ simulation implies $\varepsilon$*-simulation*, which is a widely accepted notion with interesting implications, such as WI and IIC (Input-Indistinguishable Computation). Therefore, all of our results remain valid and interesting even if we replace the term "$\mathsf{EQPT}_c$-simulatable" with "$\varepsilon$-simulatable" in all relevant theorems herein.
3. "NIC" in the last column of the fifth row stands for "non-interactive commitment."
4. It only includes results that were *explicitly* stated in the literature. For example, [2] built a PQ-MPC and thus must implicitly build a WIAoK as well; but we choose not to include such indirect results. This choice does not change the main message Table 1 is meant to convey.

5. Some rows may only contain a representative result of the same type. For example, [17] contains similar results as the sixth row in Table 1; [43,56] contain similar results as the first row in Table 1. We choose not to include them.

## 1.1 Our Results

In this work, we introduce a new primitive that we call *almost-total puzzles* (ATPs). To understand this notion, consider an interaction between a *sender* $G$ and a *receiver* $R$. At the end of their interaction, $G$ and $R$ agree on a puzzle. This puzzle is required to satisfy the following two properties:

- **Hard:** the generated puzzle must be hard to solve for any *efficient* $R$, *even if* $R$ *behaves maliciously while interacting with* $G$.
- **Almost-total:** a solution for the generated puzzle is guaranteed to exist except for with negligible probability, *even if* $G$ *behaves maliciously while interacting with* $R$.

Intuitively, the notion of ATP is useful because it sets up a hard problem for which a "trapdoor" (i.e., solution) is guaranteed to exist. As a veteran may already notice, this represents a versatile gadget that would be useful in settings like the Feige-Lapidot-Shamir (FLS) paradigm [30–32]. It is worth mentioning that we do not require (even the honest) sender $G$ to know the solution to the generated puzzle. This is because, for typical applications such as [30–32,62], the mere existence of the solution already suffices; and this indeed applies to all the scenarios considered herein.

As will be demonstrated shortly, ATPs are particularly useful when they are *public-coin* and *round-efficient*. Fortunately, we obtain such ATPs from the minimal assumption of OWFs, in both the classical and post-quantum settings:

**Theorem 1 (Informal).** *Assuming the existence of OWFs (resp. PQ-OWFs), there exists a two-round, public-coin construction of ATPs (resp. post-quantum ATPs).*

It is also worth mentioning that when we restrict an ATP to a single round and require the existence of a solution with probability 1 (as opposed to merely overwhelming probability), then it is indeed equivalent to the existence of hard-on-average **TFNP** problems.[4] It is well-established that the average-case hardness of **TFNP** can be derived from the existence of one-way permutations or collision-resistant hash functions. Furthermore, [46] demonstrated that the existence of OWFs implies the average-case hardness of **TFNP**, under an additional derandomization assumption. Whether this derandomization assumption can be eliminated remains an open question (see [34,45]).

[4] **TFNP** stands for the complexity class of "total-function" **NP**, introduced by Megiddo and Papadimitriou [57]. It is a subclass of **FNP** with the additional property of the problem being *total*, i.e., for any instance a solution is guaranteed to exist.

In this context, Theorem 1 can be interpreted as substituting the derandomization assumption with interactions. Specifically, Theorem 1 represents a relaxed version of hard-on-average **TFNP** that permits public-coin interaction while allowing for a negligible probability of no solution existing. As we will now demonstrate, this relaxed version leads to several novel results, both in the classical and post-quantum regimes.

**1.1.1 Application I: Post-quantum Simulatable Extraction in Public-Coin** As the first application, the post-quantum almost-total puzzles (PQ-ATPs) from Theorem 1 contribute positively towards addressing the earlier Question regarding public-coin simulatable extraction. In particular, we demonstrate that, at the cost of three extra rounds, public-coin PQ-ATPs imply public-coin PQ-ExtCom and PQ-WIAoK, both with $\mathsf{EQPT}_c$-simulation. In light of Theorem 1, we can derive the following corollary:

**Corollary 1.** *Assuming the existence of PQ-OWFs, there exist a PQ-ExtCom and a PQ-WIAoK, both being five-round, public-coin, and* $\mathsf{EQPT}_c$*-simulatable.*

We remark that the (relaxed) $\mathsf{EQPT}_c$ simulation notion in Corollary 1 is necessary for achieving *constant-round* PQ-WIAoK and PQ-ExtCom. This necessity arises from the aforementioned impossibility result regarding constant-round PQ-ZK protocols [18], as well as the fact that both PQ-WIAoK (see [55, Section 12]) and PQ-ExtCom (see [17, Appendix A]) imply PQ-ZK.

A noteworthy aspect of Corollary 1 is that, as shown in Table 1, prior to this work, it remained unclear whether one could construct OWF-based PQ-ExtCom/PQ-WIAoK in public-coin, *even when allowing a polynomial number of rounds.*

**1.1.2 Application II: (Classical) Public-Coin ExtCom Without Over Extraction** The construction of PQ-ExtCom from PQ-OWF in Corollary 1 also applies in the classical setting. Specifically, the same construction yields a classical ExtCom base on OWFs. Notably, the resulting ExtCom does not suffer from *over-extraction.* Over-extraction means that an extractor may extract some non-$\bot$ message from an invalid commitment instead of detecting the invalidness of the commitment (i.e., when the commitment has no valid opening).

In the classical setting, the issue of over-extraction has been observed in several prior works [35,40,50]. In fact, achieving ExtCom *without over extraction* is not particularly challenging if one is open to private-coin constructions. However, insisting on a public-coin construction necessitates stronger assumptions or super-constant rounds. Remarkably, this problem remained unresolved prior to the current work. That is, our construction is the first OWF-based ExtCom that *simultaneously* achieves public-coin and constant-round properties without over-extraction. We find this result interesting on its own:

**Corollary 2.** *Assuming the existence of OWFs, there exists a five-round, public-coin construction of extractable commitment that does not suffer from over-extraction.*

**1.1.3 Application III: Strong WI and Friends** *Strong witness indistinguishability* (sWI) is an augmented notion of WI, which requires that for two indistinguishable statement distributions $\mathcal{X}_1, \mathcal{X}_2$, a proof (or argument) for statement $x_1 \leftarrow \mathcal{X}_1$ must be indistinguishable from that for statement $x_2 \leftarrow \mathcal{X}_2$. In this work, we focus on strong WI in the *delayed-input* setting [47], where the instance is determined by the prover only in the last round of the interaction. This delayed-input notion is incomparable but yet as useful as the original notion of strong WI. For scenarios where it requires to enforce "honest behavior" on participants and only requires indistinguishability-based security, (delayed-input) strong WI can be used to replace ZK. Such a replacement could benefit from a lower round complexity, bypassing impossibility results on ZK like [6,38].

For delayed-input strong WI, [47] proposed two constructions—a two-round construction based on quasi-polynomial-time secure oblivious transfers (OTs), and a three-round construction from polynomial-time secure OTs. The requirement for super-polynomial hardness in the two-round construction appears to be necessary, as noted by [51]. Furthermore, although not explicitly discussed in the literature, we observe that it is not hard to get a four-round construction from the average-case hardness of **TFNP**. Interestingly, in this low-round-complexity regime, no constructions are known from the minimal assumption of OWFs, *particularly with the public-coin requirement.* To address this gap, we present a five-round construction of delayed-input strong WI, from the existence of OWFs. Notably, our construction is public-coin, in contrast to both constructions in [47], which are private-coin.

Our result is actually stronger—we introduce a new variant of zero-knowledge called *delayed-input non-uniform ZK* (dinuZK), in our full version [53, Section 6]. This notion differs from standard ZK in two key aspects: (1) the ZK property holds against a delayed-input (malicious) verifier, and (2) the simulator is a non-uniform machine that can depend on the verifier. This notion of dinuZK serves as a versatile alternative to standard ZK for "enforcing honest behavior" in scenarios where indistinguishability-based (IND-based) security suffices (instead of requiring the "full" simulation power of ZK). For instance, it is not hard to see that dinuZK implies both delayed-input strong WI and delayed-input WH.

We construct a compiler that converts ATPs (resp. public-coin ATPs) to dinuZK (resp. public-coin dinuZK), at the cost of three extra rounds. This compiler, combined with Theorem 1, leads to the following result:

**Corollary 3.** *Assuming the existence of OWFs, there exists a five-round, public-coin construction of dinuZKAoK (and thus a delayed-input strong WIAoK and a delayed-input WHAoK).*

**Post-quantum Setting.** Ideally, one would hope for an analogous result to Corollary 3 in the post-quantum setting. But this appears challenging (see Sect. 2.2 for related discussion). Nevertheless, we introduce yet another ZK variant called *post-quantum preprocessing ZKAoK* (PQ-ppZKAoK). This variant operates in two stages: a *preprocessing stage* and a *proof stage*, where the statement only becomes available at the beginning of the proof stage. It is worth mentioning that this preprocessing variant differs from the original delayed-input notion solely in how late the instance can be delayed—if the instance can be delayed until the last round, then it is the original delayed-input protocols; if the instance can only be delayed until some rounds before the last, it corresponds to our notion of preprocessing protocols. Regarding the notion of post-quantum AoK, we require knowledge extraction with $\mathsf{EQPT}_c$ simulation (See the full version for the formal definition [53, Section 3].).

Similar to the aforementioned dinuZK, PQ-ppZKAoK is valuable because it implies post-quantum WH and strong WI, *where the instance can be delayed until the beginning of the "on-line" (i.e., proof) stage.* We remark that these preprocessing variants could be just as useful as the (original) delayed-input protocols. This is due to the canonical "non-uniform" way in which delayed-input protocols are often utilized, as further discussed in the technical overview.

We present a compiler that converts (public-coin) PQ-ATPs to (public-coin) PQ-ppZKAoK, at the cost of three extra rounds. This compiler, together with Theorem 1, leads to the following result:

**Corollary 4.** *Assuming the existence of PQ-OWFs, there exists a five-round, public-coin construction of PQ-*ppZKAoK *(and thus a preprocessing post-quantum strong WIAoK and a preprocessing PQ-WHAoK) where the knowledge extractor is* $\mathsf{EQPT}_c$*-simulatable and the preprocessing phase has two rounds.*

#### 1.1.4 Application IV: Post-quantum Non-malleability in Public-Coin

Non-malleable commitments, introduced by [28], are a type of commitment that protects against *man-in-the-middle attacks.* Specifically, they ensure that an adversary cannot produce a commitment to a related message after seeing a commitment to another message. Non-malleable commitments are a highly versatile and useful primitive. They find applications in constructing other non-malleable primitives like coin-flipping or ZK (e.g., [7,63]). Additionally, they are also closed related to information-theoretical objects like non-malleable codes and extractors (e.g., [27,29,41]). Most significantly, they serve as a critical ingredient in resolving the exact round complexity of MPC, as well as protecting such protocols against concurrent attacks (e.g., [4,12–16,20,37,39,49,58,60,62,66,71] and more).

Although non-malleable commitments have been extensively studied in the classical setting, *post-quantum* non-malleable commitments (PQ-NMCom) manage to see interesting progress only recently. [2] constructed a constant-round PQ-NMCom w.r.t. the special case of *synchronous schedules*, assuming the super-polynomial quantum hardness of Learning with Errors. In the general (i.e., asynchronous) setting, [9] obtained the first $O(\log^* \lambda)$-round construction from the minimal assumption of PQ-OWFs. More recently, [54] eventually achieved a constant number of rounds assuming PQ-OWFs. However, all these constructions are private-coin. This is in sharp contrast to the classical setting where public-coin constructions were known, and being utilized in several scenarios, for quite a while (e.g., [24–26,35]).

As the last application, we show that our public-coin PQ-ATPs lead to the first public-coin PQ-NMCom. Our starting point is the BLS construction from [9]. We observe that their use of private coins arises primarily from three factors: (1) they employ a constant-round PQ-ZK protocol to enforce the committer's honest behavior in their small tag construction; (2) their tag amplification compiler sets up an FLS-style trapdoor in a private-coin way; (3) they rely on the private-coin ExtCom construction from [17].

The main idea underpinning our result is the observation that the PQ-ZK protocol can be replaced by an FLS-style construction, and our new PQ-ATPs can serve as a public-coin "trapdoor." This PQ-ATP must occur *at the very beginning* of the whole protocol, to enable non-uniform arguments in specific steps of the security proof. We refer to the full version of this paper [53, Section 8,9] for further details. Since public-coin PQ-ATPs follow from PQ-OWFs (and so do other components we inherited from the BLS protocol), we obtain the following result.

**Corollary 5.** *Assuming the existence of PQ-OWFs, there exists a public-coin, $O(\log^* \lambda)$-round construction of PQ-NMCom.*

## 1.2 Related Work

As will be detailed in Sect. 2.1, our construction of ATPs is inspired by the prior work of [46], where the authors showed that any average-case hard **NP** problem implies an average-case hard **TFNP** problem with non-uniform verifiers. However, we would like to emphasize that [46] is primarily a complexity-theoretic work. To the best of our knowledge, it has not been applied in cryptographic contexts, nor has it been widely recognized within the cryptography community. One of the interesting aspects of our work is the identification of a concrete cryptographic application of this idea. Moreover, our work incorporates additional non-trivial ideas beyond those in [46]. These include the introduction of the notion of preprocessing zero-knowledge, as well as a non-trivial adaptation of the non-malleable commitment scheme from [9] to obtain the first public-coin protocol.

Another related idea appears in [64, Proposition 3.2], where the authors use *infinitely often* one-way functions (OWFs) to build a public-coin "2-round puzzle." We note, however, that the notion of a "2-round puzzle" in [64] differs from ours: their construction assumes an honest puzzle generator, making it easier to guarantee the existence of a puzzle solution. Roughly speaking, their approach only requires the (honest) generator to send a randomly sampled (infinitely often) UOWHF along with a collision-target preimage. In contrast, our construction must ensure the existence of a puzzle solution even in the presence of a malicious generator, which necessitates additional technical ideas.

## 2 Technical Overview

Due to space constraints, this overview focuses only on our new notions of ATPs (in Sect. 2.1) and preprocessing ZKAoK (in Sect. 2.2), which best illustrate our ideas. We will briefly mention other results in Sect. 2.3.

### 2.1 Almost-Total Puzzle

A (post-quantum) almost-total puzzle (ATP) is an interactive protocol consisting of PPT ITMs $G$ referred as a puzzle generator and $R$ referred as a puzzle receiver. Upon execution of the protocol $\langle G, R\rangle$, a transcript $\tau$, encoding the puzzle is generated. The generated puzzle must satisfy the following properties:

- **Almost-total:** A solution for puzzle $\tau$ must exist with overwhelming probability, even if $G$ is malicious during the interaction.
- **Efficiently-verifiable:** A given solution could be certified efficiently.
- **Hard:** The solution should be hard for any efficient $R$ to solve, except for negligible probability.

An ATP is *public-coin* if $G$ sends only random bits during the interaction.

**Construction.** Our construction of ATPs makes use of *universal one-way hash functions* (UOWHFs) [59], which in turn follow from OWFs, in both the classical [67] and post-quantum [1, Section 2.1] settings. In UOWHFs, the adversary $\mathcal{A}$ must fix one preimage before the hash key $k$ is chosen, then select the other preimage after seeing $k$. The probability that the two preimages collide is negligible for any efficient adversary. Note that $k$ is randomly chosen by the challenger. See the formal definition in the full version of this work [53, Section 3].

We now present the construction of a two-round public-coin ATP, which achieves classical (resp. post-quantum) security if the underlying UOWHF is classically (resp. post-quantum) secure:

1. $R$ sends $n$ uniformly random strings $x'_1, \ldots, x'_n$ in the domain of UOWHF and send them to $G$, where $n$ depends on the security parameter $\lambda$ and UOWHF.
2. $G$ samples a uniformly random string $x$ (in the domain of UOWHF) and a hash key $k$ send them to $R$.

We say that $s$ is a solution for the ATP if there exists an $i \in [n]$ s.t.

$$(h_k(s) = h_k(x_i)) \wedge (s \neq x_i), \text{ where } x_i := x \oplus x'_i.$$

It is clear from the description that our construction is public-coin and efficiently verifiable. As for hardness, since each $x_i$ is uniformly random due to the randomness of $x$ (when $G$ is honest) and hash key $k$ is sent after $R$ sent $x'_1, ..., x'_n$, therefore we can simply reduce hardness to the security of UOWHF.

As for the almost-total property, by the compressing property of UOWHF, at least half of the target has a collision. Note that, for each fixed $x$ and $k$, $x_1, \ldots, x_n$ are independently and uniformly random. Thus, for each fixed $x$ and

$k$, at least one of $x_1, \ldots, x_n$ has a collision under $k$ except for probability $2^{-n}$. By taking the union bound over all possible $x$'s and $k$'s, the probability that $G$ can choose $x$ and $k$ in such a way that none of $x_1, ..., x_n$ has a collision is at most $2^{|x|+|k|} \cdot 2^{-n}$. So if we take $n$ sufficiently large, then the collision probability will be negligible.

Our above approach is inspired by [46], where they showed that any average-case hard **NP** problem implies average-case hard **TFNP** problem with non-uniform verifiers. Intuitively. the non-uniformity is used to hardwire the good choice of $x'_1, \ldots, x'_n$ in the above idea. Then, [46] argued how to remove the non-uniformity using an additional derandomization assumption. In our construction, it is the interactions between $G$ and $R$ that remove the non-uniformity. It is worth noting that we could instantiate the above construction with any average-case hard **NP** problem, though this offers no additional benefits since OWFs are already a necessary component for all our applications.

### 2.2 Post-quantum Preprocessing ZKAoK

We define a new notion called (post-quantum) preprocessing zero-knowledge arguments of knowledge (ppZKAoK). Essentially, ppZKAoK protocols consist of two stages: a *preprocessing stage* and a *prove stage*. During the preprocessing stage, the prover and verifier interact without any knowledge of the statement that will eventually be proven. The statement will become available at the beginning of the prove stage. This structure extends the concept of *delayed-input* protocols, and its completeness and arguments of knowledge properties are defined similarly to those in delayed-input AoK protocols.[5]

However, the ZK property is defined differently within this preprocessing framework, which we refer to as *preprocessing zero-knowledge* (ppZK)—we allow a two-stage simulator $\mathcal{S}$: an unbounded-time machine $\mathcal{S}_0$ with polynomial-size output and a QPT machine $\mathcal{S}_1$. $\mathcal{S}_0$ takes as input a transcript $\mathsf{pp}$ generated by $P$ and $V^*(\rho)$ in the preprocessing stage, and outputs $\mathcal{S}_0(\mathsf{pp})$. Once the prove stage begins, $\mathcal{S}_1$ takes both $\mathcal{S}_0(\mathsf{pp})$ and the instance $x$ as input to finish the simulation. The ppZK property requires that $\mathcal{S}_1^{V^*(\rho')}(\mathcal{S}_0(\mathsf{pp}), x)$ is indistinguishable from the output of a real execution between $P(w)$ and $V^*(\rho)$ after the prove stage.

This preprocessing zero-knowledge (ppZK) property is sufficient in various settings where the instance is provided to the verifier after preprocessing. Indeed, it implies useful properties such as strong WI and WH, *both with preprocessing* (Definition 3 and 4), as well as *standard* WI (without preprocessing). We refer the reader to Sect. 5.2 for a detailed discussion of the implications of ppZKAoK and its relationship with standard ZKAoK.

**Construction.** We show that our public-coin PQ-ATP implies a five-round, *public-coin* ppZKAoK scheme with $\mathsf{EQPT}_c$ simulation. Additionally, our construction uses Naor's commitment scheme and a PQ-WIPoK with $\mathsf{EQPT}_m$-

[5] In the post-quantum setting, we require knowledge extraction with $\mathsf{EQPT}_c$ simulation.

guaranteed-extraction property [55] (which also follow from PQ-OWFs). Let us first recall these notions.

$\mathsf{EQPT}_m$ stands for measured-runtime expected quantum polynomial-time. It is a class of quantum simulators that run for an expected polynomial number of steps when executed as follows: at each step, the simulator applies a fixed, constant-size quantum circuit $U$, followed by a measurement to determine whether to halt or perform another step. In contrast, $\mathsf{EQPT}_c$ stands for coherent-runtime expected quantum polynomial-time, which is introduced by [55] as an alternative model for post-quantum simulation. Roughly speaking, an $\mathsf{EQPT}_c$ computation can run an $\mathsf{EQPT}_m$ procedure coherently, perform some operation on the result, and then apply the inverse of the same procedure. It does not measure when it halts so that computational branches with different runtime can interfere with each other.

We say a PQ-WIPoK has $\mathsf{EQPT}_m$-guaranteed-extraction property if there exist an $\mathsf{EQPT}_m$ machine $\mathcal{GE}$ that satisfies the following property: We first run the malicious prover $P^*$ coherently and measure the decision bit of the honest verifer; if the verifer accepts, then we can run $\mathcal{GE}$ to extract a value $v$. The guaranteed-extraction property ensures that when the verifier accepts, the extracted $v$ is the a valid witness, except for with negligible probability.

With these components, our PQ-$\mathsf{ppZKAoK}$ works as follows:

1. In the preprocessing stage, prover $P$ and verifier $V$ run a PQ-ATP, with $P$ acting as the puzzle receiver $R$ and $V$ acting as the puzzle sender $G$. If the execution completes without aborting, they jointly generate a valid puzzle $\tau$;
2. In the prove stage, $P$ first sends a commitment $\mathsf{c}$ to the witness $w$ of the statement $x$, using Naor's commitment. Then, they run a PQ-WIPoK with guaranteed-extraction, where $P$ proves that either it "knows" a solution for $\tau$ or $\mathsf{c}$ is a commitment of a valid witness $w \in \mathcal{R_L}(x)$.

It is clear from the description that our protocol is complete and public-coin, and we refer the reader to Sect. 6 for a discussion about round complexity. We now focus on the preprocessing ZK and adaptive post-quantum AoK with $\mathsf{EQPT}_c$-simulation properties.

For Preprocessing ZK: By the almost-total property of ATP, a solution for $\tau$ exists with overwhelming probability. Since $\mathcal{S}_0$ is an unbounded-time machine, it can find a solution $s$ for $\tau$ with overwhelming probability. In the prove stage, $\mathcal{S}_1$ commits to 0 and uses $s$ as the witness for the PQ-WIPoK. By the (non-uniform) WI of the PQ-WIPoK and the (non-uniform) hiding property of Naor's commitment scheme, the simulated view is indistinguishable from the verifier's view in a real execution.

For Adaptive AoK with $\mathsf{EQPT}_c$-Simulation: Our goal is to construct a post-quantum witness-extended extractor $\mathcal{WE}$ that extracts the witness from any successful prover, while simulating the post-extraction state with $\mathsf{EQPT}_c$-simulation (see Definition 2 for a formal definition). Roughly speaking, machine $\mathcal{WE}$ first *coherently* runs the $\mathsf{EQPT}_m$-guaranteed-extractor $\mathcal{GE}$ we assumed from the PQ-wIPoK. That is, $\mathcal{WE}$ applies the unitary dilation $U_{\mathcal{GE}}$ of $\mathcal{GE}$, measures to obtain the witness, and then applies the inverse $U_{\mathcal{GE}}^{\dagger}$. Finally, $\mathcal{WE}$ measures and outputs the internal state of the malicious prover. By the guaranteed extraction property, the probability that the verifier accepts the proof but the extracted value is not a witness for the OR-composed language is very small. Also, by the hardness property of ATPs, the probability that the verifier accepts the proof but the extracted value is not a witness of instance $x$ is negligible. Finally, we rely on the statistical binding property of Naor's commitment, which essentially guarantees that the value extracted by $\mathcal{WE}$ is fixed with overwhelming probability. Consequently, by the gentle measurement lemma, the extraction process only negligibly alters the internal state of the malicious prover. For other nuances related to this argument, we refer readers to Sect. 6.3.

### 2.3 On Other Results

We briefly mention other results.

PQ-ppZKAoK also implies post-quantum strong WIAoK and WHAoK, *both in the preprocessing setting*, as well as standard PQ-WIAoK (i.e., in the "non-preprocessing" setting). For further details, see Sect. 5.2.

The construction of our (classical) dinuZKAoK (as per Corollary 3) follows the same construction as the above PQ-ppZKAoK, except that the PQ-WIPoK is replaced by a delayed-input WIPoK, which can be built from OWFs [52]. A formal treatment is provided in the full version of this work [53, Section 6].

Our PQ-ExtCom (see Corollary 1) is constructed by adding Naor's commitment between the preprocessing and prove stages of the PQ-ppZKAoK from Sect. 2.2, with the committer proving that it knows the value inside Naor's commitment. Roughly, the simulatable extractability follows from the AoK property of PQ-ppZKAoK, and the hiding property follows from the (non-uniform) hiding of Naor's commitment together with the ppZK property. For details, refer to Sect. 7. In the classical setting, the same construction also represents the first public-coin, constant-round ExtCom that avoids over-extraction (as per Corollary 2).

The construction of public-coin PQ-NMCom (as per Corollary 5) requires additional ideas, which are discussed in the full version of this work [53, Section 8,9] due to space constraints.

## 3 Preliminaries

We use standard notations from the (quantum) cryptography literature. Due to space limitations, we will recall only the most essential preliminaries here. Additional preliminaries are provided in the full version of this work [53, Section 3].

### 3.1 Expected Quantum Polynomial-Time Computations

We briefly review two notions of expected quantum polynomial-time: (1) measured-runtime expected quantum polynomial-time (dubbed $\mathsf{EQPT}_m$), and

(2) the coherent-runtime expected quantum polynomial-time (dubbed $\mathsf{EQPT}_c$) introduced in [55].

The definition of $\mathsf{EQPT}_m$ is rather intuitive. Suppose that we run a quantum Turing machine where we measure if it is in a "halt state" after each application of the transition unitary. We say that it is $\mathsf{EQPT}_m$ if the expected number of steps before halting is polynomial in the input length.

The definition of $\mathsf{EQPT}_c$ is more complicated. Roughly speaking, an $\mathsf{EQPT}_c$ computation does not measure when it halts so that computational branches with different runtime can interfere with each other. For the purpose of this paper, there is no need to recall the definition of $\mathsf{EQPT}_c$ in its full detail (for which we refer to [55]). We only need a special case of what can be done in $\mathsf{EQPT}_c$ as phrased in the following fact:

**Fact 2** ([55]). *Let $\Phi$ be a $\mathsf{EQPT}_m$ quantum operation and $U$ be its unitary dilation. That is, $U_\Phi$ is a unitary on the input register of $\Phi$ and an ancilla register such that $\Phi$ is equivalent to appending the ancilla register initialized to $|0...0\rangle$, applying $U_\Phi$, and discarding the ancilla. Let $M^{U_\Phi,U_\Phi^\dagger}$ be a QPT oracle machine that makes one query to each of unitary oracles $U_\Phi$ and $U_\Phi^\dagger$ where the query to $U_\Phi$ is made before that to $U_\Phi^\dagger$ and acts on the ancilla register of $\Phi$ only through access to $U_\Phi$ and $U_\Phi^\dagger$. Then an execution of $M^{U_\Phi,U_\Phi^\dagger}$ with the ancilla of $\Phi$ initialized to $|0...0\rangle$ can be done in $\mathsf{EQPT}_c$.*

## 4 Almost-Total Puzzle

We define a new notion called (post-quantum) almost-total puzzle, which will be used as a preamble in our construction of ppZKAoK in Protocol 2 and public-coin non-malleable commitment (please refer to the full version of this work [53, Section 8,9]).

**Definition 1 (Almost-Total Puzzle).** *A post-quantum almost-total puzzle (PQ-ATP) consists of a pair of PPT ITMs $\langle G, R\rangle$ and a deterministic polynomial-time algorithm* Verify *that satisfy the following syntax requirements.*

- **Puzzle Generation:** *Upon receiving the security parameter $1^\lambda$ as a common input, $G$ and $R$ interact with each other to generate a transcript $\tau$ (which encodes a puzzle). We denote this execution by $\tau \leftarrow \langle G, R\rangle(1^\lambda)$.*
- **Verification:** Verify *takes as input a transcript $\tau$ and a candidate solution $s$, and outputs a decision $d \in \{\top, \bot\}$*

*The scheme satisfies the following requirements:*

1. **Hard.** *For any non-uniform QPT puzzle receiver $\{R^*_\lambda, \rho_\lambda\}_{\lambda\in\mathbb{N}}$, the following holds:*

$$\Pr[\mathsf{Verify}(\tau, s) = \top : (\tau, s) \leftarrow \langle G, R^*_\lambda(\rho_\lambda)\rangle(1^\lambda)] \leq \mathsf{negl}(\lambda) \tag{1}$$

*where $(\tau, s) \leftarrow \langle G, R^*_\lambda(\rho_\lambda)\rangle(1^\lambda)$ denotes the procedure where $G$ and $R^*_\lambda(\rho_\lambda)$ interact to generate a transcript $\tau$ and $R^*_\lambda$ outputs a string $s$.*

*Intuitively, Inequality (1) means that no PPT/QPT malicious receiver $R^*$ could find a puzzle solution s except for with negligible probability, even if $R^*$ participates in the generation of the puzzle $\tau$.*

2. **Almost-Total.** *For any unbounded-time puzzle sender $G^*$, the following holds:*

$$\Pr[\nexists\ s\ s.t.\ \mathsf{Verify}(\tau, s) = \top : \tau \leftarrow \langle G^*, R\rangle(1^\lambda)] \leq \mathsf{negl}(\lambda). \tag{2}$$

3. **Public-Coin.** *During the puzzle generation procedure, all the messages sent by the honest puzzle sender G consist of public coins only.*

Note that Definition 1 is post-quantum; a classical almost-total puzzle (ATP) can be defined in the same manner except that the **Hard** property (i.e., Property 1) only needs to hold against non-uniform PPT (instead of QPT) adversaries.

We remark that the existence of non-interactive ATP is equivalent to the existence of average-case quantum hardness in **TFNP** w.r.t. the uniform distribution.[6] It is known that one-way permutations or collision-resistant hash functions imply average-case hardness in **TFNP** [61], and the implication trivially extends to the post-quantum setting. Thus, we have the following lemma.

**Lemma 1.** *Assuming the existence of post-quantum public-coin collision-resistant hash functions or post-quantum one-way permutations, there exists a non-interactive post-quantum public-coin almost-total puzzle.*

*Remark 2.* Unruh [69] pointed out that the "right" quantum analog of collision-resistance is what is called the *collapsing* property, which is stronger than post-quantum collision-resistance, in many settings. However, we stress that post-quantum collision-resistance, rather than the collapsing property, is sufficient in the above lemma as long as it is public-coin. We remark that post-quantum public-coin collision-resistant hash functions exist based on standard assumptions such as quantum hardness of the shortest integer solution (SIS) problem. On the other hand, there is no known candidate of post-quantum one-way permutations.

Unfortunately, it is unknown if OWFs imply average-case hardness in **TFNP**. Nonetheless, we show that OWFs imply two-round public-coin almost-total puzzles, using ideas inspired by [46]. We formalize this result as the following Lemma 2, with a constructive proof in Sect. 4.1.

**Lemma 2.** *Assuming the existence of OWFs (resp. PQ-OWFs), there exists a two-round construction of public-coin almost-total puzzles (resp. PQ-ATPs).*

[6] In the non-interactive setting, we can assume that the problem is "perfectly total," i.e., the probability in Inequality (2) is 0, without loss of generality.

### 4.1 Construction

We construct in Protocol 1 a two-round public-coin (PQ-)ATP from (PQ-)OWFs. This construction makes use of a (PQ-)UOWHF family $\mathcal{H} = \{H_\lambda\}_{\lambda \in \mathbb{N}}$ where

$$H_\lambda = \{h_k : \{0,1\}^{\ell_{\mathsf{in}}(\lambda)} \to \{0,1\}^{\ell_{\mathsf{out}}(\lambda)}\}_{k \in \{0,1\}^{\ell_{\mathsf{key}}(\lambda)}}.$$

| **Protocol 1: Almost-Total Puzzle** |
|---|
| **Parameter:** Let $n(\lambda) := \ell_{\mathsf{key}}(\lambda) + \ell_{\mathsf{in}}(\lambda) + \lambda$.<br>**Puzzle Generation:**<br>1. The receiver $R$ uniformly samples $n$ random string $x'_1 \dots x'_n$ where $x'_i \xleftarrow{\$} \{0,1\}^{\ell_{\mathsf{in}}(\lambda)}$ for each $i \in [n]$; $R$ sends them to the generator $G$.<br>2. $G$ samples a UOWHF key $k \xleftarrow{\$} \{0,1\}^{\ell_{\mathsf{key}}(\lambda)}$ and a random string $x \xleftarrow{\$} \{0,1\}^{\ell_{\mathsf{in}}(\lambda)}$ and sends them to $R$.<br>**Verification Algorithm** $\mathsf{Verify}(\tau, s)$**:**<br>1. Check the transcript $\tau$:<br>– if $R$'s message is ill-formed (i.e., it is not of the form of $(x'_1, \dots x'_n) \in (\{0,1\}^{\ell_{\mathsf{in}}(\lambda)})^{n(\lambda)}$), then output $\bot$;<br>– if $G$'s message is ill-formed (i.e., it is not of the form of $(k, x) \in \{0,1\}^{\ell_{\mathsf{key}}(\lambda)} \times \{0,1\}^{\ell_{\mathsf{in}}(\lambda)}$), then output $\top$.<br>Otherwise, parse $\tau = ((x'_1, \dots x'_n), (k, x))$.<br>2. For each $i \in [n]$, compute $x_i = x'_i \oplus x$.<br>3. If there exists an $i \in [n]$ such that $(h_k(x_i) = h_k(s)) \wedge (x_i \neq s)$, then output $\top$. Otherwise, output $\bot$. |

### 4.2 Proof of Properties

The public-coin property is straightforward from the description of Protocol 1. So, we prove the *hard* property of our protocol first, which is established by the following lemma.

**Lemma 3.** *The protocol described in Protocol 1 is hard (as per Property 1 of Definition 1).*

*Proof.* We prove Lemma 3 by contradiction. In the following, we assume for contradiction that there exists a non-uniform QPT/PPT puzzle receiver $R^* = \{R^*_\lambda, \rho_\lambda\}_{\lambda \in \mathbb{N}}$ and a function $\delta(\lambda) = 1/\mathsf{poly}(\lambda)$ such that for infinitely many $\lambda \in \mathbb{N}$,

$$\Pr[\mathsf{Verify}(\tau, s) = 1 : (\tau, s) \leftarrow \langle G, R^*_\lambda(\rho_\lambda)\rangle(1^\lambda)] \geq \delta(\lambda). \quad (3)$$

Levering this $R^*_\lambda(\rho_\lambda)$, we construct in Algorithm 4.1 a (non-uniform) QPT/PPT algorithm $\mathcal{A} = \{\mathcal{A}_\lambda, \rho_\lambda\}_{\lambda\in\mathbb{N}}$ breaking the universal one-wayness of the UOWHF $\mathcal{H}$ (see full version of this work [53, Section 3]):

**Algorithm 4.1: $\mathcal{A}$ against UOWHF**

$\mathcal{A}$ internally emulates the algorithm $R^*_\lambda(\rho_\lambda)$ (dubbed $R^*$ henceforth), while externally interacting with a challenger of the universal one-wayness of $\mathcal{H}$. In particular, $\mathcal{A}$ proceeds as follows.

1. $\mathcal{A}$ samples a string $x^* \xleftarrow{\$} \{0,1\}^{\ell_{\mathsf{in}}(\lambda)}$ and sends it to the external challenger.
2. $\mathcal{A}$ receives a hash key $k$ from the challenger.
3. $\mathcal{A}$ invokes $R^*$ internally to receive $n$ strings $x'_1 \ldots x'_n$ from $R^*$. $\mathcal{A}$ then samples $i \xleftarrow{\$} [n]$, sets $x := x^* \oplus x'_i$, and sends $(k, x)$ to $R^*$.
4. $\mathcal{A}$ receives $s$ from $R^*$ and forward it to the challenger.

Clearly, $\mathcal{A}$ runs in polynomial time, and notice that the hash key $k$ is sampled uniformly by the external challenger, and $x^*$ is sampled uniformly which implies that $x$ is also uniformly random. Therefore, from the $R^*$'s perspective, this is exactly the same execution as Protocol 1, and thus it will output a valid solution $s$ with probability at least $\delta(\lambda)$ due to our assumption in Inequality (3).

If $s$ is a valid solution, then with probability $1/n$, $\mathcal{A}$ finds a collision for $x^*$ (since we choose $i$ randomly). Namely, $\mathcal{A}$ wins the universal one-wayness game with probability $\delta(\lambda)/n$. Since $n$ is polynomial on $\lambda$, this leads to a contradiction against the security of the UOWHF $\mathcal{H}$. □

Next, we prove the *almost-total* property of our protocol, which is formalized as the following Lemma 4.

**Lemma 4.** *The protocol described in Protocol 1 is almost-total (as per Property 2 of Definition 1).*

*Proof.* For any $k \in \{0,1\}^{\ell_{\mathsf{key}}(\lambda)}$, since $h_k$ is compressing, we have:

$$\Pr_{x_i \leftarrow \{0,1\}^{\ell_{\mathsf{in}}(\lambda)}}[\exists s \neq x_i \ s.t.\ h_k(s) = h_k(x_i)] \geq \frac{1}{2}. \tag{4}$$

Thus, for any fixed $k \in \{0,1\}^{\ell_{\mathsf{key}}(\lambda)}$ and $x \in \{0,1\}^{\ell_{\mathsf{in}}(\lambda)}$, since $x_i = x \oplus x'_i$ is uniformly random when $x'_i$ is uniformly random, we have:

$$\Pr_{x'_i \leftarrow \{0,1\}^{\ell_{\mathsf{in}}(\lambda)}}[\exists s \neq x_i \ s.t.\ h_k(s) = h_k(x_i) : x_i \leftarrow x \oplus x'_i] \geq \frac{1}{2}. \tag{5}$$

Negating Inequality (5), we get

$$\Pr_{x'_i \leftarrow \{0,1\}^{\ell_{\mathsf{in}}(\lambda)}}[\forall s \neq x_i,\ h_k(s) \neq h_k(x_i) : x_i \leftarrow x \oplus x'_i] \leq \frac{1}{2}. \tag{6}$$

If we sample independently random $x_i'$ for each $i \in [n]$, then the event in the above probability is independent for each $i \in [n]$. Thus, we have

$$\Pr_{(x_1' \dots x_n') \leftarrow \{0,1\}^{\ell_{\mathsf{in}}(\lambda) \cdot n}} [\forall i \in [n], \forall s \neq x_i,\ h_k(s) \neq h_k(x_i)] \leq \left(\frac{1}{2}\right)^n, \tag{7}$$

where $x_i := x \oplus x_i'$. By taking a union bound over all possible $k \in \{0,1\}^{\ell_{\mathsf{key}}(\lambda)}$ and $x \in \{0,1\}^{\ell_{\mathsf{in}}(\lambda)}$, we have

$$\begin{aligned} &\Pr_{x_1' \dots x_n' \leftarrow \{0,1\}^{\ell_{\mathsf{in}}(\lambda) \cdot n}} \left[ \begin{matrix} \exists\ (k,x) \in \{0,1\}^{\ell_{\mathsf{key}}(\lambda)+\ell_{\mathsf{in}}(\lambda)}\ s.t. \\ \forall i \in [n], \forall s \neq x_i,\ h_k(s) \neq h_k(x_i) \end{matrix} : x_i \leftarrow x \oplus x_i' \right] \\ &\leq \frac{2^{\ell_{\mathsf{key}}(\lambda)+\ell_{\mathsf{in}}(\lambda)}}{2^n} = 2^{-\lambda}, \end{aligned} \tag{8}$$

where the last equality follows from our parameter setting $n(\lambda) = \ell_{\mathsf{key}}(\lambda) + \ell_{\mathsf{in}}(\lambda) + \lambda$. Negating Inequality (8), we have

$$\begin{aligned} &\Pr_{x_1' \dots x_n' \leftarrow \{0,1\}^{\ell_{\mathsf{in}}(\lambda) \cdot n}} \left[ \begin{matrix} \forall\ (k,x) \in \{0,1\}^{\ell_{\mathsf{key}}(\lambda)+\ell_{\mathsf{in}}(\lambda)}, \\ \exists i \in [n], \exists s \neq x_i\ s.t.\ h_k(s) = h_k(x_i) \end{matrix} : x_i \leftarrow x \oplus x_i' \right] \\ &\geq 1 - 2^{-\lambda}. \end{aligned} \tag{9}$$

In words, for at least $(1 - 2^{-\lambda})$-fraction of $(x_1', \dots x_n')$ sampled by $R$, no matter how $G^*$ chooses $(k, x)$, there is a solution $s$ such that $\mathsf{Verify}(\tau, s) = \top$ where $\tau = ((x_1', \dots x_n'), (k, x))$. This means that the almost-total property is satisfied. □

The above completes the proof of Lemma 2.

## 5 Zero-Knowledge Arguments of Knowledge with Preprocessing

In this section, we introduce the concept of interactive arguments with *preprocessing*. Essentially, these protocols are divided into two stages: a *preprocessing stage* and a *prove stage*. During the preprocessing stage, the prover and verifier interact without knowledge of the statement that needs to be proven. Once the statement is available, they engage in the prove stage to establish its truthfulness. This approach can be viewed as an extension of delayed-input protocols, where the instance is only required in the *final* round.

We first formalize the notion of zero-knowledge within this preprocessing framework, which we call *preprocessing zero-knowledge* (ppZK). We then demonstrate that ppZK leads to useful properties such as witness hiding and strong witness indistinguishability, all within the same preprocessing model.

### 5.1 Definitions

We start by formally defining interactive arguments with preprocessing.

*Syntax.* An interactive argument with preprocessing consists of PPT ITMs $P$ referred to as a prover and $V$ referred to as a verifier. The interaction between $P$ and $V$ is divided into two stages, the preprocessing stage and the prove stage. In the preprocessing stage, $P$ and $V$ take the security parameter $1^\lambda$ as input, interact with each other, and generate a transcript $\mathsf{pp}$. We write $\mathsf{pp} \leftarrow \langle P, V\rangle_{\mathsf{pre}}(1^\lambda)$ to mean this. In the prove stage, $P$ and $V$ take an instance $x$ as well as $\mathsf{pp}$ as common inputs, $P$ takes a witness $w$ of $x$ as an additional private input, and $P$ and $V$ interact with each other. At the end of the prove stage, $V$ outputs $\top$ indicating acceptance or $\bot$ indicating rejection. We write $b \leftarrow \langle P(w), V\rangle_{\mathsf{prove}}(\mathsf{pp}, x)$ to mean this where $b \in \{\top, \bot\}$ is $V$'s decision.

When we consider a malicious prover or verifier, we allow it to keep a state information from the preprocessing stage to the prove stage. Moreover, a malicious prover may adaptively choose the instance and output an arbitrary quantum state at the end of the prove stage. Specifically, for a malicious prover $P^*$ with initial state $\rho$, we write $(\mathsf{pp}, x, \rho') \leftarrow \langle P^*(\rho), V\rangle_{\mathsf{pre}}(1^\lambda)$ to mean the execution of the preprocessing stage between $P^*(\rho)$ and $V$ on the security parameter $1^\lambda$ where $\mathsf{pp}$ is the transcript of the preprocessing stage, $x$ is the statement chosen by $P^*$, and $\rho'$ as the internal state of $P^*$ at the end of the preprocessing stage, and $(\mathsf{ST}'_{\mathcal{P}^*}, b') \leftarrow \langle P^*(\rho'), V\rangle_{\mathsf{prove}}(\mathsf{pp}, x)$ to mean the execution of the prove stage between $P^*(\rho')$ and $V$ on the common inputs $\mathsf{pp}$ and $x$ where $\mathsf{ST}_{P^*}$ is the final state of $P^*_\lambda$ and $b$ is the decision output by $V$. Similarly, for a malicious verifier $V^*$ with initial state $\rho$, we write $(\mathsf{pp}, \rho') \leftarrow \langle P, V^*(\rho)\rangle_{\mathsf{pre}}(1^\lambda)$ to mean the execution of the preprocessing stage between $P$ and $V^*(\rho)$ on the security parameter $1^\lambda$ where $\mathsf{pp}$ is the transcript of the preprocessing stage and $\rho'_\lambda$ is the internal state of $V^*$ at the end of the preprocessing stage, and $\langle P(w), V^*(\rho')\rangle_{\mathsf{prove}}(\mathsf{pp}, x)$ to mean the execution of the prove stage between $P(w)$ and $V^*(\rho')$ on common inputs $\mathsf{pp}$ and $x$.

**Definition 2 (PQ-ppZKAoK with $\mathsf{EQPT}_c$-Simulation).** *A post-quantum preprocessing zero-knowledge arguments of knowledge (PQ-ppZKAoK) for an* **NP** *language $\mathcal{L}$ is an interactive argument $\langle P, V\rangle$ with preprocessing satisfying the following:*

- **Completeness:** *There exists a negligible function* $\mathsf{negl}$ *such that for any $\lambda \in \mathbb{N}$, $x \in L \cap \{0,1\}^\lambda$, and $w \in \mathcal{R}_{\mathcal{L}}(x)$, it holds that*

$$\Pr[\langle P(w), V\rangle_{\mathsf{prove}}(\mathsf{pp}, x) = \top : \mathsf{pp} \leftarrow \langle P, V\rangle_{\mathsf{pre}}(1^\lambda)] = 1 - \mathsf{negl}(\lambda).$$

- **Preprocessing Zero-Knowledge:** *There is an unbounded-time machine $\mathcal{S}_0$ with polynomial-size outputs and a QPT machine $\mathcal{S}_1$ such that for any non-uniform QPT malicious verifier $V^* = \{V^*_\lambda, \rho_\lambda\}_{\lambda\in\mathbb{N}}$ and a family $\{(x_{\mathsf{pp}}, w_{\mathsf{pp}})\}_{\mathsf{pp}}$ such that $x_{\mathsf{pp}} \in L \cap \{0,1\}^\lambda$ and $w_{\mathsf{pp}} \in R_L(x_{\mathsf{pp}})$,*[7] *it holds that*

$$\{\mathsf{OUT}_{V^*_\lambda}\langle P(w_{\mathsf{pp}}), V^*_\lambda(\rho'_\lambda)\rangle_{\mathsf{prove}}(\mathsf{pp}, x_{\mathsf{pp}}) : (\mathsf{pp}, \rho'_\lambda) \leftarrow \langle P, V^*_\lambda(\rho_\lambda)\rangle_{\mathsf{pre}}(1^\lambda)\}_{\lambda\in\mathbb{N}}$$
$$\overset{c}{\approx} \{\mathcal{S}_1^{V^*_\lambda(\rho'_\lambda)}(\mathcal{S}_0(\mathsf{pp}), x_{\mathsf{pp}}) : (\mathsf{pp}, \rho'_\lambda) \leftarrow \langle P, V^*_\lambda(\rho_\lambda)\rangle_{\mathsf{pre}}(1^\lambda)\}_{\lambda\in\mathbb{N}}.$$

[7] The subscript $\mathsf{pp}$ ranges all values that may be generated by the execution of $\langle P, V^*_\lambda(\rho_\lambda)\rangle_{\mathsf{pre}}(1^\lambda)$.

- **Adaptive AoK with $\mathsf{EQPT}_c$-Simulation** *There exists an* $\mathsf{EQPT}_c$ *oracle machine* $\mathcal{WE}$*, called the* witness-extended emulator*, such that for any non-uniform QPT machine* $\{P^*_\lambda, \rho_\lambda\}_{\lambda\in\mathbb{N}}$ *the following conditions hold:*
  1.
$$\left\{(\mathsf{ST}'_{\mathcal{P}^*}, b') : \begin{array}{l}(\mathsf{pp}, x, \rho'_\lambda) \leftarrow \langle P^*_\lambda(\rho_\lambda), V\rangle_{\mathsf{pre}}(1^\lambda); \\ (\mathsf{ST}'_{\mathcal{P}^*}, b') \leftarrow \langle P^*_\lambda(\rho'_\lambda), V\rangle_{\mathsf{prove}}(\mathsf{pp}, x)\end{array}\right\}_{\lambda\in\mathbb{N}}$$
$$\stackrel{c}{\approx} \left\{(\mathsf{ST}'_{\mathcal{P}^*}, b') : \begin{array}{l}(\mathsf{pp}, x, \rho'_\lambda) \leftarrow \langle P^*_\lambda(\rho_\lambda), V\rangle_{\mathsf{pre}}(1^\lambda); \\ (\mathsf{ST}'_{\mathcal{P}^*}, b', w') \leftarrow \mathcal{WE}^{P^*_\lambda(\rho'_\lambda)}(x)\end{array}\right\}_{\lambda\in\mathbb{N}},$$
  2. $$\Pr\left[b' = \top \ \wedge \ w' \notin \mathcal{R}_\mathcal{L}(x) : \begin{array}{l}(\mathsf{pp}, x, \rho'_\lambda) \leftarrow \langle P^*_\lambda(\rho_\lambda), V\rangle_{\mathsf{pre}}(1^\lambda); \\ (\mathsf{ST}'_{\mathcal{P}^*}, b', w') \leftarrow \mathcal{WE}^{P^*_\lambda(\rho'_\lambda)}(x)\end{array}\right] = 0.$$

*Remark 3.* In the above definition, $\mathsf{EQPT}_c$-simulation only appears in the AoK property, and the zero-knowledge property is defined by a pair of unbounded-time and (strict) QPT simulators.

## 5.2 Implications

The processing zero-knowledge property defined in Definition 2 is sufficient in many settings where an instance is given to the verifier after preprocessing. For example, it implies strong witness indistinguishability and witness hiding in the preprocessing setting as defined below:

**Definition 3 (Preprocessing Strong Witness Indistinguishability).** *An interactive argument* $\langle P, V\rangle$ *with preprocessing for an* **NP** *language* $\mathcal{L}$ *satisfies preprocessing strong witness indistinguishability if it satisfies the following:*

- **Preprocessing Strong Witness Indistinguishability:** *For any pair of families of distributions* $\{(\mathcal{X}_{0,\lambda,\mathsf{pp}}, \mathcal{W}_{0,\lambda,\mathsf{pp}})\}_{\lambda,\mathsf{pp}}$ *and* $\{(\mathcal{X}_{1,\lambda,\mathsf{pp}}, \mathcal{W}_{1,\lambda,\mathsf{pp}})\}_{\lambda,\mathsf{pp}}$ *where* $(\mathcal{X}_{b,\lambda,\mathsf{pp}}, \mathcal{W}_{b,\lambda,\mathsf{pp}})$ *is a joint distribution supported on* $\mathcal{R}_\mathcal{L} \cap (\{0,1\}^\lambda \times \{0,1\}^*)$ *and* $\{\mathcal{X}_{0,\lambda,\mathsf{pp}}\}_{\lambda,\mathsf{pp}} \stackrel{c}{\approx} \{\mathcal{X}_{1,\lambda,\mathsf{pp}}\}_{\lambda,\mathsf{pp}}$*, and for any non-uniform QPT machine* $\{V^*_\lambda, \rho_\lambda\}_{\lambda\in\mathbb{N}}$*, it holds that*
$$\left\{\mathsf{OUT}_{V^*_\lambda}\langle P(w_0), V^*_\lambda(\rho'_\lambda)\rangle_{\mathsf{prove}}(\mathsf{pp}, x_0) : \begin{array}{l}(\mathsf{pp}, \rho'_\lambda) \leftarrow \langle P, V^*_\lambda(\rho_\lambda)\rangle_{\mathsf{pre}}(1^\lambda) \\ (x_0, w_0) \leftarrow (\mathcal{X}_{0,\lambda,\mathsf{pp}}, \mathcal{W}_{0,\lambda,\mathsf{pp}})\end{array}\right\}_{\lambda\in\mathbb{N}}$$
$$\stackrel{c}{\approx} \left\{\mathsf{OUT}_{V^*_\lambda}\langle P(w_1), V^*_\lambda(\rho'_\lambda)\rangle_{\mathsf{prove}}(\mathsf{pp}, x_1) : \begin{array}{l}(\mathsf{pp}, \rho'_\lambda) \leftarrow \langle P, V^*_\lambda(\rho_\lambda)\rangle_{\mathsf{pre}}(1^\lambda) \\ (x_1, w_1) \leftarrow (\mathcal{X}_{1,\lambda,\mathsf{pp}}, \mathcal{W}_{1,\lambda,\mathsf{pp}})\end{array}\right\}_{\lambda\in\mathbb{N}}.$$

**Definition 4 (Preprocessing Witness Hiding).** *An interactive argument* $\langle P, V\rangle$ *with preprocessing for an* **NP** *language* $\mathcal{L}$ *satisfies preprocessing witness hiding if it satisfies the following:*

– **Preprocessing Witness Hiding:** *For any non-uniform QPT machine* $\{V_\lambda^*, \rho_\lambda\}_{\lambda \in \mathbb{N}}$*, there is a non-uniform QPT machine* $\{M_\lambda, \sigma_\lambda\}_{\lambda \in \mathbb{N}}$ *such that for any family of distributions* $\{(\mathcal{X}_\lambda, \mathcal{W}_\lambda)\}_\lambda$ *where* $(\mathcal{X}_\lambda, \mathcal{W}_\lambda)$ *is a joint distribution supported on* $\mathcal{R}_\mathcal{L} \cap (\{0,1\}^\lambda \times \{0,1\}^*)$*, it holds that*

$$\Pr\left[\mathsf{OUT}_{V_\lambda^*}\langle P(w), V_\lambda^*(\rho'_\lambda)\rangle_{\mathsf{prove}}(\mathsf{pp}, x) \in \mathcal{R}_\mathcal{L}(x) : \begin{array}{l}(\mathsf{pp}, \rho'_\lambda) \leftarrow \langle P, V_\lambda^*(\rho_\lambda)\rangle_{\mathsf{pre}}(1^\lambda)\\ (x, w) \leftarrow (\mathcal{X}_\lambda, \mathcal{W}_\lambda)\end{array}\right]$$
$$\leq \Pr[M_\lambda(\sigma_\lambda, x) \in \mathcal{R}_\mathcal{L}(x) : (x, w) \leftarrow (\mathcal{X}_\lambda, \mathcal{W}_\lambda)] + \mathsf{negl}(\lambda).$$

**Comparison with Definitions Without Preprocessing.** One might naturally assume sWI/WH with preprocessing are stronger notions that imply their standard counterparts, as the input can be delayed. However, in terms of existence, it turns out that standard sWI/WH are actually *stronger* than their preprocessing counterparts, contrary to intuition. If we have a standard sWI/WH protocol, we can treat all rounds as part of the prove stage, making the preprocessing stage effectively null. This would naturally imply the corresponding preprocessing sWI/WH properties. However, the converse does not hold. Consider a preprocessing sWI/WH argument: if we treat it as a standard interactive argument by combining the preprocessing and prove stages into a single stage, it does not necessarily satisfy standard sWI/WH. Intuitively, preprocessing sWI/WH only guarantees security as long as the messages in the preprocessing stage do not depend on the instance to be proven. This condition restricts the verifier's behavior, and thus the security no longer holds if the verifier's preprocessing messages are allowed to depend on the instance.

Although standard sWI/WH and preprocessing sWI/WH cannot be directly compared, we observe that a preprocessing interactive argument can be viewed as a standard interactive argument without preprocessing (We defer the formal definition to the full version of this work [53, Section 3]) by merging the preprocessing and prove stages into a single protocol. The AoK property in the preprocessing setting (as per Definition 2) implies that in the without-preprocessing setting (We defer the formal definition to the full version of this work [53, Section 3]). This is because the preprocessing AoK property is stronger, as it captures a cheating prover who adaptively selects the statement after completing the preprocessing stage. On the other hand, the preprocessing ZK property (as per Definition 2) does not imply the standard ZK property in the without-preprocessing setting, since the preprocessing part of the simulator $\mathcal{S}_0$ in our definition needs unbounded time. Nonetheless, we remark that the preprocessing ZK property (as per Definition 2) does imply witness indistinguishability in the "non-preprocessing" setting (We defer the formal definition to the full version of this work [53, Section 3]). This follows from the well-known fact that WI is equivalent to ZK with unbounded-time simulation. Based on the above observation, we have the following lemma.

**Lemma 5.** *For a PQ-ppZKAoK with* $\mathsf{EQPT}_c$*-simulation, if we regard the merge of preprocessing and prove stages as a single protocol without preprocessing, then the resulting protocol is a PQ-WIAoK with* $\mathsf{EQPT}_c$*-simulation.*

It is straightforward to see the following lemma.

**Lemma 6.** *Preprocessing zero-knowledge (Definition 2) implies preprocessing strong witness indistinguishability (Definition 3) and preprocessing witness hiding (Definition 4).*

*Proof.* Let $(\mathcal{S}_0, \mathcal{S}_1)$ be the simulator for the preprocessing zero-knowledge property. Let $\{V_\lambda^*, \rho_\lambda\}_{\lambda\in\mathbb{N}}$ be a non-uniform QPT malicious verifier. We prove preprocessing strong witness indistinguishability and preprocessing witness hiding below.

**Preprocessing Strong Witness Indistinguishability.** By the preprocessing zero-knowledge property, we have the following for $b \in \{0,1\}$:

$$\left\{ \mathsf{OUT}_{V_\lambda^*}\langle P(w_b), V_\lambda^*(\rho'_\lambda)\rangle_{\mathsf{prove}}(\mathsf{pp}, x_b) : \begin{array}{l} (\mathsf{pp}, \rho'_\lambda) \leftarrow \langle P, V_\lambda^*(\rho_\lambda)\rangle_{\mathsf{pre}}(1^\lambda) \\ (x_b, w_b) \leftarrow (\mathcal{X}_{b,\lambda,\mathsf{pp}}, \mathcal{W}_{b,\lambda,\mathsf{pp}}) \end{array} \right\}_{\lambda\in\mathbb{N}}$$
$$\overset{c}{\approx} \left\{ \mathcal{S}_1^{V_\lambda^*(\rho'_\lambda)}(\mathcal{S}_0(\mathsf{pp}), x_b) : \begin{array}{l} (\mathsf{pp}, \rho'_\lambda) \leftarrow \langle P, V_\lambda^*(\rho_\lambda)\rangle_{\mathsf{pre}}(1^\lambda) \\ (x_b, w_b) \leftarrow (\mathcal{X}_{b,\lambda,\mathsf{pp}}, \mathcal{W}_{b,\lambda,\mathsf{pp}}) \end{array} \right\}_{\lambda\in\mathbb{N}}.$$

By the assumption that $\{\mathcal{X}_{0,\lambda,\mathsf{pp}}\}_{\lambda,\mathsf{pp}} \overset{c}{\approx} \{\mathcal{X}_{1,\lambda,\mathsf{pp}}\}_{\lambda,\mathsf{pp}}$, we have

$$\left\{ \mathcal{S}_1^{V_\lambda^*(\rho'_\lambda)}(\mathcal{S}_0(\mathsf{pp}), x_0) : \begin{array}{l} (\mathsf{pp}, \rho'_\lambda) \leftarrow \langle P, V_\lambda^*(\rho_\lambda)\rangle_{\mathsf{pre}}(1^\lambda) \\ (x_0, w_0) \leftarrow (\mathcal{X}_{0,\lambda,\mathsf{pp}}, \mathcal{W}_{0,\lambda,\mathsf{pp}}) \end{array} \right\}_{\lambda\in\mathbb{N}}$$
$$\overset{c}{\approx} \left\{ \mathcal{S}_1^{V_\lambda^*(\rho'_\lambda)}(\mathcal{S}_0(\mathsf{pp}), x_1) : \begin{array}{l} (\mathsf{pp}, \rho'_\lambda) \leftarrow \langle P, V_\lambda^*(\rho_\lambda)\rangle_{\mathsf{pre}}(1^\lambda) \\ (x_1, w_1) \leftarrow (\mathcal{X}_{1,\lambda,\mathsf{pp}}, \mathcal{W}_{1,\lambda,\mathsf{pp}}) \end{array} \right\}_{\lambda\in\mathbb{N}}.$$

We remark that "$\overset{c}{\approx}$" means computational indistinguishability against *non-uniform* QPT distinguishers, and thus we can reduce the above to $\{\mathcal{X}_{0,\lambda,\mathsf{pp}}\}_{\lambda,\mathsf{pp}} \overset{c}{\approx} \{\mathcal{X}_{1,\lambda,\mathsf{pp}}\}_{\lambda,\mathsf{pp}}$ by regarding $\mathcal{S}_0(\mathsf{pp})$ as a non-uniform advice. By combining the above, preprocessing strong witness indistinguishability follows.

**Preprocessing Witness Hiding.** By the preprocessing zero-knowledge property, it holds that

$$\left| \Pr\left[ \mathsf{OUT}_{V_\lambda^*}\langle P(w), V_\lambda^*(\rho'_\lambda)\rangle_{\mathsf{prove}}(\mathsf{pp}, x) \in \mathcal{R}_\mathcal{L}(x) : \begin{array}{l} (\mathsf{pp}, \rho'_\lambda) \leftarrow \langle P, V_\lambda^*(\rho_\lambda)\rangle_{\mathsf{pre}}(1^\lambda) \\ (x, w) \leftarrow (\mathcal{X}_\lambda, \mathcal{W}_\lambda) \end{array} \right] \right.$$
$$\left. - \Pr\left[ \mathcal{S}_1^{V_\lambda^*(\rho'_\lambda)}(\mathcal{S}_0(\mathsf{pp}), x) \in \mathcal{R}_\mathcal{L}(x) : \begin{array}{l} (\mathsf{pp}, \rho'_\lambda) \leftarrow \langle P, V_\lambda^*(\rho_\lambda)\rangle_{\mathsf{pre}}(1^\lambda) \\ (x, w) \leftarrow (\mathcal{X}_\lambda, \mathcal{W}_\lambda) \end{array} \right] \right| \leq \mathsf{negl}(\lambda).$$

We define a non-uniform QPT machine $\{M_\lambda, \sigma_\lambda\}_{\lambda\in\mathbb{N}}$ as follows:

- $\sigma_\lambda := (\mathcal{S}_0(\mathsf{pp}), \rho'_\lambda)$ where $(\mathsf{pp}, \rho'_\lambda) \leftarrow \langle P, V_\lambda^*(\rho_\lambda)\rangle_{\mathsf{pre}}(1^\lambda)$;
- $M_\lambda$ takes $\sigma_\lambda = (\mathcal{S}_0(\mathsf{pp}), \rho'_\lambda)$ as advice and $x$ as input, runs $\mathcal{S}_1^{V_\lambda^*(\rho'_\lambda)}(\mathcal{S}_0(\mathsf{pp}), x)$, and outputs its output.

Clearly, the second probability in the above inequality is equal to the probability

$$\Pr[M_\lambda(\sigma_\lambda, x) \in \mathcal{R}_\mathcal{L}(x) : (x, w) \leftarrow (\mathcal{X}_\lambda, \mathcal{W}_\lambda)].$$

Thus, the preprocessing witness hiding follows. □

# 6 Post-quantum Public-Coin Preprocessing ZKAoK

We construct a *public-coin* PQ-ppZKAoK with $\mathsf{EQPT}_c$-simulation from *one-way functions* in five rounds.

## 6.1 Construction of Preprocessing ZKAoK

This protocol makes use of the following building blocks:

- A two-round public-coin PQ-ATP constructed in Protocol 1; We write $\mathsf{Verify}$ to mean its verification algorithm.
- Naor's commitment $\mathsf{Com}$; We use $\beta$ to denote the first message for Naor's commitment, and $\mathsf{Com}_\beta(m; r)$ to denote the second message where a string $m$ is committed using randomness $r$.
- A four-round public-coin PQ-WIPoK $\mathsf{WIPoK}$ with $\mathsf{EQPT}_m$-Guaranteed-Extraction (See full version of this work [53, Section 3]).

**Protocol 2: Post-Quantum Public-Coin $\mathsf{ppZKAoK}$ with $\mathsf{EQPT}_c$-simulation**

Let $\mathcal{L}$ be an **NP** language, $x \in \mathcal{L} \cap \{0,1\}^\lambda$ and $w \in \mathcal{R}_\mathcal{L}(x)$.

**Preprocessing Stage:**

1. Prover $P$ (acting as the puzzle receiver $R_{\text{PUZ}}$) sends to the verifier $V$ (acting as the puzzle sender $G_{\text{PUZ}}$) the first message of the PQ-ATP.
2. $V$ sends to $P$ the second message of the PQ-ATP, the first message $\beta$ for Naor's commitment, and the first message $v$ of $\mathsf{WIPoK}$.

Let $\tau$ be the transcript of the PQ-ATP. At this point, $P$ and $V$ share the transcript $\mathsf{pp} = (\beta, v, \tau)$ of the preprocessing stage.

**Prove Stage:**

1. **(Commit to Witness.)** $P$ samples a random tape $r$ and sends $\mathsf{c} = \mathsf{Com}_\beta(w; r)$ to $V$;
2. **(WIPoK.)** $P$ and $V$ run the rest of execution of $\mathsf{WIPoK}$ where $P$ proves to $V$ that either he "knows" a solution for $\tau$ or $\mathsf{c}$ is a commitment of a valid witness $w \in \mathcal{R}_\mathcal{L}(x)$. Formally, $P$ proves that $(\tau, \mathsf{c}) \in \mathcal{L}_{\mathsf{puz}} \vee \mathcal{L}_\beta^x$, and $\mathcal{L}_{\mathsf{puz}} \vee \mathcal{L}_\beta^x$ denotes the OR-composed language, where

$$\mathcal{L}_{\mathsf{puz}} := \{\tau \mid \exists s \ s.t. \ \mathsf{Verify}(\tau, s) = 1\}. \quad (10)$$

and

$$\mathcal{L}_\beta^x := \{\mathsf{c} \mid \exists (w, r) \ s.t. \ \mathsf{c} = \mathsf{Com}_\beta(w; r) \wedge w \in \mathcal{R}_\mathcal{L}(x)\}. \tag{11}$$

Note that $P$ uses the $(w, r)$ as the witness when executing this WIPoK.

**Theorem 3.** *Protocol 2 is a public-coin PQ-ppZKAoK with* $\mathsf{EQPT}_c$*-simulation (as per Definition 2). Its preprocessing stage is two-round and prove stage is three-round.*

Completeness, the public-coin property, and the round complexity are straightforward from the description of Protocol 2 noting that the commitment in Step 1 of the prove stage can be sent in parallel to the first message in Step 2 of the prove stage (which is the second-round message of WIPoK). The rest of the proof of Thm. 3 (preprocessing zero-knowledge and adaptive AoK with $\mathsf{EQPT}_c$-simulation) is given in Sect. 6.2 and 6.3.

By Theorem 3 and Lemma 5, we obtain the following corollary.

**Corollary 6.** *Assuming the existence of PQ-OWFs, there is a five-round public-coin PQ-WIAoK with* $\mathsf{EQPT}_c$*-simulation (See full version of this work [53, Section 3]).*

**Reducing the Round Complexity from Stronger Assumptions.** We remark that the round complexity of the preprocessing stage can be reduced by one if we use non-interactive almost-total puzzles instead of the two-round one. By Lemma 1, we have the following theorem:

**Theorem 4.** *Assuming the existence of post-quantum collision-resistant hash functions or post-quantum one-way permutations, there is a public-coin PQ-ppZKAoK with* $\mathsf{EQPT}_c$*-simulation (as per Definition 2) of which preprocessing stage is one-round and prove stage is three-round.*

Theorem 4 and Lemma 5 imply the following corollary.

**Corollary 7.** *Assuming the existence of post-quantum public-coin collision-resistant hash functions or post-quantum one-way permutations, there is a four-round public-coin PQ-WIAoK with* $\mathsf{EQPT}_c$*-simulation (See full version of this work [53, Section 3]).*

### 6.2 Proof of Preprocessing Zero-Knowledge

**Lemma 7.** *The protocol described in Protocol 2 satisfies the preprocessing zero-knowledge property.*

*Proof.* Let $V^* = \{V^*_\lambda, \rho_\lambda\}_\lambda$ be a non-uniform QPT adversary. We consider the following sequence of hybrids.

- Hybrid $H_1^{V^*}(\lambda)$: This is the real experiment that simulates the interaction between $P(x_{\mathsf{pp}}, w_{\mathsf{pp}})$ and $V^*$. That is, it runs $(\mathsf{pp}, \rho'_\lambda) \leftarrow \langle P, V^*_\lambda(\rho_\lambda)\rangle_{\mathsf{pre}}(1^\lambda)$ and $\langle P(w_{\mathsf{pp}}), V^*_\lambda(\rho'_\lambda)\rangle_{\mathsf{prove}}(\mathsf{pp}, x_{\mathsf{pp}})$ and outputs the final state of $V^*$.

– Hybrid $H_2^{V^*}(\lambda)$: This is identical to $H_1^{V^*}(\lambda)$ except that it finds the lexicographically smallest solution $s$ for $\tau$ by *brute-force* where $\tau$ is the transcript of the almost-total puzzle contained in $\mathsf{pp}$. If a solution does not exist, it outputs $\bot$, and otherwise works similarly to the previous hybrid. We note that this experiment obtains $s$ but does not use it. By the almost-total property, the probability that this hybrid outputs $\bot$ is negligible. Thus, we have

$$\{H_1^{V^*}(\lambda)\}_{\lambda\in\mathbb{N}} \overset{s}{\approx} \{H_2^{V^*}(\lambda)\}_{\lambda\in\mathbb{N}}. \tag{12}$$

– Hybrid $H_3^{V^*}(\lambda)$: This is identical to $H_2^{V^*}(\lambda)$ except that it uses $s$ obtained by brute-force as the witness in $\mathsf{WIPoK}$. By the (non-uniform) WI property of $\mathsf{WIPoK}$, we have

$$\{H_2^{V^*}(\lambda)\}_{\lambda\in\mathbb{N}} \overset{c}{\approx} \{H_3^{V^*}(\lambda)\}_{\lambda\in\mathbb{N}}. \tag{13}$$

We remark that the brute-force is done before receiving any prover message of $\mathsf{WIPoK}$ and thus we can still rely on the WI property against non-uniform adversaries by treating $\mathsf{pp}$, $s$, and the verifier's internal state right after finishing the preprocessing stage as non-uniform advice.

– Hybrid $H_4^{V^*}(\lambda)$: This is identical to $H_3^{V^*}(\lambda)$ except that it commits to 0 instead of the witness in Step 1. By the (non-uniform) hiding property of $\mathsf{Com}$, we have

$$\{H_3^{V^*}(\lambda)\}_{\lambda\in\mathbb{N}} \overset{c}{\approx} \{H_4^{V^*}(\lambda)\}_{\lambda\in\mathbb{N}}. \tag{14}$$

One can see that $H_4^{V^*}(\lambda)$ corresponds to the view simulated by the following simulator $\mathcal{S} = (\mathcal{S}_0, \mathcal{S}_1)$.

$\mathcal{S}_0(\mathsf{pp})$: Parse $\mathsf{pp} = (\beta, v, \tau)$ and find the lexicographically smallest solution $s$ of $\tau$ by brute-force. If a solution does not exist, set $s := \bot$. Output $s$.

$\mathcal{S}_1^{V_\lambda^*(\rho'_\lambda)}(s, x_{\mathsf{pp}})$: If $s = \bot$, output $\bot$. Otherwise, interact with $V_\lambda^*(\rho'_\lambda)$ in the prove stage where it uses $s$ as the witness for $\mathsf{WIPoK}$.

The computational indistinguishability between $H_1^{V^*}(\lambda)$ and $H_4^{V^*}(\lambda)$ directly means the preprocessing zero-knowledge property. This completes the proof of Lemma 7. □

### 6.3 Proof of Adaptive AoK with $\mathsf{EQPT}_c$-Simulation

**Lemma 8.** *The protocol described in Protocol 2 satisfies adaptive AoK with* $\mathsf{EQPT}_c$*-simulation.*

*Proof.* Let $\mathcal{GE}$ be the $\mathsf{EQPT}_m$ guaranteed extractor of $\mathsf{WIPoK}$ (We defer the formal definition to the full version of this work [53, Section 3]). Let $U_{\mathcal{GE}}^{P_\lambda^*}(v, a, x)$ be a unitary dilation of $\mathcal{GE}^{P_\lambda^*(\rho_\lambda)}(v, a, x)$ that acts on the prover's internal register $\mathbf{P}$ and an ancilla register $\mathbf{Anc}$. That is, it is defined in such a way that $\mathcal{GE}^{P_\lambda^*(\rho_\lambda)}(v, a, x)$ is equivalent to the following procedure:

1. Initialize **P** to be $\rho_\lambda$ and **Anc** to be $|0...0\rangle$.
2. Apply $U_{\mathcal{GE}}^{P_\lambda^*}(v, a, x)$.
3. Measure a designated subregister **W** of **Anc** to obtain $w$ and discard **Anc**.

Moreover, we assume that **W** consists of subregisters $(\mathbf{W}_1, \mathbf{W}_2)$, and if the extracted witness is $(w, r) \in \mathcal{R}_{\mathcal{L}_\beta^x}(\mathsf{c})$, then $w$ and $r$ are written in $\mathbf{W}_1$ and $\mathbf{W}_2$, respectively. Then we construct the witness-extended emulator $\mathcal{WE}$ as follows.

$\mathcal{WE}^{P_\lambda^*(\rho_\lambda)}(x)$:

1. Run the preprocessing stage with $P_\lambda^*$ while playing the role of the honest verifier. Let $\mathsf{pp} = (\beta, v, \tau)$ be the transcript of the preprocessing stage.
2. Receive $\mathsf{c}$ and the second-round message $a$ of $\mathsf{WIPoK}$ from $P_\lambda^*$.
3. Generate a uniform superposition $\sum_{r \in R} |r\rangle$ over the possible values of the third-round message of $\mathsf{WIPoK}$, and coherently run $P_\lambda^*$ to generate the fourth-round message in superposition.
4. Measure the decision of the verifier of $\mathsf{WIPoK}$ on the transcript formed by $v$, $a$, and the values in the third-round and fourth-round message registers of $\mathsf{WIPoK}$ w.r.t. the instance $(\tau, \mathsf{c})$ (without measuring the values of the third-round and fourth messages themselves). Let $b$ be the measurement outcome.
5. If $b = \bot$, then measure the transcript, let $\mathsf{ST}'_{P^*}$ be the internal state of $P_\lambda^*$ at this point, and output $(\mathsf{ST}'_{P^*}, b = \bot, w = \bot)$ and halt.
6. If $b = \top$, do the following:
   (a) Let **P** be the internal register of $P_\lambda^*$ and initalize **Anc** to be $|0...0\rangle$. Apply $U_{\mathcal{GE}}^{P_\lambda^*}(v, a, x)$.
   (b) Measure the subregister $\mathbf{W}_1$ of **Anc** to obtain $w$.
   (c) Apply $U_{\mathcal{GE}}^{P_\lambda^*}(v, a, x)^\dagger$.
   (d) Measure the transcript, let $\mathsf{ST}'_{P^*}$ be the internal state of $P_\lambda^*$ at this point, and output $(\mathsf{ST}'_{P^*}, b = \top, w)$.

Since $\mathcal{GE}$ is an $\mathsf{EQPT}_m$ machine, $\mathcal{WE}$ is an $\mathsf{EQPT}_c$ machine (Fact 2).

We say that $\beta$ is good if for any $\mathsf{c}$, there is at most one $m$ such that $\mathsf{c} = \mathsf{Com}_\beta(m; r)$ for some $r$. We denote such $m$ by $\mathsf{val}_\beta(\mathsf{c})$ where if there is no such $m$, then we define $\mathsf{val}_\beta(\mathsf{c}) := \bot$. By the statistical binding property of Naor's commitment, $\beta$ is good except for a negligible probability. We show the following claim.

**Claim 5.** *For any non-uniform QPT machine $\{P_\lambda^*, \rho_\lambda\}_\lambda$, instance $x \in \{0,1\}^\lambda$, and good $\beta$, it holds that*

$$\Pr[b = \top \wedge (w \neq \mathsf{val}_\beta(\mathsf{c}) \vee w \notin \mathcal{R}_\mathcal{L}(x))] \leq \mathsf{negl}(\lambda)$$

*where the probability is taken over the execution of $\mathcal{WE}^{P_\lambda^*(\rho_\lambda)}(x)$ with the fixed $\beta$.*

*Proof of* Claim 5. Let $\widetilde{\mathcal{WE}}^{P^*_\lambda(\rho_\lambda)}(x)$ be the same as $\mathcal{WE}^{P^*_\lambda(\rho_\lambda)}(x)$ except that it measures the whole $\mathbf{W}$ (rather than only $\mathbf{W}_1$) in Step 6b. Let $\widetilde{w}$ be the measurement outcome. By the guaranteed extraction property, it holds that

$$\Pr[b = \top \wedge \widetilde{w} \notin (\mathcal{R}_{\mathcal{L}_{\mathsf{puz}}}(\tau) \cup \mathcal{R}_{\mathcal{L}^x_\beta}(\mathsf{c}))] \leq \mathsf{negl}(\lambda) \tag{15}$$

where the probability is taken over the execution of $\widetilde{\mathcal{WE}}^{P^*_\lambda(\rho_\lambda)}(x)$. Moreover, by the hardness of the almost-total puzzle, it holds that

$$\Pr[b = \top \wedge \widetilde{w} \in \mathcal{R}_{\mathcal{L}_{\mathsf{puz}}}(\tau)] \leq \mathsf{negl}(\lambda) \tag{16}$$

where the probability is taken over the execution of $\widetilde{\mathcal{WE}}^{P^*_\lambda(\rho_\lambda)}(x)$. Indeed, this can be seen as follows: Suppose that we have $\Pr[b = \top \wedge \widetilde{w} \in \mathcal{R}_{\mathcal{L}_{\mathsf{puz}}}(\tau)] \geq 1/p(\lambda)$ for some polynomial $p$ and infinitely many $\lambda$. Since $\mathcal{GE}^{P^*_\lambda(\rho_\lambda)}(v, a, x)$ runs in $\mathsf{EQPT}_m$, a straightforward reduction gives an $\mathsf{EQPT}_m$ algorithm that solves the puzzle with the same probability.[8] By an appropriate truncation, this gives a (strict) QPT algorithm that solves the with probability at least $1/(2p(\lambda))$ for infinitely many $\lambda$. This contradicts the hardness of the almost-total puzzle. Thus, Eq. (16) holds.

Combining Eq. (15) and (16), we have

$$\Pr[b = \top \wedge \widetilde{w} \notin \mathcal{R}_{\mathcal{L}^x_\beta}(\mathsf{c})] \leq \mathsf{negl}(\lambda) \tag{17}$$

where the probability is taken over the execution of $\widetilde{\mathcal{WE}}^{P^*_\lambda(\rho_\lambda)}(x)$. By the definitions of $\widetilde{\mathcal{WE}}$ and $\mathcal{L}^x_\beta$ and the assumption that $\beta$ is good, Eq. (17) immediately implies Claim 5. □

The second requirement of the AoK with $\mathsf{EQPT}_c$-simulation property immediately follows from Claim 5 and the fact that an overwhelming fraction of $\beta$ is good. To show the first requirement, again by Claim 5 and the fact that an overwhelming fraction of $\beta$ is good, the measurement in Step 6b of the execution of $\mathcal{WE}^{P^*_\lambda(\rho_\lambda)}(x)$ results in the fixed value $\mathsf{val}_\beta(\mathsf{c})$ except for a negligible probability. Thus, by the gentle measurement lemma, Steps 6a to 6c only negligibly changes the internal state of $P^*_\lambda$. Moreover if we remove these steps, then $\mathsf{ST}'_{P^*}$ is exactly identical to that in the real execution. This implies that the first requirement is also satisfied. This completes the proof of Lemma 8. □

## 7 Public-Coin PQ-ExtCom with $\mathsf{EQPT}_c$-Simulation

We present a *post-quantum public-coin* extractable commitment from *one-way functions* in five rounds.

This protocol makes use of the following building blocks:

[8] Though $\widetilde{\mathcal{WE}}^{P^*_\lambda(\rho_\lambda)}(x)$ is an $\mathsf{EQPT}_c$ machine, we can generate $b$ and $\widetilde{w}$ from the same distribution in $\mathsf{EQPT}_m$ by running $\mathcal{GE}^{P^*_\lambda(\rho_\lambda)}(v, a, x)$ in Step 6a instead of applying its unitary dilation $U^{P^*_\lambda}_{\mathcal{GE}}(v, a, x)$. Note that we do not need to run the rest of the steps since $b$ and $\widetilde{w}$ are obtained at this point.

- A public-coin post-quantum preprocessing zero-knowledge argument of knowledge $\mathsf{ppZKAoK}$ with $\mathsf{EQPT}_c$-simulation constructed in Protocol 2. Its preprocessing stage is two-round and prove stage is three-round.
- Naor's commitment $\mathsf{Com}$; We use $\beta$ to denote the first message for Naor's commitment, and $\mathsf{Com}_\beta(m; r)$ to denote the second message where a string $m$ is committed using randomness $r$.

**Protocol 3: Public-Coin PQ-ExtCom with $\mathsf{EQPT}_c$-simulation**

**Commit Stage:** Let $m$ be the message to be committed to.

1. **(Preprocessing Stage of ppZKAoK.)** $C$ and $R$ run the preprocessing stage of $\mathsf{ppZKAoK}$ where $C$ and $R$ play the roles of the prover and verifier, respectively. Let $\mathsf{pp}$ be the transcript of the preprocessing stage.
2. **(Commit to Message)** $C$ commits to a message $m$ using Naor's commitment. Formally, $R$ samples and sends the first message $\beta$ for Naor's commitment; $C$ samples a random tape $r$ and sends $\mathsf{c} = \mathsf{Com}_\beta(m; r)$.
3. **(Prove Stage of ppZKAoK.)** $C$ and $R$ execute the prove stage of $\mathsf{ppZKAoK}$ where $C$ proves to $R$ that he "knows" the committed message $m$ in $\mathsf{c}$. Formally, $C$ proves that $\mathsf{c} \in \mathcal{L}_\beta$ where

$$\mathcal{L}_\beta := \{\mathsf{c} \mid \exists (m, r) \ s.t. \ \mathsf{c} = \mathsf{Com}_\beta(m; r)\}. \tag{18}$$

**Decommit Stage:** $C$ sends $(m, r)$. $R$ accepts if $\mathsf{c} = \mathsf{Com}_\beta(m; r)$, and rejects otherwise.

**Theorem 6.** *Protocol 3 is a five-round public-coin post-quantum extractable commitment with* $\mathsf{EQPT}_c$*-simulation (See full version of this paper [53, Section 3]).*

*Proof.* Correctness and the public-coin property are clear from the description of the protocol in Protocol 3. One can see that it runs in five rounds noting that the first message in Step 2 can be sent parallel to the final message of Step 1 (this is because we allow $(x, w)$ to depend on the preprocessing output $\mathsf{pp}$), and the second message in Step 2 can be sent parallel to the first message of Step 3. The binding property immediately follows from that of Naor's commitment.

To show the computational hiding property, we recall that the preprocessing zero-knowledge implies preprocessing strong witness indistinguishability (Lemma 6). The computational hiding is reduced to preprocessing strong witness indistinguishability in a straightforward manner since commitments to different messages are computationally indistinguishable by the computational hiding of Naor's commitment and the commitment is sent to $R$ after finishing the preprocessing stage of $\mathsf{ppZKAoK}$.

Extractability with $\mathsf{EQPT}_c$-simulation immediately follows from the adaptive AoK with $\mathsf{EQPT}_c$-simulation property of $\mathsf{ppZKAoK}$. $\square$

**Theorem 7.** *Protocol 3 is a post-quantum extractable commitment with rewinding-safe binding property (See full version of this paper [53, Section 3]).*

*Proof (Proof (Sketch)).* The binding message is the second message in Step 2, and extractability for Protocol 3 relies on the adaptive AoK with $\mathsf{EQPT}_c$-simulation property of $\mathsf{ppZKAoK}$ in Step 3. Therefore, during extraction, binding message is not rewound. □

## References


1. Aaronson, S., Christiano, P.: Quantum money from hidden subspaces. In: Karloff, H.J., Pitassi, T. (eds.) 44th ACM STOC, pp. 41–60. ACM Press, May 2012. https://doi.org/10.1145/2213977.2213983
2. Agarwal, A., Bartusek, J., Goyal, V., Khurana, D., Malavolta, G.: Post-quantum multi-party computation. In: Canteaut, A., Standaert, F.X. (eds.) EUROCRYPT 2021, Part I. LNCS, vol. 12696, pp. 435–464. Springer, Heidelberg (2021). https://doi.org/10.1007/978-3-030-77870-5_16
3. Ananth, P., Chung, K.M., La Placa, R.L.: On the concurrent composition of quantum zero-knowledge. In: Malkin, T., Peikert, C. (eds.) CRYPTO 2021, Part I. LNCS, vol. 12825, pp. 346–374. Springer, Heidelberg, Virtual Event (2021). https://doi.org/10.1007/978-3-030-84242-0_13
4. Badrinarayanan, S., Goyal, V., Jain, A., Kalai, Y.T., Khurana, D., Sahai, A.: Promise zero knowledge and its applications to round optimal MPC. In: Shacham, H., Boldyreva, A. (eds.) CRYPTO 2018, Part II. LNCS, vol. 10992, pp. 459–487. Springer, Heidelberg (2018). https://doi.org/10.1007/978-3-319-96881-0_16
5. Barak, B.: How to go beyond the black-box simulation barrier. In: 42nd FOCS, pp. 106–115. IEEE Computer Society Press (2001). https://doi.org/10.1109/SFCS.2001.959885
6. Barak, B., Lindell, Y.: Strict polynomial-time in simulation and extraction. In: 34th ACM STOC, pp. 484–493. ACM Press (2002). https://doi.org/10.1145/509907.509979
7. Barak, B., Prabhakaran, M., Sahai, A.: Concurrent non-malleable zero knowledge. In: 47th FOCS, pp. 345–354. IEEE Computer Society Press (2006). https://doi.org/10.1109/FOCS.2006.21
8. Bellare, M., Impagliazzo, R., Naor, M.: Does parallel repetition lower the error in computationally sound protocols? In: 38th FOCS, pp. 374–383. IEEE Computer Society Press (1997). https://doi.org/10.1109/SFCS.1997.646126
9. Bitansky, N., Lin, H., Shmueli, O.: Non-malleable commitments against quantum attacks. In: Dunkelman, O., Dziembowski, S. (eds.) EUROCRYPT 2022, Part III. LNCS, vol. 13277, pp. 519–550. Springer, Heidelberg (2022). https://doi.org/10.1007/978-3-031-07082-2_19
10. Bitansky, N., Shmueli, O.: Post-quantum zero knowledge in constant rounds. In: Makarychev, K., Makarychev, Y., Tulsiani, M., Kamath, G., Chuzhoy, J. (eds.) 52nd ACM STOC, pp. 269–279. ACM Press (2020). https://doi.org/10.1145/3357713.3384324
11. Blum, M.: How to prove a theorem so no one else can claim it. In: Proceedings of the International Congress of Mathematicians, pp. 1444–1451 (1986)

12. Broadnax, B., Döttling, N., Hartung, G., Müller-Quade, J., Nagel, M.: Concurrently composable security with shielded super-polynomial simulators. In: Coron, J.S., Nielsen, J.B. (eds.) EUROCRYPT 2017, Part I. LNCS, vol. 10210, pp. 351–381. Springer, Heidelberg (2017). https://doi.org/10.1007/978-3-319-56620-7_13
13. Canetti, R.: Security and composition of multiparty cryptographic protocols. J. Cryptol. **13**(1), 143–202 (2000). https://doi.org/10.1007/s001459910006
14. Canetti, R.: Universally composable security: a new paradigm for cryptographic protocols. In: 42nd FOCS, pp. 136–145. IEEE Computer Society Press (2001). https://doi.org/10.1109/SFCS.2001.959888
15. Canetti, R., Lindell, Y., Ostrovsky, R., Sahai, A.: Universally composable two-party and multi-party secure computation. In: 34th ACM STOC, pp. 494–503. ACM Press (2002). https://doi.org/10.1145/509907.509980
16. Chatterjee, R., Liang, X., Pandey, O.: Improved black-box constructions of composable secure computation. In: Czumaj, A., Dawar, A., Merelli, E. (eds.) ICALP 2020. LIPIcs, vol. 168, pp. 28:1–28:20. Schloss Dagstuhl (2020). https://doi.org/10.4230/LIPIcs.ICALP.2020.28
17. Chia, N.H., Chung, K.M., Liang, X., Yamakawa, T.: Post-quantum simulatable extraction with minimal assumptions: black-box and constant-round. In: Dodis, Y., Shrimpton, T. (eds.) CRYPTO 2022, Part III. LNCS, vol. 13509, pp. 533–563. Springer, Heidelberg (2022). https://doi.org/10.1007/978-3-031-15982-4_18
18. Chia, N.H., Chung, K.M., Liu, Q., Yamakawa, T.: On the impossibility of post-quantum black-box zero-knowledge in constant round. In: 62nd FOCS, pp. 59–67. IEEE Computer Society Press (2022). https://doi.org/10.1109/FOCS52979.2021.00015
19. Chiesa, A., Ma, F., Spooner, N., Zhandry, M.: Post-quantum succinct arguments: breaking the quantum rewinding barrier. In: 62nd FOCS, pp. 49–58. IEEE Computer Society Press (2022). https://doi.org/10.1109/FOCS52979.2021.00014
20. Choudhuri, A.R., Ciampi, M., Goyal, V., Jain, A., Ostrovsky, R.: Round optimal secure multiparty computation from minimal assumptions. Cryptology ePrint Archive, Report 2019/216 (2019). https://eprint.iacr.org/2019/216
21. Choudhuri, A.R., Ciampi, M., Goyal, V., Jain, A., Ostrovsky, R.: Round optimal secure multiparty computation from minimal assumptions. In: Pass, R., Pietrzak, K. (eds.) TCC 2020, Part II. LNCS, vol. 12551, pp. 291–319. Springer, Heidelberg (2020). https://doi.org/10.1007/978-3-030-64378-2_11
22. Chung, K.M., Liu, F.H.: Parallel repetition theorems for interactive arguments. In: Micciancio, D. (ed.) TCC 2010. LNCS, vol. 5978, pp. 19–36. Springer, Heidelberg (2010). https://doi.org/10.1007/978-3-642-11799-2_2
23. Chung, K.M., Pass, R.: Tight parallel repetition theorems for public-coin arguments using KL-divergence. In: Dodis, Y., Nielsen, J.B. (eds.) TCC 2015, Part II. LNCS, vol. 9015, pp. 229–246. Springer, Heidelberg (2015). https://doi.org/10.1007/978-3-662-46497-7_9
24. Ciampi, M., Ostrovsky, R., Siniscalchi, L., Visconti, I.: Concurrent non-malleable commitments (and more) in 3 rounds. In: Robshaw, M., Katz, J. (eds.) CRYPTO 2016, Part III. LNCS, vol. 9816, pp. 270–299. Springer, Heidelberg (2016). https://doi.org/10.1007/978-3-662-53015-3_10
25. Ciampi, M., Ostrovsky, R., Siniscalchi, L., Visconti, I.: Delayed-input non-malleable zero knowledge and multi-party coin tossing in four rounds. In: Kalai, Y., Reyzin, L. (eds.) TCC 2017, Part I. LNCS, vol. 10677, pp. 711–742. Springer, Heidelberg (2017). https://doi.org/10.1007/978-3-319-70500-2_24

26. Ciampi, M., Ostrovsky, R., Siniscalchi, L., Visconti, I.: Four-round concurrent non-malleable commitments from one-way functions. In: Katz, J., Shacham, H. (eds.) CRYPTO 2017, Part II. LNCS, vol. 10402, pp. 127–157. Springer, Heidelberg (2017). https://doi.org/10.1007/978-3-319-63715-0_5
27. Dodis, Y., Wichs, D.: Non-malleable extractors and symmetric key cryptography from weak secrets. In: Mitzenmacher, M. (ed.) 41st ACM STOC, pp. 601–610. ACM Press (2009). https://doi.org/10.1145/1536414.1536496
28. Dolev, D., Dwork, C., Naor, M.: Non-malleable cryptography (extended abstract). In: 23rd ACM STOC, pp. 542–552. ACM Press (1991). https://doi.org/10.1145/103418.103474
29. Dziembowski, S., Pietrzak, K., Wichs, D.: Non-malleable codes. In: Yao, A.C.C. (ed.) ICS 2010, pp. 434–452. Tsinghua University Press (2010)
30. Feige, U., Lapidot, D., Shamir, A.: Multiple non-interactive zero knowledge proofs based on a single random string (extended abstract). In: 31st FOCS, pp. 308–317. IEEE Computer Society Press (1990). https://doi.org/10.1109/FSCS.1990.89549
31. Feige, U., Shamir, A.: Witness indistinguishable and witness hiding protocols. In: 22nd ACM STOC, pp. 416–426. ACM Press (1990). https://doi.org/10.1145/100216.100272
32. Feige, U., Shamir, A.: Zero knowledge proofs of knowledge in two rounds. In: Brassard, G. (ed.) CRYPTO'89. LNCS, vol. 435, pp. 526–544. Springer, Heidelberg (1990). https://doi.org/10.1007/0-387-34805-0_46
33. Fiat, A., Shamir, A.: How to prove yourself: practical solutions to identification and signature problems. In: Odlyzko, A.M. (ed.) CRYPTO'86. LNCS, vol. 263, pp. 186–194. Springer, Heidelberg (1987). https://doi.org/10.1007/3-540-47721-7_12
34. Folwarczný, L., Göös, M., Hubáček, P., Maystre, G., Yuan, W.: One-way functions vs. TFNP: simpler and improved. Cryptology ePrint Archive, Paper 2023/945 (2023). https://eprint.iacr.org/2023/945
35. Garg, S., Goyal, V., Jain, A., Sahai, A.: Concurrently secure computation in constant rounds. In: Pointcheval, D., Johansson, T. (eds.) EUROCRYPT 2012. LNCS, vol. 7237, pp. 99–116. Springer, Heidelberg (2012). https://doi.org/10.1007/978-3-642-29011-4_8
36. Garg, S., Kiyoshima, S., Pandey, O.: On the exact round complexity of self-composable two-party computation. In: Coron, J.S., Nielsen, J.B. (eds.) EUROCRYPT 2017, Part II. LNCS, vol. 10211, pp. 194–224. Springer, Heidelberg (2017). https://doi.org/10.1007/978-3-319-56614-6_7
37. Garg, S., Mukherjee, P., Pandey, O., Polychroniadou, A.: The exact round complexity of secure computation. In: Fischlin, M., Coron, J.S. (eds.) EUROCRYPT 2016, Part II. LNCS, vol. 9666, pp. 448–476. Springer, Heidelberg (2016). https://doi.org/10.1007/978-3-662-49896-5_16
38. Goldreich, O., Krawczyk, H.: On the composition of zero-knowledge proof systems. In: Paterson, M.S. (ed.) ICALP 1990. LNCS, vol. 443, pp. 268–282. Springer, Heidelberg (1990). https://doi.org/10.1007/BFb0032038
39. Goyal, V.: Constant round non-malleable protocols using one way functions. In: Fortnow, L., Vadhan, S.P. (eds.) 43rd ACM STOC, pp. 695–704. ACM Press (2011). https://doi.org/10.1145/1993636.1993729
40. Goyal, V., Lee, C.K., Ostrovsky, R., Visconti, I.: Constructing non-malleable commitments: A black-box approach. In: 53rd FOCS, pp. 51–60. IEEE Computer Society Press (2012). https://doi.org/10.1109/FOCS.2012.47
41. Goyal, V., Pandey, O., Richelson, S.: Textbook non-malleable commitments. In: Wichs, D., Mansour, Y. (eds.) 48th ACM STOC, pp. 1128–1141. ACM Press (2016). https://doi.org/10.1145/2897518.2897657

42. Goyal, V., Richelson, S.: Non-malleable commitments using Goldreich-Levin list decoding. In: Zuckerman, D. (ed.) 60th FOCS, pp. 686–699. IEEE Computer Society Press (2019). https://doi.org/10.1109/FOCS.2019.00047
43. Hallgren, S., Smith, A., Song, F.: Classical cryptographic protocols in a quantum world. In: Rogaway, P. (ed.) CRYPTO 2011. LNCS, vol. 6841, pp. 411–428. Springer, Heidelberg (2011). https://doi.org/10.1007/978-3-642-22792-9_23
44. Håstad, J., Pass, R., Wikström, D., Pietrzak, K.: An efficient parallel repetition theorem. In: Micciancio, D. (ed.) TCC 2010. LNCS, vol. 5978, pp. 1–18. Springer, Heidelberg (2010). https://doi.org/10.1007/978-3-642-11799-2_1
45. Hubácek, P., Kamath, C., Král, K., Slívová, V.: On average-case hardness in TFNP from one-way functions. In: Pass, R., Pietrzak, K. (eds.) TCC 2020, Part III. LNCS, vol. 12552, pp. 614–638. Springer, Heidelberg (2020). https://doi.org/10.1007/978-3-030-64381-2_22
46. Hubácek, P., Naor, M., Yogev, E.: The journey from NP to TFNP hardness. In: Papadimitriou, C.H. (ed.) ITCS 2017, vol. 4266, pp. 60:1–60:21. LIPIcs, 67 (2017). https://doi.org/10.4230/LIPIcs.ITCS.2017.60
47. Jain, A., Kalai, Y.T., Khurana, D., Rothblum, R.: Distinguisher-dependent simulation in two rounds and its applications. In: Katz, J., Shacham, H. (eds.) CRYPTO 2017, Part II. LNCS, vol. 10402, pp. 158–189. Springer, Heidelberg (2017). https://doi.org/10.1007/978-3-319-63715-0_6
48. Katz, J., Koo, C.Y.: On constructing universal one-way hash functions from arbitrary one-way functions. Cryptology ePrint Archive, Report 2005/328 (2005). https://eprint.iacr.org/2005/328
49. Katz, J., Ostrovsky, R., Smith, A.: Round efficiency of multi-party computation with a dishonest majority. In: Biham, E. (ed.) EUROCRYPT 2003. LNCS, vol. 2656, pp. 578–595. Springer, Heidelberg (2003). https://doi.org/10.1007/3-540-39200-9_36
50. Kiyoshima, S.: Round-efficient black-box construction of composable multi-party computation. In: Garay, J.A., Gennaro, R. (eds.) CRYPTO 2014, Part II. LNCS, vol. 8617, pp. 351–368. Springer, Heidelberg (2014). https://doi.org/10.1007/978-3-662-44381-1_20
51. Kiyoshima, S.: Black-box impossibilities of obtaining 2-round weak ZK and strong WI from polynomial hardness. In: Nissim, K., Waters, B. (eds.) TCC 2021, Part I. LNCS, vol. 13042, pp. 369–400. Springer, Heidelberg (2021). https://doi.org/10.1007/978-3-030-90459-3_13
52. Lapidot, D., Shamir, A.: Publicly verifiable non-interactive zero-knowledge proofs. In: Menezes, A.J., Vanstone, S.A. (eds.) CRYPTO'90. LNCS, vol. 537, pp. 353–365. Springer, Heidelberg (1991). https://doi.org/10.1007/3-540-38424-3_26
53. Liang, X., Pandey, O., Tang, Y., Yamakawa, T.: Almost-total puzzles and their applications. Cryptology ePrint Archive, Paper 2025/949 (2025). https://eprint.iacr.org/2025/949
54. Liang, X., Pandey, O., Yamakawa, T.: A new approach to post-quantum non-malleability. In: 2023 IEEE 64th Annual Symposium on Foundations of Computer Science (FOCS), pp. 568–579. IEEE Computer Society, Los Alamitos, CA, USA (2023). https://doi.org/10.1109/FOCS57990.2023.00041. https://doi.ieeecomputersociety.org/10.1109/FOCS57990.2023.00041
55. Lombardi, A., Ma, F., Spooner, N.: Post-quantum zero knowledge, revisited or: how to do quantum rewinding undetectably. In: 63rd FOCS, pp. 851–859. IEEE Computer Society Press (2022). https://doi.org/10.1109/FOCS54457.2022.00086

56. Lunemann, C., Nielsen, J.B.: Fully simulatable quantum-secure coin-flipping and applications. In: Nitaj, A., Pointcheval, D. (eds.) AFRICACRYPT 2011. LNCS, vol. 6737, pp. 21–40. Springer, Heidelberg (2011). https://doi.org/10.1007/978-3-642-21969-6_2
57. Megiddo, N., Papadimitriou, C.H.: On total functions, existence theorems and computational complexity. Theor. Comput. Sci. **81**(2), 317–324 (1991). https://doi.org/10.1016/0304-3975(91)90200-L
58. Micali, S., Pass, R., Rosen, A.: Input-indistinguishable computation. In: 47th FOCS, pp. 367–378. IEEE Computer Society Press (2006). https://doi.org/10.1109/FOCS.2006.43
59. Naor, M., Yung, M.: Universal one-way hash functions and their cryptographic applications. In: 21st ACM STOC, pp. 33–43. ACM Press (1989). https://doi.org/10.1145/73007.73011
60. Pandey, O., Pass, R., Vaikuntanathan, V.: Adaptive one-way functions and applications. In: Wagner, D. (ed.) CRYPTO 2008. LNCS, vol. 5157, pp. 57–74. Springer, Heidelberg (2008). https://doi.org/10.1007/978-3-540-85174-5_4
61. Papadimitriou, C.H.: On the complexity of the parity argument and other inefficient proofs of existence. J. Comput. Syst. Sci. **48**(3), 498–532 (1994). https://doi.org/10.1016/S0022-0000(05)80063-7
62. Pass, R.: Simulation in quasi-polynomial time, and its application to protocol composition. In: Biham, E. (ed.) EUROCRYPT 2003. LNCS, vol. 2656, pp. 160–176. Springer, Heidelberg (2003). https://doi.org/10.1007/3-540-39200-9_10
63. Pass, R., Rosen, A.: New and improved constructions of non-malleable cryptographic protocols. In: Gabow, H.N., Fagin, R. (eds.) 37th ACM STOC, pp. 533–542. ACM Press (2005). https://doi.org/10.1145/1060590.1060670
64. Pass, R., Venkitasubramaniam, M.: Is it easier to prove theorems that are guaranteed to be true? In: 61st FOCS, pp. 1255–1267. IEEE Computer Society Press (2020). https://doi.org/10.1109/FOCS46700.2020.00119
65. Pass, R., Wee, H.: Black-box constructions of two-party protocols from one-way functions. In: Reingold, O. (ed.) TCC 2009. LNCS, vol. 5444, pp. 403–418. Springer, Heidelberg (2009). https://doi.org/10.1007/978-3-642-00457-5_24
66. Prabhakaran, M., Sahai, A.: New notions of security: achieving universal composability without trusted setup. In: Babai, L. (ed.) 36th ACM STOC, pp. 242–251. ACM Press (2004). https://doi.org/10.1145/1007352.1007394
67. Rompel, J.: One-way functions are necessary and sufficient for secure signatures. In: 22nd ACM STOC, pp. 387–394. ACM Press (1990). https://doi.org/10.1145/100216.100269
68. Unruh, D.: Quantum proofs of knowledge. In: Pointcheval, D., Johansson, T. (eds.) EUROCRYPT 2012. LNCS, vol. 7237, pp. 135–152. Springer, Heidelberg (2012). https://doi.org/10.1007/978-3-642-29011-4_10
69. Unruh, D.: Computationally binding quantum commitments. In: Fischlin, M., Coron, J.S. (eds.) EUROCRYPT 2016, Part II. LNCS, vol. 9666, pp. 497–527. Springer, Heidelberg (2016). https://doi.org/10.1007/978-3-662-49896-5_18
70. Watrous, J.: Zero-knowledge against quantum attacks. In: Kleinberg, J.M. (ed.) 38th ACM STOC, pp. 296–305. ACM Press (2006). https://doi.org/10.1145/1132516.1132560
71. Wee, H.: Black-box, round-efficient secure computation via non-malleability amplification. In: 51st FOCS, pp. 531–540. IEEE Computer Society Press (2010). https://doi.org/10.1109/FOCS.2010.87

# Foundations

# On the Limits of Non-interactive Blind Signatures

Kazuki Yamamura[1(✉)], Tetsuya Okuda[1], Eiichiro Fujisaki[2], and Masayuki Abe[1]

[1] NTT Social Informatics Laboratories, Tokyo, Japan
kazuki.yamamura@ntt.com
[2] Japan Advanced Institute of Science and Technology, Ishikawa, Japan

**Abstract.** Non-interactive blind signatures (NIBS), introduced by Hanzlik (Eurocrypt'23), enable the issuance of blind signatures on random messages without requiring interaction and have found applications in a variety of privacy-preserving protocols. Despite recent progress, all known constructions of NIBS rely on the random oracle model and/or the common reference string model, or on complexity-leveraging techniques. As a result, constructing such schemes in the plain model under standard assumptions remains an open problem.

In this work, we present new results showing that it is hard to construct NIBS in the plain model from standard assumptions, as long as the adversary is used in a black-box manner. Specifically, we first focus on black-box reductions for basing the security of *statistically blind* NIBS on any non-interactive assumption. We then extend this limitation to the *computationally blind* setting under conditions inspired by the known impossibility results for standard blind signatures, introduced by Fischlin and Schröder (Eurocrypt'10).

As an independent contribution, we study the relationship between two strong notions of blindness—strong recipient blindness and strong nonce blindness—recently introduced by Baldimtsi et al. (Asiacrypt '24). We show the separation result by constructing schemes that satisfy strong recipient blindness but not strong nonce blindness, and vice versa. Our results suggest that both notions are independently necessary for the provable security of NIBS schemes.

**Keywords:** Non-Interactive Blind Signatures · Plain Model · Impossibility

## 1 Introduction

### 1.1 (Standard) Blind Signatures

Blind signature schemes, introduced by Chaum [18], are a fundamental cryptographic primitive with numerous applications, such as e-voting [15], e-cash [17,18], and anonymous credentials [7]. A blind signature scheme can be

© International Association for Cryptologic Research 2026
G. Hanaoka and B.-Y. Yang (Eds.): ASIACRYPT 2025, LNCS 16252, pp. 447–481, 2026.
https://doi.org/10.1007/978-981-95-5125-5_15

viewed as an interactive protocol between a signer holding a signing key and a recipient holding a message, allowing the recipient to obtain a signature generated by the signer, who remains oblivious to the signed message. Blind signature schemes must satisfy two key security properties: *blindness* and *one-more unforgeability*. Informally, blindness ensures that the signer cannot learn any correlation between the interaction and the resulting message-signature pair, while one-more unforgeability guarantees that the recipient cannot generate a valid signature without interacting with the signer.

One of the main efficiency metrics for blind signatures is round complexity. A *round-optimal* blind signature scheme is a two-move protocol in which the user and the signer each send one message. Although many blind signature schemes have been proposed [1,3,10,16,18,20,23,28,30–32,39,46–49,51,52,59], all existing constructions rely on random oracles, setup assumptions, interactive assumptions, or complexity leveraging. In fact, several impossibility results for blind signatures are known [8,26,54,58].

## 1.2 Non-interactive Blind Signatures

As mentioned above, standard blind signatures inherently require interaction and necessitate that the recipient maintain state in order to successfully unblind the signer's response. However, Hanzlik [38] introduced a fascinating cryptographic protocol called a non-interactive blind signature (NIBS), which enables the creation of a blind signature without requiring online interaction between the signer and the recipient.

The key insight behind NIBS is that, although standard blind signatures allow recipient-specified messages, in the case of NIBS, the message is instead the output of the unblinding process and is therefore unpredictable to both the recipient and the signer. Nevertheless, this property is acceptable—and even desirable—in many applications, such as Privacy Pass [45], whistleblowing systems, lottery systems, and airdropping e-coins [43].

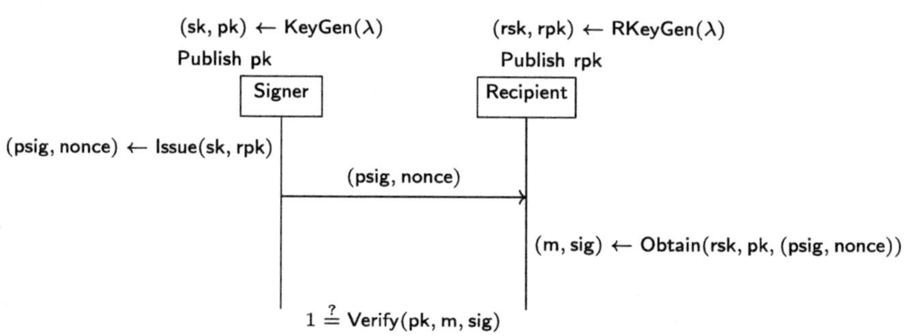


**Fig. 1.** Flow of Non-Interactive Blind Signature (NIBS)

We now provide a detailed overview of the signing procedure for NIBS. Figure 1 illustrates the flow of NIBS := (KeyGen, RKeyGen, Issue, Obtain, Verify), each component of which will be explained below. Here, $\mathsf{KeyGen}$ and $\mathsf{RKeyGen}$ denote the key generation algorithms for the signer and the recipient, respectively. Prior to the execution, unlike standard blind signatures, not only does the signer hold a secret/public key pair $(\mathsf{sk}, \mathsf{pk})$, but the recipient also holds their own secret/public key pair $(\mathsf{rsk}, \mathsf{rpk})$. First, in the $\mathsf{Issue}$ procedure, the signer generates a presignature $\mathsf{psig}$ for the recipient's public key $\mathsf{rpk}$ and a nonce $\mathsf{nonce}$ that deterministically specifies the random message to be signed, i.e., $(\mathsf{psig}, \mathsf{nonce}) \leftarrow \mathsf{Issue}(\mathsf{sk}, \mathsf{rpk})$. Next, in the $\mathsf{Obtain}$ procedure, the recipient, upon receiving the pair $(\mathsf{psig}, \mathsf{nonce})$, finalizes them into a blind signature $\mathsf{sig}$ on a random message $\mathsf{m}$ using their secret key $\mathsf{rsk}$, i.e., $(\mathsf{m}, \mathsf{sig}) \leftarrow \mathsf{Obtain}(\mathsf{rsk}, \mathsf{pk}, (\mathsf{psig}, \mathsf{nonce}))$. Finally, the signature can be verified using the signer's public key $\mathsf{pk}$: $1 \stackrel{?}{=} \mathsf{Verify}(\mathsf{pk}, \mathsf{m}, \mathsf{sig})$. The key observation here is that the recipient's public key $\mathsf{rpk}$ must be published in advance. For example, if each recipient's public key is stored in an existing PKI, then the signer can issue presignatures to a set of users without interacting with them and subsequently publish the corresponding presignatures.[1]

Like standard blind signature schemes, $\mathsf{NIBS}$ schemes must satisfy both unforgeability and blindness. In the unforgeability game, the adversary is given access to an oracle that returns a presignature-nonce pair for an adversary-specified recipient public key. In the end, the adversary must output more valid signatures than the number of oracle queries, akin to the one-more unforgeability property of standard blind signatures.

Blindness in $\mathsf{NIBS}$ consists of two distinct properties: *recipient blindness* and *nonce blindness*. Recipient blindness ensures that message-signature pairs do not leak any information about the recipient's public key, while nonce blindness guarantees that they do not reveal any information about the nonce. Formally, in the recipient blindness game, the adversary is given two honestly generated recipient public keys $\mathsf{rpk}_0$ and $\mathsf{rpk}_1$, and outputs two presignature-nonce pairs $(\mathsf{psig}_0, \mathsf{nonce}_0)$ and $(\mathsf{psig}_1, \mathsf{nonce}_1)$. These are finalized by the challenger into message-signature pairs $(\mathsf{m}_0, \mathsf{sig}_0)$ and $(\mathsf{m}_1, \mathsf{sig}_1)$. The adversary, given these two message-signature pairs in random order, is then required to distinguish which recipient creates each pair. In the nonce blindness game, the adversary is given only a single recipient public key $\mathsf{rpk}$ and must distinguish between the nonces used in the presignature-nonce pairs. Both blindness definitions do not consider aborts: if one of the signatures cannot be finalized, the adversary is given $(\perp, \perp)$ instead.

The above blindness property, introduced in [38], is referred to as *weak blindness* in this paper. In many applications, weak blindness is not sufficient,[2] and

[1] Thus, we can regard $\mathsf{NIBS}$ as a two-move protocol if the first message is a freshly generated recipient public key and the signer's response is the presignature-nonce pair.

[2] As mentioned in [6], we also remark that there exist applications where the notion of weak blindness is sufficient. As a concrete example, consider one-per-user anonymous airdrops or e-voting tokens, where only a single presignature is generated for each recipient.

NIBS schemes are therefore required to satisfy a stronger form of blindness introduced in [6]. This property, referred to as *strong blindness* in this paper, requires that the scheme satisfies both recipient blindness and nonce blindness, even in scenarios where multiple presignatures are issued.

**Table 1.** Comparisons of Existing NIBS Schemes

| Scheme | Assumption | Plain Model | Blindness |
|---|---|---|---|
| [38, Scheme 3] | InvDDH, sDDH | ✗ (ROM + GGM) | Weak* |
| [38, Scheme 5] | Generic | ✗ (ROM or CRS) | Weak |
| [6, Section 5] | Generic | ✗ (ROM + CRS) | Strong |
| [6, Section 7] | rOM-ISIS | ✗ (ROM + CRS) | Weak |
| [6, Appendix D] | Generic | ✗ (CRS) | Strong |
| [50] | CL† | ✓ | Weak |
| [40, Scheme 4] | Generic | ✗ (ROM) | Strong* |
| [40, Scheme 5] | QR, others | ✗ (ROM) | Strong |

† CL = Complexity Leveraging

* Blindness against honest-but-curious adversaries

Formally, in the strong blindness game, the adversary is given oracle access to the recipient's secret key in the form of Obtain queries. This Obtain oracle takes as input the signer's public key and a presignature-nonce pair, and returns the corresponding message-signature pair honestly finalized using the Obtain algorithm. To ensure that the game is not trivially impossible, the adversary is restricted from making Obtain queries on either of the two challenge presignatures $\mathsf{psig}_0$, $\mathsf{psig}_1$ or their corresponding nonces $\mathsf{nonce}_0$, $\mathsf{nonce}_1$. Our results focus on this strong blindness notion.

Following Hanzlik's work [38], multiple NIBS schemes have been proposed [6, 40, 50, 63]. In Table 1, we provide a comparison of these existing schemes.

To the best of our knowledge, all schemes—except [50]—are instantiated outside the plain model, meaning they rely on the Random Oracle Model (ROM) or the Common Reference String (CRS) model. However, in the trusted setup model (i.e., outside the plain model), if an authority inserts a backdoor, the scheme's security can no longer be guaranteed. In fact, [38] left the instantiation of a plain-model counterpart as an open problem. More recently, the authors of [50] presented the first NIBS scheme in the plain model. However, the scheme relies on complexity leveraging, which requires large parameters and significantly reduces efficiency. Furthermore, the scheme only satisfies *weak* blindness, leaving the instantiation of a plain-model counterpart with *strong* blindness as an open problem.

These results naturally lead to the following central question:

*Can we construct a* NIBS *scheme that achieves strong blindness from standard assumptions, without relying on the ROM or CRS?*

### 1.3 Our Contribution

Our contribution is to address the central question of whether one can construct a strongly blind NIBS scheme in the plain model. Our answer is negative. We demonstrate that constructing such a scheme is hard as long as the adversary is used in a black-box manner. Specifically,

1. We first rule out reductions that reduce the unforgeability of a *statistically* strongly blind NIBS scheme to non-interactive assumptions.
2. We then extend this result to the computational blindness setting.

We begin with the statistical setting rather than the computational one[3] because the proof outline is simpler and clarifies the approach we later adapt to the computational case[4].

Our second result, which applies to the computational setting, requires that the NIBS scheme satisfies a computational blindness property defined relative to a generic forgery oracle.[5] This blindness notion is inspired by the work of Fischlin and Schröder [26], who established an impossibility result for standard blind signatures. (We discuss this in more detail in Sect. 1.4.)

Shifting focus to the positive side, we present a non-interactive, statistically strongly blind signature scheme in the random oracle model[6]. This construction follows the generic framework of [6], representing the strongest form known to date and aligning closely with the above impossibility result for the statistical case. Furthermore, we anticipate that this construction will aid in facilitating the reader's understanding of our impossibility proof.

As an independent contribution, we focus on the definitions of strong blindness, investigating whether there is an essential difference between strong recipient blindness and strong nonce blindness. As mentioned above, strong blindness properties are necessary for many NIBS applications. However, these two notions appear to be closely related—in fact, the proofs of blindness for some existing NIBS schemes follow similar steps (e.g., [38, Scheme4], [6, Section 5, Appendix D], and [50]). This raises the following question: Is there an essential difference between strong recipient blindness and strong nonce blindness? Alternatively,

*does there exist a* NIBS *scheme that satisfies one but not the other?*

---

[3] Needless to say, proving impossibility in the computational setting is typically harder than in the statistical setting.

[4] This camera-ready version presents only the *statistical* impossibility result for *simple* reductions—i.e., reductions that run a single instance of the adversary, without concurrency or resetting. Complete proofs for both the statistical and computational settings, including the case of general (concurrent/resetting) reductions, appear in the full version.

[5] Note that this forgery oracle, which returns presignature-message pairs, is not the same as the Obtain oracle used in the strong blindness game, which returns message-signature pairs.

[6] The details of this statistically strongly blind signature scheme are given in the full version.

The analogous question for weak blindness was resolved by [50], which demonstrated a separation result between weak recipient blindness and weak nonce blindness. However, it remained unclear whether the same holds for strong blindness definitions, since the adversary in the strong blindness games clearly has more power than in the weak blindness setting. Thus, this question remained open. We resolve this question by demonstrating a separation between the two strong blindness properties. Specifically, we construct:

- a NIBS scheme that satisfies strong nonce blindness but not strong recipient blindness, and
- a NIBS scheme that satisfies strong recipient blindness but not strong nonce blindness.

This result implies that both strong recipient blindness and strong nonce blindness must be proven independently to ensure the security of NIBS schemes in practice.

### 1.4 Related Work

**Existing NIBS Schemes.** Hanzlik [38] first provided a generic construction of NIBS. They also designed an efficient NIBS scheme based on structure-preserving signatures on equivalence classes (SPS-EQ) [29,37], and a TNIBS based on tag-based equivalence class signatures [41].

Later, Baldimtsi et al. revisited the NIBS concept introduced in [38] and formalized its syntax and security definitions [6]. They particularly pointed out a weakness in Hanzlik's original blindness property, where the adversary cannot gain access to anything other than two challenge message-signature pairs. This definition fails to cover certain scenarios where a malicious signer issues multiple signatures to the same recipient. To address this limitation, [6] introduced a stronger blindness property, where the adversary is given access to a signing oracle that returns multiple message-signature pairs based on the queried signer's public key.

The authors of [6] also proposed a generic construction that satisfies strong blindness using circuit-private leveled homomorphic encryption. Their scheme achieves an optimal signature size at the cost of large public keys. Moreover, they introduced a lattice-based instantiation of NIBS that satisfies the weaker blindness notion proposed in [38]. Note that even when a NIBS scheme only satisfies such weaker blindness, it remains sufficient for applications such as one-per-user anonymous airdrops or e-voting tokens.

To apply NIBS schemes to various practical applications, recipient public keys should ideally be "wild' public keys, such as RSA or BLS [12]. However, existing constructions do not provide such wild public key formats. To address this issue, [40] introduced an efficient NIBS scheme that uses RSA keys as the recipient's keys. They specifically proposed a new generic framework for NIBS based on non-interactive oblivious transfer, enabling the construction of practical schemes with RSA wild keys.

All of these schemes are proven secure in the random oracle model (ROM) or the common reference string (CRS) model. Meanwhile, Yamamura et al. recently introduced a plain-model NIBS construction [50]. However, their scheme relies on complexity leveraging, which requires large parameters. Moreover, the scheme only achieves Hanzlik's original blindness (not the stronger notion introduced in [6]). Therefore, constructing a plain-model NIBS scheme from standard assumptions remains an open problem. In this work, we provide evidence that this goal is hard to achieve in the black-box setting.

**Separation Between Strong Blindness Definitions of NIBS.** As discussed above, NIBS schemes must satisfy two distinct notions of blindness: recipient blindness and nonce blindness. While both properties are necessary for ensuring security in NIBS applications, they appear superficially similar. This leads to a natural question: is there a fundamental difference between recipient blindness and nonce blindness? More specifically, does there exist a NIBS scheme that satisfies recipient blindness but not nonce blindness, or vice versa?

This question was recently addressed in the affirmative by [50], which demonstrated the existence of schemes that satisfy weak recipient blindness but not weak nonce blindness, and vice versa. These results imply that the two weak blindness notions are logically independent, and that both must be explicitly proven to hold in any secure NIBS scheme.

However, the work of [50] does not address the same separation question for the *strong* notions of blindness. While strong recipient blindness and strong nonce blindness appear even more closely related—since the adversary is allowed to obtain multiple message-signature pairs in the strong blindness game—their precise relationship remains unclear. In this paper, we investigate this question and show that the two strong definitions are also independent.

**The Impossibility of Standard Blind Signatures.** Several impossibility results for standard blind signatures have been established [8,26,54,58]. Lindell [54] first showed that concurrently secure blind signatures are impossible to construct in the plain model under simulation-based security notions.

Later, Fischlin and Schröder [26] demonstrated that three-move schemes in the plain model cannot be constructed from non-interactive assumptions. Their results, based on meta-reduction techniques [13], show that there is no black-box reduction from the one-more unforgeability of the scheme to the non-interactive assumption. Specifically, [26] restricted the reduction to allow running multiple instances of the adversary but prohibited "nesting" these different executions. Under this setting, they proved that there is no black-box reduction from the security of three-move (or fewer) *computationally* blind signatures to a non-interactive assumption, assuming the following conditions: (1) One can efficiently check whether a valid signature can be derived from an execution transcript (this property is called Signature Derivation Check, SDCh), (2) The blindness property holds relative to a forgery oracle, (3) One can efficiently check whether the signer's public key has a corresponding secret key (this property is called

Key Validation Check, KVCh), and (4) The reduction is restricted from running the adversary concurrently or resettably[7].

Among these, our work particularly focuses on condition (2), as our impossibility result for *computationally blind* NIBS assumes a similar but weaker condition.

Specifically, in [26], the forgery oracle takes a signer's public key pk as input and returns a corresponding secret key (uniformly chosen if multiple exist). In contrast, our oracle, tailored for the NIBS setting, takes as input both a signer's public key pk and a recipient's public key rpk, samples a secret key sk corresponding to pk, and returns a presignature-nonce pair $(\mathsf{psig}, \mathsf{nonce}) \leftarrow \mathsf{Issue}(\mathsf{sk}, \mathsf{rpk})$.

The key difference lies in that the oracle in [26] reveals the signer's secret key, while our oracle does not. Instead, it returns only a derived presignature-nonce pair. Therefore, the blindness requirement assumed in our setting is strictly weaker than that of [26]. (More details are provided in Sect. 2.2.)

Later, Pass [58] proved an impossibility result for unique blind signatures, such as Chaum's blind signature scheme, where the corresponding signature is uniquely determined by the message. This result specifically shows that there is no general reduction from the security of unique blind signatures to a non-interactive assumption, implying that the above conditions can be ruled out under the assumption of uniqueness.

Some readers might believe that the above impossibility results also apply to NIBS schemes, since NIBS can be viewed as a two-move protocol. However, as pointed out by Hanzlik [38], this connection is not straightforward and requires further investigation. This is primarily because, unlike in standard blind signature schemes, the recipient in a NIBS scheme does not choose the message being signed. Additionally, a crucial and distinguishing feature of the NIBS setting is that the recipient holds a secret key, whereas in standard blind signature settings, no such secret key exists.

In fact, our impossibility result for NIBS does not rely on certain assumptions that are necessary in [26], such as the Signature Derivation Check (SDCh) and the Key Validation Check (KVCh). This further highlights the structural differences between NIBS and traditional blind signature schemes, and underscores the need for dedicated analysis in the NIBS context.

**Meta-reduction Paradigm.** In proving our main result, we adopt the *meta-reduction* paradigm, originally introduced by Boneh and Venkatesan [13]. This paradigm aims to derive a contradiction by showing that the existence of a black-box reduction $\mathcal{R}$ breaking a cryptographic assumption $C$ would imply the existence of a PPT algorithm $\mathcal{M}$ (the meta-reduction) that also breaks $C$, using only black-box access to $\mathcal{R}$. Numerous impossibility results have since been established using this paradigm [2,4,5,9,14,19,21,24,26,27,33,36,42,44,53,55–58,60–62,64].

[7] The authors of [26] also showed that three-move *statistically* blind signature schemes cannot be constructed in the plain model if only conditions (1) and (4) are imposed.

One important challenge in the meta-reduction paradigm is handling reductions that invoke the adversary multiple times concurrently or in a resetting manner. In particular, concurrent executions may lead to *nested* invocations, a phenomenon also studied in the context of concurrent zero-knowledge [22]. If left unchecked, such nesting can lead to a super-polynomial number of rewinding steps.

To address this issue, Pass [58] proposed the *recursive rewinding strategy*. The core idea is to rewind every relevant query unless too many nested queries occur during the process. The recursion depth is geometrically reduced by a factor of $n$ at each level. Since the total number of messages is polynomial, this ensures the recursion remains within polynomial bounds. More recently, Brakerski and Medina [14] employed this strategy to prove the impossibility of adaptively secure attribute-based encryption.

An alternative and simpler technique was introduced by Morgan and Pass [56], improving upon earlier results for unique signatures [19]. Their result rules out black-box reductions (with polynomially bounded loss) from the unforgeability of unique signature schemes to interactive assumptions. Notably, their meta-reduction avoids the recursive rewinding strategy,[8] and instead rewinds the reduction only when it encounters an *end message* from which a forgery can be extracted. If a nested invocation is encountered, the meta-reduction aborts and restarts with a fresh message sequence. This bounded-rewinding strategy guarantees polynomial running time. Schäge [60] recently applied this method to rule out CCA1 security for certain ElGamal-like schemes.

These techniques [56,58] allow our result on NIBS to handle nested invocations of the adversary. However, another crucial challenge in the meta-reduction paradigm is dealing with *resetting* reductions, which can rewind the adversary with the same initial randomness. This issue did not arise in previous works [56,58], as they assume cryptographic primitives with uniqueness properties (e.g., unique signatures, unique witness-hiding proofs, or unique blind signatures), which circumvent this problem.

In contrast, NIBS schemes inherently lack such uniqueness guarantees. Therefore, in this work, we focus particularly on how to handle *resettable reductions* in the context of NIBS, extending the meta-reduction framework accordingly.

## 2 Technical Overview

In this section, we provide an overview of our results. In Sect. 2.1, we describe the idea behind our impossibility result, demonstrating the limitations of statistically strongly blind NIBS schemes in the plain model. In particular, we outline the non-existence of black-box reductions for *statistically* secure NIBS schemes through the meta-reduction paradigm. In Sect. 2.2, we shift our focus to the computational setting and describe the limits of computationally secure NIBS schemes. In Sect. 2.3, we provide an overview of our construction of a statistical

[8] The strategy of [58] does not extend directly to the unique signature setting, since repeated rewinding may bias the forgery distribution.

NIBS scheme in the random oracle model. Finally, in Sect. 2.4, we shift focus, providing an overview of our separation results concerning the definitions of strong blindness.

### 2.1 The Impossibility Results for Statistical Blind NIBS

We first present the insight behind the limitations of constructing strongly statistically blind NIBS schemes. In demonstrating our result, we follow the "meta-reduction" paradigm, originally introduced by Boneh and Venkatesan [13].

We now outline the flow of our proof using the meta-reduction paradigm. Specifically, we provide an overview of how to construct a meta-reduction that breaks a non-interactive assumption $C$ by using a black-box reduction that reduces the one-more unforgeability of NIBS to assumption $C$. In short, assuming that there exists a black-box reduction $\mathcal{R}$, which uses an adversary $\mathcal{A}$ to break the one-more unforgeability of NIBS, we can construct a PPT algorithm (i.e., the "meta-reduction") that breaks assumption $C$ by using black-box access to $\mathcal{R}$, thereby contradicting $C$.

The intuitive flow of our proof is as follows: First, we introduce an "ideal" adversary that can break the one-more unforgeability of NIBS. The term "ideal" means that this adversary is allowed to use unbounded computational power. If such an ideal adversary existed, then a reduction $\mathcal{R}$ accessing the ideal adversary in a black-box manner could break assumption $C$. Of course, this does not straightforwardly work because the ideal adversary is assumed to have unbounded computational power. Hence, we next set up a simulation of the ideal adversary using only bounded computational resources. That is, we construct a "meta-reduction" that breaks assumption $C$: if the simulation succeeds in mimicking the behavior of the ideal adversary, then the reduction $\mathcal{R}$ would be able to break $C$.

To demonstrate the indistinguishability between the ideal adversary and the simulation conducted by the meta-reduction, we rely on a new blindness property, which we refer to as Secret-Key Independence. Notably, we prove that every statistically blind NIBS scheme satisfies the Secret-Key Independence property.

**Ideal Adversary.** We now describe the specific procedure of the ideal adversary $\mathcal{A}^{\Sigma}$ against the one-more unforgeability of NIBS.[9]

Given the signer's public key $\mathsf{pk}$ from the one-more unforgeability game, the ideal adversary $\mathcal{A}^{\Sigma}$ first creates an honestly generated message-signature pair $(\mathsf{m}, \mathsf{sig})$ with the help of the game. Specifically, $\mathcal{A}^{\Sigma}$ honestly generates a recipient key pair $(\mathsf{rsk}, \mathsf{rpk})$, then outputs the public key $\mathsf{rpk}$ and obtains a message-signature pair $(\mathsf{m}, \mathsf{sig})$ from the game's response, derived from the presignature-nonce pair $(\mathsf{psig}, \mathsf{nonce})$ using the secret key $\mathsf{rsk}$.

To obtain a second valid message-signature pair without further assistance from the game, $\mathcal{A}^{\Sigma}$ enumerates all valid message-signature pairs that could be

[9] The one-more unforgeability game requires adversaries to obtain two (different) message-signature pairs while interacting with the honest signer only once.

derived from the public data $(\mathsf{pk}, \mathsf{rpk}, (\mathsf{psig}, \mathsf{nonce}))$ using unbounded computational power, and randomly selects one from this set. For readability, we model this unbounded power as an oracle, called the generic forgery oracle and denoted by $\Sigma$. Let $(\mathsf{m}', \mathsf{sig}')$ denote the second valid message-signature pair obtained via the oracle $\Sigma$, that is, $(\mathsf{m}', \mathsf{sig}') \leftarrow \Sigma(\mathsf{pk}, \mathsf{rpk}, (\mathsf{psig}, \mathsf{nonce}))$.

Some readers might worry that the message $\mathsf{m}'$ could coincide with $\mathsf{m}$, causing $\mathcal{A}^\Sigma$ to fail to win the one-more unforgeability game. However, recipient blindness and the reusability property ensure that the two messages generated by $\mathcal{A}^\Sigma$ are distinct except with negligible probability (by Corollary 1).

Thus, the ideal adversary $\mathcal{A}^\Sigma$ eventually returns the two valid message-signature pairs $(\mathsf{m}, \mathsf{sig})$ and $(\mathsf{m}', \mathsf{sig}')$ to the game and wins. Therefore, assuming the existence of a black-box reduction $\mathcal{R}$ from one-more unforgeability to a hard non-interactive problem, $\mathcal{R}$ with access to the ideal adversary $\mathcal{A}^\Sigma$ would solve the hard non-interactive problem with high probability.

**Constructing Meta-reduction for Simple Reduction.** We now describe the construction of a meta-reduction $\mathcal{M}$ that can simulate the ideal adversary without relying on the generic forgery oracle $\Sigma$ (i.e., using only bounded computational power). Here, we assume that the reduction runs the adversary a single time without rewinding. We refer to such a reduction as a *simple reduction.* (The discussion of general reductions will be provided later.)

Fig. 2 illustrates the flow of the meta-reduction $\mathcal{M}$. $\mathcal{M}$ first honestly interacts with the reduction $\mathcal{R}$ on input a hard problem instance $y$ along with initial randomness $r_\mathcal{R}$, obtaining the first message-signature pair $(\mathsf{m}, \mathsf{sig})$. This procedure follows the same steps as the ideal adversary ((1)-(5)).

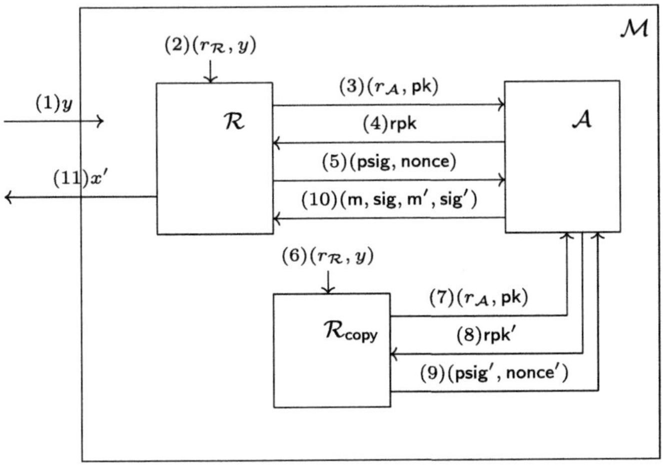


**Fig. 2.** Meta Reduction $\mathcal{M}$.

However, the approach to obtaining a second message-signature pair differs from that of the ideal adversary. The meta-reduction $\mathcal{M}$ rewinds the simple reduction $\mathcal{R}$ and interacts with it again, using a different recipient public key from the one used in the non-rewound execution, to obtain another message-signature pair $(\mathsf{m}', \mathsf{sig}')$[10] ((6)-(9)).

Thus, the meta-reduction $\mathcal{M}$ can eventually return the two message-signature pairs to $\mathcal{R}$ and obtain a putative solution $x'$ for $y$ ((10)-(11)).

**Secret-Key Independence.** We need to show that the (simple) reduction $\mathcal{R}$ cannot distinguish between the meta-reduction's simulation of the adversary and the actual behavior of the ideal adversary. To guarantee this indistinguishability, we introduce a new weaker blindness notion called *Secret-Key Independence*. This property requires that a malicious signer cannot determine which secret key the recipient used to obtain a message-signature pair.

This (artificial) notion ensures that the reduction cannot distinguish between the meta-reduction and the ideal adversary. Figure 3 provides an overview of the flow of Secret-Key Independence. Intuitively, the Secret-Key Independence game provides the adversary with two message-signature pairs $(\mathsf{m}_b, \mathsf{sig}_b)$ and $(\mathsf{m}', \mathsf{sig}')$, where $(\mathsf{m}_b, \mathsf{sig}_b)$ is honestly generated by the recipient, and $(\mathsf{m}', \mathsf{sig}')$ is derived through the generic forgery oracle $\Sigma$. This setup implies that if $b = 0$, then both pairs are derived from the meta-reduction, whereas if $b = 1$, then both pairs are derived from the ideal adversary.

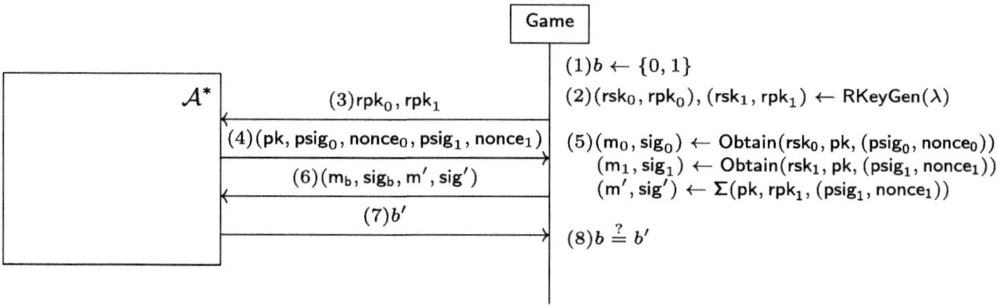


**Fig. 3.** Flow of Secret-key Independence Game.

The Secret-Key Independence property ensures that the reduction cannot distinguish between the meta-reduction's simulation of the adversary and the actual behavior of the ideal adversary. See Fig. 4, which provides an overview of the reduction from indistinguishability to Secret-Key Independence.

Given two recipient keys $\mathsf{rpk}$ and $\mathsf{rpk}'$, the reduction $\mathcal{R}^*$ runs the reduction $\mathcal{R}$ on input a hard problem instance $y$ and initial randomness $r_{\mathcal{R}}$ ((1)-(2)). The

[10] Note that the rewound reduction is provided with the same input problem instance $y$ and the same initial randomness $r_{\mathcal{R}}$ as the non-rewound reduction, ensuring that the reduction initially outputs the same public key in both executions.

reduction $\mathcal{R}$ runs the adversary $\mathcal{A}$, simulated by $\mathcal{R}^*$, on input initial randomness $r_{\mathcal{A}}$ and public key $\mathsf{pk}$, after which $\mathcal{A}$ provides a recipient public key $\mathsf{rpk}$ and obtains the first presignature-nonce pair $(\mathsf{psig}, \mathsf{nonce})$. Subsequently, the reduction $\mathcal{R}^*$ runs a copy of $\mathcal{R}$, denoted by $\mathcal{R}'$, as a subroutine to obtain a second valid presignature-nonce pair $(\mathsf{psig}', \mathsf{nonce}')$ ((3)-(9)). Note that $\mathcal{R}'$ always runs $\mathcal{A}$ (simulated by $\mathcal{R}^*$) with the same initial randomness $r_{\mathcal{A}}$ and outputs the same public key $\mathsf{pk}$ as $\mathcal{R}$, because $\mathcal{R}'$ is invoked with the same randomness $r_{\mathcal{R}}$ and problem instance $y$. The reduction $\mathcal{R}^*$ then outputs $(\mathsf{pk}, \mathsf{psig}', \mathsf{nonce}', \mathsf{psig}, \mathsf{nonce})$ to the Secret-Key Independence game and receives the message-signature pairs $(\mathsf{m}_b, \mathsf{sig}_b)$ and $(\mathsf{m}', \mathsf{sig}')$, which are then relayed to the reduction $\mathcal{R}$ ((10)-(12)). Finally, the reduction $\mathcal{R}$ outputs a solution $x$ for the instance $y$, after which the reduction $\mathcal{R}^*$ outputs a bit depending on whether $x$ is a valid solution ((13)-(14)).

We observe that when $b = 0$, the adversary $\mathcal{A}$ behaves as in the meta-reduction simulation, and when $b = 1$, it behaves as the ideal adversary, indicating that the meta-reduction faithfully emulates the behavior of the ideal adversary.

Now, the important observation is that every statistical NIBS scheme already has the secret-key independence due to Lemma 2. This means that the (simple) reduction cannot tell whether it interacts with the ideal adversary or the adversary simulated by the meta-reduction under the assumption that NIBS satisfies statistical blindness. Thus, there is proved to be no simple reduction from the unforgeability of NIBS to non-interactive assumptions.

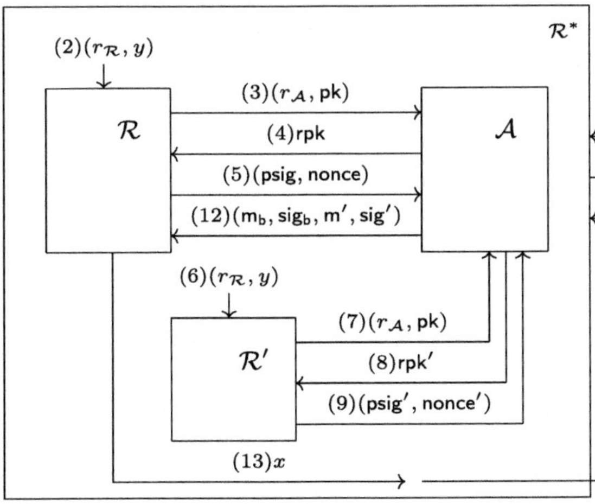


**Fig. 4.** Construction of Reduction $\mathcal{R}^*$ for Secret-Key Independence via Indistinguishability of Meta-Reduction and Ideal Adversaries.

**Toward an Impossibility Result for General Reductions.** We now consider extending the above result for simple reductions to the case of general (Turing) reductions, where the reduction $\mathcal{R}$ has access to the adversary $\mathcal{A}$ in a concurrent and resetting manner. General reductions are strictly more powerful than simple reductions; in fact, the meta-reduction strategy used for simple reductions no longer applies verbatim.

For clarity, we focus on the resettable—but non-concurrent—case: $\mathcal{R}$ may run $\mathcal{A}$ multiple times on the same signer's public key and, by rewinding, supply multiple presignature–nonce pairs to $\mathcal{A}$ across those runs, while keeping both $\mathcal{A}$'s initial randomness and the signer's public key fixed. We then build a concrete reduction $\mathcal{R}^*$ from the resulting indistinguishability task to secret-key independence, treating $\mathcal{R}$ as a black box; see Fig. 5 for an overview.

The main process is almost the same as in the simple reduction case. That is, the reduction $\mathcal{R}^*$ obtains a forgery by relaying between the reduction (and the rewound reduction) and the Secret-Key Independence game ((1)-(12)).

However, unlike the simple reduction case, if $\mathcal{R}$ rewinds $\mathcal{A}$ and provides the rewound adversary $\mathcal{A}'$ with a different presignature-nonce pair $(\mathsf{psig}'', \mathsf{nonce}'')$ from those used in the main (i.e., non-rewound) execution, namely $(\mathsf{psig}', \mathsf{nonce}')$, then the reduction $\mathcal{R}^*$ has difficulty creating a forgery because it does not possess the recipient's secret key used by the game ((13)-(15)).

However, if the game provides the reduction $\mathcal{R}^*$ with an "Obtain oracle," as in the strong blindness game, then $\mathcal{R}^*$ could obtain a valid message-signature pair ((16)-(17)).

We can prove that this "strong" Secret-Key Independence game is implied by strong recipient blindness. Thus, assuming that NIBS satisfies strong recipient blindness, we can address the issue arising from the resettable reduction $\mathcal{R}$. A formal description is provided in the full version.

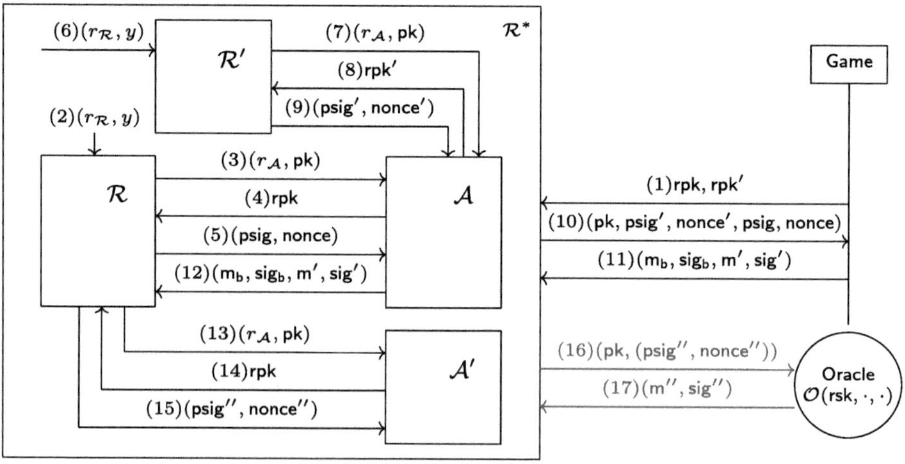


**Fig. 5.** Construction of Reduction $\mathcal{R}^*$ for Resettable Setting.

### 2.2 Extension from the Statistical Setting to the Computational Setting

We aim to extend the statistically blind NIBS result to the computational setting. As in the statistical setting, we first consider the result for simple reductions. However, unlike in the statistical case, we cannot assume unbounded computational power to ensure the distinguishability between the meta-reduction and the ideal adversary in the computational setting.

To address this limitation, we introduce a new ideal adversary $\mathcal{A}^{\Sigma_c}$ tailored for the computational setting, inspired by the work of [26].

Before presenting the procedure of the ideal adversary $\mathcal{A}^{\Sigma_c}$, we define a new generic forgery oracle $\Sigma_c$ tailored for the computational setting. Similar to the ideal adversary $\mathcal{A}^{\Sigma}$ in the statistical setting, we embed the oracle $\Sigma_c$ into the adversary, thereby constructing an ideal adversary that breaks one-more unforgeability. This generic forgery oracle $\Sigma_c$ operates as follows: Given a signer's public key $\mathsf{pk}$ and a recipient's public key $\mathsf{rpk}$ as input, it first enumerates all secret keys corresponding to $\mathsf{pk}$ using unbounded computational power. It then selects one of them at random (denoted by $\mathsf{sk}$) and returns a presignature-nonce pair by executing $(\mathsf{psig}, \mathsf{nonce}) \leftarrow \mathsf{Issue}(\mathsf{sk}, \mathsf{rpk})$. An adversary $\mathcal{A}^{\Sigma_c}$, equipped with access to the generic forgery oracle $\Sigma_c$—which we refer to as the ideal adversary—can clearly win the one-more unforgeability game.

Just like in the statistical setting, the meta-reduction in the computational setting aims to emulate the ideal adversary $\mathcal{A}^{\Sigma_c}$ by resetting the reduction. In this context, we introduce the notion of *secret-key independence* tailored for the computational setting. Intuitively, this game provides the adversary with two message-signature pairs $(\mathsf{m}, \mathsf{sig})$ and $(\mathsf{m}_b, \mathsf{sig}_b)$, where $(\mathsf{m}, \mathsf{sig})$ and $(\mathsf{m}_0, \mathsf{sig}_0)$ are honestly generated, while $(\mathsf{m}_1, \mathsf{sig}_1)$ is derived via the generic forgery oracle $\Sigma_c$.

Ideally, every computational NIBS scheme would satisfy this form of secret-key independence, as in the statistical setting. However, computational blindness alone does not suffice to guarantee this property, since we cannot simulate the generic forgery oracle $\Sigma_c$ using only bounded computational power. In other words, if the generic forgery oracle $\Sigma_c$ is explicitly provided, then simulation becomes possible even without unbounded computational power. As a result, we prove that any NIBS scheme defined relative to $\Sigma_c$ satisfies the computational version of secret-key independence. Interestingly, this blindness property relative to the generic forgery oracle is also required to achieve the impossibility result for standard blind signature schemes, as shown in [26].[11]

Thus, to summarize the discussion so far, there is no simple reduction from the one-more unforgeability of NIBS schemes that satisfy blindness relative to the generic forgery oracle $\Sigma_c$ to non-interactive assumptions.

*Remark 1.* The forgery oracle $\Sigma_c$ is a proof-technical device that enables our computational impossibility argument; it is not intended to model any realistic

[11] In contrast to [26], key-validity checks and signature-derivation checks are not required for our NIBS result.

capability. Consequently, our impossibility for the computational setting is not a fully unconditional (oracle-free) impossibility.

That said, a NIBS scheme satisfies our blindness notion tailored to the computational setting whenever the one-more unforgeability (OMUF) and blindness properties rest on *independent* assumptions. Concretely, this holds for several existing constructions, e.g., [38, Scheme 4], [6, Appendix D], and [40, Scheme 4], where the assumption used for OMUF can be independent of the one underpinning blindness. In such cases, an adversary attempting to violate our blindness cannot exploit the oracle $\Sigma_c$ in any meaningful way, and the definition is met.

Therefore, our result does not rule out *all* computationally blind NIBS in the plain model. Rather, it shows that such schemes cannot exist if OMUF and blindness are based on independent assumptions. This suggests that any plain-model computational NIBS must tie the two properties to intertwined (non-separable) assumptions.

### 2.3 Non-interactive Statistically Blind Signatures in the ROM

**Recalling Hanzlik's Generic Construction.** Before presenting our construction of non-interactive statistically blind signatures in the random oracle model, we first recall Hanzlik's generic construction of computationally blind NIBS schemes [38], in order to better contextualize our approach.

In Hanzlik's scheme, a signer's key pair consists of a standard digital signature key pair $(\mathsf{sk_s}, \mathsf{pk_s})$, while a recipient's key pair consists of a verifiable random function (VRF) key pair $(\mathsf{sk_{VRF}}, \mathsf{pk_{VRF}})$. The signer, holding the secret key $\mathsf{sk_s}$, generates a standard digital signature on the recipient's public key $\mathsf{pk_{VRF}}$ and a nonce $\mathsf{nonce}$, producing a presignature $\mathsf{psig}$. To obtain a valid message-signature pair, the recipient evaluates the VRF on the nonce $\mathsf{nonce}$ to derive the message $\mathsf{m}$. The recipient then constructs a proof that they possess a valid presignature $\mathsf{psig}$ on $(\mathsf{pk_{VRF}}, \mathsf{nonce})$, and that the message $\mathsf{m}$ is the result of applying the VRF to $\mathsf{nonce}$ under $\mathsf{sk_{VRF}}$. This proof can be interpreted as a blind signature on the message $\mathsf{m}$.

Hanzlik's scheme is setup-free and operates in the random oracle model; it does not rely on a common reference string (CRS). This is achieved using a dual-mode witness-indistinguishable proof system (NIWI) [35]. The key idea is to interpret the evaluation of the random oracle at $\mathsf{H_{crs}}(1)$ as the CRS. In the security proof for one-more unforgeability, the random oracle value $\mathsf{H_{crs}}(1)$ is set to a binding-mode value, while in the blindness proof, it is set to a hiding-mode value.

**Shifting Focus to Baldimtsi et al.'s Generic Construction.** To extend Hanzlik's scheme to achieve statistical blindness, we must avoid using a VRF, since an unbounded algorithm can break the security guarantees of a VRF. To overcome this limitation, we focus on the generic construction proposed by Baldimtsi et al. [6, Appendix D], which achieves strong blindness in the CRS model.

Notably, [6, Appendix D] does not rely on VRF. Instead, it uses only non-interactive commitment schemes and pseudo-random functions (PRF). Specifically, the recipient's secret key consists of a PRF secret key $\mathsf{sk}_{\mathsf{PRF}}$, while the public key consists of a commitment com to $\mathsf{sk}_{\mathsf{PRF}}$.

To obtain a blind signature, the recipient constructs a proof that they possess: 1. a valid presignature psig on (com, nonce), 2. a value m such that m is the result of evaluating the PRF on nonce under $\mathsf{sk}_{\mathsf{PRF}}$, and 3. a valid opening of com to the value $\mathsf{sk}_{\mathsf{PRF}}$. As a result, [6, Appendix D] shows that a secure NIBS scheme can be achieved without relying on VRF.

**Toward a Non-interactive Statistically Blind Signature.** To ensure that the scheme satisfies statistical blindness, we begin by replacing the PRF used in [6, Appendix D] with $k$-wise independent hash functions, which behave like truly random functions if used fewer than $k$ times.

Our statistically blind NIBS scheme proceeds as follows. The signer's key consists of a standard digital signature key pair, as in [6,38]. In contrast, the recipient's key pair consists of a $k$-wise independent hash function $h$ as the secret key, and a non-interactive, *statistical* hiding commitment c to $h$ as the public key. The signer generates a standard digital signature on the recipient's public key and a nonce. To obtain a valid message-signature pair, the recipient evaluates $h$ on the nonce nonce to derive the message m. The recipient then constructs a proof that they possess: 1. a valid presignature psig on (c, nonce), 2. a value m such that $\mathsf{m} = h(\mathsf{nonce})$, and 3. a valid opening of c to the $k$-wise independent hash function $h$.

In our construction, to prove these statements in the context of strong blindness, we use a *multi-theorem*, non-interactive, *statistical* zero-knowledge argument [25,34]. This NIZK system operates in either a hiding or binding mode: in the former, it provides perfect zero-knowledge and computational soundness; in the latter, it offers computational zero-knowledge, perfect soundness, and extractability (i.e., the ability to extract witnesses using a trapdoor).

The choice between hiding and binding mode depends on the CRS, whose mode cannot be efficiently distinguished. The NIZK system of [34] satisfies these properties. Specifically, the CRS is a bilinear group element: if it lies in a specific subgroup, the system is in binding mode; otherwise, it is in hiding mode. Indistinguishability between these two modes is guaranteed by the subgroup decision problem introduced by Boneh et al. [11].

To achieve setup-free capability (i.e., security in the ROM), we require the dual-mode NIZK system to have a property we refer to as *setup-free for hiding mode*. This property ensures that a CRS sampled uniformly at random from the CRS space is in hiding mode except with negligible probability. The NIZK system of [34] satisfies this, as a randomly sampled bilinear group element lies outside the specific subgroup with overwhelming probability—i.e., it is typically in hiding mode.

Therefore, by setting the CRS as an evaluation of the random oracle $\mathsf{H}_{\mathsf{crs}}$, specifically $\mathsf{crs} := \mathsf{H}_{\mathsf{crs}}(0)$, the NIZK system of [34] operates in hiding mode with high probability. Only in the one-more unforgeability proof do we use the binding mode, which is achieved by programming the value $\mathsf{H}_{\mathsf{crs}}(0)$.

### 2.4 Separation Results for Strong Blindness Definitions

**Prior Results for Weak Blindness.** We begin by recalling the recent separation result established in [50], which demonstrates the existence of NIBS schemes that satisfy weak recipient blindness but not weak nonce blindness, as well as schemes that satisfy weak nonce blindness but not weak recipient blindness. First, the existence of a NIBS scheme that satisfies weak nonce blindness but not weak recipient blindness is straightforward. Specifically, consider a secure NIBS scheme that is modified so that, during the obtaining phase, the signature additionally includes the recipient's public key. In this case, an adversary in the weak recipient blindness game can trivially link message-signature pairs to their corresponding recipient public keys. Notably, this modification does not increase the adversary's advantage in the weak nonce blindness game. The same argument can be extended to the case of strong blindness.

The work of [50] also demonstrates the existence of a NIBS scheme that satisfies weak recipient blindness but not weak nonce blindness. The idea is to modify a secure underlying NIBS scheme so that the recipient's secret key includes a random secret $s$ for use in a one-time pad. During the obtaining phase, the recipient encrypts the nonce with $s$, computing $c := \mathsf{nonce} + s$, and includes $c$ in the final signature. This construction explicitly satisfies weak recipient blindness because the one-time pad $c$ hides any correlation with the recipient's public key in an information-theoretic sense. However, weak nonce blindness is explicitly broken, since the adversary receives two ciphertexts generated using the same secret $s$ and can infer correlations between presignature-nonce pairs and the corresponding message-signature pairs.

This naturally raises the question of whether a similar separation can be achieved for strong blindness. As mentioned earlier, it is relatively easy to construct a scheme that satisfies strong nonce blindness but not strong recipient blindness. However, the strategy used in [50] does not extend straightforwardly to the converse case.

To see this, consider whether the adversary can win the strong recipient blindness game for the scheme from [50]. In fact, the adversary can always win this game. Although the signature includes a one-time pad that hides the nonce, the adversary in the strong recipient blindness game is granted access to the recipient's secret keys through the Obtain oracles. Consequently, the adversary can recover the secret key $s$ and link the nonce to the signature, thereby breaking strong recipient blindness.

**Constructing NIBS with Strong Recipient Blindness but No Strong Nonce Blindness.** In this paper, we demonstrate the existence of a NIBS scheme that satisfies strong recipient blindness but not strong nonce blindness. We now provide an overview of this scheme, which follows the approach of [50]. The construction allows an adversary in the strong nonce blindness game to extract information about the nonce from two one-time pads generated using the same secret key, while ensuring that the adversary in the strong recipient blindness game learns nothing.

Our construction relies on pseudorandom functions (or independent hash functions in the statistical case). Specifically, without loss of generality, we assume that the underlying $\mathsf{NIBS}$ scheme $\Pi$ supports multiple presignatures for a single nonce and that the signer can efficiently generate multiple presignatures for the same nonce. In fact, Hanzlik's generic constructions, which use a non-deterministic digital signature scheme as a building block, satisfy this property.

To construct our scheme, we modify the secure underlying scheme $\Pi$ by embedding a random seed $s$ for a pseudorandom function ($\mathsf{PRF}$) into the recipient's secret key. Given a presignature-nonce pair ($\mathsf{psig}, \mathsf{nonce}$), the $\mathsf{Obtain}$ algorithm adds a one-time pad to the underlying blind signature to hide the presignature. This is done by evaluating the $\mathsf{PRF}$ on input $\mathsf{nonce}$ under the secret seed $s$, i.e., $c := \mathsf{psig} + \mathsf{PRF}_s(\mathsf{nonce})$.

This construction explicitly satisfies strong recipient blindness. In the strong recipient blindness game, the adversary is not allowed to query the $\mathsf{Obtain}$ oracle with the same nonce as the challenge nonce. This restriction ensures that the secret seed $s$ used in the challenge signature is applied only once, thereby preventing the adversary from learning any correlation between the recipient public keys and the challenge signatures.

However, this scheme does not satisfy strong nonce blindness. We now present an adversary that breaks strong nonce blindness in this construction. The key observation is that the adversary is allowed to choose identical challenge nonce values. Thus, by selecting the same nonce $\mathsf{nonce}$ but distinct presignatures $\mathsf{psig}_0$ and $\mathsf{psig}_1$, the adversary can obtain two ciphertexts $c_0 = \mathsf{psig}_0 + \mathsf{PRF}_s(\mathsf{nonce})$ and $c_1 = \mathsf{psig}_1 + \mathsf{PRF}_s(\mathsf{nonce})$. These ciphertexts leak information about the shared $\mathsf{PRF}$ output, enabling the adversary to correlate the presignature-nonce pairs with their corresponding message-signature pairs.

## 3 Preliminaries

The security parameter is $\lambda \in \mathbb{Z}$. All algorithms receive $\lambda$ implicitly as input. We denote the first $N$ natural numbers by $[N] := \{1, \cdots, N\}$. For a finite set $S$, we write $x \leftarrow S$ if $x$ is sampled uniformly at random from $S$. For a probabilistic algorithm $\mathcal{A}$, we write $y \leftarrow \mathcal{A}(x)$ if $y$ is output from $\mathcal{A}$ on input $x$ with uniformly sampled initialized randomness. We write $y \leftarrow \mathcal{A}(x; \rho)$ to make the initialized randomness $\rho$ explicit, and $y \in \mathcal{A}(x)$ means that $y$ is a possible output of $\mathcal{A}(x)$. We also write $\mathcal{A}^{\mathcal{O}}(x)$ if $\mathcal{A}$ can access $\mathcal{O}$. We say that a function $f : \mathbb{N} \rightarrow \mathbb{R}_+$ is negligible in its input $n$, denoted by $f(n) = \mathsf{negl}(n)$, if $f \in n^{-\omega(1)}$. An algorithm is said to be a probabilistic polynomial time (PPT) if its running time is bounded by a polynomial in the size of its input. Moreover, we denote by $\mathsf{poly}(n)$ the set of all polynomials in $n$, and we write $k = \mathsf{poly}(n)$ to indicate that $k \in \mathsf{poly}(n)$.

We say that an algorithm is PPT if its running time can be bounded by a polynomial in its input size. In additon, we denote by $\mathsf{poly}(n)$ a set of polynomial in $n$ and denote $k = \mathsf{poly}(n)$ if $k \in \mathsf{poly}(n)$.

**Definition 1 (Hard Non-Interactive Assumption).** *A non-interactive (cryptographic) problem $P = (I, V)$ consists of two PPT algorithms:*

**Instance Generation** $I(\lambda) \to y$: *On input the security parameter $\lambda$, it outputs an instance $y$.*
**Instance Verification** $V(x, y) \to b$: *On input a value $x$ and an instance $y$, it outputs a bit $b \in \{0, 1\}$.*

*We say that $P$ is a hard non-interactive problem if it satisfies the following property:*

**Hardness** *For every PPT adversary $\mathcal{A}$, the following probability is negligible:*

$$\Pr\left[V(x', y) = 1 \mid\mid y \leftarrow I(\lambda);\ x' \leftarrow \mathcal{A}(y)\right].$$

For example, the assumption that a function $f$ is one-way is a hard non-interactive assumption. Indeed, it can be modeled as a one-round game in which the challenger sends the adversary $\mathcal{A}$ an output $y = f(x)$ for a uniformly random $x$, and $\mathcal{A}$ wins (i.e., the game outputs Accept) if it returns an $x'$ such that $f(x') = y$.

### 3.1 Black-Box Reductions

We now explain the notion of black-box reductions considered in this work. Our formulation mainly follows [58]. At a high level, we discuss what it means for one assumption to be based on another in a black-box manner. Specifically, given two assumptions $C_1$ and $C_2$, basing the hardness of $C_1$ on that of $C_2$ in a black-box way means that, given any adversary $\mathcal{A}_2$ that breaks $C_2$, one can construct a polynomial-time procedure $\mathcal{R}$ (the reduction) that breaks $C_1$ using $\mathcal{A}_2$ as an oracle.

Notably, there is no requirement that $\mathcal{R}$ invoke $\mathcal{A}_2$ only once; it may call $\mathcal{A}_2$ polynomially many times, and these invocations may even be nested. In this context, $\mathcal{A}_2$ can be viewed as a (possibly non-uniform) adversary, while $\mathcal{R}$ is the polynomial-time reduction with oracle access to $\mathcal{A}_2$.

**Definition 2 (Black-Box Reduction).** *We say that a probabilistic polynomial-time algorithm $\mathcal{R}$ is a black-box reduction from assumption $C_1$ to assumption $C_2$ if, for every deterministic adversary $\mathcal{A}$ that breaks $C_1$, the reduction $\mathcal{R}^{\mathcal{A}}$ breaks $C_2$.*

In this work, we restrict our attention to reductions where the adversary $\mathcal{A}$ accessed by $\mathcal{R}$ is deterministic (or has fixed randomness). This restriction enables the reduction to rewind or restart its adversary as needed.

Furthermore, following [56,58], we focus on fixed-parameter reductions, in which the reduction invokes its adversary using a single security parameter. That is, for security parameter $\lambda$, the reduction is allowed to run up to $M(\lambda)$ instances of the parameterized adversary $\mathcal{A}(1^\lambda)$, and the same adversary must be used in all invocations.

### 3.2 Non-interactive Blind Signature

We define non-interactive blind signature (NIBS) schemes. We adopt a simplified syntax following [6], where the nonce is viewed as the signer's public randomness.

**Definition 3**
**(Non-Interactive Blind Signature (NIBS)).** *A non-interactive blind signature scheme* NIBS = (KeyGen, RKeyGen, Issue, Obtain, Verify) *consists of the following PPT algorithms:*

KeyGen($\lambda$) $\rightarrow$ (sk, pk)*: On input the security parameter* $\lambda$*, outputs a signer's key pair* (sk, pk)*. We assume that* pk *implicitly defines a nonce space* $\mathcal{N}_{\mathsf{pk}}$.

RKeyGen($\lambda$) $\rightarrow$ (rsk, rpk)*: On input the security parameter* $\lambda$*, outputs a recipient's key pair* (rsk, rpk)*.*

Issue(sk, rpk) $\rightarrow$ (psig, nonce)*: On input the signer's secret key* sk *and the recipient's public key* rpk*, outputs a presignature* psig *and a nonce* nonce*, representing a portion of the signer's public randomness.*

Obtain(rsk, pk, (psig, nonce)) $\rightarrow$ (m, sig)*: On input the recipient's secret key* rsk*, the signer's public key* pk*, and the presignature-nonce pair* (psig, nonce)*, outputs either a valid message-signature pair* (m, sig) *or* $\perp$*.*

Verify(pk, m, sig) $\rightarrow b$*: On input the signer's public key* pk *and a message-signature pair* (m, sig)*, outputs a bit* $b \in \{0, 1\}$ *indicating whether the signature is valid.*

We require that NIBS satisfies the following properties: *correctness, reusability, one-more unforgeability, and strong nonce/recipient blindness.*

**Definition 4 (Correctness).** *A* NIBS *scheme satisfies correctness if, for all* (sk, pk) $\leftarrow$ KeyGen($\lambda$) *and all* (rsk, rpk) $\leftarrow$ RKeyGen($\lambda$)*, it holds that:*

$$\Pr\left[\mathsf{Verify}(\mathsf{pk}, \mathsf{m}, \mathsf{sig}) = 1 \;\middle|\; \begin{array}{l} (\mathsf{psig}, \mathsf{nonce}) \leftarrow \mathsf{Issue}(\mathsf{sk}, \mathsf{rpk}); \\ (\mathsf{m}, \mathsf{sig}) \leftarrow \mathsf{Obtain}(\mathsf{rsk}, \mathsf{pk}, (\mathsf{psig}, \mathsf{nonce})) \end{array}\right] = 1.$$

*Reusability* was first introduced by [6], and ensures that a recipient can obtain two distinct messages and valid signatures from presignatures generated under different nonces.

**Definition 5 (Reusability).** *A* NIBS *scheme satisfies reusability if, for every* $\lambda$*, the following probability is negligible in* $\lambda$*:*

$$\Pr\left[\mathsf{nonce}_0 = \mathsf{nonce}_1 \vee \mathsf{m}_0 = \mathsf{m}_1 \;\middle|\; \begin{array}{l} (\mathsf{sk}, \mathsf{pk}) \leftarrow \mathsf{KeyGen}(\lambda); \\ (\mathsf{rsk}, \mathsf{rpk}) \leftarrow \mathsf{RKeyGen}(\lambda); \\ \forall b \in \{0,1\}, (\mathsf{psig}_b, \mathsf{nonce}_b) \leftarrow \mathsf{Issue}(\mathsf{sk}, \mathsf{rpk}); \\ (\mathsf{m}_b, \mathsf{sig}_b) \leftarrow \mathsf{Obtain}(\mathsf{rsk}, \mathsf{pk}, \mathsf{psig}_b, \mathsf{nonce}_b) \end{array}\right].$$

Our definition of *one-more unforgeability* aligns with [6], rather than [38], since we adopt the syntax from [6][12].

**Definition 6 (One-More Unforgeability).** *A* NIBS *scheme is said to be $\ell$-one-more unforgeable if, for every PPT adversary $\mathcal{A}$, the following advantage is negligible in $\lambda$:*

$$\mathbf{Adv}^{\ell\text{-OMUF}}_{\mathsf{NIBS},\mathcal{A}}(\lambda) := \Pr\left[\ell\text{-}\mathsf{OMUF}^{\mathcal{A}}_{\mathsf{NIBS}}(\lambda) = 1\right],$$

*where the game $\ell$-*OMUF *is defined in Fig. 6. A scheme is one-more unforgeable if it satisfies $\ell$-one-more unforgeability for all $\ell = \mathsf{poly}(\lambda)$.*

*Strong blindness* is a strengthened version of the blindness property originally defined in [38], and was improved by [6] to provide more robust privacy guarantees in settings involving multiple presignatures.

| $\ell\text{-}\mathsf{OMUF}^{\mathcal{A}}_{\mathsf{NIBS}}(\lambda)$ | $\mathcal{O}_1(\mathsf{sk}, \mathsf{rpk})$ |
|---|---|
| $(\mathsf{sk}, \mathsf{pk}) \leftarrow \mathsf{KeyGen}(\lambda)$ | **if** $k$ is not initialized **then** |
| $((\mathsf{m}_1, \mathsf{sig}_1), \cdots (\mathsf{m}_\ell, \mathsf{sig}_\ell)) \leftarrow \mathcal{A}^{\mathcal{O}_1(\mathsf{sk},\cdot)}(\mathsf{pk})$ | $k := 0$ |
| **return** $(\mathsf{m}_i \neq \mathsf{m}_j$ for $1 \le i < j \le \ell) \wedge$ | $(\mathsf{psig}, \mathsf{nonce}) \leftarrow \mathsf{Issue}(\mathsf{sk}, \mathsf{rpk})$ |
| $(\mathsf{Verify}(\mathsf{pk}, \mathsf{m}_i, \mathsf{sig}_i) = 1$ for $1 \le i \le \ell) \wedge$ | $k := k + 1$ |
| $k < \ell$ | **return** $(\mathsf{psig}, \mathsf{nonce})$ |

**Fig. 6.** $\ell$-OMUF Games.

**Definition 7 (Strong Recipient Blindness).** *A* NIBS *scheme satisfies computational (resp. statistical) $q$-strong recipient blindness if, for all PPT (resp. unbounded) adversaries $\mathcal{A}$, the following advantage is negligible in $\lambda$:*

$$\mathbf{Adv}^{q\text{-rbnd}}_{\mathsf{NIBS},\mathcal{A}}(\lambda) := 2\Pr\left[q\text{-}\mathsf{RBND}^{\mathcal{A}}_{\mathsf{NIBS}}(\lambda) = 1\right] - 1,$$

*where the game $q$-*RBND *is defined in Fig. 7. The scheme satisfies strong recipient blindness if this holds for $q = \mathsf{poly}(\lambda)$.*

**Definition 8 (Strong Nonce Blindness).** *A* NIBS *scheme satisfies computational (resp. statistical) $q$-strong nonce blindness if, for all PPT (resp. unbounded) adversaries $\mathcal{A}$, the following advantage is negligible in $\lambda$:*

$$\mathbf{Adv}^{q\text{-nbnd}}_{\mathsf{NIBS},\mathcal{A}}(\lambda) := 2\Pr\left[q\text{-}\mathsf{NBND}^{\mathcal{A}}_{\mathsf{NIBS}}(\lambda) = 1\right] - 1,$$

*where the game $q$-*NBND *is defined in Fig. 7.*

A scheme is said to satisfy computational (resp. statistical) strong blindness if it satisfies both $q$-strong recipient and nonce blindness for all $q = \mathsf{poly}(\lambda)$.

$q\text{-}\mathsf{RBND}^{\mathcal{A}}_{\mathsf{NIBS}}(\lambda)$

$(\mathsf{rsk}_0, \mathsf{rpk}_0) \leftarrow \mathsf{RKeyGen}(\lambda)$
$(\mathsf{rsk}_1, \mathsf{rpk}_1) \leftarrow \mathsf{RKeyGen}(\lambda)$
$\mathcal{O} := \mathcal{O}_{\mathsf{rsk}_0,\mathsf{rsk}_1}(\cdot,\cdot,\cdot)$
$(\mathsf{pk}, (\mathsf{psig}_0, \mathsf{nonce}_0), (\mathsf{psig}_1, \mathsf{nonce}_1)) \leftarrow \mathcal{A}^{\mathcal{O}}(\mathsf{pk})$
$(\mathsf{m}_0, \mathsf{sig}_0) \leftarrow \mathsf{Obtain}(\mathsf{rsk}_0, \mathsf{pk}, (\mathsf{psig}_0, \mathsf{nonce}_0))$
$(\mathsf{m}_1, \mathsf{sig}_1) \leftarrow \mathsf{Obtain}(\mathsf{rsk}_1, \mathsf{pk}, (\mathsf{psig}_1, \mathsf{nonce}_1))$
**if** $\mathsf{sig}_0 = \perp$ or $\mathsf{sig}_1 = \perp$ **then**
  $(\mathsf{m}_0, \mathsf{sig}_0) := \perp; (\mathsf{m}_1, \mathsf{sig}_1) := \perp$
$b \xleftarrow{\$} \{0,1\}$
$b' \leftarrow \mathcal{A}((\mathsf{m}_b, \mathsf{sig}_b), (\mathsf{m}_{1-b}, \mathsf{sig}_{1-b}))$
**return** $b = b' \wedge k \leq q$

$\mathcal{O}_{\mathsf{rsk}_0,\mathsf{rsk}_1}(b, \mathsf{pk}, (\mathsf{psig}, \mathsf{nonce}))$

**if** $k$ is not initialized **then**
  $k := 0$
$(\mathsf{m}, \mathsf{sig}) \leftarrow \mathsf{Obtain}(\mathsf{rsk}_b, \mathsf{pk}, (\mathsf{psig}, \mathsf{nonce}))$
$k := k + 1$
**return** $(\mathsf{m}, \mathsf{sig})$

$q\text{-}\mathsf{NBND}^{\mathcal{A}}_{\mathsf{NIBS}}(\lambda)$

$(\mathsf{rsk}, \mathsf{rpk}) \leftarrow \mathsf{RKeyGen}(\lambda)$
$\mathcal{O} := \mathcal{O}_{\mathsf{rsk}}(\cdot,\cdot)$
$(\mathsf{pk}, (\mathsf{psig}_0, \mathsf{nonce}_0), (\mathsf{psig}_1, \mathsf{nonce}_1)) \leftarrow \mathcal{A}^{\mathcal{O}}((\mathsf{rpk}))$
$(\mathsf{m}_0, \mathsf{sig}_0) \leftarrow \mathsf{Obtain}(\mathsf{rsk}, \mathsf{pk}, (\mathsf{psig}_0, \mathsf{nonce}_0))$
$(\mathsf{m}_1, \mathsf{sig}_1) \leftarrow \mathsf{Obtain}(\mathsf{rsk}, \mathsf{pk}, (\mathsf{psig}_1, \mathsf{nonce}_1))$
**if** $\mathsf{sig}_0 = \perp$ or $\mathsf{sig}_1 = \perp$ **then**
  $(\mathsf{m}_0, \mathsf{sig}_0) := \perp; (\mathsf{m}_1, \mathsf{sig}_1) := \perp$
$b \xleftarrow{\$} \{0,1\}$
$b' \leftarrow \mathcal{A}((\mathsf{m}_b, \mathsf{sig}_b), (\mathsf{m}_{1-b}, \mathsf{sig}_{1-b}))$
**return** $b = b' \wedge k \leq q$

$\mathcal{O}_{\mathsf{rsk}}(\mathsf{pk}, (\mathsf{psig}, \mathsf{nonce}))$

**if** $k$ is not initialized **then**
  $k := 0$
$(\mathsf{m}, \mathsf{sig}) \leftarrow \mathsf{Obtain}(\mathsf{rsk}, \mathsf{pk}, (\mathsf{psig}, \mathsf{nonce}))$
$k := k + 1$
**return** $(\mathsf{m}, \mathsf{sig})$

**Fig. 7.** $q$-RBND and $q$-NBND Games.

*Remark 2.* We henceforth refer to 0-strong blindness as *weak blindness*, which corresponds to the original blindness definition by Hanzlik [38].

The following two theorems show that strong nonce blindness and strong recipient blindness are each independently necessary for the provable security of NIBS schemes.

**Theorem 1.** *If there exists a* NIBS *scheme that satisfies strong nonce blindness, then there exists a scheme that satisfies the same property but does not satisfy strong recipient blindness.*

**Theorem 2.** *If there exists a* NIBS *scheme with strong recipient blindness, then there exists a scheme which satisfies the same properties but does not satisfy strong nonce blindness.*

The proofs for the above theorems are given in the full version.

## 4 Impossibility Results for Simple Reductions

Before presenting the impossibility proof for general reductions, we first consider a simpler class of reductions, which we refer to as *simple reductions*. Formally,

**Definition 9 (Simple Reduction).** *We say that a black-box reduction $\mathcal{R}$ (with fixed parameter) is a* simple reduction *if it satisfies the following conditions:*

- *$\mathcal{R}$ executes only a single run of the adversary.*
- *$\mathcal{R}$ does not rewind the adversary.*

[12] As noted therein, the two definitions are equivalent, and this choice does not affect our impossibility results.

### 4.1 The "Ideal" Adversary

**Generic Forgery Oracle.** To define the "ideal" adversary, we introduce what it means by generic forgery oracle, which abstract the procedures associated with the unbounded power of the ideal adversary.

Informally, the generic forgery oracle $\Sigma$ takes as input a signer's public key, a recipient's public key, a presignature-nonce pair, and outputs a brute-forced message-signature pair that is potentially derived from the provided input data using its unbounded power. If multiple such message-signature pairs exist, $\Sigma$ randomly selects one and outputs it. More formally:

**Definition 10 (Generic Forgery Oracle).** *Let* $\mathsf{NIBS}$ *be a non-interactive statistically blind signature. The generic forgery oracle* $\Sigma(\mathsf{pk}, \mathsf{rpk}, (\mathsf{psig}, \mathsf{nonce}))$ *proceeds as follows:*

1. *Enumerate all recipient's secret keys* $\mathsf{rsk}'$ *such that* $(\mathsf{rsk}', \mathsf{rpk}) \in \mathsf{RKeyGen}(\lambda)$ *and all randomness* $r'$ *for algorithm* $\mathsf{Obtain}(\mathsf{rsk}', \mathsf{pk}, (\mathsf{psig}, \mathsf{nonce}; r')$ *to generate a valid message-signature pair; also store all such values.*
2. *Select a value* $(\mathsf{rsk}', \mathsf{r}')$ *randomly from the set (or return* $\perp$ *if there is no such pair); also return the valid message-signature pair* $(\mathsf{m}, \mathsf{sig}) \leftarrow \mathsf{Obtain}(\mathsf{rsk}', \mathsf{pk}, (\mathsf{psig}, \mathsf{nonce}); r')$.

*We write* $\Sigma(\mathsf{pk}, \mathsf{rpk}, (\mathsf{psig}, \mathsf{nonce})); s)$ *to make the randomness* $s$ *explicit; i.e.,* $\mathsf{rsk}'$ *and* $\mathsf{r}'$ *are deterministically selected by randomness* $s$.

**The Ideal Adversary.** We now define the *ideal adversary*, which exploits unbounded computational power to break the one-more unforgeability of a NIBS scheme.

Informally, the ideal adversary $\mathcal{A}^{\Sigma}$ obtains one message-signature pair through interaction with the one-more unforgeability game and uses the generic forgery oracle to generate a second message-signature pair. (Naturally, since the adversary is unbounded, it can internally simulate the oracle $\Sigma$.)

**Definition 11 (Ideal Adversary).** *Let* $\mathsf{NIBS}$ *be a non-interactive blind signature scheme. The ideal adversary* $\mathcal{A}^{\Sigma}$ *against one-more unforgeability proceeds as follows:*

1. *Upon receiving a public key* $\mathsf{pk}$ *from the one-more unforgeability game, sample a recipient key pair* $(\mathsf{rsk}, \mathsf{rpk}) \leftarrow \mathsf{RKeyGen}(\lambda)$.
2. *Send* $\mathsf{rpk}$ *to the game and receive a presignature-nonce pair* $(\mathsf{psig}, \mathsf{nonce})$.
3. *Compute* $(\mathsf{m}, \mathsf{sig}) \leftarrow \mathsf{Obtain}(\mathsf{rsk}, \mathsf{pk}, (\mathsf{psig}, \mathsf{nonce}))$.
4. *If* $\mathsf{Verify}(\mathsf{pk}, \mathsf{m}, \mathsf{sig}) = 1$, *then compute a second forgery*
$$(\mathsf{m}', \mathsf{sig}') \leftarrow \Sigma(\mathsf{pk}, \mathsf{rpk}, (\mathsf{psig}, \mathsf{nonce})).$$
*Otherwise, set both* $(\mathsf{m}, \mathsf{sig})$ *and* $(\mathsf{m}', \mathsf{sig}')$ *to* $\perp$.
5. *Output* $(\mathsf{m}, \mathsf{sig})$ *and* $(\mathsf{m}', \mathsf{sig}')$ *as the forgery.*

One might presume that the ideal adversary cannot win the game, since the message derived during the execution of the one-more unforgeability game may coincide with the message derived by the generic forgery oracle (i.e., $\mathsf{m} = \mathsf{m}'$). However, Lemma 1 shows that this event occurs only with negligible probability, provided that the NIBS scheme satisfies statistical (weak) blindness and reusability. This fact implies that the ideal adversary succeeds with overwhelming probability, as formally stated in Corollary 1.

**Lemma 1.** *Let* NIBS *be a non-interactive statistically blind signature scheme. For any adversary $\mathcal{A}$, the following probability is negligible in $\lambda$:*

$$\Pr\left[\begin{array}{c|l} (\mathsf{m},\mathsf{sig}) \neq \perp & (\mathsf{sk},\mathsf{pk}) \leftarrow \mathsf{KeyGen}(\lambda); \\ \wedge\ \mathsf{m} = \mathsf{m}' & (\mathsf{rsk},\mathsf{rpk}) \leftarrow \mathsf{RKeyGen}(\lambda); \\ & (\mathsf{psig},\mathsf{nonce}) \leftarrow \mathsf{Issue}(\mathsf{sk},\mathsf{rpk}); \\ & (\mathsf{m},\mathsf{sig}) \leftarrow \mathsf{Obtain}(\mathsf{rsk},\mathsf{pk},(\mathsf{psig},\mathsf{nonce})); \\ & (\mathsf{m}',\mathsf{sig}') \leftarrow \Sigma(\mathsf{pk},\mathsf{rpk},(\mathsf{psig},\mathsf{nonce})) \end{array}\right] \quad (1)$$

*Proof.* Let $p$ denote the probability in Equation (1). We construct an adversary $\mathcal{A}$ against statistical weak nonce blindness, as follows:

1. Given recipient public key $\mathsf{rpk}$ from the nonce blindness game, $\mathcal{A}$ samples $(\mathsf{sk},\mathsf{pk}) \leftarrow \mathsf{KeyGen}(\lambda)$, and computes two presignature-nonce pairs
$$(\mathsf{psig}_0,\mathsf{nonce}_0),(\mathsf{psig}_1,\mathsf{nonce}_1) \leftarrow \mathsf{Issue}(\mathsf{sk},\mathsf{rpk}).$$
It then send both pairs to the game.
2. Upon receiving challenge message-signature pairs $(\mathsf{m}_b,\mathsf{sig}_b)$ and $(\mathsf{m}_{1-b},\mathsf{sig}_{1-b})$ from the nonce blindness game, $\mathcal{A}$ computes
$$(\mathsf{m}',\mathsf{sig}') \leftarrow \Sigma(\mathsf{pk},\mathsf{rpk},(\mathsf{psig}_1,\mathsf{nonce}_1)),$$
and proceeds as follows:
   - If $\mathsf{m}_b \neq \mathsf{m}'$, then output $b' = 0$.
   - Otherwise, output $b' = 1$.

We now analyze the behavior of $\mathcal{A}$. By the correctness of NIBS, it holds that $(\mathsf{m}_1,\mathsf{sig}_1) \neq \perp$. Furthermore, by the reusability of NIBS, it holds that $\mathsf{m}_0 \neq \mathsf{m}_1$ except with negligible probability. That is, we have:

$$\begin{aligned}\Pr[b=b'] &= \Pr[b=b'\,,\,\mathsf{m}_0 \neq \mathsf{m}_1] + \Pr[b=b'\,,\,\mathsf{m}_0 = \mathsf{m}_1] \\ &= \Pr[b=b' \mid \mathsf{m}_0 \neq \mathsf{m}_1]\cdot(1-\Pr[\mathsf{m}_0=\mathsf{m}_1]) \\ &\qquad\qquad + \Pr[b=b' \mid \mathsf{m}_0 = \mathsf{m}_1]\cdot\Pr[\mathsf{m}_0=\mathsf{m}_1] \\ &= \Pr[b=b' \mid \mathsf{m}_0 \neq \mathsf{m}_1] + \mathsf{negl}(\lambda).\end{aligned}$$

We now consider the case where $\mathsf{m}_1 = \mathsf{m}'$. In the case where $b = 0$, if $\mathsf{m}_1 = \mathsf{m}'$, then it follows that $\mathsf{m}_0 \neq \mathsf{m}'$, and thus $\mathcal{A}$ outputs $b' = 0$ and wins. In the case where $b = 1$ and $\mathsf{m}_1 = \mathsf{m}'$, $\mathcal{A}$ outputs $b' = 1$ and also wins. Hence:

$$\begin{aligned}
&\Pr[b = b', \mathsf{m}_1 = \mathsf{m}' \mid \mathsf{m}_0 \neq \mathsf{m}_1] \\
&= \Pr[b' = 0, \mathsf{m}_1 = \mathsf{m}' \mid \mathsf{m}_0 \neq \mathsf{m}_1] \cdot \Pr[b = 0] \\
&\qquad\qquad + \Pr[b' = 1, \mathsf{m}_1 = \mathsf{m}' \mid \mathsf{m}_0 \neq \mathsf{m}_1] \cdot \Pr[b = 1] \\
&= \frac{1}{2} (\Pr[b' = 0 \mid \mathsf{m}_0 \neq \mathsf{m}_1, \mathsf{m}_1 = \mathsf{m}'] \cdot \Pr[\mathsf{m}_1 = \mathsf{m}' \mid \mathsf{m}_0 \neq \mathsf{m}_1] \\
&\qquad + \Pr[b' = 1 \mid \mathsf{m}_0 \neq \mathsf{m}_1, \mathsf{m}_1 = \mathsf{m}'] \cdot \Pr[\mathsf{m}_1 = \mathsf{m}' \mid \mathsf{m}_0 \neq \mathsf{m}_1]) \\
&= \frac{p}{2}.
\end{aligned}$$

We now consider the case where $\mathsf{m}_1 \neq \mathsf{m}'$. If $b = 0$, then $\mathsf{m}_0 \neq \mathsf{m}'$ so $\mathcal{A}$ outputs $b' = 0$ and wins, except with negligible probability. If $b = 1$, then $\mathcal{A}$ outputs $b' = 0$ and loses. Therefore:

$$\begin{aligned}
&\Pr[b = b', \mathsf{m}_1 \neq \mathsf{m}' \mid \mathsf{m}_0 \neq \mathsf{m}_1] \\
&= \Pr[b' = 0, \mathsf{m}_1 \neq \mathsf{m}' \mid \mathsf{m}_0 \neq \mathsf{m}_1] \cdot \Pr[b = 0] \\
&\qquad\qquad + \Pr[b' = 1, \mathsf{m}_1 \neq \mathsf{m}' \mid \mathsf{m}_0 \neq \mathsf{m}_1] \cdot \Pr[b = 1] \\
&= \frac{1}{2} (\Pr[b' = 0 \mid \mathsf{m}_0 \neq \mathsf{m}_1, \mathsf{m}_1 \neq \mathsf{m}'] \cdot \Pr[\mathsf{m}_1 \neq \mathsf{m}' \mid \mathsf{m}_0 \neq \mathsf{m}_1] \\
&\qquad + \Pr[b' = 1 \mid \mathsf{m}_0 \neq \mathsf{m}_1, \mathsf{m}_1 \neq \mathsf{m}'] \cdot \Pr[\mathsf{m}_1 \neq \mathsf{m}' \mid \mathsf{m}_0 \neq \mathsf{m}_1]) \\
&= \frac{1}{2} + \mathsf{negl}(\lambda).
\end{aligned}$$

Putting everything together:

$$\begin{aligned}
\Pr[b = b' \mid \mathsf{m}_0 \neq \mathsf{m}_1] &= \Pr[b = b', \mathsf{m}_1 = \mathsf{m}' \mid \mathsf{m}_0 \neq \mathsf{m}_1] \\
&\qquad + \Pr[b = b', \mathsf{m}_1 \neq \mathsf{m}' \mid \mathsf{m}_0 \neq \mathsf{m}_1] \\
&= \frac{p+1}{2} + \mathsf{negl}(\lambda).
\end{aligned}$$

Therefore:

$$\begin{aligned}
\mathbf{Adv}^{\mathsf{nbnd}}_{\mathsf{NIBS},\mathcal{A}}(\lambda) &:= 2\Pr[b = b'] - 1 \\
&= 2\Pr[b = b' \mid \mathsf{m}_0 \neq \mathsf{m}_1] - 1 + \mathsf{negl}(\lambda) \\
&= p + \mathsf{negl}(\lambda),
\end{aligned}$$

which implies that $p$ is negligible under the assumption of nonce blindness. □

**Corollary 1.** *The ideal adversary $\mathcal{A}^{\Sigma}$ wins the 1-one-more unforgeability game except with negligible probability. That is,*

$$\Pr\left[1\text{-}\mathsf{OMUF}^{\mathcal{A}^{\Sigma}}_{\mathsf{NIBS}}(\lambda) = 1\right] = 1 - \mathsf{negl}(\lambda).$$

### 4.2 Secret-Key Independence

We now introduce a new notion weaker than statistical recipient blindness, which is essential for demonstrating the indistinguishability between the actual behavior of the ideal adversary and the simulation produced by the meta-reduction (the details of which will be presented later). We refer to this notion as *secret-key independence.*

Informally, in the secret-key independence game, a malicious signer must distinguish whether two message-signature pairs are derived from the same or from distinct presignature-nonce pairs, using an *independent secret key.* The key observation is that each public key in a statistically blind NIBS scheme may correspond to multiple valid secret keys. More formally:

**Definition 12 (Secret-Key Independence).** *We say that a* NIBS *scheme satisfies secret-key independence if, for all adversaries $\mathcal{A}$, the following advantage is negligible in $\lambda$:*

$$\mathbf{Adv}^{\mathsf{skind}}_{\mathsf{NIBS},\mathcal{A}}(\lambda) := 2\Pr\left[\mathsf{SKIND}^{\mathcal{A}}_{\mathsf{NIBS}}(\lambda) = 1\right] - 1,$$

*where the game* $\mathsf{SKIND}^{\mathcal{A}}_{\mathsf{NIBS}}$ *is defined in Fig 8.*

$\mathsf{SKIND}^{\mathcal{A}}_{\mathsf{NIBS}}(\lambda)$

$(\mathsf{rsk}_0, \mathsf{rpk}_0) \leftarrow \mathsf{RKeyGen}(\lambda)$
$(\mathsf{rsk}_1, \mathsf{rpk}_1) \leftarrow \mathsf{RKeyGen}(\lambda)$
$(\mathsf{pk}, (\mathsf{psig}_0, \mathsf{nonce}_0), (\mathsf{psig}_1, \mathsf{nonce}_1)) \leftarrow \mathcal{A}(\mathsf{rpk}_0, \mathsf{rpk}_1)$
$(\mathsf{m}_0, \mathsf{sig}_0) \leftarrow \mathsf{Obtain}(\mathsf{rsk}_0, \mathsf{pk}, (\mathsf{psig}_0, \mathsf{nonce}_0))$
$(\mathsf{m}_1, \mathsf{sig}_1) \leftarrow \mathsf{Obtain}(\mathsf{rsk}_1, \mathsf{pk}, (\mathsf{psig}_1, \mathsf{nonce}_1))$
**if** $\mathsf{sig}_0 = \perp$ **or** $\mathsf{sig}_1 = \perp$ **then**
  $(\mathsf{m}_0, \mathsf{sig}_0) := \perp; \quad (\mathsf{m}_1, \mathsf{sig}_1) := \perp$
**else**
  $(\mathsf{m}', \mathsf{sig}') \leftarrow \Sigma(\mathsf{pk}, \mathsf{rpk}_1, (\mathsf{psig}_1, \mathsf{nonce}_1))$
$b \xleftarrow{\$} \{0, 1\}$
$b' \leftarrow \mathcal{A}((\mathsf{m}_b, \mathsf{sig}_b), (\mathsf{m}', \mathsf{sig}'))$
**return** $b = b'$

**Fig. 8.** Secret-Key Independence Game

We now show that every non-interactive statistically blind signature scheme satisfies secret-key independence.

**Lemma 2.** *If a* NIBS *scheme satisfies statistical weak recipient blindness, then it also satisfies secret-key independence.*

*Proof.* Let $\mathcal{A}$ be an adversary against the secret-key independence of NIBS. We construct a PPT algorithm $\mathcal{R}$ against statistical weak recipient blindness. The reduction $\mathcal{R}$ proceeds as follows:

1. Upon receiving the recipient public keys $(\mathsf{rpk}_0, \mathsf{rpk}_1)$ from the game, it computes
$$(\mathsf{pk}, \mathsf{psig}_0, \mathsf{nonce}_0, \mathsf{psig}_1, \mathsf{nonce}_1) \leftarrow \mathcal{A}(\mathsf{rpk}_0, \mathsf{rpk}_1),$$
and forwards the tuple $(\mathsf{pk}, \mathsf{psig}_0, \mathsf{nonce}_0, \mathsf{psig}_1, \mathsf{nonce}_1)$ to the game.
2. Upon receiving the challenge message-signature pairs $(\mathsf{m}_b, \mathsf{sig}_b, \mathsf{m}_{1-b}, \mathsf{sig}_{1-b})$ from the game, $\mathcal{R}$ proceeds as follows:
If $(\mathsf{m}_b, \mathsf{sig}_b) = \perp$, then it sets $(\mathsf{m}', \mathsf{sig}') := \perp$. Otherwise, it computes:
$$(\mathsf{m}', \mathsf{sig}') \leftarrow \Sigma(\mathsf{pk}, \mathsf{rpk}_1, (\mathsf{psig}_1, \mathsf{nonce}_1)).$$
3. $\mathcal{R}$ runs
$$b' \leftarrow \mathcal{A}(\mathsf{m}_b, \mathsf{sig}_b, \mathsf{m}', \mathsf{sig}'),$$
and finally outputs $b'$ to the game.

We now analyze the behavior of $\mathcal{R}$. When $b = 0$ in the weak recipient blindness game, the game returns $(\mathsf{m}_0, \mathsf{sig}_0, \mathsf{m}_1, \mathsf{sig}_1)$ to $\mathcal{R}$, and $\mathcal{R}$ gives $(\mathsf{m}_0, \mathsf{sig}_0, \mathsf{m}', \mathsf{sig}')$ to $\mathcal{A}$. This exactly matches the input of $\mathcal{A}$ in the case $b = 0$ of the secret-key independence game.

Similarly, when $b = 1$ in the weak recipient blindness game, the game returns $(\mathsf{m}_1, \mathsf{sig}_1, \mathsf{m}_0, \mathsf{sig}_0)$, and $\mathcal{R}$ provides $(\mathsf{m}_1, \mathsf{sig}_1, \mathsf{m}', \mathsf{sig}')$ to $\mathcal{A}$, which corresponds to the $b = 1$ case of the secret-key independence game.

Therefore, the advantage of $\mathcal{R}$ in the weak recipient blindness game is identical to the advantage of $\mathcal{A}$ in the secret-key independence game. Since the former is negligible by assumption, so is the latter. □

### 4.3 The Impossibility Result

We present a new result that rules out a simple reduction for the security of a NIBS scheme to a non-interactive assumption. More formally:

**Theorem 3.** *Let* NIBS *be a non-interactive statistically (weakly) blind signature scheme. Then, there exists no simple reduction from the one-more unforgeability of* NIBS *to a hard non-interactive assumption.*

*Proof.* Let $\mathcal{R}$ be a simple reduction that takes as input an instance $y$ of a hard non-interactive problem and has oracle access to a (non-resettable, black-box) adversary $\mathcal{A}$ against the one-more unforgeability game. The goal of $\mathcal{R}$ is to output a solution to $y$.

*Description of the Meta-Reduction.* The meta-reduction $\mathcal{M}$, on input a hard problem instance $y$, proceeds as follows:

1. $\mathcal{M}$ runs the simple reduction $\mathcal{R}$ on input $y$ with fixed randomness $r_{\mathcal{R}}$ to obtain the signer's public key $\mathsf{pk}$ (along with the initial randomness for the adversary).
2. It samples $(\mathsf{rsk}, \mathsf{rpk}) \leftarrow \mathsf{RKeyGen}(\lambda)$ and sends $\mathsf{rpk}$ to $\mathcal{R}$ to receive a presignature-nonce pair $(\mathsf{psig}, \mathsf{nonce})$.

3. $\mathcal{M}$ computes $(\mathsf{m}, \mathsf{sig}) \leftarrow \mathsf{Obtain}(\mathsf{rsk}, \mathsf{pk}, (\mathsf{psig}, \mathsf{nonce}))$. To derive a second valid message-signature pair, $\mathcal{M}$ invokes a fresh copy of $\mathcal{R}$, denoted $\mathcal{R}'$, with the same input $y$ and randomness $r_{\mathcal{R}}$, which produces the same $\mathsf{pk}$.
4. It samples a new recipient key pair $(\mathsf{rsk}', \mathsf{rpk}') \leftarrow \mathsf{RKeyGen}(\lambda)$ and sends $\mathsf{rpk}'$ to $\mathcal{R}'$ to obtain $(\mathsf{psig}', \mathsf{nonce}')$.
5. It then computes $(\mathsf{m}', \mathsf{sig}') \leftarrow \mathsf{Obtain}(\mathsf{rsk}', \mathsf{pk}, (\mathsf{psig}', \mathsf{nonce}'))$, aborts $\mathcal{R}'$, and feeds $(\mathsf{m}, \mathsf{sig})$, $(\mathsf{m}', \mathsf{sig}')$ to $\mathcal{R}$ to obtain an output $x'$. Finally, $\mathcal{M}$ outputs $x'$.

*Analysis of the Meta-Reduction.* We show that the simple reduction $\mathcal{R}$ successfully outputs a solution to $y$ with non-negligible probability. Let $\mathcal{R}^{\mathcal{A}^{\Sigma}}$ denote the reduction when interacting with the ideal adversary $\mathcal{A}^{\Sigma}$, and let $\mathcal{R}^{\mathcal{M}}$ denote the reduction when interacting with the meta-reduction $\mathcal{M}$.

Since $\mathcal{A}^{\Sigma}$ successfully outputs two valid message-signature pairs (Corollary 1), it suffices to show that the success probabilities of $\mathcal{R}^{\mathcal{A}^{\Sigma}}$ and $\mathcal{R}^{\mathcal{M}}$ are negligibly close.

To establish this, we define a reduction $\mathcal{R}^*$ from the secret-key independence game as follows:

1. $\mathcal{R}^*$ receives two recipient public keys $\mathsf{rpk}_0, \mathsf{rpk}_1$ from the game.
2. It samples $y \leftarrow I(\lambda)$ and runs $\mathcal{R}(y; r_{\mathcal{R}})$ to obtain $\mathsf{pk}$.
3. It sends $\mathsf{rpk}_0$ to $\mathcal{R}$ to obtain $(\mathsf{psig}, \mathsf{nonce})$.
4. It runs a copy $\mathcal{R}'$ with the same input and randomness to obtain $(\mathsf{psig}', \mathsf{nonce}')$ from $\mathsf{rpk}_1$.
5. It aborts $\mathcal{R}'$ and sends $(\mathsf{pk}, \mathsf{psig}', \mathsf{nonce}', \mathsf{psig}, \mathsf{nonce})$ to the game.
6. Upon receiving $(\mathsf{m}_b, \mathsf{sig}_b, \mathsf{m}_{1-b}, \mathsf{sig}_{1-b})$, it forwards them to $\mathcal{R}$ to obtain $x'$, and finally returns $b' \leftarrow V(x', y)$.

When $b = 0$, the simulation corresponds exactly to $\mathcal{M}$, and when $b = 1$, it simulates $\mathcal{A}^{\Sigma}$. Let $\mathsf{Succ}(Z)$ denote the event that $V(x', y) = 1$ for $x' \leftarrow \mathcal{R}^{Z}(y)$ and $y \leftarrow I(\lambda)$. Then:

$$\begin{aligned}\Pr[\mathsf{Succ}(\mathcal{A}^{\Sigma})] - \Pr[\mathsf{Succ}(\mathcal{M})] &= \Pr[b' = 1 \mid b = 1] - \Pr[b' = 1 \mid b = 0] \\ &= \mathbf{Adv}^{\mathsf{skind}}_{\mathsf{NIBS}, \mathcal{R}^*}(\lambda).\end{aligned}$$

By Lemma 2, statistical recipient blindness implies secret-key independence, so we have:

$$\Pr[\mathsf{Succ}(\mathcal{M})] = \Pr[\mathsf{Succ}(\mathcal{A}^{\Sigma})] + \mathsf{negl}(\lambda).$$

Moreover, Corollary 1 gives:

$$\Pr[\mathsf{Succ}(\mathcal{A}^{\Sigma})] = 1 - \mathsf{negl}(\lambda),$$

since

$$\Pr\left[1\text{-}\mathsf{OMUF}^{\mathcal{A}^{\Sigma}}_{\mathsf{NIBS}}(\lambda) = 1\right] = \Pr[\mathsf{Succ}(\mathcal{A}^{\Sigma})],$$

under the assumption that $\mathcal{R}$ is a simple reduction. Therefore, $\Pr[\mathsf{Succ}(\mathcal{M})]$ is also $1 - \mathsf{negl}(\lambda)$, which contradicts the assumption that solving $y$ is hard. □

*Remark 3.* Theorem 3 does not rule out black-box reductions that employ complexity leveraging (as in [50]). Complexity leveraging can create a computational gap between the underlying assumption and the target scheme, potentially breaking the meta-reduction. In particular, under secret-key independence, maintaining indistinguishability between the ideal adversary and the meta-reduction appears difficult once such a gap is introduced.

## References

1. Abe, M., Fujisaki, E.: How to date blind signatures. In: Kim, K., Matsumoto, T. (eds.) ASIACRYPT 1996. LNCS, vol. 1163, pp. 244–251. Springer, Heidelberg (1996). https://doi.org/10.1007/BFb0034851
2. Abe, M., Groth, J., Ohkubo, M.: Separating short structure-preserving signatures from non-interactive assumptions. In: Lee, D.H., Wang, X. (eds.) ASIACRYPT 2011. LNCS, vol. 7073, pp. 628–646. Springer, Heidelberg (2011). https://doi.org/10.1007/978-3-642-25385-0_34
3. Agrawal, S., Kirshanova, E., Stehlé, D., Yadav, A.: Practical, round-optimal lattice-based blind signatures. In: Yin, H., Stavrou, A., Cremers, C., Shi, E. (eds.) Proceedings of the 2022 ACM SIGSAC Conference on Computer and Communications Security, CCS 2022, Los Angeles, CA, USA, 7-11 November 2022, pp. 39–53. ACM (2022)
4. Bader, C., Jager, T., Li, Y., Schäge, S.: On the impossibility of tight cryptographic reductions. In: Fischlin, M., Coron, J.-S. (eds.) EUROCRYPT 2016. LNCS, vol. 9666, pp. 273–304. Springer, Heidelberg (2016). https://doi.org/10.1007/978-3-662-49896-5_10
5. Baecher, P., Brzuska, C., Fischlin, M.: Notions of black-box reductions, revisited. In: Sako, K., Sarkar, P. (eds.) ASIACRYPT 2013. LNCS, vol. 8269, pp. 296–315. Springer, Heidelberg (2013). https://doi.org/10.1007/978-3-642-42033-7_16
6. Baldimtsi, F., Cheng, J., Goyal, R., Yadav, A.: Non-interactive blind signatures: Post-quantum and stronger security. In: Chung, K., Sasaki, Y. (eds.) Advances in Cryptology - ASIACRYPT 2024 - 30th International Conference on the Theory and Application of Cryptology and Information Security, Kolkata, India, 9-13 December 2024, Proceedings, Part II. LNCS, vol. 15485, pp. 70–104. Springer (2024). https://doi.org/10.1007/978-981-96-0888-1_3
7. Baldimtsi, F., Lysyanskaya, A.: Anonymous credentials light. In: Proceedings of the 2013 ACM SIGSAC Conference on Computer & Communications Security, pp. 1087–1098 (2013)
8. Baldimtsi, F., Lysyanskaya, A.: On the security of one-witness blind signature schemes. In: Sako, K., Sarkar, P. (eds.) ASIACRYPT 2013. LNCS, vol. 8270, pp. 82–99. Springer, Heidelberg (2013). https://doi.org/10.1007/978-3-642-42045-0_5
9. Bauer, B., Fuchsbauer, G., Regen, F.: On proving equivalence class signatures secure from non-interactive assumptions. In: Tang, Q., Teague, V. (eds.) Public-Key Cryptography - PKC 2024 - 27th IACR International Conference on Practice and Theory of Public-Key Cryptography, Sydney, NSW, Australia, 15-17 April 2024, Proceedings, Part I. LNCS, vol. 14601, pp. 3–36. Springer (2024). https://doi.org/10.1007/978-3-031-57718-5_1

10. Beullens, W., Lyubashevsky, V., Nguyen, N.K., Seiler, G.: Lattice-based blind signatures: Short, efficient, and round-optimal. In: Meng, W., Jensen, C.D., Cremers, C., Kirda, E. (eds.) Proceedings of the 2023 ACM SIGSAC Conference on Computer and Communications Security, CCS 2023, Copenhagen, Denmark, 26-30 November 2023, pp. 16–29. ACM (2023)
11. Boneh, D., Goh, E., Nissim, K.: Evaluating 2-DNF formulas on ciphertexts. In: Kilian, J. (ed.) Theory of Cryptography, Second Theory of Cryptography Conference, TCC 2005, Cambridge, MA, USA, 10-12 February 2005, Proceedings. LNCS, vol. 3378, pp. 325–341. Springer (2005). https://doi.org/10.1007/978-3-540-30576-7_18
12. Boneh, D., Lynn, B., Shacham, H.: Short signatures from the Weil pairing. In: Boyd, C. (ed.) ASIACRYPT 2001. LNCS, vol. 2248, pp. 514–532. Springer, Heidelberg (2001). https://doi.org/10.1007/3-540-45682-1_30
13. Boneh, D., Venkatesan, R.: Breaking RSA may not be equivalent to factoring. In: Nyberg, K. (ed.) Advances in Cryptology - EUROCRYPT 1998, International Conference on the Theory and Application of Cryptographic Techniques, Espoo, Finland, May 31 - June 4, 1998, Proceeding. LNCS, vol. 1403, pp. 59–71. Springer (1998). https://doi.org/10.1007/BFb0054117
14. Brakerski, Z., Medina, S.: Limits on adaptive security for attribute-based encryption. In: Boyle, E., Mahmoody, M. (eds.) Theory of Cryptography - 22nd International Conference, TCC 2024, Milan, Italy, December 2-6, 2024, Proceedings, Part III. LNCS, vol. 15366, pp. 91–123. Springer (2024). https://doi.org/10.1007/978-3-031-78020-2_4
15. Canard, S., Gaud, M., Traoré, J.: Defeating malicious servers in a blind signatures based voting system. In: Di Crescenzo, G., Rubin, A. (eds.) FC 2006. LNCS, vol. 4107, pp. 148–153. Springer, Heidelberg (2006). https://doi.org/10.1007/11889663_11
16. Chairattana-Apirom, R., Tessaro, S., Zhu, C.: Pairing-free blind signatures from CDH assumptions. In: Reyzin, L., Stebila, D. (eds.) Advances in Cryptology - CRYPTO 2024 - 44th Annual International Cryptology Conference, Santa Barbara, CA, USA, 18-22 August 2024, Proceedings, Part I. LNCS, vol. 14920, pp. 174–209. Springer (2024). https://doi.org/10.1007/978-3-031-68376-3_6
17. Chaum, D.: Blind signatures for untraceable payments. In: CRYPTO, pp. 199–203 (1982)
18. Chaum, D.: Blind signature system. In: Advances in Cryptology: Proceedings of Crypto 83, p. 153. Springer (1983). https://doi.org/10.1007/978-1-4684-4730-9_14
19. Coron, J.-S.: Optimal security proofs for PSS and other signature schemes. In: Knudsen, L.R. (ed.) EUROCRYPT 2002. LNCS, vol. 2332, pp. 272–287. Springer, Heidelberg (2002). https://doi.org/10.1007/3-540-46035-7_18
20. Crites, E.C., Komlo, C., Maller, M., Tessaro, S., Zhu, C.: Snowblind: A threshold blind signature in pairing-free groups. In: Handschuh, H., Lysyanskaya, A. (eds.) Advances in Cryptology - CRYPTO 2023 - 43rd Annual International Cryptology Conference, CRYPTO 2023, Santa Barbara, CA, USA, 20-24 August 2023, Proceedings, Part I. LNCS, vol. 14081, pp. 710–742. Springer (2023). https://doi.org/10.1007/978-3-031-38557-5_23
21. Dachman-Soled, D., Kulkarni, M.: Upper and lower bounds for continuous non-malleable codes. In: Lin, D., Sako, K. (eds.) Public-Key Cryptography - PKC 2019 - 22nd IACR International Conference on Practice and Theory of Public-Key Cryptography, Beijing, China, 14-17 April 2019, Proceedings, Part I. LNCS, vol. 11442, pp. 519–548. Springer (2019). https://doi.org/10.1007/978-3-030-17253-4_18

22. Dwork, C., Naor, M., Sahai, A.: Concurrent zero-knowledge. In: Vitter, J.S. (ed.) Proceedings of the Thirtieth Annual ACM Symposium on the Theory of Computing, Dallas, Texas, USA, 23-26 May 1998, pp. 409–418. ACM (1998)
23. Fischlin, M.: Round-optimal composable blind signatures in the common reference string model. In: Dwork, C. (ed.) CRYPTO 2006. LNCS, vol. 4117, pp. 60–77. Springer, Heidelberg (2006). https://doi.org/10.1007/11818175_4
24. Fischlin, M., Harasser, P., Janson, C.: Signatures from sequential-OR proofs. In: Canteaut, A., Ishai, Y. (eds.) EUROCRYPT 2020. LNCS, vol. 12107, pp. 212–244. Springer, Cham (2020). https://doi.org/10.1007/978-3-030-45727-3_8
25. Fischlin, M., Rohrbach, F.: Single-to-multi-theorem transformations for non-interactive statistical zero-knowledge. In: Garay, J.A. (ed.) PKC 2021. LNCS, vol. 12711, pp. 205–234. Springer, Cham (2021). https://doi.org/10.1007/978-3-030-75248-4_8
26. Fischlin, M., Schröder, D.: On the impossibility of three-move blind signature schemes. In: Gilbert, H. (ed.) EUROCRYPT 2010. LNCS, vol. 6110, pp. 197–215. Springer, Heidelberg (2010). https://doi.org/10.1007/978-3-642-13190-5_10
27. Fleischhacker, N., Jager, T., Schröder, D.: On tight security proofs for Schnorr signatures. J. Cryptol. **32**(2), 566–599 (2019)
28. Fuchsbauer, G., Hanser, C., Slamanig, D.: Practical round-optimal blind signatures in the standard model. In: Gennaro, R., Robshaw, M. (eds.) CRYPTO 2015. LNCS, vol. 9216, pp. 233–253. Springer, Heidelberg (2015). https://doi.org/10.1007/978-3-662-48000-7_12
29. Fuchsbauer, G., Hanser, C., Slamanig, D.: Structure-preserving signatures on equivalence classes and constant-size anonymous credentials. J. Cryptol. **32**(2), 498–546 (2019)
30. Fuchsbauer, G., Wolf, M.: Concurrently secure blind schnorr signatures. In: Joye, M., Leander, G. (eds.) Advances in Cryptology - EUROCRYPT 2024 - 43rd Annual International Conference on the Theory and Applications of Cryptographic Techniques, Zurich, Switzerland, 26-30 May 2024, Proceedings, Part II. LNCS, vol. 14652, pp. 124–160. Springer (2024). https://doi.org/10.1007/978-3-031-58723-8_5
31. Garg, S., Gupta, D.: Efficient round optimal blind signatures. In: Nguyen, P.Q., Oswald, E. (eds.) EUROCRYPT 2014. LNCS, vol. 8441, pp. 477–495. Springer, Heidelberg (2014). https://doi.org/10.1007/978-3-642-55220-5_27
32. Garg, S., Rao, V., Sahai, A., Schröder, D., Unruh, D.: Round optimal blind signatures. In: Rogaway, P. (ed.) CRYPTO 2011. LNCS, vol. 6841, pp. 630–648. Springer, Heidelberg (2011). https://doi.org/10.1007/978-3-642-22792-9_36
33. Gentry, C., Wichs, D.: Separating succinct non-interactive arguments from all falsifiable assumptions. In: Fortnow, L., Vadhan, S.P. (eds.) Proceedings of the 43rd ACM Symposium on Theory of Computing, STOC 2011, San Jose, CA, USA, 6-8 June 2011, pp. 99–108. ACM (2011)
34. Groth, J., Ostrovsky, R., Sahai, A.: Perfect non-interactive zero knowledge for NP. In: Vaudenay, S. (ed.) EUROCRYPT 2006. LNCS, vol. 4004, pp. 339–358. Springer, Heidelberg (2006). https://doi.org/10.1007/11761679_21
35. Groth, J., Sahai, A.: Efficient non-interactive proof systems for bilinear groups. In: Smart, N. (ed.) EUROCRYPT 2008. LNCS, vol. 4965, pp. 415–432. Springer, Heidelberg (2008). https://doi.org/10.1007/978-3-540-78967-3_24
36. Guo, F., Susilo, W.: Optimal tightness for chain-based unique signatures. In: Dunkelman, O., Dziembowski, S. (eds.) Advances in Cryptology - EUROCRYPT 2022 - 41st Annual International Conference on the Theory and Applications of

Cryptographic Techniques, Trondheim, Norway, May 30 - June 3, 2022, Proceedings, Part II. LNCS, vol. 13276, pp. 553–583. Springer (2022). https://doi.org/10.1007/978-3-031-07085-3_19

37. Hanser, C., Slamanig, D.: Structure-preserving signatures on equivalence classes and their application to anonymous credentials. In: Sarkar, P., Iwata, T. (eds.) Advances in Cryptology - ASIACRYPT 2014 - 20th International Conference on the Theory and Application of Cryptology and Information Security, Kaoshiung, Taiwan, R.O.C., 7-11 December 2014. Proceedings, Part I. LNCS, vol. 8873, pp. 491–511. Springer (2014). https://doi.org/10.1007/978-3-662-45611-8_26
38. Hanzlik, L.: Non-interactive blind signatures for random messages. In: Hazay, C., Stam, M. (eds.) Advances in Cryptology - EUROCRYPT 2023 - 42nd Annual International Conference on the Theory and Applications of Cryptographic Techniques, Lyon, France, April 23-27, 2023, Proceedings, Part V. LNCS, vol. 14008, pp. 722–752. Springer (2023). https://doi.org/10.1007/978-3-031-30589-4_25
39. Hanzlik, L., Loss, J., Wagner, B.: Rai-choo! evolving blind signatures to the next level. In: Annual International Conference on the Theory and Applications of Cryptographic Techniques, pp. 753–783. Springer (2023). https://doi.org/10.1007/978-3-031-30589-4_26
40. Hanzlik, L., Paracucchi, E., Zanotto, R.: Non-interactive blind signatures from RSA assumption and more. In: Fehr, S., Fouque, P. (eds.) Advances in Cryptology - EUROCRYPT 2025 - 44th Annual International Conference on the Theory and Applications of Cryptographic Techniques, Madrid, Spain, 4-8 May 2025, Proceedings, Part II. LNCS, vol. 15602, pp. 365–394. Springer (2025). https://doi.org/10.1007/978-3-031-91124-8_13
41. Hanzlik, L., Slamanig, D.: With a little help from my friends: Constructing practical anonymous credentials. In: Kim, Y., Kim, J., Vigna, G., Shi, E. (eds.) CCS 2021: 2021 ACM SIGSAC Conference on Computer and Communications Security, Virtual Event, Republic of Korea, 15-19 November 2021, pp. 2004–2023. ACM (2021)
42. Hartmann, D., Kiltz, E.: Limits in the provable security of ECDSA signatures. In: Rothblum, G.N., Wee, H. (eds.) Theory of Cryptography - 21st International Conference, TCC 2023, Taipei, Taiwan, November 29 - December 2, 2023, Proceedings, Part IV. LNCS, vol. 14372, pp. 279–309. Springer (2023). https://doi.org/10.1007/978-3-031-48624-1_11
43. Heilman, E., Alshenibr, L., Baldimtsi, F., Scafuro, A., Goldberg, S.: Tumblebit: an untrusted bitcoin-compatible anonymous payment hub. In: 24th Annual Network and Distributed System Security Symposium, NDSS 2017, San Diego, California, USA, February 26 - March 1, 2017. The Internet Society (2017)
44. Hesse, J., Hofheinz, D., Kohl, L.: On tightly secure non-interactive key exchange. In: Shacham, H., Boldyreva, A. (eds.) CRYPTO 2018. LNCS, vol. 10992, pp. 65–94. Springer, Cham (2018). https://doi.org/10.1007/978-3-319-96881-0_3
45. IETF: Privacy Pass (privacypass). https://datatracker.ietf.org/wg/privacypass/documents/
46. Kastner, J., Nguyen, K., Reichle, M.: Pairing-free blind signatures from standard assumptions in the ROM. In: Reyzin, L., Stebila, D. (eds.) Advances in Cryptology - CRYPTO 2024 - 44th Annual International Cryptology Conference, Santa Barbara, CA, USA, 18-22 August 2024, Proceedings, Part I. LNCS, vol. 14920, pp. 210–245. Springer (2024). https://doi.org/10.1007/978-3-031-68376-3_7
47. Katsumata, S., Lai, Y., LeGrow, J.T., Qin, L.: CSI -otter: Isogeny-based (partially) blind signatures from the class group action with a twist. In: Handschuh,

H., Lysyanskaya, A. (eds.) Advances in Cryptology - CRYPTO 2023 - 43rd Annual International Cryptology Conference, CRYPTO 2023, Santa Barbara, CA, USA, 20-24 August 2023, Proceedings, Part III. LNCS, vol. 14083, pp. 729–761. Springer (2023). https://doi.org/10.1007/s10623-024-01441-7

48. Katsumata, S., Nishimaki, R., Yamada, S., Yamakawa, T.: Round-optimal blind signatures in the plain model from classical and quantum standard assumptions. In: Canteaut, A., Standaert, F.-X. (eds.) EUROCRYPT 2021. LNCS, vol. 12696, pp. 404–434. Springer, Cham (2021). https://doi.org/10.1007/978-3-030-77870-5_15
49. Katsumata, S., Reichle, M., Sakai, Y.: Practical round-optimal blind signatures in the ROM from standard assumptions. In: Guo, J., Steinfeld, R. (eds.) Advances in Cryptology - ASIACRYPT 2023 - 29th International Conference on the Theory and Application of Cryptology and Information Security, Guangzhou, China, 4-8 December 2023, Proceedings, Part II. LNCS, vol. 14439, pp. 383–417. Springer (2023). https://doi.org/10.1007/978-981-99-8724-5_12
50. Kazuki Yamamura, T.O., Fujisaki, E.: On non-interactive blind signatures in the plain model using complexity leveraging (2025). https://fc25.ifca.ai/preproceedings/59.pdf, To apper in Financial Cryptography and Data Secuirty 2025
51. Klooß, M., Reichle, M.: Blind signatures from proofs of inequality. In: Kalai, Y.T., Kamara, S.F. (eds.) Advances in Cryptology - CRYPTO 2025 - 45th Annual International Cryptology Conference, Santa Barbara, CA, USA, 17-21 August 2025, Proceedings, Part VI. LNCS, vol. 16005, pp. 157–189. Springer (2025). https://doi.org/10.1007/978-3-032-01887-8_6
52. Klooß, M., Reichle, M., Wagner, B.: Practical blind signatures in pairing-free groups. In: Chung, K., Sasaki, Y. (eds.) Advances in Cryptology - ASIACRYPT 2024 - 30th International Conference on the Theory and Application of Cryptology and Information Security, Kolkata, India, 9-13 December 2024, Proceedings, Part I. LNCS, vol. 15484, pp. 363–395. Springer (2024). https://doi.org/10.1007/978-981-96-0875-1_12
53. Lewko, A., Waters, B.: New proof methods for attribute-based encryption: achieving full security through selective techniques. In: Safavi-Naini, R., Canetti, R. (eds.) CRYPTO 2012. LNCS, vol. 7417, pp. 180–198. Springer, Heidelberg (2012). https://doi.org/10.1007/978-3-642-32009-5_12
54. Lindell, Y.: Bounded-concurrent secure two-party computation without setup assumptions. In: Larmore, L.L., Goemans, M.X. (eds.) Proceedings of the 35th Annual ACM Symposium on Theory of Computing, 9-11 June 2003, San Diego, CA, USA, pp. 683–692. ACM (2003)
55. Lu, G., Zhandry, M.: Limits on the power of prime-order groups: Separating q-type from static assumptions. In: Reyzin, L., Stebila, D. (eds.) Advances in Cryptology - CRYPTO 2024 - 44th Annual International Cryptology Conference, Santa Barbara, CA, USA, August 18-22, 2024, Proceedings, Part V. LNCS, vol. 14924, pp. 46–74. Springer (2024). https://doi.org/10.1007/978-3-031-68388-6_3
56. Morgan, A., Pass, R.: On the security loss of unique signatures. In: Beimel, A., Dziembowski, S. (eds.) TCC 2018. LNCS, vol. 11239, pp. 507–536. Springer, Cham (2018). https://doi.org/10.1007/978-3-030-03807-6_19
57. Paillier, P., Vergnaud, D.: Discrete-log-based signatures may not be equivalent to discrete log. In: Roy, B. (ed.) ASIACRYPT 2005. LNCS, vol. 3788, pp. 1–20. Springer, Heidelberg (2005). https://doi.org/10.1007/11593447_1
58. Pass, R.: Limits of provable security from standard assumptions. In: Fortnow, L., Vadhan, S.P. (eds.) Proceedings of the 43rd ACM Symposium on Theory of

Computing, STOC 2011, San Jose, CA, USA, 6-8 June 2011, pp. 109–118. ACM (2011)
59. del Pino, R., Katsumata, S.: A new framework for more efficient round-optimal lattice-based (partially) blind signature via trapdoor sampling. In: Dodis, Y., Shrimpton, T. (eds.) Advances in Cryptology - CRYPTO 2022 - 42nd Annual International Cryptology Conference, CRYPTO 2022, Santa Barbara, CA, USA, 15-18 August 2022, Proceedings, Part II. LNCS, vol. 13508, pp. 306–336. Springer (2022). https://doi.org/10.1007/978-3-031-15979-4_11
60. Schäge, S.: New limits of provable security and applications to elgamal encryption. In: Joye, M., Leander, G. (eds.) Advances in Cryptology - EUROCRYPT 2024 - 43rd Annual International Conference on the Theory and Applications of Cryptographic Techniques, Zurich, Switzerland, 26-30 May 2024, Proceedings, Part IV. LNCS, vol. 14654, pp. 255–285. Springer (2024). https://doi.org/10.1007/978-3-031-58737-5_10
61. Seurin, Y.: On the exact security of Schnorr-type signatures in the random oracle model. In: Pointcheval, D., Johansson, T. (eds.) EUROCRYPT 2012. LNCS, vol. 7237, pp. 554–571. Springer, Heidelberg (2012). https://doi.org/10.1007/978-3-642-29011-4_33
62. Wichs, D.: Barriers in cryptography with weak, correlated and leaky sources. In: Kleinberg, R.D. (ed.) Innovations in Theoretical Computer Science, ITCS 2013, Berkeley, CA, USA, 9-12 January 2013, pp. 111–126. ACM (2013)
63. Zhang, H., Chen, X., Huang, Q.: Lattice-based non-interactive blind signature schemes in the random oracle model. In: Liu, J.K., Chen, L., Sun, S., Liu, X. (eds.) Provable and Practical Security - 18th International Conference, ProvSec 2024, Gold Coast, QLD, Australia, 25-27 September 2024, Proceedings, Part I. LNCS, vol. 14903, pp. 289–308. Springer (2024). https://doi.org/10.1007/978-981-96-0954-3_15
64. Zhang, J., Zhang, Z., Chen, Yu., Guo, Y., Zhang, Z.: Black-box separations for one-more (Static) CDH and its generalization. In: Sarkar, P., Iwata, T. (eds.) ASIACRYPT 2014. LNCS, vol. 8874, pp. 366–385. Springer, Heidelberg (2014). https://doi.org/10.1007/978-3-662-45608-8_20

# New Limits for Homomorphic Encryption

Sven Schäge(✉) and Marc Vorstermans

Eindhoven University of Technology, Eindhoven, The Netherlands
{s.schage,m.h.l.vorstermans}@tue.nl

**Abstract.** We make progress on the foundational problem of determining the strongest security notion achievable by homomorphic encryption. Our results are negative. We prove that a wide class of semi-homomorphic public key encryption schemes (SHPKE) cannot be proven IND-PCA secure (indistinguishability against plaintext checkability attacks), a relaxation of IND-CCA security. This class includes widely used and versatile schemes like ElGamal PKE, Paillier PKE, and the linear encryption system by Boneh, Boyen, and Shacham (Crypto'04). Besides their homomorphic properties, these schemes have in common that they all provide efficient algorithms for recognizing valid ciphertexts (and public keys) from public values. In contrast to CCA security, where the adversary is given access to a decryption oracle, in a PCA attack, the adversary solely has access to an oracle that decides for a given ciphertext/plaintext pair $(c, m)$ if decrypting $c$ indeed gives $m$. Since the notion of IND-PCA security is weaker than IND-CCA security, it is not only easier to achieve, leading to potentially more efficient schemes in practice, but it also side-steps existing impossibility results that rule out the IND-CCA security. To rule out IND-PCA security we thus have to rely on novel techniques. We provide two results, depending on whether the attacker is allowed to query the PCA oracle after it has received the challenge (IND-PCA2 security) or not (IND-PCA1 security – the more challenging scenario). First, we show that IND-PCA2 security can be ruled out unconditionally if the number of challenges is smaller than the number of queries made after the challenge. Next, we prove that no Turing reduction can reduce the IND-PCA1 security of SHPKE schemes with $O(\kappa^3)$ PCA queries overall to interactive complexity assumptions that support $t$-time access to their challenger with $t = O(\kappa)$. To obtain our second impossibility results, we develop a new meta-reduction-based methodology that can be used to tackle security notions where the attacker is granted access to a *decision* oracle. This makes it challenging to utilize the techniques of existing meta-reduction-based impossibility results that focus on definitions where the attacker is allowed to access an inversion oracle (e.g. long-term key corruptions or a signature oracle). To obtain our result, we have to overcome several technical challenges that are entirely novel to the setting of public key encryption.

Sven Schäge: Supported by the Smart Networks and Services Joint Undertaking (EU Horizon) in the scope of the CONFIDENTIAL6G project under Grant Agreement No 101096435.

© International Association for Cryptologic Research 2026
G. Hanaoka and B.-Y. Yang (Eds.): ASIACRYPT 2025, LNCS 16252, pp. 482–515, 2026.
https://doi.org/10.1007/978-981-95-5125-5_16

**Keywords:** Impossibility · Homomorphic Encryption · IND-PCA · ElGamal Encryption · Paillier Encryption · Meta-Reduction

## 1 Introduction

Fully homomorphic encryption (FHE) is a very powerful tool that allows for conceptually elegant solutions to many challenging problems in cryptography. When using FHE in practice to design secure systems, knowing exactly what security guarantees the FHE scheme provides is of the utmost importance. Consequently, the problem of narrowing down the strongest achievable security notion for FHE has gained much attention in the last two decades [2,7,19,32,35,36,46,48], leading to both positive and negative results including proposals of new security notions on the one hand and novel attacks and impossibility results on the other hand. When we switch to the more restricted semi-homomorphic public key encryption (SHPKE) systems that only support a single homomorphic operation on encrypted plaintexts, the problem typically becomes even harder: any attack on an SHPKE scheme where the attacker only exploits one homomorphic operation on encrypted messages immediately works a forteriori if the attacker is additionally given access to a second operation. Moreover, coming up with attacks on SHPKE schemes in the first place is more challenging, precisely because the attacker only has access to a single homomorphic operation.

In cryptography, SHPKE systems like ElGamal public-key encryption (PKE) or Paillier PKE have diverse application scenarios and are widely used. Most recently, they have gained renewed attention in the realm of threshold cryptography, where their homomorphic properties allow them to combine different key shares efficiently with each other, e.g. [23,33]. Existing SHPKE schemes are typically accompanied by proofs of IND-CPA security under non-interactive security assumptions like the Decisional Diffie-Hellman assumption or the Decisional Composite Residuosity assumption. Moreover, it is well-known that they cannot achieve indistinguishability under chosen ciphertext attacks (IND-CCA2 security) because of the malleability of their ciphertexts.

The problem of whether these schemes provide IND-CCA1 (or lunchtime) security[1] – a slightly weaker notion where the attacker is not allowed to query the decryption oracle after the challenge query has been issued – has only recently been answered negatively [48]. It remains an important foundational problem to investigate the possibility to achieve weaker security notions for these widespread SHPKE schemes that lie somewhere between IND-CCA2/IND-CCA1 security and IND-CPA security. One well-known notion that can be found here is the definition of indistinguishability under plaintext checkable attacks (IND-PCA) a natural relaxation of IND-CCA security. In contrast to IND-CCA security, it only grants the attacker access to a *decision oracle* in the learning phase, that on input ciphertext/plaintext pair $(c, m)$ outputs a validity bit $w \in \{0, 1\}$ indicating whether decrypting $c$ indeed gives $m$. Since the attacker is only allowed

[1] The proof actually showed the stronger result that SHPKE schemes cannot be proven OW-CCA1 secure, a notion formally incomparable to IND-PCA security.

to query the decisional PCA oracle as opposed to having access to an inversion (decryption) oracle in the IND-CCA security game, IND-PCA security is a provably weaker notion. This has two important consequences.

First, IND-PCA security can generally be achieved more easily in constructions than IND-CCA security. As a result, IND-PCA secure PKE schemes can generally be more efficient. Moreover, since the security notion is less demanding, they may exhibit desirable features that are useful in more complex systems, like the IND-PCA secure variant of Cramer-Shoup encryption in [1] that is compatible with Groth-Sahai proofs. At the same time, despite their weaker security properties, IND-PCA secure schemes can nevertheless be very useful in practice. Remarkably, in many important PKE-based constructions, IND-PCA security is in fact sufficient. For example, as observed by [1], all the password-based security protocols in [24,25,29] that are built from IND-CCA secure PKE schemes can actually safely rely on IND-PCA secure PKE schemes.

Second, since IND-PCA is provably weaker than IND-CCA security, existing impossibility results that rule out IND-CCA security do not apply. Despite their importance in practice, until now it is thus simply unknown whether semi-homomorphic encryption schemes can achieve IND-PCA security at all.

In light of this, we investigate the following question.

*Can Semi-Homomorphic PKE be shown IND-PCA secure?*

We answer the above question negatively.

*Setting the Stage: A Weaker Security Notion.* To obtain our results, we start by introducing a security game that we call *weak* indistinguishability against plaintext checkable attacks (wIND-PCA). In contrast to the classical notion of IND-PCA security, the attacker is *not* allowed to send a plaintext to the challenger that may be used to compute the challenge ciphertext $c^*$. Instead, $c^*$ is *always* computed by encrypting a uniformly random message $m_1^*$ that has been drawn by *the challenger*. Now, $c^*$ is sent back to the attacker along with the real message $m_1^*$ (real case) or an independent random message $m_0^*$ (random case). The goal of the attacker is to distinguish the real from the random case. Since the attacker has strictly less freedom than in the IND-PCA game, the security notion for wIND-PCA is weaker and any impossibility result for wIND-PCA security immediately holds for IND-PCA security as well. Besides leading to more general impossibility results, focusing on the notion of wIND-PCA security provides a conceptual advantage: both the queries sent in the learning phase and the challenge itself consist of ciphertext/plaintext pairs. All our impossibility results consider, in fact, wIND-PCA security and thus provide a more general result that a fortiori rules out IND-PCA security.

*Agnostic Randomization with Strong Hiding.* Next, we introduce a specific randomization algorithm Randomize that, as we show, every SHPKE admits. This algorithm randomizes ciphertext/plaintext pairs $s = (c, m)$ to other pairs $s' = (c', m')$ with the crucial restriction that the validity bit remains untouched.

This means that $s'$ is a valid ciphertext/plaintext pair if and only if $s$ is valid. Remarkably, under this condition, the randomization is perfect (except with statistically low probability) and *agnostic* to the actual validity bit of the input $s$. Accordingly, if $s$ is not a valid pair, $s'$ will be distributed *uniformly* in the set $\mathsf{INV}$ of all invalid ciphertext/plaintext pairs, even for a distinguisher who knows the original $s = (c, m)$. Likewise, if $s$ is valid, then $s'$ will be distributed uniformly in the set $\mathsf{VAL}$ of valid ciphertext pairs.[2] This provides statistically strong hiding properties since any two input pairs $s, s' \in \mathsf{VAL}$ (respectively $s, s' \in \mathsf{INV}$) have the same the output distribution when applying $\mathsf{Randomize}$. It is highly useful that the algorithm $\mathsf{Randomize}$ does not need the validity bit of $s$ as input.

*Two Results.* Next, we consider two different scenarios. In the first, the attacker makes queries to the PCA oracle *after* it has received the challenges $s_1^* = (c_1^*, m_1^*), \ldots, s_p^* = (c_p^*, m_p^*)$. Making a similar distinction as between the subnotions for IND-CCA security, we refer to the resulting game as wIND-PCA2 security. In contrast, wIND-PCA1 security only considers attackers that query the oracle *before* the attacker receives the challenges. As our first result, we unconditionally rule out that SHPKE schemes achieve wIND-PCA2 security. The idea, heavily inspired by the well-known impossibility result for IND-CCA2 security, is to exploit the homomorphic properties of ciphertexts in the SHPKE scheme and randomize $s^*$ to obtain a new pair $s'^* = (c'^*, m'^*)$ that is queried to the PCA oracle. Since $\mathsf{Randomize}$ leaves the validity bit unchanged, i.e. $w'^* = w^*$, a valid response to $s'$ will immediately transfer to a valid response for $s^*$. Thus, the attacker can always win in the wIND-PCA2 security game. We believe that the impossibility of IND-PCA2 security can be shown for schemes with less demanding properties. In particular, for the result to hold, we do not need randomization algorithms with strong hiding properties, something which is required in the IND-PCA1 impossibility result.

*wIND-PCA1 Security.* Settling the question of whether SHPKE schemes are wIND-PCA1 secure is much more complicated. To answer it, we follow the meta-reduction methodology introduced by Boneh and Venkatesan [8]. The central idea is to describe an ideal successful attacker $A$ that can be efficiently simulated by a meta-reduction $M$ towards the reduction $B$. Meta-reduction $M$ rewinds $B$ to simulate the ideal attacker. As a consequence, the combination of $M$ and $B$ can be used to break the security assumption that the reduction reduces to. This approach yields strong impossibility results that do not idealize mathematical structures in contrast to, for example, the generic group model [37,50] or the generic ring model [30]. The only restriction we make is that the reduction uses inefficient attackers in a black-box way. Intuitively, our idea to efficiently simulate the ideal attacker is to exploit that the meta-reduction can rewind the reduction. Similar to before, the goal of $M$ is to randomize the challenge $s$ and send the result $s'$ as a query in the learning phase. However, to make sure that the reduction accepts this rewound query, we not only have to make sure that

[2] We assume that $\mathsf{VAL} \cap \mathsf{INV} = \varnothing$.

the query is distributed like any other query in the learning phase. Since general reductions can rewind the attacker, we also have to make sure that the entire *behavior* of the simulated attacker $M$ is indistinguishable from that of $A$, even if $B$ can rewind the attacker and run several attacker instances concurrently. To do this, we have to overcome several obstacles that we describe in more detail shortly. Our main result shows the impossibility of general reductions from the wIND-PCA1 game with $3\kappa(2t + 2\kappa + 2u)$ PCA queries to any $t$-interactive complexity assumption ($t$ICA). Here $\kappa$ is the security parameter and $u$ is the maximum number of attacker instances that may be run by $B$. In the full version, we also provide an impossibility result with quantitatively better bounds that, however, only holds for simple reductions. In contrast to general Turing reductions, simple reductions only execute the attacker once and without rewinding.[3] Let us now describe several challenges that we have to overcome to obtain our impossibility result for wIND-PCA1 security.

*Rewound Queries Must not Disturb External ICA Communication.* After our meta-reduction receives the challenge statement $s^* = (c^*, m^*)$, it rewinds the reduction back to the learning phase with the aim of exploiting the reduction itself to provide the answer to $s^*$. To ensure that the meta-reduction cannot immediately be distinguished from the ideal attacker, $s^*$ needs to be randomized to look like a new ciphertext/plaintext pair. Moreover, it is highly important that the additional query sent to the reduction after the rewinding will, with non-negligible probability, not disturb $B$'s overall interaction with the interactive complexity assumption. In particular, we have to make sure that this rewound query will not make $B$ query its ICA-challenger at all to avoid any influence of the rewinding on the overall number of queries made to the ICA-challenger. This is important to guarantee that ideal attacker and meta-reduction remain indistinguishable from the viewpoint of the reduction.

*Dealing with Correlated Validity Bits.* It turns out, that solving this problem is much harder than in previous results like [48] where the challenge $s^*$ and the randomized statement $s'^*$ are statistically independent. In our setting, a major problem is that, even though $s'^* = (c'^*, m'^*)$ is a 'good' randomization of $s^* = (c^*, m^*)$, the two values have the same validity bit and thus are highly correlated. Any reduction that recognizes that the *validity bit of both statements is equal* can thus base its behavior in some subtle way on this fact. This is problematic as the reduction may specifically choose a strategy where external queries to the ICA-challenger are, for example, *always* made by the reduction if the queried pair has validity bit $w = 0$. If the reduction now produces challenge $(c^*, m^*)$ with validity bit $w^* = 0$ as well, the meta-reduction cannot successfully use a naive rewinding approach because randomizing $(c^*, m^*)$ to $(c'^*, m'^*)$ will

[3] Although simple reductions are widespread in cryptography, focussing on them restricts the freedom of the reduction considerably. Moreover, there are important classes of reductions that are not simple like classical proofs of knowledge in zero-knowledge protocols that rely on rewinding.

leave the validity bit unchanged and querying $(c'^*, m'^*)$ to $B$ will *always* disturb the interaction between $B$ and the interactive complexity challenge. If the meta-reduction rewinds the reduction and sends $s'^* = (c'^*, m'^*)$ in the learning phase, reduction $B$ will thus always invoke an external query and *never* respond to the query $s'^*$ without using an additional external query.

*Statistical Solution for Correlated Validity Bits and Multiple Attacker Instances.* We solve this problem statistically. To this end, we describe an algorithm RSample that can be used by the ideal attacker to draw the corresponding validity bits $w$ in its queries *uniformly at random* although the sets INV and VAL can have vastly different sizes. Half of the overall $y$ queries that the attacker makes thus have $w = 0$ (or 1) on average. Hoeffding's inequality assures that with overwhelming probability the actual number of validity bits that are equal to 0 (or 1) is very close to the average $y/2$. Luckily and similar to Randomize, we are able to show that every SHPKE encryption scheme in fact gives rise to such an algorithm RSample. Intuitively, we use this to guarantee that the probability of having more than $t+u$ and fewer than $y-(t+u)$ queries in the learning phase (before rewinding) be equal to 0 is overwhelming. (Symmetrically, the probability that at least $t+u$ and at most $y-(t+u)$ values equal 1 is overwhelming.) We set up the parameters such that there is always one query, a so-called useful rewinding spot, with the property that when the reduction $B$ delivers the response to the query i) $B$ has not made a new query to its ICA-challenger (that only accepts $t$ queries in total), and ii) $B$ has not requested any of the other $u-1$ attacker instances to output an answer to their challenge. While the first condition effectively guarantees that the interaction of the reduction with its $t$ICA challenger does not get disturbed, the second condition guarantees that the runtime of the meta-reduction does not blow up exponentially. The underlying problem is well-known in the realm of zero-knowledge proofs [9,10,15,44,47]. In a nutshell, the challenge is that the reduction could wait until all other attacker instances have successfully delivered solutions to their challenges before it finally outputs its response to the rewound query. Since each of these solutions can only be obtained by the meta-reduction via rewinding, the rewinding success of the $u$ attacker instances could depend on each other in a way that increases the runtime exponentially. However, once a useful rewinding spot exists, the meta-reduction $M$ can, with non-negligible success probability, guess when it occurs and send the rewound query. The response $w'^*$ to $s'^*$ is also a solution $w^*$ to the challenge $s^*$. Validity bit $w^*$ will be sent back to the reduction $B$ and, by assumption, the reduction breaks the $t$ICA. Since $B$ and $M$ are efficient, this would break the assumed security of the $t$ICA, which ultimately shows that $B$ cannot exist.

*Dealing with Rewinding Reductions and Incorrect Responses.* Another central problem that we have to overcome when dealing with general Turing reductions is that a naïve meta-reduction is not able to verify the responses of the reduction [48] *after rewinding*. Before rewinding, in contrast, both the ideal attacker and meta-reduction can easily verify the responses of the reduction if they produce the queries that they sent to $B$ themselves and thus know their validity bits. However, in the rewinding phase, the meta-reduction is *not* able to verify the responses of the reduction as it does not know the validity bit of the challenge statement. (This is what the meta-reduction aims to reveal in the first place.) This is problematic, for example when faced with a rewinding reduction that always responds to any query with an incorrect answer first. Observe that such a reduction is still efficient: if the attacker aborts because of an incorrect response, the reduction can simply rewind the attacker and send a correct response instead. The meta-reduction's inability to recognize incorrect responses after rewinding could now be used by the reduction to tell the ideal attacker and meta-reduction apart, because the ideal attacker (that does not use rewinding) always knows the correct response and thus may always abort if it is given an incorrect response.

*Solution: Adding Redundancy.* To overcome this problem, we implement an additional mechanism such that the meta-reduction can recognize if the response of the reduction is incorrect – *even if it does not know the validity bit of the challenge.* To achieve this in our setting, we develop entirely novel techniques. Technically we proceed as follows. First, we consider a security game that is even weaker than wIND-PCA security where queries are vectors, that consist of $3\kappa$ pairs $(c_1, m_1), \ldots, (c_{3\kappa}, m_{3\kappa})$. This game keeps the overall number of statements of the wIND-PCA game, such that the resulting game is simply less adaptive than the wIND-PCA1 game and thus provably weaker. The vectors are carefully constructed as follows: first, we draw a random bit $w$. Next, we construct three random pairs $s_1 = (c_1, m_1)$, $s_2 = (c_2, m_2)$, and $s_3 = (c_3, m_3)$ conditioned on the fact that $s_1$ has validity bit 0, $s_2$ has validity bit 1, and $s_3$ has validity bit $w$. Finally, we randomize each $s_i$ a total of $\kappa$ times to obtain $3\kappa$ new pairs in total. As a last step, we permute these $3\kappa$ pairs with a secret random permutation to obtain $(c_1, m_1), \ldots, (c_{3\kappa}, m_{3\kappa})$. The reduction will now have to provide as a response all the $3\kappa$ validity bits in the correct order (exactly 2/3 of them have value $w$). The ideal attacker knows, as well as the meta-reduction *before* it rewinds $B$, the validity bit of each ciphertext/plaintext pair in the vector. In the rewinding phase, the meta-reduction essentially sets $s_3 = (c^*, m^*)$ to be equal to the challenge statement such that $w$ is determined by the validity bit of the challenge $s^* = (c^*, m^*)$. However, this validity bit is unknown to the meta-reduction. We show, however, that the only way for the reduction to successfully output an incorrect response now is by flipping *all* the validity bits at the positions with randomizations of $s_3$. In all other cases, the meta-reduction will notice that the response is incorrect: for 2/3 of the components the meta-reduction knows what the validity bit is and where it should occur (those based on $s_1$ and $s_2$). Only for the validity bits derived from $s_3$ the meta-reduction does not know what the validity bit is. However, it knows where these derived components will be and that they must all have the same validity bit. Moreover, due to the hiding properties of $\mathsf{Randomize}$ the exact positions that belong to $s_3$ are *perfectly* hidden in a subvector of size $2\kappa$. This subvector consists of all pairs that have the validity bit that is more frequent overall. To only flip the validity bits that correspond to $s_3$, the best the reduction can do is thus correctly guess which $\kappa$ of the $2\kappa$ pairs with validity bit $w$ belong to $s_3$ since the random permutation is kept secret. The probability for this is $\binom{2\kappa}{\kappa}^{-1}$ which is statistically small. We obtain the following theorem.

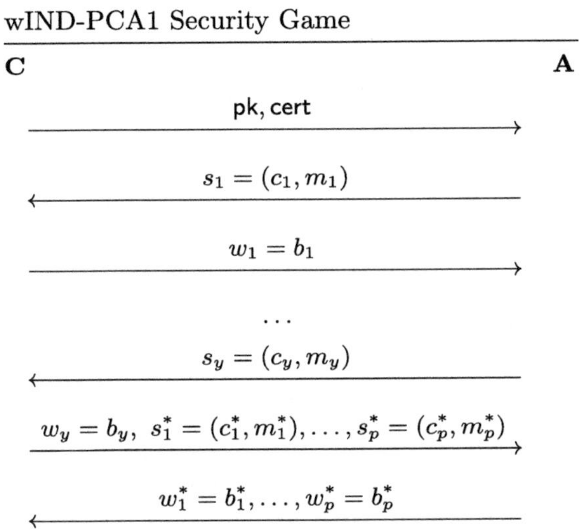


**Fig. 1.** The wIND-PCA1 security game between challenger **C** and attacker **A**. On initialization, a public key pk together with a certificate cert of an SHPKE are sent to the attacker. The attacker may query $y$ PCA queries of the form $s_i = (c_i, m_i)$ for $i \in [y]$. The challenger will respond with $w_i = 1$ if $s_i$ is a valid ciphertext/plaintext pair for the SHPKE. Otherwise, **C** responds with bit $w_i = 0$. After $t$ queries, the attacker is given $p$ challenge statements $s_1^* = (c_1^*, m_1^*), \ldots, s_p^* = (c_p^*, m_p^*)$, for which it has to determine the corresponding validity bits $w_1^*, \ldots, w_p^*$.

**Theorem 2 (Second Main Result, Informal).** *Let* PKE *be an SHPKE with security parameter $\kappa$. There exists no PPT reduction $B$ that, while creating at most $u$ attacker instances, reduces the security of the wIND-PCA1 security game with $3\kappa(2t + 2\kappa + 2u)$ adaptive PCA queries to the security of any $t$-interactive complexity assumption* ICA.

*Related Work.* We add new results to the line of work in [4,16,17,20–22,41,42,49] that focuses on the (in)feasibility of cryptographic primitives. In contrast to previous meta-reduction-based works like [3,11,27,28,31,38,48] that tackle inversion-type security notions, we concentrate on the *decisional* problem of recognizing valid ciphertext/plaintext pairs. In this way, our work complements the recent results of [48] that focuses on the computational problem of computing plaintexts from ciphertexts. However, there are major differences in the two settings, and we have to develop novel solutions to new problems: in our setting we do not need to consider the re-randomizability of witnesses since the witness,

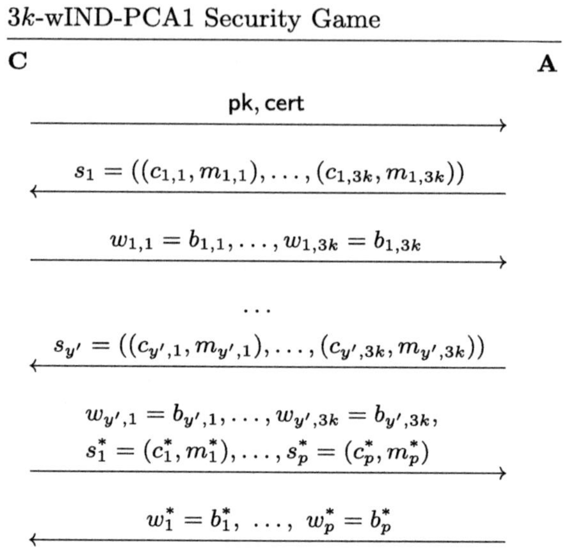


**Fig. 2.** The $3k$-wIND-PCA1 security game between challenger **C** and attacker **A**. On initialization, a public key pk together with a certificate cert of an SHPKE are sent to the attacker. The attacker may query $y'$ $3k$-PCA queries of the form $s_i = ((c_{i,1}, m_{i,1}), \ldots, (c_{i,3k}, m_{i,3k}))$ for $i \in [y']$. The challenger will respond with $w_{i,j} \in \{0,1\}$ for each pair $(c_{i,j}, m_{i,j})$. After $y'$ queries, the attacker is given $p$ challenge statements $s_1^* = (c_1^*, m_1^*), \ldots, s_p^* = (c_p^*, m_p^*)$, for which it has to determine the corresponding validity bits $w_1^*, \ldots, w_p^*$. Since it is less adaptive, this security notion is weaker than the wIND-PCA security game that admits $y$ queries in the learning phase in case $y = 3ky'$. In our final proof we will set $k$ to equal the security parameter $k = \kappa$.

i.e. the validity bit, is unique.[4] In this sense, our work is closer to earlier works on meta-reductions that entirely rely on unique witnesses like [11,28]. Moreover, our randomization technique is very different from the one used in [48]. Whereas their randomization produces derived statements and witnesses that are independent of the challenge statement and witness, our statement randomization technique does not change the witness at all. We thus have to introduce novel statistical techniques to make sure that this correlation between challenge and derived statements is not problematic overall. Finally, since we only consider a decisional PCA oracle that outputs a single bit, we cannot rely on existing techniques to deal with rewinding reductions via algebraic one-time MACs. Instead we use an entirely novel technique that considers $3\kappa$ ciphertext/plaintext pairs per query.

[4] For re-randomizable relations there exist efficient algorithms that can be used to uniformly draw from the class of witnesses for some statement once a single witness has been obtained. This makes sense if there is more than one witness per statement to begin with.

*Restrictions.* To obtain our impossibility result, our definition of SHPKE schemes requires that valid ciphertexts (and valid public keys) can efficiently be recognized using public values. Existing PKE schemes that provide strong security guarantees like IND-CCA2 security, usually do not provide such algorithms. On the contrary, their security arguments often rely on the very fact that it is hard to separate valid from invalid ciphertexts [12]. Taking this one step further, the recent technique of Libert [32] specifically introduces restrictions on the message space of existing SHPKE schemes, that always (artificially) partition the ciphertext space into valid and non-valid ciphertexts, thus sidestepping our results.

## 2 Preliminaries

*Definitions and Notation.* We let $\kappa$ denote the security parameter. Let $\mathcal{PK}, \mathcal{SK}$ be the public-key space and secret-key space respectively. Let $\mathcal{C}$ be the set of ciphertexts and let $\mathcal{M}$ be the set of plaintexts. Let $s = (c, m) \in \mathcal{C} \times \mathcal{M}$ be a ciphertext/plaintext pair, which we often refer to as a statement. The corresponding witness to a statement $s = (c, m) \in \mathcal{C} \times \mathcal{M}$ is denoted by $w \in \{0, 1\}$. We often refer to $w$ as the validity bit of $(c, m)$. The validity bit is 1 if $c$ decrypts to plaintext $m$, otherwise it is set to 0. We let $\mathsf{VAL}$ denote the set of ciphertext/plaintext pairs that for a given public key are valid. Correspondingly, the set of invalid ciphertext/plaintext pairs is denoted $\mathsf{INV}$. We denote vectors of statements of size $k$, i.e. $s = ((c_1, m_1), ..., (c_k, c_k))$ as $(c, m)_k$. Similarly, we denote the (corresponding) vector containing validity bits by $(w)_{3\kappa} = (w_1, w_2, ..., w_{3\kappa})$. We assume that for both $\mathcal{C}$ and $\mathcal{M}$, there exist efficient public memberships tests to check whether $c \in \mathcal{C}$ and $m \in \mathcal{M}$. The notation $[k; n]$ for $k, n \in \mathbb{N}$ and $k \leq n$ will be used to denote the set of natural numbers $k, k + 1, \ldots, n$. For simplicity of notation, we use $[n]$ to denote $[1; n]$.

*Algorithms.* Let $A$ be a probabilistic algorithm. We use the notation $y = A(x; r)$ to say that algorithm $A$ takes as input $x$ and randomness $r$ while outputting $y$. In this way, $A$ can be understood as a deterministic algorithm with explicit coins $r$. The randomness is taken from a set $D = \{0, 1\}^l$ with some polynomial $l = l(\kappa)$. Of course, we can also make the random coins implicit. In this case, we assume the random coins $r \in D$ are drawn uniformly at random. In the remainder of the paper, we assume that any probabilistic algorithm uses random coins in $D = \{0, 1\}^l$ unless explicitly specified otherwise. When $T$ is a set, we use $t \leftarrow T$ to denote that $t$ is drawn uniformly random from $T$.

*Reductions.* To define reductions, we mainly follow the work of [43]. A black-box reduction is a probabilistic polynomial-time (PPT) oracle algorithm. We use black-box reductions to base the security of some cryptographic primitive $X$ on the hardness of some other cryptographic primitive $Y$. A black-box reduction $B$ breaks the security of $Y$ using an attacker $A$ (we denote this by $B^A$), whenever $A$ breaks the security of $X$. The security games are played between a challenger and an attacker. For each security game, the necessary conditions will be defined to express when the attacker has successfully broken the security game. We distinguish interactive and non-interactive oracles and generally consider oracles to be deterministic. At the beginning of the security game, oracles can be given random coins as input to model probabilistic behavior. Whenever $B$ gives new random coins to an oracle $A$, we consider this as $B$ *creating an instance* of $A$. We require that simple reductions can only provide their oracles with randomness once – at the start of the security game. General Turing reductions, in contrast, may do this several times. This models that general reductions can rewind their oracles. All algorithms are considered to be uniform in this work. In the following, we often refer to the notion of a *spot*. A spot is a state in the execution of the security game when the attacker is expected to send a query to the reduction.

*Success Probability after Rewinding.* An important tool to analyze the success probability of the meta-reduction after rewinding, is the splitting lemma [45]. We use the splitting lemma to lower bound the probability that the reduction will not abort after rewinding.

**Lemma 1 (Splitting Lemma).** *Let $X$ and $Y$ be finite sets. Let $G \subseteq X \times Y$ be the set containing 'good' elements. For any element $(x, y) \in X \times Y$, we define $k_x$ to be the number $y' \in Y$ such that $(x, y') \in G$. Assume there exists some $\epsilon \in [0, 1]$ such that $|G| \geq \epsilon|X \times Y|$. Let $G' = \{(x, y) \in G \mid k_x \geq \epsilon/2\ |Y|\}$, the set of so called 'super-good' elements. It holds that*

$$|G'| \geq \epsilon/2\ |X \times Y|.$$

*Hoeffding's Inequality.* Another tool that we require is Hoeffding's inequality. It will later be used to show the existence of a useful rewinding spot. We introduce a variant for Bernoulli random variables.

**Lemma 2 (Hoeffding's Inequality).** *Let $X_1, ..., X_n$ be independent Bernoulli random variables. We consider their sum $S_n = \sum_{i=1}^{n} X_i$. Then the following inequality holds*

$$\mathsf{Pr}[|S_n - E[S_n]| > t] \leq 2e^{-2t^2/n}.$$

*Here $E[S_n]$ denotes the expected value of $S_n$.*

## 3 Notions for PKE

In this section, we introduce the notion of semi-homomorphic public-key encryption, as well as the associated security notions that we need to prove our impossibility result. This includes the formal security notions of wIND-PCA1 and wIND-PCA2 as well as a weaker security notion that we denote by $3k$-wIND-PCA1. This weaker security notion is used to show our second main result. For completeness, we also provide definitions for the classical IND-PCA notions in Sect. 3.4.

### 3.1 Public-Key Encryption

Let us start by providing a formal notion of a public-key encryption system. A public-key encryption (PKE) system $\mathsf{PKE} = (\mathsf{PKE.KGen}, \mathsf{PKE.Enc}, \mathsf{PKE.Dec})$ consists of three algorithms.

1. $\mathsf{PKE.KGen}(1^\kappa)$. Algorithm $\mathsf{PKE.KGen}$ is a probabilistic algorithm that takes as input the security parameter in unary and outputs an asymmetric key pair $(\mathsf{pk}, \mathsf{sk}) \in \mathcal{PK} \times \mathcal{SK}$. Algorithm $\mathsf{PKE.KGen}$ is called the key-generation algorithm.
2. $\mathsf{PKE.Enc}(\mathsf{pk}, m)$. Algorithm $\mathsf{PKE.Enc}$ is a probabilistic algorithm that takes as input the public key $\mathsf{pk} \in \mathcal{PK}$ and a message $m \in \mathcal{M}$ and outputs some ciphertext $c \in \mathcal{C}$. Algorithm $\mathsf{PKE.Enc}$ is called the encryption algorithm.
3. $\mathsf{PKE.Dec}(\mathsf{sk}, c)$. Algorithm $\mathsf{PKE.Dec}$ is a deterministic algorithm that takes as input the secret key $\mathsf{sk} \in \mathcal{SK}$ and some ciphertext $c$ (not necessarily in $\mathcal{C}$). It either outputs a message $m \in \mathcal{M}$ if $c \in \mathcal{C}$ or a dedicated error symbol $\perp$ if $c \notin \mathcal{C}$. Algorithm $\mathsf{PKE.Dec}$ is called the decryption algorithm.

We say that a $\mathsf{PKE}$ is perfectly correct if for all keypairs $(\mathsf{pk}, \mathsf{sk}) \leftarrow \mathsf{PKE.KGen}(1^\kappa)$, we have for all $m \in \mathcal{M}$ that $\Pr[\mathsf{PKE.Dec}(\mathsf{sk}, \mathsf{PKE.Enc}(\mathsf{pk}, m)) = m] = 1$. In the remainder of the paper, we only consider perfectly correct PKEs. Next, a PKE scheme is said to be certified if i) it can be efficiently verified whether $\mathsf{pk} \in \mathcal{PK}$ and ii) we have that $[\mathsf{PKE.KGen}(1^\kappa; D)]_1 = \mathcal{PK}$. In other words, we can efficiently recognize the set of public keys that is output by the key generator. In general, we assume that a certificate $\mathsf{cert}$ is distributed together with the public key that proves this fact with perfect soundness. (This requirement might be relaxed to statistical soundness but for simplicity, we refrain from doing this.) It is well-known that ElGamal, Paillier [40], and Damgård-Jurik [14] are either certified or can easily be made certified [33]. In the following, we will use $w := (m \stackrel{?}{=} \mathsf{PKE.Dec}(\mathsf{sk}, c))$ to denote the process of assigning 1 to $w$ in case $m = \mathsf{PKE.Dec}(\mathsf{sk}, c)$ and 0 otherwise.

### 3.2 Semi-homomorphic PKE

Our results follow directly from the properties of a semi-homomorphic PKE scheme. We formally introduce the notion in this section. A public key encryption scheme $\mathsf{PKE} = (\mathsf{PKE.KGen}, \mathsf{PKE.Enc}, \mathsf{PKE.Dec})$ is said to be homomorphic if the following properties are fulfilled.

1. For any security parameter $\kappa$ and all secret key/public key pairs $(\mathsf{pk}, \mathsf{sk}) \leftarrow \mathsf{PKE.KGen}(1^\kappa)$, it is possible to define finite, cyclic groups $(G, +)$ and $(H, \cdot)$ such that the $G = \mathcal{M}$, the plaintext space, and $H = \mathcal{C}$, the ciphertext space. Also, both $G$ and $H$ have an efficient membership test.
2. The set $G$ grows exponentially in the security parameter $\kappa$.
3. There exists an efficient algorithm that draws integer $t$ uniformly at random from $t \leftarrow [|G|]$ with only statistically small error probability $\delta$.

4. Let $m, m' \in G$ and take any scalar $t \in [|G|]$. Then it holds that

$$\begin{aligned}\mathsf{PKE.Dec}(\mathsf{sk}, \mathsf{PKE.Enc}(\mathsf{pk}, m') \cdot \prod_{i=1}^{t} \mathsf{PKE.Enc}(\mathsf{pk}, m)) &= m' + \sum_{i=1}^{t} m \\ &= m' + tm.\end{aligned}$$

5. For every $\mathsf{pk} \in \mathcal{PK}$ and each ciphertext $c \in \mathcal{C}$, there exists a plaintext $m$ and randomness $r$, so that $c = \mathsf{PKE.Enc}(\mathsf{pk}, m; r)$. In other words, we have that $\mathcal{C} = \mathsf{PKE.Enc}(\mathsf{pk}, \mathcal{M}; D)$.
6. If $m \in \mathcal{M}$ and $r \in D$ are taken uniformly random, then $\mathsf{PKE.Enc}(\mathsf{pk}, m; r)$ is distributed like a uniformly sampled ciphertext $c \in \mathcal{C}$.

As pointed out in [48], the third property is useful to model setups like Paillier PKE. These properties are fulfilled by ElGamal PKE, Paillier PKE, Damgård-Jurik PKE and the linear encryption system introduced by Boneh, Boyen, and Shacham [6] as well as its generalizations based on arbitrary Matrix-DDH assumptions [18]. Since we only consider certified and perfectly correct PKEs, our requirement in 1. and 5. guarantee that we can always efficiently check from the public parameters whether a purported ciphertext $c$ indeed decrypts to some (unique) message $m \in \mathcal{M}$.

As such, our definition does not cover schemes like Damgård's ElGamal PKE [13,34] or (the lite version of) the Cramer-Shoup PKE [12] where efficient public membership tests for recognizing valid ciphertexts do not exist. Similarly, the schemes considered in the recent work of Libert [32] sidestep our requirements. Essentially, this is because the variants in [32] require that ciphertexts are only decrypted in case the plaintext has a specific format (e.g. if it lies in some small interval). However, whether this is true cannot be recognized efficiently via public parameters only. We believe that it is possible to relax our rather strict requirements (including perfect correctness) to hold with all but statistically low error probability without violating our impossibility results, albeit under some well-defined conditions only. Specifically, we have to require that whenever an error event happens (e.g. where $\mathsf{pk} \notin \mathcal{PK}$ or $c \notin \mathcal{C}$ will remain unrecognized), the attacker can always efficiently break the security of the scheme. Jumping ahead, our impossibility result should still hold then, since for each error we then have an efficient attack that *both* ideal attacker and meta-reduction can launch. As a consequence, error events can efficiently be simulated by the meta-reduction as well.

### 3.3 Algorithms for Randomization, Sampling, and Random Sampling

Let us now also define two algorithms for generating and randomizing (in)valid ciphertext/plaintext pairs in SHPKE schemes. Their properties readily follow from the properties of the SHPKE. These algorithms will later be used by the attacker and meta-reduction as described in Sect. 6.

*Randomization.* The probabilistic randomization algorithm $\mathsf{Randomize}$ takes as input the public key $\mathsf{pk}$, a ciphertext $c$, and a plaintext $m$. Let $w$ be the validity bit of $(c, m)$. The output of $\mathsf{Randomize}(\mathsf{pk}, c, m)$ is a ciphertext/plaintext pair $(c', m')$ with validity bit $w'$, such that $w = w'$. The randomization algorithm guarantees that $(c', m')$ is indistinguishable from any uniformly random pair $(c'', m'')$ with equal validity bit (so $w' = w''$). Let us describe the randomization algorithm concretely. Let $\mathsf{pk} \in \mathcal{PK}$. For any pair $(c, m)$, we perform the following.

- We generate uniformly random $r \leftarrow G$ and uniformly random $s \leftarrow [|G|]$ with overwhelming probability $1 - \delta$ (according to Property 3).
- We set $c' = c^s \cdot \mathsf{PKE.Enc}(\mathsf{pk}, r)$ and $m' = sm + r$.
- Finally, we output $(c', m')$.

The validity of the ciphertext/plaintext pairs is preserved by the properties of the SHPKE scheme: if $w = 1$, i.e. $(c, m)$ is a valid ciphertext/plaintext pair, we have $c' = \mathsf{PKE.Enc}(\mathsf{pk}, m)^s \cdot \mathsf{PKE.Enc}(\mathsf{pk}, r)$ and $m' = sm + r$. Thus we have $w' = 1$ as well. Similarly, if $w = 0$, we have that $c' = \mathsf{PKE.Enc}(\mathsf{pk}, m)^s \cdot \mathsf{PKE.Enc}(\mathsf{pk}, r)$ and $m' = s(m + z) + r = (sm + r) + sz$ for some $z \neq 0$. Since $s \in [|G|]$ we have in particular $s \neq 0$. Thus $zs \neq 0$ and $w' = 0$ as well. Moreover, as both $r$ and $s$ are chosen independently and uniformly at random (with overwhelming probability), we have that $c', m' \in \mathcal{C} \times \mathcal{M}$ is a uniform random element in $\mathsf{VAL}$ if $w = 1$ with probability at least $(1 - \delta)$, because $c'$ is ranging over every possible ciphertext. Similarly, if $w = 0$, then $(c', m')$ is a uniform random element in $\mathsf{INV}$. In this case, we have that $c' = \mathsf{PKE.Enc}(\mathsf{pk}, m)^s \cdot \mathsf{PKE.Enc}(\mathsf{pk}, r)$ and $m' = s(m + z) + r = (sm + r) + sz$ for some $z \neq 0$. Since both $r \in G$ and $s \in [|G|]$ are drawn at random and since in particular $s \neq 0$, we have that $c'$ ranges over all possible ciphertexts and $m'$ ranges over all possible plaintext conditioned on the fact that $(c', m')$ is an invalid ciphertext/plaintext pair.

*Sampling and Random Sampling.* Let us now introduce two probabilistic algorithms $\mathsf{Sample}$ and $\mathsf{RSample}$ that we will often make use of in the following.

The algorithm $\mathsf{Sample}$ takes as input public key $\mathsf{pk}$ and bit $w$. To evaluate $(c, m) \leftarrow \mathsf{Sample}(\mathsf{pk}, w)$ it executes the following steps.

1. First, it draws two messages $m', m'' \in \mathcal{M}$ uniformly at random.
2. After that, it draws fresh random coins $r$ and computes the ciphertext $c = \mathsf{PKE.Enc}(\mathsf{pk}, m'; r)$. If $w = 1$, it sets $m = m'$. Otherwise, it sets $m = m''$.
3. Finally, it draws fresh random coins $r'$ and outputs $\mathsf{Randomize}(\mathsf{pk}, c, m; r')$[5] and $w$.

Using $\mathsf{Sample}$, we can produce ciphertext/plaintext pairs $(c, m)$ with a given validity bit $w$ such that $(c, m)$ are drawn uniformly random in the set $\mathsf{VAL}$ or $\mathsf{INV}$ depending on $w$.

[5] Since $m', m''$ are drawn randomly, applying $\mathsf{Randomize}$ is not strictly necessary. However, it simplifies the analysis later as now all queries sent to the reduction, before and after the rewinding, have been output by $\mathsf{Randomize}$.

The probabilistic random sampling algorithm RSample, takes as input the public key pk. It creates a ciphertext/plaintext pair together with its validity bit $(c, m, w) \leftarrow \mathsf{RSample}(\mathsf{pk})$, such that the probability of the event $w = 1$ is $1/2$. The algorithm generates these values by drawing $w \leftarrow \{0, 1\}$ and simply outputting $(c, m) \leftarrow \mathsf{Sample}(\mathsf{pk}, w)$ together with $w$. This shows that independent of the sizes of VAL and INV we can draw statements uniformly from either set with probability $1/2$. Observe that Sample and RSample use Randomize, which fails with statistically low probability $\delta$. They thus also have overwhelming success probability $(1 - \delta)$.

### 3.4 IND-PCA, wIND-PCA, and 3k-wIND-PCA1 Security

We introduce the classical IND-PCA security notion: Indistinguishability under plaintext checkable attacks [1]. Next, we present two progressively weaker versions of this security notion called weak IND-PCA security (wIND-PCA) and $3k$-wIND-PCA1 security. The corresponding security games for the weaker versions are given in Fig. 1 (wIND-PCA1), Fig. 2 ($3k$-wIND-PCA1), and Fig. 3 (wIND-PCA2). Let us begin with the notion for IND-PCA security.

1. The challenger $C$ computes $(\mathsf{pk}, \mathsf{sk}) \leftarrow \mathsf{PKE.KGen}(1^\kappa)$ and sends pk to the attacker $A$.
2. The attacker $A$ may (adaptively) query up to $y'_1$ queries to $C$. Each query consists of a ciphertext/plaintext pair $s_i = (c_i, m_i) \in \mathcal{C} \times \mathcal{M}$ for $i \in [y'_1]$.
3. The challenger $C$ responds to each query with the truth value $w_i := (m_i \stackrel{?}{=} \mathsf{PKE.Dec}(\mathsf{sk}, c_i))$.
4. The attacker computes $p$ plaintexts $\hat{m}^*_{1,1}, \ldots, \hat{m}^*_{1,p}$ and sends them to the challenger.
5. Challenger $C$ determines $p$ challenge statements as follows. For each $j \in [p]$, $C$ draws random message $\hat{m}^*_{0,j}$ and a random bit $w^*_j$ and computes $c^*_j \leftarrow \mathsf{PKE.Enc}(\mathsf{pk}, \hat{m}^*_{d,j})$ with $d = 1 - w^*_j$. Next, $C$ sets $m^*_j = \hat{m}^*_{0,j}$ and outputs $s^*_j = (c^*_j, m^*_j)$ to the attacker $A$.
6. The attacker $A$ may (adaptively) query up to $y'_2$ queries to $C$. Each query consists of a ciphertext/plaintext pair $s_i = (c_i, m_i) \in \mathcal{C} \times \mathcal{M}$ for $i \in [y'_2]$.
7. $A$ responds with bits $w'^*_1, \ldots, w'^*_p$.

We say the attacker wins if $\bigwedge_{i=1}^{p} (w'^*_i = w^*_i)$. Moreover, we say that the PKE scheme is IND-PCA secure if the *advantage*

$$\left| \Pr\left[ \bigwedge_{i=1}^{p} (w'^*_i = w^*_i) \right] - 1/2^p \right|$$

is negligible for any PPT $A$. We also say the attacker breaks the security of a PKE scheme if its advantage is non-negligible. Additionally, we say that the PKE scheme is wIND-PCA secure if we collapse Steps 4. and 5. of the IND-PCA game and substitute it by the following step, as depicted in Fig. 1.

4*. Challenger $C$ determines $p$ challenge statements as follows. For each $j \in [p]$, $C$ draws two random messages $\hat{m}^*_{0,j}$ and $\hat{m}^*_{1,j}$ and a random bit $w^*_j$ and computes $c^*_j \leftarrow \mathsf{PKE.Enc}(\mathsf{pk}, \hat{m}^*_{1,j})$. Challenger $C$ sets $m_j{}^* = \hat{m}^*_{w^*,j}$ and outputs $s^*_j = (c^*_j, m^*_j,)$ to the attacker $A$.

As is common, we introduce subnotions, making distinctions between IND-PCA1 and IND-PCA2 security on the one hand and wIND-PCA1 and wIND-PCA2 on the other hand. In traditional notions like IND-CCA security, $p$ is usually set to $p = 1$. Having $p > 1$ generalizes this concept, making it harder for the attacker since it has to deliver several correct solutions at the same time.[6] The advantage takes into account that, for any $p$, the attacker might just guess the validity bits. Practically, this has been used in modelling the threat of mass surveillance [5]. Using established terminology, this results in the natural AND notion [5] for suitable parameter choices. In case the attacker cannot reveal the challenge bits of any of the challenges, this is polynomially equivalent to other notions like LORX, RORX, UKU. Interestingly, as our proofs show, the techniques we use can vary in the range of parameters for $p$ that they support. In particular, the full version of this work also provides an IND-PCA1 impossibility result for simple reductions that, however, requires $p$ to be a constant, whereas our more general result in Sect. 6 supports arbitrary polynomial $p$. Depending on whether we have at least one IND-PCA2 query per challenge or not, we consider the following cases.

- In the IND-PCA2 game, we have that $y'_2 \geq p$.
- In the IND-PCA1 game, we have that $y'_2 < p$ but $y'_1 \geq 1$.

For convenience, we call $s^*$ challenge (statement), $c^*$ challenge ciphertext, $m^*$ challenge plaintext, and $w^*$ challenge bit. We call $w'^*$ the (attacker's) guess and $\hat{m}^*_0$ and $\hat{m}^*_1$ candidate plaintexts. If $b := (m \stackrel{?}{=} \mathsf{PKE.Dec}(\mathsf{sk}, c))$ we also say that $b$ is the *validity bit* of $s = (c, m)$. Moreover, we often refer to the interaction in Steps 1, 2, and 3 as the learning phase of the security game.

It is easy to see that the wIND-PCA security game is weaker than IND-PCA security: in contrast to classical indistinguishability attacks, $A$ cannot even provide a candidate plaintext. Instead, it is entirely chosen by the challenger. Since wIND-PCA security is weaker than IND-PCA security it is also weaker than IND-CCA security. This is because the attacker obtains less information in the PCA learning phase than in the CCA learning phase. Instead of decryption queries, the attacker can now only make PCA queries that solely output a single bit. Put differently, a decryption oracle can easily be used to implement a PCA oracle. We show our impossibility result for wIND-PCA.

We remark that the *weakest* variant of the wIND-PCA1 security game with $y' = y'_1 + y'_2$ queries overall is in case $y'_2 = 0$. This is because in this game the attacker cannot rely on the knowledge of the challenge when computing any of its queries. For more generality, we will thus in the following only consider

[6] This is different from classical, hybrid arguments where the reduction expects the attacker to deliver a solution for one instance (out of many).

this variant. In particular, when introducing our next security notions, we will not consider scenarios where the attacker makes queries after the challenge and always implicitly assume that $y'_2 = 0$.

This shows that our final new security notion, $3k$-wIND-PCA1 security, as depicted in Fig. 2, is provably weaker than wIND-PCA security in case the attacker is allowed to send the *same overall number of ciphertext/plaintext pairs* to the challenger. In contrast to the wIND-PCA game, $3k$ of these pairs have to be sent at a time. This makes the $3k$-wIND-PCA1 game simply less adaptive. We refer to these queries as $3k$-PCA queries. In our result, we will set $k = \kappa$.

It is clear that this game is weaker than wIND-PCA1 security if $y \geq 3ky'$: any attacker $A$ that is able to efficiently break the $3k$-wIND-PCA1 security of some PKE scheme with $y'$ $3k$-PCA queries, is immediately able to efficiently break its wIND-PCA1 security with $y$ PCA queries as well in case $y \geq 3ky'$.

## 4 Interactive Complexity Assumptions

*t-Interactive Complexity Assumptions.* Our impossibility result excludes reductions that reduce wIND-PCA security to that of arbitrary *interactive* complexity assumption. We adopt the general notion of a $t$-interactive complexity assumption ($t$ICA) from [48], which is based on the formulation in [3]. We almost take the definition in verbatim. A $t$ICA consists of $t + 3$ Turing machines, given by $\mathsf{ICA} = (\mathsf{ICAGen}, \mathsf{ICAVer}, \mathsf{ICATriv}, \mathsf{ICAQuery}_1, \ldots, \mathsf{ICAQuery}_t)$. We provide a description for each of these Turing machines.

- $\mathsf{ICAGen}$. Algorithm $\mathsf{ICAGen}$ is an efficient probabilistic instance generator. As input it takes the security parameter $\kappa$ and it outputs a problem instance $c$ and an initial state $st_0$.
- $\mathsf{ICAQuery}_1$– $\mathsf{ICAQuery}_t$. Algorithm $\mathsf{ICAQuery}_i$, given as input the $i$-th query $q_i$ and state $st_{i-1}$ for $i \in [t]$, efficiently outputs a response $p_i$ and state $st_i$. We consider the set of all $\mathsf{ICAQuery}_i$ algorithms as a stateful algorithm $\mathsf{ICAQuery}$.
- $\mathsf{ICATriv}$. Algorithm $\mathsf{ICATriv}$, given a problem instance $c$ and $t$-time oracle access to $\mathsf{ICAQuery}$, uses a trivial attack strategy to efficiently determine a candidate solution $s$ to $c$.
- $\mathsf{ICAVer}$. Algorithm $\mathsf{ICAVer}$, given a problem instance $c$, the final state $st_t$, and a solution $s$, outputs a bit $b$. If $\mathsf{ICAVer}(c, st_t, s) = 1$, then $s$ is a valid solution to problem instance $c$. If the $\mathsf{ICAVer}$ algorithm is efficient, then $\mathsf{ICA}$ is said to be falsifiable.

*Security Games for tICAs.* Let $A$ be the attacker and $N$ be a $t$-interactive complexity assumption. We present a general description for a security game $\mathsf{ICA}_N^A$.

1. The game starts by running $(c, st_0) \leftarrow \mathsf{ICAGen}(1^\kappa)$.
2. Attacker $A$ is given $c$, together with $t$-time oracle access to $\mathsf{ICAQuery}$.
3. The attacker $A$ outputs a candidate solution $s$.
4. The experiment returns $\mathsf{ICAVer}(c, st_t, s)$.

We provide a definition for breaking the security of $t$ICA. Intuitively, attacker $A$ wins the security game if it returns a valid candidate solution $s$ with a probability non-negligibly better than any trivial attack. Moreover, $A$ has to provide $s$ in polynomial time. An example of such a trivial attack is simply guessing $b \in \{0,1\}$, which gives the trivial advantage of $1/2$ in an indistinguishability-based security game.

**Definition 1.** *Let $A$ be an attacker. Attacker $A$ is said to efficiently break $t$ICA* ICA *if $A$ has a polynomial running time and if the advantage*

$$|\mathsf{Pr}[\mathsf{ICA}^{A}_{\mathsf{ICA}}(1^{\kappa}) \Rightarrow 1] - \mathsf{Pr}[\mathsf{ICA}^{\mathsf{ICATriv}}_{\mathsf{ICA}}(1^{\kappa}) \Rightarrow 1]| = \epsilon$$

*is non-negligible. The probability is taken over the random coins used by the probabilistic algorithms* ICAGen, ICATriv, ICAQuery, *as well as $A$. A $t$ICA* ICA *is said to be secure if no probabilistic polynomial algorithm can break* ICA.

## 5 Impossibility of wIND-PCA2 Security

As warm-up, let us first investigate wIND-PCA2 security for SHPKE schemes.

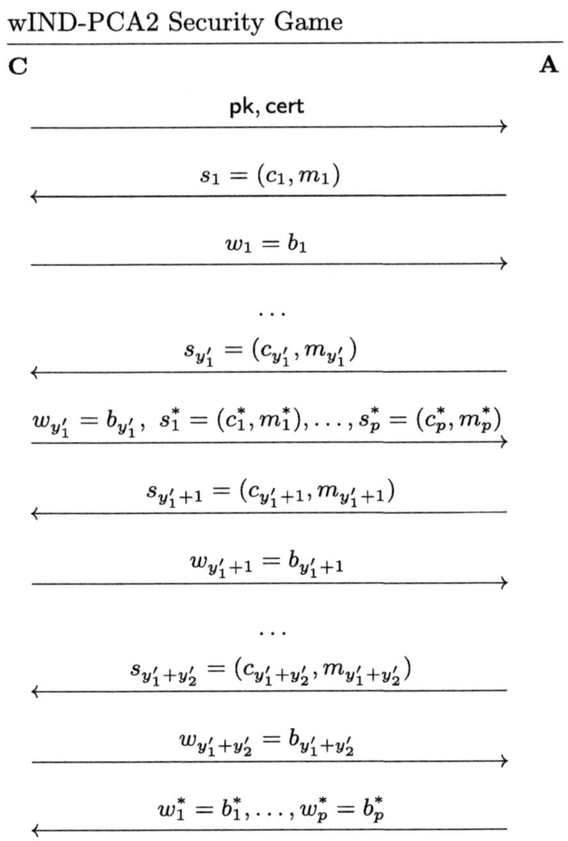


**Fig. 3.** The wIND-PCA2 security game between challenger **C** and attacker **A**.

**Theorem 1.** *There is no SHPKE scheme that is wIND-PCA2 secure.*

The proof of this theorem follows ElGamal's well-known IND-CCA2 impossibility result. In contrast to the existing impossibility result, we not only exploit the malleability of the ciphertexts. We rather rely on the fact that in SHPKE schemes ciphertexts and plaintext pairs can be randomized without changing the validity bit. To this end we can use the Randomize procedure that works for *pairs* of ciphertexts and plaintexts. Moreover, we have to consider that the attacker has to provide answers to $p$ queries overall.

*Proof.* Let $\mathsf{PKE} = (\mathsf{PKE.KGen}, \mathsf{PKE.Enc}, \mathsf{PKE.Dec})$ be an SHPKE scheme. Consider the following wIND-PCA2 attacker $A$. Assume $A$ receives the public key $\mathsf{pk}$ from the challenger $C$. The attacker $A$ makes $y_1'$ arbitrary PCA queries and receives the corresponding responses. (For example, the attacker could send the pair $(c, m)$ a total of $y_1'$ times to the challenger where $c$ is the encryption of random message $m$.) When $A$ receives the challenges $s_1^* = (c_1^*, m_1^*), \ldots, s_p^* = (c_p^*, m_p^*)$, the attacker $A$ computes $(c_i', m_i') \leftarrow \mathsf{Randomize}(\mathsf{pk}, c_i^*, m_i^*)$ to generate $p$ derived statements $s_i' = (c_i', m_i')$ for $i \in [p]$. Next, $A$ sends $s_1', \ldots, s_p'$ to $C$ one after the other. Since in the wIND-PCA2 game we have $y_2' \geq p$, the attacker can always do this by using up the $y_2'$ queries available after the challenges have been received. To each $s_i' = (c_i', m_i')$, the challenger responds with the corresponding validity bit $b_i'$. Because Randomize produces outputs that have the same validity bit as the input, $b_i'$ is also a correct validity bit for $s_i^*$. If $y_2' > p$, $A$ makes $y_2' - p$ additional arbitrary queries to $C$ and receives back the responses. Finally, $A$ sends $b_1', \ldots, b_p'$ to $C$. In this way, the attacker will always win in the security game. Observe that all arguments are independent of the concrete value of $y_1'$. □

In this proof, we rely on the Randomize algorithm that we have defined before. This is for simplicity. We remark that the strong hiding property of Randomize (outputs are always uniformly random in the set VAL respectively INV and thus only provide very limited information on the input statement) is not necessary. Indeed, it seems the proof can rely on Property 4. and Property 5. as given in the general definition of SHPKE in Sect. 3.2. Also, observe that the proof essentially relies on the fact that all derived statements can be sent to the challenger *after* the challenge has been received. This strategy does not work in the case of wIND-PCA1 security. We present the following corollary, which is a direct result of Theorem 1 since IND-PCA2 security implies wIND-PCA2 security.

**Corollary 1.** *There is no SHPKE scheme that is IND-PCA2 secure.*

## 6 Impossibility of wIND-PCA1 Security

Let us now consider the more challenging case of wIND-PCA1 security. In our second main result, we rule out that SHPKE schemes can be shown $3\kappa$-wIND-PCA1 secure via general Turing reductions. We use this result to finally rule out provable wIND-PCA1 security for SHPKE schemes. Since wIND-PCA1 is weaker than IND-PCA security, the impossibility result immediately transfers to IND-PCA security as well.

**Theorem 2.** *Let $\kappa$ be the security parameter. Let* PKE *be a certified SHPKE. Let $p$, the number of challenges statements that the attacker must solve in the $3\kappa$-wIND-PCA1 security game, be polynomial. Then, there exists no PPT reduction $B$ that reduces the $3\kappa$-wIND-PCA1 security of* PKE *with $2t + 2\kappa + 2u$ adaptive PCA queries to the security of any $t$ICA, while creating no more than $u$ attacker instances for $t + u < O(\kappa^2)$.*

In the full version, we present a more restricted but conceptually much simpler result that rules out simple reductions. This result has better quantitative bounds. On the other hand, however, it only applies to scenarios with a constant number of challenges $p$. Intuitively, the underlying reason is that when dealing with simple reductions, our meta-reduction simply hopes that the reduction only provides correct responses in the learning phase after it rewinds the reduction. However, the meta-reduction cannot check if this is actually true. Nevertheless, with non-negligible probability this is bound to happen for a single challenge since the reduction has, by assumption, non-negligible success probability. In this way, the first challenge $w_1^*$ can easily be computed by the meta-reduction with non-negligible probability. However, the meta-reduction uses this process for all other challenges as well and the overall probability that the reduction always provides correct answers after all the rewindings diminishes exponentially in $p$. This problem does not occur in the proof of Theorem 2 since after each rewinding we can actually check with *overwhelming probability* whether the reduction has output a correct response to our rewound query. A simple application of Bernoulli's inequality shows that the overall probability remains overwhelming after polynomially many challenges.

*Remaining Challenges.* To prove Theorem 2, we have to find solutions for the following challenges when dealing with general Turing reductions $B$.

1. $B$ may rewind the adversary $A$.
2. $B$ may communicate externally with the $t$ICA challenge (at most $t$ times).
3. $B$ may initiate $u$ attacker instances of $A$.
4. $B$ may provide incorrect responses.

In the introduction, we have already sketched how we deal with the latter three challenges. It remains to describe how we deal with rewinding reductions more generally. Essentially, the main idea is to make the ideal attacker behave deterministically towards the reduction. Since the meta-reduction controls the reduction, it can always simulate such a behavior by proper bookkeeping. If the ideal attacker $A$ behaves deterministically (in the initially provided random coins), any reduction that rewinds $A$ to some earlier point will receive the same queries as before in the learning phase. This limits the benefits that the reduction obtains by being able to rewind the attacker. The only way a reduction can change the attacker's behavior in the learning phase at all is by either creating a new instance of $A$ (via new initial randomness) or by responding incorrectly to some of the queries. However, slightly jumping ahead, we will have that, by setup, the ideal attacker knows the correct responses to begin with. To make the attacker deterministic, we follow previous works like [38,39,43] that give $A$ access to some (private) random oracle $h(\cdot)$. We assume that each instance of $A$ is given some initial random coins $r$ (by $B$) at the beginning. Every instance of $A$ will now apply $h(\cdot)$ to their transcript so far of sent and received messages to generate fresh random coins for all the randomized algorithms it uses next. We will not make this explicit. However, we emphasize that for each query sent by $A$ in the learning phase, there is only a single correct validity bit that $B$ can send without the attacker aborting. Therefore, the entire learning phase is now essentially fixed for each attacker instance when it receives the initial randomness.

*Stateless Attackers: The Next-Message Function.* As is common in meta-reduction-based results, we will model the attacker as a stateless next-message function that is given as input the entire communication transcript so far (including the initial randomness). Intuitively, this outsources the state management to the reduction. Moreover, it gives her full control of the state that the adversary should be in next via a single interface. Creating new instances corresponds to using new initial randomness. However, to make sure that the attacker only accepts plausible transcripts, we require it to check all the steps in the transcript by recomputing its values. If the transcript does not correspond to a plausible transcript the attacker aborts. Otherwise, it outputs the next message, which can either be the next query in the learning phase or the response to the challenge. This modeling simplifies arguments about the view and behavior of the reduction: essentially view and behavior can now not depend on a state that $A$ is in, simply because $A$ is stateless. To be consistent with this modeling, we assume in the following that $B$ sends entire transcripts to $A$. For simplicity, we will often not consider this mechanism explicitly and instead view the attacker as stateful.

*Useful Rewinding Spot.* Our proof strategy is centered around the idea of guaranteeing that a useful rewinding spot exists. By this, we refer to a state in the learning phase of $B$ that the meta-reduction rewinds $B$ back to. More precisely, this is a state of $B$ immediately before $A$ outputs a new query to the reduction. A useful rewinding spot has the following properties: i) no external queries are made to the $t$ICA by $B$ before it responds to $A$'s query, ii) the response of $B$ is correct, and iii) $B$ does not wait for any of the other $u-1$ attacker instances to respond to a challenge statement before $B$ outputs the response to $A$'s query.

*Sampling Vectors of Ciphertext/Plaintext Pairs.* To prepare our description, let us now describe a probabilistic algorithm $\mathsf{VectorSample}$ that, given input pair $(c, m) \in \mathcal{C} \times \mathcal{M}$, outputs $3k$ ciphertext/plaintext pairs $(c_1, m_1), \ldots, (c_{3k}, m_{3k})$ together with the description of a random permutation $\pi$ on the set $\{1, \ldots, 3k\}$. In the following, assume that $w$ is the validity bit of $(c, m)$. We stress however, that $w$ is not given as input to $\mathsf{VectorSample}$. The algorithm works as follows:

1. First, $\mathsf{VectorSample}$ generates two additional ciphertext/plaintext pairs that are computed via $(c_1', m_1') \leftarrow \mathsf{Sample}(\mathsf{pk}, 1)$ and $(c_2', m_2') \leftarrow \mathsf{Sample}(\mathsf{pk}, 0)$. By construction, the first pair has validity bit 1 while the second has validity bit 0. Additionally, $\mathsf{VectorSample}$ sets $(c_3', m_3') := (c, m)$.
2. Next, $\mathsf{VectorSample}$ creates $3k$ pairs $(c_1'', m_1''), \ldots, (c_{3k}'', m_{3k}'') \in \mathcal{C} \times \mathcal{M}$ by calling $(c_i'', m_i'') \leftarrow \mathsf{Randomize}(\mathsf{pk}, c'_{\lceil i/k \rceil}, m'_{\lceil i/k \rceil})$ for all $1 \leq i \leq 3k$. Intuitively, this creates $3k$ random pairs such that the first $k$ (for $1 \leq i \leq k$) of them have validity bit 1, the central $k$ pairs (for $k+1 \leq i \leq 2k$) have validity bit 0, and the last $k$ pairs (for $2k+1 \leq i \leq 3k$) have the same validity bit as the input pair, i.e. validity bit $w$.
3. In the last step, $\mathsf{VectorSample}$ draws a random permutation $\pi$ on $[3k]$.
4. Finally, $\mathsf{VectorSample}$ outputs $(c_1, m_1), \ldots, (c_{3k}, m_{3k})$ together with $\pi$ where the positions of the $(c_j, m_j)$ are permuted according to $\pi$ as follows: $(c_j, m_j) := (c''_{\pi(j)}, m''_{\pi(j)})$.

When $((c_1, m_1), \ldots, (c_{3k}, m_{3k}), \pi) \leftarrow \mathsf{VectorSample}(\mathsf{pk}, c, m)$ is called, we always have by the properties of $\mathsf{Randomize}$ that exactly 2/3 of the $(c_i, m_i)$ have validity bit $w$. Moreover, using $\pi$ we can always determine which of the pairs $(c_i, m_i)$ have been derived from $(c_1', m_1')$ and $(c_2', m_2')$ and accordingly, what their validity bit is. Also, we can compute all the $(c_i, m_i)$ that have been derived from the input pair. Importantly, all these pairs must always have the same validity bit.

*Testing Vectors of Ciphertext/Plaintext Pairs.* This gives rise to an efficient deterministic validity test $\mathsf{VectorTest}$ that on input $(c_1, m_1), \ldots, (c_{3k}, m_{3k}) \in \mathcal{C} \times \mathcal{M}$, permutation $\pi$ on $[3k]$, and the purported vector of validity bits $w_1, \ldots, w_{3k} \in \{0, 1\}$, tests whether all the $w_i$ indeed correspond to the validity bits of $(c_i, m_i)$. To compute bit $b \leftarrow \mathsf{VectorTest}(\mathsf{pk}, (c_1, m_1), \ldots, (c_{3k}, m_{3k}), w_1, \ldots, w_{3k}, \pi)$, the algorithm $\mathsf{VectorTest}$ does the following:

1. It computes the three index sets $I_j = \{\pi(\ell) | 1 + (j-1)k \leq \ell \leq jk\}$ for $j = 1, 2, 3$.
2. Next, $\mathsf{VectorTest}$ checks whether it holds for all positions $i \in I_1$ that $w_i = 1$.
3. After that, it checks whether for all positions $i \in I_2$ it holds that $w_i = 0$.
4. Finally, $\mathsf{VectorTest}$ checks whether for all positions $i \in I_3$ it holds that the $w_i$ are all equal, i.e. if $|\{w_i | i \in I_3\}| = 1$.
5. If all the checks in Steps 2, 3, and 4 are successful, $\mathsf{VectorTest}$ outputs 1. Otherwise, it outputs 0.

We observe that in case $((c_1, m_1), \ldots, (c_{3k}, m_{3k}), \pi)$ is the output of $\mathsf{VectorSample}$, there are at most two possible bit vectors $w_1, \ldots, w_{3k}$ that make the invocation of $\mathsf{VectorTest}((c_1, m_1), \ldots, (c_{3k}, m_{3k}), \pi, w_1, \ldots, w_{3k})$ output 1. These two vectors differ exactly in the $k$ positions $i \in I_3$. One of these vectors contains all the correct validity bits. The other one has all the validity bits $w_i$ with $i \in I_3$ flipped. (Otherwise the check in Step 4 of $\mathsf{VectorTest}$ would fail.) Moreover, given only $(c_1, m_1), \ldots, (c_{3k}, m_{3k})$, it is hard to compute $I_3$. To see this, assume that 2/3 of the $(c_i, m_i)$ have validity bit 1. (The argument for $w = 0$

works analogously.) Information-theoretically, this decreases the set of possible indices that $I_3$ may contain to $2k$ candidates. This set of candidates not only consists of the pairs that have been derived from $(c'_3, m'_3)$ but also of those that have been derived from $(c'_1, m'_1)$ when executing $\mathsf{VectorSample}$. However, since the output of $\mathsf{Randomize}$ is always uniformly random in $\mathsf{VAL}$ the pairs at positions $i \in I_1$ are distributed exactly like those that are located at positions $i \in I_3$. Thus, the best the reduction can do is to guess the $k$ positions of $I_3$. However, this has statistically low success probability $\binom{2k}{k}^{-1}$.

### 6.1 The Ideal Attacker

In this section we present the ideal attacker $A$ for the $3\kappa$-wIND-PCA1 security game. Let $C$ be the challenger of the security game. Let $u$ be the maximum number of attacker instances the reduction is allowed to initiate. For simplicity of notation, let $y = 2t + 2\kappa + 2u$.

1. *Initialization.* On initialization, the challenger sends a public key $\mathsf{pk}$ and a proof $\mathsf{cert}$, together with random coins $r$, to $A$. The ideal attacker $A$ checks whether $\mathsf{pk}, \mathsf{cert}$ are valid. If not, $A$ aborts. Otherwise, it computes $(c, m, w) \leftarrow \mathsf{RSample}(\mathsf{pk})$. Then, it calls the algorithm $\mathsf{VectorSample}$ to compute $((c_1, m_1)_{3\kappa}, \pi_1) \leftarrow \mathsf{VectorSample}(\mathsf{pk}, c, m)$. Finally, it sends $(c_1, m_1)_{3\kappa}$ to $C$.
2. *Verifying Responses of B.* If $A$ receives an input of the following form $T = (\mathsf{pk}, \mathsf{cert}, r, (c_1, m_1)_{3\kappa}, (w'_1)_{3\kappa}, \ldots, (c_i, m_i)_{3\kappa}, (w'_i)_{3\kappa})$ for $i \in [y-1]$, $A$ checks whether $T$ is plausible. To this end, it computes all the $(c_i, m_i)_{3\kappa}$ and checks whether they are equal to the values in $T$. To recompute $(c_i, m_i)_{3\kappa}$, $A$ proceeds as before. It calls $(c, m, w_i) \leftarrow \mathsf{RSample}(\mathsf{pk})$ and after that $((c_i, m_i)_{3\kappa}, \pi_1) \leftarrow \mathsf{VectorSample}(\mathsf{pk}, c, m)$. (Recall that implicitly the randomness used in the probabilistic algorithms is actually derived deterministically.) If any of the recomputed values is different from the one in $T$, $A$ aborts. At the same time, $A$ verifies if the received validity bits are indeed correct. To this end, it checks for each $i$ whether, $\mathsf{VectorTest}(\mathsf{pk}, (c_i, m_i)_{3\kappa}, \pi, (w'_i)_{3\kappa}) = 1$. Moreover, $A$ checks if the $j$-th component of $(w'_i)_{3\kappa}$ for $j = \pi(2\kappa + 1)$ is equal to $w_i$. On failure, attacker $A$ aborts. Finally $A$ computes a new query $(c_{i+1}, m_{i+1})_{3\kappa}$ as before and sends it to the challenger.
3. *Computing the challenge validity bits.* If $A$ receives an input of the following form $T = (\mathsf{pk}, \mathsf{cert}, r, (c_1, m_1)_{3\kappa}, (w'_1)_{3\kappa}, \ldots, (c_y, m_y)_{3\kappa}, (w'_y)_{3\kappa}, s^*_1, \ldots, s^*_p)$, the attacker $A$ first checks, in the same way as before, whether the transcript prefix $T' = (\mathsf{pk}, \mathsf{cert}, r, (c_1, m_1)_{3\kappa}, (w'_1)_{3\kappa}, \ldots, (c_y, m_y)_{3\kappa}, (w'_y)_{3\kappa})$ is plausible. Next, $A$ uses its unbounded computational resources to compute the validity bits $w^*_1, \ldots, w^*_p$ for the challenges $s^*_1, \ldots, s^*_p$. To this end, it can, for example, find for each $s^*_i$ the randomness $r_i$ such that $(s^*_i, w^*_i) \leftarrow \mathsf{RSample}(\mathsf{pk}; r_i)$. Finally, $A$ outputs $w^*_1, \ldots, w^*_p$.

We remark that $A$, due to having unbounded computational resources, wins the security game with overwhelming probability.

### 6.2 The Meta-reduction

In this section, we present the meta-reduction that simulates the ideal attacker. Notation-wise, the $z$-th instance of $A$ is denoted by $A[z]$. Any variable $x$ belonging to the communication between $B$ and $A[z]$ is denoted by $x[z]$. We require that $A[z]$ can store the internal state of $B$ to allow $M$ to rewind $B$.

As sketched before, we exploit that $M$ runs $B$ and thus can easily simulate the deterministic behavior of $A[z]$ by proper bookkeeping. As an example, $M$ may use precomputations to generate all random values (that are computed by the ideal attacker via $h(\cdot)$) beforehand and keeps track of their usage in a table. In this way, they can be used consistently. In the following, we will assume that the meta-reduction will do this implicitly throughout the entire simulation.

The meta-reduction $M$ will, in each simulated attacker instance, receive the initial values from the reduction and start to generate $3k$-PCA queries. To each query, it receives the corresponding response from the reduction. This will continue until for one of the $u$ instances, say instance $z \in [u]$, $A[z]$ has to provide a response to its challenges. As a response, $M$ will repeatedly rewind $B$, to obtain valid responses stepwise for all the $s_i^*[z]$ with $i \in [p]$. For each $i$ the meta-reduction sends a ciphertext/plaintext pair to $B$ that is derived from $s_i^*[z]$. This derived statement is sent at a random position in the learning phase of instance $z$. The meta-reduction hopes that this position turns out to be a useful rewinding spot. In this case instance $z$ will receive back a response that is correct while no other instances have been asked by to provide challenges and no query has been asked to the $t$ICA. All these three conditions can efficiently be checked by $M$ since it controls the execution of $B$. Moreover, to make sure the response is correct, it can apply $\mathsf{VectorTest}$. If the output is 1, then $M$ has that with overwhelming probability, the response is indeed correct. If $M$ does not find a useful rewinding spot, it repeats the process, starting with a fresh randomization of $s_i^*$.

Let us present the construction of meta-reduction $M$ more formally. For simplicity of notation, let $y = 2t + 2\kappa + 2u$.

0. The meta-reduction $M$ receives the $t$ICA instance $c$ and relays it to $B$ along with random coins $r_B \in D_B$.
1. *Initialization.* On initialization of some attacker instance $z$, $B$ sends a public key $\mathsf{pk}[z]$ and a proof $\mathsf{cert}[z]$, together with random coins $r[z]$, to $A[z]$. Then, $A[z]$ checks whether $\mathsf{pk}, \mathsf{cert}$ are valid. If not, $M$ aborts the simulation of $A[z]$. Otherwise, $A[z]$ computes $(c_1[z], m_1[z], w_1[z]) \leftarrow \mathsf{RSample}(\mathsf{pk})$. Then, it calls $((c_1, m_1)_{3\kappa}[z], \pi_1[z]) \leftarrow \mathsf{VectorSample}(\mathsf{pk}[z], c_1[z], m_1[z])$. Note that $M$ keeps track of the number of attacker instances that have been initiated by $B$. For rewinding purposes, $M$ stores the execution state of $B$ as $\mathsf{state}_1[z]$. Next it sends $(c_1, m_1)_{3\kappa}[z]$ to $B$.
2. *Verifying responses of $B$.* For attacker instance $z$, if $A[z]$ receives input value $T[z] = (\mathsf{pk}[z], \mathsf{cert}[z], r[z], (c_1, m_1)_{3\kappa}[z], (w_1')_{3\kappa}[z], \ldots, (c_j, m_j)_{3\kappa}[z], (w_j')_{3\kappa})[z]$ for $j \in [y-1]$, $A[z]$ checks whether $T[z]$ is plausible. To this end, it computes all the $(c_i, m_i)_{3\kappa}[z]$ with $i \in [j]$ on its own and checks whether they are equal to the values in $T[z]$. To recompute $(c_i, m_i)_{3\kappa}[z]$, $A[z]$ proceeds as the ideal attacker. It calls $(c[z], m[z], w_i[z]) \leftarrow \mathsf{RSample}(\mathsf{pk}[z])$ and uses

the result to compute $((c_i, m_i)_{3\kappa}[z], \pi_i[z]) \leftarrow \mathsf{VectorSample}(\mathsf{pk}[z], c[z], m[z])$. If one of the recomputed values is different from the one in $T[z]$, $M$ aborts the simulation of $A[z]$. At the same time, $A[z]$ verifies if the received validity bits are indeed correct. To this end, it checks for each $i$ whether $\mathsf{VectorTest}(\mathsf{pk}[z], (c_i, m_i)_{3\kappa}[z], \pi_i[z], (w_i')_{3\kappa}[z]) = 1$. Moreover, $A[z]$ checks if the $\pi(2\kappa+1)[z]$-th component of $(w_i')_{3\kappa}[z]$ is equal to $w_i[z]$. If this check fails, $A[z]$ aborts. Next, $A[z]$ generates a new query $(c_{i+1}, m_{i+1})_{3\kappa}[z]$ in the same way as before. For rewinding purposes, $A[z]$ stores the execution state of $B$ as $\mathsf{state}_{i+1}[z]$. Finally, it sends $(c_{i+1}, m_{i+1})_{3\kappa}[z]$ to $B$.

3. *Computing the challenge validity bits.* If $A[z]$ receives an input of the following form $T[z] = (T'[z], s_1^*[z], \ldots, s_p^*[z])$ where for the prefix $T'[z]$ we have $T'[z] = (\mathsf{pk}[z], \mathsf{cert}[z], r[z], (c_1, m_1)_{3\kappa}[z], (w_1')_{3\kappa}[z], \ldots, (c_y, m_y)_{3\kappa}[z], (w_y')_{3\kappa}[z])$, the simulated attacker $A[z]$ first checks whether the prefix is plausible in the same way as before. If not, $M$ aborts the simulation of $A[z]$. Next, the execution state of $B$ is stored by $M$ as $state^*[z]$. Now, $A[z]$ will rewind $B$ to obtain the validity bits for the challenge statements. For each challenge statement $s_i^*[z] = (c_i^*[z], m_i^*[z])$ with $i \in [p]$, $A[z]$ executes the following procedure.

3.$i$.1. $M$ iterates through all possible states $\mathsf{state}_n[z]$ for $n \in [y]$.

3.$i$.$n$.1. $M$ rewinds $B$ back to $\mathsf{state}_n[z]$. Similar to the first run, $M$ calls $((c_i', m_i')_{3\kappa}[z], \pi_i'[z]) \leftarrow \mathsf{VectorSample}(\mathsf{pk}[z], c_i^*[z], m_i^*[z])$ but now uses the challenge $(c_i^*[z], m_i^*[z])$ as input to $\mathsf{VectorSample}$. Attacker $A[z]$ sends the query $(c_i', m_i')_{3\kappa}[z]$ to $B$.

3.$i$.$n$.2. We abort the execution at $\mathsf{state}_n[z]$, and go to Step 3.$i$.$n+1$.1. if $n < y$ and either one of the following cases occurs: i) $B$ sends an external query to its $t$ICA challenger before it sends its response $(w_i')_{3\kappa}[z]$ (to query $(c_i', m_i')_{3\kappa}[z]$) to $A[z]$, or ii) $B$ requires a response to a challenge query of another attacker instance $z' \neq z$ before it sends its response to $A[z]$, or iii) $B$'s response $(w_i')_{3\kappa}[z]$ will make $\mathsf{VectorTest}(\mathsf{pk}[z], (c_i', m_i')_{3\kappa}[z], (w_i')_{3\kappa}[z])$ output 0 (which means that one of the validity bits send by $B$ is invalid). If either of the three cases occurs and $n = y$, we return to Step 3.$i$.1. and repeat the entire computation using fresh randomness.[7]

3.$i$.$n$.3. We set $w_i^*$ to be the $j$-th component of $(w_i')_{3\kappa}[z]$ where we set $j = \pi_i'(2\kappa+1)[z]$. If $i < p$, we proceed to Step 3.$i+1$.$n$.1. If $i = p$, then we go to step 4.

4. $M$ loads state $state^*[z]$ and sends the validity bits $w_1^*, \ldots, w_p^*$ to $B$.
5. If at any point, $B$ makes a query that is directed to its $t$ICA challenger, $M$ relays this query to the $t$ICA challenger and the response back to $B$.

[7] This is very similar to the check before rewinding except that now we do not know what the third validity bit is.

### 6.3 Proof of Theorem 2

We now provide a series of lemmas that will ultimately be used to prove Theorem 5. For these lemmas, we consider $A$ to be the ideal attacker as described in Sect. 6.1, and $M$ to be the meta-reduction as described in Sect. 6.2. We let $B$ be a rewinding reduction, reducing the $3\kappa$-wIND-PCA security of some SHPKE scheme to the security of some $t$ICA. Assume that when given access to the successful attacker $A$, $B$ breaks the underlying $t$ICA with probability $\epsilon$.

First, we apply the splitting lemma to determine the probability that the randomness $r_B$ given to $B$ admits many different runs of $A$ that make $B$ accept. In other words, $r_B$ is super-good, using the terminology of the Splitting Lemma. To this end let us first introduce configurations. For attacker instance $z$, a configuration is defined to be a sequence of queries $(q_1[z], ..., q_i[z])$ for $i \in [y]$. For all attacker instances $1, ..., u$, a configuration has the following form $((q_1[1], ..., q_{i_1}[1]), ..., (q_1[u], ..., q_{i_u}[u]))$, i.e. in attacker instance $u' \in [u]$, queries $q_1[u'], ..., q_{i_{u'}}[u']$ have been sent by $A[u']$. Note that for at least one of the attacker instances, we must have that $i_j = y$ for $j \in [u]$ as otherwise, $A$ would never have to solve any challenge statement. (In this case, $B$ could break the $t$ICA without the help of $A$ contradicting the security of the $t$ICA.)

**Lemma 3.** *With probability $\epsilon/2$, the randomness $r_B$ given to $B$, will make $B$ accept a total of $\epsilon/2$ of all configurations.*

*Proof.* For simplicity of notation, we denote a $3\kappa$-PCA query by $q_i = (c_i, m_i)_{3\kappa}$. Let us first provide an argument to show that $B$ accepts many configurations. We define the set $Q'$ to be the set containing all configurations that could potentially get accepted by $B$ before breaking the $t$ICA.

Now we apply the splitting lemma on set $Q'$, to show that the randomness $r_B$ makes $B$ accept at least a fraction $\epsilon' = \epsilon/2$ of the configurations $q' \in Q'$. We set $X = D$, the set containing the possible randomness of $B$, and set $Y = Q'$. We let $G$ be the set of all pairs $(r_B, q) \in D \times Q'$ that lets $B$ break the $t$ICA. As we assume that $B$ breaks the underlying $t$ICA with probability $\epsilon$, we have that $|G|/|D \times Q'| \geq \epsilon$. Thus, the randomness $r_B$ is considered to be super-good (according to our terminology for the splitting lemma). □

Therefore, in the next proofs (of Lemmas 4–8), we assume that $B$ uses fixed randomness $r'$ and assume that it is always super-good. Moreover, we will accordingly consider $B$ to have success probability $\epsilon' = \epsilon/2$ from now on. However, for simplicity we make this implicit. In all cases, these adaptions only account for a non-negligible decrease in success probability or a polynomial increase in running time overall.

**Lemma 4.** *For our construction of meta-reduction $M$, there always exists a useful rewinding spot with overwhelming probability.*

*Proof.* We show, using Hoeffding's inequality (see Lemma 2), that there exists a useful rewinding spot with overwhelming probability. In particular, we apply Hoeffding's inequality to show that there exists a rewinding spot such that i) the query has the same validity bit as the challenge statement, ii) the reduction does not start a new attacker instance or perform an external query, and iii) the reduction sends a correct response. Let us consider conditions i) and ii) first. Then, we argue why case iii) must occur as well for some spot. More concretely, we show now that there are no fewer than $t+u$ and no more than $y-(t+u)$ queries in the first run that share a validity bit with the challenge statement. This allows cases i) and ii) to occur for at least one slot, concluding the existence of a good rewinding spot.

Let $X_i$ be the discrete boolean event such that *the i-th query shares the validity bit with the challenge statement.* Let $S_y = \sum_1^y X_i$. We determine the probability of the following events: i) $S_y$ is less than $t+u$ or ii) $S_y$ is more than $y-(t+u)$. Observe that $E[S_y] = \frac{y}{2} = \kappa + t + u$. We obtain

$$\mathsf{Pr}[S_y < t+u] = \mathsf{Pr}[E[S_y] - S_y > \kappa].$$

For the second case, we use that $y = 2t + 2\kappa + 2u$ to obtain

$$\mathsf{Pr}[S_y > y-(t+u)] = \mathsf{Pr}[S_y - E[S_y] > \kappa].$$

We combine these probabilities and apply Hoeffding's inequality to obtain that

$$\mathsf{Pr}[|S_y - E[S_y]| > \kappa] \leq 2e^{-2\kappa^2/(2t+2\kappa+2u)}.$$

For $t+u < O(\kappa^2)$, we have that this probability is negligibly small in $\kappa$. Therefore, with overwhelming probability, in the first run, there are more than $t+u$ or fewer than $y-(t+u)$ queries that share the same validity bit. Thus, there exists at least one query in the first run that shares the validity bit with the challenge statement, for which $B$ did not invoke an external query nor initiate a new attacker instance. As the queries made by $A[z]$ during rewinding are distributed exactly like those of the ideal attacker (except with statistically low error $\delta$), we conclude that this spot is a good candidate for a useful rewinding spot. The error probability $\delta$ reflects the fact that in the rewinding phase VectorSample is *given* the challenge as input whereas the ideal attacker generates the input to VectorSample by calling RSample. However, RSample has failure probability $\delta$.

Lastly, we analyze the probability that $B$ can send an invalid response in this candidate spot (during the rewinding phase) that $A$ will not notice. (Otherwise, $A$ simply aborts.) The meta-reduction can use VectorTest to verify whether the response $B$ is valid or not. By the construction of VectorTest, $B$ has to guess which of the $\kappa$ statements $(c_i, m_i)$ (out of $2\kappa$, as there are $2\kappa$ statements in a $3\kappa$-PCA query sharing a validity bit) correspond to the challenge statement. It should then flip all validity bits for these statements. The probability of $B$ succeeding in this is given by $\binom{2\kappa}{\kappa}^{-1} \leq 2^{-\kappa}$, which is negligible in $\kappa$. This probability is still negligible taken into account that $B$ may rewind $A[z]$. This concludes that a useful rewinding slot exists. □

Now let us analyze the running time of the meta-reduction.

**Lemma 5.** *$M$ has expected polynomial running time (in $\kappa$).*

*Proof.* We show that the meta-reduction $M$ has an expected polynomial running time. Most steps are efficient by construction. We have to analyze the running time of the rewinding phase, which is dominated by steps 3.1.1.1 – 3.$p$.$y$.3. We show that the expected number of jumps within these steps is polynomial. For an attacker instance $z$, we define $E_{i,n}$ as *the event, that after sending a* $3\kappa$-*PCA query to* $B$ *in* $\mathsf{state}_n$, *the meta-reduction receives a response* $w_i^*$ *while* $B$ *did not perform an external query, nor did it send a challenge statement for another* $z' \neq z$ *instance, nor did* VectorTest *output 0 for the response of* $B$. By Lemma 3, it follows that $B$ accepts an arbitrary configuration with probability $\epsilon'$. Let $z$ be the attacker instance. Let $(q_1[z], ..., q_y[z])$ be the configuration that has been sent in the first run. Then, we know that this configuration is accepted by $B$. Otherwise, the rewinding procedure would not have been started. Any individual statement $q_i$ will be responded to with probability at least $\epsilon'$. Assume that we load the internal state $\mathsf{state}_n$ of $B$ in order to find the validity bit of $w_i^*$ for $i \in [p]$. Then, the configuration will be of the following form $q_1, ..., q_{n-1}, q_i'$ where $q_i'$ is a randomization of challenge statement $s_i^*$. This configuration is distributed in the same way as the one from the ideal attacker $A$, except with probability $\delta$. This is because the ideal attacker uses RSample to generate the input to VectorSample. But RSample has success probability $1 - \delta$. Since we know that among the $y$ queries there always exists a useful rewinding spot, we have $\mathsf{Pr}[E_{i,n}] \geq (\epsilon' - \delta)/y$. Of course, the same lower bound holds if we consider the event $E_i$ that for at least one of the possible rewinding spots, $B$ will accept the configuration, i.e. $\mathsf{Pr}[E_i] = \mathsf{Pr}[E_{i,1} \vee ... \vee E_{i,y}] \geq (\epsilon' - \delta)/y$. Therefore, the running time of the meta-reduction for finding a validity bit for challenge $s_i^*$ is $x_i = O(1/\mathsf{Pr}[E_i])$, which is polynomial. As we can verify the responses of $B$ immediately after we receive them (using VectorTest), we repeat this argument $p$ times, once for each challenge statement. Therefore, the expected number of jumps that are made to answer all challenge statements is polynomial as well. This shows that the expected running time for attacker instance $z$ is polynomial. Observe that the argument in the proof is independent of the choice of $z$. Therefore, the overall running time of $M$ is expected to be polynomial time. □

The next two lemmas focus on the success probability of the meta-reduction $M$ when rewinding the reduction $B$.

**Lemma 6.** *If* $M$ *does not abort early on, it outputs validity bits* $w_1^*, \ldots, w_p^*$ *that are valid with a probability that is non-negligibly better than* $1/2^p$.

*Proof.* In Lemma 4, we have shown that there exists a useful rewinding spot. In Lemma 5, we have shown that the running time of $M$ is polynomial. Therefore, by our construction, if $M$ and $B$ do not abort the security game, then $M$ outputs a sequence of validity bits $w_1^*, ..., w_p^*$.

The fact that the validity bits $w_1^*, ..., w_p^*$ output by $M$ are valid with overwhelming probability is a direct consequence of Lemma 4 and the fact that the validity bits are not changed when applying Randomize. Thus the response received by $M$ is valid with probably non-negligibly better than $1/2^p$. □

We apply Lemmas 4 and 6 to show that $B$ is not able to distinguish the ideal attacker $A$ from the meta-reduction $M$ with probability statistically close to 1.

**Lemma 7.** *The reduction $B$ is not able to distinguish $A$ and $M$ with probability statistically close to one.*

*Proof.* We show that reduction $B$ cannot distinguish the ideal attacker $A$ and meta-reduction $M$ with a probability statistically close to 1. In the first run, both $A$ and $M$ behave similarly. Reduction $B$ may only spot a difference in behaviour if $M$ fails to extract valid witnesses during rewinding. This may either be because i) $B$ delivered an invalid witness without $M$ noticing, or ii) $B$ has aborted during the second run. For the first case, we have seen that this probability is at least $1/2^{\kappa}$ (see Lemma 4), which is statistically small in $\kappa$. For the second case, we observe that a query made by $M$ is distributed statistically close to a query by the ideal attacker $A$. Each $3\kappa$-PCA query consists of $3\kappa$ individual statements. However, the only difference in the way they are generated is the way in which the input to VectorSample is generated. All other computations remain the same. Thus, for each rewinding, the queries are equally distributed except with probability $\delta$ so $B$ cannot distinguish $A$ and $M$ with a probability statistically close to 1. □

Finally, we analyze the number of queries that $M$ has to make to the ICA challenger throughout a run.

**Lemma 8.** *$M$ will make at most $t$ queries to the ICA challenger.*

*Proof.* By our construction, meta-reduction $M$ simply relays queries from the reduction to $t$ICA without allowing the reduction to execute more of such queries. By carefully searching for useful rewinding spots, $M$ actively prevents $B$ from making additional queries because of the rewinding. Therefore, the meta-reduction does not make more than $t$ queries to the $t$ICA challenger. □

Using these lemmas, we can finally prove Theorem 2.

*Proof of Theorem* 2. Using the previous lemmas we have established that i) $M$ runs in expected polynomial time, ii) $B$ cannot distinguish $A$ from $M$, and iii) $M$ outputs the correct responses to the challenges for every attacker instance. However, the combination of $B$ and $M$ efficiently break the security of the $t$ICA. So, under the assumption that $t$ICA is secure, $B$ cannot exist. □

Since $3k$-wIND-PCA security is weaker than wIND-PCA security for the same overall number of queried ciphertext/plaintext pairs and as the attacker in the $3\kappa$-wIND-PCA game queries $3\kappa(2t + 2\kappa + 2u)$ such pairs, we immediately obtain the following result.

**Theorem 3.** *Let $\kappa$ be the security parameter. Let $p$, the number of challenge statements that the attacker must solve in the wIND-PCA1 security game, be polynomial. Then, there exists no PPT reduction $B$ that reduces the wIND-PCA1 security of a certified semi-homomorphic PKE with $3\kappa(2t + 2\kappa + 2u)$ adaptive PCA queries to the security of any $t$-interactive complexity assumption, while creating no more than $u$ attacker instances, for $t + u < O(\kappa^2)$.*

### 6.4 Applications of Theorem 3

We can now immediately present some important applications of Theorem 3. We begin with a corollary stating that ElGamal PKE cannot be proven IND-PCA1 secure. Next, we present a similar result for Paillier PKE.

**Corollary 2.** *Let $\kappa$ be the security parameter. Let $p$, the number of challenge statements that the attacker must solve in the IND-PCA1 security game, be polynomial. Then, there exists no PPT reduction $B$ that reduces the IND-PCA1 security of ElGamal PKE with $3\kappa(2t + 2\kappa + 2u)$ adaptive PCA queries to the security of any $t$-interactive complexity assumption, while creating no more than $u$ attacker instances for $t + u < O(\kappa^2)$.*

**Corollary 3.** *Let $\kappa$ be the security parameter. Let $p$, the number of challenge statements that the attacker must solve in the IND-PCA1 security game, be polynomial. Then, there exists no PPT reduction $B$ that reduces the IND-PCA1 security of Paillier PKE with $3\kappa(2t + 2\kappa + 2u)$ adaptive PCA queries to the security of any $t$-interactive complexity assumption, while creating no more than $u$ attacker instances for $t + u < O(\kappa^2)$.*

### 6.5 Impact, Interpretation, and Limitations

We present new impossibility results for the IND-PCA security of a class of well-known semi-homomorphic cryptographic schemes under a very liberal notion of reduction. Switching perspectives, our results more generally provide a simple method to identify whether it is impossible to prove a semi-homomorphic PKE scheme secure under IND-PCA attacks (or any other strictly stronger notion). Of course, all our results transfer to schemes that additionally support the homomorphic evaluation of a second operation, making them a valuable tool in the design of FHE schemes. At the same time, our impossibility results require several restrictive assumptions to hold. Crucially, these assumptions imply the existence of reliable membership tests for valid public keys and ciphertexts that only work on public parameters. In contrast to this, existing schemes (even without homomorphic properties) that provably provide stronger security guarantees (e.g. IND-CCA2), usually do not provide such algorithms. On the contrary, their security arguments often rely on the very fact that it is hard to separate valid from invalid ciphertexts [12].

Finally, we observe that since the recent notion of indistinguishability against verified chosen ciphertext-attack (vCCA) by Manulis and Nguyen implies IND-CCA1 security (and thus also IND-PCA1 security) [36], our results are meaningful as well. Interpreted accordingly, our result shows that the class of schemes we consider in this work cannot provide IND-vCCA security.

It is well known that when using programmable random oracles (pROs), meta-reduction-based impossibility results can be sidestepped [26]. Essentially, this is due to the fact that pROs allow the construction of cryptographic primitives that are non-committing for the reduction. Transferred to our setting, such a reduction could only decide on-the-fly whether a ciphertext/plaintext pair has validity bit 0 or 1 by programming the pRO correspondingly. Problematically, the challenges output by the reduction could have undefined validity bits. Furthermore, and in a similar way, our results do not immediately extend to general setup routines that establish non-certified common reference strings.

In the full version, we also provide an impossibility result for the much more restricted class of simple reductions. Although the considered type of reductions is restricted, it provides better quantitative bounds on the number of IND-PCA queries for otherwise equal parameters, applying already in case the attacker only makes $2t + 2\kappa$ PCA-queries as opposed to $3\kappa(2t + 2\kappa + 2u)$ queries. It is unclear whether these bounds are optimal.

## References

1. Abdalla, M., Benhamouda, F., Pointcheval, D.: Public-key encryption indistinguishable under plaintext-checkable attacks. In: Katz, J. (ed.) PKC 2015. LNCS, vol. 9020, pp. 332–352. Springer, Heidelberg (2015). https://doi.org/10.1007/978-3-662-46447-2_15
2. Akavia, A., Gentry, C., Halevi, S., Vald, M.: Achievable CCA2 relaxation for homomorphic encryption. In: Kiltz, E., Vaikuntanathan, V. (eds.) TCC 2022, Part II. LNCS, vol. 13748, pp. 70–99. Springer, Cham (2022). https://doi.org/10.1007/978-3-031-22365-5_3
3. Bader, C., Jager, T., Li, Y., Schäge, S.: On the impossibility of tight cryptographic reductions. In: Fischlin, M., Coron, J.-S. (eds.) EUROCRYPT 2016. LNCS, vol. 9666, pp. 273–304. Springer, Heidelberg (2016). https://doi.org/10.1007/978-3-662-49896-5_10
4. Baldimtsi, F., Lysyanskaya, A.: On the security of one-witness blind signature schemes. In: Sako, K., Sarkar, P. (eds.) ASIACRYPT 2013. LNCS, vol. 8270, pp. 82–99. Springer, Heidelberg (2013). https://doi.org/10.1007/978-3-642-42045-0_5
5. Bellare, M., Ristenpart, T., Tessaro, S.: Multi-instance security and its application to password-based cryptography. In: Safavi-Naini, R., Canetti, R. (eds.) CRYPTO 2012. LNCS, vol. 7417, pp. 312–329. Springer, Heidelberg (2012). https://doi.org/10.1007/978-3-642-32009-5_19
6. Boneh, D., Boyen, X., Shacham, H.: Short group signatures. In: Franklin, M. (ed.) CRYPTO 2004. LNCS, vol. 3152, pp. 41–55. Springer, Heidelberg (2004). https://doi.org/10.1007/978-3-540-28628-8_3
7. Boneh, D., Segev, G., Waters, B.: Targeted malleability: homomorphic encryption for restricted computations. In: Goldwasser, S. (ed.) Innovations in Theoretical Computer Science 2012, Cambridge, MA, USA, 8–10 January 2012, pp. 350–366. ACM (2012). https://doi.org/10.1145/2090236.2090264
8. Boneh, D., Venkatesan, R.: Breaking RSA may not be equivalent to factoring. In: Nyberg, K. (ed.) EUROCRYPT 1998. LNCS, vol. 1403, pp. 59–71. Springer, Heidelberg (1998). https://doi.org/10.1007/BFb0054117
9. Canetti, R., Goldreich, O., Goldwasser, S., Micali, S.: Resettable zero-knowledge (extended abstract). In: 32nd ACM STOC, pp. 235–244. ACM Press, Portland, OR, USA (2000). https://doi.org/10.1145/335305.335334
10. Canetti, R., Lin, H., Pass, R.: Adaptive hardness and composable security in the plain model from standard assumptions. In: 51st FOCS, pp. 541–550. IEEE Computer Society Press, Las Vegas, NV, USA (2010). https://doi.org/10.1109/FOCS.2010.86

11. Coron, J.-S.: Optimal security proofs for PSS and other signature schemes. In: Knudsen, L.R. (ed.) EUROCRYPT 2002. LNCS, vol. 2332, pp. 272–287. Springer, Heidelberg (2002). https://doi.org/10.1007/3-540-46035-7_18
12. Cramer, R., Shoup, V.: A practical public key cryptosystem provably secure against adaptive chosen ciphertext attack. In: Krawczyk, H. (ed.) CRYPTO 1998. LNCS, vol. 1462, pp. 13–25. Springer, Heidelberg (1998). https://doi.org/10.1007/BFb0055717
13. Damgård, I.: Towards practical public key systems secure against chosen ciphertext attacks. In: Feigenbaum, J. (ed.) CRYPTO 1991. LNCS, vol. 576, pp. 445–456. Springer, Heidelberg (1992). https://doi.org/10.1007/3-540-46766-1_36
14. Damgård, I., Jurik, M.: A generalisation, a simplification and some applications of Paillier's probabilistic public-key system. In: Kim, K. (ed.) PKC 2001. LNCS, vol. 1992, pp. 119–136. Springer, Heidelberg (2001). https://doi.org/10.1007/3-540-44586-2_9
15. Deng, Y., Goyal, V., Sahai, A.: Resolving the simultaneous resettability conjecture and a new non-black-box simulation strategy. In: 50th FOCS, pp. 251–260. IEEE Computer Society Press, Atlanta, GA, USA (2009). https://doi.org/10.1109/FOCS.2009.59
16. Dodis, Y., Oliveira, R., Pietrzak, K.: On the generic insecurity of the full domain hash. In: Shoup, V. (ed.) CRYPTO 2005. LNCS, vol. 3621, pp. 449–466. Springer, Heidelberg (2005). https://doi.org/10.1007/11535218_27
17. Dodis, Y., Reyzin, L.: On the power of claw-free permutations. In: Cimato, S., Persiano, G., Galdi, C. (eds.) SCN 2002. LNCS, vol. 2576, pp. 55–73. Springer, Heidelberg (2003). https://doi.org/10.1007/3-540-36413-7_5
18. Escala, A., Herold, G., Kiltz, E., Ràfols, C., Villar, J.: An algebraic framework for diffie-hellman assumptions. In: Canetti, R., Garay, J.A. (eds.) CRYPTO 2013. LNCS, vol. 8043, pp. 129–147. Springer, Heidelberg (2013). https://doi.org/10.1007/978-3-642-40084-1_8
19. Fauzi, P., Hovd, M.N., Raddum, H.: On the IND-CCA1 security of FHE schemes. Cryptography **6**(1), 13 (2022) https://doi.org/10.3390/CRYPTOGRAPHY6010013
20. Fischlin, M., Fleischhacker, N.: Limitations of the meta-reduction technique: the case of Schnorr signatures. In: Johansson, T., Nguyen, P.Q. (eds.) EUROCRYPT 2013. LNCS, vol. 7881, pp. 444–460. Springer, Heidelberg (2013). https://doi.org/10.1007/978-3-642-38348-9_27
21. Fleischhacker, N., Jager, T., Schröder, D.: On tight security proofs for Schnorr signatures. In: Sarkar, P., Iwata, T. (eds.) ASIACRYPT 2014. LNCS, vol. 8873, pp. 512–531. Springer, Heidelberg (2014). https://doi.org/10.1007/978-3-662-45611-8_27
22. Garg, S., Bhaskar, R., Lokam, S.V.: Improved bounds on security reductions for discrete log based signatures. In: Wagner, D. (ed.) CRYPTO 2008. LNCS, vol. 5157, pp. 93–107. Springer, Heidelberg (2008). https://doi.org/10.1007/978-3-540-85174-5_6
23. Gennaro, R., Goldfeder, S., Narayanan, A.: Threshold-optimal DSA/ECDSA signatures and an application to bitcoin wallet security. In: Manulis, M., Sadeghi, A.-R., Schneider, S. (eds.) ACNS 2016. LNCS, vol. 9696, pp. 156–174. Springer, Cham (2016). https://doi.org/10.1007/978-3-319-39555-5_9
24. Gennaro, R., Lindell, Y.: A framework for password-based authenticated key exchange. In: Biham, E. (ed.) EUROCRYPT 2003. LNCS, vol. 2656, pp. 524–543. Springer, Heidelberg (2003). https://doi.org/10.1007/3-540-39200-9_33, https://eprint.iacr.org/2003/032.ps.gz

25. Groce, A., Katz, J.: A new framework for efficient password-based authenticated key exchange. In: Al-Shaer, E., Keromytis, A.D., Shmatikov, V. (eds.) ACM CCS 2010, pp. 516–525. ACM Press, Chicago, Illinois, USA (2010). https://doi.org/10.1145/1866307.1866365
26. Guo, F., Chen, R., Susilo, W., Lai, J., Yang, G., Mu, Y.: Optimal security reductions for unique signatures: bypassing impossibilities with a counterexample. In: Katz, J., Shacham, H. (eds.) CRYPTO 2017. LNCS, vol. 10402, pp. 517–547. Springer, Cham (2017). https://doi.org/10.1007/978-3-319-63715-0_18
27. Hofheinz, D., Jager, T., Knapp, E.: Waters signatures with optimal security reduction. In: Fischlin, M., Buchmann, J., Manulis, M. (eds.) PKC 2012. LNCS, vol. 7293, pp. 66–83. Springer, Heidelberg (2012). https://doi.org/10.1007/978-3-642-30057-8_5
28. Kakvi, S.A., Kiltz, E.: Optimal security proofs for full domain hash, revisited. In: Pointcheval, D., Johansson, T. (eds.) EUROCRYPT 2012. LNCS, vol. 7237, pp. 537–553. Springer, Heidelberg (2012). https://doi.org/10.1007/978-3-642-29011-4_32
29. Katz, J., Vaikuntanathan, V.: Round-optimal password-based authenticated key exchange. In: Ishai, Y. (ed.) TCC 2011. LNCS, vol. 6597, pp. 293–310. Springer, Heidelberg (2011). https://doi.org/10.1007/978-3-642-19571-6_18
30. Leander, G., Rupp, A.: On the equivalence of RSA and factoring regarding generic ring algorithms. In: Lai, X., Chen, K. (eds.) ASIACRYPT 2006. LNCS, vol. 4284, pp. 241–251. Springer, Heidelberg (2006). https://doi.org/10.1007/11935230_16
31. Lewko, A., Waters, B.: Why proving HIBE systems secure is difficult. In: Nguyen, P.Q., Oswald, E. (eds.) EUROCRYPT 2014. LNCS, vol. 8441, pp. 58–76. Springer, Heidelberg (2014). https://doi.org/10.1007/978-3-642-55220-5_4
32. Libert, B.: Leveraging small message spaces for CCA1 security in additively homomorphic and BGN-type encryption. In: Fehr, S., Fouque, P. (eds.) EUROCRYPT 2025, Part II. LNCS, vol. 15602, pp. 34–63. Springer, Cham (2025). https://doi.org/10.1007/978-3-031-91124-8_2
33. Lindell, Y.: Fast secure two-party ECDSA signing. In: Katz, J., Shacham, H. (eds.) CRYPTO 2017. LNCS, vol. 10402, pp. 613–644. Springer, Cham (2017). https://doi.org/10.1007/978-3-319-63715-0_21
34. Lipmaa, H.: On the CCA1-security of Elgamal and Damgård's Elgamal. In: Lai, X., Yung, M., Lin, D. (eds.) Inscrypt 2010. LNCS, vol. 6584, pp. 18–35. Springer, Cham (2010).https://doi.org/10.1007/978-3-642-21518-6_2
35. Loftus, J., May, A., Smart, N.P., Vercauteren, F.: On CCA-secure somewhat homomorphic encryption. In: Miri, A., Vaudenay, S. (eds.) SAC 2011. LNCS, vol. 7118, pp. 55–72. Springer, Heidelberg (2012). https://doi.org/10.1007/978-3-642-28496-0_4
36. Manulis, M., Nguyen, J.: Fully homomorphic encryption beyond IND-CCA1 security: integrity through verifiability. In: Joye, M., Leander, G. (eds.) EUROCRYPT 2024, Part II. LNCS, vol. 14652, pp. 63–93. Springer, Cham (2024). https://doi.org/10.1007/978-3-031-58723-8_3
37. Maurer, U.: Abstract models of computation in cryptography. In: Smart, N.P. (ed.) Cryptography and Coding 2005. LNCS, vol. 3796, pp. 1–12. Springer, Heidelberg (2005). https://doi.org/10.1007/11586821_1
38. Morgan, A., Pass, R.: On the security loss of unique signatures. In: Beimel, A., Dziembowski, S. (eds.) TCC 2018. LNCS, vol. 11239, pp. 507–536. Springer, Cham (2018). https://doi.org/10.1007/978-3-030-03807-6_19

39. Morgan, A., Pass, R., Shi, E.: On the adaptive security of MACs and PRFs. In: Moriai, S., Wang, H. (eds.) ASIACRYPT 2020. LNCS, vol. 12491, pp. 724–753. Springer, Cham (2020). https://doi.org/10.1007/978-3-030-64837-4_24
40. Paillier, P.: Public-key cryptosystems based on composite degree residuosity classes. In: Stern, J. (ed.) EUROCRYPT 1999. LNCS, vol. 1592, pp. 223–238. Springer, Heidelberg (1999). https://doi.org/10.1007/3-540-48910-X_16
41. Paillier, P., Vergnaud, D.: Discrete-log-based signatures may not be equivalent to discrete log. In: Roy, B. (ed.) ASIACRYPT 2005. LNCS, vol. 3788, pp. 1–20. Springer, Heidelberg (2005). https://doi.org/10.1007/11593447_1
42. Paillier, P., Villar, J.L.: Trading one-wayness against chosen-ciphertext security in factoring-based encryption. In: Lai, X., Chen, K. (eds.) ASIACRYPT 2006. LNCS, vol. 4284, pp. 252–266. Springer, Heidelberg (2006). https://doi.org/10.1007/11935230_17
43. Pass, R.: Limits of provable security from standard assumptions. In: Fortnow, L., Vadhan, S.P. (eds.) 43rd ACM STOC, pp. 109–118. ACM Press, San Jose, CA, USA (2011). https://doi.org/10.1145/1993636.1993652
44. Pass, R., Venkitasubramaniam, M.: On constant-round concurrent zero-knowledge. In: Canetti, R. (ed.) TCC 2008. LNCS, vol. 4948, pp. 553–570. Springer, Heidelberg (2008). https://doi.org/10.1007/978-3-540-78524-8_30
45. Pointcheval, D., Stern, J.: Security proofs for signature schemes. In: Maurer, U. (ed.) EUROCRYPT 1996. LNCS, vol. 1070, pp. 387–398. Springer, Heidelberg (1996). https://doi.org/10.1007/3-540-68339-9_33
46. Prabhakaran, M., Rosulek, M.: Homomorphic encryption with CCA security. In: Aceto, L., Damgård, I., Goldberg, L.A., Halldórsson, M.M., Ingólfsdóttir, A., Walukiewicz, I. (eds.) ICALP 2008. LNCS, vol. 5126, pp. 667–678. Springer, Heidelberg (2008). https://doi.org/10.1007/978-3-540-70583-3_54
47. Richardson, R., Kilian, J.: On the concurrent composition of zero-knowledge proofs. In: Stern, J. (ed.) EUROCRYPT 1999. LNCS, vol. 1592, pp. 415–431. Springer, Heidelberg (1999). https://doi.org/10.1007/3-540-48910-X_29
48. Schäge, S.: New limits of provable security and applications to ElGamal encryption. In: Joye, M., Leander, G. (eds.) EUROCRYPT 2024, Part IV. LNCS, vol. 14654, pp. 255–285. Springer, Cham (2024). https://doi.org/10.1007/978-3-031-58737-5_10
49. Seurin, Y.: On the exact security of Schnorr-type signatures in the random oracle model. In: Pointcheval, D., Johansson, T. (eds.) EUROCRYPT 2012. LNCS, vol. 7237, pp. 554–571. Springer, Heidelberg (2012). https://doi.org/10.1007/978-3-642-29011-4_33
50. Shoup, V.: Lower bounds for discrete logarithms and related problems. In: Fumy, W. (ed.) EUROCRYPT 1997. LNCS, vol. 1233, pp. 256–266. Springer, Heidelberg (1997). https://doi.org/10.1007/3-540-69053-0_18

# MicroCrypt Assumptions with Quantum Input Sampling and Pseudodeterminism: Constructions and Separations

Mohammed Barhoush[1(✉)], Ryo Nishimaki[2], and Takashi Yamakawa[2]

[1] Université de Montréal (DIRO), Montréal, Canada
mohammed.barhoush@umontreal.ca
[2] NTT Social Informatics Laboratories, Tokyo, Japan
{ryo.nishimaki,takashi.yamakawa}@ntt.com

**Abstract.** We investigate two natural relaxations of quantum cryptographic primitives. The first involves quantum input sampling, where inputs are generated by a quantum algorithm rather than sampled uniformly at random. Applying this to pseudorandom generators (PRGs) and pseudorandom states (PRSs), leads to the notions denoted as $\mathsf{PRG}^{\mathsf{qs}}$ and $\mathsf{PRS}^{\mathsf{qs}}$, respectively. The second relaxation, $\bot$-pseudodeterminism, relaxes the determinism requirement by allowing the output to be a special symbol $\bot$ on an inverse-polynomial fraction of inputs.

We demonstrate an equivalence between bounded-query logarithmic-size $\mathsf{PRS}^{\mathsf{qs}}$, logarithmic-size $\mathsf{PRS}^{\mathsf{qs}}$, and $\mathsf{PRG}^{\mathsf{qs}}$. Moreover, we establish that $\mathsf{PRG}^{\mathsf{qs}}$ can be constructed from $\bot$-PRGs, which in turn were built from logarithmic-size PRS. Interestingly, these relations remain unknown in the uniform key setting.

To further justify these relaxed models, we present black-box separations. Our results suggest that $\bot$-pseudodeterministic primitives may be weaker than their deterministic counterparts, and that primitives based on quantum input sampling may be inherently weaker than those using uniform sampling.

Together, these results provide numerous new insights into the structure and hierarchy of primitives within MicroCrypt.

## 1 Introduction

The search for the minimal assumptions required for quantum cryptography was triggered with the astonishing discovery that pseudorandom states (PRSs) [23] may exist even when quantumly-evaluable[1] one-way functions (OWF) do not, relative to an oracle[2] [25]. PRSs serve as the quantum analog to PRGs, outputting

M. Barhoush—Part of this work was done while visiting NTT Social Informatics Laboratories as an internship.

[1] In this work, all primitives including OWFs and PRG, refer to the quantum-evaluable versions, unless stated otherwise.

[2] Note that one-way functions and pseudorandom generators are equivalent.

© International Association for Cryptologic Research 2026
G. Hanaoka and B.-Y. Yang (Eds.): ASIACRYPT 2025, LNCS 16252, pp. 516–548, 2026.
https://doi.org/10.1007/978-981-95-5125-5_17

a state instead of a classical string. Critically, this difference does not prevent PRSs supporting some applications similar to those enabled by PRGs, such as commitments, one-time signatures, and one-way state generators (OWSG)s [2, 29].

This separation naturally raised questions on the minimal assumptions required to build quantum cryptographic primitives. Addressing this question has fueled significant research, leading to a variety of quantum assumptions. Different assumptions provide a different balance between how well they replicate OWFs in cryptography and how strong of an assumption they constitute. The resulting assumptions are intricately related in what has now came to be known as *MicroCrypt.* This field comprises various assumptions derived from OWFs, but where the other direction is not known. Despite substantial progress, numerous questions remain unanswered. What is clear, however, is that MicroCrypt is significantly more intricate than its classical counterpart.

Several of the MicroCrypt assumptions introduced parallel their classical counterparts but incorporate quantum elements. For instance, quantum unpredictable state generators [31] and one-way state generators [29] yield quantum outputs, similar to PRSs. Additionally, assumptions such as $\bot$-PRG [4] and one-way puzzles [24] involve only classical communication but rely on quantum computation. These quantum elements are believed to make the assumptions weaker.

Despite advances, using general PRSs as a complete replacement for PRGs in cryptographic applications has been challenging. Some progress has been made in the specific case of logarithmic-size pseudorandom states, which we denote by *short* PRS *(*SPRS*)* as in [3], where tomography can transform the state into a classical pseudorandom string [3]. However, tomography is not deterministic, resulting in what has been termed *pseudodeterministic* PRG. This roughly means that on $1 - 1/\mathsf{poly}(n)$ fraction of inputs, the output is the same except with negligible probability [3]. While these generators proved useful in various applications, the pseudodeterminism is sometimes problematic when using them in place of traditional PRGs. This obstacle motivated a follow-up work [4], that introduced an intermediate notion called $\bot$-PRG, which is built from pseudodeterministic PRGs. With $\bot$-PRGs, the non-deterministic outcomes can be detected and replaced with $\bot$, allowing many PRG applications to proceed by handling $\bot$ cases separately. This approach enabled significant applications, such as many-time digital signatures and quantum public-key encryption with tamper-resilient keys, which had eluded MicroCrypt.

While these applications are powerful, $\bot$-PRGs and SPRSs have not been black-box separated from OWFs[4], which somewhat limits the significance of these results. In fact, most MicroCrypt assumptions, such as pseudorandom function-like states with proofs of destruction [8] and efficiently verifiable one-way puzzles (Ev-OWPuzzs) [15,24], have been conjectured to be weaker than (quantum-

[3] "Pseudodeterminism" is sometimes defined differently in other works [5–7]. We follow the definition given in [3].

[4] Notably, the separation between PRS and OWFs [25] only applies to linear-sized PRSs and not to SPRS.

evaluable) OWFs, but their separability has not been established. Understanding which assumptions are separated from OWFs and, more generally, the relations among different MicroCrypt primitives is an important goal in the field.

### 1.1 Our Work

Traditionally, many cryptographic primitives such as PRGs and PRSs rely on inputs sampled uniformly at random. The main idea of our work is that sampling inputs with a quantum procedure, instead of at random, yields fundamentally different primitives. We denote the resulting primitives with a superscript such as $\mathsf{PRG}^{\mathsf{qs}}$s and $\mathsf{PRS}^{\mathsf{qs}}$s.

To clarify, a pair of QPT algorithms $(\mathsf{QSamp}, G)$ is a $\mathsf{PRG}^{\mathsf{qs}}$ if $\mathsf{QSamp}(1^\lambda)$ samples a $\lambda$-bit input, which is then mapped by $G$ to an output of length $\ell > \lambda$, and the following security condition is satisfied: For any QPT adversary $\mathcal{A}$,

$$\left| \Pr_{k \leftarrow \mathsf{QSamp}(1^\lambda)} [\mathcal{A}(G(k)) = 1] - \Pr_{y \leftarrow \{0,1\}^\ell} [\mathcal{A}(y) = 1] \right| \leq \mathsf{negl}(\lambda).$$

Naturally, we also require that $G$ is *almost-deterministic*, meaning that it returns the same output on a fixed input except with negligible probability. Notice that this notion differs from a traditional PRG, where the above security condition is guaranteed if the input $k$ is sampled uniformly at random. Similarly, a $\mathsf{PRS}^{\mathsf{qs}}$ consists of a pair of algorithms $(\mathsf{QSamp}', G')$ such that for an input $k \leftarrow \mathsf{QSamp}'(1^\lambda)$, polynomial copies of $|\psi_k\rangle \leftarrow G'(k)$ are indistinguishable from polynomial copies of a Haar random state.

While variants of MicroCrypt primitives based on quantum input sampling have been considered before for notions such as OWSGs and PRSs [12,24,30], the fundamental distinction between primitives based on quantum versus uniform input sampling has not been previously recognized.

Note that any classical input sampling algorithm can be derandomized and replaced with uniform key sampling. Therefore, using a classical input sampling algorithm is unnecessary. However, a quantum procedure cannot be derandomized and might include non-deterministic quantum computations. Postponing such computations to the evaluation or state-generation phase can result in different outcomes across executions, which is problematic for deterministic primitives such as PRSs and PRGs.

Before moving to a detailed explanation, we first list a brief high-level description of the main contributions of this paper. For the sake of simplicity, this summary is somewhat weaker than what we actually accomplish. We show the following:

- The pseudodeterminism error in $\perp$-PRGs can be eliminated if quantum input sampling is allowed. In particular, $\perp$-PRG imply $\mathsf{PRG}^{\mathsf{qs}}$. This stands in contrast to the fact that $\perp$-PRG are not known to imply PRG.
- Primitives with quantum input sampling behave differently from their uniform input sampling counterparts. In particular, we realize that $\mathsf{PRG}^{\mathsf{qs}}$,

bounded-copy $\mathsf{SPRS}^{\mathrm{qs}}$, and $\mathsf{SPRS}^{\mathrm{qs}}$ are all equivalent under a certain parameter regime. Such an equivalence is not known to exist in the uniform input sampling setting.

- While PRGs trivially imply $\mathsf{PRG}^{\mathrm{qs}}$s, we show that the reverse implication is unlikely by showing that there is no black-box construction of PRGs from a pseudorandom function with quantum key sampling ($\mathsf{PRF}^{\mathrm{qs}}$s) see Definition 13, even with unitary and inverse access to the $\mathsf{PRF}^{\mathrm{qs}}$. In addition, we provide more fine-grained black-box separations: separating PRG from $\bot$-PRG, and $\bot$-PRG from $\mathsf{PRG}^{\mathrm{qs}}$, albeit within a weaker oracle access model. Thus, we establish a hierarchy among uniform input sampling, pseudodeterministic, and quantum input sampling primitives within MicroCrypt.

**Quantum Input Sampling.** In the first part of this work, we introduce natural variants of MicroCrypt primitives that incorporate quantum input sampling, and demonstrate how this framework helps address the issue of pseudodeterminism.

Recall that [4] extended the applicability of SPRS by converting them into $\bot$-PRGs, which inherit many of the useful properties of PRGs. However, $\bot$-PRGs still exhibit a form of non-determinism due to the possibility of outputting $\bot$, which may be problematic in certain applications. Specifically, for a $\bot$-PRG, there exists a set of "good" inputs, that produce deterministic outputs, and an inverse-polynomial fraction of inputs termed "bad" inputs, that may yield $\bot$. To address this non-determinism, a natural solution is to test inputs during the sampling process to ensure that only good inputs are selected. We show that this technique can be used to construct a $\mathsf{PRG}^{\mathrm{qs}}$ from a $\bot$-PRG, thus resolving the pseudodeterminism issue. Note that this approach necessitates a quantum input sampling procedure instead of traditional uniform input sampling, since the $\bot$-PRG itself may be a quantum algorithm.

We utilize this result, along with other key insights, to establish the following relationships among primitives with quantum input sampling. Specifically, we show fully black-box constructions for the following:

1. $\mathsf{PRG}^{\mathrm{qs}}$ from bounded-copy $\mathsf{SPRS}^{\mathrm{qs}}$ ($\mathsf{BC\text{-}SPRS}^{\mathrm{qs}}$).
2. $\mathsf{SPRS}^{\mathrm{qs}}$ from $\mathsf{PRG}^{\mathrm{qs}}$.
3. $\mathsf{BQ\text{-}PRU}^{\mathrm{qs}}$[5] from $\mathsf{PRG}^{\mathrm{qs}}$.
4. $\mathsf{PRU}^{\mathrm{qs}}$ from $\mathsf{PRF}^{\mathrm{qs}}$.

The last two results are only shown in the full paper. These findings mean that $\mathsf{PRG}^{\mathrm{qs}}$, $\mathsf{BC\text{-}SPRS}^{\mathrm{qs}}$, and $\mathsf{SPRS}^{\mathrm{qs}}$ can all be built from one another under a certain parameter regime. This relationship is surprising, as it is not known to hold in the uniform input sampling setting. Specifically, it is not known how to construct a PRG from a SPRS, nor how to build a SPRS from a bounded-copy SPRS.

[5] This stands for bounded-query pseudorandom unitaries with quantum key sampling and is defined in the full paper.

Furthermore, as a direct consequence of these results, we obtain both a method to reduce the output length of a $\mathsf{SPRS}^{\mathsf{qs}}$ and a way to transform a SPRS into a $\mathsf{SPRS}^{\mathsf{qs}}$ with a longer output length.

**Separations.** In the second part of our work, we extend our analysis with separation results that highlight the distinctions between quantum input sampling and uniform input sampling and between $\perp$-pseudodeterminism and determinism.

Our separation results demonstrate the impossibilities of certain types of black-box constructions. There are different variants of black-box constructions in quantum cryptography (see [16] for an exposition). We informally define the two variants considered in this work.

**Definition 1 (Informal version of Definition 5).** *A QPT algorithm* $G^{(\cdot)}$ *is a* fully black-box construction of a primitive $Q$ from a primitive $P$ with inverse access *if there is a QPT algorithm* $S^{(\cdot)}$ *such that for every unitary implementation* $U$ *of* $P$*:*

- $G^{U,U^{-1}}$ *is an implementation of* $Q$*.*
- *Every attack* $\mathcal{A}$ *that breaks the security of* $G^{U,U^{-1}}$*, and every unitary implementation* $\tilde{\mathcal{A}}$ *of* $\mathcal{A}$*, it holds that* $S^{\tilde{\mathcal{A}},\tilde{\mathcal{A}}^{-1}}$ *breaks the security of* $U$*.*

We also consider a less general notion limited to *completely-positive-trace-preserving (CPTP) maps.* These are quantum channels that are not necessarily unitary.

**Definition 2 (Informal version of Definition 6).** *A QPT algorithm* $G^{(\cdot)}$ *is a* fully black-box construction of $Q$ from CPTP access to $P$ *if there is a QPT algorithm* $S^{(\cdot)}$ *such that for every CPTP implementation* $\mathcal{C}$ *of* $P$*:*

- $G^{\mathcal{C}}$ *is an implementation of* $Q$*.*
- *Every attack* $\mathcal{A}$ *that breaks the security of* $G^{\mathcal{C}}$*, it holds that* $S^{\mathcal{A}}$ *breaks the security of* $U$*.*

Since CPTP maps are not necessarily unitary and cannot be purified or inverted, Definition 2 only includes constructions that do not assume purified/inverse/unitary access. On the other hand, Definition 1 includes constructions that use such access, thus covering a broader range of constructions. We discuss these distinctions more thoroughly in Sect. 1.1, but for now, we state the results.

Our first and main separation is between PRGs and $\mathsf{PRF}^{\mathsf{qs}}$s, with inverse access.

**Theorem 1 (Informal version of Theorem 10).** *There does not exist a fully black-box construction of a* PRG *from a (quantum-query-secure)* $\mathsf{PRF}^{qs}$*s with inverse access.*

Given that $\mathsf{PRF}^{\mathsf{qs}}$s inherits many applications of PRFs, we obtain other new separations as a corollary.

**Corollary 1.** *There is no fully black-box construction of a* PRG *from the following primitives with inverse access:*

1. $\mathsf{PRG}^{qs}$, $\mathsf{SPRS}^{qs}$, *linear-sized* $\mathsf{PRS}^{qs}$, *and* $\mathsf{PRU}^{qs}$.
2. *Statistically-binding, computationally hiding bit commitments with classical communication (BC-CC).*
3. *Existentially unforgeable message authentication codes of classical messages with classical communication (EUF-MAC).*
4. *CCA2-secure symmetric encryption with classical keys and ciphertexts (CCA2-SKE).*
5. *EV-OWPuzzs.*

We present another two separations that are only proven in the full paper, but we describe the results here. Our second separation is between $\bot$-pseudodeterministic notions and deterministic ones, but with CPTP access.

**Theorem 2.** *There does not exist a fully black-box construction of a* OWSG *from CPTP access to a* $\bot$-PRG.

Note that the OWSGs considered in this paper are those with pure-state outputs and with uniform key generation. Our separation is further emphasized by the fact that a OWSG is considered weaker than a PRG, since PRSs imply OWSGs and PRGs are separated from PRSs [25]. As $\bot$-PRGs have broad applicability [4], this result yields additional separations as corollaries.

**Corollary 2.** *There does not exist a fully black-box construction of a* OWSG*s from CPTP access to:*

1. $\bot$-PRF*s.*
2. *(Many-time) existentially unforgeable digital signatures of classical messages with classical keys and signatures (EUF-DS).*
3. *CPA-secure quantum public-key encryption of classical messages with tamper-resilient keys and classical ciphertexts (CPA-QPKE).*

Our third separation shows that CPTP access to $\mathsf{PRF}^{\mathsf{qs}}$s is insufficient for constructing $\bot$-PRGs. Recall that our second separation establishes a gap between PRGs and $\bot$-PRGs. Taken together, this means the third separation strengthens the first by demonstrating a separation between $\mathsf{PRF}^{\mathsf{qs}}$ and $\bot$-PRG. However, this result is more limited in scope, as it only applies to CPTP access.

**Theorem 3.** *There does not exist a fully black-box construction of a* $\bot$-PRG *from CPTP access to a (quantum-query-secure)* $\mathsf{PRF}^{qs}$*s.*

We obtain other new separations as a corollary.

**Corollary 3.** *There does not exist fully black-box constructions of* $\bot$-PRG*s or* SPRS*s from CPTP access to:*

1. $\mathsf{PRG}^{qs}$, $\mathsf{SPRS}^{qs}$, *linear-sized* $\mathsf{PRS}^{qs}$, *and* $\mathsf{PRU}^{qs}$.
2. *BC-CC.*
3. *EUF-MAC and CCA2-SKE.*
4. *EV-OWPuzzs.*

Note that separations listed in Corollaries 1 to 3 were not known prior to this work. This highlights how $\perp$-PRGs and $\mathsf{PRG}^{\mathsf{qs}}$ not only aid in building applications for SPRS, but also in establishing separations among well-studied MicroCrypt assumptions that may be difficult to separate otherwise. For instance, EV-OWPuzzs have been studied and introduced as a potentially weaker replacement to (quantum-evaluable) OWFs, but no separation existed prior to our work.

Our results give a natural hierarchy in MicroCrypt as depicted in Fig. 1.

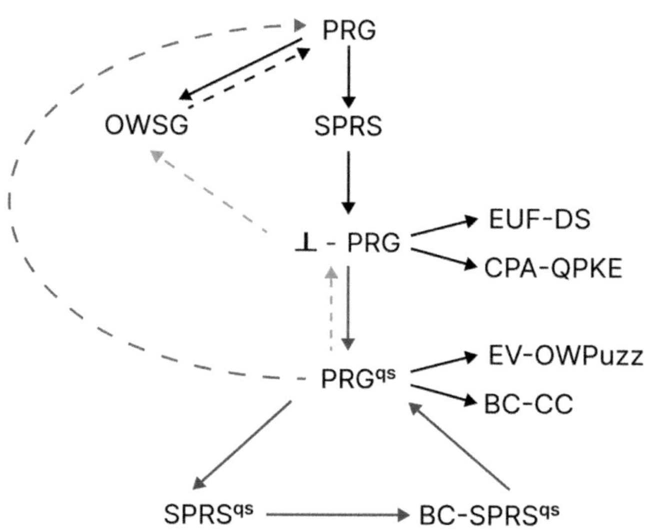


**Fig. 1.** The black straight arrows indicate implications that are trivial or from previous works [3,4,29]. The black dotted arrow indicates a separation from previous work [25]. The blue straight arrows are implications from this work. The red dotted arrow is a separation under inverse access from this work. The orange dotted arrows are separations under CPTP access from this work.

**Discussion of Separations.** Separation results make use of the fact that fully black-box constructions relativize [16,22]. In particular, to establish the non-existence of black-box constructions granting unitary/inverse access in the plain model (Definition 5), it is sufficient to show that there does not exist such constructions relative to a unitary oracle with inverse access. Similarly, to rule out black-box constructions with CPTP access (Definition 6), it is sufficient to show that no such constructions exist relative to a CPTP oracle.

In particular, our first separation (Theorem 1), separating PRG from inverse access to $\mathsf{PRF}^{\mathsf{qs}}$s, is achieved by demonstrating the unattainability of such constructions relative to a unitary oracle with inverse access. Advantageously, this separation precludes black-box constructions that use purified/inverse/unitary versions of the adversary. Certain reductions, such as in quantum proofs of knowledge [34,35] and quantum traitor tracing [38], rely on inverse access to the adversary.

On the other hand, the second and third separations (Theorems 2 and 3) are proven by demonstrating the impossibility relative to CPTP oracles, which are not unitary and cannot be purified or inverted. As a result, these separations are weaker as they only preclude black-box constructions that do not assume access to purified/inverse/unitary versions of the adversary.

However, in many black-box constructions, such strong forms of access (e.g., purification, unitarization, or inversion of the adversary) are unnecessary. Indeed, many known black-box constructions in this domain, such as $\mathsf{PRG} \to \bot\text{-}\mathsf{PRG}$, $\bot\text{-}\mathsf{PRG} \to \mathsf{PRG}^{\mathsf{qs}}$, and $\mathsf{PRG} \to \mathsf{OWSG}$ do not require such strong access. Hence, we believe that separations based on CPTP oracles still yields meaningful results. Notably, prior works [19,20] have also considered CPTP oracle separations.

That said, we also investigated whether the second and third separations could be based on unitary oracles. For the separation between deterministic and psuedodeterministic primitives, specifically OWSGs and $\bot$-PRG, doing so appears particularly challenging: our separation strategy relies on inherent randomness in the oracle to achieve a level of pseudodeterminism, which is critical to ensuring that the oracle cannot be leveraged to build deterministic primitives such as OWSGs, while still being useful in building $\bot$-PRGs. Yet, another difficulty emerged when attempting to separate $\bot$-PRG from $\mathsf{PRF}^{\mathsf{qs}}$ using a unitary oracle, due to the pseudodeterminism of $\bot$-PRG, as we shall discuss in Sect. 1.3. An interesting avenue for future work is to strengthen the second or third separation by basing them on unitary oracles.

### 1.2 Relation to Previous Work

We discuss relation to previous work.

- Prior research has typically defined PRSs and OWSGs with uniform input sampling. However, some works have defined them with quantum input sampling, such as [24,30]. Nevertheless, the relations among certain MicroCrypt primitives with quantum sampling and the advantage of quantum sampling in yielding potentially weaker assumptions have not been previously recognized. The latter insight is crucial for known MicroCrypt primitives as well, enabling us to identify multiple new separations, as outlined in the previous section (Corollaries 1 and 3). None of the separations mentioned were known prior to this work.

- Previous research did not establish a connection between quantum input sampling and $\perp$-pseudodeterminism. This connection enabled us to address the pseudodeterminism inherent in $\perp$-PRGs (built in [4] from SPRS) by converting them to $\mathsf{PRG}^{\mathsf{qs}}$s.
- It may seem that EV-OWPuzzs can be viewed as a one-way function with a quantum input sampler. However, critically, these puzzles are non-deterministic. In fact, [15] use this property to show that uniform and quantum sampling versions of these puzzles are equivalent. Hence, quantum input sampling seems more interesting to study in deterministic notions such as PRGs.
- All definitions in this work consider quantum-evaluable algorithms, and we never require any algorithm to be classically-evaluable. This is noteworthy since, very recently, [26] used a classical oracle to show a separation between classically-evaluable OWFs and quantumly-evaluable OWFs. Our separations are not comparable with theirs. However, as a direct result, they find that classically-evaluable OWFs are black-box separated from many cryptographic applications of quantum-evaluable OWFs, such as EUF-MAC and CCA2-SKE. Given that many of these applications can be built from $\mathsf{PRF}^{\mathsf{qs}}$ in the same way, our separations imply that even OWSGs are separated from these applications under CPTP access, and (quantum-evaluable) OWFs are separated from these applications under inverse access.

### 1.3 Technical Overview

We now describe our results in more detail.

**Quantum Input Sampling.** Our study reveals surprising equivalences among several variants of MicroCrypt primitives utilizing quantum input sampling.

$\mathsf{BC\text{-}SPRS}^{\mathsf{qs}}$*s imply* $\mathsf{PRG}^{\mathsf{qs}}$*s.* Our first result is that *bounded-copy* $\mathsf{SPRS}^{\mathsf{qs}}$ imply $\mathsf{PRG}^{\mathsf{qs}}$s. Prior works [3,4] demonstrated that SPRSs enable $\perp$-PRGs. We first extend this result by showing that bounded-copy SPRSs (BC-SPRS) suffice for this construction.

At first glance, using BC-SPRS appears infeasible because each evaluation of the $\perp$-PRG exhausts several copies of the SPRS and the adversary has access to arbitrarily many evaluations in the security experiment. However, the $\perp$-PRG only uses these copies to perform tomography and extract a classical string. Crucially, the extracted strings remain largely consistent across evaluations. Thus, the information gained through multiple evaluations can be simulated with only a limited number of SPRS copies. By formalizing this observation, we construct a $\perp$-PRG from a BC-SPRS.

Our next idea is to show that $\perp$-PRGs imply (deterministic) $\mathsf{PRG}^{\mathsf{qs}}$s, thereby showing that quantum input sampling resolves the pseudodeterminism problem. The idea is simple: to construct a $\mathsf{PRG}^{\mathsf{qs}}$ from a $\perp$-PRG, we search for a good input for the $\perp$-PRG during the input sampling phase and use this input during evaluation. However, this approach sacrifices uniform input sampling, which compromises the security reduction given in [3,4], thereby only giving a *weak* $\mathsf{PRG}^{\mathsf{qs}}$. Standard amplification techniques are then applied to achieve strong security. Hence, we obtain $\mathsf{PRG}^{\mathsf{qs}}$ from BC-SPRS.

Finally, since we are allowed to use a quantum input sampler for a $\mathsf{PRG}^{\mathsf{qs}}$, we can perform the same conversion starting instead with a $\mathsf{BC\text{-}SPRS}^{\mathsf{qs}}$. Therefore, we obtain $\mathsf{PRG}^{\mathsf{qs}}$s from $\mathsf{BC\text{-}SPRS}^{\mathsf{qs}}$.

*$\mathsf{PRG}^{\mathsf{qs}}$s imply $\mathsf{SPRS}^{\mathsf{qs}}$s.* We also establish the converse: $\mathsf{SPRS}^{\mathsf{qs}}$s can be built from $\mathsf{PRG}^{\mathsf{qs}}$s. This follows in the same way as the construction of PRSs from PRFs given in [23], but instantiated with a polynomial-domain PRF. Note that $\mathsf{PRF}^{\mathsf{qs}}$ with polynomial domain can be trivially derived from $\mathsf{PRG}^{\mathsf{qs}}$s[6].

*Modifying the Size of* SPRS. By leveraging the above equivalence, we obtain a way to decrease the output length of a $\mathsf{SPRS}^{\mathsf{qs}}$. Simply convert a $\mathsf{SPRS}^{\mathsf{qs}}$ into a $\mathsf{PRG}^{\mathsf{qs}}$, and then convert this back into a $\mathsf{SPRS}^{\mathsf{qs}}$. Due to the change in parameters during this conversion, the resulting $\mathsf{SPRS}^{\mathsf{qs}}$ is smaller in size. Interestingly, a similar result is not known for SPRS.

Furthermore, these equivalences can also be leveraged to increase the output length of a SPRS. Note that it is trivial to extend the output length of a $\perp$-PRG by composition. For instance, if $G_\lambda$ is a $\perp$-PRG mapping $\{0,1\}^\lambda$ to $\{0,1\}^{2\lambda}$, i.e. with expansion factor of 2, then the composition $G_{2\lambda} \circ G_\lambda$ is a $\perp$-PRG with expansion factor 4. Hence, starting with a SPRS, building a $\perp$-PRG, extending the output length of the $\perp$-PRG sufficiently through composition, building a $\mathsf{PRG}^{\mathsf{qs}}$, and finally converting this to a $\mathsf{SPRS}^{\mathsf{qs}}$, we obtain a method to convert a SPRS into a $\mathsf{SPRS}^{\mathsf{qs}}$ with larger output length.

*Other Constructions.* On the downside, we face an obstacle in the quantum input sampling regime when attempting to build a $\mathsf{PRF}^{\mathsf{qs}}$s from $\mathsf{PRG}^{\mathsf{qs}}$s. While a $\mathsf{PRG}^{\mathsf{qs}}$ with sufficient expansion easily implies a $\mathsf{PRF}^{\mathsf{qs}}$ with polynomial domain, it is not clear if a $\mathsf{PRG}^{\mathsf{qs}}$ can be used to build full-fledged $\mathsf{PRF}^{\mathsf{qs}}$ with exponential domain. Note that the standard conversion of a PRG to a PRF [21], and its quantum adaption [37], both implicitly use the uniform input sampling property of PRGs. Hence, adapting this conversion to the quantum input sampling setting is an interesting open question.

Fortunately, $\mathsf{PRF}^{\mathsf{qs}}$ with polynomial domain can still be useful. Using domain extension techniques [18], we convert them into *bounded-query* $\mathsf{PRF}^{\mathsf{qs}}$s with exponential domain. These, in turn, enable the construction of bounded-copy linear-length $\mathsf{PRS}^{\mathsf{qs}}$ and bounded-query $\mathsf{PRU}^{\mathsf{qs}}$, following a similar approach outlined in [23,27] for the uniform sampling setting, and is given in the full paper.

**Separation Results.** We present three separation results in this work that complement the positive results discussed above. We only provide a simplified overview of the core ideas of the separations and many technical considerations are not discussed here to maintain clarity.

[6] The output of the $\mathsf{PRG}^{\mathsf{qs}}$ can be interpreted as the complete description of a $\mathsf{PRF}^{\mathsf{qs}}$ with polynomial domain.

*Separating* PRGs *from* $\mathsf{PRF}^{\mathsf{qs}}$*s.* Our first and main separation is between PRGs and $\mathsf{PRF}^{\mathsf{qs}}$s. This separation is established using a unitary oracle with access to the inverse. As discussed in Sect. 1.1, this precludes a wide class of black-box constructions.

We define three oracles based on a pair of random functions $(O, P)$:

- $\mathcal{C}$: An oracle for membership in a PSPACE-complete language.
- $\sigma$: A unitary "flip" oracle that swaps the state $|0^{2n}\rangle$ with the state $|\psi_n\rangle = \sum_{x\in\{0,1\}^n}|x\rangle|O(x)\rangle$ and acts as the identity on all other orthogonal states[7].
- $\mathcal{O}$: Unitary of the classical function that maps $(x, y, z)$ to $P(x, z)$ if $O(x) = y$ and to $\perp$ otherwise.

It is straightforward to construct a $\mathsf{PRF}^{\mathsf{qs}}$ relative to these oracles. The quantum key generation algorithm of the $\mathsf{PRF}^{\mathsf{qs}}$ queries $\sigma(|0^{2n}\rangle)$ and measures the response in the computational basis to obtain a pair $(x^*, O(x^*))$, which serves as the secret key. On input $z$, the evaluation algorithm computes $\mathcal{O}(x^*, O(x^*), z) = P(x^*, z)$ and outputs the result $P(x^*, z)$. Since the same key is reused across evaluations, this yields deterministic outputs. Furthermore, given that a quantum-accessible random oracle acts as a (quantum-query-secure) PRF [33], it is not difficult to show that this construction constitutes a $\mathsf{PRF}^{\mathsf{qs}}$.

The more difficult part is showing that PRGs cannot exist relative to these oracles. Our strategy is to show that any candidate generator must be independent of the oracles $(\sigma, \mathcal{O})$ in order to establish that it can be broken using $\mathcal{C}$. In particular, measuring $\sigma(|0^{2n}\rangle)$ returns a different pair $(x, O(x))$ each time, and $\mathcal{O}$ then evaluates a different function $P(x, \cdot)$ depending on the value of $x$. On the other hand, a PRG should produce almost-deterministic outputs, meaning that it cannot depend on this inconsistent randomness.

To make this rigorous, we make small modifications to the oracle and argue that the generator's output should remain stable under such perturbations. The main idea is that a PRG cannot distinguish between oracles that differ only negligibly in the states they produce. Given that a PRG produces deterministic classical values, this implies that its output must remain invariant under such small perturbations. By applying this reasoning inductively, we conclude that the generator's output must remain stable even if the oracles are replaced entirely.

This, in turn, implies that the oracles can be simulated using internal randomness, effectively yielding a PRG that does not require oracle access. In other words, since the PRG's output is the same regardless of the oracle, we can simulate its computation by sampling random strings directly, rather than querying the oracles. But a PRG that does not use oracle access to $(\sigma, \mathcal{O})$ can easily be broken with a PSPACE oracle. Thus, we establish that relative to the unitary oracles $(\sigma, \mathcal{O}, \mathcal{C})$, there is no fully black-box construction of a PRG from a $\mathsf{PRF}^{\mathsf{qs}}$ with inverse access. Given that fully black-box constructions relativize, we obtain the impossibility of such constructions in the plain model.

*Separating* OWSGs *from* $\perp$-PRGs*.* We show that there does not exist a fully black-box construction of a OWSG from CPTP access to a $\perp$-PRG. This result

[7] Similar "flip" oracles were used in recent works: [9,11,14].

is only given in the full paper, but described informally here. We prove this by demonstrating the separation relative to a CPTP oracle. This result is somewhat surprising, since OWSGs are considered weaker than PRGs, as evidenced by existing separations between them [25]. Instead, our separation emphasizes the distinction in determinism to separate OWSGs from $\perp$-PRGs. Recall, a $\perp$-PRG is the same as a PRG except on a $1/\mathsf{poly}(n)$ fraction of inputs, the algorithm may return $\perp$ sometimes.

Our separation leverages two oracles. The first oracle is for membership in a PSPACE-complete language, used to break any OWSG. The second oracle, denoted $\mathcal{O}$, is a modified quantum random oracle with an abort mechanism. This oracle exhibits inherent $\perp$-pseudodeterminism, making it well-suited for constructing $\perp$-PRGs but unsuitable for deterministic primitives like OWSGs. One downside of this design is that it complicates lifting the oracle to a unitary map.

The oracle $\mathcal{O}$ operates as follows: on input $x \in \{0,1\}^n$, it computes $(a_x, b_x, c_x) \leftarrow O(x)$, where $O$ is a random function mapping $n$-bits to $3n$-bits and $a_x, b_x, c_x \in \{0,1\}^n$. The first component, $a_x$, determines whether $x$ is a "good" (deterministic) or "bad" (may evaluate to $\perp$) input. If $x$ is deemed bad, which occurs with $1/\mathsf{poly}(n)$ probability, then $\mathcal{O}$ outputs $c_x$ with probability $1 - \frac{b_x}{2^n}$ and $\perp$ with $\frac{b_x}{2^n}$ probability, where $b_x$ is interpreted as an integer. Otherwise, if $x$ is deemed good, $\mathcal{O}$ outputs $c_x$ with probability 1. It is easy to verify that $\mathcal{O}$ behaves as a valid $\perp$-PRG.

The challenge lies in showing that $\mathcal{O}$ cannot be used for constructing OWSGs. Formalizing this requires some effort, but the main idea is that a generator, relying on $\mathcal{O}(x)$ for some $x$, cannot infer whether $x$ is good or bad with certainty, given that the error probability (i.e., the chance of receiving $\perp$) can be very small. When $x$ is bad, small changes in the error probability cannot be distinguished in polynomial time. As a result, the generator's output must remain stable under such small variations. Extending this reasoning, we show that the output must remain unchanged even when $\mathcal{O}(x)$ always returns $\perp$. Informally, this implies that the generator's output is independent of $\mathcal{O}$. This independence allows us to construct an OWSG that does not use $\mathcal{O}$. But since OWSGs cannot exist relative to a PSPACE oracle [13], we reach a contradiction. Hence, no fully black-box construction of an OWSG from a $\perp$-PRG is possible in this setting.

*Separating* $\perp$-PRG*s from* $\mathsf{PRF}^{\mathsf{qs}}$*s.* Our third result separates $\perp$-PRGs from CPTP access to a $\mathsf{PRF}^{\mathsf{qs}}$s. This result is only given in the full paper, but described informally here. This separation, like our first, hinges on the distinction between quantum and classical input sampling procedures. We use a similar oracle setup—$(\sigma, \mathcal{O}, \mathcal{C})$—but in this case, $\sigma$ is defined as a CPTP map that samples $x$ uniformly at random and outputs the pair $(x, O(x))$.

Constructing a $\mathsf{PRF}^{\mathsf{qs}}$ relative to these oracles proceeds analogously to the first separation and is relatively straightforward. The more involved part is proving that $\perp$-PRGs cannot exist relative to this oracle setup. Intuitively, since $\sigma$ outputs fresh, random pairs $(x, O(x))$ with each call, every evaluation of the $\perp$-PRG interacts with an essentially independent instantiation of $\mathcal{O}$. Because

$\bot$-PRGs are expected to exhibit some degree of determinism, they cannot depend on these inconsistent oracle outputs. More precisely, we show that the behavior of the $\bot$-PRG can be simulated by replacing oracle access with sampling random strings directly.

Consequently, there would exist a $\bot$-PRG that operates without oracle access yet remains secure against adversaries with access to a PSPACE oracle, which is a contradiction.

Importantly, this argument breaks down if $\sigma$ were defined as in the first separation. In that setting, $\sigma$ is a unitary map, so its outputs are no longer distinct. Furthermore, unlike in the first separation, we cannot argue that the $\bot$-PRG output remains invariant under small perturbations to the oracle responses: slight variations in $\sigma$ could induce slight differences in the probability of returning $\bot$. Consequently, the set of "bad" inputs as well as the evaluations on this set can change across different oracles. To avoid this issue, we require that $\sigma$ yield classical outputs, ensuring that different evaluations receive completely independent query results.

## 2 Preliminaries

### 2.1 Notations

We let $[n] = \{1, 2, \ldots, n\}$, $[n : n+k] = \{n, n+1, \ldots, n+k\}$, and $y_{[n:n+k]} = y_n y_{n+1} \cdots y_{n+k}$ for every $n, k \in \mathbb{N}$ and string $y$ of length at least $n+k$. Furthermore, we let $\mathsf{negl}(x)$ denote any function that is asymptotically smaller than the inverse of any polynomial.

We let $x \leftarrow X$ denote that $x$ is chosen from the values in $X$, according to the distribution $X$. If $X$ is a set, then $x \leftarrow X$ simply means $x$ is chosen uniformly at random from the set. We say $(a, \cdot) \in X$ if there exists an element $b$ such that $(a, b) \in X$. We let $\Pi_{n,m} = (\{0,1\}^m)^{\{0,1\}^n}$ denote the set of functions mapping $n$-bits to $m$-bits, and $\Pi_n$ denote the set of permutations on $n$-bits.

We refer the reader to [32] for a detailed exposition to preliminary quantum information. We let $\mathcal{S}(\mathcal{H})$ and $\mathcal{U}(\mathcal{H})$ denote the set of unit vectors and unitary operators, respectively, on the Hilbert space $\mathcal{H}$ and let $\mathsf{Haar}(\mathbb{C}^d)$ denote the Haar measure over $\mathbb{C}^d$ which is the uniform measure over all $d$-dimensional unit vectors. We let $d_{\mathsf{TD}}$ denote the total trace distance between two density matrices or two distributions.

We follow the standard notations to define quantum algorithms. We say that a quantum algorithm $A$ is *QPT* if it consists of a family of quantum algorithms $\{A_\lambda\}_\lambda$ such that the run-time of each algorithm $A_\lambda$ is bounded by some polynomial $p(\lambda)$. Furthermore, we say that a quantum algorithm $A = \{A_\lambda\}_\lambda$ is *almost-deterministic* if there exists a negligible function $\epsilon$, such that for every $\lambda \in \mathbb{N}$ and every input $x$ in the domain of $A_\lambda$, there exists an (possibly quantum) output $y$ satisfying $\Pr[A_\lambda(x) = y] \geq 1 - \epsilon(\lambda)$. We also avoid using the $\lambda$ subscript in algorithms to avoid excessive notation.

We say $A$ has *quantum-query access* to a classical function $P$ to mean that it is given polynomial quantum queries to the unitary map $U_P : |x\rangle \rightarrow |x\rangle|P(x)\rangle$.

### 2.2 Black-Box Separation

The notion of oracle black-box separations was first considered in [22] and later formalized in the quantum setting in [16]. We just recall the definitions relevant for this work from [16].

**Definition 3.** *A* primitive *$P$ is a pair $P = (\mathcal{F}_P, \mathcal{R}_P)$*[8] *where $\mathcal{F}_P$ is a set of quantum channels, and $\mathcal{R}_P$ is a relation over pairs $(G, \mathcal{A})$ of quantum channels, where $G \in \mathcal{F}_P$.*

*A quantum channel $G$ is an* implementation *of $P$ if $G \in \mathcal{F}_P$. If $G$ is additionally a QPT channel, then we say that $G$ is an* efficient implementation *of $P$. A quantum channel $\mathcal{A}$ $P$-*breaks *$G \in \mathcal{F}_P$ if $(G, \mathcal{A}) \in \mathcal{R}_P$. We say that $G$ is a* secure implementation *of $P$ if $G$ is an implementation of $P$ such that no QPT channel $P$-breaks it. The primitive $P$* exists *if there exists an efficient and secure implementation of $P$.*

We now formalize the notion of constructions relative to an oracle.

**Definition 4.** *We say that a primitive $P$ exists relative to an oracle $\mathcal{O}$ if:*

- *There exists QPT oracle-access algorithm $G^{(\cdot)}$ such that $G^{\mathcal{O}} \in \mathcal{F}_P$.*
- *The security of $G^{\mathcal{O}}$ holds against all QPT adversaries with access to $\mathcal{O}$ i.e. for all QPT $\mathcal{A}$, $(G^{\mathcal{O}}, \mathcal{A}^{\mathcal{O}}) \notin \mathcal{R}_P$.*

We are now ready to define the notion of fully black-box construction. We define two versions: under unitary/inverse access and under CPTP access.

**Definition 5.** *A QPT algorithm $G^{(\cdot)}$ is a fully black-box construction of $Q$ from $P$* ***with inverse access*** *if the following two conditions hold:*

1. *For every unitary implementation $U$ of $P$, $G^{U,U^{-1}} \in \mathcal{F}_Q$.*
2. *There is a QPT algorithm $S^{(\cdot)}$ such that, for every unitary implementation $U$ of $P$, every adversary $\mathcal{A}$ that $Q$-breaks $G^{U,U^{-1}}$, and every unitary implementation $\tilde{\mathcal{A}}$ of $\mathcal{A}$, it holds that $S^{\tilde{\mathcal{A}},\tilde{\mathcal{A}}^{-1}}$ $P$-breaks $U$.*

The following result from [16] shows the relation between fully black-box constructions and oracle separations.

**Theorem 4 (Theorem 4.2 in [16]).** *Assume there exists a fully black-box construction of a primitive $Q$ from a primitive $P$ with inverse access. Then, for any unitary $\mathcal{O}$, if $P$ exists relative to $(\mathcal{O}, \mathcal{O}^{-1})$, then $Q$ exists relative to $(\mathcal{O}, \mathcal{O}^{-1})$.*

We now consider the setting of CPTP oracles.

**Definition 6.** *A QPT algorithm $G^{(\cdot)}$ is a fully black-box construction of $Q$ from* ***CPTP access*** *to $P$ if the following two conditions hold:*

---

[8] We can think of $\mathcal{F}_P$ to mean the "correctness" conditions of $P$ and $\mathcal{R}_P$ to mean the "security" conditions of $P$.

1. *For every CPTP implementation* $\mathcal{C}$ *of* $P$, $G^{\mathcal{C}}$ *is an implementation of* $Q$.
2. *There is a QPT algorithm* $S^{(\cdot)}$ *such that, for every CPTP implementation* $\mathcal{C}$ *of* $P$, *every adversary* $\mathcal{A}$ *that* $Q$*-breaks* $G^{\mathcal{C}}$, *it holds that* $S^{\mathcal{A}}$ $P$*-breaks* $\mathcal{C}$.

We also obtain a relationship between fully black-box constructions and oracle separations in the CPTP setting.

**Theorem 5.** *Assume there exists a fully black-box construction of a primitive* $Q$ *from CPTP access to* $P$. *Then, for any CPTP oracle* $\mathcal{O}$, *if* $P$ *exists relative to* $\mathcal{O}$, *then* $Q$ *exists relative to* $\mathcal{O}$.

The proof of the above result follows in the same way as the proof of Theorem 4.2 in [16].

### 2.3 MicroCrypt Primitives

We recall several MicroCrypt assumptions relevant to this work. First, we define pseudorandom states (PRSs), first introduced in [23].

**Definition 7 (Pseudorandom State Generator).** *Let* $\lambda \in \mathbb{N}$ *be the security parameter and let* $n = n(\lambda)$ *be polynomial in* $\lambda$. *An almost-deterministic QPT algorithm* $\mathsf{PRS}$ *is called a* $n$-pseudorandom state generator ($\mathsf{PRS}$), *if it generates* $n$*-qubit pure-states and the following holds:*

*For any polynomial* $t(\cdot)$ *and QPT distinguisher* $\mathcal{A}$:

$$\left| \Pr_{k \leftarrow \{0,1\}^{\lambda}} \left[ \mathcal{A}\left( \mathsf{PRS}(k)^{\otimes t(\lambda)} \right) = 1 \right] - \Pr_{|\phi\rangle \leftarrow \mathsf{Haar}(\mathbb{C}^n)} \left[ \mathcal{A}\left( |\phi\rangle^{\otimes t(\lambda)} \right) = 1 \right] \right| \leq \mathsf{negl}(\lambda).$$

*We divide* PRS *into three regimes, based on the state size* $n$:

1. $n = c \cdot \log(\lambda)$ *with* $c \ll 1$.
2. $n = c \cdot \log(\lambda)$ *with* $c \geq 1$, *which we call* short pseudorandom states (SPRSs).
3. $n = \Omega(\lambda)$, *which we call* long pseudorandom states (LPRSs).

We will also recall the standard definition for PRGs.

**Definition 8 (Pseudorandom Generator).** *Let* $\lambda \in \mathbb{N}$ *be the security parameter and let* $n = n(\lambda)$ *be polynomial in* $\lambda$. *An almost-deterministic QPT algorithm* $G$ *mapping* $\{0,1\}^{\lambda}$ *to* $\{0,1\}^n$ *is called a* $n$-pseudorandom generator (PRG), *if* $n > \lambda$ *for all* $\lambda \in \mathbb{N}$ *and for any QPT distinguisher* $\mathcal{A}$:

$$\left| \Pr_{k \leftarrow \{0,1\}^{\lambda}} [\mathcal{A}(G(k)) = 1] - \Pr_{y \leftarrow \{0,1\}^n} [\mathcal{A}(y) = 1] \right| \leq \mathsf{negl}(\lambda).$$

### 2.4 Pseudodeterministic Pseudorandom Strings from Pseudorandom States

We describe the procedure given in [3] to extract classical pseudorandom strings from pseudorandom states. The original procedure is, for some states, pseudo-deterministic meaning that running this procedure on the same state may yield different outcomes each time. We first recall the notion of tomography, which is used to extract a classical approximate description of a quantum state.

**Lemma 1 (Corollary 7.6 [1]).** *For any error tolerance $\delta = \delta(\lambda) \in (0, 1]$ and any dimension $d = d(\lambda) \in \mathbb{N}$ using at least $t = t(\lambda) := 36\lambda d^3/\delta$ copies of a d-dimensional density matrix $\rho$, the process $\mathsf{Tomography}(\rho^{\otimes t})$ runs in polynomial time with respect to $\lambda$, $d$, $1/\delta$ and outputs a matrix $M \in \mathbb{C}^{d\times d}$ such that*

$$\Pr\left[\|\rho - M\| \leq \delta : M \leftarrow \mathsf{Tomography}(\rho^{\otimes t})\right] \geq 1 - \mathsf{negl}(\lambda).$$

We now recall how Tomography is used to extract pseudorandom strings in [3].

**Construction 1. (Extract [3]).** *Let $\lambda \in \mathbb{N}$ be the security parameter. The algorithm Extract is defined as follows:*

- *Input: $t := 144\lambda d^8$ copies of a d-dimensional quantum state $\rho$.*
- *Perform $\mathsf{Tomography}(\rho^{\otimes t})$ with error tolerance $\delta := d^{-5/6}$ to obtain a classical matrix $M \in \mathbb{C}^{d\times d}$.*
- *Run $\mathsf{Round}(M)$ to get $y \in \{0, 1\}^{\ell}$. Output $y$.*

$\mathsf{Round}(M)$: Input: Matrix $M \in \mathbb{C}^{d\times d}$.

- Define $k := d^{5/6}$, $r := d^{2/3}$, and $\ell := d^{1/6}$.
- Let $p_1, \ldots, p_d$ be the diagonal entries of $M$.
- For $i \in [\ell]$:
  1. Let $q_i := \sum_{j=1}^{r} p_{(i-1)r+j}$.
  2. Define $b_i := \begin{cases} 1 & \text{if } q_i > r/d \\ 0 & \text{if } q_i \leq r/d. \end{cases}$
- Output $b_1 \| \ldots \| b_\ell$.

This extraction procedure was shown to satisfy the following two lemmas.

**Lemma 2 (Lemma 3.6 in [3]).** *If Extract is run on a Haar random state, then $d_{\mathsf{TD}}((q_1, \ldots, q_\ell), Z/(2d)) \leq O(k/d) + O(\ell/\sqrt{r})$ where $Z$ is a random variable in $\mathbb{R}^{\ell}$ with i.i.d. $\mathcal{N}(2r, 4r)$ entries. In other words, $Z/(2d)$ has an i.i.d. $\mathcal{N}(r/d, r/d^2)$ entries.*

**Lemma 3 (Claim 3.7 in [3]).** *Define*

$$\mathcal{G}_d := \left\{ |\psi\rangle \in \mathcal{S}(\mathbb{C}^d) : \forall i \in [\ell], \left|q_i - \frac{r}{d}\right| > 2/d \right\}.$$

*Then,*

1. $\Pr\left[|\psi\rangle \in \mathcal{G}_d : |\psi\rangle \leftarrow \mathit{Haar}(\mathbb{C}^d)\right] \geq 1 - O(d^{-1/6})$.
2. *There exists a negligible function* $\mathsf{negl}(n)$ *such that for any* $|\psi\rangle \in \mathcal{G}_d$*, there exists a string* $y$ *such that* $\Pr\left[y \leftarrow \mathit{Extract}(|\psi\rangle^{\otimes t})\right] \geq 1 - \mathsf{negl}(\lambda)$.

### 2.5 Pseudodeterministic Primitives in MicroCrypt

We introduce $\perp$-PRGs from [4]. Note that it is easy to distinguish $\perp$ evaluations from random. However, it is sufficient to only require indistinguishability for non-$\perp$ evaluations. This is incorporated in the security game by providing $\perp$ in the truly random case as well. See [4] for a more in-depth discussion.

**Definition 9 (Is-$\perp$).** *We define the operator*

$$\mathsf{Is}\text{-}\perp(a, b) := \begin{cases} \perp & \text{if } a = \perp \\ b & \text{otherwise.} \end{cases}$$

**Definition 10 ($\perp$-Pseudorandom Generator).** *Let* $\lambda \in \mathbb{N}$ *be the security parameter and let* $m = m(\lambda)$ *be polynomial in* $\lambda$*. A QPT algorithm* $G$ *mapping* $\{0,1\}^\lambda$ *to* $\{0,1\}^m \cup \{\perp\}$*, is a* $(\mu, m)$-$\perp$-pseudodeterministic pseudorandom generator ($\perp$-PRG) *if:*

1. (Expansion) $m(\lambda) > \lambda$ *for all* $\lambda \in \mathbb{N}$.
2. (Pseudodeterminism) *There exist a constant* $c > 0$ *such that* $\mu(\lambda) = O(\lambda^{-c})$ *and for sufficiently large* $\lambda \in \mathbb{N}$ *there exists a set* $\mathcal{G}_\lambda \subseteq \{0,1\}^\lambda$ *such that the following holds:*
   *(a)*
   $$\Pr_{x \leftarrow \{0,1\}^\lambda}\left[x \in \mathcal{G}_\lambda\right] \geq 1 - \mu(\lambda).$$
   *(b) For every* $x \in \mathcal{G}_\lambda$ *there exists a non-*$\perp$ *value* $y \in \{0,1\}^m$ *such that:*
   $$\Pr\left[G(x) = y\right] \geq 1 - \mathsf{negl}(\lambda). \tag{1}$$
   *(c) For every* $x \in \{0,1\}^\lambda$*, there exists a non-*$\perp$ *value* $y \in \{0,1\}^m$ *such that:*
   $$\Pr\left[G(x) \in \{y, \perp\}\right] \geq 1 - \mathsf{negl}(\lambda). \tag{2}$$
3. (Security) *For every polynomial* $q = q(\lambda)$ *and QPT distinguisher* $\mathcal{A}$*, there exists a negligible function* $\epsilon$ *such that:*

$$\left| \Pr\begin{bmatrix} k \leftarrow \{0,1\}^\lambda \\ y_1 \leftarrow G(k) \\ \vdots \\ y_q \leftarrow G(k) \end{bmatrix} : \mathcal{A}(y_1, ..., y_q) = 1 \right] - \Pr\left[\begin{matrix} k \leftarrow \{0,1\}^\lambda \\ y \leftarrow \{0,1\}^m \\ y_1 \leftarrow \mathsf{Is}\text{-}\perp(G(k), y) \\ \vdots \\ y_q \leftarrow \mathsf{Is}\text{-}\perp(G(k), y) \end{matrix} : \mathcal{A}(y_1, \ldots, y_q) = 1 \right] \right| \leq \epsilon(\lambda)$$

$\perp$-PRGs were constructed from SPRSs in [4].

**Lemma 4 (Corollary 1 [4]).** *If there exists* $(c \log \lambda)$-SPRS *for some constant* $c > 12$*, then there exists a* $(O(\lambda^{-c/12+1}), \lambda^{c/12})$ - $\perp$-PRG.

# 3 Definitions: Cryptography with Quantum Input Sampling

We present definitions for various known cryptographic primitives but with quantum input sampling algorithms. First of all, we define PRS with quantum input sampling.

**Definition 11 (Pseudorandom State Generator with Quantum Input Sampling).** *Let $\lambda \in \mathbb{N}$ be the security parameter and let $n = n(\lambda)$ and $m = m(\lambda)$ be polynomials in $\lambda$. A pair of QPT algorithms ($\mathsf{QSamp}, \mathsf{StateGen}$) is called a $(m, n)$-*PRS with quantum input sampling ($\mathsf{PRS}^{qs}$)*, if the following conditions hold:*

- $\mathsf{QSamp}(1^\lambda)$ : *Outputs a string $k \in \{0,1\}^m$.*
- $\mathsf{StateGen}(k)$ : *Takes a $m$-bit string $k$ and outputs a $n$-qubit pure-state.*
- (Determinism) *For every $k \in \{0,1\}^m$, there exists a $n$-qubit state $|\psi_k\rangle$, such that the following condition is satisfied over the distribution of inputs:*

$$\Pr_{k \leftarrow \mathsf{QSamp}(1^\lambda)} [\mathsf{StateGen}(k) = |\psi_k\rangle] \geq 1 - \mathsf{negl}(\lambda).$$

- (Security) *For any polynomial $t(\cdot)$ and QPT distinguisher $\mathcal{A}$:*

$$\left| \Pr_{k \leftarrow \mathsf{QSamp}(1^\lambda)} \left[ \mathcal{A}\left( \mathsf{StateGen}(k)^{\otimes t(\lambda)} \right) = 1 \right] - \Pr_{|\phi\rangle \leftarrow \mathsf{Haar}(\mathbb{C}^n)} \left[ \mathcal{A}\left( |\phi\rangle^{\otimes t(\lambda)} \right) = 1 \right] \right| \leq \mathsf{negl}(\lambda).$$

*In the case where security only holds for $t \leq q$ for some polynomial $q = q(\lambda)$, then we call this $(q, m, n)$-*bounded-copy $\mathsf{PRS}^{qs}$ ($\mathsf{BC\text{-}PRS}^{qs}$)*. If $n = c \cdot \log(\lambda)$ with $c > 1$, then we call this* $\mathsf{SPRS}^{qs}$ *and if $n = \Omega(\lambda)$, then we call this* $\mathsf{LPRS}^{qs}$.

We now introduce PRG with quantum input sampling and PRF with quantum key generation. As far as we know, these notions has not been defined previously.

**Definition 12 (Pseudorandom Generator with Quantum Input Sampling).** *Let $\lambda \in \mathbb{N}$ be the security parameter and let $n = n(\lambda)$ and $m = m(\lambda)$ be polynomials in $\lambda$. A pair of QPT algorithms ($\mathsf{QSamp}, G$) is a $(m, n)$-*PRG with quantum input sampling ($\mathsf{PRG}^{qs}$) *if:*

1. $\mathsf{QSamp}(1^\lambda)$ : *Outputs a string $k \in \{0,1\}^m$.*
2. $G(k)$: *Takes an input $k \in \{0,1\}^m$ and outputs $y \in \{0,1\}^n$*
3. (Expansion) $m(\lambda) < n(\lambda)$ *for all $\lambda \in \mathbb{N}$.*
4. (Determinism) *For every $k \in \{0,1\}^m$, there exists a string $y_k \in \{0,1\}^n$, such that the following condition is satisfied over the distribution of inputs:*

$$\Pr_{k \leftarrow \mathsf{QSamp}(1^\lambda)} [G(k) = y_k] \geq 1 - \mathsf{negl}(\lambda).$$

5. (Security) *For any QPT distinguisher $\mathcal{A}$, there exists a negligible function $\epsilon$ such that:*

$$\left| \Pr_{k \leftarrow \mathsf{QSamp}(1^\lambda)} [\mathcal{A}(G(k)) = 1] - \Pr_{y \leftarrow \{0,1\}^n} [\mathcal{A}(y) = 1] \right| \leq \epsilon(\lambda).$$

*We say that $G$ is a $\mathsf{PRG}^{qs}$ if for every QPT $\mathcal{A}$, $\epsilon$ is a negligible function. We say that $G$ is a* weak $\mathsf{PRG}^{qs}$ *if for every QPT $\mathcal{A}$, $\epsilon \leq \frac{1}{p}$ for some polynomial $p$.*

**Definition 13 (Pseudorandom Function with Quantum Key Generation).** *Let $\lambda \in \mathbb{N}$ be the security parameter and let $n = n(\lambda)$ and $m = m(\lambda)$ be polynomials in $\lambda$. A pair of QPT algorithms $(\mathsf{QSamp}, F)$ is called a $(m,n)$-*$\mathsf{PRF}$ with quantum key generation ($\mathsf{PRF}^{qs}$)*, if:*

1. $\mathsf{QSamp}(1^\lambda)$ : *Outputs a key $k \in \{0,1\}^m$.*
2. $F_k(x)$: *Takes a key $k \in \{0,1\}^m$ and an input $x \in \{0,1\}^n$ and outputs a string $y \in \{0,1\}^n$*[9].
3. (Determinism) *For every $k \in \{0,1\}^m$ and $x \in \{0,1\}^n$, there exists a string $y_{k,x} \in \{0,1\}^n$ such that for all $x \in \{0,1\}^n$, the following is satisfied over the distribution of keys:*

$$\Pr_{k \leftarrow \mathsf{QSamp}(1^\lambda)} [F_k(x) = y_{k,x}] \geq 1 - \mathsf{negl}(\lambda).$$

4. (Security) *For any QPT distinguisher $\mathcal{A}$:*

$$\left| \Pr_{k \leftarrow \mathsf{QSamp}(1^\lambda)} [\mathcal{A}^{F_k}(1^\lambda) = 1] - \Pr_{O \leftarrow \Pi_{n,n}} [\mathcal{A}^{O}(1^\lambda) = 1] \right| \leq \mathsf{negl}(\lambda)$$

*where $\Pi_{n,n}$ is the set of permutations on $\{0,1\}^n$. We say a $\mathsf{PRF}^{qs}$ is* quantum-query-secure *if the above holds even if $\mathcal{A}$ is given quantum-query access to $F_k$ and $O$. Furthermore, in the case where security only holds for $t \leq q$ queries for some polynomial $q = q(\lambda)$, then we call this a $q$-query $\mathsf{PRF}^{qs}$.*

# 4 Relations Among Primitives with Quantum Input Sampling

In this section, we explore relations among MicroCrypt primitives with quantum input sampling algorithms. In summary, we find that there exists black-box constructions for the following:

1. $\mathsf{PRG}^{\mathsf{qs}}$ from $\perp$-$\mathsf{PRG}$.
2. $\mathsf{PRG}^{\mathsf{qs}}$ from $\mathsf{BC}$-$\mathsf{SPRS}^{\mathsf{qs}}$.
3. $\mathsf{SPRS}^{\mathsf{qs}}$ from $\mathsf{PRG}^{\mathsf{qs}}$.

We also discuss how these results can be used to modify the output size of a $\mathsf{SPRS}$ in Sect. 4.3. In the full paper, we also show how to construct $\mathsf{BQ}$-$\mathsf{PRU}^{\mathsf{qs}}$ from $\mathsf{PRG}^{\mathsf{qs}}$.

[9] For simplicity, we only consider $\mathsf{PRF}^{\mathsf{qs}}$s with the same input and output lengths. All our results easily generalize to $\mathsf{PRF}^{\mathsf{qs}}$s with different input and output lengths.

### 4.1 $\mathsf{PRG}^{\mathsf{qs}}$ from $\perp$-PRG

We show how to build $\mathsf{PRG}^{\mathsf{qs}}$s from $\perp$-PRGs. First, we build a weak $\mathsf{PRG}^{\mathsf{qs}}$, and then amplify security to achieve a standard $\mathsf{PRG}^{\mathsf{qs}}$.

**Construction 2.** *Let $m$ be a polynomial on the security parameter $\lambda \in \mathbb{N}$ such that $m > \lambda$. Let $\mu = O(\lambda^{-c})$ for some constant $c > 0$. Let $G$ be a $(\mu, m)$-$\perp$-PRG. The construction for a weak $(\lambda, m)$-$\mathsf{PRG}^{qs}$ is as follows:*

- $\mathsf{QSamp}(1^\lambda)$ : *For $i \in [\lambda]$ :*
  1. *Sample $k_i \leftarrow \{0,1\}^\lambda$.*
  2. *For each $j \in [\lambda]$, compute $y_{i,j} \leftarrow G(k_i)$.*
  3. *If $\mathsf{vote}_\lambda(y_{i,1}, \ldots, y_{i,\lambda}) \neq \perp$[10], then output $k_i$.*

  *Otherwise, output $\perp$.*
- $\mathsf{PRG}(k)$ :
  1. *If $k = \perp$, output $0^m$.*
  2. *For each $j \in [\lambda]$, compute $y_j \leftarrow G(k)$.*
  3. *If $y_j = \perp$ for all $j \in [\lambda]$, then output $\perp$.*
  4. *Otherwise, output the first most common non-$\perp$ value in $(y_1, \ldots, y_\lambda)$.*

**Lemma 5.** *Construction 2 is a weak $(\lambda, m)$-$\mathsf{PRG}^{qs}$ assuming the existence of a $(\mu, m)$-$\perp$-PRG.*

We prove Lemma 5 in the full paper but the idea is described in Sect. 1.3. Next, it was shown in [17] that a weak PRG can be upgraded to a strong PRG through a standard amplification argument, increasing the input length from $\lambda$ to $\lambda^2$. This argument applies to $\mathsf{PRG}^{\mathsf{qs}}$s, giving the following result.

**Theorem 6.** *If there exists $(\mu, m)$-$\perp$-PRG where $m > \lambda^2$ and $\mu = O(\lambda^{-c})$ for some constant $c > 0$, then there exists a $(\lambda^2, m)$-$\mathsf{PRG}^{qs}$ satisfying strong security.*

### 4.2 $\mathsf{PRG}^{\mathsf{qs}}$ from BC-$\mathsf{SPRS}^{\mathsf{qs}}$

In this part, we show that BC-$\mathsf{SPRS}^{\mathsf{qs}}$ can be used to construct $\mathsf{PRG}^{\mathsf{qs}}$s using properties of pseudorandom states described in Sect. 2.4.

**Construction 3.** *Let $\lambda \in \mathbb{N}$ be the security parameter and let $n = c \cdot \log \lambda$, $d = \lceil \lambda^c \rceil$, and $m := \lceil \lambda^{c/12} \rceil$, where $c > 24$ is a constant. Let $(\mathsf{QS}, \mathsf{PRS})$ be a $(500\lambda d^8, \lambda, n)$-BC-$\mathsf{SPRS}^{qs}$. The construction for a weak $(\lambda, m)$-$\mathsf{PRG}^{qs}$ is as follows:*

- $\mathsf{QSamp}(1^\lambda)$ : *For each $i \in [\lambda]$ :*
  1. *Sample $s_i \leftarrow \mathsf{QS}(1^\lambda)$.*
  2. *Extract $t := 144\lambda d^8$ copies of pseudorandom state $\rho_i^{\otimes t}$ using $\mathsf{PRS}(s_i)$.*
  3. *Run $M_i \leftarrow \mathsf{Tomography}(\rho_i^{\otimes t})$.*

[10] $\mathsf{vote}(a_1, \ldots, a_\lambda)$ outputs the first most common element in the tuple $(a_1, \ldots, a_\lambda)$.

*4. If $M_i \in \mathcal{G}_\lambda$*[11]*, then output $k := s_i$.*
*Otherwise, output $\bot$.*
- *$G(k)$ :*
  1. *If $k = \bot$, then output $\bot$.*
  2. *Extract $t := 144\lambda d^8$ copies of pseudorandom state $\rho^{\otimes t}$ using $\mathsf{PRS}(k)$.*
  3. *Compute $y \leftarrow \mathsf{Extract}(\rho^{\otimes t})$.*
  4. *Output $y$.*

**Lemma 6.** *Construction 3 is a weak $(\lambda, m)$-$\mathsf{PRG}^{qs}$ assuming the existence of a $(500\lambda d^8, \lambda, n)$-$\mathsf{BC\text{-}SPRS}^{qs}$.*

*Proof.* We first show that the determinism condition of a $\mathsf{PRG}^{\mathsf{qs}}$ is satisfied (see Definition 12).

Assume for contradiction that the determinism condition is not satisfied. Then, there is a non-negligible probability such that sampling a key $k \leftarrow \mathsf{QSamp}(1^\lambda)$ and evaluating $G(k)$ twice yields distinct values. We obtain a contradiction as follows.

By Lemma 3, there is negligible probability that $\mathsf{QSamp}(1^\lambda)$ outputs $\bot$. The other possibility is that $\mathsf{QSamp}(1^\lambda)$ outputs a key $k = s$ satisfying $M_s \in \mathcal{G}_\lambda$ where $M_s \leftarrow \mathsf{Tomography}(\rho^{\otimes t})$ and $\rho \leftarrow \mathsf{PRS}(s)$. Therefore, with non-negligible probability, $k = s$ satisfies $M_s \in \mathcal{G}_\lambda$ but two evaluations of $G(k)$ yield distinct values.

Then, we construct a distinguisher $\mathcal{D}$ that breaks the security of $\mathsf{BC\text{-}SPRS}^{\mathsf{qs}}$ as follows. $\mathcal{D}$ receives $500\lambda d^8 > 3t$ copies of a state $\rho$ and needs to distinguish whether $\rho \leftarrow \mathsf{PRS}(k)$ for $k \leftarrow \mathsf{QS}(1^\lambda)$ or $\rho \leftarrow \mathsf{Haar}(\mathbb{C}^n)$ is a Haar-random state. $\mathcal{D}$ computes $M \leftarrow \mathsf{Tomography}(\rho^{\otimes t})$ with the first $t$ copies, $y_1 \leftarrow \mathsf{Extract}(\rho^{\otimes t})$ with the second $t$ copies, and $y_2 \leftarrow \mathsf{Extract}(\rho^{\otimes t})$ with the last $t$ copies. If $y_1 \neq y_2$ and $M \in \mathcal{G}_\lambda$, then $\mathcal{D}$ guesses that $\rho$ is a $\mathsf{BC\text{-}SPRS}^{\mathsf{qs}}$ i.e. outputs 1. Otherwise, $\mathcal{D}$ outputs 0. By our assumption, $y_1 \neq y_2$ and $M \in \mathcal{G}_\lambda$ occurs with non-negligible probability if $\rho$ is generated using $(\mathsf{QS}, \mathsf{PRS})$. On the other hand, Lemma 3 states that this occurs with negligible probability when $\rho$ is a Haar-random state. It is clear that $\mathcal{D}$ has non-negligible advantage in distinguishing $\mathsf{BC\text{-}SPRS}^{\mathsf{qs}}$ from Haar-random states using only $3t$ copies of the state, which contradicts the security condition of $\mathsf{BC\text{-}SPRS}^{\mathsf{qs}}$. Therefore, $(\mathsf{QSamp}, G)$ satisfies the correctness condition of a $\mathsf{PRG}^{\mathsf{qs}}$.

Next, we need to show security. Specifically, we need to show that for any QPT distinguisher $\mathcal{A}$:

$$\left| \Pr_{k \leftarrow \mathsf{QSamp}(1^\lambda)} [\mathcal{A}(G(k)) = 1] - \Pr_{y \leftarrow \{0,1\}^m} [\mathcal{A}(y) = 1] \right| \leq O(1/d^{1/6}).$$

The proof is through a hybrid argument:

- $\mathsf{H}_0$:

[11] This step just involves checking the values of the diagonal entries as defined in Lemma 3.

1. Sample $k \leftarrow \mathsf{QSamp}(1^\lambda)$.
2. Compute $y \leftarrow G(k)$.
3. Run $\mathcal{A}(y)$ and output the result.

- $\mathsf{H}_1$: The same as $\mathsf{H}_0$, except we modify the $\mathsf{PRG}^{\mathsf{qs}}$ algorithms by extracting a classical string from the pseudorandom states during input sampling instead of during evaluation.
  - $\mathsf{QSamp}_{\mathsf{H}_1}(1^\lambda)$ : For each $i \in [\lambda]$ :
    1. Sample $s_i \leftarrow \mathsf{QS}(1^\lambda)$.
    2. Extract $t := 144\lambda d^8$ copies of pseudorandom state $\rho_i^{\otimes t}$ using $\mathsf{PRS}(s_i)$.
    3. Run $M_i \leftarrow \mathsf{Tomography}(\rho_i^{\otimes t})$.
    4. If $M_i \in \mathcal{G}_\lambda$, then compute $y_i \leftarrow \mathsf{Round}(M_i)$.
    5. Output $k := y_i$.

    Otherwise, output $\perp$.
  - $G_{\mathsf{H}_1}(k)$ : Output $k$.
- $\mathsf{H}_2$: Same as $\mathsf{H}_1$, except we modify the $\mathsf{PRG}^{\mathsf{qs}}$ algorithms by using random Haar states instead of pseudorandom states.
  - $\mathsf{QSamp}_{\mathsf{H}_2}(1^\lambda)$ : For each $i \in [\lambda]$ :
    1. Sample $t := 144\lambda d^8$ copies of a random Haar state $\rho_i^{\otimes t}$ from $\mathsf{Haar}(\mathbb{C}^d)$.
    2. Run $M_i \leftarrow \mathsf{Tomography}(\rho_i^{\otimes t})$.
    3. If $M_i \in \mathcal{G}_\lambda$, then compute $y_i \leftarrow \mathsf{Round}(M_i)$.
    4. Output $k := y_i$.

    Otherwise, output $\perp$.
  - $G_{\mathsf{H}_2}(k)$ : Output $k$.
- $\mathsf{H}_3$: Same as $\mathsf{H}_2$, except we modify the $\mathsf{PRG}^{\mathsf{qs}}$ algorithms by removing the condition on the random Haar states.
  - $\mathsf{QSamp}_{\mathsf{H}_3}(1^\lambda)$ :
    1. Sample $t := 144\lambda d^8$ copies of a random Haar state $\rho^{\otimes t}$ from $\mathsf{Haar}(\mathbb{C}^d)$.
    2. Run $M \leftarrow \mathsf{Tomography}(\rho^{\otimes t})$.
    3. Compute $y \leftarrow \mathsf{Round}(M)$.
    4. Output $k := y$.
  - $G_{\mathsf{H}_3}(k)$ : Output $k$.
- $\mathsf{H}_4$: Same as $\mathsf{H}_3$, except we sample a random string instead of extracting randomness from the Haar random states.
  - $\mathsf{QSamp}_{\mathsf{H}_4}(1^\lambda)$ : Sample a random string $y \leftarrow \{0,1\}^m$. Set $k = y$.
  - $G_{\mathsf{H}_4}(k)$ : Output $k$.

First of all, hybrid $\mathsf{H}_0$ is statistically indistinguishable from hybrid $\mathsf{H}_1$, since we just move a step from the evaluation phase to the input sampling phase.

$\mathsf{H}_1$ is computationally indistinguishable from hybrid $\mathsf{H}_2$ because any QPT adversary that can distinguish between these hybrids can be used to break $\mathsf{BC\text{-}SPRS}^{\mathsf{qs}}$ security.

Next, if $M \in \mathcal{G}_\lambda$ in $\mathsf{QSamp}_{\mathsf{H}_3}$ in hybrid $\mathsf{H}_3$ and $M_1 \in \mathcal{G}_\lambda$ in $\mathsf{QSamp}_{\mathsf{H}_2}(1^\lambda)$ in $\mathsf{H}_2$, then it is clear that $\mathsf{H}_2$ and $\mathsf{H}_3$ are statistically indistinguishable. This scenario occurs with $O(d^{-1/6})$ probability by Lemma 3.

Finally, the variational distance between hybrids $\mathsf{H}_3$ and $\mathsf{H}_4$ is at most $O(d^{-1/6})$ by Lemma 2.

All in all, by the triangle inequality:

$$\begin{aligned}&\left|\Pr_{k\leftarrow \mathsf{QSamp}(1^\lambda)}[\mathcal{A}(G(k))=1]-\Pr_{y\leftarrow\{0,1\}^m}[\mathcal{A}(y)=1]\right|\\&=\left|\Pr_{y\leftarrow \mathsf{H}_0}[\mathcal{A}(y)=1]-\Pr_{y\leftarrow \mathsf{H}_4}[\mathcal{A}(y)=1]\right|\\&\leq O(d^{-1/6}).\end{aligned}$$

□

Recall that weak $\mathsf{PRG}^{\mathsf{qs}}$ can be upgraded to a strong $\mathsf{PRG}^{\mathsf{qs}}$ following the same argument in [17]. Hence, we obtain the following result.

**Theorem 7.** *If there exists $(500\lambda d, \lambda, n)$-$\mathsf{BC}$-$\mathsf{SPRS}^{qs}$, then there exists a $(\lambda^2, m)$-$\mathsf{PRG}^{qs}$ satisfying strong security.*

### 4.3 $\mathsf{SPRS}^{\mathsf{qs}}$ from $\mathsf{PRG}^{\mathsf{qs}}$

In this section, we show that $\mathsf{PRG}^{\mathsf{qs}}$s can be used to build $\mathsf{SPRS}^{\mathsf{qs}}$.

**Construction 4.** *Let $\lambda \in \mathbb{N}$ be the security parameter and let $c > 12$ be a constant. Let $m = m(\lambda)$ be polynomial on $\lambda$ such that $m > \lambda^{2c+1}$. Let $(QS, G)$ be a $(\lambda, m)$-$\mathsf{PRG}^{qs}$. Let $N = \lceil \lambda^c \rceil$ and $\mathcal{X} = \{1, \ldots, N\}$. The construction for a $(\lambda, c \cdot \log \lambda)$-$\mathsf{SPRS}^{qs}$ is as follows:*

- *$\mathsf{QSamp}(1^\lambda)$ : Sample $s \leftarrow \mathsf{QS}(1^\lambda)$. Output $k = s$.*
- *$\mathsf{StateGen}(k)$ :*
  1. *Compute $y \leftarrow G(k)$.*
  2. *Interpret $y$ as a function $f_y : \mathcal{X} \to \mathcal{X}$[12].*
  3. *Output*

$$|\psi_k\rangle := \frac{1}{\sqrt{N}} \sum_{x\in\mathcal{X}} \omega_N^{f_y(x)} |x\rangle.$$

**Theorem 8.** *Construction 4 is a $(\lambda, c \cdot \log \lambda)$-$\mathsf{SPRS}^{qs}$ assuming the existence of a $(\lambda, m)$-$\mathsf{PRG}^{qs}$ where $m > \lambda^{2c+1}$.*

Theorem 8 follows directly from [23]. Specifically, [23] shows that a $n$-$\mathsf{PRS}$ can be built from a $\mathsf{PRF}$ with domain size $2^n$. This conversion applies to the quantum input sampling regime as well. Then, Theorem 8 follows by setting $n := c \cdot \log \lambda$ and noting that $f_y$ in Construction 4 is computationally indistinguishable from a random function by the security of $\mathsf{PRG}^{\mathsf{qs}}$s.

Theorem 7 states that we can construct a $\mathsf{PRG}^{\mathsf{qs}}$ from any $\mathsf{SPRS}^{\mathsf{qs}}$. On the other hand, Theorem 8 state that we can construct a $\mathsf{SPRS}^{\mathsf{qs}}$ from a $\mathsf{PRG}^{\mathsf{qs}}$. Applying these two results consecutively, we get a method to shrink the size of a $\mathsf{SPRS}^{\mathsf{qs}}$.

---

[12] For $i \in \mathcal{X}$, $f_z(i) := z_{[it:(i+1)t]}$, where $t := \lceil \log N \rceil$.

**Corollary 4.** *For any constant* $c > 36$*, and any constant* $0 < m < c/36$*,* $(\lambda, c\log\lambda)$-$\mathsf{SPRS}^{qs}$ *implies* $(\lambda, m\log\lambda)$-$\mathsf{SPRS}^{qs}$.

Furthermore, by starting with a SPRS, building a $\perp$-PRG (Lemma 4), amplifying the output length sufficiently[13], building a $\mathsf{PRG}^{\mathsf{qs}}$ (Theorem 6), and finally a $\mathsf{SPRS}^{\mathsf{qs}}$ (Theorem 8), we obtain a $\mathsf{SPRS}^{\mathsf{qs}}$ of larger size.

**Corollary 5.** *For any constant* $c > 36$*, and any constant* $m > c$*,* $(\lambda, c\log\lambda)$-SPRS *implies* $(\lambda, m\log\lambda)$-$\mathsf{SPRS}^{qs}$.

## 5 Separating PRG from $\mathsf{PRF}^{\mathsf{qs}}$

In this section, we show that there does not exist a fully black-box construction of a PRG from a $\mathsf{PRF}^{\mathsf{qs}}$ with inverse access. We show this by demonstrating the result relative to a unitary oracle with inverse access. We first introduce some preliminary information for the proof.

We present $s$-PRG security relative to an oracle $\mathcal{T}$ in the form of an experiment to simplify notation later on.

$\mathsf{Exp}^{\mathsf{PRG}}_{\mathcal{A}^{\mathcal{T}},G^{\mathcal{T}}}(1^\lambda)$:

1. Sample $k \leftarrow \{0,1\}^\lambda$ and $b \leftarrow \{0,1\}$.
2. If $b = 0$, generate $y \leftarrow G^{\mathcal{T}}(k)$. Else, sample $y \leftarrow \{0,1\}^s$.
3. $b' \leftarrow \mathcal{A}^{\mathcal{T}}(y)$.
4. If $b' = b$, output 1. Otherwise, output 0.

We define the advantage of the adversary in this experiment as follows. It is clear that PRG security implies that this advantage should be negligible.

$$\mathsf{Adtg}^{\mathsf{PRG}}_{\mathcal{A}^{\mathcal{T}},G^{\mathcal{T}}}(1^\lambda) := \Pr\left[\mathsf{Exp}^{\mathsf{PRG}}_{\mathcal{A}^{\mathcal{T}},G^{\mathcal{T}}}(1^\lambda) = 1\right] - \frac{1}{2}.$$

We will use the following result from [14].

**Theorem 9 (Theorem 2.6 in [14]).** *Let* $T, n \in \mathbb{N}$*,* $\epsilon > 0$*, and* $|\psi\rangle$ *be a real-valued* $n$*-qubit state orthogonal to* $|0^n\rangle$*. Let* $U_{|\psi\rangle}$ *be a unitary that flips* $|0^n\rangle$ *with* $|\psi\rangle$ *and acts as the identity on all other orthogonal states. For any oracle algorithm* $\mathcal{A}$ *making* $T$ *queries to* $U_{|\psi\rangle}$*, there exists an algorithm* $\tilde{\mathcal{A}}$ *with access to* $O(\frac{T^2}{\epsilon^2})$ *copies of* $|\psi\rangle$ *that outputs a state that is* $\epsilon$*-close in terms of trace distance.*

Note that Theorem 2.6 in [14] is more involved than Theorem 9 since it deals with *complex-valued* quantum states. Our version is limited to real-valued states.

Also, note that [37] shows that any computationally unbounded adversaries cannot distinguish quantum-query-access to a randomly sampled polynomial of degree $(2r-1)$ and a random function given only $r$ quantum queries. Given

[13] It is easy to amplify the output length of a $\perp$-PRG by re-applying the algorithm on the output, at the cost of increasing the pseudodeterminism error.

that this result holds for computationally unbounded adversaries, it holds for adversaries with access to a PSPACE-oracle. We now describe the oracles used in the separation.

**Construction 5.** *For $n \in \mathbb{N}$, let $O_n \leftarrow \Pi_{n,8n}$ and $P_n \leftarrow \Pi_{2n,n}$ be random functions. Let $\mathcal{T} := (\sigma, \mathcal{O}, \mathcal{C})$ be a tuple of oracles, where $\sigma = \{\sigma_n\}_{n\in\mathbb{N}}$, $\mathcal{O} := \{\mathcal{O}_n\}_{n\in\mathbb{N}}$, and $\mathcal{C} := \{\mathcal{C}_n\}_{n\in\mathbb{N}}$ are defined as follows:*

1. *$\mathcal{C}$ is for membership in a PSPACE-complete language.*
2. *$\sigma_n$: Unitary that swaps $|0^{9n+1}\rangle$ with the state $|\psi_n\rangle := \frac{1}{\sqrt{2^n}}|1\rangle \sum_{x\in\{0,1\}^n} |x\rangle|O_n(x)\rangle$ and acts as the identity on all other orthogonal states.*
3. *$\mathcal{O}_n$: Unitary of the classical function that maps $(x, y, a)$, where $x, a \in \{0,1\}^n$ and $y \in \{0,1\}^{8n}$, to $P_n(x, a)$ if $O_n(x) = y$ and to $\perp$ otherwise.*

Notice that the unitary oracles above are self-inverse, so our separation is relative to a unitary oracle with access to the inverse.

We introduce some notation for the proof. Let $\mathbb{T}$ denote the set of all possible oracles and let $\mathcal{T} \leftarrow \mathbb{T}$ denote sampling an oracle in the way described in Construction 5. For any oracle $\mathcal{T}$ and integer $m \in \mathbb{N}$, let $\mathcal{T}_{\leq m}$ denote the sequence of oracles $(\sigma_n, \mathcal{O}_n)_{n\leq m}$ and let $\mathbb{T}[\mathcal{T}_{\leq m}]$ denote the set

$$\mathbb{T}[\mathcal{T}_{\leq m}] := \{\tilde{\mathcal{T}} \in \mathbb{T} : \tilde{\mathcal{T}}_{\leq m} = \mathcal{T}_{\leq m}\}.$$

**Theorem 10.** *There does not exist a fully black-box construction of a* PRG *from a (quantum-query-secure)* $\mathsf{PRF}^{qs}$ *with inverse access.*

*Proof.* For simplicity, we only prove the theorem for $(9n, n)$-$\mathsf{PRF}^{\mathsf{qs}}$ i.e. for $\mathsf{PRF}^{\mathsf{qs}}$s with $9n$-bit keys and $n$-bit inputs. However, the proof easily generalizes to other parameters by modifying the parameters of the oracles.

Assume, for the purpose of obtaining a contradiction, that $\tilde{G}^{F,F^{-1}}$ is a black-box construction of a PRG, from any $(9n, n)$-$\mathsf{PRF}^{\mathsf{qs}}$ $F$. First, we show that there exists a $\mathsf{PRF}^{\mathsf{qs}}$ relative to $\mathcal{T}$. Intuitively, $\mathsf{QSamp}(1^n)$ simply outputs a sample $(x, y) \leftarrow \sigma_n(|0^{9n+1}\rangle)$, while the evaluation algorithm with key $(x, y)$ and input $z$, outputs $\mathcal{O}(x, y, z)$. It is not difficult to see that this acts as a $\mathsf{PRF}^{\mathsf{qs}}$, but the proof is given in the full paper.

**Lemma 7.** *There exists a (quantum-query-secure) $(9n, n)$-$\mathsf{PRF}^{qs}$ relative to $\mathcal{T}$ for any $O$ and with probability 1 over the distribution of $P$. Furthermore, correctness is satisfied for any oracle $\mathcal{T}$.*

By Lemma 7 and the assumed existence of a black-box construction $\tilde{G}$, there exists an algorithm $G^{\mathcal{T}}$ that is a PRG with probability 1 over the oracles $\mathcal{T}$ and satisfies correctness for any oracle $\mathcal{T} \in \mathbb{T}$. Let $s = s(\lambda)$ be a polynomial denoting the output length of $G$.

**Claim 1.** *For any QPT adversary $\mathcal{A}$:*

$$\Pr_{\mathcal{T}\leftarrow\mathbb{T}}\left[\mathsf{Adtg}^{\mathsf{PRG}}_{\mathcal{A}^{\mathcal{T}},G^{\mathcal{T}}}(1^\lambda) \leq O\left(\frac{1}{\lambda^4}\right)\right] \geq \frac{3}{4}.$$

*Proof.* If this does not hold, then there exists a QPT adversary $\mathcal{A}$ such that

$$\Pr_{\mathcal{T} \leftarrow \mathbb{T}}\left[\mathsf{Adtg}^{\mathsf{PRG}}_{\mathcal{A}^{\mathcal{T}}, G^{\mathcal{T}}}(1^\lambda) > \frac{1}{\lambda^5}\right] > \frac{1}{4}$$

for infinitely many $\lambda \in \mathbb{N}$.

By a variant of Borel-Cantelli Lemma (Lemma 2.9 in [28]), this means $\mathcal{A}$ is successful in breaking the security of $G^{\mathcal{T}}$ with probability $\frac{1}{4}$ over the oracle distribution. Therefore, $G^{\mathcal{T}}$ is not a PRG with probability $\frac{1}{4}$ over the oracle distribution, giving a contradiction. □

Let $r = r(\lambda)$ denote the maximum run-time of $G$ and $m = m(\lambda) := 10(r\lambda)^4 + \lambda$. Hence, $G$ makes at most $r$ queries to the oracles.

Fix an oracle $\mathcal{T}$. We will need to show the following lemma.

**Lemma 8.** *For large enough $\lambda$ and any $k \in \{0,1\}^\lambda$,*

$$\Pr_{\mathcal{T}', \mathcal{T}'' \leftarrow \mathbb{T}[\mathcal{T}_{\leq \log(2\,m)}]}\left[G^{\mathcal{T}'}(k) = G^{\mathcal{T}''}(k)\right] \geq 1 - \frac{r}{m}.$$

*Proof.* Let $\mathcal{T}' := (\sigma', \mathcal{O}', \mathcal{C})$ and $\mathcal{T}'' := (\sigma'', \mathcal{O}'', \mathcal{C})$ be two oracles sampled from $\mathbb{T}[\mathcal{T}_{\leq \log(2m)}]$ and determined by the functions $(P', O')$ and $(P'', O'')$, respectively, as described in Construction 5. Fix $k \in \{0,1\}^\lambda$.

We will now describe how to construct a sequence of oracles $\mathcal{T}^i = (\sigma^i, \mathcal{O}^i, \mathcal{C})$, starting with $\mathcal{T}'$ and ending with $\mathcal{T}''$, such that $G^{\mathcal{T}^i}(k)$ is invariant (to some degree) as we move along the sequence. Note that $\mathcal{T}'_n$ and $\mathcal{T}''_n$ only differ for $\log(2m) < n < r$. For such a value of $n$, let $x^* \in \{0,1\}^n$ be an arbitrary string.

- $\mathcal{T}^1$: This is the same as $\mathcal{T}'$. Define

$$|\psi^1_n\rangle := \frac{1}{\sqrt{2^n}}|1\rangle \sum_{x \in \{0,1\}^n} |x\rangle|O'_n(x)\rangle.$$

- $\mathcal{T}^2$ : Same as $\mathcal{T}^1$, except we change $\sigma^2_n$ to be the unitary that swaps $|0^{9n+1}\rangle$ with

$$|\psi^2_n\rangle := \frac{1}{\sqrt{2^n - 1}}|1\rangle \sum_{x \in \{0,1\}^n \setminus \{x^*\}} |x\rangle|O'_n(x)\rangle.$$

- $\mathcal{T}^3$ : Same as $\mathcal{T}^2$, except for any $a \in \{0,1\}^n$, we set $\mathcal{O}^3_n(x^*, O'_n(x^*), a)$ to $\perp$ and, then, we set $\mathcal{O}^3_n(x^*, O''_n(x^*), a)$ to $P''_n(x^*, a)$.
- $\mathcal{T}^4$ : Same as $\mathcal{T}^3$, except $\sigma^4_n$ is the unitary that swaps $|0^{9n+1}\rangle$ with

$$|\psi^4_n\rangle := \frac{1}{\sqrt{2^n}}\left(|1\rangle \sum_{x \in \{0,1\}^n \setminus \{x^*\}} |x\rangle|O_n(x)\rangle + |1\rangle|x^*\rangle|O''_n(x^*)\rangle\right).$$

We perform these modifications for every input $x^*$ of length $n$ for every $\log(2m) < n < r$, one input at a time, until the oracle $\mathcal{T}'$ is completely replaced with $\mathcal{T}''$ on inputs of length less than $r$. What remains to show is that $G$ is invariant to some degree under these modifications.

**Claim 2.** *For large enough* $\lambda$,

$$d_{TD}\left(G^{\mathcal{T}^1}(k), G^{\mathcal{T}^2}(k)\right) \leq \frac{3}{\lambda}.$$

*Proof.* In the oracles $\mathcal{T}^1$ and $\mathcal{T}^2$, only $\sigma_n^1$ and $\sigma_n^2$ differ. Both these oracles are unitaries that swap two states and, thus, have the structure required to apply Theorem 9. Specifically, setting $T = r$ and $\epsilon = \lambda$ in Theorem 9, we get that there exists an algorithm $\tilde{G}^{\mathcal{T}^1 \setminus \sigma_n^1}(k, |\psi_n^1\rangle^{\otimes q})$ that simulates $G^{\mathcal{T}^1}(k)$ without oracle access to $\sigma_n^1$, given $q := O(\frac{T^2}{\epsilon^2}) = O(r^2\lambda^2)$ copies of $|\psi_n^1\rangle$, yielding an output that is $(\frac{1}{\lambda})$-close in trace distance. Similarly, $\tilde{G}^{\mathcal{T}^2 \setminus \sigma_n^2}(k, |\psi_n^2\rangle^{\otimes q})$ simulates $G^{\mathcal{T}^2}(k)$ without oracle access to $\sigma_n^2$, given $q$ copies of $|\psi_n^2\rangle$, yielding an output that is $(\frac{1}{\lambda})$-close in trace distance.

Given that, for large enough $\lambda$,

$$d_{\mathsf{TD}}\left(|\psi_n^2\rangle^{\otimes q}, |\psi_n^1\rangle^{\otimes q}\right) \leq \frac{q}{m} < \frac{1}{\lambda},$$

and noting that $\mathcal{T}^1 \setminus \sigma_n^1$ is equivalent to $\mathcal{T}^2 \setminus \sigma_n^2$, we get

$$d_{\mathsf{TD}}\left(\tilde{G}^{\mathcal{T}^1 \setminus \sigma_n^1}\left(k, |\psi_n^1\rangle^{\otimes q}\right), \tilde{G}^{\mathcal{T}^2 \setminus \sigma_n^2}\left(k, |\psi_n^2\rangle^{\otimes q}\right)\right) \leq \frac{1}{\lambda}.$$

Therefore, by the triangle inequality, we have that for large enough $\lambda$,

$$d_{\mathsf{TD}}\left(G^{\mathcal{T}^1}(k), G^{\mathcal{T}^2}(k)\right) \leq \frac{3}{\lambda}.$$

□

**Claim 3.** *For large enough* $\lambda$,

$$\Pr_{\mathcal{T}',\mathcal{T}'' \leftarrow \mathbb{T}[\mathcal{T}_{\leq \log(2m)}]}\left[d_{TD}\left(G^{\mathcal{T}^2}(k), G^{\mathcal{T}^3}(k)\right) \geq \frac{1}{2^{2n}}\right] \leq 1/2^{2n}.$$

*Proof.* Notice $\sigma^2 = \sigma^3$ and $\mathcal{O}^2$ only differs from $\mathcal{O}^3$ on inputs starting with $(x^*, O'(x^*))$ or $(x^*, O''(x^*))$. Crucially, $O'(x^*)$ and $O''(x^*)$ are distributed uniformly at random and are of length $8n$. Therefore, to distinguish these two oracles, $G$ needs to do unstructured search for an input starting with $x^*$ that maps to a non-$\perp$ element.

The lower bound for unstructured search [10,36] states that $G$ cannot distinguish these two oracles with better than $O(\frac{r^2}{2^{8n}}) \leq \frac{1}{2^{4n}}$ probability for large enough $\lambda$. This probability is over the oracle distributions of $\mathcal{T}', \mathcal{T}''$ as well. The Markov inequality then gives for large enough $\lambda$:

$$\Pr_{\mathcal{T}',\mathcal{T}'' \leftarrow \mathbb{T}[\mathcal{T}_{\leq \log(2m)}]}\left[d_{\mathsf{TD}}\left(G^{\mathcal{T}^2}(k), G^{\mathcal{T}^3}(k)\right) \geq \frac{1}{2^{2n}}\right] \leq 1/2^{2n}.$$

□

**Claim 4.** *For large enough* $\lambda$,

$$d_{TD}\left(G^{\mathcal{T}^3}(k), G^{\mathcal{T}^4}(k)\right) \leq \frac{3}{\lambda}.$$

*Proof.* This follows in the same way as Claim 2. □

As a result of the past three claims and the triangle inequality, with probability $1 - \frac{1}{2^{2n}}$ over the distributions $\mathcal{T}', \mathcal{T}''$, we have for large enough $\lambda$,

$$\Pr\left[G^{\mathcal{T}^1}(k) = G^{\mathcal{T}^4}(k)\right] \geq 1 - \frac{7}{\lambda}. \quad (3)$$

We now argue that this inverse-polynomial difference must in fact be negligible. Notice that $\mathcal{T}^4 \in \mathbb{T}$ so by Lemma 7, $G^{\mathcal{T}^4}$ satisfies the correctness condition of a PRG. In other words, it is almost-deterministic, meaning it must output a fixed value except with negligible probability. Combining this with Eq. (3), we get that, with probability $1 - \frac{1}{2^{2n}}$ over the oracle distributions, $G^{\mathcal{T}^1}(k)$ and $G^{\mathcal{T}^4}(k)$ agree except with negligible probability.

Performing the same changes on every $\log(2m) < n < r$ and $x^* \in \{0,1\}^n$, we reach $\mathcal{T}''$. The union bound gives us that with probability

$$1 - \sum_{\log(2m)<n<r} \left( \sum_{x^* \in \{0,1\}^n} \frac{1}{2^{2n}} \right) > 1 - \sum_{\log(2m)<n<r} \frac{1}{2^n} > 1 - \frac{r}{2m}.$$

over the distribution of oracles $\mathcal{T}', \mathcal{T}''$, $G^{\mathcal{T}'}(k)$ and $G^{\mathcal{T}''}(k)$ agree except with negligible probability. More formally,

$$\Pr_{\mathcal{T}',\mathcal{T}'' \leftarrow \mathbb{T}[\mathcal{T}_{\leq \log(2m)}]}\left[G^{\mathcal{T}'}(k) = G^{\mathcal{T}''}(k)\right] \geq \left(1 - \frac{r}{2m}\right)(1 - \mathsf{negl}(\lambda)) \geq 1 - \frac{r}{m}.$$

*Remark 1.* It may seem problematic that our argument involves exponentially many hybrids, where each differs from its neighbor with some negligible error. Why don't the errors accumulate and become non-negligible? This issue is mitigated by the almost-determinism property of PRGs, which guarantees that the most likely output must be produced with $1 - \mathsf{negl}(\lambda)$ probability. As a result, the output cannot be gradually altered across the hybrids.

□

By Lemma 8, for any $k \in \{0,1\}^\lambda$, there exists a string $y_k^{\mathcal{T}_{\leq \log(2m)}}$, such that

$$\Pr_{\tilde{\mathcal{T}} \leftarrow \mathbb{T}[\mathcal{T}_{\leq \log(2m)}]}\left[G^{\tilde{\mathcal{T}}}(k) = y_k^{\mathcal{T}_{\leq \log(2m)}}\right] \geq 1 - \frac{r}{m} \geq 1 - \frac{1}{\lambda^4}. \quad (4)$$

Furthermore, note that $G$ should not depend on $\mathcal{C}$, since the $\mathsf{PRF^{qs}}$ given in Lemma 7 does not rely on $\mathcal{C}$ (only on $\mathcal{O}$ and $\sigma$) and $G$ is based on a black-box construction from this $\mathsf{PRF^{qs}}$.

We now consider a generator $\overline{G}$ that does not depend on the oracles, and is defined as follows on inputs of length $\lambda + 16m^3$:

$\overline{G}(k)$:

- Parse $k$ as $(k_1, k_2)$ where $k_1 \in \{0,1\}^\lambda$ and $k_2 \in \{0,1\}^{16m^3}$.
- Construct functions $(\sigma_n^{k_2}, \mathcal{O}_n^{k_2})_{n \le \log(2m)}$ in the same way as Construction 5 but with the randomness determined by $k_2$.
- For $j \in [\lambda]$ :
  1. For each $\log(2m) \le i \le r$, sample uniformly at random two $2r$-degree polynomials $\tilde{O}_i : \mathbb{F}_{2^i} \to \mathbb{F}_{2^{8i}}$ and $\tilde{P}_i : \mathbb{F}_{2^{2i}} \to \mathbb{F}_{2^i}$. Let $(\tilde{\sigma}_i, \tilde{\mathcal{O}}_i)$ be the resulting oracles.
  2. Run $G(k_1)$ and answer the queries as follows:
     (a) For a query $x$ of length $n \le \log(2m)$, respond using $(\sigma_n^{k_2}, \mathcal{O}_n^{k_2})$.
     (b) For a query $x$ of length $n > \log(2m)$, respond using $(\tilde{\sigma}_n, \tilde{\mathcal{O}}_n)$.
  3. Let $y_j$ be the result of $G(k_1)$.

  [1.]
- Set $y = \mathsf{vote}_\lambda(y_1, \ldots, y_\lambda)$.
- Output $(y, k_2)$.

Now consider the following variants of PRG security experiment.

- $\mathsf{Exp}_1^{\mathcal{A}}(\lambda)$:
  1. Sample oracle $\mathcal{T}$ as in Construction 5.
  2. $b \leftarrow \mathsf{Exp}^{\mathsf{PRG}}_{\mathcal{A}^{\mathcal{T}}, G^{\mathcal{T}}}(1^\lambda)$.
  3. Output $b$.
- $\mathsf{Exp}_2^{\mathcal{A}}(\lambda)$:
  1. Sample oracle $\mathcal{T}$ as in Construction 5.
  2. $b \leftarrow \mathsf{Exp}^{\mathsf{PRG}}_{\mathcal{A}^{\mathcal{T}_{\le \log(2m)}, \mathcal{C}}, G^{\mathcal{T}}}(1^\lambda)$. *Notice that $\mathcal{A}$ only has access to $\mathcal{T}_{\le \log(2m)}$ in this experiment.*
  3. Output $b$.
- $\mathsf{Exp}_3^{\mathcal{A}}(\lambda)$:
  1. $b \leftarrow \mathsf{Exp}^{\mathsf{PRG}}_{\mathcal{A}^{\mathcal{C}}, \overline{G}}(1^\lambda)$.
  2. Output $b$.

By Claim 1, for any QPT adversary $\mathcal{A}$,

$$\Pr_{\mathcal{T} \leftarrow \mathbb{T}} \left[ \mathsf{Adtg}^{\mathsf{PRG}}_{\mathcal{A}^{\mathcal{T}}, G^{\mathcal{T}}}(1^\lambda) \le O\left(\frac{1}{\lambda^4}\right) \right] \ge \frac{3}{4}.$$

Therefore, for large enough $\lambda$,

$$\Pr\left[\mathsf{Exp}_1^{\mathcal{A}}(\lambda) = 1\right] - \frac{1}{2} \le \frac{1}{4} \cdot \frac{1}{2} + \frac{3}{4} \cdot \frac{1}{\lambda^3} \le \frac{1}{4} + \frac{1}{\lambda^2}.$$

Next, the only difference between $\mathsf{Exp}_1^{\mathcal{A}}(\lambda)$ and $\mathsf{Exp}_2^{\mathcal{A}}(\lambda)$ is that $\mathcal{A}$'s oracle access to $\mathcal{T}$ is restricted. Hence, for any QPT adversary $\mathcal{A}$, there exists a QPT $\mathcal{B}$ such that $\Pr\left[\mathsf{Exp}_2^{\mathcal{A}}(\lambda) = 1\right] \le \Pr\left[\mathsf{Exp}_1^{\mathcal{B}}(\lambda) = 1\right]$.

Finally, we need to relate the success probabilities of $\mathsf{Exp}_2^{\mathcal{A}}$ and $\mathsf{Exp}_3^{\mathcal{A}}$.

**Claim 5.** *For any QPT adversary $\mathcal{A}$ and large enough $\lambda$, there exists a QPT algorithm $\mathcal{B}$ such that*

$$\Pr\left[\mathit{Exp}_3^{\mathcal{A}}(\lambda) = 1\right] \leq \Pr\left[\mathit{Exp}_2^{\mathcal{B}}(\lambda) = 1\right] + \frac{1}{\lambda^4}.$$

*Proof.* Fix an adversary $\mathcal{A}$ in $\mathsf{Exp}_3^{\mathcal{A}}(\lambda)$. We construct an algorithm $\mathcal{B}$ in $\mathsf{Exp}_2^{\mathcal{B}}(\lambda)$ as follows.

In $\mathsf{Exp}_2^{\mathcal{B}}(\lambda)$, a random input $k_1 \leftarrow \{0,1\}^\lambda$ and a random bit $b \leftarrow \{0,1\}$ are sampled. Then, let $y_0 \leftarrow G^{\mathcal{T}}(k_1)$ and $y_1 \leftarrow \{0,1\}^s$. $\mathcal{B}^{\mathcal{T}_{\leq \log(2m)},\mathcal{C}}$ receives $y_b$ and must guess $b$.

$\mathcal{B}^{\mathcal{T}_{\leq \log(2m)},\mathcal{C}}$ commences as follows. For every $n \leq \log(2m)$, it queries $\sigma_n(|0^{9n+1}\rangle)$ $4m^2$ times and measures the result in the computational basis. This allows $\mathcal{B}$ to obtain all the evaluations of $O_n$ and learn the function entirely, except with negligible probability. Next, for each $n \leq \log(2m)$, $\mathcal{B}$ uses $O_n$ and the oracle $\mathcal{O}_n$ to learn $P_n$ entirely, which requires at most $2m$ queries.

$\mathcal{B}$ encodes $(P_n, O_n)_{n \leq \log(2m)}$ into a string, say $k_2$, of length less than $16m^3$. $\mathcal{B}$ runs $\mathcal{A}^{\mathcal{C}}$ on $(y_b, k_2)$ and receives a response $b'$. $\mathcal{B}$ outputs $b'$.

As long as $\mathcal{B}$ encodes $(P_n, O_n)_{n \leq \log(2m)}$ correctly (which occurs with $1 - \mathsf{negl}(\lambda)$ probability) and $\overline{G}(k_1, k_2) = y_0$ (which occurs with probability $1 - 2r/m$ by Eq. (4)), then it is clear that $\Pr\left[\mathsf{Exp}_2^{\mathcal{B}}(\lambda) = 1\right]$ is at least $\Pr\left[\mathsf{Exp}_3^{\mathcal{A}}(\lambda) = 1\right]$. Therefore,

$$\Pr\left[\mathsf{Exp}_2^{\mathcal{B}}(\lambda) = 1\right] \geq \Pr\left[\mathsf{Exp}_3^{\mathcal{A}}(\lambda) = 1\right](1 - \mathsf{negl}(\lambda))\left(1 - \frac{2r}{m}\right),$$

which implies, for large enough $\lambda$,

$$\Pr\left[\mathsf{Exp}_3^{\mathcal{A}}(\lambda) = 1\right] \leq \Pr\left[\mathsf{Exp}_2^{\mathcal{B}}(\lambda) = 1\right] + \frac{1}{\lambda^4}.$$

□

To sum up, for any QPT adversary $\mathcal{A}$, there exists a QPT algorithm $\mathcal{B}$ and large enough $\lambda$ such that

$$\Pr\left[\mathsf{Exp}_3^{\mathcal{A}}(\lambda) = 1\right] \leq \Pr\left[\mathsf{Exp}_2^{\mathcal{B}}(\lambda) = 1\right] + \frac{1}{\lambda^4} \leq \frac{3}{4} + \frac{1}{\lambda^2} + \frac{1}{\lambda^4} \leq \frac{3}{4} + \frac{1}{\lambda} \quad (5)$$

Notice that $\mathsf{Exp}_3^{\mathcal{A}}(\lambda)$ is just the PRG security experiment for $\overline{G}$ against $\mathcal{A}^{\mathcal{C}}$. On the other hand, there exists a trivial search attack, using a PSPACE oracle, against PRG security, given that any polynomial-space quantum computations with classical inputs can be simulated using a PSPACE oracle. In particular, there exists an adversary $\overline{\mathcal{A}}$ such that

$$\Pr\left[\mathsf{Exp}_3^{\overline{\mathcal{A}}}(\lambda) = 1\right] \geq 1 - \mathsf{negl}(\lambda).$$

contradicting Eq. 5 above.

Therefore, there does not exist a fully black-box construction of a PRG from a $\mathsf{PRF}^{\mathsf{qs}}$. □

**Acknowledgment.** AI (ChatGPT) was used for basic language editing such as correcting grammar and spelling.

## References


1. Ananth, P., Gulati, A., Qian, L., Yuen, H.: Pseudorandom (function-like) quantum state generators: new definitions and applications. In: Theory of Cryptography: 20th International Conference, TCC 2022, Chicago, IL, USA, November 7–10, 2022, Proceedings, Part I, pp. 237–265. Springer (2022). https://doi.org/10.1007/978-3-031-22318-1_9
2. Ananth, P., Lin, Y.T., Yuen, H.: Pseudorandom strings from pseudorandom quantum states. In: arXiv preprint arXiv:2306.05613 (2023)
3. Ananth, P., Qian, L., Yuen, H.: Cryptography from pseudorandom quantum states. In: Advances in Cryptology–CRYPTO 2022: 42nd Annual International Cryptology Conference, CRYPTO 2022, Santa Barbara, CA, USA, August 15–18, 2022, Proceedings, Part I, pp. 208–236. Springer (2022). https://doi.org/10.1007/978-3-031-15802-5_8
4. Barhoush, M., Behera, A., Ozer, L., Salvail, L., Sattath, O.: Signatures from pseudorandom states via $\perp$-PRFs. arXiv:2311.00847 (2024)
5. Bartusek, J.: Secure quantum computation with classical communication. Cryptology ePrint Archive, Paper 2021/964 (2021). https://eprint.iacr.org/2021/964
6. Bartusek, J., Brakerski, Z., Vaikuntanathan, V.: Quantum state obfuscation from classical oracles. In: Proceedings of the 56th Annual ACM Symposium on Theory of Computing, pp. 1009–1017 (2024)
7. Bartusek, J., Kitagawa, F., Nishimaki, R., Yamakawa, T.: Obfuscation of pseudo-deterministic quantum circuits. In: Proceedings of the 55th Annual ACM Symposium on Theory of Computing, pp. 1567– 1578 (2023)
8. Behera, A., Brakerski, Z., Sattath, O., Shmueli, O.: Pseudorandomness with proof of destruction and applications. In: Cryptology ePrint Archive (2023)
9. Behera, A., Malavolta, G., Morimae, T., Mour, T., Yamakawa, T.: A new world in the depths of microcrypt: separating OWSGs and quantum money from QEFID. In: Annual International Conference on the Theory and Applications of Cryptographic Techniques, pp. 23–52. Springer (2025). https://doi.org/10.1007/978-3-031-91098-2_2
10. Bennett, C.H., Bernstein, E., Brassard, G., Vazirani, U.: Strengths and weaknesses of quantum computing. SIAM J. Comput. **26**(5), 1510–1523 (1997)
11. Bostanci, J., Chen, B., Nehoran, B.: Oracle separation between quantum commitments and quantum one-wayness. In: Annual International Conference on the Theory and Applications of Cryptographic Techniques, pp. 3–22. Springer (2025). https://doi.org/10.1007/978-3-031-91098-2_1
12. Brakerski, Z., Shmueli, O.: Scalable pseudorandom quantum states. In: Annual International Cryptology Conference, pp. 417–440. Springer (2020). https://doi.org/10.1007/978-3-030-56880-1_15
13. Cavalar, B., Goldin, E., Gray, M., Hall, P., Liu, Y., Pelecanos, A.: On the computational hardness of quantum one-wayness. arXiv preprint arXiv:2312.08363 (2023)
14. Chen, B., Coladangelo, A., Sattath, O.: The power of a single Haar random state: constructing and separating quantum pseudorandomness. arXiv preprint arXiv:2404.03295 (2024)

15. Chung, K.M., Goldin, E., Gray, M.: On central primitives for quantum cryptography with classical communication. In: Annual International Cryptology Conference, pp. 215–248. Springer (2024). https://doi.org/10.1007/978-3-031-68394-7_8
16. Coladangelo, A., Mutreja, S.: On black-box separations of quantum digital signatures from pseudorandom states. arXiv preprint arXiv:2402.08194 (2024)
17. Dodis, Y., Impagliazzo, R., Jaiswal, R., Kabanets, V.: Security amplification for *interactive* cryptographic primitives. In: Reingold, O. (ed.) TCC 2009. LNCS, vol. 5444, pp. 128–145. Springer, Heidelberg (2009). https://doi.org/10.1007/978-3-642-00457-5_9
18. Döttling, N., Malavolta, G., Pu, S.: A combinatorial approach to quantum random functions. In: Moriai, S., Wang, H. (eds.) ASIACRYPT 2020. LNCS, vol. 12492, pp. 614–632. Springer, Cham (2020). https://doi.org/10.1007/978-3-030-64834-3_21
19. Fefferman, B., Kimmel, S.: Quantum vs classical proofs and subset verification. arXiv preprint arXiv:1510.06750 (2015)
20. Goldin, E., Morimae, T., Mutreja, S., Yamakawa, T.: CountCrypt: quantum cryptography between QCMA and PP. arXiv preprint arXiv:2410.14792 (2024)
21. Goldreich, O., Goldwasser, S., Micali, S.: How to construct random functions. J. ACM **33**(4), 792–807 (1986). https://doi.org/10.1145/6490.6503
22. Impagliazzo, R., Rudich, S.: Limits on the provable consequences of one-way permutations. In: Proceedings of the Twenty-First Annual ACM Symposium on Theory of Computing, pp. 44–61 (1989)
23. Ji, Z., Liu, Y.-K., Song, F.: Pseudorandom quantum states. In: Shacham, H., Boldyreva, A. (eds.) CRYPTO 2018. LNCS, vol. 10993, pp. 126–152. Springer, Cham (2018). https://doi.org/10.1007/978-3-319-96878-0_5
24. Khurana, D., Tomer, K.: Commitments from quantum onewayness. In: Proceedings of the 56th Annual ACM Symposium on Theory of Computing, pp. 968–978 (2024)
25. Kretschmer, W.: Quantum pseudorandomness and classical complexity. In: 16th Conference on the Theory of Quantum Computation, Communication and Cryptography (2021)
26. Kretschmer, W., Qian, L., Tal, A.: Quantum-computable one-way functions without one-way functions. arXiv preprint arXiv:2411.02554 (2024)
27. Ma, F., Huang, H.Y.: How to construct random unitaries. arXiv preprint arXiv:2410.10116 (2024)
28. Mahmoody, M., Mohammed, A., Nematihaji, S., Pass, R., et al.: A note on black-box separations for indistinguishability obfuscation. In: Cryptology ePrint Archive (2016)
29. Morimae, T., Yamada, S., Yamakawa, T.: Quantum unpredictability. Cryptology ePrint Archive, Paper 2024/701 (2024). https://eprint.iacr.org/2024/701
30. Morimae, T., Yamakawa, T.: One-wayness in quantum cryptography. arXiv preprint arXiv:2210.03394 (2022)
31. Morimae, T., Yamakawa, T.: Quantum commitments and signatures without one-way functions. In: Advances in Cryptology–CRYPTO 2022: 42nd Annual International Cryptology Conference, CRYPTO 2022, Santa Barbara, CA, USA, August 15–18, 2022, Proceedings, Part I, pp. 269–295. Springer (2022). https://doi.org/10.1007/978-3-031-15802-5_10
32. Nielsen, M.A., Chuang, I.L.: Quantum Computation and Quantum Information. Cambridge University Press, New York (2000). https://doi.org/10.1017/CBO9780511976667
33. Saito, T., Xagawa, K., Yamakawa, T.: Tightly-secure key-encapsulation mechanism in the quantum random oracle model. In: Nielsen, J.B., Rijmen, V. (eds.) EURO-

CRYPT 2018. LNCS, vol. 10822, pp. 520–551. Springer, Cham (2018). https://doi.org/10.1007/978-3-319-78372-7_17
34. Unruh, D.: Computationally binding quantum commitments. In: Fischlin, M., Coron, J.-S. (eds.) EUROCRYPT 2016. LNCS, vol. 9666, pp. 497–527. Springer, Heidelberg (2016). https://doi.org/10.1007/978-3-662-49896-5_18
35. Unruh, D.: Quantum proofs of knowledge. In: Annual International Conference on the Theory and Applications of Cryptographic Techniques, pp. 135–152. Springer (2012). https://doi.org/10.1007/978-3-642-29011-4_10
36. Zalka, C.: Grover's quantum searching algorithm is optimal. Phys. Rev. A **60**(4), 2746 (1999)
37. Zhandry, M.: How to construct quantum random functions. In: IEEE 53rd Annual Symposium on Foundations of Computer Science, pp. 679–687. IEEE (2012)
38. Zhandry, M.: Schrödinger's pirate: how to trace a quantum decoder. In: Theory of Cryptography: 18th International Conference, TCC 2020, Durham, NC, USA, November 16–19, 2020, Proceedings, Part III 18, pp. 61–91. Springer (2020). https://doi.org/10.1007/978-3-030-64381-2_3

# Game-Theoretically Fair Coin Toss with Arbitrary Preferences

Forest Zhang and Ke Wu(✉)

University of Michigan, Ann Arbor, USA
{forestz,kewucse}@umich.edu

**Abstract.** Fair multi-party coin toss protocols are fundamental to many cryptographic applications. While Cleve's celebrated result (STOC'86) showed that strong fairness is impossible against half-sized coalitions, recent works have explored a relaxed notion of fairness called Cooperative-Strategy-Proofness (CSP-fairness). CSP-fairness ensures that no coalition has an incentive to deviate from the protocol. Previous research has established the feasibility of CSP-fairness against majority-sized coalitions, but these results focused on specific preference structures where each player prefers exactly one outcome out of all possible choices. In contrast, real-world scenarios often involve players with more complicated preference structures, rather than simple binary choices.

In this work, we initiate the study of CSP-fair multi-party coin toss protocols that accommodate arbitrary preference profiles, where each player may have an unstructured utility distribution over all possible outcomes. We demonstrate that CSP-fairness is attainable against majority-sized coalitions even under arbitrary preferences. In particular, we give the following results:

- We give a reduction from achieving CSP-fairness for arbitrary preference profiles to achieving CSP-fairness for structured split-bet profiles, where each player distributes the same amount of total utility across all outcomes.
- We present two CSP-fair protocols: (1) a *size-based protocol*, which defends against majority-sized coalitions, and (2) a *bets-based protocol*, which defends against coalitions controlling a majority of the total utilities.
- Additionally, we establish an impossibility result for CSP-fair binary coin toss with split-bet preferences, showing that our protocols are nearly optimal.

**Keywords:** Coin-toss protocol · game-theoretic fairness

## 1 Introduction

Good friends Alice and Bob want to spend Christmas together in 2025. They are deciding between three locations: Los Angeles (Alice's city), New York (Bob's

---

The full version of this paper is available on Cryptology ePrint Archive.
Author order is randomized.

© International Association for Cryptologic Research 2026
G. Hanaoka and B.-Y. Yang (Eds.): ASIACRYPT 2025, LNCS 16252, pp. 549–581, 2026.
https://doi.org/10.1007/978-981-95-5125-5_18

city), and Dallas (midpoint). However, due to the long flight, their preferences differ: Alice prefers Los Angeles over Dallas over New York, while Bob ranks them in the reverse order. To ensure fairness, they agree to select a destination via a random ternary coin toss: 0 for Los Angeles, 1 for Dallas, and 2 for New York. But how can they remotely decide a *fair* ternary coin?

The problem of fairly tossing a coin among multiple players is formulated as *coin toss protocol*. A rich body of work [2,7,8,10,12,17,18,22,23,33] has focused on achieving *strong fairness* in coin toss protocols, which guarantees that an adversary controlling a set of corrupted players cannot bias the outcome towards *any* direction by a non-negligible amount. It is well known that when the adversary controls less than half of the players, strong fairness is attainable via standard multi-party computation [21,32,37]. However, the impossibility result by Cleve [17] showed that strong fairness becomes impossible if the adversary controls half of the players. Specifically, in Alice and Bob's case, if either deviates from the protocol, they always have a strategy to bias the outcome.

Fortunately, this is not the end of the story. Despite Cleve's impossibility result, Alice and Bob can still use a variant of Blum's coin toss protocol [11]: They each flip a private uniform ternary coin and post the commitments of the private coin to a public bulletin board (such as blockchains). Then they each open the commitments, and the outcome is the sum of the two coins modulo 3. If either fails to post a commitment or opens its commitment incorrectly, they forfeit, and the outcome defaults to the city where the other player lives. While this protocol does not achieve strong fairness since a player can always refuse to open its commitment and bias the outcome, it does achieve meaningful fairness in a *game-theoretic* sense: A rational player has no incentive to deviate from the protocol, as doing so only reduces their utility.

*Game-Theoretic Fairness.* Surprisingly, this natural notion of game-theoretic fairness was only recently formalized by Chung, Guo, Lin, Pass, and Shi [16]. They introduced *Cooperative-strategy-Proofness*, or CSP-fairness for short. Specifically, they considered $N$-party binary coin toss where each of the $N$ players has a *publicly known* preference for either heads or tails. Each player gets utility 1 if the outcome matches their preference and 0 otherwise. CSP-fairness requires that any $t$-sized coalition cannot increase its expected utility compared to the honest behavior by deviating from the prescribed protocol. Previous works characterized (in)feasibility of CSP-fairness for binary [16,36] and multi-sided coin toss [35], where each player has a public preference of *exactly one* outcome. It is observed that while CSP-fairness is achievable against half or more-sized coalitions, the landscape is starkly different from that of strong fairness. The coalition resilience of CSP-fairness heavily relies on the actual preferences of the players: If all but one players share the same preference, CSP-fairness can be achieved against any $(N-1)$-sized coalition; if every outcome is preferred by the same number of players, only a half-sized coalition can be tolerated.

*Our Work: Arbitrary Preference Profile.* In many practical applications, players do not simply prefer one outcome; rather, they have ranked or even arbitrary utilities across outcomes. For example, imagine a community wishing to jointly decide on a random facility location from $m$ candidates. Instead of preferring only one location, each member ranks different locations based on distance: the closer the facility, the higher the utility they get. Another example is on-chain roulette, where players stake bets on specific outcomes. Each player may put varying bets on different outcomes and receive different payoffs depending on their stake allocation. In all these examples, players' preferences are public and non-binary. To capture these practical applications, we initiate the study of CSP-fairness for arbitrary preferences and address the following question:

*Can we build CSP-fair multi-party coin toss protocols for arbitrary preference profiles against majority-sized coalitions?*

### 1.1 Our Contributions

Our work initiates the study of game-theoretic fairness for arbitrary preferences, making both conceptual and technical contributions. On the conceptual side, we introduce two formulations of preferences that capture natural preference structures, and show that each formulation can be reduced to the other when it comes to achieving CSP-fairness against majority-sized coalitions. On the technical side, we give two multi-sided coin toss protocols: One achieves CSP-fairness against majority-sized coalitions and the other against coalitions controlling a majority of total utility. Additionally, we establish an impossibility result for binary coin toss protocols to better characterize the landscape of CSP-fairness.

To describe our main results, we briefly introduce the model. Consider $N$ number of players jointly tossing a uniform $m$-sided coin. Each player $i$'s preference $\mathbf{p}_i$ is a vector of length $m$, the $\ell$-th entry of which is player $i$'s utility if the outcome is $\ell$. We also say that a player places $x$ *bets* on an outcome $\ell$ if the player gets utility $x$ when the protocol outputs $\ell$. In this paper, we may use *bets* and utility interchangeably. We also assume non-negative integer utilities (see Sect. 1.2 for a discussion of generalizing to negative or fractional utilities). A preference profile is thus all players preferences $(\mathbf{p}_1, ..., \mathbf{p}_N)$. A player's total bet is the sum of its bets across all outcomes.

Some players together form a coalition $\mathcal{C}$, and their joint utility is the sum of every coalition member's utility. A coalition prefers an outcome if its joint utility on that outcome exceeds its honest expected joint utility. We say that a protocol is CSP-fair for a preference profile $\boldsymbol{\mathcal{P}}$ iff any $t$-sized coalition cannot increase their expected utility by a non-negligible amount compared to their honest expected utility.

Designing CSP-fair protocols for arbitrary preference profiles against majority-sized coalitions is inherently challenging, as no structure can be assumed on the profile. To address this, we showed that designing CSP-fair protocols for arbitrary preference profiles can be reduced to designing CSP-fair protocols for well-structured preference profiles. Formally, we define:

- **Arbitrary-bet** $\mathcal{F}_{\mathsf{arb}}(N, m)$: In this formulation, each of the $N$ players can put arbitrary non-negative integer bets on different outcomes $\{0, ..., m-1\}$.

- **Split-bet** $\mathcal{F}_{\mathsf{split}}(N, m)$: In this formulation, each player has $B$ total bet that can be distributed across the $m$ possible outcomes.

The preference profiles considered in previous works are a specific example of split-bet where $B = 1$. A direct generalization would be *unit-split* where each player chooses $B$ out of $m$ possible outcomes, and gets utility 1 for each chosen outcome and 0 otherwise. Another concrete example is *ranked preference profiles*, which are also captured by the split-bet framework with $B = m(m-1)/2$: Each player assigns $m-1$ utility on the most preferred outcome, $m-2$ to the second preference, until 0 on the least preferred outcome.

**Theorem 1.1** (Reducing arbitrary preference profile to split-bet). *Fix any $N$ and $m$. There is an efficient mapping $\mathcal{T} : \mathcal{F}_{\mathsf{arb}}(N, m) \mapsto \mathcal{F}_{\mathsf{split}}(N, m)$ such that for any arbitrary-bet preference profile $\mathcal{P} \in \mathcal{F}_{\mathsf{arb}}(N, m)$, a CSP-fair protocol $\Pi$ for $\mathcal{P}$ against $t$-sized coalition exists if there is a CSP-fair protocol $\Pi'$ for $\mathcal{T}(\mathcal{P})$ against $t$-sized coalition.*

By Theorem 1.1, we only need to focus on building CSP-fair protocols for split-bet profiles. We use *cumulative bet* of an outcome $\ell$ to denote the sum of all players' bets on $\ell$. Without loss of generality, we assume that 0 is the least preferred outcome, i.e., 0 has the lowest cumulative bet.[1] Our main result shows that, except in the special case where all outcomes receive exactly the same cumulative bet, CSP-fairness is attainable against $N/2$-sized coalitions.

**Theorem 1.2** (CSP-fairness, informal). *Assuming the existence of oblivious transfer (OT). There exists a CSP-fair $m$-sided $N$-party coin toss protocol for split-bet preference profile against $t$-sized malicious coalitions. Unless all outcomes are equally preferred, $t \geq N/2$.*[2]

To achieve the above coalition resilience, we present two protocols: the *size-based protocol*, which achieves CSP-fairness against coalitions based on their size, and the *bets-based protocol*, which achieves CSP-fairness against coalitions based on their total bet. While these two metrics are equivalent for split-bet preference profiles, each protocol outperforms the other in different scenarios depending on the preference structure. Below, we first give the general coalition resilience achieved by both protocols and compare their performance on the concrete unit-split and ranked preference profiles for a better understanding.

*Size-Based Protocol.* Let $n_j$ be the number of players with $j$ bets on outcome 0 and $\mu = \frac{B}{m}$ be the honest expected utility of each player. Then $N_0 = \sum_{i>\mu} n_i$ represents the number of players who prefer outcome 0, called the 0-supporters, and $N_{\mathsf{oth}} = \sum_{i\leq\mu} n_i$ is the number of players who prefer other outcomes, called

[1] When there are multiple least preferred outcomes, break ties arbitrarily. All our protocols and fairness guarantees hold regardless of which one is chosen.

[2] In rare cases, $t = \lfloor N/2 \rfloor$ for odd $N$ due to rounding effects. This happens only when the cumulative bets on all outcomes are almost the same. Similar rounding effects have also been observed in [35,36].

the oth-supporters. We sort the 0-supporters and the oth-supporters separately based on the decreasing order of their bets on 0 (break ties arbitrarily).

Let $S$ denote the set of $0 \leq \gamma \leq N_{\mathsf{oth}}$ such that the last $N_{\mathsf{oth}} - \gamma$ number of oth-supporters together with all $N_0$ number of 0-supporters do *not* prefer 0. Let $\gamma_0 = N_{\mathsf{oth}}$, and $\gamma_i = \gamma_{i-1} - n_{i-1}$ be the sequence of "margins" among the oth-supporters. See Fig. 1 for an illustrative example.

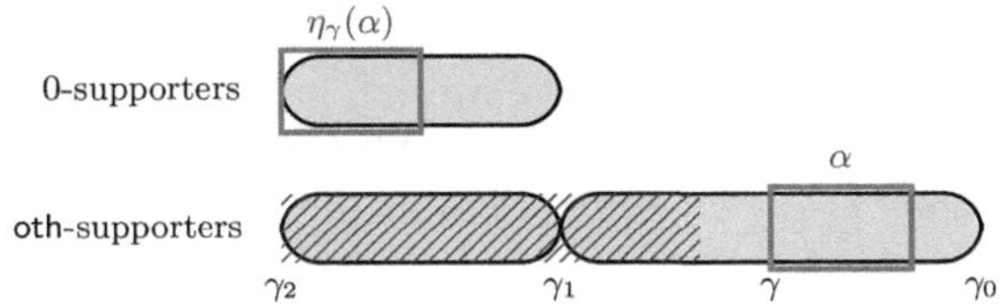


**Fig. 1.** Illustration of a split-bet preference profile with $B = 2$. The green and orange bar each sorts the 0- and oth-supporters according to their bets on 0 in the decreasing order, respectively. Each chunk represents players with the same bets on 0. The first orange chunk bets 1 on outcome 0, and the last chunk puts no bets on 0. The $\gamma_i$' (Color figure online)s are the margins of these chunks. The shaded area represents the set $S$. A coalition containing all players in the two blue rectangles does not prefer 0.

Let $\eta_\gamma(\alpha)$ be the largest number such that the first $\eta_\gamma(\alpha)$ number of 0-supporters together with the $(\gamma+1)$-th to the $(\gamma+\alpha)$-th oth-supporter does *not* prefer 0, as illustrated in Fig. 1. We set $\eta_\gamma(\alpha) = \infty$ if all $N_0$ of the 0-supporters together with the $(\gamma+1)$-th to the $(\gamma+\alpha)$-th oth-supporter do not prefer 0. Let $\mathsf{opt}(\gamma) := \arg\min_\alpha |N_{\mathsf{oth}} + \frac{N_0}{2} - \frac{\gamma}{2} - 2\alpha - \eta_\gamma(\alpha)|$.

**Theorem 1.3** (Feasibility against corrupted size). *Assume oblivious transfer (OT) exists. If $\eta_0(\lfloor N_{\mathsf{oth}}/2 \rfloor) > N_0/2 + 1$, there exists a CSP-fair $m$-sided coin toss protocol against any $t$-sized malicious coalitions where*

$$N/2 \leq t = \max_{\gamma_i \in S} \left\{ \left\lfloor N_{\mathsf{oth}} + \frac{N_0}{2} - \frac{\gamma_i}{2} - \mathsf{opt}(\gamma_i) \right\rfloor \right\}. \quad (1)$$

As illustrated in the ternary ranked preference example in Table 6, the optimal resilience is achieved at different $\gamma_i \in S$, depending on the actual profiles. Therefore, no single $\gamma^*$ universally maximizes the coalition resilience across all possible preference profiles.

In the above theorem, the condition $\eta_0(\lfloor N_{\mathsf{oth}}/2 \rfloor) > N_0/2 + 1$ intuitively means that the first half of 0-supporters and the first half of oth-supporters together do *not* prefer 0. This generally holds except when there is a large number of "swing" oth-supporters whose bets on 0 are close to $\mu$. In such cases, this protocol may only defend against minority-sized coalitions. Later comparisons show that when the number of swing oth-supporters is large, this protocol is no better than the bets-based protocol described below.

While we follow the traditional threshold-based model for coalition tolerance, our protocol can in fact tolerate larger-sized coalitions as long as the coalition members' preferences satisfy certain structural conditions. The formal structural characterization is given in Constraints 5.5.

*Bets-Based Protocol.* An alternative approach is to measure coalition resilience based on the total bet controlled by the coalition rather than the number of players. A coalition's total bet is the sum of all members' total bet. A protocol is CSP-fair against coalitions of total bet $\beta$ if any coalition controlling at most $\beta$ total bet cannot increase its expected joint utility by deviating. We use $B_\ell$ to represent the cumulative bet on outcome $\ell$ and $B_{\mathsf{oth}} = \sum_{\ell \neq 0} B_\ell$ represents the sum of the cumulative bet on all other outcomes. As before, without loss of generality, we assume 0 is the least preferred outcome, i.e., $B_0 \leq \frac{1}{m-1} B_{\mathsf{oth}}$.

**Theorem 1.4** (Feasibility against corrupted bets). *Assuming the existence of oblivious transfer (OT). There exists a CSP-fair $m$-sided coin toss protocol against any malicious coalition controlling at most $\beta$ total bet, where*

$$\beta = \begin{cases} B_{\mathsf{oth}} + \left\lceil \frac{1}{2} B_0 \right\rceil - (m-1) B_0, & \text{if } B_{\mathsf{oth}} \geq \frac{4m-3}{2} B_0 \\ \left\lfloor \frac{m}{2m-1} B_{\mathsf{oth}} + \frac{m}{2(2m-1)} B_0 \right\rfloor, & \text{otherwise.} \end{cases} \quad (2)$$

*Unless the profile is perfectly balanced, $\beta \geq (B_0 + B_{\mathsf{oth}})/2$.*

*For a split-bet preference profile where each player has $B$ total bet, this protocol defends against any $t$-sized coalition where $t = \lfloor \beta / B \rfloor$.*

The bets-based protocol can be used directly on arbitrary preference profiles to defend against coalitions controlling majority bets. However, if used directly, it may fail to tolerate majority-*sized* coalition since a few players with large bet could collectively control more than $\beta$ total bet. Therefore, to achieve CSP-fairness against majority-sized coalitions for arbitrary preference profiles $\mathcal{P}$, one should first transform $\mathcal{P}$ to a split-bet profile $\mathcal{T}(\mathcal{P})$ as in Theorem 1.1 and then apply one of our two protocols on $\mathcal{T}(\mathcal{P})$.

Similar to our size-based protocol, this bets-based protocol can in fact achieve fairness against coalitions controlling more bets than the above stated threshold as long as the coalitions members' bets satisfy certain structural conditions, as formally stated in Constraints 6.4.

*Comparison of the Two Protocols.* When the number of swing oth-supporters is small relative to the total number of players, the size-based protocol offers stronger resilience. However, when many swing oth-supporters are present, the bets-based protocol provides better resilience. Below, we give the resilience of both protocols for some concrete examples for comparison.

**Unit-split.** Each player chooses $B < m$ out of $m$ outcomes and gets utility 1 on each chosen outcome. In this case, we have $B_0 = N_0$ and $B_{\mathsf{oth}} = B \cdot N - N_0$. For unit-split, the size-based protocol is always better than the bets-based protocol (Table 1), as this formulation has no swing oth-supporters. The coalition resilience is always at least $N/2$.

**Ternary ranked preference.** Each player has a rank over the three possible outcomes. Each player gets utility 2 on the most preferred outcome, utility 1 on the second preferred outcome, and 0 on the least preferred outcome. Recall that

$n_i$ is the number of players with bets $i$ on outcome 0. Here, the $n_1$ players with bets 1 on outcome 0 are those swing oth-supporters.

From Table 2, one can see that when $n_0$ is much larger than $n_1 + n_2$, the size-based protocol performs better; when $n_0 \leq n_1 + n_2$, the bets-based protocol achieves better resilience.

**Table 1.** Optimal resilience for unit-bet.

| Case | Size-based protocol (Theorem 1.3) | Bets-based protocol (Theorem 1.4) |
|---|---|---|
| $N_{\mathsf{oth}} \geq \frac{4m-3B}{2B} N_0$ | $N_{\mathsf{oth}} + \lceil \frac{2B-m}{2B} N_0 \rceil$ | $N_{\mathsf{oth}} + \lfloor \frac{2B-2m+1}{2B} \rfloor N_0$ |
| Otherwise | $\lfloor \frac{m}{2m-B} N_{\mathsf{oth}} + \frac{m}{2(2m-B)} N_0 \rfloor$ | $\lfloor \frac{m}{2m-1} N_{\mathsf{oth}} + \frac{2m-m/B}{2(2m-1)} N_0 \rfloor$ |

**Table 2.** Optimal resilience for ternary ranked preference.

| Size-based protocol (Theorem 1.3) | | Bets-based protocol (Theorem 1.4) | |
|---|---|---|---|
| Case | resilience | Case | resilience |
| $n_0 \geq \frac{5}{2} n_2 - \frac{1}{2} n_1$ | $\lfloor n_0 + \frac{1}{2} n_1 - \frac{1}{2} n_2 \rfloor$ | $n_0 \geq \frac{5}{6} n_1 + \frac{8}{3} n_2$ | $\lfloor n_0 + \frac{1}{6} n_1 - \frac{2}{3} n_2 \rfloor$ |
| $n_1 + n_2 \leq n_0 < \frac{5}{2} n_2 - \frac{1}{2} n_1$ | $\lfloor \frac{2}{3} n_0 + \frac{1}{3} n_1 + \frac{1}{3} n_2 \rfloor$ | Otherwise | $\lfloor \frac{3}{5} n_0 + \frac{1}{2} n_1 + \frac{2}{5} n_2 \rfloor$ |
| Otherwise | $\lceil N/2 \rceil - 1$ | | |

*Impossibility.* To complement our protocols, we also give an impossibility result for binary split-bet preference profiles. As before, without loss of generality, we assume that 0 is the least preferred outcome.

**Theorem 1.5** (Impossibility for binary split-bet). *Let $N_0$ and $N_1$ denote the number of 0-supporters and 1-supporters, respectively. Given a preference profile $\mathcal{P} \in \mathcal{F}_{\mathsf{split}}(N, 2)$, there is no CSP-fair binary coin toss protocol against t-sized semi-malicious coalition for*

$$t \geq \max\{N_1 + \lceil N_0/2 \rceil - \theta^*, \gamma' + \lceil N_0/2 \rceil\},$$

*where $\gamma'$ is smallest value such that $\eta_0(\gamma') > N_0/2$, and $\theta^*$ is the maximum number such that $2\theta + \lceil (\eta_\theta(\theta) + 1)/2 \rceil \leq N_1$.*

When $N_1$ is much larger than $N_0$, this impossibility result is tight except for a gap of at most $\lceil \theta^*/2 \rceil + 2$. Specifically, our impossibility is optimal when the first $2\theta^* + 2$ number of 1-supporters have the same bets on 0. In the worst case, it is tight up to only a constant multiplicative factor.

### 1.2 Applicability of Our Model.

Our model aims to initiate a formal understanding of CSP-fairness for general preference structure in settings where (1) each player has a non-negative integer utility for each outcome, and (2) a coalition's utility is the sum of its members' utilities. We believe these assumptions capture many practical settings. Below, we elaborate on the modeling choices and their implications.

- **Extension to negative or fractional utilities**: Our non-negative integer utility assumption reflects many practical scenarios where utility represents divisible resources—such as tokens, currency, or physical items with minimal granularity. Meanwhile, our results can be extended to a broader range of utilities as long as the linear transformation $\mathcal{T}$ in Theorem 1.1 can be efficiently computed. This only requires the utilities to be encoded using a polynomial number of bits, allowing negative or fractional utilities.
- **On coalition's joint utility**: Like prior works, we adopt the model where a coalition's joint utility is the sum of its members' utilities. This additive view again fits the settings where utilities correspond to divisible and transferable goods, such as monetary rewards or stake outcomes. In such cases, a coalition aims to increase its total utility to redistribute the total wealth to make every member strictly happier.
  This approach inherently emphasizes the numerical scale since players with higher bets contribute more to the coalition's joint utility. In contrast, there are contexts where players express normalized or ordinal preferences and scale invariance is desired. We emphasize that our framework can accommodate such settings through rescaling. If all players are to be treated equally, utilities can be transformed into a split-bet profile where each player distributes an equal total bet across outcomes. We leave the complete characterization of fairness under alternative notions of coalition utility that may enforce scale invariance or other desiderata as a promising future direction.

### 1.3 Additional Related Work

Game-theoretic fairness has also been studied in the context of leader election [14,15,26,28] where $N$ players want to jointly elect a random leader. Previous work [15,16,26,28,36] also studied another form of game-theoretic fairness called maximin fairness, which requires that the coalition cannot harm honest users. With the recent progress on blockchains and decentralized finance, another line of work has focused on financial fairness [3,6,9,13,20,29–31], where players' collateral is used to punish misbehavior. Interestingly, our work and previous works on game-theoretic fairness achieve fairness without collateral.

The connection between game theory and multi-party computation is not new [1,4,5,19,24,25,27,34]. However, this line of work considers a rather different utility structure: it assumes that players prefer to get the correct outcome and learn others' secrets without leaking their own secrets.

**Organization.** In Sect. 2, we give a technical overview. The preliminaries and formal model are introduced in Sect. 3. In Sect. 4, we establish a reduction from arbitrary preference profiles to split-bet preferences. We present our two CSP-fair coin toss protocols in Sect. 5 and Sect. 6. Section 7 gives the characterization for some concrete examples. The impossibility result and upgrade to malicious security are given in the full version.

## 2 Technical Overview

In this section, we outline the main techniques for achieving CSP-fairness against semi-malicious coalitions using a binary coin toss as an example. All of our feasibility results can be generalized to multi-sided coin tosses with techniques from [35]. A semi-malicious coalition can program its randomness used in the protocol or abort early, but otherwise follows the protocol honestly. Our protocols against semi-malicious adversaries achieve information-theoretic security, and can be upgraded to malicious security using standard cryptographic techniques.

We organize this section as follows. Section 2.1 explains how to reduce arbitrary preferences to split-bet preferences. We then illustrate the high-level idea of the two protocols and the technical challenges in Sect. 2.2 and Sect. 2.3. The impossibility is discussed in Sect. 2.4.

*Notations.* We use $N_0$ to denote the number of 0-supporters who prefers outcome 0 and $N_1$ denote the number of 1-supporters who do not prefer 0. We also use $B_0$ and $B_1$ to denote the cumulative bet on 0 and on 1, respectively. Additionally, $B$ is used to denote the total bet each player can distribute. For a player $i$, we use $\mathbf{p}_i = (\mathsf{bet}_i(0), \mathsf{bet}_i(1))$ to denote player $i$'s preference where $\mathsf{bet}_i(b)$ is player $i$'s bets on outcome $b$. A preference profile $\mathcal{P} = (\mathbf{p}_1, ..., \mathbf{p}_N)$ is the preference of all $N$ players. We will sort the 0-supporters and 1-supporters separately in decreasing order based on their bets on 0, breaking ties arbitrarily.

### 2.1 Reducing Arbitrary Preference To Split-Bet

Given an arbitrary preference profile $\mathcal{P}$, our goal is to find an efficient transformation $\mathcal{T}$ that maps $\mathcal{P}$ to a split-bet preference profile such that we can build CSP-fair protocols for $\mathcal{P}$ from any CSP-fair protocol for $\mathcal{T}(\mathcal{P})$ while maintaining the same coalition resilience.

A naive approach is to map a 0-supporter's preference to $(1, 0)$ and a 1-supporter's preference to $(0, 1)$, and then apply the protocol from [36]. However, this fails to preserve coalition preferences, which is crucial for CSP-fairness. Consider a preference profile $\mathcal{P} = ((1, 0), (1, 0), (0, 4))$ of two 0-supporters and one 1-supporter as an example. If mapped naively, the resulting profile would be $\mathcal{P}' = ((1, 0), (1, 0), (0, 1))$. However, a coalition $\mathcal{C}$ containing the 1-supporter and one of the 0-supporters will prefer outcome 1 in $\mathcal{P}$ but does not prefer any outcome in $\mathcal{P}'$. Consequently, a CSP-fair protocol for $\mathcal{P}'$ could allow $\mathcal{C}$ to bias the outcome towards 1 without violating fairness, but such a strategy will surely increase the coalition's expected utility with respect to $\mathcal{P}$.

Therefore, to ensure fairness, the transformation must preserve every coalition's preference. We achieve this by enforcing *linearity*. Specifically, each player's preference profile $\mathbf{p}_i$ is mapped to

$$\mathbf{p}'_i = 2 \cdot \mathbf{p}_i + \mathbf{b}_i.$$

Here, 2 is a global scaling factor across all players and $\mathbf{b}_i$ is a length-2 shift vector where each entry equals $b_i$, the maximum total bet among all players minus player $i$'s total bet. Intuitively, linear transformations preserve coalition preferences because a coalition's joint preference is fundamentally a linear combination of all coalition members' preferences. We choose 2 as the global scaling factor to guarantee that all players' total bets after the mapping become the same, since the shift vector $\mathbf{b}_i$ increases player $i$'s total bet by $2 \cdot b_i$ (for general $m$-sided coin toss, this scaling factor will be $m$). After the transformation, every player's total bet becomes $2\cdot$(maximum total bet among all players in $\mathcal{P}$). For example, $\mathcal{P} = ((1,0),(1,0),(0,4))$ will be mapped to $\mathcal{P}' = ((5,3),(5,3),(0,8))$. Unlike the naive approach, this transformation ensures that every coalition's preference remains consistent between $\mathcal{P}$ and $\mathcal{P}'$. With this preference-preserving transformation, we design CSP-fair protocol $\Pi$ for $\mathcal{P}$ as follows: the $N$ players together run a CSP-fair protocol $\Pi'$ for $\mathcal{P}' = (\mathbf{p}'_1, ..., \mathbf{p}'_N)$ where each player $i$ acts as if its preference is $\mathbf{p}'_i$. Since the transformation preserves coalition preferences, protocol $\Pi$ achieves CSP-fairness against any $t$-sized coalition for $\mathcal{P}$ if $\Pi'$ defends against any $t$-sized coalition for $\mathcal{P}'$.

### 2.2 CSP-Fairness Against Corrupted Size

Now we only need to focus on constructing CSP-fair protocols for split-bet profiles where each player distributes $B$ total bet across different outcomes. A natural starting point is to generalize the protocol from [36], which works for the special case of $B = 1$. They partition players into two groups: Group $G_0$ of the 0-supporters and $G_1$ of the 1-supporters. Each group runs the following sub-protocol $\mathsf{size\text{-}GroupToss}^G[k]$ to decide a coin $s_b$ for $b \in \{0,1\}$, where $G$ denotes the group running this sub-protocol and $k$ is a parameter to be specified later. The final outcome is then determined by the value of $s_0$ and $s_1$.

Several technical challenges arise when extending this protocol to general split-bet preference profiles:

- *Characterizing coalition preference.* In the special case where $B = 1$, a coalition's preference is $b$ iff $b$-supporters dominate in the coalition. However, for general split-bet profiles, a 1-supporter may also put bets on 0 and vice versa. Thus, a coalition's preference is no longer determined solely by the number of corrupted $b$-supporters but also by their bet distributions.
- *Partition of $G_0$ and $G_1$.* The trivial partition that places all $b$-supporters into group $G_b$ does not always give the optimal resilience. Instead, we need

to assign some of the "swing" 1-supporters to $G_0$. Swing 1-supporters are players who prefer outcome 1 but still put significant bets on 0. We revise the partition to ensure that players in $G_1$ are aggressive 1-supporters truly opposed to outcome 0. As we will later explain, this is crucial to achieve CSP-fairness against large coalitions.
- *Optimal choice of parameters.* We need to optimize the parameter $k$ in $\mathsf{size\text{-}GroupToss}^G[k]$ and the number of swing 1-supporters in $G_0$ to achieve the best coalition resilience. This results in a rather involved integer optimization problem, as we will elaborate on later.

Below, we describe the protocol and show how to address these challenges.

$\mathsf{size\text{-}GroupToss}^G[k]$ sub-protocol

**Sharing Phase.** Each player $i$ chooses a random coin $\mathsf{coin}_i \xleftarrow{\$} \{0,1\}$ and shares it using $(k+1)$-out-of-$|G|$ Shamir secret sharing into $\{c_{i,j}\}_{j \in G}$. Send $c_{i,j}$ to player $j$. If any players abort, remove them from $G$.

**Reconstruction Phase.** Every player $i$ computes the sum of the shares it received $c_i := \sum_{j \in G} c_{j.i}$ and broadcasts $c_i$. Players use the broadcast shares to reconstruct $s = \oplus_{i \in G} \mathsf{coin}_i$. If the reconstruction fails, set $s = \perp$; otherwise, output $s$.

By the security of Shamir secret sharing, this sub-protocol satisfies the following properties against coalition $\mathcal{C}$.

- *Binding.* The sharing phase uniquely binds to a secret $s$, such that the reconstruction either succeeds and outputs $s$, or it fails and outputs $\perp$.
- *Knowledge threshold.* If $|\mathcal{C}| \geq k+1$, the coalition can completely control value $s$ during the sharing phase. Otherwise, the secret $s$ looks uniformly random to the coalition.
- *Liveness threshold.* If $|\mathcal{C}| \geq |G| - k$, the coalition can cause the reconstruction to fail and output $\perp$. Otherwise, the reconstruction phase must succeed.

CSP-fair coin toss against coalition size

**Sharing phase**: $G_0$ runs the sharing phase of $\mathsf{size\text{-}GroupToss}^{G_0}[k_0]$. Then $G_1$ runs the sharing phase of $\mathsf{size\text{-}GroupToss}^{G_1}[k_1]$.

**Reconstruction phase**: $G_0$ runs the reconstruction phase of $\mathsf{size\text{-}GroupToss}^{G_0}[k_0]$ to reconstruct $s_0$. If $s_0 = \perp$, set $s_0 = 0$. Then $G_1$ runs the reconstruction phase of $\mathsf{size\text{-}GroupToss}^{G_1}[k_1]$ to reconstruct $s_1$. If $s_1 = \perp$, output 0. Otherwise, output $s_0 \oplus s_1$.

Roughly speaking, this protocol achieves CSP-fairness by disincentivizing $G_1$ from hampering the reconstruction of $s_1$. If $G_1$ fails to reconstruct $s_1$, the protocol will output 0 as a punishment. This ensures that rational players in $G_1$ have no incentive to fail the reconstruction of $s_1$.

As long as the following three conditions are satisfied, the above protocol achieves CSP-fairness against any coalition of size no more than $t = t_0 + t_1$ where $t_b$ denotes the number of corrupted players in group $G_b$ for $b \in \{0,1\}$.

(C1) *$\mathcal{C}$ cannot control both coins.* Equivalently, $t \leq k_0 + k_1 + 1$. Otherwise, $\mathcal{C}$ can force the outcome to be whatever the coalition's overall preference is.
(C2) *If $\mathcal{C}$* controls $s_1$*, then it cannot fail the reconstruction of* $s_0$. That is, $t \leq |G_0| - k_0 + k_1$. Otherwise, $\mathcal{C}$ can fail the reconstruction of $s_0$ and force the outcome to be $s_1$ it determines.
(C3) *If $\mathcal{C}$ can fail the reconstruction of $s_1$, then it must NOT prefer 0.*

Here, condition (C3) guarantees that any coalition is not incentivized to fail the reconstruction of $s_1$. Conditioned on $s_1$ being successfully reconstructed, condition (C1) and (C2) together guarantee that at least one of $s_0$ or $s_1$ is uniformly random. Consequently, the final outcome must also be uniformly random. Therefore, these three conditions together ensure CSP-fairness of the protocol.

*Characterizing Preference.* For any fixed group partition $G_0$ and $G_1$, we only need to choose $k_0$ and $k_1$ such that the above three conditions are satisfied to achieve CSP fairness. Observe that the first two conditions are independent of player preferences once $G_0$ and $G_1$ are fixed. However, the third condition heavily depends on player preferences and cannot be simply captured by the number of $b$-supporters in the coalition, as we explained in the technical challenges above.

Recall that 0- and 1-supporters are sorted by decreasing bets on 0. Let $\eta(x) < N_0$ be the maximum number such that the first $\eta(x)$ number of 0-supporters together with the first $x$ number of 1-supporters in $G_1$ does *not* prefer 0. If all $N_0$ number of 0-supporters together with the first $x$ number of 1-supporters in $G_1$ does not prefer 0, we set $\eta(x) = \infty$. Then (C3) can be expressed as $t \leq (|G_1| - k_1) + \eta(|G_1| - k_1)$. This is to guarantee that *any* coalition with $|G_1| - k_1$ number of 1-supporters and $\eta(|G_1| - k_1)$ number of 0-supporters—even if they are the ones with the most bets on 0—does not prefer 0. Specifically, if $\eta(|G_1| - k_1) = \infty$, failing the reconstruction of $s_1$ never benefits the coalition, regardless of how many 0-supporters are corrupted.

Given $G_0$ and $G_1$, the problem boils down to the following optimization:

$$\begin{aligned}
&\text{Maximize } t \text{ subject to}\\
&0 \leq k_0 \leq |G_0| - 1, 0 \leq k_1 \leq |G_1| - 1,\\
&t \leq \min\{k_0 + k_1 + 1, |G_0| - k_0 + k_1, (|G_1| - k_1) + \eta(|G_1| - k_1)\}.
\end{aligned}$$

*Partition of $G_0$ and $G_1$.* To maximize coalition resilience, we must carefully decide the partition $G_0$ and $G_1$, since the naive approach of assigning all $b$-supporters to $G_b$ is not necessarily optimal for general split-bet profiles. For example, consider a profile $\boldsymbol{\mathcal{P}}^* = \{2@(3,0), 2@(1,2), 5@(0,3)\}$ of 9 players. This notation means that the profile contains two players with preference $(3,0)$, two with $(1,2)$, and five with preference $(0,3)$. Using the naive partition $G_0 = \{2@(3,0)\}$ and $G_1 = \{2@(1,2), 5@(0,3)\}$, we can defend against at most $t = 4$ by choosing $k_0 = 1$, $k_1 = 3$. However, if we move the two swing 1-supporters with preference $(1,2)$ to $G_0$, now the new $G_0 = \{2@(3,0), 2@(1,2)\}$ and $G_1 = \{5@(0,3)\}$, which allows us to defend against $t = 5$ by picking $k_0 = 2$, $k_1 = 3$.

Why is this new partition better? Recall that the crux of the protocol is to output 0 as a punishment if the reconstruction of $s_1$ fails. To make this punishment effective, $G_1$ should consist only of aggressive 1-supporters who strongly oppose outcome 0. In the example of $\mathcal{P}^*$, the two $(1, 2)$ players are swing 1-supporters: they prefer outcome 1 but also place bets on outcome 0. If they collude with any 0-supporter, the coalition actually prefers outcome 0. Thus, to ensure that $G_1$ only contains aggressive 1-supporters, we move swing 1-supporters into $G_0$ to improve coalition resilience.

In general, we use $\gamma$ to denote the number of 1-supporters in group $G_0$. These players will be the $\gamma$ number of 1-supporters with the most bets on 0. Then $|G_0| = N_0 + \gamma$ and $|G_1| = N_1 - \gamma$. We redefine $\eta_\gamma(x)$ to be the maximum number of 0-supporters such that the first $\eta_\gamma(x)$ number of 0-supporters together with the first $x$ number of 1-supporters in $G_1$ do *not* prefer 0. As before, if all $N_0$ number of 0-supporters together with the first $x$ number of 1-supporters in $G_1$ do not prefer 0, we set $\eta_\gamma(x) = \infty$. The problem then becomes

$$\begin{aligned}&\text{Maximize } t \text{ subject to}\\ &0 \leq \gamma < N_1, \quad 0 \leq k_0 \leq N_0 + \gamma - 1, \quad 0 \leq k_1 \leq N_1 - \gamma - 1,\\ &t \leq \min\{k_0 + k_1 + 1,\ N_0 + \gamma - k_0 + k_1,\ (N_1 - \gamma - k_1) + \eta_\gamma(N_1 - \gamma - k_1)\}. \quad (3)\end{aligned}$$

*Solving the Optimization.* Let $\alpha := |G_1| - k_1$. We explain how to solve the above optimization, allowing non-integer solutions in the overview. The formal proof is given in the full version. Observe that the optimal solution of $k_0$ is always $|G_0|/2 = (N_0 + \gamma)/2$. Substituting this back to Eq. 3, the problem reduces to finding the optimal $\gamma$ and $\alpha$ to maximize $t$, subject to the constraint

$$t \leq t(\gamma, \alpha) := \min\{c_1(\gamma, \alpha), c_2(\gamma, \alpha)\},$$

where $c_1(\gamma, \alpha) = \frac{(N_0 - \gamma)}{2} + N_1 - \alpha$ and $c_2(\gamma, \alpha) = \eta_\gamma(\alpha) + \alpha$. Here, $\eta_\gamma(\cdot)$ has been extended naturally to allow both non-integer input and output.

Let $\mathsf{opt}(\gamma)$ be the optimal choice of $\alpha$ given any fixed $\gamma$. From the feasible region depicted in Fig. 2, $\mathsf{opt}(\gamma)$ is either $f(\gamma)$ or $h(\gamma)$[3] where:

$$\begin{aligned}f(\gamma) &:= \alpha \text{ such that } c_1(\gamma, \alpha) = c_2(\gamma, \alpha) \text{ if such } \alpha \text{ exists.}\\ h(\gamma) &:= \text{the minimum } \alpha \text{ such that } \eta_\gamma(\alpha) = \infty \text{ if such } \alpha \text{ exists.}\end{aligned}$$

We analyze $t(\gamma, \mathsf{opt}(\gamma))$ for the two cases separately.

**If** $\mathsf{opt}(\gamma) = f(\gamma)$: we show that $t(\gamma, f(\gamma))$ is a decreasing function in $\gamma$ by analyzing $\eta_\gamma(\cdot)$.

**If** $\mathsf{opt}(\gamma) = h(\gamma)$: we show that $t(\gamma, h(\gamma)) \leq \max\{t(\gamma_0, h(\gamma_0)), t(\gamma_1, h(\gamma_1))\}$, where $\gamma_0$ and $\gamma_1$ are the two margins of $\gamma$ after we group players with same bets on 0 into the same chunk, as depicted in Fig. 3.

We use a sliding window technique to prove this claim. Let $S_\gamma$ be the set of the first $h(\gamma)$ number of players in $G_1$. By definition of $h(\gamma)$, players in $S_\gamma$ should

[3] There are corner cases where $\mathsf{opt}(\gamma) = N_1 - \gamma$, we leave it to the full proof.

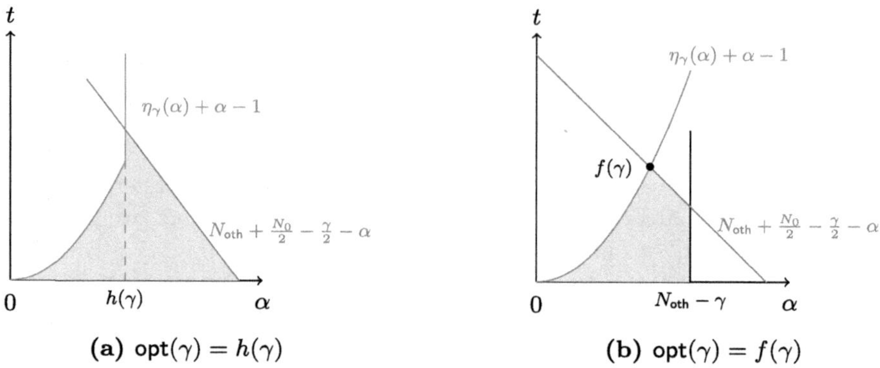


**Fig. 2.** The orange shaded area represents the feasible region of $(\alpha, t)$ for any fixed $\gamma$. Here, the orange and green line represent $c_1(\gamma,\alpha)$ and $c_2(\gamma,\alpha)$, respectively. (Color figure online)

exactly "cancel out" all 0-supporters' joint preference on 0: when $S_\gamma$ collude with all $N_0$ number of 0-supporters, their average expected utility on outcome 0 is exactly $B/2$, the honest expected utility. That is, $h(\gamma)$ is the number of players needed to fail the reconstruction of $s_1$ such that the coalition never prefers 0.

Based on the above argument, the average utility $\overline{\mu}(\gamma)$ of players in $S_\gamma$ must satisfy the following invariant for any $\gamma$:

$$(B/2-\overline{\mu}(\gamma))\cdot h(\gamma)=C,$$

where $C$ is a constant that only depends on all 0-supporters' total bet on 0. Therefore, we have

$$\begin{aligned}\frac{B}{2}(h(\gamma_0)-h(\gamma)) &= \overline{\mu}(\gamma_0)\cdot h(\gamma_0)-\overline{\mu}(\gamma)\cdot h(\gamma)\\ &= x\cdot(\gamma-\gamma_0)-x'(\gamma+h(\gamma)-\gamma_0-h(\gamma_0)),\end{aligned} \tag{4}$$

where $x$ and $x'$ are the average utility of players in the green block and blue block in Fig. 3, respectively. Figure 4 follows directly by observing that $\overline{\mu}(\gamma)\cdot h(\gamma)$ is the joint utility of players in $S_\gamma$. This allows us to relate changes in $h(\gamma)$ with respect to changes in $\gamma$. We can thus compare $t(\gamma,h(\gamma))$ for $\gamma$ and $\gamma_0$ (respectively $\gamma_1$) since the difference between $t(\gamma,h(\gamma))$ and $t(\gamma_0,h(\gamma_0))$ is exactly $\frac{1}{2}(\gamma-\gamma_0)+(h(\gamma)-h(\gamma_0))$.

Putting the two cases together, a careful case analysis shows that the global optimal choice of $\gamma$ must be one of the margins, with $\mathsf{opt}(\gamma)$ being $f(\gamma)$ if it exists, or $h(\gamma)$ otherwise. This depends on the actual preference profiles. Our concrete example in Table 6 implies that each margin could potentially be the optimal choice. The full analysis and the integer solution are available in the full version.

### 2.3 CSP-Fairness Against Corrupted Bets

Another natural approach is to consider coalition resilience in terms of the total bet controlled by a coalition. In a split-bet preference profile where each player

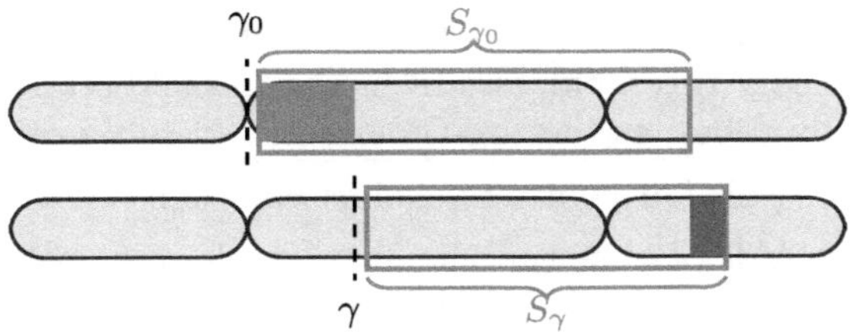


**Fig. 3.** Illustrative explanation of Eq. 4. Specifically, $x$ and $x'$ are the average utility of players in the solid green and blue blocks.

holds exactly $B$ total bets, defending against coalitions by corrupted size is equivalent to defending against coalitions by corrupted bets.

Recall that $B_0$ and $B_1$ denote the cumulative bet on outcome 0 and 1, respectively. Each player can be interpreted as $B$ number of "virtual players", each holding one bet. Specifically, player $i$ controls $\mathsf{bet}_i(0)$ number of virtual players with preferences $(1,0)$ and $\mathsf{bet}_i(1)$ with preference $(0,1)$. For example, consider $\widehat{\mathcal{P}} = ((0,3),(2,1),(2,1))$ where $B=3$. This profile can be viewed as a preference profile with 9 virtual players, four with $(1,0)$ and five with $(0,1)$. Thus, defending against a coalition based on the number of virtual players is equivalent to defending based on the total bet they control.

Rather than directly applying the protocol from [36] to the $B \cdot N$ number of virtual players, we use weighted threshold secret sharing. This allows the protocol to work seamlessly even for arbitrary preference profiles.

In our scheme, each player participates in two sub-protocols to generate coins $s_0$ and $s_1$. In the sub-protocol for coin $s_b$, players run a weighted threshold secret sharing protocol where each player's weight equals their bets on outcome $b$. For example, under profile $\widehat{\mathcal{P}}$ above, the first player has weight 3 while the other two players have weight 1 in the sub-protocol determining $s_1$. The secret $s_b$ can only be reconstructed from players controlling enough total weights. More formally, the access structure of the secret sharing is $\Gamma = \{S \subseteq [n] : \mathsf{bet}_S(b) \geq k+1\}$ where $\mathsf{bet}_S(b)$ is the total bet of set $S$ on outcome $b$. In other words, any set with $k+1$ or more bets on outcome $b$ can reconstruct the secret, while any set with fewer than $k+1$ bets on outcome $b$ learns nothing about the secret.

$\mathsf{bet\text{-}GroupToss}^b[k]$ sub-protocol

Let $\mathcal{O}$ be the set of players remain online. $\mathcal{O}$ is initialized as $[N]$.

**Sharing Phase.** Each player $i$ chooses a random coin $\mathsf{coin}_i \xleftarrow{\$} \{0,1\}$. Player $i$ shares $\mathsf{coin}_i$ into $N$ shares with an access structure $\Gamma = \{S \subseteq [N] : \mathsf{bet}_S(b) \geq k+1\}$. Denote the set of shares as $\{c_{i,j}\}_{j\in[n]}$. Send $c_{i,j}$ to player $j$. If any player aborts, remove them from $\mathcal{O}$.

**Reconstruction Phase.** Every player $i$ broadcast the shares $\{c_{j,i}\}_{j\in\mathcal{O}}$ it has received from players in $\mathcal{O}$. Players use $\{c_{j,i}\}_{j\in\mathcal{O}}$ to reconstruct $\{\mathsf{coin}_i\}_{i\in\mathcal{O}}$. If any $\mathsf{coin}_i$ failed to be reconstructed, output $c=\perp$; otherwise, output $(\oplus_{i\in\mathcal{O}}\mathsf{coin}_i)$.

By the property of weighted secret sharing, this sub-protocol also satisfies the binding, knowledge threshold, and liveness threshold properties with respect to the corrupted total bet, as the size-GroupToss$^G[k]$ sub-protocol.

CSP-fair coin toss against coalition bets

**Sharing phase**: All players run the sharing phase of bet-GroupToss$^0[k_0]$ and then the sharing phase of bet-GroupToss$^1[k_1]$.

**Reconstruction phase**: All players run the reconstruction phase of bet-GroupToss$^0[k_0]$. Let $s_0$ be the reconstructed outcome. If $s_0 = \perp$, set $s_0 = 0$. Then players run the reconstruction phase of bet-GroupToss$^1[k_1]$. Let $s_1$ be the reconstructed outcome. If $s_1 = \perp$, output 0. Otherwise, output $s_0 \oplus s_1$.

Consider a coalition that controls $\beta$ total bets, out of which $\beta_b$ is the corrupted bets on outcome $b$ for $b \in \{0, 1\}$. By a similar argument before, the above protocol achieves CSP fairness against any coalition controlling $\beta$ total bet as long as the following three conditions are satisfied:

(C1′) *$\mathcal{C}$ cannot control both coins.* Equivalently, $\beta \leq k_0 + k_1 + 1$.
(C2′) *If $\mathcal{C}$ controls $s_1$, then it cannot fail the reconstruction of $s_0$.* That is, $\beta \leq B_0 - k_0 + k_1$.
(C3′) *If $\mathcal{C}$ can fail the reconstruction of $s_1$, then it must NOT prefer 0.* That is, if $\beta_1 \geq B_1 - k_1$, then $B_0 \leq B_1$.

The problem then becomes maximizing $\beta$ subject to constraints (C1′), (C2′), and (C3′). The optimal resilience is given by

$$\beta = \begin{cases} B_1 - \left\lfloor \frac{B_0}{2} \right\rfloor, & \text{if } B_1 \geq \frac{5}{2} B_0 \\ \left\lfloor \frac{2}{3} B_1 + \frac{1}{3} B_0 \right\rfloor, & \text{otherwise.} \end{cases}$$

Equivalently, this protocol tolerates $\left\lfloor \frac{\beta}{B} \right\rfloor$-sized coalition for split-bet profiles.

## 2.4 Impossibility

Our impossibility result adopts a similar approach in [16,35,36] but with more involved optimization techniques. The core idea is to transform an $N$-party CSP-fair protocol $\Pi$ for profile $\boldsymbol{\mathcal{P}}$ to a three-party protocol $\Pi^*$ as follows: The $N$ parties are partitioned into the three supernodes. Each supernode emulates the execution of the players it contains. Messages between players in the same supernode are dealt with internally, and those between players in different supernodes will become messages between supernodes. Then the protocol $\Pi$ naturally transforms to a three-party protocol $\Pi^*$. The goal is to find a partition of the $N$ players, such that if $\Pi$ achieves CSP-fairness against any $t$-sized coalition, then the resulting $\Pi^*$ satisfies the following three properties:

(C1″) *Lone-wolf condition:* $\mathcal{S}_1$(or $\mathcal{S}_3$) cannot bias the output towards any direction.

(C2″) *Wolf-minion condition:* $\mathcal{S}_1$(or $\mathcal{S}_3$) and $\mathcal{S}_2$ cannot bias the output towards 1.

(C3″) $\mathbf{r}_2$-*equity condition:* for all but a negligible fraction of $\mathcal{S}_2$'s randomness $\mathbf{r}_2$, the value $|F(\mathbf{r}_2) - \frac{1}{2}|$ is negligible, where $F(\mathbf{r}_2)$ denotes the expected coin outcome in an honest execution where $\mathcal{S}_2$ 's randomness is fixed to $\mathbf{r}_2$.

However, no three-party protocol satisfies the above three conditions simultaneously. Therefore, no CSP-fair protocol defend against $t$-sized coalition for $\boldsymbol{\mathcal{P}}$.

Following this framework, we focus particularly on optimizing the partition of players into supernodes. To convey the main idea, we use $\boldsymbol{\mathcal{P}}^* = \{2@(3,0), 2@(1,2), 5@(0,3)\}$ as an example. Recall that our feasibility from Sect. 2.2 gives a CSP-fair protocol for $\boldsymbol{\mathcal{P}}^*$ against any 5-sized coalition. We will show that this is tight: no protocol is CSP-fair against 6-sized coalition for $\boldsymbol{\mathcal{P}}^*$.

In the partition, $\mathcal{S}_1$ and $\mathcal{S}_3$ each contain $\{1@(3,0), 1@(1,2), 1@(0,3)\}$ and $\mathcal{S}_2$ contains the remaining three 1-supporters $\{3@(0,3)\}$. Assuming for the sake of contradiction that there is a CSP-fair protocol $\Pi$ against 6-sized coalition, then with the above partition, the resulting three-party protocol $\Pi^*$ should satisfy

1. *Lone-wolf condition:* $\mathcal{S}_1$ cannot bias the output towards 1 directly by CSP-fairness. If it can bias the outcome towards 0, then $\mathcal{S}_1$ can collude with the 0-supporter in $\mathcal{S}_3$ to form a coalition of size four that prefers 0. This would allow the coalition to bias the outcome towards 0, which contradicts CSP-fairness. The same argument holds for $\mathcal{S}_3$.
2. *Wolf-minion condition:* $\mathcal{S}_1$(or $\mathcal{S}_3$) and $\mathcal{S}_2$ cannot bias the output towards 1 by CSP-fairness, since this coalition controls 6 players and prefers 1.
3. $\mathbf{r}_2$-*equity condition:* Since $\mathcal{S}_2$ prefers 1, for all but a negligible fraction of $\mathbf{r}_2$, $F(\mathbf{r}_2)$ must not bias towards 1. Since $\mathbb{E}[F(\mathbf{r}_2)] = 1/2$ when everyone behaves honestly, it must be that $F(\mathbf{r}_2)$ cannot bias towards any direction.

But this is impossible. Thus, no protocol is CSP-fair for $\boldsymbol{\mathcal{P}}^*$ against $t = 6$.

To generalize this argument for split-bet, we parametrize the partition as follows. For simplicity, we assume $N_0$ is even here. At a high level, $\mathcal{S}_1$ and $\mathcal{S}_3$ each contains half of 0-supporters and $\theta$ number of 1-supporters. $\mathcal{S}_2$ contains the remaining 1-supporters. However, we cannot simply put the first half of 0-supporters in $\mathcal{S}_1$ and the rest in $\mathcal{S}_3$. To get a tighter bound, we need to make the total bet on 0 in $\mathcal{S}_1$ and $\mathcal{S}_3$ as balanced as possible, as in the above example of $\boldsymbol{\mathcal{P}}^*$. Therefore, we will partition as follows (See Fig. 4 for an example).

Let $\mathbf{P}_0$ and $\mathbf{P}_1$ be the 0- and 1-supporters after sorting, respectively. Let $\eta_1 = \eta_0(\theta) + 1$ and $\eta_3 = \eta_\theta(\theta) + 1 \geq \eta_1$ where $\eta(\cdot)$ is defined in Sect. 2.2. Intuitively, $\eta_i$ represents the minimum number of 0-supporters such that the 1-supporters in $\mathcal{S}_i$ together with $\eta_i$ number of 0-supporters prefers 0 for $i \in \{1, 3\}$.

- $\mathcal{S}_1$ contains the first $\theta$ number of 1-supporters $\mathbf{P}_1[1, \theta]$, and half of 0-supporters:

$$\mathbf{P}_0\left[1, \lceil \eta_1/2 \rceil\right] \bigcup \mathbf{P}_0\left[\eta_1 + 1, \eta_1 + \lceil \eta_3/2 \rceil - \lceil \eta_1/2 \rceil\right] \bigcup \mathbf{P}_0\left[N_0/2 + (\lceil \eta_3/2 \rceil), N_0\right]$$

- $\mathcal{S}_3$ contains the remaining 0-supporters and the next $\theta$ number of 1-supporters $\mathbf{P}_1[\theta + 1, 2\theta]$.

– $\mathcal{S}_2$ contains the remaining 1-supporters.

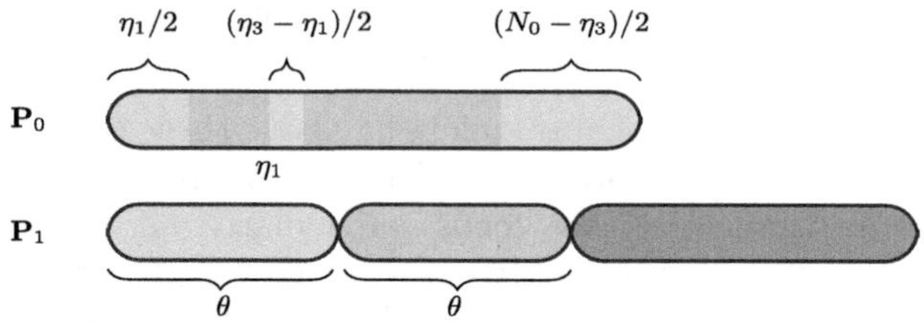


**Fig. 4.** Illustration of partition. For simplicity, we omit the rounding in the figure. The players marked by orange are partitioned into $\mathcal{S}_1$, those marked by green are partitioned into $\mathcal{S}_3$, and those marked by blue are put into $\mathcal{S}_2$. (Color figure online)

With this partition, we require $\theta$ to satisfy the following. Let $\gamma'$ be the minimum number such that $\eta_0(\gamma') > N_0/2$, i.e., any $\gamma'$ number of 1-supporters together with the first half or 0-supporters do *not* prefer 0. As indicated by the concrete example with $\boldsymbol{\mathcal{P}}^*$ above, the main constraints are posed by the lone-wolf condition and the wolf-minion condition.

1. *Non-negativity:* $0 \leq 2\theta \leq N_1$ to ensure that the partition is well-defined.
2. *Lone-wolf condition:* For $i \in \{1,3\}$, we need to build two coalitions $\mathcal{C}$ and $\mathcal{C}'$, both containing $\mathcal{S}_i$ and both have size no more than $t$ such that $\mathcal{C}$ prefers 0 and $\mathcal{C}'$ prefers 1. For this, we need 1.) $t \geq |\mathcal{S}_i| + \lceil \eta_i/2 \rceil$ to construct coalition $\mathcal{C}$ containing $\mathcal{S}_i$ and $\lceil \eta_i/2 \rceil$ number of 0-supporters outside $\mathcal{S}_i$ to prefer 0; and 2.) $t \geq |\mathcal{S}_i| + \gamma' - \theta$ to construct $\mathcal{C}'$ containing $\mathcal{S}_i$ and $\gamma' - \theta$ number of 1-supporters outside (if necessary) to prefer 1.
3. *Wolf-minion condition:* We need $t \geq |\mathcal{S}_i| + |\mathcal{S}_2|$ for $i \in \{1,3\}$. In case $\mathcal{S}_i$ together with $\mathcal{S}_2$ does not prefer 1, we also require $t \geq N_0/2 + \gamma'$ to form a coalition $\mathcal{C}$ containing $\mathcal{S}_i$ and $\mathcal{S}_3$, as well as $\gamma' - (N_1 - \theta)$ number of 1-supporters outside such that $\mathcal{C}'$ that prefers 1.

Combining all these constraints, the impossibility result reduces to yet another optimization problem of minimizing $t$ subject to the above non-negativity, lone-wolf condition, and the wolf-minion condition. The optimal $t$ is given by

$$t = \max\{N_1 + N_0/2 - \theta^*, \gamma' + \lceil N_0/2 \rceil\},$$

where $\theta^*$ is the maximum number such that $2\theta + \lceil (\eta_\theta(\theta)+1)/2 \rceil \leq N_1$. The formal proofs can be found in the full version.

## 3 Preliminaries and Model

*Notations.* We use $\mathbb{Z}_{\geq 0}$ for non-negative integers and $[N]$ for the set of integers $\{1,\ldots,N\}$. Similarly, we use $[m]_0$ for set of integers $\{0,\ldots,m-1\}$. Additionally, $[i,j]$ denotes the set of all numbers between $i$ and $j$, both ends included.

We use boldface letters to denote vectors. All vectors are 1-indexed. For a vector $\mathbf{V}$ and $i, j \in [|\mathbf{V}|]$, let $\mathbf{V}[i]$ denote the $i$-th entry and $\mathbf{V}[i, j]$ denote the $i$-th to $j$-th entry, both sides included.

We use $\lambda$ as the security parameter. Each player is modeled as probabilistic polynomial time (ppt) Turing machines and receives $1^\lambda$ as an additional input.

## 3.1 Coin Toss Protocol

In an $N$-party coin toss protocol, $N$ players want to jointly decide a random $m$-sided coin. We use the term "party" and "player" interchangeably. Players can communicate with each other through pairwise private channel as well as a broadcast channel. All the communications are authenticated, i.e., each message carries the identity of the true sender. In this work, we assume that the network is synchronous, and the protocol proceeds in rounds. At the end of the protocol, the final coin outcome is a deterministic, polynomial-time computable function based on the whole broadcast history. Since players are computationally bounded, we require $m$ and $N$ to be at most $\mathsf{poly}(\lambda)$ for some polynomial function $\mathsf{poly}(\cdot)$.

**Correctness.** In an $m$-sided coin toss protocol, the outcome must be a uniformly random $m$-sided coin if every player behaves honestly.

**Preferences and utilities.** In an $m$-sided coin toss protocol, each player has a utility function that maps each of the $m$ outcomes $\{0, \dots, m-1\}$ to a non-negative integer units of utility. In this paper, we use *bet* or utility interchangeably to describe each player's utility associated with each outcome. For example, a player with bet 5 on outcome 3 will receive 5 units of utility if the protocol outputs 3. We use $\mathsf{bet}_i(\ell)$ to denote player $i$'s bet on outcome $\ell$. A player $i$'s *preference* $\mathbf{p}_i$ is simply the vector of its bet on all possible outcomes: $\mathbf{p}_i = (\mathsf{bet}_i(0), \dots, \mathsf{bet}_i(m-1))$. We also define the *total bet* of a player $i$ as $\mathsf{total}(\mathbf{p}_i) = \sum_{\ell=0}^{m-1} \mathsf{bet}_i(\ell)$. As before, for each player $i$, we have $\mathsf{total}(\mathbf{p}_i) \leq \mathsf{poly}(\lambda)$ for some polynomial function $\mathsf{poly}(\cdot)$. A *preference profile* is then a list of all of the players' preferences $\boldsymbol{\mathcal{P}} = (\mathbf{p}_1, \dots, \mathbf{p}_N)$.

Some of the players may form a coalition, also referred to as the adversary in our cryptography analysis. A coalition's utility is the sum of all the coalition members' utility. Specifically, for a coalition $\mathcal{C}$, its utility when the final outcome is $\ell$ equals $\mathsf{bet}_\mathcal{C}(\ell) = \sum_{i \in \mathcal{C}} \mathsf{bet}_i(\ell)$. The preference of a coalition $\mathcal{C}$ is defined analogously as $\mathbf{p}_\mathcal{C} = (\mathsf{bet}_\mathcal{C}(0), \dots, \mathsf{bet}_\mathcal{C}(m-1)))$. Similarly, $\mathsf{total}(\mathbf{p}_\mathcal{C}) = \sum_{\ell=0}^{m-1} \mathsf{bet}_\mathcal{C}(\ell)$.

We say that a coalition "prefers" an outcome $\ell$, if the coalition's utility on outcome $\ell$ is greater than the honest expected utility, i.e., a coalition $\mathcal{C}$ prefers outcome $\ell$ iff $\mathsf{bet}_\mathcal{C}(\ell) > \frac{1}{m}\mathsf{total}(\mathbf{p}_\mathcal{C})$. If player $i$ prefers $\ell$, we call $i$ an $\ell$-supporter.

We use *cumulative bet* of an outcome $\ell$ to denote the sum of all players' bets on the outcome $\sum_{i=1}^{N} \mathsf{bet}_i(\ell)$. The least preferred outcome is the one with the least cumulative bet. In this paper, we only consider *non-degenerate* preference profiles, where there is at least one $\ell$-supporter for every outcome $\ell \in [m]_0$. For degenerate preference profiles, the protocol from Thyagarajan, Soni, and Wu [35] achieves CSP fairness against $(N-1)$-sized coalition.

**Strategies.** A strategic coalition can perform a *rushing attack*. In each round $r$, the coalition can wait for messages from honest players and then decide what messages to send in round $r$. Additionally, a *semi-malicious* coalition can perform semi-malicious strategies, which includes the following types of deviations: 1.) program the randomness used in the protocol after observing honest players' messages; 2.) abort the protocol in some round $r$, after observing the honest players' messages in round $r$. Once a player aborted, it does not participate in future rounds. A *malicious* coalition can perform the above two kinds of strategies, as well as sending arbitrary messages.

**CSP fairness.** Recall that *Cooperative-strategy-proofness* (or "CSP-fairness" for short) requires that no coalition can increase its own expected utility no matter what strategy the coalition utilizes.

**Definition 3.1** (CSP-fairness [16]). A coin toss protocol $\Pi$ satisfies *CSP-fairness* against any $t$-sized coalitions with respect to preference profile $\boldsymbol{\mathcal{P}}$ iff for all coalitions $\mathcal{C} \subseteq [N]$ such that $|\mathcal{C}| \leq t$, for any non-uniform ppt strategy $S'_{\mathcal{C}}$, there is a negligible function $\mathsf{negl}(\cdot)$ such that

$$U_{\mathcal{C}}(S'_{\mathcal{C}}, S^H_{-\mathcal{C}}) \leq \frac{\mathsf{total}(\mathbf{P}_{\mathcal{C}})}{m} + \mathsf{negl}(\lambda),$$

Where $U_{\mathcal{C}}(S'_{\mathcal{C}}, S^H_{-\mathcal{C}})$ is the expected joint utility of coalition $\mathcal{C}$ in an execution of $\Pi$ when using strategy $S'_{\mathcal{C}}$ while the rest players behaves honestly.

### 3.2 Different Formulations

In this work, we consider the following two formulations. In the full version, we also introduce some other natural formulations and their relationship with arbitrary-bet preferences. A *formulation* is the set of all feasible preference profiles. Here, we only consider atomic formulations where each player's preference is restricted in the same way and independent of other players' preferences.

*Arbitrary-bet.* The most general formulation allows each player to have an arbitrary non-negative integer utility on each of the $m$ possible outcomes. Formally, each player's preference can be described as $\mathbf{p} \in \mathbb{Z}^m_{\geq 0}$. This formulation is simply

$$\mathcal{F}_{\mathsf{arb}}(N, m) := (\mathbb{Z}^m_{\geq 0})^N.$$

*Split-bet.* This is a rather restricted formulation where each player has the same total bet of $B$ that can be split across the $m$ possible outcomes. In this formulation, each players' preferences can be described as a vector $\mathbf{p} = (b_0, \ldots, b_{m-1})$ such that $\sum_{\ell=0}^{m-1} b_\ell = B$ for the same $B$. Formally,

$$\mathcal{F}_{\mathsf{split}}(N, m) := \{(\mathbf{p}_1, \ldots, \mathbf{p}_N) \in (\mathbb{Z}^m_{\geq 0})^N \mid \mathsf{total}(\mathbf{p}_i) \text{ are the same for all } i \in [N]\}.$$

# 4 Reducibility Between Formulations

In this section, we show that the problem of achieving CSP-fairness against $t$-sized coalitions for a particular arbitrary-bet preference profile is reducible to the achieving CSP-fairness against $t$-sized coalitions for a particular split-bet preference profile and vice versa.

For a preference profile $\mathcal{P}$ and a protocol $\Pi$, let $t(\mathcal{P}, \Pi)$ be the maximum value $t$ such that when the players with preferences $\mathcal{P}$ run the protocol $\Pi$, the protocol achieves CSP fairness against any $t$-sized coalitions. We use $\mathbf{1}_m$ to denote the vector $(1, \ldots, 1)$ of length $m$.

**Definition 4.1** (Reducibility). Fix any $N$ and $m$ Given two formulations $\mathcal{F}_1(N, m)$ and $\mathcal{F}_2(N, m)$, we say that a formulation $\mathcal{F}_1$ is *reducible* to $\mathcal{F}_2$ iff there is an efficient transformation $\mathcal{T} : \mathcal{F}_1(N, m) \mapsto \mathcal{F}_2(N, m)$, such that for any protocol $\Pi_2$ for $\mathcal{F}_2(N, m)$, we can build a protocol $\Pi_1$ for $\mathcal{F}_1(N, m)$ satisfying the following:

- On any $\mathcal{P} \in \mathcal{F}_1(N, m)$, protocol $\Pi_1$ runs $\Pi_2$ on $\mathcal{T}(\mathcal{P})$;
- The size of the coalition $\Pi_1$ can tolerate satisfies that $t(\mathcal{P}, \Pi_1) = t(\mathcal{T}(\mathcal{P}), \Pi_2)$.

The existence of a transformation that satisfies Definition 4.1 is non-trivial. As explained in Sect. 2.1, the transformation must preserve the relative preference of all possible coalitions. This would guarantee that if the coalition can increase its expected utility in $\Pi_2$ run on $\mathcal{T}(\mathcal{P})$, then it must be able to increase its expected utility in $\Pi_1$ run on $\mathcal{P}$.

**Definition 4.2** (Preference-preserving transformation). Fix $N$ and $m$. We say that a transformation $\mathcal{T} : \mathcal{F}_1(N, m) \mapsto \mathcal{F}_2(N, m)$ is *preference preserving* iff for a preference profile $\mathcal{P} = (\mathbf{p}_1, \ldots, \mathbf{p}_N) \in \mathcal{F}_1(N, m)$, the transformation maps each player's preference $\mathbf{p}_i$ in to $a\mathbf{p}_i + \mathbf{b}_i$ where $a \in \mathbb{Z}_{>0}$ is the same constant scalar across all $i \in [N]$ and $\mathbf{b}_i = b_i \cdot \mathbf{1}_m \in \mathbb{Z}^m_{\geq 0}$ is a length $m$ vector where all entries equals some $b_i \geq 0$.

Intuitively, for each player or coalition, preference-preserving transformations maintain the differences between bets on each outcome by some scalar factor.

**Lemma 4.3** (Transitivity of preference-preserving transformation). *Fix $N$ and $m$. If there exists a preference transformation $\mathcal{T} : \mathcal{F}_1(N, m) \mapsto \mathcal{F}_2(N, m)$ and another preference-preserving transformation $\mathcal{T}' : \mathcal{F}_2(N, m) \mapsto \mathcal{F}_3(N, m)$, then there is a preference-preserving transformation $\widetilde{\mathcal{T}} = \mathcal{T}' \circ \mathcal{T}$ that maps formulation $\mathcal{F}_1(N, m)$ to $\mathcal{F}_2(N, m)$, where $\circ$ means functional composition.*

*Proof.* By definition, given a $\mathcal{P} = (\mathbf{p}_1, \ldots, \mathbf{p}_N) \in \mathcal{F}_1$, the transformation $\mathcal{T}$ maps each player's preference $\mathbf{p}_i$ into $\mathbf{p}'_i = a\mathbf{p}_i + \mathbf{b}_i$. Similarly, $\mathcal{T}'$ will then maps each $\mathbf{p}'_i$ to $\widetilde{\mathbf{p}}_i = a'\mathbf{p}'_i + \mathbf{b}'_i$. Thus, the composition $\widetilde{\mathcal{T}}$ will map $\mathbf{p}_i$ into $a \cdot a'\mathbf{p}_i + (a' \cdot \mathbf{b}_i + \mathbf{b}'_i)$. By definition, this is still a preference-preserving transformation. $\square$

**Lemma 4.4.** *Fix $N$ and $m$. A formulation $\mathcal{F}_1(N, m)$ is reducible to $\mathcal{F}_2(N, m)$ if there exists an efficient transformation $\mathcal{T} : \mathcal{F}_1(N, m) \mapsto \mathcal{F}_2(N, m)$ that is preference-preserving.*

The proof of this Lemma is given in the full version.

*Reducibility Between Split-bet and Arbitrary-bet.* With the above lemma, we only need to build preference-preserving transformations between both formulations. Below we give the formal proof that the split-bet and arbitrary-bet formulations are reducible to each other.

**Theorem 4.5.** *For any $N$ and $m$, $\mathcal{F}_{\mathsf{split}}(N, m)$ and $\mathcal{F}_{\mathsf{arb}}(N, m)$ are reducible to each other.*

*Proof.* Showing that $\mathcal{F}_{\mathsf{split}}(N, m)$ is reducible to $\mathcal{F}_{\mathsf{arb}}(N, m)$ can be done using the identity transformation $\mathcal{I}(\boldsymbol{\mathcal{P}}) = \boldsymbol{\mathcal{P}}$ because $\mathcal{F}_{\mathsf{split}}(N, m) \subset \mathcal{F}_{\mathsf{arb}}(N, m)$.

By Lemma 4.4, to show $\mathcal{F}_{\mathsf{arb}}(N, m)$ is reducible to $\mathcal{F}_{\mathsf{split}}(N, m)$, we only need to give a transformation $\mathcal{T}_{\mathrm{as}} : \mathcal{F}_{\mathsf{arb}}(N, m) \mapsto \mathcal{F}_{\mathsf{split}}(N, m)$ that is preference-preserving. Consider the transformation $\mathcal{T}_{\mathrm{as}}$, on input $\boldsymbol{\mathcal{P}}$, that maps player $i$'s preference $\mathbf{p}_i$ to $\mathbf{p}'_i$:

$$\mathbf{p}'_i = m \cdot \mathbf{p}_i + (B(\boldsymbol{\mathcal{P}}) - \mathsf{total}(\mathbf{p}_i))\, \mathbf{1}_m, \tag{5}$$

where $B(\boldsymbol{\mathcal{P}}) = \max_{j \in [n]}\{\mathsf{total}(\mathbf{p}_j)\}$. Clearly, $\mathcal{T}_{\mathrm{as}}$ can be efficiently computed.

**Claim 4.6.** *If $\boldsymbol{\mathcal{P}} \in \mathcal{F}_{\mathsf{arb}}(N, m)$, then $\mathcal{T}_{\mathrm{as}}(\boldsymbol{\mathcal{P}}) \in \mathcal{F}_{\mathsf{split}}(N, m)$ and each player's total bet is $m \cdot B(\boldsymbol{\mathcal{P}})$.*

*Proof.* Suppose the transformation $\mathcal{T}_{\mathrm{as}}$ maps $\mathbf{p}_i$ is mapped to $\mathbf{p}'_i$ according to Eq. 5. Then

$$\mathsf{total}(\mathbf{p}'_i) = m \cdot \mathsf{total}(p_i) + m \cdot (B(\boldsymbol{\mathcal{P}}) - \mathsf{total}(\mathbf{p}_i)) = m \cdot B(\boldsymbol{\mathcal{P}})$$

This value is the same for all players in the transformed preference profile. □

Thus, by Lemma 4.4 we have shown that $\mathcal{F}_{\mathsf{arb}}(N, m)$ is reducible to $\mathcal{F}_{\mathsf{split}}(N, m)$. □

## 5 Size-Based Protocol for Split-Bet Formulation

In this section, we give a CSP-fair coin toss protocol for split-bet preference profiles against semi-malicious coalitions. By Theorem 4.5, this also yields a protocol for arbitrary-bet preference profiles. Since Blum's coin toss protocol [11] achieves CSP fairness for two-party case against one corrupted player, we will focus on the case where $N \geq 3$. Without loss of generality, let 0 be the outcome with the least bets. Throughout this section, we will use a running example preference profile $\boldsymbol{\mathcal{P}}^*$ for binary coin toss to help understand the protocol construction and the parameter optimization. The preference profile

$$\boldsymbol{\mathcal{P}}^* = ((3,0),(3,0),(1,2),(1,2),(0,3),(0,3),(0,3),(0,3),(0,3)) \in \mathcal{F}_{\mathsf{split}}(9, 2).$$

We also use an abbreviation as $\{2@(3,0), 2@(1,2), 5@(0,3)\}$ to indicate that there are two players with preference $(3,0)$, two players with preference $(1,2)$, and the rest five players with preference $(0,3)$. Recall that $N_0$ denotes the number of 0-supporters who prefer outcome 0, and $N_{\mathsf{oth}}$ denote the number of the rest players who do not prefer outcome 0. For the specific example $\boldsymbol{\mathcal{P}}^*$, we have $N_0 = 2$ and $N_{\mathsf{oth}} = 7$.

As discussed in Sect. 2.2, we do not simply partition players based on whether they prefer 0 or not. Instead, our group $G_0$ contains all the 0-supporters and some swing oth-supporters. The rest aggressive oth-supporters goes to group $G_{\mathsf{oth}}$. Each group $G_b$ for $b \in \{0, \mathsf{oth}\}$ will decide a random coin $s_b$ using Shamir secret sharing. The final outcome is then the sum of $s_0$ and $s_{\mathsf{oth}}$. Specifically, if the reconstruction of $s_0$ fails, we simply output $s_{\mathsf{oth}}$; but if the reconstruction of $s_{\mathsf{oth}}$ fails, we will output 0 as a punishment.

### 5.1 sizeGroupToss$^G[k]$ Sub-Protocol

Consider the size-GroupToss$^G[k]$ sub-protocol defined below where $G$ is the set of players running the protocol and $k$ is a threshold parameter to be determined later. Specifically, the size-GroupToss$^G[k]$ sub-protocol run among the players in $G$ to decide a coin $c$ while players outside $G$ audit the protocol by observing the broadcast messages.

**Protocol 5.1.** size-GroupToss$^G[k]$ **sub-protocol (Semi-Malicious)**
Let $\mathcal{O}$ be the set of online players, initialized as $G$.

**Sharing Phase.** Each player $i$ chooses a random coin $\mathsf{coin}_i \xleftarrow{\$} [m]_0$ and shares it using $(k+1)$-out-of-$|G|$ Shamir secret sharing into $\{c_{i,j}\}_{j \in G}$ among the players in $G$. Send $c_{i,j}$ to player $j$. If any players abort, remove them from $\mathcal{O}$.

**Reconstruction Phase.** Every player $i$ computes the sum of the shares it received $c_i := \sum_{j \in \mathcal{O}} c_{j.i}$ and broadcast $c_i$. Players use the broadcast shares to reconstruct $s = \sum_{i \in \mathcal{O}} \mathsf{coin}_i$. If the reconstruction fails, set $s = \bot$; otherwise, output $s \mod m$.

**Lemma 5.1** Lemma 4.2 of [35] size-*GroupToss*$^G[k]$ *satisfies the following properties for any coalition* $\mathcal{C}$ *due to the property of Shamir secret sharing.*

- *Binding. The sharing phase uniquely binds to a secret $s$, such that the reconstruction phase either succeeds and outputs $s$, or it fails and outputs $\bot$.*
- *Knowledge threshold. If $|\mathcal{C}| \geq k+1$, the coalition can completely control binded value $s$ of the sharing phase. Otherwise, the binded secret $s$ looks uniformaly random to the coalition.*
- *Liveness threshold. If $|\mathcal{C}| \geq |G|-k$, the coalition can cause the reconstruction to fail and output $\bot$. Otherwise, the reconstruction phase must succeed.*

### 5.2 Final Protocol for Coalition-Size

*Protocol Parameters.* Given a preference profile $\mathcal{P}$, we define some parameters that will be used in the protocol. The parameter selection is given in the full version. Recall that we partition players into two groups $G_0$ and $G_{\mathsf{oth}}$ such that players in $G_{\mathsf{oth}}$ have "strong" preference against 0. We use $\gamma$ to denote the number of oth-supporters that will be put into $G_0$. Therefore, we have

$$|G_0| = N_0 + \gamma, \qquad |G_{\mathsf{oth}}| = N_{\mathsf{oth}} - \gamma.$$

Given a preference profile $\mathcal{P}$, group $G_0$ consists of all 0-supporters and the $\gamma$ number of oth-supporters who have the most bet on 0, breaking ties arbitrarily. In the example where $\mathcal{P}^* = \{2@(3,0), 2@(1,2), 5@(0,3)\}$, we will pick $\gamma^* = 2$, separating players into $G_0^* = \{2@(3,0), 2@(1,2)\}$ and $G_{\mathsf{oth}}^* = \{5@(0,3)\}$. The coin toss protocol works as follows with the parameters $k_0, k_{\mathsf{oth}}$ and $\gamma$ to be specified later.

**Protocol 5.3 Size-based protocol (semi-malicious)**
**Input**: The preference profile $\mathcal{P}$. **Sharing phase**:

1. $G_0$ runs the sharing phase of $\mathsf{size\text{-}GroupToss}^{G_0}[k_0]$. $G_{\mathsf{oth}}$ audits.
2. If $G_{\mathsf{oth}}$ is non-empty, $G_{\mathsf{oth}}$ runs the sharing phase of $\mathsf{size\text{-}GroupToss}^{G_{\mathsf{oth}}}[k_{\mathsf{oth}}]$. $G_0$ audits.

**Reconstruction phase**:

1. $G_0$ runs the reconstruction phase of $\mathsf{size\text{-}GroupToss}^{G_0}[k_0]$ while $G_{\mathsf{oth}}$ audits. Let $s_0$ be the outcome of this protocol.
2. If $G_{\mathsf{oth}}$ is non-empty, $G_{\mathsf{oth}}$ runs the reconstruction phase of $\mathsf{size\text{-}GroupToss}^{G_{\mathsf{oth}}}[k_{\mathsf{oth}}]$ while $G_0$ audits. Let $s_{\mathsf{oth}}$ be the outcome of this protocol. If $G_{\mathsf{oth}}$ is empty, let $s_{\mathsf{oth}} = 0$.
3. If $s_{\mathsf{oth}} = \bot$, output 0. Otherwise, if $s_0 = \bot$, set $s_0 = 0$ and output $(s_0 + s_{\mathsf{oth}}) \mod m$.

*Coalition Resilience.* For any fixed parameter $k_0, k_{\mathsf{oth}}$, and $\gamma$, we can decide the coalition resilience of Protocol 5.3. Consider a coalition $\mathcal{C}$ that controls $t = t_0 + t_{\mathsf{oth}}$ players where $t_0$ and $t_{\mathsf{oth}}$ denote the number of corrupted players in group $G_0$ and $G_{\mathsf{oth}}$, respectively.

If $\gamma = N_{\mathsf{oth}}$, i.e., $G_{\mathsf{oth}}$ is empty, the protocol degrades to a standard single-shot secret sharing and can tolerates only less than half corrupted players (and achieves strong fairness). In the following analysis, we focus on $\gamma < N_{\mathsf{oth}}$.

For a group $G_b$ for $b \in \{0, \mathsf{oth}\}$ and any integer $0 \leq x \leq |G_b|$, let $\overline{M}(G_b, x)$ denote the $x$ number of players with the most bet on 0 in $G_b$, breaking ties arbitrarily. For instance, when $G_0^* = \{2@(3,0), 2@(1,2)\}$, we have $\overline{M}(G_0^*, 3) = \{2@(3,0), 1@(1,2)\}$.

**Definition 5.4.** For any fixed $0 \leq \gamma < N_{\mathsf{oth}}$, define $\eta_\gamma(\cdot)$ as:

$$\eta_\gamma(y) = \begin{cases} \max\left\{x \in [N_0] \mid \overline{M}(G_0, x) \bigcup \overline{M}(G_{\mathsf{oth}}, y) \text{not prefer } 0\right\} & \text{if } \overline{M}(G_0, N_0) \bigcup \overline{M}(G_{\mathsf{oth}}, y) \text{ prefers } 0 \\ \infty & \text{otherwise.} \end{cases}$$

Let $\alpha = |G_{\mathsf{oth}}| - k_{\mathsf{oth}}$ be the number of corrupted oth-supporters needed to fail the reconstruction of $s_{\mathsf{oth}}$. Intuitively, $\eta_\gamma(\cdot)$ is defined such that if a coalition controls more than $\eta_\gamma(\alpha)$ number of 0-supporters and $\alpha$ number of oth-players, then the coalition is able to fail the reconstruction of $s_{\mathsf{oth}}$ while still preferring 0. Such coalition could break the CSP-fairness. However, if the coalition only contains $\eta_\gamma(\alpha)$ number of 0-supporters and $\alpha$ number of oth-players, then this coalition does not prefer 0, and it is not incentivized to fail the reconstruction of $s_{\mathsf{oth}}$. If $\eta_\gamma(\alpha) \geq N_0$, that implies if a coalition controls $\alpha$ number of oth-supporters, it shall never prefer 0.

**Constraints 5.5.** *To achieve CSP fairness, $t = t_0 + t_{\mathsf{oth}}$ needs to satisfy the following conditions:*

($C1$) *$\mathcal{C}$ cannot control both coins. Equivalently, either $t_0 \leq k_0$ or $t_{\mathsf{oth}} \leq k_{\mathsf{oth}}$. Otherwise, $\mathcal{C}$ can force the outcome to be whatever the coalition's overall preference is.*

($C2$) *If $\mathcal{C}$ controls $s_{\mathsf{oth}}$, then it cannot fail the reconstruction of $s_0$. That is, if $t_{\mathsf{oth}} > k_{\mathsf{oth}}$, then it must be that $t_0 < |G_0| - k_0$. Otherwise, $\mathcal{C}$ can control the outcome to be the $s_{\mathsf{oth}}$ coin it decides by failing the reconstruction of $s_0$.*

($C3$) *If $\mathcal{C}$ can hamper the reconstruction of $s_{\mathsf{oth}}$, then it must NOT prefer 0. That is, if $t_{\mathsf{oth}} \geq |G_{\mathsf{oth}}| - k_{\mathsf{oth}}$, then $t_0 \leq \eta_\gamma(t_{\mathsf{oth}})$. Otherwise, $\mathcal{C}$ can fail $s_{\mathsf{oth}}$'s reconstruction to force the outcome 0, benefiting $\mathcal{C}$ compared to honest behavior.*

**Lemma 5.6.** *If ($C1$), ($C2$), ($C3$) are satisfied, then Protocol 5.3 achieves CSP-fairness against any coalition controlling no more than $t = t_0 + t_{\mathsf{oth}}$ players.*

*Proof.* By Lemma 5.1, for a coalition to fail the reconstruction of $s_{\mathsf{oth}}$, we it must have $t_{\mathsf{oth}} \geq |G_{\mathsf{oth}}| - k_{\mathsf{oth}}$. Thus, condition ($C3$) implies that if the coalition fails the reconstruction of $s_{\mathsf{oth}}$, the coalition's utility must be no more than its honest expected utility by the definition of $\eta_\gamma(\cdot) \geq t_0$. Therefore, any coalition is incentivized to successfully reconstruct $s_{\mathsf{oth}}$.

Conditioned on $s_{\mathsf{oth}}$ being reconstructed, if the coalition controls the value of $s_{\mathsf{oth}}$, i.e., $t_{\mathsf{oth}} \geq k_{\mathsf{oth}} + 1$, then by Condition ($C1$), $t_0 \leq k_0$. By Lemma 5.1, this means the $s_o$ coin's value must be uniformly random to the coalition. Furthermore, ($C2$) stipulates that $t_0 < |G_0| - k_0$, so by Lemma 5.1, the coin $s_0$ is successfully reconstructed. Therefore, the protocol outcome must be uniformly random. If $t_{\mathsf{oth}} \leq k_{\mathsf{oth}}$, then $s_{\mathsf{oth}}$ must be a uniformly random coin to the coalition and successfully reconstructed. Thus, the outcome again is uniformly random, whether $s_0$ is successfully reconstructed or not. □

**Constraints 5.7. Coalition Size Parameter Constraints**
Let $\alpha := |G_{\mathsf{oth}}| - k_{\mathsf{oth}}$.
$0 \leq \gamma < N_{\mathsf{oth}}, 0 \leq k_0 \leq N_0 + \gamma - 1,\ 1 \leq \alpha \leq N_{\mathsf{oth}} - \gamma$

(C1*) $t \leq k_0 + (N_{\mathsf{oth}} - \gamma - \alpha) + 1$.
(C2*) $t \leq N - \alpha - k_0$.
(C3*) If $\eta_\gamma(\alpha) < N_0$ then $t \leq \eta_\gamma(\alpha) + \alpha$.

**Lemma 5.8.** *Protocol 5.3 with parameters $k_0, k_{\mathsf{oth}}$, and $\gamma$ achieves CSP fairness against any size-$t$ coalition where $t$ satisfies Constraint 5.7.*

*Proof.* We only need to show that Constraint 5.7 imply $(C1)$, $(C2)$, $(C3)$. Recall that $k_{\mathsf{oth}} = N_{\mathsf{oth}} - \gamma - \alpha$. Constraint (C1*) implies Condition $(C1)$ as in order to control both coins, a coalition would need at least $k_0 + k_{\mathsf{oth}} + 2$ parties. Similarly, constraint (C2*) implies Condition $(C2)$ as in order to control the $s_{\mathsf{oth}}$ coin and fail the $s_0$ coin, the coalition would need at least $(N_{\mathsf{oth}} - \gamma - \alpha + 1) + (N_0 + \gamma - k_0) = N - \alpha - k_0$ parties. We now focus on proving that (C3*) implies $(C3)$.

Observe that if $\eta_\gamma(\alpha) \geq N_0$, then when $t_{\mathsf{oth}} \geq \alpha$, it must be that $\eta_\gamma(t_{\mathsf{oth}}) \geq N_0 \geq t_0$. Therefore, Condition $(C3)$ is satisfied. On the other hand, if $\eta_\gamma(\alpha) < N_0$, the constraint implies that $t \leq \eta_\gamma(\alpha) + \alpha$. Therefore, it must be that when $t_{\mathsf{oth}} \geq \alpha$, we have $t_0 \leq t - t_{\mathsf{oth}} \leq t - \alpha \leq \eta_\gamma(\alpha) \leq \eta_\gamma(t_{\mathsf{oth}})$. □

The optimization and the proof of Theorem 1.3 is given in the full version.

## 6 Construction by Coalition Bet

Another natural construction goal is to achieve fairness against coalitions based on the total bet of the coalition. In this section, we present a protocol that achieves CSP fairness against any coalition with total bet no more than $\beta$.

Given a preference profile $\boldsymbol{\mathcal{P}}$, we use $B_0$ and $B_{\mathsf{oth}}$ to respectively denote the cumulative bet on outcome 0 and on all other outcomes. Formally,

$$B_0 = \sum_{i=1}^{\ell} \mathsf{bet}_i(0), \qquad B_{\mathsf{oth}} = \sum_{i=1}^{n} \sum_{\ell=1}^{m-1} \mathsf{bet}_i(\ell).$$

We also use $\mathsf{bet}_i(\mathsf{oth}) = \sum_{\ell=1}^{m-1} \mathsf{bet}_i(\ell)$ to denote the sum of player $i$'s bets on all non-0 outcomes.

In this protocol, we will use weighted secret sharing to defend against coalition in terms of corrupted bets. Weighted secret sharing has an access structure of the secret sharing is $\Gamma = \{S \subseteq [n] : \mathsf{bet}_S(b) \geq k+1\}$ where $\mathsf{bet}_S(b) = \sum_{i \in S} \mathsf{bet}_i(b)$ is the total bet of set $S$ on outcome $b$. In other words, any set with $k+1$ or more bets on outcome $b$ can reconstruct the secret while any set with less than $k+1$ bets on outcome $b$ learns nothing about the secret. In our protocol, weighted secret sharing can be instantiated using Shamir's secret sharing in a straightforward manner: Each secret is split into $B_b$ shares for $b \in \{0, \mathsf{oth}\}$, and each player $i$ gets $\mathsf{bet}_i(b)$ number of shares.

### 6.1 $\mathsf{betGroupToss}^b[k]$ Sub-Protocol

Similar to Protocol 5.3, the bets-based protocol runs two sub-protocols $\mathsf{bet\text{-}GroupToss}^b[k]$ for $b \in \{0, \mathsf{oth}\}$ and decide two coins $c_0$ and $c_{\mathsf{oth}}$. Here, $k \in [B_b]$ is the threshold parameter to be chosen later. The final outcome will be determined by the value of $c_0$ and $c_{\mathsf{oth}}$. The sub-protocol $\mathsf{bet\text{-}GroupToss}^b[k]$ runs a weighted secret sharing among all $N$ players, where each player's weight is associated with its bets.

> **Protocol 6.1.** $\mathsf{bet\text{-}GroupToss}^b[k]$ **sub-protocol (Semi-Malicious)**
> Let $\mathcal{O}$ be the set of online players, initialized as $[n]$.
>
> **Sharing Phase.** Each player $i$ chooses a random coin $\mathsf{coin}_i \xleftarrow{\$} [m]_0$. Player $i$ shares $\mathsf{coin}_i$ among $[n]$ with an access structure $\Gamma = \{S \subseteq [n] : \mathsf{bet}_S(b) \geq k+1\}$. Denote the set of shares as $\{c_{i,j}\}_{j\in[n]}$. Send $c_{i,j}$ to player $j$. If any player aborts, remove them from $\mathcal{O}$.
> **Reconstruction Phase.** Every player $i$ broadcast the shares $\{c_{j,i}\}_{j\in\mathcal{O}}$ it has received from players in $\mathcal{O}$. Players use $\{c_{j,i}\}_{j\in\mathcal{O}}$ to reconstruct $\{\mathsf{coin}_i\}_{i\in\mathcal{O}}$. If any $\mathsf{coin}_i$ failed to be reconstructed, output $c_b = \bot$; otherwise, output $(\sum_{i\in\mathcal{O}} \mathsf{coin}_i) \mod m$.

**Lemma 6.2** (Lemma 4.2 of [35]). *The above* $\mathsf{bet\text{-}GroupToss}^b[k]$ *protocol satisfies the following properties due to the property of Shamir secret sharing.*

- *Binding. The sharing phase uniquely binds to a secret $s$, such that the reconstruction phase either succeeds and outputs $s$, or it fails and outputs $\bot$.*
- *Knowledge threshold. If a coalition $\mathcal{C}$ controls bets $\mathsf{bet}_{\mathcal{C}}(b) \geq k+1$, the coalition can completely control the binded value $s$ of the sharing phase. Specifically, the coalition can reconstruct the values of $\mathsf{coin}_i$ from honest players and choose their value of $\mathsf{coin}_j$ for $j \in \mathcal{C}$ accordingly. Otherwise, the secret $s$ looks uniformly random to the coalition.*
- *Liveness threshold. If a coalition $\mathcal{C}$ controls bet $\mathsf{bet}_{\mathcal{C}}(b) \geq B_b - k$, the coalition can cause the reconstruction to fail and output $\bot$. Otherwise, the reconstruction phase must succeed.*

### 6.2 Bets-Based Protocol

The full protocol runs a $\mathsf{bet\text{-}GroupToss}^0[k_0]$ and a $\mathsf{bet\text{-}GroupToss}^{\mathsf{oth}}[k_{\mathsf{oth}}]$ as follows where $k_0$ and $k_{\mathsf{oth}}$ are parameters that will be determined later.

> **Protocol 6.3 Bets-based protocol (semi-malicious)**
> **Sharing Phase**
>
> 1. All players run the sharing phase of $\mathsf{bet\text{-}GroupToss}^0[k_0]$.
> 2. All players run the sharing phase of $\mathsf{bet\text{-}GroupToss}^{\mathsf{oth}}[k_{\mathsf{oth}}]$.
>
> **Reconstruction Phase**
>
> 1. Run the reconstruction phase of $\mathsf{bet\text{-}GroupToss}^0[k_0]$. Let $s_0$ be the outcome of the sub-protocol.

2. Run the reconstruction phase of bet-GroupToss$^{\mathsf{oth}}[k_{\mathsf{oth}}]$. Let $s_{\mathsf{oth}}$ be the outcome of the sub-protocol.
3. If $s_{\mathsf{oth}} = \perp$, output 0; Otherwise, if $s_0 = \perp$, set $s_0 = 0$ and output $(s_{\mathsf{oth}} + s_0) \mod m$.

**Constraints 6.4.** *Consider a coalition $\mathcal{C}$ that controls $\beta = \beta_0 + \beta_{\mathsf{oth}}$ total bet, where $\beta_0$ and $\beta_{\mathsf{oth}}$ denote the bets on 0 and on* oth. *That is, $\beta_0 = \mathsf{bet}_{\mathcal{C}}(0)$ and $\beta_{\mathsf{oth}} = \mathsf{bet}_{\mathcal{C}}(\mathsf{oth})$. To achieve CSP-fairness, we must choose $k_0$ and $k_{\mathsf{oth}}$ such that the following hold.*

($C1'$) *$\mathcal{C}$ cannot control both coins. Equivalently, either $\beta_0 \leq k_0$ or $\beta_{\mathsf{oth}} \leq k_{\mathsf{oth}}$. Otherwise, $\mathcal{C}$ can force the outcome to be whatever the coalition's overall preference is.*

($C2'$) *If $\mathcal{C}$ controls $s_{\mathsf{oth}}$, then it cannot fail the reconstruction of $s_0$. That is, if $\beta_{\mathsf{oth}} > k_{\mathsf{oth}}$, then it must be that $\beta_0 < B_0 - k_0$. Otherwise, $\mathcal{C}$ can control the outcome to be the $s_{\mathsf{oth}}$ coin it decides by failing the reconstruction of $s_0$.*

($C3'$) *If $\mathcal{C}$ can hamper the reconstruction of $s_{\mathsf{oth}}$, then it must NOT prefer 0. That is, if $\beta_{\mathsf{oth}} \geq B_{\mathsf{oth}} - k_{\mathsf{oth}}$, then $\beta_0 \leq \frac{\beta}{m}$. Otherwise, $\mathcal{C}$ can fail the reconstruction of $s_{\mathsf{oth}}$ to force the outcome 0, benefiting $\mathcal{C}$ compared to honest behavior.*

**Lemma 6.5.** *If conditions ($C1'$), ($C2'$), ($C3'$) are satisfied, then Protocol 6.3 achieves CSP-fairness against any coalition controlling $\beta$ total bet.*

*Proof.* Condition ($C3'$) implies that if the coalition fails the reconstruction of $s_{\mathsf{oth}}$, requiring $\beta_{\mathsf{oth}} \geq B_{\mathsf{oth}} - k_{\mathsf{oth}}$ by Lemma 6.2, the coalition's utility $\beta_0$ must be no more than its honest expected utility $\frac{\beta}{m}$. Therefore, any coalition is incentivized to successfully reconstruct $s_{\mathsf{oth}}$.

Conditioned on $s_{\mathsf{oth}}$ being reconstructed, if the coalition controls the value of $s_{\mathsf{oth}}$, i.e., $\beta_{\mathsf{oth}} \geq k_{\mathsf{oth}} + 1$, then by Condition ($C1'$), $\beta_0 \leq k_0$. Thus by Lemma 6.2, the coin $s_0$ must be uniformly random to the coalition. Furthermore, ($C2'$) stipulates that $\beta_0 < B_0 - k_0$, so by Lemma 6.2, the $s_0$ coin is successfully reconstructed. Therefore, the protocol outcome must be uniformly random. If $\beta_{\mathsf{oth}} \leq k_{\mathsf{oth}}$, then $s_{\mathsf{oth}}$ must be a uniformly random coin and successfully reconstructed. Thus, the outcome again is uniformly random, whether $s_0$ is successfully reconstructed or not. □

**Constraints 6.6. Coalition Bet Parameter Constraints**
Assume $0 \leq k_0 \leq B_0$, $0 \leq k_{\mathsf{oth}} \leq B_{\mathsf{oth}}$

(C1*) $\beta \leq k_0 + k_{\mathsf{oth}} + 1$
(C2*) $\beta \leq k_{\mathsf{oth}} + B_0 - k_0$
(C3*) if $B_{\mathsf{oth}} - k_{\mathsf{oth}} < (m-1)B_0$, then $\beta \leq \frac{m}{m-1}(B_{\mathsf{oth}} - k_{\mathsf{oth}})$

**Claim 6.7.** *Constraint 6.6 imply ($C1'$), ($C2'$), ($C3'$).*

*Proof.* The first two are straightforward and follow the same proof structure as Lemma 5.8, so we only focus on proving the third one condition. If $B_{\mathsf{oth}} - k_{\mathsf{oth}} \geq (m-1)B_0$, then if a coalition can fail the reconstruction of $s_{\mathsf{oth}}$, it must be the case that $\beta \geq m \cdot \beta_0$ since $\beta_0 \leq B_0 \leq \frac{1}{m-1}\beta_{\mathsf{oth}}$. In this case, the coalition must not prefer 0. On the other hand, if $B_{\mathsf{oth}} - k_{\mathsf{oth}} < B_0$, then the constraint requires $\beta \leq \frac{m}{m-1}(B_{\mathsf{oth}} - k_{\mathsf{oth}})$. This guarantees that if $\beta_{\mathsf{oth}} \geq B_{\mathsf{oth}} - k_{\mathsf{oth}}$, i.e., if the coalition can fail the reconstruction of $s_{\mathsf{oth}}$, then $\beta_0 = \beta - \beta_{\mathsf{oth}} \leq \frac{1}{m-1}\beta_{\mathsf{oth}}$, which implies that $\beta_0 \leq \frac{\beta}{m}$. □

Below, we give the optimal parameters and coalition resilience of 6.3 (Tables 3, 4 and 7).

**Table 3.** Optimal resilience of Protocol 6.3 against semi-malicious adversary.

| Case | $k_0$ | $k_{\mathsf{oth}}$ | $t$ |
|---|---|---|---|
| If $B_{\mathsf{oth}} \geq \frac{4m-3}{2}B_0$ | $\lfloor \frac{B_0}{2} \rfloor$ | $B_{\mathsf{oth}} - (m-1)B_0$ | $\lceil \frac{B_0}{2} \rceil + B_{\mathsf{oth}} - (m-1)B_0$ |
| Otherwise | $\lfloor \frac{B_0}{2} \rfloor$ | $\lfloor \frac{m}{2m-1}B_{\mathsf{oth}} - \frac{m-1}{2(2m-1)}B_0 \rfloor$ | $\lceil \frac{B_0}{2} \rceil + \lfloor \frac{m}{2m-1}B_{\mathsf{oth}} - \frac{m-1}{2(2m-1)}B_0 \rfloor$ |

## 7 Concrete Examples

While the above optimization describes the optimal solution, it is hard to give a closed form optimal resilience since Protocol 5.3 aims for a rather general preference profile. In this section, we give a closed form for some concrete examples and compare the coalition resilience of both protocols.

*Unit-Split.* In this sub-formulation of split-bet, for each player $i$'s preference, we have $\mathbf{p}_i \in \{0,1\}^m$. That is, each player chooses $B < m$ out of $m$ possible outcomes, and gets utility 1 for each chosen outcome. Without loss of generality, we assume that 0 is the least preferred outcome, i.e., 0 has the cumulative bet. In this case, the expected honest utility of each player is $\mu = \frac{B}{m} < 1$. One can see that when $B = 1$, this downgrades to the special case considered in previous works where each player prefers a specific outcome. Each player either gets utility 0 on outcome 0 or utility 1 on outcome 0. Therefore, the optimal choice of $\gamma$ is either $\gamma = 0$ or $\gamma = N_{\mathsf{oth}}$.

In Table 5, we give the comparison of both protocols on unit-split. Specifically, the size-based protocol is always at least as good as the bets-based protocol. For the specific case where $B = 1$, both protocol achieves the same resilience.

**Table 4.** Optimal resilience of Protocol 5.3 for the unit-bet against semi-malicious adversaries.

| Case | $\gamma$ | $k_0$ | $k_{\text{oth}}$ | $t$ |
|---|---|---|---|---|
| $N_{\text{oth}} \geq \frac{4m-3B}{2B} N_0$ | 0 | $\lfloor \frac{N_0}{2} \rfloor$ | $N_{\text{oth}} - \left\lceil \frac{(m-B)N_0}{B} \right\rceil$ | $N_{\text{oth}} + \lceil \frac{2B-m}{2B} N_0 \rceil$ |
| Otherwise | 0 | $\lfloor \frac{N_0}{2} \rfloor$ | $\left\lfloor \frac{m}{2m-B} N_{\text{oth}} - \frac{m-B}{2(2m-B)} N_0 \right\rfloor$ | $\left\lfloor \frac{m}{2m-B} N_{\text{oth}} + \frac{m}{2(2m-B)} N_0 \right\rfloor$ |

**Table 5.** Comparison of the optimal resilience for the unit-bet formulation. Here, the size-based protocol is always at least as good as the bets-based protocol.For the specific case where $B = 1$, both protocol achieves the same resilience.

| Case | Size-based protocol Protocol 5.3 | bets-based protocol Protocol 6.3 |
|---|---|---|
| $N_{\text{oth}} \geq \frac{4m-3B}{2B} N_0$ | $N_{\text{oth}} + \lceil \frac{2B-m}{2B} N_0 \rceil$ | $N_{\text{oth}} + \lfloor \frac{2B-2m+1}{2B} \rfloor N_0$ |
| Otherwise | $\left\lfloor \frac{m}{2m-B} N_{\text{oth}} + \frac{m}{2(2m-B)} N_0 \right\rfloor$ | $\left\lfloor \frac{m}{2m-1} N_{\text{oth}} + \frac{2m-m/B}{2(2m-1)} N_0 \right\rfloor$ |

*Ranked Preference.* Next, we give the optimization for another concrete example of split-preference called the ranked preference profile. Specifically, we will give the characterization for $m = 2$ and 3 for better understanding. Instead of preferring certain outcomes, the players now have a rank over all possible outcomes and gets utility $m - i$ on the $i$-th preferred outcome. We use $\ell \succ \ell'$ to represent that a player ranked $\ell$ over $\ell'$. For example, in a ternary ranked preferences, some players' rank is $2 \succ 0 \succ 1$, while some other players' rank is $1 \succ 2 \succ 0$. Each player gets utility 2 on its highest-ranked preference, 1 on the medium-ranked preference and 0 utility on its lowest-ranked preference. Note that when $m = 2$, this ranked preference boils down to the standard binary coin toss. The table below presents the optimal parameter choices for $m = 2$ and $m = 3$. Since $k_0$ is simply $\lfloor \frac{N_0+\gamma}{2} \rfloor$, we omit $k_0$ in the table.

**Table 6.** Coalition resilience of Protocol 5.3 for ranked preference.

| # sides | Cases | $\gamma$ | $k_{\text{oth}}$ | $t$ |
|---|---|---|---|---|
| $m = 2$ | $n_0 \geq \frac{5}{2} n_1$ | 0 | $n_0 - n_1$ | $n_0 - \lfloor \frac{1}{2} n_1 \rfloor$ |
| | otherwise | 0 | $\lfloor \frac{2}{3} n_0 - \frac{1}{6} n_1 \rfloor$ | $\lfloor \frac{2}{3} n_0 + \frac{1}{3} n_1 \rfloor$ |
| $m = 3$ | $n_0 \geq \frac{5}{2} n_2 - \frac{1}{2} n_1$ | $n_1$ | $n_0 - n_2$ | $\lfloor n_0 + \frac{1}{2} n_1 - \frac{1}{2} n_2 \rfloor$ |
| | $n_1 + n_2 \leq n_0 < \frac{5}{2} n_2 - \frac{1}{2} n_1$ | 0 | $\lfloor \frac{1}{3} n_0 + \frac{2}{3} n_1 + \frac{1}{6} n_2 \rfloor$ | $\lfloor \frac{2}{3} n_0 + \frac{1}{3} n_1 + \frac{1}{3} n_2 \rfloor$ |
| | otherwise | $n_1 + n_0$ | N/A | $\lceil \frac{1}{2} n_0 + \frac{1}{2} n_1 + \frac{1}{2} n_2 \rceil - 1$ |

Below, we give the resilience of both protocols for ternary ranked preference, since binary ranked preference is equivalent to unit-split with $B = 1$.

**Table 7.** Comparison of the optimal resilience for the ternary ranked preference. When $n_0$ is much larger than $n_1 + n_2$, the size-based protocol performs better; when $n_0 \leq n_1 + n_2$, the bets-based protocol achieves better resilience.

| Size-based protocol Protocol 5.3 | | Bets-based protocol Protocol 6.3 | |
|---|---|---|---|
| Case | Resilience | Case | Resilience |
| $n_0 \geq \frac{5}{2}n_2 - \frac{1}{2}n_1$ | $\lfloor n_0 + \frac{1}{2}n_1 - \frac{1}{2}n_2 \rfloor$ | $n_0 \geq \frac{5}{6}n_1 + \frac{8}{3}n_2$ | $\lfloor n_0 + \frac{1}{6}n_1 - \frac{2}{3}n_2 \rfloor$ |
| $n_1 + n_2 \leq n_0 < \frac{5}{2}n_2 - \frac{1}{2}n_1$ | $\lfloor \frac{2}{3}n_0 + \frac{1}{3}n_1 + \frac{1}{3}n_2 \rfloor$ | | |
| Otherwise | $\lceil N/2 \rceil - 1$ | Otherwise | $\lfloor \frac{3}{5}n_0 + \frac{1}{2}n_1 + \frac{2}{5}n_2 \rfloor$ |

## References


1. Abraham, I., Dolev, D., Gonen, R., Halpern, J.: Distributed computing meets game theory: robust mechanisms for rational secret sharing and multiparty computation. In: PODC (2006)
2. Alon, B., Omri, E.: Almost-optimally fair multiparty coin-tossing with nearly three-quarters malicious. In: TCC (2016)
3. Andrychowicz, M., Dziembowski, S., Malinowski, D., Mazurek, u.: Secure multi-party computations on bitcoin. Commun. ACM **59**(4), 76–84 (2016). https://doi.org/10.1145/2896386
4. Asharov, G., Canetti, R., Hazay, C.: Towards a game theoretic view of secure computation. In: Eurocrypt (2011)
5. Asharov, G., Lindell, Y.: Utility dependence in correct and fair rational secret sharing. J. Cryptology **24**(1) (2011)
6. Aumayr, L., Thyagarajan, S.A., Malavolta, G., Moreno-Sanchez, P., Maffei, M.: Sleepy channels: bi-directional payment channels without watchtowers. In: Proceedings of the 2022 ACM SIGSAC Conference on Computer and Communications Security, pp. 179–192. CCS '22, Association for Computing Machinery, New York, NY, USA (2022). https://doi.org/10.1145/3548606.3559370
7. Beimel, A., Haitner, I., Makriyannis, N., Omri, E.: Tighter bounds on multiparty coin flipping via augmented weak martingales and differentially private sampling. SIAM J. Comput. **51**(4), 1126–1171 (2022)
8. Beimel, A., Omri, E., Orlov, I.: Protocols for multiparty coin toss with a dishonest majority. J. Cryptol. **28**(3), 551–600 (2015)
9. Bentov, I., Kumaresan, R.: How to use bitcoin to design fair protocols. In: CRYPTO, pp. 421–439 (2014)
10. Berman, I., Haitner, I., Tentes, A.: Coin flipping of any constant bias implies one-way functions. J. ACM (JACM) **65**(3), 1–95 (2018)
11. Blum, M.: Coin flipping by telephone a protocol for solving impossible problems. SIGACT News (1983)
12. Buchbinder, N., Haitner, I., Levi, N., Tsfadia, E.: Fair coin flipping: tighter analysis and the many-party case. In: Proceedings of the Twenty-Eighth Annual ACM-SIAM Symposium on Discrete Algorithms, pp. 2580–2600. SIAM (2017)
13. Chung, H., Masserova, E., Shi, E., Thyagarajan, S.A.: Rapidash: foundations of side-contract-resilient fair exchange. Cryptology ePrint Archive, Paper 2022/1063 (2022). https://eprint.iacr.org/2022/1063

14. Chung, K.M., Chan, T.H.H., Wen, T., Shi, E.: Game-theoretic fairness meets multi-party protocols: The case of leader election. In: CRYPTO (2021). https://eprint.iacr.org/2020/1591
15. Chung, K.M., Chan, T.H.H., Wen, T., Shi, E.: Game-theoretic fairness meets multi-party protocols: the case of leader election. In: Malkin, T., Peikert, C. (eds.) Advances in Cryptology - CRYPTO 2021, pp. 3–32. Springer International Publishing, Cham (2021)
16. Chung, K.M., Guo, Y., Lin, W.K., Pass, R., Shi, E.: Game theoretic notions of fairness in multi-party coin toss. In: TCC (2018)
17. Cleve, R.: Limits on the security of coin flips when half the processors are faulty. In: Proceedings of the eighteenth annual ACM symposium on Theory of computing, pp. 364–369 (1986)
18. Dachman-Soled, D., Lindell, Y., Mahmoody, M., Malkin, T.: On the black-box complexity of optimally-fair coin tossing. In: Theory of Cryptography Conference, pp. 450–467. Springer (2011)
19. Dodis, Y., Rabin, T.: Cryptography and game theory. In: AGT (2007)
20. Dziembowski, S., Eckey, L., Faust, S.: Fairswap: How to fairly exchange digital goods. In: Proceedings of the 2018 ACM SIGSAC Conference on Computer and Communications Security, pp. 967–984. CCS '18, Association for Computing Machinery, New York, NY, USA (2018). https://doi.org/10.1145/3243734.3243857
21. Goldreich, O., Micali, S., Wigderson, A.: How to play any mental game, or a completeness theorem for protocols with honest majority. In: STOC (2019)
22. Haitner, I., Omri, E.: Coin flipping with constant bias implies one-way functions. SIAM J. Comput. **43**(2), 389–409 (2014)
23. Haitner, I., Tsfadia, E.: An almost-optimally fair three-party coin-flipping protocol. In: Proceedings of the forty-sixth annual ACM symposium on Theory of computing, pp. 408–416 (2014)
24. Halpern, J., Teague, V.: Rational secret sharing and multiparty computation. In: STOC (2004)
25. Katz, J.: Bridging game theory and cryptography: recent results and future directions. In: TCC (2008)
26. Klein, O., Komargodski, I., Zhu, C.: On the (im) possibility of game-theoretically fair leader election protocols. In: Theory of Cryptography Conference, pp. 383–412. Springer (2024)
27. Kol, G., Naor, M.: Cryptography and game theory: Designing protocols for exchanging information. In: TCC (2008)
28. Komargodski, I., Matsuo, S., Shi, E., Wu, K.: log*-round game-theoretically-fair leader election. In: Dodis, Y., Shrimpton, T. (eds.) Advances in Cryptology - CRYPTO 2022, pp. 409–438. Springer Nature Switzerland, Cham (2022)
29. Kosba, A.E., Miller, A., Shi, E., Wen, Z., Papamanthou, C.: Hawk: the blockchain model of cryptography and privacy-preserving smart contracts. In: IEEE Symposium on Security and Privacy, SP 2016, San Jose, CA, USA, May 22–26, 2016, pp. 839–858. IEEE Computer Society (2016)
30. Kumaresan, R., Bentov, I.: How to use bitcoin to incentivize correct computations. In: Proceedings of the 2014 ACM SIGSAC Conference on Computer and Communications Security, Scottsdale, AZ, USA, November 3-7, 2014, pp. 30–41. ACM (2014)
31. Kumaresan, R., Vaikuntanathan, V., Vasudevan, P.N.: Improvements to secure computation with penalties. In: ACM CCS (2016)

32. Micali, S., Goldreich, O., Wigderson, A.: How to play any mental game. In: Proceedings of the Nineteenth ACM Symposium on Theory of Computing, STOC, pp. 218–229. ACM New York, NY, USA (1987)
33. Moran, T., Naor, M., Segev, G.: An optimally fair coin toss. J. Cryptol. **29**(3), 491–513 (2016)
34. Ong, S.J., Parkes, D.C., Rosen, A., Vadhan, S.P.: Fairness with an honest minority and a rational majority. In: TCC (2009)
35. Thyagarajan, S.A., Soni, P., Wu, K.: Game-theoretically fair distributed sampling. In: Annual International Cryptology Conference, pp. 207–239. Springer (2024)
36. Wu, K., Asharov, G., Shi, E.: A complete characterization of game-theoretically fair, multi-party coin toss. In: Dunkelman, O., Dziembowski, S. (eds.) Advances in Cryptology - EUROCRYPT 2022, pp. 120–149. Springer International Publishing, Cham (2022)
37. Yao, A.C.: Protocols for secure computations. In: FOCS (1982)

# Game Changer: A Modular Framework for OPRF Security

Karla Friedrichs(✉), Anja Lehmann, and Cavit Özbay

Hasso Plattner Institute, University of Potsdam, Potsdam, Germany
{karla.friedrichs,anja.lehmann,cavit.oezbay}@hpi.de

**Abstract.** Oblivious pseudorandom functions (OPRFs) allow the blind evaluation of a pseudorandom function, which makes them a versatile building block that enjoys usage in numerous applications. So far, security of OPRFs is predominantly captured in the Universal Composability (UC) framework, where an ideal functionality covers the expected security and privacy properties. While the OPRF functionality appears intuitive at first, the ideal-world paradigm also comes with a number of challenges: from imposing idealized building blocks when building OPRFs, to the lack of modularity, and requiring intricate UC knowledge to securely maneuver their usage. Game-based definitions are a simpler way to cover security properties. They model each property in a single game, which grants modularity in formalizing, proving, and using OPRFs. Interestingly, the few game-based works on OPRFs each re-invent the security model, with considerable variation. Thus, the advantages of the game-based approach remain out of reach: definitions are not easily accessible and comparability across works is low. In this work, we therefore systematize all existing notions into a clear, hierarchical framework. We unify or separate properties, making hidden relations explicit. This effort reveals the necessity of two novel properties: an intermediate privacy notion and a stronger unpredictability notion. Finally, we analyze the two most prominent constructions in our framework: HashDH and 2HashDH. The former does not achieve UC security, but has advantages in applications that require key rotation or updatability; yet it lacks a security analysis. We show that it achieves most security properties in our framework. We also observe that HashDH and 2HashDH do not satisfy our strongest privacy notion, indicating that the guarantees by the UC functionality are not as well understood as we might expect them to be. Overall, we hope that our framework facilitates the usage and design of OPRFs.

**Keywords:** OPRFs · provable security · game-based model · HashDH

## 1 Introduction

Oblivious pseudorandom functions (OPRFs) [18,29] allow two parties, an evaluator holding a secret key $k$ and requester holding a private input $x$, to jointly compute a pseudorandom value $y = F(k, x)$. The obliviousness thereby guarantees that the evaluator does not learn anything about the input $x$ nor output $y$

© International Association for Cryptologic Research 2026
G. Hanaoka and B.-Y. Yang (Eds.): ASIACRYPT 2025, LNCS 16252, pp. 582–613, 2026.
https://doi.org/10.1007/978-981-95-5125-5_19

for which the PRF is computed. At the same time, the requester can only learn as many PRF values as the evaluator agrees to. These properties make the OPRF a powerful building block, and they enjoy wide-spread usage in privacy-preserving protocols (e.g., [27,32,38,39]) and protocols for the secure key management and user authentication (e.g., [7,15,20,26,33,35]). The two most prominent applications are Privacy Pass [22], ensuring privacy-preserving access control through blindly issued one-time tokens, and OPAQUE [36], the first strongly secure asymmetric PAKE. Both are standardized in the IETF [13,19], and also the underlying OPRF – 2HashDH – is part of an IRTF RFC [21] that covers practical instantiations of oblivious PRFs from prime-order groups.

**OPRF Functionalities.** The most established way to define the security of OPRFs is through modelling their behavior as an ideal functionality $\mathcal{F}_{\mathsf{OPRF}}$ in the Universal Composability (UC) framework [17] (e.g., [6,10,33,34]). The ideal OPRF functionality receives all private inputs and then internally enforces the desired behavior. Here, this desired functionality would be a consistent mapping from arbitrary inputs to pseudorandom outputs, where the evaluator only learns that a query was made, but nothing about the in- or output. Thus, the ideal world makes capturing the combination of (perfect) privacy and consistency trivial. When designing protocols relying on OPRFs, one uses $\mathcal{F}_{\mathsf{OPRF}}$ instead of the concrete instantiation, thereby abstracting from any particular OPRF design choice. In theory, UC promises a simple usage with strong guarantees under arbitrary composition. In practice, however, this approach comes with a number of challenges, outlined in the following.

*Multitude of Monolithic Functionalities.* There is no single, standardized definition for $\mathcal{F}_{\mathsf{OPRF}}$ – in fact, many applications introduce tailored ideal functionalities for their protocols (e.g., [7,12,14,33–36,40,41]). Consequently, security proofs must be redone from scratch, even when two OPRF instantiations are very similar. The tailored design and the monolithic nature of ideal functionalities also make a comparison of their implied guarantees challenging.

*(Too) Strong Requirements.* Further, realizing UC functionalities usually requires idealized primitives to provide the extractability and simulatability needed for the security proof. For OPRFs, this is easily achieved by using the 2HashDH construction $F(k, x) = H_2(x, H_1(x)^k))$, where the outer hash function provides both capabilities in the random oracle model. However, this outer hash takes away any "direct access" to the PRF key $k$, and protocols that require such access, e.g., for key rotation [25] or key homomorphic properties [42], had to revert to HashDH and ad-hoc defined security guarantees.

*Functionalities Abstract All Crypto.* UC functionalities can be too abstract, in that they do not expose cryptographic values. For $\mathcal{F}_{\mathsf{OPRF}}$, there are no cryptographic messages sent or received by the evaluator, which prevents protocols from incorporating these values into a larger design, ultimately hindering modularity. For instance, Faller et al. [26] require the output of an OPRF to be signed by a server – but since no evaluator output is modeled, the authors resort to using 2HashDH instead of a substitutable $\mathcal{F}_{\mathsf{OPRF}}$. Consequently, their proof cannot rely on any of the ideal properties. Similarly, Backendal et al. [4] build 2HashDH as the only non-generic component into their cloud encryption protocol because their security proof requires the outer random oracle.

*The UC Divide.* Finally, UC proofs and functionalities often remain inaccessible to a large part of the cryptographic community, especially its more applied side. Quoting Bellare et al. [8]: "There is a divide, in the cryptographic community, between those who speak and use the language of UC, and those who don't." In fact, even the eponymous property of composability has its pitfalls: It only holds if the composed building blocks are fully independent. For instance, the OPAQUE protocol was proven secure for a single user only, relying on UC self-composition for scaling the protocol to multiple users. This requires using independent OPRF instances for all users. In the OPAQUE IRTF draft [13], however, re-using related OPRF keys was suggested, which not only invalidates the proven security guarantees but can also lead to actual attacks [23].

**Game-Based OPRF Definitions.** Game-based definitions offer a more established and accessible approach for modelling and applying security guarantees. Each security game addresses a particular property where an attacker with a set of abilities tries to perform a particular attack. A construction is deemed secure if the game cannot be beaten by any efficient attacker. Splitting the model into such elementary properties allows to compose an analysis for an arbitrary set of aspects. Especially compared to UC ideal functionalities, this facilitates reusable protocols by breaking down complex proofs into manageable steps and allowing for easy comparison of achieved properties across constructions. Furthermore, the game-based approach requires a concrete, algorithmic representation of the construction, exposing key material and cryptographic components – which enhances modularity in protocol design compared to abstract UC interfaces.

*In Search of a Standard Definition.* While there is some previous work on security games for OPRFs [1,3,8,25,42,45], contributions are overall scarce. Strikingly, instead of an agreed-upon definition, each work comes up with their own syntax and properties of OPRFs, often tailored to a specific construction. To a wider audience, it is desirable to have definitions readily available, especially considering that OPRFs are often just one building block in larger applications. Unfortunately, at the time of writing, some definitions overlap or are equivalent, others use strikingly different approaches to express the same property. Being aware of the variants and selecting one becomes a tedious task. This issue even seems to extend to more expert readers: looking ahead, some property relations turn out intricate and non-trivial to prove.

Overall, in the current state of research, the advantages of game-based over UC definitions cannot take effect: Accessibility of models is low, the proven security from different works is hard to compare and protocols cannot be designed in a modular way as long as the modules lack clear relations.

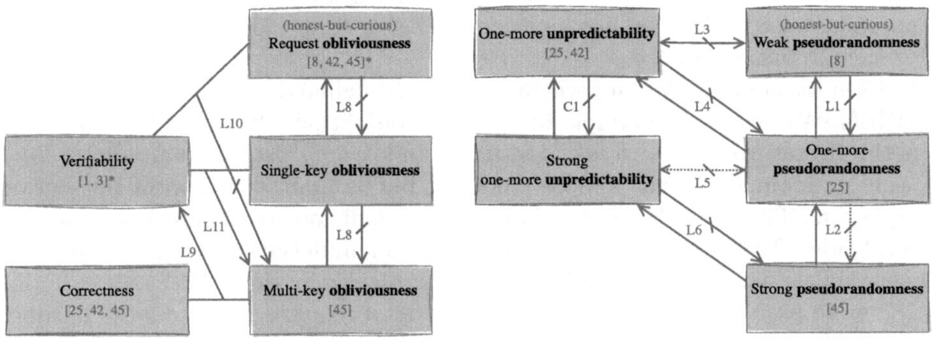


**Fig. 1.** Overview of our definitional framework. Here we cite the definitions we adapted or modified (*), more related works are discussed in the corresponding section. Arrows are implications, barred arrows are separations shown in our work, labelled with the corresponding lemma or corollary. Relations with a dotted line require additional assumptions. All lemmas are new except for L4, which has been stated before by [25], and L8 which was informally treated by [45].

## 1.1 Our Contributions

In this work we propose a hierarchical framework for game-based security of OPRFs, systematizing and extending the scattered definitional landscape. Our framework provides a new formal foundation for this powerful primitive, and discovers a number of gaps and challenges when dissecting the concrete properties of OPRFs. An overview of all definitions and shown relations is depicted in Fig. 1. Our game-based approach enables to capture the different levels of security and privacy, and their necessity when designing protocols. This provides a more granular understanding of OPRFs and hopefully simplifies the quest of finding quantum-safe instantiations, which still proves to be a challenge when aiming at full UC security [2,5,10,12]. We also analyze the two most prominent OPRF instantiations, HashDH and 2HashDH, particularly focusing on the security properties HashDH can provide without the burden of UC security. In more detail, our work comprises the following contributions.

*Security: Unpredictability and Pseudorandomness.* The intuitive security properties expected from OPRFs are *unpredictability* and *pseudorandomness*. For the former, we first recap the existing notion of *one-more unpredictability*. We stress that this sole available formalization is insufficient for one of the most prominent applications of OPRFs, Privacy Pass: therein, OPRF outputs are employed as access tokens, essentially providing a verification oracle to users. Therefore, we propose *strong one-more unpredictability* that reflects this adversarial ability. Looking ahead, the property also turns out necessary in a generic compiler for strongly pseudorandom OPRFs. Interestingly, unpredictability is a notion that has not been captured as a stand-alone goal within the UC formalization, and our game-based definition now provides an easier target for OPRFs that are used for such applications.

Pseudorandomness is surprisingly tricky to define due to the blind nature of OPRFs. We restate and adapt three type of definitions that have been proposed in the literature before: *weak*, *one-more* and *strong pseudorandomness*. Weak pseudorandomness is the simplest notion, but is limited to honest-but-curious requesters. The two other notions allow for a malicious requester, but have their own trade-offs: The strongest one reverts to a simulation-based game, and thus likely relies strongly on idealized building blocks in the OPRF construction. One-more pseudorandomness on the other hand requires more tailored hardness assumptions in the security proofs.

*Privacy: Obliviousness.* For privacy, the expected property is *obliviousness*, meaning that the evaluator must not learn anything about the values it blindly computed the PRF for. We capture this privacy property through three obliviousness definitions, with increasing strength. Our first notion *request obliviousness* assumes an honest-but-curious evaluator and implies the three obliviousness notions proposed before [8,42,45], albeit being simpler than any of the existing models. A stronger notion with an actively malicious evaluator, *multi-key obliviousness*, is also found in the literature [45]. The challenge thereby is how to prevent trivial wins, when the adversary evaluates different requests with different public keys. As OPRFs are classically secret-key primitives, they typically do not come with public verifiability. And in fact, the strongest notion multi-key obliviousness requires some form of *implicit verifiability* that allows the requester to check that they received a correctly computed response. We formally define this verifiability property and show that it is implied by multi-key obliviousness. While prior work [45] successfully builds a multi-key oblivious OPRF by adding implicit verifiability to a request-oblivious construction, it has gone unnoticed that formally, something stronger than request obliviousness is needed for the base construction. Therefore, we introduce an intermediate obliviousness property called *single-key obliviousness*.

*Security Analysis of (2)HashDH.* To showcase our framework, we conduct a security analysis of the ubiquitously used OPRFs HashDH and 2HashDH. HashDH does not achieve UC security, but has the advantage of preserving the group structure, thus enabling features such as key rotation or key homomorphism. We present the first formal analysis of HashDH and show that this simpler construction is still surprisingly strong, as it achieves single-key obliviousness on the privacy side, and strong one-more unpredictability as well as one-more pseudorandomness on the security side. We also provide evidence that HashDH *cannot* satisfy strong pseudorandomness, by proving that such a security proof implies breaking a natural CDH-related assumption. This stronger pseudorandomness notion is achieved by 2HashDH, and we show that applying an outer hash function generally lifts strong one-more unpredictability to strong pseudorandomness, adapting a similar result recently shown by Beullens et al. [10] in the UC framework.

We also show that neither HashDH nor 2HashDH satisfy our strongest privacy notion of multi-key obliviousness, as they do not come with any verifiability. While this might not be surprising per se, it does show that the UC definitions might not be as well-understood as we would expect them to be. Therein, privacy is often guaranteed towards malicious evaluators, too, indicating equivalence with our strongest privacy notion, yet the 2HashDH construction is used which does not satisfy this property. We show that multi-key obliviousness can be achieved for (2)HashDH via a simple zero-knowledge proof.

*Comparison with Related Work.* Our work performs a thorough survey of existing game-based OPRF definitions [1,3,8,25,42,45], making implicit knowledge explicit. We relate the final framework to these previous works in depth in the respective section for each property. For a high-level summary of the related work we refer to the full version of the paper [30]. The focus of our work is to provide a simple and well-analyzed framework for the core security and privacy properties of OPRFs. Extensions to cover more functionality, such as partial obliviousness or threshold evaluation, as well as a formal study to compare our framework to the UC definitions are beyond the scope of our work, and interesting open problems.

## 2 Preliminaries

This section introduces the writing conventions and building blocks used in the rest of the work.

*Game-Based Models.* We follow Shoup's [44] formalization for game-based models, and use Bellare and Rogaway's [9] notation to indicate failure events via a flag $\mathsf{bad}$. We make some further simplifications to reduce syntactic clutter: Adversaries are expected to respect domains with their inputs. Variables and public parameters are initialized at the beginning of a definition, and assumed to be accessible as a shared game state. Finally, we use $\Pr\left[\mathsf{Game}^{\mathsf{X}}(\lambda)\right]$ as a standard shorthand for the event that game $\mathsf{Game}^{\mathsf{X}}$ terminates with output 1.

*Pseudorandom Functions.* A PRF is a function $\mathsf{F} : \mathcal{K} \times \mathcal{X} \rightarrow \mathcal{Y}$. The computation of $\mathsf{F}$ is efficient and deterministic, and *pseudorandomness* ensures that without knowledge of the key the output is indistinguishable from random.

*Zero-Knowledge Proofs (ZKPs).* They allow to prove statements without disclosing anything else than the fact that the statement is true. We use the Camenisch and Stadler notation [16] to denote non-interactive zero-knowledge proofs (NIZK). Therein, proof statements are written in the form of

$$\pi \leftarrow_{\$} \mathsf{NIZK}\{(\alpha, \beta, \gamma) : y = g^{\alpha} h^{\beta} \wedge \tilde{y} = \tilde{g}^{\alpha} \tilde{h}^{\gamma}\}(ctx)$$

which expresses a zero-knowledge proof of secret values $\alpha, \beta, \gamma$ for the well-formedness of $y, \tilde{y}$ w.r.t. the group elements $g, h, \tilde{g}, \tilde{h}$. The proof can additionally be bound to a context message $ctx$, which usually comprises all public values the proof should be bound to. Any proof written in such an abstract form can be easily realized through a Schnorr-based instantiation via the Fiat-Shamir transform. We require the NIZK to be *correct*, *zero-knowledge* and *sound*.

*DH-based Assumptions.* The security of the (2)HashDH OPRF constructions is based on several CDH and DDH assumptions we state informally in the following. We consider hardness relative to a group generation algorithm $\mathsf{GGen}$, from which initially a prime order group $(\mathbb{G}, q, g)$ of order $q$ and with generator $g$ is sampled and given to the adversary. The full paper [30] presents the assumptions in detail and discusses their relations to standard assumptions.

**(Gap-)OM-CDH:** Given $g^x$ for $x \leftarrow\!\$\, \mathbb{Z}_q$, random challenges $Y_i \leftarrow\!\$\, \mathbb{G}$ and $\ell - 1$ "hints" $Y_i^x$, it is computationally infeasible for an efficient adversary to output $Y_i^x$ for $\ell$ challenges (even with access to a DDH oracle that upon an input $A, B, C$ returns 1 if $\log_g(C) = \log_g(A) \cdot \log_g(B)$).

**Hint-CDH:** Given a challenge $Y^* \leftarrow\!\$\, \mathbb{G}$ and a hint $Y^x$ for a $x \leftarrow\!\$\, \mathbb{Z}_q$ and an adversary-chosen base $Y \in \mathbb{G}$, it is computationally infeasible for an efficient adversary to output $(Y^*)^x$.

**DDH-Mult:** Given $g^x$ for $x \leftarrow\!\$\, \mathbb{Z}_q$ and multiple challenges of either two random elements $(Y, Z \leftarrow\!\$\, \mathbb{G})$, or $(Y \leftarrow\!\$\, \mathbb{G}, Y^x)$, depending on a global $b \leftarrow\!\$\, \{0,1\}$, it is computationally infeasible for an efficient adversary to guess $b$.

**OM-DDH:** Given $g^x$ for $x \leftarrow\!\$\, \mathbb{Z}_q$ and $\ell - 1$ queries to a CDH oracle that upon input $Y$ returns $Y^x$, it is computationally infeasible for an efficient adversary to guess $b_i$ for $\ell$ challenges of either two random elements $(Y, Z \leftarrow\!\$\, \mathbb{G})$, or $(Y \leftarrow\!\$\, \mathbb{G}, Y^x)$, where each challenge randomly takes one of the two cases.

## 3 OPRF Syntax

This section presents a syntax of OPRFs, for which we state formal definitions of the core properties in the following two sections. An OPRF is an interactive protocol run between two parties: the *requester* and the *evaluator*. The evaluator holds a PRF secret key $\mathsf{sk}$. The requester wants to learn the evaluation of the PRF, $y \leftarrow \mathsf{Eval}(\mathsf{sk}, x)$, for an input $x$ without revealing any information about $x$ or $y$ to the evaluator.

*Setup and KGen.* Before the protocol, a $\mathsf{Setup}$ algorithm generates the public parameters $pp$. The evaluator then generates its key pair as $(\mathsf{pk}, \mathsf{sk}) \leftarrow\!\$\, \mathsf{KGen}(pp)$. Thus, we provide our definition in a *public-key* setting. The public key is required for an implicit form of *verifiability*, allowing the requester to verify whether a blind evaluation was performed honestly. It can simply be set to $\mathsf{pk} = \bot$ when this feature is not needed. However, this verifiability is in fact necessary to obtain any reasonably strong form of privacy for the requester as proven for our framework in Sect. 5.3.

*(Blind) Evaluation.* We make the standard PRF evaluation $y \leftarrow \mathsf{Eval}(\mathsf{sk}, x)$ explicit in our syntax, following [1,25,42,45], as this will be helpful in the definition of the security model.

The core of the OPRF is the interactive evaluation protocol, and we formalize the round-optimal version which consists of three algorithms Request, BlindEval, and Finalize. Initially, the requester runs $(\overline{x}, \mathsf{st}) \leftarrow\$ \mathsf{Request}(\mathsf{pk}, x)$ to obtain a blinded version $\overline{x}$ of the value $x$ it wants to query the PRF on. The algorithm also outputs a state st which will be needed to unblind the response. The requester then sends $\overline{x}$ to the evaluator who returns $\overline{y} \leftarrow\$ \mathsf{BlindEval}(\mathsf{sk}, \overline{x})$. Finally, the requester can obtain the unblinded response by running $y \leftarrow \mathsf{Finalize}(\overline{y}, \mathsf{st})$. Correctness requires that $y \leftarrow \mathsf{Eval}(\mathsf{sk}, x)$. A visual overview of the exchange is given in the full version [30].

Note that we already include pk in the Request algorithm, as this is required in some lattice-based schemes, e.g., [1]. We do not provide pk again in Finalize since it can be passed into the Finalize algorithm as part of the state st. Our modelling also ensures that both algorithms are invoked on the same key.

More formally, an OPRF is defined as follows:

**Definition 1 (OPRF Scheme).** *An oblivious pseudorandom function for input space $\mathcal{X}$ is a scheme $\Pi$ with the following algorithms:*

- **$\mathsf{Setup}(\lambda) \xrightarrow{\$} pp$ :** *On input of a security parameter $\lambda$ generates public parameters $pp$. We make $pp$ only explicit in* KGen, *and assume it as an implicit input in all other algorithms.*
- **$\mathsf{KGen}(pp) \xrightarrow{\$} (\mathsf{pk}, \mathsf{sk})$ :** *On input of the public parameters $pp$ outputs the PRF key* sk *and a public verification key* pk.
- **$\mathsf{Eval}(\mathsf{sk}, x) \rightarrow y$ :** *Evaluates the underlying PRF non-interactively for secret key* sk *and input $x$.*
- **$\mathsf{Request}(\mathsf{pk}, x) \xrightarrow{\$} (\overline{x}, \mathsf{st})$ :** *Prepares a blind request for input $\overline{x}$ to be evaluated by the* sk *belonging to* pk, *outputs a blinded input $\overline{x}$ and state* st.
- **$\mathsf{BlindEval}(\mathsf{sk}, \overline{x}) \xrightarrow{\$} \overline{y}$ :** *Evaluates the blind request $\overline{x}$ with secret key* sk, *returning the blind response $\overline{y}$.*
- **$\mathsf{Finalize}(\overline{y}, \mathsf{st}) \rightarrow y/\bot$ :** *Unblinds the blind response $\overline{y}$ using the state* st *(which contains* pk *in the implicitly verifiable case). It returns the PRF evaluation $y$ if it succeeds. Otherwise, it returns $\bot$.*

*Correctness.* Correctness provides a guarantee for *honest* execution of the protocol, i.e., honest executions of the oblivious and standard evaluation to have identical results, and is defined in the full version [30].

## 4 Security of OPRFs

This section models the core security properties of an OPRF: unpredictability and pseudorandomness. Unpredictability demands that the requester cannot learn more OPRF evaluations than the number of interactions with the evaluator. This property is sufficient in applications such as Privacy Pass [22], where requesters run the protocol to obtain one-time tokens they can redeem later for accessing a service. In contrast, applications using the OPRF output as a cryptographic key require the stronger notion of pseudorandomness. While the property is trivial to define for standard PRFs, the blind nature of OPRFs makes this surprisingly challenging in the game-based manner. Our work recaps different ways to address this challenge and analyzes their relation.

We present two variants for unpredictability notions: the known *one-more unpredictability* and a new *strong one-more unpredictability*, that will be necessary for applications that implicitly provide a sk-based verification check, such as Privacy Pass. For pseudorandomness we restate and adapt three types of definitions that have been proposed in the literature before: *weak*, *one-more* and *strong pseudorandomness*. Weak pseudorandomness assumes an honest-but-curious requester, while the other two accommodate malicious requesters with different trade-offs in their game design. Finally, we present a thorough analysis of the relations among this set of different notions, as depicted in Fig. 1.

### 4.1 Unpredictability

Unpredictability seems to be the most well-understood property, with the works by Everspaugh et al. [25] and Lehmann [42] proposing very similar definitions for the variant of *one-more unpredictability*. It clearly resembles one-more unforgeability for blind signatures, but while unforgeability asks the adversary to produce a signature that *validates*, we ask for the unique value that is *correct*.

We define two types of unpredictability: The first is standard one-more unpredictability [25,42]. Interestingly, this definition – the only existing definition of unpredictability at the time of writing – is insufficient for one of the most prominent applications of OPRFs, Privacy Pass. Privacy Pass uses OPRF outputs as one-time access tickets to a service, which implicitly allows users to check the validity of a PRF tuple $(x, y)$. This ability is not captured in one-more unpredictability, so our proposed second definition grants the adversary a sk-verification oracle. Looking ahead, the novel property will also be needed for our generic strongly pseudorandom OPRF compiler.

We state both security games in Fig. 2, and define unpredictability as follows:

**Definition 2 ((Strong) One-more Unpredictability).** *We call an OPRF protocol $\Pi$ (strongly) one-more unpredictable if $\forall$ PPT adversaries $\mathcal{A}$ the following advantage is negligible:*

$$\mathsf{Adv}_{\Pi,\mathcal{A}}^{\mathsf{(str\text{-})unpred}}(\lambda) := \Pr\left[\mathsf{Game}_{\Pi,\mathcal{A}}^{\mathsf{(str\text{-})unpred}}(\lambda)\right]$$

**One-More Unpredictability (unpred).** Intuitively, the goal is to ensure that an adversary cannot predict a fresh OPRF evaluation without the help of the evaluator. The adversary may interact with the evaluator multiple times to learn some evaluations, but must not win by reusing these evaluations. As in blind signature unforgeability, this is enforced via a one-more style game: The adversary must produce more evaluations than the number of interactions performed.

The basic unpredictability game first generates a key pair, which is used to answer any $\mathcal{O}_{\mathsf{BlindEval}}$ queries. The adversary finally outputs $\ell$ input-output pairs, which must surpass the number of blind evaluations (counted by $c_{\mathsf{BE}}$) and be distinct. $\mathcal{A}$ wins if all $\ell$ evaluations are correct under the set key.

| $\mathsf{Game}^{\mathsf{unpred}}_{\Pi,\mathcal{A}}(\lambda)$, $\mathsf{Game}^{\mathsf{str\text{-}unpred}}_{\Pi,\mathcal{A}}(\lambda)$ | $\mathcal{O}_{\mathsf{BlindEval}}(\overline{x})$ | $\mathcal{O}_{\mathsf{Vf}}(x, y)$ |
|---|---|---|
| $pp \leftarrow\!\!\$\ \mathsf{Setup}(\lambda)$; $(\mathsf{pk}, \mathsf{sk}) \leftarrow\!\!\$\ \mathsf{KGen}(pp)$; $c_{\mathsf{BE}} := 0$ | $c_{\mathsf{BE}} := c_{\mathsf{BE}} + 1$ | **return** $y \stackrel{?}{=} \mathsf{Eval}(\mathsf{sk}, x)$ |
| $((x_1, y_1), \ldots, (x_\ell, y_\ell)) \leftarrow \mathcal{A}^{\mathcal{O}_{\mathsf{BlindEval}}, \mathcal{O}_{\mathsf{Vf}}}(pp, \mathsf{pk})$ | **return** $\mathsf{BlindEval}(\mathsf{sk}, \overline{x})$ | |
| **if** $\ell \leq c_{\mathsf{BE}} \ \vee\ \exists \alpha \neq \beta : x_\alpha = x_\beta$ : **return** 0 | | |
| **return** $\forall \alpha : \mathsf{Eval}(\mathsf{sk}, x_\alpha) \stackrel{?}{=} y_\alpha$ | | |

**Fig. 2.** Security games for (strong) one-more unpredictability.

**Strong Unpredictability (str-unpred).** In practical applications, malicious requesters might be given another capability we have not modeled so far: If an application prompts users to provide their OPRF evaluation, as, e.g., in Privacy Pass, then the application only accepts correct values and reject others. Thus, the application essentially provides a sk-based verification function, where the user can provide values $x, y$ and learns whether $y = \mathsf{Eval}(\mathsf{sk}, x)$. As OPRFs implement a *deterministic* evaluation function, such verification can only be done in the canonical way, i.e. by computing $y' \leftarrow \mathsf{Eval}(\mathsf{sk}, x)$ and checking whether $y = y'$.

Our strong unpredictability definition models this accordingly through an additional Vf oracle that takes an input-output pair $x, y$ and returns a single bit signaling correctness, determined through canonical verification. The recent work by Beullens et al. [10] also introduces a $(n, q)$-unpredictability notion that comes with such a verification oracle. They keep their definition intentionally weak, though, to capture the minimal requirements needed for their 2Hash transform, whereas our notion yields a strong stand-alone property that will suffice for a broad class of applications.

Interestingly, this additional verification ability is not obsolete as it would be for related unforgeable primitives like signatures or MACs, which we show in Sect. 4.3. For some intuition of why one-more unpredictability does not trivially imply the strong version, observe that we cannot know what exactly an adversary learns from a response given out by $\mathcal{O}_{\mathsf{BlindEval}}$. Consequently, we cannot simulate a verification oracle as we would for MACs by approving exactly the evaluations we know $\mathcal{A}$ obtained during the game.

Adding a non-blind Eval oracle to the definition would not change its strength though, as we show in the full version of the paper [30], so we omit it.

**Unpredictability in the UC Framework.** UC ideal functionalities typically assume the OPRF evaluations to be assigned through a random function. Thus the UC definition is aiming at the stronger pseudorandomness property, which implies unpredictability as it eliminates any prediction strategy besides guessing. While (one-more) unpredictability is then implied by any UC secure construction, it takes away the possibility to aim at a construction that fails to achieve this strong notion, but still guarantees the weaker unpredictability guarantee. As we will see in Sect. 6.1, the HashDH construction is such an example.

Another notable observation is that, to the best of our knowledge, there is no ideal functionality that permits the requester to sk-verify input-output pairs, as we do in our strong unpredictability notion. This makes the existing UC definitions unsuitable for one of the most widely-used applications of OPRFs, Privacy Pass, which provides such verification.

## 4.2 Pseudorandomness

For stronger security, we may not only want evaluations to be unpredictable, but even hard to tell apart from truly random values. This property known as *pseudorandomness* adds versatility, as such OPRF evaluations may be used in place of random values in larger protocols.

Although pseudorandomness is well understood for standard PRFs, applying it to OPRFs surprisingly turned out a challenge. Recall that pseudorandomness for regular PRFs is defined roughly as follows: An adversary is given an oracle that either returns the PRF evaluation of an input or a truly random value. We call the former case the *real world* and the latter the *random world*. Introducing blind evaluations to this game, however, is non-trivial. Since we cannot observe what inputs an adversary hides in a blind request, a BlindEval oracle risks to be inconsistent with the random-world challenges output by the standard Eval oracle, making the two worlds easily distinguishable. There is no easy fix, and related works take different approaches to this problem, each with their own advantages and disadvantages. Looking ahead, a stronger attacker model is only addressed by either deviating from the above structure or resorting to a simulation-based definition.

We first present the weaker, but significantly simpler notion we call *weak pseudorandomness*, slightly modifying the approach of *OPRF-PR* by Bellare et al. [8] to use only a single evaluation key instead of many, for consistency within our framework. We then formalize *strong pseudorandomness*, for which we choose the *POPRF* notion from Tyagi et al. [45], and finally *one-more-pseudorandomness* as proposed by Everspaugh et al. [25].

The security games for all three definitions are given in Fig. 3, and we define the various levels of pseudorandomness as follows:

**Definition 3 (Pseudorandomness).** *We call an OPRF protocol* $\Pi$ $\mathsf{x}$*-pseudorandom for* $\mathsf{x} \in \{\mathsf{weak}, \mathsf{str}, \mathsf{om}\}$*, if* $\forall$ *PPT adversaries* $\mathcal{A}$*, there exists a simulator* $\mathsf{S} = (\mathsf{S.Setup}, \mathsf{S.BlindEval}, \mathsf{S.Prim})$ *such that the following advantage is negligible:*

$\mathsf{Game}^{\mathsf{weak\text{-}prnd}}_{\Pi,\mathcal{A}}(\lambda)$

$pp \leftarrow\!\!\$\ \mathsf{Setup}(\lambda)$
$(\mathsf{pk}, \mathsf{sk}) \leftarrow\!\!\$\ \mathsf{KGen}(pp)$
$\mathsf{f} \leftarrow\!\!\$\ \mathsf{RandFnGen}(pp)$
$\mathsf{E} := [];\quad b \leftarrow\!\!\$\ \{0,1\}$
$b' \leftarrow \mathcal{A}^{\mathcal{O}_{\mathsf{Eval}}, \mathcal{O}_{\mathsf{BlindEval}}}(pp, \mathsf{pk})$
$\textbf{return } b' \stackrel{?}{=} b$

$\mathcal{O}_{\mathsf{Eval}}(x)$

$\textbf{if } x \notin \mathsf{E}:$
$\quad \textbf{if } b = 0: \quad$ // random
$\qquad \mathsf{E}[x] \leftarrow \mathsf{f}(x)$
$\quad \textbf{else}: \quad$ // real
$\qquad \mathsf{E}[x] \leftarrow \mathsf{Eval}(\mathsf{sk}, x)$
$\textbf{return } \mathsf{E}[x]$

$\mathcal{O}_{\mathsf{BlindEval}}(x)$

$\textbf{if } x \in \mathsf{E}: \textbf{return } \bot$
$\omega \leftarrow\!\!\$\ \Omega \quad$ // fix randomness
$(\overline{x}, \mathsf{st}) \leftarrow \mathsf{Request}(\mathsf{pk}, x; \omega)$
$\overline{y} \leftarrow\!\!\$\ \mathsf{BlindEval}(\mathsf{sk}, \overline{x})$
$\mathsf{E}[x] \leftarrow \mathsf{Finalize}(\overline{y}, \mathsf{st})$
$\textbf{return } (\overline{x}, \overline{y}, \mathsf{E}[x], \omega)$

---

$\mathsf{Game}^{\mathsf{str\text{-}prnd}}_{\Pi,\mathcal{A},\mathsf{S}}(\lambda)$

$pp \leftarrow\!\!\$\ \mathsf{Setup}(\lambda)$
$(\mathsf{st}_{\mathsf{S}}, \mathsf{pk}_0) \leftarrow\!\!\$\ \mathsf{S.Setup}^{\mathcal{O}_{\mathsf{LimEval}}}(pp)$
$\mathsf{st}_{\mathsf{Prim}} \leftarrow\!\!\$\ \mathsf{Prim.Setup}(pp)$
$(\mathsf{pk}_1, \mathsf{sk}) \leftarrow\!\!\$\ \mathsf{KGen}(pp)$
$\mathsf{f} \leftarrow\!\!\$\ \mathsf{RandFnGen}(pp)$
$b \leftarrow\!\!\$\ \{0,1\};\quad c_{\mathsf{BE}}, c_{\mathsf{S}} := 0$
$b' \leftarrow \mathcal{A}^{\mathcal{O}_{\mathsf{Eval}}, \mathcal{O}_{\mathsf{BlindEval}}, \mathcal{O}_{\mathsf{Prim}}}(pp, \mathsf{pk}_b)$
$\textbf{return } b' \stackrel{?}{=} b$

$\mathcal{O}_{\mathsf{Eval}}(x)$

$\textbf{if } b = 0: \quad$ // random
$\quad \textbf{return } \mathsf{f}(x)$
$\textbf{else}: \quad$ // real
$\quad \textbf{return } \mathsf{Eval}(\mathsf{sk}, x)$

$\mathcal{O}_{\mathsf{LimEval}}(x)$

$c_{\mathsf{S}} := c_{\mathsf{S}} + 1$
$\textbf{if } c_{\mathsf{S}} \leq c_{\mathsf{BE}}:$
$\quad \textbf{return } \mathcal{O}_{\mathsf{Eval}}(x)$
$\textbf{return } \bot$

$\mathcal{O}_{\mathsf{BlindEval}}(\overline{x})$

$c_{\mathsf{BE}} := c_{\mathsf{BE}} + 1$
$\textbf{if } b = 0: \quad$ // random
$\quad (\overline{y}, \mathsf{st}_{\mathsf{S}}) \leftarrow\!\!\$\ \mathsf{S.BlindEval}(\overline{x}, \mathsf{st}_{\mathsf{S}})$
$\textbf{else}: \quad$ // real
$\quad \overline{y} \leftarrow\!\!\$\ \mathsf{BlindEval}(\mathsf{sk}, \overline{x})$
$\textbf{return } \overline{y}$

$\mathcal{O}_{\mathsf{Prim}}(x)$

$\textbf{if } b = 0: \quad$ // random
$\quad (y, \mathsf{st}_{\mathsf{S}}) \leftarrow\!\!\$\ \mathsf{S.Prim}(x, \mathsf{st}_{\mathsf{S}})$
$\quad \textbf{return } y$
$\textbf{else}: \quad$ // real
$\quad \textbf{return } \mathsf{Prim.Eval}(x, \mathsf{st}_{\mathsf{Prim}})$

---

$\mathsf{Game}^{\mathsf{om\text{-}prnd}}_{\Pi,\mathcal{A}}(\lambda)$

$pp \leftarrow\!\!\$\ \mathsf{Setup}(\lambda);\quad (\mathsf{pk}, \mathsf{sk}) \leftarrow\!\!\$\ \mathsf{KGen}(pp)$
$\mathsf{f} \leftarrow\!\!\$\ \mathsf{RandFnGen}(\lambda)$
$c_{\mathsf{Chal}}, c_{\mathsf{BE}} := 0;\quad \boldsymbol{b} := []$
$(i_1, \ldots, i_\ell, b') \leftarrow \mathcal{A}^{\mathcal{O}_{\mathsf{Chal}}, \mathcal{O}_{\mathsf{BlindEval}}}(pp, \mathsf{pk})$
$\textbf{if } \ell > c_{\mathsf{Chal}} \lor \ell \leq c_{\mathsf{BE}} \lor \exists \alpha \neq \beta : i_\alpha = i_\beta : \textbf{return } 0$
$\textbf{return } b' \stackrel{?}{=} \bigoplus_{\alpha=1}^{\ell} \boldsymbol{b}[i_\alpha]$

$\mathcal{O}_{\mathsf{Chal}}(x)$

$c_{\mathsf{Chal}} := c_{\mathsf{Chal}} + 1$
$\boldsymbol{b}[c_{\mathsf{Chal}}] \leftarrow\!\!\$\ \{0,1\}$
$\textbf{if } \boldsymbol{b}[c_{\mathsf{Chal}}] = 0 : \textbf{return } \mathsf{f}(x)$
$\textbf{else} : \textbf{return } \mathsf{Eval}(\mathsf{sk}, x)$

$\mathcal{O}_{\mathsf{BlindEval}}(\overline{x})$

$c_{\mathsf{BE}} := c_{\mathsf{BE}} + 1$
$\textbf{return } \mathsf{BlindEval}(\mathsf{sk}, \overline{x})$

**Fig. 3. Top:** Security game for weak pseudorandomness. The adversary is passive. **Middle:** Security game for strong pseudorandomness. The adversary is active. **Bottom:** Security game for one-more pseudorandomness. The adversary is active.

$$\mathsf{Adv}^{\mathsf{x\text{-}prnd}}_{\Pi,\mathcal{A},\mathsf{S}}(\lambda) := 2 \cdot \Pr\left[\mathsf{Game}^{\mathsf{x\text{-}prnd}}_{\Pi,\mathcal{A},\mathsf{S}}(\lambda)\right] - 1$$

**Weak Pseudorandomness (weak-prnd).** The weakest notion of pseudorandomness circumvents the challenge of dealing with blind evaluations by assuming an honest-but-curious attacker model for the requester. This is captured by forcing the adversary to send $x$ in plain to the $\mathcal{O}_{\mathsf{BlindEval}}$, and blinding happens within the oracle prior to the blind evaluation. Although this notion offers no security against misbehaving requesters, it gives the simplest model of pseudorandomness, and it has been used by Lehmann [42], and Bellare et al. [8].

For weak pseudorandomness, we adapt Bellare et al.'s definition with small changes. The adversary has access to an Eval and a BlindEval oracle. The behavior of $\mathcal{O}_{\mathsf{Eval}}$ depends on a random bit $b$: It returns either PRF evaluations ($b = 1$) or random values ($b = 0$). For the latter, we assume there is an algorithm $\mathsf{RandFnGen}(\lambda)$ that randomly selects a function $\mathsf{f}$ with deterministic, but truly random outputs of matching size.

The blind evaluation oracle $\mathcal{O}_{\mathsf{BlindEval}}$ always runs the blind OPRF evaluation protocol, but for a plain input value $x$. To provide the same view as if the adversary was running the algorithm themselves, we first fix some randomness by sampling $\omega \leftarrow\$ \Omega$ and then apply the $\omega$ to a probabilistic algorithm. Thus a probabilistic $\mathsf{Request}(\mathsf{pk}, x)$ becomes a deterministic $\mathsf{Request}(\mathsf{pk}, x; \omega)$ which can be re-computed identically if $\omega$ is known.

The oracle blinds the input, evaluates the blinded input and finalizes it with the kept state. Finally, it outputs all values $(\overline{x}, \overline{y}, y, \omega)$, including the internal randomness $\omega$. (We show in the full version [30] that omitting the randomness or at least the blinding state $\mathsf{st}$ results indeed in a weaker definition.) As in Bellare et al., at the first query of some $x$ at either oracle, one fix $y$ is assigned for the whole game, preventing trivial wins. At the end of the game, the adversary outputs their guess $b'$ and wins if $b = b'$.

Bellare et al. model their game for multiple evaluators as their work considers concrete security. We leave this feature out for consistency among our definitions, but one can prove that the two versions are equivalent via a hybrid argument.

**Strong Pseudorandomness (str-prnd).** We now strengthen the attacker model by allowing an attacker to maliciously blind requests. When allowing blind requests, the adversary may send the same inputs to $\mathcal{O}_{\mathsf{Eval}}$ and $\mathcal{O}_{\mathsf{BlindEval}}$. This is fine for the real world, since standard and blind evaluations are consistent in correct schemes. But in the random world, $\mathcal{O}_{\mathsf{Eval}}$ assigns truly random values to each input and in $\mathcal{O}_{\mathsf{BlindEval}}$, facing potentially information-theoretic blinding, it seems impossible to consistently match the response to the same value.

Tyagi et al. [45] and Lehmann [42] therefore resort to a simulation-based approach for their pseudorandomness property: The simulator takes care of blind evaluations in the random world and restores consistency later in the protocol, before the requester has finished finalizing the evaluation. Its exact strategy is highly OPRF-dependent, but the simulator obviously requires additional idealized powers such as programming a random oracle. We adopt Tyagi et al.'s game as *strong pseudorandomness* for our framework.

The overall structure of the game is similar to weak pseudorandomness and tasks the adversary to determine whether it is in the real or random world. Now, the $\mathcal{O}_{\mathsf{BlindEval}}$ oracle does no longer always return real protocol values, but returns simulated ones via $\mathsf{S.BlindEval}$ in the random world, i.e. when $b = 0$. The simulator's additional powers are modeled via an ideal primitive oracle $\mathcal{O}_{\mathsf{Prim}}$ that it controls in the random world. Clearly, to restore consistency, the simulator $\mathsf{S}$ also needs access to the non-blind evaluation, which is modeled by giving the

$\mathsf{S}$ access to $\mathcal{O}_{\mathsf{LimEval}}$ model. Following Tyagi et al., this oracle is limited to one query per $\mathcal{O}_{\mathsf{BlindEval}}$ query that $\mathsf{S}$ processes. This controlled access guarantees that the simulator does not leak more than one evaluation per $\mathsf{BlindEval}$ call.

While this approach cleverly modifies the established pseudorandomness paradigm, it also inherits the disadvantages of simulation-based security. Security guarantees of a strongly pseudorandom OPRF now depend on a variable simulator and thus become less concrete. Moreover, as we will see later, strong pseudorandomness fails to do what we wanted to achieve with a game-based alternative to UC security: It seems once more to require an idealized outer structure and thus inhibits a proof for HashDH. Finally, since the simulator cannot succeed without additional powers, the definition is bound to the Ideal Primitive model [31] – essentially, a generalization of the random oracle model – making proofs less flexible in comparison with the other notions.

**One-More Pseudorandomness (om-prnd).** Everspaugh et al. [25] go a different route, avoiding the simulator at the cost of switching to a non-standard game structure. The authors accept that $\mathcal{A}$ may cross-check challenges between $\mathcal{O}_{\mathsf{Eval}}$ at $\mathcal{O}_{\mathsf{BlindEval}}$. Instead of fixing consistency at $\mathsf{BlindEval}$, they draw each $\mathcal{O}_{\mathsf{Eval}}$ challenge either from the real or random world, count the uses of $\mathcal{O}_{\mathsf{BlindEval}}$ and then ask $\mathcal{A}$ to guess the world of *one more* challenge.

In the game, the adversary chooses $\ell$ distinct challenges themselves to answer, but at least one more than they made calls to $\mathsf{BlindEval}$. Their guess is a single bit, which must be the world of each of the $\ell$ challenges combined via the exclusive or. This trick ensures that from knowing the correct bits for $\ell - 1$ evaluations, the adversary learns nothing about the final output.

One-more pseudorandomness is perhaps the most straightforward strengthening of one-more unpredictability. On the downside, the one-more paradigm makes the relation to other properties less tight and security analyses likely require tailored versions of computational assumptions.

**Pseudorandomness in the UC Framework.** In the UC framework, pseudorandomness is typically captured by having ideal evaluations be some truly random function tables (e.g., [7,35]), and security is expressed through the existence of an efficient simulator that makes the real and ideal world indistinguishable. This aspect is thus similar to the strong pseudorandomness notion. The UC definition also comes with a one-more aspect, which is most apparent in works that use a "ticket counter" (e.g., [33]). Such a counter increases every time the evaluator agrees to an evaluation, and the requester is allowed to retrieve one OPRF output for each ticket they possess. Intuitively, UC security is closest to strong pseudorandomness due to the reliance on the simulator in that definition, but also integrates aspects of the one-more notion, and a formal analysis is an interesting open problem.

### 4.3 Relations Among Security Properties

We now analyze the formal relations between the various unpredictability and pseudorandomness properties we saw so far.

**Unpredictability Relations.** We first show that our strong one-more unpredictability notion is indeed strictly stronger than the version that does not grant a sk-verification oracle. In fact, we get the relation as a corollary of Lemmas 4 and 5 below; additionally we provide a direct proof in the full version [30].

**Corollary 1.** str-unpred *is strictly stronger than* unpred.

**Pseudorandomness Relations.** Weak, one-more and strong pseudorandomness form a clear hierarchy. We start by showing that one-more pseudorandomness is strictly stronger than weak pseudorandomness, and then prove that strong pseudorandomness is strictly stronger than the one-more variant. Comparing one-more and weak pseudorandomness, while both games pose real-or-random challenges, we clearly strengthened the adversary in one-more pseudorandomness, where malicious BlindEval requests are allowed.

**Lemma 1.** om-prnd *is strictly stronger than* weak-prnd.

*Proof (sketch).* It is easy to see that weak pseudorandomness does not imply one-more pseudorandomness. One can define a scheme that becomes insecure upon rogue requests, e.g., BlindEval might reveal the secret key if some flag is set in the request. Such a change does not affect weak pseudorandomness, since the adversary is allowed only honest requests, but an active attacker can exploit this and trivially win the one-more pseudorandomness game.

Proving the inverse implication turns out rather tedious and untight due to the non-standard one-more paradigm, where the adversary must solve a single, fresh challenge instead of multiple challenges from one, consistent, world. The detailed proof is given in the full version [30], and the high-level idea is below.

Our goal is to make the weak pseudorandomness attacker $\mathcal{A}_{\mathsf{weak\text{-}prnd}}$ solve a single fresh one-more challenge – so we need to tame the $q$ challenges $\mathcal{A}_{\mathsf{weak\text{-}prnd}}$ actually receives from $\mathcal{O}_{\mathsf{Eval}}$. We do this in $q$ steps; transitioning from the random to the real case of $\mathsf{Game}_{\Pi,\mathcal{A}}^{\mathsf{weak\text{-}prnd}}$, in each intermediate game we switch one of $q$ $\mathcal{O}_{\mathsf{Eval}}$ challenges to *real.* Thus, if some distinguisher is able to distinguish between two adjacent games, they actually solve exactly one real-or-random challenge. So we bound each game hop via one-more pseudorandomness, providing the remaining random challenges with a self-picked random function and the other real challenges from the BlindEval oracle of $\mathsf{Game}_{\Pi,\mathcal{A}}^{\mathsf{om\text{-}prnd}}$.

Moving on, we show that strong pseudorandomness implies one-more pseudorandomness. It remains an open question whether it is a strict strengthening, although Sect. 6.1 provides evidence that HashDH is one-more, but not strongly pseudorandom, which suggests this relation.

**Lemma 2.** str-prnd *implies* om-prnd *(in the Ideal Primitive model).*

*Proof (sketch).* Our strategy will be to modify the one-more pseudorandomness game into an impossible-to-solve version where all challenges are random, and show that this game is in fact indistinguishable from the original $\mathsf{Game}^{\mathsf{om\text{-}prnd}}_{\Pi,\mathcal{A}}$, unless $\mathsf{Game}^{\mathsf{str\text{-}prnd}}_{\Pi,\mathcal{A},\mathsf{S}}$ can also be won. In detail, we replace any *real* challenges from $\mathcal{O}_{\mathsf{Eval}}$ to outputs of a second random function $\mathsf{f}_1$, and let a simulator operate $\mathcal{O}_{\mathsf{BlindEval}}$ and an ideal primitive $\mathcal{O}_{\mathsf{Prim}}$ to be consistent with $\mathsf{f}_1$.

With this setup, we can reduce one-more to strong pseudorandomness as follows: $\mathcal{A}_{\mathsf{str}}$ simulates one-more pseudorandomness by forwarding $\mathcal{O}^{\mathsf{om}}_{\mathsf{BlindEval}}$ and $\mathcal{O}^{\mathsf{om}}_{\mathsf{Prim}}$ queries to their own oracles, and for $\mathcal{O}^{\mathsf{om}}_{\mathsf{Eval}}$ either runs a random function $\mathsf{f}_0$ or forwards the query to their own $\mathcal{O}_{\mathsf{Eval}}$. Depending on $\mathcal{A}_{\mathsf{str}}$'s world, either the original $\mathsf{Game}^{\mathsf{om\text{-}prnd}}_{\Pi,\mathcal{A}}$ or the random version is simulated. The two cases must be indistinguishable if a scheme is strongly pseudorandom. Moreover, the random game described above does not give $\mathcal{A}_{\mathsf{om\text{-}prnd}}$ any advantage over a random guess. The full proof is given in the full version [30].

Additionally, we provide a direct treatment of the relation between strong pseudorandomness and the weaker properties in the full version [30], avoiding the lossy intermediate step of one-more pseudorandomness.

**Pseudorandomness vs. Unpredictability.** For classic PRFs, pseudorandomness clearly implies unpredictability. For OPRFs, however, we introduced different levels for both notions, and thus it is interesting to analyze how they relate to each other on the same level and across. Surprisingly, we find some orthogonality, both between the weakest version of each property and between strong one-more unpredictability and one-more pseudorandomness.

**Lemma 3.** weak-prnd *and* unpred *are orthogonal properties.*

*Proof (sketch).* OPRFs whose evaluations include some non-random part, let us say a fixed first half of zeroes, are clearly not pseudorandom, but may still have a second unpredictable half that makes them fulfill one-more unpredictability. Because of our decision to limit weak pseudorandomness to passive adversaries, it is not stronger than unpredictability though.

The one-more pseudorandomness property overcomes the constraint of weak pseudorandomness and implements an active attacker model, therefore surpassing weak one-more unpredictability. Everspaugh et al. [25] provide a proof sketch of the following lemma, which immediately holds for our definitions, too:

**Lemma 4.** om-prnd *is strictly stronger than* unpred.

When we move to our stronger unpredictability definition, this implication no longer holds. Strong unpredictability added a capability that is not reflected in the one-more pseudorandomness game: a canonical verification oracle for the PRF evaluation, which we can now exploit to separate the two notions.

Designing a scheme that satisfies one-more pseudorandomness but not strong unpredictability is challenging. We present such a scheme, $\Pi'$, which builds upon an existing OPRF $\Pi$. Our analysis demonstrates that if $\Pi$ is strongly pseudorandom – implying both one-more pseudorandomness and strong unpredictability – then $\Pi'$ achieves one-more pseudorandomness, but not strong unpredictability.

Somewhat unusually, this incomparability result relies on the existence of a strong pseudorandom OPRF $\Pi'$. This is necessary due to a technical subtlety in the formal proof. Given that Beullens et al. [10] showed that existence of a strongly unpredictable OPRF implies the existence of a pseudorandom OPRF in the ROM, our assumption is a reasonable one. While showing this incomparability without such an additional assumption is an interesting open problem, our result is still enough to justify that the verification oracle of str-unpred makes the unpredictability definition meaningfully stronger.

**Lemma 5.** *If there exists a* str-prnd *OPRF, then* str-unpred *and* om-prnd *are orthogonal properties.*

*Proof (sketch).* As shown in Lemma 3, it is easy to construct an OPRF that is unpredictable but not pseudorandom. For a construction that is one-more pseudorandom, but not strongly unpredictable, we exploit the fact that a $\mathsf{Game}^{\mathsf{str\text{-}unpred}}_{\Pi,\mathcal{A}}$ adversary $\mathcal{A}_{\mathsf{str\text{-}unpred}}$ can distinguish between a correct and an incorrect evaluation, but a $\mathsf{Game}^{\mathsf{om\text{-}prnd}}_{\Pi,\mathcal{A}}$ adversary $\mathcal{A}_{\mathsf{om\text{-}prnd}}$ cannot.

The high-level idea is to embed a special string $s^*$ into an OPRF which allows to obtain two evaluations from a single request, but we carefully hide $s^*$ such that it is only observable by $\mathcal{A}_{\mathsf{str\text{-}unpred}}$. By appending an index $i$ to a blind request, the $i^{th}$ bit of $s^*$ is leaked in a circumscribed way: The returned response contains the evaluation of the input $x = s^*_i \| i$. Thus, one learns the bit $s^*_i$ only if one can distinguish the evaluation of $0\|i$ and of $1\|i$. While $\mathcal{A}_{\mathsf{str\text{-}unpred}}$ may use $\mathcal{O}_{\mathsf{Vf}}$ to check, $\mathcal{A}_{\mathsf{om\text{-}prnd}}$ is in trouble: $\mathcal{O}_{\mathsf{BlindEval}}$ requests are costly in the one-more paradigm, and $\mathcal{O}_{\mathsf{Eval}}$ will in 1/2 of the cases return a useless random value. A concrete construction and its justification is given in the full version [30].

On the other hand, strong pseudorandomness does not "penalize" $\mathcal{O}_{\mathsf{BlindEval}}$ calls in the same way one-more pseudorandomness does – the strong notion allows the adversary to make unlimited calls to the oracle without the challenge getting harder every time. Thus, a verification oracle becomes simulatable in this version of pseudorandomness.

**Lemma 6.** str-prnd *is strictly stronger than* str-unpred.

*Proof (sketch).* Let $G_0$ be as the strong unpredictability game but with an ideal primitive oracle. We transition to a game $G_1$ where the OPRF is replaced by a truly random function $\mathsf{f}$: the verification oracle checks input-output pairs against this function $\mathsf{f}$, $\mathcal{O}_{\mathsf{BlindEval}}$ and $\mathcal{O}_{\mathsf{Prim}}$ are run by a simulator. If a scheme $\Pi$ is strongly pseudorandom, these two games are indistinguishable. But winning $G_1$ clearly requires guessing a truly random value, so we conclude that any strongly pseudorandom OPRF must also be strongly unpredictable. For the inverse implication, a standard argument can be made that not every unpredictable ORPF is also pseudorandom. We give the full proof in the full version [30].

# 5 Privacy of OPRFs

We now turn to the privacy property expected from OPRFs: The evaluator should learn nothing about the input $x$ or the output $y$ during the exchange. This is essential for privacy-preserving application such as Privacy Pass, or when the OPRF is used to derive keys from low-entropy inputs such as a password.

We capture this privacy property through three obliviousness definitions, with increasing strength. Our first notion *request obliviousness* captures the same privacy guarantees as has been formalized in three different manners in the works by Lehmann [42], Tyagi et al. [45], as well as Bellare et al. [8]. This notion assumes an honest-but-curious evaluator though, and we therefore also propose definitions where the adversary can be actively malicious: *Single-key obliviousness* ensures privacy against an adversary that is malicious but does not use rogue keys, and *multi-key obliviousness* protects against malicious adversaries without the latter restriction.

We then observe that *multi-key obliviousness* implies *implicit verifiability*; the requester must be able to check that they received a correctly computed response for a targeted public key pk. To emphasize this need, we formally define this verifiability property and show that it is implied by multi-key obliviousness and also lifts single-key obliviousness to this stronger form.

$\mathsf{Game}^{\mathsf{obliv\text{-}req}}_{\Pi,\mathcal{A}}(\lambda)$, $\mathsf{Game}^{\mathsf{obliv\text{-}1k}}_{\Pi,\mathcal{A}}(\lambda)$, $\boxed{\mathsf{Game}^{\mathsf{obliv\text{-}k+}}_{\Pi,\mathcal{A}}(\lambda)}$

$pp \leftarrow\!\!\$\ \mathsf{Setup}(\lambda)$
$c_{\mathsf{req}} := 0;\ b \leftarrow\!\!\$\ \{0,1\}$
$b' \leftarrow \mathcal{A}^{\mathcal{O}_{\mathsf{Request}}, \boxed{\mathcal{O}_{\mathsf{Finalize}}}}(pp)$
$\textbf{return } b \stackrel{?}{=} b'$

$\mathcal{O}_{\mathsf{Request}}(\mathsf{pk}, x_0, x_1)$

$c_{\mathsf{req}} := c_{\mathsf{req}} + 1;\quad x_{c_{\mathsf{req}},0} := x_0;\quad x_{c_{\mathsf{req}},1} := x_1$
$(\overline{x_b}, \mathsf{st}_{c_{\mathsf{req}},b}) \leftarrow\!\!\$\ \mathsf{Request}(\mathsf{pk}, x_b)$
$(\overline{x_{1-b}}, \mathsf{st}_{c_{\mathsf{req}},1-b}) \leftarrow\!\!\$\ \mathsf{Request}(\mathsf{pk}, x_{1-b})$
$\textbf{return } (\overline{x_b}, \overline{x_{1-b}})$

$\mathcal{O}_{\mathsf{Finalize}}(\overline{y}', \overline{y}'', i, \mathsf{sk})$

$\textbf{if } i > c_{\mathsf{req}} : \textbf{return } \bot$
$y_b \leftarrow \mathsf{Finalize}(\overline{y}', \mathsf{st}_{i,b})$
$y_{1-b} \leftarrow \mathsf{Finalize}(\overline{y}'', \mathsf{st}_{i,1-b})$
$\textbf{if } y_0 \neq \mathsf{Eval}(\mathsf{sk}, x_{i,0}) \vee y_1 \neq \mathsf{Eval}(\mathsf{sk}, x_{i,1}) :$
$\quad \textbf{return } \bot$
$\boxed{\textbf{if } y_b = \bot \vee y_{1-b} = \bot : \textbf{return } \bot}$
$\textbf{return } (y_0, y_1)$

**Fig. 4.** Games for request, single-key, and multi-key obliviousness. The first property assumes an honest-but-curious adversary, the other two a malicious adversary. Highlighted code is exclusive to the respective game.

## 5.1 Obliviousness

Obliviousness is similar to blindness for blind signatures, and accordingly obliviousness definitions borrow the concept of left-or-right indistinguishability: A malicious evaluator chooses two inputs $x_0, x_1$, which are blinded and returned in random order, and they have to tell which blind request belongs to which input.

Our three variants of obliviousness definitions are formally defined through security games in Fig. 4 and each notion's advantage is defined as follows:

To address different adversarial models, we will motivate three definitions, with increasing strength: *request obliviousness* ensures privacy against an honest-but-curious adversary, *single-key obliviousness* ensures privacy against an adversary that is malicious but does not use rogue keys, and *multi-key obliviousness* protects against malicious adversaries without the latter restriction.

**Definition 4 (Obliviousness).** *We call an OPRF protocol $\Pi$ $\mathsf{x}$-oblivious for $\mathsf{x} \in \{\mathsf{req}, \mathsf{1k}, \mathsf{k+}\}$, if $\forall$ PPT adversaries $\mathcal{A}$ the following advantage is negligible:*

$$\mathsf{Adv}^{\mathsf{obliv\text{-}x}}_{\Pi,\mathcal{A}}(\lambda) := 2 \cdot \Pr\left[\mathsf{Game}^{\mathsf{obliv\text{-}x}}_{\Pi,\mathcal{A}}(\lambda)\right] - 1$$

**Request Obliviousness (obliv-req).** Our first notion assumes that the evaluator is honest-but-curious. This might be a reasonable assumption in some scenarios. For instance, a requester that trusts the evaluator may still want to ensure that the transcript of the blind evaluation does not leak information to third parties who eavesdrop on their communication.

We find three related works employing the same model, even though, at first glance, they differ strongly in how the challenges look and how much control the adversary has over evaluation keys. Lehmann [42] (in a property called *obliviousness*) provides the attacker with a single request as the left-or-right challenge, while Tyagi et al. [45] (*POPRIV*) as well as Bellare et al. [8] (*input indistinguishability*[1]) provide the challenges via a transcript oracle, which upon two inputs returns not only the request, but also blind and cleartext evaluation of the given inputs. Concerning the keys used in generating the challenges, Lehmann and Tyagi et al. fix a key pair, while Bellare et al. offer a key generation oracle so that the adversary can obtain honest keys and query challenges for many different key pairs.

Somewhat surprisingly, the transcript oracles do not result in a stronger definition, so we propose the simpler game titled *request obliviousness.* To see why the full transcript is redundant, note how the adversary is in possession of the secret key and can compute both the blind response and the cleartext evaluation themselves – in other words, after receiving the request, for a protocol-following evaluator the rest of the exchange does not bear new information.

Thus, the adversary is merely given a $\mathsf{Request}$ oracle, where they can repeatedly obtain left-or-right challenges consisting of the blinded inputs. We adopt Bellare et al.'s choice of letting the adversary use arbitrary evaluation keys, which seems the strongest variant. Instead of an oracle, our passive attacker model captures implicitly that key generation is honest.

Formally, we can show our definition is equivalent to each of the related works. The proofs to the following lemma are given in the full version [30].

---

[1] Input indistinguishability is a generic property for two-party-computation, but plugging in OPRFs with the evaluator as the corrupt party, we get request obliviousness.

**Lemma 7.** obliv-req *is equivalent to obliviousness in [42], POPRIV1 in [45] and input indistinguishability in [8].*

**Single-Key Obliviousness (obliv-1k).** While omitting the finalized evaluations in the game does not matter when considering only honest-but-curious adversaries, this no longer holds when we switch to an active attacker model: The adversary may send maliciously crafted responses, and the finalization failing or returning an incorrect value can then reveal information about the associated input. A malicious evaluator could also handle each request with a different key, and later, by inspecting under which key an evaluation is valid, link it to the evaluation process. We refer to this strategy as a *multi-key* attack.

We partially capture the aforementioned attacks by granting the adversary a Finalize oracle that takes two blinded responses and finalizes them. It only returns the final outputs if they are both correct, i.e. valid under the same secret key. The same approach is taken in definitions of signature blindness, where this check is straightforward due to the public verifiability. For OPRF, we (generally) lack a public verification mechanism though, so we force the adversary to specify the secret key used during blind evaluation. Since we are limiting the adversary to one key pair per challenge, we call our property *single-key obliviousness.*

The Finalize oracle might appear rather useless, given that it returns nothing but two correct evaluations – which the adversary could compute themselves as $\mathsf{Eval}(\mathsf{sk}, x)$ for any input $x$. But in fact, $\mathcal{O}_{\mathsf{Finalize}}$ provides one bit of extra information: The adversary can test whether some malicious evaluation finalizes into the correct value with respect to the $i^{th}$ request. Thus, single-key obliviousness covers bugs in the Finalize algorithm that could leak some information on the output. Additionally, active attacks on the Request algorithm are addressed. These two details fill an important gap between request obliviousness and the strongest obliviousness notion, as we will see in Sect. 5.3.

**Multi-key Obliviousness (obliv-k+).** The single-key definition still implicitly requires some honest behavior. In particular, it takes multi-key attacks out of the equation by enforcing the adversary to use the same key for both evaluations. Thus, our strongest notion of obliviousness aims to prevent multi-key attacks.

Tyagi et al. [45] propose such a stronger property as *POPRIV2*, where they relax the restrictions within $\mathcal{O}_{\mathsf{Finalize}}$ to refuse garbage data that makes the finalization fail, but do not impose a single key pair. We adopt Tyagi et al.'s definition and call it *multi-key obliviousness.*

However, the property is now so strong that standard OPRFs such as HashDH or 2HashDH do not achieve it. Intuitively, in these constructions the requester simply has no way of ensuring that a consistent key is used. The only fix is to introduce a mechanism of implicit verifiability to allow Finalize to refuse rogue key evaluations. Indeed, any multi-key oblivious OPRF is also verifiable. We prove this relation in Sect. 5.3 after formally introducing verifiability.

**Obliviousness in the UC Framework.** Obliviousness is typically captured in an ideal functionality by giving the input $x$ and output $y$ exclusively to the requester and no other party (e.g., [34]). The only information the evaluator gets is that a function query is made. Once the evaluator approves the query, the functionality directly responds with a random value to the requester. The exact level of obliviousness captured by the ideal functionalities is not entirely clear. Many UC definitions follow the approach by Jarecki et al. [34], where corrupt evaluators can point to a different function table for each query, that is then consistently filled with random values. The adversary still does not learn any information on the requester's input or output. Thus, the functionality gives a corrupt evaluator the freedom to use inconsistent keys, but still requires their outputs to be indistinguishable from random values. Analyzing a clear connection between the various UC functionalities and our three levels of obliviousness is an interesting open problem. In particular, if the UC functionality can be shown to be equivalent to our multi-key obliviousness notion, then the 2HashDH instantiation that is typically used for the functionality would *not* be secure. Moreover, asking for random outputs even for a malicious evaluator once again suggests an outer random oracle is mandatory – whereas we are able to also prove a verifiable HashDH multi-key oblivious (Corollary 2).

### 5.2 Verifiability

We saw in the previous section how malicious responses may violate the requester's privacy, e.g., plain evaluations become linkable through a multi-key attack. This is because in standard OPRFs, the requester essentially has to trust the evaluator about the blind evaluation; they have no means of knowing what the evaluator did as long as the finalization does not fail.

To provide protection against malicious evaluators, we introduce an extension: implicit verifiability. This introduces a mechanism for the requester to verify that the blind evaluation was performed honestly with the targeted *public key*. The verification is implicitly performed during Finalize, so in a verifiable scheme, we expect Finalize to fail upon any dishonest response if the result is not correct w.r.t. the public key the requester has chosen in their Request algorithm.

| $\mathsf{Game}^{\mathsf{vf}}_{\Pi,\mathcal{A}}(\lambda)$ | $\mathcal{O}_{\mathsf{Request}}(\mathsf{pk}, x)$ | $\mathcal{O}_{\mathsf{Finalize}}(\overline{y}, i)$ |
|---|---|---|
| $pp \leftarrow\!\!\$\ \mathsf{Setup}(\lambda);\quad c_{\mathsf{req}} := 0$ | $c_{\mathsf{req}} := c_{\mathsf{req}} + 1$ | $\mathbf{if}\ i > c_{\mathsf{req}} : \mathbf{return}\ \bot$ |
| $(\mathsf{sk}, j, \overline{y}) \leftarrow \mathcal{A}^{\mathcal{O}_{\mathsf{Request}}, \mathcal{O}_{\mathsf{Finalize}}}(pp)$ | $\mathsf{pk}_{c_{\mathsf{req}}} := \mathsf{pk};\quad x_{c_{\mathsf{req}}} := x$ | $\mathbf{return}\ \mathsf{Finalize}(\overline{y}, \mathsf{st}_i)$ |
| $y' \leftarrow \mathsf{Finalize}(\overline{y}, \mathsf{st}_j)$ | $(\overline{x}, \mathsf{st}_{c_{\mathsf{req}}}) \leftarrow\!\!\$\ \mathsf{Request}(\mathsf{pk}, x)$ | |
| $\mathbf{if}\ \mathsf{public}(\mathsf{sk}) \neq \mathsf{pk}_j \vee y' = \bot : \mathbf{return}\ 0$ | $\mathbf{return}\ \overline{x}$ | |
| $\mathbf{return}\ y' \overset{?}{\neq} \mathsf{Eval}(\mathsf{sk}, x_j)$ | | |

**Fig. 5.** Security game for verifiability.

We capture implicit verifiability in the game shown in Fig. 5, where a malicious evaluator tries to generate a response that yields an incorrect result with respect to the target key. The game allows the adversary to pick a challenge request and target key pair themselves, and to test their responses at a Finalize oracle. At the end of the game, the adversary selects a $j^{th}$ request as their challenge, outputs their rogue response $\overline{y}$ and reveals the purported evaluation key sk. It is checked that the public counterpart of sk is indeed the public key $\mathsf{pk}_j$ that the $j^{th}$ request was bound to, and that the finalization of $\overline{y}$ does indeed not fail. If these conditions are met and the resulting value is still incorrect, the adversary wins. For checking correctness of the public key, we introduce a function public(sk) $\rightarrow$ pk$'$ which computes the corresponding public key from sk, and checks it against the provided value pk. Thus, our definition implicitly assumes unique public keys, which holds trivially for DL-based constructions, but will be challenging for lattice-based constructions. Asking the adversary to output the secret key might appear like a strong request. This can be realized by using an extractable zero-knowledge proof as part of the public keys in the construction. We have opted for our model for the sake of simplicity.

**Definition 5 (Verifiability).** *We call an OPRF protocol $\Pi$ verifiable, if $\forall$ PPT adversaries $\mathcal{A}$ the following advantage is negligible:*

$$\mathsf{Adv}^{\mathsf{vf}}_{\Pi,\mathcal{A}}(\lambda) := \Pr\left[\mathsf{Game}^{\mathsf{vf}}_{\Pi,\mathcal{A}}(\lambda)\right]$$

Significant prior work on implicit verifiability comes from Albrecht et al. [1,3] and Tyagi et al. [45], from whom our definition takes inspiration. Albrecht et al. weaken the adversary slightly by forcing them to commit to a challenge before getting access to the oracles, and do not pose any limitations on the evaluation keys, which unfortunately leaves room for a trivial attack (shown in the full version of our paper [30]) where the attacker announces a key pair with public and secret key that are not matching. Tyagi et al. define a slightly different notion *uniqueness*, which ensures that malicious evaluators cannot make the requester accept two distinct evaluations to the same input. The game structure and adversarial abilities are similar, but the goal is slightly weaker. Informally, verifiability implies uniqueness, since the adversary can *exclusively* output the honest response. But uniqueness does not imply verifiability: Even if the adversary cannot provide more than one response that is accepted by Finalize, this one response could still be dishonest.

**Verifiability in the UC Framework.** Two examples of UC-based works defining a verifiable OPRF are Jarecki et al. [33] and Boneh et al. [12]. Both capture verifiability in a subtle way: Evaluators must initially register a function table from which during the interaction any evaluation is drawn. This seems a more limited guarantee than what $\mathsf{Game}^{\mathsf{vf}}_{\Pi,\mathcal{A}}$ expresses: Jarecki et al. state explicitly that pseudorandomness cannot be ensured, so while a malicious evaluator cannot dynamically forge evaluations, they still have some head space and could register a faulty table initially. In contrast, the game-based notion promises that a requester who (1) honestly executes their own algorithms and (2) verifies the blind evaluation will receive the unique correct PRF evaluation at the end.

### 5.3 Relations Among Privacy Notions

Our obliviousness notions successively increase the privacy requirements, where request obliviousness only ensures the input is securely blinded, single-key obliviousness adds a key-restricted Finalize oracle, and multi-key obliviousness gives full freedom in key usage. Unsurprisingly, this results in a clear hierarchy among the definitions. The proof of Lemma 8 is given in the full version [30].

**Lemma 8.** obliv-k+ *is strictly stronger than* obliv-1k*, which in turn is strictly stronger than* obliv-req.

Multi-key obliviousness demands that a malign response might trigger an error during finalization, but can never change the result in any way that would allow linking. Thus, the only blind responses any evaluator can create are *expected* ones. The similarity of this requirement to implicit verifiability is apparent, and as already noted by Tyagi et al. [45], multi-key obliviousness indeed requires a verifiable scheme. For preciseness, we add that this holds only for correct schemes: Consider an OPRF where Finalize simply outputs a completely random value. This OPRF is multi-key oblivious – there is no way to link the outputs to the blind evaluation – without being verifiable.

**Lemma 9.** *Correctness and* obliv-k+ *imply* vf.

The inverse is not true, i.e. implicit verifiability is not sufficient for multi-key obliviousness. Verifiability provides only a guarantee for honest blind evaluation; requester privacy could still be completely broken if the blinding or finalization algorithms are flawed. This is where our newly introduced single-key obliviousness property comes into play: combining implicit verifiability and request obliviousness is explicitly not sufficient to achieve the strongest obliviousness notion, since it lacks active security of the blinding and does not cover the Finalize algorithm, but single-key obliviousness provides the missing guarantee.

**Lemma 10.** obliv-req *and* vf *do not imply* obliv-k+.

**Lemma 11.** obliv-1k *and* vf *imply* obliv-k+ *(in the Knowledge of the Secret Key Model [11]).*

The Knowledge of the Secret Key (KOSK) model of Lemma 11 is needed due to a technicality: We reduce to single-key-obliviousness and verifiability, where adversaries must explicitly output secret keys. Therefore, we need access to the multi-key-obliviousness adversary's secret key, which the KOSK model solves generically. We formally prove Lemmas 9 to 11 and show that implicit verifiability does not imply multi-key obliviousness in the full version [30].

As a final note, for some applications neither multi-key obliviousness nor verifiability might be desirable, because the evaluator must use different keys for protocol-internal reasons and the requester should not be able to tell which key is used for what evaluation.

# 6 Security and Privacy of the (2)HashDH OPRFs

To showcase our framework, we conduct a security analysis of two widely used OPRFs. HashDH and 2HashDH achieve almost all properties, with HashDH lacking strong pseudorandomness and both constructions requiring an additional proof of honest behavior for implicit verifiability and multi-key obliviousness.

## 6.1 Analysis of HashDH

The non-blind DH-based PRF $\mathsf{F}(\mathsf{sk}, x) := \mathsf{H}(x)^{\mathsf{sk}}$ was first introduced by Naor et al. [43], and is secure under the DDH assumption if H is a random oracle. The PRF is easily made interactive by blinding $\mathsf{H}(x)$ exponentially[2].

**Definition 6 (HashDH).** *The HashDH OPRF is defined as follows, with group generation* $(\mathbb{G}, q, g) \leftarrow\$ \mathsf{GGen}(\lambda)$ *and hash function* $\mathsf{H} : \{0,1\}^* \to \mathbb{G}$.

$\mathsf{Setup}(\lambda) : (\mathbb{G}, q, g) \leftarrow\$ \mathsf{GGen}(\lambda);$ **return** $(\mathbb{G}, q, g)$
$\mathsf{KGen}(pp) :$ *parse* $(\mathbb{G}, q, g) = pp;$ $\mathsf{sk} \leftarrow\$ \mathbb{Z}_q;$ $\mathsf{pk} := \bot;$ **return** $(\mathsf{pk}, \mathsf{sk})$
$\mathsf{Request}(\mathsf{pk}, x) : r \leftarrow\$ \mathbb{Z}_q \setminus \{0\};$ $\overline{x} := \mathsf{H}(x)^r;$ $\mathsf{st} := r;$ **return** $(\overline{x}, \mathsf{st})$
$\mathsf{BlindEval}(\mathsf{sk}, \overline{x}) : \overline{y} := \overline{x}^{\mathsf{sk}};$ **return** $\overline{y}$
$\mathsf{Finalize}(\overline{y}, \mathsf{st}) :$ *parse* $r = \mathsf{st};$ $y := \overline{y}^{(1/r)};$ **return** $y$

Correctness is straightforward and shown in the full version [30]. Note that we require the blinding exponent $r$ explicitly to be non-zero, as otherwise the scheme is no longer perfectly correct. Despite its simplicity, HashDH achieves strong security and privacy guarantees. We start with unpredictability and pseudorandomness; here the only missing property is strong pseudorandomness, for which HashDH lacks an outer idealized primitive.

**Unpredictability.** Everspaugh et al. [25] show one-more unpredictability for a pairing-based version of HashDH, and we show that this proof can be adapted for HashDH as well. The security of HashDH is proven under the OM-CDH assumption, which tasks the adversary to solve $q+1$ CDH challenges after being able to learn at most $q$ CDH solutions of their choice. For strong unpredictability, the CDH assumption is not enough to simulate the canonical verification oracle, which essentially requires solving DDH for each verification query. In order to satisfy this extra need, we prove the strong one-more unpredictability under the gap-OM-CDH assumption, which extends the OM-CDH assumption with such a DDH oracle. Note that using a gap assumption in non-gap groups is a common approach to prove the security of (2)HashDH or related constructions [15,33,45]. The full proof of Theorem 1 is given in the full version [30].

**Theorem 1.** *If* H *is a random oracle, then HashDH is:*

- unpred *if the* OM-CDH *assumption holds for* GGen,
- str-unpred *if the* gap-OM-CDH *assumption holds for* GGen.

[2] For both HashDH and 2HashDH we use exponential blinding. While multiplicative blinding has performance advantages, it opens new attack vectors [24,37].

**Weak Pseudorandomness.** Our weakest pseudorandomness notion now requires that the OPRF outputs must be indistinguishable from random. This notion assumes an honest-but-curious requester, which essentially simplifies the proof to showing that the non-blind version is secure. The proof requires a little more care though. Intuitively, a DDH assumption typically lets the adversary distinguish between a real world, in which they receive DH pairs $Y, Y^x$, and a random world, in which they receive an independent, random pair $Y, Z$. In contrast, during the weak pseudorandomness game, the adversary also has the BlindEval oracle, which always hands out "real" DH values. We handle this via an intermediate game hop between the real and the random world: We initially supply both $\mathcal{O}_{\mathsf{Eval}}$ and $\mathcal{O}_{\mathsf{BlindEval}}$ queries with DDH challenges, and then move to a game where only $\mathcal{O}_{\mathsf{BlindEval}}$ is returning DDH challenges, whereas $\mathcal{O}_{\mathsf{Eval}}$ samples random responses. Finally, to simplify the proof, we follow Bellare et al. [8] and employ a variation of the classic DDH assumption with multiple challenges that is equivalent to DDH. The full proof is given in the full version [30].

**Theorem 2.** *HashDH is* weak-prnd *if* H *is a random oracle and the* DDH-mult *assumption holds for* GGen.

**One-More-Pseudorandomness.** We show that HashDH is also one-more pseudorandom by adapting the proof of Everspaugh et al. [25]. They gave a proof for a pairing-based variant of HashDH via a tailored one-more DDH assumption, which we adapt to standard groups in the full version [30]. This assumption provides multiple real-or-random challenges and a CDH helper oracle. The adversary therein wins if they can break more DDH challenges than they made queries to the CDH oracle. While this assumption allows for a simple proof that we give in the full version [30], it leaves us with a specialized assumption, and further investigation of the hardness of that assumption is desirable.

**Theorem 3.** *HashDH is* om-prnd *if* H *is a random oracle and the* OM-DDH *assumption holds for* GGen.

**Strong Pseudorandomness.** We have already mentioned that the simulation-based nature of strong pseudorandomness imposes similarly strong constraints as a UC definition, in particular, it seems to impose the need for an *outer* idealized primitive. We now provide strong evidence that HashDH is indeed not strongly pseudorandom due to the lack of the outer hash. We prove this by showing that a simulator needed in the strong pseudorandomness proof would allow to break a reasonable CDH-related assumption. While our assumption is novel, we show that it is implied by the DL assumption in the AGM in the full version [30].

**Theorem 4.** *If* hint-CDH *holds, HashDH is not* str-prnd.

*Proof (sketch).* The proof is rooted in the observation that a simulator needed in the strong pseudorandomness proof for HashDH obtains a request blinded by an unknown $r$ and a randomly chosen evaluation $y$, and then has to generate some response $\overline{y}$ such that $y^r = \overline{y}$. Essentially, it is solving a CDH challenge for the exponent $r$ and the base $y$.

Concretely, the following simple attack cannot be averted by any efficient simulator (without invalidating a CDH-based assumption): An adversary $\mathcal{A}_{\mathsf{prnd}}$ queries the ideal primitive oracle $\mathcal{O}_{\mathsf{Prim}}$ (modeling the hash function) on some input $x$, and then sends a blinded request to $\mathcal{O}_{\mathsf{BlindEval}}$, and checks whether the result is consistent with $\mathcal{O}_{\mathsf{Eval}}(x)$.

In the real world, the two oracles' outputs are always consistent, but in the random world, they differ unless the simulator solves a CDH-type challenge. We construct a CDH adversary that forwards the CDH challenge to the simulator upon its $\mathcal{O}_{\mathsf{LimEval}}$ query. To simulate the blinded response correctly, the simulator must raise this challenge to the unknown $r$, enabling the CDH adversary to win.

As a technicality, we have to consider that the simulator sees $\overline{x}$, which is the value returned from $\mathcal{O}_{\mathsf{Prim}}$ raised to $r$. We accommodate this detail by resorting to a new hint-CDH assumption. The formal definition of hint-CDH assumption and the full proof of Theorem 4 are given in the full version [30].

Turning to our privacy properties, the standard construction of HashDH satisfies request obliviousness and single-key obliviousness.

**Request Obliviousness.** Request and single-key obliviousness are achieved directly from the exponential blinding. We start with the weaker property, which does assume an honest-but-curious evaluator, and is expressed through the indistinguishability of honest requests. We follow the proof by Bellare et al. [8] showing how the blinding is almost, but not perfectly hiding.

**Theorem 5.** *If* H *is a random oracle, then HashDH is* obliv-req.

The exponential blinding yields perfect privacy, as it produces a uniformly random group element. However, as Bellare et al. [8] point out, the hash function introduces a subtlety: If the H returns the identity element 1 for some $x_i$, then any blinding $\mathsf{H}(x_i)^r = 1$ fails to hide the input. Fortunately, this exception happens rarely for a secure hash function and large group size, which is what we capture through the random oracle assumption for convenience. The actual requirements are more relaxed: We need neither programmability nor observability, not even true randomness, it only should be hard to find a map to 1. Standard hash-to-curve algorithms with appropriate group sizes $q$ fulfill this condition: The probability of a random input being mapped to 1 is roughly $1/q$ and finding such an input is deemed "computationally infeasible" [28]. The full proof is in the full version of our paper [30].

**Single-Key Obliviousness.** In single-key obliviousness, we also consider malicious adversaries and model access to a Finalize oracle that checks whether two blind responses finalize correctly under a given secret key. We argue that for the case of HashDH, this attacker model is equivalent to request obliviousness, and thus single-key obliviousness is implied by request obliviousness. The full proof of the following theorem is in the full version [30].

**Theorem 6.** *If* H *is a random oracle, then HashDH is* obliv-1k.

*Proof (sketch).* We want to show that an adversary $\mathcal{A}_{\text{obliv-1k}}$ has identical abilities to an adversary in the request obliviousness game. First, $\mathcal{O}_{\text{Request}}$ is identical, and $\mathcal{A}_{\text{obliv-1k}}$ gains no advantage from becoming active, either: They could send a rogue pk, but the key is not used in HashDH's Request algorithm. Secondly, there is the additional $\mathcal{O}_{\text{Finalize}}$ in $\mathcal{A}_{\text{obliv-1k}}$, which tells whether two given responses result each in the correct evaluation of the associated input. However, observe that HashDH's Finalize is a bijection. Consequently, the only $\overline{y}$ that will finalize into the correct one is the *honest* blind evaluation. But $\mathcal{A}_{\text{obliv-1k}}$ can check trivially themselves whether $\overline{y}$ is the honest blind evaluation of some $\overline{x}$ by checking whether $\overline{x}^{\text{sk}} = \overline{y}$ – so there is nothing to be learned from $\mathcal{O}_{\text{Finalize}}$.

**No Multi-key Obliviousness.** Standard HashDH achieves neither multi-key obliviousness nor implicit verifiability: A blind evaluation is not bound to a key and the Finalize algorithm accepts arbitrary input. Requester privacy is therefore fully compromised by a malicious evaluator. In particular, using the multi-key attack, the evaluator can later link every plain evaluation they see to the specific OPRF session by checking under which key it verifies. We describe this attack formally in the full version [30].

**Theorem 7.** *HashDH is not* obliv-k+ *and not* vf.

**Vf-HashDH: Achieving Multi-key Obliviousness and Verifiability.** We established in Sect. 5.3 how multi-key obliviousness requires a mechanism of implicit verification for the requester. Therefore, we need to modify HashDH accordingly, using the well-established approach of adding a zero-knowledge proof of correct evaluation. We first modify key generation to now output a public key $\text{pk} := g^{\text{sk}}$. In addition, the evaluator must provide a proof $\pi$ of correct computation of $\overline{y}$ as: $\pi \leftarrow\!\$\ \text{NIZK}\{(\text{sk}) : \text{pk} = g^{\text{sk}} \wedge \overline{y} = \overline{x}^{\text{sk}}\}(g, \text{pk}, \overline{x}, \overline{y})$. The requester verifies the proof while finalizing. To this end, Finalize needs the public values pk and $\overline{x}$, so we store both in the state st during Request. This has already been used in a number of works, e.g., [15,22,33]. We thus do not claim any novelty for this extension, but merely want to point out its necessity for achieving the stronger – and intuitively expected – privacy guarantees.

**Definition 7 (Vf-HashDH).** *The vf-HashDH OPRF is defined analogously to HashDH, using an additional NIZK as follows.*

$\text{Setup}(\lambda) : (\mathbb{G}, q, g) \leftarrow\!\$\ \text{GGen}(\lambda);$ **return** $(\mathbb{G}, q, g)$
$\text{KGen}(pp) :$ *parse* $(\mathbb{G}, q, g) = pp;\ \text{sk} \leftarrow\!\$\ \mathbb{Z}_q;\ \text{pk} := g^{\text{sk}};$ **return** $(\text{pk}, \text{sk})$
$\text{Request}(\text{pk}, x) : r \leftarrow\!\$\ \mathbb{Z}_q \setminus \{0\};\ \overline{x} := \text{H}(x)^r;\ \text{st} := (\text{pk}, \overline{x}, r);$ **return** $(\overline{x}, \text{st})$
$\text{BlindEval}(\text{sk}, \overline{x}) : \overline{y} := \overline{x}^{\text{sk}};\ \pi \leftarrow\!\$\ \text{NIZK}\{(\text{sk}) : \text{pk} = g^{\text{sk}} \wedge \overline{y} = \overline{x}^{\text{sk}}\}(g, \text{pk}, \overline{x}, \overline{y}),$
  $\overline{y}' := (\overline{y}, \pi);$ **return** $\overline{y}'$
$\text{Finalize}(\overline{y}', \text{st}) :$ *parse* $(\text{pk}, \overline{x}, r) = \text{st}$ *and* $(\overline{y}, \pi) = \overline{y}'$; *verify* $\pi$ *w.r.t.* $(g, \text{pk}, \overline{x}, \overline{y})$.
  *If* $\pi$ *fails,* **return** $\perp$; *else* $y := \overline{y}^{(1/r)}$; **return** $y$

Vf-HashDH achieves the same properties as HashDH if the NIZK is correct, sound and zero-knowledge. For single-key obliviousness, which we use in the following, we provide some argumentation in the full version [30].

**Theorem 8.** *Vf-HashDH is* obliv-1k *if* H *is a random oracle.*

Next, we show how the additional proof of honest blind evaluation corrects the unwanted malicious linkability of the standard HashDH OPRF.

**Theorem 9.** *Vf-HashDH is* vf *if the NIZK is sound.*

Verifiability follows directly from the soundness of the employed NIZK scheme, and we state the simple proof in the full version [30]. Multi-key obliviousness then follows according to Lemma 11.

**Corollary 2.** *Vf-HashDH is* obliv-k+ *if* H *is a random oracle and the NIZK is sound.*

### 6.2 Analysis of 2HashDH & Generic Compiler

We now analyze 2HashDH, which is the stronger variant of HashDH. It was proposed by Jarecki et al. [33] as a UC-secure OPRF, by adding an outer hash to HashDH. We also observe that adding this outer hash yields a generic transform that allows to lift any strongly one-more unpredictable OPRF into a strongly pseudorandom one.

**Security and Privacy of 2HashDH.** 2HashDH is defined through the blind evaluation of $\mathsf{2HashDH.Eval}(\mathsf{sk}, x) := \mathsf{H}_2(x, \mathsf{H}_1(x)^{\mathsf{sk}})$. It achieves all security and privacy properties of our framework, although multi-key obliviousness and implicit verifiability once more require the extension by a proof of honest blind evaluation. In the full version [30], we formally state the construction as well as its verifiable variant before giving a full security analysis. We point to and adapt existing game-based proofs where possible. Notably, our work closes the gap for the yet unaddressed properties (strong) one-more unpredictability, single-key obliviousness, and verifiability, showing the following:

**Theorem 10.** *If* $\mathsf{H}_1$ *is a random oracle, then 2HashDH is*

- str-prnd, om-prnd, weak-prnd, *and* str-unpred *if* $\mathsf{H}_2$ *is a random oracle and* gap-OM-CDH *holds for* GGen
- unpred *if* $\mathsf{H}_2$ *is a random oracle and* OM-CDH *holds for* GGen
- obliv-req
- obliv-1k *if* $\mathsf{H}_2$ *is collision resistant.*

*With a secure NIZK, vf-2HashDH achieves all of the above and is additionally*

- vf *and* obliv-k+ *if the NIZK is sound.*

**Generic Transform.** The pseudorandomness proofs of 2HashDH (see the full version of the paper [30] and *3HashSDHI* OPRF by Tyagi et al. [45] give rise to a generic construction of pseudorandom OPRFs. In fact, Beullens et al. [10] recently demonstrated that a universally composable OPRF can be obtained by applying an outer hash to an unpredictable OPRF. Their unpredictability notion was kept weak on purpose to examine minimal properties needed for that transform. We now show that a similar result holds for transforming a strongly unpredictable OPRF into a strongly pseudorandom one. Thus, our result complements [10] in the game-based model and holds for an underlying OPRF with a meaningful stand-alone property. We begin by presenting the generic construction.

**Definition 8.** *Let $\Pi_{\mathsf{unpred}}$ be an OPRF and* $\mathsf{H}$ *be a hash function mapping from the output space of $\Pi_{\mathsf{unpred}}$ to strings of length $n$. Let $\Pi_{\mathsf{prnd}}$ be identical to $\Pi_{\mathsf{unpred}}$ except the following algorithms:*

$\mathsf{Eval}'(\mathsf{sk}, x)$ : **return** $\mathsf{H}(x, \mathsf{Eval}(\mathsf{sk}, x))$
$\mathsf{Request}'(\mathsf{pk}, x)$ : $(\overline{x}, \mathsf{st}) \leftarrow\$ \mathsf{Request}(\mathsf{pk}, x)$; **return** $(\overline{x}, (\mathsf{st}, x))$
$\mathsf{Finalize}'(\overline{y}, \mathsf{st})$ : *parse* $(\mathsf{st}', x) = \mathsf{st}$; $y' \leftarrow \mathsf{Finalize}(\overline{y}, \mathsf{st}')$; *if* $y' = \bot$ : **return** $\bot$; **elsereturn** $\mathsf{H}(x, y')$

Intuitively, $\Pi_{\mathsf{prnd}}$ is secure in the ROM as the outputs of $\mathsf{H}$ are indistinguishable from truly random values to an adversary that is unlikely to *predict* the input value $\mathsf{H}$ is invoked on. This is exactly what the input $\mathsf{Eval}(\mathsf{sk}, x)$ of the underlying strongly unpredictable OPRF will provide.

The privacy properties of $\Pi_{\mathsf{prnd}}$ can be analyzed by relying on the corresponding properties of the underlying $\Pi_{\mathsf{unpred}}$ as well. We show this for the multi-key obliviousness explicitly, the other implications follow similarly. The full proof of Theorem 11 is given in the full version [30].

**Theorem 11.** *If $\Pi_{\mathsf{unpred}}$ is* str-unpred *and* obliv-k+, *and* $\mathsf{H}$ *is a random oracle, then $\Pi_{\mathsf{prnd}}$ is* str-prnd *and* obliv-k+.

**Acknowledgments.** This research was partially funded by the HPI Research School on Systems Design.

## References

1. Albrecht, M.R., Davidson, A., Deo, A., Gardham, D.: Crypto dark matter on the torus. In: Joye, M., Leander, G. (eds.) EUROCRYPT 2024, pp. 447–476. Springer, Cham (2024)
2. Albrecht, M.R., Davidson, A., Deo, A., Smart, N.P.: Round-optimal verifiable oblivious pseudorandom functions from ideal lattices. In: Garay, J.A. (ed.) PKC 2021. LNCS, vol. 12711, pp. 261–289. Springer, Cham (2021). https://doi.org/10.1007/978-3-030-75248-4_10

3. Albrecht, M.R., Gur, K.D.: Verifiable oblivious pseudorandom functions from lattices: Practical-ish and thresholdisable. In: Chung, K.M., Sasaki, Y. (eds.) ASIACRYPT 2024, pp. 205–237. Springer, Singapore (2024)
4. Backendal, M., Davis, H., Günther, F., Haller, M., Paterson, K.G.: A formal treatment of end-to-end encrypted cloud storage. In: Advances in Cryptology – CRYPTO 2024, pp. 40–74. Springer, Cham (2024). https://doi.org/10.1007/978-3-031-68379-4_2
5. Basso, A.: A post-quantum round-optimal oblivious PRF from isogenies. Cryptology ePrint Archive, Paper 2023/225 (2023). https://eprint.iacr.org/2023/225
6. Baum, C., et al.: Efficient maliciously secure oblivious exponentiations. IACR Commun. Cryptol. **1**(3) (2024). https://doi.org/10.62056/a66cy7qiu
7. Baum, C., Frederiksen, T., Hesse, J., Lehmann, A., Yanai, A.: Pesto: proactively secure distributed single sign-on, or how to trust a hacked server. In: 2020 IEEE European Symposium on Security and Privacy (EuroS&P). IEEE (2020). https://doi.org/10.1109/eurosp48549.2020.00044
8. Bellare, M., Ranjan, R., Riepel, D., Aldakheel, A.: The concrete security of two-party computation: simple definitions, and tight proofs for PSI and OPRFs. In: Chung, K.M., Sasaki, Y. (eds.) ASIACRYPT 2024, pp. 328–362. Springer, Singapore (2024)
9. Bellare, M., Rogaway, P.: Code-based game-playing proofs and the security of triple encryption. IACR Cryptology ePrint Archive 2004/331 (2004). https://eprint.iacr.org/2004/331
10. Beullens, W., Dodgson, L., Faller, S., Hesse, J.: The 2hash OPRF framework and efficient post-quantum instantiations. In: Fehr, S., Fouque, P.A. (eds.) EUROCRYPT 2025, pp. 332–362. Springer, Cham (2025)
11. Boldyreva, A.: Threshold signatures, multisignatures and blind signatures based on the gap-Diffie-Hellman-group signature scheme. In: Desmedt, Y.G. (ed.) PKC 2003. LNCS, vol. 2567, pp. 31–46. Springer, Heidelberg (2003). https://doi.org/10.1007/3-540-36288-6_3
12. Boneh, D., Kogan, D., Woo, K.: Oblivious pseudorandom functions from isogenies. In: Moriai, S., Wang, H. (eds.) ASIACRYPT 2020. LNCS, vol. 12492, pp. 520–550. Springer, Cham (2020). https://doi.org/10.1007/978-3-030-64834-3_18
13. Bourdrez, D., Krawczyk, H., Lewi, K., Wood, C.A.: The OPAQUE Augmented PAKE Protocol. Internet-Draft draft-irtf-cfrg-opaque-18 (2024). https://datatracker.ietf.org/doc/draft-irtf-cfrg-opaque/18/, work in Progress
14. Camenisch, J., De Caro, A., Ghosh, E., Sorniotti, A.: Oblivious PRF on committed vector inputs and application to deduplication of encrypted data. In: Goldberg, I., Moore, T. (eds.) FC 2019. LNCS, vol. 11598, pp. 337–356. Springer, Cham (2019). https://doi.org/10.1007/978-3-030-32101-7_21
15. Camenisch, J., Lehmann, A., Neven, G.: Optimal distributed password verification. In: Proceedings of the 22nd ACM SIGSAC Conference on Computer and Communications Security, CCS 2015, pp. 182–194. ACM (2015). https://doi.org/10.1145/2810103.2813722
16. Camenisch, J., Stadler, M.: Proof systems for general statements about discrete logarithms. Technical report (1997). https://doi.org/10.3929/ETHZ-A-006651937
17. Canetti, R.: Universally composable security: a new paradigm for cryptographic protocols. In: Proceedings 42nd IEEE Symposium on Foundations of Computer Science, pp. 136–145 (2001). https://doi.org/10.1109/SFCS.2001.959888
18. Casacuberta, S., Hesse, J., Lehmann, A.: SoK: oblivious pseudorandom functions. In: 2022 IEEE 7th European Symposium on Security and Privacy (EuroS&P), pp. 625–646 (2022). https://doi.org/10.1109/EuroSP53844.2022.00045

19. Celi, S., Davidson, A., Valdez, S., Wood, C.A.: Privacy Pass Issuance Protocols. RFC 9578 (2024). https://doi.org/10.17487/RFC9578. https://www.rfc-editor.org/info/rfc9578
20. Das, P., Hesse, J., Lehmann, A.: Dpase: distributed password-authenticated symmetric-key encryption, or how to get many keys from one password. In: Proceedings of the 2022 ACM on Asia Conference on Computer and Communications Security. ASIA CCS 2022. ACM (2022). https://doi.org/10.1145/3488932.3517389
21. Davidson, A., Faz-Hernandez, A., Sullivan, N., Wood, C.A.: Oblivious Pseudorandom Functions (OPRFs) Using Prime-Order Groups. RFC 9497 (2023). https://doi.org/10.17487/RFC9497. https://www.rfc-editor.org/info/rfc9497
22. Davidson, A., Goldberg, I., Sullivan, N., Tankersley, G., Valsorda, F.: Privacy pass: bypassing internet challenges anonymously. Proce. Priv. Enhancing Technol. **2018**(3), 164–180 (2018). https://doi.org/10.1515/popets-2018-0026
23. Dayanikli, D., Lehmann, A.: (Strong) apake revisited: capturing multi-user security and salting. In: 2024 IEEE 9th European Symposium on Security and Privacy (EuroS&P), pp. 415–439 (2024). https://doi.org/10.1109/EuroSP60621.2024.00030
24. Dong, M.: Multi-point hashdh OPRF using multiplicative blinding with application to private set intersection. IACR Cryptology ePrint Archive 2022/1482 (2022). https://api.semanticscholar.org/CorpusID:253205196
25. Everspaugh, A., Chaterjee, R., Scott, S., Juels, A., Ristenpart, T.: The Pythia PRF service. In: 24th USENIX Security Symposium (USENIX Security 2015), pp. 547–562. USENIX Association, Washington, D.C. (2015). https://www.usenix.org/conference/usenixsecurity15/technical-sessions/presentation/everspaugh
26. Faller, S., Handirk, T., Hesse, J., Horváth, M., Lehmann, A.: Password-protected key retrieval with(out) HSM protection. In: Proceedings of the 2024 on ACM SIGSAC Conference on Computer and Communications Security, CCS 2024, pp. 2445–2459. Association for Computing Machinery, New York (2024). https://doi.org/10.1145/3658644.3690358
27. Faust, S., Hazay, C., Venturi, D.: Outsourced pattern matching. Int. J. Inf. Secur. **17**, 327–346 (2013). https://api.semanticscholar.org/CorpusID:2486674
28. Faz-Hernandez, A., Scott, S., Sullivan, N., Wahby, R.S., Wood, C.A.: Hashing to Elliptic Curves. RFC 9380 (2023). https://doi.org/10.17487/RFC9380. https://www.rfc-editor.org/info/rfc9380
29. Freedman, M.J., Ishai, Y., Pinkas, B., Reingold, O.: Keyword search and oblivious pseudorandom functions. In: Kilian, J. (ed.) Theory of Cryptography, pp. 303–324. Springer, Heidelberg (2005)
30. Friedrichs, K., Lehmann, A., Özbay, C.: Game changer: a modular framework for oprf security. Cryptology ePrint Archive, Paper 2025/1565 (2025). https://eprint.iacr.org/2025/1565
31. Gaži, P., Tessaro, S.: Secret-key cryptography from ideal primitives: a systematic overview. In: 2015 IEEE Information Theory Workshop (ITW), pp. 1–5 (2015). https://doi.org/10.1109/ITW.2015.7133163
32. Hazay, C., Lindell, Y.: Efficient protocols for set intersection and pattern matching with security against malicious and covert adversaries. In: Canetti, R. (ed.) Theory of Cryptography, pp. 155–175. Springer, Heidelberg (2008)
33. Jarecki, S., Kiayias, A., Krawczyk, H.: Round-optimal password-protected secret sharing and T-PAKE in the password-only model. In: Sarkar, P., Iwata, T. (eds.) ASIACRYPT 2014. LNCS, vol. 8874, pp. 233–253. Springer, Heidelberg (2014). https://doi.org/10.1007/978-3-662-45608-8_13

34. Jarecki, S., Kiayias, A., Krawczyk, H., Xu, J.: Highly-efficient and composable password-protected secret sharing (or: How to protect your bitcoin wallet online). In: 2016 IEEE European Symposium on Security and Privacy (EuroS&P). IEEE (2016). https://doi.org/10.1109/eurosp.2016.30
35. Jarecki, S., Kiayias, A., Krawczyk, H., Xu, J.: Toppss: cost-minimal password-protected secret sharing based on threshold OPRF. In: Gollmann, D., Miyaji, A., Kikuchi, H. (eds.) Applied Cryptography and Network Security, pp. 39–58. Springer, Cham (2017)
36. Jarecki, S., Krawczyk, H., Xu, J.: OPAQUE: an asymmetric PAKE protocol secure against pre-computation attacks. In: Nielsen, J.B., Rijmen, V. (eds.) EUROCRYPT 2018. LNCS, vol. 10822, pp. 456–486. Springer, Cham (2018). https://doi.org/10.1007/978-3-319-78372-7_15
37. Jarecki, S., Krawczyk, H., Xu, J.: On the (in)security of the Diffie-Hellman oblivious PRF with multiplicative blinding. In: Garay, J.A. (ed.) PKC 2021. LNCS, vol. 12711, pp. 380–409. Springer, Cham (2021). https://doi.org/10.1007/978-3-030-75248-4_14
38. Jarecki, S., Liu, X.: Efficient oblivious pseudorandom function with applications to adaptive OT and secure computation of set intersection. In: Reingold, O. (ed.) Theory of Cryptography, pp. 577–594. Springer, Heidelberg (2009). https://iacr.org/archive/tcc2009/54440575/54440575.pdf
39. Jarecki, S., Liu, X.: Fast secure computation of set intersection. In: Garay, J.A., De Prisco, R. (eds.) Security and Cryptography for Networks, pp. 418–435. Springer, Heidelberg (2010). https://link.springer.com/content/pdf/10.1007/978-3-642-15317-4_26.pdf
40. Kaluderovic, N., Cheng, N., Mitrokotsa, A.: A post-quantum distributed OPRF from the legendre PRF. IACR Cryptology ePrint Archive 2024/544 (2024). https://api.semanticscholar.org/CorpusID:269045259
41. Kolesnikov, V., Matania, N., Pinkas, B., Rosulek, M., Trieu, N.: Practical multi-party private set intersection from symmetric-key techniques. In: Proceedings of the 2017 ACM SIGSAC Conference on Computer and Communications Security, CCS 2017, pp. 1257–1272. Association for Computing Machinery, New York (2017). https://doi.org/10.1145/3133956.3134065
42. Lehmann, A.: ScrambleDB: oblivious (chameleon) pseudonymization-as-a-service. Proce. Priv. Enhancing Technol. **2019**(3), 289–309 (2019). https://doi.org/10.2478/popets-2019-0048
43. Naor, M., Pinkas, B., Reingold, O.: Distributed pseudo-random functions and KDCs. In: Stern, J. (ed.) Advances in Cryptology — EUROCRYPT 1999, pp. 327–346. Springer, Heidelberg (1999). https://link.springer.com/content/pdf/10.1007/3-540-48910-X_23.pdf
44. Shoup, V.: Sequences of games: a tool for taming complexity in security proofs. IACR Cryptology ePrint Archive 2004/332 (2004). https://api.semanticscholar.org/CorpusID:13341188
45. Tyagi, N., Celi, S., Ristenpart, T., Sullivan, N., Tessaro, S., Wood, C.A.: A fast and simple partially oblivious PRF, with applications. In: Dunkelman, O., Dziembowski, S. (eds.) EUROCRYPT 2022, pp. 674–705. Springer, Cham (2022)

# Author Index



© International Association for Cryptologic Research 2026
G. Hanaoka and B.-Y. Yang (Eds.): ASIACRYPT 2025, LNCS 16252, pp. 615–616, 2026.
https://doi.org/10.1007/978-981-95-5125-5

GPSR Compliance

*The European Union's (EU) General Product Safety Regulation (GPSR) is a set of rules that requires consumer products to be safe and our obligations to ensure this.*

*If you have any concerns about our products, you can contact us on ProductSafety@springernature.com*

In case Publisher is established outside the EU, the EU authorized representative is:

Springer Nature Customer Service Center GmbH
Europaplatz 3
69115 Heidelberg, Germany

**Batch number: 10607174**

Printed by Printforce, the Netherlands